THE
ENCYCLOPEDIA
of the
CHINESE
OVERSEAS

ADVISERS AND EDITORIAL CONSULTANTS

PANEL OF ADVISERS

Wang Gungwu
Director
The East Asian Institute

Philip A. Kuhn
Francis Lee Higginson Professor of History and
Professor of East Asian Languages and Civilization
Harvard University

J. A. C. Mackie
Professor Emeritus
Australian National University

Tu Wei-ming
Professor of Chinese History and Philosophy
Harvard University

Wang Ling-Chi
Professor of Ethnic Studies
University of California

Friedrich Wu
Vice-President and Head of Economic Research
Development Bank of Singapore

Zhou Nanjing
Professor of Afro-Asian Studies
Beijing University

EDITORIAL CONSULTANTS

George Hicks
Economist and Writer

Leo Suryadinata
Associate Professor of Political Science
National University of Singapore

First published in 1998 by Landmark Books Pte Ltd,
5001, Beach Road, #02-73/74, Singapore 199588
and Editions Didier Millet, 593 Havelock Road #02-01,
Singapore 229672, *for the* Chinese Heritage Centre,
Nanyang Drive, Nanyang Technological University,
Singapore 639798.

CONTRIBUTORS

PAUL BAILEY, Senior Lecturer in East Asian History, University of Edinburgh, Scotland
JOHN CAYLEY, Founder and publisher, Wellsweep Press, London, England
SCARLET CHENG, Freelance journalist, Hong Kong
CHOI KWAI KEONG, Research Fellow, Chinese Heritage Centre, Singapore
FLEMMING CHRISTIANSEN, Senior Lecturer, East Asian Studies, University of Leeds, England
GLORIA DAVIES, Senior Lecturer, Department of Asian Languages and Studies, Monash University, Australia
LEO M. DOUW, Lecturer in Modern Chinese History and Society, Vrije Universiteit Amsterdam and Universiteit van Amsterdam, the Netherlands
PAUL HANDLEY, Freelance journalist, Bangkok, Thailand
KAREN LEIGH HARRIS, Senior Lecturer in History, University of South Africa, South Africa
MARY SOMERS HEIDHUES, Author, *Southeast Asia's Chinese Minorities* and *Bangka Tin* and *Mentok Pepper: Chinese Settlement on an Indonesian Island,* Germany
HENG PEK KOON, Senior Research Associate, Institute for Pacific Rim Studies, Temple University, Japan and Adjunct Associate Professor, School of International Service, The American University, USA
MARLOWE HOOD, Freelance journalist, Paris, France
EVELYN HU-DEHART, Chair of Department of Ethnic Studies, University of Colorado, Boulder, USA
CHRISTINE INGLIS, Director, Multicultural Research Centre, University of Sydney, Australia
MANYING IP, Senior Lecturer in Chinese Studies, University of Auckland, New Zealand
KWOK KIAN WOON, Lecturer, Department of Sociology, National University of Singapore, Singapore
KYO SYUKUSHIN, Professor of International Relations between Japan and China, Setsunan University, Osaka, Japan
WALTON LOOK LAI, Lecturer in History, University of the West Indies, St Augustine, Trinidad-Tobago
HIM MARK LAI, Adjunct Professor, San Francisco State University, USA
LEE SEOK CHEE, Member of the Advisory Panel, Singapore Art Museum and the Asian Civilizations Museum, Singapore
TANA LI, Lecturer, Department of History and Politics, University of Wollongong, Australia
LIANG XIUJING, PhD candidate, School for Postgraduate Interdisciplinary Research on Interculturalism and Transnationality, Aalborg University, Denmark
LIM BEE LENG, Research Assistant, Chinese Heritage Centre, Singapore
ROSEMARY LIM, Editor, Singapore
LINDA LIM YUEN-CHING, Director, Southeast Asia Business Program, University of Michigan Business School, USA
BERTIL LINTNER, Correspondent, *Far Eastern Economic Review*, Bangkok, Thailand
LIVE YU-SION, Maître de conférences en Sociologie, Faculté des Lettres et des Sciences Humaines, Université de la Réunion, France
HUGUETTE LY-TIO-FANE PINEO, Author, *Lured Away: The Life History of Indian Cane Workers in Mauritius* and *Chinese Diaspora in Western Indian Ocean*, Mauritius
ALEXEI A. MASLOV, Professor of Far Eastern Studies, Department of East Asian Spiritual Civilization Studies, Russian Academy of Sciences, Moscow, Russia
J. A. C. MACKIE, Professor Emeritus, Australian National University, Canberra, Australia
THOMAS MENKHOFF, Author, *Trade Routes, Trust and Trading Networks: Chinese Small Enterprises in Singapore* and *Chinese Non-Contractual Business Relations and Social Structure: The Singapore Case*, Kuala Lumpur, Malaysia
NG BEOY KUI, Senior Lecturer, Nanyang Business School, Nanyang Technological University, Singapore
NG SHUI MENG, Project Officer, United Nations Children's Fund, Beijing, China
NG WING CHUNG, Assistant Professor of History, The University of Texas, San Antonio, USA
NIEW SHONG TONG, Senior Lecturer, Department of Public Policy and Administration, University Brunei Darussalam, Brunei
ELLEN OXFELD, Associate Professor of Anthropology, Middlebury College, Vermont, USA
LYNN PAN, Founding Director, Chinese Heritage Centre, Singapore and author, *Sons of the Yellow Emperor,* Shanghai, China
PANG CHENG LIAN, First Vice-President of United Overseas Bank Group, Singapore
DAVID PARKER, Lecturer, Department of Cultural Studies, University of Birmingham, England
FRANK PIEKE, Lecturer in Chinese Politics and Society, The University of Oxford, England
ANTHONY REID, Professor of Southeast Asian History, Research School of Pacific and Asian Studies, Australian National University, Canberra, Australia
SHIM JAE HOON, Correspondent, *Far Eastern Economic Review*, Seoul, South Korea
ELIZABETH SINN, Lecturer, Department of History, The University of Hong Kong, Hong Kong
RONALD SKELDON, Author, *Population Mobility in Developing Countries: A Reinterpretation* and *Population Migration and Development: A Global Perspective*, Hong Kong
MICHAEL R. J. VATIKIOTIS, Bureau Chief, *Far Eastern Economic Review*, Bangkok, Thailand
WANG GUNGWU, Director, The East Asian Institute, Singapore
VIVIENNE WEE, Programme Director, Engender, Singapore
EDGAR WICKBERG, Emeritus Professor of History, University of British Columbia, Vancouver, Canada
W. E. WILLMOTT, Professor of Sociology, University of Canterbury, Christchurch, New Zealand
ALIZA S. WONG, PhD candidate, University of Colorado, Boulder, USA
ZENG LING, Research Fellow, Centre for Chinese Language and Culture, Nanyang Technological University, Singapore
ZHENG DEHUA, Associate Professor, Institute of Chinese Studies, University of Macao, Macao
ZHUANG GUOTU, Professor of History, Xiamen University, Xiamen, China

THE ENCYCLOPEDIA
of the
CHINESE OVERSEAS

General Editor
LYNN PAN

Harvard University Press
Cambridge, Massachusetts
1999

Library of Congress Cataloging-in-Publication Data

The encyclopedia of the Chinese overseas / edited by Lynn Pan.
      p.   cm.
Includes bibliographical references and index
ISBN 0-674-25210-1
1. Chinese—Foreign countries. 2. China—Emigration and immigration.
I. Pan, Lynn. II. Chinese Heritage Centre (Singapore)
DS732.E53 1999
304.8'0951—DC21   98-35466

FOREWORD

This encyclopedia is compiled and published under the aegis of the Chinese Heritage Centre, which was set up in Singapore in 1995. The establishment of this centre has made it possible to study overseas Chinese globally, rather than as separate communities. Thus this book is not only the first major project of the centre but the first to look at overseas Chinese communities across the world so comprehensively. Bringing many communities together between the covers of a single volume helps to reveal the contacts that these communities have established both among themselves, and between themselves and the wider world. And such contacts are crucial in a world increasingly linked and shrunk by information technology.

The purpose of both this book and the Chinese Heritage Centre is to meet the increasing demand for information on the overseas Chinese, interest in whom has waxed and waned through the years but which has patently grown with China's expanding openness to the world. There is no doubt that the overseas Chinese have played an important part in the ties which China has forged with its neighbours in Asia and with the West over the centuries. These ties have been forged for the most part around trade, but they have also been enriched by the flow of ideas and culture.

The Chinese Heritage Centre aims to contribute to such exchanges. It does so as a repository of materials on overseas Chinese settled across the globe. This information bank will expand through both its own efforts and through cooperation with research institutions sharing its interests throughout the world. It is helped in this endeavour by its location in Singapore, a place with a sizeable population of Chinese descent and strong telecommunications infrastructure.

The centre was founded by the Singapore Federation of Chinese Clan Associations, but it is housed in a building leased from the Nanyang Technological University. It is deeply in the debt of these two organizations, but it could not have embarked on the encyclopedia without the support of many individuals located outside Singapore. Specifically, I want to record my thanks to the international Board of Governors and to all those donors whose generous financial assistance brought both the centre and this volume into being. I am also grateful to the international Panel of Advisers for their wise counsel. We recognize that the book is only the first step on a long journey for the Chinese Heritage Centre. But we are confident of steady progress towards our goal of being the world's premier centre for the study of the Chinese overseas.

WEE CHO YAW
Chairman, Board of Governors
Chinese Heritage Centre

CONTENTS

GUIDE TO THE USE OF THE ENCYCLOPEDIA AND EDITORIAL CONVENTIONS

TYPES OF MATTER

The encyclopedia contains signed articles by the authors named in the List of Contributors. The articles are of two kinds: main-text essays and boxed features. The boxed features, indicated by a square sign in the Table of Contents, allow certain topics or illustrative examples to be treated with a degree of focus that would otherwise interrupt the narrative or analytical flow of the main text. Each signature relates to all the text that appears between it and the preceding signature, however many separate sections that text may contain.

Cross-references, indicated by the title of the section into which the point referred to falls, or its page number, help the reader to locate earlier or later mentions of a particular subject. A further aid to locating information is the detailed Index.

Copious photographs apart, the pictorial material consists of maps, figures and tables. For the maps, the intention has been to mark and name only those places mentioned in the accompanying text, with just a few additional places indicated for purposes of context and reference. The key to the symbols used in all the maps is as follows:

▨	Area/areas under discusssion	——————	International boundary
☐	Area/areas beyond scope of discussion	–·–·–	Provincial/state boundary

Supplementary materials at the back of the book include Timelines of important economic, political and social events in China. This is a selective chronology, listing events judged to have a particularly significant bearing on the history of the overseas Chinese. In addition, a bilingual, alphabetically arranged Chinese Character List is provided. This comprises the personal name of every Chinese individual mentioned in the text for which the Chinese characters are known. The names appear in either their regional speech-based spelling or romanized Mandarin, or both. The list also includes Chinese place names, institutions with Chinese names, Chinese words, phrases and idioms.

The Bibliography contains two kinds of material: first, titles referred to in the text, tables, figures and maps; second, a selection of the sources used by the authors. Rather than being consolidated into a single list, the titles are grouped according to the five Parts into which the main text falls, namely 'Origins,' 'Migration,' 'Institutions,' 'Relations' and 'Communities.' This means that some titles appear more than once.

LANGUAGES AND ROMANIZATION

The editorial approach has been to use English as far as possible. However, the nature of the material is such that romanized non-English vocabulary, including Chinese terms and idioms with no exact or appropriate English equivalents or are in wide use in their romanized form, occasionally appears. Besides Chinese, there is a sprinkling of Bahasa Indonesian, Burmese, Dutch, French, Italian, Japanese, Malay, Spanish, Tagalog, Thai and Vietnamese terms.

Chinese personal names appear in the forms by which their referents are most widely known. The requirement to adopt local names in some places means that these forms may be Indonesian, Japanese or Thai rather than Chinese. Where they are Chinese, they usually appear in romanized forms based on their regional-speech pronunciation rather than on Mandarin. Such transliterations are rarely standardized and they often reflect the way the names were pronounced and spelt by the particular colonial authority, whether British, Dutch, French or Spanish, under which they were initially adopted. With few exceptions, their equivalents in Mandarin and Chinese characters may be found in the Chinese Character List. The exceptions are those for whom the original Chinese has proved difficult to identify. Mandarin is rendered in the Pinyin system of romanization officially adopted by the People's Republic of China. Chinese personal names are given surname first if that is the order followed by their bearers, but not if the norm is to give it after the forename (as it is in America and Europe).

For two Chinese place names, the Pinyin forms are not provided; these are Canton and Taipei, the one an old English spelling, the other based on the Wade-Giles system of transliteration. For three others — Amoy, Quemoy and Swatow — both the old English spelling, familiar to many English-language readers, and the Pinyin romanization more widely used in modern times (Xiamen, Jinmen and Shantou), appear, with either one or the other form sometimes given in parentheses as a reminder to the reader.

The names of the chief Chinese languages — or dialects, as they are commonly called — spoken by overseas Chinese are mostly given in the established dialect spelling (examples include Hokkien and Hakka). So also are the names of the groups which speak them. One, Cantonese, appears in the old English spelling. Where it is judged helpful to the reader, the dialect-based form is followed in parentheses by the Pinyin spelling, or vice versa; one example of the latter is Fuqing (Hokchia).

Chinese expressions are spelt in Pinyin with few exceptions. The exceptions — *sinkeh*, *towkay*, *sinseh* and *cukong* — appear in the dialect spelling that has become established. Syllable combination and division in romanized Chinese terms, which are represented by discrete, monosyllabic characters in the Chinese original even when the terms themselves are multi-syllabic compounds, follows semantic and grammatical principles.

In Pinyin, hyphens are not used to join syllables, and the hyphens which appear in this book are used in a coupling which reflects the way the Chinese sometimes refer to two places in the same breath by taking one syllable from each name and running the two together. Thus 'Chao-Shan,' for example, stands for the area encompassed by Chaozhou and Shantou, while 'Nan-Shun' is short for Nanhai and Shunde.

The spelling of English words is based on the eighth edition of *The Concise Oxford Dictionary of Current English*, which does not regard as foreign, and therefore does not italicize, many words — including 'mestizo,' 'yin' and 'yang' and 'kung fu' — absorbed from other languages.

LIST OF FIGURES, TABLES AND MAPS

Square brackets enclose place names which do not appear in the tables themselves.

INTRODUCTION

The peopling of the earth has been an enduring part of human history. From very early times, individuals, families and tribes moved from place to place whenever necessary in search of abundance and safety. When the urge to migrate for the sake of survival or for a better livelihood was strong, it could only be halted or slowed down by territorial constraints supported by superior arms. After technological changes made the agricultural revolution possible, long-term settlement became the norm. The surpluses that this produced made possible the growth of towns, cities, kingdoms and empires, and of institutions that kept their own people in and foreign peoples out. In China, this led to the growth of one of the most stable political systems ever recorded. Its success led China to become, for thousands of years, a major attraction for immigrants and a meagre source of emigrants. Until the 19th century, almost all voluntary migration happened within the borders of the empire.

The population of China doubled from about 50 million between the first century and the 11th, and doubled and redoubled to about 400 million by the beginning of the 19th century. Increasingly, official demographic policies, and the search for agricultural land or urban employment, led to massive internal migrations. Alongside these movements of people, merchants ventured forth to trade, some travelling to markets beyond China's borders. They were held back not only by the needs of security and foreign relations, but also by social and cultural injunctions not to leave home. Trading overseas particularly was actively discouraged for long periods. It was not until the 19th century that Chinese people left the country in large numbers to find work in distant foreign lands. This new phenomenon of emigration marks the beginning of agrarian China's response to the industrial revolution. Its leaders took a while to realize what this involved, but a series of defeats by the Great Powers made it inevitable that China would have to join the race for modernization. Today, with emigrant communities in every continent and many of them playing a dynamic part in the global economy, the Chinese overseas have a remarkable story to tell. This volume is the first attempt to provide a comprehensive account of that transformation.

Initially, all migrations involve pull or push factors. China experienced some of the cruellest forms of both sets of factors during the 19th century. War and famine within the country drove many abroad, and the dire need for cheap labour by some of the newly industrializing powers opened up opportunities for China's poor. From one point of view, only the slave trade from Africa was more tragic than the fates of the thousands of coolies who were transported around the world. From another, emigration offered life and hope. These Chinese met the challenge with a fortitude and enterprise that confounded everyone, even their own governments and élites back in China. To understand this, we need to link their story to the nature of Chinese culture and history, but the heart of the story lies with the varied responses the sojourners made to the conditions they found abroad. In particular, the experiences they had that led many of them to decide to settle and not return to China shaped the kind of communities they established. This in turn determined the future they hoped their descendants would have in their adopted countries.

There is a tendency among many Chinese to attribute every success they have to the uniqueness and superiority of Chinese culture. This is sometimes exaggerated to the point of incredulity, notably by those with chauvinist or nationalist agendas. Such efforts to use Chinese values to explain what the Chinese have or have not achieved abroad should be made with caution, and full weight must be given to vital factors of economic and political change both in China and elsewhere. On the other hand, it is not possible to avoid the question of Chinese culture. Those who minimize, or even dismiss, factors of culture, and invariably attribute all significant developments to the forces of modernization, are also guilty of oversimplification. Much depends on what is being described. To believe that all factors causing change or resistance to change stem from rational choice and universal human traits is no less a narrowing of one's ability to explain. Migration involves multiple responses to alien stimuli, and the way Chinese sojourners and migrants managed new environments deserves closer attention than we have given it so far.

As the accounts in this volume show, culture and history do matter in the way migrant communities are formed and evolved. It is not enough to say that Chinese immigrants are industrious, practise thrift and make sacrifices for their families, value education and social mobility, and organize themselves for effective defence and action. Many others do the same. How the Chinese have sustained what they do, however, does reflect their cultural origins and their uniquely structured history. The earliest traders in Southeast Asia clung to a sojourning pattern, and their appeals to distinctive family, religious and other customary ties determined the way their small communities survived. The later labouring classes that were transported around the world, especially those among them who did not return to China, strengthened the resistance to assimilation among those who had chosen to settle. They were followed in the 20th century by several waves of better educated teachers, journalists, students and refugees. Many of these brought new communication and organizational skills that connected the emergent communities with a modernizing China, including some underlying political and cultural changes which either attracted the Chinese diaspora or repelled them. These changes in turn influenced the way the Chinese responded to new economic opportunities both within China and in their host countries.

In the end, immigrants representing a great multiplicity of origins were neither colonists backed by their country's expanding power, nor slaves to circumstances or economic forces bound to a particular place and occupation. They had varying capacities to choose and varying degrees of freedom to act. The factors behind each migration were never constant, the contexts were always important. Both could be more decisive than the cultural baggage the Chinese carried with them. As the essays in the volume show, *when* the Chinese left home and *where* they went to played extremely important parts in shaping the communities they formed outside China. Over time, these two questions help us group the Chinese around the world in three broad ways. The first group consists of the large majority who are located in lands in the neighbouring region where the Chinese first went and continued to go to; the second, those who are scattered among developing countries around the world in small numbers; and the third, those who have moved to the industrializing West, especially the recent exodus to the migrant states of North America and Australasia.

When the Chinese migrate is important because this highlights the conditions under which they leave China and are received abroad. The timing not only gives precedence to those who settled in areas close to China but also emphasizes the depth of their ethnic identity if they choose to assert it. It reminds us not to assume that questions of Chinese identity are simply matters of policy and personal choice.

Some 80 per cent of Chinese who live outside China (that is, the People's Republic, Hong Kong and Taiwan) belong to the first group. Many of those who had traded there since earlier times had assimilated to the local population (mostly in Korea, Japan and mainland Southeast Asia), but others have remained Chinese and are conscious of living among peoples who have long trading links with China. This is particularly true of those descended from southern Chinese who had migrated across the South China Sea since the 19th century. They still rely on the economic roles they can play in future relations between their adopted countries and a China seeking to regain its historic place in the region. Even in Singapore where ethnic Chinese can form an independent government and Malaysia where they are the largest minority, their economic function is primary. Only if they perform that role successfully can they ensure a continued political, social and cultural position in those societies. Wherever the countries in the region trade closely with China, the reliance of their Chinese on commercial success is even more obvious. This is not without cost. Having a spotlight shone on the wealth of the successful few could threaten the safety of the many who try to live normal lives among their indigenous fellow nationals. The phenomenon reminds us how important China's proximity to the region is. It is one that must invariably call for care and sensitivity among all concerned.

For the second group, the formation of scattered communities in the developing nations of Africa, Latin America and the rest of Asia came about largely during the 20th century. The Chinese there have been too few in number to play significant roles and, therefore, are prone to assimilate or re-migrate if their population is not augmented by new immigration. They too have depended on trading skills to sustain their small communities. There has been little prospect of political activity and, for their social and cultural life, they have had to depend on new technologies to reduce the distances between them and similar communities elsewhere. But if China does eventually become the economic giant predicted for it, every Chinese community, however small today, would have the opportunity to expand its trading role and strengthen its links with people not only in China but with ethnic Chinese in their respective regions. This presupposes a long-term and wider acceptance of multi-ethnic tolerance in the new states. In any case, in an era of capitalist globalization, there are other options. If necessary, many would seek to move to centres where wealth-making is perceived as easier and safer.

As for the third and growing group in the West, theirs is a history filled with contradictions. Most of the early miners and coolie labour who went to the English-speaking migrant states were forced to return to China. Those who remained had turned to a limited number of trades and a few eventually acquired enough education to join the professions. But, after World War II, there was a reversal of immigration policies which transformed conditions almost beyond belief. Today, these migrant states, notably the United States, Canada and Australia, receive more immigrants directly from Chinese territories than from anywhere else in the world. To their weak and scattered communities that had been declining surely and steadily during the first half of the 20th century, there came new waves of immigrants from Taiwan, Hong Kong and more recently the Chinese mainland. Increasingly, they came as families, with many headed by those who were educated and who chose to migrate to a particular country in search of even better education and opportunities for themselves and their children.

Among the newcomers were many who could be described as refugee élites intent on playing a part in the modernization of China. They have been compared with the élite literati who left to learn from the West, and those who, since the beginning of the 20th century, have brought Nationalist and Communist organizations and education ideals to their compatriots abroad. But in terms of numbers, including many who had studied in the West and turned their backs on one Chinese regime or another, such movements of élite families were unprecedented.

Their impact on earlier layers of Chinese settlers, however, is uncertain. They are still mobile and could readily re-migrate if necessary. Their ties with China remain emotionally and culturally strong, and already some have returned to Taiwan, Hong Kong and the mainland. Such loyalties as they have to things and matters Chinese will vary from individual to individual, but much will depend on the future development of the Chinese polity. The future moves of these new émigrés are unpredictable and no doubt these will be carefully monitored by Chinese and non-Chinese alike. But it is likely that most of them will remain abroad as diaspora communities in those countries where legal and political conditions permit them to do so.

In an era of expanded global relationships, the three distinctive groups described above are now less likely to develop apart. Many are already interacting with parts of China whenever feasible, and many do so with one another across the various regions. Unlike in the past when such connections were primarily commercial, modern communications enable them to be multi-dimensional and much more entwined. There will emerge many kinds of political and community leaders to cope with rapidly changing local environments. Their visions of the future will be couched in increasingly modern terms. As they become more articulate and convincing, they could lead the Chinese in several different directions. And when, as many would expect, China joins the mainstream of the nation-state system in some future modified form, the alternatives will become clearer. Some leaders will ask their communities to emphasize their Chinese identities, or offer to take their followers home to China. Others will persuade theirs to disappear as Chinese, give total loyalty to their adopted homes and, wherever possible, participate fully in the lives of their fellow nationals. Yet others will seek one of the many positions in between and, from past experience, it would seem likely that the numbers of these will remain large. For them, the meaning of Chineseness will be found along a spectrum, and the length and breadth of that spectrum will be determined by local needs and the place of China in the region and the world.

Throughout China's history, there have been peoples who have become Chinese as well as Chinese who have become other peoples, both within and outside China's long and moveable borders. Never, however, have the numbers of Chinese ready to become other peoples been so great as during the 20th century. Never before has there been the perception that Chinese civilization itself was being threatened. What the story in this volume brings to the fore is that the unique challenge of global modernization has changed the conditions under which Chinese people move out of China and move back in again. This has also ensured that the impact of China on the world will remain strong. If the transformation within China is successfully managed, and its rejuvenated civilization greatly enhanced, all Chinese will look at the Chinese diaspora depicted here with different eyes. They will see that many people of Chinese descent have made significant contributions to the countries in which they have settled. They will better acknowledge that such achievements have been an inspiration to those who stayed home during the past hundred years or more.

Wang Gungwu

SYMBOLIC REPRESENTATION OF VARIETIES OF CHINESE

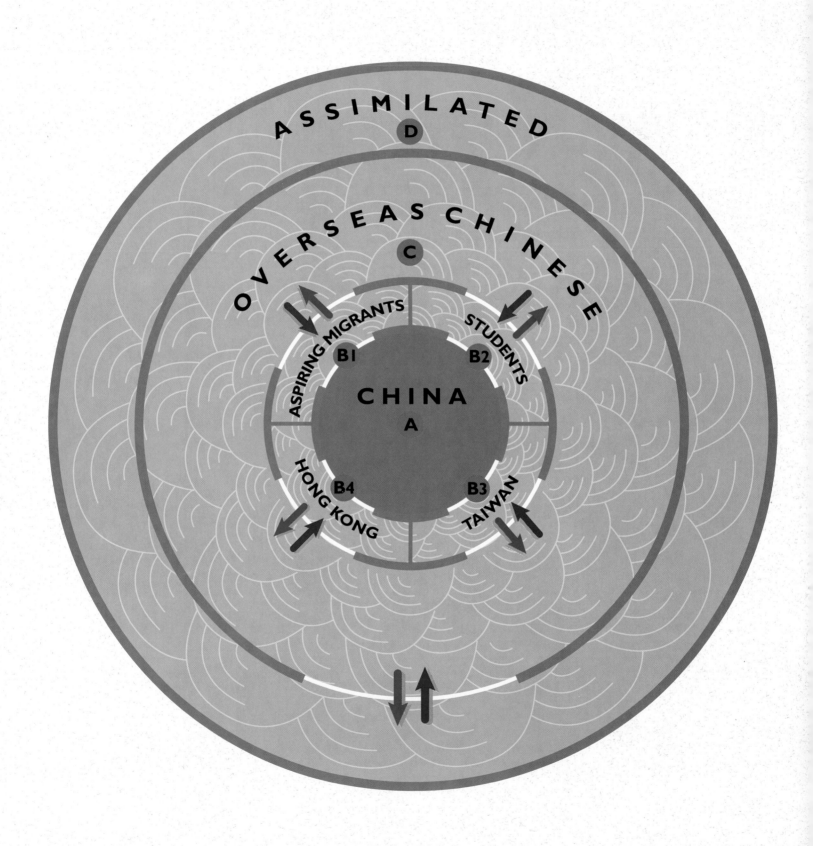

DEFINITIONS

VARIETIES OF CHINESE

Who are the Chinese with whom this book is concerned? There are many ways of slicing the melon of 'Chinese.' One way is to divide those who live in China from those who live outside it. The focus of this book is on most, but not all, of the Chinese in the latter category.

What distinguishes the most from the all? A first step in answering this question is to provide an abstract representation of all those who call themselves Chinese, one where varieties of Chinese are visualized in four concentric circles, with the boundary lines broken in some places to suggest a measure of permeability. As with all symbolic representations, the distinctions are not watertight, nor are the dimensions drawn to scale. However, they do serve as a guide to categories too often muddily described.

The innermost circle, A, represents those Chinese who live permanently in the People's Republic of China and who belong to the group of Chinese nationals conventionally designated 'Han.' Numbers of these may be temporarily resident abroad, as diplomats, representatives of China-based companies, visiting scholars and so on.

The next circle, B, is segmented into:

(1) nationals of China living abroad; of these, many are aspiring migrants who may or may not return to China, and who may, once settled and naturalized in their country of adoption, be assimilated to circle C.

(2) nationals of China studying abroad; many of these, too, are aspirant foreign Chinese who may choose to settle and become naturalized in the country where they are pursuing their studies – in which case they would move into circle C.

(3) Chinese who live in Taiwan and who think of themselves as Taiwan People. By no means all are exclusively nationals of the Republic of China; those who have acquired foreign citizenship would be better placed in circle C.

(4) Chinese who call themselves Hong Kong People. Subjects of the Hong Kong Special Administrative Region (and no other jurisdiction) would remain in B, but the many who are simultaneously permanent residents of Hong Kong and naturalized Britons, Canadians, Australians, Americans, Singaporeans and so on would more properly belong in C.

The outer circle, C, encompasses those unequivocally identified as 'overseas Chinese' (or 'Chinese overseas'). Examples of these are the so-called 'hyphenated' Chinese: Sino-Thais, Chinese Americans and so on; people who are Chinese by descent but whose non-Chinese citizenship and political allegiance collapse ancestral loyalties. If this book may be said to have a constituency, these foreign Chinese are it.

The outermost circle, D, involves those of Chinese ancestry who have, through intermarriage or other means of assimilation, melted into another people and ceased to call themselves Chinese. Whether they will call themselves Chinese at some future date must be left an open question, however, because it has been known to happen.

The 'overseas Chinese' with whom this book is chiefly concerned are those represented by circle C. But while one may focus on one area, to understand it in any depth one must be acutely conscious of the whole penumbra. This is why the diagram shows a perspective wide enough to take in all four circles.

Huaqiao

Unfortunately, not everyone draws the same lines around 'overseas Chinese.' The category is made murky by those who indiscriminately lump B and C under it, and also by those who translate the Chinese term 'Huaqiao' by it.

'Hua' is a name the Chinese have long used of their country, the character appearing in such compounds as Huaren ('Hua people' or 'Chinese'), Huayi ('Hua descendants' or 'people of Chinese descent') and Huayu ('Chinese speech' or 'Mandarin').

The word with which it is combined, *qiao,* means chiefly 'to stay away from home somewhere temporarily.' So far as the word's usage is concerned, that somewhere can be within China or outside it. Nevertheless, the name Huaqiao, 'Chinese sojourner,' is always understood as implying a stay outside China. This goes also for two other compounds of note: *qiaoxiang*, 'sojourner's home village,' or, more broadly, the homeland of the absentee emigrant; and *qiaohui*, the sojourner's remittances home.

Qiao is also to be found combined with the words *gui* ('return') and *juan* ('dependants') to mean 'former overseas Chinese' (Guiqiao) and 'dependants of overseas Chinese' (Qiaojuan). Guiqiao and Qiaojuan are official labels for people who live in China but whose identification as a category for purposes of policy-making is bound up with residence abroad.

'Huaqiao,' a term dating from the late 19th century, can be considered with or without its heavy emotional semantic freight. With it, the term is nuanced in ways not completely captured by its English rendering of 'Chinese sojourner.' For one who has left China for good and become a foreign subject, the term 'Chinese sojourner,' with its suggestion of transience, is clearly not the happiest. But it is the one which, until its usage was formally narrowed in 1957, China was using for *all* Chinese abroad from the 1910s onwards. What makes the term all the more unhappy is its implication that all Chinese were part of the Chinese nation, that remaining Chinese mattered, and that a special relationship existed between China and the overseas Chinese.

Without its semantic freight, it means, according to the definitions China proclaimed in 1957 and 1984, a citizen of the People's Republic of China resident abroad – one of those to be found in the segment designated 'aspiring migrants,' in other words. In principle, the government in Taiwan, by contrast, continues to see a special relationship between itself and foreign Chinese.

A Huaqiao is distinguished in official labelling and attendant administrative policies from a Tongbao ('consanguine'), a term normally rendered as 'Compatriot' and commonly prefaced by either 'Taiwan' or 'Gang-Ao' ('Hong Kong-Macao').

Nanyang Chinese

Nanyang, the literal rendering of which is 'Southern Ocean,' is the Chinese term for what we now call Southeast Asia. But the two are not exact equivalents. 'Nanyang' used to mean the region immediately to the south of China, which includes the Philippines, the Dutch East Indies, Malaya and Borneo, Siam, Indochina, Burma, and sometimes even Ceylon and India. But when one speaks of the Nanyang Chinese today, one has in mind Chinese settled in Malaysia, Singapore, the Philippines and Indonesia – places reached by sea, in other words, specifically the South China Sea. One does not, on the whole, mean those Chinese who moved overland to Vietnam, Laos, Cambodia, Burma and Thailand from neighbouring Chinese provinces at various points in history.

DIASPORA

The terms for the people with whom this book is concerned seem to come only in degrees of badness. As if 'overseas Chinese' and 'Huaqiao' were not troublesome enough, there is 'diaspora.'

Surely, some analysts say, it is unwise to call the overseas Chinese the 'Chinese diaspora,' when the word 'diaspora,' meaning 'dispersal' in Greek, has been reserved historically for the Armenian, Greek and, in particular, the Jewish communities settled outside their original homelands? Yet, just as surely, since the 1990s many scholars have been tearing down the intellectual fences surrounding the term, and to describe African Caribbean people, Italians, Indians and many others as people 'in diaspora' is no longer to make an *outré* generalization.

One who understood the word in its broad sense long before the call came to free it from its Jewish trappings was the historian Arnold Toynbee. A question he posed in his monumental *A Study of History* was: in what chunks, if not in units of nation-state, should he look at mankind's history? The 'intelligible unit of study,' he concluded, was civilization, and the 'models' for histories of civilizations, he went on to say, were the Hellenic, the Chinese and the Jewish. The Jewish community, he wrote, was only the most famous specimen of a more comprehensive genus: the diaspora-type of community represented also by, among others, the Scots, the Lebanese, the Parsees and the Chinese. Indeed, he extended the expression 'global diasporan community' even to people held together by bonds of common profession or concern – to the world's physicists, say, or the world's musicians. And he suggested that such worldwide diasporas, rather than national states, are the wave of the future.

GREATER CHINA

The term has been used with varying degrees of imprecision by journalists, academics and pundits. Some have taken it to mean the 'South China–Hong Kong–Taiwan Economic Circle,' an economically integrated area lumping the 150 million inhabitants of Hong Kong, Macao, Taiwan and the southern coastal provinces of Guangdong and Fujian. (By the two commonly employed touchstones of bilateral trade and investment, these places have indeed achieved a high degree of economic integration.) Other commentators have used it of a larger entity, a future China enfolding Hong Kong, Macao and Taiwan. An idea more grandiose is that of Greater China as a transnational 'Chinese business circle' embracing all 'ethnic Chinese,' both within and outside China. This raises fears of Chinese expansionism and evokes suspicions about the loyalties of overseas Chinese towards their countries of residence.

Another conception of transnational Chinese integration is cultural rather than economic or political. Here the chief proponent is the scholar Tu Wei-ming, who defines the membership of what he calls a global 'Cultural China' as comprising not only all those of Chinese descent but also non-Chinese 'scholars, teachers, journalists, industrialists, traders, entrepreneurs and writers, who try to understand China intellectually and bring their conceptions of China to their own linguistic communities.'

GENERATIONS

In theory, immigrants to a country are 'first generation' if they are born in the home country. Children born to them in the destination country are 'second generation,' while their children's children are 'third generation.' In practice, and in the case of the Chinese, the matter of generations is somewhat more complicated. It being common for Chinese emigrants to maintain wives and families at their native place, to which they would return from time to time, a Chinese family may have been established in the destination country for generations and yet be made up entirely of members born in China.

ORIGINS

Chinese
South China Chinese
South China Chinese from Guangdong
South China Chinese from Cantonese-speaking area of Guangdong
South China Chinese from Siyi-dialect area of Cantonese-speaking area of Guangdong

In a sequence like this, we see how a person's origin can proceed from the general to the particular. We begin with China as a whole, then move to a particular region and onward to a particular speech area within that region. The final steps take us into the domain of local and sub-local identity.

For many Chinese pondering their origins, 'China' is too great a generality. Staggering in the length of its recorded history, it is also mammoth in size and population. Something on a lower scale of inclusiveness is necessary. For the bulk of the world's overseas Chinese, that something boils down to coastal South China. In this section we consider Fujian, Guangdong, Hainan and Zhejiang as places of overseas Chinese origin.

For each of the first three, themselves large enough areas to warrant subdivision, we select certain component localities for closer focus.

Places of emigrant origin are distinctive by virtue of the mansions which native families build to advertise their members' overseas success. Thus Longdu, a Teochiu-speaking district in Guangdong province, is home to the 540-room mansion of Chen Cihong, the patriarch of a clan with branches and businesses in Thailand and Hong Kong.

ORIGINS

OVERVIEW

What does it mean to originate from China? An overseas Chinese claim to an origin in China is a claim that requires some elaboration, or refinement, because China as just a territory – let alone as a historical homeland or a source of heritage – can be conceived of in so many ways.

China can be thought of in terms of territorial civil administration. In late imperial China, the administrative ordering would have run from province to prefecture to *xian* (usually rendered as 'counties' or 'districts'). Today China is divided into 23 provinces (with Taiwan counted as one of the 23 and, since 1988, Hainan as another), five Autonomous Regions and four central-level Municipalities, namely Beijing, Chongqing, Shanghai and Tianjin. In 1997 the hitherto British-run Hong Kong reverted to Chinese sovereignty as a Special Administrative Region of the People's Republic of China.

Under the provinces come districts (*diqu*) and cities. Districts are divided into counties (*xian*) and towns and, further down the pecking order, counties subdivide into villages (*xiang*) and townships (*zhen*). What sometimes makes for confusion is that the same place-name could stand for both an administrative unit (say, county) and the capital of that administrative unit.

Such administrative divisions are clearly germane to the overseas Chinese who claim, as they often do, that their forebears hailed from Fujian or Guangdong, the two provinces that have produced the largest number of emigrants; or who name their native place of origin as, say, Putian (a county in Fujian) or Taishan (a county in Guangdong). They also bear on those students of history or anthropology who try to count heads and analyze information in ways independent of locality and find that, even if they wanted to, they cannot ignore the conceptual barbed wires that have grown up around the administrative entities. China is too vast a territory not to be broken up into local units and subcultures. The units and subcultures do not always coincide.

A second way of dividing China is along boundaries dictated by geography. The scholar G. William Skinner, for example, suggests that we would understand China better if we divided it into large physiographic macroregions defined in terms of drainage basins and economic integration. Each of these units, embracing parts of several provinces, experienced its own internal cycle of development and decline. Each had a central area where resources of all kinds (principally arable land) were concentrated, and a periphery towards which such resources thinned. Skinner's framework is useful to the study of mobility, to understand which we need to dissolve the provincial barriers into more inclusive entities, and to think of Chinese history not in national terms, nor in provincial terms, but in terms of the logic of the terrain

Map 1.1

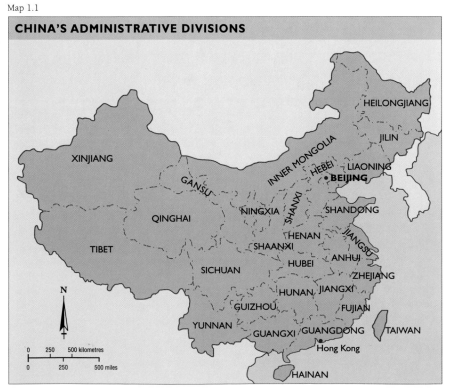

CHINA'S ADMINISTRATIVE DIVISIONS

Figure 1.1

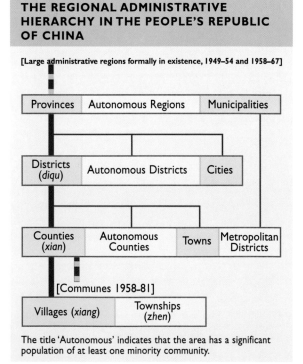

THE REGIONAL ADMINISTRATIVE HIERARCHY IN THE PEOPLE'S REPUBLIC OF CHINA

The title 'Autonomous' indicates that the area has a significant population of at least one minority community.

Source: Goodman (1989).

Map 1.2

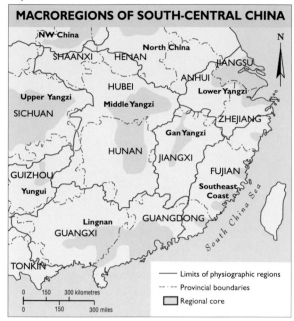

MACROREGIONS OF SOUTH-CENTRAL CHINA

Limits of physiographic regions
Provincial boundaries
Regional core

Source: Leong (1997).

and the economy. The administrative partition of space between Fujian and Guangdong provinces obscures, as macroregional boundaries do not, the regional systems in which some migration stories unfolded.

From the political, economic and cultural standpoint, the two most important macroregions are north China and the Lower Yangzi. But the two that mean most to overseas Chinese mindful of their origins are Lingnan, consisting of the province of Guangdong, minus its easternmost corners, and Guangxi; and the Southeast Coast, comprising Fujian, southern Zhejiang and east Guangdong. Lingnan is the drainage basin that includes the West, North and East Rivers, astride whose confluence stands Canton, the port city to which, before the advent of modern transport and communications, all roads in Lingnan led. The Southeast Coast includes the basins of the rivers that run from the Wuyi mountains: the Ou, at whose estuary stands Wenzhou (in Zhejiang province); the Min, with Fuzhou as its delta city; the Jiulong River system, watering Zhangzhou and Quanzhou; and the Han, with its outlet at Shantou (Swatow in the old Western spelling) in Guangdong province.

A third way of thinking about China is with reference to the traditional Chinese differentiation between China proper as the 'inner territories,' and the periphery as the areas 'beyond the borders.' The precise boundaries between the inner and outer regions varied over the centuries, but were generally understood to be those enclosing the Chinese heartland, where settled agriculture was the norm and people were Chinese. In the border zone, beyond the pale of Chinese civilization, lived non-Chinese; the demarcation was thus not simply geographical but also ethnic and cultural, and helped to give the Chinese their self-definition.

To name one's place of origin as China is to state an uncontroversial fact. But to imply by this that one is Chinese is less straightforward. For not all denizens of China are 'Chinese,' as that term is generally understood. One of the many different ways of dividing up the population of the nation-state we know as China is to distinguish ethnically between Han Chinese, the over-

whelming majority, and the rest. The rest is made up of Tibetans, Uighurs, Dai, Miao, Yao and about 50 other ethnically defined groups of non-Han Chinese nationals. It would thus be more accurate, if pedantic, to style the Chinese who form the subject of this book 'Han Chinese overseas.'

The areas where ethnic minorities predominate lie mostly outside China proper, away from China's heart. These areas form the last remnants of a history marked by the expansion of the territory settled or colonized by the Han Chinese.

A fourth notion useful in imagining China is that of core and periphery. In the Chinese tradition, Han Chinese people spread out from the civilized core of the Central Plains to the less fortunate lands of the barbarian periphery. Self-styled Hua or Xia, these Chinese tamed and absorbed non-Chinese tribes as they staked themselves out from north China, making 'barbarians' Chinese. It was a cultural transformation that, no 'right-thinking' Chinese need add, could only be for the better.

The ancient peoples of the Yangzi valleys lost their savagery early, but the barbarians of the deep south did not become acceptably Chinese until the Tang dynasty (618–907). This was the period when the number of northern Chinese flocking to the south increased sharply.

Women belonging to a non-Han minority in southwestern China.

To this moment may be traced the self-styling of coastal southerners as Tangren ('Tang people'); their home region as Tangshan, ('Tang hills'); and the dubbing of Chinatowns all over the world as Tangrenjie, ('street of Tang people'). This last expression is still widely heard, but 'Tangren' and 'Tangshan,' while not altogether obsolete, have an old-fashioned ring to them.

It was people from the coastal communities of southeast China, men living on the geographical and cultural periphery of the Chinese heartland, who emigrated overseas in the largest numbers. Indeed, the fact of their being peripheral is integral to the identity of the Chinese who form the subject of this book.

Being peripheral could come in one of several different ways. The non-Han minorities who inhabit Inner Mongolia or Tibet are peripheral in one way, while the coastal communities of south China are peripheral in another. What also distinguishes the latter is the fact of their being maritime. A difference of periphery and core is, to put it another way, a difference of coast and inland. The Southeast Coast and Lingnan communities lie close enough to the sea to have had a pathway to the wider world. They may be places on the fringe, but far from being on the outside looking in, they have long looked out.

Fifth and no less pertinently, China can be conceived of linguistically. Chinese is classified within the Sino-Tibetan family of languages, one which occupies a solid bloc covering the bulk of China, Tibet, Thailand, Laos, Vietnam and most of Burma. Speakers of the language

Map 1.3

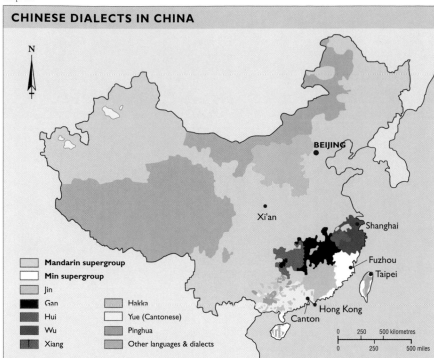

CHINESE DIALECTS IN CHINA

N

BEIJING

Xi'an

Shanghai

Fuzhou
Taipei

Hong Kong
Canton

0   250   500 kilometres
0   250   500 miles

Mandarin supergroup
Min supergroup
Jin
Gan
Hui
Wu
Xiang
Hakka
Yue (Cantonese)
Pinghua
Other languages & dialects

Source: Wurm and Li (1987).

Ancestral hall with tablets (right).

In another scheme, that proposed by Jerry Norman (1988), the dialects are divided into three categories: the Northern type, embracing all the Mandarin dialects; the Southern type, grouping Yue, Min and Kejia; and a type transitional between the two (Wu would belong to this type).

The linguistic diversity of south China is particularly marked. It is hard for a southerner to make himself understood by another southerner living in the next town, let alone by a northerner speaking Mandarin. 'Of all the officials of every grade who come for audience,' goes an imperial edict issued in 1728, 'it is only those from Fujian and Guangdong who when they speak have accents so strong that We cannot understand them.'

China as ancestral homeland

In earlier times, people did not move around much. They lived out their lives in one place with parents, grandparents, uncles and cousins either in the same hamlet or at the next bend of the river. They did not need to wonder where they came from or to be curious about their roots. Mobility altered all that. As people began to live away from home, so ties grew fragile and, in many cases, were severed altogether. Time was when we knew someone as his father's son, his grandfather's grandson and so on. Today, for large numbers of people, it is hard to put a name to every one of the four grandparents, let alone to all eight of the great-grandparents.

People who have left home to settle in another country are all the more distanced from their family pasts. And if first-generation immigrants are distanced, how much more so must be the second and third generations that come after them? And yet, against the odds, it would seem, ancestry continues to matter. The term by which most Chinese overseas may be described, Huayi, 'people of Chinese descent,' is itself retrospective in connotation, tracing a bloodline back to a Chinese ancestor. Historically, the Chinese have always distinguished their place of birth from *jiguan*, 'native place,' the latter being the home of their forebears.

Centuries of 'ancestor worship,' as it is loosely known in English, have left their ancient stamp on families. In the traditional Chinese home Grandfather or Great-Grandfather remained a fixture dead or alive, and the filial piety due to fathers in their lifetime was due no less to forefathers after death. As well as seeing to the needs of his parents and producing offspring to carry on the ancestral line, a filial son performed ancestral rites. The reverence due to ancestors extended to the place wherein the souls of the departed dwelt. Regular sacrifices were made at graves, and rituals were conducted in a shrine in the home or, if there was wealth enough to maintain one, in an ancestral hall on the family grounds housing the wooden ancestral

ancestral to the modern Chinese dialects have inhabited the northern plains around the middle reaches of the Yellow River since the earliest days of recorded history. In the centuries just before and just after the birth of Christ, these people spread by conquest, colonization and migration, carrying their language with them to areas where aboriginal languages were spoken. In the course of this expansion, the languages mixed and differences came to mark the speech of the north from that of the south, giving rise to local, mutually unintelligible varieties of the source language. These varieties, which are usually but not altogether accurately called 'dialects,' differ as much from each other as do the Romance languages of Europe. Yet they are all called 'Chinese.'

Of these Chinese languages, one stands out by virtue of the fact that it is spoken by more people than any other language in China – or in the world, for that matter. This is Modern Standard Chinese, which is derived from the speech of Beijing and which, whether it is called Mandarin, Hanyu, Putonghua, Guanhua (officials' speech) or Huayu, enjoys the prestige of being the language of officialese and the medium of instruction in Chinese schools almost everywhere.

Research by the Chinese linguistics specialist Li Rong has shown that, Mandarin apart, nine other Chinese languages are spoken in China:

Language	Main speech area
Jin	Shanxi
Wu	Shanghai area
Hui	Anhui
Gan	Jiangxi
Xiang	Hunan
Min	Fujian
Yue	Guangdong
Pinghua	Guangxi
Kejia	pockets of Guangdong, Guangxi and Fujian

tablets on which the names of the honoured dead were inscribed. Such practices, repeated generation after generation, conflated the bonds of family, home and place, and intensified loyalties to clan and village. The link between people from the same native place was all the stronger for the fact that their respective ancestors were buried in the same soil.

Ancestors' names were carefully collected in written genealogies, which set forth the recognized lines of descent of the family, or rather the family writ large in the lineage. The genealogical tables attest to the lineage's unity and continuity, its endurance beyond the transitory life of individual men. But it would be wrong to suppose that they have a utility as great as that of a telephone directory, for black sheep were apt to find their names and the names of their children erased from the tables. As Wolfram Eberhard wryly observes in his study, *Social Mobility in Traditional China*, genealogical records are no place to look for data on Chinese criminality. For Chinese genealogists as for genealogists everywhere, the temptation to cover up undesirable connections has been as hard to resist as the temptation to provide proof of superior pedigree or racial purity. There are any number of Li's claiming kinship with Li Shimin (598–649), the founding emperor of the Tang dynasty. And the myth to beat all genealogical myths is the tracing of Chinese descent to the pseudo-historical Huangdi, Yellow Emperor.

Many overseas Chinese have had reason to ponder the matter of ancestry because of their membership of the so-called clan associations, where people could fraternize with those of the same surname, if not of the same kinship group (see Part III). These associations kept up the fiction that people bearing the same surname are genealogically related, descended on the father's side from a common ancestor. Another thing these associations drove home to their members was that to forget their forebears was to fly in the face of hallowed Chinese precedent.

Several generations of overseas settlement later, and an interest in genealogy still persists. Cultural hangover doesn't explain it all. The reasons are probably bound up in complex and intricate ways with affluence, mobility, politics and the modern condition of worrying about who one is.

Cultural origins

An overseas Chinese who thinks of himself as Chinese may do so with a sense of his origin in China and of his having inherited bits of tradition handed down from the Chinese past. Tradition lives on in every society, and many areas of past Chinese experience have an ongoing existence in the present, not only in China itself but in overseas Chinese communities. What these areas are might stand a better chance of elucidation if Chinese tradition itself were *one* thing rather than several. Similarly, if Chinese tradition were one thing rather than several, we would better understand how these areas are transformed by modern challenges, by exposure and adaptation to non-Chinese experience and by their having been selectively and unevenly inherited in the first place, or selectively conserved or restored for economic or political ends. As it is, the cloth out of which

today's shapes were cut makes available many, even conflicting, options. Confucians, for example, may want to keep the supernatural at a distance, but anyone who looks into the world of popular 'Chinese culture' will discover an obsession with gods and goddesses, ghosts and spirits.

Those invoking 'Chinese culture' as an explanation for present behaviour may pick any one of a whole range of traditions which that culture flexibly makes available. They may pick something out of the Confucian world of thought and action, or alternatively choose some strain of Daoism or Buddhism or of various superstitious cults and practices that might claim connection to either of these two traditions, both, or neither. The imperial Chinese state, with its penchant for control and order, did not preclude its alternatives, such as violent and subversive popular organizations like the network of 'secret societies' that called themselves Triads, Heaven and Earth Society (Tiandi Hui) and many other names.

Hoary roots in the Chinese past have been cited to account for a particular habit or turn of mind today but also for their exact opposites. China's slowness to modernize has been attributed to the Confucian heritage; but so has the alacrity with which Hong Kong, Taiwan and Singapore have used capitalist methods to develop modernized industrial economies. Is it the case, as some argue, that different strains of Confucianism are involved, one predisposing its carriers to capitalism, the other against it? Yet to argue in this way is still to leave unanswered the question of why one strain should emerge and not the other.

So the act of locating an overseas Chinese's cultural antecedents in the traditions of China contains at least three question marks: Which tradition? Which strain of tradition? Why that tradition instead of all the others? Chinese culture is richly varied, contradictory and protean. Selected fragments may be used to build a new identity, but the new identity is not the old one, and to claim that it is would be a pretence.

REGIONAL ORIGINS

To say that someone is from China is simply to name the most inclusive of a succession of regional and local origins. These origins are nested one within the other. A native of Taishan, for instance, is simultaneously a belonger to Siyi (the so-called 'four districts' of which Taishan is one), and a man of Guangdong, the province which encompasses Siyi. He is also a denizen of the Siyi speech area, which is encapsulated within Yue, the language known in English as Cantonese.

Local origin and dialect (the two frequently overlap) define the boundaries between self and other, us and them. The Cantonese, say, have some sense of peoplehood, common language and heritage that they do not share with Fujianese or Sichuanese. More than just a place-name, 'Guangdong' defines an identity, connoting meanings far beyond its administrative and geographical referent.

Snippets from the rich cloth of Chinese tradition: the yin yang *symbol surrounded by the Eight Diagrams used in divination (above left) and the mythological demon chaser Zhongkui, whose image has been popularly fixed on walls in the belief that it will dispel evil influences.*

The idea of native place looms large in traditional Chinese consciousness. If regional origin was not the first or second piece of personal information to be asked of a Chinese by another Chinese at their first encounter, it would certainly be the third. A tombstone would not be a Chinese tombstone if the name of the deceased's native county did not appear on it. In China a person's native place defined him almost as much as his surname: one was a Lin or a Wang but, almost as importantly, one was a Lin or a Wang from so-and-so county.

If a person moved to a new place of residence, his bond of identification with his native place went with him. Any children and grandchildren born to him in his new place of residence would not acquire a new native place but would inherit the native place of their father and grandfather. Even the soul, goes a popular Chinese expression (*hun hui gutu*), returns to the native place. 'Home' was where one's father came from, but it was also where one returned to for burial. The dead, without any question, should be buried in ancestral soil, and tablets for them set up on the family altar so that their spirits could receive the sacrifices and solicitude of later generations.

Regional differences are inevitable in a land the size of China, all the more so for its being an agrarian society with rooted peasant communities and unmechanized transport until very recent times. Indeed, such variations have long been recognized by Chinese officialdom; the distinct 'folkways' of each region is a standard entry in officially authorized local gazetteers. A consideration of what it means for an overseas Chinese to trace his origins to China, then, should properly include a look at regional culture and history.

Speech areas

Language and dialect signal geographical origin and regional identity: to the question, 'Where are you from?'

what can provide a clearer answer than speech? To a Chinese sojourner abroad, 'home' or 'native place' may not be 'China' so much as the county or village in Fujian where Min is spoken – and not just Min either, but the particular variety or dialect of Min which he and his parents speak. In the overseas communities, too, the traditional divisions in the pattern of Chinese society have been nowhere more conspicuous than in those separating one speech group from another. A feeling of us versus them has very often been founded on an opposition between one local language and another.

Of the speech groups into which the overseas Chinese fall, the three largest are Min, Yue (also known as Cantonese) and Kejia (pronounced Hakka in the local dialect). According to Jerry Norman (see p 22), Min, Cantonese and Hakka were once more similar to one another than they are today and they can be regarded as having a common historical source. Norman calls this source Old Southern Chinese, a language which, spoken by the descendants of Chinese who migrated to the south in the Han dynasty (206 BC to AD 220) and before, departed from northern speech some time long before the 7th century.

From Old Southern Chinese, the Min, Cantonese and Hakka groups of dialects developed in different directions depending on their exposure to the aboriginal language spoken in the migrants' area of settlement and to the influence of the Mandarin dialects brought by new waves of migration from the north. In the course of these developments, the original unity of Min, Cantonese and Hakka became obscured.

Min is a 'supergroup,' varieties or dialects of which are spoken in Fujian, Taiwan, eastern Guangdong and Hainan. Min divides into eight subgroups:

1. Minnan (southern Fujian), also known as Hokkien, which subdivides into three subgroup speech areas:

* Quan-Zhang	Quanzhou, Zhangzhou, Xiamen (Amoy), Jinmen, Tongan, Jinjiang, Dehua, Taiwan among other areas
* Datian	Datian
* Chao-Shan	Chaozhou, Shantou, Chenghai, Jieyang, Chaoyang, among other areas
2. Pu-Xian	Putian and Xianyou, previously subsumed under the prefectural name Xinghua
3. Eastern Min	
* Houguan	Houguan, Fuzhou, Changle, Fuqing, Longxi, among other areas
* Fu-Ning	Fu'an, Shouning, Zhouning, among other areas

4. Northern Min
5. Central Min
6. Qiong-Wen, commonly called Hainanese
7. Leizhou   Leizhou Peninsula
8. Shaojiang

Map 1.4

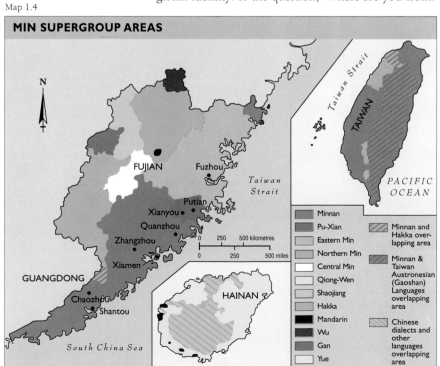

MIN SUPERGROUP AREAS

Legend:
- Minnan
- Pu-Xian
- Eastern Min
- Northern Min
- Central Min
- Qiong-Wen
- Shaojiang
- Hakka
- Mandarin
- Wu
- Gan
- Yue
- Minnan and Hakka overlapping area
- Minnan & Taiwan Austronesian (Gaoshan) Languages overlapping area
- Chinese dialects and other languages overlapping area

Source: Wurm and Li (1987).

Map 1.5

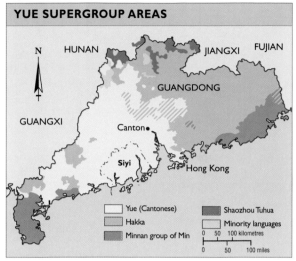

YUE SUPERGROUP AREAS

HUNAN JIANGXI FUJIAN

GUANGDONG

GUANGXI

Canton

Siyi

Hong Kong

Yue (Cantonese) | Shaozhou Tuhua
Hakka | Minority languages
Minnan group of Min

0 50 100 kilometres
0 50 100 miles

Source: Wurm and Li (1987).

Yue, colloquially termed Cantonese, is a supergroup that divides into seven dialect areas in Guangdong province, most of them in the Pearl River Delta and western Guangdong:

1. Guangfu (the speech of Canton)
2. Yongxun
3. Gaoyang
4. Siyi ('four districts')
5. Goulou
6. Wuhua
7. Qinlian

Hakka may be divided into these main dialect areas, the first four (1–4 below) in Guangdong province, the fifth in Fujian, the sixth in Jiangxi, the seventh and eighth in Jiangxi and Hunan.

1. Yuetai
   - Jiaying — Meixian and other areas
   - Xinghua — Dabu and other areas
   - Xinhui — Huiyang and other areas
   - Shaonan
2. Yuezhong — Boluo and other areas
3. Huizhou
4. Yuebei
5. Tingzhou — Yongding and other areas
6. Ninglong
7. Yugui
8. Tonggu

Wu, of which 'Shanghainese' is the best known, divides into six dialect areas:

1. Taihu — Shanghai, Ningbo, among other areas
2. Taizhou
3. Oujiang (Ou River) — Wenzhou, Qingtian, among other areas
4. Wuzhou
5. Chuqu
6. Xuanzhou

The speech groups most frequently encountered among the people who form the subject of this book are:

Super-group	Dialect group	Dialect	Conventional identification
Min	Minnan	Quan-Zhang	*Hokkien
		Chao-Shan	*Teochiu
	Pu-Xian		*Henghua
	Eastern Min	Fuzhou	*Hokchiu or Foochow
		Fuqing	*Hokchia
	Qiong-Wen		Hainanese
Yue	Guangfu		Cantonese
	Siyi		Szeyap
Wu	Taihu		Shanghainese
	Oujiang	Wenzhou	Wenzhounese
		Qingtian	

*Hokkien, Teochiu, Henghua, Hokchiu and Hokchia are the local pronunciations respectively of 'Fujian,' 'Chaozhou,' 'Xinghua,' 'Fuzhou' and 'Fuqing.'

It is clear that Chinese belonging to the same language group do not always share a common regional or local identity. Thus Minnan speakers (Hokkiens) from Quanzhou or Zhangzhou are often unaware that Teochius (the natives of Chaozhou, or Teochiu in the local pronunciation) are classed by linguistics specialists as Minnan speakers too. From this it can be seen that 'Hokkien' is more of a native-place definition than a strictly linguistic one. Similarly, the terms 'Teochiu,' 'Hainanese' or 'Henghua' define native-place identities. The only exception is 'Hakka.'

Hakkas

Hakkas, whose name means 'guest people' or 'newcomers,' are a speech group with a difference. First, while

Map 1.6

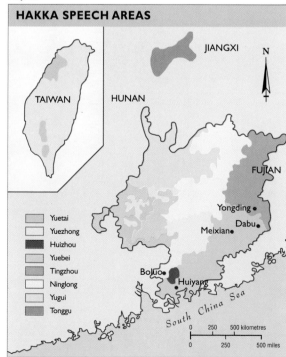

HAKKA SPEECH AREAS

JIANGXI N

TAIWAN HUNAN

FUJIAN

Yongding

Dabu

Meixian

Yuetai
Yuezhong
Huizhou
Yuebei
Tingzhou
Ninglong
Yugui
Tonggu

Boluo

Huiyang

South China Sea

0 250 500 kilometres
0 250 500 miles

Source: Wurm and Li (1987).

Hakka homes reflect the group's defensiveness.

Seal of the kingdom established by Taiping rebels.

Sea lapping the shores of many Fujian emigrant communities (bottom right).

other groups claim a coherent homeland of their own, Hakkas live with few exceptions in dispersion, as minorities scattered around southern China. Viewed in terms of the regional systems developed by the scholar G. William Skinner, they were a people who, alone of all Chinese groups, 'had no drainage basin to call their own' (as he puts it in his paper, 'Regional Systems in Late Imperial China'). Second, whereas no particular stigma attaches to the other groups, the Hakkas' lowly status in the Chinese social hierarchy has traditionally been a marker of their identity. Third, the Hakkas are sojourners and migrants *par excellence*, rarely hesitating to pull up stakes and move on to another destination, whether within or outside China. Fourth, the typical Hakka habitat is the remote, marginal highland or frontier, the peripheries of macroregions (see pp 20–21) other Chinese spurned: as a Chinese saying puts it, 'He is not a Hakka who is not on a hill, there is no hill but has Hakkas on it' (*wu ke bu shan, wu shan bu ke*). Indeed, when it came to opening up marginal hillsides and clearing them for cultivation, Hakkas were hard to beat. Land apart, mineral deposits and timber forests drew these itinerant workers travelling in search of work along routes in mountainous peripheries.

Every other piece of writing about the Hakkas describes them as having originated in the Central Plains, the historical heartland in northern China, as though other southern Chinese, whether Cantonese or Fujianese, did not also trace their ancestry to north China. The importance Hakkas attach to an origin in the core area of Chinese civilization is perhaps a way of laying a claim to a Chineseness which other Chinese groups have begrudged them. Indeed, some of these other Chinese have denied it to them altogether, supposing Hakkas to have been aborigines who had been assimilated by the Chinese; for example, textbooks published during the first two decades of the 20th century characterized them as non-Han Chinese, prompting a flurry of research by Hakka intellectuals to prove otherwise. Many Hakka writers perpetuated the group's 'origin myth,' including the dubious notion that the Hakka language was an extension of northern Chinese (rather than a variety of Old Southern Chinese, see p 24). Scholars such as Sow-Theng Leong and Chen Zhiping have corrected many

of the misconceptions purveyed by Luo Xianglin's *Kejia yanjiu daolun* (*Introduction to the Study of the Hakkas*), the standard work which, Leong says, is in fact partly 'ethnic rhetoric.'

Leong sees Hakka migrations unfolding in ways best explained by reference to economic upturns and contractions in the cores and peripheries of the Lingnan, Southeast Coast and Gan Yangzi macroregions (see p 21). Hakkas moving into areas occupied by the Punti (*bendi* in Mandarin), 'natives,' during a downturn in these regional cycles were bound to be greeted with animosity, and this would doubtless have raised their ethnic consciousness. It was where they came into conflict with the lowland natives in Lingnan that the label 'Hakka' first emerged.

Beyond Lingnan, the usage 'Hakka' was not heard before the 20th century. Instead, people were bracketed by the designation Pengmin, 'shed people' pejoratively named after the rudimentary style of their dwellings. Not all 'shed people' were Hakka, but the majority of them were. These groups 'seem to have been singled out,' write Susan Naquin and Evelyn Rawski, 'because they were seasonal migrants and escaped normal household registration.'

Hakkas are found today in parts of Guangdong, Jiangxi and Fujian, and in pockets in Sichuan, Hunan, Guangxi, Yunnan, Hainan and Taiwan. From the 16th century, they came to identify Meixian and its purlieus (formerly known as Jiaying Prefecture) – at the conjunction of the Lingnan, Gan Yangzi and Southeast Coast macroregions – as their homeland. For nearly two centuries before that time, this upland area was isolated from the valleys, and it was during this 'incubation' period, Leong argues, that Hakka adaptation to a marginal, hilly environment was completed. In the process they appeared to have borrowed certain economic and cultural practices from the aboriginal inhabitants with whom they shared their mountain habitat, the She. Certainly, like the She, their women worked in the fields and did not bind their feet.

Their exceptional sense of solidarity, a response to the hostility of neighbouring Chinese groups, may be seen in the unusual and defensive style of their dwellings: circular, multi-storey structures with hundreds of rooms arranged round a communal space and surrounded by a mud wall.

The brutal competition between the Hakkas and the settled Punti inhabitants for scarce land turned their villages into ethnically separated armed camps. Hakkas

who took up tenancies from Cantonese lineages in the 18th century lived amicably with their landlords at first, even in the same villages. With growing prosperity, they started to buy land and expand. Ominously and inexorably, hatred began building up between Punti tenants and Hakka landlords, or between Hakka tenants and Punti landlords, until all quarrels came down to the final primitive determination: kill or be killed. The climax of the successive outbreaks of violence was the large-scale wars of the West River region in the 1850s.

It was in the context of Hakka-Punti fighting, itself linked to a downturn in the Lingnan regional economy, that the Society of God Worshippers evolved (see p 56). Started by Hakka converts to a new kind of Christianity, the society met the needs of embattled, dispossessed Hakkas. It became militarized and grew into the revolutionary army that swept through China in the 1850s in the guise of the famous Taiping Rebellion, heralding, in the words of Susan Naquin and Evelyn Rawski, 'the greatly magnified power of ethnicity combined with religion, a power that almost ended the life of the dynasty.'

THE CONCEPT OF *QIAOXIANG*

Asked for his place of local origin, a Huaqiao (see p 16) was apt to name one or another of the places the Chinese call *qiaoxiang*. Literally 'sojourner's village,' *qiaoxiang* are villages with extensive and, until the 1950s, intensive Huaqiao connections and large numbers of Guiqiao (former Huaqiao or returned Chinese sojourners) and Qiaojuan (kin or dependants of Huaqiao). These communities are to be found preponderantly in Guangdong and Fujian. A typical *qiaoxiang* is Meixian (see p 26), where (according to figures published in 1957) Guiqiao and Qiaojuan were a third of the population.

There is no hard and fast rule for determining which is a *qiaoxiang* and which is not. One would go by the number of Chinese who have migrated abroad if such figures were reliable or even available. Statistics for returned Huaqiao and their dependants are no less patchy. But, for what it is worth, to the right is a map of towns and counties in Guangdong where, according to figures published in 1957, returned Chinese Huaqiao and their dependants were more than 10 per cent of the population.

In most cases, a high proportion of Guiqiao and Qiaojuan implies a high proportion of Huaqiao, but the fit is by no means exact. Look, for example, at the next map, which is based on figures published for Fujian in 1958 and where towns and counties are considered *qiaoxiang* only if the ratio of their Huaqiao to their population is above 10 per cent. Putian is counted as a *qiaoxiang*, but it would not be if the percentage of Guiqiao and Qiaojuan (9.1) were used instead of the percentage of Huaqiao (11.37). An even better illustration is Zhaoan, whose Huaqiao were more than 28 per cent of the population but whose Guiqiao and Qiaojuan added up to only 8 per cent.

Qiaoxiang are 'emigrant communities,' a term researchers use to refer to any town or village which, for various ecological and historical reasons, specializes in sending men abroad and which relies on regular remittances for at least half of its regular income. Though

Map 1.7

PLACES IN GUANGDONG WHERE HUAQIAO AND THEIR DEPENDANTS EXCEEDED 10% OF POPULATION, 1957

Map 1.8

PLACES IN FUJIAN WHERE HUAQIAO EXCEEDED 10% OF POPULATION, 1958

remittances can be domestic, originating within the country from, say, rural men who have gone to work on building sites or in factories in the city, the term 'emigrant community' is usually reserved for places with a high degree of *overseas* migration.

Places with a tradition of emigration range from the West Indian island of Montserrat, a sender of emigrants to Britain in the 1950s and 1960s, to the southern Italian town of Torregreca, the source of hundreds of thousands of 'guest workers' in Germany. Through 'migration chains,' fellow villagers or townsmen join migrant pioneers who have established bridgeheads abroad (see Part II). In this way, strong financial, social, cultural and psychological networks build up between the home locality and the community established by its denizens abroad. A chain, for example, links Jinjiang (a *qiaoxiang* in Fujian) with the Philippines (see below). For the first generation, at least, the overseas settlement becomes an extension of the home community, one having minimal contact with the host population.

At the home end, the chain focuses large numbers of people on overseas emigration. Indeed emigration becomes part of the very fabric of society. After the initial outflow, emigration often becomes routinized and the sending village or town switches to a remittance economy. People leave not for the reasons which

GUANGDONG *QIAOXIANG* ARCHITECTURE

Remittances and overseas savings find their most conspicuous expression in the houses emigrants build back home. A housing boom at home is a typical consequence of emigration, as is the adoption of architectural styles imported from the places of overseas settlement. This can be seen in the thousands of homes, schools, libraries and other public buildings erected in Guangdong *qiaoxiang* during the housing boom of the first two decades of the 20th century. Apart from using imported materials and furnishings, builders married local Chinese traditions (the residential quadrangle of the 'courtyard' layout; the circular-walled communal Hakka structure; roof tiling) to European forms and ornamentation (Doric orders, domed roofs, towers, pinnacles).

The aggrandizement of their own lineage apart, fortified mansions with watchtowers bear witness to Huaqiao's concern to protect life and property during times of civil disorder in the two decades following the collapse of the Qing dynasty. Secret-society supporters of Sun Yat-sen's revolutionary movement against the Qing dynasty, warlords, Kuomintang factions, disbanded soldiers, defeated remnants of Communist forces, brigands, pirates – each group added its quotient to the lawlessness. Overseas money paid not only for the castles but for guns and the policing of the home community.

1, 2, 3, 4. Named Lianfanglou, this house was built by the Indonesian Chinese Qiu Linxiang and his six brothers in Meixian in 1931–34. Despite the European-style façade, with its porches, arched balconies and window pediments, the house is structured in the distinctly Hakka way, with its front, sides and back enclosing a compound.

5, 6, 7. Built in 1930–40, this 540-room home in Chenghai, Shantou, belonged to Thai Chinese Chen Cihong. Its traditional Chinese 'courtyard' layout is combined with foreign window decoration, balconies and balusters, while local Teochiu wood carving and ceramic inlay craftsmenship went into ornamenting its eaves, door and window arches, and winding corridors.

8, 11. Thousands of homes in Siyi stand like forts against the looting and disorder that plagued the area in the 1920s and 1930s. Rich returned migrants were particularly vulnerable. These are among the 18 that stand in two rows in Nanhua Village in Taishan.

9, 10, 12. Named Fengcaitang, this building in Kaiping (erected in 1906–14) incorporates European tracery, Palladian motifs and Chinese brick carving.

13. The modernist Kaiping Huaqiao Middle School was built in 1933 by Kaiping migrants in the US and Canada, notably Wu Zaimin.

14. A Huaqiao home aspiring to be a castle in Kaiping.

Zheng Dehua

Japanese officials wrest territorial rights from Chinese delegates at Shimonoseki.

compelled the earlier emigrants, such as political strife or economic need, but because emigration has become a way of life. The shortage of labour created by the departures is filled, paradoxically, by immigrants from other parts of the country. With so many absentee men, emigrant communities typically show a predominance of women and children. The low birthrate, another feature of emigrant communities, gave rise in earlier times to the popular practice of buying or adopting sons.

But emigrant communities are not necessarily moribund. The men might be gone but, collectively and cumulatively, they send plenty of money back. Many home societies have a look of prosperity about them, with opulent modern houses paid for with remittances by emigrants who have made good abroad (see box pp 28–29). The anthropologist James L. Watson, who studied migration to Britain from the rural New Territories of Hong Kong in the early 1970s, reports that in the emigrant communities there, these homes were called 'sterling houses,' after the British currency; and that in India they were known as '*pakka* [brick-built or good] houses.' Nor is the money fuel for construction booms only, since many emigrants return for a visit or to retire, bringing their earnings with them to spend on goods and services at home. The community profits from their overseas members in other ways too – in the charitable donations they make and the investment capital they provide. The issue of overseas Chinese remittances and investment has kept quite a few scholars busy and still confronts us with its tricky problems of definition and calculation (see Part IV).

Returned emigrants and the families of emigrants fared badly as members of the landlord class targeted by communist land reform in China in the early 1950s. They suffered further discrimination during the Cultural Revolution (1966–76), when they were branded as spies, traitors and counter-revolutionaries and persecuted. Restitution, including return of confiscated properties, was made after 1979, the great turning point in Chinese government policies (see Part IV).

Emigrant communities in Fujian

Small as it is, the province known to many Chinese as Min, and Fujian to the rest of the world, is not hard to find in an atlas of China, for it is not tucked away in the heart somewhere, but lies instead on a perimeter. Indeed the fact that it is located on a periphery lapped by the sea is one of Fujian's chief characteristics, setting it on its path to maritime trade. One of those pithy phrases to which the Chinese are much given says as much: 'Sea,' it tells you, 'is paddy to the Fujianese.'

Then there is topography. 'Circled by mountains and girded by seas,' *jinshan daihai*, is another one of those Chinese clichés describing Fujian. Highland covers as much as 95 per cent of the total area, leaving little room for coastal plains and river valleys, and limiting

Tea pickers on the slopes of Fujian.

the average acreage. What added to the tiller's woes was that the soil itself was not all that fertile. Little wonder that down the ages, lamenting the pressure of population on cultivated land has become a stock comment on Fujian. By Chinese standards the population was not large, but it was certainly large enough for the size of Fujian: 7.6 million in 1749, 8.1 million in 1771, 11 million in 1776, 15.9 million in 1819 and 20 million in 1851. The distress of empty bellies may easily be imagined from such dispassionate data as the occurrences of famine in Fujian in the 17th, 18th and 19th centuries: 228, 158 and 101 times respectively.

New World food crops, brought along well-trodden routes from Southeast Asia and adopted in the 16th century, put taro and sweet potato on dinner tables along with rice, the age-old southern Chinese staple. In the latter Fujian was chronically deficient, as these two statistics will suffice to illustrate: the prefectures of Fuzhou, Xinghua, Zhangzhou and Quanzhou needed to import up to two million *dan* (1 *dan* = about 184.5 pounds) of rice a year by the early 18th century, as did 46 counties out of the province's 61 in the 19th. The rice was imported from Zhejiang, Taiwan and Southeast Asia – one more tie fastening the Fujianese to seaborne commerce.

Sea and slope: these are the topographical features which shaped Fujian's livelihoods. With the Taiwan Strait in front, and the South China Sea (Nanhai) and the East China Sea lying in an arc all around, the Fujianese came to be famous maritime merchants, known for their success up and down the China coast, as well as on the trading circuits of Korea, Japan and Southeast Asia. Merchant junks crowded the quays of their seaports – first Quanzhou, then Zhangzhou, Fuzhou and Amoy

(Xiamen) – where goods were shipped or trans-shipped to the markets of the world. As well as offering a vocation to Fujian merchants, the sea also gave a living to fishermen, shipbuilders and salt producers. By the mid-18th century, the China coast and nearby waters were providing a livelihood to at least 100,000 sailors and fishermen. As the provincial governor observed, 'The Fujianese on the coast are largely dependent upon overseas trading. When their ships returned, not only is rice available everywhere, but also money and goods fill up the shops.'

Looking to the sea one way, the Fujianese looked to the hills the other. Tea shrubs cladded the slopes of celebrated northern Fujian mountains like the Wuyi (Bohea Hills), and gave to the province a native product sought after the world over – it was no accident that when the Chinese word *cha* entered the English language, it did so in its Min form, *te*. Tea apart, the upland areas supported mushroom and bamboo growing, indigo, forestry, paper making and printing. There were also the kilns of Dehua, whose pure white porcelain, described as 'lard white' by Chinese and called *blanc de Chine* by European buyers, found markets far beyond Fujian.

One way of distinguishing the Han inhabitants of Fujian was by speech; this would set Minnan, southern Fujian areas like Amoy and Quanzhou, apart from eastern Min, whose denizens spoke the dialects of Fuzhou and Fuqing (Hokchiu and Hokchia in the local pronunciation). Another is by ethnicity. Fujian was home to the She, an aboriginal group of hunters and slash-and-burn farmers who tended to move along mountain peripheries. They had to share their borderland habitat with the incoming Hakkas, two of whose identifying

characteristics were mobility and marginality and who supplied the labour needed to open up hillsides and clear them for cultivation (see p 26). Men moving in search of work came from inside as well as outside Fujian. Migrants from the neighbouring province of Jiangxi were especially hard to miss, seen working as tailors and barbers in one county, and as carpenters, masons, bamboo workers, blacksmiths and tea pickers in another. All in all, there was considerable mobility in search of work and markets within Fujian. Many Fujianese went one further, and crossed over to Guangdong. Others went further still – to Taiwan, to Japan, to Korea, to Southeast Asia.

The island of Taiwan (Formosa) was part of Fujian for about 200 years, from 1683 to 1885. Inhabited by aboriginal people of Malayo-Polynesian stock, it was colonized by Chinese from the mainland braving the short 145-kilometre sea passage across the Taiwan Strait. An important intermediary port for Chinese trade with Japan and other Asian countries, Taiwan came briefly under Dutch rule in the 17th century.

During that period it offered a haven to the many Fujianese who travelled, traded and settled abroad in defiance of their country's closed-door policy (see p 58). Most of these were Hokkien-speaking emigrants from Quanzhou and Zhangzhou, with a smaller proportion of Hakkas (who became some 16 per cent of Taiwan's population by the 1920s). Much of the island was too mountainous for easy settlement, but its extensive alluvial lowlands to the west and south proved a great draw to migrants prepared to brave the resistance of the aborigines to develop rice and cane sugar production for export to the mainland. Migration accelerated when the island came under the control of the anti-Qing forces of Zheng Chenggong (see p 49), for whom it served as a refuge. The island was named a full province in 1885, and ceded to Japan by the terms – so disastrous for the defeated China – of the Treaty of Shimonoseki, 1895.

As an emigrant source, Fujian is second to Guangdong, its natives estimated in 1955 to constitute a little over 30 per cent of all overseas Chinese in Southeast Asia (3.7 million out of 12 million). The distribution of the Fujianese diaspora further distinguishes it from Guangdong: whereas the vast majority of Chinese in America came from Guangdong, Fujian sent most of its sons to Southeast Asia. In 1955, for example, Fujianese in Indonesia and Malaya were 50 and 40 per cent respectively of the Chinese populations of those countries, while in the Philippines their proportion was as much as 82 per cent. In 1986–90 they were said to be 55 per cent of all Chinese in Indonesia, 37 per cent of all Chinese in Malaysia, 42 per cent of all Chinese in Singapore, and no less than 90 per cent of all Chinese in the Philippines.

Although most Chinese abroad frequently take 'Fujianese' to denote Hokkien Chinese, the province is in fact home to other varieties of regional speech; eastern and northern Min dialects apart, it harbours settlements of Hakka speakers. Yongding, for example, is predominantly Hakka speaking, just like its neighbours Dabu and Meixian. Many Yongding natives have ventured abroad, taking ship at Shantou or Xiamen for ports in Nanyang or, in a smaller number of cases, travelling overland by way of the southwestern Chinese provinces

Yongding Hakka, Aw Boon Haw of Burma and Singapore.

of Guangxi and Yunnan to Vietnam and Burma. Arguably the best-known overseas Chinese of Yongding origin was Aw Boon Haw (Hu Wenhu). Born to the owner of a Chinese herbal medicine shop in Burma, he made a fortune with Tiger Balm, an ointment which became a household name in the Chinese world. Relocated to Singapore, Aw expanded into newspaper publishing and banking.

Within Fujian, *qiaoxiang* differ in the size of their emigrant population. A survey published in 1958 showed that of all the various administrative centres (cities and counties), Jinjiang sent the largest number of people (220,000) abroad. For this reason Jinjiang will be looked at more closely below. Then, we turn our attention to the sender of a remarkably large number of migrants in the 1980s and 1990s: the area around Fuzhou.

Editor

Jinjiang

Jinjiang, with a population of 951,900 in 1993, or 3 per cent of the total population of Fujian province, was designated a 'city' in 1992, elevated from the lesser status of 'county.' As a typical *qiaoxiang*, its townships and villages harbour sizeable numbers of Guiqiao (returned overseas Chinese) and Qiaojuan (dependants of overseas Chinese), the proportions of which in the local population could be as high as 50–80 per cent (it was 69 per cent in 1987). According to a count that year, Jinjiang County, as it was then designated, had 944,500 natives overseas, distributed across more than 50 countries or territories, but mostly concentrated in Southeast Asia, with the Philippines hosting the largest settlement of all.

In common with other *qiaoxiang*, remittances shaped the economy, enabling a large proportion of recipients to live without working and stimulating the growth of consumer production and spending. Furthermore, overseas Chinese donations supported nine-tenths of the 200 primary and five secondary schools in Jinjiang before the Communist takeover of China in 1949. Such overseas Chinese money as came in the form of investments was mainly invested as follows: in 1889–1918,

A steel factory in Fujian started by Philippine Chinese investors.

in pawnshops, 'letter offices' handling remittances (see Part IV), gold shops, seafood and cotton goods; in 1919–27, in transport services; in 1927–37, in electric power, flour mills, textiles, real estate; in 1937–46, in commercial undertakings; in 1946–49, in industry and commerce.

However, such industry as was introduced was small-scale and Jinjiang remained an agricultural economy right up to the time of China's 'reforms and opening' in 1979 (see p 58). Thereafter, Jinjiang's economy experienced a remarkable shift in the balance between industry and agriculture, from 17:83 in 1949 to 90:10 in 1992. This shift can only be understood in relation to the transformation of Fujian as a whole. Before 1979, Fujian was way below the national average in most economic and social indicators (such as GNP per capita, foreign investment, trade, annual wage, employment). Although the central government privileged Fujian by allowing it, along with Guangdong, to embark on market reforms and to open up to the world, the province, with its poor infrastructure, remained unattractive to foreign investors and these indicators did not improve until 1988, when the government in Taiwan began to lift restrictions on its people visiting and trading with the mainland (via a third country). Fujian beckoned to Taiwan as a site for relocating labour-intensive industries. And Taiwan responded to the privileges granted to foreign investors in the cities favoured by the government's preferential economic policies. Along the development corridor between Fuzhou to the northeast and Zhangzhou to the southwest, growth rates accelerated. By 1993, Fujian's GNP per capita, which was less than 73 per cent of the national average in 1978, had out-stripped the national average by more than 26 per cent.

Jinjiang, located in this development corridor, has been a beneficiary of this growth spurt, particularly since 1992. From rural township enterprises, it evolved intermediate processing joint ventures with foreign partners, whose investments amounted to US$134.73 million in 1992 and US$206.14 million in 1993. All this is reflected in the per capita GNP, which rose from 1,541 yuan in 1990 to 6,874 yuan in 1993. It is clear, though, that Jinjiang's new-found prosperity cannot be separated from Fujian's growth story as a whole. This may be seen even in the timing of the overseas Chinese donations Jinjiang received; funds for improving its infrastructure and public utilities, and for various educational, health and cultural causes began to increase largely after 1988.

Although Jinjiang's links to its emigrants have become more tenuous with the passing of the first generation, considerable numbers of Chinese of Jinjiang origin have come to visit after China's opening. Nor has the traffic been one-way. In 1993–96, some 20,000 Jinjiang natives emigrated, largely to the Philippines. But instead of settling there, many of them returned to pursue business opportunities in Jinjiang once they had acquired a foreign passport and established the right overseas contacts. Many relocated to Hong Kong for family reunion and business reasons; after the initial outflow, the rate of such departures has stabilized to about 1,000 a year since 1993.

Zeng Ling

Fuzhou

In their book on the Fujianese diaspora, Yang Li and Ye Xiaodun estimate that about 78 per cent of overseas Fujianese in the world in 1990 traced their origins to southern Fujian (Xiamen, Zhangzhou, Quanzhou and their environs). Fuzhou and its surrounding counties were a much smaller fount of emigration, accounting for just under 10 per cent. Why we single the latter out for discussion here, however, is that the post- 'reforms and opening' migration to the United States of rural Fuzhounese is unique: never in the Chinese immigrant experience have so many from a single locale moved so far by clandestine means within such a short period of time.

Between 1979 and 1995, 300,000 to 400,000 people found their way by some combination of air, land and sea routes to the lower east side of Manhattan and from there to individual fates ranging from persistent penury and drudgery to extravagant wealth (see Part V: The United States). Tens of thousands more remained in limbo, waiting in dozens of way stations around the globe for their chance to slip into the promised land, while others set out on their difficult voyages only to wind up back where they started from. And no one knows how many hundreds perished in transit or upon arrival, victims of disease, accidents and the violence inherent in the organized criminal enterprise which has facilitated this extraordinary passage.

In this discussion 'Fuzhounese' refers to the inhabitants of not only Fuzhou City but also the surrounding counties under its jurisdiction, namely Changle, Fuqing (better known in Southeast Asia in its local pronunciation, Hokchia) and Lianjiang, among others. Like other cities in southern and coastal China today, Fuzhou, with 1.5 million registered inhabitants and a 'floating population' (see p 47) of about 250,000, throbs with economic activity, part of the free-wheeling capitalist growth characteristic of Guangdong and Fujian as a whole. The scarcity of large state-run industry is not an accident but the result of a deliberate Maoist-era strategy designed to deprive a hostile Nationalist regime, a scant 100 kilometres away in Taiwan, of military targets. No small irony, given that the post-Mao industrial and commercial boom in the Fuzhou region has been fuelled in large measure by investment from and trade with the Taiwanese.

But Taiwan's role in the Fuzhou-US migration extends well beyond helping to shape the economic environment in which it became possible for individuals to undertake the journey of a lifetime halfway around the globe. Indeed, the connection to Taiwan has been at the core of the worldwide clandestine transportation network through which the traffic in smuggled human beings has flowed.

Relatively few of the US-bound migrants originate from Fuzhou City itself, the vast majority coming instead from greater Fuzhou and the surrounding counties, particularly Changle. Fuqing natives head for Japan (see Part V: Japan), while inhabitants of Pingtan Island go to Taiwan, both on smuggling boats owned and operated for the most part by Taiwanese.

The migration to the US can be roughly divided into five stages. Before World War II, Fuzhounese men, almost all seamen, stole into the US – virtually one by one

Duck farm in Fuqing, or Hokchia to Southeast Asians.

– in gradually increasing numbers. By 1970, they had established themselves in New York and graduated from labourers in Cantonese businesses to entrepreneurs in their own right. It was at that point, having accumulated sufficient capital to bring their immediate families to join them, that the second phase began, facilitated by small-scale organized migrant smuggling by way of Central and South America and across the Mexican border. The process of family reunification gathered momentum in tandem with the growth in scope and sophistication of the smuggling business, and surged exponentially during the years 1979–82, at which point the number of illegal entries dropped sharply. The reasons were simple: the original seed population had depleted much of its liquid assets in transporting their nuclear families, and the new 'seed migrants,' most of whom arrived in the space of three years, had not yet saved enough money to begin the cycle anew.

The third stage, from 1982–86, was thus another period of capital accumulation, with less than 5,000 Fuzhounese leaving for and arriving in the US every year. During the fourth phase, 1986–94, a series of US government policy actions related to immigration, several specifically directed to citizens of the People's Republic of China, coincided with the transformation of smuggling by organized crime into a worldwide, multi-billion dollar business. The result was a massive exodus of approximately 200,000 Fuzhounese to the US during 1991–93. The amnesty provisions of the 1986 Immigration Reform and Control Act, implemented over a two-year period, granted employment authorization, the right to travel and permanent residence to a large segment of the Fuzhou community in the US. Likewise, a Presidential Executive Order signed in the wake of the June 4, 1989 massacre gave the right of abode to Chinese who had arrived on or prior to April 11, 1990. Even many of those who didn't qualify managed nonetheless to secure a berth with the help of false or illegally procured documents.

By 1994, migration had again dropped off dramatically, marking what some analysts see as a terminal stage characterized by the arrival of older women and young children. Many villages in the Fuzhou region had by that time reached a kind of equilibrium, with up to half the population living in the US, and the rest remaining in China. (In one extreme case, Houyu in Changle county, as much as 80 per cent of the village population has found its way to New York and its environs.) While even a cursory tour through Lianjiang, Changle and Minhou leaves no doubt that there are still many people

'Resolve to put an end to clandestine migration,' reads a poster in a village in Fuzhou (top right). Opium den in Canton, 1900.

eager to go to America, it is likely that migration from Fuzhou to the US has begun to reach its natural limits. It is estimated that 15,000 Fuzhounese went to the US in 1994, and 5,000 in 1995, a fraction of the number in previous years.

The Fuzhou exodus falls within the broad pattern of Chinese emigration. Whether driven primarily by calamity, colonialism, world capitalism or the simple desire for economic betterment, once the flow of migrants begins from a given community, evidence points to a predictable dynamic rooted in family ties that itself becomes a powerful engine for migration. The Fuzhou emigration to the US appears to have been governed by such an internal logic, even as it has adapted to fluctuating economies and shifting government policies. The hopes of earlier migrants to bring their families over to their countries of settlement, frustrated for the first three decades of Communist rule by a virtual ban on emigration, lay dormant until a confluence of factors opened the doors to those seeking passage overseas.

At first glance, there would seem to be more reasons for rural dwellers to stay put than to pay a fortune (US$35,000 in 1996), risking life and limb, to be ferried to a distant and inhospitable land for the privilege of working 12 hours a day in a sweatshop or a Chinese take-out restaurant for years on end. Fujian's economy – and with it the general standard of living – has improved dramatically since the 1980s, while the governments of host countries have actively discouraged the arrival of immigrant workers. Average farmer income has increased several fold during this period, and is now dominated by earnings derived from private businesses and employment in township and village enterprises. But, as many locals would point out, it is only when the income differential between China and the overseas destination becomes 1:2 rather than 1:15 or 1:20 that Fuzhounese would stop leaving and even start to come back. In 1996, in terms of income potential for the average worker, one year in the US equalled 15 Chinese years.

While only a partial answer, this is the one most often proffered by those explaining why they have gone or are seeking to go abroad: to make money. What stands out on Fuzhou's horizon is the tangible success of those who have sent back enough of their earnings from the US to enable immediate family – once smuggling debts are cleared – to build palatial four- and five-storey houses that rise like advertisements from the rice fields at the edge of nearly every village in the region. Likewise relatives returning from abroad to visit or do business, whose occasional admonishments not to follow in their footsteps – 'It's too hard' – are belied by the gold draped around their necks and the US$1,000 mobile phones clipped to their belts.

In assessing their quality of life, dozens of migrants and aspiring migrants interviewed for this article take their measure not against the objective yardstick of a poorer past, but their subjective expectations for the future. Such thinking is not, of course, unique to Fuzhou – it is a hallmark of China in the reform era. But the ambition to improve the family fortune that burns at almost every level of Chinese society, restrained only by a sense of the possible, became one of the driving forces once migration to the United States entered that realm of feasibility.

Yet not all villages are equally big emigrant senders. The case of Luxia, a village at the outer edge of Fuzhou's expanding suburbs, is illustrative. A villager interviewed there, the 28-year-old Liu Keguang, had decided against going to America as of mid-1996, though he bought a passport and an exit visa in case he changed his mind. He chose to remain because business – a backyard rubber thong factory employing a dozen migrant workers from Sichuan and Jiangxi – was pretty good, and likely to expand. Very few of his 4,000 co-villagers, in fact, opted to emigrate, making Luxia an exception worthy of scrutiny.

The place is close enough to Fuzhou to profit easily from proximity to a big city. More crucial still, perhaps, has been an extremely effective Party leader who also happens to be the most successful entrepreneur in town. Independently wealthy political leadership does not need to rely on bribes for income and can thus genuinely serve common interests, which included, in the case of Luxia,

Map 1.9

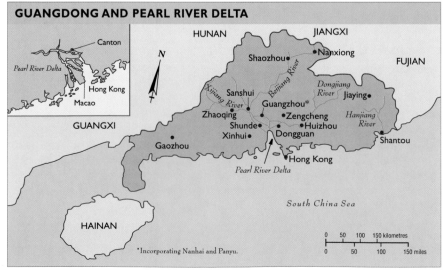

GUANGDONG AND PEARL RIVER DELTA

Source: Faure (1989).

building a new road to a collectively owned plastics factory. Moreover, two of the villagers who did go to the US travelled on the *Golden Venture*, the cargo freighter that ran aground near New York City on June 6, 1993. The fact that ten of its passengers died, 47 were deported back to China, and most of the rest were still in American jails three years later seemed to have dampened enthusiasm in Luxia for sending its sons abroad.

Luxia stands in sharp contrast to Changxian, a village just outside Changle. As of mid-1996, virtually every household in Changxian had at least one family member in the US – typical for the entire Changle area. One such emigrant is a woman who had, a year earlier, joined her husband in New York where he had been working for five years in a garment factory. In May 1996, she sent a letter to her family explaining that the reunited couple were looking for someone to transport – for a fee of US$1,000 – their newborn daughter to China so that the mother could continue working. Many elderly couples in the Fuzhou region are raising grandchildren whose parents are absent. 'If we had had a son, I would have been satisfied with one child, but now we will have to try again,' the letter continued, distilling in a few words another core motive for venturing across the Pacific: the absence of a one-child policy in America.

The fact that daughters marry *out* in China, combined with the rarity of retirement pensions in the countryside, has created an overwhelming incentive not just to have male offspring obliged to support their parents but to direct them towards maximum income-earning situations. Thus it is often parents who effectively send their adult male children abroad and undertake to borrow the vast sums required to do so. (This is also why most rural families in China are willing to absorb exorbitant fines or pay bribes to circumvent the one-child policy.) Working overseas is an especially lucrative option that happened, almost by historical accident, to be more open to Fuzhounese than some other regional groups in China who share the same imperatives. That New York is the address abroad, if not accidental, is certainly incidental.

Unlike Luxia, where virtually every household operates a factory (there are more migrant labourers from central China in the village than native residents), Changxian's 'only industry is overseas Chinese,' as some of the inhabitants note wryly. Its officials are also profoundly venal and consistently filch funds intended for collective use, according to these villagers. Corruption is also an important contributing factor to migration. Its obvious role is in facilitating Chinese citizens' organized, illegal exit, an exodus that the local government has very little incentive to stop, and arguably a good reason to tolerate given the vast amount of remittances flowing back into the region, US$100 million annually according to Changle officials. Corruption that takes the form of arbitrary fines, illegal exactions and outright violence by local officials is another factor pushing people to seek their fortunes elsewhere. Only when people-smuggling became an international embarrassment were forces mobilized to halt the practice, and half-heartedly at that.

Marlowe Hood

Emigrant communities in Guangdong

The sailor navigating the South China Sea coast of Guangdong province, at the southernmost edge of the Chinese land mass, comes upon an opening in the long shoreline and, turning northwards – past an island called Hong Kong to his right and a spit named Macao to his left – he enters a great estuary. This, the Pearl River estuary, he discovers to be the mingling of the North and East Rivers (Beijiang and Dongjiang), astride whose confluence with each other and with a third waterway, the West River (Xijiang), there stands the port city and provincial capital of Canton.

In the late imperial period numerous foreign countries and their merchant companies transacted 'China trade' business at Canton, where Western traders were allowed to erect their *hongs* or 'factories' (historically, a factory was a merchant company's foreign trading station) on a small strip of land along the Pearl River; in no other Chinese port, according to a decree in 1757, might they legally do so. All along the coastline smuggling gave livelihoods to many. Out of a variety of merchandise, one came to be the largest single article of commerce anywhere in the world: opium. Enormous fortunes were made by the illicit dealers on both sides, British and Chinese.

Canton is in the heart of the Pearl River Delta country, where a web of interconnected creeks and tributaries fragment the land into what seems like a quilt-pattern of polders. Nowhere in Guangdong is more thickly settled or richer in cultivated land. Studded with villages, in the late imperial period it came under the jurisdiction of two prefectures, Canton and Zhaoqing. Under the purview of the first came Xinning (later known as Taishan) and Xinhui, among other counties; while under the second, the counties of Kaiping, Enping and Heshan, among others. The world at large called the inhabitants of these places Cantonese, after their language. But Cantonese is a language with many local dialects, some of

Home of a Guangdong native who made good in America (top) and a township in Taishan specializing in sending men abroad.

Procession to mark opening of school funded by Taishan emigrant.

Banknote issued by British trading company in Swatow in the 1880s.

which are so different from the rest as to be unintelligible to speakers of the standard variety, that heard in Canton itself. ('Cantonese' is also the self-designation of most of the Chinese in Hong Kong and Macao.)

Shaded by camphor, pine and Chinese banyan, Guangdong was home to many products – Canton's lychee and *longan* being two of the best known, as well as the tangerine it introduced to the world. Seaward-looking, considerable numbers of Cantonese lived by entrepôt trade. Besides importing rice from Southeast Asia and exporting sugar to Amsterdam, Nagasaki and India, Guangdong sold silk, porcelain and tea to Europe.

In common with Fujian and Guangxi, Guangdong was once inhabited only by aboriginal tribes, remnants of whom – the Zhuang, Dai, the Yao and the Li – are still to be found in the region today. The southward migration of Han Chinese from the north, a movement which got into its stride from about the 10th century, resulted either in these aborigines becoming sinicized or driven into the highlands where they succeeded in living in isolation from the Han population and in preserving their distinctive speech and customs (see p 21).

Guangdong, then, was a 'colonial' area – that is, an area little inhabited until the Chinese came. Being intermixed with the local aboriginal groups both ethnically and linguistically, and therefore of only partial Han ancestry, Guangdong people assert their Chinese racial and cultural purity all the more defensively, calling themselves Tangren ('people of Tang culture').

The mix of peoples in the delta included Hakka migrants and also Tanka boat people. The latter, described as 'a tribe of Yao barbarians' by an 18th-century imperial edict, were brought into the Chinese fold by the assimilative policies of the Qing, but their name has continued to carry an ethnic slur.

One other group inhabited the coasts, a seafaring people commonly referred to in Cantonese by the rather derogatory term Hoklo, 'Men from Fujian.' Otherwise called Teochius (see p 25), they are Min speakers settled around Chaozhou (pronounced 'Teochiu' in local speech) in eastern Guangdong. Their boats were distinctive by virtue of the eyes painted on their bows.

Guangdong has supplied the world's largest number of overseas Chinese, estimated at 8.2 million in 1957, 68 per cent of the total. In terms of distribution, figures compiled by researchers in China for that year show that some 7.9 million people of Guangdong origin, or just over 68 per cent of all overseas Chinese, were settled in East and Southeast Asia. There they rubbed shoulders with many Fujianese, but they accounted for 99 per cent of Chinese settled in the Americas in the year in question.

Editor

Taishan

The main emigrant communities of the Pearl River Delta region are: Taishan, Xinhui, Kaiping, Enping, Panyu, Nanhai, Shunde, Zhongshan (previously named Xiangshan), Chixi and Baoan (formerly Xin'an). The first four are collectively named Siyi (Szeyap in Cantonese), 'four districts'; or Wuyi, 'five districts,' if Heshan is included. The next three communities, lying to the east of Siyi, are collectively known as Sanyi (Samyap in Cantonese), 'three districts.' The affinity of the counties of 'four districts' to each other cuts across administrative lines and rests on dialect, which is unintelligible to the people of 'three districts.'

Taishan alone supplied an estimated 60 per cent of the Chinese population of the United States in the 19th century, while the rest of Siyi sent another 20 per cent. The remaining 20 per cent hailed from 'three districts,' namely Zhongshan, Chixi and Baoan, the last two counties supplying small contingents of Hakkas.

Siyi, the pre-eminent sending area, is poorly endowed with arable land, much of the terrain being either rocky or swampy. Sealed off from the country on three sides by mountains and traditionally scorned as a remote and lawless place only suitable for exiled criminals, it has long looked to the open sea. Its denizens were among the first Chinese to have any dealings with Europeans – the first of these to appear, the Portuguese, occupied an island just off the coast in the 16th century. Written records also attest to Siyi natives' activity in Southeast Asia in the 18th century.

Siyi was inhabited by Cantonese speakers who called themselves Punti (*bendi*, 'native' or 'local') as well as Hakkas (whose number rose with immigration, until it was a third of the population of Xinning by 1850). The feuding between the two groups escalated into the protracted and bloody Punti-Hakka war of 1854–67 (see p 26). Eventually, intervention by the governor of Guangdong led to a truce and to the administrative separation of Chixi, a Hakka stronghold, from Xinning (Taishan). Chixi became an exclusively Hakka settlement, a sort of reservation segregated from its neighbour by a dividing mountain wall. The devastation wrought by the war formed part of the background of exoduses from Siyi.

Taishan took on the trappings of an 'emigrant community' in the last two decades of the 19th century, following the waves of emigration propelled by the discovery of gold in California – frequently referred to as *jinshan,* meaning 'Gold Mountain' – and the building of the American transcontinental railway (see Part V: The United States). Local records speak of migrants bringing money home from abroad to build new homes, while 'men working as woodcutters and tillers barely numbered two or three out of ten.' One index of higher purchasing power is the spread of market centres in the county, rising from 52 in 1821–50 to 74 by 1893. There, signs of a 'consumer society' could be seen in the proliferation of Chinese-style banks (*qianzhuang,* also called *jinshanzhuang,* meaning 'Gold Mountain banks'), jewellery shops, stores selling fabrics and

numerous other items, suppliers of building materials and so on.

Another symbol of 'emigrant community' was the ninefold growth in the number of schools, from only five before 1850 to 47 by 1911. Native sons who had 'made it' abroad showed that they were spreading their good fortune around at home through such typical forms of overseas Chinese philanthropy as orphanages, hospitals, assembly halls and *yizhuang* (farmsteads leased to others with the rental collected used for the relief of the needy among one's own lineage). The fashionable adoption of certain Western styles of clothing and food and some Western words further proclaimed the county's links to the outside world.

Remittances reached staggering levels by the 1920s and 1930s, while funds raised among emigrants paid not only for new roads and bridges but a railroad, the 138-km Xinning Railway. Completed in 1920, the railway aimed to capture the trade that normally flowed from Enping to the Pearl River Delta through Kaiping. The improvement of transport links by road and sea quickly followed, while the founding of successive market centres crystallized the growth of commerce.

Another thing overseas money paid for was a new kind of periodical, the sort that kept emigrants abreast of developments at home. The first to appear in Taishan was the *Xinning Magazine*, founded in 1909. Some 122 periodicals were published in the county in 1909–49.

Taishan fell to the Japanese invaders in 1941. Remittances were cut off, spelling destitution to many. Taishan experienced a sharp drop in population and untold suffering. Within a matter of a few years, deaths from famine alone numbered 145,825. Resumed when war ended, remittances amounted to more than US$14.2 million in 1946. A sizeable proportion of this money went into acquiring land. This proved a liability when the Communists took over and instituted land reform, and several thousand 'Huaqiao households' were branded as landlords in 1951 and expropriated. These households' 'overseas connections' proved no less a liability during the autarkic Cultural Revolution.

When ties were restored at the onset of China's 'reforms and opening' in the late 1970s, emigration resumed, with 70,000 people leaving Taishan in 1978–89 and thousands marrying Chinese of foreign nationality. Money flowed in from Hong Kong and elsewhere to renovate schools and hospitals. But the direct foreign investment coming in to start factories and processing plants had to do with the relocation of Hong Kong's manufacturing to cheaper sites in the hinterland and did not involve the old migrant connections to America.

Chaozhou–Shantou

To the east of the Pearl River Delta, near Guangdong's border with Fujian province, lies the second most populous cluster of settlement and cultivation in the province. This is the delta and valley of the Han River, at whose mouth stands Guangdong's other great port, Shantou (Swatow). To Shantou's north stands the city (formerly prefecture) of Chaozhou, the local pronunciation of which, Teochiu, is the name by which the inhabitants of the area, and also their speech, are commonly known. Today's Teochius are the descendants of people who started to migrate from the Quanzhou-Zhangzhou area in southern Fujian in the 9th century.

Administratively, the area at the turn of the century comprised not only the prefecture of Chaozhou but also the counties of Haiyang (renamed Chaoan in the Republican period), Chaoyang, Jieyang, Raoping, Huilai, Chenghai, Puning, Dabu and Fengshun. But administrative boundaries do not necessarily coincide with linguistic and cultural ones, and the last two counties, namely the Hakka-speaking Dabu and Fengshun, would have to be excluded if the area were to be delimited as a Teochiu homeland. Chaozhou was eclipsed by Shantou after the latter was opened to Western trade and residence as a Treaty Port (see p 55) in 1860. As well as funnelling huge numbers of emigrants from its hinterland overseas, Shantou rose in importance as a trading port, with shipping tonnage figures for the 1930s showing it to be China's third busiest trading port after Shanghai and Canton.

Portrait of Chaozhou family sent to relatives in Singapore, 1957.

Easy communication by water facilitated both external trade and overseas geographical mobility. From Shantou sailed merchant-migrants of an important Teochiu network, the Hong Kong–Singapore–Siam–Shantou trade. The earliest notable example was Chen Xuanyi, the founder of Hong Kong's first general import-export company, Kin Tye Lung (Qiantailong), the parent of the Siam-based firm Wanglee (see Part V: Thailand). Lineage members pooled resources and fellow-Teochius at home and abroad maintained trading relations cemented by kinship and native-place ties. A notable item of commerce was rice, imported from Siam since the Qing dynasty to supply Shantou's hinterland, a grain-deficit area. Closely interwoven with Siam's pre-eminence as a Teochiu emigrant destination was the fact that during the first three decades of the 20th century, more than 90 per cent of all Siam's import-export trade with China went through Shantou's port.

It was not only traders who embarked at Shantou but also labourers (1.51 million in 1876–98). A centre of the notorious coolie trade (see Part II), Shantou had 23 barracoons by 1872. Nor was it only departees who took ship at Shantou: return migration was voluminous, with arrivals between 1869 and 1934 numbering 4.15 million – a figure which, when subtracted from departures totalling 5.55 million, points to a net migration of 1.4 million. Returns exceeded departures in 1931–33, the Depression years.

As an emigrant community, the Chaozhou area received considerable sums of remittance money. If the years 1931–35 are any guide, they were a fifth of China's total, with 50 per cent originating from Thailand, 30 per cent from Malaya, 10 per cent from Vietnam, 6 per cent from the Dutch Indies, and the rest from other countries. Before 1949, nowhere else in Guangdong did 'letter offices' (small remittance banks) operate on so large a scale. A drying up of remittances caused by Shantou's fall to the Japanese army in 1939 resulted in staggering hardship among their regular recipients. While investments by overseas Chinese in the area petered out after the Communist takeover in 1949, remittances continued to find their way in to support home-bound kin. After China's switch to the 'reforms and opening' policy in 1979, the sums mounted, and that recorded for 1980, US$57 million, was the highest in local history.

Overseas Chinese largesse paid for welfare and educational causes. Shantou's first university, the foundation stone of which was ceremoniously laid in 1984, was built with funding by a single Teochiu billionaire resident in Hong Kong, Li Ka Shing.

Shantou, rather than the rural home localities, received the bulk of overseas Chinese investments, accounting for two-thirds of all investments in the

Building housing Hakka association in Malaysia (top) recalls typical layout of village homes and clan halls in Meixian.

Map 1.10

Chaozhou area in the periods 1889–1919, when such investments began; 1919–27, when they grew; 1927–37, when they peaked; 1937–45, when they dwindled; and 1945–49, when they started climbing again and then ceased altogether. Bearing considerable risk, overseas Chinese capital financed the city's first modern enterprises and public utilities; its waterworks and electric light company were started by a Japan-educated overseas Chinese, Gao Shengzhi, whose father had made money in Nanyang (Southeast Asia).

Public transport, steam navigation and rail were all developed with overseas Chinese capital investment. The best known of these projects, the Chaozhou-Shantou railway, involved prominent Chinese in the Netherlands Indies – Zhang Yunan (Tjong Yong Hian), his brother Zhang Hongnan (Tjong A Fie), and their cousin Zhang Bishi, who probably urged it on them. The two brothers were born in Meixian, and so were Hakkas; while Zhang Bishi hailed from the Hakka-speaking Dabu, and so was a Chaozhou (Teochiu) native if not a Teochiu speaker. The building of the 24-mile line, begun in 1904, was a troubled affair, with violent opposition by local inhabitants, who objected to its passage through their ancestral graves and to its Japanese construction crew. Eventually, the problems raised by the murder of two Japanese workers, the huge cost overruns and nationalist student protests were overcome and the railway was completed.

Since 1980, when Shantou was opened as a Special Economic Zone, there has been a resumption of overseas Chinese investment, 80 to 90 per cent of it from Teochiu speakers. While, among source territories, Thailand led in the first half of the 20th century, since 1979 it has been Hong Kong. In the 1980s, these two sources accounted for about 80 per cent of all foreign direct investments, followed by Malaysia and Singapore.

Meixian

The scholar Luo Xianglin reckoned that 17 of Guangdong's counties were purely Hakka in population and 44 mixed Hakka and other groups. Among the exclusively Hakka counties, Meixian, known as Jiaying

Prefecture until the 20th century, stands out, recognized by all as the Hakka 'capital.' It lies in an area generally referred to as the 'Hakka heartland': the 32 purely Hakka counties located in the mountains between western Fujian, eastern Guangdong and southern Jiangxi (see p 26). With a population of around half a million in the 1930s and 1940s, Meixian exhibited many of the environmental features Luo identified as being typical of Hakka country: it was hilly, poor, isolated, handicapped for trade by difficult communications and bad transport links, and it had mines (in this case coal mines).

It was a Meixian emigrant, Luo Fangbo, who established the Lanfang Kongsi (shareholding group) of gold miners in Borneo in 1778 (see Part V: Indonesia). Meixian natives were also among the pioneer colonizers of Taiwan. Population pressure was no doubt a triggering factor in emigration: between 1818 and 1847, numbers increased by 78 per cent, from 150,273 to 268,193.

Emigrants left via Shantou, but also via Canton, Macao and Hong Kong. Recruiters (*shuike*), with their knowledge of the logistics and procedures, helped overcome the practical difficulties posed by the county's relative isolation from the outside world. It was recruiters, too, who were entrusted with finding wives back home for Meixian men abroad – a practice common in the first half of the 20th century and encapsulated in the local saying, 'taking a woman to wife across the mountain.' The recruiters were organized in a guild started by an Indonesian Chinese of Meixian origin, Liang Jianmao.

Homeward investments were small, though overseas Meixian migrants opened five mining companies (the Xietai Coal Mining Company, the Yangwen Coal Mining Company, among others) in their native place between 1911 and 1928. During the Japanese war Meixian benefited from investments in flight from places in China which had fallen to the invading army. In the 1950s, property-owning Guiqiao (returned Huaqiao) or Qiaojuan (Huaqiao dependants) were adversely affected by

the agrarian reforms instituted by the Chinese Communist Party. It was still worse to be so labelled during the Cultural Revolution (1966–76), when having overseas connections was tantamount to counter-revolutionary activity, and Guiqiao or Qiaojuan properties were expropriated or forcibly occupied.

Following China's transition from socialism, Hakkas at home appealed to Hakkas abroad for investment capital of the kind other places in Guangdong and Fujian were attracting. Hakkas at home are noticeably more reticent about being Hakka than their cousins abroad, but the renewal of contacts with the outside world – with thousands of overseas Hakkas coming to China to look for their roots – has reawakened their need to assert their distinctive identity. As signs of a Hakka revivalism attest, the construction of such an identity is underway. Among other manifestations of this was Meixian's appeal for overseas funding for urban renewal, a Hakka folk festival and a proposed museum with a section devoted to Hakka history. Hakkaology, a newly named academic field, was launched in December 1989. Meixian hosted an international conference, conducted in Hakka, and used overseas support to upgrade the local teachers college into Jiaying University.

Zheng Dehua

Wenzhou, emigrant community in Zhejiang, makes everything from buttons to lighters.

Emigrant communities in Zhejiang

Zhejiang province, lying in the lower Yangzi region to the north of Fujian, has not been a major source of emigrants, but one part of it has been: the valley of the Ou River with its delta city of Wenzhou. Those who think of China as being divided into macroregions defined in terms of drainage basins and economic integration (see pp 20-21) would dissolve the provincial boundary and assimilate this area to its southern neighbour Fujian. Much of the surrounding terrain is mountainous, with

Blots on the Qingtian landscape: mansions built by returned migrants.

Family grave of Qingtian emigrant who had 'made it' abroad.

ranges to the north and south of the River Ou isolating the area culturally as well as economically. This is reflected in the speech of the Wenzhou region, which belongs to the Wu group of dialects but is altogether unintelligible to Wu speakers elsewhere.

From the most remote villages in mountainous Wencheng County to downtown Wenzhou's booming waterfront, the region is permeated by its overseas – mostly European – connections. Rural and urban landscapes alike have been transformed by remittances, export earnings and donations from wealthy overseas compatriots. The Chinese transliterations for European cities roll off the tongues of pedlars and pedicab drivers as easily as the names of neighbouring counties, even if 'Haiya' (The Hague) or 'Duling' (Turin) remain abstractions despite a steady stream of letters from the relatives who have made homes in these places. Almost every township has native sons and daughters abroad, even if only a handful of locales have become famous *qiaoxiang*, or emigrant communities.

A person from this region might broadly identify himself as 'Wenzhounese' when, at a lower level of territorial identity, he would be regarded as a native of one of Wenzhou's subservient counties (such as Wencheng and Rui'an) or, on an even narrower basis of identification, as belonging to Yuhu (which comes under Wencheng's administration) or Li'ao (which comes under Rui'an's administration). Wenzhou's history as an active port dates back a millennium to the Song dynasty and includes, in 1876, its forced opening to foreign ships and commerce, an event that engendered regular contact with the West even if concomitant trade was not on a par with other major entrepôts.

In the 1990s urban Wenzhou is famous within China as a beehive of small-scale entrepreneurship, one where tens of thousands of private and nominally collective enterprises dominate the local economy and attempt to corner national markets in products ranging from buttons to lighters to electric light switches. Physically isolated from the rest of China – the first-ever rail link to the region was not scheduled for completion until 1998, and its first airport opened only in 1990 – the city provides a commercial lifeline to a constellation of county capitals. And yet this apparent integration obscures regional divergence: between the wealth of suburban Wenzhou and the precarious poverty of mountain regions less than 50 kilometres distant, between pockets of semi-literacy and areas of ample access to education. There is, for example, little industry and even less agriculture in Qingtian county, a major emigrant source lying about 50 kilometres upstream from Wenzhou on the northern bank of the Ou River.

Whether it is in spite of or because of their shared isolation, the inhabitants of the region have ventured outside their home areas in exceptionally large numbers. Not only have some 300,000 Wenzhounese labourers and entrepreneurs sought their fortunes abroad,

Carving of deer and cranes from soapstone quarried in Qingtian.

another million have also set up manufacturing and commercial outposts throughout China, most notably in a southern suburb of Beijing known as 'Zhejiang Village.'

According to internally published official statistics, there were approximately 240,000 Wenzhounese and 60,000 natives of Qingtian living abroad by the end of 1995. Because these estimates are based on the issuance of passports and exit permits, the actual number is certainly higher, since many of those entering Europe overland by clandestine means do not bother with costly exit procedures. It is likely, then, that 5 to 6 per cent of greater Wenzhou's seven million registered inhabitants reside overseas, with sub-regional concentrations closer to Qingtian's 15 per cent and a few townships reaching levels above 50 per cent. If the total numbers overseas are underestimated, the official breakdown by destination country is probably accurate in terms of percentage distribution, and corroborates research by Chinese and foreign researchers indicating that 75 to 80 per cent of the overseas population live in western Europe, especially France, Italy, Spain and the Netherlands.

The saga of migration from the region to the West began in the 19th century. Local chronicles tell of a Mr Tian from Yongjia, one of Wenzhou's subservient counties, setting up a business in Germany in the 1870s. To judge by the epitaph on the gravestone of a Lin Maoxiang from Shankou, a village in Qingtian, one native, at least, ventured as far as America in 1888. At the turn of the century, no more than a trickle of traders and labourers found their way to Europe. The numbers increased from a handful to several thousand during the 1920s and 1930s, some going by ship from Shanghai directly to Mediterranean ports, others by boat to Port Arthur and from there across Russia on the Trans-Siberian railroad, which opened in 1904. In 1930 the Qingtian community in Europe was 20,000 strong, several times the number from Wenzhou. It was also, between the World Wars, more widely dispersed, with sizeable enclaves not just in France, but in Italy, the Netherlands, Germany and, at least into the 1920s, Russia and then the Soviet Union. Numbers escalated steadily until the onset of World War II.

One reason is engraved in stone – engraved, that is, 10,000 times over in pieces of the semi-precious soapstone extracted from Qingtian's otherwise unyielding mountains, and which dozens of generations of carvers have fashioned into landscapes, insects and figures from Chinese mythology. According to local historians, one day in 1884 a Qingtian carver named Chen Yuanfeng, employed at the time as a servant in a gentry family, had occasion to display his work at Putuoshan, an island off the coast of Zhejiang, where a group of foreign sightseers purchased some carvings at inflated prices. The promise of a new, lucrative market, the story goes, inspired a small group of carvers and traders, including Chen, to embark for Europe in 1893 on a French boat leaving from Vietnam. By 1900, enough Qingtian natives were making the trip for one of them to operate a hotel in Marseilles to accommodate new arrivals and a parallel business recruiting sailors for European shipping companies. It is surely no coincidence that the townships and villages closest to the soapstone deposits – Fangshan, Youzhu, Shankou – have consistently had the highest rates of emigration from Qingtian.

Two other factors fuelled migration to Europe during the early 20th century, one a natural disaster and the other a man-made one. The latter was World War I. In 1917 France and England recruited more than 100,000 labourers (see p 64) – 2,000 from Qingtian – to support their war efforts. When the fighting was over, part of the Qingtian contingent stayed behind. They were later joined by relatives, and by compatriots fleeing the second disaster, a drought in 1929 that wiped out a grain harvest which, even in a good year, only met a fraction of Qingtian's consumption needs.

The onset of World War II effectively froze further emigration to Europe, with many Wenzhounese and Qingtian natives actually returning home in the late 1930s. After the war, during the first three decades of Communist rule, what had been an increasing flow of out-migration was reduced to a tiny trickle. Most Wenzhounese arriving in Europe in the 1950s and 1960s came from elsewhere in Asia – especially Singapore, Taiwan and Hong Kong – or as merchant marines who jumped ship.

As the Cultural Revolution's mixture of autarky and anarchy yielded in the mid-1970s to the juggernaut of externally oriented development, a wave of pent-up demand to reunite long-disrupted families and to seek economic opportunity abroad was released. Relatives in Europe of would-be migrants from Wenzhou and Qingtian had already been abroad in significant numbers for decades, during which time many had started successful businesses and accumulated capital that could be used for the new migrants' transportation costs. The fact that most western European nations established diplomatic relations with China at the time of or before its admittance to the United Nations in 1971 also opened the way for legal, albeit highly selective, family reunification. Finally, the contiguous land mass between China and western Europe had a profound impact on the extent and nature of the movement, which grew exponentially in the mid-to-late 1980s as chain migration reached a peak even as European Union countries beset with unemployment moved to close their doors to foreign labour.

The added option of travelling by land, generally through the former Soviet Union, opened up the market for smuggling services to a much wider field of small-scale criminal entrepreneurs. It also made it possible for smuggled migrants to proceed in stages to their destination as immigration policies in Europe shifted – stopping along the way to earn money or, in some cases, changing plans and settling down.

Because urban Wenzhou has enjoyed an economic boom since the late 1970s, by the early 1990s very few of its residents sought to make their way abroad illegally; indeed, it has itself become a recipient of migrants from such inland Chinese provinces as Sichuan, Guizhou and Jiangxi. Those residents who did go went to do business more often than to earn hourly wages in a garment factory or restaurant. The income gap that once made European sweatshops beckon has diminished for urban Wenzhounese. But in the surrounding suburbs and countryside, the lure of pay cheques equivalent to 10,000 yuan per month was still very powerful in the 1990s.

Less than a dozen kilometres from downtown Wenzhou is the island of Qidu, a flat, dreary township composed of six villages all dotted with outsized and ostentatious tile and concrete houses perched at the edge of tiny rice fields and their drainage ditches. Qidu's out-migration started in the 1930s, and even though more than 50 per cent of its 7,000 inhabitants are in France and the United States – unusually, in roughly equal numbers – many still try to find passage abroad.

Likewise for Li'ao, another of Wenzhou's famous *qiaoxiang*, in nearby Rui'an. Though the township has clearly prospered, and enjoys the munificence of returned compatriots in the form of 12 kilometres of new roads, seven bridges, ten schools, a freshwater reservoir, a clinic and – appreciated above all by Li'ao's youth – a palatial movie

Deck-hands playing mahjong in coastal Zhejiang, 1987.

Coconut plantation in Wenchang on Hainan Island.

trade diasporas in the Ming dynasty but accelerating from the mid-19th century onwards, with annual rates reaching 10–20,000 in 1884–98. By 1856, Singapore already had an association of Hainanese sojourners, the Qiongzhou Huiguan. Outflows remained abundant in the first four decades of the 20th century, reaching an unprecedented total of 48,744 persons in 1927. The outbreak of the war with Japan prompted a rise from 33,000 in 1936 to 44,000 in 1937, with even greater numbers leaving when the Japanese overran Hainan. Still later, the civil war caused further departures.

Emigration rates were clearly affected by both domestic exigencies and external factors (see Part II). Natural calamities, even a fall in boat fare, could swell departures, as could an increase in manpower needs abroad arising from, for example, railroad building in Thailand in 1892 and the construction of a naval port in Singapore in 1927. As for the sex-mix of emigrants, consider 1921 North Borneo (now Sabah, Malaysia), where the ratio of male to female was 1,000:106. Today about two million Chinese of Hainan origin live in more than 50 countries, the bulk of them in Southeast Asia, principally Thailand and Indonesia.

Remittances from these overseas Hainanese made their way back to the native places through couriers (*shuike*) or specialized banks called 'letter offices' – of which there were 55 in 1937. Of their investments before 1949, the largest part went into real estate, Haikou being the preferred location rather than the places of local origin, no doubt because, as the provincial capital, it was commercially livelier and properties there offered a higher return on capital. It was thanks to the overseas Hainanese that rubber, pepper, pineapple, cocoa, palm oil and lemon grass were introduced to the island and commercially produced there. And overseas Hainanese donations have helped to build or maintain schools, libraries and hospitals.

theatre, it is taken for granted by the few young men between 20–30 still at home that they are Europe-bound. In mountainous Wencheng, Yuhu and neighbouring townships are poor, have virtually no level ground for planting crops, and speak distinct dialects poorly understood by urban Wenzhounese. Li Minghuan, who conducted fieldwork in Wencheng in 1996, was shocked to discover that Lishan, a small remote village of about 1,000 inhabitants, had 700–800 adult natives making a living abroad, most of them in the Netherlands, France and Italy.

In Qingtian, too, one is hard put to it to find someone of any age who doesn't have an immediate relative in France, Italy, Spain, Austria or Holland. By 1995, Qingtian had 60,000 of its natives in 50-odd countries, with another 80,000 living at home as returnees (Guiqiao) and 'dependants of overseas Chinese' (Qiaojuan). Material obtained from the local Overseas Chinese History Exhibition Hall shows that Qingtian natives are settled in places as far-flung as Ecuador and the Congo.

Marlowe Hood

Emigrant communities in Hainan

Once a part of Guangdong, the island of Hainan is now a province in its own right. To mainland Chinese, it has long connoted remoteness and backwardness, an outback to which criminals and officials were banished in earlier times. Development came late to Hainan, and it was to lift it from its backwardness that the central government opened it up as a Special Economic Zone and elevated it to provincial status in 1988. Rapid growth followed, attracting considerable inflows of migrants from the mainland. Officially, Hainan's population at the end of 1993 was just over seven million, with the proportion of Han Chinese estimated in 1990 at 83 per cent and that of the main aboriginal group, the Li, at 16 per cent.

Long a recipient of migrants from the mainland (Hakkas displaced by the 19th-century wars with the Punti Cantonese, for example, were relocated there by the authorities), the island has also been a source of overseas emigration. Its outflows began later than those of mainland Guangdong and Fujian, starting with small

A returned overseas Chinese (top right) and market in Hainan.

Foreign capital inflows from a range of sources, not necessarily overseas Hainanese, greatly increased with the improvement in Hainan's investment climate in the 1980s and 1990s. Among 1992 investors Hong Kong predominated by dollar value, followed by Taiwan, Japan and the United States. Some of the investment from Singapore and Thailand – which, among countries, ranked sixth and seventh – will have been by their resident Hainanese.

Almost all emigrant areas lie in the northeastern quadrant of the island. By volume of historical out-migration, Wenchang and Lehui (absorbed into Qionghai in 1958) lead. Most of the 52,117 Hainanese counted in Singapore in 1947, for example, were of either Wenchang or Lehui origin. Of 52 Hainanese questioned in Labuan, Sabah, in 1970, 62 per cent traced their local origin to Wenchang, the rest to Haikou, Qiongshan, Wanning and Danxian. Similarly, of the 103 Hainanese questioned in Sabah's capital Kota Kinabalu, 59 per cent were found to have originated in Lehui and 27 per cent in Wenchang.

Almost every one of the 22 townships administratively embraced by Wenchang has sent people overseas. The *qiaoxiang* of *qiaoxiang* is Huiwen Township, whose returned Huaqiao and Huaqiao dependants number some 25,660 people, amounting to nearly 92 per cent of a total population of 28,000. Prospective emigrants embarked at the port of Qinglan, either sailing by steamship directly to their Southeast Asian destinations, or alternatively trans-shipping at Haikou, Zhanjiang or Hong Kong.

More than 98 per cent of Wenchang's population was rural before 1949, though urbanization has since risen, and 1990 figures put the proportions of rural and urban population at 81 and 12.8 per cent respectively. Wenchang has long experienced grain shortage, which has been aggravated by typhoons and drought and has had to be offset by imported Thai rice. However, Wenchang is China's prime producer of coconut, one of a range of tropical plantation crops – rubber, pepper and coffee – which overseas Hainanese have had a hand in developing.

With its scenic attractions, Wenchang has benefited from the local government's keenness to develop the tourist industry; and hotels, karaoke bars and resort facilities have been built with Thai, Malaysian and Singaporean money. Overseas Chinese money is also evident in a new 'Huaqiao street' in a commercial area in Huiwen Township. One of three thoroughfares in this centre, it boasts more than 100 shops and 20 eating places, the majority of which represent overseas Chinese investments. Just the names some of these establishments bear are suggestive – Huaqiao Hotel, Nanyang Garden, Singapore Teahouse, Xingzhou ('Singapore') Store, and so on.

A tract of what used to be wasteland in Wenchang harbours a 'Huaqiao state farm,' one of China's many receiving stations for overseas Chinese expelled from their host countries. About half of the 2,000-odd Huaqiao came from Indochina. They live by afforestation; by growing padi, peanuts, sugar cane and coconut; raising pigs and, since 1989, farming freshwater fish with the help of a grant from the United Nations High Commissioner for Refugees.

As a *qiaoxiang*, next to Wenchang in importance is Qionghai, a county with emigrants scattered in 28 countries, principally Singapore, Malaysia, Indonesia and Thailand, in that order. Its 181,936 returned Huaqiao and Huaqiao dependants were 44.3 per cent of its total population in 1990. It has a 'Huaqiao farm,' set up in Bincunshan in 1960, for those expelled from Indonesia and Vietnam.

Leather factory in Qionghai county.

From 1859, local opera troupes began to perform in Southeast Asia, and a renowned singer, Li Fenglan, became the first woman to emigrate from Qionghai when, after travelling with a troupe, she decided to settle in Southeast Asia. There were Qionghai natives among the 8,319 people of Hainan origin counted in Singapore in 1881, but it was in the first four decades of the 20th century that emigration developed momentum. Many of those who left for Southeast Asia between the end of the 1920s and beginning of the 1930s were revolutionaries fleeing the country. In the civil war period of the 1940s, many left to escape conscription. After 1949, small numbers left to be united with their families abroad; such departures increased from 1980.

Qionghai is overwhelmingly agricultural. It was Huaqiao from Malaysia who introduced tropical crops like rubber and pepper. Today, overseas Hainanese are involved in developing profitable agriculture. In 1994, for example, the Malaysian Chinese Chen Yeliang and fellow investors started an agricultural development company, introducing new technology and new varieties of pea, bamboo shoot and other economic crops from Europe and America. There is Malaysian and Singaporean Chinese investment also in the light industrial sector, including food processing, and in services, including particularly hotels.

Choi Kwai Keong

Logo of Qiongzhou (Hainan) Huiguan in Singapore.

Border regions

Whether a pioneer pushed north, south, east or west, if he travelled by land he would sooner or later arrive at an extremity. In the story of Chinese migration the most important of these extremities have been Manchuria in the northeast and Yunnan province in the southwest. Proximity to Russian territories in the one case, and to mainland Southeast Asia (Burma, Cambodia, Laos and Vietnam) in the other, has made these regions places of frontier ambiguity, with fluid populations and a mingling of sojourning peoples, languages, customs and currency. As the overland channels of trade with their neighbouring nations, they have also been the borderlands of migrant seepage.

However, by and large they are not the places meant when the terms 'emigrant community' or 'sending society' are used. In the story of Chinese movement beyond national borders, migration across land frontiers has been but a sub-plot.

Editor

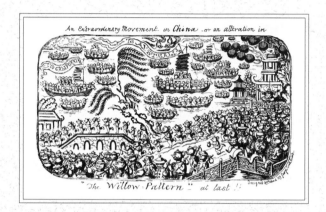

An Extraordinary Movement in China or an alteration in

"The Willow Pattern" at last!

PART II

MIGRATION

THE PEOPLING OF THE AMERICAS and Australasia, the Vietnamese push into Cham and Khmer territory, transfers of people to colonize the Chinese empire's frontier territories – these are all migration stories. Clearly migration comes in many kinds, from the mass movement of whole tribes in ancient times to the seasonal sojourning of traders and labourers.

We begin by briefly considering internal movements within China, then turn to cross-border migration overseas. Emigration is a concomitant of economic, social and political changes; and we look at the concatenation of these in China and the world at large in order to arrive at an understanding of the contexts in which the history of Chinese migration has been enacted.

This calls for a study of the different types of migrant, from the sojourning trader and the indentured labourer to the cosmopolitan entrepreneur and student-turned-settler.

The phrase 'an extraordinary movement' on this engraving (published in the Comic Almanack *in 1853 by George Cruikshank, the best-known British caricaturist of his time) is an apt description of the waves of migration that crested with the high tide of European imperialism, taking the Chinese far from their homeland.*

MIGRATION

MIGRATION IN CHINA

A distinction has often been made between internal and international migration. The migration undergone by the Chinese with whom this book is chiefly concerned is of the latter type; in other words, theirs was a move abroad from Chinese soil. The distinction is useful so far as it goes, but stops us from seeing migration out of China as having aspects of mobility within China. Comparing the internal with the overseas reveals many similarities, whether it is a question of the social infrastructure of migration (migration mechanisms and associations), native-place identity or minority-majority relations. And in China, as elsewhere, internal migration is sometimes a first step to emigration.

In late imperial China internal migration, as Chinese scholars like Guo Songyi have shown, was related to declines in land per capita. The degree of population pressure on land, giving rise to the mobility of people within China, may be seen in one scholar's estimate of the fall in per capita cultivated land: from 4 *mu* per capita in 1753 to 2.36 *mu* per capita in 1812 (one *mu* is about 733 square yards). Yet land shortage cannot be isolated from the other forces setting migration in motion. As Philip A. Kuhn observed in 1997, 'Studies of late imperial society now generally recognize the intricate synergy that moved Chinese society at that time: the interaction among population increase, commercialization, migration, and external trade. Both commercialization and migration can be seen as adaptations to population growth, and both provided the economic means for further growth. Silver coming in from foreign trade further monetized the economy, and the West contributed new food plants that made possible more migration and larger population.' Such a synergy was similarly at work in overseas migration.

Refugees from the countryside converge on Shanghai (top), there finding work as rickshaw pullers.

Colonization and resettlement

Flows of population punctuate China's long history. If not to colonize virgin frontiers newly opened for cultivation, people moved to resettle land wasted by calamities. The peopling of Chinese borderlands resulted not only from spontaneous migration but from conscious government efforts to relieve demographic pressure in the crowded Chinese heartland by encouraging and in some cases compelling relocation. Into these places moved soldiers, colonists and refugees. Some were exiles, deported to the far frontiers in accordance with the ancient tradition of banishing troublemakers to the outlying regions of the empire.

While they occurred in all periods, these shifts of population were at their most pronounced in the wake of military unrests and in times of widespread disturbance. Guangdong and the rest of the southeast coast, for example, were filled up by southward shifting migrants during the break-up of the Tang empire and the retreat of the Song from its northern tribal neighbours.

Sojourning

Migrants are people who change their place of residence. A migrant is usually understood to be someone who has, figuratively speaking, taken a one-way passage to a place and is there 'for good.' A sojourner, on the other hand, is understood to be a temporary resident who is at his new place of abode 'for the time being.' In fact, sojourners often end up by becoming settlers, as in the case of guest workers who stay on.

Consider 19th-century Jiangsu province, poor to the north and prosperous to the south, at whose sea outlet stands the great port of Shanghai. Not surprisingly, the north became a notorious producer of migrants to the south and to Shanghai. A flood or simply the slack winter season would see them leaving their homes for the south, there to cultivate land too poor to interest the natives. Others headed for the cities, lured there by the job opportunities ushered in by industrialization. Forming an underclass, they worked as coolies, pulled rickshaws, collected garbage and nightsoil, while their women migrated seasonally to find jobs as domestic servants. The natives kept them at arm's length, calling them 'guest people' or 'vagabonds' to mark them off from themselves.

In Shanghai, where population grew spectacularly from immigration, many newcomers arrived with the help of kinsmen and fellow villagers. Indeed it was native-place ties that chiefly shaped the recruitment and patterns of labour in the city. Single male workers would go home to their villages to marry, leaving their wives behind upon returning to Shanghai. These newcomers were not exactly people passing through, nor were they exactly transients, but they were not natives in their place of sojourn either. Shanghai was a place of temporary abode that was on its way to being a home. These incomers were sojourners, perhaps one day to become permanent residents.

'Sojourning' is a concept well served by the Chinese lexicon, which possesses many terms to express the ideas of roving, lodging and being away from home temporarily. Indeed the sojourner has long been a familiar figure in the Chinese landscape. As G. William Skinner puts it in 1977: 'The simple fact is that aside from the peasantry large numbers of men in traditional China pursued their occupational calling away from home; they were sojourners, and [the places] where they sojourned were typically more urban than the native places where they still maintained their residence.'

Skinner has described a particular type of sojourning, one implying the export of local skills and occupational specialities. A region's craft speciality might be reflected in the speciality of its sojourning artisans. Ningbo, a traditional producer of wood furniture, might export not furniture but cabinet-makers to the nearby big cities. However it might have arisen, a specialization encouraged the local people in the belief 'that they had a good thing going for them that was peculiarly theirs.'

Pursuing that calling away from home, in places offering richer rewards, was a 'mobility strategy'; 'the success of even one native son in a distant city could initiate the chain migration that eventually led to dominance of the occupation in that particular city.' The sojourner's continued link to his home community was important; as Skinner puts it in 1976, it was 'precisely because those who left could be counted on to return that a man with aspirations to get ahead could expect support from members of his local [community] beyond the limits of family and lineage.'

Examples of speciality exports are plentiful. Finding their *métier* in trade, Hokkien merchants hailing from southern Fujian exercised their entrepreneurial prowess in cities beyond their home region whenever local opportunities lessened. With each wave of emigration, Hokkien merchants enlarged their inter-regional and overseas trading networks and increased the number of ports where their trading firms were represented.

Another illustration is provided by the famously entrepreneurial merchants of Huizhou, in Anhui province. What follows is a description of how a boy from that area was groomed for a career as a sojourning merchant in Zhejiang or Jiangxi, but it would do just as well for a young Fujianese headed for Singapore or the Philippines:

When a family in our region has two or more sons, only one stays home to till the fields. The others are sent out to some relative or friend doing business in some distant city. Equipped with straw sandals, an umbrella and a bag with some food, the boy sets out on the journey to some place in Chekiang [Zhejiang] or Kiangsi [Jiangxi], where a kind relative or friend of the family will take him into his shop as an apprentice. He is about 14 years old at this time. He has to serve an apprenticeship of three years without pay, but with free board and lodging. Then he is given a vacation of three months to visit his family, who in the meantime have arranged his marriage for him. When he returns to his master he leaves his wife in his old home . . .

(Skinner, 1976, 345)

'Floating populations'

The packed masses in front of the railway stations in Beijing, Shanghai and Canton show these big cities to be very much at the receiving end of the migratory impulse bringing unemployed job seekers from the countryside. The movement of peasants from the land is an inescapable part of economic development – a development hastened in China in the 1980s by the decollectivization of agriculture, the opening of the economy to trade and foreign investment and the growth of non-state industry. Structural mass migration has been

'Floating population' seeking work in Beijing.

one of the genies sprung from the bottle of uneven economic progress. Such migration shows its face in the so-called 'floating population' of drifters looking for work outside the *hukou* or 'household registration' system – that is, in places where these people have no official rights of residence. In China, only movements to places where

Map 2.1

INTER-PROVINCIAL 'FLOATING POPULATION' FLOWS, 1985–90

N

Heilongjiang
Jilin
Liaoning
Xinjiang
Gansu
Inner Mongolia
Beijing
Tianjin
Hebei
Shanxi
Ningxia
Shandong
Qinghai
Shaanxi
Henan
Jiangsu
Tibet
Hubei
Anhui
Shanghai
Sichuan
Zhejiang
Hunan
Jiangxi
Guizhou
Fujian
Yunnan
Guangxi
Guangdong
Taiwan
Hainan

Volume of flows (in 1000s)

→ 50–100

→ 101–200

→ 201–400

0   250   500 kilometres
0   250   500 miles

Source: Chan (1996).

one has a permanent *hukou* is considered 'migration'; all the rest is *liudong*, 'floating,' or what Western migration specialists call 'circulation.' Published projections for the eruption of further surplus labour in China's countryside in the late 1990s spoke of up to 150 million in the succeeding decade.

EMIGRATION FROM CHINA

Contexts: 1100s–1910s

The story of Chinese overseas migration between the 12th and 20th centuries unfolds in a series of interlocking frameworks. No one framework alone adequately explains the movement. Although, for analytical purposes, we treat each context as distinct, it must be remembered that in 'real' historical time they interacted with one another. Nevertheless, the frameworks had different time-scales, beginning at different times and following different trajectories.

The first of these frameworks is China's naval, maritime and commercial development. The second is China's interactions with Southeast Asia. A third is the growth of Chinese population. A fourth framework lumps together events in the world at large, notably Western military and industrial expansion. The fifth flows from the fourth and is more narrowly focused on the European impact on China and Southeast Asia. A sixth context is China's domestic disruption.

Maritime and commercial development

Chinese migration abroad was interwoven with the comings and goings of traders. Seaborne trade and travel were inseparable. China's overseas trade hinged on the import of primary produce from Nanyang, modern Southeast Asia. As well as pepper and spices it encompassed a cornucopia of every luxury item from rhinoceros horns to aromatic plants. To conceive of this trade, one might usefully imagine two sectors, formal and informal. With neighbours like Korea, Burma, Siam, Vietnam and Ryukyu Islands (Okinawa), China conducted a formal trade through official delegations called 'tribute missions.' Away from the court, down by the coasts, local officials and private traders conducted an informal trade with foreign merchants.

Informal trade in Nanyang had its heyday in China's maritime age. That age began after the Southern Song dynasty was forced south in 1127 to Hangzhou and became more dependent on sea trade. The Southern Song was not a mercantile empire – no Chinese empire was that – but it was less land-bound, more in touch with the sea than any of its predecessors. The government created a navy, built harbours and sponsored foreign commerce. Shipbuilding made great strides, and China produced technologically superior vessels and larger fleets than contemporary Europe: the junks of the time were big sailing ships with four or six masts, a dozen sails and room for about a thousand men.

Inland, an enormous network of canals and navigable riverine waterways bore traffic of a density unmatched anywhere in the world. An identifiably urban character was already apparent in the cities; a commercial class

The pepper plant keenly sought by traders (top) and Southern Song battleship (bottom).

Ming dynasty coin (above right).

Zheng He's ship was more than four times the size of Columbus's Santa Maria.

had burgeoned. The growing sophistication of what would be called urban middle-class tastes today went hand in hand with an efflorescence of inter-regional and overseas trade. Chinese foreign trade was of course a function of the expansion of domestic trade. It was merchant venturing on land and sea that brought luxury goods and exotic merchandise into the homes of the rich; and merchant venturing easily transmuted into sojourning. There were traders from the port of Quanzhou who stopped abroad for the winter, for a year or even ten years – in a form of sojourning referred to in Chinese records as *zhudong* ('staying the winter') or *zhufan* ('residing abroad'). The monsoon pattern gave an annual and seasonal rhythm to long-haul navigation, obliging voyagers to tarry at their port of call, eventually forming colonies.

All this continued into the Yuan, the Mongol dynasty that brought the Southern Song to an end. Chinese maritime energies strengthened under Mongol aegis, given further scope by the Yuan's global ambitions. Great fleets set out to challenge Japan and Java. By such expeditions, and by virtue of the sheer span of the Mongol domain, Chinese contacts with foreign lands were markedly widened. There were Chinese troops on the expeditionary forces to Java, for example, who thought they could save themselves the discomforts of the return journey by staying behind, creating Chinese settlements. The Mongol annexation of Yunnan also brought Chinese frontiers within hailing distance of overland neighbours in Indochina. Chinese quarters are said to have existed in even Moscow and Novgorod in the 14th century.

Haunted by the Yuan, the first emperor of the succeeding dynasty, the Ming, sought to restore order and security by bringing the economy under government control. This entailed reducing the volume of foreign trade and subjecting it to the state system of trading through tribute missions sent by foreign countries. 'Not an inch of plank,' it was decreed, should go down to the sea. The policy cramped the style of those who had been profiting from private trade, both Chinese and foreign. Quite naturally, these people resorted to trading illegally through smuggling and piracy.

The succeeding reign, that of the Yongle emperor, lowered the maritime barricades, reversing the earlier policy of sealing China off from foreign incursion and foreign commerce. Indeed, under Yongle Chinese sea-power was supreme. Between 1405 and 1433 Chinese fleets commanded by the eunuch admiral Zheng He vis-

ited the countries of East and Southeast Asia, and crossed the Indian Ocean to reach Ceylon, the Persian Gulf and the east coast of distant Africa. Excavations at a shipyard at Nanjing in the 1960s confirmed the figures given in the official Ming history for the ships' stupendous dimensions. Zheng He's 'treasure ships' inspired awe and his epic voyages entered the folk memory of half the world almost a century before the great age of European exploration and expansion. Yet at this moment, in the plenitude of its naval majesty, the Ming government withdrew from the sea. No other Chinese emperor had so interested himself in Southeast Asia, but when Yongle shifted his capital northwards, from Nanjing to Beijing, he was recognizing the more vital security claim of the northern frontier, with its Mongol threat, upon his concern and attention.

The reign of Yongle apart, the Ming was not much interested in southern sea contacts. With the barricades up once more, to pursue overseas commerce outside the tribute system was to engage in smuggling. The saturation of commerce by contraband marked the maritime climate of the 16th century, when the world of the overseas trader was tangled up with that of the coastal pirate. Piracy was rife, with the so-called Wokou (*wo*, 'dwarves' was the Chinese name for the Japanese) and their Chinese collaborators terrorizing and wreaking havoc all along the coasts. And mixed up in all this was the arrival of the Portuguese. That these newcomers were a sign of things to come, pioneers of a Western intrusion that would presently rejig the map of Southeast Asia, was not realized by anyone. So far as the government was concerned, the scourge called for coastal defence, and coastal defence implied banning overseas trading. The ban made an outlaw of every Chinese who ventured overseas. Many a profit-seeker abroad preferred to stay away, finding a perch in Taiwan and trading posts in Southeast Asia.

But economic realities and the appeals of those coastal Chinese whose livelihoods and profits were at stake prompted a change of policy, and informal overseas trading was legalized in 1567. A tectonic shift was underway in China during the 16th century: Chinese society was being subjected more intensely than ever before to the play of market forces. The commercialization of agriculture, the expansion of rural and urban handicraft production, the growth of trade and competition, heightened social mobility – all these pointed to the government taking its hand off the economy. Export trade flourished; Japanese and Mexican silver flowed into the empire. Junks going to Southeast Asia and Japan reinforced the impression that the focus of Chinese trade had turned from Central Asia to the southeast coast, where there was no shortage of intermediaries for commerce with East and Southeast Asia. The Hokkiens, in particular, were a trading force *par excellence*.

Among them, the figures of Zheng Zhilong and his son Koxinga (Zheng Chenggong) loomed large. This family, based in Amoy (Xiamen), had naval capability enough, and entrepreneurial energy enough, to command a virtual maritime empire, with trading networks extending from Manila to Nagasaki. After the Ming house was toppled by the Manchus, who inaugurated the Qing dynasty in 1644, the elder Zheng went over to the victor's side but the son remained doggedly loyal. Amoy

Koxinga.

was a bastion of resistance, but also became, under Koxinga, an international entrepôt of great commercial consequence. In its turn, Taiwan came under Koxinga's control and became a link in the chain of trade and Chinese settlement. Indeed, Koxinga is honoured still in today's Taiwan, as a founder and local hero.

Guessing that Koxinga's resistance depended on the trade in which the maritime provinces were involved, the Manchus moved to cut off that trade in the expectation that without it, he could not hold out for long. Maritime trade barriers were cranked up accordingly, and in 1662 the Manchu ordered the coasts to be devastated and forcibly depopulated. This cruel exercise destroyed homes, burned villages, parted families and made migrants of many. From Amoy the coastal evacuation policy was extended to Guangdong and parts of Zhejiang. Koxinga died shortly afterwards, but his son held out in Taiwan until 1683, when the Qing finally annexed Taiwan and made it a prefecture of Fujian.

About trade and travel, the Manchus remained ambivalent. They lifted the maritime ban in 1684 but emigrants were not to have it all their own way. In 1717, a government ban on maritime intercourse in the South China Sea (but not the East China Sea) specifically prohibited emigration. Despite a relaxation of controls in 1723, the restrictions on foreign travel from Guangdong and Fujian remained in place. Although largely a dead letter by then, the ban on emigration was not lifted until 1860 and not officially revoked until September 13, 1893.

Editor

Map 2.2

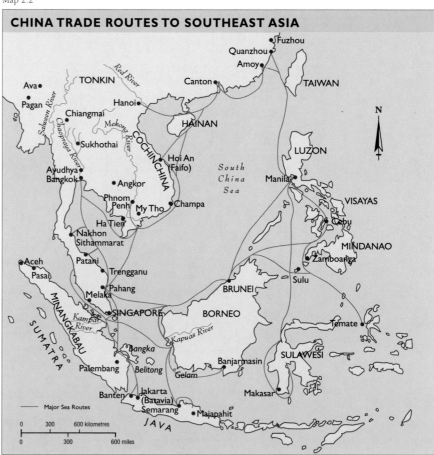

Source: Reid (1996).

Chinese and Southeast Asian interactions

The stops and starts of Chinese imperial policy provide the rhythm behind the historical interaction of China and Southeast Asia. The southward movement of Chinese derived from both peaceful private trade and political intervention, and came in a series of bursts.

The first recorded burst followed Mongol interventions in the 13th century. Faring badly at Mongol hands, the established 'classic' empires of Pagan, Angkor, Champa and Java were all hastened to their demise. Their decline cleared a path for a series of Tai kingdoms to emerge in mainland Southeast Asia. The earliest of these, at Sukhothai, appeared to have good relations with China, with a steady flow of missions in both directions in the period 1296–1323.

A Mongol force of 20,000 soldiers sent to Java in 1293 to punish King Kertanegara for his insolence had profound if unintended consequences. Kertanegara's son-in-law, Wijaya, was able to manipulate the Chinese troops to his own advantage and then harry them out of Java, leaving him on the throne. Thousands of Chinese soldiers reportedly died in Java, but many must have been captured by the Javanese or stayed behind voluntarily to avoid the rigours of a return journey. This episode not only marked the rise of the new dynasty of Majapahit, but also brought a major injection of Chinese technology to Java, notably in shipbuilding techniques and coinage.

Chinese ceramics – 14th-century flask found in Indonesia (top) and 15th-century jar found in Borneo – attest to commerce between Ming China and Southeast Asia.

Chinese map of the 'barbarian states of the southeastern seas,' from a 16th-century Chinese book.

The Chinese or Sino-Indonesian communities left behind by the Mongol invasion may have played a longer-term role in stimulating commerce. Java's rapid rise as a maritime power almost certainly relied on incorporating under Majapahit's hegemony the seamen, pilots and shipowners who already plied these routes. Predominant among these were Chinese-descended sailors and traders who had made local bases in the Archipelago, and Muslim merchants spreading eastward from their centres in Pasai (northern Sumatra) and eastern Java.

Under the Yongle emperor (1403–24) in the early Ming, Chinese interactions with Southeast Asia were intense as never before. In total nine Chinese imperial missions went to Champa, eight to Siam, six each to Malacca and Samudra-Pasai and ten to Java in the first 11 years of the Yongle reign. Each let it be known that missions of tribute to the imperial court would be welcomed and rewarded with trade goods. The imperial avowal 'to protect the weak and deter the greedy' in Southeast Asia was not just rhetoric but a claim to effective suzerainty over the whole region.

The port-states that most successfully exploited the opportunities offered by the new Chinese dynasty were Ayudhya, Malacca and Brunei. Their alacrity in sending tribute missions that included royalty gained these states protection from more powerful neighbours. Above all they became the key Southeast Asia entrepôts collecting tropical goods for despatch to China and selling Chinese manufactures to traders from the region. Uthong, the founder of Ayudhya according to Thai chronicle

traditions, was certainly a merchant 'outsider,' probably from a Chinese background, and possibly a first-generation Chinese. Malacca's rise in the period 1403–14 was inextricably tied to its relationship with the Yongle emperor's energetic state diplomacy.

In the Philippines and Borneo the symbiosis was still more unbalanced between the world's most powerful ruler and coastal chieftains who were just beginning to see how to turn their territories into states. The important point to note is that the number of Chinese who found themselves in the Nanyang, as well as the opportunities for them to become indispensable to rising rulers by arranging their affairs with the Chinese court, increased dramatically as a consequence of the intense early Ming activity. The 70 Chinese missions sent to Southeast Asian rulers during the Yongle reign evoked twice as many tribute missions in return.

For Java and Sumatra there is clear evidence of strong Chinese commercial communities in the early 15th century. The intense interaction with imperial fleets and envoys must have placed Chinese in key positions in Southeast Asian trade and statecraft. Embassies to China were made possible by ethnic Chinese or Sino-Southeast Asians domiciled in Nanyang. In this lively diplomatic and commercial activity, the locally domiciled Chinese, Southeast Asian and Sino-Southeast Asian élites and seamen who made up the cosmopolitan port communities of 15th-century Southeast Asia, all had a part to play.

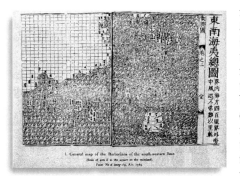

I. General map of the Barbarians of the south-western Seas
(Scale of 400 li to the square on the mainland)
From Yü-ti tsung-tú, A.D. 1564

The Zheng He expeditions marked the starting point of Southeast Asia's 'age of commerce' (see p 48). His fleets stimulated the production of pepper, clove, nutmeg and sappanwood, and the distribution networks that brought these items to the major entrepôts and took cloth, rice and manufactured goods in exchange to the production centres. Demand for Southeast Asian products in China leapt, with pepper and sappanwood becoming for the first time items of mass consumption in the15th century.

The diplomatic and commercial roles of some Sino-Southeast Asian cultural brokers extended to the establishment of the first known diplomatic contacts between Southeast and Northeast Asia in the 15th century, between Siam and Java on one side and Japan and Korea on the other. Another role played by the Southeast Asian Chinese was in maintaining a lively indirect commerce with China and Japan through the Ryukyu (Okinawa) kingdom – most intensively in the latter two-thirds of the 15th century. Ryukyu became a major entrepôt between Northeast and Southeast Asia by using its tributary relations with China to circumvent the Ming ban on private trade. The earliest contacts between Ryukyu and Southeast Asia were with Siam, and after that with the Chinese community of Palembang. After Chinese-ruled Palembang had sent an exploratory ship to Japan and Ryukyu, the Ryukyu state opened commercial relations with it in 1428 and with (eastern) Java in 1430. Sino-Southeast Asian merchants probably managed the reception of Ryukyuan vessels and the accompanying correspondence in Chinese.

After 1450 Ming interest in Southeast Asia reached a low-water mark. Between then and 1520, China-based ships still sailed illegally to the closer ports in Vietnam, Champa and Siam, but scarcely at all to the islands of Southeast Asia. The extensive trade between the Archipelago and China took place primarily through intermediate ports. Malacca was the most important, followed, after its fall, by Johor and Patani, but Ayudhya and Champa also continued to be major entrepôts for the China trade. During this period of relative isolation the overseas Chinese effectively merged into the cosmopolitan society of the Southeast Asian ports, so that at the time of the arrival of the Portuguese (1509) they were no longer perceived as a separate group in island Southeast Asia, and only as a very minor community in Malacca.

In 1567 China first legalized private trade to Southeast Asia by licensing 50 junks a year to trade. The rapid expansion of trade and emigration thereafter gave rise to a new set of Southeast Asian port-cities comparable to those that had emerged in the early 1400s. Manila, whose economic viability is inconceivable without the junk trade, is a striking case in point. Others are Hoi An (Faifo to Europeans), the commercial lifeline of the southern Vietnamese state known to Europeans as Cochinchina; Phnom Penh, Patani, the pepper port of Banten (in west Java) and to some extent even Banten's rival in west Java, the Dutch port of Batavia. The most lucrative aspect of the trade with the mainland ports was, or soon became, commerce with Japanese ships, which brought large quantities of silver to Southeast Asian ports in the first three decades of the 17th century, in exchange largely for Chinese silk.

The boom years of the age of commerce occurred from about 1570 to 1640, as silver poured into the region from Japan, Mexico and Europe, while Japanese, Chinese, Europeans and Indians all competed for their share of the valuable Southeast Asian trade. The Chinese junk trade flourished as never before and hundreds of Chinese disembarked every season at the major ports of Southeast Asia.

Arriving in about 1600, the Dutch and English found large and very distinct colonies of Chinese in Asian ports such as Hoi An, Patani, Banten and Phnom Penh, as well as Manila. In Hoi An there were reckoned to be four to five thousand Chinese by 1642, and they were assuming commercial dominance with the withdrawal of the Japanese. Some 2,000 Chinese freebooters had made Patani their commercial base in the 1560s, and by 1600 they had extended their trade network throughout the Archipelago, notably to Brunei. In Banten the Chinese numbered about 3,000 in 1600, living in a separate quarter outside the city wall.

The change of dynasty from Ming to Qing produced a different kind of migratory spurt, for the first time interested in building (pro-Ming) Chinese polities in Nanyang. Chinese-led states arose in the southern part of the Indochinese peninsula. In 1679 there arrived in Hoi An some 3,000 soldiers of the demoralized Koxinga forces seeking an alternative to Qing subjugation (see p 49). The Nguyen ruler of the southern Vietnamese state, no doubt concerned at the force they represented, sent them to the Mekong delta area, where Cambodian rule was in disarray through the rivalry of

three candidates for the throne. The Chinese eventually settled the Saigon and My Tho areas and turned them into bustling markets much frequented by Malays, Cambodians and Europeans as well as Vietnamese. In effect they formed an autonomous satrapy that pushed back the Khmer but was not fully absorbed into the Vietnamese administration until 1732 (see Part V: Cambodia and Vietnam).

Further west on the Cambodian coast a similar role was played by Mac Cuu, who had fled his native Guangdong in 1671 to serve as a commercial official of the court at Phnom Penh. In about 1700 he obtained from the Khmer ruler the farm of gambling revenues at the port of Ha Tien. He flourished, attracting many Hainanese and Cantonese as well as Vietnamese and Khmers fleeing from dynastic troubles, and built a little state embracing a string of ports along the eastern shore of the Gulf of Siam.

Despite the continued difficulties in trade between China and Southeast Asia, the Chinese profile in many parts of Southeast Asia rose rapidly in this period. One reason was the decline of most of the alternative foreign trading groups. European, Indian Muslim and Japanese traders largely withdrew from Siam, Vietnam and Cambodia in the last decades of the 17th century for a variety of reasons. Access to Canton after 1684 gave Europeans an alternative to buying Chinese goods in Southeast Asian ports. Peace between the rival Vietnamese kingdoms after 1680 reduced their need for European military technology and allowed them to return to their systematic discouragement of traders other than Chinese. There and in Siam, Chinese had become the overwhelming dominant factor in both internal and external trade by 1740. In Mindanao, the sultan pursued a deliberate policy of attracting Chinese immigrants, even learning their language. In Java and the Philippines, Chinese spread from the European enclave cities, where they had been concentrated, to dominate internal trade throughout the islands.

The middle years of the 18th century marked a watershed in the triangular relationship of Southeast Asians, Chinese and Europeans. As global commerce quickened in the second half of the 18th century, an

Qing dish, Swatow ware.

Picture by Dutch artist of mosque in Java displaying Chinese features, 17th century.

Trading vessel crewed by Chinese entering port in Sulu, late 1830s.

implicit partnership developed between the Chinese junk trade, now accepted and even reinforced by imperial authority, and the remaining centres of independent Southeast Asian power.

While the European traders became more hostile to the Chinese, the independent Southeast Asian states became yet more dependent upon them. Though a declining presence in Batavia and Manila, the Chinese junk trade flourished elsewhere as never before. It became the lifeline of independent states from Siam to Sulu.

The major Southeast Asian centre for the junk trade was Siam. After its capital at Ayudhya fell to the Burmese in 1767, Siamese fortunes were restored by King Taksin, son of a Teochiu-speaking Chinese immigrant father and a Thai mother, though brought up in the household of a Thai nobleman. He fled the Burmese advance to the southeast, where Teochiu immigrants were principally concentrated, rallied support to drive the Burmese out, and founded a new capital at Thonburi. During his reign, and that of his successor and son-in-law, Rama I, also half-Chinese, at Bangkok, Chinese shippers, shipbuilders and traders were particularly encouraged to settle. Bangkok probably replaced Batavia as the leading port of Southeast Asia in this period. Some 11,500 seamen were engaged in Bangkok's maritime trade, almost all of them of Chinese descent. The flourishing trade was accompanied by very correct and profitable relations with Beijing. This successful Thai-Chinese partnership made Bangkok a dominant power extending its suzerainty to the Lao principalities in the north and to Kedah and Trengganu in the south.

For the border states, Burma and Vietnam, Chinese influence was necessarily a more mixed blessing. Border skirmishes followed by unsuccessful punitive Chinese expeditions were eventually settled and the peace signed between the antagonists in 1769 laid the basis for an unusually cordial century of caravan trade and tribute between Burma and China. When the powerless Le emperor of Vietnam fled to China before the rebellious Tayson forces in 1788, the Chinese emperor intervened to attempt to restore him to the throne (see Part V: Vietnam). The results were similar to those in Burma – an ignominious Chinese withdrawal followed by the restoration of exceptionally warm relations. The Tayson ruler of the north, Nguyen Hue, expressed his apologies and submission and travelled in person to Beijing in 1790 to attend the celebrations of the emperor's 80th birthday. Tribute missions were sent in every year of Tayson's rule in Hanoi. When the Nguyen dynasty succeeded in returning to power and unifying the country in 1802, the French soldiers who had assisted Gia Long to power were gradually removed and an unprecedentedly orthodox replica of a Chinese regime created. From then until the rise of Singapore, Vietnam's foreign trade was almost exclusively with China and carried in Chinese junks.

The states of the Archipelago were always more open to foreign trade of every kind than were the larger kingdoms of mainland Southeast Asia. States such as Riau, Palembang, Trengganu, Sambas, Brunei and Sulu were able to establish a new revenue base through the 18th-century influx of Chinese miners (of gold and tin) and planters (of pepper and gambier).

Anthony Reid

Demographic changes

At the inception of the 17th century China was the world's largest empire, with a population already past the 100 million mark, a figure far higher than that of all the European countries combined. Between about 1620 and 1670, foreign invasion, civil war, outbreaks of rebellion, natural calamities and epidemics cut the population down by perhaps as much as 50 million. Thereafter it rose again, and by 1800 it had tripled. But because the opening up and settling of new lands succeeded only in doubling the acreage of arable land during that period, the size of individual holdings actually shrank and contention for land and work steepened. By 1850, the already awesome numbers had probably increased to 430 million.

It would help if technology and organization kept pace with the mounting numbers, but China's population was already swamping the capacity of society to cope. At the end of the day, one cannot long escape the simple logic of demography: the press of numbers, no less than merchant venturing, made migrants of the many Chinese who subsisted on farming.

Developments in the world at large

International labour migration as we know it is the direct result of the post-1500 globalization of the west European economies, in both their pre-industrial and industrial phases. Prior to the 16th century, migratory movements within Asia or elsewhere were relatively small scale in nature, and limited in geographic scope. Thus transnational mercantile or religious travel, regional displacement cycles (caused by political, religious or ethnic conflict), rural to urban transitions, even traditional forced labour movements, were overshadowed from the 16th century by massive transcontinental movements of settlers and labourers to newly conquered countries, in addition to regional migrations towards newly resurgent traditional economies stimulated by Western market demands. The numbers and origins of the migrants, their numerous destinations, the roles they played in their new environments, the communities they did or did not form, all have as their historical backdrop the progressive expansion of Western overseas trade, colonization and settlement in their pre-industrial and industrial stages.

Significant mercantile (and religious) mobility within the Asian region predate the arrival of Western commercial interests in the 16th century, but it is impossible to separate the creation of overseas Chinese communities within Southeast Asia from the impact of Western commercial interests since that time. The first significant overseas community in Manila dates from the 1560s, and is directly connected to the China-Manila-Acapulco trade connection established by the Spanish. Certainly, Chinese migration beyond Asia proper, which began in the 19th century, was the direct result of the Western impact during its industrial expansionist phase.

Chinese emigration can thus be separated into three distinct phases: the pre-16th century or traditional phase; the 16th to 19th century phase, when migration was directed mainly to Southeast Asia, and when European expansionism in the East was more commercial than annexationist (annexationism being confined mainly to the Americas); and the 19th century period when migration ventured beyond Asia, and Western commercial-industrial expansion and territorial annexation (political imperialism) went largely hand in hand, not only in Asia but also in Africa and the Pacific. Today there is a fourth new period, one which began in the 1950s and 1960s. Here the migration is directed mainly to the cities of the metropolis, the 'centre,' rather than to the developing outer regions, the 'periphery.' Here moreover the primary impetus seems to be the need for multi-class and multi-skilled labour rather than just unskilled labour, more brain and brawn drain than pure brawn drain.

Slave auction in Chicago, 1852.

Our concern here is with the second and third phases, when much of the Chinese diaspora was born. During the second phase, which coincides with the history of colonial America, the transcontinental migration of settlers and labourers was firmly established. Whole new colonial societies linked to the emerging transatlantic economic complex were created on the ruins of the old. In the process, the Mediterranean was replaced by the Atlantic; ancient America was virtually obliterated from history; massive transcontinental migration filled the vacuum; and new socio-racial hierarchies were created (the black–white schism). The new migrants were masters, slaves and small settler-farmers; chattel-slaves, indentureds and free, and they came mainly from Europe and Africa. Wherever native America was not obliterated or marginalized, its traditional hierarchies were forcibly levelled out and whole communities were brutally incorporated into the lowest rungs of the colonial labour force.

During this colonial-American and global pre-industrial phase, Asian transcontinental migration was virtually non-existent, but the principles and practices were already being laid in this period for a later Asian (mainly Chinese and Indian) involvement after the 1850s. Even so, a trickle of Chinese (and Malay) labourers found their way into the life of early America. The trade nexus which had been established between Manila in the Philippines and Acapulco in New Spain in the 16th century had facilitated the arrival of small numbers of Chinese sailors and labourers in New Spain. There are authorized reports of Chinese servants, textile workers, farmers and barbers in Mexico City, Acapulco, and the state of Michoacan in the early 17th century.

Chinese from the Philippines also found their way into the woollen textile mills of Peru in the 17th century. Chinese were recorded as engaged in shipbuilding in Spanish-controlled lower California as early as the late 16th and 17th centuries, and they accompanied the Spanish in their early northward expeditions to upper California in the late 1700s. Even in the gold mines of Minas Gerais in Portuguese Brazil, there were reports of Chinese in the early 1700s, brought there no doubt via Macao. The writer Alexander von Humboldt, who travelled to Latin America between 1799 and 1804, also encountered Chinese in Cuba who had gone there on the Manila galleons. This was a full 50 years before the mass migrations to the Americas of the 1850s and beyond.

The first Chinese diaspora was created not in the heart of this transatlantic economy, but in its Eastern extensions. If one wing of the new transatlantic economy could be described as post-Columbus, the other was clearly post-da Gama. Throughout this period, the regional Asian economy maintained its traditional autonomy, with the newcomers from Europe providing a complex new presence on two fronts: within the intra-Asian trade itself, and as a dynamic market extension for regional products (East–West trade). The new global economy, with its heartbeat located within the transatlantic complex, intruded but did not fundamentally transform regional economic traditions. However, the Chinese communities which formed themselves in the wake of the European entry into Asia clearly were creations and beneficiaries of this new presence: as servants and labourers, but more importantly as merchant middlemen and seafaring carriers of people and goods.

Then, between 1763 and 1815 came the British Industrial Revolution, the British defeat of the French in the war for domination of the colonial enterprise, the

Figure 2.1

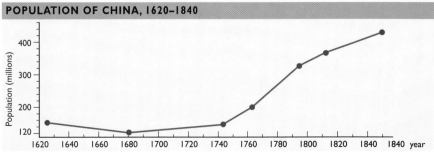

POPULATION OF CHINA, 1620–1840

Source: Gernet (1982).

Arrivals at pier of Pacific Mail Steamship Company, San Francisco.

conquest of Bengal, and the loss of the 13 colonies in North America. Ten years later came the independence of most of Spanish and Portuguese America, already de facto economically dependent on northwest Europe, particularly Britain.

Not only had British productive powers been unleashed beyond anything that had been possible before, but the new political-military developments led to a gradual shift of Empire focus from the West to the East. The prospect of new markets and new spheres of influence inside and outside the Empire gave new life to an industrially vitalized Britain. With the conquest of India, colonialism in the East assumed new annexationist ambitions. Countries which had confined the Western presence to coastal trading enclaves found themselves being annexed or indirectly controlled by aggressive new rulers, led by Britain.

The Industrial Revolution also created an expanding domestic market for a range of food products and industrial raw materials, and this in turn stimulated a global boom scenario, as old and new countries, colonies and ex-colonies, in the West and the East, vied to tap into the needs of this market. Add to this the critical labour situation in the Americas, with the end of the slave trade and slavery, and the vigorous opening up of new frontiers and new economies. Add to this also the continuing displacement of peasant and artisan labour in industrializing Europe, the degeneration occurring in British India and imperial China largely as a result of the new Western aggressiveness, the easier linking of physical space made possible by the use of steamers in international trade from the 1860s, and the framework was laid for a whole new global labour migration, free and semi-free, in the mid-19th century. Thus began the renewal of European immigration, from old and new sources, and to many new destinations. Thus began also the involvement of millions of Asians (Indians, Chinese, Indonesians, even Japanese) into the network of transcontinental and intra-Asian labour migration, and the creation in the 19th century of new Asian diasporas worldwide.

Walton Look Lai

Western expansion into China and Southeast Asia

The arrival of European shipping in the South China Sea was the prologue to a profound change of scene on the world historical stage. Heralding their countries' imperial adventures, pioneer European merchants linked ports to sea routes westward and made the inter-Asian trade an arm of the world market. The flags raised, the territories claimed and the settlements attempted by these newcomers gave to the Chinese at home and abroad new troubles no less than new opportunities. As well as trading under their own steam, the Chinese abroad became agents and partners of the Europeans; indeed they became a sort of neutral service industry. To the European bases (whether these were newly established entrepôts like Singapore or Treaty Ports like Amoy and Canton), flocked thousands of internal and cross-border migrants. Chinese migration not only increased in volume and variety but went from being regional to being global.

The opening of the Suez Canal in 1869 was a turning point, accelerating the force of the Western penetration of Asia and its commercialization under Western direction. In Southeast Asia new export industries rose, acting as an economic engine that was also a labour pump, sucking in workers and pouring them through the wheels of agriculture and industry. Migration to and within the area fed the pump. In the long run, European penetration had subtle ramifications like modernization, the transfer of technology and institutions (including, most importantly, law) and the rise of nationalism.

Among European ships the first to drop anchor in Asian waters were those of the Portuguese. In search of mace and nutmeg, they were headed for the Spice Islands to the east of Sumatra when they broke into the busy Southeast Asian carrying-trade with its main entrepôt at Malacca. They seized the port, and found there the Chinese junk traders to lead them to China. In 1557 they built a permanent trading station on a tiny tongue of land sticking out of the Pearl River Delta to the south of Canton. This small port eventually became the city of Macao. An imperial ban of direct trade by Chinese

Painting of trading station established by Western merchant companies in Canton, circa 1820.

A Cohong merchant in Canton, circa 1840.

Trace left by China–Mexico trade: Mexican vase decorated with Chinese sailor.

Lithograph of early Malacca (above left).

By 1759 the Qing court had restricted all European trade to the one port of Canton. There, Chinese merchants formed their own monopolistic guild known to the Europeans as the Cohong (*gonghang*, 'combined merchant companies'). Europeans must channel all their business through the Cohong, and the Cohong alone; and only during the trading season, which ran each year from October to March, were these foreigners allowed to reside in Canton. So specified the imperial edict, ushering in the 'Canton system.' Especially irksome to British traders, the system took a war – the Opium War – to undo.

What attracted the foreign merchants like flies to a honey pot was Chinese tea, the thirst and vogue for which had become particularly great in England. In time the trade was to produce a great new social evil, the import of Indian opium. It was this that the English, after years of casting around for something to sell to the Chinese, finally found as payment for their tea purchases. The first Chinese to acquire the opium-smoking habit were probably sojourning traders and sugar plantation labourers in Java. The southeast coast of China introduced it to the rest of the mainland and disseminated it along domestic trading networks. By the 1830s the rapid rise in opium imports had reversed China's balance of trade, producing an outflow of silver and severe currency problems to add to the dire social effects of drug addiction.

Imperial efforts to cut off imports met British resistance. The two sides clashed at Canton. The First Opium War (1840–42) was followed by a second still fiercer conflict in 1856–60. The Treaty of Nanjing that ended the first war ceded Hong Kong Island outright to Britain, opened five Treaty Ports – Amoy, Canton, Fuzhou, Ningbo and Shanghai – to foreign consuls, traders and missionaries and enforced the adoption by China of the most-favoured nation principle in diplomatic agreements with Western countries. The Convention of Beijing that concluded the second war brought the British the southern tip of the Kowloon Peninsula. Later the British were able to acquire extensions to their colony at Hong Kong and Kowloon; called the New Territories, these were leased by China to the British for a period of 99 years, ending in 1997.

The convention also stipulated that the Chinese emperor would allow any Chinese wishing to work in British colonies or other foreign parts to do so, and to take ship with their families at any of the open ports of

merchants with Japan created a commercial vacuum into which the Portuguese were pleased to step, becoming middlemen. In exchange for the Chinese silks they shipped to Japan, they got silver from Japanese mines.

Nor was Japanese silver the only bullion streaming into China. There was the silver from the mines of Mexico and today's Bolivia, flowing to China in a returning tide across the route of the Manila galleons bearing Chinese silks and other rich commodities to Europe by way of the Americas. In the 1570s the Spanish conquerors of Mexico established a colony at Manila, in the Philippines, which became a link in the global chain of East-West trade. Freighted in the Manila galleons, reaching Europe by way of the Americas, both the goods and the silver were handled by Chinese traders who, following their noses, congregated in Manila. The Spaniards called the Manila galleon *nao de la China*, 'the ship of China.'

The Dutch now entered the picture, challenging the Portuguese domination of the spice trade with the incorporation in 1602 of the Dutch East India Company. By 1619 they had begun to settle the island of Java, establishing their headquarters at Batavia. In 1624 they built a trading post on Formosa (Taiwan), from which island they were eventually to be expelled by the forces of the Ming loyalist Koxinga. Both here and in Batavia they would find many uses for Chinese settlers. Indeed, to people their colonies, they were not above sending fleets to coastal China to shanghai Chinese men, women and children to the Indies.

The Dutch ousted the Portuguese in Malacca and also proved a match for the somewhat late-arriving English, who were after a base around the fringes of the Dutch ambit in Southeast Asia as a forward position for improved commercial access to China, a purpose for which their bases in India were too distant. Southeast Asia lay athwart the routes from the West to China: it was not the terminus of the long Western quest for a foothold in China. The founding of a British settlement at Penang in 1786 produced one more destination for Chinese immigration but did not help crack the China market – nor, for that matter, did Singapore, founded as yet another way station to Canton.

British man-of-war as seen by 19th-century Chinese artist.

A Boxer rebel.

China. The terms were secured by France and Spain as well, and by the United States eight years later. The agreement signed with the latter provided for the emperor's recognition of 'the inherent and inalienable right of man to change his home and allegiance, and also the mutual advantage of the free migration and emigration of their citizens and subjects respectively from one country to the other for purposes of curiosity, trade or as permanent residents.'

The 19th century was the era of large-scale international migration. The movement of population and capital from countries where they were relatively abundant to countries where they were relatively scarce was a necessary condition of the expansion of the international economy. And here was China, bursting to discharge its surplus peasants into the world labour market. Hinterlands were being opened up under colonial aegis in Southeast Asia, natural resources were being exploited. Elsewhere, the abolition of human slavery and the freeing of African bondmen created a manpower shortage that cried out to be corrected. Against all this grew Chinese labour migration.

Domestic dislocation and instability

When a gathering disorder is getting too close for comfort, people rush for the door. The refugee fleeing turbulence in times of flux and crisis or dynastic transition is a familiar figure in Chinese history. When the Song dynasty collapsed at the end of the 13th century, for example, some Chinese took refuge in Annam. The Mongol conquest of China prompted an exodus of Chinese to Vietnam, Cambodia, Siam and Indonesia. After the Qing forces' pacification of Taiwan, many who had supported the Ming cause fled to ports where they had traded in Southeast Asia, becoming emigrants.

In the Qing dynasty, foreign aggression combined with internal stresses ushered in a generation of rebellion. The cycle of history that began with the Opium Wars was punctuated by waves of domestic unrest. Imperial authority was repeatedly threatened by popular risings, which culminated in the mid-19th century in four major rebellions, at least one of which, the

Taiping rebels quelled by imperial troops in Nanjing.

Taiping (1850–64), almost toppled the dynasty. Originating in the poor Guangxi countryside and led by a possibly mad Hakka utopian dreamer and convert to fundamentalist Christianity, this upheaval resulted in dreadful carnage, with the loss of perhaps 20 million lives (see p 27). Genealogies found in Guangxi tell of rebels fleeing to California, Vietnam and Singapore or being shipped off as coolies to Cuba and the Dutch East Indies following the defeat of the uprising. It was with Hakkas, too, that the Cantonese of Guangdong fought in the devastating inter-ethnic wars of 1854–68, wars which put many villagers in the Pearl River Delta to flight and migration (see p 27).

Another outbreak to take the torch to the dynasty was the Nian movement (1851–68), which emerged in the area between the Huai and Yellow Rivers. When hardship turned to desperation, peasants and salt smugglers joined with roving bands of armed bandits connected to Triad societies to plunder towns and villages. Two other rebellions, both led by Muslims, broke out in the far southwest and northwest in the mid-1800s. The Qing survived this tidal wave of popular insurrection, but while the dynasty had a reprieve and a chance to rally its forces with Western help, its defeat in two brief yet shattering wars – one with the French and the other with the Japanese – exposed the crisis and impotence at its heart. With China beaten, the stage was set for the cutting up of 'the Chinese melon' by foreign powers.

Profound anti-foreign feeling found an outlet in the Boxer movement, which erupted in 1900 and expressed itself in attacks on Western missionaries and Chinese Christians. The Boxers drew their martial practices from folk religion and secret-society lore. With its ranks swollen by canal boatmen, vagrants, dismissed soldiers and peasants made desperate by drought and flood, the movement climaxed in the famous siege of the Beijing Legations. Though it was suppressed by foreign force, the emerging impulses of Chinese nationalism it represented were to bring the long Manchu travail to an end.

The monarchy fell in 1911, but though the revolution that brought this about was singularly unviolent, disorder was not at an end. Warlordism, revolution, external aggression and civil war subjected the Chinese who lived through this period to an experience of turbulence unexampled in earlier eras of China's history. The Japanese invasion of China in 1937 prompted much emigration, as did the Communist victory in 1949. China's search for a new order, unity and a revival of national vigour was to prove a long and frustrating process, and was to appear at times like either a struggle up a cul-de-sac or an exercise in terror and self-destruction.

BETWEEN DEPARTURE AND ARRIVAL

By the mid-1860s sail had yielded to steam, and scheduled steamer services were running between south China and the ports of Southeast Asia. Departures and arrivals were made up not only of emigrants but also returnees. Indeed some of those taking ship at the ports might be called commuters; termed 'old guests' in Chinese, they were seasoned enough migrants to become recruiters of new migrants ('new guests' in Chinese) for jobs in their country of sojourn. Such people acted as couriers as well, travelling to Southeast Asia once every three or

Amoy sea front.

four months in the early decades of the 20th century to provide services like writing and delivering letters for illiterate Chinese and handling remittances from overseas senders to their families back home (see p 109). Recruiter-couriers typically sourced prospective emigrants from their own native place or its environs. Contracts entered into by the emigrant and the recruiter, who advanced the passage money and travelling expenses, were commonly guaranteed by friends or relatives from the same native place.

While awaiting departure in a Chinese port, prospective emigrants would stay at a local inn. Most inn operators were from the same place of origin as the lodgers. The coast sprouted with inns which proclaimed their native-place affiliation by carrying door signs that read 'Fuqing Inn,' 'Quanzhou Inn' and so on. They also specialized by their guests' destination: some put up departees for Thailand, for example, while others housed men bound for Malaya.

The inns made it their business to buy blocks of boat tickets from shipping brokers. These they sold to the recruiter-couriers with whom they worked closely or, in some cases, had entered into partnerships. In another less common arrangement, the inns extended loans to the prospective emigrants directly, bypassing the recruiter-courier and using a guarantor instead. The recruiter-couriers themselves would lodge in the same inn as their charges while awaiting the ship to their overseas destination.

Disputes arising between the inn and the recruiter-courier would be mediated by an institution (which might itself be an inn) known as the Gonghe Society. This was a body with branches in the main overseas destinations (such as Singapore, Penang, Vietnam and Luzon) and a handful of officers at home who kept records of each loan statement and guarantee document drawn up.

Upon landing at the overseas destination, staff from the inn contacted by the recruiter prior to departure met the arrivals and arranged for their accommodation and onward travel (many arrivals in one overseas port – Singapore, for instance – were in transit to another destination). The recruiter delivered the arrivals to their employer or to the friends or relatives who had sent for them. From these he received payment for his services and expenditure, while those of his charges who were without such sponsors would repay him with interest by instalment from their earnings.

The main ports of embarkation were Amoy, Shantou and Hong Kong. Amoy, the home of seamen whose sea-going experience was once unrivalled in Chinese waters, was the emigration hub of Fujian. As such, it was the conduit of departees and returnees originating in Zhangzhou, Quanzhou, Xinghua (Henghua), Fuzhou, Fuqing and other centres in the province. In the early decades of the 20th century prospective migrants from these places would typically sail down coastal waters in sampans or small steamboats to board a scheduled sea-going vessel at Amoy. Some would have travelled by foot from their village to the nearest county town (see figure).

The quays of Shantou funnelled emigrants bound for Thailand, the Straits Settlements and other destinations in Southeast Asia. These emigrants would have travelled there from the counties round about, many of them across a large enough distance to necessitate an overnight stay in one of the inns in the port. In the early decades of the 20th century Shantou had 60 such inns, a third of the number boasted by Amoy.

From Hong Kong's busy harbour, many Cantonese, travelling by boat from

Figure 2.2

THE JOURNEY OF A RECRUITED EMIGRANT, 1914–40			
Day	**Journey**	**Items**	**Expenses (yuan)**
July 1	Fuqing–Fuzhou	pillow	1.50
	(by foot)	grass mat	0.30
		food	0.30
July 2	Staying in Fuzhou	food and rent	1.50
		sundries	0.30
July 3	Boat ride to Amoy	sampan ride	0.10
		fare to Amoy	3.00
July 4	Arriving in Amoy	sampan ride	0.10
		rent	1.20
July 5	Staying in Amoy	food (2 days)	0.50
		sundries & boat fare	0.40
July 6	Boat ride to Singapore	boat ticket	10.00
	Boat tickets may cost		
	8–15 yuan		
July 13	Arriving in Singapore	sundries on boat	1.00
		sampan ride	0.15
July 14	Staying in Singapore	rent and food	1.30
July 15		(2 days)	
Total			14.55

The amounts were those prepaid by recruiter–couriers. They charged the emigrant twice or in some places three times these amounts.
Source: Hicks (1993).

Canton and other points in the Pearl River Delta, took ship for scheduled sea voyages in huge numbers to North America and Southeast Asia. Other departures from Hong Kong had originated from Hainan Island, and even from Amoy and Shantou, themselves emigration ports. As a regular port of call on sailing routes between south China ports and Southeast Asian destinations like Saigon, Medan, Penang, Rangoon and Manila, Hong Kong was a convenient transit point for changing vessels.

Contexts: Post-World War II

By the outbreak of World War II, between 8.5 and 9 million Chinese were living outside the borders of China, the vast majority in Southeast Asia. By about 1990, it has been estimated that some 30.7 million Chinese were living outside Greater China (comprising mainland China, Hong Kong and Taiwan), up from 21.8 million around 1980.

The period from the 1930s to the late 1970s was one of extremely limited migration from China, though movements from peripheral Chinese territories, Hong Kong and Taiwan, had begun from the 1960s or earlier. After the long period of quiescence, Chinese migration began again in earnest in the late 1970s. It did so in the context of a profound political and economic shift in China on the one hand, and of broader changes in the wider world on the other.

China's 'reforms and opening'

When the People's Liberation Army of Mao Zedong defeated Chiang Kai-shek's Nationalists in 1949, the losers fled to Taiwan. As the Chinese Communist Party's grip on the Chinese mainland tightened over the next few years, hundreds of thousands more people headed south for the British colony of Hong Kong. Emigration in the old sense, however, all but ended with the birth of the People's Republic.

Several times in its short life, Maoist China was shaken to the core. Of these instances, the Great Leap Forward (1958) and the Cultural Revolution (1966–76) were the most dramatic. A hardening of attitudes attendant upon the failure of the Leap and the Sino–Soviet split was accompanied by an inward turn towards the old do-it-yourself ideal of self-reliance, and followed by the reign of terror of the Cultural Revolution. The introversion and xenophobia as good as ended emigration.

With the death of the old guard in 1976, the stage was set for the dramatic policy turnaround of 1978–79. Hard as it was to think of a label more sneering than 'capitalist roader' in Mao Zedong's day, Deng Xiaoping, emerging triumphant from the succession power struggle, launched China on its 'reforms and opening' – that is, tilting it towards a market economy and opening it to trade and foreign investment – in effect redefining

Mao Zedong (top).

Target of attack in China's Cultural Revolution.

Deng Xiaoping (left) and wife (right) with US President Jimmy Carter and wife.

the Chinese revolution.

In a coastal arc stretching from Hainan Island through Guangdong (adjacent to Hong Kong) and on to Fujian (opposite Taiwan), five Special Economic Zones (Amoy, Shantou, Shenzhen, Zhuhai and Hainan) and 14 'Open Coastal Cities' were established to experiment with open-door economic freedoms. Amidst the appearance of shop-front capitalism, entrepreneurial peasants and such totems of a rising middle class as portable telephones and karaoke bars, restrictions on travel, both at home and abroad, were eased. The economic reforms and the 'open door' bore fruit in not only an explosive economic boom and a less equitable distribution of income, but also an outflow of Chinese in quest of jobs from countryside to city, and from city to destinations abroad.

The increase in income disparities between rural and urban areas has been a spur to country–city migration, as have the inroads of mechanization, the wish of peasants to escape gruelling work and the lure of what appear to be brighter prospects in the city. Once he finds himself there, many a rural arrival then uses the city as a stepping-stone to international migration. Indeed, one of China's many flourishing private-sector businesses is the shipping of clandestine emigrants to Europe and America.

Emigration responds to change, real or anticipated, from a previously accepted status quo. Any number of developments could encourage people to move, but the disruption of past livelihoods by industrialization, economic liberalization, commercialization of agriculture (making superfluous a large proportion of the rural population) and the lifting of barriers to the transport of goods (including labour) is the most crucial. Such transformations provide the context for much Chinese emigration in the 1980s and 1990s.

Editor

Globalization

Migration is part of that modern pattern in which goods, capital, people, communications, knowledge, fashions, culture and crime flow ever more readily across national and territorial boundaries. Global in scale, the pattern is one in which events in one part of the world can have significant consequences for people and societies in other, quite distant parts. The term 'globalization' is used to define the process by which this interconnectedness is intensified. Because the fates of individual national communities are increasingly bound together by globalization, it is more and more difficult to understand migration without reference to international forces.

Three interrelated factors drove the new migrations in the post-World War II period: first, the increasing development and prosperity of Asian societies in general and Chinese societies in particular; second, the ageing of European societies and their transition from being sources of migrants to North America and Australasia to being recipients of migrants from Africa, the Middle East and Asia; and, third, the major shifts in immigration policy in the dominantly white settler societies of Australia, Canada, New Zealand and the US that turned a predominantly European immigration into one of largely Asian and Latin American origin.

The numbers of migrants from China, Hong Kong and Taiwan may be small compared with the historical migrations out of Europe, but what counts is not so much the quantity as the quality of the movers and their control of resources. While not all Chinese migrants are extremely wealthy, some are, and large numbers are armed with education and capital. For example, Hong Kong and Taiwan migrants have dominated the business immigration programmes of Canada, Australia and New Zealand. Hong Kong and Taiwan migrants accounted for nearly two fifths of all the entrepreneurs who entered Canada during the 1980s; and the 11,000 admitted to that country between 1987 and 1990 brought an estimated C\$14.3 billion and created 48,000 jobs. In the decade to 1987 in the US, the number of Chinese-owned businesses tripled to some 90,000, with annual receipts of US\$9.6 billion.

One of the characteristics of the international migration system today is the growing circulation of skilled and entrepreneurial groups centred upon the world's largest cities, the so-called 'global cities.' Chinese migration is primarily urban-oriented, directed towards the largest urban centres in Canada, the US and Australia.

A fundamental generalization on migration, proposed over a century ago by Ernest George Ravenstein, the father of modern migration studies, is that for every stream of migrants there is a counter-stream. One of his famous 'laws' of migration, this finds illustration in the reverse flows from the major cities in North America and Australasia back to Chinese cities, particularly Hong Kong and Taipei, but also other major cities in East and Southeast Asia. Much of this movement is within networks established by transnational companies, the headquarters of which are in the global cities; some of the movement is of Chinese returning to their home places either independently or through their employment in transnational companies.

The family is often left behind at the destination in an almost 'reverse sojourner' pattern of migration, with the husband, and sometimes the wife as well, returning to maintain or take up jobs in Asia. Leaving the family at the destination rather than the origin appears to represent a new form of mobility, one found among peoples other than the Chinese. Chinese cases of transnational households may be found among Malaysians and Singaporeans in London and Perth; and Hong Kongers and Taiwanese in Vancouver, Los Angeles, Sydney or Auckland.

This type of mobility has resulted in large numbers of female-headed households in the destination communities. With the husbands back in the origin areas and the wives

struggling to bring up the children in a culturally unfamiliar environment, social problems inevitably arise. So do questions of national identity. The settler-destination societies wish to admit people who will become Canadians, Australians or New Zealanders. Yet, where the head of the household, joined in some cases by the spouse, spends most of his time in the origin society, new transnational identities may emerge.

Since more boys than girls are sent abroad to continue their education, a higher proportion of males among the destination's school-age population is also part of the pattern. Overseas study is a widespread practice among upwardly mobile East Asians. Students often pioneer population movements from a particular country. In the early 1990s, students from China, Taiwan and Hong Kong represented almost a quarter of all foreign students in degree courses in the US and accounted for some 95,710 students in 1993–94. There were 14,148 students from these three areas in higher education in Australia in 1994, 10,340 at universities in Canada in 1992 and over 25,000 students from China alone in post-secondary education in Japan in the early 1990s.

Many of the students appear to stay on as settlers; this was the case with the more than 27,000 from China for whom Australia became home after the Tiananmen killings in June 1989. But many also return to their place of origin: in the 1960s, only about 5 to 10 per cent of the students who left returned to Taiwan; by the 1980s, this proportion had increased to about 25 per cent. The fact that Taiwan emerged as one of the newly industrialized economies (NIEs) in the interim cast some doubt on the supposedly damaging effects of the brain drain.

Ageing Europe's shift from a point of origin to a destination is the second factor driving the new migrations in the global system. While this has impacted on Chinese migrations directly, its indirect effect has been even more important. The direct effect may be seen in the small but increasing flow of Chinese migrants to that continent. Initially the movement was primarily from the New Territories of Hong Kong, but this has been replaced by a flow from China's Zhejiang province.

As for the indirect effect, this stems from the fact that, as the growth of European native labour forces began to slow with sustained declines in fertility, the continent could no longer supply migrants to the Americas and Australasia. To maintain the dynamism of their economic and demographic growth, these areas turned to other sources of supply for their settler populations. Thus, the changes in Europe indirectly engendered change in other parts of the global migration system.

The third factor affecting international migration has been the relaxation of restrictions on Asian entrants by the predominantly white settler states. In the late 1950s, migrants from Asian origins accounted for less than 8 per cent of the migration to the United States and around 3 per cent of that to Canada and Australia. By the early 1990s, these proportions had increased to about 48 per cent of the annual immigration to Canada, 38 to the US and 46 per cent of the immigration to Australia. The absolute number of Asian immigrants entering the US

Migration today is part of the global interconnectedness symbolized by mobile phone and laptop.

Table 2.1

CHINESE SETTLER MIGRATION TO THE THREE MAIN OVERSEAS DESTINATION COUNTRIES				
UNITED STATES				
	1982–87	1987–92	1992–93	1993–94
China	79,385	116,057	57,761	47,694
Hong Kong	54,325	69,216	14,010	11,949
Taiwan	81,230	76,397	15,736	11,157
AUSTRALIA				
	1982–87	1987–92	1992–93	1993–94
China	4,887	6,242	1,665	1,915
Hong Kong	21,635	61,881	8,111	4,075
Taiwan	2,315	12,300	1,389	779

CANADA					
	1982–86	1987–91	1992	1993	1994
China	11,788	31,737	10,429	9,447	12,250
Hong Kong	34,221	110,960	38,910	36,510	43,651
Taiwan	2,782	15,211	7,456	9,842	7,328

Canada compiles its immigration data for calendar year; the United States and Australia employ fiscal or financial years which are from different mid-year dates for each country.
Sources: Yearbook and immigration statistics published by the respective governments, various years.

in 1990 alone was around 256,000, with some 91,000 entering Canada and 56,000 entering Australia in that same year. It is virtually impossible to calculate accurately the number of Chinese as information on ethnicity is rarely collected as part of the data on immigration. Obviously, the overwhelming majority of migrants from China, Taiwan, Hong Kong and Singapore in recent years have been Chinese, but large numbers of those from Vietnam, Laos and Cambodia, as well as Malaysia and the Philippines, were also ethnic Chinese.

To take only the heartland of Chinese emigration – China, Taiwan and Hong Kong – the marked increases in migration during the decade of the 1980s are clear (see table 2.1). As foreign trade, foreign investment and the market economy burgeoned in China, so emigration accelerated. Some 57,761 entered the United States in the fiscal year 1992–93 alone, compared with just under 80,000 for the five years from 1982 to 1987. Hong Kong's trend is equally clear (see p 69). In Taiwan, the downturn following the rise in emigration is almost certainly associated with its transition to a labour-deficit economy. In this shift from emigration to immigration, Taiwan mirrors Korea.

But statistics on legal entrants reflect only part of the total migrant flows. In addition to settlers – and these normally include those accepted through humanitarian resettlement programmes – there are several types of non-permanent migrants, namely students, highly skilled workers and low-skilled contract workers, as well as large numbers of clandestine or illegal migrants (see p 63). These migrant flows are not only interrelated but also linked to the whole process of development in the areas of both origin and destination.

In many countries in the Asian region, governments have tried to capitalize on their available or surplus manpower by sending labourers overseas. The Chinese government, too, is an exporter of migrant labourers – people whose absence, it hopes, would help relieve domestic unemployment and whose remittances home would add to China's foreign exchange reserves. In the decade from 1983 to 1993 the number of labourers sent overseas increased almost sixfold to 173,654, generating over US$6.8 billion. The majority of these labourers were males from southern China going on construction contracts for one to two years. In the early 1990s they were employed in over 100 countries.

Ronald Skeldon

PATTERNS OF MIGRATION

Chinese migration has not been all of a piece; on the contrary, it has been immensely varied. At one extreme were emigrants who left home out of despair; at the other were those driven by calculated ambition. Emigration has been both necessity and advantage, both exile and opportunity. To do justice to the variety, writers have used terms like chain migration, forced migration, labour migration, free migration, student migration, seasonal migration, illegal migration, return migration, secondary migration (or re-migration) and so on. Nor are the categories mutually exclusive; to complicate matters, an individual can undergo several kinds of migration within a lifetime. Indeed the movements of Chinese across the world bear witness to a general observation in the way we conceive of migration by any people: that it is a multi-directional and continuing movement incorporating both onward relocation and repatriation.

Trade diasporas

Before the birth of the industrial age, long-distance trade along sea routes required someone to go abroad and become a foreigner. Over a long period of world history, trade diasporas were the dominant institutional form in cross-cultural trade. Merchants would physically move themselves from their homeland to reside in a town on an alien shore. Some moved back and forth; others settled; in some places the merchants stayed so long that they seemed almost like natives. A string of such settlements might arise, forming a trade network or, to borrow the Greek word for scattering (as in the sowing of grain), a trade diaspora. Trans-shipment centres were where merchant communities clustered. British Singapore, for example, was a major node in many resident trade diasporas: Arabs, Parsees, Klings, Bugis, Javanese, above all Chinese. For such Chinese, a trading voyage from the home port would become in effect a series of stages from one settlement of Chinese merchants to the next. At each settlement, a kinsman or a fellow-countryman would act as the trader's local agent.

It would be wrong, however, to suppose that as it was then, so it is now. Trade at a distance today does not

(From left) Foreign trader, his wife, and another foreign trader going about their business in Banten.

require anyone to migrate and set up home abroad. Yet the increased mobility of people, one of the many economic goods that have become globalized – capital, knowledge, management – is a concomitant of the expansion of international trade and business.

Labour migration

Trade diasporas could be the first stage of a much larger movement of people. Chinese merchants investing in plantations or tin mines in colonial Southeast Asia, for example, recruited labour by sponsoring contract workers from their home country. In the days when the sun never set on their empire, the British imported Tamils and Chinese to work in their colonies. Poor countries have always provided the sinews for rich ones to make the economic strides that would otherwise be hobbled for lack of manpower.

The 'guest worker' system was often run on the erroneous assumption that the foreign migrant labourers, having earned enough to improve their position in their country of origin, would quietly pack up and go home. But wholesale international labour migration has led to settlement and to the development of ethnic minorities in the recipient countries. Immigrant labourers tend to become a permanent part of the workforce because they perform socially undesirable and low-paying jobs that indigenous workers spurn, even during recessions. In retrospect, mass importation of foreign labour may be seen as merely the first phase of the entire migratory process.

The coolie trade

One way of looking at the rise of the notorious coolie trade is to see it as the replacement of one system of forced labour, African slavery, by another, namely Chinese contract or indentured labour. In the 19th century many places needed more Chinese workers than they could recruit. Between 1845, when the traffic began, and 1874, when it began to tail off, shiploads of Chinese were transported across long distances to ease labour shortages in Southeast Asia and halfway round the world in Hawaii, North and Central America and Africa. One estimate (that of the scholar Chen Hansheng) puts the volume of traffic between the 18th and 20th centuries at six to seven million people. Another reckons that between 1801 and 1925 about three million contract labourers were shipped out of China.

Men could migrate in one of three ways. They could pay their way. They could have the passage money advanced to them by a sponsor (who could be a kinsman, a local Chinese broker or an established Chinese immigrant based in the destination country) and repay that loan with interest after arrival; this was the so-called credit-ticket system that took Chinese to Australia, Canada, Southeast Asia and the United States. The third means was that of contract or indentured migration; indenture contracts were what bound thousands of Chinese to harsh labour worsened by physical brutality on the plantations of Cuba, Peru and the British West Indies.

The hub of the coolie business was first Amoy, then Macao. There, Western merchants such as Messrs Tait & Co. and Messrs Syme, Muir and Co. set up agencies to conduct recruitment operations with the help of Chinese brokers (called *ketou* in Chinese), who in turn used local crimps (press-gangers) with underworld connections to gather fodder for the barracoons (stockades). Of those put on board coolie ships, which were virtual 'floating hells,' many had been abducted, decoyed, tricked or terrorized into leaving China. Not all contractors were private speculators. Some recruiters were state agencies: the British government, for example, ran operations in Hong Kong, Canton and Swatow (Shantou) to recruit labour for its colonies in consultation with the Chinese authorities. The majority of Chinese indentured labourers returned to China when their contracts ended, but some stayed on to earn a living as small traders.

Indentured labour is a thing of the past but China continues to be a source, albeit on a considerably diminished scale, of organized migrant labour – batches of 'guest workers' have been recruited through government channels to work abroad. Fujian's Anxi County, for example, sent 1,042 of its people to labour in the US, Singapore and elsewhere between 1985 and 1990; of these, more than 100 became permanent residents of Singapore, many joined by their families.

Sojourning and chain migration

Once settled in the destination country, migrants become part of overseas networks that would welcome future arrivals from their places of origin; they provide the bridgeheads for the migration of their relatives, friends or fellow-townsmen. They become like links in a long chain; finding one link brings the others into view.

Colonial plantations, here of Javanese coffee, typically used imported labour.

Chinese coolies crowd deck of coastal vessel leaving probably from Amoy for Singapore.

This social infrastructure of migration has usually sprung up wherever sizeable numbers of immigrants have gathered. Since most migrants have traditionally relied on people from the same native place already settled in their destination countries to help them adjust and find work, a strong correlation exists between the choices of destination of emigrants and the locations of their fellow-townsmen.

It has long been common in China for young able-bodied single men from rural areas to earn their livelihoods in urban centres away from home and to think of their new places of abode as temporary. These centres might be in China, but they might equally be overseas. They would go home to their villages to marry, leaving their wives behind upon returning to the city. They would also help their kinsmen and fellow-villagers to find work in their own place of sojourn, where they themselves would be part of a native-place network of shelter and succour.

An aspect of their sojourning was the geographical spread of the members of their immediate family, some resident at the native place, others at the place of sojourn. The more successful would have secondary wives at their host location, and offspring from such liaisons would in some cases be sent back to the native place to be brought up and educated (see p 78).

Student migration

People entering a country on student visas to receive further education without envisaging long-term residence are usually placed in a different category from 'ordinary' immigrants, but the lines are in fact blurred and the categories fluid. Whatever the original intention, time alone tells who does return home and who does not.

I. M. Pei (b.1917), the most internationally accomplished architect of his generation, is one of many Chinese to embody the transition from student to immigrant. Arriving as a 17-year-old in the US from Shanghai, the young Pei had planned to return to China after graduating from the MIT (Massachusetts Institute of Technology) in 1940. But his father dissuaded him (Japan had attacked China) and he went on to study with Walter Gropius, the founder of Germany's avant-

University students in Canada.

garde Bauhaus, at Harvard. A thesis he did for Gropius, consisting of pen-and-ink drawings and a beautiful balsa wood model of a two-storey art museum (with pavilions and a stream running through a tea garden) for Shanghai, showed that he still had it in mind to apply his skills to China. 'It was a struggle with myself when to return,' he said, 'and then it eventually became should I return' In 1955 he became a US citizen.

American investigations, such as were reported by David Zweig and Chen Changgui in their 1995 monograph *China's Brain Drain to the United States*, show a difference between those who went in the early 1980s and the succeeding generation of overseas Chinese students. While many of the first group returned to China, large numbers of the second group look set to stay. Taiwan suffered a low rate of return in the 1960s – of the 80,000 university graduates who left for overseas study in 1950–80, only 5 per cent returned. However, returned PhDs in Taiwan grew as work conditions became more attractive.

Return migration and re-migration

Return migration is a theme in all emigrant histories, whether Chinese, Irish or Italian. Return migration has been both voluntary and induced. Many Chinese have been induced to return by political changes, persecution or other forms of inhospitality in their adopted countries. In the 1950s and 1960s deportees and repatriates from Malaya, Burma, Indonesia, Cambodia, India and Vietnam filled the so-called Overseas Chinese Farms, places for resettling colonies of returnees to China.

Not all returnees, called Guiqiao in China, have ended up in their own hometown. A sub-theme of return migration is resettlement in a non-native town or city. To give one example out of many, the Kwok (Guo) family, natives of Xiangshan in Guangdong province, returned to China from Australia to open the famous Wing On Department Store and to live, not in their native Guangdong, but in Hong Kong (1907) and Shanghai (1918). A variant of return migration, then, is re-migration. Another illustration is the 100,000-odd Indonesian Chinese who returned to China in 1960; disenchanted with life there, large numbers of these repatriates moved to Hong Kong in the 1970s.

Onward relocation is the recourse of the affluent and mobile, open to the choice of migrating a second or third time in quest of still wider options. When a Chinese achieves the international standing and autonomy of

Table 2.2

ESTIMATED POPULATION OUTFLOWS FROM CHINA, 1801–1925 (THOUSANDS)							
YEAR	**1801–1850**						
REGION	SOUTHEAST ASIA	CUBA	PERU	AUSTRALIA	UNITED STATES	WEST INDIES	OTHERS	SUB-TOTAL
Number	200	17	10	10	18	15	50	320
YEAR	**1851–1875**						
REGION	WEST INDIES	BRITISH GUYANA	CUBA	PERU	PANAMA	UNITED STATES	CANADA	AUSTRALIA
Number	30	20	135	110	25	160	30	55
YEAR	**1851–1875**						
REGION	NEW ZEALAND	HAWAII	PHILIPPINES	MALAY PENINSULA	EAST INDIES	OTHERS	SUB-TOTAL
Number	5	25	45	350	250	40	1280
YEAR	**1876–1900**						
REGION	UNITED STATES	HAWAII	MALAY PENINSULA	EAST INDIES	AUSTRALIA	CANADA	PHILIPPINES	OTHERS	SUB-TOTAL
Number	12	5	360	320	8	4	20	21	750
YEAR	**1901–1925**						
REGION	SOUTH AFRICA-TRANSVAAL	EUROPE, BRITAIN, NORTH AFRICA	MALAY PENINSULA	EAST INDIES	OTHERS	SUB-TOTAL
Number	55	150	125	300	20	650

Source: Zhu (1994).

someone like the painter Zhang Daqian (1899–1983), for example, he encounters few barriers to movement. Born in Sichuan province and a student in Kyoto, Zhang was widely travelled in China itself, spending formative years in Shanghai and periods of work and residence in Suzhou, Nanjing and Dunhuang (in the Gobi Desert). Leaving China for good in 1949, he lived successively in Hong Kong, Brazil and California before finally settling in Taiwan.

Like Zhang Daqian, many educated Chinese in the late 20th century move not just once but again and again. Such experimental sojourning is part of a wider pattern of increased mobility in a global economic system in which productive capital, finance and trade flow ever easier and faster across national boundaries. This newer way of long-term foreign residence poses a challenge to older ideas of permanent settlement and assimilation, and prompts a redefinition of the meaning of migration.

Editor

Clandestine migration

Wherever there is migration, there are strategies for dealing with the obstacles erected against migration. These have developed in tandem with the growth within modern nation-states of formal structures to control migration, institutions which paradoxically come to enhance the significance of the human movement they were created to control. Where such controls as border patrols, fines on employers of illegal immigrants and close examination by immigration officials at detention centres (notably Angel Island in San Francisco Bay) prove ineffective, what has been called 'undocumented migration' and 'alien smuggling' occurs.

Though barred from the United States by the exclusion laws it passed in the late 19th century, thousands of Chinese workers still entered the country. One way was to enter as a 'paper son,' using the slot created when a Chinese-American citizen eligible for re-entry to the US announced the birth of a fictitious child after a visit to China. But as well as the effectiveness or otherwise of these controls, domestic changes in the sending country also affect the volume of illegal migration, just as they do legal movement. For example, Hong Kong experienced a deluge of what it calls II's ('illegal immigrants') from China in 1979 and 1980, with daily

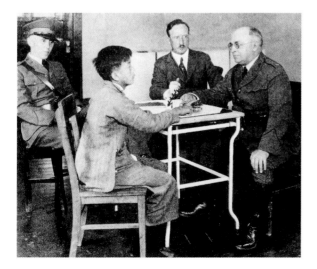

arrivals averaging 528 and 411 respectively, or about 10 to 20 times the number of previous and succeeding years. This was clearly linked to China embarking upon its 'reforms and opening' policy in 1979.

The 'paper son' racket apart, cases of illicit migration in the early part of the 20th century include those from the Fuzhou and Wenzhou areas (see pp 33, 40). A pedlar seeking passage abroad from Wenzhou in 1920, say, could pay a fee, often through an intermediary in or connected to a secret society, to be smuggled as a stowaway or a crew member to his destination, where he could then hope to be delivered into the hands of established immigrants from his home region. Alternatively, those travelling legally but still in need of assistance with contacts or financing could turn to unlicensed banks. These operations were interrupted first by the onset of war in the late 1930s, and finally ruptured altogether by the Communist victory in 1949.

When flows resumed in the late 1970s, they were much greater in volume. What the US government calls 'alien smuggling' is not unique to China but is, rather, a worldwide trend involving the increasingly organized illegal movement of people from Africa, Latin America, South and East Asia, the former Soviet Union and central Europe to the US, Canada, western Europe and Japan. More and more would-be immigrants seeking entry into highly developed countries – some fleeing war, poverty or persecution, others simply searching for economic opportunity – combined with constricting avenues of legal immigration have created a tremendous demand for the services of professional, generally intra-ethnic migrant traffickers.

In 1996, the going rate for a one-way excursion to the US from the Fuzhou area – which probably accounts for 95 percent of US-bound illegal emigration from China since 1970 – was US$34,000 to US$38,000. Recent clandestine passage to western Europe has been similarly though somewhat less dominated by a single source, the Wenzhou area, and costs about half as much as from Fuzhou. Exactly how many people have been smuggled half-way around the world for a fee from these two regions in the 25 years preceding the mid-1990s is impossible to say, but fragmentary data suggest, conservatively, that 300,000 have gone from Fuzhou, and 200,000 from Wenzhou.

A virtual ban on emigration during the first three decades of Communist rule ensured that smuggling networks

Figure 2.3

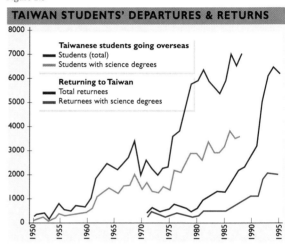

TAIWAN STUDENTS' DEPARTURES & RETURNS

Taiwanese students going overseas
— Students (total)
— Students with science degrees

Returning to Taiwan
— Total returnees
— Returnees with science degrees

Source: National Youth Commission and Ministry of Education, Taiwan.

Branch of Kwok family at home in Shanghai (top).

Zhang Daqian (above).

Chinese arrival at Angel Island being interrogated by US immigration officers (left).

RECRUITMENT OF WORKERS FOR BRITAIN AND FRANCE

One of the least-known episodes of World War I was the recruitment of indentured Chinese labour by Britain, France and Russia, the result of formal agreements entered into with Chinese authorities. The model for these contract agreements was the Anglo-Chinese Convention of 1904, which governed the recruitment and treatment of Chinese workers contracted to work on the Transvaal gold mines between 1904 and 1906 (see Part V: South Africa).

Between 1916 and 1920 approximately 150,000 Chinese workers were employed by the British and French governments, while Russia recruited more than 50,000 between 1915 and 1917. The Russian recruitment is covered elsewhere in the book (see Part V: Russia) and this article is concerned only with France and Britain.

The French dealt with the ostensibly private Huimin Company. In reality the company was under the control of Liang Shiyi, a government minister and close confidant of Yuan Shikai, who had emerged as president of the Chinese Republic established following the overthrow of the Qing dynasty. Liang, like other officials, was enthusiastic about the project; he believed that Chinese workers in France would learn skills that might in the future contribute to China's industrial development and hoped that supplying labourers for the Allied cause would enhance China's status at a future peace conference.

By May 1916 a contract had been signed with the Huimin Company (which came under the control of the Bureau for Overseas Chinese Workers when China officially entered the war in 1917). Recruiting centres were established in Tianjin, Qingdao and Pukou; a number of skilled artisans were also recruited from the French Concession area in Shanghai. The British government recruited directly (through Chinese agents) from its leasehold territory of Weihaiwei, just as it had done in 1904–06. Notices were posted in a variety of places, including teahouses. The first group of workers the French recruited (totalling 1,700) arrived in France in August 1916, while the first British contingent (totalling 1,000) arrived in Plymouth in April 1917 before being transported to France.

Eventually there were to be 100,000 workers under British control and 35,000 under French control. Most came from impoverished peasant families in the north (particularly Shandong province), although one Chinese observer noted the presence amongst their ranks of students, unemployed minor officials and those who had obtained lower-level degrees under the old civil service examination system (which had been abolished in 1905). Figures provided by the French Ministry of War in 1922 on the Chinese workers under French employ noted that 31,409 came from northern China, 4,024 from the south, 1,066 from Shanghai and 442 from Hong Kong.

Chinese workers (referred to as 'coolies' in the contract) recruited by Britain were to replace British dock and transport workers in France so that they could be released for work in Britain. After passing a medical examination and signing the contract (usually by means of a thumbprint since many recruits were illiterate), each member of the Chinese Labour Corps, as they would come to be called, was awarded an embarkation payment of 20 Mexican dollars; identification tags recording a worker's allotted number, name and next of kin were attached to the worker's wrist. During their stay in France they would be paid one franc (US$19.30) for a ten-hour day (about half the daily wage for a British army private), although foremen would receive two to five francs per day. Meanwhile a monthly payment of ten Mexican dollars (US$5.40) would be awarded their next of kin in China. There was no provision for sick pay (other than continued free food and lodging); more drastically still, if a worker was sick for more than six weeks the monthly allotment payment was to cease. Although the contract specifically stated that workers were not to be involved in 'military operations,' they would still be subject to martial law.

Billeted in camps that were located along France's western coast as well as in the northwest (some of which comprising more than 3,000 men), the Chinese Labour Corps by 1918 was engaged in trench-digging, burying war dead, and building aerodromes from Arras to Cambrai. Significantly, the Chinese Labour Corps was to form the largest contingent of foreign workers employed by Britain during the war (which included Indians, black South Africans, Egyptians and West Indians).

Workers recruited by the French government had five-year contracts with the option of staying on (in which case their return home would not be paid). A report by the French Interior Ministry in 1925 was to note the continued presence in France of 3,000 Chinese workers and apprentices. Initially under

the control of the Colonial Labour Service established by the War and Colonial Ministries, and later of the Labour Ministry, these workers were more widely dispersed throughout the country in smaller camps situated near rural settlements. From Brest in the north to Marseilles in the south, French-employed Chinese labourers were sent to work in government munition factories as well as in privately owned metallurgical, chemical and construction firms.

In contrast to those under British employ, these workers constituted a smaller proportion of the total number of foreign workers recruited by France during the war (36,941 out of a total of 662,000). Also, in order to pre-empt the accusations of French trade unions that their government was importing cheap labour, French-employed Chinese workers were paid more than their counterparts in the Chinese Labour Corps; in addition to the provision of food, clothing and lodging they were paid 2.5 francs per day. Whereas the highest wage a British-employed Chinese worker could earn was five francs a day (for a Class I interpreter), head machinists recruited by the French in Shanghai could earn 8.25 francs a day. Furthermore, it was stipulated that French-employed Chinese workers were to receive the same amount of bonuses as their French counterparts in the same occupations. They were also to receive 50 centimes daily sick pay for up to six weeks. Interestingly, although both British and French employed workers were entitled to one day off per week (in addition to French national holidays), the latter were also entitled to have time off for Chinese national holidays. In the event of death or permanent disablement both the British and French contracts stipulated a payment of 150 Mexican dollars to the worker's family.

It was also made clear that the Chinese labourers recruited to work in France were not to be regarded as combatants. Yet they were still exposed to considerable risk. Some of the earlier groups were transported via the Suez Canal and the Mediterranean (later groups went via the Cape of Good Hope or via the Pacific and then overland across Canada and by sea across the Atlantic), where the transport ships they were on were subject to German submarine attacks. One such ship, the *Athos*, was torpedoed in the Mediterranean in February 1917, resulting in the deaths of 540 Chinese workers. After August 1917 (when China declared war on Germany), Chinese workers in French employ were expected to work near the battle lines, exhuming and reburying war dead. Those working in Calais and Dunkirk were especially vulnerable to air attack (eight were killed by a bomb dropped on Calais), a fact attested to by the British prime minister David Lloyd George in his memoirs. An article in *The Times* of December 28, 1917 reported that Chinese workers were actually bringing up ammunition to the front line and that they remained in the trenches repairing dugouts and keeping machine-gun emplacements in order. During the course of the war, nearly 2,000 Chinese workers perished as a result of illness or enemy attack.

The European attitudes towards them were either racist or condescending. A report appearing in *The Times* on December 27, 1917, for example, declares that, 'The Chink, like the Kaffir, has to be kept under ward when he is not working. He gives little trouble if rightly managed, gambles a good deal, but does not get drunk or commit crimes of violence and is docile and obedient.' Another paper observes that 'they are only great big boys, and whatever their age may be, they are none of them older than ten years in character.'

In fact Chinese workers were not as docile and compliant as their British and French employers assumed (and wanted) them to be. They often protested against breaches in their contracts, the dangerous nature of their work, and the harsh treatment they at times received. Scuffles between French and Chinese workers occurred at war plants in Le Creusot in 1916 and in the gasworks of St Denis in 1917. Companies employing Chinese dock workers in Bordeaux and Nantes complained that they were intractable. In September 1917 a strike amongst

Chinese workers in Dunkirk protesting against their exposure to German air attack led to armed clashes with French guards during which two workers were killed. Between 1916 and 1918 there were 25 disturbances (riots and strikes) involving Chinese workers. Significantly, after May 1918 Chinese workers employed by the French were made subject to military discipline.

While in France Chinese workers formed mutual self-improvement associations which organized night classes (often taught by Chinese members of the YMCA or Chinese work-study students who arrived in France after 1919), as well as emphasizing the need to correct unseemly behaviour such as gambling, drinking and fighting. Such associations drew up elaborate rules of etiquette and daily living so that their members would not become the target of abuse and ridicule, a fate that had often befallen their compatriots in North America. Workers were told that it was their patriotic duty to save money and study. In fact, a growing sense of national consciousness and even politicization did occur amongst Chinese workers. When news of the (ultimately abortive) attempt in 1917 by the warlord Zhang Xun to restore the Qing monarchy reached France, protesting telegrams were sent in the name of 'Chinese workers, merchants and students residing in France.' Chinese workers at a factory in southern France embroidered a national flag in October 1919 to commemorate the outbreak of the 1911 Revolution that had overthrown the monarchy. Perhaps most significantly of all, when floods engulfed the metropolitan province of Zhili in 1918, Chinese workers in France donated funds for famine relief.

The Chinese workers recruited by Britain were repatriated in 1920, while many of those under French employ returned home in 1922. Their role during the war was fulsomely praised by some contemporary observers. Manico Gull, the British commander of the second group of workers transported to France as part of the Chinese Labour Corps, commented in 1918 that 'their emigration from the shores of Shandong will take its place certainly as one of the most important aspects of the Great European War,' while the French socialist politician, Marius Moutet, observed: 'What is worth remembering of this experience is the undoubted goodwill of the Chinese government to take an active part in the conflict in which the very existence of France was at stake. This assistance was valuable. Thousands of Chinese workers in our factories allowed us to spare an equal amount of French workers for military service.' There was also the hope expressed by some French politicians that the returning Chinese workers would contribute to the increase of France's economic and cultural influence in China.

Nevertheless, the hopes Chinese delegates had at the 1919 Versailles Peace Conference that the contribution of Chinese indentured labour to the Allied war effort might bring about an improvement of China's international position went unfulfilled. Except for the minor concessions granted China after it had declared war on Germany in 1917, the unequal treaty system imposed on China by the powers during the 19th century was not dismantled. Japan was allowed to retain the former German leasehold territory of Qingdao (along with its mining and railway concessions) that it had appropriated in 1914; Weihaiwei was to remain a British leasehold territory until 1930.

Finally, in 1925 the General Association of Chinese Workers in France, which had been established in 1919 and represented those who had remained after 1922, requested that the French government mark the contribution made by Chinese workers during World War I by erecting a commemorative monument and establishing a national cemetery for all those who had died in France. It also suggested that Boxer indemnity funds owed France (for damages wreaked by Boxer rebels upon French life and property in China) might be used to finance repatriation of Chinese workers still living in France. All these requests were turned down by the French authorities.

Paul Bailey

Chinese workers in their dormitory in France (far left). Graveyard in France where Chinese casualties of war lie buried.

through the 1970s remained limited in scope. To the US, clandestine migrants from Fuzhou – typically joining US-based family units established by stowaways – travelled without papers by boat to central America. From there they were ushered across the US-Mexican border by autonomous smuggling operations based at first in the Cantonese communities that had been in the region for generations, and later by Taiwanese residents who settled in Latin America during the 1960s and 1970s. To Europe, migration from China came to a virtual standstill during those years, picking up again in the late 1970s.

Aspiring migrants have been moved by plane, boat and land through an ever-shifting transportation network spanning every continent and at least 60 countries. Structured as a vertically organized chain linked by regional and criminal connections, this network is composed of recruiters (called *shetou* or 'snake heads' in Fuzhou, and *huangniu bei* or 'ox's back' in Wenzhou), corrupt officials, travel agents, document forgers, lawyers, hotel and ship owners, debt collectors, money launderers and even consular officials. An example of this last group was a senior American veteran, an officer of the US Immigration and Naturalization Service, who was arrested in July 1996 for delivering forged Honduran passports to Hong Kong.

Cover of Chinese book on human smuggling with picture of the Golden Venture *and her passengers.*

Regardless of whether 'smugglees' travel on a direct flight from Shanghai to Los Angeles or through a dozen countries during a year-long journey, the nodes controlling their movement are located in Central and South America for traffic to the US, and in Wenzhou and central Europe for traffic to France, Spain, Italy, Austria, Germany and northern Europe.

The process of illegally transporting people from China to the US or Europe can be broken down into three phases (1) leaving China, including required preparations; (2) transit between China and the country of destination; and (3) arrival. There is enormous variation within each phase, some of which is reflected in the stories of Zhang, Chen and Hu (not their actual names), whose real-life experiences are woven into the schematic descriptions below.

Once the decision to go abroad is made, an individual contacts a smuggling broker and negotiates the price and terms of passage. Chen, a 23-year old man from Changle (Fujian) who went to the US in 1991, signed a typical contract: he agreed to pay US$25,000, 10 per cent before departure and the balance within three days of passing through American immigration control or, in case of detention, three days after his release. The smuggler's obligation was to get Chen to the US within three months, and to cover all basic costs – food, transport and lodging – along the way.

Most brokers, including Chen's, provide the further service – for an additional fee of several thousand dollars – of securing a People's Republic of China passport and exit permit. Alternatively, the client can pay the necessary bribes to secure these documents independently, or he can exit with an escort overland via

Burma to Thailand and beyond, or via Russia to Europe, thus obviating the cost of Chinese travel documents altogether.

Zhang, a 28-year old woman from Lianjiang county, opted for the cheapest method of transport, one that required no travel documents whatsoever – by boat. In December 1992, she and several dozen others boarded a small fishing vessel in southern Fujian that transferred them to the *Eastwood*, a bulk cargo ship. With 527 Chinese nationals crammed into its refitted hold, the *Eastwood* sailed for the US west coast, and might have made it if the crew had not disabled and abandoned the vessel after a conflict with criminal enforcers on board. The passengers were repatriated to China after the US Coast Guard towed the ship to a US naval base on Kwajalein Island. Unable (and unwilling) to cancel her smuggling contract, Zhang embarked again, except this time she travelled, and arrived, on commercial airlines using forged documents. (One individual from the village of Houyu near Changle tried six times before succeeding.) By mid-1994 the three-year wave of long-distance boat traffic – which never, in any case, comprised more than 10 per cent of the total flow – had virtually come to a halt.

With enough money (about US$50,000) and, more critically, the right connections, a very small percentage of 'smugglees' have been able to travel 'first class' with the kind of passport used by government officials. Issued by the Foreign Ministry rather than the Public Security Bureau, these documents are rarely challenged by immigration authorities in the US or Europe.

The second phase revolves around the network of transit points between China and the US or Europe; this spans dozens of countries and is in constant flux, shifting in response to law enforcement efforts and national policies. Chen, whose broker proved incompetent, waited two months in the 'Thaibei Hotel,' a notorious Bangkok smuggling safe house, before receiving a stolen Japanese passport with his picture spliced inside, only to be stopped by Thai police at the airport and thrown in jail where he languished in horrid conditions for another two months. Once released, he left Thailand with a Singapore passport and passed through Sri Lanka, Hong Kong, Nepal, India, Karachi, Kuala Lumpur and London – handled along the way by sub-contractors in the smuggling network – before finally landing in New York, more than a year after setting out. (Average transit time to the US is about four weeks, to Europe three.) In the mid-1990s, Vietnam and Cambodia also became well-travelled way stations.

Most traffic to the US flows in the other direction, through Latin America. On her second and successful attempt, Zhang hopscotched by air to Belize, and then proceeded as part of a group of 30 over land through Mexico and across the US border at night. Other transit points in the region included the Bahamas and the Dominican Republic, from where the eastern US seaboard and Florida are accessible by small boats. The fact that 'every country in Central America plays a significant role' in migrant trafficking, in the words of an American government report published in 1995, is due to staggering levels of corruption – the immigration directors of Panama, Belize and Guatemala were all fired in the early 1990s for accepting bribes from Chinese smugglers – and the fact that as of 1996 nowhere except in Honduras is alien smuggling a crime.

Hu, a 38-year old man from Qingtian, in Zhejiang province, flew in 1994 from China to Moscow, where he likewise waited several months before securing falsified documents that would allow him to proceed by train through central Europe to Prague, and from there to his final destination, Paris. By 1995 sizeable enclaves of Chinese had formed in Budapest, Bucharest and Kiev, some waiting to move on, others apparently settled, legally or illegally.

Unlike smuggling to the US, transport to Europe is more decentralized, with many migrants finding their way to Romania, the Czech Republic and Hungary with legitimate visas, and then paying traffickers from there to proceed further west. It is also more diversified, at least as pertains to eastern Europe: a 1995 study by the International Organization for Migration suggested that there were more Chinese immigrants in the three above-cited countries from the Beijing area than from Zhejiang and Fujian combined, though the sampling cited was very small. Further complicating the picture is the fact that many Chinese intending to proceed to western Europe have stayed in central Europe instead or even returned there to start businesses after stints as wage labourers in European Union nations. Even within western Europe there is a higher degree of mobility, with clandestine workers moving away from countries cracking down on illegal immigration (such as France) towards those with enhanced opportunities for permanent residence or employment (such as Italy).

The third phase begins with arrival. Zhang entered the US without papers, whereas Chen attempted to enter with a falsified passport. Chen was caught, but was soon released 'on parole' with an appointment to appear before an immigration judge because there was no place to detain him. Both Chen and Zhang were taken into another form of custody – criminally operated 'safe houses' – in the New York area and held by members of the Fuk Ching (Fuqing) gang until the balance of their smuggling debts were paid off by relatives, in the US and in China respectively. Virtually all 'clients' pass through such safe houses, and some are tormented and tortured to encourage prompt remuneration. For the few who cannot pay, they can either be forced into servitude – as gang members if they are men, as prostitutes if women – or held until relatives can raise the cash.

Once payment is made, the relationship with the criminal organization that facilitated entry is terminated. Most migrants know very little about how the smuggling network is structured, and make little attempt to find out. Their legal status after arrival depends on whether they passed through immigration inspection, and on what policies are in force at any given time. Those without any papers, like Zhang and Hu, must work in the black market while seeking to regularize their situation through false documentation and/or amnesties. In Europe and especially the US, seeking political asylum was a common means to gain at least temporary work authorization and eventually, in many cases, permanent residence. Most applications of this kind were based on false claims of religious persecution or, for those seeking

A hairdresser's named Fuzhou Queen in New York.

asylum in the US, claims of persecution under China's 'one-child-only' birth-control policy, though a small minority legitimately qualified for such status.

Marlowe Hood

The case of Hong Kong

The island of Hong Kong was ceded to Britain in 1842. In 1898 the British extended their scope of control by leasing for 99 years an adjacent area of the Chinese mainland called the New Territories. Since its foundation as a British colony, Hong Kong has been an important point of origin for the Chinese going overseas. However, its position as a destination for migration, from China itself and from overseas, has been just as significant. It is this role, as a continuing centre of population interchange, that gives Hong Kong its unique place in the study of the Chinese overseas. Returned to Chinese sovereignty in 1997, Hong Kong connects China to the international ¡community, serving as a key node linking Chinese, overseas Chinese and other ethnic groups in a complex web of human circulation.

A place of transit

From shortly after its establishment as a British colony until 1939, over six million Chinese passed through Hong Kong on their way overseas. Although its relative degree of barrenness in pre-colonial times is debated, there can be little dispute that Hong Kong was not a major centre under the Qing, and the vast majority of later migrants came not from there but from a broad hinterland that stretched westwards into the Pearl River Delta and eastwards along the coast of Guangdong into Fujian. This shows the difficulty of assigning a definite point of origin to much of the migration from Hong Kong. While the majority of Chinese going overseas from Hong Kong were simply in transit, others had worked in the city, perhaps on more than one occasion, before going overseas.

Even today, many of those going overseas from Hong Kong have their origins in other parts of China, primarily Guangdong. They have come in three major waves of movement: first, immediately after the foundation of the People's Republic of China in 1949; second, in 1961–62, following the famine brought on by the Great Leap Forward; and third, in 1977–79, immediately prior to Deng Xiaoping's 'reforms and opening.' As late as 1981, only 2.4 per cent of the ethnic Chinese population of Hong Kong considered themselves to be of 'Hong Kong origin.' In 1991 some 40 per cent still had been born outside Hong Kong. Many of the older migrants had come as refugees from China, and a 'refugee mentality' has generated a creative tension that has contributed as much to the city's prosperity as to any desire to leave. Thus, compared to the Chinese populations of other places of origin, Hong Kong's is more fluid, has shallower roots and attachment to place, and is more predisposed to move again.

Rural origins of Hong Kong migration

A migration truly of Hong Kong origin took place from the villages of the New Territories mainly during the 1950s and 1960s. This migration, primarily to the United Kingdom, developed from a unique combination of factors. From the second half of the 1950s, the indigenous rice economy was undermined by rising urban labour costs and found itself uncompetitive against cheap imported rice. Britain, to which all Commonwealth citizens were allowed free access, was one of the few overseas destinations open to ethnic Chinese in the immediate post-World War II period.

The movements in and out of the colony resulting from the Japanese Occupation and the founding of the People's Republic of China made for a confusion in which only indigenous New Territories villagers could demonstrate conclusively that they had been born on British-administered territory, and hence were Commonwealth citizens. In Britain itself, the growing popularity of Chinese restaurants and takeaways offered opportunities to the inflows of migrants from the New Territories. By the early 1980s, however, British immigration controls had reduced migration from Hong Kong to a trickle. But by this time Hong Kong had become an origin for migration to other destinations.

Emigration and the transition to Chinese sovereignty

In the late 20th century, outflows tended to be linked to the return of the British colony to Chinese sovereignty on July 1, 1997. The international media saw the movements to Canada in particular, but also to Australia, the US and New Zealand, as streams of wealthy capitalists fleeing the transition to Communist control. While there is an element of truth in this viewpoint, it is also deceptive. Nervousness about 1997 unquestionably made reluctant exiles of many, but broader geographical and historical factors were also important.

The more recent migration from Hong Kong can be dated to the late 1960s and early 1970s and was the direct consequence of the major shifts in North American and Australasian immigration policies. Ending decades of discriminatory bias in immigrant selection, Canada in 1962, the US in 1965, Australia in 1973 and finally New Zealand in 1978 opened their borders to migrants from non-European, non-white sources. As a result, significant Asian and Latin American inflows into these settler countries came to rival and surpass the

movements from Europe. The international migration system came to be dominated by transpacific rather than transatlantic movements. It took several years for the impact of these policy changes to be manifest in actual flows from Hong Kong (see table 2.3).

Although there was a short surge of emigration out of Hong Kong to Canada in the early to mid-1970s, the movements were fairly steady until 1986–87. From that year, total departures accelerated from around 20,000 a year to over 60,000 within three years, and they have remained more or less at that level since then. Unlike the earlier emigrants, the vast majority of these came from Hong Kong's middle-income professional and entrepreneurial groups. This migration was overwhelmingly urban in origin. The exodus of these migrants raised enough public concern about the potential loss of skills and capital to the economy for a special government task force set up in 1988 to monitor the situation.

The 1997 factor alone does not fully explain the outflow. The time emigration began to accelerate, the period 1986-87, also saw the North American and Australasian economies emerge from the severe recession of the early to mid-1980s. The recurrent low fertility in those societies, and the change in their economies towards flexible production and labour systems, favoured the importation of labour from overseas. This labour was at two different levels: low-skilled workers to fill jobs spurned by native workers; and highly skilled, entrepreneurial workers to enhance native skills and stimulate the economy. The Hong Kong Chinese clearly fell into the latter category, and they have dominated the business migration programmes to Australia, Canada and New Zealand. Hence the emigration needs to be seen not just in terms of anxiety at home but also of opportunity abroad. Hong Kong migrants are as much bold pioneers in transnational commerce as they are reluctant exiles. The emigrants are part of a global movement of the highly skilled that is linking centres of economic dynamism around the world (see p 59).

The impact of migration

The vast majority of Hong Kong's population have no wish to move. A survey conducted in 1991, shortly after concerns about the future had been high, showed that only 5.6 per cent of the population would 'definitely move' before 1997, with a further 7.4 per cent saying they would 'probably move.' Most lack the resources and overseas contacts that would facilitate a move. However, the departure of the minority which did move was seen at one time to erode the 'functional core' of the labour force. Nevertheless, until mid-1996, no measurable impact on productivity or production could be solely or directly attributed to the emigration of this sector of the population. The stock of the highly educated and skilled actually increased in Hong Kong during the period of maximum emigration.

It is virtually impossible to isolate emigration as a factor of change in a complex matrix of transformation that has seen the restructuring of the Hong Kong economy in the 1980s and 1990s, from one based on labour-intensive industrialization to one based on services. With the transfer of its industrial base to southern China, Hong Kong has become a key service provider to a huge urban complex that stretches across the Pearl River Delta and includes Macao, Canton, the surrounding towns and the Special Economic Zones of Shenzhen and Zhuhai. Opportunities created by Hong Kong capital have prompted a massive internal migration southwards from many parts of China.

That Hong Kong is an area of significant immigration explains why emigration has had little effect. Even during the period of accelerating emigration, 1986–97, there was only one year in which it registered a negative net-migration, that is, when emigration exceeded immigration. That was in 1990, when there was a net balance of −15,700 at the end of the year, hardly significant in terms of the total population. By end-1995, net migration had increased to +120,600 and the annual rate of growth at 2.6 per cent was the highest in almost two decades. The British officials having increased the quota of those entitled to enter Hong Kong to avoid a surge after July 1,1997, much of the immigration was of dependants from China. Many, however, came to participate in the boom economy: the skilled from developed countries in Asia, Europe, North America and Australia, lower-skilled domestic workers from the Philippines, and labourers from China and elsewhere in Asia.

Emigration, return migration and circulation

A significant, but quantitatively unknown, component in the immigrant flows is the return of those who had previously left Hong Kong. In fact, many of those who left did so with the thought of return. Their sojourn overseas was aimed solely at fulfilling the residence requirements for a foreign passport, which was sought as an insurance policy against things going wrong after 1997.

Owing to its more flexible immigration policies, Australia has received more of this type of migrant than either Canada or the US, though this kind was almost certainly found in all emigrant flows from Hong Kong. Those who composed the flow to Australia were not only much more highly educated and skilled than those headed for the other major destinations, but they also

Table 2.3

IMMIGRANTS FROM HONG KONG				
YEAR	AUSTRALIA	CANADA	UNITED STATES	NEW ZEALAND (FROM 1980)
1960	na	1,146		
1961	na	710		
1962	na	426		
1963	na	1,008		
1964	na	2,490		
1965	na	4,155	75,007	
1966	na	3,710	(1961–70)	
1967	na	5,767		
1968	na	7,594		
1969	na	7,306		
1970	na	4,509		
1971	na	5,009	7,960	
1972	715	6,297	10,916	
1973	734	14,661	10,300	
1974	1,130	12,704	10,700	
1975	1,593	11,132	12,547	
1976	1,302	10,725	16,950	
1977	1,633	6,371	12,272	
1978	2,313	4,740	11,145	
1979	1,836	5,966	16,838 *	
1980	2,822	6,309	na	263
1981	1,960	6,451	na	351
1982	2,414	6,542	11,908	401
1983	2,756	6,710	12,525	292
1984	3,691	7,696	12,290	361
1985	5,136	7,380	10,795	462
1986	4,912	5,893	9,930	397
1987	5,140	16,170	8,785	445
1988	7,942	23,281	11,817	579
1989	9,998	19,908	12,236	1,081
1990	11,538	29,261	12,853	2,029
1991	16,747	22,340	15,564	2,492
1992	15,656	38,910	16,741	3,331
1993	8,111	36,510	14,010	2,780
1994	4,075	43,651	11,949	3,016

*Includes transition quarter June to Sept in realigned year.
Australia's statistics are for the financial year July 1–June 30. Canada's statistics are for calendar years. Immigrants to the US were admitted for the fiscal year July 1–June 30 in 1970–75 and from Oct 1 to Sept 30 in 1977–89.
Sources: Statistics published by respective governments. New Zealand data supplied by R. D. Bedford.

represented a much higher incidence of return. The return need not be permanent, nor need it involve complete family groups. Two patterns are common. In the 'astronaut' pattern, a family emigrates but the chief breadwinner, usually the husband, returns to Hong Kong, leaving wife and children at the new destination and flying in to visit periodically (hence frequently airborne, like an astronaut). In the 'parachute kid' pattern, both husband and wife return, leaving the children at the destination in the care of a relative or the eldest child.

Hong Kong's pattern shows clear parallels with other Chinese areas in Southeast Asia and Taiwan, but in its polarized distribution of migrants, it is much more like that of other global cities such as New York, London or Tokyo. There is immigration and emigration of the highly skilled or the high-earning, the 'new aristocracy of labour'; and there is immigration of the lower-skilled. Moreover, there is a continuous flow of population within the transnational networks established by the migrants, with family members virtually commuting across the Pacific, forming a new kind of extended family, one extended in physical space rather than across generations.

In the early 1990s there were probably around 585,000 Hong Kong people at overseas destinations. This estimate includes the Hong Kong-born as well as those born in China who had migrated to, and lived in, the city before going overseas. The figure, compiled from stock figures from the destination countries, excludes Taiwan where there may be some 60,000 Hong Kong people, and also children born overseas to Hong Kong parents. All but 2 to 3 per cent of this number would be ethnic Chinese. Almost 90 per cent of the total were to be found in the three principal destinations of Canada, the US and Australia, with most of the balance in New Zealand, Great Britain and Singapore. Thus, about 10 per cent of Hong Kong's resident population in 1990–91 was overseas, a fairly substantial proportion.

In the mid-1990s, emigration appeared to have declined slightly and to have stabilized; immigration continued to increase. Given the large number of foreigners in Hong Kong, estimated at 415,400 at the end of 1995, and an unknown number of people with foreign passports or residence rights overseas, anywhere between 11 and 16 per cent of the total population, or 700,000 to 1 million people, could leave quickly if faced with a disaster scenario.

Ronald Skeldon

Patterns of Chinese migration to Europe

Europe, unlike the USA, has no core history of Chinese immigration: Chinese immigrants are scattered and diverse, and there is no central narrative (like the migration to the West Coast and the early settlement in San Francisco's Chinatown) to capture one's imagination. James Watson's 1975 study of emigration from Hong Kong apart, major research on overseas Chinese has not been carried out on Chinese in Europe until the 1990s. The appearance in 1998 of *The Chinese in Europe*, a collection edited by Gregor Benton and Frank N. Pieke, was thus a landmark.

Chinese are not equally distributed among the various countries, and immigration waves took place at different times. Population statistics are unreliable, but it can safely be said that, taken as a whole, the rate of growth of Europe's Chinese numbers exceeded those of all other continents in the 1960s and 1970s. What also makes Europe's Chinese settlements distinctive are their spatial and relational dimensions. The country-by-country approach typical of the study of overseas Chinese – and adopted by this volume – seems even less satisfactory in the case of European nation-states than elsewhere in the world. Core communities in some countries do exist, as the chapters on Britain, France and the Netherlands in Part V attest, but Chinese immigration in the 1980s and 1990s conjures up images of a fanning out across national borders towards new frontiers. Most communities are best understood if considered transnationally, each connected to the other through a range of cross-border migratory and organizational linkages. Such linkages may or may not have been affected by the integrative emphasis of a Europe headed for economic and political union.

In Europe, as elsewhere, the pattern of migration may be analyzed in terms of source (or native-place origin) and timing. The main points of origin are Hong Kong,

especially the New Territories; Zhejiang, especially Wenzhou and Qingtian (see p 39); and French Indochina. In numerical terms Taiwanese immigrants would not be worth mentioning were it not for their disproportionately substantial economic impact, the majority of them being representatives of large Taiwanese firms who have used the contacts gained in Europe to set up their own businesses in Britain, the Netherlands and Germany.

In terms of timing, the earliest group came not, as is commonly believed, from Zhejiang but from Siyi ('four districts') in Guangdong. Other early immigrants were those originating from Guangdong's Dongguan and Baoan, particularly Dapeng in the latter county; and from Zhejiang. Yet others, contract workers in the first case (see pp 61 and 64) and seamen and service suppliers in the second, were brought over in connection with the two world wars. The 1960s saw inflows and chain migration of Hakkas from the New Territories. The biggest waves date from the inception of China's 'reforms and opening' in 1978 and its relaxation of emigration policy in 1985.

Independently of these inflows, there were trickles of individuals in the pre-World War I period: acrobats and circus artists who settled; small groups of human exhibits in fairgrounds who married Europeans; intellectuals, students, Christian clergy and artists who became sojourners then and later. After the Chinese Communist Party's crackdown on intellectuals in 1957–58 and during the Cultural Revolution in 1966–76, small numbers of highly educated Chinese arrived in Europe as refugees along the most extraordinary routes, and later taught Chinese and related subjects at European universities.

But analysis in terms of origin and timing leaves out too much that is significant about Chinese immigration to Europe. That story could conceivably be fleshed out by tracing the threads that run through it. The first of these threads is shipping. The majority of the early Siyi people came as seamen on European shipping lines, many to Liverpool and some to London. So did those who arrived in Holland from Dongguan and Baoan, hired as strike breakers by Dutch shipping companies (see Part V: The Netherlands). London, Liverpool, Amsterdam, Rotterdam, Antwerp and Hamburg were all ports harbouring small Chinatowns, where lived Chinese sailors and people who serviced their needs. Hamburg's Chinese Seamen's Club (Hanbao Zhonghua Haiyuan Zhi Jia) still exists.

During World War II, with all available hands diverted to battleships, the demand for seamen to work on merchant fleets rose steeply; the allied nations needed to keep the route between Britain and North America open for a massive transfer of goods. Liverpool became the centre for the Chinese Merchant Sailors Pool, the numbers of which rose to tens of thousands. After the war, some American Navy units were relocated from the Far East to Europe, and groups of Chinese suppliers, especially tailors, followed them to, and eventually settled in, various European countries.

The second thread is the colonial connection. Hakkas in the New Territories were admitted to Britain because, born on British territory, they were counted as Commonwealth citizens. Similarly, the many Siyi people who

Masthead of the Europe Journal.

Advertisement of Chinese shopping centre in Paris.

had migrated to the Australian and British South Pacific protectorate of Nauru to work in phosphate mines there in the early 20th century came to England when Nauru became independent. It was also to the metropolitan country that the Dutch-educated Peranakan Chinese of the Netherlands East Indies came when the latter gained independent nationhood. Likewise, the Netherlands was the metropolitan country of the Chinese immigrants from the former Dutch colony of Surinam. France received the bulk of the ethnic Chinese forced out of its former colonies in Indochina in the mid-1970s (though Denmark also took a couple of thousand following its rescue of Chinese boat people in international waters).

The third thread is the quite singular European focus of the culture of emigration in Wenzhou and Qingtian. How poor Qingtian people walked through Siberia or along the Silk Road, clad in rags and clutching small carved stone figurines to sell in Europe in the late 19th and early 20th centuries, is a story still told today (see p 40). Of the World War I contract workers mentioned earlier, 2,000 were from Qingtian, and of these 1,000 remained in France after the war. It is certain that, given the right economic and political conditions, a few pioneers can set off large-scale chain migration; and this seems to have happened with Qingtian natives. A leader of a Chinese organization in the Netherlands told the authors of this article that after his own arrival in 1965, he brought over his family and enabled the migration of between 100 to 200 people from Qingtian.

Since 1990 immigration from the Qingtian and Wenzhou areas has surged, rapidly producing communities in France, Italy (see Part V: Italy), Spain, Portugal and Scandinavia. How rapidly may be seen, for example, in Belgium, where Qingtian immigrants doubled in 1990–96, from 1,450 to 3,000. Similarly, Spain's Chinese population rose from 300–500 in the 1960s and 1970s to 30,000 in the mid-1990s, the overwhelming majority of them from Qingtian and Wenzhou.

The fourth thread is intra-Europe secondary migration. For some Chinese restaurateurs in Britain, the Netherlands was a new frontier. Later, grasping job opportunities offered by Chinese restaurants opening further afield, both British and Dutch Chinese moved to Germany, especially the Rhineland. Among Chinese interviewed by the authors was a descendant of Yuan Yang, a Dapeng native whose business it had been to bring large numbers of Dapeng sailors to the Netherlands. After Yuan relocated to the Rhineland, he helped British and Dutch Chinese, and some Chinese coming directly from Hong Kong, to go to Germany.

Much such re-migration stemmed from differential immigration policies. French restrictions, for example, diverted illegal Chinese migrants to Italy, Portugal and Spain, where the authorities were laxer and the chances of amnesty higher. One great funnel of re-migrants has been Hungary, which the nationals of the People's Republic of China initially did not require a visa to enter, and which saw its Chinese population leap from only nine before 1990 to more than 27,000 in 1991. After the introduction of a visa requirement in 1992, Chinese numbers plummeted, with many of those who escaped deportation re-migrating, often illegally, to Italy and other parts of Europe.

A fifth strand is student migration. As a place of higher learning where educational transients may subsequently become permanent residents, Europe may not be as popular as English-speaking destinations like North America and Australia, but its universities are some of the world's most advanced and prestigious, and many Chinese from China and Southeast Asia have completed their tertiary education or training in Europe. British educational establishments, for example, have graduated many Hong Kong, Malaysian and Singaporean Chinese, numbers of whom have stayed on. After 1979, many students from the Chinese mainland came to Europe to study, supported either by government grants or by their own means.

One such student was Zhao Liang, who arrived in Berlin in 1983 as a student financed by the Beijing government. Upon gaining his doctorate, he started his own business in Berlin. Only four of the 78 government-supported Chinese students who arrived in Germany at the same time as Zhao returned to China before graduating. Most remained in Germany, or else moved on to the US, Canada or Australia after gaining their degrees.

But return rates from Europe are higher than those from the US. In general, visiting scholars and students are supposed to leave the country at the end of their studies, and they are not normally given permanent resident visas. Rules vary by country, the British ones being very strict. Nevertheless, around the core of those granted 'exceptional leave to stay' after the events of June 4, 1989 and those whose academic excellence won them employment, an exile community has emerged in Britain. Depending on personal circumstances, growing numbers get visa extensions and permanent residence status. A special case of student migration is that of the exchange students Taiwan sent to Spain after the latter restored relations with the government in Taipei in the 1950s. Most of these students became permanent residents in or citizens of Spain, and some later moved to other parts of Europe.

Flemming Christiansen and Liang Xiujing

Chinese restaurant owners (top) and chef (bottom) in Holland.

Started in 1923, Belgium's first Chinese restaurant is called Huaqiao, or Wah Kel in the local spelling.

PART III

INSTITUTIONS

THIS SECTION REVIEWS basic overseas Chinese institutions. We are concerned here with the grounds for association and assistance by people who left their homes to work in a foreign environment, the historical and contemporary networks that have knitted clusters of overseas Chinese together. Because these did not spring out of thin air but were adumbrated in the Chinese homeland, we begin with an account of how the fundamental structures and hierarchies of traditional Chinese society fitted together.

We move on to an overview of the entire spectrum of overseas Chinese institutions, beginning with the family. Then we turn from the human realm to the supernatural to examine the form of Chinese religious worship and its place in the modern world. Next we survey the entire spectrum of non-profit ethnic Chinese associations in both the past and the present.

Finally we look at the growth of formal economic organization, showing how overseas Chinese businessmen have financed and managed their enterprises. To this survey is appended a debate on the popular perceptions of business connections between ethnic Chinese in different parts of the world.

Singapore's Chinese Chamber of Commerce, founded in 1906 by the men pictured here, exemplified the range of business, cultural, political, religious, educational and recreational organizations which overseas Chinese, drawing upon both Chinese and foreign models, established in their countries of settlement.

INSTITUTIONS

Learning how an overseas Chinese community fits together as a whole is a key to understanding how it works. This entails grasping the forms and bases of its togetherness and division. The forms and bases are changeable, and more or less adaptable to new circumstances. Indeed, even at their most pristine overseas Chinese associations were a reconstitution on new soil of older patterns. For they did not spring out of thin air, but were adumbrated in the Chinese homeland.

Emigration turns a new page in the life of an individual, but the page, when held up to the light, is found to be not all that new. Of course this is not to say that Chinese organizations abroad replicate Chinese society at home, or that precursors in the place of origin alone provide a standard or model of comparison. Nevertheless, not to portray the precursors is to tell only one side of the story. The differences are made more striking by the similarities.

THE ORDER OF THINGS IN CHINA

A Chinese at the dawn of the 19th century stood bounded by circles of social control extending from family elders to the remote structure that, though it affected him in barely comprehensible ways, he knew to be surmounted by the emperor. If he lived in a peasant village, he was one of at least 340 million who did – out of a population of perhaps 360 million. A millennium of tradition and an officialdom that was perhaps the world's most bureaucratized governed the Chinese millions. The state's business was done both centrally, in the capital in Beijing; and in the field, in provinces, prefectures, sub-prefectures and counties. In the field, officialdom was arranged in a pyramid descending from the provincial governor at the top, down through the prefects in the main towns, to the magistrates in the counties.

Between the magistracy and the mass of the peasantry was an informal tier of local government conducted by a local élite whose dual make-up is better captured by its Chinese name, *shenshi*, 'official and scholar,' than by its English translation, 'gentry.' It was officials retired or temporarily out of office, local scholars (degree-holders) and notables from the great clans in the local community who made up this class, seen by many as the mainstay of orderly society.

Officials were barred by the so-called law of avoidance from serving in their own native provinces lest they be tempted into collusion with kinsmen. They were recruited through regular civil service examinations, whose arrangement was a ladder which candidates had to scale to rise from the lowest, local-level degree to the highest, one competed for in metropolitan Beijing itself. Higher degrees being a prerequisite for office and the begetter of prestige and power, the examination ladder was good for other kinds of climbing as well, social no less than pecuniary. At each level, a system of quotas prevailed, with the number of degrees to be awarded set in advance to ensure a balanced representation among provinces and counties. Such quotas did not, however, prevent the over-representation of men among the highest degree-holders from one part of China, the lower Yangzi.

The possibility of acquiring degrees by purchase gave a measure of flexibility to the system. Designated as such, purchased degrees admitted some men of wealth, chiefly merchants and landlords, to the charmed circle of those who saw themselves (and were seen) as the bearers of Chinese civilization, if not to office. In China as in other societies, money bought class.

The millennium of tradition referred to earlier was founded on a body of text, the Classics that embodied the essence of Confucianism and formed the subject matter of the state examinations. Memorizing the canon, as boys in well-to-do families were obliged to do, was a process of socialization and ideological indoctrination in the conventional Confucian ideals. It was a means, in other words, by which the norms of the imperial bureaucracy, norms believed to be essential to good government and social order, were more or less internalized.

As administered by the learned officials, the Confucian order of things subordinated youth to age; female to male; individual to family; merchant, peasant, soldier and artisan to scholar; and all to imperial supremacy. Of course the foregoing sentence is a purist statement of Confucian social theory, and reality frequently contradicted rhetoric – how could it not? If the classical pecking order that consigned merchants to the bottom produced any reluctance on the part of the Chinese to seek the most lucrative investments for their capital, it did not do so for long. Such Confucian prejudices as impeded their ascendancy were brushed aside by the merchants hitching a ride up the social escalator on the back of their wealth. The real gauges of upper-class status were, learning and bureaucratic position apart, family connections and money.

Wealth was founded, above all, on the possession of land. Land might be worked for rich absentee landlords living in towns by tenant farmers in the countryside, though the complexity of China's rural structure was such that to picture all landowners as a clean scissored cut above the peasantry would be grossly to oversimplify. The rich town-dwelling landowner was merely at one end of a spectrum that, at its farther end, included the countless peasant proprietors who owned a tiny bit more land than they needed for subsistence and so hired

Book learning underpinned upward social mobility in Confucian China.

casual labour to help till it, as well as those who owned less than they needed and either leased extra acreage or hired themselves out as short-term labour during busy seasons.

If rents and profits from landed estates represented one means to enrichment, returns on investment in commerce were another. Substantial fortunes were made in inter-regional and international trade, signs of whose briskness may be found wherever the historian chooses to look. Great distances were crossed by the flows of traded merchandise, which comprised not only luxury items and the regional products in which each locality specialized, but even essentials such as rice, soya bean and cotton.

Between buyer and seller, goods moved by land and water, crossing provincial as well as national borders. Trade, commercialization and urbanization had loosened social categories and heightened upward mobility; but traders remained a lesser breed in the hierarchy of power, if only because the indulgence and protection of the Confucian-educated mandarin continued to matter to their business success. There was still no questioning the notion that if anything fitted a person for laying down prescriptions – the dos and the don'ts – for the rest of society, classical education did. And though models are not supposed to be true, merely the way things ought to be, most Chinese could be persuaded to take the Confucian one on board – if not in whole, then at least in part – and to believe that somehow that was what being Chinese was about.

Rural society

The Chinese Everyman lived in a rural village and worked the land. The subject of a realm that was nothing if not agrarian, he was sustained by an economy based on intensive agriculture. The importance of growing grain to Chinese life had the absoluteness of immemorial dogma. Land was cultivated by the individual farming family, owner or tenant.

Chinese scholars distinguish between lineage lands (that is, estates corporately held by a lineage) and other holdings, such as private plots owned by the heads of households. The lineage is a group that traces its ancestry through the male line to a common patriarch, the first forebear to settle in a particular locality. Of particular interest to some observers is the type of property called ancestral or 'sacrifice land' (*jitian* or *zhengchangtian* in Chinese), a family trust set up to provide sacrifice for ancestors. Shared property, the income from which went to support education, philanthropy and rites, was what made a lineage a lineage.

Broadly speaking, lineages were not unknown in north China, but they became more numerous and their role appeared greater as one went south. Indeed they were hard to ignore in the rural villages of Fujian and Guangdong, not least because, if they could make their power felt, they did. For the way some of them behaved, Fortress Family might not be an inappropriate epithet. To tangle with a strong lineage was unwise, unless one were as powerful oneself. Big was better than small where lineages were concerned, for clearly the weight of numbers counted, translating as it did into economic and social muscle. A *daxing* ('big surname,' meaning a large

lineage) commanded respect from lesser bodies.

There were villages – albeit not in the majority – where one surname did for all; where, in other words, the settlement and the lineage were one and the same. This need not imply that the members were in every case related by blood and marriage. For the sake of self-protection or aggrandizement, a lineage might bring its size and status into line with its pretensions by merging with another, resorting to putative genealogies. 'Clan' is the word used by Western anthropologists for an alliance of this kind. Not that there is a parallel precision in Chinese usage; the Chinese frequently understand 'family' figuratively, and in documents dating from the Ming and Qing dynasties, *zu* (commonly rendered as 'lineage') is often interchangeable with *jia*, usually translated as 'family.'

Any individual might be expected to do better with the full weight of his backers behind him; that backing might be the Church or the guild, or law and the enforcement machinery of the state. But what else could it be in the villages of rural southern China if not the family? Of course there is no reason to suppose that the Chinese family was any more united than families elsewhere, or that it was any less riven by fraternal rivalry. Few large families could escape quarrels and recriminations over inheritance and money. There was no shortage of cases where the richer and more predatory branch of a family bullied and exploited the poorer and weaker. Yet, as against all this, there was the practice of lineage allying with lineage the better to fend off adversaries. That union was strength was well understood by the local alliances of interdependent groups bearing different surnames.

Groups had reason to build up power by confederating because a running theme of life in south China was armed feuding (called *xiedou* in Chinese). Such mayhem was reported in southern Fujian in the 18th century, but became endemic also in Guangdong in the 19th century. Vendettas shattered whole districts into fragments of self-arming and self-authorizing warring bands. One place where *xiedou* caught on particularly virulently was Taiwan.

The sounding of a gong; the gathering of leaders in the ancestral hall, which doubled as the military headquarters; the mustering of spears, iron-tipped carrying poles, clubs, knives and firearms; the enlisting of mercenaries; the swearing of oaths; the massing of men running at times to a hundred thousand and more – all these were signs that one of these bloody affrays was about to break out. The pitched battles showed men in their beastliest aspects; if they settled any dispute over land, water, honour or the boundaries of fields and graveyards, they never did so without violence. All in all, southern Fujian was no place for the squeamish. So thoroughly ingrained was its unruliness that observers speak of the region as having a tradition of violence.

In a place and time of such fierce rivalries, a family needed no

Portrait of Confucius.

Emigration was often an alternative to land-bound labour.

Entrance to ancestral hall of Li lineage in Fujian.

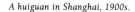

Statue of Tianhou, also known as Mazu, in Taiwan.

Confucian urging to attach importance to progeny. It was a popular practice in Fujian to increase family size by buying young boys for adoption. The custom of acquiring brides as children – the 'little-daughter-in-law' form of marriage where a girl was raised in the household of her future husband from childhood – was also quite common. Men of means would have secondary wives beside their principal partner, while indigence put the bride price beyond the reach of others and so condemned them to bachelorhood and childlessness. Concubinage and the custom of property partition among male heirs were factors accounting for a trend noticed by many, which was that here as elsewhere in China a family was inclined to go down in the world rather than up in succeeding generations.

The Confucian stereotyping of moral relations between the sexes, between parents and children, and between brothers held good for many families. In the 17th and 18th centuries, numbers of Fujian's childless widows won admiration and their place in local history for publicly committing suicide to demonstrate their wifely devotion and chastity. Memorial arches were raised to such women here as elsewhere in China. Indeed, erecting these was one of the arts of one-upmanship practised by men of substance.

It was such men, too, who took turns to build, maintain and renovate temples, a focus of local community beyond the kin group. No neighbourhood was without its cult, and deities, surrounded by accretions of local lore and legend, had shrines dedicated to them in both town and country. The authorities did not smile on all of them – 'secret sect' was an official label serving to discredit the heterodox.

Others were favoured with imperial recognition. To name just two, Guandi, the God of War, was admitted to the official pantheon, as was Tianhou, 'Empress of Heaven,' or Mazu to many Fujianese. Her cult is said to have started in Putian county, Fujian province, in the 10th century, when a woman the locals called Lin Dagu, or Aunt Lin, came to be deified as a supernatural being whose spirit guided seamen safely home through storms. The cult caught on all along the coast, and, upgraded as Empress of Heaven, Aunt Lin has been a fixture in the folk traditions of south China, Taiwan and Chinese communities in Southeast Asia ever since. As the patron goddess of fishermen, mariners and seafaring traders, she was a symbol around which sojourning merchants could especially rally.

Temples were but one form of social organization. The secret society was another. By whichever name it is known – Hongmen, Triads – one of the earliest such brotherhoods was the Tiandi Hui (Heaven and Earth Society). The Tiandi Hui was founded at the Goddess of Mercy Pavilion (Guanyin Ting) in Zhangzhou prefecture (southern Fujian) around 1761, and then exported to Guangdong and other parts of China. Kinship (usually fictive), common local origin, secret signs and passwords, initiation rituals, sworn brotherhood, an origin myth, lore, the bonding of worker to contractor – permutations of these made for tight comradeship in the Triads. The Triad-type organization made itself felt in several guises, the best known of which came to be the criminal gang with its unsavoury reputation for opium smuggling, racketeering and other familiar underworld businesses. As mutual-aid support groups, these associations proved particularly useful to persons who moved from place to place to fill the ranks of casual labour.

Many casual labourers mixed farming with mining, but considerable numbers of men made mining a profession and travelled from workings to workings in bands under leaders. Such men were in the habit of forming brotherhoods, an institution so common that it was a saying in Yunnan province, China's largest producer of copper in the 18th century, that no mine might open without an oath being sworn. A miner's life was hazardous and hard. Of no fixed abode, he lived in a hastily constructed shack wherever he went, and where he went was all too often a remote, backward and mountainous region. He no doubt felt stronger and more secure for being a member of a brotherhood.

Mining communities seemed to have an egalitarian side to them. Having chosen a mine to operate, a leader would gather together a group of miners to work on a profit-sharing basis. If the start-up money had been raised by getting people to chip in, then the profits would be divided according to how much each partner had put in. In an overseas setting, this brotherhood-partnership structure would, give or take an adaptation or two, assume the shape of the *kongsi*.

Urban society

To understand overseas Chinese urban communities, it helps to look at late imperial Chinese cities. This is because they grew out of similar migrations. Although every Chinese city had residents who thought of themselves as natives of the place, 'it is easy to get the impression,' writes G. William Skinner in 1977, 'that in late imperial times most urbanites were sojourners.' Place of origin (or regional identity) was the first of the markers of difference among these sojourners. And since sojourners from specific regions in China tended to specialize in one or more trades, Chinese urban society exhibited an 'ethnic division of labour.' Furthermore, neighbourhoods were linguistic enclaves, each inhabited by people from a particular region in China.

Occupational and native-place affiliations found organizational forms in *gongsuo, huiguan, bang, tongxiang-hui* and *hui* – Chinese terms that are sometimes used interchangeably.

Gongsuo: Only partially translated by 'guild' and 'chamber of commerce,' this was a commercial or craft association with its own building. Though *gongsuo* were

A huiguan in Shanghai, 1900s.

organized on the whole along lines of trade specialization rather than regional origin, the distinction was by no means always clear.

Huiguan: This was a formal association of sojourning persons from the same native place. The term refers both to the building in which the association conducted its business and to the body of people it housed. The word is hard to distinguish from *gongsuo* because of the overlapping of local origin with trade speciality. To translate it, scholars have used 'guild' or '*landsmannschaften*,' the latter term chosen by Ho Ping-ti in his classic study of Chinese regional associations, whose origins he traces to 16th-century hostels specializing in housing imperial examinations candidates at the capital, as well as expectant officials awaiting assignment to bureaucratic office.

A lodger of a particular regional origin would stay in the hostel identified with that region, one using the dialect and serving the cuisine of that region. Wealthy sojourning merchants came to use the hostels' facilities, and by and by the merchant element began to predominate and region-specific mercantile associations evolved.

Many purposes were served by *huiguan*: sentimental, religious, cultural and instrumental. To further group interest, to facilitate networking, to honour the home region's own local gods, to provide coffins or cemetery space for fellow-provincials lacking the means for home burial – all these were important *huiguan* concerns.

Sojourning groups differed in their degree of success and power, and their *huiguan* buildings, some very splendid indeed, had to reflect this. The one which sojourning merchants from Fujian built in 18th-century Shanghai, for example, was lavish in scale, with courtyards and temple features like altars (one dedicated to Tianhou, the other to Guandi) and a stage for theatrical performances.

Bang: A generic term derived from the word for convoys of boats tied together for mooring. Originally describing the mutual-protection associations of boatmen, it could, used loosely of a variety of groupings, refer to a trade or occupational group without a fixed meeting place or, if it did have permanent premises, to the group rather than to its building.

Though widely used of lower-class groups such as coolies, dock workers and gangs, the term could just as well be applied to businessmen and wielders of financial or political power (in which case it takes on the connotations of 'clique'). It can also refer to associations based on common trade and local origin like *gongsuo* and *huiguan*, with which it is often used interchangeably. (Among overseas Chinese it commonly denotes dialect-based groupings.) When combined with the character *hui* (see below), as *banghui*, it becomes a term for gangs and secret societies.

Tongxianghui: A post-1911 term which may be translated as 'association of fellow-regionals,' this denotes a more modern form of native-place association, one with a constitution, elected office bearers and public meetings. In theory, though not perhaps always in practice, *tongxianghui* opposed themselves to the traditionalism of *huiguan*.

Hui: This is another form of voluntary association. It could be a religious society or a criminal gang. Like *bang*, it does not designate a corporate body so much as a grouping of people with a common, sometimes secret, interest. Another designation for gangs was *tang*, literally 'hall,' which was sometimes a *hui* or *bang* by another name.

Editor

THE OVERSEAS CHINESE FAMILY

Consider a family comprising a man, his wife, two sons and two daughters. They all live in one household in rural China. As the children grow up, the daughters marry out and one of the sons also weds. The daughter-in-law comes to live under the same roof as her husband and his parents, and participates in the household's economic activities. The second son, still single, leaves home to seek work in the city. He sends his earnings back to be used to repair his natal home and to supplement its income. He returns to marry a girl chosen by his parents but goes back to the city shortly after the wedding, leaving the bride behind. On his visits he fathers children on her. A second generation born to the two brothers grows up in the same home. The parents die, and the two conjugal units continue to live together for a while, but eventually the brothers divide the estate and what was one household becomes two.

We need alter only one detail of this sketch of a rural Chinese household to make it relevant to a discussion of the overseas Chinese family: change the second son's migrant destination from 'the city' to 'overseas.' In all other important respects, it sums up the family arrangements of Chinese sojourning overseas in the 19th and early 20th centuries. The remittances sent home, the wife left behind, the maintenance of a claim to an equal share of the patrimony – all these were aspects of the overseas Chinese sojourner's relationship to his family in China. On the whole women did not emigrate, but sons would join fathers in the latter's place of sojourn as chain migrants.

Departures from the pattern were few. One was that countless men were too poor to send back money, to undertake the periodic homeward journeys, to marry and to perpetuate their line. To quote Daniel Kulp, who studied an emigrant village in south China in the 1920s: 'Not a few persons are forced to live from hand to mouth, finally returning broken in productive efficiency, a charge upon their families, or dying miserable deaths away from home with none to burn the candles.' In China, too, access to women was unequal, but it was even more so in the 'bachelor society' in which the overseas migrants found themselves. The total absence of family life turned the mass of the overseas plantation and mining workers and coolies to the surrogate solace of prostitutes.

The second departure was that some men married, or formed liaisons with, local non-Chinese women abroad, siring children of mixed parentage. These children were called mestizos in the Philippines, *lukjin* in Siam, *gwe chia* in Burma, Minh Huong in Vietnam and so on. Some locally born Chinese in the Straits Settlements are descended from Chinese-Malay unions, but by no means all Babas, as the

Prostitute in San Francisco's Chinatown.

Offspring of locally born Singaporean Chinese.

Su Manshu.

locally born Chinese are called, are of mixed blood.

Elsewhere, such as in the United States, anti-miscegenation attitudes and legislation worked against inter-racial unions. Intermarriage in some instances entailed conversion to a religion: Islam in Malaya and Catholicism in Mauritius, to cite two examples. In mixed marriages, there tended to be more equality between the sexes and, especially if they were foreign-educated, more independence on the part of the women. The scholar Chen Ta tells of a 1930s Baba girl married to a Singapore Chinese migrant who, in less than 20 days after her arrival on a visit to her husband's ancestral village near Shantou, succeeded in persuading him, greatly to the consternation of his uncle, the patriarchal head of the family, that the property held in common for three generations should be divided so that she and her husband could have the wherewithal to set up home on their own.

By and large the offspring of mixed marriages was brought up as Chinese, and one or more sons were commonly sent back to be educated in the home village. For instance, the writer Su Manshu, born to a Cantonese merchant and a Japanese woman in Yokohama in 1884, began his study of the Chinese Classics as a seven-year-old at the village school in his father's native Guangdong province.

Su Manshu's father did nothing out of the ordinary for a man of his means in acquiring a Japanese concubine in addition to his Chinese first wife and Chinese concubines. Polygyny was a custom both in China and abroad. As practised by an emigrant, it could take a form of family organization which Chen Ta has named the 'dual family system.' Under this arrangement, a man maintained two homes, one in his place of sojourn and the other in his place of origin. In a more complex variation of the system (see figure 3.1), a man might have a first wife in his home village, the first of his concubines (a local woman) with him in his adopted country, his second concubine in his home village and his third and fourth concubines, both Chinese, in his overseas home. As is indicated in the figure, of the children born to these wives, most were resident in Thailand; others appeared to prefer Shantou, which was the nearest urban centre to the home village.

Many of the best-known overseas Chinese of the period had multiple wives: Tan Kah Kee (of Singapore) had four wives and 18 children; Aw Boon Haw (of Burma and then Singapore) had four wives and nine children; Oei Tiong Ham (of the Dutch Indies) had five wives and 26 children. In families this large, dissension among wives and their children could not have been avoidable. If this was bad enough during the patriarch's lifetime, it could get far worse at his death, which was often the prelude to a protracted wrangling among kin over their share of the inheritance.

In China the status of concubines, who were generally bought from poor or lowlier families and taken into the household without ritual recognition, was deemed inferior to that of the wife. But before the law, their offspring had the same rights as those of the principal wife. In practice, though, widely accepted custom often prevailed over the letter of the law and far from inheriting equally with the principal wife's offspring, the concubine's children frequently suffered discrimination at the hands of their half-brothers.

Judicial institutions were stronger in the European colonies where overseas Chinese settled, and there it was not unknown for Chinese women to take their polygynous husbands to court on a charge of bigamy. And whereas in China, concubines had an inferior position in the family, they were not always so regarded by the colonial courts of places such as the Straits Settlements (Malacca, Penang and Singapore). This may be illustrated by the famous Six Widows Case. Choo Eng Choon, a Straits-born Chinese, died intestate in Singapore. After hearing the case over a four-year period from 1905, the courts decided to treat the widows, whether 'principal' or 'inferior,' as equal for purposes of succession and legitimacy and the distribution of Choo's considerable estate.

Inheritance was further complicated by the fact that while patrilineal transmission of property was standard in China, such custom did not necessarily mesh with the foreign jurisdictions under which overseas Chinese lived. Oei Tiong Ham's wish to bequeath the ownership of his business empire to nine of his 13 sons, disinheriting his 13 daughters, was thwarted by Dutch law, under which daughters had the right to inherit. His relocation to Singapore was partly prompted by the fact that the English law which prevailed there allowed him to disinherit some of his children.

Far outnumbered by men, wives were sometimes valued and respected to a higher degree abroad than they might have been at home. But this is not to say that they were free from male violence – in San Francisco, for example, Christian mission homes provided a sanctuary for Chinese women fleeing domestic lives made intolerable by the husband's physical abuse, or by his opium smoking, drinking, polygamy or negligence in providing for the family. The balance of women's dependency on men did not shift until wider social and economic changes transformed marriage and family in the early decades of the 20th century. In the transformation, Western influences played a part, but so did revolutionary and anti-traditionalist ideas wending their way from a faraway modernizing China and given voice in the Chinese periodicals published in the overseas communities.

Figure 3.1

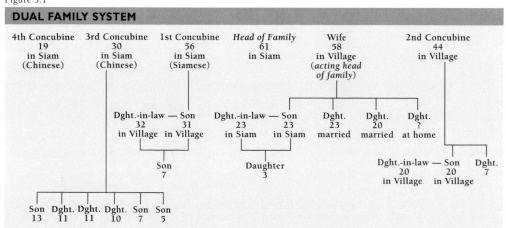

DUAL FAMILY SYSTEM

| 4th Concubine 19 in Siam (Chinese) | 3rd Concubine 30 in Siam (Chinese) | 1st Concubine 56 in Siam (Siamese) | *Head of Family* 61 in Siam | Wife 58 in Village (*acting head of family*) | 2nd Concubine 44 in Village |

Dght.-in-law — Son
32 — 31
in Village — in Village

Dght.-in-law — Son
23 — 23
in Siam — in Siam

Dght. 23 married   Dght. 20 married   Dght. ? at home

Dght.-in-law — Son — Dght.
20 — 20 — 7
in Village — in Village

Son
7

Daughter
3

Son 13   Dght. 11   Dght. 11   Dght. 10   Son 7   Son 5

Source: Chen (1940).

THE CHINESE FAMILY IN THE STRAITS SETTLEMENTS

For some overseas Chinese, the maintenance of Chinese marriage and family rituals became a prime marker of a Chinese identity otherwise culturally thinned by local adaptation. The Babas, who spoke Malay rather than Chinese, provide a good example of this. Behind the centrality of ancestor worship in Baba life lay the conflation of family ritual and Chinese identity. Since language and perhaps other forms of Chinese culture were lost, it became all the more important to maintain ancestor worship as a marker of Chinese identity. This perhaps explains why ancestor worship should remain important to someone as far removed from his roots as the Malacca-born Tan Cheng Lock (1883–1960), a fourth-generation Chinese who was apt to quote Jane Austen, Shakespeare and Victor Hugo to his children. So appalled was Tan to learn that his children had got themselves baptized as Christians while living in England that he wrote them a letter running to 12 foolscap pages reprimanding them; by embracing a faith which considered ancestor worship idolatrous, he thought, they had denied their culture.

How some Baba families lived may be glimpsed in such homes as have been preserved in places like Heeren Street in Malacca and Emerald Hill in Singapore. These are usually terraced houses on two floors, with the sleeping quarters located in the upper storey. Much has been written about these houses from an architectural point of view. Their mix of Chinese, local and European features does indeed give concrete form to Baba acculturation; but here we are interested in the house as an embodiment of Baba domesticity. This may be conjured up from the floor plan (see figure 3.2), the way domestic space was divided and allocated and the way furniture was arranged. From these it may be seen that, as in China, interior space was functionally separated and used for domestic and ritual practices, while furnishings and decorations signalled not only class and status but also the family's aesthetic preferences.

The front entrance led to the main hall, where the dominant note was struck by the household altar bearing images of Guandi (the God of War) or Guanyin (the Goddess of Mercy), the deities favoured by Babas. As the room was also where guests were received and where, if there was a death in the family, the coffin was placed for the duration of the funeral, the space served both social and ritual purposes. In some homes the next room was the offering hall containing a teak ancestral altar; in others the ancestral altar was absent, and only on feast days and death anniversaries was a temporary one set up to the right of the household deity in the first hall. Domestic offerings to the ancestors included food, which was prepared and served for both the dead and the living. Beyond the second hall was the air well, a feature that may be interpreted in straightforwardly functional terms, as a receptacle for rainwater and a way of keeping the house open to light and ventilation, but which also recalls the courtyard common to dwellings in China.

The kitchen was located at the back of the house. This was the women's domain, the site of production of *Nyonya ware teapot.*

Nyonya cuisine, a distinct style of cooking blending Malay, Indian and Chinese influences. The crockery found in a well-stocked Baba home would include dinner services of brightly coloured Chinese porcelain originally referred to as 'Shanghai ware' (but now called 'Nyonya ware') – Shanghai being where orders for them were placed by the families who imported them. These wares, whose decoration came in colour mixes – olive green, pink, mustard, brown, powder blue – that departed distinctly from Chinese taste, are now much sought after by art collectors as embodiments of the Baba aesthetic.

Another female domain was the bridal chamber, where elaborate wedding rites of part-Chinese derivation were performed. The sumptuously decorated marital bed would have symbols for fertility, wealth and longevity – blessings immemorially wished for by Chinese – placed beneath it; but instead of the familiar Chinese ones, the emblems were, respectively, yam tuber, banana and lemon grass. In cases where the groom was of humble means, the marriage would be matrilocal, with the husband residing in the bride's home after the wedding. Marrying their daughters to them was one way in which wealthy Baba families absorbed and influenced new immigrants. The bride would be dressed in a heavily embroidered wedding robe which, for all its allusions to Manchu costume, was unlike any that a contemporary bride in China would wear. On other, everyday occasions the Nyonya would wear Malay costume and be adorned with jewellery. This last was an artefact no well-to-do household would be without. Conspicuous consumption was crucial to the sustaining of the Baba identity.

As a frame and a showcase for these and other elements of Baba material culture, the well-to-do family home and its significations marked out the Baba way of life from those of the *sinkeh*, the new immigrants from China. Its function as a shelter could not be separated from its symbolic meanings. While helping to maintain its occupants' Chinese identity, however hybridized, the Baba family home simultaneously made distinctions and established boundaries between them and the upstart newcomers.

Editor

Figure 3.2

FLOOR PLAN OF A STRAITS CHINESE HOUSE IN MALACCA

Street

First Floor

KEY

1cm = 300cm
b : bedroom
d : drain
e : entrance
g : deity's altar
m : main entrance
s : bathroom
t : toilet
v : verandah
w : window
---- : split level
⌐ : stairway

Ground Floor

roofed extension

Source: Tan (1988).

For many women, such as those in the US, being mobilized for participation in the labour force during World War II was a still greater step towards independence. And with more and more women proving themselves professionally, women's identities came to be formed outside the confines of marriage and motherhood. Later, the possibility of divorce and alterations in women's fertility patterns gave rise to further flexibility within marriage. Partners came to be personally and relatively freely chosen on the basis of mutual attraction. Family size shrank.

In overseas Chinese populations as a whole, the greatly expanded volumes of female and family migration in the first half of the 20th century put paid to the 'bachelor society' of earlier generations. But in an ironic twist to the previous dual family arrangement, much late-20th century migration has also involved residential separation. This time the wife is left, not at home, but as the lone head of the family in the destination country, while the husband returns to his job or business in the place of origin (notably Hong Kong), coming to visit periodically – thereby spending much time in the air – in what is called the 'astronaut' migration pattern. Anecdotal evidence suggests that the risk of family breakdown is increased by the extended periods of the couple's physical separation and the difficulties of lone parenthood.

Meanwhile, the 'Chinese family' has emerged as a key element in the late-20th century way of talking, thinking or representing overseas Chinese business. In this

Chinese woman offers burning incense in temple in Vietnam.

Almanac marked with auspicious or inauspicious days.

Chinese remember ancestors on feast-day in Singapore.

discourse (see p 125), 'Chinese family values,' variously said to include paternalism, nepotism, cohesiveness and discipline, and frequently conflated with 'Confucian values' and 'Asian values,' are sometimes seen as a help to Chinese business advancement, and sometimes a hindrance. These putatively Chinese values were viewed as cultural assets conducive to the Chinese embrace of global capitalism during Asia's boom in the 1980s and first half of the 1990s, but were seen to be liabilities, inviting cronyism and corruption, when the boom turned to bust in 1997.

Choi Kwai Keong

RELIGION

The form of religion most widely practised in both historical and contemporary overseas Chinese communities is Chinese Religion (also called Chinese Popular Religion elsewhere in this book), sometimes referred to by its practitioners simply as 'worshipping the Gods' or *baishen*. Often mistakenly labelled 'Buddhism,' Chinese Religion is based on a heterogeneous mixture of ancestor worship with elements deriving from Buddhist, Daoist and Confucian sources as well as from traditional Chinese folklore and religious practices indigenous to the places where the Chinese have established communities. Despite differences in interpretation and practice between individual communities, Chinese Religion shows a remarkable degree of consistency in its basic form and content across overseas Chinese communities.

While social and cultural differences between sites of overseas Chinese settlement have helped to produce a range of distinctive versions of Chinese Religion, these versions have at least four salient features in common: a belief system founded on the assumption that gods and ghosts not only exist but possess the power to influence human affairs; the mapping of a non-human realm mirroring the hierarchy and practical conditions of traditional Chinese social life; subscription to the notion that fate (*ming*) and luck (*yun*) are the key determinants of life and that the effects of luck can be manipulated with the help of gods and ghosts to modify the otherwise absolute nature of fate; the assumption that the human soul has two discrete components, namely regenerate and personal soul-portions, which become separated at the time of death.

Influenced by Hindu and orthodox Buddhist notions of karma, Chinese Religion essentially pursues the practical outcome of achieving peace and avoiding suffering either in this life or the next, depending on the circumstances of the individual. Peace takes the form of *haoming* (a good life) and *fuqi* (one's allotted happiness) in this life, and of a good rebirth and tranquil happiness through attainment of godhead in the next. Suffering in this life is the reverse of *haoming* and *fuqi*, while in the next life, it takes the form of torture in the Underworld and rebirth as an animal. It goes without saying that as Chinese Religionists grow older, the focus of their concerns shifts from this life to the next.

For the Chinese Religionist, peace and suffering in this life are the result of fate, and since fate is understood as being both absolute and knowable only in retrospect, not only is one powerless to bring about radical changes to one's life but one cannot be certain whether fate has dealt one a good or poor hand until one's life ends. This predisposition towards fatalism imposes limitations on the range of possible religious actions available to practitioners of Chinese Religion, while providing the very basis for their religious activity in the first place.

Thus, Chinese Religion is centred on divinatory practices by means of which an individual formulates and deploys strategies for coping with his or her perceived lot in life with the aid of gods and ghosts. Concerns with good versus evil and truth versus falsehood, prominent in Christian theology, are largely absent from Chinese Religion. The utilitarian focus of Chinese Religion militates against such metaphysical enquiry. Rather, what it provides is a range of simple but extremely versatile blueprints for practical action which can be implemented to a greater or lesser degree by practitioners across different socio-economic classes and educational levels.

In their earliest days, all overseas Chinese communities practised one or another version of Chinese Religion. For the bulk of Chinese immigrants, who were largely rural in origin, illiterate and accompanied in few cases by women, religious practice generally took the form of worship of various gods and ghosts organized along clan and native-place lines as well as according to the ritual prescriptions of secret societies. In Western countries, where migrant Chinese workers often faced extreme racial hostility and were largely alienated from the dominant white society, Chinese Religion was practised largely in private, in exclusively Chinese places separated from the wider community. Chinese Religion as practised in larger overseas Chinese settlements in Southeast Asia, however, was widely visible in society through the dominant presence of Chinese temples and the public conduct of funeral and other religious ceremonies.

Any attempt to define Chinese Religion in theological terms is fraught with risks since it is non-canonical and relies primarily on the carrying out of symbolic action or ritual (as opposed to the knowledge and interpretation of scripture) for its substance. It belongs to a Little Tradition, as opposed to the Great Tradition represented by canonical Buddhism and other scripture-based sectarian religions. The tremendous importance accorded learning and thus textual authority in traditional Chinese culture is the reason many Chinese Religionists label themselves 'Buddhists' despite having little or no knowledge of the Buddhist canon. What they are signalling in this context is their respect for the superior authority of Buddhism as a Great Tradition. Similar respect is given to the texts which make up the Confucian and Daoist canons.

In many ways, the rituals and symbolic values of Chinese Religion are simply direct extensions of conventions and protocols within traditional Chinese culture. Ancestor worship, for instance, derives part of its legitimacy from the importance attached to filial piety in Confucian orthodoxy. In Chinese Religion, the sanctity of filial piety is translated into rituals – rituals which help consolidate the collective identity of the family and the clan by symbolically bridging the gap between the human realm of living descendants and the non-human realm of departed ancestors.

By such means, social relations within the extended family are regularly renewed and affirmed as constitutive of a group entity comprising both human and non- or superhuman members. For instance, when Chinese Religionists make offerings to dead family members, they treat them as if they were still alive by offering them their favourite kinds of food, and by interpreting the results of divination connected with such rituals in terms of how they remembered the person before he or she became an ancestral ghost. If the divining blocks used to indicate whether the ancestor has finished eating the ritual offerings keep showing a negative answer, the worshipping descendants are apt to make remarks such as 'Grandmother was always a slow eater; we'd better not rush her.'

The assumption that human and non-human realms can be bridged through appropriate rituals is fundamental to Chinese Religion. It provides the comforting narrative of a universe made up of a vast and ordered network of complementary relationships by which all human lives are ultimately guided. What is more, this network is imagined to be ever-expanding and changing as a consequence of human action and historical events.

The tremendous investment of effort made by Chinese Religionists in worshipping, and thus communing, with gods and ghosts is a form of pragmatic optimistic faith in the latter's power to meet the practical needs and desires of the living within the fixed parameters of their individual fates. Chinese Religion is constitutively open to interpretation, and indeed positively

encourages modification and adaptation through interpretation, as it is not bound to a given scripture (like the Bible or the Koran) but to the notion that wherever one is situated, there are always beneficial relationships to be discovered or even created between humans, gods and ghosts.

Such relationships can be accessed through ritual for alleviating suffering and solving problems as these arise in the course of one's life. Chinese Religion's characteristic pragmatism springs undoubtedly from the generally adverse conditions under which the majority of ordinary Chinese lives, both historical and contemporary, take place. In this context, it is worthwhile noting that Chinese Religion is conducive to an attitude of equanimity towards the experience of hardship, failure or personal tragedy. If one suffers despite ongoing rigorous attention to religious practice, this is generally interpreted as an outcome of one's predestined lot in life, a lot which even the gods and ghosts are unable to ameliorate. One thus accepts one's poor fate without, however, abandoning the hope of a good rebirth or the possibility of capitalizing on the temporary good luck which might unexpectedly come one's way.

Traditional Chinese cosmology's ordering of the universe in a series of hierarchical relationships, as various permutations of yin (female/dark) and yang (male/light) forces and as combinations of the five elements of metal, wood, water, fire and earth, provides the basic paradigm for a range of divinatory practices in Chinese Religion. Gods and ghosts are similarly hierarchized according to their perceived importance within specific domains of influence. In the Heavenly hierarchy the Jade Emperor (Yu Huang), who is sometimes merged with the Hokkien God Supreme Grandfather Heaven (Tian Gong) in Singaporean Chinese Religion; Sakyamuni Gautama (or Fo, Buddha, as he is commonly referred to in Chinese); and the Goddess of Mercy Guanyin are assigned the top three or four positions, while Emperor Yanluo is deemed to be the highest god of the Underworld.

There is also a range of gods on Earth who are generally divided into the two categories of: first, the attached *shen* (spirit/essence) of Earthly objects such as mountains, seas, areas of land, trees and even man-made objects; and second, the Earthly manifestations of the gods of Heaven and the Underworld as

Paper model of Mercedes Benz for use by deceased person in other world (left).

Tian Gong shrines on street pillar in Singapore (above).

Statue of Guanyin.

Night fair organized by Chinese association in Indonesia for the benefit of unemployed Chinese, 1934.

free *shen* made manifest in the material form of an image or a spirit medium.

In Chinese Religion, free *shen* are considered to be more powerful than attached *shen* because the former is eternal whereas the latter is not. Chinese Religionists tend on the whole to turn more often to free *shen* than to attached *shen* for help because free *shen* are believed, among other things, to be more compassionate, possibly from having been human or at least animal previously. In the case of Guanyin, it is assumed that the free *shen*, or essence of this deity, materializes in different ways through different images, as if each image contained its own specific bounded portion of the Guanyin essence as a whole. Thus, as Guanyin Dashi Ye (Most Powerful Grandfather Guanyin), the deity is represented as male and plays custodian to the ghosts who roam on Earth during the seventh lunar month. In the more common female manifestations of the deity, Guanyin is worshipped for her compassionate and merciful aspects.

Chinese Religionists overseas have consistently incorporated local religious elements into their practice. In Singapore and Malaysia, indigenous Malay animism is acknowledged and affirmed in Chinese Religion by the presence of Datuk Gong (Lord/Grandfather) shrines, which were set up for the purposes of addressing and worshipping the local spirit of a particular area. Offerings made to such shrines would not include pork, in deference to Islam, the canonical religion of the Malays. Also in deference to Islam, seldom are there images made of Datuk Gong. The gods held in the highest regard, however, remain ethnically Chinese ones or ones deriving from Indian Buddhist and Hindu sources, such as Gautama, Hanuman (the Monkey God) and Guanyin (originally Avalokitesvara), which have long been incorporated into traditional Chinese lore and adapted for Chinese religious worship.

Chinese Religion is arguably at its most versatile as practised in Singapore. Since the 19th century, its places of worship there have included Malay-influenced animistic shrines, Hindu temples, a range of sectarian Buddhist temples (Theravada, Vajrayana and so forth) and even the Catholic Saint Alphonsus (Novena) Church. This highly syncretic approach to worship is facilitated by the utilitarian, opportunistic and adaptive logic of Chinese Religion on the one hand, and by the multiethnic and multi-religious nature of Singapore society on the other.

As migrants, the Chinese overseas drew nourishment from the oral rather than canonical tradition of their homeland, for the former enabled relationships to be ritually formalized between person and place in the here-and-now. Whether one was in one's home village in China or in a Chinese settlement in Singapore, the oral tradition provided the means by which an individual could find his bearings by adapting family, clan, village or regional customs, beliefs, values and rituals to suit local conditions.

The high rate of literacy among Chinese overseas of the 1990s has contributed significantly to the decline of Chinese Religion and to the concomitant rise of canonical religions, in particular Christianity and Buddhism. The global dominance of Western cultural and politico-economic forces in the 20th century has led to strong associations being assumed between Christianity, on the one hand, and modernity and progress on the other.

Furthermore, as overseas Chinese communities now comprise a large majority of secondary- and tertiary-educated people born overseas, people whose everyday lives and experiences have little in common with those of their migrant forebears, systematic religions which provide explanations of life through textual sources as well as ritual have a greater appeal. The religious canon satisfies the desire of the educated for knowledge through study, and provides a range of sophisticated interpretations which the Western-educated, rationalist mind would find more plausible than the arbitrary (albeit highly inventive) narratives of Chinese Religion. Indeed, the emphasis on textual interpretation has produced a strong reformist trend within existing canonical Buddhism, resulting in the emergence of new forms of Buddhism, such as Nichiren Shoshu, which is increasingly popular among young Singaporean Chinese.

What rapid modernization and greatly increased literacy have also produced among the Chinese overseas is the phenomenon of secular materialism. Because secular materialism underpins government and socio-economic management in modern society, it is readily granted institutional legitimacy. Similarly, the priority accorded by this world-view to rational science as the sole appropriate measure of life (seen as spiritless, calculable, divisible matter) resonates with authority in modern public culture everywhere. The advocacy of Confucianism by a number of Asian governments as a transcultural code of ethics appropriate to late 20th-century social conditions is part of this secular materialistic enterprise (see p 126). The quest for money and material wealth integral to the utilitarian logic of Chinese Religion, coupled with its seeming 'irrational' belief in gods and ghosts, does not appeal to the sophisticated sensibilities of well-educated professionals among the Chinese overseas. But it should be noted in conclusion that the rise of secular materialism and systematic religions has resulted in the loss of a sense of spiritual connectedness fundamental to Chinese Religion, between people and the places they inhabit.

Vivienne Wee and
Gloria Davies

The Yeoh Clan Temple in Penang.

OVERSEAS CHINESE ORGANIZATIONS

General

Overseas ethnic Chinese organizations, in this discussion, are taken to be non-profit associations with ethnic Chinese membership and concerns. Their range is quite wide: in size, from a dozen members to several thousand; in focus and function, from simple to multi-faceted and complex; in life span, from temporary crisis bodies to associations with a century or more of history; and in prosperity, from clubs with no fixed address and precarious existence to thousand-member organizations with wealthy leaders, elaborate annual banquets and corresponding social influence.

Organizations have been and continue to be important to Chinese abroad. They provide assistance to new immigrants, and social life, companionship and emergency aid to members. They are conduits and reference points for business connections as well as avenues of communication with local governments and with China. For this last reason, they are also important to China, which has utilized them for both political support and the recruitment of trade and investment.

Two broad conditions shape Chinese organizations overseas: first, everywhere, outside Singapore, ethnic Chinese are minorities in host societies with whose non-Chinese governments and non-Chinese populations they must deal; and second, in most cases, especially since 1900, Chinese overseas live in cities. Their organizations, then, are those that best fit living as cultural minorities in urban environments.

Before World War II, membership in organizations might be essential to an individual's survival and welfare, offering needed protection and solidarity. More recently, membership is usually voluntary and it often happens that, of, say, 1,000 persons eligible for membership in a given society, only 100 join and only 30 of those are active.

On the other hand, exclusive membership in a single society has rarely been the rule. It is common for an individual to belong simultaneously to several organizations for which he is eligible. Indeed, it is the overlapping and interlocking memberships of so many associations that make possible what is often called 'Chinatown politics,' where Chinese community leaders are typically those who hold leadership positions in several interlocking and leading organizations.

Ethnic Chinese organizations are highly diverse and a variety of classificatory schemes has been applied to them. Some analysts focus on the ascriptive principle by which members are eligible for recruitment – for example, kinship (real or fictive), as in surname or 'clan' associations; or territoriality, as in eligibility according to ancestral home in China. Others classify by function: What are the major purposes and activities of a given association, and what needs does it serve? Still others divide into 'traditionist' or 'China-referent' associations, and 'modernist' or non-traditional and local community-oriented associations. Yet another method, used here, is a distinction between two broad types of organization: those based on experience in China and those drawing upon non-Chinese models. All analysts, however, see a major divide between the organizational scene before World War II and that after it.

Pre-World War II

Organizations in this period were based largely on models known about by immigrants from examples in the urban centres of their ancestral part of China. The immigration of this era took the form of a large flow to Southeast Asia and a much smaller flow elsewhere, particularly to North America. Migrants were usually single males and, whether intentionally or not, were usually sojourners. Most were engaged in commerce or trades or were labourers. Usually they were subject to restrictions on their activities and suspicion on the part of dominant non-Chinese in their host countries. One other major shaping force on organizations after 1900 was China – its politics and its defence against Japanese invasion.

Faced with basic needs for mutual aid and interest articulation, migrant Chinese created clan and native-place associations, or *huiguan*, on Chinese models. These provided social services, rituals of cultural expression and retention, negotiation and protection against competing or threatening forces from the outside, and – for

Inside a Chinese Christian church in Victoria, Canada, 1890s.

Document with chop of Indonesia's Tiong Hoa Hwee Koan (Zhonghua Huiguan).

their leaders – opportunities for participation in the local Chinese political and business systems. Their principles were ancestral and patriarchal, focusing upon patrilineal ancestral kinship – whether real or fictive (surname or 'clan' associations) – and locality of ancestral origin in China ('native-place' or 'district' associations). *Huiguan* were the core organizations of pre-1945 Chinese communities. Initially, they were usually territorially and linguistically based and known as *bang*. As immigration increased the size and complexity of a given local Chinese population, its *huiguan* segmented into more narrowly defined bodies. Thus, a district association focused on a given county in Fujian might hive off a smaller body limited to only those of Tan (Hokkien pronunciation for Chen) surname in that county, which might then further segment into associations of Tans from each of several sub-county units.

Alongside the *huiguan*, frequently, were trade guilds, monopolizing one or another kind of Chinese business. Although these often included kin and native-place dimensions, their basis was traditional skills and thereby occupational interest. In the 20th century these were replaced by modern Chinese-style trade associations (*tongye gonghui*). By the end of World War I another form of occupation-related association, the modern Chinese labour union, appeared in many places overseas.

A third type of association was the brotherhood, frequently spoken of as the 'secret society.' Brotherhoods could include anything from martial arts and Chinese musical societies to various kinds of organization in the Hongmen tradition, including Triads. Most had at least some political dimensions, both with reference to local Chinese society and to China. The earliest overseas Chinese political parties also fit into this fraternal-political category. These included the Baohuang Hui of Kang Youwei, Sun Yat-sen's early Tongmeng Hui, the Kuomintang, the (Hongmen) Zhigong Tang, and local left-wing groups associated with the Chinese Communist Party.

In the late 19th and early 20th century a new type of organization appeared, what analysts call the 'umbrella organization.' These are overarching bodies that federate existing organizations under their leadership and serve as both the dominating body of the local Chinese community and the spokesman for that community to the outside world. Usually, a combination of internal and external stresses produced these organizations. Internal competition and violence among existing Chinese associations was paralleled by the growing interest of both host governments and China in having some kind of representative body to speak for local Chinese. Most often these were called Chinese Benevolent Associations (Zhonghua Huiguan) or Chinese Chambers of Commerce (Zhonghua Shanghui). Others might be called simply The Chinese Association (Zhonghua Zonghui). Still others began as boards of directors of a Chinese charitable association or hospital, subsequently expanding their duties.

Besides their mediating and negotiating functions, they were responsible for promoting economic welfare, providing social services and encouraging cultural maintenance, especially in the form of Chinese schools, whose work they supervised. Umbrella organizations were usually headed by executive committees, whose members, chosen from the leaders of the most important associations under the umbrella, were the political élite of Chinatown. Their broad functions made these organizations like super *huiguan*. They did everything a *huiguan* did, but at a community-wide level.

Religious organizations included those typical of the Fujian or Guangdong localities of origin of the Chinese settlers. There were temples enshrining the more generally popular deities such as Guanyin, Mazu (Tianhou), Guan Gong (or Guandi), and Tudi Gong; there were also gods who were the focus of local cults. In some overseas sites some deities were associated with particular native-place *huiguan* and housed in their buildings; elsewhere, their temples and temple organizations were separate bodies. There were Buddhist temples and organizations, and there were Catholic and Protestant churches with entirely Chinese congregations, especially in North America and the Philippines, and especially in the 20th century.

Cultural, educational and recreational organizations were numerous and varied. Some cultural and recreational bodies, like those of Chinese music, theatre and martial arts, were sometimes also political, lending their performances to political causes, both within the community and in relation to China. In the latter case, it was particularly theatrical groups who staged fund-raising performances in support of China's defence against Japanese threats. In the course of the early 20th century certain Western sports became popular in some communities. YMCAs were established and, in the Canadian case, young ethnic Chinese, rejecting non-Chinese operation of these centres, established their own, Chinese-run YMCAs.

Chinese schools were a major part of Chinese life from 1900 onward. Sometimes they were established and operated by the community as a whole. Often, however, they were funded and operated by individual *huiguan*, fraternal-political organizations or religious bodies, primarily for the benefit of members' children, but frequently open to others as well. School curriculum was a contentious issue among community organizations because it involved different opinions about use of Mandarin versus use of regional dialect, conformity to standards in China versus more local interests, and courses with political content that might favour one or another group or viewpoint.

By the 1930s the Overseas Chinese Affairs Commission in China provided funds, textbooks and teachers to overseas schools that needed help, but some saw the price of such aid as the loss of political autonomy. In Southeast Asia, Chinese schools were comprehensive, meeting on a full-day schedule and teaching Chinese language and culture along with other school subjects. Outside Southeast Asia, Chinese schools tended to be supplementary, offering only Chinese language and culture courses, and these only outside school hours. Where population warranted it in Southeast Asia, there were Chinese secondary schools as well as elementary ones; elsewhere, structures were less formal and well developed.

Besides the foregoing list of regular types of organization, there were ad hoc or single-issue ones that waxed and waned with the issue, whether local or referring to China. In the latter case, some examples are: associations to resist Japanese encroachment on China, which appeared with each crisis from 1915 onward; associations to provide disaster relief for China; and fund-raising associations in support of schools or other modernizing projects in early 20th-century China. In the case of local needs in the country of residence, these included: disaster relief, participation in civic celebrations of the host country; support for 'worthy causes' in general; and participation in that country's defence against Japan or other common enemies.

Post-World War II

This period can be divided into two: 1945-70 and post-1970. In the first part (1945-70), direct emigration from mainland China was slight. Migration from and through Hong Kong continued but at a much reduced volume. Chinese communities in Southeast Asia, unreplenished by significant new immigration, came to be societies of mostly local-born ethnic Chinese. Elsewhere, Chinese communities expanded slowly by immigration but mostly by natural increase of existing populations. Everywhere, economic growth was the rule and local Chinese populations benefited by it in terms of new opportunities. At the same time, however, nationalism in the newly independent states of Southeast Asia placed new restrictions on some Chinese activities and opportunities. The Cold War cut off overseas communities and their organizations from direct contact with ancestral districts in China.

Organizations on the Left in overseas communities – or those allegedly so – were forced to shut down or go underground, and in Southeast Asia Chinese organizations in general were suspected by local governments of disloyalty to host countries merely by their encouragement of Chinese cultural activities.

In the second half (post-1970) four major changes took place. First, new migration opportunities for Chinese opened up in North America, Australia, New Zealand and Europe. Second, with the waning of the Cold War mainland China opened up to expanded foreign trade, investment and emigration. Third, the first postwar generation of locally born ethnic Chinese reached maturity. And fourth, a revolution in communications technology made possible globalization of many aspects of life.

Migration assumed new forms. Postwar economic and educational growth everywhere had created a new middle class of ethnic Chinese with international-level educational and cultural skills. Many of these moved, as families, either from Hong Kong (and, after 1985, Taiwan as well) to some overseas locale, or else from one overseas site to another. Non-middle-class Chinese, too, became more mobile, rejoining other family members overseas. China's opening created both business opportunities and ancestral-district attractions for Chinese overseas. That opening – and the continued absence of large Chinese immigration to the region – also reduced Southeast Asian suspicions about the 'subversiveness' of Chinese organizations, and made possible a revival of China-related associations. The rise of local-born ethnic Chinese generations was followed by their assertive commitment to the lands of their birth, and to organizations reflecting that commitment. In North America and Australia their identities were influenced by governments' multicultural policies, which allowed for integration without assimilation. Global communications technology made possible international and regional organizations and meetings on a scale of frequency never before possible.

Over the entire period since 1945 several new organizational developments and trends are visible. There has been a general proliferation of organizations, especially in North America and Europe, where much of the new migration has gone. A comprehensive study (by Li Minghuan) of Chinese diaspora organizations published in 1995 estimates there are about 9,000 ethnic Chinese organizations outside China. But this source excludes political bodies from its coverage. A Taiwan source (*The Republic of China Yearbook 1995*) also estimates 9,000, but is probably also incomplete in its coverage. Part of the increase is due to internal processes. Organizations continue to segment in various ways. Regional branches, for example, are created in distant cities of a given country. These are then federated with one another and with the original, capital city-based branch, thus creating several new, semi-autonomous organizations. In some cases, branching, segmenting and federating even lead to the construction of elaborate pyramids of organizations, as in Malaysia and the Philippines.

Pre-war type organizations have con-

Symbols of nationalism in newly independent states: flags of Malaysia (top) and Singapore.

Textbooks used in overseas Chinese schools in Singapore.

tinued to exist by adapting to changing conditions and needs. Meanwhile, new 'modern' associations have sprung up around them. These draw upon models derived from Western experience and, typically, are Chinese middle-class organizations. Their members are drawn from both middle-class immigrants and middle-class local-borns. Membership eligibility is based not on traditional Chinese norms of ancestral origin or craft skills but on standards of educational, professional or business achievement. Unlike *huiguan*, whose membership includes both the successful and the unsuccessful, these are peer-group associations of achievers. Compared to *huiguan,* they are democratically operated. In many such organizations women play a leading role, again quite unlike the case of traditional Chinese associations.

Some of these organizations are alumni or school-support bodies focused on their school of reference, or social service agencies that provide professional assistance to new immigrants and underachievers, sometimes including non-Chinese as well as Chinese. Middle-class organizations also include various kinds of cultural association. Some of these, in countries where host government policies or local conditions make it seem possible, are devoted specifically to the goal of socio-political integration with the mainstream society but with Chinese cultural retention.

Cultural associations serve many purposes. Within a local Chinese community they encourage cultural maintenance and, addressing younger generations, promote pride in their Chinese heritage. Activities may include language and cultural arts courses and displays, organized group trips to China, sponsorship of visiting Chinese cultural groups, and attention to the history of the Chinese in the country of the association's location. This last may include promotion of historical publications and creation of museums of local ethnic Chinese history. Here, as in some of their other activities, these cultural associations address both local ethnic Chinese and non-Chinese. In the latter case, the objective is to explain Chinese culture and also to educate non-Chinese in the contributions of local Chinese to the host society. Examples of these kinds of cultural organization may be observed in Singapore, Kuala Lumpur, Manila, Kobe, Melbourne, Vancouver, San Francisco, New York and elsewhere.

Yet another kind of Western-derived organization popular in overseas Chinese communities since the 1940s is the service club, Rotary and Lions clubs being the most salient. Chinese Lions clubs, in particular, have proliferated rapidly in parts of Asia and North America. Like other 'modern' associations, these are peer group bodies that perform social services but are also excellent vehicles for business and social networking.

In the postwar period the rise of local-born generations and the relative inaccessibility of mainland China for so long have resulted in an increased organizational focus upon the local Chinese community itself and its host country. Another influence in that direction has been the increased intrusiveness of most governments into local Chinese affairs since 1945. Chinese organizations have now become less abstracted from their mainstream environ-

Acrobats from China at performance organized by Singapore Federation of Chinese Clan Associations.

Cover of newsletter keeping Lee clan in touch with each other.

ment, and much more than before required to know about local government policies and mainstream society's practices. Organizations' statements of goals now more frequently than before include references to such ideas as aiding the economic growth of the host country and promoting its good relations with China.

In the Cold War era and since, ethnic Chinese organizations have perpetuated the Left-Right political split found in most overseas communities since the 1920s. Organizations had always tended to line up on one side or the other, bundling their concerns about China's politics with those about local Chinatown politics. During the Cold War, Left organizations ceased to exist or went underground, while in those countries that recognized Taiwan, Kuomintang-related bodies, including some specifically anti-Communist ones, thrived. In recent years, the split has re-emerged, but issues are now more regularly focused on Chinatown needs than China's needs (see box p 88).

Since 1970 new immigrant groups have appeared. From the late 1970s ethnic Chinese from Indochina, mostly Teochius, have scattered to other parts of Asia and to Australia, North America, France and elsewhere. Most — on arrival at least — are not middle class, and they tend to settle on the edges of existing Chinatowns, forming their own associations. Second-country overseas Chinese are another group. Like the Indochina Chinese, these form organizations that refer to their previous country of residence (or, when they have passed through several, their most recent country), further defining themselves, at times, by sub-ethnic segmentation. Thus, in Vancouver, there are associations of Hokkien

Chinese from the Philippines and Cantonese Chinese from the same place.

This phenomenon may result in some difficulty in identifying the membership of organizations by their names. A 'Hokkien Association' may be made up of mainland Fujianese, or its members may be Taiwanese who do not wish to be part of a general Taiwan association, or they may be Hokkiens from any given migrant-sending country that has Hokkiens in its Chinese population. The 'Hokkien Association' in Vancouver may thus have an entirely different kind of membership from the ones in Paris or in northern California.

Taiwan migrants are both a long-term and a recent phenomenon. Since the 1960s sizeable numbers of Taiwan Chinese have remained in the United States after completing higher education there. Recently, large numbers of family immigrants, many of them middle class, have moved from Taiwan to the United States and Canada. Alongside the otherwise Cantonese cultural environment of North American Chinese communities they have formed their own business associations, schools and cultural and social service bodies. There is one other new addition to all this diversity now found in many countries of the diaspora: the newest wave of Chinese intellectuals abroad. These are graduate students, scholars and political exiles from mainland China living in several countries where there are Chinese populations. Their organizations on the one hand support political hopes for China and research and commentary on Chinese culture in the modern world, and on the other hand provide networks for sharing of information about employment in their countries of residence.

Another new development is the willingness of many Chinese organizations to serve non-Chinese and even to allow them to become association members. In many countries Chinese schools now admit non-Chinese, sometimes allowing them to avoid taking Chinese language courses. Chinese-sponsored hospitals and clinics provide services to non-Chinese patients. In Manila Chinese Fire Brigades serve neighbourhoods, not ethnic groups. Some North American Chinatown neighbourhood improvement groups have included non-Chinese participants. Mainstream fund-raisers in host countries find that appeals to Chinatown organizations are more fruitful than ever. Thai-Chinese business associations accept non-Chinese as members. So do a variety of associations in the Philippines and Singapore. Sometimes non-Chinese members have limited rights; often, however, they are fully empowered. Some Chinese cultural organizations allow non-Chinese members, in some cases even as members of the executive board. In some places Chinese Dragon Boat festivals include both Chinese and non-Chinese organizers and participants.

Yet another trend is internationalization (which includes regionalization). This is not entirely a postwar phenomenon. Early in the century some fraternal-political organizations – the Kuomintang and some of the Hongmen organizations – had begun to do this. So had Hakka organizations. When ethnic Chinese began to create their own Lions and Rotary club units they joined existing international networks of non-Chinese units. In the postwar era Taiwan took the lead in sponsoring international federations of clan associations, usually with headquarters in Taipei.

After 1970, as the Chinese diaspora developed, accompanied by the communications revolution, the pace of internationalization increased, as did the variety of internationalizing organizations. Not only clans, but native-place associations also created international federations. Some were at the level of the *bang* (for example, Hokkien regional and global federations); others, at the county level (Hokkien Ann Kway World Convention). Indochina Chinese have established a world federation.

Religious organizations have followed the migration of their members. Sometimes this is planned as a global enterprise from the beginning, as in the case of the Chinese Coordination Centre of World Evangelism (CCCOWE) based in Hong Kong. In other cases, it is an ad hoc linking of newly established Buddhist temples or Christian churches in various parts of the world. Alumni of famous universities in Asia – St John's (Shanghai), Lingnan (Canton), Nanyang (Singapore) – have formed transregional linkages. Even high school support associations in Asia have their branches in North America.

Business globalization has produced a Taiwan-sponsored international Chinese business association. And, most prestigiously, there is the World Chinese Entrepreneurs Convention which, since 1991, has periodically brought together 1,000 or so major business figures (and some aspirants to that status) to exchange business information and create or renew business ties. Four meetings have been held so far, in Singapore, Hong Kong, Bangkok and Vancouver. In Europe two federations of European Chinese organizations (one pro-Taiwan, the other pro-mainland China) have been established since 1975. In North America, where national-level organizations were rarely successful before 1945, there are now national federations of Chinese organizations concerned with such issues as discrimination and political rights and participation.

Organizations already existing in 1945 have undergone changes in order to survive. *Huiguan* may now do less to help new immigrants. In Southeast Asia the immigrant flow, and hence the demand for services, is less. In North America the burden is lightened because other agencies supply so much aid and because many transcultural middle-class immigrants need no organized assistance. Where their help is needed, North American *huiguan* have often shifted the nature of their aid from basic housing and employment introductions to job-training programmes.

Generally, *huiguan* have had to adapt to the change from serving societies of single male sojourners to that of meeting the needs of family settlers. Although they remain basically male organizations, they have long since established women's subgroups and, as recruitment of youth has become a problem, youth activity subgroups as well. They have a new role as one of the conduits for overseas Chinese investment in ancestral districts in China. Some *huiguan*, in order

2000年在温哥华举行
下届南大校友联欢会
将由美加校友会联办

第7届全球南大校友联欢会将在公元2000年，在加拿大温哥华举行。下一届的盛会将由加拿大温哥华南大校友会与美国南大校友会联合主办，到了2002年才由新加坡南大毕业生协会接办，今 面，在货币贬值，股市下跌的一连串风暴中，每个人或多或少都有损失。现在，看见大家喜气洋洋地欢聚在一起，证明了大家处理经济危机的应变能力很强，正所谓冬天来了，春天还会远

Headline reads, 'Next meeting of Nanyang University Alumni to be organized by US–Canada Alumni.'

Non-Chinese join Chinese in Lunar New Year celebrations in Paris.

CHINESE PAN-EUROPEAN ORGANIZATIONS

This discussion is based on written sources as well as on interviews conducted by the authors in the 1990s. The basis of association of Pan-European Chinese community organizations (that is, organizations which seek to include overseas Chinese in all parts of Europe in an echo of the integrative thrust of that continent) is by definition transnational. But that is not their only notable characteristic. Also notable is their clear political leaning, either towards Taipei or mainland China. The great majority of overseas Chinese organizations in European countries lean towards mainland China, but the *European* overseas Chinese bodies first emerged among those leaning towards Taipei. Here we set out the main frontier-crossing institutions Chinese have established to co-operate on a Europe-wide basis.

Organizations with a Taiwan affiliation

Founded in 1975, the Taipei-oriented Conference of the Overseas Chinese Federations in Europe (Ouzhou Huaqiao Tuanti Lianyihui), or Annual Conference (Ou Hua Nianhui) for short, was the first overseas Chinese pan-European organization to be established. David Ting (Ding Dawei) of Bologna tells how some Chinese tailors arrived in Europe with American troops just after 1949 and how, after settling in various European countries, they decided to meet once a year, rotating the gatherings among the countries, giving birth to the Annual Conference. Ting's account is contradicted by Chie Nun (Xu Neng) of Munich, who took part in the preparations for the first gathering and who suggests a different course of events: when Chiang Kai-shek, president of the Republic of China, died in 1975, Chinese in Europe came together in mourning, then decided to gather in a European country every year on rotation. The preparatory meeting in Hamburg, which became known as 'The First Annual Conference,' was followed by a gathering in Belgium. Official historiography claims that the preparatory meeting was held under the auspices of the *Chinesischer Verein* in Hamburg, the Chinese Association of Hamburg, Germany (Deguo Hanbao Zhonghua Huiguan), though its present president claims that it was convened in a restaurant.

The majority of the original participants were opposed to an organization with a permanent secretariat, agreeing instead on devolving responsibility for each conference to the country to which it rotated. By 1997, the meeting had been held in 14 different European countries, with high-ranking officials from the Overseas Chinese Affairs Commission and the government in Taipei participating every year. It is generally believed that the institution's longevity and relative success is owed to its loose structure. From just a couple of dozen delegates, it has grown to almost a thousand-strong today.

A 12-point document sets out the institution's objectives:

(1) To express patriotism by hoisting the national flag, singing the national anthem and listening to public readings of messages of greeting from the President of the Republic, the President of the Executive Yuan and from the Minister in charge of Overseas Chinese Affairs

(2) To proclaim the policies of the government

(3) To discuss matters affecting the well-being of overseas Chinese compatriots

(4) To promote mutual understanding through the sharing of experiences

(5) To recognize talent among overseas Chinese (the pursuit of which aim may be seen in the fact that the resident personnel of the Overseas Chinese Affairs Commission in Europe and other office bearers have virtually all emerged from the ranks of the participants at the Annual Conference)

(6) To display strength in the anti-Communist cause

(7) To promote the nation's foreign affairs in order to enhance the status of overseas Chinese

(8) To collaborate closely with the government's overseas representatives and to promote unity among overseas Chinese organizations

(9) To encourage overseas Chinese compatriots' accomplishments in artistic endeavours and sport

(10) To support and initiate other activities

(11) To further mutual contact and understanding at home and abroad

(12) To promote the establishment of related organizations.

Out of the conference a number of other European organizations have emerged. One is the Women's Association (Funü Lianyihui), the European branches of which form part of a world organization initiated by Soong Mei-ling, the widow of Chiang Kai-shek. The pan-European meeting of this organization is held in tandem with the Annual Conference, and the chair woman is invariably the wife of the head of the Taipei representative office.

Another is the Association of Overseas Chinese Chambers of Commerce in Europe (Ouzhou Huashang Jingmao Xiehui), which was brought into being by a decision of the Annual Conference in 1987. Aimed at promoting overseas Chinese trade and economy, this was to come into conflict with the Council of Taiwanese Chambers of Commerce in Europe (Ouzhou Taiwan Shanghui Lianhe Zonghui) when the latter emerged in 1994 (see below). In some countries a merger took place between the two organizations; this is exemplified in Belgium by the Association Belgo-Chinoise et Taiwanaise pour le Développement Economique (Bihua Taishang Jingmao Xiehui), which in turn joined the global organization of the World Taiwanese Chambers of Commerce (Shijie Taiwan Shanghui Lianhe Zonghui). A third, established in 1985, is the Dr Sun Yat-sen Society (Zhongshan Xuehui), of which there is one in every country, the whole incorporated in an umbrella organization (with its own permanent secretariat) at the European continental level.

The Council of Taiwanese Chambers of Commerce in Europe, mentioned above, was established in 1994 at the urging of the Taipei government to unite the strengths of Taiwanese business circles by establishing Chambers of Commerce everywhere. In tandem with the flow of Taiwanese investments into Germany, a Chamber of Commerce opened there in 1989, but proved inefficient. It was not until President Lee Teng-hui called for a united force of Taiwanese traders in 1994 that the Taiwanese Chamber of Commerce in Germany was established, alongside the Council of Taiwanese Chambers of Commerce in Europe and the World Taiwanese Chambers of Commerce. The structure of these organizations is similar all over the world, with the chairmen and board directors appointed for one year only. The streamlined organization, high-tech image and economic strength, as well as the political importance attached to it by the Taipei government, have contributed to a schism between the new Taiwanese traders it represents and the overseas Chinese traders of old.

Finally, there is the organization which the Overseas Chinese Affairs Commission in Taiwan set up – at the national, European and world levels – to coordinate the flight and resettlement of ethnic Chinese from Vietnam, Cambodia and Laos in the mid-1970s (see Part V: Vietnam, Cambodia, Laos). Following an inaugural meeting in Paris in 1992, delegates from all over the world met annually in the next couple of years. However, by 1996 the enthusiasm of both the Taipei officialdom and the local organizations had waned, with some

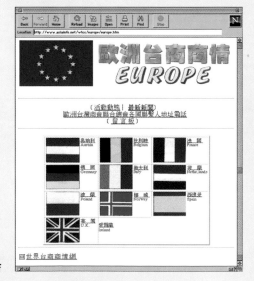

of the latter, like the one in Italy, becoming almost extinct. Observers thought that Taipei had shifted its priorities towards the Council of Taiwanese Chambers of Commerce in Europe.

Organizations inclined towards mainland China

The chief of these is the European Federation of Chinese Organizations (Ouzhou Huaqiao Huaren Shetuan Lianhehui), or EFCO (Ouhua Lianhui) for short. The idea to found it was proposed during a meeting of the Association des Chinois Resident en France in Paris in September 1983 – a meeting attended also by invitees resident in countries other than France. The idea received general support, and in June the following year, delegates from Spain, Britain, France, Belgium, Sweden, the Netherlands, Austria, Luxembourg and Portugal met in Madrid at a second preparatory meeting. On this occasion official observers from China took part. The third preparatory meeting was held in the Netherlands in August 1991 and was attended by delegates from 26 organizations in ten countries.

Officially established in Amsterdam in May 1992, by 1996 EFCO had developed from 22 member organizations in 11 countries to more than 50 member organizations in 13 countries. Its objectives may be summarized as follows:

(1) To foster cooperation between overseas Chinese organizations in Europe

(2) To promote the economic advancement of overseas Chinese in Europe

(3) To encourage the overseas Chinese to abide by the laws and regulations of their host countries and to take the initiative to join local mainstream society.

EFCO pledges itself to raise European Chinese awareness of the political, economic, social and cultural dimensions of their host countries and of Europe as a whole, and to adjure its members to participate in local and national elections as well as elections for the European Parliament. The contrast these objectives pose to those of the Taiwan-oriented organization – the one urging integration with the host society, the other reminiscent of the old Kuomintang nationalism – is noteworthy.

Internal disagreements over appointments and responsibilities slowed EFCO's progress towards these goals in the first few years of its existence. When it did act in 1996, it was to join with other organizations – the Landelijke Federatie van Chinese Organisaties in Nederland, or the Federation of Chinese Organizations in Holland (QuanHe Huaren Shetuan Lianhehui), and other Dutch overseas Chinese organizations – in convening a conference on Chinese mother-tongue education in Europe. The concern of that and subsequent conferences to promote Chinese-language education has gained the support of the Overseas Affairs Office of the State Council of the People's Republic of China.

An organization which may have no political commitment to the People's Republic of China, but whose ties are by definition to the Chinese mainland, is the native-place association of migrants from Qingtian (in Zhejiang province). As with all such organizations, the place of origin in China is the chief component of its identity. The largest and newest such organization in Europe is the Association of Qingtian Townsmen in Europe (Ouzhou Qingtian Tongxianghui). Although immigration from Qingtian to Europe has a long history, the Qingtian native-place associations in various European countries only began to emerge in the late 1980s (the oldest organization, in Belgium, was established in 1988).

It was at the inaugural meeting in 1996 of the Association des Compatriotes de Qing Tian en France (Lü Fa Qingtian Tongxianghui), to which Qingtian Chinese living in other European countries were invited, that the idea of the continent-wide Association of Qingtian Townsmen in Europe was mooted. Duly founded in Paris on March 4, 1996, the organization had the head of the French association, Yen Chih Chao (Yan Zhizhao), for its first chairman. Thereafter the chairmanship will rotate.

As a footnote, individual native-place and clan organizations like the Lam Chuen Overseas Chinese Community in Europe (Lü Ou Lincun Tongxianghui) and the Man Clan Association, Europe (Lü Ou Wenshi Zongqinhui) should be mentioned. The former's basis of association is common origin in a village in the New Territories, while the latter's focus of identification is the surname Man. Such organizations have small numbers of members spread over Europe, but their organization is mainly established in one country (in the case of the two organizations just mentioned, in Britain), and the majority of their members live in that country.

Others

Finally, integration of a less formal character rates a mention. Each year since 1991, Chinese have held a European Karaoke Competition (Ouzhou Huayi Xinxiu Gechang Bisai). Sporting events where Chinese in different countries compete against each other are held on occasion, and since the early 1980s different associations have organized pan-European Miss Chinatown competitions. Some organizations have also discussed the possibility of running overseas Chinese summer camps in Europe as an alternative to the costly practice of sending children to China during school vacations. In all these ways, Chinese across Europe come together at the grassroots level. Finally, the Association of Chinese Scholars in Europe (Ouzhou Huaren Xuehui) joins together Chinese scholars working in individual European countries. Though this body has little or no contact with other overseas Chinese organizations on a group level, individually many members participate in local Chinese affairs, often as unofficial consultants.

Liang Xiujing and Flemming Christiansen

(Facing page) Newspaper reporting on declaration of annual conference of the Overseas Chinese Federations in Europe (top). Web page of European chapter of World Taiwanese Chambers of Commerce.
Chiang Kai-shek and Soong Mei-ling (top). Web page of Overseas Chinese Affairs Commission (left).

Book on internal dissension in Singapore Chinese Chamber of Commerce.

to attract middle-class women and youth, offer them immediate opportunities to be association officers. In some places *huiguan* officer lists have been greatly expanded to include large numbers of honorary officers or advisers. These are usually wealthy businessmen who contribute financial support in exchange for such a listing. Both organization and individual businessman are thereby given enhanced status, and an ever-growing pool of would-be community leaders is thus accommodated.

Trade associations continue to exist, as constituent members of Chinese Chambers of Commerce or Benevolent Association umbrella organizations. Alongside them, associations of newer, non-traditional trades have sprung up. More important, the professional association – Chinese physicians, dentists and the like – is a definite growth area. Brotherhoods continue to exist, especially in the Philippines, and some fraternal-political associations (for example, some Hongmen bodies) now focus more on local issues rather than on China. Meanwhile, as many more Chinese are now citizens of their country of residence, they participate in political parties appropriate to that country's politics, whose members, in most cases, include non-Chinese as well.

'Chinatown politics' continues, but at least some of its organizational players are new. Among religious organizations, the expansion of Buddhist associations everywhere and evangelical Protestant Christian churches, especially in North America, are notable. Religious institutions respond to the need of migrants for stability, solace and meaning in a world of change and material striving. They also, as in some places in North America, may be the only Chinese organization in a given locality, and hence centres of not only Christian fellowship but social networking and community life as well.

Pre-1945 umbrella organizations have lost much of their power in many places. This is especially so in North America, where new immigration and the rise of local-born generations have created both new social needs and new associations to meet them. Even in Southeast Asia it is now difficult for a single organization to maintain its status as omni-competent leader of a united Chinese community and spokesman for it to the outside world. Umbrella organizations' functions – business promotion, social service, cultural maintenance and internal/external mediation – now tend to be distributed among three or more organizations. The original body may hold on to a kind of business promotion activity, while three other organizations lead the way in the three other functions. Chinese communities have become so diverse in member backgrounds, experiences and skills, and there are now so many other ways for members to accomplish things that the original umbrella body has lost its monopoly. In some instances, some specialization in community social service leadership has long been the case: for example, the Shanju Gongsuo in Manila and the numerous *shantang* in Thailand. But much of this segmentation is postwar, either through leadership-created federations of clan associations with a cultural mandate, as in the Philippines and Singapore, or on independent, middle-class initiative.

Chinese schools have been under pressure for several decades. In Southeast Asia governments have restricted them in one way or another. In North America, until the 1980s, the problem has been the apathy of local-born generations who found new opportunities in fields not requiring knowledge of Chinese language and culture. Since the 1980s, the opening of China has stimulated interest everywhere – among non-Chinese as well as Chinese – in learning something of Chinese language and culture. There is now a problem of how to teach the language to those for whom it has become no longer a native tongue. In some places there are new organizations to address that problem: school parents' associations and teachers' associations. Some of the former exist even where Chinese children attend a non-Chinese school but the parents wish to promote the best possible education for them.

Traditional Chinese cultural arts, such as music, opera, calligraphy and painting, are revived abroad by new immigrants and by cultural centre classes. Martial arts clubs proliferate. Social clubs for ethnic Chinese at North American universities segment according to student background (Hong Kong, Taiwan or local-born) and

Hawaiian variant of the 'shophouse,' the most widespread form of overseas Chinese business.

sometimes beyond that by religion or other distinction. Here, as everywhere else, organizations reflect the basic changes in immigrant and settler populations that have taken place: from single male sojourners to family settlers; from encapsulated community to society of families with many options for occupation and education; from outpost of China to special sector of local host society.

Edgar Wickberg

CHINESE BUSINESS ORGANIZATIONS

Two forms of overseas Chinese business have attracted much attention in recent years, the large-scale enterprises described either as 'conglomerates' or 'business groups,' and the much vaunted business networks linking overseas Chinese firms within the various countries of Southeast Asia and internationally (see box p 94).

But before we discuss these forms, a key question must be asked: How should we define or identify overseas Chinese business organizations? If they are merely firms whose ownership and control rest in the hands of a Chinese, then the defining criterion is simply ethnicity, in which case it would be no more useful to speak of a 'Chinese firm' than of a Malay or English or any other ethnically defined firm. Yet 'the Chinese firm' is often written about as though it were a category with distinctive cultural/organizational features of its own. Furthermore, much of the writing on 'the Chinese firm' actually draws on examples in Taiwan, Hong Kong and China, whose ethnic homogeneity makes it hard to make intra-territory, cross-cultural comparisons.

The ethnic heterogeneity of the countries where overseas Chinese are settled, on the other hand, offers the chance to compare enterprises cross-ethnically, producing answers to questions such as: How different are 'Chinese firms' from those owned and controlled by other ethnic groups based in the same country? How different are they from local firms whose ownership and control are not ethnically based? However, the available literature offers little in the way of answers to these questions.

If identification were simply by ethnicity, then we would have to include Singapore's 'government-linked companies,' the controllers of which are virtually all ethnic Chinese. Yet the writing on 'Chinese business' excludes such organizations, suggesting a measure of inconsistency in definition. Some joint-stock companies in Malaysia and the Philippines may pose a problem too, since they have such an ethnic diversity of owners that it may be inaccurate to categorize them as 'Chinese.' Nor do commentators distinguish clearly between China-based and overseas businesses, and indeed the trend in the scholarship is to treat them as if they were the same animal.

Much of what is written about Chinese business is not fully spelt out, but the underlying drift seems to be this: family-mindedness and particularism are features of traditional Chinese culture, and this leads to a preference on the part of the Chinese entrepreneur for family ownership rather than partnerships or joint-stock companies. In reality, partnerships are just as 'traditional' a form of Chinese enterprise as family firms. In imperial China, the classic type of partnership was one where profits were divided according to the percentage of capitalization put up by each investing partner.

A form developed in China and adapted to the tough, frontier conditions of Southeast Asia in early Chinese overseas settlement was the partnership known as *kongsi* (see p 76). The best-known examples were those involved in gold and tin mining and in plantations in various parts of Southeast Asia in the 18th and 19th centuries. These were groups of men who supplied their own capital and equipment, and got their return not in wages but in shares of ore sales.

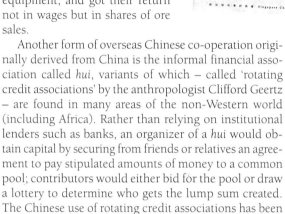

Brochure for the first World Chinese Entrepreneurs Convention.

Another form of overseas Chinese co-operation originally derived from China is the informal financial association called *hui*, variants of which – called 'rotating credit associations' by the anthropologist Clifford Geertz – are found in many areas of the non-Western world (including Africa). Rather than relying on institutional lenders such as banks, an organizer of a *hui* would obtain capital by securing from friends or relatives an agreement to pay stipulated amounts of money to a common pool; contributors would either bid for the pool or draw a lottery to determine who gets the lump sum created. The Chinese use of rotating credit associations has been documented in America and Southeast Asia.

Asked to identify a Chinese business during the first half of the 20th century, the man in the street in many sites of overseas Chinese settlement would most likely point to a small shop. The most widespread type of Chinese firm throughout much of the world, and particularly in Southeast Asia, was indeed the 'shophouse' found in small and large towns, or its rural equivalent (called *toko* or *warung* in Indonesia and *sari-sari* store in the Philippines).

Most of these were based on the work-unit not so much of the family as the household, if 'family' is understood to consist of father, mother and children, since Chinese sojourning was typically a masculine affair and unless intermarriage with local women took place, there were no wives or children. However, the proprietor usually sent for his son or a young relative from his home village in China, the latter to serve as an apprentice in his shop. Thus 'family firms,' such as were found in China and indeed throughout the world, did not exist in their ideal-typical form in the early overseas Chinese communities.

Apprentices did not expect to remain permanently as apprentices, aspiring on the contrary to set up business on their own account eventually. One of the stories told of the entrepreneur Thio Thiau Siat (Zhang Bishi), for example, is that his rise to riches began with his becoming apprenticed to a dealer in sundries in Batavia. The 19th-century magnate Loke Yew also started out as an apprentice in a shop (in Singapore) before opening his own provisions store. Observers have noted Chinese apprentices' unusual zeal to set up on their own as soon as possible, often with the backing of their master, even if they were going into competition with him.

Stained glass panel with Chinese character for 'commerce' in Oversea-Chinese Banking Corporation branch, Singapore.

The evolution of the Chinese family-owned, family-run business firm has been outlined by the sociologist Wong Siu-lun, in whose model the firm undergoes four phases – what he calls the emergent, centralized, segmented and disintegrative stages. The first two refer to the way in which businesses start and come under the paternalistic authority of the founder-head. According to Wong, the segmentation and disintegration are closely bound up with a traditional Chinese practice, that of equal inheritance by sons. Equal inheritance, by contrast with primogeniture (by which the right of succession and the deceased's estate pass to the eldest son), conduces to fission and the family firm's disintegration in the third generation, when further division of assets will have taken place on the basis of partible inheritance.

This model can only be partially tested in overseas Chinese businesses, however, because most of the ones studied by academics so far (generally the large conglomerates) are still controlled by first- or second-generation families and so have not yet developed beyond the segmented phase. The conglomerates built, for example, by Liem Sioe Liong and Mochtar Riady of Indonesia; Robert Kuok, Lim Goh Tong and Vincent Tan of Malaysia, Lucio Tan of the Philippines and Thaksin Shinawatra of Thailand are still headed by the founder, and even older firms like the Lee Rubber OCBC (Oversea-Chinese Banking Corporation) group, founded by Lee Kong Chian of Singapore, and the Bangkok Bank founded by Chin Sophonpanich of Thailand (see Part V: Thailand) are

Loke Wan Tho, 1947.

only into their second generation.

One third-generation firm, the Singapore-based Cathay Organization, departs from the model altogether. Its history began with Loke Yew, but Cathay Organization itself was started by Loke's fourth wife and a number of partners. The film production and distribution business greatly expanded under the stewardship of Mrs Loke's son Loke Wan Tho. When the childless Loke died tragically in an air crash, the business passed to his brother-in-law, Choo Kok Leong. In 1984, Choo's daughter, Meileen, took over as Chairman and Chief Executive Officer. Nor is it only in its female leadership that the business runs counter to the Chinese pattern; far from 'disintegrating,' it has thrived in the third generation.

Writers on overseas Chinese business have generally cited problems over leadership change and generational succession as the most serious weaknesses of the Chinese family firm. They note that, while these are often handled successfully in the transition from the first to the second generation, they are likely to prove more difficult later for the reasons set out by Wong Siu-lun. But, as noted earlier, the generational shallowness of most overseas Chinese firms makes these observations hard to test (see box p 94).

Consider the Oei Tiong Ham business empire in the Netherlands Indies. The trading company from which the empire grew was founded by Oei Tiong Ham's father; thus Oei himself represented the second generation and his heirs the third. Despite a smooth transition to Oei Tjong Hauw, one of his more capable sons, the business did decline in the third generation. But was this caused by internal factors such as the failure to separate management from family ownership, or Oei Tjong Hauw's sudden early death, or did it come of the profound change in the business climate resulting from the country's independence and tilt towards socialism? The Japanese scholar Yoshihara Kunio observes that 'The most serious change for Oei Tiong Ham Concern was government interference in the economy.' Comparing it to the Japanese *zaibatsu* (business combine) Mitsui, he points out that the latter's long life was ensured by its practice of using professional managers, but adds that this practice was one which had evolved over several centuries and was not a tradition one could yet expect of so young a conglomerate as Oei Tiong Ham's (even though it already employed Dutch accountants, lawyers and engineers).

Much has been made by commentators of the extent to which Chinese family firms exemplify 'familism,' 'paternalism,' 'patrimonialism' and 'personalism' as characteristic Chinese business practices. These characteristics are contrasted, moreover, with the presumed economic rationality of Western business organizations. In China (including Taiwan, where much of the research on the subject is based), small business dealings did depend greatly on personalistic connections and a local reputation for trustworthiness that made possible the securing and extension of credit. Creditors and debtors knew each other by reputation, and financial relationships were regulated by unofficial rather than legal sanctions. People were discouraged from defaulting on their commitments by their need to safeguard their reputation and to avoid nastiness – creditors could resort to strong-arm tactics to exact payment. In the absence of a system of law that transcended state authority to protect purely commercial transactions, Chinese turned to their merchant guilds more readily than to the courts to settle a dispute. In many overseas settings, Chinese businessmen felt – and still feel – scarcely better protected. Under the circumstances – these could range from anti-Chinese discrimination or corrupt government officials – their inclination towards unofficial, uninstitutionalized styles of business is hardly surprising.

Network organizations

Much of the literature describes Chinese businesses as 'networks' ('bamboo network enterprises' in one formulation). It is hard to know what a 'network' is exactly, since Chinese businessmen themselves do not use this term – *wangluo*, the Chinese translation of the English word, is adapted from electrical vocabulary. It seems to refer to practices of which one concrete historical manifestation has been the domination of particular trades by particular speech groups, or *bang*, in several cross-border markets. *Bang* domination suggests numerous 'closed' systems operating on the basis of native-place ties (hence particularistic) rather than purely commercial contractual and 'rational' linkages. To put it in another way, if it is a Teochiu who exports Thai rice from Bangkok and it is a Teochiu who imports it in Hong Kong, then something other than a purely formal commercial relationship is assumed to be at work. What is at work may be little more than an informal, personal connection founded on a common place of origin.

The organizational basis for merchant guilds (*huiguan* and *gongsuo*) in China was a voluntary group whose common interest could rest on craft, trade or occupation as well as on place of origin. This puzzled and frustrated Western observers, for whom the term 'guild' denoted an essentially economic organization, one which did not signify an overlap of trade association with particularistic connections. But it seemed to fit in well with a trend in Western scholarship (inspired by Max Weber) which emphasizes the particularism of Chinese business ties and which links China's failure to achieve capitalism and modernity with its failure to develop economically 'rational' associations.

Today's commentators have, however, reversed this argument, asserting that 'Chinese networks' play an important role in advancing overseas Chinese business by facilitating inter-regional integration. Through their far-flung networks, overseas Chinese are said to be particularly well-placed to meet the needs of globalization. Contrary to the earlier Western view, particularism is seen to be a help rather than a hindrance. Yet what has not changed is the perception that business ties based on personal trust rather than legal obligations are a mark of 'Chinese culture' and somehow peculiarly Chinese.

Conglomerates

Several hundred large Chinese business groups have become prominent in Thailand, Malaysia, Singapore, Indonesia and the Philippines since about 1970. Many smaller multi-firm groups, with essentially similar features to the large conglomerates, may also be included in this category. Although sometimes categorized erroneously as variants of 'Chinese networks,' it must be stressed that conglomerates are definitely not a form of network. They are tightly controlled structures, whereas networks are intrinsically loose and personalistic.

Most are owned or controlled by a single individual, the founder, or his family, usually through a holding company through which the family retains a dominant stake. By this means a tight grip is maintained over the many subordinate companies. Some parts of these groups have been floated on the stock exchange as public companies – although never the holding company or core assets, usually the most profitable ones – and outside directors are becoming more numerous than they used to be. Yet they remain essentially family-owned enterprises. Only in the rare cases where conflicts have occurred within the dominant family has control been imperilled or lost.

Most of these groups are highly diversified, relatively few of them having concentrated primarily on one field of business activity, or established vertical chains of manufacturing enterprise. Nearly all have some stake in property development, or banking and financial services, or the many other fast-growing urban services of the modern sector. Only a few are heavily involved in either heavy industry, plantation agriculture or mining, all of which require long gestation periods for any investment.

One reason for this is that diversification entails spreading their risks more widely (in high-risk environments); another is that they have been quick to move into the most profitable, fast-growth niche markets opening up in the economies of Southeast Asia. Some of the foremost of them do retain a basic core activity, however – for example, banking and financial services in the case of Thailand's Bangkok Bank and George Ty's Metrobank group in the Philippines, agro-industry in the case of Thailand's Charoen Pokphand (see p 113) and the Indonesian Sinar Mas palm oil group, and automobiles and motorcycles in the case of Astra in Indonesia. On the other hand, the Robert Kuok business empire has spanned sugar trading and cultivation, shipping and heavy industry, and hotels and property, while that of the Indonesian-Chinese tycoon Liem Sioe Liong has included flour milling, cement, food processing, banking, automobiles and much else.

Professional managers and technical experts from outside the family have been brought into senior managerial positions in more and more of these groups, while promising members of the family have been sent overseas for higher education. Some of the latter have returned to take control of parts of the family firm and are being groomed or tested for the top leadership in due course. A few groups have already been successful in making the transition from old-style autocratic systems of management and control towards more modern decision-making methods and business strategies, while others are following down the same path.

In the late 1990s the slowdown of the economies in which Chinese companies mainly operate may force changes in the way they are managed. In any case, the effect of an increasing globalization may be to reduce the heterogeneity of management styles across the world.

J. A. C. Mackie

James Riady helps run the family-owned conglomerate Lippo.

CHINESE BUSINESS NETWORKS:
A HYPOTHETICAL DIALOGUE

To make sense of the decade (mid 1980s–90s) of unprecedented growth in East and Southeast Asia, scholars and journalists homed in on Chinese entrepreneurs and brandished them as the crucial agents of regional market expansion and transnational integration. They saw Hong Kong, Taipei, Canton, Singapore, Kuala Lumpur, Jakarta, Bangkok, Manila, Vancouver and other cities with Chinese communities as nodes in a global network of Chinese business, allocating a variety of goods and services from sharks' fins and PC components to funds and information among participants tied by personal bonds and trust relations. Every age has its own way of looking at things, and with the financial calamities of the late 1990s came a less rosy view of overseas Chinese business. But what of the views during the boom years? For a summary, listen to a debate between two hypothetical specialists – Dr A, best-selling author of *Confucius, Chinese Connections and the Ancient Way of Global Networking in the Asia–Pacific*, and Dr B, one of his critics.

Dr B: It is clear from your writings that you see the economic and social intercourse of the peoples of China, Hong Kong and Taiwan as facilitating the integration of Greater China. You connect this with the Chinese in Southeast Asia to conjure up a regional-going-on-global Chinese network of companies, clans and ancestral hometowns linked by blood and roots. Your books are trendy, feeding not only the increasing fascination which businessmen, the media and academia have for the economic success of ethnic Chinese in East and Southeast Asia and for the so-called Pacific Century, but also the revival of ethnicity around the world, a phenomenon echoed, incidentally, by the debate on 'Asian Values' and the 'Asian Renaissance.' But aren't you being a bit *passé*? It is true that networking on the basis of kinship, ethnicity and common place of origin is one of Chinese trade history's most familiar stories. But isn't the story over?

Dr A: Just look at the facts. Many overseas Chinese are doing business with people and towns in China with whom they have family or social connections (*guanxi*) or linguistic affinities. Guangdong province is where Hong Kong's Cantonese originated, where they have relatives and where the bulk of their investments in China has gone. Fujian is both the ancestral homeland of the majority of Taiwanese and the favoured destination of Taiwanese investments. Singapore's government-linked companies, almost

entirely run by ethnic Chinese, have also invested in China. The Charoen Pokphand Group of Thai Chinese billionaire Dhanin Chearavanont has businesses in China ranging from petrochemicals to Kentucky Fried Chicken outlets. Malaysia's Sugar King Robert Kuok, whose business empire encompasses plantations, sugar refining, shipping, property, insurance and hotels, was one of the first overseas Chinese investors in China. He is well known to have good *guanxi* (connections) with the government in Beijing. One of his earliest regional partners was Indonesia's Liem Sioe Liong, whose Salim Group accounts for an estimated 5 per cent of Indonesia's GDP. Besides investing in China, Liem has partnered Dhanin Chearavanont in joint ventures.

Dr B: You suggest that these people invest in China because they are Chinese, but surely it makes more sense to explain their moves in terms of China's lures to investors: its market reforms and opening for a start, its establishment of Special Economic Zones (in Guangdong and Fujian), its growth rates (among the world's highest) and the usual enticements like tax breaks? The character of foreign investments in China was heavily influenced by central government policies and by the focus and scope of reforms. You must remember that there were two waves of ethnic Chinese investment. The first wave saw the relocation of export processing factories from Hong Kong to Guangdong. But while the tycoons bought goodwill with *donations* – but not investments – in their ancestral hometowns, they remained on the sidelines. Not until certain policy changes had occurred did they seriously come in: these included a shift of the open door policy into a higher gear, the opening of previously closed sectors to the foreign investor, and the easing of controls on the sale and transfer of land-use rights to foreign buyers. Their coming in represented the second wave, one characteristic of which was that the investment destinations were no longer limited to special zones or coastal cities, but spread over the hinterlands. Doesn't all this show that policy changes explain the influx of overseas Chinese capital far better than ethnic feeling or linguistic affinity? Look at the Singaporean Chinese. Coming late to China, at a time when the hinterland has opened up, these people invested in Jiangsu and Shandong, pastures well beyond the main ancestral province of Fujian.

Dr A: You can't tell me that historical ties, a common language and cultural heritage aren't comparative advantages overseas Chinese have when

it comes to penetrating China's and Southeast Asia's markets. Ethnicity as the basis of networking is not history, it is now. Think of the World Chinese Business Network, the web site of Chinese businesses on the Internet set up by the Singapore Chinese Chamber of Commerce and Industry in December 1995. The Confucian idea that relatives must help each other means that familism remains important in network construction and the formation of business alliances. Many Chinese entrepreneurs married daughters of fellow-regionals from Fujian or Guangdong who helped them to extend their business networks by introducing them to their wealthy relatives. Without their wives many Chinese tycoons would never have been able to tap other clusters of relationships. I can cite any number of transnational conglomerates that are controlled by Chinese business families. They may employ professional managers but never at the cost of diluting family control. Such autocratically owner-managed family firms can respond quickly to changing economic and political conditions.

Deals struck between overseas Chinese businessmen over a game of golf took a beating in the Asian currency crisis and economic slowdown that cast doubt on the supposed advantages of an autocratic style of managing economies.

Dr B: I know from your writings that you believe there is something culturally distinct about Chinese business; indeed, you posit a 'Chinese capitalism' epitomized by the Chinese family business, which you counterpoint to the Korean *chaebol* and the Japanese *keiretsu* as the dominant form of overseas Chinese business. But you betray an ignorance of Chinese history when you posit the family business as a traditional Chinese form. In fact partnerships are just as traditional a form of Chinese business as family firms. Most new businesses in the US are also family owned, but to remain profitable and competitive, families take on outside investors and, as a result, give up some control over the business. You say that Chinese family businesses don't give up control. But then nor would the first Henry Ford, who passed his business to his son Edsel — whose failure to talk his father into modernizing the company must ring a few bells — and it wasn't until the firm was well into its third generation, Henry Ford II, that Lee Iacocca was brought in. You have left out the factor of generational depth. With Chinese businesses, we're still talking first or second generation. You contrast generationally shallow businesses with generationally mature ones — failing to compare like with like, in other words — and put the difference down to familism. How can I accept that? You should talk to a few Chinese and find out what they really think about 'family.' In China the conventional wisdom is that the last place an overseas Chinese invests in is his hometown, because no sooner is your factory built than a whole queue of putative kinsmen turns up expecting jobs and handouts. Kinship reciprocity tends to limit economic options: kinsmen often claim favours such as lower prices and delayed payments.

Dr A: Yet one fact remains: the Chinese lack of trust in groups outside their own, which holds them back from doing business with non-Chinese. How often do you hear of two Chinese strangers successfully clinching a business deal without having first committed time to establishing personal trust relations? To understand how Chinese business really works, you have to understand how the moral order — that is, the values and belief system of Chinese businessmen — regulates social and business behaviour and strengthens cohesion among members of the business community. To be 'embedded' in such moral economies is to be subject to sanctions against unpredictable behaviour and breaches of trust. Those who violate the moral order by failing to fulfil relationship obligations risk losing resources provided by the network, itself an important element of one's social capital.

Dr B: But the moral order is 'socially constructed,' to echo sociologists who show that areas of social life understood to be fixed or given have in fact been shaped in concrete social situations and historical contexts. You overlook such structural factors as state economic policies geared to enhancing entrepreneurship. The notion of a global Chinese network underpinned by values derived from remote traditional China assumes first, that these values have persisted into late-modernity; second, that they may be generalized across Chinese communities in environments as widely different as Indonesia and the USA. But I don't see how you can make these assumptions. Simply comparing Hong Kong and Singaporean Chinese is enough to indicate how different one Chinese community is from another.

Dr A: Still, blood is thicker than water. Political sensitivities in Southeast Asia keep alive the vulnerability the Chinese have long felt as minorities. Combined with their strong ethnic identity and sense of mutual dependency and trust, this keeps them functioning as a group which maintains the flow of resources such as capital, manpower, market information or social support within its own, exclusively Chinese, channels. It is hard for outsiders to break into a Chinese network.

Dr B: To break into established networks is difficult for all businessmen. A Chinese network is in no way exceptional. Indeed cross-cultural studies examining how white and Asian businessmen use social networks have shown more common traits than differences. Businessmen who rely on tribal networks and ethnic resources alone for the partners and capital they need end up under-utilizing opportunities offered by regional integration and globalization. Successful global corporations tend to be culturally more diverse from having to adapt to local conditions. I am sure that the new generation of Chinese entrepreneurs, with their MBA degrees from Western universities and work experience in Western and Japanese companies, would subscribe to the view that entrepreneurs with a tribal mentality are anachronistic in the age of information superhighways.

Dr A: You suggest that Chinese businesses are shifting from kin obligations, nepotism and patronage towards non-kin ties and 'modern' management patterns. Can you prove that?

Dr B: Yes and no. But then your picture of culturally distinct Chinese networking along ethnic lines is not validated by empirical research either. Indeed, the evolution of Chinese conglomerates in Asia shows how important *non-Chinese* connections have been. Liem Sioe Liong's success hinges on his connections to Indonesia's military-bureaucratic élite. Business partnerships with non-Chinese enabled him to build a global empire with interests in Africa, Europe and America. Robert Kuok was networking with Malay political leaders and Europeans before the term became a buzzword. But if I take you up on the sweeping nature of your writing, it is not only for scholarly reasons. What also troubles me is the practical harm it can do. Indeed, by perpetuating the popular image of rich homogeneous Chinese communities as 'closed' systems of business network relationships — relationships which look like cartels or mafias to non-Chinese — you play to the prejudices of those who scapegoat the Chinese. We ought to be careful that we don't exacerbate racial stereotyping and ethnic tensions.

Thomas Menkhoff

Figure 3.3

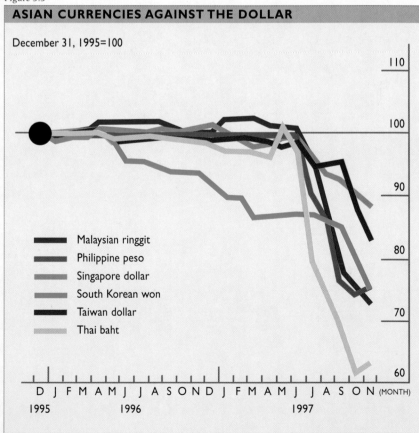

ASIAN CURRENCIES AGAINST THE DOLLAR

December 31, 1995=100

- Malaysian ringgit
- Philippine peso
- Singapore dollar
- South Korean won
- Taiwan dollar
- Thai baht

D J F M A M J J A S O N D J F M A M J J A S O N (MONTH)
1995 · 1996 · 1997

Source: The Economist, Nov 22, 1997.

PART IV

RELATIONS

THE TWO THEMES OF THIS PART – overseas Chinese relations with China, and overseas Chinese relations with non-Chinese – are aimed at illuminating that most complex of questions, the identities of the overseas Chinese. For those identities are formed and transformed in a continuous dialogue with China and with the surrounding non-Chinese social and cultural systems.

The first sub-section considers China's policies towards the overseas Chinese, the politicization of overseas Chinese identification by nationalism, Hong Kong's role in the relationship between China and the overseas Chinese, and overseas Chinese remittances and investments in the home country.

The second sub-section turns to interactions with the non-Chinese world. A discussion on ethnicity is followed by one on what it means to be an overseas Chinese living in a modern and progressively globalized world. For the term 'non-Chinese' is to be taken in the broadest sense, as encompassing those processes summed up by the term 'modernity.' To give the reader some sense of how these abstract discussions relate to concrete situations, features on visual artists, writers and people working in the cinema interleave the text. Finally, we look at the ways in which overseas Chinese have worked and competed with others in the commercial expansion of their host economies.

This painting (The Last Banquet, 1989) by the Chinese American Zhang Hongtu shows that the artist's reference points and images are both Chinese (Mao Zedong) and European (Leonardo da Vinci's The Last Supper). So are those of most overseas Chinese, pulled at by China and by the non-Chinese world at once.

RELATIONS

RELATIONS WITH CHINA

Overseas Chinese relations with China today still bear the marks of a chequered history. China's modern view of the overseas Chinese, and vice versa, is necessarily refracted through the prism of this history, which colours that view in various ways. But 'China' – whether as an original homeland (see Part I) or basis of identity, as a source of tradition or 'historical capital' – does not impact upon overseas Chinese in isolation. When affecting how overseas Chinese relate to it, it is always part of a wider mix. That mix includes ideology, particularly in the days of the Cold War; technological and economic changes; diplomatic relations with other nations and so on.

Carved Chinese characters denote 'Seal of the Grand Marshal,' namely Koxinga.

China's policies towards overseas Chinese

Until the Qing dynasty (1644–1911), the Chinese government's policies towards Chinese overseas were basically an aspect of its policies towards overseas trade. Neither foreign trade nor foreign travel was subject to restrictions under any of the dynasties preceding the

more autocratic Ming (1368–1644). With the exception of the reign of the Yongle emperor, the Ming was, until 1567, antagonistic to private maritime commerce. The lifting of the imperial ban that year opened the way to overseas Chinese residence. But the fundamental bias against emigration was continued by the Qing dynasty that succeeded the Ming; the government allowed localized foreign trading but banned overseas residence. Indeed, from 1717, the court issued a series of decrees prohibiting its subjects from leaving the country and re-entering it.

By and large Chinese abroad had an 'image problem' in China, seen as deserters, traitors, rebels and conspirators. By leaving home, they left their filial duties undone – their parents unattended, their forefathers' graves unswept, their ancestral sacrifices unoffered. Whereas working the land has been a paramount Chinese virtue since the earliest times, the overseas Chinese sought profit in trade. As the emperor put it in a decree in 1727, 'I believe that the majority of those who go overseas are undesirable elements. If they are allowed to go as they wish without any time limit, they will become more undesirable, and will encourage more people to follow suit.' Down by the Treaty Ports, in Canton and Amoy, they betrayed their race by conniving with foreign opium smugglers. They further aroused suspicion by their links to secret societies.

The imperial Qing view of overseas Chinese as rebels and subversives hatching conspiracies abroad is not surprising either. In challenging the Qing conquest, Koxinga's resistance (see p 49) drew on naval and financial resources outside China. Even after Koxinga was defeated, the court remained uneasy, fearing that remnants of his forces taking sanctuary in Southeast Asia might foment plots against the dynasty. A wish to counter such challenges lay behind the series of imperial edicts, issued between 1656 and 1712, which made overseas travel and residence a capital crime punishable by beheading. Chinese sojourners overseas were thus criminal by definition. The legal sanctions against them had never been stricter or more comprehensive. Local officials, though opened to the heaviest penalties themselves if they did not enforce the decrees assiduously, were often tempted to extortion and arbitrary proceedings against the vulnerable returnees.

China's defeat in the Opium Wars brought the foreign world within its maritime gates. Among other things, that world wanted cheap labour. This it gained through the coolie trade, by which huge numbers of Chinese were transported between 1845 and 1874 (see p 61). The abuses which characterized this trade eventually forced themselves upon the blind eye turned to it by the local Chinese officials, and in 1860, under pressure by Britain and France, China agreed to the right of its subjects to work and live abroad. A clause to that

---

THE CHINESE OVERSEAS CYCLE

Under the heading 'the Chinese overseas cycle,' the historian Wang Gungwu has summarized the interactions between Chinese governments and the Chinese overseas during alternating periods of national strength and weakness in the following manner:

1. Strong and prosperous Qing empire from 1680s to 1840s.
   Chinese government (CG) neglectful of, and indifferent to, the fates of the Chinese overseas;
   Chinese overseas (CO) faced great obstacles, but learned to be self-sufficient and independent, and increasingly successful in commerce.

2. The Hundred Years' weakness and poverty, 1840s to 1949 (the weak and poor Qing empire followed by a republic divided by civil wars and invaded by Japan).
   CG offered recognition of, and support to, the CO, but expected political loyalty from them, and also economic investments from the rich CO;
   CO numbers grew rapidly but the Huaqiao were responsive to China's needs and were, on the whole, caring; they continued to be economically prosperous but were also angry and ashamed at the failure of successive Chinese governments.

3. The Mao era of strength and promise unfulfilled, 1949–76: strong country, poor people, living under the shadow of the Cold War and the US–Soviet 'central balance.'
   CG impervious but constrained, forced by diplomatic isolation and ideology to ineffectual policies amounting to a return to neglect of, if not indifference to, the CO;
   CO faced new obstacles and relearned how to be self-sufficient and economically autonomous; became politically localized and naturalized, if not still divided by the forces of China politics.

4. The reforming People's Republic of China since 1978 has become potentially strong and prosperous relative to China's neighbours and its place in the world, but is still on the margins of Third World poverty.
   CG returns to recognition and modest support of the CO, but defensively, welcoming investments but not expecting loyalty;
   CO once again grow fast but they remain sympathetic, even caring; being better educated, they adapt to conditions abroad more easily and are divided in the ways they are attracted to the promise of Greater China but dismayed by China's political system.

effect was included in the Beijing Conventions it signed with Britain and France.

If, as traders and rebels, the Chinese overseas aroused distrust in China, they provoked sympathy and dismay as downtrodden coolies. Travelling abroad, Chinese diplomats noted the hardship and discrimination suffered by China's subjects overseas. When the news was brought home, it wrought quite a change in the attitudes prevailing in official circles. It fell to people like Li Hongzhang (1823–1901), who was governor-general at Tianjin but who acted as China's de facto foreign minister, to improve the wretched lot of the overseas coolies. As part of a new stage of foreign-policy activism over which Li presided, investigation commissions were sent to Cuba in 1873 and Peru the following year to report on the conditions of life and work for Chinese labourers there.

The findings were horrifying enough to radically change the official Chinese stance on the overseas Chinese. The disclosures of the commission's reports left no doubt that the abduction and forcible transportation of Chinese coolies across the seas were prologues to hideous atrocities perpetrated in the destination country. The revelations came at a time when a Peruvian plenipotentiary was negotiating a treaty with Li Hongzhang for augmenting the supply of Chinese coolie labour to Peru. Such abuses, Li made clear to the Peruvian, could not be countenanced, nor would he agree to the treaty without some reassurance of justice for the victims. To be sympathetic to and even protective of the Chinese abroad was a new departure for a government whose stance had been for so long to denigrate, dismiss and punish them.

The right of Chinese to emigrate, to visit or return to their homeland at will was formally recognized in 1893, with the lifting of the old ban on emigration. Prime movers in the abolition were Xue Fucheng, the Chinese minister to England, and Huang Zunxian, the Chinese consul-general to the Straits Settlements (Malacca, Penang and Singapore). These men saw the gains to be had in harnessing the economic strengths of the overseas Chinese to the cause of China's modernization. Earlier, in 1877, the first Chinese consulate had been established in Singapore, with Hu Xuanze, better known as Hoo Ah Kay, as consul. By its demise, the Qing had established 46 consulates, a great part of whose concern was to recruit overseas Chinese merchant support for China's economic development; among other things, these consulates promoted Chinese education and the setting up of Chambers of Commerce in the overseas communities.

Widely publicizing the change of policy in local Chinese newspapers in Singapore, Huang Zunxian offered visas to those who wished to return to China, visas which obliged Chinese officials to protect the returned subjects. Yet the returnee could not always be sure that the new rules would be effectively and coherently applied at the local level by officials at the ports in Guangdong or Fujian. There remained an overhang of prejudice from the days when overseas residence was tantamount to desertion.

The Merchants Protection Bureau, a new body proposed by the governor of Fujian and duly created there and in Guangdong with the blessing of the court, was to see to it that returned overseas Chinese were registered and looked after. But it did not live up to its name, and many overseas Chinese merchants still found themselves prey to local harassment and extortion. Indeed, the local gentry who ran the bureaus were themselves corrupt and predatory. All in all, an overseas Chinese merchant contemplating business investments in his hometown would have little reason to believe that either he or his money was safe. The Ministry of Commerce tried to intervene, but the tricky central–local balance of power made this another case of uncooperative local government thwarting central authority.

Chinese imperial administrators were grappling with what China under Deng Xiaoping a century later would call 'modernization.' Modernization implied industrialization. And it was here (again anticipating the China of the 1980s) that the overseas Chinese came into play: they were a source and conduit of much needed capital and entrepreneurial skills. The Qing court was aggressive in its bid to attract overseas Chinese capitalists. For the latter, association with the imperial bureaucracy conferred mandarin status of the kind denied them in their overseas commercial setting. Their eagerness for the traditional Chinese indices of prestige showed itself in their purchase of Qing official titles and honorary ranks.

Modernization also implied a degree of Westernization. Here again, overseas Chinese could make an impression, as a source and conduit of 'Western learning.' Li Hongzhang, the leading modernizer of the day, brought into his entourage of experts a number of overseas Chinese, Yung Wing (Rong Hong) and Wu Tingfang being two of the best known (see box p 100). These were men with experience of the West. Ever since then, overseas Chinese have been viewed as assets to China.

China's interest in Huaqiao (Chinese sojourners abroad) found legal expression in the Nationality Law, China's first, promulgated by the Qing government in 1909. This was based on the principle of *jus sanguinis*: any person born of a Chinese father or mother (if the

Li Hongzhang (top) and Hoo Ah Kay.

Double allegiance of Chinese in colonial Singapore: to Queen Victoria, and to the Chinese empire.

THREE BEARERS OF 'WESTERN LEARNING'

Numerous Chinese overseas embodied the 'Western learning' which China needed to modernize. One of the many who lent their skills was **Yung Wing** (Rong Hong, 1828–1912). Educated in missionary schools in his birthplace Macao and also in Hong Kong, Yung went on to study at Yale and, upon gaining his degree there in 1854, became the first Chinese to graduate from an American university. Back in China, he worked as a translator for the Shanghai customs service and travelled to the West as an appointee of the Qing government to buy machinery for an arsenal the latter was establish-

ing in a bid to strengthen itself militarily and politically. It was also at Yung's instigation that a group of Chinese boys were sent to study in Hartford, Connecticut (see Part V: The United States). One of the teachers at Hartford, Mary Kellogg, would eventually become his wife. In Shanghai he helped start a modern-style periodical and acquire Western equipment for the city's first modern textiles factory. He died an American citizen and a supporter of Sun Yat-sen's revolution.

Another Chinese bearer of 'Western learning' was **Wu Tingfang** (1842–1922). Born the son of a merchant in Singapore and therefore a British subject, Wu received a classical Chinese education in his native Guangdong

province. He was then sent, aged 14, to study at Hong Kong's St Paul's College, on whose graduates English culture rubbed off to a greater or lesser degree. Beginning his working life in the British colony, Wu was part of an Anglo-Chinese world that included his brother-in-law, the businessman and civic leader Ho Kai (He Qi); Tong King-sing (Tang Tingshu), the head comprador of the British firm Jardine, Matheson and Company; and Sir Robert Hotung (He Dong), the half-Chinese millionaire businessman.

Following a stint as an interpreter in the Hong Kong courts, Wu went on to study law at Lincoln's Inn in London and was called to the Bar in 1877, the first Chinese to become a barrister. Back in Hong Kong, he became the first Chinese to practise law, to be a magistrate and

to serve on the Legislative Council.

In 1882, the Chinese statesman Li Hongzhang hired him as an aide and Wu moved to China, where he lived first in Tianjin, then in Beijing and finally in Shanghai. In between he was twice Minister to the United States. There he found himself helpless to avert American persecution of Chinese immigrants and the extension of the notorious Chinese exclusion laws (see Part V: The United States). A bitter lesson he learned was that his own capabilities counted for little when the country he represented stood so low in the ranking of nations. Back in China, he helped shape the 1905 movement to boycott American goods in protest against US mistreatment of American Chinese, a movement some historians see as the first concerted expression of modern Chinese nationalism.

Wu's nationalist sentiments were complexly mixed with a belief, rooted in his own training, that British legal and judicial institutions were the best in the world and that China should ultimately adopt them as a crucial step in its modernization. He devised China's first code of commercial law, but in legal reform, as in diplomacy, his efforts met frustration and he accomplished little; too many forces, both petty and political, worked against him. He remains an interesting exemplar, nonetheless, of that first generation of overseas Chinese who were in the front line of contact with the West and who urged selective Westernization upon China. That generation would not be the last.

Bearer of 'Western learning' of another sort was **Wu Lien-teh** (Wu Liande, 1879–1960), who was born the son of a Cantonese goldsmith in Penang and became the first Chinese student to study medicine at Cambridge University, England. While practising medicine in Penang, Wu campaigned hard

against opium addiction, treading on the toes of many vested interests, which retaliated by getting him unfairly convicted for possessing a tincture of opium in his dispensary. He thus needed little persuasion to accept an invitation from Tianjin's governor, Yuan Shikai (one day to rise to the presidency of the Republic of China), to become the vice-director of the Imperial Army Medical College there.

In 1910–11 a pneumonic plague epidemic swept Manchuria. It was as the physician chiefly responsible for stamping out this plague that Wu most heroically distinguished himself in China. Arriving in Harbin in December 1910, he noted that 'There were no hospitals, laboratories, or disinfection stations, and only a plague house . . . existed into which suspected patients, that is, those who coughed, vomited blood or suffered from headache of any kind, were indiscriminately thrown.' One decisive step he took was to set fire to 2,000 coffins. The second time an outbreak occurred (in Manchuria and Siberia in 1920–21), the plague prevention service he had established was there to contain it.

It was also thanks to his energy and dedication that the Chinese Medical Association was founded, Chinese medical services were modernized and Chinese medical education improved. The anti-opium cause continued to interest him; expressing gratification at the international recognition of his efforts on behalf of that cause, he said, 'The earlier work was for a community; this one concerns a whole nation.'

Returning to Malaya in 1937, the year the Japanese invaded China, he chose to live in relative obscurity as a doctor in private practice in Ipoh. Epidemiologist, microbiologist, pathologist and medical historian, he was also to become an autobiographer, publishing his *Plague Fighter: The Autobiography of a Modern Chinese Physician* in England in 1959. His decades in China had demanded enormous courage, but also faith, needed because, as he himself put it, 'without it during those troublous times one would simply have to throw up one's hands in despair.'

Editor

father were unknown) was a Chinese citizen regardless of birthplace.

Meanwhile, as the dynasty began to crack, reformists and revolutionaries, followers respectively of Kang Youwei and Sun Yat-sen (see box at right), cultivated supporters among the overseas Chinese, many of whose children were inculcated with nationalistic sentiments at the overseas schools the two camps influenced. Liu Wu-chi reports in his book on the half-Japanese writer Su Manshu (see p 78 and Part V: Japan) that at the Chinese school the latter attended in Yokohama, slogans like this were chanted regularly:

> *Our national humiliation has not been avenged,*
> *And the people's life is still full of hardships.*
> *Do not forget it every time you take your meals.*
> *Oh, young men, exert yourselves diligently!*

Interest in Huaqiao became still stronger under the Republican government ushered in by Sun Yat-sen's 1911 revolution. This was in keeping not only with Sun's thinking on Huaqiao but with the fact that the new ruling party, the Kuomintang, had been helped to power by ardent Huaqiao. Under new laws, Huaqiao could send six representatives to the newly elected Parliament. The Kuomintang's loss of power to Yuan Shikai, the military leader, did not diminish the government's interest in *qiaowu*, 'overseas Chinese affairs.' In addition to passing laws and regulations relating to overseas Chinese labour, repatriation, investment and education, Yuan Shikai's regime established a machinery for overseeing such affairs. This took form locally, as the Jinan Bureau in Fujian ('Jinan' is an allusion to 'Nanyang'), and then at the level of the central government.

The first coherent policy towards overseas Chinese was laid down by the Nationalist government which a newly triumphant Kuomintang inaugurated in Nanjing in 1927. That year the government established an Overseas Chinese Affairs Bureau in Shanghai. In 1929 the government adopted the Nationality Law first enacted by the Qing in 1909; this law has remained in force in Taiwan. In 1932 the Overseas Chinese Affairs Commission became what it has continued to be in Taiwan, a ministry under the Executive Yuan with nationwide responsibilities. Its counterpart in the Kuomintang party was the so-called 'No.3 Section,' an organ, renamed the Overseas Work Committee in 1972, whose work is often hard to tell apart from the Overseas Chinese Affairs Commission's. At the local government level, eight *qiaowu* bureaus or departments were set up in either emigrant areas or at ports of entry or exit regularly used by Huaqiao. In 1931–48, the Nationalist government promulgated scores of laws and regulations dealing with overseas Chinese education, investment, migration, and overseas Chinese voluntary associations, and setting out the rules to be observed by consular and diplomatic representatives in the management of Huaqiao educational affairs.

The importance which the government attached to the whole Huaqiao policy area was reflected not only in the fact that the various laws and regulations left no stone unturned but in the panoply of machinery set up to administer them. What gave an added stamp of legality to the rights of the overseas Chinese was the in-

SUN YAT-SEN

Nationalist sentiment fuelled the revolution identified with the leadership of Sun Yat-sen (1866–1925). Born a Cantonese, Sun went to school at the age of 13 in Honolulu, joining his elder brother there. (Like thousands of poor Cantonese, some of the Suns had emigrated.) In Hawaii, Sun picked up ideas about democracy and republican government as well as an interest in Christianity. Sent home to his native Guangdong lest he became too Westernized, he wound up as a student at Hong Kong's College of Medicine.

In 1894 he offered his services to the Qing statesman Li Hongzhang, who at that moment was too preoccupied to take any notice of him. Turning towards revolution, Sun established a secret society in Hawaii, the Revive China Society, to work for the overthrow of the Qing dynasty. In Hong Kong he plotted with secret societies near Canton to stage a military uprising. The ill-hatched revolt ended in failure and flight to Japan. From there Sun's travels took him eventually to London, where he read widely in Western political and economic theory and where the Chinese legation's failed attempt to kidnap him for execution in China, widely publicized in the Western press, made a celebrity of him.

Sun's call for revolution was opposed by a more cautious campaign for reform. Reform was advocated by two fellow-Cantonese: the scholar and political organizer Kang Youwei (1858–1927) and Kang's best student Liang Qichao (1873–1929). Kang was for constitutional monarchy, but the reforms he had persuaded the young Guangxu emperor to decree in the summer of 1898 had been scuppered by the emperor's aunt, the Empress Dowager Cixi, whose antagonism to Kang had made an exile of him. Wandering from country to country, Kang sought support among the overseas Chinese for the Emperor Protection Society (Baohuang Hui), the political organization he founded on the symbolism of a *modern* Chinese emperor.

Sun competed for the same support. He had come to appreciate the financial backing rich overseas Chinese could give him. The revolutionists vied with the reformists for influence and control in overseas Chinese schools and social organizations (in Singapore and Malaya the turf fought over included the Chinese Chambers of Commerce and Anti-Opium Societies). Infiltrators from one camp worked to outflank the other. Each camp had its own periodical press to wage a war of words for the hearts and minds of the overseas Chinese.

Kang's cause was the more popular, until the tide began to turn around 1900. Sun's revolutionary message found takers among the Chinese studying in Japan, and in 1905 he joined his revolutionary organization to other radical groups to form the Revolutionary Alliance, Tongmeng Hui, in Tokyo. This signalled the start of a united revolutionary movement, one of whose new directions was the expansion of the Alliance's branches in overseas Chinese communities. By 1909, Sun was in the ascendant. Funds raised by the Chinese abroad helped finance the insurrections which culminated in the toppling of the Qing dynasty in 1911. So crucial to his triumph did Sun deem the backing of the overseas Chinese that he dubbed them, famously, 'the mother of the revolution.'

Editor

clusion of articles providing for their protection and political participation in the country's draft constitution. The overall thrust of the policies was the 'care' of the 'transplants.' Uppermost on the government's agenda by 1937 was education, a matter covered by the largest number (at least 16) of regulations governing Huaqiao. At that time, there were more than 2,000 overseas Chinese schools to serve as vehicles for strengthening the emigrants' cultural, sentimental and even patriotic ties to China.

Another major preoccupation was to work with overseas community associations to enhance the sway of the Kuomintang, branches of which were established in many places of overseas Chinese settlement until, on the eve of the outbreak of China's war with Japan, they were to be found across the entire diaspora. The com-

Yuan Shikai.

Flag of Nationalist China hoisted on street in Amsterdam on National Day, 1931.

Zhou Enlai, 1954 (top) and Liao Chengzhi, 1976.

munity associations and overseas Chinese recruits to the party did fall very much under the Kuomintang government's influence. That influence explains the strength of Huaqiao's reaction to Japan's invasion of China and the enthusiasm with which they contributed to the war effort and the 'national salvation movement.' After the war ended, the Kuomintang and the Chinese Communist Party carried their battle into the overseas Chinese arena, where each vied for supremacy in the schools and community organizations and among Huaqiao generally. That rivalry continues today despite the ending of the Cold War.

The period immediately after the Communist triumph in China was a time of stocktaking for those in charge of overseas Chinese matters in Taiwan. Protection of overseas Chinese remained a concern; proof of this was the responsibility Taiwan took for evacuating overseas Chinese from war-torn Korea in 1950 and for relocating North Vietnamese Chinese to South Vietnam in 1954 and 1955 (see Part V: Korea, Vietnam). Education continued to be a major preoccupation, one index of which is the fact that in 1951–60 more than 14,000 overseas Chinese students enrolled in institutions of higher learning in Taiwan. But what had assumed overarching importance, though, was anti-Communism work among what the Kuomintang saw as its overseas constituencies.

On the mainland, the Communist Party, while not exactly starting from scratch, certainly had less of a *qiaowu* tradition than the Kuomintang. In 1949–54 its policies were basically modelled on those of its predecessor, regarding Chinese residents abroad as citizens of China by descent, including them (in the 1954 Constitution) among groups eligible to send representatives to the National People's Congress (without, however, specifying the number of deputies), and stipulating that publications and education among overseas Chinese enjoined allegiance to the Chinese state and nation. Similarly, the Overseas Chinese Affairs Commission it set up was based on the Kuomintang prototype.

However, at the first Afro–Asian Conference in Bandung (Indonesia) in 1955, the Communist government, represented by Premier Zhou Enlai, showed itself willing to renounce its claim to overseas Chinese who wished to opt for local nationality. This was a gesture of goodwill towards the newly independent Asian countries, where overseas Chinese communities were feared as sources of subversion and a fifth column. It would be best, China suggested, if overseas Chinese were to comply with the laws and customs of their adopted countries. The Kuomintang government in Taiwan denounced this as a sell-out. But to a Beijing bent on gaining the widest diplomatic recognition, continued claim to jurisdiction over Chinese of foreign residence could prove a foreign policy impediment. China, it seems, would sacrifice the interests of the overseas Chinese should these conflict with higher national priorities.

From the signing in 1955 of the Sino-Indonesian Dual Nationality Treaty (recognizing the right of overseas Chinese to choose the nationality they preferred), there began a process which the scholar Stephen Fitzgerald has termed 'decolonization.' This did not mean an entirely 'hands-off' stance, only that a measure of restraint would be exercised. A 'special relationship,' similar to what Britain and France have forged with their former colonies would prevail.

In China *qiaowu* comprises two aspects: external and internal, the one relating to Chinese resident abroad and the other to 'domestic overseas Chinese.' The latter consists of returnees, the dependants of overseas Chinese, and overseas Chinese students studying in China. The majority of them were recipients of remittances from kin abroad. Remittances constituted one of the two chief concerns (the other being nationality) of the overseas Chinese policy of the Chinese Communist Party in the early years of its rule. Initially singled out for preferential treatment as part of the Communist Party's united front work, domestic overseas Chinese were to suffer increasing discrimination as China's preoccupation with go-it-alone development climaxed in the autarky of the Cultural Revolution. Once lauded, their overseas connections became a political liability to them during the mid-1960s and early 1970s, when they were seen as links to foreign conspiracies.

The mass organization representing their interests, the Association of Returned Overseas Chinese, was disbanded, only to be revived in 1978. That year saw radical changes across a gamut of policy areas, including *qiaowu*. The Overseas Chinese Affairs Office (as the Commission was now called) was also resuscitated. The heads of this organization, commonly referred to as Qiaoban, have come from a family with impeccable revolutionary credentials: first He Xiangning, the wife of Liao Zhongkai, one of Sun Yat-sen's comrades-in-arms; then her son Liao Chengzhi and then, after his death, *his* son Liao Hui. Coming directly under the State Council, Qiaoban has branches in almost every province.

Large numbers of domestic overseas Chinese quit the country when China's doors opened. Yet, it cannot be said that *qiaowu* has become a less important policy area. On the contrary, China is keener than ever to rally overseas Chinese investments and expertise in its dash towards prosperity and modernity. Nor is its interest in them purely economic: the question of Taiwan remains very much on the agenda. Unlike Taiwan, though, mainland China has repudiated the *jus sanguinis* principle in defining Chinese citizenship: its 1980 Nationality Law states that 'Any Chinese national who has settled abroad and who has been naturalized there or has acquired foreign nationality of his own free will automatically lose Chinese nationality.'

While China is aware of the distinction between Huaqiao and Huaren (ethnic Chinese), in practice its *qiaowu* work concerns itself with both groups. Moreover, the external aspect of *qiaowu* is seen to be facilitated by attentiveness to its internal dimension – in 1990, for example, the National People's Congress passed a law protecting returned overseas Chinese and overseas Chinese dependants, the first such law enacted by the People's Republic of China.

Zhuang Guotu

Nationalism among the overseas Chinese

Nationalism arose among the Chinese as a political awakening to modern foreign invasion from another world. It was different from their reactions when their tribal neighbours like the Mongols and the Manchus conquered China. In particular, when the Manchus adopted Confucian principles of government and co-opted Han Chinese élites to support the new imperial house, the Chinese accepted their Qing dynasty as having received the Mandate of Heaven. Such a traditional response was based on Confucian culturalism and earlier xenophobic feelings were suppressed. Western naval victories on the China coast during the 19th century initially provoked similar responses. But extensive contacts with Western political ideas and institutions made the Chinese aware that the overall military and technological superiority their ancient empire encountered was a greater challenge than anything China had ever known. A consciousness of a profound foreign threat to Chinese civilization developed among those who had most to do with these powerful foreigners, especially Chinese in the coastal provinces and among the overseas Chinese. This planted the seeds of modern nationalism.

The climax of this first phase of awareness of a threat to national sovereignty came with the Japanese defeat of China in 1894–95. The responses to that defeat laid the foundations of nationalism among the Chinese abroad; these Chinese saw that China's weakness lowered their status, especially among the Europeans; the Confucian state needed thorough reform; the Manchu rulers were themselves invaders and the time had come to overthrow them; and learning from the advanced West was the road to wealth and power. All these culminated in the growing support for Sun Yat-sen's idea of revolution and the establishment of the Republic in 1911.

The second phase followed in the 1920s. It marked the full flowering of modern nationalism which spread quickly among the younger generation of the educated. They had concluded that economic penetration inland from the Treaty Ports, with growing foreign dominance of trade and industry, constituted a form of invasion. With the introduction of modern schools and newspapers among the Chinese overseas, this view was readily accepted by those with first hand knowledge of Western power.

Japanese troops marching into village in Manchukuo.

But it was the actual loss of large parts of Chinese territory that raised the nationalism to a high pitch. This began with the Japanese Occupation of China in Shandong and the Jinan Incident in 1928 (in which Chinese forces clashed with troops sent by Japan). In 1931, the three northeastern provinces were turned into the Japanese puppet state of Manchukuo. Finally, in 1937, there followed the full-scale invasion that placed half the population of China under various forms of Japanese control. The years 1928–45 brought a new kind of emotional experience to all Chinese people. For those overseas, the occupation of their home provinces of Fujian and Guangdong highlighted the extent of the disaster to national pride. The willingness of these Chinese to participate in patriotic activities grew. These activities included direct involvement in the political struggles of China and the extensive establishment of party organizations among the immigrant communities. In Southeast Asia, this provoked great alarm and resentment among both colonial administrations and indigenous leaders. An unexpected effect was that Chinese nationalism played an important part in the develop-

ZOU RONG (1885–1905)

One of the themes which linked China to the Chinese overseas was a racial conception of the nation, with its emphasis on a people united by common Han ancestry. A nationalist who embodied that theme was Zou Rong, an 18-year old student who had studied in Japan and who lived in the foreign-concession area of Shanghai. Zou put together his anti-Manchu ideas in a tract called *The Revolutionary Army* (1903). In stirring language, he called on his countrymen to reject the Manchu yoke and seize their own destiny.

'The reason why our sacred Han race, descendants of the Yellow Emperor, should support revolutionary independence,' he said, 'arises precisely from the question of whether

our race will go under and be exterminated.' Repeatedly reprinted in China, copies of this short book were widely distributed in overseas Chinese communities in America and Southeast Asia. Indeed, much of the reprinting was done by Sun Yat-sen's supporters in Hong Kong and Japan. With his grasp of the book's propagandist value, Sun was assiduous in getting copies to those he was wooing to his cause of revolution. Zou Rong was charged with distributing inflammatory writings and jailed. He fell ill in prison and died, aged only 19. Young as he was, he had already stoked patriotic and revolutionary heat among the overseas Chinese and made a mark on his times.

Editor

ment of local nationalist movements.

This second phase remained powerful until the 1950s when nationalism became a much more complex phenomenon. The Chinese Communist Party's victory and the dependent status of Nationalist China brought the Cold War to all Chinese communities. The retreat of the West from Southeast Asia where more than 90 per cent of overseas Chinese lived exposed these communities to the new forces of anti-colonial nationalism. By the end of that decade, all these Chinese had to make decisions about whether to stay or return to China, whether to identify with the new nations or retain their Chinese nationality.

The third period during which most Chinese made their choices lasted through the 1970s. Many did go back to the new China, but the majority chose to become nationals in their adopted homes. Most of them were local-born and cared much less about their origins. The earlier nationalism of a weak and divided China was now more abstract. It had been softened by Japan's defeat, and the unification of mainland China by a strong regime further rendered it unnecessary. As trading communities, the Chinese overseas saw no future for them in revolutionary socialism. The global struggle between capitalism and communism further reduced the appeal of Chinese nationalism. The new nations in Southeast Asia, in varying degrees, showed that they were prepared to accept Chinese minorities as economically valuable citizens. Many gave ethnic Chinese room to play their part in nation-building. Most Chinese found the conditions acceptable and stopped calling themselves temporary residents, 'Huaqiao.'

China's shift away from internationalist rhetoric during the 1980s has brought a new emphasis to patriotism in China itself. How will this affect those of Chinese descent who have adopted foreign nationalities but still regard themselves as ethnic Chinese? The challenge in the 21st century is to remain loyal to their new homes, while building on their trading links with a China that is poised to play a vital role in the region. Also relevant are the aspects of economic globalization that are undermining the idea of the nation-state. Can the Chinese overseas keep their adopted national identities separate from the pull of China? If modern nationalism remains a reactive and defensive product of China's weakness, then it should have less appeal when China regains its wealth and power.

In the past the Chinese did not see themselves as a nation. Those abroad had a sense of a common cultural identity but, as sojourners, they were never homogeneous. From the beginning they kept strong links through dialect and clan groupings and non-kin trade organizations and secret societies. Only when attacked did they feel that they were Chinese, often only for short periods of time. The gradual politicization of those who felt discriminated against when Qing China became obviously feeble made them respond warmly to a common identification as Huaqiao at the beginning of the 20th century. This gave them, for the first time, the embracing idea of being of one nation. The new generation of Chinese political leaders demonstrated that modernity required nationhood. To belong to a nation assumes the protection of that nation's embassies; to register as nationals made them feel that they were merely temporarily overseas.

But not all Chinese felt equally keen about that identity which was at one end of a wide spectrum. There were large numbers of the local-born in Southeast Asia who had begun to accept their position as potential nationals in their respective adopted countries. This was particularly true of those who had intermarried and of their descendants. While still proud enough of their Chinese ancestry to keep up certain cultural practices, they felt no affinity with the politics of China. Some sought colonial recognition, while others stressed their links with the local peoples. But during the height of anti-Japanese nationalism, the pressure to conform with the majority was so strong that they suppressed their real feelings. It was not until the 1950s that their preference for a local identity came to the surface again.

The decade of the 1950s was the great period of change for all Chinese. The strong push to be patriotic Chinese was still there, and those who considered themselves Huaqiao were keen to demonstrate their ties with China, whether Nationalist or Communist. But these became fewer in number as many of them returned to China. Today, those who had stayed abroad no longer share their feelings of patriotism. Strictly, the term 'Huaqiao' can only be used for those who carry the passports of the People's Republic of China or Taiwan.

At the other end of the spectrum, those who did not see themselves as Huaqiao had the choice of either going to the West when the colonial rulers left, or adopting the identities offered to them in the new nations. Those who stayed tended to participate in local and national politics. Their economic and political activities would often demand that they took up their social responsibilities as members of an ethnic minority. Many were ready to merge with the local populace, but whether they could do so depended on when the political majority would accept them as full nationals of the adopted country. In the meantime, those whose loyalty to the country are not in question may be described as Huayi, those of Chinese descent.

This group is still relatively small. As for the majority of those who have become local citizens, they sought more practical positions across the middle ranges of the

Bangkok Bank founder Chin Sophonpanich (left), applauding as a Thai prince opens his bank, 1955, was one of many Thai Chinese to be accepted by the political majority.

spectrum. While they accepted the new citizenship rights and duties, they continued to maintain their sense of being culturally Chinese. They did so for a variety of reasons. They were economically active and found their social and cultural identity to be an asset, not only in their adopted country, but also for doing business with Chinese communities elsewhere, including with China and territories like Hong Kong and Taiwan. They were, on the whole, politically passive and did not need to identify further than necessary with the indigenous majorities. In some cases, they were also resigned to the fact that their host nation intended to treat them as an ethnic minority indefinitely.

There is much confusion in identifying this large group and finding an appropriate name to describe them. There is no single term that could cover the wide range of people in these situations. Identifying them with their countries of adoption would be the most accurate way, but this can be very clumsy, as can be seen in many 'hyphenated' versions like Sino-Thai, Chinese Americans, Malaysian Chinese and so on. Also, it fails to convey the fact that they also have much in common when engaged in business and professional pursuits. Thus, for foreigners and most Chinese, they are 'overseas Chinese,' or *haiwai huaren* when translated into Chinese, or *huaren* (ethnic Chinese) for short. The poverty of language to convey the richness and complexity of the reality is here to stay. Only scholars and those concerned for the niceties of legal and political usage can avoid the misunderstandings which necessarily flow from such misleading terms.

Wang Gungwu

Hong Kong's role in the relationship between China and the overseas Chinese

Almost as soon as Hong Kong became a British colony in 1843, it became involved with Chinese emigration and overseas Chinese. For many Chinese who went abroad, Hong Kong was the first stop to the rest of the world, and the last stop before re-entering China. For them, Hong Kong acted as the bridge with the motherland in a variety of ways throughout their sojourn.

Hong Kong was able to play this bridging role for many reasons. It was a free port with an open economy, and relatively free and fast access to information about China and the world beyond. It was the converging point of riverine, coastal and ocean shipping, located on the doorstep of Guangdong, one of the two great senders of Chinese overseas, and also near enough to Fujian, the other great emigrant source. Moreover, as a British colony and operating under a separate jurisdiction from China, Hong Kong was free from many of the legal and political constraints of the mainland. Thus it became an entrepôt for not only goods but people, letters and remittances, and less tangible things such as information, ideas and culture.

Remittances

One of Hong Kong's major roles was being the centre for overseas Chinese remittances. Whatever the means used to convey and deliver them – whether by courier or returned emigrants; or through remittance houses, private postal exchanges or banks – the funds almost invariably made a stop in Hong Kong before continuing their journey into China. Sometimes, the foreign currency, whether in cash or remittance notes, would be changed into Hong Kong dollars or Hong Kong dollar remittance drafts before being carried by returnees or couriers to China. In other cases the foreign currency would be converted to Hong Kong dollars, and then into the particular currency of the province of the recipient. This explains why the money exchanges overseas and in Chinese cities such as Xiamen (Amoy) usually quoted rates in Hong Kong's money market.

Services provided by the Canton Bank of San Francisco included American-Chinese remittances to China.

The major banks in Hong Kong became the main remittance clearing houses. In the 19th and early 20th centuries, the field was dominated by the Hongkong & Shanghai Bank; other banks active in remittance transactions included the Chartered Bank, Mercantile Bank, German-Asian Bank, Banque de l'Indochine, Chase Manhattan Bank, Dutch Indies Commercial Bank and the Bank of Taiwan. These banks exercised direct influence on the exchange process and profited greatly from foreign exchange dealings. By the early 20th century, Chinese merchants, who began to see the opportunities in this line of business also founded modern banks. The first Chinese-owned modern bank in Hong Kong, the Bank of Canton, was started by overseas Chinese from San Francisco particularly to deal in foreign exchange and remittances from the United States.

Ordinary Chinese in this period still largely depended on remittance agencies rather than modern bank services because of their low education level; but remittance agencies relied on banks. Hong Kong's open economy and relative lack of government interference helped to make it an ideal exchange centre. At the same time, its exchange infrastructure – composed of modern banks, Chinese 'native banks' (known in Guangdong as *yinhao* and in the north as *qianzhuang*), money exchange shops and remittance houses – accumulated valuable experience in handling a wide range of foreign currencies and the international movements of funds.

It was also the case that many Chinese returning from Southeast Asia with foreign currencies came first to Hong Kong to sell them for currencies circulating in their home provinces. In the 1930s, there were about 50 money exchange shops in Hong Kong, dealing mainly in the currencies of Southeast Asia, the region with the highest concentration of overseas Chinese. These all helped to enhance Hong Kong's position as a remittance centre.

In addition, there was a brisk traffic in gold and other coins from the start. From the Blue Books of Hong Kong, we can see records of over 23,000 taels of gold, 9,005 sovereigns and 600,000 dollars brought through Hong Kong by returning Chinese emigrants in 1865.

Things changed considerably from the late

(Top) Label of Hong Kong's Kin Tye Lung, a trading company which also handled remittances. (Bottom) Tin Fook, the San Francisco goldsmith shop where Chinese miners left their gold to be made into objects they could carry home to China.

1940s. The establishment of the People's Republic, the achievement of independence in the main host countries of overseas Chinese (namely Indonesia, the Philippines, Malaysia and Singapore) and the Cold War led to a drop in remittances. Despite the difficulties, however, Hong Kong remained the remittance centre. Stephen Fitzgerald estimates that about 95 per cent of remittances in the 1960s passed through Hong Kong. An economist claims that about US$25–30 million entered China through Hong Kong annually. In fact, this sum was only a fraction of the total amount of US$90–100 million remitted by overseas Chinese, as some US$40 million of the funds was invested quite deliberately in Hong Kong in their name. Without Hong Kong overseas Chinese trading and dealing in Chinese goods, either directly with China's state trade corporations or with non-official companies, might have found it that much harder to conduct their business from their countries of residence. Fitzgerald puts matters into perspective by stating, 'The point about Hong Kong is that it is not indispensable to China's financial and commercial contacts with overseas Chinese but it does provide a very great convenience.'

Up to the early 20th century, a Hong Kong institution which played a major part in channelling remittances for individuals to China was the Tung Wah Hospital. The model for the Nanhua Hospital in Penang and the Tung Chai (Tongji) Hospital in Singapore, this institution was also instrumental in organizing and collecting funds raised by overseas Chinese communities for relieving various disasters on the mainland. Founded in 1869 as a hospital for Chinese by leaders of the Chinese community in Hong Kong, the Tung Wah soon offered a wide range of services to overseas Chinese as well (see below). Another group of institutions in Hong Kong which helped overseas Chinese maintain ties with their native places were the *tongxianghui* (native-place associations).

Returning through Hong Kong

Hong Kong was the last stop for the returning Chinese sojourner before entering the motherland. As early as 1865, for instance, while 6,859 Chinese were recorded as having emigrated from China through Hong Kong, the number of returnees through Hong Kong was 6,026.

For the independent and healthy, returning to China was a private concern. However, not all returnees were independent and healthy, and soon organizations in Hong Kong were called upon to help those who needed assistance – the destitute, the sick, the disabled and victims of kidnapping and other emigration-related abuses and disasters. Much of the repatriation work was done by the Tung Wah Hospital. Soon after it was founded, it repatriated about 50 victims of a disaster on board an emigrant ship; besides raising a subscription it also had to send their names, places of origin and other personal particulars to another charitable organization in Canton before the actual repatriation could begin. The hospital persuaded a steamship company to charge only half-fare and the remainder of the donation was distributed among the men.

One particular group of returnees were Chinese prostitutes, many of whom were forcibly repatriated when the United States began in the 1870s to exclude Chinese women who emigrated for 'immoral reasons.' Other women were repatriated from places such as Singapore; when victims of kidnapping or decoying were discovered by officials, they were sent back on compassionate grounds. After receiving such women, the Tung Wah sent them home, but in cases where the hospital's directors suspected that a woman's family might actually sell her again or mistreat her, they would arrange for her to be married in Hong Kong. After 1878, much of the hospital's women-related work was taken over by the newly founded Po Leung Kuk (Society for the Protection of Women and Girls), which, like the Tung Wah, soon became the model for Chinese charitable organizations in China as well as overseas.

In most cases the Tung Wah Hospital would receive requests from Chinese voluntary associations abroad, or the Chinese consuls, to receive and repatriate returnees who needed assistance, and it arranged for their safe passage home. It was a complicated process because the returnee's home could be remote, and many persons and institutions had to be contacted to ensure that on each leg of the journey, the returnee would be handed to the right party. One may imagine the complex social network that must exist to make this kind of work possible. It was a network which extended into vast parts of China on the one hand, and to overseas Chinese communities throughout the world on the other. It was precisely because the Tung Wah Hospital occupied a pivotal position in that network, or series of networks, that it was able to perform such functions so effectively.

In the 20th century, various governments and large companies became involved in formal repatriation, but the Tung Wah was often doing the actual repatriation work. For instance, in 1914, to repatriate decrepit men and destitutes from North Borneo, the British North Borneo government appointed Messrs Gibb, Livingston as agents in Hong Kong. But it was the Tung Wah which arranged for the men to be met on arrival and sent on to their homes, with Gibb, Livingston reimbursing it for the expenses incurred. The scale of repatriation could be immense, especially during the years of the Depression. In 1931, for instance, a total of 28,314 persons were repatriated to Hong Kong. Some batches numbered over 1,000 persons at a time and each one of these would be met, housed and, with his passage paid, sent on his way home with some money.

In the 1950s, under a totally different set of circumstances, Hong Kong continued to be the gateway to China. Overseas Chinese prevented from visiting their native place by the fact that their host countries did not recognize the People's Republic of China often found their way there through Hong Kong, a place they were allowed to enter. Some organizations in Hong Kong seem to have been particularly equipped to facilitate this kind of 'unrecorded' travel. The Fujianese Association, for instance, enabled overseas Chinese to meet their family members in southern Chinese border towns such as Jiangmen and Shenzhen.

Returning the dead

It is well-known that almost all sojourners yearned to grow old and die in the home village, and even for those unfortunate enough to die abroad, efforts would be made

Stamps commemorating the 100th anniversary of Tung Wah Hospital.

to send their coffins or bones home for interment. Native-place associations often provided the network for the trans-shipment of human remains, and those in Hong Kong were particularly crucial. For instance, the Jishan Tang was established in Hong Kong in the late 19th century, by the Changhou Tang, an association of Panyu natives in San Francisco, specifically to receive exhumed bones. From Hong Kong the Jishan Tang would redistribute the bones for re-interment in various localities in Panyu county. The Tung Wah Hospital also received and trans-shipped coffins and bones from overseas localities regardless of native-place affiliation. The large coffin depository it ran catering largely for overseas Chinese testifies to the scale of its service. As late as the 1970s, coffins from Southeast Asia destined for China still went through Hong Kong.

Communications

An open city with an effective communications infrastructure, Hong Kong also acted as a conduit of letters overseas Chinese sent to China. China did not become a full member of the Universal Postal Union until 1914: before that date there were only post offices in the Treaty Ports, and even after 1914 many parts of China had no postal service. Letters were often transmitted to persons or institutions in Hong Kong for distribution to different parts of the country, however remote. After 1949 Hong Kong again became the place of postal transit; overseas Chinese in countries without direct postal links with China first sent their letters to friends or institutions in Hong Kong for redirection to destinations in China.

Apart from forwarding personal letters, Hong Kong acted as a channel of information between overseas Chinese and their homeland by virtue of the fact that its newspapers, which publicized such information, were widely circulated in south China. For instance, advertisements placed in Hong Kong newspapers in the 1870s and 1880s warned prospective emigrants of anti-Chinese riots in their destination country, or informed them of new immigration legislation.

Hong Kong's role as a bridge and interface continued into the years of the People's Republic. Even when circumstances changed drastically, such as when the Cultural Revolution (1966-76) erupted, Hong Kong's role continued and at times became even more vital. In a sense Hong Kong was neutral territory, since the British government allowed Communist agencies to operate there openly, and it was relatively easy for overseas Chinese of any country to visit Hong Kong, whereas this was certainly not the case with Communist China.

In addition, Hong Kong was an outlet for Communist and pro-Communist propaganda. The existence there of mainland-affiliated film companies and cinemas, department stores and exhibitions and official agencies of the Chinese government further enabled overseas Chinese to catch a glimpse of China. Non-Communist newspapers published in Hong Kong were also important channels of news about China. On a subnational level, the publications of Hong Kong's *tongxianghui* reported on conditions in the native place, and these, when distributed by their overseas counterparts, became another means of keeping overseas Chinese abreast of conditions in the home country.

Post Office in Hong Kong (building on right near tree) channelled letters between emigrant destinations and home districts.

Culture

To many overseas Chinese, Hong Kong was a source of Things Chinese. It supplied typical Chinese foodstuffs to importers in many overseas Chinese communities. The *jinshanzhuang* ('California traders'), which had thrived until the late 1940s, were based on the sale of Chinese foodstuffs and other consumer goods to immigrants in the United States. We can also see how Hong Kong served overseas Chinese as a supplier of cultural materials in the request sent by a Chinese association in Kobe in 1899 to the Tung Wah Hospital, asking it to find funeral workers who were familiar with Chinese practices to exhume and clean the bones of deceased Chinese in Japan.

With China becoming increasingly inaccessible and inscrutable from the 1950s, Hong Kong's cultural role assumed new dimensions. In the 1960s, one way for Chinese children in Thailand and Vietnam to get a Chinese education was to attend schools in Hong Kong. On another level, Cantonese opera troupes and other artistes from Hong Kong were invariably warmly received when on tour in Southeast Asia and North America. From the 1960s onwards, we can see Hong Kong's impact grow through the proliferation and export of Hong Kong films, television programmes, magazines, popular music and martial arts fiction to overseas Chinese communities. As aspects of Hong Kong's cultural business attained sophistication, their appeal to overseas Chinese widened. The largely Cantonese works it produced appealed particularly to the Cantonese-speaking overseas Chinese, but even in non-Cantonese speaking communities, its television drama series were promptly dubbed into other languages and Mandarin.

Not only have Hong Kong's cultural products provided entertainment; they have also been perceived as representative of Chinese culture. Enjoying and consuming them has been a means of maintaining links to the ancestral land. As elements of Chinese culture, they have added to the cultural capital of overseas Chinese. For some of the younger generation, popular magazines and movies from Hong Kong have provided ideas of how modern Chinese should behave.

Elizabeth Sinn

(Top) Hong Kong film periodical International Screen. (Bottom) Video CD sleeve of Hong Kong movie 'God of Gamblers.'

BANK OF CHINA

Money transfers were accompanied by letters (top) or else were handled by the Bank of China, among others.

Overseas Chinese remittances

Sending money back to relatives in the village of origin has been an obligation borne by all but the destitute. Indeed, the overseas Chinese's remittance obligations are, together with the notion of eventual return to their families (with whom they must hold their place even while abroad), part of the migrant ideology. As a business, remittance transfers were one of a range of international linkages – trading networks, native-place ties, labour recruitment agencies – which connected Chinese emigrants with China and with other Chinese in the diaspora.

The available data on the amounts remitted are rough indicators of trends rather than precise calculations. C. F. Remer, who published a book on foreign investment in China, obtained his figures by extensively interviewing bankers in the 1928–31 period. Others arrived at their totals by multiplying an estimated average amount of remittances per head by the number of overseas Chinese. The imperial government officially sanctioned remittances in the 1860s, and between that time and the 1930s, their flow increased steadily with the rise in migration volume.

The Japanese researcher Fukuda Shozo put the total at 2,336 million yuan for the years 1922–31. The high tides were from the 1910s to the Sino–Japanese War (1937–45) and the years after 1980, with peaks in 1921, 1924, 1929–31 and 1938–39. Fluctuations in the price of silver (China was on a silver standard up to 1935) affected the amounts remitted; silver price appreciation resulting from World War I led to a dip in the flow in 1916–18, while a dramatic fall in price following the world economic crisis explains the peak in 1929–31. Fukuda Shozo claimed that where remittances rose, they did so by a proportion greater than the fall in silver; from this we may suppose that the increases were not only a question of differences in exchange rate.

Remittances were interrupted by the Japanese Occupation of Hong Kong and Southeast Asia, much to the distress of families dependent on them. They resumed when war ended, the country's financial chaos notwithstanding. Nor did they cease with the Communist takeover of China in 1949, though on the whole they declined, to pick up again after 1972. The Bank of China was able to keep track of official inflows but not, obviously, of the value of the currency smuggling that clearly went on. After 1981 data again proved hard to obtain because remittance transactions were decentralized and more and more people personally carried money to their relatives in China.

The remittance business
Money could be remitted in a variety of ways. It was brought home in person or carried to the recipient by privately hired couriers. The latter could be friends or fellow-villagers the senders trusted, or traders (and smugglers) whose business involved travel to south China. After the 1870s, to meet the needs of a larger flow of money, professionally organized institutions arose to take over the business, largely replacing the earlier forms of transaction. But the provincial gazetteers of Fujian report that the older practice of delivering money in person has made a comeback since the 1980s.

The most widely used system was through the so-called 'letter offices,' private postal exchanges named *minxinju* and *pixinju* in Chinese. They worked in the following way: the money to be remitted was brought to one of their offices either by the sender himself or by a collecting agent; there, a letter was attached stating the amount of the remittance and the name, address and occupation of the remitter (the envelope, which bore the name and address of the recipient, would be sent back with a receipt in it after the funds had been delivered). The office sent the money to the head office, where it was changed into Chinese currency and despatched, along with the letter, to one of the exchange's branches in south China. From there, it was delivered to the remitter's family by a courier. The volume of business was such that instead of despatching the remittances individually, the exchanges would send them in large batches, often in the form of remittance drafts bought from (and sold to) the Hongkong & Shanghai Bank or the Chartered Bank. While waiting for the remittances to pile up, the letter office would sometimes lend them out for short terms. As well as the interest earned on them, the letter office would profit from currency conversions.

From the 1920s onwards, remittances were increasingly channelled through public post offices and modern banks; but the bulk of the business remained in the hands of the letter offices. The latter's tradition of personal service based on trust made them attractive to humble, illiterate remitters who relied on them to write the letters accompanying the transfers. However, for big amounts, banks were preferable. Apart from the two mentioned earlier, the main banks handling overseas Chinese remittance transfers were the Bank of China and the Oversea-Chinese Banking Corporation. Better known today as the OCBC, the latter was founded in Singapore and operated through branches in the Straits Settlements (Malacca, Penang and Singapore), Indonesia, Thailand, Hong Kong and Shanghai. The remittance business was a major stimulus for the development of the banking sector in centres such as Xiamen (Amoy) and Shantou.

Transfers were made in certain circumstances in the form of goods, which could either be consumed by the receiver or sold on for cash. In cases where letter offices were simultaneously trading houses, the money to be remitted might be used to buy export goods for sale in China, the proceeds of which would then be despatched to the remittance's intended receiver. Rice was certainly one of these commodities, the trade in which was at times a widely used channel for transferring remittances to Shantou.

In tandem with China's socialist transformation, remittance transactions were brought under centralized management. Initially the letter offices continued to operate, but later they were collectivized into various new institutions: 'joint management offices' (*lianying chu*), established in 1955; 'joint sending offices' (*lianhe paisong chu*), in 1957; and 'foreign private remittance service offices' (*haiwai siren huikuan fuwu chu*), in 1974. In 1958 the remittance business was brought under state-private joint ownership (*gongsi heying*); and in 1975, the remittance offices installed a year before were nationalized and brought under the control of the People's Bank of China. In 1981, the handling of transfers from abroad was decentralized to lower administrative levels, but the Bank of China remained in overall charge. Money often took a circuitous route – notably through Hong Kong – because of foreign exchange controls in the countries of overseas settlement: the US made it illegal, for example, to remit funds to the People's Republic of China.

Impacts on the recipients

The impacts which remittances had at the level of the receiving family, the local community and the nation will be considered separately. To begin with the first level: for the most part, remittances enhanced the receiving families' material welfare. Throughout the period they have flowed, between 60 to 80 per cent of the amounts have been spent on food, clothes and housing. Receiving families have had a higher visibility in the community because remittances have enabled them to achieve not only a higher standard of living but, thanks both to their higher cash incomes and to the foreign influences channelled through their relatives abroad, also a distinct lifestyle (involving such new items of consumption as foreign fashion, foreign-style housing, and coffee and milk). Remittances have characteristically paid for conspicuous consumption, with sumptuous funerals and weddings – attended by the entire community – giving evidence of the recipient families' wealth. Such social display, based on a high surplus income enabling families to indulge in patterns of consumption designed to impress others, has made a comeback in China, as field research in Wenzhou, the sender of many new waves of emigrants, makes clear.

In their wish to show that they have 'made it' abroad, many returnees are tempted to flashy display and luxurious styles of living, falling to the normal diversions of what is imagined to be the life of the idle rich – feasting, gambling and entertaining. But many overseas senders no doubt saw remittances as contributing to the savings that would secure them a comfortable retirement when the time came for them to return home. If part of the funds paid for immediate consumption, a portion was earmarked for 'pensions.'

However, if buying land and building a house on it were by way of providing for the family, they could also be a form of investment, or even speculation. Such investments were low before 1949, amounting to about 3 per cent of total remittances; thereafter they rose to a much higher percentage. The 'business' and 'family' purposes of remittances are hard to distinguish, however, and rather than trying to do so, it would be as well to remember that families in rural China were economic units of which the emigrant sons remained members (see p 77). C. F. Remer has argued that remittances should be seen in most cases as profits and income from property transferred back home. As an example, he cites the case of a man from a village near Shantou who ran his family's business in Siam; the man did this for more than 30 years before his son took over; the money remitted from Siam to China, then, was simply business profits from an enterprise owned by a 'transnational' family.

Remittance obligations frequently extended beyond wife and children, as may be seen in this letter addressed to Ho-mou, a Chinese laundry man in the US, by his brother-in-law in 1939 (quoted in Paul C. P. Siu's book): 'Your letter arrived January 12 with a cheque for three hundred and twenty dollars Hong Kong currency. Of this amount you allotted fifty dollars to Mother Wo [Ho-mou's mother], fifty dollars to Older Brother Ho-yin [Ho-mou's brother], ten dollars to Cousin Wai-wah, ten dollars to Nephew Kwong-pui, and the rest to Second Sister. I have divided it as you wished and I take this opportunity to thank you for them.'

Some emigrants resented their remittance obligations and sent home their earnings reluctantly. In the course of investigating emigrant communities in the 1930s, Chen Ta heard a retired miner from Malaya say, 'The joint family is an obnoxious social institution. When a member of such a family earns money he is obliged to support all the rest of it and to carry a heavy economic burden. I have had very bitter experience and always feel that I am virtually a slave of the family. They are of no help to me at all.' Those who lived off money from abroad all too often developed dependency, a habit they would need to lose, usually painfully, when remittances dried up.

Not just at the level of the family, but the community as a whole could turn into a dependent remittance economy, one highly susceptible to recessions in the emigrants' destination countries. But while a dwindling of homeward flows could leave it high and dry, the receiving community also benefited from such demonstrations of migrant success as public philanthropy. Money remitted by emigrants for raising or improving schools, libraries, temples and public amenities in the native village took some 15 to 20 per cent of total remittances both before and after 1949. Their philanthropy sometimes earned the richer of the overseas Chinese donors a place among the local political élite. The ancestral hall of one clan in south Fujian, reported Chen Ta in the 1930s, served as the seat of local government, the budget of which – the salaries of the officers, the costs of training and equipping guards and police to defend the community against robbery and banditry – were largely met by remittance money from clan members in Penang.

In the post-1949 socialist state, the possibility of influencing local power structures diminished considerably. But since the 1980s, a different picture has emerged,

A well-heeled Indonesian Chinese disembarking at Xiamen Airport is stared at by locals as though he were a man from another planet.

Villager looks up at portraits of overseas Chinese benefactors as he once did at those of Marx, Engels, Stalin and Mao.

with rich overseas Chinese reinstating their ancestral halls and contributing significantly to community development in their native villages. By doing so, overseas contributors aspired to local prestige, or else they sought a return on their donations: this was the case, for example, with the for-profit schools set up in Jinjiang in the early 1990s by Philippine Chinese.

Remittances have had an impact beyond the local level. We have already seen how they stimulated the development of modern banking. Aside from this, they would hardly have been of so much interest to successive Chinese governments had they not been of direct financial benefit to the country. Data for the years 1871–1931 show that of all China's sources for keeping its international balance of payments in equilibrium, overseas Chinese remittances (accounting for 41 per cent of all receipts, according to Fukuda Shozo) were the most important.

That overseas Chinese were its best hopes of gaining foreign exchange was well recognized by the Chinese Communist Party, whose only source of sizeable foreign credits at the time it came to power was the Soviet Union. If remittances were to flow as abundantly as they did before the war, and to do so through official channels, that would assure the new government of an annual net gain in foreign exchange well beyond the amount it could obtain from the Soviet Union. What was more, this was 'foreign aid' that did not have to be repaid. However, as remittances dwindled with the cessation of emigration and attenuation of family obligations, the financial usefulness of overseas Chinese declined. China's interest in attracting overseas Chinese capital never disappeared, but when its economic policy took a turn away from central planning towards capitalist-style growth generation in the late 1970s, that capital would come in the form of direct foreign investment rather than as family remittances.

Leo M. Douw

Overseas Chinese investments in China

Between the 19th century and *circa* 1980

Lin Jinzhi of Xiamen University has studied Huaqiao's pre-1949 investments in the two main emigrant-sending provinces, Guangdong and Fujian, as well as in Shanghai, not a notable source of emigrants but a significant destination for emigrant investments. Of his findings, one set is summarized in table 4.1.

Guangdong ranked first in volume of investments because it had the largest number of natives abroad, but while it and Fujian hosted mostly small and medium-sized enterprises, the large-scale ones preferred Shanghai, the country's prime manufacturing, commercial and financial centre. Even within Guangdong and Fujian, investments headed not for *qiaoxiang*, the emigrants' ancestral areas, but the provinces' big ports or cities, namely Shantou, Canton and Xiamen (Amoy).

In both Guangdong and Fujian the bulk of the investments went into property, followed by commercial enterprises, and then transport (roads, railways and shipping). Shanghai presents a marked contrast: there virtually no money went into property, and it was industry (tobacco, textiles, sugar production), followed by commercial enterprises and finance, that attracted the largest proportion of investments. For Guangdong and Fujian, inflows reached a peak in 1927–37, representing capital in flight from countries badly hit by the 1929 world Depression on the one hand, and in search of exchange-rate advantages resulting from a fall in the price of silver on the other (China was on a silver standard). The years 1945–49, an interlude between the end of World War II and the triumph of the Chinese Communist Party, saw another surge. Thereafter investments dwindled.

On how Huaqiao investments fared in the 87 years between 1862 and 1949, the record is decidedly dismal. Indeed, Lin Jinzhi calls it a 'grievously painful' history. Hardly any Huaqiao investor saw a return on his money, least of all those who had put it in the transport sector. Some businesses no doubt owed their failure to internal weaknesses, but most found themselves disabled by the unstable political and bureaucratic environment.

In the 1950s the Chinese government established Overseas Chinese Investment Corporations to serve as a channel for incoming money. The corporations guaranteed annual dividends, but the Marxist-Leninist cast of China's political economy would have persuaded few investors to loosen their purse-strings. It took a redefinition of 'socialism' in the 1980s – one incorporating a large measure of capitalism – to turn China into a popular destination for foreign direct investment. But when overseas Chinese investments resumed, it was thanks to changes not only in China but in the world at large. For this reason, direct investment by overseas Chinese has to be seen in the context of inter-regional and global trade and investment.

Editor

Trade and investment between Southeast Asia and Greater China, 1980s and 1990s

When it was revealed that Hong Kong accounted for more than half of the direct investment flows into China in the 1980s, and that Taiwan and Southeast Asian Chinese were also investing in Guangdong and Fujian, the world's press portrayed this as a case of 'Chinese' money heading for 'home' (see figure 4.1). Some observers even spoke of an ethnic Chinese 'transnational economy'; others of a borderless 'Chinese economic sphere.' Money was defined by ethnicity rather than nationality.

More serious scholars have taken issue with the casual

lumping of Taiwan and Hong Kong money with that of Southeast Asian Chinese under the rubric of 'overseas Chinese capital.' This is because its effect is not only to make Southeast Asian Chinese seem more powerful, numerically and economically, than they really are, but to imply that they still feel the sentimental pull of the place their ancestors came from when their loyalties should have long transferred to their adopted countries. It did not help matters that these countries were already worried about China getting the largest share of the regional and global capital for which they themselves were competing.

These commentators are right to warn against the tarring of Southeast Asian Chinese with the brush of Hong Kong and Taiwan money. But where trade and investment flows are concerned, distinguishing one sort of Chinese from another is tricky. Data for Hong Kong investments in China are widely believed to include Taiwan and Southeast Asian investments routed through Hong Kong. Data for Hong Kong and Singapore include Malaysian and Indonesian investments in China, in their own countries and other Southeast Asian economies. For example, First Pacific, the Hong Kong-based investment vehicle of Indonesia's Salim Group (Indonesian-Chinese tycoon Liem Sioe Liong's conglomerate), invests in 25 countries, with a concentration in Asia, including China, the Philippines and Indonesia itself.

To reiterate, then, the issue of overseas Chinese investment has to be seen in the context of global trade and investment flows. These have exploded since the 1980s in response to several worldwide developments: multilateral and regional trade and investment liberalization, capital market deregulation, major exchange-rate realignments and associated shifts in comparative advantage, market-oriented economic reforms in emerging and transitional economies, and the progressive globalization of corporations in industrialized and newly industrialized countries.

Much of this rapid expansion in global trade and investment was concentrated in East and Southeast Asia, home to the world's most dynamic economies in the 1980s and early 1990s. Their fast growth was largely based on openness to trade and capital flows. Trade and direct investment linkages between China, Taiwan and Hong Kong on the one hand, and Southeast Asia on the other, and among the Southeast Asian countries themselves, grew dramatically from the mid-1980s.

Between 1981 and 1995, the two-way trade of these economies increased tenfold in absolute dollar terms and more than doubled as a share of their total trade. The bulk of this trade consisted of the exchange of machinery and other manufactures, though China and countries like Thailand, Indonesia and Malaysia are also major exporters of food and primary products to their more industrialized neighbours.

The investment picture is even more dramatic. In the mid-1980s direct investment by these economies in each other was negligible. A decade later, Taiwan had invested some US$60 billion in its neighbours, Hong Kong another US$60 billion, and Singapore US$36 billion. About half of Taiwan's outward direct investment in Asia went to China, the rest to Southeast Asia. By 1995, Taiwan was the single largest foreign investor in Vietnam. It ranked second in China and Malaysia, third in the Philippines and Laos, and fourth in Thailand.

Hong Kong was by far the largest external investor in China. It ranked among the top five investors in Vietnam, Thailand and the Philippines. That Singapore ranked fifth in China and among the top five investors in other Southeast Asian countries is remarkable given its small domestic economy. Although the individual country totals were relatively small, total ASEAN (the Association of Southeast Asian Nations, comprising Brunei, Indonesia, Malaysia, Philippines, Singapore and Thailand) foreign direct investment in China had exceeded US$10 billion by 1995.

The data on investment should be interpreted with care, however. Official figures very likely understate the true extent of regional investment flows. Many small and medium-sized enterprises invested abroad without seeking home or recipient government approval. To avoid bureaucratic controls, they disguised their investments as local projects undertaken by recipient-country partners with whom they might have had personal connections. Local investors may also have brought their money out of a country only to re-enter it as 'foreign' capital eligible for special investment incentives. Facilitated by the open capital markets and sophisticated financial services of Hong Kong and Singapore, such 'round-tripping' exaggerated the amount of foreign investment that actually originated in these cities.

These intra-regional flows of largely ethnic Chinese money do not represent all or even most of the region's international trade and investment. Japan and the US were still the largest trade partners of China and the ASEAN countries, especially if entrepôt trade through Hong Kong and Singapore were excluded. In cumulative terms, they were also the largest foreign investors in ASEAN.

The sectoral distribution of intra-Asian Chinese investment was varied. Most of Taiwan's investments in China and ASEAN were in labour-intensive light manufacturing. But there were some large capital-intensive projects in steel, chemicals and infrastructure. Investments from Hong Kong and Singapore were mostly in light manufacturing, property development, distribution and infrastructure. Investments originating in the other ASEAN countries included agribusiness and natural resource-based projects. The vast majority of investments was undertaken by private enterprises, though government-linked and state-owned enterprises were also important in investments originating in Taiwan, Singapore and China.

Several factors – geography, growth and open borders – converged to produce these burgeoning flows. As in North America and western Europe, trade liberalization and physical proximity caused trade with near neighbours to increase

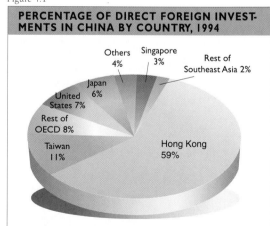

Figure 4.1

PERCENTAGE OF DIRECT FOREIGN INVESTMENTS IN CHINA BY COUNTRY, 1994

Others 4%
Singapore 3%
Rest of Southeast Asia 2%
Japan 6%
United States 7%
Rest of OECD 8%
Taiwan 11%
Hong Kong 59%

Source: State Statistical Bureau, China, 1995.

Table 4.1

HUAQIAO INVESTMENTS IN YUAN			
RECIPIENT	YEAR	ANNUAL RATE	INVESTMENT PER ENTERPRISE
Guangdong	1862–1949	4,438,731	18,157
Fujian	1871–1949	1,784,484	34,325
Shanghai	1900–1949	2,146,940	574,049

Source: Lin (1994).

faster than with the rest of the world. Many doors broke down in the 1980s: China and socialist Southeast Asian nations pursued liberal economic reforms, Taiwan relaxed restrictions on cross-Strait relations with China at the same time as it pursued a 'Go South' policy that encouraged investment in Southeast Asian countries, which themselves reduced trade and investment barriers, including specific restrictions on relations with China.

Physical proximity has also encouraged trade and investment relations by limiting transportation costs and information barriers. Although outward investments from the region by ethnic Chinese investors showed a substantial and increasing flow to farther-flung, non-Asian locations, until the currency crisis of 1997 the size, dynamism and proximity of Asian countries made them the dominant recipient locations for ethnic Chinese foreign investment.

Macroeconomic imbalances also motivated foreign investment. Rapidly rising incomes and high savings rates in Taiwan and Singapore resulted in the accumulation of large capital surpluses that investors in these economies were anxious to invest in more capital-scarce countries offering higher returns. China and the ASEAN countries fitted the bill here, with their huge appetite for capital to fuel their rapid economic growth. They thus attracted the lion's share of portfolio (short-term liquid investments in securities and bank deposits) as well as direct (long-term fixed) investment capital flows from their richer neighbours.

Yet another motivating factor for direct investment was the lure of cheap labour and big markets. Trade and investment also resulted from complementarities in resource endowments and differential income levels. Taiwan, Hong Kong and Singapore are poor in natural resources, high in income, industrially developed and technologically advanced. They thus buy food, petroleum and other raw materials from their larger and resource-rich but less-developed neighbours like China, Indonesia and Thailand, selling industrial goods and machinery in return. Hong Kong and Singapore are also major international and regional financial and commercial service centres which act as intermediaries for much of China's and ASEAN's trade and capital flows.

Between the mid-1980s and mid-1990s, sharply rising wages and severe land and labour shortages in all three newly industrialized economies, and appreciating currencies in Taiwan and Singapore, caused these places to lose cost competitiveness in the labour-intensive export manufacturing industries which had fuelled their earlier rapid growth. But firms in these economies still retained industry-specific competitive advantages in technology, management, marketing and distribution.

Singaporeans deal with China at central government level (top), while Philippine investor in small factory (bottom) at local, native-place level.

They responded to their home economies' changing comparative advantage by relocating labour-intensive manufacturing to lower-wage locations nearby. The textile and garments manufacturers among them had already invested in operations in other countries in response to Multi-Fibre Arrangement (MFA) quotas imposed by importing countries. Manufacturers of footwear, accessories, toys, electrical appliances, consumer electronics and other labour-intensive products have since followed in their path.

Overall, ethnic Chinese direct and portfolio investors were not much different from those of advanced industrialized countries like Japan and the US in choosing recipient locations for economic and strategic reasons rather than for reasons of ancestrally based 'ethnic pull.' These locations have a comparative advantage in sectors in which ethnic Chinese have a competitive advantage – mainly light manufacturing and property development.

What does make a difference is that many overseas Chinese in Southeast Asia have long been an envied or suspect minority. Although any gains which result from their outward investments benefit both the recipient locations and the source countries, historically rooted political sensitivities and economic rivalries with their host communities complicate this calculus.

If ethnic Chinese accounted for a sizeable chunk of portfolio and direct investments in East and Southeast Asia, this was largely because these Chinese had high incomes, high savings rates and a high share of the business of each locality. But political insecurity – particularly among Chinese Indonesians, and Hong Kong and Taiwan investors – also had a hand in directing such flows into political 'safe havens' like Singapore. The acquisition of major listed companies in Singapore by Chinese-Indonesian interests, for example, may have stemmed from jitters about a future Indonesia without President Suharto, whose family has long been pleased to do business with the local Chinese minority.

The large inflow of foreign Chinese capital increases the visibility of ethnic Chinese, as well as such perceptions of their business dominance as are already held by the indigenous peoples of ASEAN countries. If foreign Chinese investors choose local Chinese rather than indigenes as partners and managers, the latter may take this to signify racist exclusivity. A Taiwanese investor in a factory in Indonesia, say, by unknowingly offending against Javanese etiquette, may increase cultural conflict in the workplace and confirm indigenous suppositions of 'Chinese' insensitivity. Even where labour–management conflict is not cultural in origin, it can worsen local inter-ethnic relations.

Local Chinese themselves do not necessarily welcome the business competition brought by foreign Chinese investors. They resent the foreign investment incentives that foreign Chinese businesses can claim, and believe that it does them little good to have their ethnically tinged economic profile raised by an infusion of Taiwan, Hong Kong or Singaporean Chinese money.

In any event, there is less cultural affinity between different sorts of Chinese than non-Chinese think. Local Chinese strongly acculturated to their Southeast Asian countries are thought 'different' by foreign Taiwan Chinese, who are in turn deemed 'arrogant' by the locals. Finding themselves uncompetitive against Japanese and Western investors who are larger, more capital-intensive and technologically sophisticated and thus enjoy greater government incentives, some small and medium-sized Taiwan companies in Malaysia fled failing investments, leaving in the lurch local partners and workers, many of whom are ethnically Chinese.

Linda Yuen-Ching Lim

CHAROEN POKPHAND'S INVESTMENTS IN CHINA

As the first official foreign investor to come in through China's open door after it embarked on its 'reforms and opening' in 1979, the Thailand-based agribusiness and industrial conglomerate Charoen Pokphand (CP) took foreign investment certificate No. 0001 in the Shantou and Shenzhen Special Economic Zones. By 1996 CP had operations in every single Chinese province and had become arguably the largest of all foreign investors in China. Known there as the Zhengda group, it had more companies and more types of business than anyone else in the country.

CP was started by Chia Ek-chor (Xie Yichu, 1896-1983), a native of Chenghai, a Teochiu-speaking county near Shantou. In 1922 Chia, following a wave of migration from the Teochiu area, arrived in Bangkok carrying, so the story goes, 'a shop signboard, some advertisements, a ledger and an assortment of seeds' to set up the Chia Tai (Zhengda) shop. The Chia Tai shop apparently thrived supplying seeds grown in the family garden back in China, and later other supplies, to the ethnic Chinese-dominated market-garden industry around the Thai capital. In a typical sojourner pattern, Chia Ek-chor left a brother and other members of his family in charge of the Bangkok shop while he returned to develop the seeds farm in Chenghai.

There he remained until the late 1950s (though he passed World War II in Singapore and Malaysia).

Today the business is run by the chairman of CP Group Co Ltd, Dhanin Chearavanont (Xie Guomin, b. 1939), Chia Ek-chor's fourth son (born of his first wife). Born and raised in Bangkok, where he attended a Catholic school, Dhanin joined his father in Shantou when he was 14 years of age to complete his schooling. After five years there, Dhanin returned in 1958 to join the family business in Bangkok, while his father left China for good the same year. Working side by side with Dhanin is group president Sumet Jiaravanon (Xie Zhongmin, b. 1931), Chia Ek-chor's third son (born of a second wife). Chia Ek-chor's first and second sons still take part in managing the business, but are more or less semi-retired.

In the 1960s Chia Tai, now using its Thai name Charoen Pokphand, expanded and diversified into other agribusiness areas. Run by Dhanin's elder brothers and cousins, the business expanded in Southeast Asia, Hong Kong and Taiwan, moving vertically from producing and trading the ingredients for animal feeds, to raising chickens for meat and eggs, slaughtering and processing them and later exporting them around the region. It expanded sideways as well into related businesses, such as chemicals and pharmaceuticals for agribusiness. By the early 1980s it had applied this approach to other livestock, shrimp farming, and fruits and vegetables. And extending the vertical integration theme a step further, it launched Kentucky Fried Chicken restaurants in Thailand using its own chickens, as well as developing other franchise-based fast food outlets under its own brands.

By the mid-1980s, then, CP was well-placed to be the master of Asia's kitchens, involved in every step in the chain of food production to feed the on-the-go urban Asian middle class. It had production units in over a dozen countries in Asia, Europe and North America, and trading offices in most of the major cities of the globe. However, despite the fact that it had publicly listed arms in Thailand, Indonesia, Taiwan, Hong Kong, Shanghai, London and New York, its size was nearly impossible to estimate; typically, operations were woven through hundreds of mostly privately held operating and shell companies. Still, in the mid-1990s the overall group turnover was estimated to be as high as US$7 billion, and growing at 10-15 per cent annually.

The lion's share of that growth was coming from CP's massive China operations, by 1995 already larger than the group's business in Thailand. Starting with animal feed plants and chicken plants, Dhanin strove to reproduce in China the agribusiness that was the launchpad for CP's growth elsewhere. China was the place where CP, already outgrowing Thailand, could make a stand as *the* overseas Chinese conglomerate. With the agribusiness smoothly growing on its own strengths in nearly every Chinese province, CP moved into motorcycle production (Ek-Chor Industries, named after the father), real estate, oil refining and distribution, retailing,

telecommunications, construction materials, banking and other industries. The group even added basic capabilities in music, television and film production, and sponsored the most popular television programme in China of the early 1990s, Zhengda Zongyi, a variety show.

The focus of CP's China efforts, aside from agribusiness, has not been Shantou but Shanghai and the northern cities of Tianjin and Shenyang. In these heavy-industry areas, the group was getting more ambitious by the mid-1990s, investing (or co-investing) in automobile parts and assembly (as also in Thailand), chemicals manufacturing and electronics.

Although Dhanin never spelt out his goals exactly, it was clear that he saw expansion in China as the way to turn CP into a world-size conglomerate. In a rare interview in 1994, he noted that South Korea's Samsung, Hyundai, and Daewoo were very small after World War II; now, with government support, they had become huge global players. On the other hand the Thai government, he complained, 'is afraid that a large company will create problems. If CP is only in Thailand, then it cannot be big.'

Besides his astute understanding of consumer demographics, building and working connections is arguably Dhanin's greatest talent. After his return from China, the family placed him as their liaison in the state monopoly slaughterhouse, where he worked directly with the most politically powerful army and police generals of the country, all of whom were on the board of directors of the lucrative business. CP is, Thai political analysts say, the biggest contributor to all Thai political parties. The company puts on its payroll the top active and former politicians, soldiers, diplomats and civil servants.

CP's ties in China probably date back to the agricultural trade it conducted in the 1950s. By cloning the feedmill and poultry business throughout most Chinese provinces, CP forged essential friendships with local administrators around the country, and impressed Beijing leaders to boot: CP's efforts helped boost farm incomes, an exceptional achievement among foreign investors, most of whom simply set up export processing factories in coastal provinces.

Dhanin's awesome ties to the Chinese leadership were firmly cemented by his response to the Tiananmen crisis in 1989. While other investors paused to see which way the wind would blow, CP refused to panic, telling its scores of Thai and Taiwanese staff in China to remain in place and keep investing. Today, when Dhanin goes to Beijing, his access appears to be better than a Southeast Asian prime minister's. His close links range from Zhao Ziyang (the former premier ousted in the Tiananmen convulsions) to retired army boss General Yang Shangkun.

His traditional Chinese beliefs still permeate the conglomerate's operations, though he rarely lets them get in the way of a real deal. He is known to screen top managers and executives - uniformly of Chinese extraction - through Chinese facial analysis. His building sites are all assessed by a prominent *fengshui* (geomancy) specialist of Taiwan origin. His Chineseness has been the butt of constant Thai criticism, as has the group's intense corporate secretiveness and political manipulations. The most common criticism is that CP, with its mysteriously endless fount of capital and its near-monopoly of agribusiness and other sectors, is an agent of the Beijing (or Taipei) government. Dhanin has not done much to dispel this image, sponsoring visits by Chinese opera and other cultural groups to Thailand and acting as a diplomatic go-between to help resolve problems between Bangkok and Beijing. Such criticisms cannot be brushed aside because ethnic Chinese in Thailand are still viewed by many as having uncertain loyalties.

CP made a stab at combating that impression when, officially launching several projects in China in August 1996, it pointedly declared itself a Thai conglomerate in its press announcement. It arranged for the Thai monarch's popular daughter, Princess Sirindhorn (herself a Chinese speaker), to go to Shanghai to inaugurate the projects. 'Wherever CP Group goes to invest,' the announcement claimed, 'we raise the Thai national flag to display our pride of being Thai.'

In the late 1990s, CP's headlong growth was halted by Asia's financial crisis. It had borrowed heavily to extend its reach in China, but with the Asian liquidity crunch has come the need to draw in its horns and to sell stakes in some of its subsidiaries.

Paul Handley

RELATIONS WITH NON-CHINESE

Ethnicity

A sense of one's own Chineseness may have had its beginning from the moment of one's first exposure to non-Chinese and to Chinese from elsewhere in the coastal ports of emigration. Once overseas, other groups were encountered, often in a competitive context. It was also apparent that some peoples enjoyed more opportunities or power than others. That stimulated a sense of difference and inequality, which in turn led to such considerations as: What were the differences? What characteristics made one 'Chinese'? Where were the boundaries between Chinese and non-Chinese? Who was Chinese and who was not became an important question, as it would not have been in one's ancestral village. Developments in the host country and in China continued to raise such questions.

A hypothetical new immigrant of the pre-1950s era might go through several adaptive stages, each with its own ethnicity dimensions. If he moved to where Chinese were already present, his initial needs after arrival (basic housing, employment, protection and support-group needs) would all be met from within local Chinese society. His social relationships would be entirely Chinese. His external ties would be only to relatives left behind in China, to whom he would send remittances.

In a second stage the new immigrant has become a resident. He is established in business and has joined one or more ethnic Chinese organizations. Although his meaningful relationships are almost all with other Chinese, his business interests have forced him to learn something of local non-Chinese languages and customs. While continuing to send remittances to his relatives in China, he may attempt to bring some or all of his family to where he is. Our Immigrant Everyman now reaches a critical point.

Relations with non-Chinese probably began for many early emigrants at port of departure (top) but remained impersonal if they mixed only with other Chinese in Chinatown (bottom).

If his business does not prosper he remains in stage two, living in Chinatown or, if outside, in his shop in isolation from the non-Chinese around him. An example of the latter case, the Chinese laundryman or convenience store operator found in North American cities of the early 20th century, was famous for his ability to maintain arm's-length, impersonal relations with his non-Chinese customers. And if his children did not attend school, the whole family might remain at arm's length for two or more generations.

But if, instead, our immigrant's business flourished, he would reach a third, or settler stage. He may now be a leader in Chinatown, which implies some responsibility to think about what is 'true' Chinese culture, or at least the right kind of culture for Chinatown and for China. More personally pressing, he has become concerned about Chinese cultural maintenance for his own children. His business may now have outgrown Chinatown bounds and Chinese personal bonds. Like his children's Chineseness, his own has become complicated and different from his memories of Chineseness in China. But his Chineseness is also different from his children's.

If the family business continues to prosper and opportunities for expansion are available, the family may, over the next two generations, gradually separate itself from the core of the local Chinese community. Residential separation may be part of it; but there may be also a declining frequency of participation in community rituals and other activities. The Chineseness of the family may then become, more than ever, a purely family affair. Written language skills in Chinese may be lost, though possibly regainable with great effort. Spoken language may or may not be retained. And the original values of family goals, discipline and mutual support are likely to persist.

The foregoing story illustrates several points. The first is about Chineseness, or Chinese ethnicity. Ethnicity can be understood as having two levels, ethnic culture and ethnic identity. Applied to Chinese, the first of these – ethnic culture – refers to the cultural dimensions of individuals or groups of Chinese background. It is about the clusters of emphasized values and habits – often exhibited unconsciously by the individuals or groups themselves – that shape their daily lives. It is what Chinese migrants take with them as 'cultural baggage.' The second level – Chinese ethnic identity – is the conscious cultural definition of self or others and includes affiliation with ethnically defined groups. It is what individuals and groups do when confronted with others that appear to be somehow different. It is a process of defining and redefining self and group in contrast to other selves and groups, a boundary-marking and defending exercise, but one with the potential also – through re-definition – of modifying, or even dissolving, boundaries between one's own group and another. Where 'ethnic culture' is simply 'lived Chineseness,' ethnic identity is 'expressed or asserted Chineseness.' We know most about the former from observing the latter.

Ethnicity, including Chinese ethnicity, is not a single, unchanging entity. It is regularly modified by the interaction of individuals and groups with environments and experiences, and their subsequent reflections thereon. It is as various as the experiences and adapta-

tions of the individuals and groups that we see as somehow 'Chinese.' And, for mobile Chinese, it is in constant flux, as new environments, experiences, and adaptations lead to new cultural modifications and reconstructions. In short, ethnicity is a construction. The more mobile the individual or group, the more intense the process of construction and reconstruction. The story of the Immigrant Everyman finds him forced to question his idea of Chineseness even in the coastal emigration port, where he encounters Chinese unlike himself. This kind of encounter we now understand better than before because of recent studies of ethnic and regional variation within China. But Chinese ethnicity overseas is no mere carry-over of domestic Chinese ethnicity. The overseas Chinese migrant is in an environment of mostly non-Chinese, full of new and frequent non-Chinese experiences – ones which require of him new kinds of cultural combinations and compromises. Wherever they have gone, Chinese have proved themselves to be among the most adaptable of peoples and that very adaptability has now created a great many varieties of Chineseness in the world.

It is the varieties and the constructed nature of ethnicity that should cause us to rethink some of our assumptions and concepts. Though it is common, for example, to speak of individuals or groups of Chinese as being 'more Chinese' or 'less Chinese' than some others, the degrees of Chineseness are difficult to measure and may be less significant than the kinds of Chineseness. The image of a powerful and continuous tradition in China may encourage us to think that Chinese everywhere carry with them some irreducible core of an eternal Chineseness, but the variations that are visible make that proposition difficult to defend. It is clear also that attempting to capture overseas Chinese ethnicity by reference only to residential or political commitments ('roots' and 'loyalties') does not do justice to the complexity of the phenomenon. Nor does the concentration on such terms as integration and assimilation. These describe only certain aspects of the ethnic situation: broad political circumstance, as in the first term; or an extreme case, as in the second.

Generality is, however, inevitable in a short treatment. In what follows an historical treatment will be used to illustrate some cultural generalities about the Chinese abroad. Before doing so, however, one last look at the Immigrant Everyman. Two more 'lessons' might be drawn from the story as a whole. The first is that Chinese, like other immigrants, seek success. But paradoxically, it is often the case that the greater the success the more the immigrant is drawn into the world of the non-Chinese, and thereby the more difficult it may be to control which kinds of Chineseness are maintained and in what forms. That was true in grand fashion for the most successful Chinese in Thailand in the two hundred years since the end of the 18th century. There, the more successful one became the greater the likelihood of being co-opted into the ruling Thai élite. On a more modest scale, the early 20th century 'mayor of Chinatown' in a North American city was usually a local Chinese with well-developed cross-cultural brokerage skills. The better he became at expressing Chinese interests the more likely he was to be appointed to general race relations and brotherhood committees of pri-

Interaction with non-Chinese, often colonial, environment (here Singapore) modified Chinese ethnicity.

mary interest to the mainstream society.

The second 'lesson' is this: the Chinese family is the origin and focus of overseas ambitions. It may also be the ultimate unit of persistence of both ambitions and visible ethnicity. Chinese core values taken abroad by pre-20th century emigrants were particularly those centred on ancestral locality versions of Chinese familism as they had developed by the late imperial era and as they were understood and practised in southeast China. These included ancestral and filial principles, with emphasis upon both ancestry by genealogy and by place. Family discipline and mutual support, and the importance of education were other values. Goals focused themselves upon familial achievement and prosperity. Beyond the family, there was a stress on personal relationships and networks of social reciprocity. Although migrants were usually from rural areas, they often had an awareness of practices in nearby towns and the cities of coastal Guangdong and Fujian. Since overseas migration was so often a local or even family tradition, they also had had contact with returnees who had overseas experience.

The history of the Chinese abroad before the 1970s may serve to illustrate the importance of such factors as demography, opportunities – for business and for contact with non-Chinese – and relations with China in shaping ethnicities. The themes are those of constant adaptation, redefining and reconstructing, and the crossing of ethnic boundaries.

From the 16th to the 19th centuries, migration was from China to other parts of Asia. Most migrants were from Fujian and Guangdong, but in some cases – Japan, for instance – an important group came from the lower Yangzi region. Although there were rural Chinese residents, more often they were concentrated in cities. Most Chinese were single male

A Chinese gone native in Siam.

Culturally adapted Chinese: trainer at the Singapore Turf Club.

Colonial social contexts, in Singapore as elsewhere, shaped some Chinese adaptations.

Chinese Filipino, 1920s, represents one local version of Chineseness.

sojourners but they were usually part of all-Chinese settlements, such that the group helped maintain the individual's Chineseness, while he contributed that to the Chineseness of the whole. Within the group Chinese saw themselves as subdivided into *bang* (see p 77), usually based on common language ('dialect'). In some places, notably Vietnam and Cambodia, colonial authorities recognized *bang* as formal instruments of government. Formalized or not, *bang* were an important intermediate identity focus – between ancestral village at one extreme, and pan-Chinese identity at the other.

But even sizeable urban concentrations of Chinese in Southeast Asia were numerical and cultural minorities in terms of the broader colonial social context. As such they were aware of their vulnerability to political persecution should they freely express themselves culturally. Their condition was that of economic salience and power combined with cultural and political vulnerability. There was no mistaking the feelings behind violent massacres or sweeping expulsions of Chinese groups. Restrictions on the interaction of Chinese and non-Chinese were common in colonial Indonesia and the Philippines. Chinese were often segregated in quarters of their own. There were sometimes limits on where Chinese could travel or live. Restrictions or threats from frequently hostile non-Chinese might encourage the Chinese to pull together into a unit, emphasizing their pan-Chinese rather than *bang* identities. More accepting attitudes had the opposite effect. The *ways* in which local Chinese saw themselves – as Chinese – were also influenced by what was said about them by local non-Chinese governments and people. That included labels and accompanying stereotypes – *sangley, lukjin,* Baba – and extended to views of China as well as the local Chinese. None of that could be ignored: one had to react to it in some way; and all of it shaped what local Chinese thought and said about themselves. Being Chinese had to do not merely with memories and images from China, or comparisons with other local Chinese; it was also influenced by the labels and terms applied by non-Chinese. It was, in addition, shaped by their own stereotypes. Since commerce was the dominant overseas Chinese occupation, Chinese leaders represented themselves as merchants and, before 1900, were so called – Huashang (Chinese merchants) – by China. As late as the l970s Chinese in one Philippine city took 'merchant'

to be synonymous with 'Chinese.'

In the 19th century the volume of emigration from China greatly increased, as did both the number of source areas in China and the number of destinations overseas. More variety in source locales meant a greater variety of *bang* and other localized identities in Chinese settlements around Asia. But the spread of *bang* was uneven across Southeast Asia. The competing varieties of Chineseness were numerous in Malaya and Indonesia. In Thailand, where Teochius dominated, and the Philippines, where Hokkiens ruled, there was no question which version set the standard. New destinations included Australia/New Zealand, the Western Hemisphere, and parts of Africa and western Europe. Some new immigrants went to mines, plantations and other non-urban destinations; others joined earlier migrants in the cities.

Since the 16th century Chinese migration to Southeast Asia had proceeded in waves. Each new wave brought renewed sinicization, but also at least a small cultural gap between old-timers (*laoke*) and newcomers (*sinkeh*). An old timer understood the local context and how to cope with it. He had already made his adaptations and compromises. To an old-timer, a new immigrant did not yet know how to act. The latter's Chineseness was not the right kind for local conditions. He needed tutoring by the old-timer.

A third cultural dichotomy, to add to those of *bang* and old-timer/newcomer, was that between – using the Indonesian terms – Peranakan and Totok. As each migratory wave receded it left behind a residue of creolized Chinese. These were a locally adapted group, eventually numerous enough to form a unique society that was intermediate between the Chinese and the indigenous societies. Examples are the Peranakans of Indonesia, the Babas of Malaya and Singapore, and the mestizos of the Philippines. Despite – in two of the three cases – governmental attempts to keep Chinese and non-Chinese apart, single Chinese males and non-Chinese women found each other and intermarriage was common. The resulting societies created new versions of transcultural Chineseness. Members of these groups generally acquired the languages and cultural skills of the non-Chinese groups in their country of residence. They saw themselves as separate from the Totoks (pure-blooded, China-born Chinese) and their relations with them were often ambivalent. When the next wave of immigration from China brought 'real Chinese' (Totoks), the contrast was readily apparent to each side and it was much greater than the old-timer/newcomer difference. Creole cultures were blends of Chinese and local cultural elements. To a Totok, a Peranakan seemed not very Chinese – or even not Chinese at all.

The fates of these creolized societies varied. The Babas, a small, highly Malayanized and Anglicized group, but preservers of much of Chinese culture, moved eventually in the 20th century towards resinicization and membership in local Chinese society. The Peranakans of Indonesia, with Dutch encouragement, remained apart from both Chinese and non-Chinese. The mestizos of the Philippines joined in the 19th century with a rising class of Filipinos to create a modern Philippine culture, which these two groups would then lead as the new élite of the country.

In the late 19th century China's political influence began to be felt in overseas Chinese societies. China had always been a factor, though often in the background: China as memories and images of ancestral district and family, and China as a political entity with various levels – local, provincial and national. All contributed to the sense of oneself as Chinese. Now, in the late 19th century, China established consulates to protect the lives and property of the Chinese abroad. Wealthy Southeast Asian Chinese now purchased the honours and titles offered them by the Chinese government, and these political connections implied the possibility of a place in the Chinese polity for Chinese overseas.

In local Chinese societies around the world, leaders now saw the desirability of forming Chinese groups into Chinese communities, with themselves as leaders. There were two main reasons. In several countries there was now more broadly based anti-Chineseness than heretofore. The defence against this, and also the way to negotiate with local Chinese consuls, seemed to be internal unity. To achieve this leaders began to form federating 'umbrella' organizations – benevolent or charitable associations and, somewhat later, Chinese Chambers of Commerce. The purpose was for the leaders to act as spokesmen for the newly created 'community' to the local host society government and to the government of China and its representatives. To be effective, leaders had to speak for a united community. That meant reducing internal disputes as much as possible and creating a kind of cultural unanimity that was acceptable to China.

In the early 20th century the various local versions of Chineseness that had existed abroad began everywhere to experience the superimposition of unifying 'national' versions, defined for them by China and its representatives. Officially, the Chinese government labelled the Chinese abroad 'Huaqiao.' Popularly, a common view in China was that the wealth and skills of the overseas Chinese were needed by China for its modernization. But those Chinese were seen as culturally denatured and in need, as quid pro quo, of re-infusions of true Chinese culture from its only source, China itself. Accordingly, China took a keen interest in the curriculum of the overseas Chinese schools now being established. From China's perspective, the goal of the schools – besides their locally focused interests – should be to prepare overseas youth to be citizens of a new, modern Chinese nation. That goal, as China came under severe pressure from Japan in the 1930s, increasingly was urged as more important than all others. In and out of the schools, Chinese overseas were urged to put the defence of China ahead of all other concerns and to subordinate regional and local cultures of all kinds to the 'higher' national culture of China.

These developments brought China's politics and ideologies to the overseas world. Previous cultural divisions were now to be further complicated and deepened by partisan political views of culture and education. As Chinese governments changed rapidly in the early 20th century, so did their visions of what a modern China should be. The one thing they agreed upon with respect to Chinese culture was that it had to be modern. Thus, modernity became a new and essential element in the thinking of Chinese overseas (and has continued to be so ever since). Cities like Shanghai, Xiamen (Amoy) and Canton were now taken as models of what was both modern and Chinese. In the schools, teachers coming from China introduced the intellectual currents of the day, along with the Mandarin language. By the 1930s and 1940s local Chinese leaders in North America (Qiaoling, 'overseas Chinese leaders') were associating themselves with the Chinese government-approved version of Chinese culture and using it to maintain both their position and the unity of the 'community.'

In the early 20th century immigration to Southeast Asia continued its general increase, but immigrant flows to North America and to Australia/New Zealand declined. This was because of regulations strictly limiting, or completely cutting off, Chinese immigration. The general pattern of increasing urbanization of Chinese populations continued. Those who were not part of this urban concentration had more opportunities for interaction with non-Chinese. One such type, the only Chinese person in a remote town on the Canadian Prairies, would frequently be drawn into relationships with his customers and ultimately, perhaps, intermarriage and a place in local society. On the whole, however, an increasing number of Chinese women were now going abroad, thereby reducing the frequency of intermarriage in most host countries.

The larger number of women resulted in more all-Chinese family life overseas. That, in turn, may have stimulated more religious observance. Since at least the 19th century the tutelary deities of popular religion in China have been exported overseas and given new protective mandates. Sometimes they have been syncretically identified with deities of local religions. In the Philippines, for example, the protecting goddess Mazu is identified with several versions of the Virgin Mary. Chinese Buddhist temples have flourished in many parts of Southeast Asia. By the early 20th century, Christian missionary enterprise on coastal China had won to the faith a number of families that had overseas members. This, and local missionary efforts overseas, had an effect, especially in North America, where the growing numbers of all-Chinese families often centred their lives and social activities on a church.

More children meant more demands for education overseas that would be suitable to Chinese economic goals and cultural maintenance. In Asia these were met by the creation and expansion of comprehensive, full-time Chinese schools. These taught necessary life and business skills, and also Chinese language and culture. Chinese

Shanghai was a model for Singaporean woman reading popular Shanghai periodical Liang You.

Indonesian magazine satirizes politics in China (left).

Ivory figure of Virgin, 17th-18th century, carved by Chinese shows Chinese cast to her facial features.

Chinese children being initiated into Christian ways at the Good Shepherd Mission in Vancouver, 1920.

Transcultural reading matter: Chinese kung fu novels in Bahasa Indonesia (below and facing page).

in Asia thus had a unitary experience: both job-training and cultural education were taught in the same school from the same perspective. Not so for North American Chinese. Their experience was usually dual: in a mainstream school and in an after-school Chinese school. Each of these schools gave them both culture and job-training; but the time available was much less for the Chinese school than for the mainstream school. Chinese children in North America grew up in a culturally divided world. Their English school prepared them for life in a Western-dominated world they could only partly enter. Their Chinese school gave them the language and cultural skills needed for Chinatown jobs – the only ones they could get. It also prepared them for Chinatown lives, the kind they likely would live. This dual education provided some training in North American mainstream culture, as did church affiliation. But contact with non-Chinese remained, in this period, at arm's length. This North American 'creolized' small group was different from its parents but lived most of its life in Chinatown and in all-Chinese churches.

Whether in North American Chinatowns or in Southeast Asia, the frequency of occupational monopolies had a strong bearing on the possibilities of contact with non-Chinese. In such cases, one simply had no workmates or other business contacts who were not of the same ethnicity. If the job were a Chinese monopoly there was that much greater an incentive, if there were any choice at all, to 'staying Chinese' in culture.

These demographic and opportunity considerations – and others – urged the formation of other Chinese community institutions that would both serve ethnic Chinese economic goals and insure the maintenance of Chinese culture. The annual rituals of the Chinese ethnic organizations that emerged were not only a reminder of China, they were a reaffirmation of dissimilarity and separateness from the often hostile non-Chinese society surrounding them. What the early 20th-century Chinese

schools and homes taught was not only the cultural skills needed by the local-born Chinese for 'Chinese' jobs in the 'Chinese' sector of the local economy, it was lessons in the stereotypes of difference. The 'rags to riches' folklore of Chinese overseas enterprise was promoted as basic truth, with just enough examples to verify it. The formula to realize that dream was hard work and self-denial – presented as if eternal Chinese values, rather than ones learned in overseas practice. Industrious, self-denying Chinese were contrasted, explicitly or implicitly, with lazy, self-indulgent non-Chinese locals. Thus, by the early 20th century, Chinese community organizations and institutions had become devices that limited interaction with non-Chinese and thereby maintained individuals' and families' continued focus on the goals of overseas effort and the ways to achieve them. They also became part of the discourses of ethnic Chinese among themselves about themselves. These involved not merely contrasts between Chinese and non-Chinese; there was also an internal discourse about the differences among Chinese themselves: sub-ethnic or *bang* differences, differences between old-timers and newcomers, and differences between generations.

Some differences between Southeast Asia and North America – the two areas of greatest Chinese presence – became increasingly apparent. These reflected two very different ethnic and political histories. Southeast Asian immigration was a centuries-old series of waves, the most recent of which was still on the upswing. North American Chinese immigration dated only from the 1850s and its upward swing had been arrested by restrictions starting in the 1880s and intensifying by the 1920s. The creolized Peranakan analogue in North America was, for some time, too small to form a separate, self-conscious society. Its members were the children of a small number of all-Chinese families: intermarriage in North America had been slight and geographically dispersed. There were no *bang* in its heritage: North America was an exclusively Cantonese frontier and its emerging Chinatown culture was a locally adapted version from the Siyi region of Guangdong. When the Hong Kong 'Totoks' rushed in after 1970, these 'Creoles' (or old-timers) spoke modestly of their Chinese language as 'village dialect' – not the usages of Canton, let alone ambitiously modern Hong Kong.

By the 1950s and 1960s North American ethnic Chinese began to find voices – in English and in Chinese. The English writers, local-born Chinese intellectuals of the 1960s, set out to explain ethnic Chinese cultural and economic history in America. That would be a more difficult and painful task than the Southeast Asian case would have been. The Chinese of the 1960s in Southeast Asia might feel culturally vulnerable; but they could take pride in a history of economic success and pre-eminence. North American Chinese were conscious of being marginal in both areas. Theirs appeared to be a history of unrelieved failure. The generation of the 1960s pointed to the importance of racist rejection by mainstream society in making their ancestors into involuntary sojourners and marginalized denizens of a pathetic ethnic sector of the general economy.

The most striking things about this argument, and the way it was put forward, are its entirely positive view of the ideals of North American culture and its seemingly alienated stance in relation to Chinese culture. The argument took place as part of the general debates of the 1960s in American society. The atmosphere was one of generational challenge to the existing order and the revival and expression of ethnic interests. Like that of its co-generational cohort in the mainstream, the ethnic Chinese argument was completely domestic: America should live up to its own traditions and those who wish to be American should not be rejected, whatever their physical appearance and cultural heritage.

Contrast this with Southeast Asia where, from the 1880s onward, Indonesian Peranakans had developed a transcultural literature of their own and sought political and social organization to match. In Indonesia, Singapore and Malaya, where (among other reasons) the large Chinese share of the population gave some confidence to cultural expression, the Chinese written language was maintained better than elsewhere in Southeast Asia, and a literature in Chinese, only partly about Southeast Asia, flourished. There were also writings in Malay and Indonesian by ethnic Chinese and translations from Chinese into those languages. In the 1950s pro-China political activism was common in the Chinese schools of Indonesia and Singapore. But by the 1960s Chinese culture was forcibly suppressed in Indonesia, and in Singapore English-educated Chinese were winning the domestic political competition against the Chinese-educated. In Malaysia communalism ruled. In Thailand, by the 1960s, many Sino-Thai, or *lukjin*, had become deeply involved in Thai politics. Meanwhile, the local-born Chinese of the Philippines were arguing against assimilation and for integration: participation in the Philippine polity but with acceptance and maintenance of their Chinese heritage. In short, where North American Chinese culture appeared to be losing some of its Chinese dimensions, Southeast Asia showed a mixed picture of Chinese cultural maintenance.

After World War II Chinese overseas became more settled for a time (1945–70). A trend towards family reunifications in Southeast Asia had begun in the 1930s. The thought of an overseas site as a 'second home' was beginning to be entertained in some places. In the years immediately after the war, family reunifications continued. This was facilitated in some cases by local governments' policies. But the largest consideration was the political change of 1949 in mainland China which ended the old easy in-and-out flow of migrating Chinese and their unregulated investments. Cold War political and economic barriers added to the difficulties. Reunification overseas or in Hong Kong now became the dominant trend.

The cultural consequences were important. The old single-male sojourner immigrant societies were being replaced by settled family societies. A larger number of families overseas meant a larger number of local-born descendants who would have different cultural experiences from those of their immigrant parents. Indeed, in many overseas Chinese societies, by the 1960s local-born Chinese with a local frame of cultural reference made up a substantial and increasing proportion of the population. Reunifications in Hong Kong meant a Hong Kong cultural experience, often of some duration, for a number of families, who then took that experience with them wherever they settled overseas. The principal par-

ticipants in emigration from Hong Kong in these years were Cantonese, whose overseas destinations were largely North American. Emigration to Southeast Asia remained slight. Thus the positions of the two areas were reversed from what they had been before the War. At that time Southeast Asian Chinese settlements were constantly resinicized by new immigrants from China, while North American Chinatowns, by the 1920s, were left almost without further newcomers. In the postwar era, Southeast Asian societies grew mostly through natural increase of local-borns, or, as they were later called, Huayi. Meanwhile, in North America small but growing numbers of immigrant Cantonese were adding to the complexity of Chinese societies there.

In Southeast Asia the independence of new states completely changed the relationship between Chinese and non-Chinese. The colonial rulers had served as cultural models and political referees. Now that they were gone it was simply the Chinese and locals in confrontation and interaction. The Chinese had now to redefine themselves as participants within a new national context. Citizenship became critical, since many new policies that affected ethnic Chinese were established on that basis. The Cold War complicated matters. China was seen as nearby and, to some Southeast Asians, threatening. Among Southeast Asian governments and non-Chinese Southeast Asians there was a persistent tendency in these years to conflate Chinese ethnicity and ethnic expression with political loyalty to China. The fervent interest of Chinese schools and their students in the affairs of China served to encourage this belief.

Some Southeast Asian states were focusing much of their nationalism upon reducing the economic power of the local Chinese through restrictive legislation and policy. That tended to maintain cultural separation and increase the sense of vulnerability the Chinese felt. Occupational restrictions were placed upon the Chinese in the Philippines and Indonesia. Citizenship for Chinese was difficult to obtain in the Philippines, and remained an extremely confusing and complicated issue in Indonesia. In Thailand Chinese schools were brought under control and their Chinese curriculum limited. By the end of the 1960s the Philippines was heading in the same direction. In Malaysia the formal structures of communalism kept Chinese and non-Chinese apart. The New Economic Policy, the result of ethnic clashes in 1969, exacerbated the differences. In Indonesia Baperki, a Peranakan-led party that generally favoured integration over assimilation, aligned itself with the government. But it, and almost everything else about Chinese

Young Chinese bloodied in a mob attack in Indonesia, 1965.

culture, disappeared after the bloody coup attempt and massacre of 1965.

Despite these difficulties, there were opportunities. In Southeast Asia the rapidly growing universities generally did not deny entry to ethnic Chinese, thus allowing them to acquire new skills and cultural outlooks. The economies of Southeast Asian countries also generally grew in the 1950s and 1960s, offering new, unregulated opportunities for the Chinese. By the 1960s a Chinese middle class, similar in education and in some of its tastes and interests to the growing non-Chinese middle class, was beginning to appear. The broader experiences and outlooks of these Chinese began to give them some new perspectives on – and new choices about – their ethnicity.

Some of that was reflected in the literature that developed. Chinese increasingly wrote in local languages and about local themes – most importantly about their own cultural and social situation. In one instance, the Philippines, a group of local-born Chinese created a new label for themselves, drawing upon Tagalog slang to do so. The name Tsinoy combines Tsino, for Chinese, with Pinoy, for Filipino.

In North America discriminatory laws and practices were terminated (although discriminatory attitudes did not change immediately), and opportunities of all kinds opened up for Chinese. 'Hyphenated' identities (for example, Chinese American) became acceptable in American popular discourse and – somewhat later – in Canada, where the adoption of multiculturalism as a national policy presented Chinese there with a new identity possibility. That government policy proved to be a defining point in a long-standing post-war debate in the Chinese newspapers of Vancouver. The contestants in this internal discourse were chiefly those local-born youth who had not deserted Chinatown and newcomer-youth from Hong Kong.

Here, unlike the highly audible English-language expressions of the American local-borns that recounted a history of racism before a wide English-reading audience – including educational and other policy-makers – the stress in this temperate Chinese-language discourse was on self-definitions for the present era and the audience was purely internal, limited to readers of Chinese. Much of the discussion was about Chineseness or, more particularly, Chinese-ness appropriate

Becoming a naturalized American citizen.

to living in Canada. The scene recalls those played out so often in Southeast Asia, between Peranakans and Totoks, old-timers and newcomers. But here the terms of the discourse were influenced by a host government's formal change in its cultural policy. That change made it possible for the local-born youth, in the Peranakan or old-timer position, to argue decisively that the right kind of Chineseness for the situation was the kind that used the government-approved 'hyphenated' identity label, 'Chinese Canadian': in other words, the kind which best described them. Parenthetically, it remains to be investigated whether a parallel internal discourse appeared in American Chinese-language newspapers, presumably with a very different content, given the radically different American context.

Meanwhile, enrolment declined in Canada's Chinese schools. As new job opportunities opened for ethnic Chinese, the schools lost half of their function. They could, as before, provide for cultural maintenance; but they had lost their job function in a time and place when more Chinese were acquiring needed job skills in the public schools and the universities. Even the kind of Chineseness they taught came under attack, in a generational assault on the 'overseas Chinese leaders' (Qiaoling) and their cultural hegemony. The younger generation did this with a symbolic opposition of mainland China's modern Chineseness to the Taiwan-sponsored Chineseness of the Qiaoling. Such a device would have been risky in many parts of Southeast Asia at the time. In that region, the Taiwan version was most salient in the countries where American influence was strongest: the Philippines, South Vietnam and Thailand. The mainland version was strong until 1965 in Indonesia. Malaysia and Singapore were zones of contest. But in North America China was distant and the symbolic use of mainland culture, in the context of the 1960s, was not unduly dangerous.

These two discourses on ethnicity in Canada illustrate some interesting points. One is that when China itself is not the issue, the debate on Chineseness is likely to be about Chineseness at the site of the debate: the kind of Chineseness suitable to where we are. The other point is that, even in internal discourses on Chineseness, the debate involves not only influences from China but, inevitably, relations with the local non-Chinese.

From about 1970 major changes in the world brought on a new age for the Chinese overseas. A revolution in communications technology made possible international business and social interaction on a scale and at a speed hitherto impossible. A global ethnic revival was part of the ferment of the 1960s. It encouraged the maintenance of ethnicities and the role of ethnicity in politics. The United States, Canada, Australia and New Zealand changed their immigration policies to ones that encouraged settlement by migrant Chinese, especially those with needed skills, entrepreneurial talents and investable funds. Meanwhile, growing economies in several Asian countries had produced new middle classes, many of whose members were ethnic Chinese. Some of them, perceiving political instability in Asia, were prepared to accept the new opportunities for migration. China's opening to international business in the late 1970s also attracted the interest of Chinese abroad, both in its economic and cultural dimensions. Thus, after two decades of settlement and stability overseas, and the cultural consequences thereof, some of the Chinese overseas were once again becoming mobile, but this time in different ways and in a different context.

Edgar Wickberg

Being Chinese in the modern world

In an essay published in 1994, Wang Gungwu writes:

Many mirrors, some less distorting than others, intervene when a Chinese abroad constructs his composite image of what it means to be Chinese. Sooner or later, it is impossible to avoid asking what being among foreigners does to one's perception of being Chinese. To look different, to speak differently, to be regarded as Chinese by others, leads naturally to an awareness of what is or is not Chinese. That awareness may be simple or superficial; it may also be deliberate, even assertive. . . . For most Chinese abroad, it is the non-Chinese environment that impinges on their lives most directly.

This essay does not aim to pin down 'what is or is not Chinese.' Indeed it is written out of a distrust that such an exercise were possible. As Wang suggests, identities are not things we are born with, but are constructed in relation to representation ('mirrors'). A Chinese American, say, only knows what it is to be Chinese because of the way 'Chineseness' or 'non-Chineseness' has been represented by other Chinese Americans, by non-American Chinese, by white or black Americans and other non-Chinese.

This article focuses on the late-modern period, a time when the question of identity is being vigorously debated, the debate itself being part of a wider process of transformation generally labelled 'globalization.' It interests itself in what 'being among foreigners' does to one's sense of Chineseness while remaining alert to what it means to be Chinese in China. Indeed, it is scarcely possible to understand the overseas Chinese's experience of modernity without reference to that of the latter.

For both we may take the mid-19th century expansion of Western colonial power over the non-Western world – propelling the globalization of capitalism – as a critical turn in the Chinese path to modernity. For Chinese in China, modernity came to be experienced from that time on as a series of revolutions (most notably the ones that took place in 1911 and 1949) and as repeated assaults on, and rejections of, Chinese tradition (the May Fourth Movement in 1919 and the Cultural Revolution, 1966–76). For the Chinese overseas the period marked the beginnings of a mass emigration that released new energies and brought individuals into proximity with the disciplines that drove the engines of capitalism. Moving out of China and into the arena of Western imperialist expansion, Chinese overseas inserted themselves into the niches of an emerging global capitalism – from the mines and plantations of Southeast Asia to those of the Americas.

For the most part, they *bypassed* the Chinese revolution on the mainland. They were, to quote from another essay by Wang Gungwu, '*outside* the Chinese revolution,'

Young Singaporean Chinese being 'modern,' 1920s.

that is, 'both outside China and outside the idea of revolution as the Chinese have conceived it.' This fact has crucial and paradoxical implications for the question of Chineseness. Away from China, the migrants sidestepped the iconoclastic assaults on traditional culture on the mainland. This enabled many Chinese overseas to sustain certain traditional forms of Chineseness, especially familial organization and folk religion, which were rejected as feudal and backward in China but which provided some cultural continuity as Chinese overseas faced the challenge of new environments. At the same time, in leaving China, the migrants were freed from the confines of traditional culture and, while they carried Chinese social experiences and cultural practices with them, they were faced with newer and more plural milieux than had been encountered back home.

Theirs was a different kind of revolution, 'a smaller revolution,' as Wang puts it, 'cumulatively a series of little modernizations' that may have been even more revolutionary if seen as doing the work of global capitalism in their various places of settlement. There they became, in Lynn Pan's words, 'a kind of foil to earthbound China, part of the oceanic influence pulling the country into the ambit of modern exchange systems, values and technology.'

Being among foreigners, then, has been more than a question of living among Malays or Peruvians or whatever; it has also been to experience the West in its guise as global capitalism. In other words, the Chinese overseas experienced the capitalist path to modernity – Western-led modernity – for a longer sustained period than the Chinese in China.

Varieties of Chineseness

To quote Wang Gungwu again, overseas Chinese ethnic awareness 'may be simple or superficial; it may also be deliberate, even assertive.' A simple starting point for understanding Chineseness is to separate out this awareness into three interrelated levels. At the primary level of everyday life, Chineseness is lived out in the family milieu and expressed in ordinary habits, attitudes, idioms and gestures that are rooted in Chinese traditions

Jardine Matheson trademark symbolizes global capitalism.

American-Chinese TV producer Felicia Lowe visits the land of her forefathers.

include language, religion, institutions, beliefs, practices and so on – are what people think of themselves as being part of, so when overseas Chinese identify themselves as Chinese, it must be supposed that it is to Chinese culture that they think of themselves as belonging. Yet if one asks some overseas Chinese what marks them off from people belonging to other cultures, it is not obviously their possession of, or familiarity, with the Chinese language, Chinese beliefs, history and all the rest of it. Thus a claim of identity is not always a claim of culture. And to conflate identity with cultural content obscures rather than illuminates our understanding of 'Chineseness.' To see how complex the issue is, let us look at three pairs of individuals as contrasting examples of how the process of identifying oneself as Chinese can vary not only from setting to setting but from person to person.

transmitted over time. Hence, even when third-generation overseas Chinese families begin to lose a strong hold of the language, their sense of being Chinese may be sustained in varying degrees by everyday mores. Chineseness is alive and well when it is taken for granted and woven into the fabric of everyday life. This is particularly true of family life, a private sphere that can be relatively unaffected by the larger, non-Chinese environment, even as Chinese adapt or assimilate to the latter.

However, to say, as we did above, that the sense of being Chinese may be sustained 'in varying degrees' begs a question: At what bottom degree does one move from being Chinese to being 'unChinese'? To ask that question is to shift the issue of identity to another level. People are often described as being 'more' Chinese than others, or 'less.' One who feels himself 'less' Chinese than others, or even 'unChinese,' is often led to the 'search for roots.' Chineseness, at this level, is no longer taken for granted but is considered a *personal* problem which, unless some solution can be found for it, puts one at risk of having an incomplete or incoherent sense of self.

That quest for a meaningful sense of self, however, frequently occurs in a larger social context in which individual identity is not merely a personal matter. At this third level, the question of identity is tied to what has been called 'the politics of recognition' or 'politics of difference.' In modern political systems, the principle of the equality of citizens has generated the demand for public recognition of the particular identities of diverse minority groups, groups which believe themselves oppressed by non-recognition or mis-recognition – that is, by prevailing distorted or negative public perceptions. In such a situation, identity becomes a kind of social resource. As such, and feeling itself threatened or suppressed, Chineseness (or non-Chineseness) becomes all the more purposefully maintained, defended, displayed and asserted.

It is not clear, however, that in the 'politics of difference,' the difference that is demanding to be recognized is necessarily a cultural one. Cultures – whose forms

In November 1996 Gary Locke (b. 1950) was elected governor of Washington, the first Chinese American to become state governor in US history and the first Asian American to win that position outside Hawaii. Locke's immigrant background drew a great deal of attention in the American media, with many reporters portraying his success as the realization of 'the American dream,' one achieved, moreover, against the discrimination suffered by Asian-American minorities in the past. The January 15, 1997 edition of the *San Francisco Chronicle* quoted him as saying, 'We have been an integral part of American history…. We helped to build this country with our blood, our sweat and our tears. Now, it is time for us to share in governing it.'

Locke's grandfather, who had arrived in the US from Taishan in Guangdong province, served as a houseboy in Olympia, Washington, before returning to China to start a family. Gary Locke's China-born father, who migrated to Seattle and settled there, served in the US Army during the 1944 Normandy invasion. As well as his membership of a minority, Locke's Chinese ancestry became 'a big part of his political persona' during his election campaign. It was further highlighted during his first official trip to China in October 1997; reported by the *Seattle Times* on September 28, 1997 as 'both personal and symbolic,' this included a visit to Jilong, his ancestral village.

The trip certainly had different layers of meaning. For the state of Washington, it betokened the expansion of ties with China, a large economy on the other side of the Pacific Rim, through the symbolic intermediary of the Chinese-American governor. For the people of Taishan and Jilong, it signified the return of a descendant to the land of his forefathers. For Chinese Americans, it meant American recognition of their eth-

Gary Locke.

nic roots at a time when they have arrived on the national stage and China has arrived on the global one. For Locke, it no doubt had some personal significance.

'I am proud to be Chinese. But I am thoroughly American,' that article in the *Seattle Times* quoted him as declaring. What is of interest is the ease with which foreign descent and ethnic background can be invoked – indeed celebrated – by US citizens and minorities. The recognition of cultural diversity has been a basic principle in the multiculturalism of the United States. In many cases, the constitutional guarantee of civil rights and the expansion of opportunities for minorities have been accompanied by the assertion of ethnic identity as a resource. The principle of cultural diversity is used to mark out a legitimate space – and even to enlarge that space – for minority citizens in the public sphere and in national life.

But Locke's public declaration of ethnic pride is a luxury that only the citizens of a liberal democracy could indulge. Contrast it with the statement (quoted by the *Straits Times* on May 16, 1997) of the prominent Indonesian-Chinese businessman Liem Sioe Liong. The latter found it necessary to declare that he was 'more Indonesian than Chinese.' At the time he was 82 years of age and had lived for 61 years in Indonesia, a country which has repeatedly persecuted its Chinese minority and suppressed the Chinese language and identity. 'I have,' he said, 'more than 225,000 employees. Only a small percentage of them are Chinese. I am proud to be an Indonesian and I am a patriot.'

Yet he also noted that most ethnic Chinese went into business because they had no opportunities in the public sector, adding, 'If a Chinese person wants to work in a government office, would he be allowed to?' Thus, at the same time as he asserted his Indonesian identity, Liem did not shy away from reminding his audience that Chinese origin was a source of discrimination in Indonesian society. But then Liem was exceptional: most Indonesian Chinese would think twice about voicing their grievances in public. Yet paradoxically, the question of being Chinese is kept alive by its being muted. Given the contours of national politics, one is Chinese in having to declare that one is Indonesian. And being Indonesian means having to downplay and even hide Chineseness.

For our second illustration we turn to two artists. The Fujian-born See Hiang To (Shi Xiangtuo, 1906–90) was a Shanghai-trained painter who migrated to Singapore in 1938 and taught at the Nanyang Academy of Fine Art there. In an article written in 1949, See spoke of the need for Chinese artists to accept the challenge and influence of 'international art.' Only through the upheaval of a direct encounter with the latter, he insisted, could traditional Chinese art be rejuvenated. In subsequent decades, See and his colleagues were to create the Nanyang School and produce works of art whose Chinese roots were obvious, but whose mixed styles and subject matter reflected their relocation to Southeast Asia.

See's art, showing a continuity of Chineseness, contrasts sharply with the work of Yeoh Jin Leng, a locally born Malaysian. Yeoh, whose paternal great-grandmother was Malay, comes from a Peranakan family assimilated over five generations to local society. He trained in Britain in the 1950s. He would have come into contact with the artists of the Nanyang School, who were dominant in local circles, but he felt himself more foreign to their work than to the modernist movements he encountered in his years in Britain. 'The Chinese Mandarin world,' he said in an interview he gave in 1994, 'was a world of its own, an enclave accessible to Chinese who speak the language only.' And the Nanyang Academy was 'a Chinese institution and, like the Great Wall of China, impenetrable, standing aloof from the mainstream movement of art fired by a national consciousness for nation building.'

The Nanyang artists, while intentionally positioning themselves in relation to the mainstream tradition of Chinese art, experimented with modern Western styles and attempted to localize their art in a manner which Yeoh completely bypassed. Yeoh did not have to struggle with the question of Chinese identity until it was forced upon him by the race riots which erupted in Malaysia in May 1969. Suddenly, he discovered that he was 'a Malaysian of a different class,' one 'made to feel a foreigner' in a country he and his ancestors had called their own. His Chineseness, in other words, was not a self-identification but an identification imposed by others. The painful realization that he had been thrust into a cultural limbo induced an identity crisis so profound that he was unable to paint for three years.

An artist different again is Zhang Hongtu (see his work, *Last Banquet*, on p 96). Zhang left China in 1982 when he was 37 to live in New York. He had been there nearly a decade when he was asked by an interviewer, Jonathan Hay, how his long absence from China had affected his ability to think of himself as Chinese. Being Chinese, he replied, meant being tightly bound to Chinese culture in mind and spirit. But 'Chinese culture' in this case meant more than the high art which concerned See and his colleagues; it meant such life experiences – shared by the post-1970s emigrants from China – as having to remember that 'when you buy lunch you have to pay ration coupons,' and having to put up with enormous political pressure in your day-to-day existence.

'Malay Man with Wayang Kulit,' painting by See Hiang To, 1977, Chinese ink and colour, 83 x 36 cm.

Installation by Yeoh Jin Leng, 'Of Humans, Icons and Precious Earth,' 1991-92.

Singaporeans of Chinese descent on Chinese soil – and smelling it.

If the image of Chinese culture remains clear to him, it is not only because he continues to read and think about it, but because living abroad has allowed him to compare it with Western culture. Indeed, it has become clearer to him by virtue of this contrast – to illustrate this, he quotes the poet Su Dongpo (1036–1101), '*Bu shi Lushan zhen mianmu/ Zhi yuan shen zai ci shan zhong.* Which means,' he explains, 'one can't see the image of Mount Lu because one is inside the mountain. Now that I'm outside of this mountain . . . I understand Chinese culture better . . . I have also come to understand myself as a Chinese person better than nine years ago.'

Contrast Zhang with William Yang, a third-generation Chinese Australian photographer for whom the question, 'Am I Chinese?' has been an abiding dilemma. Yang felt he had to deal, as he put it in an article published in *Art and Asia Pacific* in 1994, with 'the tyranny of appearance': 'It is my fate to be born with a Chinese face and to live among Westerners, to share their identity yet to look different. I have absorbed the Australian identity as a natural process because I have been born into it, yet somehow I feel alien from it.' But being Chinese too was foreign to his upbringing, his mother wanting her children to be assimilated. On being called 'Ching Ching Chinaman' once when he was growing up, he asked his mother if he was Chinese and when told that he was, he 'knew that being Chinese was a terrible curse.' He was what many others like him have been called – a 'banana,' yellow on the outside, white inside. Perhaps Peranakans in Southeast Asia have it easier because physically Chinese do not stick out there.

The upshot of all this was that Yang began to discover his 'Chinese heritage through philosophy and art.' He went to China in 1989 and described the experience as being 'very powerful': 'It had to do with feeling you were standing on the soil of your ancestors and feeling that the blood of China ran through your veins.' His friends called him a 'born-again Chinese' and he acknowledged his own zealousness in taking up 'traditional values' – even to the point of rejecting his earlier work. Indeed, he has 'made a career of being Chinese' and concluded, 'I now feel more complete and able to draw on two worlds, getting the best from both.'

His Chineseness, though, must surely be different from that of Zhang Hongtu: the one earned almost instantaneously by a first visit to China; the other enhanced only after nearly a decade of absence from the homeland. Yang took a shortcut to Chineseness, while Zhang had to come at it the long way round. While those like Zhang may take their links to China for granted, the notion that one can feel 'the blood of China' running through one's veins can perhaps only be entertained by those for whom such links have had to be recovered. The impulse to do so and make complete one's identity is akin to a religious conversion, and this is indeed what the metaphor of being 'born again' suggests.

Concerns of the kind Yang exemplifies have grown in a world increasingly globalized. Globalization has been centuries in the making. But its pace and scale has increased dramatically with the expansion of corporate capitalism and the revolution in information technology and mass communications since the 1970s. Apart from the widespread emergence of consumer society, this has led to the transmission, through the mass media, of a profusion of symbols and images that are received almost instantaneously in different parts of the world. To be in such a world is to experience what has been called 'the postmodern condition.'

In such a world, which is more interconnected economically and technologically but more fragmented ('pluralized') culturally, identities are less anchored in locality or territoriality. For example, whereas their ancestral speech area would have been an important component of the identity of overseas Hokkiens or Cantonese of an earlier generation, people now find their focus of identification in a global marketplace of disconnected and shifting cultural markers in a 'pick and choose' and 'mix and match' manner. Hence the bicultural or even multiple identities claimed by many overseas Chinese. In defining people's consciousness and identity, styles of consumption (of products homogenized across the world) become more important than venerable traditions and symbols. At the same time, troubled by the feeling of dislocation and discontinuity, many Chinese appeal to a fixed, or at any rate stable, notion of Chineseness as a kind of cultural essence uniting Chinese across the globe.

Discourse on Chineseness

Views of Chineseness are historically specific. The springs of the late 20th-century view can probably be located to the late 1970s, and factors such as the opening of China to world capitalism under Deng Xiaoping, the return of Hong Kong to Chinese sovereignty, the rapid growth of East Asian and some Southeast Asian economies and the ethnicization of the ways in which we look at the world (as exemplified by Samuel Huntington's book *The Clash of Civilizations*, 1996) all had a part to play.

By the close of the century, a discourse on Chineseness

had developed and become influential in many circles. By 'discourse on Chineseness' we refer to the combination of ways in which Chinese identity is defined and represented in the public arena, building upon certain underlying concepts and assumptions. In the process of formulation and circulation, such concepts and assumptions become increasingly accepted, acquiring the status of conventional wisdom. In a discourse, the words tell one not so much 'this is how things are' as 'this is how you should look at it.' By limiting and influencing the terms in which Chineseness is viewed, discourses close off alternative ways of seeing the Chinese.

The discourse on Chineseness emerged out of a spate of writings by American social scientists highlighting the economic rise of the East Asian region. Against the background of Japan's postwar boom, followed by the rapid growth of the newly industrializing economies of South Korea, Taiwan, Hong Kong and Singapore, scholars such as Herman Kahn (in 1979) and Roderick MacFarquhar (in 1980) put forward the idea of a 'post-Confucian challenge,' suggesting that certain 'Confucian' values were conducive to industrial capitalist development.

Their idea was taken up by a large number of scholars and popular commentators seeking to explain modernization in terms of such cultural values as diligence, frugality, filial piety, paternalism, collectivism, regard for education, and pragmatic reliance on personal relations and networking. Identified as 'Confucian,' these values were interpreted as positive predispositions to modern economic enterprise. From this it was but a short step to identifying Chineseness with an intrinsic aptitude for capitalist endeavour – as though four decades of socialism in China counted for nothing. The irony of it is that earlier scholars had pointed to Confucianism as one of the *hindrances* to modernization in Asia.

Those who reject cultural explanations direct attention instead to the social and political conditions Chinese face in their adopted countries. If Chinese business practices in some Southeast Asian countries revolved around informal networks of partnership and credit and social relations based on trust, it was because, as the Malaysian scholar K. S. Jomo argues (1997), Chinese 'could not rely on the colonial state to provide the legal enforcement necessary for business transactions.' In post-colonial Malaysia, such practices continued in response to the discrimination embodied in the New Economic Policy, the government's affirmative action programme favouring indigenous Malays. A 'Chinese business idiom,' therefore, observes Jomo, 'is based on a kind of resistance to state control and the sense that ethnic discrimination is either an existing or at least a potential threat.'

What *is* congenial to capitalist enterprise are rational business practices undergirded by a legal framework. But when such institutions are absent or underdeveloped, as they are in China and other parts of Asia, businessmen fall back on personal relations, old boy networks called *guanxi* in Chinese. The continuity into the present of personalism and other values found in premodern (not just Chinese) societies is not an indication of 'culture' persisting autonomously but is rather the result of having to adapt to prevailing political-economic structures. Yet the discourse of the 1990s almost

Western popular culture represented by Michael Jackson rubs off on Chinese early.

always describes *guanxi* relationships as though they were an intrinsic aspect of Chinese identity.

Among the strands that made up the discourse was Joel Kotkin's book *Tribes: How Race, Religion, and Identity Determine Success in the New Global Economy* (1992). The Chinese figure in the book as a 'global tribe,' one which, like Jews, Japanese and Indians, have among other things 'a global network based on mutual trust that allows the tribe to function collectively beyond the confines of national or regional borders.' Overseas Chinese are portrayed as part of an 'empire of *guanxi*' and the mainland as 'the repository of virtually all the cultural heritage of the tribe.'

Kotkin's book was followed by John Naisbitt's *Global Paradox* (1994) and Sterling Seagrave's *Lords of the Rim* (1995). The former referred to 'Greater China and the global Chinese tribe' and borrowed the term 'Chinese Commonwealth' from John Kao, a Chinese-American professor at the Harvard Business School, to refer to the worldwide network of Chinese entrepreneurs. In a similar vein, Seagrave speaks of the overseas Chinese as part of 'invisible China,' a 'separate world force ... an empire without borders, national government or flag.' Then came Samuel Huntington's influential and widely debated article published in 1993 and follow-up book published three years later, advancing the thesis that it is culture and cultural identities that are dividing humankind and shaping the patterns of cooperation and conflict in the post-Cold War world. One of the cultural identities he names is that based on the 'Sinic civilization' that has China as its 'core state.' This he presumes is shared by all Chinese across the world; in one passage, he writes, 'Chinese throughout East Asia identify their interests with those of the mainland.'

Not the least of the contributors to the discourse are overseas Chinese themselves. For example, addressing the 1993 World Chinese Entrepreneurs Convention in Hong Kong, Lee Kuan Yew drew from Joel Kotkin's book and said, 'What ethnic Chinese from

李光耀的「亞洲價值」

李

Headline reads: 'Lee Kuan Yew's "Asian Values".'

Hong Kong, Macao and Taiwan did [in investing in China] was to demonstrate to a sceptical world that *guanxi* through the same language and culture can make up for a lack in the rule of law, and transparency in rules and regulations'

It was under Lee Kuan Yew that Singapore advocated Confucianism in the 1980s as a bulwark against the moral fallout of fast-paced modernization. By the early 1990s, this had given way to the promotion of 'Asian values,' counterpointed by leaders like Lee and Mahathir Mohamed to the universality of such 'Western' values as individualism and an emphasis on civil rights and freedom. In the terms of the discourse on 'Asian values' (under which 'Chinese' values are subsumed), Chineseness is said to be incompatible with modern political values; for one thing, the Chinese respect for authority is thought to sit uneasily with the general sense of individual self-sufficiency required by direct democracy.

But go to the heartlands of democracy, and a different picture emerges. Consider the exercise of constitutional rights and democratic procedures by Chinese settled in countries like the US, Canada and Australia. Finding themselves in liberal democracies where national goals and symbols are not reserved exclusively for the majority (unlike, say, in Indonesia), the resident Chinese have formed pressure groups and mobilized support from not only within their communities but cross-communally (with other Asians and even with whites) to fight on issues affecting their interests. If overseas Chinese are widely – and stereotypically – seen to be apolitical, that is sometimes because, as Kasian Tejapira has pointed out in relation to Thai nationalism, official accounts of political activity leave them out, denying the *lukjin* (Sino-Thai), for example, their place in the story.

What discourses obscure is one of the most important aspects of cultural identity: how it changes. And the cultural inheritances on which identities are based never operate in isolation. Even more than that of the Chinese in China, overseas Chinese identity is the product of several interlocking histories and cultures and is not and will never be unified.

Kwok Kian Woon

Business relations with non-Chinese

Through the centuries, Chinese have journeyed to truck, produce and exchange for profit among non-Chinese

Chinese employee (far right) of Western merchants at European trading establishment in Yokohama, 19th century.

abroad. This article will briefly consider their relationship to the Japanese and Korean markets, but will focus mainly on Southeast Asia because only in that region have Chinese business activities been an enduring force of consequence.

East Asia

Outside the framework of tributary trade (see p 48), Chinese and Japanese were fellow-freebooters in the endemically piratical, smuggler-ridden character of East Asian maritime commerce in the Ming dynasty (1368–1644). Relations between many of these extra-tributary traders were close, so close that the mid-16th century raids on the Chinese coasts were joint Chinese–Japanese endeavours. Chinese merchants had also to ally themselves with the Portuguese (who had established a base in Macao) to conduct trade in the teeth of Chinese imperial proscription.

Japan itself was closed in 1639 by the Tokugawa shogunate's national exclusion policy, which allowed only Chinese and Dutch to trade in Nagasaki. Direct contact with Japanese lessened from 1688 to the middle of the 19th century, when Chinese merchants were confined to an enclosed Chinese compound and liaised with the host society through a Chinese commissioner.

After Japan's opening to the West in the 1850s, the arrival of Western merchants who had been working in China's Treaty Ports was followed by that of their Chinese compradors and independent merchants. Japanese inexperienced in foreign trade believed themselves disadvantaged by the Westerners and the Chinese compradors with whom they transacted business. These Japanese resented the Chinese for their business acumen as well as for the status they enjoyed as privileged business associates of Western merchants.

Chinese and Japanese merchants were key commercial players – and competitors – in the Korean market after Pusan, Wonsan and Inchon opened as international ports in the 1880s. Both Chinese and Japanese traders were better able to cater to Korean tastes than their European counterparts, and between them they monopolized the foreign trade of Korea. But both here and in Japan, a series of international developments starting with China's defeat in the Sino–Japanese war of 1895 marked the decline of the resident Chinese trading communities.

Southeast Asia

In the pre-colonial era, non-Chinese rulers and traders in Southeast Asian ports related to the transient Chinese as they did to such other trade diasporas as Indians or Arabs. Those with whom Chinese did business included the resident Japanese communities (*nihommachi*) which, because Chinese law kept Japanese out of China after 1547, had come seeking trade in the various ports of Southeast Asia, as well as the Portuguese, the Dutch and the English, who at first operated on a scale no greater than that of their Asian counterparts.

This pattern changed with European colonization, not least because of the growth of settled Chinese communities and their differentiation into locally born Chinese (mestizos in the Philippines and Peranakans in Batavia, for example) and, after the 1860s, rising numbers of China-born immigrants. The diversity and complexity of relations further increased as colonial rule spread and intensified over the 19th century. The changes were gradual until the last quarter of the century, when European capital investment in plantation crops, mining, banking and commerce started and the economic transformation of the region accelerated rapidly. Until then, Chinese relations with Western colonial authorities and traders had been far less unequal. For example, in the early stages of the sugar industry in Java (1830–70), Chinese contractors were almost as numerous and prominent as Dutch in running the government-sponsored sugar mills.

After the 1880s, Chinese rarely competed as equals with the British or Dutch. The diversified, sugar-based Oei Tiong Ham group in the Netherlands East Indies was unique in all Southeast Asia in taking on and outstripping the Dutch at their own game. Oei used modern technology and European technicians, lawyers and banks. His relations with the Dutch authorities were not very close or dependent: he seemed not to have cultivated them more than he had to and to have sometimes imitated them with flamboyant gestures.

In the largest Chinese communities, many Chinese could prosper through trading with China and other Chinese, maintaining minimal business contact with non-Chinese. But in all other communities, the Chinese mainstay was trading with non-Chinese, whether European agency houses, local rulers or officials or indigenous villagers. Relations were broadly those of the market-place, but these would eventually take on a political and ethnic edge as rising local nationalism began to colour Chinese-indigenous economic competition. Out of the complex of economic interactions between the colonial masters, Chinese and indigenous peoples, ethnic stereotypes arose – especially of the Chinese shopkeeper or revenue farmer as a rapacious middleman whose relationship to local villagers was egregiously exploitative. But relations with villagers were often cordial, the latter appreciative of the services or loans which, had the Chinese not provided them, would not have been accessible.

Chinese business relationships with non-Chinese broadened even further in the post-1945 period. As colonial rule crumbled in the 1940s–50s, Chinese had to forge intricate relationships with the indigenous élites of the newly independent countries. Relations followed changing patterns in the larger economic and political environment. At first they were highly tentative, ambivalent and complex, but gradually they settled down into some fairly stable patterns.

The post-colonial nationalism of indigenous governments entailed policies aimed at shrinking Chinese and foreign enterprise and promoting indigenous activity. Restrictive licences, protective tariffs, ownership limitations, preferential credit allocations to indigenous groups and outright bans of Chinese activity in particular sectors were common. These discriminatory measures elicited a range of adaptive responses from Chinese forming the so-called Ali-Baba ventures fronted by the indigenous sleeping partner (Ali, a nickname for the indigene) and run by Chinese (Baba); giving bribes to government officials to circumvent restrictions or secure protection; cultivating powerful indigenous political

European colonization (here of Penang) changed the pattern of Chinese business.

patrons and sponsors.

A major change which has influenced business relations profoundly has been the rise of the most successful Chinese to the economic heights once occupied by Westerners. Whereas only a few Chinese – like Tan Kah Kee (Singapore), Oei Tiong Ham (Dutch East Indies) or Loke Yew (Malaya) – had ranked among the wealthiest property owners in the colonies, large numbers of them became so between the 1950s and 1980s. Insofar as a distinctive capitalist class was developing throughout those years, wealthy Chinese were now the core element of it.

But at first they were regarded as mere 'pariah capitalists,' highly dependent on the protection they received from indigenous patrons (particularly political leaders, bureaucrats or military officers). That term was becoming increasingly outdated by the late 1980s, and the dependent status of Chinese business people has become considerably attenuated, especially in Thailand. They are still highly vulnerable to political pressures, however, but as they have become wealthier and the economies of the region more internationalized, they have found many more options open to them, and much greater bargaining power. The emergence of many Chinese-owned conglomerates (that is, multi-firm enterprises or business groups) in Thailand, Malaysia and Indonesia, and a few in Singapore and the Philippines, has also altered their bargaining power. Both foreign multinational companies and the local governments need their help and cooperation as much as vice versa. However, this remains true for only as long as overall economic growth stays healthy. As the financial crisis of the late 1990s triggered rioting in Jakarta, the scapegoating of Indonesian Chinese was a stark reminder of how vulnerable they remain. In the turmoil which brought down Suharto, tens of thousands of Chinese ran for cover as mobs looted their shops, gang-raped their women and set fire to their homes and cars. As always, the worst hit were the small businesses, owners of the 'shophouse' rather than the conglomerate. The latter would have parked much of their money abroad, but the anger which poor ethnic Indonesians felt towards them was taken out against those with far fewer resources for shielding themselves against plunder.

J. A. C. Mackie

Revenue farmer in the Dutch East Indies.

Oei Tiong Ham.

MULTI-LAYERED IDENTITIES: OVERSEAS CHINESE ARTISTS IN THE 20TH CENTURY

In diverse ways, 20th-century overseas Chinese artists have learned to balance a known or imagined Chinese past with a culturally hyphenated present. Many works exploring the individual's interaction with society suggest the artists' need to resolve underlying dilemmas of identity. Whether to assert or surrender their Chineseness as they integrate into their host societies is a question they have to deal with in art no less than in life. Thus, while the works project a highly personal vision, they may also express cross-cultural experiences unique to the Chinese diaspora.

A generation or more may separate these émigrés. Since the 1920s, artists born in China have found their way to Europe, North America, Japan and Southeast Asia, going initially as students or teachers, eventually becoming settlers. Those of the pre-Communist era were largely in search of new artistic horizons. Swept along by the thrust towards modernization in China, they hoped to reconcile Eastern and Western approaches in their work. In contrast, post-1949 émigrés sought freedom from political control, leaving to explore avant-garde approaches and to taste an untrammelled lifestyle. Both groups took with them not only their brushes and painting materials but also a significant amount of cultural baggage.

A third group are the foreign-born, those distanced from their ancestral culture by not only space but time. Awareness of cultural displacement has impelled a significant number of these artists to undertake a psychological, if not physical, journey to recover their 'lost' heritage.

ARTISTS BORN IN CHINA

C. C. Wang/Wang Jiqian (b. 1907)

Such is his eclecticism that C. C. Wang, the acclaimed artist, teacher and connoisseur, appreciates the bold spontaneity of forms as divergent as Japanese prints and New York subway graffiti. Coming from an old scholarly family in Suzhou, Wang emigrated to the US in 1949, ahead of the Communist takeover of China. A characteristic receptivity to contemporary ideas drew him to Abstract Expressionism and Action Painting, the study of which lent a fresh approach to his art. Nevertheless, it was to the early pioneers of Chinese landscape painting that Wang turned for his primary inspiration. Within the works of 10th-century masters, rather than those of later painters, he found the clues he sought to convey the monumentality and enduring grandeur of earth forms. Though he belongs to a generation schooled in traditional disciplines, Wang possesses a refreshingly modern, free-ranging mind and personality, uncircumscribed by history or geography.

Lee Man Fong (1913–88)

In Lee Man Fong's ability to draw sustenance from separate artistic traditions, we see an illustration of the cultural balance developed for survival by many first-generation Chinese migrants to Southeast Asia. Court painter to President Sukarno of Indonesia in the 1960s, and the most prominent Indonesian Chinese artist of his time, Lee adapted with ease to a succession of cultural environments.

At the age of two, Lee arrived in Singapore from Canton with his father. In

1932 he moved to Indonesia, where he worked as a commercial artist and as the editor of a Chinese daily. A self-taught painter, he found his greatest inspiration in the exotic landscape and people of Bali. Awarded a Dutch government scholarship to study in Holland, he returned to Indonesia in 1952 with a deeper affinity for European art. His best-known works in oils were executed in a lyrical impressionistic style that is recognizably Western in origin. However, he also painted ink and brush works that exuded the vigour and spontaneity of the *xieyi* (freehand brushwork) style favoured by Chinese scholars.

Cheong Soo Pieng (1917–83)

Cheong Soo Pieng, who had migrated from Fujian province in 1946, was one of a few Singaporean artists of his generation to achieve international recognition. Until 1961, he taught at the Nanyang Academy of Fine Arts, where Mandarin was the main language of instruction and where the students were largely Chinese-educated. Cheong himself would retain a Chinese lifestyle and outlook till his last years, but his art permitted no cultural boundaries. He found an endless array of themes in the vibrant tropical environment, and explored them with enthusiasm, employing Western as well as Chinese media. A restless innovator, Cheong exploited the artistic possibilities of various materials to forge one fresh and surprising style after another. Drawing initial inspiration from the vocabulary of Western artists like Gauguin, Picasso and Matisse as well as that of traditional Chinese art, he succeeded, through brilliant experimentation, in creating a distinctive pictorial language.

The empathy he felt with the people of Nanyang underlies the sensitively conceived composition *Drying Salted Fish*. While impassioned colour and bold strokes characterized many works of the 1950s, the gentle restraint seen here foreshadows his lyrical last works – works hauntingly reminiscent of Chinese literati paintings.

Zao Wou-ki/Zhao Wuji (b. 1921)

Zao Wou-ki epitomizes the fortunate emigrant who has successfully melded his personal and artistic identities, achieving an enviable international reputation. Born into a Beijing family that traces its ancestry to the Song dynasty, he was well-versed in ancient ink traditions. In 1948 he left for Paris

Cheong Soo Pie[ng], *Drying Salted Fi[sh]*, c. 1960s, Chinese [ink] & colour, 55.5 x [...] cm (Singapore A[rt] Museum).

(*Far left*) C. C. Wang, *Landscap[e]*, 1986, ink & colo[ur] on paper, 62 x 66 [cm] (Hong Kong Mus[eum] of Art).

(*Below*) Lee Man Fong, *The Developers*, oil [on] board, 58 x 120 [cm] (Singapore Art Museum).

to pursue an interest in contemporary Western art, and was persuaded by its heady artistic atmosphere to settle there. Paradoxically, the intellectual stimulation he found among the community of Western artists in Paris brought him to a fresh appreciation of his own artistic heritage.

His early European oils were pictorial and specific, but he soon turned to an abstractionist style for the freedom he required to express inner feelings and universal truths. Large and dynamic works which employ colour with a Western facility also project a calligraphic power derived from the Chinese literati tradition. Beneath the celebratory warmth and vibrancy of a work like *Juin-octobre 85* are glimpses of the swirling mists and timeless spaces that appear in classical Chinese landscapes. Zao's sensibilities have indubitably been honed by his long residence in France, where he feels very much at home. However, embedded in his consciousness is a reverence for the cyclical rhythms of nature, an ancestral legacy brought West by the artist.

Zao Wou-ki, *Juin-octobre 85*, 1985, oil on canvas, 280 x 1000 cm (Raffles City Pte Ltd).

(Right) Tseng Yuho, *An Autumn Monument*, 1991, paper & acrylic, 60 x 120 cm.

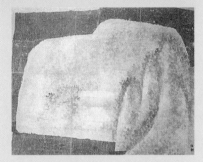

(Left) Hung Liu, *Judgement of Paris*, 1992, oil on canvas with lacquered wood, 182.9 x 243.8 x 12.1 cm.

(Below) Gu Wenda, *The Dangerous Chessboard Leaves the Ground*, 1987, installation: Toronto, Canada, 270 x 1000 x 1000 cm.

Tseng Yuho/Zeng Youhe (b. 1925)

Subjected, as few Beijing women of her generation still were, to footbinding as a child, Tseng took a crucial first step towards freedom when she unbound her feet at the age of 14. In 1945, when she was 20, she made a further break with tradition by marrying a foreigner, the eminent German art historian Gustave Ecke; and moved with him a few years later to Hawaii. Reacting to a strange and radically different environment, Tseng asserted her Chinese identity more strongly through the years. Expanding on her knowledge of ancient techniques in scroll-mounting, she created subtle compositions by intricately juxtaposing and layering handmade papers and other materials. Her 'dsui hua,' as she calls them, are intimate personal adventures, in which she has seemingly layered and transmuted her memories, hopes, thoughts and experiences into poetic visual images. Today, Tseng still practises her quiet meditative art in a mountain-top house she designed in Oahu. Incorporating ancient Chinese cosmic beliefs in its plan, the house, like her art, is intended to express the intangible and to order the irrational and unpredictable in life.

Hung Liu/Liu Hong (b. 1948)

Born in Manchuria, Hung Liu spent her student days producing Cultural Revolution banners and murals. She left for America in 1984, and four years later acquired the official Green Card verifying her double status as Alien and Resident. To protest this contradictory characterization of her identity, she painted an enlarged version of the offending document, replacing her name with *Cookie, Fortune*, a pointed reference to the Chinese-American confection made for American consumption.

The age-old suppression of women is an issue of great concern to this painter and installation artist. In *Judgement of Paris*, she depicts a pair of young women posing in a pseudo-Western setting by adapting turn-of-the-century photographs of Chinese prostitutes. On a large porcelain vase is pictured bare-breasted Greek goddesses purveying their charms in a beauty contest. Their shameless seductiveness is in sharp contrast to the demure pose struck by the Chinese prostitutes. Clearly ironic, the painting's message is that bold or coy, occidental or oriental, women are the mere playthings of men.

Gu Wenda (b. 1955)

From monumental calligraphic works based on Chinese traditional ink painting, Gu Wenda has turned to provocative installations using bodily secretions and shed tissue (notably human hair). Reacting to the banning of his radical works in China, Gu left for North America in 1987 in search of greater tolerance. Acclaimed in the West as one of the most original of China's post-Mao artists, the uncompromising Gu succeeds in shocking even those accustomed to avant-garde defiance. He has produced installations incorporating blood-soaked articles which even Western galleries are reluctant to exhibit. In this he shows himself to be a child of Maoist iconoclasm.

Startling red splashes are an obsessively recurring motif in his work. The colour red is traditionally associated in China with happiness and good fortune, but it is more likely to serve in Gu's work as a disturbing metaphor for blood, violence or death. Viewers of *The Dangerous Chessboard Leaves the Ground,* his first installation abroad, were encouraged to don long red robes and breathe in the menacing, ritual-like atmosphere evoked by the minimalist colour scheme and highly charged setting. Man's fears and conflicts, his strategies, victories and defeats in the Game of Life are some of the complex themes addressed.

ARTISTS BORN ABROAD

Georgette Chen/Zhang Liying (1906 or 1907–93)

The forthright and unwavering glance of the subject of this portrait (top left) projects the strong character of the artist herself. Born as Zhang Liying into a prominent Shanghainese family in France with business interests in Paris, she spent her years shuttling between China and France. Later married to the Chinese Foreign Minister Eugene Chen (see p 253), she was equally at ease in formal diplomatic circles and the casual Bohemian fraternity of Left-Bank artists.

Interned during World War II and widowed by its end, she sought a new life in Southeast Asia, settling in 1954 in Singapore, where she taught at the Nanyang Academy of Fine Arts. With renewed creative energy, she incorporated the intense colour and light of the tropics into her oils and pastels. Rambutans and other exotic fruit filled her canvases, but mooncakes and other Chinese festival forms continued to appear, evoking a Chinese past and palette. Significantly, she chose as a pen-name the Malay name for the fragrant sandalwood tree, *Chendana* – a term prefixed to her familiar signature 'Chen.' This was undoubtedly intended to symbolize the meshing of her own identity with that of her adopted environment .

Tan Swee Hian (b. 1943)

Writer, poet and choreographer as well as painter, the Indonesian-born but Singapore-based Tan Swee Hian served as Cultural Attaché in the French Embassy for many years. Winnowing dreams, Western poetry and fables as well as esoteric oriental philosophy and religious texts, he employs surrealist imagery to summon an awareness of the insignificance of material existence. For this self-taught artist, man's spiritual rather than temporal identity is the overriding concern. To Tan, art is another form of the meditation he practises as a staunch Buddhist: he contends that it is imperative to transcend the bondage imposed by our senses, and thus break free from the *maya*, or illusion, of the material world. Painted in 1996, Tan's six-panel series, comprising *The Six Indriyas* (or senses), was inspired by Hindu–Buddhist writings. The imaginative evocation of the sense of smell by the panel *The Wind Has a Nose* mirrors his belief that 'what we perceive should only be a point of departure for us to explore.'

Sanit Khewhok (b. 1944)

A third-generation Thai Chinese, Sanit Khewhok grew up speaking Thai in a household that continued to adhere to Confucian values and observe traditional south Chinese customs and rituals. Influenced by an early journey to Italy to train as an art conservator and restorer, and by his subsequent relocation to Hawaii, he was also spiritually and creatively shaped by a pivotal inner journey – a period of meditation in a Thai-Buddhist monastery. *The Journey of the Copper Ant,* a metaphor for man's uncertain progression through life, is indicative of Sanit's approach in its refinement, its quiet humour and its sense of tensile strength. While a gentle whimsy pervades paintings inspired by the Hawaiian landscape, his three-dimensional works attest to a conservator's respect for his material, a typically south Chinese skill in maximizing the resources at hand, and a Buddhist compassion for nature's lesser creatures. With their carefully wrought framework, his small-scale sculptures express his belief in the necessity of discarding superfluities accumulated in the cycle of existence in order to attain a delicate emotional balance.

Chong Fah Cheong (b. 1946)

A Political Science and Philosophy graduate from the University of Singapore, Chong Fah Cheong is a self-taught sculptor who likes to work in natural materials like wood and stone. An art teacher in Singapore schools for several years, he now lives with his family in Canada. The sense of alienation he felt there convinced him of the need to maintain his Straits Chinese roots by making periodic trips back. However, he believes that immersion in another culture has contributed substantially to his personal growth, broadening his social perspective and deepening his tolerance. Ranging from easily recognizable objects to near-abstract forms, his sculptures embody

quietly astute observations about life or the natural world. *Third Auntie's Birthday,* depicting pairs of shoes and slippers untidily deposited on a low flight of steps, is disarmingly simple in concept yet strangely poignant. Combining nostalgia with a touch of whimsy, it commemorates the Southeast Asian custom of removing footwear before entering a village house, an ingrained practice still faithfully followed in Western-style high-rise flats today.

Lao Lian Ben (b. 1948)

The works of this Filipino-Chinese painter provide salient clues to his identity as an artist of his generation, positioned in a Southeast Asian society

Georgette Chen,
Self-Portrait, 1946,
oil on canvas,
22.5 x 17.5 cm
(Singapore Art Museum).

(Right) **Tan Swee Hian,**
The Six Indriyas #3, The Wind Has a Nose, 1996,
Chinese ink & acrylic on ricepaper, 69 x 138 cm
(Singapore Art Museum).

(Below) **Sanit Khewhok,**
The Journey of the Copper Ant, 1988,
mixed media,
90 x 90 x 30 cm.

long swept by influences from the East and West. Reflecting the modernist search for meaning in the non-industrial environment, Lao's early assemblages incorporated reminders of Filipino folk culture and unspoilt nature. He made extensive use of scraps of Manila hemp, pebbles and other discarded fragments – materials which had perhaps served magical or ritualistic functions in a primitive society. The charred twigs appearing in his assemblages are accusatory fingers pointing silently to man's thoughtless destruction of the natural world. His later works show a deliberate paring of all extraneous or distracting material. His canvases have been purified down to a basic palette, and the forms which surface tantalize because they are half-hidden and mysterious. The restrained treatment of his *Zen Master* series and his occasional employment of calligraphic signs and images are implicit references to an ancient Asian heritage. Within the timeless minimalist world of *Tryst*, he envelopes the viewer in the calmness of one who has returned to his philosophical roots.

Wong Hoy Cheong (b. 1960)

Wong Hoy Cheong was born in Penang, the grandson of an immigrant from south China who married into a well-to-do Straits Chinese family. Occasionally painting quiet, introspective works, he is best known for paintings and performances which are overtly political. The ambivalence of the transplanted Chinese psyche comes through in touching works like *Aspirations of the Working Class*, portraying a couple and their two children posing stiffly in a curious combination of Chinese and Western clothes. Non-Chinese elements surrounding the little family point up their cultural vulnerability and isolation. When focused on the affluent middle class, Wong's commentary is touched with acidity. In *The Nouveau Riche, the Elephant, the Foreign Maid, or the Discreet Charm of the Bourgeoisie*, the artist has trained a satirical lens on the Malaysian tendency to ape an imported lifestyle. While his subjects are ethnically ambiguous, their unconscious mimicking of fashionable Western postures and pastimes is unmistakable. Despite the distinctly Malaysian content of his work, Wong regards himself as a relative outsider in his own country. Having long lived abroad, he has the sharp, unclouded vision of those who have learned to view themselves and their compatriots with a merciless objectivity from prolonged exposure to a different culture.

Baet Yeok Kwan (b. 1961)

A young Singaporean, Baet Yeok Kwan offers the viewer of his untitled painted montage a visual inventory of the discordant and incongruous images he encounters in daily urban life. Some are metaphors for his overseas Chinese background, others point to the encroachment of Western or technological presence in the city: scattered on a paint-splotched wall, a rough Chinese bowl and chopsticks as well as Chinese line drawings of the human anatomy are curiously juxtaposed with a cinema poster and a head adapted from a computer school logo. The large central image which rivets the eye is an elaborate red-and-gold swing door. Though clearly associated with upper-class Straits Chinese homes in Singapore, this gateway also suggests the push-pull ambiguity of contemporary existence. Inescapably, the viewer is led to wonder: Is the door a symbol of entry (and re-entry) into the security of a familiar Chinese environment, or does it conversely denote an exit or means of escape from the world of traditional Chinese life and values – a milieu perhaps outdated and irrelevant to younger Singaporeans?

Goh Ee Choo (b. 1960)

For this bilingual third-generation Singaporean, true self-identity is linked to the understanding and acceptance of universal truths. A graduate of both Singapore's Nanyang Academy and the Slade School of Art in London, he has been moulded by his immersion in Buddhism and Daoism and the Chinese aesthetic principle of *qiyun* (resonance or energy). He employs installation and performance art to tap into that creative energy in the universe which he believes can dissolve man's anger and dissension. In early two-dimensional works, natural forms like dried lotus buds, twigs or sea shells denoted intuitive points in carefully manipulated compositions. In more recent works, structured, symmetrical forms contain the underlying flow of psychic energy. A triangle may symbolize a mountain; its convergence, man's quest for emotional harmony. Dramatically inverted in *The Word*, a meticulously executed ink drawing, the triangle unfolds and vibrates with a mesmerizing, pulsating rhythm, radiating an intensity that derives from the artist's approach to life.

Lee Seok Chee

Lao Lian Ben, *Tryst, acrylic and oil on wood, 122 x 122 cm (Singapore Art Museum).*

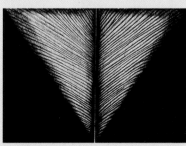

Goh Ee Choo, *The word*, 1991, *pigment ink on paper, 113 x 153 cm (Singapore Art Museum)*

(Left) **Chong Fah Cheong,** *Third Auntie's Birthday*, 1986, *wood and bronze (Singapore Art Museum).*

Wong Hoy Cheong, *The Nouveau Riche, the Elephant, the Foreign Maid, or the Discreet Charm of the Bourgeoisie,* 1991, *mixed media, 228 x 304 cm (Singapore Art Museum).*

Baet Yeok Kwan, *Untitled (door),* 1988, *mixed media, 183 x 183 cm (Singapore Art Museum).*

CROSS-CULTURAL CINEMA

At the close of the 20th century, Chinese cinema and those working in it broke out of the boundaries of the Chinese-speaking world. The change was dramatic. Even at the beginning of the 1990s, Westerners would have been hard pressed to name a Chinese film-maker or actor, with the possible exception of kung fu cult hero Bruce Lee. In Hollywood, world Mecca of film, Asian roles had remained largely stereotyped or negligible since the early days of silent film. Today, such names as Jackie Chan (the leading actor of 'Rumble in the Bronx') and Gong Li (the leading actress of 'Raise the Red Lantern'), who are still based in Asia; and John Woo (director of 'Broken Arrow') and Ang Lee (director of 'Wedding Banquet'), who are based abroad, have become not only familiar but box office draws in North America and Europe.

Several factors have contributed to this trend. To take first the non-Chinese side of the story, three may be identified. First, rapidly increased travel and trade as well as the incursion of a 'world media' (particularly through film, television, music and advertising) to all corners of the globe, has served to breach cultural borders. The growing cultural pluralism of modern society – and the recognition of such plurality – has opened up perspectives on minority groups, be they feminists, gays or ethnic minorities. In fact, Ang Lee's first major hit, 'The Wedding Banquet', a social comedy wherein a Chinese yuppie in New York has to hide his homosexuality and live-in Caucasian boyfriend from visiting parents, played right into this pluralism. This counter-stereotyped and cleverly constructed film delighted a European audience, winning it the Berlin Film Festival's top prize. It was later hailed by *Variety*, the important American trade publication, as being 'the most profitable film in the world in 1993' (that is, profitable as a percentage of production costs).

The second factor has been changing demographics. Immigration has increased Asian populations in the West, creating both a larger audience for Asian films there, as well as new subject matter for film-makers. Witness the Chinese–American themes in such films as Wayne Wang's 'Chan Is Missing,' Peter Wang's 'A Great Wall' and 'The Joy Luck Club' (adapted from Amy Tan's best-selling novel).

Thirdly, the emergence of China, long a source of fascination and curiosity to Westerners, has resulted in a new valuation of things Chinese. In 1984 Chen Kaige's 'Yellow Earth' proved the international debut of the post-Cultural Revolution Chinese film-makers, announcing the arrival of the New Chinese Cinema. Subsequent films such as Zhang Yimou's 'Raise the Red Lantern' and Chen Kaige's 'Farewell My Concubine' intrigued foreign audiences hungry to glimpse the inner workings of a culture long cut off from the world and now entering the 20th century in fits and starts.

Related to that is the West's incessant appetite for novelty and trendiness. In recent decades, for example, Western cinephiles have been successively enamoured of French New Wave films, Japanese films and Australian films. The 1990s seemed the decade of the Chinese film, with Chinese films *de rigueur* at film festivals from Venice to Vancouver, and often picking up prizes where prizes are given out. Furthermore, when certain mainland China films were banned domestically, such controversy made these films all the more alluring for foreigners. Of course, these films have been promoted not only for their educational or political value: they are also making money. Often produced on low budgets, they can reap great financial rewards when internationally appealing and marketed correctly.

Meanwhile, in Asia, the Chinese side of the story has revolved around other factors. First, the rapid economic growth of the East Asia region has created both affluence and an expanded sense of opportunity – that is, both the means and the yearning for creative pursuits. Since the 1970s, a number of Chinese youths from Hong Kong and Taiwan have gone abroad to study film, particularly in the US and London. Ang Lee and Terence Chang, the producer of John Woo's films, trained at New York University; Hong Kong directors Ann Hui ('Boat People,' 'Summer Snow') and Yim Ho ('The Day the Sun Turned Cold') studied at the London Film School; actress Vivian Wu ('The Pillow Book,' 'The Soong Sisters') has taken acting workshops in Los Angeles.

Secondly, political censorship of varying degrees at home has pushed film-makers to seek both funding and distribution elsewhere. In the People's Republic of China films must be submitted for official approval from scripting to final cut, and many a finished movie has been banned there for broadly defined offences of subversion, indecency and so on. The doors opened in China are also escape hatches for artists, though what they seek is often not so much freedom of creative expression as opportunity.

The film industries of China, Hong Kong, and Taiwan face shrinking domestic demand for their films as well as limited distribution abroad. By contrast, the opportunities for working abroad are plentiful. More than ever, film is an international business which plucks talent from the world over to make one motion picture. Thus, in the 1990s directors like the Vietnam-born, American-educated and Hong Kong-based Tsui Hark were chosen to shoot films with international action star Jean Claude Van Damme in North America and Europe. Hong Kong's Ronny Yu, who has migrated to Australia, was tapped by an American-based film company to direct an action fantasy, 'Warriors of Virtue,' that was shot in Beijing and Vancouver. The cast was American and Chinese. The Malaysian-born, British-educated and Hong Kong-based Michelle Yeoh became what one headline (*Far Eastern Economic Review*, January 1, 1998) called '007's New Knockout' when she played the Bond girl in the James Bond feature 'Tomorrow Never Dies.' Similarly, the British-raised but Hong Kong-based Maggie Cheung has moved into cross-cultural cinema, appearing in the French film 'Irma Vep' and with the British actor Jeremy Irons in 'The Chinese Box.'

All these factors, inseparable in reality, have helped to internationalize Chinese working in cinema. Many Chinese film-makers and actors are turning overseas for their future, with the United States a favoured destination. Obviously, they have differing experiences of transition, but their paths have parallels. Usually the launch of an American career comes slowly and gradually, and the migrants have to overcome language barriers, disparate acting and film-making techniques, as well as very real cultural differences in working with people in an intensely people-oriented business. While obviously adaptation to all these elements is the key to working successfully in the new environment, the individual must also offer something unique to producers and casting directors in an intensely competitive business.

(Left, top to bottom) Bruce Lee movie screens in Singapore; 'The Wedding Banquet,' a hit with Western audiences; Jackie Chan in one of his movie stunts. (Facing page, clockwise) Terence Chang; Vivian Wu; Michelle Yeoh; John Woo. (Facing page, centre) Ang Lee directing 'Sense and Sensibility.'

Some come, stay a year or so but fail to make a go of it in America, then return to Asia to restart their careers. This was the case with Chen Kaige and actress Lin Ching Hsia ('Peking Opera Blues,' 'Swordsman II'). Others come and stay, such as Shanghai-born actresses Joan Chen ('The Last Emperor,' 'Heaven and Earth') and Vivian Wu. Still others come but have not had much luck breaking into the system – examples include the legendary directors King Hu ('Dragon Gate Inn,' 'Touch of Zen') from Taiwan and Wu Tianming ('Old Well') from China. The age factor must be noted here as both Hu and Wu belong to an older generation and began their film careers in the 1960s. Also, there are far fewer opportunities for directors than for actors – a feature film has a cast of many but only one director. Professionally, the first hurdle has been language. Even though Wu Tianming has been in the United States since 1989, he could not get a single film made until he went back to China in 1995. By all accounts, English was a problem for him, and the film-making system was overly complex compared to the studio system he knew in China.

Language was not a problem for Terence Chang, who had studied English in his hometown of Hong Kong. He went to the US to study in 1968, then returned to Hong Kong in 1978 for a jump-start on a film career. At that time Hong Kong needed young talent, and he quickly landed a job with the company Golden Harvest. Later, he hopscotched through several production and marketing positions in television and film companies before entering a partnership with director John Woo in 1990. Producing such bullet-drenched, cops-and-gangsters action films as 'The Killer' and 'Hard-boiled,' both international cult hits, gained him notice abroad. Chang could see the possibility of working elsewhere, and in 1990 he emigrated to Canada (he became a citizen in February 1995).

Because of language, John Woo was initially frustrated by not being able to follow meetings with Hollywood executives, then later determined to study English when he became serious about making an American film. At first he was offered mostly low-budget action films to helm. Then Universal Pictures offered him what was a 'reasonable' budget at the time – US$20 million – to direct 'Hard Target' with Jean Claude Van Damme in the US. He became the first Chinese director to do a major studio film – and a non-Chinese film at that – and its success made him one of the hottest directors around, sought after by the likes of A-list actors Sylvester Stallone and Sharon Stone.

However, all has not been smooth sailing. Chang cites cultural differences in working. When he was working in Hong Kong, 'All the energy was about making that film, but here producing involves a lot of bullshit. People here have huge egos.' While the major American studios offer huge production and promotion budgets, they also have an entrenched bureaucracy which must be placated.

Ang Lee, too, faced work style differences while directing the screen adaptation of Jane Austen's classic of 18th-century British manners and mores, 'Sense and Sensibility,' for Columbia Pictures. His first three projects had been independent films made on small budgets provided by Central Motion Pictures of Taiwan and featured largely Chinese casts. In preparation for the British film, he studied the period closely and was helped by a highly professional British cast and crew and historical consultants.

Emma Thompson, lead actress and also scriptwriter, suggests in her published diary that at first there were frictions between cast and director, who was initially put off by their suggestions. 'Here, making movies takes a lot of discussion,' Lee observed during an interview on the film set in England. 'In Chinese movies you just tell people what to do. Nobody questions, they just do it. Here – actors, camera crew, art department – everyone gets involved. You have to verbalize, and there's more collaboration.' The movie won seven Academy Award nominations in 1996, though none for the director.

Chinese actors and actresses seeking work in North America have similar adjustments to make, though with variations. Some arrive with romantic notions fuelled by Hollywood mythology. As a child in Shanghai, for example, Vivian Wu imagined Hollywood as a kind of enclosed fairyland with palm trees and a gigantic main gate. When she arrived she was disappointed to find that there was no fairyland, no gate, just the uncontrolled urban sprawl of Los Angeles.

Wu played the lead in Peter Greenaway's avant-garde meditation on love, death, and calligraphy, 'The Pillow Book.' Incredibly enough, in all these years she has never, unusually for a Chinese actress in America, been asked to play a prostitute. Contrast that with the slew of stereotyped China Doll/Dragon Lady parts that Joan Chen, who is only a few years older and broke into Hollywood in the 1980s, had to take on to survive in the system. The lack of role choices has driven Chen to directing her own feature project.

Obviously, few creative people want to be limited to ethnic labels. Major barriers were broken in 1995 when John Woo made the blockbuster action thriller 'Broken Arrow,' starring John Travolta, and Ang Lee made 'Sense and Sensibility.' In the same year the Hong Kong-born but US-based director Wayne Wang went one step further and worked with the American author Paul Auster in producing two quirky, independent films depicting the goings-on at a Brooklyn tobacco store, 'Smoke' and 'Blue in the Face.' The central character in both was the owner of a store (Harvey Keitel), and the people who revolve around him are an idiosyncratic collection of neighbourhood chums and customers – as far from China or Chinatown as one can get. Both films were warmly received by the critics, impressed by their slice-of-life quality.

Scarlet Cheng

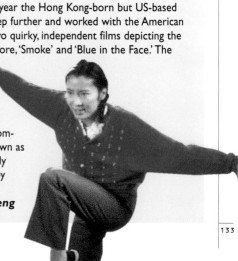

CONTEMPORARY ÉMIGRÉ WRITERS

This article confines itself to poetry and fiction written by overseas Chinese in Chinese or the language of their adopted country, pre-eminently English. As autobiographical or non-fiction works fall outside its scope, it does not consider published émigré writers like Jung Chang (British-Chinese author of the spectacularly successful *Wild Swans*), Liu Binyan (a US resident who produced some of the best reportage of the post-Mao period), or Lynn Pan (British-Chinese author of *Sons of the Yellow Emperor* and other books).

WRITING IN CHINESE

Two groups linked by their common experience of expatriation may be distinguished: writers who left the Chinese mainland during the liberalizations of the 1980s, many of them centred around the magazine *Today* (*Jintian*) and acquainted with each other; and an earlier generation of writers who ended up in America via the territories 'in between,' namely Taiwan and Hong Kong.

Originally published in China, *Today* was relaunched in 1990, still in the Chinese language, but with its office in Stockholm, Sweden. Its initial intention was simply to provide an outlet for Chinese émigré writers and a potential focus, as the academic Gregory Lee puts it in 1993, for a 'free association of writers for whom not conformity but a human and humanizing culture for China would be the aim.' But it became much less of an émigré magazine when, later, it decided to include material from writers based in China.

Many of those writing from outside China may be identified with the condition of exile. Exile has its terrors, especially if it is exile from one's own language, but it also provides writers with what may prove a necessary distance from their native culture. With this comes the possibility of greater self-consciousness in relation to one's profession, and a more universal perspective on literary art. If there is an exile literature (*liuwang wenxue*, as the Chinese call it), then its most conspicuous practitioner is the poet Yang Lian – though he himself resents the term *liuwang*, 'exile,' preferring *piaobo* (or 'floating') instead. Yang acquired New Zealand nationality when he was living there, but he is now settled in Britain, where he continues his grand poetic projects, the rediscovery of universal poetic values through the individual's exploration of tradition.

One of the founders of *Today*, Bei Dao, is an acknowledged leading voice of his generation, fantastically popular with Chinese readers in the 1980s. The figurehead of the so-called 'Misty' group of poets who pioneered a language of individual, sometimes obscure, modernist imagery, he was exiled in Britain and now lives in America. Expatriation marked a new path for Duoduo, a poet and short story writer who left China in 1989 and now lives in the Netherlands with Canadian citizenship, but only after he had put what he called his 'exile phase'

behind him. On the other hand, for Gu Cheng, an other-worldly poet, foreign residence in New Zealand was brought to a shockingly tragic end when he died aged 37 by his own hand in 1993.

Other well-known émigré voices published in *Today* include the playwright Gao Xingjian (resident in France), the author of an important novel, something of a Chinese *Magic Mountain*, *Ling shan*; the fiction writer Liu Suola (previously a resident of Britain, now of the US), who is representative of a type of writing new to China, one reminiscent of punk in Western popular culture; and A Cheng (now in the US), a fine storyteller of the 'lost' Cultural Revolution generation who achieved his greatest popularity with the publication of *Three Kings* (*San wang*), novellas which spell human depths out of quiet, simple narratives.

The earlier generation of writers arrived in America at a time, from the 1950s to the 1970s, when it was more or less politically impossible for the English-speaking world to receive Chinese literary figures from anywhere other than Taiwan or Hong Kong. These writers' inclination was generally homewards, China-wards, harkening back longingly to particular places of origin or 'golden' times in the modern, Republican period. In the short stories of the China-born but Taiwan-raised Bai Xianyong, for example, a past of real or imagined glory lives on in the characters, haunting them. Openly gay, Bai wrote his first novel, *Niezi* (*Crystal Boys*), about a group of homosexuals in Taiwan, after emigrating to the United States.

Fiction-writing seemed to dry up for the finest novelist of her generation, Zhang Ailing (Eileen Chang), whose literary career continued in Hong Kong but whose most important work was done before she left Shanghai. After moving to the US, she turned away from fiction and became famous for her reclusiveness, a symbol perhaps of the ultimate effects of displacement. In her last home in Los Angeles, she holed herself up in an isolation so complete that, when she died in 1995, it was a week before anyone discovered her. Breaking in, the police found an apartment with neither table, desk nor even bed.

Unlike Zhang Ailing, the US-based Nie Hualing produced her best work (*Sangqing yu Taohong*, about an illegal immigrant with a split personality) after she left Taiwan. Yu Lihua, who was born in Shanghai and educated in Taiwan and the United States, now her permanent home, has also created displaced, immigrant Chinese characters in her fiction – such as in her novel *You jian zonglü, you jian zonglü* (*To See the Palm Tree Again, To See the Palm Tree Again*); indeed she is said to be a spokesperson for what has been called the 'Rootless Generation.'

Published in Hong Kong, Taiwan and increasingly in China, works in Chinese by writers settled in the West can only be known to those amongst whom they live through translation. English is the language into which a writer in Chinese has to be translated if he is to acquire international recognition. Chinese admits one to its own symbolic world of meaning; English, to a universe of meaning whose reach is increasingly global. Yet not many writers are well-served by their translators; non-Chinese readers have

to take it on faith, for example, that Zhang Ailing was a fine writer, since none of her works available in English reveals anything of the quality of her Chinese. Even good translations find it hard to reach an audience beyond the specialist circles of Western sinologists and academics. If the translations do see the light of day, it is usually thanks to the academic or specialist press rather than to a general, trade imprint. Among émigré writers, one who has broken through into 'mainstream' publishing is the British-based Hong Ying, whose novel (described by an English reviewer as a 'candid, carnal little tale' unfolding in the shadow of the Tiananmen Square killings) was brought out in an English translation entitled *Summer of Betrayal* in 1997 by the British publishing house Bloomsbury.

WRITING IN NON-CHINESE LANGUAGES

Reference is made elsewhere in this volume to the body of Peranakan literature produced in Malay by Chinese acculturated to Indonesian society. We are told by the scholar Claudine Salmon that the number of literary works in Malay written by Chinese between the 19th century and early 1960s is larger than that by indigenous Indonesians. Few Chinese wrote as prolifically in the language of their adopted country as the Java-born Kwee Tek Hoay (1886–1951), whose work spans a wide array of genres, including one he is said to have pioneered himself, that of the 'occult novel.' The occult elements are there, moreover, not only because they interested him but because they appealed to his readers.

Inevitably, the best-known of those expressing themselves in the language of their adopted country are those writing in English. The reputations of writers such as Timothy Mo in Britain (*Sour Sweet*), and Maxine Hong Kingston (*The Woman Warrior*) and Amy Tan in America, are not, in theory, founded on their 'Chineseness' but on their accomplishments as novelists, as stylists in English. Nonetheless their books tackle Chinese themes. While Tan's novels focus on the Chinese family, its special histories and its particular engagements and disengagements with modern Western society, Hong Kingston, who also implicates Chinese family histories, provides a window onto the world of Chinese mythology and fantasy. Hong Kingston is more self-consciously literary and intellectual, but is still caught up within her own myths of Chinese identity. Timothy Mo's subjects too have included the position of Chinese immigrants in Western society, Chinese family life and social relations and, in *An Insular Possession*, Chinese history and its clashes with imperialism.

A newer writer is Fae Myenne Ng (*Bone*), who was selected as one of the 'best of young American novelists' by the highly regarded publication *Granta*. Ng seems still to be bound to her own and her family's immigrant experiences, and one reason her work finds an audience is that it is read, not simply as literature, but because it offers to tell Western readers something about the strangely attractive and exotic culture of China, once distant but now brought closer by the immigrant presence. This is the kind of thing Edward Said is analyzing in his book *Orientalism* ('Orientalism' is a discourse of an exoticized 'Other' that influences the way the West perceives the

(Clockwise from bottom left) Bai Xianyong, Eileen Chang, Hong Ying, Timothy Mo and Maxine Hong Kingston.

non-Western world). Even the popular Canadian-Chinese Emily Lau (*Runaway: Diary of a Street Kid*), whose searching fiction and confessional poetry on contemporary Western street life and sexuality bear no relation to China, has had her work presented as 'Chinese.'

The complex relationship which writers of Chinese origin have with their Western audiences is pointed up by the meeting of Hong Kingston and Bei Dao at an international literary festival in Britain in 1995. Typically, such a meeting will be programmed as an occasion for reading 'Chinese writing' in a public context, to give it a wider recognition, as well as to try and probe identity issues that trouble contemporary Western literary culture. Ironically, despite the way such encounters are framed, the audience of a literary festival is supposed to focus on *literary* values. How is this possible? At the present time, it simply doesn't happen. Chinese writing is still sold to its Western readers first as 'Chinese' and then as 'writing.'

In the case of this meeting, what does 'Chinese' mean? Consider the sharp differences between Hong Kingston and Bei Dao. One writes in her first language, English, and her books come to life as works of English literature. The other was raised in northern China and came to maturity during the Cultural Revolution. He now lives permanently abroad but, although widely translated, he continues to compose poetry in Chinese with little regard for Western literary fashion. The two are brought together as 'Chinese writers,' but they demonstrate clearly that their 'being Chinese' is much less meaningful than what they do share: their profession of literature and the recognition of their literary accomplishments, which have a real potential to reach out of their specific cultures and touch readers everywhere.

John Cayley

PART V

COMMUNITIES

CHINESE ARE SETTLED in more communities than are surveyed in this section, but the ones presented are here either because they are – or used to be – sizeable (in terms of absolute number or as a proportion of the total national population) or because they have attracted scholarly study by anthropologists and historians. These include communities which have since dwindled or dispersed. The word 'community' is used in the sense of a body of people living in a specific locality, without any suggestion that the inhabitants have to be of a minimum number or that they should have anything in common other than their Chinese ancestry. Indeed, far from being unified or integrated communities, all of this section's entries are highly divided internally.

The articles are grouped by region and arranged country by country except where it makes sense to adopt a unit of treatment greater than that of the nation-state. There is no perfect way of dividing the clusters of Chinese overseas, and to do so in nation-bound components is merely to follow academic research convention and work with ready-made categories.

The gates to San Francisco's Chinatown lead to a concentration of Chinese settlement, an ethnic quarter of the kind found in Chinese communities the world over. In the image of Chinatown many immigrant themes coalesce: landfall, ghettoization, sojourning, ethnic trading, generational change and cultural maintenance.

BRUNEI

Two historical relics attest to Brunei's early contacts with China. The first is a Chinese tombstone unearthed in Brunei in 1972. Dating from 1264, the stone marked the grave of an official (possibly a Muslim, in the opinion of a scholar who studied it, Wolfgang Franke) from the Fujian port of Quanzhou. The second is a tomb, discovered in 1958 in the Chinese city of Nanjing, of a king of Brunei who travelled to China with his family and who died there shortly after his arrival. The king, Maharaja Karna, had gone to China to pay homage to the Yongle emperor, who was gratified enough to write a poem and inscription praising his loyalty. The restored tomb in the Yuhuatai area of Nanjing is approached through a Spirit Way guarded by stone carvings of men and animals.

As a tributary of Ming China, the port-state of Brunei, on the island of Borneo, enjoyed much commercial consequence gathering tropical merchandise for despatch to China and selling Chinese goods to the region's traders. According to one legend, the royal family in Brunei originated in the marriage of a sultan and a Chinese princess. Another legend traces the ancestry of the Dusun indigenes of what is today's Sabah to the union of a Brunei princess and a local Chinese ruler.

Brunei's consequence did not survive European incursion, however. Parts of its territory were lost to James Brooke (see Part V: Malaysia) and Britain in the 19th century, and between 1888 and 1906 the sultanate came under increasing British protection. Today it is a fraction of its former self. A fully independent state since 1984, its chief claim on international attention has been its oil wealth and the reputation its reigning sultan enjoys as the richest man in the world. Of the country's ethnic groups, Muslim Malays predominate (at well over 60 per cent of the population), followed by Chinese (at 15 per cent).

Chinese settlement

During Brunei's golden age in the first half of the 16th century, a resident Chinese community conducted trade between China and Southeast Asia. Brunei's gold, pepper and other spices no doubt accounted for the large Chinese community settled there in the 1600s, until local disorder drove away both Chinese junks and settlers in the latter part of that century. However, Chinese were once again established there in the early part of the 1700s, building junks and planting the pepper on which Brunei chiefly relied for its revenue throughout that century.

The first population census shows that there were 736 Chinese in 1911 (see table 5.1). By the 1920s, the number had nearly doubled. A contemporary account, Peter Blundell's *The City of Many Waters* (1923), portrays the Chinese trader of the time in a familiar guise: 'The Malay cuts down the sago palms in the swamps, brings the trunks up to Brunei, rasps them into powder, and treads and washes out the raw sago for shipment to Singapore. The Chinese advances the money while he is doing his work, takes over the sago in exchange, and reaps the profits on the sale.'

It was with the discovery and exploitation of oil in 1929 that Chinese immigration steepened, the rate of population increase rising by more than 200 per cent in 1931–47. During this period many technically qualified Chinese from Sarawak, Singapore and Hong Kong came to Brunei to take up jobs in the oil industry. Other Chinese settlers pursued agriculture in rural areas. Immigration continued to rise in the post-World War II period, spurred by the employment opportunities created by Brunei's quickened development and infrastructure construction. While absolute numbers were no match for those of countries like Malaysia and Thailand, in terms of proportion the Chinese were as much as a fifth of Brunei's small population in 1947–81.

Thereafter arrivals slowed, their decline particularly marked in 1981–91. Closer examination reveals that in 1991 almost half the Chinese were temporary residents with one- to three-year work permits – upon whose expiry the holders were required to leave the country. Out of the 52 per cent that were permanent residents, only 23 per cent were citizens. The remaining 29 per cent did not possess Brunei nationality, to qualify for which aliens have to have had 20 years' residence in Brunei and to pass Malay language tests. Some Chinese thus became re-migrants, moving to Australia and Canada.

Map 5.1

Table 5.1

BRUNEI'S CHINESE POPULATION			
	NUMBER	INCREASE	% INCREASE	% OF TOTAL
1911	736	–	–	3.4
1921	1,423	687	93.3	5.6
1931	2,683	1,260	88.5	8.9
1947	8,300	5,617	209.4	20.4
1960	21,795	13,495	162.6	26.0
1971	31,925	10,130	46.5	23.4
1981	39,461	7,536	23.6	20.5
1991	40,621	1,160	2.9	15.6
1995	45,800	5,179	12.7	15.5

Sources: Population censuses, 1981 and 1991; Brunei Darussalam Key Indicators, 1995/96.

Table 5.2

GEOGRAPHICAL DISTRIBUTION OF CHINESE POPULATION						
DISTRICT	1960	%	1991	%	1995	%
Brunei/Muara	6,476	29.7	24,300	59.8	27,600	60.9
Belait	14,149	64.9	13,739	33.8	14,900	32.9
Tutong	881	4.0	2,080	5.1	2,300	5.1
Temburong	289	1.3	502	1.2	500	1.1
Total	21,795	100	40,621	100	45,300	100

Sources: Population censuses and estimates.

Chinese are concentrated mainly in the Brunei–Muara district, the centre of government, business and commerce; and in the Belait district, where the oilfields are (see table 5.2). Belait's Chinese population has waned since the 1950s and 1960s, owing possibly to the re-migration of its residents, many of them employees of the oil industry, to judge by the industry's loss of technically qualified Chinese staff in the 1990s.

The preference of overseas Chinese for urban residence is particularly marked in Brunei, with 82 per cent living in towns and cities (in 1991), the bulk of them in Bandar Seri Begawan, Kuala Belait, Seria and Tutong.

Community life

The Chinese community is made up of Hokkiens, particularly those from Quemoy (Jinmen), Cantonese, Hakkas, Hainanese, Teochius, Henghua (Xinghua) and others. There is a degree of territorial separation among these groups, with Quemoy Hokkiens concentrated in the capital, and Hakkas, Cantonese and Hainanese in Belait District. The diverse origins of the community are reflected in the range of place-of-origin associations: the Belait District Hainanese Association, the Brunei Hainan Huiguan, the Belait District Fuzhou Association, the Belait District Hakka Association, the Brunei Guangdong–Huizhou–Zhaoqing Association, the Brunei Dabu Association (*tongxianghui*) and the Chinese Taipei Sojourners Society. These associations were not directly responsible for establishing the eight Chinese-language schools (five primary and three secondary) Brunei boasts today, but they make annual donations to the schools, and many of their office bearers sit on the schools' boards of directors.

Other organizations started by Chinese concern themselves with charity, mutual aid and welfare, religion, recreation and sport. In addition, there are a number of associations based on common type of work; notable among these is the Chinese Engineering Association in Kuala Belait. Established in 1930 and now housed in its own building, it has served the interests of its members by, among other things, seeking price reductions in building materials and appealing to the government to ease restrictions on the import of labour. While community service is not its rationale, it has nonetheless supported educational and charitable causes.

An important focus of religious life has been the Buddhist Tengyun Temple, built by Quemoy Hokkiens in 1918. Before that date religious festivals were marked by regional opera performances on a makeshift stage. When the temple was rebuilt and expanded in 1960, donations from Chinese in Sarawak and British North Borneo (today's Sabah) supplemented local funding.

Economic profile

In the early years of the 20th century, Chinese lived either by agriculture or by running small businesses. In the 1960s, when Brunei stepped up its infrastructural development, the range of Chinese occupations widened with the influx of engineers, technicians, mechanics, professionals, sales personnel, and construction workers and managers. The distribution of Chinese by sector shows that in 1981 the largest proportion (25 per cent) worked in the construction industry, followed by the wholesale, retail, catering and hotel sector at 23 per cent. However, by 1991 the latter had become more important, accounting for 36 per cent of total Chinese employment, with construction coming second at 20 per cent. A major source of Chinese employees in the construction industry, many of them temporary residents, has been East and West Malaysia. Chinese construction companies built some of Bandar Seri Begawan's most imposing edifices: the sultan's old palace, the Brunei Museum, the Parliament building, the Supreme Court, the Omar Ali Saifuddien Mosque, the Royal Regalia Museum (formerly the Winston Churchill Memorial Building), the sports stadium and the Sheraton Hotel, among others.

What is also noteworthy is that from 1981 to 1991, the number of Chinese working in finance, insurance, property and commercial services jumped by 113 per cent. Responding to government calls in the 1980s to diversify the economy and reduce its heavy reliance on oil and natural gas production, Chinese have additionally branched out into manufacturing.

Their small size notwithstanding, Chinese have contributed significantly to Brunei's prosperity. In recognition of this, the sultan has bestowed titles on a number of community leaders. At a ceremony in May 1996, for example, five Chinese – Lim Teck Hoo, Pang Boon Ting, Ng Teck Hock, Onn Siew Siong and Lim Jock Seng – were so honoured, awarded titles such as Pehin Datu Temenggong, Pehin Kapitan China Kornia Diraja and Pehin Orang Kaya Pekerma Dewa.

Niew Shong Tong

Inside a Chinese home in Brunei.

BURMA (MYANMAR)

Burmese call the Chinese who live among them *paukphaw*, or 'next of kin.' This implies some recognition of blood affinity, and closeness of a kind is certainly inevitable given the geographical proximity of Burma and China, between which runs a common land border of 2,171 kilometres.

Across that border, between the neighbouring Chinese province of Yunnan and the northeastern parts of Burma, have flowed streams of trade and people since early times. The existence of that frontier, no less than its ambiguity, has given a special cast to the history of the Chinese in Burma. Overland border crossings, inextricably linked to the caravan trade along the highways between Yunnan and Bhamo, gave rise to the seasonal migration and settlement of the Mountain Chinese – so called to distinguish them from the later arrivals by sea, the Maritime Chinese from Guangdong and Fujian.

Table 5.3

CHINESE POPULATION IN BURMA (THOUSANDS)						
YEAR	1931	1941	1953	1961	1973	1983
Total	14,670	16,824	19,100	21,530	28,921	35,307
Chinese	194a	—	300 b	350	227	234
Chinese as % of total	1.3	—	1.6	1.6	0.8	0.7

a) About 54 per cent born in Burma.
b) Influx of Kuomintang troops fleeing Yunnan accounts for much of the sharp rise. In 1950 half the population lived in and around the Irrawaddy Delta. The breakdown by speech was roughly 40 per cent Hokkien, 25 per cent Cantonese, 20 per cent Yunnanese, 8 per cent Hakka and 3 per cent Hainanese.

Table 5.4

NUMBER OF CHINESE REGISTERED AS FOREIGNERS COMPARED WITH INDIANS						
YEAR	1961	1970	1975	1981	1991	1994
Chinese	81,766	128,052	114,666	99,296	70,558	57,785
Indians	108,738	81,301	58,740	55,840	40,956	36,590
Total	226,753	253,285	179,863	186,786	131,883	113,718

Further reflecting the diversity of the Chinese population are the so-called Kokang Chinese, the Panthays and the regiments of beaten Kuomintang soldiers who, cut off from the main force that had left the Chinese mainland for Taiwan, streamed south from Yunnan into the hills of northeastern Burma in the 1950s (see boxes pp 141 and 142). Kokang and Yunnanese Chinese are said to account for about 30 to 40 per cent of all Chinese in Burma in the 1990s.

Local Burmans have also distinguished between *Leto* (literally 'short sleeve') and *Letshe* ('long sleeve') Chinese, the one a rubric for coolies, carpenters and farmers; the other, for traders, bankers and brokers. The distinction by occupation is also a distinction by regional origin: *Leto* Chinese are by and large from Guangdong, while *Letshe* Chinese are chiefly Fujianese.

In the absence of reliable statistics, it is hard to say how many people of Chinese descent are to be found in Burma today. Estimates vary from 1 to 2 or 3 per cent of a total population of 45 million. Under the country's draconian laws, full citizenship is granted only to those who can prove that their families were living in Burma before the outbreak of the first Anglo-Burmese War in 1824. Others have to apply for a special Foreigners' Registration Card, which entitles the holder to live in the country but not to enjoy equal rights with 'indigenous' peoples – Burmans, Karens, Kachins, Shans, Mons, Karennis and Chins. The way around this is obviously to buy citizenship papers, which many have done.

Historical profile

The first Chinese to settle in Burma were jade merchants who arrived several centuries ago in the hills near Hpakan in today's Kachin State in the far north of the country, the world's only source of the green, imperial jade so prized by Chinese. Old Amarapura near Mandalay has the ruins of a Chinese temple bearing the names

Map 5.2

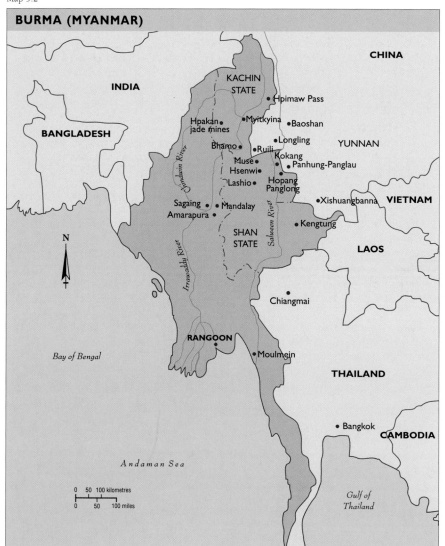

BURMA (MYANMAR)

CHINA

INDIA

KACHIN STATE

Hpimaw Pass

Hpakan jade mines • Myitkyina • Baoshan

BANGLADESH

Bhamo • Ruili • Longling YUNNAN

Muse • Kokang

Hsenwi • Panhung-Panglau

Lashio • Hopang Panglong

Sagaing • Mandalay

Amarapura • Xishuangbanna VIETNAM

• Kengtung

SHAN STATE

LAOS

Chingmai

RANGOON

Bay of Bengal • Moulmein

THAILAND

• Bangkok

CAMBODIA

Andaman Sea

Gulf of Thailand

Chindwin River

Irrawaddy River

Salween River

N

0 50 100 kilometres
0 50 100 miles

of 5,000 prominent jade-seeking Chinese merchants who perished in Burma during the 19th century alone.

While Chinese migration from Yunnan forms part of the history of the caravan trade, the movement of Hokkien and Cantonese speakers by way of Singapore and other ports paralleled the migration of Chinese across the whole of Southeast Asia.

The first Cantonese merchant in the old, pre-British royal capital of Mandalay arrived in 1861 by way of Singapore. But Chinese immigration only got into its stride with the extension of the British Raj over the whole of Burma by 1895. The British already held the port city of Rangoon (now Yangon), and once they succeeded in annexing the Burmese kingdom of Mandalay to British India, the way was open for large-scale immigration by sea via the Straits Settlements.

Nearly all the Cantonese and Hokkien immigrants settled in the urban areas. But the Chinese were never as numerous, nor as poor, as the hundreds of thousands of Indians brought in by the British to work as coolies, stevedores, rickshaw-wallahs, gardeners and watchmen. Before World War II, Rangoon's population was 45 per cent Indian. Indeed the city was dominated by Indians, Chinese and Europeans, while the Burmese themselves lived mostly in the countryside or in up-country towns.

Among the Chinese, speech divisions and occupations overlapped: the Cantonese were carpenters, shoemakers and skilled artisans, while the Hokkiens ran shops and small businesses. According to the 1931 census, the occupational breakdown of the Chinese was as follows: traders and merchants, 41 per cent; carpenters and workers in metal and leather, 38 per cent; semi-skilled workers, 9 per cent; and agriculture and forestry, 6 per cent. Almost no town or city was without its Chinese general merchandise store.

Anti-Chinese sentiments prevailed in the 1930s, though Burmese nationalist activity and violence were targetted at Indians rather than Chinese. If the early independence movement campaigned against the British, it fought still more fiercely against Indian moneylenders and Indians working in the colonial administration. As a much smaller minority, the Chinese did not arouse such fear and ill-feeling, even though many were wealthy and the nationalist movement had definite Marxist leanings. Chinese numbers rose quickly during the 1930s, and had reached 194,000–300,000, or 1 per cent of the total population, by the time war broke out. They had their own newspapers, schools and organizations.

They contributed greatly to the development of Rangoon, and indeed of Burma as a whole before independence. Sir Lee Ah Yain, the first Chinese to hold high office in the country, was Minister of Forests during the governorships of Sir Harcourt Butler and Sir Charles Innes. Ah Shark, a Chinese contractor who had arrived in Burma as an impoverished carpenter, built the premises of the Legislative Council as well as the barracks of the cantonment at Mingaladon, immediately to Rangoon's north. Chan Chor Khine, a rich Chinese businessman, financed a gymnasium and an open-air theatre at Rangoon University.

Following Burma's independence in 1948, the pursuit of nationalization and indigenization policies affected the Chinese less than the Indians. With the latter quitting the country in increasing numbers, a clearer field was left for Chinese shopkeepers.

In 1950, there were four Chinese-language dailies and three weeklies published in Rangoon, and well over 200 Chinese vernacular schools in Burma. As was the case in other overseas Chinese communities, both the periodicals and schools were split along pro-Beijing or pro-Taipei lines.

In 1962, following a *coup d'état* staged by General Ne Win, the army captured state power. Burma was declared a socialist state and, under the banner of 'the Burmese Way to Socialism,' the government established a system in which 23 (and later 22) military-run corporations took control of the economy. The military takeover of private enterprise led to an exodus of businessmen and merchants, most of whom were non-Burmese. More than

A villager living near the Burma-Thai border.

KOKANGESE AND PANTHAYS

Burma is unique in Southeast Asia in having not just immigrant Chinese but its own indigenous Chinese minority. These are Chinese who have ended up on the Burmese side of the border with China, in Kokang, by an accident of history.

A mountainous area in the northern Shan States, Kokang has always been a buffer zone (or link) between Yunnan and Burma. Although it remained a part of China for centuries, its location in a remote corner of Yunnan made it impossible for the central government to exercise control over the area. To the west, the deep Salween gorge formed a natural barrier between Kokang and the Shan principalities. Kokang was left alone and, over generations, grew a strong sense of independence. The area was consolidated into a single political entity by the Yang clan, to whom were given hereditary rights to rule Kokang as a vassal of the Chinese emperor.

As trade between Yunnan and British Burma flourished, some of the local Chinese chieftains in Kokang prospered. This border buffer was home to both valuable opium and reputedly the best tea in the region. For economic and strategic reasons, the British became increasingly interested in Kokang, and the area was formally incorporated into British Burma by the Anglo-Chinese Treaty of February 4, 1897, although its inhabitants were almost exclusively Chinese of Yunnanese stock.

Nevertheless, the British were no more successful than the Chinese empire before them in establishing central, governmental control over this remote region. Theirs was, at best, indirect rule through the British-advised Shan prince of Hsenwi, to whom the local, hereditary ruler of Kokang now paid tribute instead of to the Chinese emperor. Even today, the people of the area refer to themselves as 'Kokangese' or 'Kokang Chinese,' and few of the local farmers know a word of Burmese.

Related to, but distinct from, the people of Kokang are the Panthay, said to be descendants of Kublai Khan's Arab and Tartar soldiers who settled in the Dali area of western Yunnan and married local women. In 1855, the Panthays rose in rebellion against the Chinese emperor in Beijing. The fighting blocked Yunnan for nearly two decades, and it was eventually crushed with a heavy loss of life.

Tens of thousands of Yunnanese Muslims were butchered when Beijing reasserted control over the area, and many survivors migrated across the mountains into the northeastern Shan States. Speaking the same dialect as the Kokang Chinese, they settled in the vicinity, mainly in the Hopang-Panglong area immediately south of Kokang proper. Deprived of land to cultivate, the Panthays of Panglong became traders. Since their arrival there more than a century ago, they have acquired a reputation as first-class muleteers and opium smugglers. In China they are known as Hui and classified as a non-Han ethnic minority.

Early morning in Kokang.

Kuomintang base in the Shan states, 1960s.

IN THE SHADOW OF BIG-POWER RIVALRIES

Kokang and other areas along the Yunnan frontier became war zones after Chiang Kai-shek's troops were defeated and the Chinese civil war ended. Kuomintang troops separated from the main force regrouped and rebuilt their regiments there with the help of the Taiwan government and American intelligence agencies, and tried on a number of occasions to re-enter China, only to be driven back again.

For years, the Burmese army fought bitter battles in the northeast to dislodge the uninvited intruders. Success eluded the Burmese until the early 1960s. Even today, many remnants of the Kuomintang's 'secret army' remain in the area, where they have settled down as traders in towns and villages. Politically and culturally, links with Taiwan remain strong.

In the 1960s and 1970s communist China gave massive support to the Communist Party of Burma. It is probably safe to assume that what lay behind Chinese assistance – which included vast quantities of munitions as well as vehicles, uniforms, food, medicines and military advisers and other 'volunteers' – was not merely a desire to export revolution. Hardly by coincidence, when the Chinese-trained Burmese communists streamed across the border, they made straight – as their Chinese instructors had told them to – for the well-known bases of the powerful intelligence network of the Kuomintang forces along the Yunnan frontier.

The Burmese communists found radio transmitters, code books and other secret documents from Taiwan when some of the bases were captured. They also apprehended Taiwan agents and turned them over to the Chinese communist authorities across the border, where they were most probably summarily executed. Most of them had come from the Baoshan area in western Yunnan, a long-time stronghold of various Kuomintang warlords.

Among the Chinese émigrés in northern Burma was one who had become a prominent businessman as well as a staunch supporter of the Nationalist cause: Liu Binghong. The former Kuomintang mayor of Longling, near Baoshan, Liu commanded what amounted to a secret society in the small market towns between the Yunnan frontier and Lashio.

The remote mountains of northeastern Burma became the arena of little-known battles between communist and Nationalist Chinese forces, although these were not the first ones. In fact, parts of the common border had remained undemarcated throughout the British time and it was not until 1960 that tough and protracted negotiations between the governments in Rangoon and Beijing settled the matter. China recognized de facto Burmese sovereignty over areas which it had claimed in northern Kachin State, while Burma in return agreed to cede to China two small village clusters, one at Hpimaw Pass in Kachin State and the other at Panhung–Panglau in the Wa Hills. Since this border agreement was signed with the government of Beijing,

it remains unrecognized by Taipei: official maps of the Republic of China continue to mark the whole area north of Myitkyina as Chinese territory.

What was not announced, however, was that Burma had also agreed secretly to allow Chinese forces to enter Burma and attack the Kuomintang in the eastern Shan States. On January 26, 1961, three divisions of regulars from the People's Liberation Army, a total of 20,000 men, crossed the frontier between Xishuangbanna in Yunnan and Kengtung state in Burma, and swept down across the hills in waves. The campaign, code-named 'the Mekong River Operation,' broke the back of the Kuomintang in northeastern Burma. Beaten Nationalist soldiers retreated towards Thailand, where many remain in small villages along the Thai–Burmese border.

Before the operation could be completed, however, the military coup of 1962 occurred. It was the insurgent Communist Party of Burma, backed by the Chinese, that dealt the final blow to the Kuomintang's military foothold. In the process it created even sharper divisions between those Sino–Burmese who still supported the Kuomintang and those who rallied behind the pro-Beijing Communist Party of Burma.

This divide – and the curious twists of it – became especially obvious in Kokang, where the local militia commander, Luo Xinhan (who had close connections with Taiwan), now sided with the Burmese government. Another Kokang faction, led by the brothers Pheung Kya-shin (Peng Jiasheng) and Pheung Kya-fu (Peng Jiafu), received support from the Communist Party of Burma, whom they helped to take over Kokang in 1968.

The years wrought few changes to the insurgency, relations with China or the status of the Sino-Burmese community. The rebels, including the Kokang Chinese, fought on and the Chinese merchants in the urban areas made money by importing contraband consumer goods from Thailand and export-ing precious stones, jade and opium. However, as the old, hardline Maoists lost the struggle for power in Beijing to Deng Xiaoping and his fellow-reformers in the late 1970s, China began to downgrade its support of the Communist Party of Burma.

In 1989, the rank and file of the Communist Party of Burma's army mutinied and drove its ageing, Burmese Maoist leadership into exile in China. The army broke up into four local forces along ethnic lines – including one of the Kokang Chinese – and subsequently made peace with the government in Rangoon. By the terms of the ceasefire agreement, the former rebel forces are allowed to maintain their forces, control their respective areas and engage in any kind of business.

The result is that the previously closed border with Yunnan is now open for business, and an official border-trade agreement signed with Beijing. The Chinese frontier town of Ruili has been given special status as a free economic zone, and the guns are silent.

300,000 Indians and perhaps as many as 100,000 Chinese left during the years between 1963 and 1967. All Indian and Chinese schools and newspapers had to close.

The Burmese Way to Socialism spawned a huge black market, known initially as Corporation No. 24 and later as No. 23. It was Indians and Chinese who ran Corporation 24. Of the Chinese who left, many became prosperous in their new domicile. An example is the Ho family, owners of the biggest gem and jewellery empire in Southeast Asia, a symbol of whose remarkable success is the 55-storey Jewellery Trade Centre on Silom Road in Bangkok, owned by one of the sons, Henry Ho. Bangkok apart, Singapore received many Chinese departees from Burma, followed by Australia and southern California. Another outflow of Chinese occurred in 1982, when new citizenship legislation discriminating against people of foreign origin made life harder for the Chinese and many left the country to resettle in Taiwan, Hong Kong, Australia and America.

In between, there were the violent anti-Chinese riots of June 1967. Angry mobs went on a rampage through Rangoon's Chinatown. Chinese shops and homes were ransacked and looted, and many Sino-Burmese were killed. Breaking out in several cities, the riots were said to be a reaction to the reverberations of the Cultural Revolution among the China-oriented groups of Chinese in Burma. But they also came at a time when the country was facing an acute shortage of rice, and it was widely suspected that the riots were instigated by the authorities to deflect attention from their inability to deal with the crisis. The authorities did not intervene until mob violence got out of hand and even the Chinese Embassy in Rangoon was attacked.

Post-1988 developments

In 1988, anti-government demonstrations shook Burma. Conspicuous by their absence from the street protests were the urban Chinese, who, wise from their bitter experiences in the 1967 riots, chose to hang back, though most of the material support for the anti-government movement came from Chinese merchants who evidently hoped it would bring an end to the prevailing system. Success was only partial, though the new junta, the State Law and Order Restoration Council, did abolish the Burmese Way to Socialism in favour of an open, market economy.

The Chinese have taken full advantage of the turnaround, as may be seen in their strong showing in the commercial life of Rangoon (one example is the city's largest supermarket, a Chinese operation). Many of the Chinese resettlers in Thailand, Singapore and elsewhere, with contacts and perhaps relatives still in Burma, have also come back to do business.

The overall pattern of Chinese settlement in Burma remains more or less as it was. The Cantonese and the Hokkien continue to dominate the urban Chinese population in Rangoon, where most of them are engaged in both small-scale business and bigger enterprises, often in collaboration with Chinese investors from Singapore, Hong Kong and Taiwan. The Kokang Chinese, along with their Muslim Panthay cousins, continue to dominate the Yunnan border areas, but they too have been able to invest in Rangoon, Mandalay and other towns since the cease-fire came into effect in 1989.

However, a significant influx of Chinese, primarily from Yunnan, in the 1990s has threatened to upset the demographic balance in the north. When a person in Mandalay dies, his death is not reported to the authorities. Instead, that person's relatives send his identity card to a broker in Ruili or some other border town in Yunnan. There, the identification papers are sold to anyone willing to pay the price. The Chinese buyer's photo is substituted on the card, and he can then move to Mandalay as a Burmese citizen.

In this way, thousands of Yunnanese have entered towns in northern Burma, bought property and set up businesses. Their partners are often Kokang Chinese, who are bona fide citizens and, of course, speak the same dialect as the Yunnanese immigrants. The latter now pervade commercial life in Mandalay, including the trade in precious stones, jade and narcotics. The presence of almost unlimited quantities of drug money, which have to be laundered, has pushed up prices of real estate beyond the means of most ordinary Burmese. Not surprisingly, this new wave of Chinese immigration has re-ignited old anti-Chinese sentiments among many Burmese, feelings reflected in cartoons and short stories in local Mandalay publications.

But the neo-nationalist publications, which are not sanctioned by the authorities, tend to overlook the diversity of the Chinese communities in Burma. The drug-lords and noveau-riche immigrants from Yunnan represent only a small portion of a larger community whose presence goes back well over a century.

Having remained beyond the control of any central government in Rangoon, the Yunnanese are the least assimilated. The urban Sino-Burmese, especially those who have intermarried, are almost indistinguishable from other Burmese. Only a red paper streamer by the doorpost, or a family shrine on the floor inside their homes, reveals that they are not ordinary Theravada Buddhists (though their business connections still make them stand out).

The loyalties of the various communities vary. Former Kuomintang soldiers and their children, as well as many old-time merchants in market towns in the north, think of Taiwan as their homeland. The people along the common border are closer to China, where many of them have relatives, while the urban communities, especially that of Rangoon, look to Singapore not only as a place to do business, but also as a place to visit and to send their children for higher education.

Bertil Lintner

Selling to tourists in Rangoon's main market.

Trade with China thrives in Lashio.

CAMBODIA

Section of a bas-relief on the Bayon (Angkor Thom) showing a Chinese merchant sitting in his home or shop surrounded by his family and servants, early 13th century. The wooden rafters are used to hang hams and other dried goods.

Cambodia was once a harmonious 'plural society.' 'Plural society,' a concept developed by J. S. Furnivall, a British colonial officer in Burma, defines those colonial societies where class and ethnic boundaries coincide. Furnivall was thinking of places where commerce was entirely dominated by Chinese or Indian immigrants, ethnically distinct from indigenous élites and peasants. He believed that such a society could exist only if a colonial power held it together. Another student of minorities in Southeast Asia, W. F. Wertheim, suggests that ethnic conflict arises when similar economic classes exist in both ethnic groups, in direct competition with each other. This was true in early 20th-century Java, earlier in Manila, whereas Cambodian history was free of anti-Chinese incidents until 1970 – the start of 20 years of great tragedy and terror.

Early history before the French Protectorate

The historical record of relations between Cambodia and China goes back at least to the third century AD, but until the Yuan dynasty (1279–1368) contact was lim-

ited to occasional two-way official missions and a small amount of trade carried in non-Chinese ships. In 1296, one such mission brought the Chinese chronicler Zhou Daguan to Angkor city. From his account we learn of Chinese merchants and carpenters living there, some of them with children from Khmer wives (see box p 145). It is evident that some had settled down permanently and were engaged in trade with China. Chinese trade goods were mainly luxury and ritual objects, primarily for the court. In return, China imported fisher-martin fur, rhinoceros horn and beeswax.

While there may have been a few score Chinese living in the successive capitals of Angkor, significant Chinese settlement probably dates from the establishment of Phnom Penh as the capital of Cambodia in 1434. Situated at a river crossroads, Phnom Penh was a trading city *par excellence*, and it quickly attracted a heterogeneous population of Chinese, Malays, Indians, Annamese and Japanese. Chinese preponderance in trade is indicated by the adoption of Chinese measures for silver (*tael*) and grain (including the Chinese word, *dou*), and the inclusion in the Khmer language of the Cantonese numbers for multiples of ten from 30 to 90 and the Cantonese word for 10,000.

In 1606 a Portuguese visitor reported 3,000 Chinese living in Phnom Penh. At that time, the king governed the foreign communities through a system of indirect rule, appointing a leader (*chautéa*) for each – a precursor of the system later used in Vietnam by the Nguyen emperor Gia Long and adopted by the French (see below and Part V: Vietnam).

The first Chinese settlers may have been Hokkien, but two major groups of Ming patriots fleeing the victorious Manchu armies at the end of the 17th century brought Cantonese and Hainanese into the region. In 1679 General Yang Yandi led several thousand Cantonese to My Tho, later moving to Saigon-Cholon; some of these people went up the Mekong into Cambodia. About the same time, a young patriot from Hainan, Mac Cuu (Mo Jiu), settled in Cambodia, rising quickly in the feudal hierarchy to become a provincial governor of the coastal region, where he encouraged Hainanese settlement and established Cambodia's major port at Ha Tien. When Saigon eclipsed Ha Tien at the end of the 18th century, the Hainanese turned from trade to cultivating pepper. Thus, Kampot province became a major producer of pepper for European markets.

During the 19th century, these speech groups were joined by Teochiu and Hakka migrants, so that at the advent of the French Protectorate in 1864, five speech groups were present in Phnom Penh, each with its own association (*huiguan*). Hokkiens and Cantonese predominated in the city until the 20th century, but Teochius gradually outnumbered them in small centres and in the rural areas.

Map 5.3

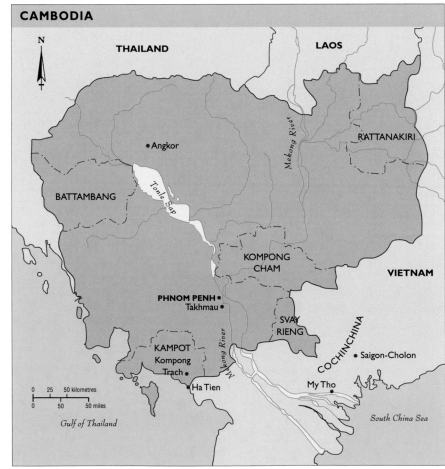

CAMBODIA

N

THAILAND

LAOS

Mekong River

•Angkor

RATTANAKIRI

Tonle Sap

BATTAMBANG

KOMPONG CHAM

VIETNAM

PHNOM PENH•
Takhmau •

SVAY RIENG

COCHINCHINA

• Saigon-Cholon

KAMPOT
Kompong Trach •

Mekong River

• Ha Tien

My Tho •

0   25   50 kilometres
0   50   50 miles

Gulf of Thailand

South China Sea

French Protectorate, 1864–1953

The advent in the mid-19th century of steam navigation and of French colonial rule in Cochinchina gave the Cantonese community in Saigon-Cholon dominance over all Cambodian trade. Previously, dried fish was the major export item, but by the beginning of the 20th century rice had taken over. No Chinese was growing rice in Cambodia then, but Chinese monopolized its trade at all levels – from the rural Teochiu storekeeper who bought it in the field, through the Hokkien and Cantonese merchants who collected and transported it, to the wealthy Cantonese millers in Cholon who sold it to the French exporters. Kampot pepper production and commerce were in the hands of Hainanese.

In 1864, King Norodom acceded to a French Protectorate over Cambodia to dispel the threat of Thai annexation. French economic priorities remained in their Vietnamese colonies, however, and they saw Cambodia primarily as a strategic buffer against rising British influence in Thailand. Consequently, Cambodia's economy was little affected by French rule, and the Chinese continued to dominate trade.

In Cochinchina, the French adopted the Nguyen emperor Gia Long's pattern of indirect rule through *huiguan*. Each speech group was defined as a *congrégation* (Chinese: *bang*), and a *chef de congrégation* (*bangzhang*) was appointed to govern it. This system was applied to Cambodia in 1891, when *congrégations* were established for the five speech groups then present: Cantonese, Hokkien, Teochiu, Hainanese and Hakka. By then, the Chinese numbered some 20,000 in Phnom Penh. Each speech group was a discrete social unit, the constituency for business relationships, marriage arrangements, voluntary associations and dealings with the French administration. Each group nominated a *chef*, who was then appointed by the *Résident-Supérieur*. Supported by French authority and the approval of the leading Chinese, the *chef* exercised considerable power, including control over immigration and emigration, business licences and movement between cities.

The *chef's* ability to frustrate any attempt to build alternative associations meant that the Chinese community structure became thoroughly hierarchical rather than competitive, distinctively different from Chinese communities elsewhere in Southeast Asia. Secret societies such as the Hongmen disappeared early in the 20th century, and the Kuomintang did not emerge until after the Sino-Japanese war. Such organizations as schools, temples and cemeteries, musical and cultural societies all fell under the direction of the *huiguan* committees. The five *huiguan* were thus corporate groups that satisfied the extra-familial needs of the Chinese community and embraced every Chinese in the country. None could escape their jurisdiction.

At the pinnacle of this arrangement was a committee of the ten *chefs* and *sous-chefs*, chaired by the Teochiu *chef* and known unofficially as the Wu Bang Gongsuo, an organization that actually predated the *congrégation* system. It met regularly to consider deportation appeals, although not with official French sanction until 1944. It also organized such pan-Chinese projects as the Chinese Hospital established in Phnom Penh in 1906, the annual celebration of Yuanxiao (see box p 146) and a reconciliation commission to settle inter-group disputes. This committee became known as the Zhonghua Huiguan and was housed in the Wu Bang Gongsuo temple.

Prior to 1920, Chinese immigrants to Cambodia were almost entirely men, many of whom married Khmer women and therefore had Sino-Khmer children. Some of the boys were sent to China for a Chinese education. Beginning in about 1923, women and children also migrated from China, drastically changing the nature of the Chinese community, especially in education. The first Chinese school in Cambodia was established in Kompong Cham in 1901, and Teochius in Phnom Penh founded a school in 1907 that became the Duanhua Middle School in 1914. With the emergence of Chinese families, however, the number of Chinese

Chinese pedlar in Phnom Penh, 1928.

EXCERPTS FROM ZHOU DAGUAN'S *NOTES ON THE CUSTOMS OF CAMBODIA*, (1296)

On Chinese immigrants:

Chinese sailors coming to the country note with pleasure that it is not necessary to wear clothes, and, since rice is easily had, women easily persuaded, houses easily run, furniture easily come by, and trade easily carried on, a great many sailors desert to take up permanent residence.

Generally speaking, the people of Cambodia are very simple. On seeing a Chinese they show him timid respect and call him 'Buddha,' throwing themselves on the ground before him and bowing low. An increasing number, however, are learning to outwit the Chinese and doing harm to a great many of our countrymen who have visited there.

My compatriot, Mr Hsieh [Xue] ... spent 35 years in this country.

On trade:

In Cambodia it is the women who take charge of trade. For this reason a Chinese, arriving in the country, loses no time in getting himself a mate, for he will find her commercial instincts a great asset.

[Chinese goods] most in demand are gold and silver; next come figured silk fabrics ... tin ware from Chen-chou [Zhenzhou], lacquered trays from Wen-chou [Wenzhou], green porcelains (celadon) from Ch'üan-chou [Quanzhou], mercury, vermilion, paper, sulphur, saltpeter, sandalwood, angelica-root, musk, linen, *huang-ts'ao* [huangcao] cloth, umbrellas, iron pots, copper trays, fresh-water pearls, tung oil, bamboo nets, basketry, wooden combs, and needles ... What the Cambodians most urgently need are beans and wheat, but export of those from China is forbidden.

On agriculture:

In fertilizing the fields and growing vegetables no use is made of (human) dung, which they look on as an impure practice. Chinese who travel to this country never mention the use of dung in China, for fear of rousing Cambodian scorn ... After visiting the privy [Cambodians] always wash themselves, using only the left hand ... When they see a Chinese cleaning himself with paper at the privy, they jeer at him and indicate their unwillingness to have him enter their homes.

On the dead:

[The Cambodians] carry the corpse outside the city to some lonely place, abandon it there, and go home after seeing that the vultures, dogs, and other beasts are coming to devour it ... There is a slowly increasing number of those resorting to cremation – mostly descendants of Chinese.

On bathing:

On days of leisure, the Chinese often treat themselves to the spectacle [of mixed nude bathing in the river]. In fact, I have heard it said that many of them enter the water to take advantage of whatever opportunity offers.

Green glaze on Khmer bottle dating from 11th to 12th century may signify Chinese influence.

schools rose rapidly to reach 95 by 1938, including two secondary schools. By 1942, each of the five *huiguan* ran a secondary school for their own speech group. Many Chinese schools were co-educational by this time.

After independence, 1953–70

For two decades (1950–70), Prince Norodom Sihanouk dominated Cambodian politics. After Cambodian independence in 1953, Sihanouk developed cordial relations with the People's Republic of China, and his domestic policies did not threaten Chinese predominance in the Cambodian economy. As in neighbouring Thailand, quite a large number of the political élite were of mixed parentage, in this case Sino-Khmer. With wealth and influence protecting and enabling the Chinese community, Chinese social organization reached its zenith during this period.

Large-scale immigration following World War II brought the number of Chinese to over 400,000 – roughly just under 10 per cent of the estimated total population – by the time immigration dried up in the early 1950s. A third lived in Phnom Penh itself, while some of the remainder were scattered in smaller towns. Over a third lived in the countryside, however, almost all of them Teochiu except for the Hainanese pepper farmers in Kampot. The rural Teochius were engaged in retail and rice trade as well as providing credit to Khmer peasants. There were also Teochiu market gardeners who grew vegetables for the urban markets.

In the cities, Chinese dominated retail, the restaurant and hotel business, export-import trade (including rice) and light industry, including food processing, soft drinks, printing and machine shops. Chinese banks emerged after the war, although French banks continued to dominate finance. A law passed in 1956 to nationalize some occupations by excluding aliens was frustrated by the fact that many Chinese had taken out Cambodian citizenship by then. The richest men during this period were Chinese of Cambodian nationality.

After independence, the *congrégation* system collapsed, as did the Wu Bang Gongsuo. A profusion of Chinese voluntary associations then emerged, including clan or same-surname associations, native-place associations (*tongxianghui*), sports and cultural clubs. The Kuomintang came briefly into prominence, especially among the Cantonese – the Cantonese school, temple and youth organizations were pro-Kuomintang groups. However, a new organization which soon became the major opposition to the Kuomintang was established among Teochiu proletarians called the Lianyou Mutual Aid Society (Lianyou Huzhu She). In 1956, when Cambodia established diplomatic relations with the People's Republic of China, Kuomintang power faded rapidly, and its leaders were continually harassed by the Cambodian police.

Chinese language and education flourished, with five daily newspapers and 170 Chinese schools providing a vehicle. Of the over 50 Chinese schools in Phnom Penh, six were 'public' in the sense that they were run by school boards responsible to the broader community. There were only three Chinese middle schools, because many Chinese families sent their children to state secondary schools to acquire literacy in Khmer. After about 1950, all Chinese schools taught in Mandarin, although Teochiu was the most commonly spoken language, and one could hear Cantonese, Hokkien, Hainanese and Hakka spoken in the streets and shops, notably by older Chinese; younger Chinese often spoke Mandarin or Khmer. The Chinese were clearly distinguished from other ethnic groups by religious ritual (temples, household shrines, funerals, burial) and by their festivals.

With many associations and competing centres of power, the Chinese community in Phnom Penh began to resemble overseas Chinese communities elsewhere in its complexity and conflicting loyalties. As the proportion of Cambodian-born Chinese grew, the five distinct speech groups that previously provided organizational diversity were now complicated by differing cultural identities. Furthermore, Cambodian nationalism competed with Chinese nationalism among Chinese, some of whom had Khmer mothers. The Cantonese enjoyed historical and ongoing connections with the Chinese community in Saigon, while wealthy Teochiu were more closely associated with families in Bangkok.

With the exception of the Kuomintang associations, Chinese associations were integrated by their cross-cutting memberships, which provided effective informal mechanisms for resolving conflicts. The Chinese Hospital Committee served as an informal executive for the entire community, its membership comprising representatives from the five *huiguan* and the Lianyou

YUANXIAO

In Cambodia, the celebration of Yuanxiao, otherwise known as the Lantern Festival, was unique in its annual Procession of the Gods (*youshen*). On the 14th and 15th day of the lunar year, a parade of 60 to 80 possessed mediums paraded with their cortèges along the river front to the Royal Palace, then snaked through the streets of the Chinese section of the city. All five of the *huiguan* temples were represented by mediums, and many others came from rural temples, both Chinese and Vietnamese. Mediums became possessed early in the afternoon and remained in a trance state until late at night, when the cortèges returned to their home temples, the idols were repositioned on their altars, and the spirits were allowed to leave their mediums for another year.

At the head of the procession were many large paper lanterns carried on long poles and shaped as fish, flowers, birds and lions. They were followed by orchestras, dragon and lion teams, opera troupes in costume, and teams of dancing girls. Then came a long string of temple cortèges, each with its idol sitting in a brightly coloured sedan chair and a possessed medium standing behind dressed in a colourful costume and surrounded by costumed attendants, dancers and musicians. The mediums flagellated themselves with spiked balls on chains or cut their tongues with sharp swords. Some mediums sat on chairs of knives or nails, others had skewers or spears through their cheeks and lips; all were bloody.

As the cortèges wound through the city streets during the evening, some stopped in front of Chinese businesses, where the mediums danced among exploding firecrackers and cut their tongues to wipe blood onto paper charms. Crowds lined the pavements, noisily joining in the celebrations, and the entire city was forced to a standstill for two evenings. This flamboyant Procession of the Gods reached its climax in 1963, after which it declined in size and support until it ended in 1968.

W. E. Willmott

Medium with spear through cheek in Yuanxiao procession, 1963.

Table 5.5

ECONOMIC CLASSES IN CAMBODIA, 1963					
ECONOMIC CLASS	CHINESE NUMBER	%	ALL CAMBODIA NUMBER	%	CHINESE AS % OF TOTAL
Peasants & fishermen	—	—	4,950,000	86.2	—
Working, of which:	64,000	15.1	209,000	3.6	30.6
industrial	24,000	5.6	54,000	0.9	44.4
commercial	30,000	7.1	42,000	0.7	71.4
rural	2,000	0.5	102,000	1.8	2.0
service*	8,000	1.9	11,000	0.2	72.7
Commercial, of which	359,000	84.5	379,000	6.6	94.7
urban	186,000	43.8	196,000	3.4	94.9
rural	173,000	40.7	183,000	3.2	94.5
Professional, civil	2,000	0.5	202,000	3.5	1.0
Total	425,000	100	5,740,000	100	7.4

Including restaurant workers.

Mutual Aid Society. This body made decisions for the Chinese community as a whole in such matters as Chinese participation in national events and the annual Yuanxiao procession.

In the smaller towns, a single speech group tended to predominate, such as the Hainanese in Kampot, the Hakka in Rattanakiri, or the Hokkien in Battambang. Most ran cemeteries and had temples, many to the god Bentougong but sometimes to a god specific to the speech group. Almost every community supported a Chinese primary school. More homogeneous and smaller, these communities were more tightly organized than in Phnom Penh, with the school committee serving as the local *huiguan* and a single leader dominating the structure. Community boundaries were not as clear-cut, however, as they experienced far more social interaction with the local Khmer population, who comprised their customers and neighbours; and many more spoke Khmer as their household language.

Chinese exploitation of the indigenous peasantry produced no anti-Chinese feeling because there were no Khmer merchants in competition with them and peasants depended on Chinese commerce and services. No less than 95 per cent of the commercial class was Chinese, and if commercial workers are included, over 90 per cent of the Chinese were involved in commerce around 1965 (see table 5.5).

When the Cultural Revolution in China began to spark radical Chinese nationalism in 1967, Sihanouk closed all the Chinese newspapers and clamped down on school curriculum. Newspapers gradually reappeared, however, and apart from swearing an oath of allegiance 'to the Prince and fatherland,' Chinese students continued their education uninterrupted.

The international situation reinforced the relatively favourable position of the Chinese. In attempting to keep Cambodia out of the Vietnam War, Sihanouk tried to balance American and Chinese influences in his country, and as the American presence grew in Vietnam, he leaned even further towards the Chinese. For the local Chinese community, this translated into official tolerance and commercial advantage. That all changed in 1970.

The Lon Nol regime, 1970–75

Taking advantage of Prince Sihanouk's absence from the country on a diplomatic mission to Europe in early 1970, General Lon Nol led a coup and established a right-wing government, cut links with China and sought help from the American and South Vietnamese governments. This had major repercussions on the Chinese, whom he neither trusted nor supported and who began to experience repression and discrimination.

Lon Nol closed Chinese schools and newspapers because they were 'spreading communist propaganda.' At this time, guerrilla forces led by the Khmer Rouge under Pol Pot had established a base in Battambang province, strengthened in 1967 by a number of urban leftists who defected from Sihanouk's government, including some radical Chinese youth. By 1970 its control had enlarged to the remote southwestern region of the country. After Lon Nol's coup, several of its leaders petitioned Sihanouk, then exiled in Beijing, to join them in a struggle against Lon Nol's government. He agreed, and together they formed the United Royal Government of Kampuchea (known as GRUNK from its French acronym), which gained the support of many patriotic Cambodians. American attempts to destroy the Khmer Rouge by carpet-bombing the Cambodian countryside only strengthened its support.

In his campaign against the growing influence of the Khmer Rouge, Lon Nol encouraged anti-Chinese sentiment by accusing Chinese of undermining Khmer culture and morality. Together with widespread and increasing economic hardship, this sparked anti-Chinese riots in Phnom Penh, Battambang and Svay Rieng, where Chinese shops were torched and several Chinese traders killed.

Such riots, unprecedented in Cambodian history, frightened Chinese into abandoning such signs of their cultural distinctiveness as community associations and language. They tried to avoid speaking Chinese, and Chinese education became an underground activity in their homes.

To control the Chinese, Lon Nol established the Federated Association of Chinese in Cambodia to replace any community structure that had previously existed. His government issued special Chinese identity cards and levied special taxes on them. In addition, wealthy Chinese were expected to contribute heavily towards campaigns for national defence.

At the same time, the massive American bombing campaign in 1970–73 destroyed the Chinese communities outside the main cities. Many Chinese temples and schools were razed, along with most other rural buildings, and Chinese joined the thousands of refugees who moved to the cities to avoid the bombs. By 1975, very few Chinese remained in the countryside apart from those radicals who had joined the Khmer Rouge guerrillas. Although some wealthy Chinese benefited financially from Lon Nol's civil war, the rapidly deteriorating urban conditions caused disease and hardship among Chinese and Khmer alike. But worse was yet to come with the advent of Democratic Kampuchea in April 1975.

The Khmer Rouge, 1970–78

In the regions controlled by the Khmer Rouge, Chinese schools at first remained open and the Chinese were not subject to special attention, either negative or positive, from the authorities. After Sihanouk joined the

Victims of the Pol Pot regime.

rebels in 1971, Overseas Chinese Associations were established in the 'liberated zones' to support the rebel government that he headed.

Without adopting any explicitly anti-Chinese policy, the communists disrupted the economic base of the rural Chinese by eliminating local markets, either through drastically reducing prices or by actually destroying the market stalls. This was another reason for most rural Chinese residents to flee to the cities, where they were also free from the American bombing.

In their policy towards the Chinese (and other ethnic minorities), the Khmer Rouge appeared to change drastically in 1974. Until then, they had emphasized the multi-ethnic nature of their support, but now their propaganda stressed the Khmer identity of the revolution and explicitly warned against other ethnic groups 'splitting' the revolutionary forces. Chinese began to experience discrimination; they fearfully hid their Chinese identity whenever possible, and Chinese associations disappeared from GRUNK areas. This mono-ethnic policy led to the extreme repression instigated after the Khmer Rouge came to power in April 1975 as Democratic Kampuchea.

It has been estimated that the Chinese population of Cambodia fell from 400,000 to 200,000 during less than four years of Democratic Kampuchea, the so-called Pol Pot regime. There is little evidence that the regime singled out the Chinese for special treatment, certainly not in its early years, but its obsessive elimination of all social inequality and all Vietnamese 'traitors' redounded tragically on the Chinese.

Faced with two million refugees in Phnom Penh without food, and ferociously committed to national self-reliance, the Khmer Rouge summarily emptied the cities into the countryside, forcing the urban population, including almost all the Chinese, to become peasants overnight, many of them in undeveloped regions without arable land. One consequence of this move was the widespread starvation and misery of those who could not adapt; this included the Chinese, none of whom had been peasants.

The totalitarian regime's commitment to instant equality went to such extremes in some areas that anyone suspected of middle-class origins was eliminated. The repression was harshly reinforced by a growing paranoia about the Vietnamese threat. In the campaign to eliminate 'traitors,' thousands of Khmer Rouge supporters, including some of their top leadership, were tortured and killed, among them Hu Nim, Hou Yuon and other Sino-Khmer.

Furthermore, in some localities, leaders applied the Khmer Rouge mono-ethnic policy by taking draconian measures against the Chinese, not only forbidding them to speak Chinese or practise any Chinese customs, but executing them if they did not conform. In a few areas, however, Chinese were able to maintain their Chinese identity without reprisal, suffering only economic hardship along with everyone else.

Since China was in the throes of the Cultural Revolution, the Chinese in Democratic Kampuchea received no support from China's representatives in Cambodia. Indeed, overseas Chinese in China were castigated as 'evil capitalists' and China advisers in Cambodia simply enjoined 'forbearance.'

The People's Republic of Kampuchea

In the final years of Democratic Kampuchea, 1977–78, anti-Chinese incidents increased considerably, so much so that many Chinese welcomed the Vietnamese invasion in 1979 that ended the Pol Pot regime and inaugurated the pro-Vietnamese government of the People's Republic of Kampuchea under Heng Samrin.

Their troubles were not over, however, for owing to China's support of Pol Pot and Vietnamese antagonism towards China, the new regime was anti-Chinese. The Chinese invasion of Vietnam in 1979 reinforced this attitude, and Cambodia's Chinese continued to suffer discrimination and repression. Vietnamese authorities attempted to keep Chinese from returning to urban trading, and many Chinese therefore fled the country to join the refugees in Thai camps or boat people braving the oceans to distant shores. Many of those who failed to leave were rusticated once again. Since those registered as Chinese suffered discrimination in business and other aspects of public life, fearful Chinese opted to hide their identity. Many tried to pass themselves off as Khmer or bribe the registrars into leaving them off the roll. Many had their dead cremated rather than buried in order to appear more Khmer.

The anti-Chinese policy gradually mellowed in the final years of the Republic, 1986–89. A Chinese association was able to operate in Kampot, informally as a welfare agency from 1986 and formally as the Chinese Association of Kampot in 1988. A Chinese coffin shop opened in Phnom Penh in 1986, and the famous Chinese Buddhist temple at Takhmau reopened in 1987. Not until 1989, however, with the establishment of the State of Cambodia, did a Chinese cultural renaissance commence.

Contemporary Cambodia

With the withdrawal of the Vietnamese forces and the establishment of the State of Cambodia in 1989, things began to improve rapidly for the Chinese. Relations between Phnom Penh and Beijing were normalized in 1990, and Chinese in Cambodia began to feel more secure about their identity. By that time, Chinese had established themselves in all areas of the internal economy, notably in retail, restaurant and hotel, mechanics and repairs, light manufacturing and import businesses in Phnom Penh.

In 1990, the government established the Association of Chinese Nationals in Cambodia (Jianpuzhai Huaren Lishihui), which has a cultural mandate and is forbidden to engage in politics. This association is for Cambodian citizens of Chinese descent. Eleven local Chinese merchants were appointed to its board, whose first priority was reopening Duanhua School. Chinese were again permitted to celebrate Chinese festivals and follow their religious practices, and Chinese New Year was celebrated in Phnom Penh in 1991 for the first time in almost 20 years. That same year, Sihanouk returned to Cambodia as king, an event many Chinese consider as the turning point in their cultural freedom.

Today the Chinese population of Cambodia numbers about 350,000, although it is difficult to provide an accurate estimate of total numbers because the boundaries

Association of Chinese Nationals in Cambodia, nor do they have much to do with the other Chinese associations. As yet, no association has emerged specifically for the thousands of recent immigrants from China. Chinese associations no longer define the boundaries of the Chinese community as they did prior to 1970.

Over three-quarters of the Chinese in Cambodia today are Teochiu, with lesser proportions of Cantonese, Hainanese, Hokkien and Hakka, in that order. There is some economic specialization among these speech groups, with Teochius more widely spread through commerce generally. Cantonese are concentrated in the mechanical and repair trades, while Hainanese are found in cooking and baking, Hokkiens in clerical occupations and government service. Hakkas, the smallest speech group, run food stalls and peddle fruit.

Since 1990, a major resurgence of Chinese culture and community organization has occurred, with many residents keen to reassert their Chinese identity and to re-establish the institutions that express that identity and carry

Tall block in Phnom Penh street represents a Singaporean investment.

of the Chinese community are less clear-cut than before, with many Chinese speaking Khmer and a growing rate of intermarriage, especially in the rural areas. This figure suggests a remarkably rapid recovery of the Chinese community from the two decades of repression. It includes many Chinese returnees and a growing number of newcomers from China, Hong Kong and Taiwan.

The Chinese population of Phnom Penh, now about 200,000, is more heterogeneous than ever before. The five traditional speech groups have been joined by recent arrivals from other parts of China, such as dentists and doctors from Shanghai, doctors and architects from Taiwan and businessmen from Hong Kong. Chinese have also come from other parts of Southeast Asia, including doctors from Singapore and local representatives of companies investing in Cambodia.

Ninety per cent of foreign investment in Cambodia comes from companies owned by Chinese in Southeast Asia and China. Malaysian companies have invested the most (75 per cent), with lesser amounts from Singapore (9 per cent), China (3.5 per cent), Taiwan, Thailand and Hong Kong. All these companies, from whatever country, have personnel living in Phnom Penh, but since they are not citizens of Cambodia, they do not belong to the

it forward into the next generation. In Phnom Penh, the five Chinese *huiguan* have been resurrected, commencing with the Cantonese *huiguan* in 1991, the other four in the following year. These associations are also renovating their temples and cemeteries where possible. Each is centred on its temple, as before, and each runs a school. Gradually reclaiming much of the property that was appropriated by successive antagonistic regimes, they are now once more well endowed.

The five *huiguan* facilitate links with Chinese of the same speech groups elsewhere in Southeast Asia and in China. For example, the Hokkien *huiguan* was successful in attracting Hokkien support from Malaysia, Singapore, Thailand and Canada for refurbishing the Xietiangong Temple. Similarly, the Duanhua School built an annex with assistance from Teochius in Thailand, and the Hakka school was renovated with donations from Hakkas in Hong Kong, Canada, Thailand and Malaysia.

The Chinese presence is evident in various ways. Many of the shops in Phnom Penh and other cities bear Chinese signs. Chinese films and performances from Hong Kong and China are popular with both Chinese and Khmer audiences. Similarly, Chinese restaurants attract a cosmopolitan clientele. Two Chinese daily newspapers serve Cambodia, the *Huashang ribao* and

Two ways of celebrating Chinese New Year in Phnom Penh: lion dance (top) and open-air disco (bottom).

Yazhou ribao, the latter a local edition of a Thailand paper. Both cover local events, including news of Chinese schools, associations and delegations from Taiwan or the People's Republic of China as well as Khmer festivals and cultural events. Chinese culture, history and literature are presented in features.

Many Chinese schools have re-opened, notably the 'public schools' in Phnom Penh but also middle schools in several provincial towns. The largest and most prestigious Chinese school, Duanhua, has nearly 10,000 students, including extensive night classes. Chinese schools now accept Khmer pupils, who comprise nearly 10 per cent of their student bodies. Many Khmer families recognize the importance of Mandarin as an international language and are keen for their children to learn it. Provincial branches of the Association of Chinese Nationals in Cambodia form the umbrella organizations for the Chinese communities in smaller towns, where speech-group differences are likely to be ignored because the numbers are small and there is more reliance on Khmer as the common language. In many towns Chinese organized community mutual aid societies in the late 1980s to assist with such funeral expenses as payment for coffins and ritual objects. Some also began to reconstruct their local Bentougong temple and to renovate their cemetery. These societies became the nuclei for local chapters of the national association when it was established.

Despite the destruction of populations and infrastructure by 20 years of civil war, some Chinese rural communities survived or have been re-established in Cambodia. Many are of the same speech groups as before, Teochiu in most places, Hainanese in Kampot province (notably at Kompong Trach, though no longer farming pepper). These communities now have closer relations with the local Khmer, including intermarriage and considerable ritual and social interaction at the village level.

Younger rural Chinese now speak Khmer most of the time, only the older generation maintaining their Chinese languages. Chinese funerals and weddings include Khmer rituals, and mixed couples usually live in the bride's home, a Khmer custom that contradicts traditional Chinese patriarchal marriage patterns. More Chinese now worship at the local Khmer *wat* (temple), and many Khmer villagers now attend ceremonies at the Bentougong temples. Some Chinese now cremate their dead, while others continue to bury them in Chinese cemeteries.

W. E. Willmott

INDONESIA

Demography

With five to six million people, Indonesia's Chinese minority is, among Southeast Asian Chinese, second only to Malaysia's in number. Proportionately, they are not comparable at all; Chinese form somewhat less than 3 per cent (some sources say 2.5 per cent) of the total population. The Indonesian government has not kept official statistics on numbers of people of Chinese descent for some decades, so even these figures represent rough estimates.

Why, then, do some people think the Chinese are more numerous than even five million? To begin with, Chinese are a highly visible minority. They live mostly in urban areas, often in business or residential districts that are almost exclusively Chinese, and they engage in activities that bring them into public view: shop owning, trading, industry, banking, real estate development, the professions. They appear to have a controlling position in the modern economy. Most large corporations are in ethnic Chinese hands. Ethnic Indonesians fear that widespread illegal immigration of Chinese still threatens and some even believe that high birth rates are enabling the Chinese to increase faster than the indigenous or *pribumi* population. In reality, illegal immigration cannot be more than a trickle, while the growth rate of the Chinese minority, given widespread access to birth control and some trend towards emigration, is probably less than that of the *pribumi* Indonesians.

The 1930 colonial census offers the last 'hard' statistics about the ethnic Chinese, and later figures are just estimates. Then, 1,233,000 Chinese lived in the Dutch East Indies, slightly less than half of them on the island of Java, the rest in the so-called Outer Islands. Many of the Chinese outside Java, perhaps 77,000 of them in 1930, were contract 'coolie' labourers and transients; others were short-term migrants. The decade prior to 1930 was a time of rapid economic growth and high demand for labour, and the Chinese population grew by an average of 4.3 per cent annually between 1920 and 1930. Population increase among the Chinese slowed dramatically after that, and many areas experienced net emigration because of the Depression. Import of contract labourers from China never resumed, and, although some immigration of Chinese continued during the 1940s, since the 1950s Indonesia has not admitted Chinese immigrants; consequently the growth rate has fallen. In 1960, some 100,000 people of Chinese origin left Indonesia for China, and unknown numbers have departed since then, some to China, but the majority to North America, Australia, New Zealand or Europe.

Indonesia is a huge nation and the geographic dispersal of the Chinese is very uneven. Chinese range from nearly one-fourth of the population of the island of Bangka, to less than 2 per cent in the eastern part of the Archipelago. In Jakarta, they may be about 10 per cent of the city's population; in Medan (Sumatra), they are less than 13 per cent (in 1930 they were nearly 36 per cent); in Pontianak, at most, 30 per cent.

In addition, Indonesian traditions and beliefs exercised a strong influence over those who resided for generations in the Archipelago, especially in Java, but also in some parts of other islands like Sulawesi or West Sumatra. As a result, many local communities have become culturally bifurcated between the long-resident Peranakans (in the past, they were also known as 'Baba,' as were the Chinese of the Straits Settlements, see Part V: Malaysia and Singapore), who spoke Indonesian or a local language in daily life, and the more 'pure' Chinese, called Totoks (which means 'pure' in Indonesian), who were usually immigrants or their children, and who usually used a Chinese language. Since both geographical and historical experiences differed greatly because of Indonesia's diversity, the three major groups of Indonesia's Chinese will be discussed separately here: the Peranakans, who live mostly in Java; the Totoks of Java, especially its business community; and the Outer Islands communities, where Chinese languages also persist, but which underwent a different historical development, resulting in special kinds of accommodation to the local societies.

Map 5.4

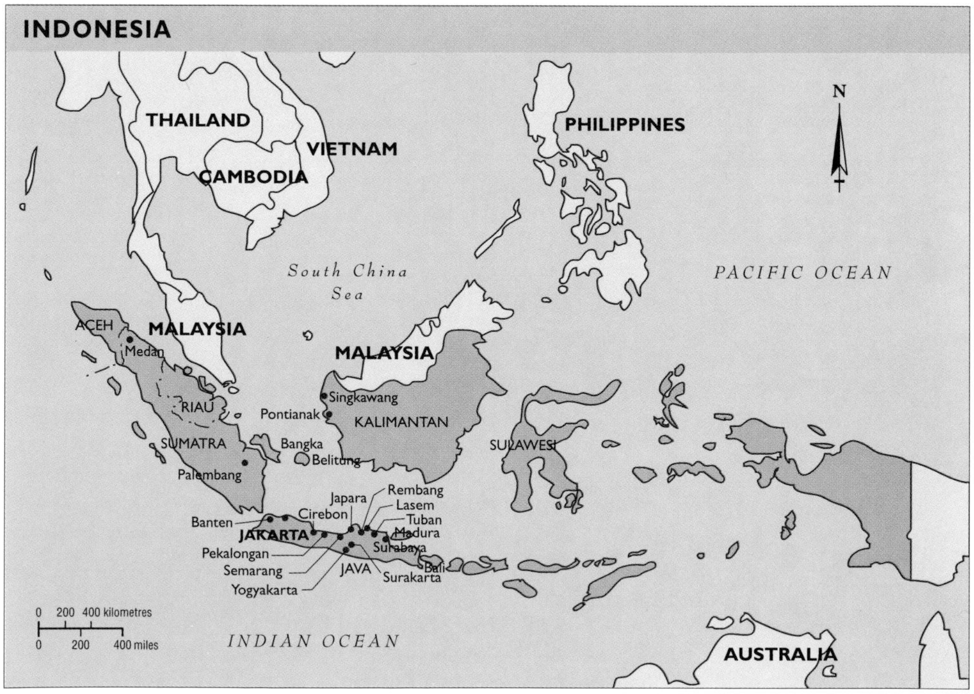

INDONESIA

Chinese trading pepper (in bag hanging from scales) in Banten.

Early history of Chinese settlement

Hundreds of years ago, Chinese visitors already used the Indonesian Archipelago as a way station for their trade with India and the Middle East. Later they began collecting its exotic products for their medicine chests and their kitchens: aromatic resins, marine products, birds' nests and rare items from the animal world. Gradually, small settlements built up at major ports and groups of traders and craftsmen – and sometimes nests of pirates – took root. Chinese visitors also provided the earliest written accounts of the Archipelago.

By the time Europeans reached the Indies in the 16th century, substantial settlements existed in many local port cities, and there were even some rural communities of Chinese in areas surrounding these towns. In native harbour cities, resident Chinese often took the role of *syahbandar*, master of the port, collecting dues and supervising traffic in the name of the ruler. Some were close to the rulers, becoming Muslims, acquiring official titles, and intermarrying with the local élite.

The sultanate of Banten, for example, which dominated western Java in the 16th century, had a substantial *pacinan* or Chinese quarter, which was its market centre, separate from the politico-religious centre with the sultan's court and mosque. Banten's Chinese merchants, together with others from India, the Malay Peninsula or the Archipelago, traded in pepper and other goods, as well as exchanging products brought from elsewhere in Asia, and were already well established when the Dutch arrived. In time, it would be Dutch policy towards the Chinese which would shape the minority in important cultural, economic and political ways.

Batavia: a Chinese city

If Chinese were important figures in native-dominated ports like Banten, they became essential to the operation of Batavia, now the capital city known as Jakarta. When Jan Pieterszoon Coen of the Dutch East India Company (Verenigde Oost-Indische Compagnie, VOC) selected the location in 1619, on the site of a native settlement called Jakarta (or Jayakerta), he planned to develop this new harbour, which was strategically located between the South China Sea and the Indian Ocean, to gain a dominant position in the valuable Indies trade. He soon recognized that his grand plan would need Chinese labour and commerce to make it work.

Batavia soon became the major entrepôt for the China trade in the Archipelago, with the VOC offering wares

from India and spices and tin from the Archipelago in exchange for Chinese goods, which it traded to Europe and elsewhere. The port was not really an administrative city or a colonial capital, nor was it an emporium for products from Java. These roles would come only in the 19th century.

Chinese quickly provided much of the human infrastructure for the town. In fact, it was – and is – the largest Chinese community in the islands. They were the various merchants, the provisioners to the Dutch, and shopkeepers. A colony of Chinese agriculturalists in the nearby countryside, outside the walls, provided fresh foods for the town; in the 18th century they also planted sugar in the environs of Batavia, distilling it into rum or arrack. Harbour coolies, virtually all Chinese, moved the freight; many artisans were Chinese. Chinese contractors and their labourers dug Batavia's famous canals and built most of its houses, and, for a time, even minted its coins. Soon Chinese were half of the civilian population of the multi-ethnic town.

Chinese settlements, whether under native rulers or under the VOC, were organized (as were other settlements of foreigners) in groups under their own headmen, a policy which continued into the 20th century. The headman was responsible to the VOC for the behaviour of his group of Chinese, and often for collecting its taxes; otherwise the community managed its own affairs. Usually these early headmen or officers were called Kapitan (or in Dutch, *kapitein*); such Chinese officers were the richest and most influential men in their own community, but they had to get along with the Dutch as well.

Another colonial policy which began in early Batavia was a system of farming out revenue. The farmer would collect taxes or tolls, turning over the proceeds to the government. What he collected over and above the sum he paid to the government was his profit. From the earliest times, Chinese dominated these so-called revenue farms (discussed below).

The Chinese population of Batavia continued to grow rapidly in the following years, Chinese junks came annually to the harbour, and Chinese settlers increasingly spilled over into the countryside of Java, out of the control of the few Europeans living in the walled town, and largely free of the influence of the Chinese Kapitan. The sugar boom was partly responsible for uncontrolled immigration, but when economic difficulties resulted in the closing of the mills, unemployed Chinese from the countryside, unregistered and uncontrollable, revolted against VOC authority, attacking the town.

The Europeans of Batavia, outnumbered by the immigrant Chinese in a larger, for the most part hostile, Javanese environment, responded in their panic with an orgy of killing. Most of the Chinese within the city paid with their lives, nearly all of them paid with their property, in the 1740 massacre. One estimate is that two-thirds of the 15,000 Chinese inhabitants of the environs of Batavia died. The ensuing conflict spread to involve the local rulers of neighbouring territories, resulting finally in an extension of Dutch power along the entire northern coast of Java. In China, the Qianlong emperor, informed by a repentant Dutch governor-general of the massacre of his subjects, blamed the victims: the Chinese of Batavia were law breakers who

Dutch ship decorates Chinese porcelain for the VOC market.

should never have settled away from the homeland. Dutch relations with the Chinese empire remained unaffected by what the Dutch called the 'Chinese murder.'

Yet the Chinese community showed, as it would time and again in later years, remarkable resilience. Almost at once VOC officials, almost helpless without a Chinese population, began encouraging immigration again, and the Chinese emperor's subjects responded gladly to the invitation. By the end of the 18th century, the Chinese were again the largest group in the city; their economic role was indispensable.

The Peranakan Chinese of Java

Batavia was not the only Chinese settlement on Java; all along the north coast of the island, the Pasisir, in trading ports like Cirebon, Semarang and Surabaya, and in smaller concentrations like Pekalongan, Tuban, Rembang or Japara, Chinese settlements formed. As VOC rule was extended to their area, on the pattern of Batavia, they, too, acquired their own Kapitans, or in smaller towns, lieutenants.

Initially, Chinese immigrants were males and they took local women; if they were not Muslims, they often took non-Muslim women like Balinese slaves. But if early settlers married natives, succeeding generations often tried to maintain their Chinese character, if their means allowed. The existence of substantial Chinese communities in the towns made it possible for most children born there to remain 'Chinese,' and the sons, raised in a Chinese way, could succeed to the professions of their fathers. Although, like other Chinese societies, that of Java placed a premium on male descendants, the daughters, usually sequestered from public view, would be a valuable asset, given the scarcity of Chinese women. Giving them in marriage strategically would seal business and political alliances. Records show that families of Chinese officers in Java intermarried. Probably, the lower classes imitated this pattern, reserving their daughters for marriage to other Chinese. There was some assimilation to native status among the very poor or otherwise isolated, but it was probably not the rule, though occasionally converts to Islam entered the local élite.

An important reason for the maintenance of the Chinese community was that Dutch power enforced separation of the Chinese and wanted them to remain distinct. After all, Chinese paid more taxes than did natives, and they provided a lion's share of the VOC's internal revenues. Repeatedly, colonial regulations emphasized their separateness; they had to live in separate quarters, dress in a Chinese way, and, in 1717 and again in 1766, the authorities expressly prohibited Chinese from marrying outside their own group. Even Chinese who converted to Islam were not necessarily 'natives.'

At the same time, in the towns, cultural influences met and mixed. The word 'Peranakan,' which comes from the Malay *anak*, child, contains a suggestion of mixed racial origin: somewhere in the past, Peranakans may have had *pribumi* mothers. The early use of the term, however, may actually have referred to Muslim Chinese, who formed a separate group from other Chinese with their own headman until 1827. Later, in the 20th century, the colonial government used the word simply to mean Indies-born, reflecting the distinction between immigrants, who were aliens, and local-born, who were Dutch subjects. For most scholars of recent generations, following the example of G. William Skinner (1996), 'Peranakan' implies adoption of a creolized or mestizo culture with strong Indies influences, and possibly racial mixing as well. The most important characteristic of Peranakans in this sense is their use of an Indonesian language in the family.

Chinese pedlar accompanied by his coolie.

Peranakan Chinese men were addressed as Baba, married women known as Nyonya. Many of them were ignorant of Chinese, except for some Hokkien kinship, religious or culinary expressions. Their typical low or 'bazaar' Malay was the lingua franca of the Indies, not only in the market-places, but between European colonial officials and virtually all other peoples of the Indies. Living mostly in the colonial-dominated towns, the Peranakans rapidly began to express themselves in Malay; those who lived in other settlements often used the regional language.

Although Peranakan culture has attracted considerable comment, little of it deals with the bifurcation of Peranakan culture according to gender. It was the women who, especially in the 19th century, adopted a special form of Malay dress, using colours and patterns influenced by Chinese taste. Men stayed with Chinese dress or, in the early 20th century, donned Western clothing. Only later did women adopt Western dress too. Peranakan women also borrowed food and table habits from local life; a few generations ago, most of them chewed betel. Women had more freedom than in traditional Chinese society, although not as much as many native women did. A distinctive culture resulted, with certain factors, such as colonial law and Chinese religion and family life, combining to keep the Peranakans separate from native society. Peranakans were a special kind of Chinese, they thought of themselves as Chinese, and others regarded them as Chinese.

Most Peranakans were of Hokkien origin. Hokkien was still spoken in the small, traditional Chinese schools, used for kinship and religious expressions, and sometimes it was the language of business. Although Chinese society in Javanese towns was almost constantly replenished by immigrants from China, in a generation or two their descendants became part of Peranakan society. Only after 1850 did changes in immigration patterns bring about a new situation. Peranakans then found that they were only one part of Chinese society, and the first efforts began to make them conform more to a 'Chinese' cultural model.

Peranakan culture: literature

In the second half of the 19th century, Peranakan culture began to express itself in literature, theatre and art. Over the following decades, an extensive body of writings produced by the Chinese, but written in Malay, appeared. In addition, publishing houses brought out a substantial number of Malay-language newspapers and magazines, directed primarily, although not exclusively, to a reading public of Chinese descent. The literary texts included novels, short stories and storytelling poems called *syair*. The topics show great variety: there are translations from Chinese classics or popular adventure stories like the *Romance of the Three Kingdoms* (*San guo yanyi*), original works dealing with local Chinese society or native society, thinly veiled fictionalizations of recent events, religious or didactic works, and translations or adaptations of Western writings. Readers and listeners (for some texts were read and told aloud to the non-literate public) included Chinese and non-Chinese. Especially popular were *cerita silat*, adventure stories from Chinese tradition, amply spiced with virtuous bandits and amazing kung fu masters.

These works were written in the ordinary Malay of the Indies. Because this language was the everyday language of the cities, and within the cities, of the Chinese, it is often called *Melayu Tionghoa* or *Melayu Cina*, Chinese Malay. However, except for a few loan words from Chinese, and some variation in syntax, nothing about 'Chinese Malay' is uniquely Chinese. The language was simply low, bazaar Malay, the common tongue of Java's streets and markets, especially of its cities, spoken by all ethnic groups in the urban and multi-ethnic environment. Because Chinese were a dominant element in the cities and markets, the language was associated with them, but government officials, Eurasians, migrant traders, or people from different language areas, all resorted to this form of Malay to communicate.

However, the modern Indonesian national language derives not so much from the urban street-level Malay, but from the supposedly more 'pure,' courtly Malay spoken especially in the Riau Archipelago, as it developed in the late colonial period for official purposes. Colonial language authorities sometimes heaped scorn on Chinese-Malay literature and its language, however popular it was with the reading public. The colonial government propagated standard Malay, and Indonesian nationalists found it to be 'Indonesian.' After World War II and Indonesian independence, bazaar Malay died out as a literary language, and most ethnic Chinese now speak standard Indonesian. Their contemporary literature is a part of Indonesian literature, but only since the 1970s has the contribution of Chinese-Malay literature to the development of Indonesian language and literature begun to be appreciated.

Peranakan culture: dress

Peranakan Chinese women, probably following the example of the Indo-European wives of Dutch officials, chose to dress in the local way, but in their own typically 'Chinese' pattern. Although the items of clothing women wore were virtually the same, the patterns and cut identified a woman as Chinese. Her sarong (a wrapped, tubular skirt stitched together at the ends, with a special, contrasting pattern at the *kepala* or head of the skirt) or *kain* (a length of unsewn cloth, wrapped as a skirt) would be in a multicolored pattern; sometimes she had a silver belt around her waist. Her patterned, embroidered, or lace-trimmed *kebaya* (a jacket or coat-

like garment, which varied in length), fastened by jewelled clasps (if she was well-off) often had a distinctive form too. On the Nyonya's feet were slippers she may have embroidered and beaded herself, in a typically Chinese technique, and she often added golden hairpins to her hair. Until Confucian reformers castigated the practice at the end of the 19th century, many women chewed betel, another Southeast Asian borrowing.

During the 20th century, young Peranakan women began to wear Western dress. Although for a time in the 1920s and 1930s, some appeared on formal occasions in the cheongsam or *baju Shanghai* (Shanghai dress), as it was known in the Indies, Western dress has prevailed. Nowadays, only grandmothers wear the *sarong-kebaya*, but batik is popular in other forms, integrated into Western dress. Ethnic Chinese men often appear on social occasions in batik shirts, especially if they are mixing with *pribumis*. A few Peranakan women may wear Indonesian dress for special events.

Peranakan culture: batik

Peranakan Chinese adopted Indonesian resist-dyed batik as fashion, as industry, and as art. Originally, batik was produced by repeated dyeings, with the pattern drawn and redrawn in wax by hand on the cloth before it was dipped into its dyes, usually indigo blue and a natural brown or red tone. The ultimate inspiration for this technique may have come to Pasisir villages from southern China, where minority peoples also use wax-resist methods to decorate cloth, but Indonesians think of it as a typical feature of Indonesian, especially Javanese, culture. In any case, it bloomed along the Pasisir in a multi-ethnic environment.

In the 18th century, locally produced patterned textiles began to replace the more expensive cloths imported from India; probably they were first produced in the cities of Java's north coast. Pasisir batik, inspired by many cultures, may actually be older than the 'classic' Central Javanese batiks of the courts of Yogyakarta and Surakarta, with their subdued brown-and-blue colouring and stylized motifs.

By the beginning of the 20th century, Chinese businessmen (and sometimes business women) who engaged in batik production had changed it from a handmade product for an élite public to a semi-industrial ware for mass consumption. Chinese let out production of the batik by financing home producers, mostly women, who drew the patterns in wax on the cloths; then they began small-scale production of the textiles in their own workplaces, for example, concentrating the dyeing of the cloth. They began to utilize a *cap*, or stamp, which enabled a skilled (male) worker to apply wax to several pieces in the time a craftswoman would produce a single hand-drawn cloth. Around 1890, new synthetic dyes made possible a wide range of bright colours, while tastes began to run to patterns borrowed from China: clouds and rocks, flowers and mythical animals. The most elegant Pasisir batiks used hand painting to reproduce the

Cotton batik from Java, 1930-35 (top) and 1900-10 (bottom).

fine details of their figures. Probably the technique of batikking on silk, known in Lasem and Rembang, was also Chinese-inspired.

The new designs were widely popular among Peranakan Chinese, and they spread beyond Java to the Outer Islands and the Straits Settlements, but other consumers began to favour them, too. In addition, the batik made with a *cap* was cheaper, so such textiles were no longer confined to the upper classes. The expansion of the large-scale batik industry had a negative effect on the indigenous batik producers, who might themselves be dependent on Chinese traders for supplies of synthetic dyes, paraffins or textiles. Their resistance to Chinese competition in batik, and also in the Javanese *kretek* cigarette industry, laid the grounds for an Islamic traders' union (Sarekat Dagang Islam), which in turn developed into Indonesia's first popular nationalist organization, the Sarekat Islam (Islamic Union) in 1912.

Today some batik firms run by ethnic Chinese are in the forefront of the contemporary industry, employing hundreds of workers. They have introduced printing of the typical batik patterns, an even cheaper operation than the *cap,* suited to mass production and especially for colouring synthetic fabrics (which do not take wax, as do cotton and silk). They have also expanded their products to include items like ready-made clothing, tablecloths and household items, and souvenirs stitched from batik.

Interest in indigenous arts was not merely for industrial purposes. The close proximity of some ethnic Chinese in Central Java to Javanese culture and even court life also awakened their interest in Javanese art forms, including the rather different, more sombre batik of Yogyakarta and Surakarta. Some Peranakan Chinese became adepts of the courtly cultures of Central Java, gaining an understanding of Javanese philosophy, music and dance. Others have been attracted to modern Indonesian art, or to Balinese traditions, becoming collectors of contemporary works. Still others are now modern fashion designers and artists, drawing their inspiration from many cultures.

Peranakan society and its institutions

Institution-building seems to thrive in Chinese communities abroad, and the Peranakan Chinese were no exception. In Batavia, as early as 1640, the Dutch created an official body to look after the inheritances (and the debts) of deceased Chinese, manned by prominent Chinese. From the proceeds of this endeavour, the community supported a Chinese hospital and an orphanage. It quickly established Chinese schools, on a community or private basis; Dutch sources refer to a school in 1729, and there is every reason to believe that wealthy families engaged tutors for their sons much earlier.

In Batavia and other major settlements, the pinnacle of community organization was the college or board of Chinese officers, later called the Kong Koan (*gongguan*). This body managed community temples and graveyards, and it organized the important community festivals. After 1740, the board was charged with acting as a civil registry. Probably these institutions gave wealthy Chinese officers an unofficial venue for their business negotiations as well, for sons of prominent families often worked their way up through the inheritance board to a position as Chinese officer.

Hokkien was the language of the Kong Koan in the 18th and 19th centuries; in this century, the board began to use Malay for its discussions. Only in 1878, when immigration patterns had changed and more people from Guangdong were entering Batavia, did the Dutch require that three of the ten members of the Kong Koan be Hakkas or Cantonese, while two would be immigrant Hokkiens and five Peranakans.

Temples were an important early focus of community activity – as they still are. Jakarta had, as late as the 1970s, two Chinese temples dating from the 1660s and several more from the late 18th century, although temple-building really took off with the rapid growth of the community after about 1850. While the Kong Koan looked after community temples, many surname organizations or professional guilds maintained their own places of worship.

Officers

The Chinese Kapitans soon acquired assistants, like Lieutenants, and in 1829 the first Major was appointed in Semarang. In Surabaya (1834) and Batavia (1837), other majors, placed above the Kapitans, followed. Officers were servants of both the government and the community. Since Dutch officials, only a few of whom ever learned Chinese, preferred partners who were fluent in Malay, officers were usually Peranakans, although sometimes a well-regarded immigrant might succeed to the office. Chinese officers were unsalaried, although they received a monthly allowance, and usually personal wealth was a prerequisite for office. The result was the formation of an élite of settled families, where offices sometimes passed from father to son, and which intermarried among themselves; they were the *cabang atas*, the 'upper branch' of Java's Chinese society. New members might be admitted from among the most successful immigrants. Closely linked to the Dutch authorities, officers were the first Chinese permitted to send their children to schools for Europeans, and, although the officers initially had worn Mandarin garb, by the 20th century they were decked out in official uniforms with plenty of gold braid to emphasize their status.

An elderly officer might retire from his duties but keep his rank as a 'titular' Major or Kapitan. The early officers were supposed to be men of reputation whose influence in the community would be beyond challenge. Their financial interests, as tax collectors, holders of monopolies and revenue farms, or as owners of the so-called private lands, as well as their duties, kept them close to the colonial power. Revenue farms were an important source of income for Chinese officers, and they were exempt from onerous provisions like the head tax on all Chinese.

During the 20th century, criticism of the institution of Chinese officers became widespread, both within the Chinese community and outside it. Many Western-educated Chinese saw the officers as an anachronism and felt they could deal with the administration without their help; others criticized them for corruption and abuse of authority; to the new immigrants, beginning to be influenced by Chinese nationalism, they seemed irrelevant. The colonial officials were eager to rationalize the ad-

Major Khouw Kim An (top) and Kapitan Lie Hin Liam.

ministration, and the Kapitans seemed old-fashioned and inefficient. In 1934, the Chinese officer position was abolished in Java and Madura, although not in Batavia. Elsewhere in the Indies, those who died in office were simply not replaced.

Revenue farms

One of the most-criticized institutions of Dutch Indies society was that of the revenue farms, which were closely linked to the Chinese, though they were a colonial institution, not a Chinese one. Especially after the VOC was abolished in 1799, the government depended on such farms for much of its financing, and, given the small size of its administration, letting out tax collection and revenue generation saved personnel and expense.

The first farms taxed mainly Chinese activities such as slaughtering pigs, gambling, smoking opium and distilling alcoholic beverages; the collection of head tax also applied only to ethnic Chinese. As the government needed even more funds, it extended monopolies and taxes to the natives of Java, and some Chinese gained a key economic position in rural areas as a result of their monopolies, holding licenses, in the 18th and early 19th century, for toll-gates, ferries, markets and slaughtering cattle, all activities which reached into the daily lives of the rural people. Sometimes, native rulers had also made use of Chinese as tax and toll collectors, but under colonial rule, it became a widespread system, backed if necessary by the force of colonial power.

The most controversial farm was the opium monopoly, not least because of its effects on the Javanese population. Whereas in the Outer Islands, opium use was a 'Chinese vice,' practised by many of the coolies working in mines and plantations there, the opium farms of Central and East Java were so lucrative because opium use penetrated to many members of the Javanese élite and even to the large village population, although they usually consumed the drug in small amounts. In other, strongly Islamic areas like the Priangan (West Java except for the coast) or Banten, opium sales were illegal. In fact, after 1820, Chinese were not even allowed to settle in the Priangan. As a result of these limitations, the opium farms of the Batavia area were less significant than those of Central and East Java. By the 1870s opium use was widespread in other parts of Java, where well-managed farms might bring in enormous profits.

Potential farmers often combined in a syndicate or *kongsi* (see Part III: Institutions) to bid for the farms, pooling their capital and, at the same time, involving potential opponents in the fate of the venture, thereby keeping their rivals from undermining the farm by smuggling. Of course such combinations might reduce the colonial government's profit from the farm, if the combination kept the price of the farm low and shut out other bidders at the auctions. On the other hand, a bidding war might raise the price of the farm so high that the farmer was unable to pay the price he originally bid. By the end of the century, the outcry against opium and opium addiction forced the government to change its policies and establish a government-run monopoly of opium sales in Java beginning in 1904, and in the Outer Islands a few years later. With that the Chinese officers and other members of the mainly Peranakan Chinese élite lost a major source of their income.

A wealthy Chinese carried by Javanese in a palanquin, 18th century.

Chinese and landowning

The Dutch and – during the British interregnum in the Indies in 1811–16 – the British authorities, needing cash, also began to sell tracts of land along the north coast of Java to private persons, for the most part Europeans or Chinese. Thousands of hectares of these so-called 'private lands' passed into the hands of wealthy purchasers. While European private lands were often run as plantations, Chinese sometimes acquired large properties that were inhabited by native farmers. Private lands were an important source of wealth for the officers of Batavia, where the revenue farms were not as profitable as elsewhere in Java. In the last quarter of the 19th century, for example, Chinese-owned properties accounted for nearly 40 per cent of all private lands in the residency of Batavia.

In East Java, too, leading Chinese families of Surabaya obtained agricultural estates for growing rice or sugar. Owners of these lands were free to exploit them – and the people who lived on them – with little interference from the government. Because of abuses, counter-movements soon began: by 1910, the government had repurchased many of the private lands, especially from Chinese, and none survived after Indonesian independence. While some prominent Chinese were able to move their capital into more modern activities, after the abolition of revenue farming and the repurchase of the private lands, like sugar-milling, other old, wealthy families faded from their previous high status.

Colonial policy: legal segregation of natives and Chinese

That Indonesia has a group of Peranakans of Chinese descent and not, as in Thailand or the Philippines, a group of mestizos or assimilated descendants of Chinese immigrants, is largely a result of colonial policy. Colonial policy vacillated between two extremes of either using the Chinese to increase economic activity, and therefore, revenue, or trying to limit or isolate the Chinese from the native population. An early but recurring question was whether it was desirable to have these Asiatic foreigners in the Indies at all. The answer was – and has remained to this day – twofold. On the one hand, the presence of Chinese facilitated the activities of the VOC and later of the colonial state, contributed to the development of new economic activities, and even encouraged new directions among the native groups. On the other, the Chinese sometimes competed with Westerners, they took advantage of the financially less clever natives, they appeared to combine for conspiratorial purposes and to reject the political authority of others, and their numbers grew at times so rapidly that alarmed authorities feared a wave of immigrants might engulf the Archipelago. An ongoing concern was to limit the numbers of Chinese admitted to long-term residence, to limit their political activities and to 'protect' the natives from their competition.

In colonial law, Chinese were 'Foreign Orientals' (or 'Asiatics'), a category which initially included people from elsewhere in the Archipelago (like migrants from Sulawesi), but after 1818 the term applied to Chinese (who were about 90 percent of all Foreign Orientals), Arabs and Indians. Initially, their status was considered to be similar to that of natives, but gradually it became more like that of Europeans. Only in 1920 was their tax status equal, as it was in general business matters. In 1917, European family law was extended to Chinese; in Java (and in the Outer Islands a few years later); marriages had to be registered with the general civil registry to be recognized as legal. But full equality with Europeans in all matters of law remained elusive (although it was extended to Japanese in 1899, and later to Thais and Filipinos). Criminal cases involving Chinese were tried in courts for natives, where legal processes were rudimentary, and this offended the sensibilities of many educated Peranakans. Although some Chinese attained assimilation to legal European status by petitioning for it (this was called *gelijkstelling*), most remained in their ambiguous situation, sharing some privileges and some disadvantages with both groups.

During the 19th century, two regulations taken together particularly galled the Chinese: the so-called pass and quarter system. The authorities introduced the pass system to limit travel to the countryside – a Chinese desiring to visit the next town had to apply in advance for a travel pass. Regulations also required all Foreign Orientals to live in special quarters or zones within the towns. Chinese could thus only reside where there was a Chinese quarter, and officials might force those who lived elsewhere to move to a quarter.

In 1866, new regulations softened the provisions of the law to permit Chinese to reside elsewhere if necessary for purposes of agriculture or industry. The most important exceptions to the pass and quarter systems were for revenue farmers and their agents in pursuit of business – one estimate is that this opened some 30,000 villages to residence by ethnic Chinese, provided they were associated with the revenue farms. When the farms were abolished at the turn of the century, many of these people were stranded.

Also important in limiting Chinese activity were laws to prevent the Chinese from acquiring agricultural land; after 1870, only natives could obtain titles to ordinary farming land. Landowners of the private lands could retain what they already held, and Foreign Orientals, like Europeans, could own land in urban areas. The purpose of the legislation was clear: Chinese entering rural areas should have no chance of buying or seizing the natives' land, or cheating them of it.

As a result of this law, which remained in effect until the 1960s, a landlord class of Chinese descent never arose on Java as it did in the Philippines and southern Vietnam. If Chinese traders lent money to farmers, the farmers would use their still-growing crops as collateral, and the influence of the traders was great enough that most farmers turned over the ripe crops as agreed, even if the price was not favourable. Outside Java, where Chinese farming communities existed, some exceptions to the law permitted Chinese engaged in small-scale agriculture to acquire farm land on a lease or other basis. Usually only European individuals or companies acquired long-term, large-scale leases for growing plantation crops. Not having the freedom of owning agricultural land or other supposed advantages natives had, many Chinese felt they had the worst of both worlds. Some of these tensions would awaken feelings of Chinese nationalism in the Peranakan community.

Immigrant and Totok Chinese in Java

The bifurcation of the Chinese society in Java between Totok and Peranakan was a development of the last decades of the 19th century. The Chinese immigrant or *xinke* (newcomer) who reached Java before that time might seek a Peranakan wife if he were successful enough to impress her parents, or he might find a local woman. Bringing a wife from China was virtually out of the question, and his descendants, speaking local languages easily and adapted to the environment around them, would melt into Peranakan society.

In the late 19th century, however, changes in patterns of immigration, in numbers of arrivals and especially the introduction of steamships, made it easier to bring Chinese brides to Java and facilitated travel to the homeland for those with means. New migrants could establish families which were more purely Chinese (Totok), retaining Chinese language, dress and customs. They might keep their mainland Chinese culture over generations, and children might even spend time in their fathers' home villages in China. In addition, modern Chinese schools (discussed below), a Chinese-language press with a large number of daily and weekly publications, reading material from China, as well as some locally published material in Chinese, helped maintain a society literate in Chinese. Many Totoks lived in Chinatowns, where the culture was typically theirs, for in the 20th century, as restrictions on residence of Chinese relaxed, many Peranakans – at least the better-off –

Totok men in Java, 19th century.

Glodok, Jakarta's Chinatown.

Rachman Halim, an Indonesian-Chinese businessman of Hokchia (Fuqing) origin.

were putting Chinatown behind them for newly developing areas of the cities.

In northern Jakarta's Chinese area the Chinese left their stamp on the houses of Glodok and Pintu Kecil. Even today, typical shophouses are still to be found there, as well as temples and churches which cater to Chinese. Other cities had similar Chinatowns.

Also significant was the expansion of a dynamic Chinese business community among the new immigrants. Whereas the Peranakan élite had been landowners, revenue farmers, sugar planters and officials, the Totoks forged into the expanding retail and intermediate trade, spreading moneylending activities into rural areas of Java, which opened up to Chinese settlement after the restrictions on Chinese were lifted in 1919. Very soon the Peranakans began to feel inadequate to face the competition with the more vigorous Totoks, and this in turn affected community solidarity. As Skinner put it, 'Totoks more than Peranakans value wealth, frugality, work, self-reliance, and "nerve." Peranakans more than Totoks value the enjoyment of life, leisure, social standing, and security.'

To the present, the Totoks have continued to emphasize business and self-employment, while the Peranakans drift, if they can, into white-collar occupations. In colonial times, if natives were favoured for government positions, Peranakans found themselves as office employees of private firms, foremen for mines and plantations, and, with the expansion of the Western education system, in the professions.

Totok organizations

An early and important institution among the immigrants was that of the sworn brotherhood (see Part III). In fact, the evidence for the existence of such brotherhoods, usually called 'secret societies,' goes back to early colonial days. During the late 19th century, the societies were very strong among coolie populations in Sumatra and Bangka, and the colonial government gave much attention to their influence, especially where they appeared to be responsible for rebellion and violence among the coolies of Bangka and Sumatra or the former gold miners of Kalimantan. In 1851, secret societies had been forbidden by law in the Dutch Indies. Officials were well-informed about the ceremonies of the brotherhoods and

easily recognized society paraphernalia. Members were, of course, sworn to secrecy in dealing with authorities and investigators, but in reality the Dutch usually managed to find someone to keep them informed about what was happening.

In time, however, colonial officials became convinced that the societies most often functioned as organizations of mutual help, especially for immigrants far from their homes and families. As long as the societies did not engage in open violence and intimidation, officials were inclined to tolerate them, seeing them as a kind of semi-benevolent Asiatic version of Freemasonry. Some societies continued to exist openly in this century as burial associations, their members known to the authorities. The Hoo Hap (Hehe) of Java, originally a secret society, openly staged an all-Java congress in 1935, announcing plans to become a political organization. Probably many of its members were Peranakans. The authorities nevertheless also knew that many apparently harmless societies continued to maintain a core of non-official members who acted as 'enforcers' or thugs to protect the interests of the more powerful members if necessary, and the societies often engaged in illegal gambling and extortion, for example.

Other typically Totok organizations were those associated with home places in China: those of speech groups, areas or even villages of origin, and, in some cases, surname associations (see Part III). Some of these associations maintained their own schools or temples. The close linkage with China and, sometimes, with relatives there made the associations less attractive to Peranakans, although most were open to them.

Totok business culture

By the 1960s, probably about 40 per cent of the Chinese in Java, including many local-born ones, were Totoks. While Peranakan culture evolved among almost purely Hokkien settlers, with only a minority from other groups, the Totoks were varied in their place of origin. In Java, the Hokkiens were still an important element, but Hakkas were also numerous, especially in Jakarta and West Java; in the 1960s the Hakkas were said to be the largest group there.

Since Totoks retained their Chinese language, speech-group identification was important in the Totok community, and as elsewhere certain speech groups became influential in certain businesses. Groups from around Hokchia (Fuqing) in northern Fujian operated bicycle repair shops, and many Hokchias, for example, penetrated the villages as itinerant pedlars and moneylenders – *tukang mindering*, from the Indonesian for 'pedlar' and the Dutch word for 'instalment payments.' Travelling on foot or by bicycle, they brought credit or small amounts of consumer goods and supplies to the people in the villages, in return taking agricultural crops from the farmers, whose indebtedness kept them bonded to the Chinese traders. Living close to the native population, some Hokchia men married Javanese women. That the numbers of Chinese speakers were proportionately higher in inland Java than along the Pasisir or coast (where most of the old Peranakan settlements were) shows that it was the Totoks who were penetrating the interior of Java in the 1920s.

Indonesian nationalist legislation has changed the

lives and occupations of Totoks, and itinerant rural moneylenders are a thing of the past. Many Chinese fled rural areas because of violence against them during the Japanese occupation (1942–45) and Indonesian revolution (1945–49). In 1959, a regulation forbade aliens (and all Chinese not born in Indonesia were aliens, as were many others) from engaging in retail trade outside major cities; later an extension made it illegal for aliens even to reside in rural areas. As a result, Chinese traders have concentrated their business in the towns; Chinese farmers (in the Outer Islands) usually located in the environs of the cities. In Java, cooperatives have replaced Chinese intermediate traders, while in the Outer Islands, Chinese traders rely either on native traders at the village level, or make use of trucks and boats to compensate for not residing near their sources. Internal migration, as Chinese move from the Outer Islands to the centres of economic activity, has added to Java's Totok communities, especially around Jakarta.

Totok culture persists, especially among businessmen. Some sources estimate that 75–80 per cent of the largest businesses are in the hands of ethnic Chinese and the great majority of these men (women are not represented at this level) are Totoks; many were born or educated in China, most of them speakers of Chinese. They outshine the Peranakans in importance in the business world; Indonesian Chinese business culture seems to be almost a Totok monopoly.

Restrictions on economic activity of foreigners – and virtually all Totoks were non-citizens in the 1950s and 1960s – however forced Chinese to seek alliances with *pribumi* businessmen. While some of the earliest 'Ali–Baba' connections (Ali being the *pribumi*, Baba the Chinese) linked Chinese importers and *pribumi* front men with ties to the influential political parties, after the shift of power to the military towards the end of the 1950s, Chinese-military linkages became more significant. Some of these alliances went back to the Indonesian Revolution when units of the military often had to support themselves. Smuggling of raw materials like rubber, copra and sugar, usually to Singapore, became a necessary source of income to pay the troops, buy arms and maintain operations. Contacts with Chinese businessmen facilitated access to Singapore's markets. Because of high inflation and the devaluation of the Indonesian rupiah, many provincial units remained dependent on this kind of 'guerrilla' financing, and Jakarta was unable to intervene.

Alliances formed in early days continue into the present. In Java, the Hokchias, with their history of petty trade in rural areas, seem to have been especially suited to forming links with the military. Sudono Salim, usually known by his Chinese name Liem Sioe Liong (Lin Shaoliang), became a business associate of President Suharto when the latter was commander of the forces in Central Java, an association that continued after Suharto became president. Mohamad 'Bob' Hasan, in addition to being a 'timber baron' with a dominant position in Indonesia's timber and plywood industry, holds key offices in a number of foundations run by the president. A younger businessman with political links is Prajogo Pangestu, also a lumberman, born in a Hakka-speaking area of West Kalimantan. In some cases, influential *pribumi* are shareholders in these enterprises; in others,

it suffices to name them as 'consultants.' Sometimes, a Baba–Ali situation arises, in which a *pribumi* who has money invests it with a Chinese, without necessarily revealing his own interest; in this case he is the stronger of the two associates, for he provides the capital.

Indonesia has developed rapidly since the end of the 1960s. Initially, extractive industries like petroleum, other raw materials and lumber (apart from foreign aid) led growth and financed government expenditures. Chinese enterprises participated in lumber, but extractive industries were almost all state-run or joint ventures between the state and foreign companies. In other fields, however, ethnic Chinese proved to be highly desirable partners for investors from East Asia or other regions.

Some Chinese business grew by benefiting from monopoly concessions for the importing or processing of imported and local products. Sometimes tariffs on imports were so high as to provide almost total protection for local industries, even where imports were needed in other areas of local processing. A well-known example was the concession for flour milling, awarded to a businessman with close ties to powerful military figures, a pattern of cooperation which earned for the Chinese partners the name of *cukong*. *Cukongs* were active in the 1970s in a number of other fields, but international donors and advisers have pointed out the disadvantages to the economy at large which result from monopoly concessions of this kind, and have pressed the Indonesian government to withdraw such privileges.

The decline in raw material prices, especially for Indonesia's major export, petroleum, at the end of the 1980s forced economic policy-makers to turn to export-oriented production as an engine of economic growth. As a result, industries which make use of Java's ample supply of low-cost, relatively unskilled labour, especially for textile and shoe manufacturing, have grown enormously since the 1980s. The key industrialists in these endeavours are usually ethnic Chinese, who can collaborate well with foreign suppliers and buyers in East Asia and the developed countries, and who have good access to financing, including financing from abroad. *Pribumi* connections remain important for these businesses too, for example, in facilitating granting of licenses and permits or in controlling the labour force, so close relations with power holders are still desirable.

Since then, ethnic Chinese entrepreneurs have also expanded into activities like banking and real estate. Indonesia has seen an enormous growth of private banking in the past decade – many of the larger of which, like Liem Sioe Liong's Bank Central Asia or Mochtar Riady's (Li Wenzheng) Lippo Bank, are in ethnic Chinese hands. This in turn has opened new, private sources of capital for Chinese firms. Chinese businessmen have opened shopping malls in major cities, and they have started housing developments, especially around Jakarta, acquiring large tracts of land around the city.

Although Chinese have certainly expanded urban residential and commercial landholdings in recent decades, there is little evidence that they are buying up farm land, something which, in Java, remains a prerogative of *pribumis*. Not only are they present, or even dominant, in many commercial sectors, their scale of activities may be highly diversified. As a result, the rather

Liem Sioe Liong.

Prajogo Pangestu.

pejorative *cukong* has fallen into disuse: with reference to these multi-faceted industries, many speak of the big businessmen simply as *konglomerat*, conglomerates.

Ownership of many conglomerates may be dispersed among ethnic Chinese businessmen, individuals in politically influential positions or in the military, and so-called foundations, which maintain links to powerful figures or to the military. Nevertheless, executive authority in most conglomerates is in individual or family hands. Given the limitations of this form of enterprise, especially the problem of maintaining control when future generations succeed to power, some diversification is taking place. Since 1989, some major firms have offered shares for sale to the public, although controlling interest usually remains with the family of the leading entrepreneur.

The fact that most large-scale ethnic Chinese businessmen are conversant in Chinese (usually Mandarin or Hokkien) facilitates their access to capital and business connections abroad; many of them consciously cultivate facility in Chinese. But as a result, members of the Totok business culture, however close their links to power, and however much they draw the interest of the press, remain suspect to many Indonesians. As room for financial engagement in China has opened, many ethnic Chinese businessmen have invested there. Many Indonesians see this as transferring money earned in Indonesia elsewhere, while the investors themselves look upon it as another investment promising high returns. In addition, both China and an ASEAN newcomer like

Vietnam can undercut Indonesia's already low wages, but ethnic Indonesians tend to regard transfer of investments to these countries as proof of the opportunism and essential untrustworthiness of ethnic Chinese businessmen. Such negative appraisals affect both popular attitudes and government policies (see below).

Chinese in the Outer Islands

Most of the Indonesian islands outside Java came under colonial rule later than Java did, some only at the beginning of the 20th century. Native rule persisted and, in the absence of Europeans, the Chinese often formed alliances with local rulers, finding niches in both the pre-colonial and later in the colonial economy. Furthermore, Chinese in these areas display greater diversity than those in Java, as their accommodations to local conditions differed widely. Unlike those in densely populated Java, who often acted as middlemen for the colonial economy, Chinese elsewhere were labourers and small farmers, traders and artisans, filling a variety of functions and having a variety of class statuses. Above all, a high proportion immigrated during the 20th century: in 1930, only about one-fifth of the Chinese in Java were born in China, but over half of those in the Outer Islands were.

Some areas of the Outer Islands do have Peranakan concentrations. Where Chinese settled in the Indies over a long time, where large numbers of immigrants did not arrive prior to the 1870s, where intermarriage with native women was common and immigrant Chinese women were few, Chinese usually began to use the local language or Malay in preference to a Chinese language. Such was the case in Chinese concentrations in west Sumatra, north and south Sulawesi, south and east Borneo (Kalimantan) and in some of the small communities farther east. The majority of Chinese in the Outer Islands, however, tended to retain their Chinese language, and before 1942, in the largest settlements, the foreign-born had a dominant influence.

The four major concentrations of Chinese in the Outer Islands, in 1930, were along the eastern coast of Sumatra, on the islands of Bangka and Belitung, in the Riau Archipelago, and in West Kalimantan. These settlements are grouped around Singapore, which was the hub of much of their economic activity and, with the exception of eastern Sumatra, they existed long before Singapore was founded in 1819. In fact, they go back to the mid-18th century. In these four concentrations, Chinese were a substantial proportion of the total population: 44 per cent in Bangka–Belitung (47 per cent in Bangka, 40 per cent in Belitung), 14 per cent in West Kalimantan and 11 per cent in Riau and in eastern Sumatra. In 1920, in all these areas, over 90 per cent of the ethnic Chinese claimed they spoke some kind of Chinese as their daily language. A substantial part of these Chinese lived in rural areas, in contrast to Java's almost exclusively urban Chinese minority. Unlike the Chinese of Java, who were concentrated in commercial activities, those of the four settlements engaged primarily, in one way or another, in the production of raw materials.

One important area of settlement was the gold mining area to the north of Pontianak in the present Indonesian province of West Kalimantan. There, in the mid-

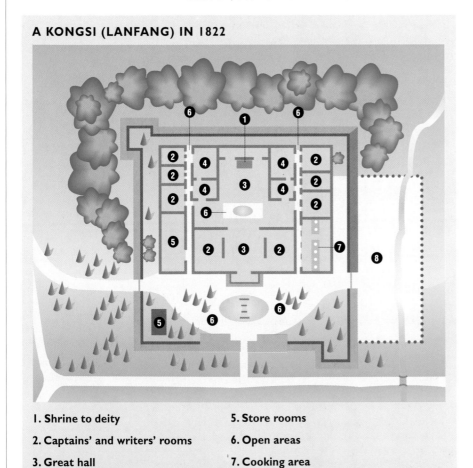

A KONGSI (LANFANG) IN 1822

1. Shrine to deity
2. Captains' and writers' rooms
3. Great hall
4. Guest rooms
5. Store rooms
6. Open areas
7. Cooking area
8. Sleeping quarters

18th century, local sultans invited the Chinese to work the deposits of gold on their account. Living in relatively isolated and self-sufficient settlements, the Chinese miners formed *kongsis* to share their work and profits. Originally these *kongsis* were probably shareholding groups of gold miners; in time they grew larger and more powerful, several *kongsis* combining and becoming completely independent of the sultans' authority, taking on the attributes of states. The Dutch, welcomed by the sultans, gradually extended their power in the area after 1819. In stages, as gold sites were exhausted and the *kongsis* fell into debt or mutual fighting, they forced the *kongsis* to surrender and disband. By 1885, all Chinese living on the west coast of Kalimantan were under the direct rule of the colonial power, supported by a corps of Chinese officers who were, however, little more than tax collectors.

During the 20th century, this important settlement, which may have had 400,000 Chinese in 1990, continued to grow even though the gold mines were played out. Kalimantan had large expanses of land, some of it well-suited for sedentary agriculture, and the Chinese took advantage of its availability. Chinese early introduced wet-rice farming to the area, as well as engaging in cultivation of vegetables and fruits. When cash crops like coconut and especially rubber opened up, Chinese migration to the area surpassed that of gold rush times, and the population grew rapidly, reaching almost 108,000 in 1930. Many Chinese engaged in trade; they spread rubber cultivation to the interior, awakening the interest of other ethnic groups in planting rubber. The Hakkas especially were intrepid upland traders, giving credit, selling consumer goods, and buying up rubber and jungle produce. The town of Pontianak, dominated by Teochius, became a centre for processing and exporting rubber and copra; later it also became a centre of the timber industry.

Chinese came first to Bangka in the early 18th century, responding to the desire of the sultan of Palembang to have them work his tin mines there. Thanks to their technology, an improvement on native methods, and to their ability to assemble and control large numbers of workers, keeping them constantly at work in the mines, they greatly improved tin production for the sultan. He then sold the metal to the Dutch East India Company, which in turn traded much of the tin via Batavia to China. Mining on Bangka thus began long before colonial rule took over on the island and, in the course of time, it underwent a transition from native to Chinese to Western methods, although Chinese continued to dominate the labour force up to World War II. Chinese labourers, who initially organized themselves in shareholding *kongsis*, smaller and less powerful than those of Kalimantan, gradually lost control of the enterprises as the Dutch extended their influence, and by the second half of the 19th century, they were little more than powerless coolies.

By the time the Dutch took control of Bangka and its mines in 1816, Chinese were so firmly in control of the industry that the Dutch contented themselves with the sultan's previous role of supervisor, creditor and purchaser. Chinese bosses controlled not only production of the tin but the crucial supply of labourers, most of whom came from China under a system which bound them to work to repay their passage money and then allowed them, once debt-free, to become shareholders in their mine. By the mid-19th century, however, advances in mining technology in Europe, shortages of replacement coolies, and the threat of declining supplies of tin led the colonial authorities to assume more and more responsibility for the day-to-day operation of the mines. During the 20th century, Bangka Tin became a fully state-owned enterprise. The Depression of the 1930s hit Bangka hard, and many coolies returned to China. Only after World War II, however, did Chinese coolies become superfluous, their physical labour being replaced by machines with native operators.

By nature coolies were a transient population, but in Bangka some stayed on as settlers. The island proved well-suited for production of pepper, which Chinese planters cultivated intensively, turning the product into the aromatic white pepper for which Bangka became known. To a lesser extent, some miners also settled more permanently in Belitung, where a private company had begun mining in earnest in 1860.

Bangka still shows Chinese influence in many aspects of its culture, but that influence is declining. Coolies no longer arrive; instead, many Bangka Chinese have left the island for Java and abroad, and the Chinese are now probably well under 25 per cent of the total population of Bangka, even less on Belitung. This decline is less a decline in absolute numbers than in proportions. It results from selective emigration, higher birth rates among native Indonesians and especially from the internal migration of ethnic Indonesians from elsewhere in the country.

The character of the concentrations in Kalimantan and Bangka was nevertheless quite different from that of Java. For one thing, most of the Chinese in Bangka, Belitung and West Kalimantan were of Hakka origin, and Hokkiens were a small minority, mostly engaged (as far as Bangka and Belitung are concerned) in the pepper trade. The Hakkas seem to have associated easily with the native peoples and adjusted to the tropical rhythm of agriculture, but they stubbornly retained their language and many of their customs, even though these areas already had a high proportion of third-generation residents in 1930. These long-term residents were, in G. William Skinner's words (1996), more 'locally rooted' than 'Peranakan,' but they were not quite Totoks either, and a difference from the new arrivals from China remained noticeable.

Riau, with its predominantly Hokkien and Teochiu Chinese population, seems at times to have been a doorstep to Singapore. But this area, too, was settled before Singapore's founding, when Chinese began planting gambier and pepper on the islands during the 18th century. As in the mines, the Chinese were able to import groups of labourers and keep them working in the gambier plantations, tending the crops and preparing them laboriously for market. Only the exhaustion of the natural base, including the essential wood supply, forced the gambier producers to move onward. Many Chinese

Leaders of a revolt of Chinese tin miners in Bangka, 1899.

remained in Riau as smallholders, fishermen and petty traders. Here, too, the proportion of Chinese has declined in recent decades, and the development of some parts of the Riau Archipelago as an industrial zone in connection with Singapore and Johor is changing the basis of the local economy.

In these three areas, it was Chinese entrepreneurship which brought changes to the local economy, although European capital later took over capital-intensive mining. Eastern Sumatra was an area of dominance of Western capital, and the Chinese only migrated there, at first mostly as coolies, when Europeans began to open up the area after the 1860s and the European-owned tobacco plantations became desperate for unskilled labour. Over the next decades, thousands of Chinese coolies arrived in this frontier area, living and working in barely human conditions. But imported Chinese labour became too costly for the plantation owners, who later expanded to rubber and oil palm as well as the special cigar wrappers for which the Deli area near Medan was famous. As a result, unskilled contract labourers from Java – including women for the finer work – began to replace Chinese coolies, and in 1932 labour recruitment in China for Sumatra completely ceased.

The coolies were of mixed origins. One source mentions Hakkas from the hinterlands of Swatow (Shantou), a mostly Teochiu-speaking area, as preferred labourers, but many were Hokkiens. Medan, a city which grew up with the plantations, has a Hokkien majority (and close links with Penang in Malaysia, also a Hokkien concentration). As elsewhere, the influence of Chinese, numerically and otherwise, has fallen. In 1930, at nearly 36 per cent of Medan's ethnically heterogeneous population, Chinese were a dominant group in the city; in 1981, the proportion had fallen, in spite of a growth in their absolute numbers, to less than 13 per cent.

In spite of this evidence of decline in numerical influence, and replacement of Chinese by indigenes in the field of labour, Chinese still dominate the market economy of the major Outer Islands. Chinese also predominate as urban businessmen and artisans. They play a major role in industry, trade and banking. Although since the 1960s, they have ceased to collect export crops in the interior, most exports like rubber, copra and pepper still pass through the hands of Chinese in the cities, who are ultimately responsible for processing and putting them on the world market. One notable change, however, is that the economies of these areas (except perhaps Riau) are increasingly focused on Jakarta and not, as in the past, on Singapore as entrepôt for raw material exports.

Kang Youwei with Chinese schoolgirls.

Religion

Scholars often describe traditional Chinese religion as a mixture of Buddhism, Confucianism and Daoism. Peranakans, for the most part, perpetuated popular Chinese beliefs in their new homeland, constructing temples and celebrating the festivals they knew in China, although over the years, some of these beliefs became mixed with local devotions and practices. Three impulses brought about a reconsideration of Chineseness and Chinese religion in the late 19th and early 20th centuries. The first was the greater influx of immigrants. Peranakans, on the one hand, felt they were 'Chinese,' because that was what the colonial government insisted they were: they still bore Chinese names before the 20th century, they wore Chinese dress (in the case of the women a form of Indonesian dress which was peculiarly 'Chinese'), even down to pigtails for Chinese men, and they lived for the most part in Chinese quarters or Chinatowns. The new arrivals confronted the Peranakans with a different kind of Chinese culture: they spoke Hokkien or other Chinese languages, some could read and write Chinese; some Totok women, who wore drab trouser suits, even had bound feet! Where, then, was the essence of 'Chineseness' to be sought? Would Peranakans have to become like these people?

A second impetus came from Dutch Protestant missionaries, who were – in small numbers – active in Java from the 1850s on. Because European schools were closed to most Chinese, some children attended schools run by Christian missionaries, only to find their teachers scornful of Chinese 'superstitious beliefs.' In time, some influential Peranakan authors began to assert Confucianism as a rational, intellectually honourable form of Chinese religion.

Finally, colonial policy, beginning with new laws in 1854, began to separate the Chinese (or Foreign Orientals) more and more consistently from the natives. Consciousness of ethnicity grew, and among the influential Peranakans a fear arose that their community had already gone too far in adopting the local culture: conversions to Islam threatened its continued existence and syncretistic religious practices were widespread.

Early signs of a Confucian revival were the temples built for venerating ancestors, in particular those dedicated to a particular surname or group of names. A number of collective temples for ancestor veneration date from the second half of the 19th century, as do some associations for the 'purification' of wedding and funeral practices from supposedly non-Chinese elements. The Boen Bio (*Wen miao*) of Surabaya is an interesting relic of this movement; founded on the site of an earlier temple to the god of literature (Boen Tjhiang Soe, Wenchang Ci), it was dedicated to Confucius himself in 1899, the only such house in all of Southeast Asia.

In another important development, the writings of Lie Kim Hok (himself a former pupil of missionaries) and other initiatives led, in 1900, to the founding of the Tiong Hoa Hwee Koan (Zhonghua Huiguan, Chinese Association) in Batavia. The primary purpose of the new association was to purge local – that is, Peranakan – Chinese customs of what it saw as unorthodox elements. Among its goals were: 'to improve the customs of the Chinese, insofar as possible in keeping with those principles of the prophet Confucius so necessary to civilized conduct, and to broaden the knowledge of the Chinese in language and literature.' That Confucius was a 'prophet' or *nabi* shows how strong the influence of the Islamic environment on the founders of the association was. On the other hand, ideas of mainland Chinese reformers like Kang Youwei had begun to reach the Indies and interest in the Confucian classics (in Malay translation) grew.

Challenged to suggest appropriate funeral arrangements for a deceased father, a Tiong Hoa Hwee Koan committee compiled a list of practices, both Southeast Asian and Chinese in origin, condemned by the sage, some undesirable because he did not mention them, and others thought impractical, unhealthy or otherwise inappropriate, such as gambling. Those who tried to introduce the simplified ceremony, however, were accused of being unfilial, filiality being one Confucian virtue known to virtually all Peranakans. Thus, although 'modernists' welcomed the suggestions, they were only partly successful. The association soon turned its attention from the purification of rites to its second goal, that of improving knowledge, and soon it established the first of hundreds of modern Chinese schools, opening branches throughout Java and on other islands.

With the association now concentrating on education, Confucianism gradually began to take on some of the characteristics of an organized religion. Confucian societies grew up throughout Java, propagating their beliefs through publication and proselytizing. Confucianism is today represented in Indonesia by a council called MATAKIN (Majelis Tertinggi Agama Khonghucu Indonesia, Supreme Council of Confucian Religion in Indonesia). Its religious hierarchy includes priests, lay preachers and elders, and it has a repertoire of liturgies, a creed and, of course, holy books in the form of the Classics. Most adherents are Peranakans, probably because it now represents a conservative, restorationist movement, a reaction against Western influences. MATAKIN professes monotheism, uses the Indonesian language in its meetings, and is concerned to attract non-Chinese believers. Confucianism in Indonesia today is thus an organized, doctrinal, monotheistic religion in the pattern of Christianity or Islam, not the Confucianism of China, but that of Indonesia.

Partly an outcome of the early Confucianists' reference to Christianity, these developments are also a response to Indonesia's contemporary policy on religion. The Indonesian government expects all citizens to have a religion; anyone who 'does not yet' adhere to a religion is automatically suspected of being pro-Communist, which is interpreted as being disloyal to the state. However, the government usually recognizes only five religions as fulfilling the criteria of monotheism, having a scripture and a prophet, and not being limited to a single ethnic group: Islam, Protestant Christianity, Catholicism, Hinduism and Buddhism. Despite efforts to obtain official recognition, Confucianism, while not persecuted, is called a 'belief' (although not by its adherents), and its status is ambiguous. Officially, therefore, most Chinese who are not convinced Confucianists, Muslims or members of a Christian church, give their religion for official purposes as Buddhist, and follow Buddhist ceremonies for weddings and funerals.

Despite the importance of Buddhism among Chinese in contemporary Indonesia, little literature exists about either history or practice. The movement is, of course, not new: in the 1930s, the Peranakan writer Kwee Tek Hoay (Guo Dehuai) published a ten-volume work on Buddhism and a Buddhist revival of sorts followed. Most Chinese temples contain Buddhist and other figures; some juxtapose, for example, Guandi, a historical figure who could be called Daoist, and Guanyin, a Bodhisattva. Kwee himself promoted a mixture of the three Chinese strands of belief, Sam Kauw (*san jiao*, three religions) or, as it is now called, Tri Dharma. The Tri Dharma organization is affiliated with the Indonesian Buddhist Council, so it qualifies as one branch of Buddhism, but other Buddhist organizations are influential among Chinese as well. There is also a tendency to press Buddhism to a Theravadan mould, although Chinese Buddhism is of the Mahayana variety, and to insist that Buddhist practices conform to the officially sanctioned monotheism.

Another aspect of Chinese religion in contemporary Indonesia is the influence of both security forces and of the Ministry of Religion, which sometimes interfere in the public practice of worship, especially in its more Chinese forms. Whereas formerly events like Chinese New Year, the Hungry Ghosts Festival (called Rebutan in Indonesia), or the Dragon Boat Festival were public occasions attracting onlookers and even participants from all communities with their public processions, dispensing of favours and open pageantry, these public festivals are a thing of the past. Chinese religious events are supposed to take place within the temple precincts or within family dwellings. In Singkawang, famous for its showy commemoration of Tjap Go Meh (the 15th day of the New Year), the celebration was prohibited for years, although it resumed in the mid-1990s.

Apart from reasons of public order, Indonesian officials argue that such festivals as Chinese New Year or the Dragon Boat Festival are not Buddhist festivals and therefore have no *raison d'être*. Nevertheless, in spite of the reserved and often hostile attitude of some authorities, many Chinese temples exist throughout the Archipelago, some couched behind Sanskrit names like *vihara* but others openly displaying Chinese characters. Many show evidence of recent renovations, a sign that Chinese beliefs are still current, and some festivals are still celebrated, if not with the lavishness they previously displayed. Similarly, although in the large cities many Chinese are resorting to cremation because of a shortage of burial places, in less-crowded areas, large Chinese cemeteries still exist.

Christianity, in its Catholic and Protestant forms, has

Members of the Board of Tiong Hoa Hwee Koan.

Chinese cemetery in Java.

appealed greatly to the Chinese because of its modern schools. Even today, many parents who are not Christians try to send their children to religious-run schools, which they believe offer the best education. Some of the children finally adopt Christianity, but Chinese parents are usually prepared to tolerate religious deviation within the family, especially because many Christian Chinese will still join in traditional Chinese rituals like ancestor veneration, some churches tolerating the practice. In general, because of their history, many Protestant churches were exclusively Chinese, and some still hold services using the Chinese language, but they are members of the Union of Protestant churches in Indonesia. Christianity does not seem to be an alien religion; in some areas, Chinese Christians were converted by other Chinese. For a time, some Catholic and Protestant missionaries were Chinese mainlanders, although none have been admitted to work in Indonesia since the 1960s, and their number was small compared to that of Western missionaries.

The Catholic church has strongly supported Indonesianization since the 1960s and discouraged exclusively Chinese activities. Although some parishes are, by reason of their location, still largely Chinese, the church does not desire ethnic separation, and the liturgy is in Indonesian or a regional language.

For most ethnic Indonesians, the most important religion is Islam, to which well over 80 per cent claim allegiance. In the past, some ethnic Chinese who came to the Archipelago were already Muslims, others converted to Islam, and the Islamic art and architecture of the Pasisir show strong evidence of Chinese influences. Especially in the Outer Islands, Chinese closely involved with native courts tended to adopt Islam and to marry local women; in Java, conversion was also a path to high office and noble titles. In Malay-influenced areas of Sumatra, Bangka and Kalimantan, a Chinese family might give a daughter in adoption to a native family, and the girl would be raised as a Muslim, completely assimilated to native society, a practice still known in recent times.

Conversion might, thus, mean assimilation to native society, or it might remain in a Chinese cultural con-

text. Although colonial policy discouraged conversion to Islam, a few Chinese were prominent Muslims, and Chinese-Islamic organizations were formed in various places. Some Muslims, like the family of Tjan Tjoe Som, a Sinologist, and his brother Tjan Tjoe Siem, a Javanologist, viewed their religion as completely compatible with their Chinese identity.

More recently, the active leadership of Haji Junus Jahja, a Dutch-educated economist (formerly Lauw Chuan Tho), who converted to Islam in 1979, gave a new impetus to propagation of Islam among Chinese. While the number who have adopted Islam is a small percentage of all Chinese, some prominent converts see, as does Junus, their conversion as a final step in the process of assimilating to Indonesian society and losing their Chinese identity. Although some observers have been sceptical about the process, certainly some converts are now accepted as both true believers and true Indonesians.

Modern schools

If religion was an area for skirmishing about Chinese identity, modern schools were a battleground. At the end of the 19th century, there were, on the one hand, some 200 old-fashioned Chinese schools in Java (and over 150 outside Java), and on the other a few mission schools, with a handful of children of the most wealthy and prominent ethnic Chinese being admitted to publicly supported Western schools. To this unsatisfactory state of affairs, the Tiong Hoa Hwee Koan schools, unquestionably Chinese, unquestionably modern, and open to all, offered a dynamic alternative.

These schools, the first of which opened in Jakarta in 1901, broke with tradition in three ways: within a few years, the language of instruction was Mandarin and not Hokkien or another southern Chinese language; second, they derived their curriculum from modern Western education as it was taught in modern Chinese and Japanese schools, and not the classics and the Chinese imperial examination system; third, classes for girls soon opened and, in 1928, the Batavia school went co-educational. They also broke, a few years later, with Confucianism, when Chinese secular nationalism condemned the teachings – and the influence – of the sage. By 1908 there were 75 modern Chinese schools in the Indies (not all of them officially affiliated with the Tiong Hoa Hwee Koan), with an estimated 5,500 pupils. As the nationalistic content of their instruction became evident (the schools even taught English in preference to Dutch), the colonial government reacted by finally opening Western education to ethnic Chinese children with the founding of the HCS or Dutch-Chinese Schools (Hollands-Chinese School).

The Tiong Hoa Hwee Koan schools, which had no monopoly of Chinese-language education, many schools being run by native-place associations or other private bodies, had drawn Totok and Peranakan children. With the opening of the HCS, which were Chinese in student body but completely Dutch in curriculum, Peranakan children whose parents could afford it streamed to the new schools. In general the poorer Peranakans tended to remain in the Chinese-language schools, to attend native schools or, in the late 1930s, to go to a few schools

Performance marking festival at Tiong Hoa Hwee Koan.

for Chinese taught in Malay. The Peranakan élite, for all its conservatism, responded enthusiastically to the opening of Dutch education; in a short time, Dutch became the language of the upper classes of Peranakans. The most successful graduates of the schools went for secondary education to Dutch schools and some had the opportunity to study in the Netherlands, becoming doctors, lawyers, pharmacists and engineers or, when higher education became available in the colony, to attend the university there. As a result, leadership of the Peranakan community passed to the Western-educated.

Graduates of Chinese schools, by contrast, travelled different paths. If they did not attend the few secondary schools in the colony, the children had to look to China for continuing education. And for tertiary education, although a handful of successful graduates were admitted to universities in the English-speaking world, for others, the only possibility for most was to go to China, sometimes a dangerous alternative during times of disorder in the motherland. Furthermore, many discovered that their knowledge of Mandarin was not good enough for continuing education in China; they had to attend special schools for Chinese from overseas. Although Peranakans and Totoks served on the school boards of Chinese schools, some of these same Peranakans sent their children to the HCS! Furthermore, the Chinese schools tended to be strongly nationalistic, drawing the disapproval of the colonial regime. After the HCS caught on, the Chinese community of Java was not one, but two. Although the press in the 1920s and early 1930s frequently reiterated the necessity for Chinese to form one single society and to stick together, the reality was otherwise.

The bifurcation of Chinese society in Java was evident not only in education and choice of language. For the Dutch, all Chinese born in the Indies were Dutch subjects, and they repeatedly intervened to insist on that status when officials from China, for example, tried to apply to the Indies-born the Chinese nationality law recognizing all descendants of Chinese fathers as Chinese nationals.

In the interwar period, as Chinese nationalism became a dominant force in the Chinese-language schools and press; most Totoks followed events in China and felt that they were somehow part of them, as indeed they were, for nearly all were, in both Dutch and Chinese law, nationals of China. Businessmen for a time boycotted Japanese goods and all elements of the community, including many Peranakans, supported relief efforts in China during the early years of World War II. Politically, some Totoks supported a small, often internally divided Kuomintang, while some labour organizers or Chinese school teachers fuelled a small, left-wing movement with anti-Kuomintang sympathies.

Most tried to stay clear of politics. On the Peranakan side, the influential Malay-language Batavia daily *Sin Po*, which also published a Chinese-language edition (*Xin bao*), fought to keep the Peranakans as Chinese as possible, rejecting Dutch education and cooperation with the colonialists. A small, conservative political group, the Chung Hua Hui (Zhonghua Hui) chose to identify with the colonial power. Critics called its wealthy members the 'Packard Club,' after a luxury limousine of the time. Another political association was the Partai

Tionghoa Indonesia (Chinese-Indonesian Party), composed of Peranakans who supported Indonesian nationalism and expected to become part of Indonesia.

Since the Islamic-inspired batik boycotts, Indonesian nationalism had spread from Islamic to ethnic and secular nationalists. The idea of an independent Indonesia, however, still seemed remote when Japanese forces occupied the Archipelago in March 1942. The new masters outlawed Dutch education and language, and many Peranakans found they had to learn, however laboriously, to write Chinese – at least their names – while Peranakan children who continued to attend school now went to Chinese schools. The net effect of the war years was, politically and culturally, a certain level of resinicization, dividing the Chinese from the ethnic Indonesians. Not a few welcomed the return of the Dutch in 1945 and when, during the Indonesian revolution, Chinese were victims of violence in various parts of the Archipelago, many began to view the Dutch as guarantors of their security. Many Chinese left rural areas at this time to reside in cities, which were, until 1949, controlled by Dutch forces.

Graduates of Chinese schools in Indonesia looked to China for continuing education: at the Jinan School, Nanjing, 1907.

Independent Indonesia

During the revolution, some political leaders made efforts to gain the support of minority communities like the Chinese for the Indonesian Republic. At the same time, they were sometimes ambivalent about the loyalty of the Chinese and were unable to restrain irregular forces responsible for most of the anti-Chinese violence. A Peranakan Chinese, Siauw Giok Tjhan (Xiao Yucan), became Minister without Portfolio in one of the revolutionary cabinets. When the Dutch recognized Indonesian independence at the end of 1949, the euphoria over the new status of China as a power after 1945 and the widespread sympathy for the People's Republic of China after its proclamation in October 1949 complicated the question of the minority's allegiance.

The effect of colonial and post-colonial legislation was to make the majority of ethnic Chinese aliens, and Indonesian authorities seemed reluctant, for the most part, to see this group enjoy the status of citizens. In addition, Indonesian citizens of Chinese descent were citizens of China by Chinese law, thus they were 'dual nationals.' When the People's Republic of China indicated an interest in remedying this situation by an act of choice, the Indonesians limited the act to those already holding Indonesian citizenship. There was a small loophole allowing people who had been minors in 1949–51, and whose parents had rejected their Indonesian citizenship,

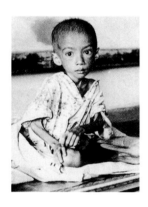

Indonesian-Chinese refugees arriving in Hong Kong en route *to China, 1966.*

A starving Chinese child in a refugee camp in Kalimantan, 1967.

to acquire Indonesian citizenship by choice when they came of age. When the choice was carried out, in 1960–62, the majority elected to be Indonesian citizens, but about one-third opted for Chinese citizenship, thus raising the numbers of aliens. Only a few individuals were ever naturalized as citizens, so over 60 per cent of the ethnic Chinese in Indonesia remained aliens up to the 1980s. There was some emigration of this group to China, but most found themselves permanent residents of a land that did not appear to want them.

From the 1950s onward, the Indonesian government adopted various measures to limit the economic role of non-citizens and of dual nationals, or it simply continued colonial policies to restrict the role of ethnic Chinese in, for example, landholding. It used a restrictive citizenship policy to keep the Chinese minority from enjoying equal rights with native Indonesians.

Yet having such a large population of aliens was not desirable either. China maintained a large embassy in the former home of a Chinese officer in Jakarta's Chinatown, and opened a number of consulates. Its diplomats actively sought contacts with residents of Chinese origin, Chinese literature from China circulated freely, and Chinese schools, which mushroomed after 1945, closely followed China curricula, again promoting resinicization and, it was thought, alien loyalties. A steady stream of young people moved to China to continue their education. Still, most alien Chinese expected to continue to live in Indonesia and the Indonesian government became aware that it could not expect to expel hundreds of thousands of people, not least because China (and also Taiwan) was not willing to take them in. In 1957, Indonesian citizens were required to attend Indonesian schools, while schools sympathetic to the Kuomintang were closed outright, and several hundred thousand pupils left the Chinese-language schools. Their number declined from 1,800 to about 510, but this still left some 120,000 pupils in Chinese schools.

The anti-Communist violence surrounding the purported coup of September 30, 1965 took a strong anti-Chinese turn by late 1966. Chinese were driven from areas like Aceh, in north Sumatra, or the rural areas of west Kalimantan. Diplomatic relations with China were frozen. Chinese schools were closed, all children had to move to instruction in Indonesian, Chinese newspapers were prohibited, except for one produced by the government. Public display of Chinese characters, even on Chinese temples, was curtailed or forbidden; printed material in Chinese could not normally be imported. This harassment has led some commentators to perceive the violence and killings of hundreds of thousands of people as an anti-Chinese pogrom. While it is true that some thousands of Chinese lost their lives, the number killed was proportionately less than the number of ethnic Indonesians. The violence of 1965–67 was directed against Communists or suspected Communists, not against ethnic Chinese.

Concurrently, the Indonesian government began to adopt assimilation as the appropriate policy for dealing with the minority. In addition to curtailing the influence of Chinese culture, the government encouraged, sometimes with more than gentle pressure, Chinese to adopt Indonesian-sounding names, something which had been illegal, under a colonial law, until the 1960s. Peculiarly Chinese organizations were disbanded, whether those of Totoks like the place-of-origin societies, or those of Peranakans like Baperki, an organization to promote Indonesian citizenship and defend minority interests (it was both too left-wing and too Chinese), or even non-political associations. In time, however, Chinese temples, at first hard hit by the prevailing atmosphere, recovered their position, and with growing prosperity after the 1970s, many were remodelled and refurbished. Other Chinese associations persist in the form of clan or burial societies.

President Suharto, preparing the way for defrosting relations with China in the late 1970s, finally opened the way for most aliens to acquire Indonesian citizenship without going through a costly and difficult process of naturalization. Ethnic Chinese who gave evidence of having adjusted to an Indonesian lifestyle, either by local birth, by their occupation (farmers and fishermen, for example), by having assumed Indonesian names, or in other ways, could qualify for this simplified procedure, and apparently many did. Official statistics do not count numbers of ethnic Chinese, but they do list Chinese nationals, and those numbers decreased rapidly after the president's instruction. Probably well under 10 per cent of all ethnic Chinese in Indonesia are now non-citizens, and, since many of these are old people born in China, the proportion will surely decline in the future. For many, the decision to become citizens was based on practical and not sentimental reasons, but it ended their status as aliens and Chinese nationals.

Relations with non-Chinese, anti-Chinese sentiments

Many pressures on Indonesian citizens of Chinese descent result from the feeling that they are 'economically strong' while *pribumis* are 'weak,' that they profited from the colonial period or from more recent corrupt activities to establish superior wealth, and that they are not really loyal to Indonesia as their homeland, not only cherishing ties to China, but being ready to emigrate to any land that offers them a chance for economic gain. All these sentiments contain a grain of truth, but are, in the end, distortions of reality. More and more, *pribumis* have access to wealth, while many Chinese have little income; not the old families of revenue farmers and Chinese officers are dominant among the wealthy, but those who have made their fortunes since the 1960s. Although ethnic Chinese show more readiness to emigrate than do ethnic Indonesians, many young Chinese feel as loyal to Indonesia as do their fellow citizens. Such preconceptions do, however, provide rationalizations for official and non-official measures ranging from petty corruption – someone who looks Chinese or has a Chinese name can expect to pay a higher bribe than does a native – to massive government intervention.

As in citizenship – extending rights to Chinese, but still limiting them – the Indonesian government limits the opportunities of most ethnic Chinese in the economy at the same time as it extends them for certain large entrepreneurs of Chinese origin. Government and the military service are the prerogatives of *pribumis*. *Pribumis* have taken over jobs in the unskilled and semi-skilled labour force, and cooperatives or individual *pribumi* traders have displaced the Chinese intermediate traders in rural areas. Authorities constantly urge Chinese businessmen to employ *pribumis*. Prasetya Mulia, a foundation set up by some of the large Chinese businessmen in 1980, also supports business education for *pribumis*. At the same time, few Chinese are admitted to public university education; many choose the expensive private universities or, if their parents can afford to send them, go abroad.

In 1990, President Suharto announced a scheme to encourage large businesses which had recently gone public to turn over part of their shares to cooperatives, especially in rural areas. On another occasion, prominent businessmen – most but not all of Chinese origin – were called to Bali to initiate a project to divert some of their profits to support small and medium enterprises. In December 1996, the president reiterated his demand that the major taxpayers contribute 2 per cent of their profits to the poor through semi-official charitable foundations. The method thus chosen by the Indonesian authorities to achieve a better distribution of wealth – pressuring large entrepreneurs for 'voluntary' contributions – probably arouses consciousness of the unequal distribution of wealth more than it remedies it.

Many observers believe this awareness contributes to the violence that has shaped Indonesia's relations with its Chinese minority to a shocking degree. Sometimes only a trivial incident or an unfounded rumour seems enough to set off large-scale and sustained rioting against Chinese, resulting in destruction of property and sometimes injuries and deaths. Revolutionary violence and that associated with the change of power in 1965–67 has been mentioned above. Political, religious, and locally aroused tensions have led to other outbreaks; these seem to have become more frequent since the 1960s.

Changes in society: outlook

Two relationships affect the outlook for the ethnic Chinese of Indonesia: the mutual relations of Peranakan and Totok, the mutual relations of the minority and ethnic Indonesians. One issue is the direction of cultural change. The dichotomy between Peranakan and Totok explains much about the Chinese minority in Indonesia, including why the dream of a united Chinese community proved impossible to realize. But these two groups are hardly opposites, nor are they always sharply defined today. Many Peranakans have one or more Totok relatives; the fact that Indonesian is or is not the language of the family does not mean that Totoks do not understand and speak Indonesian well; some Peranakans may be proficient in Hokkien or Mandarin.

Furthermore, because education in Indonesian and Indonesian citizenship are now nearly universal, the result may be a trend to Peranakanization, with both elements of the community drawing closer at that level. Certainly use of Indonesian is now nearly universal among ethnic Chinese, even if many still speak a Chinese language at home, or with the older generation of the family. Immigration is a thing of the past and ties to the homeland have weakened as family ties become more distant. Like Peranakans, Totoks were urged to take on Indonesian names, and many have complied.

More than the Peranakans, however, Totoks experience the pull between Indonesian society's demands for adaptation and the attractions of an international society of ethnic Chinese. Travel to China is now relatively easy, so it is possible to reassert ties with the ancestral homeland. While some parents, especially Totoks or those in the Outer Islands with connections to Singapore and Malaysia, urge children to learn Mandarin and even send them abroad to improve their Chinese, most appear to accept at least superficial Indonesianization.

During the 1960s, a movement for assimilation took root among a small group of Peranakan Chinese. Since then, the Indonesian government has adopted assimilation of the Chinese minority as official policy. Often, this policy provides an excuse for forbidding displays of Chinese culture – visiting Chinese opera troupes, lion dances, theatre performances. Many of these are very meaningful for Totoks, but such official interventions are not especially effective in isolating the Chinese minority from cultural influences of a Chinese character, given Indonesia's location in Southeast Asia in an era of porous borders.

In the end, it may be their economic interests, and not cultural sentiments, which lead some people to emphasize Chineseness. Since government jobs go to ethnic Indonesians, Chinese have to look to private enterprise for their chances. Totoks tend to favour going into business themselves, but they need networks to obtain capital, suppliers and buyers, and expertise. Sometimes these networks extend beyond national borders. On the other hand,

Locally born Chinese well-adjusted to Indonesian lifestyle.

Epitaph refers explicitly to mixed Chinese-Indonesian intermarriage, 1980s.

Peranakans, seeing some lines of work or study closed to them, and now having difficulty in being admitted to some of the professions, may turn to large Chinese-owned enterprises for employment.

As far as relations of ethnic Indonesians with the minority are concerned, the above discussion has tended to separate the ethnic Chinese as if they were incompatible with the Indonesian majority, but that is not necessarily the case. Some older people recall a time when Chinese visited Indonesian neighbours and friends at Lebaran, the end of the Islamic fasting month, while ethnic Indonesians paid visits and exchanged gifts at Chinese New Year, but they now see this practice falling into disuse. They remember a society in which Chinese – or at least Peranakan – culture was part of the Indies cultural scene. Nowadays, thanks to both political and economic changes, ethnic consciousness and separateness may be increasing.

Nevertheless, today some ethnic Chinese have no special desire to be recognized as 'Chinese.' They speak Indonesian, have been educated as Indonesians, live in neighbourhoods with ethnic Indonesians and associate with them freely. Intermarriage has also increased slightly. Although Indonesian marriage law restricts inter-religious marriages, intermarriage among Christians is possible and some Chinese have converted to Islam and married *pribumi* Muslims. In certain occupations, above all among academics, both groups mix freely in the workplace and even socially. For some of these individuals, assimilation is a real possibility; its success depends on the day-to-day reactions of the majority and on the health of the economy, as was borne out by the persecution of the Chinese in the upheavals of 1998 proved.

For the minority as a whole assimilation seems a much less realistic alternative. Most occupations are still ethnically determined. Often neighbourhoods are predominantly Chinese – certainly Indonesians are not found living in shophouses and Chinese are usually not rural villagers; nor are they, usually, urban slum dwellers. Some new housing developments around Jakarta are almost exclusively Chinese in composition. Chinese children generally tend to attend private schools, and parents still exercise a great deal of authority over their children's education. Many Chinese families have relatives who live abroad, opening perspectives which are closed to most Indonesians.

China and Chinese minorities in neighbouring countries play a role in the new consciousness of many. Satellite dishes and imported videos bring influences of strongly Chinese art, culture and public life to living rooms in the Archipelago. As so often happened in the past, a consequent trend to resinicization may gradually bring more of the minority into a Chinese orbit.

If the outcome of assimilation is uncertain, it can nevertheless only be an attractive solution if all citizens indeed are treated equally, but this is exactly what Indonesian authorities seem reluctant to do. They still fear unfair competition from the Chinese, or they think the minority has enjoyed advantages which must be compensated for by discrimination. Many are directly suspicious of Chinese culture, and indeed, Chinese contributions to Javanese culture and religion are given little play, while the Indian contribution to Indonesian culture is known to all.

Some ethnic Chinese who would like to melt into Indonesian society see themselves unable to do so, as authorities insist on entering special codes in their identity papers or in querying whether they have had a Chinese name in order to treat them separately. On the other hand, other Indonesians of Chinese descent would like to see Indonesian authorities put the national motto, Bhinneka Tunggal Ika (Out of Many, One), into practice by recognizing the contributions of ethnic Chinese and of Chinese culture to modern Indonesia and permitting them to retain that culture while being loyal Indonesians.

Mary Somers Heidhues

As Indonesia's economic crisis worsened in 1998, rioters brought down Suharto and scapegoated the Chinese community, torching their shops and homes, gang-raping their women and subjecting them to other atrocities.

LAOS

Pre-colonial history

Laos, once known as the 'land of a million elephants' (Langxang), shares its northern border with China's Yunnan province. Proximity to China ensured that Langxang came within the fold of China's tributary states. Missions bearing gifts of elephants, rhinoceros, horses, silver and gold to the Yongle emperor of the Ming dynasty were recorded as early as 1403. Continuing intermittently during the Qing dynasty, these official contacts waned in the mid-19th century as Laos came increasingly under the influence of Siam.

As was the case elsewhere, tribute relations did not give rise to significant Chinese settlement in Laos. Itinerant traders from Yunnan and, further to the east, Guangxi province, represented the only Chinese presence there until the late 19th century, when some Chinese traders from mainly Vietnam and Thailand started to set up homes in Vientiane and Luang Prabang. In his book *Travels in Siam, Cambodia and Laos 1858–1860*, Henri Mouhot, a French natural scientist, observes:

> Little commerce is carried out in this part of Laos. The Chinese inhabiting Siam do not come as far, owing to the enormous expense of transporting all their merchandise on elephants. Nearly every year a caravan arrives from Yunnan and Quangsee [Guangxi], composed of about 100 persons and several hundred mules. Some go to Kenne Thao, others to M. Nane and Chieng Mai. They arrive in February, and leave in March or April.

Inaccessible by sea, far removed from major trade routes, made up of small riverine plains separated by large tracts of mountainous and inhospitable terrain, Laos has throughout history held little attraction for migrants.

From the colonial period until the present

Two distinct periods of Chinese migration may be identified: during the French colonial period, and after independence in 1954. In 1893, Laos became part of French Indochina. France had already established control over Tonkin, Annam, Cochinchina (present-day Vietnam) and Cambodia. With the complete annexation of Laos, the entire area east of the Mekong and south of Yunnan came under its sway, leaving only Siam as a buffer state between French-ruled Indochina and British-controlled Burma and Malaya. Chinese migration into Indochina, including Laos, was part of that larger movement prompted by the new economic opportunities which

Market in Laos thronged by traders, including those from China.

imperialist Western powers, including France, created when they extended their reach in Southeast Asia.

As a practical and cost-cutting measure, the French colonial government brought in people from its colonies in Indochina – especially from Tonkin, Annam and Cochinchina – to staff the administrative and military services in Laos. Later it also offered incentives like land grants and tax concessions to encourage people to open up new lands to production and business. As a result, some Chinese earlier settled in Indochina, especially Cochinchina and Cambodia, moved to Laos. While a small number worked in the French colonial service, the majority came to set up small businesses, to engage in the cross-border trade along the Mekong, or to work in the towns.

But French Indochina, especially Laos, was not the favoured destination of Chinese migrants, who preferred Singapore, Malaya, Thailand and Indonesia. The number of Chinese in Laos at no time exceeded 2 per cent of the population. In absolute terms the number of Chinese who made their homes in Laos was also small.

As a landlocked country, Laos was seldom the Chinese migrants' first planned destination. Most incomers were in fact secondary migrants from Vietnam, Cambodia and Thailand. The

Map 5.5

LAOS

CHINA

CHINA

VIETNAM

BURMA

Dien Bien Phu

LUANG PRABANG

HOUA PHAN

XIENG KHOUANG

N

Gulf of Tonkin

VIENTIANE

Paksan

VIENTIANE

Thakhek

SAVANNAKHET

THAILAND

Pakse

0   50   100 kilometres

0   50   100 miles

only direct migrants were people from Yunnan and Guangxi. However, their number was small, accounting for less than 1 per cent of the total Chinese migrant population.

Though begun in the late 19th century, Chinese settlement did not really grow into sizeable communities until the mid-20th century. In 1921, of the 355,000 Chinese found in Indochina, only 5,000 were settled in Laos. The Depression years of the 1930s saw a decline of Chinese to only 3,000 people. Although numbers increased in succeeding years, at no time did they exceed 65,000. Official estimates actually put the figures closer to between 40,000 and 45,000.

When the French took control at the end of the 19th century, Laos had an estimated population of only 500,000 people, thinly scattered over an area of more than 230,000 square kilometres. When the French left in 1954, Laos's population numbered about two million, of whom only 30,000 were Chinese.

The second and larger wave of Chinese migration came in the wake of independence in 1954. The period spanning the 1960s and early 1970s was the 'golden age' of the Chinese in Laos. Fearful that Laos would fall into Communist hands, just as North Vietnam did, after the French defeat in Dien Bien Phu, the Americans poured aid into Laos to shore up the Royal Lao government against the North Vietnam-allied Pathet Lao. Commercial opportunities increased, and trade with Thailand and places beyond boomed. This prompted a new influx of Chinese, largely from Thailand, into Laos, especially to the towns along the Mekong River. They established thriving businesses in Vientiane, Savannakhet and Pakse. In the 1970s, the number of Chinese was estimated to be 45,000–50,000 people, or nearly 2 per cent of Laos's total population.

The Chinese community in Laos suffered a major setback in 1975. In December of that year, following the defeat of South Vietnam by North Vietnam in April, the Lao People's Revolutionary Party (as the Pathet Lao was officially called), came out of their revolutionary bases in northern Laos and declared the establishment of the Lao People's Democratic Republic. The large outflow of refugees this triggered mirrored the departures from Vietnam and Cambodia. In all, some 300,000 Laotians (or about 10 per cent of the population) left between 1975 and 1982. Among them were nearly all the Chinese in the country. By the mid-1990s, only an estimated 5,000 to 6,000 Chinese, or between 800 and 850 families, were left in Laos.

In 1979, China sent troops across the border to teach the Vietnamese a lesson after the latter invaded and evicted the Chinese-supported Khmer Rouge from Cambodia. As a close ally of Vietnam, Laos was bound to be affected, and as a result its own relations with the Chinese government were strained to breaking point. To the Chinese living in Laos at the time, the daily and increasingly vociferous denouncements of China must have sounded like a death knell. Already fearful of a socialist future, between 90 to 95 per cent of the Chinese were pro-

Li Peng met by Laos Premier upon arrival in Vientiane, 1990.

pelled by the added political tensions to quit the country. Those who stayed were mostly people over 40 or the very young.

Matters improved only after the Fourth Party Congress in 1986, when political tensions between Laos and China eased and the country began to embark cautiously upon an open-door policy. The former Chinese sections of town slowly returned to life. A few shops reopened; some of the premises whose owners lacked capital or manpower to resume business were let or sold to new investors. Chinese schools reopened when teaching staff gradually became available once more.

For the Chinese community, the visit of Chinese Premier Li Peng to Vientiane in December 1990 was a turning point. His visit was followed by the 1991 Fifth Party Congress, in which the Lao Communist Party fully endorsed the transition to a market economy. With the opening of the economy to domestic and foreign investment, confidence has gradually returned to the Chinese community, and Chinese associations are slowly being revived. But the community remains a pale shadow of what it was in its heyday.

Internal differentiation and geographical distribution

Most of the Chinese trace their origins to Guangdong province, particularly Teochiu-speaking Shantou, Hakka-speaking Meixian, and the island of Hainan. As in Thailand, Teochiu speakers predominate, accounting for 85–90 per cent of all Chinese. Hakkas come a distant second, followed by Hainanese. Hokkien and Cantonese are spoken by a very small minority, as is Yunnanese, whose speakers, numbering no more than between 150 and 200, are found mainly in Xieng Khouang, Houa Phan and Luang Prabang.

Though much reduced in size, the Chinese community remains unchanged in geographical distribution. The Chinese were and still are almost exclusively town dwellers. Almost all Chinese remaining in Laos are to be found in Vientiane, Pakse, Savannakhet and Luang Prabang, cities where more than 95 per cent of the Chinese used to live (see table 5.6).

Small though their numbers were, in the early half of the 1970s the Chinese actually made up a sizeable proportion of the towns' populations, ranging from 10 to 30 per cent of the total. Smaller Chinese communities such as those in Thakhek, Paksan and Xieng Khouang – numbering anywhere from more than a thousand to a few hundred members – have almost completely disappeared.

Chinese organization, culture and education

As elsewhere, the Chinese were organized along regional speech lines. In Vientiane, they had two associations; the bigger and more prominent Teochiu association; and a smaller Hakka association, to which all the other speech groupings (Hainanese, Cantonese and Hokkien) also belonged. Pakse, similarly, had two associations, one Teochiu, the other Hakka. Savannakhet and Thakhek had only one Chinese association each; while Luang Prabang had two, Teochiu and Hainanese. Xieng Khouang had a Yunnanese association.

Table 5.6

ESTIMATED CHINESE POPULATION IN LAOS		
	1975	1996
Vientiane	45,000	3,000
Pakse	10,000	1,000
Luang Prabang	5,000	550
Savannakhet	3,000	650
Thakhek	1,500	under 100
Total	64,500	under 5,300

Active and vibrant, these organizations represented the interests of the community vis-à-vis the local government. They ensured that their members abided by the laws of the country, and intervened on their behalf when they ran foul of the local authorities. They provided advice on business matters, as well as welfare services and shelter for newcomers and those in need. They also acted as keepers of Chinese customs and religion by organizing cultural activities and religious ceremonies around the major Chinese festivals. In the bigger cities of Vientiane, Savannakhet and Pakse, the Chinese also had their own temples, but in smaller cities like Luang Prabang and Thakhek, they worshipped alongside the Buddhist Lao in the *wat*.

Most important of all, the Chinese associations promoted Chinese education by setting up Chinese schools: in Pakse in 1929; in Vientiane in 1937; in Thakhek in 1939; in Savannakhet in 1940; and in Luang Prabang in 1943. Student enrolment, small to start with, increased with the growth of the community.

The Vientiane Chinese School, for example, had an enrolment of more than 5,000 students in 1970. This has shrunk to 1,000, of whom nearly 400 are children of Chinese descent and the rest are Lao, Vietnamese and Thai. The school's 69-strong staff comprises 40 Chinese teachers, 21 Lao teachers, and 8 administrative and general employees. It depends for its funds on school fees as well as donations by parents and the Chinese business community. Running classes at both the primary and junior middle-high levels, the school now follows the national curriculum, and Chinese is taught alongside Lao. In order to graduate, every pupil must take the nationally administered primary and junior middle school leaving examinations in addition to the school's own Chinese language exam.

It was not only schools that declined in the post-1975 period. The Chinese associations' other activities came almost to a standstill too, while their buildings and temples were left to deteriorate for lack of maintenance. The Chinese who remained behind in Laos stayed out of harm's way by keeping a low profile. Caution being the better part of valour, Chinese signs were largely replaced with Lao ones. Since businesses were shut down, many shophouses in the main town area were boarded up and occupied by a few elderly housekeepers. If Chinese festivals were at all observed, they were observed behind closed doors. Written or spoken forms of Chinese were avoided and never used in front of strangers.

Relations with China and the host people

Laos's geographical position made it physically hard for Chinese migrants to maintain close contact with their relatives in China. Very few ordinary Chinese made return visits to their ancestral homes in coastal China once they had settled in landlocked Laos.

The Laotian government's political stance was another deterrent. In parallel with the strong anti-Communist sentiments of the Royal Lao government in the post-1954 period, the Chinese community took pains to distance itself from direct contact with mainland China. Instead, relations with Taiwan became closer. Such relations were actively fostered by the Taiwan government, using vehicles like the Chinese associations and Chinese schools. Not only did teachers from Taiwan come to staff these schools, but pupils were sent to Taiwan for further study.

The post-1975 Sino-Vietnam split made it unwise for the Chinese in Laos to maintain links with either China or Taiwan. Only when Laos and China became friendlier neighbours did a new chapter open in the community's relations with China.

The Chinese are very well integrated into Lao society, and under normal conditions their relations with the host people are excellent. It was common for the early Chinese migrants, mostly single males, to intermarry with local Lao women. The post-1954 migrants, mainly from Thailand, brought with them Thai or Thai-Chinese wives who were already well integrated into local society. The Chinese have almost all adopted Lao or Thai names and the everyday lingua franca is Lao. The blurring of social distinctions between Chinese and Lao is particularly evident among Lao-born second and third-generation Chinese.

Economic livelihood and adjustment

Up until 1975, the Chinese were dominant in the commercial and industrial sectors. In line with the underdevelopment of the Lao economy and market, their enterprises were relatively small or medium-sized. Nonetheless, they controlled most of the import-export trade, owned most of the rice mills, saw mills and breweries, and held monopolies in the soft drink bottling, tobacco and cigarette enterprises. They also owned most of the dry-goods stores, bakeries, car and bicycle repair shops, and restaurants in all the main cities.

Only a few small-scale businesses – eateries, dry-goods stores and construction companies – have survived the events of 1975 as scaled-down versions of their former selves. In the early 1980s, the parts of town once dominated by Chinese businesses took on a deserted look. More than a decade later, an 81-year-old resident, Lim Seng Huat, remembers: 'All the shops along the main streets of Samsenthai, Setthathirath, and Chao Anou were owned by the Chinese. They were filled with goods and these streets were always full of bustling crowds. It is completely different now. Very few Chinese are left now; they are all gone – gone to Thailand or to France or America.'

But as Laos moved towards the market economy in the 1990s, new opportunities opened up for the Chinese. They have reasserted their dominance in the construction business; in import-export trade, especially in machinery and motorcars; and in wood processing and furniture. There are also signs of some tentative return flow of investment from a few Chinese who had fled earlier.

Ng Shui Meng

MALAYSIA

PENINSULAR MALAYSIA

Proportionately, Peninsular Malaysia has the largest Chinese minority of all the countries in Southeast Asia. Totalling 4,251,000 in 1991, Chinese formed 29.4 per cent of the country's population, compared to 58.3 per cent Malays, 9.5 per cent Indians and 2.8 per cent Malaysians of other descent. Chinese experiences in Peninsular Malaysia (known as Malaya in the period before the formation of Malaysia in 1963) can be divided into six phases: (1) Malacca sultanate, (2) British colonial rule, (3) Japanese Occupation, (4) decolonization and independence, (5) the Alliance coalition government, and (6) the National Front coalition government.

Baba and Nyonya on their wedding day, 1950.

Early migration and settlement: the Malacca sultanate

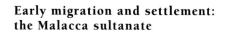

The earliest recorded Chinese settlement in Malaya was a small community established in Malacca around 1400 by Hokkien traders who came to engage in the thriving maritime trade of the sultanate, the region's busiest entrepôt before the arrival of the Europeans a century later. Baba Chinese (or male Straits Chinese; females are referred to as Nyonya), the progeny of intermarriage between Hokkien males and local females, constitute a tiny minority within the Malaysian Chinese population today, residing primarily in Malacca and Penang. Baba culture is predominantly Chinese, but overlaid

Malacca, 1629.

with Malay and British features. The Babas have integrated Malay speech, attire and diet into a style of everyday life that is governed largely by Chinese religious, cultural and familial practices. Few have converted to Islam. During the colonial period, most Babas gained fluency in English and adopted Western styles of dressing and recreational habits.

The Babas were the earliest mercantile and professional class within the Malaysian Chinese community. When the British established their presence in Penang in 1786 and Singapore in 1819, Malacca Baba merchants moved to the new settlements. There they were instrumental in financing the gambier and pepper plantations pioneered by Chinese immigrant labour in Singapore and Johor, and the sugar industry of Penang and Province Wellesley. Baba capital from Malacca, Singapore and Penang was also heavily invested in tin mines and rubber plantations, the mainstay industries of colonial Malaya.

The British colonial era

Chinese settlement in Malaya was relatively insignificant until after the early 19th century. Mass immigration was prompted by new economic opportunities created by the British mercantile and administrative presence in the Straits Settlements (Penang, Malacca and Singapore, established in 1826) and in the Malay states (after 1874), as well as by adverse economic and political conditions in China. The flows of new immigrants (*sinkeh*, 'newcomers'), accompanied by steady capital accumulation, soon eclipsed Baba numerical and economic predominance in the Straits Settlements. At the same time, the Babas became resinicized, and biological and social assimilation into Malay society virtually ceased.

Most Chinese immigrants were illiterate or poorly educated peasants and coolies who came through the credit ticket system or, in fewer cases, had their journeys financed by kinsmen already resident in Malaya. In this they differed from the Tamil labour recruited by the colonial authorities from south India to work in the rubber

Map 5.6

plantations. Contracted out to work off their debts to *kheh-tau* (labour brokers) who had prepaid their passage, *sinkeh* were commonly exploited until the Chinese Protectorate was established in 1877. Enactment of the Immigrants' Ordinance in 1880 further curbed the abuses of the credit ticket system.

The free flow of *sinkeh* to Malaya continued unabated until the Immigration Restriction Ordinance (1929) and the Aliens Ordinance (1933) were promulgated. These ordinances, by staunching the flow of male immigrants but allowing unrestricted entry for females and children, led to the emergence of a sexually balanced community. A second generation came into being, and by 1947 the local-born had reached almost 63 per cent of the total.

Social organization

Chinese social organization was based on institutional prototypes in China. Here as elsewhere, common surname, locality, dialect or craft were all bases for association. These organizations catered to the general economic, social and recreational needs of members by organizing ancestor and deity worship, overseeing burials and upkeep of cemeteries, settling disputes, providing mutual aid and maintaining schools. The principal common-origin associations were the Guangdong Association, Fujian Association, Teochiu Association and Hakka Association. The most important pan-dialect organizations were the Chinese Chambers of Commerce.

The tightly organized, all-male secret society, whose membership normally came from the same speech group, was particularly effective at controlling the flow and disposal of labour, and in directing back-breaking pioneering work in the tin mines and plantations. 'Secret societies' in Malaya were neither secret nor anti-government until they were banned in 1890. While they were initially indispensable to the British authorities in facilitating pioneering work and maintaining law and order in their respective territorial preserves, their drawbacks eventually outweighed their usefulness. Outbreaks of secret society feuding, caused usually by economic rivalries, frequently disrupted the peace of the Straits Settlements and the Malay states. In fact, the Hai San and Ghee Hin societies' embroilment in Malay internecine feuds arising from rival claims to the Perak sultanate caused such severe economic and social disruption that the British finally intervened in 1874. With the conclusion of two agreements, one with the Malay chiefs (known as the Treaty of Pangkor) recognizing Raja Muda Abdullah as the new sultan, and the other with the secret societies' headmen giving them a role in the state politics of Perak, the British took the first step in their colonial advance into the Malay states.

Today the more than 4,000 Chinese associations play a diminished role but retain their relevance, particularly for the Chinese-educated born before the war. The continued importance of organizations based on common place of origin has meant the persistence of divisions along speech lines, but economic cooperation across such lines has been successfully promoted by the Chinese Chambers of Commerce. Since its formation in 1947, the Associated Chinese Chambers of Commerce has served not only as the bastion of pan-Malaysian Chinese capitalist interests, but has also sought to advance Chinese political and educational welfare by

PATTERNS OF CHINESE SETTLEMENT

Originating mainly from Guangdong and Fujian, the Chinese population is divided into five major speech groups: Hokkien (37 per cent), Hakka (22 per cent), Cantonese (19 per cent), Teochiu (12 per cent) and Hainanese (4 per cent). Each speech group is further divided by dialect. Most Chinese practise Buddhism overlaid with Confucian and Daoist beliefs (88.5 per cent), a minority is Christian (7.8 per cent), and less than 1 per cent is Muslim.

As a result of chain migration, the various speech groups are not randomly distributed in the peninsula. Hokkiens and Teochius are generally located along the coastal, southern and northern regions, while Cantonese and Hakkas are found in inland regions. The Chinese population is predominantly urban: in 1980, Chinese formed 50.4 per cent of the urban population (the Malay proportion was 37.9 per cent) and 23.3 per cent of the rural population (the Malay proportion was 66.8 per cent). Different dialect groups predominate in different cities: Kuala Lumpur is largely Cantonese, Malacca and Penang are Hokkien, and Johor Bahru is Teochiu.

The Chinese New Village population is a distinguishing Malaysian demographic feature. Most of the New Villages are located along the west coast, where most Chinese immigrants have settled. Fifty-seven per cent of New Villages, and 76 per cent of New Village residents were originally located in the three states of Perak, Johor and Selangor.

At the time of independence, Chinese formed the majority populations in the states of Penang, Perak and Selangor: today they constitute a majority population only in Penang.

Heng Pek Koon

working closely with Chinese political parties, in particular the Malaysian Chinese Association.

Leadership and political mobilization

Leadership of the Chinese community had, for the most part, been exercised by successful merchant-entrepreneurs (*towkays*) drawn from the mining, plantation, small-scale manufacturing and retail and distribution sectors. The fact that the merchant, rather than the intelligentsia or any other class, assumed the role of leader is consistent with the primacy of wealth as a criterion of leadership in immigrant societies.

For most of the 19th century, secret society heads were the acknowledged leaders of the Chinese community. With considerable financial and manpower resources at their disposal, the most powerful of these men became the business partners and political allies of local Malay chiefs who conferred formal leadership status on them. Recognized as Kapitan Cina (Chinese Captain), these men were appointed to State Councils and charged with the jurisdiction of their local Chinese population. Yap Ah Loy, Malaysia's most famous Kapitan Cina and head of the Hai San society in the state of Selangor, rose to fame by siding with Sultan Abdul Samad in the succession war during the 1860s. Under Yap Ah Loy's leadership, tin mining and other commercial activities in the Kuala Lumpur area developed rapidly, thereby transforming an erstwhile backwater into the country's leading commercial centre and capital city.

In the first few decades of colonial rule, the British continued to rely on the Kapitan Cina/secret society leadership system to administer revenue farms (opium, spirits, gambling), develop the tin and plantation industries and keep the peace among Chinese. However, as the colonial administration became more established, Chinese increasingly came under direct British jurisdiction. Banned in 1890, the secret societies degenerated into underworld gangs engaged in organized crime, drug-trafficking, extortion and prostitution.

By the early 20th century, when the colonial government had finally acquired sufficient administrative capacity – mainly through Chinese Advisory Boards

Seal of Ghee Hin society.

Yap Ah Loy.

Amoy members of the Chinese élite were the office-bearers of the Anti-Opium Association of Penang, 1905–06.

Tan Cheng Lock.

established in 1890 to keep the government informed of developments within the Chinese community – the Kapitan Cina system was abolished, first in Selangor in 1902 and shortly after in Perak. However, the system survived unofficially until the 1930s when the last Kapitan Cina in the country relinquished his office in Pulai in the state of Kelantan.

From the 1900s until the outbreak of World War II, the mantle of Chinese leadership passed from the Kapitan Cina with secret society links to merchant-entrepreneurs heading the voluntary associations. The colonial administration legitimized the position of these men by appointing them to Chinese Advisory Boards and legislative councils in the Straits Settlements and Malay states. However, Chinese leaders continued to exercise considerable autonomy in local matters, especially in the area of education. Chinese schools were funded and managed through resources provided by the local community, with rich merchants serving as benefactors and patrons.

During the interwar years, new élite groups, drawn mainly from the ranks of the locally educated Chinese intelligentsia, emerged to challenge the merchant leadership. Modern Chinese education, which saw Mandarin replacing regional speech as the medium of instruction, was introduced to Chinese schools in Malaya at a time when nationalist and anti-imperialist sentiments were strong in China. Chinese schoolteachers and students were politicized and radicalized by events such as the 1911 Revolution and the subsequent ideological contest between the Kuomintang and the Communist Party of China.

The new Chinese-educated intelligentsia was organized in the Kuomintang Malaya (KMTM, formed in 1913) and Malayan Communist Party (MCP, formed in 1930). Both groups were deeply immersed in the dramatic events in China, but the Communist leadership, with its anti-imperialist stance, also concerned itself with local issues, espousing the cause of Malayan self-rule. Radical MCP activists began organizing trade unions and fomenting industrial unrest in the 1930s as a prelude to the creation of a Communist state in Malaya.

The KMTM and MCP leadership, in appealing to the wellspring of China-centred patriotism, as well as speaking out forcefully against discriminatory colonial practices in the areas of Chinese education and treatment of Chinese labour, gained the respect of the community. Moreover, as the first generation of an educated class, these locally bred political activists claimed a leadership status that would have been theirs in traditional Chinese society (which looked up to scholars).

In their rivalry for Chinese hearts and minds, the MCP won the support of most of the Chinese schools and labour organizations. The KMTM, on the other hand, received greater backing from the more conservative merchant leadership of the Chinese associations. Although the colonial government attempted to control both parties, subjecting the Communists in particular to severe reprisals, it failed to curb the spread of anti-imperialist and China-centred nationalist sentiments within the community. During the late 1930s, KMTM-MCP cooperation in the National Salvation Movement to mobilize Chinese financial and manpower backing for the anti-Japanese campaign in China brought Chinese nationalism in Malaya to its peak.

A third group of Chinese political leaders who emerged during the colonial period was organized in the Straits Chinese British Association, formed in 1900 to represent the minority interests of English-educated professionals and entrepreneurs within the Baba population. The association's leaders, especially Tan Cheng Lock, were the first Chinese leaders in Malaya to argue that Chinese in Malaya needed to be weaned from China-centred preoccupations and inculcated with a Malaya-centric outlook. Tan urged the British to adopt policies that would foster loyalty to Malaya among the three races to prepare the country for eventual self-rule.

World War II and the Japanese Occupation

Japan's invasion and occupation of Malaya (December 1941–August 1945) opened a new chapter in Malayan history by setting in motion the chain of events which resulted in independence in 1957. At the same time, it produced fundamental changes in the power structure of the Chinese community.

While all Malayans suffered during the war, Chinese were the most harshly treated by the Japanese military regime for having supported the anti-Japanese campaign in China. Some 40,000 Chinese were killed in purges. Chinese associations were replaced by the Japanese-sponsored Overseas Chinese Associations. These were ordered to collect a 'gift' of 50 million Malayan dollars and other 'voluntary donations' as Chinese 'atonement,' and to conduct a Grow More Food campaign. Thousands of Chinese urban dwellers were relocated to rubber plantations and jungle land to cultivate food crops.

The KMTM disintegrated when the Japanese invaded. Several pro-KMTM merchant leaders collaborated with the Japanese to protect their families and their business interests. Although some KMTM leaders went underground and organized the Overseas Chinese Anti-Japanese Army, the movement was ineffective. Comprising some 400 men and operating in the remoter parts of northern Malaya, the army occasionally engaged in looting and plundering in the same manner as other gangs of common bandits from secret societies and criminal groups.

The MCP, in contrast, organized the only effective

anti-Japanese resistance. Its 7,000-strong military wing, the Malayan People's Anti-Japanese Army, engaged Japanese troops in skirmishes throughout the length of the peninsula. The MCP also drew support through a number of affiliated organizations, the most important of which was the Malayan People's Anti-Japanese Union. Although set up to cultivate multiracial backing for the Communist resistance, it attracted little Malay backing; Chinese made up almost all of its membership.

Decolonization and independence

With the Japanese surrender, the MCP emerged as the ascendant political force in Malaya. When the British returned and set up the British Military Administration (BMA) in September 1945, MCP-sponsored People's Committees had been established in some 70 per cent of the country's towns and villages. For several months, the MCP operated as an alternative government alongside the BMA. It formed organizations for youths, women, farmers, artisans and other functional groups in a move to restructure Chinese social organization along Communist principles.

The BMA initially accommodated the MCP, but as British rule became more firmly entrenched, it neutralized the Communist movement, first by disbanding the Malayan People's Anti-Japanese Army in December 1945, and secondly by reviving the conservative merchant leadership. When the BMA's successor civilian administration, the Malayan Union (inaugurated in April 1946), began to remove Communist leaders from representative bodies, the MCP opted to seek power through insurrection. In June 1948, in its war to regain control of the country, the British government declared a state of Emergency in Malaya.

Symbolizing left-wing Chinese ambitions of political dominance, the ascendancy of the MCP, though short-lived, was nonetheless a landmark in the development of Chinese politics in Malaya. While the party was theoretically committed to the establishment of a multiracial Communist state, its sinocentric outlook and policies held little appeal for non-Chinese. For example, during the debate in May 1946 arising from the Malayan Union proposal to grant equal citizenship rights to Chinese in Malaya, the MCP, while welcoming the move, urged that Chinese in Malaya be entitled to dual Malayan and Chinese citizenship. More damaging to its image in the eyes of Malays was its contention that while dual citizenship obliged Chinese to be loyal to Malaya and China, ultimate allegiance should be owed to China in the event of a conflict between the two countries.

From the onset of mass migration until World War II, the Chinese in Malaya, having experienced considerable independence in running their community affairs, developed strong habits of autonomous cultural and social behaviour. The network of voluntary associations, together with the hundreds of schools established and maintained by local private enterprise, served as potent transmitters of Chinese values. On the eve of independence, this culturally distinctive Chinese population, which also formed the majority population in many urban centres and settlements along the west coast, demonstrated a strong desire for an independence arrangement that would make them the political equals of

CHINESE ECONOMIC ACTIVITIES

During the colonial period, Chinese business activities were concentrated mainly in the production of tin and rubber, in haulage and transportation, light manufacturing, rice milling and food processing, and in the distributive and service trades. Because the Chinese economic role was both diverse and widespread, it gave rise to the misconception that they dominated the economy. While it is true that the Chinese economic role was much bigger than that of Malays, who were mainly subsistence rice farmers and rubber smallholders, and Indians, who were mainly rubber plantation workers, Chinese played a subordinate role to Western, primarily British, capital. The large majority of Chinese were lowly paid wage earners employed in tin mines, rubber plantations and urban sector jobs. A minority were self-employed small proprietors and even fewer were affluent capitalists.

British firms dominated the colonial economy, especially the import-export sector and the two mainstay tin and rubber industries. Chinese entrepreneurs were mostly British-appointed middlemen and compradors, collecting produce for exports and distributing and retailing imports. As late as 1970, 13 years after independence, British capital still dominated the Malaysian economy: foreign (mainly British) ownership of corporate equity in Peninsular Malaysia was 63.3 per cent, the non-Malay was 34.3 per cent (27.2 of which was Chinese), and the Malay share was 2.4 per cent. Since the Malay Reservations Enactment of 1913 restricted Chinese access to agricultural land, few Chinese became rice farmers. At the same time, Chinese had little incentive to put their savings in land as it was more profitable to invest in enterprises with a quick turnover. Wage earners with sufficient savings turned to trade because it presented opportunities for self-employment and upward mobility, and for keeping capital liquid for handy remittance to China.

Compared to the Malays, Chinese had superior access to capital and credit through their associations. Based on common surname, speech and regional origins, these associations served as networks for members to gather and exchange information on market conditions, and as sources of credit and capital for starting or expanding one's business.

Regional origin (or speech group) to some extent defined trade and occupational specialization. For example, Hokkiens dominated the rubber trade; Teochius were heavily engaged in rice trading; Cantonese ran most of the gold shops, printing presses and restaurants; Fuzhou speakers mostly owned coffee shops; Hakkas managed pawnshops and worked on construction sites; and Hainanese worked as cooks and in the hotel industry. Chinese-owned banks with a regional speech-based clientele were also prominent. Until recently, the Kwong Yik Bank was a Cantonese bank, and the Penang-based Ban Hin Lee Bank was Hokkien. However, with rapid economic modernization, lines of speech-occupational specialization are disappearing.

Independence brought unprecedented opportunities for the expansion and diversification of Chinese economic activities. From the mid-1950s to the late-1960s, in the context of import substitution industrialization pursued by the *laissez-faire* Alliance coalition government, small- and medium-sized Chinese entreprises established a strong presence in light manufacturing, food processing, and production of household consumer goods. Rapid urban expansion resulted in active Chinese participation in the real estate and construction industries. At the same time, Chinese entrepreneurs expanded their networks in traditional stronghold industries such as distribution and retail, and transportation services. The era of unimpeded Chinese economic expansion in Peninsular Malaysia ended in 1970 when the New Economic Policy was enacted (see p 180).

Statistics released in 1995 on Chinese occupations in Malaysia (including Sabah and Sarawak) give the following proportions: 36 per cent in production, manufacturing and

transportation; 19.3 per cent were sales workers; 11.2 per cent were clerical workers; 11 per cent were in agriculture and fisheries; 8.9 per cent were professional and technical workers; 7.8 per cent were service workers; and 4.5 per cent were administrative and managerial workers.

Heng Pek Koon

Chinese mining tin.

Tunku Abdul Rahman.

Tan Siew Sin.

(Above right) Chinese voluntary associations like this one (founded by Hakkas in Malacca) were supporters of the MCA.

Chin Peng.

Malays. However, independence paradoxically brought significantly less 'self-rule' for the Chinese as it ended the autonomy they had during the colonial period.

For a brief period during the first phase of decolonization (1946–47), it appeared that Chinese might be granted equal political and economic rights through the Malayan Union. This plan sought to centralize the three administrative units of the Straits Settlements, the Federated Malay States and the Unfederated Malay States, and to create a common citizenship giving equal rights to Malays and non-Malays as a first step towards self-government. However, the British government was forced to abandon its plan in the face of unyielding Malay opposition led by the newly formed United Malays National Organization (UMNO). The Malayan Union idea was unacceptable to Malays, who feared it would enable the Chinese population – which, with Singapore, exceeded Malays by 2 per cent in 1941 – to dominate the new nation both politically and economically.

The British government replaced the Malayan Union with the Federation of Malaya Agreement in February 1948. The new arrangement satisfied the British objective of bringing the Straits Settlements, Federated Malay States and Unfederated Malay States under a centralized federal system. At the same time, it met UMNO requirements for safeguarding Malay sovereignty, the special position of Malays, stringent citizenship requirements for non-Malays, and the exclusion of Chinese-dominated Singapore from the new federation.

The Malayan Chinese Association, the Emergency and independence

The colonial administration actively encouraged the formation of the Malayan Chinese Association (MCA, known as the Malaysian Chinese Association from 1963) to mobilize Chinese support behind the government's campaign to defeat the MCP, as well as to assist UMNO

in setting the terms of Malayan independence. Formed in February 1949, the MCA brought together, for the first time, three strains of Chinese conservative leadership: pro-KMTM merchant leaders representing the Chinese associations, Chinese educationists, and English-educated professionals. Founder-leaders of the MCA included Tan Cheng Lock (who served as the party's first president); his son, Tan Siew Sin (who became Malaya's first Minister of Finance); H. S. Lee (who helped form the Associated Chinese Chambers of Commerce and served as its first chairman); and Leong Yew Koh (who became the first governor of Malacca).

The MCA was an effective facilitator of counter-insurgency policies because it was strongly supported by the Chinese voluntary associations and Chambers of Commerce. Its primary objective during the Emergency was to conduct welfare work among the 570,000 Chinese 'squatters' forcefully resettled in 480 fortified New Villages by the British so as to deny the MCP access to supplies, recruits and intelligence among the rural Chinese. The MCA organized welfare assistance to the beleaguered New Village residents, and sought just treatment for the thousands of detainees threatened with deportation to China for alleged ties to the MCP. By 1955, the MCP was defeated, and its remnants, led by Chin Peng, retreated to the Malayan–Thai border, where they languished until they accepted a government amnesty and surrendered in 1989.

More important than the MCA's Emergency welfare work was its pivotal role in the independence process. The party represented Chinese interests in independence discussions with the British government, the Malay sultans and UMNO, and with the Malayan Indian Congress (MIC), which represented the Indians. The British made it clear that power would be devolved only to an indigenous conservative, multiracial leadership. The first generation of top-ranking leaders of UMNO, MCA and MIC had in common an English-educated background, and a mutual desire to achieve independence at the earliest possible time. The three parties attained their objective of becoming the first government of independent Malaya by winning the country's first general election in 1955, and by successfully negotiating an independence blueprint.

The Alliance coalition emerged from the UMNO–MCA joint contest of the 1952 Kuala Lumpur municipal elections. Joined by the Malayan Indian Congress in 1955, the Alliance has since facilitated political cooperation at the élite level while allowing the component parties to mobilize support along ethnic lines. The Alliance's early electoral victories were facilitated by MCA financial resources and UMNO organizational skills, as well as the latter's larger electoral support base.

The MCA made major constitutional concessions to UMNO in the following areas: recognition of Islam as the state religion and Malay as the sole national language; lack of official status for Mandarin; and special rights for Malays. The MCA had little choice but to accommodate UMNO, since the Federation of Malaya Agreement of 1948 had already discriminated against Chinese interests by guaranteeing Malay special rights and restricting non-Malay access to citizenship. The MCA made the attainment of citizenship based on *jus soli* (determined by place of birth) its overriding objective on the grounds that without citizenship, post-independence generations of Chinese would be denied a legitimate role in the political process. At the same time, to safeguard Chinese commercial interests against erosion by Malay special rights, the MCA had insisted on the inclusion in the constitution of Article 153, which reads: 'Nothing in this Article shall empower Parliament to restrict business or trade solely for the purpose of reservations for Malays.'

There was, however, widespread Chinese dissatisfaction with the MCA-negotiated deal. Party leaders who supported the deal were characterized as self-serving *towkays* who sold out Chinese interests, and who were willing to act as UMNO lackeys in order to reap the spoils of political office. Chinese opposition to the constitutional proposals coalesced in the formation of an MCA breakaway movement called the Council of Representatives of Chinese Guilds and Associations led by Chinese-educated merchant Lau Pak Khuan, who sought a new deal containing equal citizenship rights and official language status for Mandarin. Stonewalled by UMNO and rebuffed by the British, the breakaway movement could not but be ephemeral and futile. However, Chinese dissatisfaction with the MCA's brokering of the agreement contributed significantly to the party's declining popularity after independence.

The Alliance coalition government, 1957–69

Because Westminster-style democracy and *laissez-faire* capitalism were favoured by Prime Minister Tunku Abdul Rahman, who headed the first Alliance coalition government, the Chinese enjoyed meaningful political participation while making significant economic gains. Chinese political parties, with the exception of those suspected of ties to the MCP, had freedom of political expression and unimpeded political mobilization.

Since independence, the Chinese have been represented by at least one government party (primarily the MCA), and one or more Chinese-based opposition parties (primarily the Labour Party until the 1960s and after that the Democratic Action Party, or DAP). Whether as part of the ruling coalition or in opposition, Chinese political parties have sought to represent the community's bedrock interests: rights of full citizenship, opportunity for economic advancement, preservation of the Chinese language and schools, and outlets for public cultural expression. The pursuit of these objectives reflects not only a desire to participate fully in the Malaysian polity but also a need to preserve the cultural autonomy that they had had.

The MCA served as the sole Chinese representative in the 1957–69 period. While clearly subordinate to UMNO, it nonetheless played a key role in shaping economic policies: party president Tan Siew Sin was Minister of Commerce and Industry during 1957–61, and Minister of Finance in 1961–74. The MCA's influence in the Alliance government stemmed from Tan Siew Sin's strong personal relationship with Tunku Abdul Rahman, as well as the latter's belief that MCA leaders, the majority of whom were entrepreneurs, could more competently chart the country's economic course than UMNO leaders with landed aristocratic, bureaucratic or educationist backgrounds.

As Finance Minister, Tan Siew Sin prevailed on Tunku Abdul Rahman to be gradualist and minimalist when it came to pursuing preferential policies favouring Malays. In return, he backed two key pieces of UMNO-led legislation: the 1961 Education Act, and the 1967 National Language Bill. The first bill ended state funding for Chinese education beyond the six years of primary instruction and permitted conversion of Chinese-language primary schools, known as National Type Schools, into National Schools with Malay as the medium of instruction. The second bill established Malay (Bahasa Malaysia) as the sole official and national language.

Under the Tunku-Tan partnership, Chinese economic interests made steady gains. While the income gap between Chinese and Malays at the time of independence was already considerable, it widened even more between 1957 and 1969: in 1957, the Chinese and Malay mean monthly household incomes stood at US$108.8 and US$57.6 respectively; by 1970, the figures were $157.6 and $68.8. However, Tan Siew Sin's apparent neglect of Chinese cultural interests, particularly Chinese education and language, was to cost the party the support of the Chinese associations and other powerful pressure groups, including the Chinese press and Chinese education bodies (especially the Dongjiaozong, United Chinese School Teachers and School Committees Association).

Lim Lian Geok, president of the United Chinese School Teachers' Association, 1954–61.

The rise of Chinese opposition politics

Chinese-based opposition parties were formed and led mainly by English-educated political activists aggrieved by the preferential policies favouring Malays. During the colonial period, English-educated Chinese had enjoyed unhindered access to higher education and public service employment. The gradual curtailment of educational and employment opportunities for non-Malays after independence did not bother the Chinese-educated Chinese to the same degree since they already faced discrimination in public sector employment before independence. However, the majority Chinese-educated population was deeply disappointed by the MCA's lacklustre record on Chinese education and language.

While the primary appeal of Chinese-based opposition parties lay in their assertive championing of Chinese interests, their ideological orientation to the Left of the MCA was also important in attracting Chinese votes, especially from lower-income groups.

The most significant Chinese-based opposition

Lau Pak Khuan.

Textbook used in Chinese school in Malaya.

Lim Kit Siang.

Dr Lim Chong Eu.

Chinese shophouses torched in Kuala Lumpur during the May 13 riots.

party during the late 1950s and early 1960s was the Labour Party. Founded in 1954 by a multiracial, but largely Chinese, English-educated leadership that espoused a moderate socialist programme, it moved further towards the Left during the 1960s, when a group of radical Chinese-educated leaders gained control of the party. In the 1959 general election, the party gained the New Village Chinese vote that was won by the MCA in the 1955 election.

Two smaller regional Chinese-based opposition parties competed with the Labour Party for the Chinese vote during this period: the Perak-based People's Progressive Party (PPP) and the Penang-based United Democratic Party (UDP). Although led by two Sri Lankan brothers, D. R. and S. P. Seenivasagam, the PPP successfully capitalized on issues which affected the disgruntled Chinese majority electorate of the Kinta region. The UDP was formed by Lim Chong Eu, a former MCA president who left the party after failing to extract from UMNO a number of political and cultural concessions for the Chinese in July 1959.

No serious Chinese opposition challenge to the MCA existed until the formation of Malaysia and the inclusion of Singapore in the new federation in 1963. The leadership style of Singapore's Lee Kuan Yew and his articulation of egalitarian principles under the 'Malaysian Malaysia' slogan – that Malays and non-Malays should enjoy equal political and cultural rights – appealed greatly to Chinese voters. Lee Kuan Yew's People's Action Party was viewed as a party led by competent and principled intellectuals, and its leaders commanded a level of moral authority within the Chinese community higher than that enjoyed by other contemporary groups of Chinese leaders.

The deep racial polarization created by the 'Malaysian Malaysia' debate and the threat posed to the MCA by the People's Action Party led to Tunku Abdul Rahman's decision to ask Singapore to leave Malaysia in 1965. However, the People's Action Party's equal rights crusade was picked up by the newly formed Malaysian-based Democratic Action Party (DAP). Seen to be the People's Action Party's successor, Lim Kit Siang's party remains dedicated to a 'free, democratic and socialist Malaysia, based on the principles of racial equality and social and economic justice.' Malays, however, have equated the championing of 'social justice,' 'racial equality' and other egalitarian principles by the DAP (and other Chinese-based opposition parties) with the fight for Chinese rights. The DAP has sought to represent Chinese in lower socio-economic groups, particularly in the New Villages. At the same time, it has also drawn considerable Chinese urban middle-class support.

To compete with the DAP for the Chinese opposition vote, Gerakan Rakyat Malaysia (Malaysian People's Movement) was formed in 1968 by a multiracial leadership of trade unionists, professionals and university lecturers, which included former MCA and UDP leader Lim Chong Eu and former Labour Party leader Tan Chee Khoon. Conceived as a moderate social reform party working for the principles of social justice, human rights and an open democratic system, Gerakan has been more committed than other Chinese-based parties to a multiracial integrationist approach to Malaysian politics.

In the 1959 and 1964 general elections, the MCA

fended off the Chinese opposition by relying on pro-UMNO Malay votes to augment its minority share of Chinese votes in racially mixed constituencies. However, in 1969, Chinese voters deserted the MCA. The party was trounced by the DAP and Gerakan, holding on to only 13 out of 33 contested seats. The Chinese opposition gained 26.2 per cent of the total vote (compared to the MCA share of 13.5 per cent) and 25 parliamentary seats. UMNO also suffered significant electoral losses (though less than the MCA) at the hands of its major rival, the Pan-Malaysian Islamic Party. The latter had successfully appealed to Islamic sentiments and capitalized on widespread Malay discontent with the apparent failure of UMNO's Malay special rights programme to deal with Malay economic backwardness. Despite the sharp drop in popular support and loss of its two-thirds parliamentary majority, the Alliance still controlled a comfortable majority (66 out of 104 seats) in the House of Representatives, the lower house of the Malaysian parliament.

Stung by the rejection of the Chinese voters and by UMNO criticisms of its poor performance, the MCA leadership decided to pull out from the government, but not from the Alliance. The MCA's decision exacerbated tensions already caused by the DAP victory parade in Kuala Lumpur. At a counter-demonstration organized

by UMNO activists on May 13, racial violence broke out. In the several days of rioting which followed, some 6,000 Kuala Lumpur residents, about 90 per cent of whom were Chinese, lost home and property. Official statistics claimed a death toll of 196, while non-government sources judged the figure to be much higher.

From the bitter experience of the riots, the Chinese learned hard lessons. The indisputable fact of a superior Malay power backed by Malay-controlled military and police forces meant that, in a showdown, they lacked the means to impose their will on any issue of fundamental concern to Malays. This realization resulted in a lowering of expectations and a gradual acceptance of their politically subordinate position in a Malay-dominated state after 1969.

The National Front coalition government

Chinese political marginalization

Emergency rule by the UMNO-dominated National Operations Council replaced parliamentary democracy in the country for 20 months in 1969–70. In September 1970, Tun Abdul Razak, who replaced Tunku Abdul Rahman as Prime Minister, reintroduced the multiracial coalition in the form of the expanded National Front, or Barisan Nasional.

Constitutional amendments enacted in 1971 effectively ended the Alliance coalition era of liberal political expression and mobilization, and concentrated power in UMNO, the backbone of the National Front. The new amendments prohibited any act, speech or publication on 'fundamental issues' that would incite racial animosity (in other words, Malay special rights, non-Malay citizenship rights, the position of Islam and the status of Malay as the sole national language).

A second measure used by UMNO to tighten Malay control over the political process was the creation of constituencies which inflated the strength of the Malay rural vote. In 1959 the percentage of Chinese voters and Chinese-majority parliamentary constituencies proportionately reflected their numbers in the total population: 36 per cent and 36.5 per cent respectively. Though the principle of weightage for rural areas established by the independence constitution, which set a limit on rural over-representation at 15 per cent, was removed in 1962, Malay voting strength was inflated after the riots, particularly during the 1984 apportionment which resulted in Malays forming a majority in 70 per cent of parliamentary constituencies. The disproportion between the largest (mainly Chinese urban) and smallest (Malay rural) constituencies is so great that some non-Malay majority constituencies have more than three times the population of the smallest Malay-majority constituency.

To overcome the problem of Malay economic weakness, the root cause of the 1969 racial rioting, UMNO implemented the New Economic Policy, or NEP (see box p 180). This also significantly concentrated power in UMNO. While the NEP institutions established by the UMNO-dominated legislative and executive branches of government were primarily aimed at acquiring economic resources on behalf of Malays, the scope of Malay affirmative action maximized Malay opportunities in almost every sphere of Malaysian life. Chinese political expression was thus concomitantly circumscribed.

Rebuilding the MCA

The sobering experience of the riots motivated a number of opposition parties to respond to the UMNO call to cooperate in rebuilding racial harmony. With the entry of Gerakan and the PPP into the National Front, the MCA was no longer the sole government party representing Chinese interests, and the DAP was left as the only significant Chinese opposition party. Increased representation in the National Front paradoxically weakened Chinese bargaining strength, as UMNO could play the parties off against each other and reward the one that came closest to its own point of view. However, the MCA has remained as the stronger partner since the Gerakan has yet to expand beyond its stronghold in the state of Penang.

The MCA claims a membership of 600,000, making it the world's third largest ethnic Chinese party, after the Communist Party of China and the Kuomintang in Taiwan. Following its poor electoral performance in 1969, and in the face of profound political and economic restructuring in the country, the MCA leaders worked, with mixed results, to change the party's *towkay* image and to widen its popular appeal.

In the early 1970s, the party launched a Chinese Unity Movement to generate Chinese political solidarity under its leadership. The campaign, especially the activities of the MCA Perak Task Force, drew enthusiastic backing from diverse Chinese socio-economic groups: English-educated professionals, Chinese educationists, *towkays* and thousands of youths from the New Villages. Unfortunately the movement's very success brought about its demise. While UMNO undoubtedly wanted a Chinese coalition partner which had credibility with Chinese, it perceived the chauvinistic overtones of the campaign to be dangerously inflammatory. In June 1973, a newspaper blackout on the campaign was imposed. Soon after, Tan Siew Sin expelled the movement's Young Turks leaders, many of whom defected to Gerakan.

When ill health caused Tan Siew Sin to resign as party leader and Finance Minister in 1974, the MCA became less relevant to Chinese business interests. From that time, Chinese business leaders increasingly found it more advantageous to deal directly with Malay patrons in UMNO, the royal families and the upper reaches of the bureaucracy. Succeeding Tan Siew Sin as party president, Lee San Choon initiated several ambitious projects to address Chinese concerns. Apart from the NEP, a New Educational Policy and a National Cultural Policy also adversely affected Chinese interests. In 1970, the New Educational Policy made Malay the main language of instruction in state schools and universities, implemented in stages from 1971 to 1983, and restricted Chinese access to university placements and scholarships. The National Cultural Policy, introduced after 1971, aimed at propagating a Malaysian national culture based almost exclusively on Malay and Islamic elements.

Two out of three of Lee San Choon's most ambitious projects during his tenure of

Chinese sundry goods 'shop' on bicycle, 1970s.

THE NEW ECONOMIC POLICY (NEP), 1970-90

The NEP was an affirmative action plan aimed first at eradicating poverty, and secondly at eliminating 'the identification of race with economic function' – that is, at producing numerical parity of representation of Bumiputra ('sons of the soil' or, in effect, Malays) throughout the economy. These objectives were translated into quantifiable targets in the four development plans drawn up for Peninsular Malaysia from 1970. The targets were to be met within two decades, that is, by 1990.

In 1970 it was estimated that more than 63 per cent of share capital in limited companies was held by foreigners; more than 34 per cent by 'other Malaysians,' chiefly Chinese; and only 2.4 per cent by Malays. The government used six measures to increase the Malay stake in the economy. One, the takeover of foreign tin and plantation companies such as London Tin and Sime Darby boosted national (read Malay) corporate ownership without reducing that of the Chinese. Though uncontroversial, the acquisitions were seen by some taxpayers as an inappropriate use of public funds which, given the secular decline of commodity prices, did not redound profitably to the country.

Two, the Foreign Investment Committee and the Capital Issues Committee were set up to ensure that acquisitions of assets or interests by the private sector, both foreign and domestic, conformed with the NEP. In particular, private companies listing on the Kuala Lumpur Stock Exchange had to have 30 per cent of their share capital in Malay hands. Three, under the Industrial Coordination Act, 1975, licences would be issued only to those manufacturers who met the NEP's requirement of 30 per cent Malay equity and employment.

Four, the government used trust agencies to mobilize resources and accumulate share capital on behalf of the Malays. Two well-known examples of such enterprises were Permodalan Nasional Berhad (National Equity Corporation) and Perbadanan Nasional (Pernas, or National Corporation). Five, Malay entrepreneurship was fostered through vehicles like MARA (Council of Trust for Indigenous People). Lastly, the government set up numerous state enterprises, including 13 state economic development corporations, to expand Malay share ownership and employment. Massive allocations of government funds to these organizations resulted in the staggering growth of the public sector.

Of all constraints on Chinese business, the Industrial Coordination Act was the most dire. Tightly knit small and medium Chinese family businesses

Lim Goh Tong.

Vincent Tan.

built up through years of hard work and risk-taking were particularly loathe to share the fruits of their success with Malay partners. Chinese resistance and circumvention took several forms: scaling down investment at home, investment abroad, a shift from manufacturing to real estate, the use of figurehead Malay partners to secure licences, contracts or other advantages in the so-called Ali-Baba arrangement (where a Malay, Ali, would secure the licence or contract for the Baba, a loose synonym for a Chinese, for a commission or share of the profits). As a group, the Chinese tried to dilute the effect of the NEP by the establishment of the ill-fated Multi-Purpose Holdings (see p 181).

To judge the NEP's success in meeting its target of 30 per cent Malay corporate ownership is to enter a contested terrain. Officially the Malay share was still below target by the end of 1990, having reached 20.3 per cent against a Chinese share of 44.9 per cent. But a number of commentators have argued that the Malay share had been grossly underestimated, pointing out that substantial Malay equity held by nominee and locally controlled companies had been relegated to the non-Malay and Chinese shares. An analysis based on market capitalization as at

September 30, 1988 shows that Malays owned 34.5 per cent of the total market value of companies listed on the Kuala Lumpur Stock Exchange, compared to 33.3 per cent for other Malaysians and 32.2 per cent for foreigners. There is no doubt that a Malay business élite has emerged, one which blurs the categories of state, party and private capital.

To elucidate the complex ways in which Chinese big business adapted to the NEP, it is useful to distinguish between those groups which made their money before 1970 ('old money') and those who flowered after that date ('new money'). Peter Whitford Searle, whose 1994 doctoral dissertation made this distinction, judged some representatives of old money more adaptable than others. By way of example, he showed how Robert Kuok (Perlis Plantations) and Lim Goh Tong (Genting) went from strength to strength by intensifying and broadening their links to the government.

The distinction between old and new is by no means hard and fast, but what does distinguish the latter – of whom Vincent Tan (Berjaya) and Quek Leng Chan (Hong Leong) are cited as examples – is the degree to which their capital became enmeshed with that of government, UMNO and private Malay interests. Indeed, it was the post-NEP nexus between government and business that provided the context for the rise of new Chinese wealth. Malaysian business had previously been described as though Malay and Chinese capital were separate, competing entities. But after two decades of the NEP, ethnic boundaries no longer equal business borders.

Corporate ownership apart, the NEP worked to restructure employment and occupation. Between 1970 and 1977, 60 per cent of new jobs in the public sector went to Malays; this rose to 80 per cent between 1977 and 1980, when there was a sizeable expansion of the public sector. In the private sector, too, Malay representation increased rapidly, and there was a net transfer of Malay labour from agriculture to modern industry. In the registered professions, figures for 1995 still show a higher proportion of Chinese accountants, architects, dentists, engineers and lawyers; but Malays were better represented than Chinese among doctors, surveyors and veterinary surgeons. The overall trend, though, is a decline in the Chinese share of these professions since 1980.

Preferential policies in the form of quotas were also vigorously pursued in university enrolment, and in the award of government grants and scholarships for local and overseas study. To cite just one example, nine out of ten students given scholarships to study abroad were Malay. At home, the government established higher education institutions such as the International Islamic University and the MARA Institute of Technology almost exclusively for Malays, while it rejected a Chinese community bid to set up a private Chinese university.

What of the poor, the improvement of whose lot was one of the two main goals of the NEP? Before the NEP was implemented, the poverty incidence among Malay, Chinese and Indian households was 65, 26 and 39 per cent respectively. Sizeable allocation of public funds to rural development, plus generous subsidies to Malay farmers and smallholders, helped to reduce the incidence of Malay poverty. Rural Chinese (those living in the New Villages) did not receive anything like the same degree of government funding. Yet a startling finding is that the betterment of the poor was more marked among Chinese than Malays: while the incidence of Malay poverty shrank threefold from 65 per cent in 1970 to just under 21 per cent in 1990, that of the Chinese poor dropped four and a half times, from 26 per cent to 5.7 per cent. Chinese mean monthly household income rose from US$158 in 1970 to US$633 in 1990. But the ratio of Chinese household incomes to the national average fell during that period (see table 5.7).

The NEP provided an expanding pie within which Malays and Chinese realized benefits, albeit at different rates. (The prosperity of the NEP years bypassed the Indians, whose share of wealth remained more or less unchanged between 1970 and 1990, at about 1 per cent.)

A severe recession in the mid-1980s spurred a reorientation in economic policy. The redistributive aims of the NEP gave way to an emphasis on growth. In 1991, the NEP was replaced by the National Development Policy (NDP), a ten-year programme less concerned than its predecessor with ethnically defined proportionality.

Ng Beoy Kui

office (1974–83) – the establishment of Tunku Abdul Rahman College, and the building of a new multi-storeyed party headquarters – were realized. The College has enabled thousands of Chinese secondary school graduates unable to gain admission to state universities to obtain a tertiary education. From 1975 to 1995, the institution produced more than 40,000 graduates.

The third project, the Multi-Purpose Holdings Berhad business conglomerate, in contrast, fared poorly. The company was formed in 1975 as a communally based corporate strategy to meet the challenge of state-sponsored economic institutions. The MCA urged under-capitalized Chinese family businesses – which then constituted more than three-quarters of Chinese enterprises – to pool their resources and to transform themselves into modern corporations. Chinese Chambers of Commerce and associations were also exhorted to form investment arms to engage in business. During the mid- to late-1970s, the MCA corporatization initiative led to the formation of some two dozen small- to medium-sized holding companies by regional-origin associations and trade guilds, the largest of which was UNICO, the investment arm of the Associated Chinese Chambers of Commerce. However, by 1986, it was obvious that the MCA's 'communal' route of meeting the NEP challenge was ineffective. Mismanagement and over-rapid expansion undermined the Multi-Purpose Holdings' ability to weather the ongoing recession.

When Lee San Choon stepped down as president, the party was seriously weakened by a destructive 20-month long leadership struggle between Neo Yee Pan and Tan Koon Swan, as well as the failure of several MCA-sponsored loans and savings cooperatives (known as Deposit Taking Cooperatives). In 1986, Ling Liong Sik, the new party chief, divested the MCA of its business holdings in Multi-Purpose Holdings, and focused party attention on Chinese education and cultural issues to rebuild party support.

The issue of Chinese education, in particular, has remained of fundamental concern to the Chinese community. About 85 per cent of Chinese parents still send their children to Chinese Primary National Type Schools. In the absence of state financing at the secondary level, some 60 schools supported by private funding currently exist to meet the demand for Chinese secondary education. Chinese-educated voters remain the most important constituency for Chinese political parties, although the numbers of younger generations of Malay-educated but Chinese-speaking voters are fast expanding.

Table 5.7

MEAN MONTHLY HOUSEHOLD INCOME

| | CURRENT PRICES | | | AS RATIO OF MEAN INCOME | | |
	1970	1976	1990	1970	1976	1990
MALAYSIA						
Overall	na	505	1,167	na	1.0	1.0
Bumiputra	na	339	928	na	0.7	0.8
Chinese	na	796	1,631	na	1.6	1.4
Indians*	na	537	1,201	na	1.1	1.0
Others	na	996	3,292	na	2.0	2.8
PENINSULAR MALAYSIA						
Overall	264	na	1,163	1.0	1.0	1.0
Bumiputra	172	na	931	0.7	0.7	0.8
Chinese	394	na	1,582	1.5	1.5	1.4
Indians	304	na	1,201	1.2	1.2	1.0
Others	813	na	3,446	3.1	3.1	3.0
SABAH						
Overall	na	513	1,148	na	1.0	1.0
Bumiputra	na	344	895	na	0.7	0.8
Chinese	na	1,191	2,242	na	2.3	2.0
Others	na	1,415	2,262	na	2.8	2.0
SARAWAK						
Overall	na	427	1,208	na	1.0	1.0
Bumiputra	na	288	932	na	0.7	0.8
Chinese	na	708	1,754	na	1.7	1.5
Others	na	2,913	4,235	na	6.8	3.5

* Peninsular Malaysia only.
Source: Government of Malaysia, Second Outline Perspective Plan, 1991–2000.

While Ling has appealed to Chinese communal sentiments to cultivate Chinese support, primarily through an ambitious expansion programme for Tunku Abdul Rahman College, he has also steered the party towards a hitherto untrodden multiracial path. In 1993, he launched the party's 'One Heart, One Vision' campaign to encourage Malaysian Chinese to be more multiculturally orientated. Pointing to evidence of a slow but steady process of inter-ethnic acculturation, as reflected by the blending of flavours in Malaysian cuisines and reciprocal participation in each other's festivals, Ling argued that the different races have not become 'less Malay, or less Indian or less Chinese but all have become more Malaysian.' In 1994, the MCA made its first meaningful move away from Chinese exclusivity when party rules were amended to admit members of mixed ethnic descent, so long as one parent is Chinese. By breaching the exclusive Chinese political culture of the MCA, Ling's call to Chinese to adopt a multicultural Malaysian identification represents an important milestone in the maturation of MCA politics.

Chinese opposition politics

In five general elections (1974, 1978, 1982, 1986 and 1990) before its severe setback in 1995, the DAP's share of the Chinese vote was larger than the MCA's or Gerakan's. Lim Kit Siang led the party to its greatest electoral performance in 1986 when the party won 24 seats, capturing 21 per cent of the popular vote (about two-thirds of the total Chinese vote).

The DAP demonstrated spirited leadership on Chinese issues, as well as calling for more press freedom, less corruption and more accountability from government leaders. In contrast, as members of the ruling coalition, the MCA and Gerakan generally held back from

Ling Liong Sik (third from left) and former Deputy Prime Minister Anwar Ibrahim (second from left) hold up banner reading 'We are all one family.'

UMNO assembly, 1995.

pragmatic growth-oriented Malay leadership holds the reins of power, fundamental Chinese political, economic and cultural concerns will be accommodated. Although UMNO has responded to the pressures of the Islamic opposition by introducing Islamic elements into public policies – as evidenced by the establishment of an Islamic university and Islamic bank – and a closer foreign policy alignment with the Islamic world, its leadership has eschewed a doctrinaire rigidity harmful to the interests of non-Muslims. From the Chinese perspective, the worst-case scenario would be if UMNO's pragmatism were overcome by Islamic doctrinaire fundamentalism, whether by the Parti Islam or the Muslim revivalist groups that have gained ground within the Malay community since the 1970s. The Islamicizing mission of the Parti Islam state government in Kelantan since 1990 has resulted in stronger Chinese political support for the existing secular UMNO-dominated political system.

Another problematic scenario for Malay-Chinese relations would be if Malaysia were to experience a prolonged recession. The NEP succeeded primarily because the wealth produced by the country's robust growth rates enabled both Malays and Chinese to move forward. As the mid-1980s recession showed, economic deterioration threatened inter-ethnic relations.

Most Chinese in Peninsular Malaysia currently see the decommunalization of Malaysian politics as the only viable means for placing Malay-Chinese relations on a solid footing in the long term. They also realize that they lack the means to initiate such a process and must wait for Malay leaders to break the old mould and set up a new multiracial political configuration in which non-Malays would be invited to participate as co-equals.

Heng Pek Koon

publicly criticizing UMNO policies deemed detrimental to Chinese interests. While the DAP's vocal watchdog role won it the Chinese protest vote, the party leadership frequently found itself in trouble with the authorities. Party chief Lim Kit Siang was incarcerated under the Internal Security Act twice, after the 1969 racial riots and in 1987.

Although the DAP has consistently won a majority share of Chinese votes until the 1995 general elections, it has never succeeded in capturing enough votes to exercise power at the state level, unlike the Malay opposition party, Parti Islam, which has enjoyed several terms of power in Kelantan. The DAP's failure in the 1995 election revealed a sea change in Chinese voting behaviour brought about primarily by the successful economic performance of the National Front government, and also by the realization that accommodation was the only feasible option for Chinese political participation.

In 1991, the NEP was replaced by the less racially divisive National Development Policy. MCA and Gerakan electoral successes in 1995 (the former scored its largest ever gains, winning 31 out of 36 contested seats) were, in effect, endorsement for Prime Minister Datuk Seri Dr Mahathir Mohamad's growth-oriented and income-raising policies. Mahathir's call for Malaysia to become a fully developed country by the year 2020, in particular, offered the promise that Chinese business interests would be actively involved.

While obviously still committed to increasing the Malay share of national wealth, Mahathir appeared to have moved beyond Malay exclusivity with his call for a 'nation at peace with itself, territorially and ethnically integrated, living in harmony and in full and fair partnership, made up of one Bangsa Malaysia [Malaysian Nation].' While cynics dismiss Mahathir's sentiments as mere rhetoric, others see in his pragmatic policies a central role for continued Chinese economic participation.

After being forced to lower their horizons by the NEP, the Chinese are hopeful that, as long as a secular and

Chinese and Malay New Year jointly celebrated, 1996.

SABAH

Once the domain of the sultans of Brunei and Sulu, Sabah, or North Borneo as it was called, was ceded to the British North Borneo (Chartered) Company in 1881 and became a British colony in 1946. Following independence, it became a state within the Federation of Malaysia in 1963.

Census figures for 1995 put the size of the Chinese community at 225,000, or 12.5 per cent of a population numbering 1.8 million. A plural society, Sabah is also home to Dusuns, Bajaus, Kadazans, Muruts, Malays and, more recently, immigrants from Indonesia and the Philippines.

Migration history

Within a century of their arrival in the 18th century, the earliest Chinese settlers had ceased to speak Chinese and had melted into the local culture. Along with the mid-19th century Hakka migration into Bau (see p 184) was a much smaller movement into Sabah, particularly into Papar. The late 19th century saw the beginnings of Western attempts to settle Chinese along the coasts. An American attempt to set up a plantation-style colony at Kimanis with about 60 Chinese ended in failure. Scarcely more successful was the British Chartered Company's scheme for bringing Chinese from Hong Kong and the Straits Settlements to settle Sandakan, on the east coast. The first governor of North Borneo, William Hood Treacher, had been encouraged by the experience of Sarawak; he had appointed Sir Walter Medhurst, the Commissioner for Chinese Immigration of the Chartered Company, to bring in Chinese to meet the manpower needs of plantations. The migrants did not take kindly to their new undeveloped habitat, however, and many fled back to where they came from. It was only with the import of hardy Hakka cultivators from rural Guangdong that enduring Chinese settlements were created.

The arrival of the mostly Christian Hakkas was organized by Medhurst and a missionary named Rudolph Leschler, who had a church in Hong Kong. Leaving for Borneo could have got the Hakkas out of harm's way; large numbers of their kind had been casualties in the wars with the Punti (see p 26). The district they settled, Kudat, was reported to be well cleared by the mid-1880s, with maize, coconut, coffee, tea, pepper, fruits, vegetables and rice grown on hills and valleys. Through the Basel Mission Society, more Hakka Christians were brought in during 1913–14.

At about the same time the Chartered Company arranged for the immigration of more than 400 people from a part of northern China recently devastated by Yellow River floods. These settlers in Penampang, in the outskirts of Jesselton (now called Kota Kinabalu), are popularly referred to as 'Shandong people,' though most in fact originated in another Chinese province, Hebei. Today, what has come to be called 'Shandong Settlement' still has about 1,000 inhabitants, representing a rarity in Southeast Asia: a Chinese community of northern origin.

Plans to lay a railroad from Jesselton to Beaufort and Tenom prompted the import of more than 2,000 Chinese – Hakka and Cantonese – to the west coast in the early years of the 20th century. Numbers were rapidly augmented in the 1920s and 1930s by voluntary migration, the volume of which far exceeded that of organized migration (see table 5.8).

Since the 1960s, the Chinese population as a proportion of the total has steadily decreased. This is not only because the fertility rate of the Chinese has fallen while that of the indigenous peoples has risen, but also because large influxes of immigrants from Indonesia and the Philippines have altered the population composition, reducing even the chief ethnic group, the Dusuns, to only 12 per cent of the total.

Chinese family (Elizabeth Choy, first right and younger siblings) in British Borneo, circa 1916.

Distribution by speech group and place of settlement

The community is overwhelmingly Hakka, who for 40 years have accounted for more than half of all Chinese (see table 5.9). Next come the Cantonese, followed by Hokkiens and trailed by other much smaller speech groups. Hakka predominance is undoubtedly the outcome of earlier migration policies. Their numbers were given a particular boost after the 1920s by the government encouragement of family migration. Hakka is the lingua franca of the Chinese in Sabah, rather like Cantonese in Hong Kong.

Though mainly cultivators in earlier times, they have entered urban trades in large numbers following the rapid development of Kota Kinabalu (the state capital),

Table 5.8

Year	Number	Increase	Growth rate (%)	% of total population
1891*	7,156	—	—	11
1901*	12,282	5,126	71.6	12
1911	27,801	15,519	126.4	13
1921	39,256	11,455	41.2	15
1931	50,056	10,800	27.5	18
1951	74,374	24,318	48.6	22
1960	104,542	30,168	40.5	23
1970	139,509	34,967	33.4	21
1980	164,000	24,491	17.6	16
1991	218,200	54,200	33.0	16

*Excluding the population of Labuan Island.
Sources: Population censuses of North Borneo and Malaysia.

Table 5.9

DISTRIBUTION OF CHINESE BY REGIONAL SPEECH GROUP, 1991

Speech group	Number	% of total Chinese population
Hakka	113,628	57.0
Cantonese	28,769	14.4
Hokkien	26,303	13.2
Teochiu	10,350	5.2
Hainanese	6,939	3.5
Fuzhou	4,789	2.4
Guangxi	615	0.3
Henghua	459	0.2
Others	7,288	3.7
Total	199,140	100

Source: State Population Report: Sabah, 1991.

Table 5.10

TEN MAIN DISTRICTS OF CHINESE CONCENTRATION, 1991		
DISTRICT	**NUMBER OF CHINESE**	**% OF TOTAL CHINESE POPULATION**
Kota Kinabalu	57,864	26.5
Sandakan	45,637	20.9
Tawau	35,097	16.1
Penampang	14,129	6.5
Lahad Datu	8,080	3.7
Keningau	6,906	3.2
Kudat	6,323	2.9
Papar	4,886	2.2
Tenom	4,304	2.0
Tuaran	3,865	1.8

Source: State Population Report: Sabah, 1991.

Sandakan and other towns. Statistics for 1991 show that, of the more than 110,000 Hakkas in Sabah, 68 per cent were urbanites. Despite their occupational mobility, however, they have remained dominant in agriculture, constituting 60 per cent of all Chinese cultivators in 1991.

The Chinese are concentrated in three towns: Kota Kinabalu, Sandakan and Tawau (see table 5.10). Before 1970, Kota Kinabalu had fewer people than Sandakan, but the rapid development of the timber and other industries and an accelerated growth in other sectors of the economy turned Kota Kinabalu into Sabah's premier business centre, with opportunities which beckon to Chinese from all over the state. The timber business bolstered the growth of Sandakan, whose Cantonese emphasis has earned it the epithet of Little Hong Kong.

Economic adjustment

The early settlers worked on tobacco plantations and grew padi. Then rubber became important from the early 20th century. Welcomed by the British, Chinese energies underpinned the development of North Borneo's economy.

Occupational mobility became apparent from the 1960s, with the Chinese making their mark in wholesale, retail, manufacturing, construction and the service industry. Many Chinese rode on the state's economic expansion in the 1970s to become either wealthy timber merchants in Sandakan or cocoa planters in Tawau (the Chinese in Tawau, where cocoa plantations are concentrated, were well placed to benefit from the rise of cocoa prices on the world market).

But an economic challenge to the Chinese was posed by the New Economic Policy (see p 180). In addition local Chinese interests were affected by new players in Sabah like West Malaysian and Taiwan investors. Downstream timber industries are now under the control of Taiwan capital, while many palm oil and cocoa plantations are operated by West Malaysian businessmen. The government prohibition of log exports in 1993 dealt a further blow to the local Chinese. They remain strong in the service sector – in wholesale and retail, in import-export trading, hotels, restaurants and property development. But in other sectors they are up against stiff competition from newcomers from outside Sabah.

Organization

The oldest of the Chinese business associations is the Sandakan Chinese Chamber of Commerce, founded in 1891; but each of the dozen-odd towns in Sabah has one. They joined together to form the Sabah United Chinese Chambers of Commerce in 1955. Business networking apart, the various Chambers of Commerce concern themselves also with education. The one in Kota Kinabalu, for example, has singly established five Chinese-medium schools and helped to found a sixth.

Politically the Sabah Chinese are not at one. Some are members of the multi-ethnic Parti Bersatu Sabah; others have joined the predominantly Chinese Sabah Progressive Party (CSPP), the Liberal Democratic Party or the Malaya Chinese Association. The CSPP is a member of the ruling United Front. In May 1996, the post of Chief Minister, rotated every two years, fell on a Chinese, Yong Teck Lee, the chairman of the CSPP. Three of his fellow party members also became State Ministers: Tham Nyip Shen, Minister of Industrial Development; Raymond Tan, Minister of Social Services, and Michael Lim, Deputy Minister of Local Government and Housing.

Niew Shong Tong

SARAWAK

The Chinese are multi-ethnic Sarawak's second largest ethnic group, surpassed only by the Ibans (Sea Dayaks), but numbering more than the Bidayuh (Land Dayaks), Melanau, Malay and other minorities.

The island of Borneo, of which Sarawak forms a territorial part, appears in early Chinese sources as Poni, Poli or Polo. Trade and tribute relations between the island and China go back 1,500 years, but only with the arrival of pioneering Hakka gold-mining partnerships and brotherhoods in the mid-18th century could one speak of Chinese settlement. Grouped into frontier organizations called *kongsi* (see Part III) – of which two of the best known were Lanfang and Dagang (Ta-kong) – these miners were located at first in areas beyond the boundaries of today's Sarawak, but began moving into the latter's Bau, Simanggang and Engkilili districts with the founding of the Brooke dynasty in 1841.

A war in 1857 between the Bau *kongsi* and James Brooke, the first White Rajah, marked the onset of po-

Chinese gold miners in Bau.

litical and economic changes which saw Hakka miners shifting to gambier and pepper planting. The number of Chinese remained small until the start of the 20th century (see table 5.11).

An agreement between Charles Brooke, the second Rajah, and Wong Nai Siong, a Fuzhou Methodist minister, to start a colony of Fuzhou men, women and children brought the first big wave of Chinese immigrants to Sarawak, principally to Sibu (New Fuzhou, as it is still known). The second batch, led by a Cantonese called Tang Kung Suk, was of Chinese from Guangdong. They too were brought to open up the land around Sibu to cultivation. The third batch, headed for the same area, was brought by the Reverend Dr William Brewster from Henghua (Xinghua) in Fujian.

As Sarawak needed manpower also for its coal mines, agents were appointed to recruit Chinese indentured labourers through Singapore. Mainly Cantonese and Hakka, these arrivals also included smaller numbers of Teochius and Hainanese. Chinese labour, sourced in Singapore, southeastern China and Hong Kong, was also brought in to work the oilfields in Miri.

The 1950s saw the slowing of immigration in response to restrictive policies. Thereafter the Chinese population grew by natural increase. The falling proportion of Chinese in the total population has come of a lower fertility rate than that of the indigenes.

Distribution by speech group and place of settlement

Hakkas predominated until 1980, when Fuzhou speakers surpassed them (see table 5.12). Hakka immigration predated that of the other speech groups, but the Fuzhou community overtook them in size by virtue of immigration volume as well as a rate of increase made faster by economic advancement. The fact that these two groups make up more than 65 per cent of the total indicates both their importance in the community and the head start they had over others in the timing of their immigration.

A noteworthy feature in the growth of the Fuzhou community is its geographical spread from Sibu to the Rajang River valley, where it opened up Sarikei, Kanowit, Kapit and other frontiers. Subsequently it spread to the area administratively known as the Fourth Division, specifically the towns of Bintulu, Miri and Marudi, though its presence remains strongest in Sibu and Sarikei, which together account for 56 per cent of all Fuzhou settlers. It is in Miri, Bintulu and Kuching, however, that it has grown the fastest. Indeed, no major town in Sarawak is without Fuzhou-speaking merchants or professionals.

The history of Chinese migration, the economic pursuits of the Chinese, and regional development (in particular urban growth) are three factors making for an uneven geographical distribution (see table 5.13). The first factor may be seen in the preponderance of Chinese in Kuching and Sibu: these were the destinations of the early pioneers. The second is borne out by the Chinese numbers in Miri, whose oilfields have provided livelihoods for many. Third, if the Chinese are at the most numerous in Kuching, Sibu and Miri, it is also because these are the three largest cities in Sarawak.

Economic activity

Speech group differentiation closely mirrors the division of Chinese economic activity into agriculture, manufacturing and services. Starting out as agriculturalists – growing padi, vegetables, rubber and pepper – Fuzhou people turned to urban commerce when land became scarce after the 1960s. With their own bank, the Hock Hua Bank, as a source of credit, they branched out successfully into trading activities, and by the 1970s had established themselves in finance, trading, wholesale, hostelry and other services. The greatest shift was into forestry, and today they virtually control the lumber industry. The well-known timber kings Tiong Xiao King and Lau Hui Kang, for example, are both of Fuzhou origin.

Agriculture has traditionally been, and still is, dominated by the Hakkas, who represented 75 per cent of all Chinese engaged in pepper, rubber, coconut, fruit and vegetable farming in the 1970s. By another indicator, namely the proportion of rural dwellers in the total Chinese population, Hakkas again predominate: 45 per cent in 1991 as against Fuzhou speakers' 30 per cent.

In trade too, specialization and speech-group membership overlap. A pawnshop or a herbal medicine is likely to have a Hakka owner, while grocery stores and shops selling local Chinese specialities are usually run by Teochius. The Cantonese are not so specialized, as may be seen from their jewellery shops, shoe shops and sundry stores. Fuzhou interests are particularly well represented in banking and finance, import and export trade, hardware and, latterly, the timber business. In Sarawak as elsewhere, Hainanese work chiefly in the catering trade. Equally specialized are the Henghua (Xinghua) speakers. They were the fishermen and rickshaw pullers of the pre-war era, and are now drivers of buses and taxis.

In manufacturing and the service sector, the Chinese are better represented than any of the other ethnic groups. This is particularly pronounced in commerce, over 80 per cent of which appears to be in Chinese hands. Similarly, a majority of the interests in transport and construction are Chinese. Given their economic pursuits, it is not surprising that the Chinese are so highly urbanized.

Organization

Of Sarawak's Chinese associations, more than 200 are based on common trade, over 90 are based on common geographic origin, and some 50 are same-surname groupings. Quite a few go back to the 19th century: the Teochiu Association, for example, was founded in 1864, while

Table 5.11

GROWTH OF SARAWAK CHINESE POPULATION

YEAR	NUMBER	GROWTH RATE (%)	% OF TOTAL POPULATION
1841	1,000	—	—
1857	4,000	300.0	—
1871	4,947	23.6	3.5
1877	7,000	41.5	3.0
1909	45,000	542.8	10.8
1939	123,626	174.7	25.2
1947	145,158	17.4	26.6
1960	229,154	57.9	30.8
1970	293,949	28.3	30.1
1980	385,200	31.0	29.5
1991	475,800	23.5	28.0

Sources: Runciman (1960); Purcell (1951); Baring-Gould and Bampfylde (1909); Report on the Population Census, 1947, 1960, 1970, 1980 and 1991.

Table 5.12

CHINESE POPULATION BY REGIONAL SPEECH GROUP

SPEECH GROUP	1980	%	1991	%
Fuzhou	126,346	32.8	149,293	33.5
Hakka	124,805	32.4	142,743	32.0
Hokkien	51,617	13.4	59,322	13.3
Teochiu	33,127	8.6	36,062	8.1
Cantonese	23,882	6.2	27,485	6.2
Henghua	13,097	3.4	14,567	3.3
Hainan	7,704	2.0	7,898	1.8
Others	4,622	1.2	8,178	1.8
Total	385,200	100.0	445,548	100.0

Source: Ko (1986).

Table 5.13

MAIN DISTRICTS OF CHINESE CONCENTRATION, 1991		
DISTRICT	NUMBER OF CHINESE	% OF TOTAL CHINESE POPULATION
Kuching	154,113	32.4
Sibu	97,663	20.5
Miri	51,707	10.9
Sarikei	21,367	4.5
Bintulu	20,711	4.4
Maradong	11,194	2.4
Serian	10,197	2.1
Marudi	9,282	2.0
Simanggang (Sri Aman)	8,703	1.8
Bau	8,605	1.8

Source: Population Census, 1991.

the Hokkien Association began in 1871. Business interests are advanced through bodies such as the Kuching Chinese General Chamber of Commerce (the earliest such association, founded in 1930) and the Associated Chinese Chambers of Commerce and Industry of Sarawak. These organizations were headed by wealthy and locally influential merchant–entrepreneurs like Ong Tiang Swee (1864–1950) and Wee Kheng Chiang (see box below). Smaller associations have also banded together to form federations based on the local catchment area – the Federation of Sibu Division Chinese Associations and the Federation of Miri Chinese Associations being two ex-amples. These in turn have federated into a state-wide association, the Federation of Sarawak Chinese Associations.

Chinese political interests are organized into the Sarawak United People's Party (SUPP), which was formed in 1959 when three groups came together: the traditional merchant-entrepreneur (*towkay*) class, a new generation of Chinese with advanced English education, and left-wingers with a grassroots following. Despite its multi-ethnic membership, the SUPP is all but perceived as an ethnically based Chinese political party. Another political party, the Sarawak Chinese Association, was established in the 1962, but it failed to attract and hold interests and was disbanded in the 1970s. In 1970 the once left-wing SUPP became part of the establishment by joining the state coalition government, and many of the state cabinet ministers were drawn from the SUPP membership.

Niew Shong Tong

Wee Kheng Chiang (1890-1978).

WEE KHENG CHIANG (1890–1978)

So influential was the Sarawak Chinese businessman Wee Kheng Chiang that Lady Sylvia Brooke, the wife of Rajah Vyner Brooke, called him the 'Uncrowned King of Sarawak' in her 1970 autobiography, *Queen of the Head-Hunters*.

His was the proverbial rags to riches story. In her book Sylvia Brooke wrote that he was 'a brilliant and ambitious man with the lined face of one who has had to work hard for everything. He amassed great riches, became very powerful, and eventually owned vast properties and a bank. I . . . often told him he was a rascal and a rogue, and this delighted him so much that he would send for a bottle of champagne and drink to it.'

Born in Kuching in July 1890, he was the second son of Wee Tee Yah, an immigrant from the village of Eng Khee in Quemoy (Jinmen), China. Although he already had a wife in Quemoy, Wee Tee Yah married a Hakka widow, Song Kim Keow, in Kuching.

Wee Tee Yah died in 1899 of illness, leaving behind three sons and a daughter. His widow, who already had two children by her first marriage, found it difficult to raise six children on her meagre earnings as a Chinese *sinseh* (medical practitioner). So the 11-year-old Kheng Chiang and his two brothers were sent to Quemoy to live with their father's first wife and their maternal grandparents.

Wee's brothers did not adapt well to their new surroundings and returned to Kuching within a year. However, Wee stayed on until 1906 when a plague broke out in the village. Concerned for Wee's health, his father's first wife sent him back to Kuching – a prudent move, as her own death from the plague shortly thereafter proved.

The gangling teenaged Wee enrolled at the Anglican, English-medium St Thomas's Secondary School. His knowledge of the English language was undoubtedly a tremendous asset in his adulthood, for it opened doors to the English-speaking community and the palace of the White Rajahs. At the same time, his Chinese education in Quemoy facilitated his contacts with the Chinese business community in Sarawak.

Wee's superior mind and determination to succeed caught the attention of the most influential Chinese businessman in Sarawak, Kapitan China Ong Tiang Swee. So impressed was Ong that he decided to betroth his eldest

daughter, Siew Eng, to Wee despite the latter's humble background. And when his eldest son died, Ong appointed Wee as the new manager of his bank, the Sarawak Chinese Bank.

In 1914 Rajah Brooke set up the Sarawak Farms Syndicate, a joint venture between the government and Chinese businessmen, to run the lucrative gambling and opium monopolies and the arrak distilleries. As Kuching's richest man, Ong became chairman of the new syndicate, and the bilingual Wee was made manager.

The job brought Wee into contact with the higher echelons of government as well as Sarawak's leading Chinese businessmen. As the man in charge, Wee was also very often the first man to know if any shareholder wanted to sell his interest in the company. By purchasing such interests, Wee became a substantial shareholder of the syndicate.

He was relieved of his duties as manager when, following the outlawing of opium sale by the Geneva Convention, Rajah Brooke dissolved the syndicate in 1924. Having already started the Bian Chiang Bank four years earlier, Wee now set up his own distillery. In addition, he owned a pig farm; operated an import-export company, a grocery company and a coconut oil mill. Bit by bit he also acquired some of the choicest properties in Kuching.

Following in the footsteps of his father-in-law and the other leading Chinese businessmen, he began to play an active role in the community. Besides contributing generously to the Chinese schools, to his alma mater and to local charities, he assumed leadership roles in the Chinese civic organizations.

In 1930, when the Chinese General Chamber of Commerce was founded, Wee was its treasurer. He succeeded his father-in-law as chairman of the Chamber when the latter decided not to stand for re-election after his first term. Similarly, when Ong stepped down as chairman of the Hokkien Association, Wee took his place. His social status rose further when Rajah Brooke appointed him to the Council Negri, an advisory body of which the only other Chinese member was Ong. Later, in recognition of his contributions to the state, the Sarawak government honoured him with the Panglima Negara Bintang Sarawak award and the Officer of the Star of Sarawak medal.

In the 1930s Wee extended his business activities to Singapore. There he started first a commodities firm, Chop Bian Hong, which was subsequently renamed Kheng Leong Pte Ltd, and then, in 1935, he founded the United Chinese Bank (now the United Overseas Bank). The next 40 years saw him travelling frequently between Sarawak and Singapore to oversee his business empire.

Before his death after a long illness in his beloved Kuching home on April 12, 1978, he left the running of his Sarawak interests and Bian Chiang Bank to his third son, Hood Teck, and the Singapore interests and United Overseas Bank to Cho Yaw, the eldest son of his Quemoy-born wife.

Pang Cheng Lian

THE PHILIPPINES

Demography

There are no firm figures for the number of Chinese in the Philippines. Estimates range from 800,000 to 1,200,000, the most common being 1,000,000, or less than 2 per cent of the total population of the Philippines. Half or more reside in Metro Manila. Much smaller clusters are found in such provincial cities as Cebu and Davao. The trend has been towards concentration in larger cities. Population growth has been rapid in recent decades: as late as 1950 there were only about 120,000 Chinese. Most of the growth has been by natural increase. Chinese immigration has been quite restricted for several decades and legal immigrants have been relatively few. There is an undetermined body of illegals, but the total of legal and illegal immigrants is believed to be no more than 100,000 in the early 1990s.

The population is now young and mostly local-born. Citizenship roughly parallels birthplace or very long residence: an estimated 90 per cent of Chinese are citizens of the Philippines. Despite centuries of immigration from China, generational depth in today's Chinese society is relatively slight. Until the 1940s a sojourning pattern of prolonged stay but ultimate return to China prevailed. Third-generation members are now quite common, but anything beyond that much less so. In recent decades some middle-class Chinese emigration (not necessarily permanent) has occurred, to such destinations as the United States, Canada and Singapore.

Demographically, Hokkiens overwhelm, at 85–90 per cent of the population. Cantonese are the only other group. Sizeable Hokkien immigration began in the 16th century from ports in the regions of Zhangzhou and Quanzhou. Over the centuries, Zhangzhou people lost their original pre-eminence in the Philippines and Quanzhou migrants became numerically and culturally dominant. Within the Quanzhou region, migration to the Philippines became increasingly concentrated so that today people from the Jinjiang and Shishi area are said to make up at least 60 per cent of the Philippine Chinese population. Important numbers of Hokkiens also come from Nan'an county, the Tongan-Xiamen area and the Zhangzhou region.

The Cantonese began to come to the Philippines only in the 19th century. Their origins are the same as those Cantonese who migrated to the Western Hemisphere: the Siyi counties west of the Pearl River Delta, especially Taishan and Kaiping, and the counties around Canton and the delta itself. The Cantonese population does not appear to be growing and there may be some decline because of migration to places where Cantonese are the majority.

Both Hokkiens and Cantonese have been motivated to migrate to the Philippines by the influences common to emigrant regions in southeast China: population pressure and economic and political difficulties in the home region. But the Hokkiens, in addition, are the heirs to a centuries-old, once-prosperous trading connection and a long-standing near-monopoly of the Philippines as a Hokkien hinterland of jobs and remittances. Chain migration of individual family members from Fujian was the principal historical feeder of the Philippine Chinese population.

Historical outline

Though Chinese trade with the Philippines began much earlier, our knowledge of Chinese residence there dates only from the 16th century. Spanish colonial settlement in the 1570s and the development of a lucrative connecting trade between Manila and Mexico stimulated a much enlarged Chinese settlement. By 1600 there were 20,000 Chinese, mostly in the Manila area, and a level of settlement of 20–30,000 was maintained for much of the 17th century.

Not only did Chinese provide silk and porcelain goods, which they exchanged in Manila for American silver from Mexico; Chinese also created and monopolized new commercial and service occupations of all

Map 5.7

THE PHILIPPINES

kinds, meeting the needs of Manila and other urban settlements.

Before long they had become indispensable to local economies and societies. Along with their indispensability there arose suspicions. The Chinese greatly outnumbered the Spaniards, who feared their economic power, cultural difference, and the possibility they might seek aid from nearby China to overthrow Spanish rule in the Philippines. The Chinese resented their treatment by the Spanish colonial government: restrictions of residence and economic opportunity, discriminatory and burdensome taxation, forced labour drafts, and pressures to convert to Catholicism. As the Spaniards suspected revolt, the Chinese suspected preventive massacre. Both took place. In 1603 and again in 1639 there were uprisings/massacres in which 20,000 or more Chinese lost their lives. Yet the Chinese still returned to the Philippines and its – even with restrictions – economic opportunities.

The early pattern of rising suspicions, resentments and fears, culminating in crises and bloodshed, was repeated in 1662, 1686, and 1762. There were also attempts to limit the number of Chinese residents by immigration controls and by expulsions, the largest of the latter taking place in the mid-1700s. There were further extensions of the pattern of indispensability combined with restriction and mutual mistrust: Chinese bribed Spaniards to circumvent restrictions and Spaniards accepted and expected bribes. Meanwhile, in the colonial learning situation, Filipinos observed and learned, finding themselves sometimes on the side of the Chinese but as often not. José Ignacio Paua, an ethnic Chinese, is now seen as a hero of the Filipino Revolution of the 1890s, and Chinese financial and other contributions to that movement are recognized. But in the uprisings/massacres of earlier years, Chinese and Filipinos were often on opposite sides.

From the 1760s onward, sanguinary episodes involving the Chinese became less frequent and smaller in scale. After the expulsions of 1755 and 1766, the level of Chinese population remained low – in the range of 5,000–10,000 – for many decades. The expulsion of 1766 followed the involvement of the Chinese on the side of the British in 1762–64. Then, beginning in the mid-19th century, as Spain opened the Philippines to world trade and promoted economic growth, Chinese were allowed to immigrate in greater numbers than ever. By 1898, when the United States assumed colonial rule over the Philippines, Chinese numbered approximately 100,000. Moreover, Chinese were now settled in every part of the Philippines and had entered many new lines of work: collectors and distributors of export crops and imported goods, rice and corn millers, labour contractors, and operators of small *sari-sari* (miscellaneous goods) retail stores in remote villages.

Under American rule, Chinese immigration was somewhat restricted but by 1939 the population had grown to just under 120,000. The Chinese continued to enter new occupations. And, as in the late 19th century, they developed both new community institutions and enhanced relationships with China. The American promise of eventual independence for the Philippines encouraged the development of Filipino nationalism, which was partly directed against the Chinese. This was particularly so during the era of the semi-independent Philippine Commonwealth, 1935–41, when a number of anti-Chinese measures were passed by the Commonwealth government.

There followed the short but terrifying Japanese Occupation of the Philippines, 1942–45. The Philippine Chinese were now face to face with those they had tried to keep out of China. Throughout the 1930s, as Japan had advanced in China, the Philippine Chinese had been among the most ardent overseas Chinese contributors of funds, manpower and propaganda to the cause of China's resistance. All this the Japanese knew. In the face of the occupation, some Chinese collaborated; but many went into hiding or joined one of the several Chinese guerrilla units that sprang up, fighting the Japanese for China but also for their future in the Philippines.

When the Philippines became independent in 1946, Filipinos fully assumed the rulers' heritage and dilemma. The Chinese were indispensable to the desired national economic development. But they seemingly were alien at a time when nationalism was at its height. National economic development, it was felt, should mean economic development by and for Filipinos. Beginning in 1954, several nationalist laws were passed aimed at the economic power – present and anticipated – of the Chinese. Retail trade was to be limited to citizens, thereby excluding the Chinese, nearly all of whom were non-citizens. The rice and corn business was handled in the same way. And, in anticipation of the future, Chinese (the only major non-citizen group in the Philippines) were forbidden to practise the professions.

The passing of these laws caused an economic crisis for the Chinese. They responded either by organizing group efforts to negotiate for softening the application of the laws, or else by individually using various evasive measures. Some Chinese who had the means to do so shifted their operations from retail to wholesale, or from commerce to manufacturing. But for those who could

Chinese Filipina, Manila, 1880s.

not shift, the 20 years from 1954 to 1975 were a time of difficulty and limited achievement.

Philippine Chinese relations with China now became closer than ever. The 'China,' in this case, was the Republic of China (ROC) on Taiwan. Philippine law effectively required nearly all the local Chinese to be citizens of the ROC. And the Cold War made allies of the ROC and the Philippines under the American anti-Communist alliance umbrella.

The Chinese entered a new era in the 1970s. President Ferdinand Marcos, as a preliminary to switching diplomatic recognition from Taipei to Beijing, took two important steps. He filipinized the Chinese schools, greatly reducing their Chinese language and cultural content. He also, in 1975, facilitated mass naturalization for the Philippine Chinese. Most of the local ethnic Chinese who were eligible to do so applied for naturalization and the majority of the Chinese population now became citizens of the Philippines rather than, as they otherwise would have become, citizens of the People's Republic of China.

The Chinese were now formally equal to all others in the Philippines. The economic opportunities denied them by the nationalist laws were now theirs as citizens. So were political rights, and over the next two decades the Chinese increasingly participated in national and local political affairs. Since the Chinese were now Philippine citizens and the Cold War alliance of the Philippines with Taiwan had been terminated, the political influence of 'China' receded. Philippine governments now dealt with both mainland China and Taiwan at arm's length, with emphasis on economic issues. For their part, the Philippine Chinese, while maintaining economic and familial interests in China, focused increasingly upon their future in the Philippines.

Reception: excluded or included?

The shaping forces of Philippine-Chinese society may be said to have been: demography, opportunities, community institutions and relations with China (see Part IV). 'Demography' refers to the size, concentration and generational character of the Chinese population. 'Opportunities' in the Philippines refers to questions of participation in the economy, society and politics of the country. 'Community institutions' are those organizations that may hold the Chinese together as a group (or allow them to bridge the gap between themselves and Malay Filipinos). 'Relations with China' are personal, familial and 'home' regional on the one hand, and broadly economic, political and cultural on the other.

These forces work themselves out historically in a general pattern as follows: expansion of Chinese population and its economic activities leads to Filipino reaction in the form of anti-Chinese sentiment; that, in turn, encourages the formation and maintenance of Chinese institutions in local Chinese society, and an inclination to seek China's aid when it is available.

It has been argued that the relationship of the Chinese to Philippine society has been an occasionally

Chinese merchants, or sangley.

oscillating one, as follows: (1) excluded, 1570–1750; (2) included, 1750–1850; (3) excluded, 1850–1930; (4) artificially excluded, 1930–75; (5) potentially included, 1975–present.

In the first period, 1570–1750, Chinese monopolization of economic activities, their cultural alienness, apparent ties to a nearby and powerful China and the obvious mutual antipathies of Spaniards and Chinese led Filipinos to adopt Spanish stereotypes and to despise the Chinese as a pariah group. Although the Spaniards called the early Chinese residents *sangley*, a word referring to their mercantile character, Filipinos had their own term. The Filipino word *intsik*, originally carrying polite connotations, became a term of opprobrium, equivalent to that of 'Chink' in North America. Spanish policy segregated the Chinese in residence, the most famous place of these being a Chinese quarter called the Parián, where non-Chinese might go to shop but not to live. For their part, the Chinese, mostly sojourners, followed the custom of China by referring to non-Chinese – whether Filipinos or Spaniards – as 'barbarians,' or *hoan-a* in the Hokkien version.

In the second period, 1750–1850, expulsion of non-Catholics had drastically reduced the number of Chinese and their population remained at a low level of 5–10,000, nearly all converted Catholics and all in the Manila area. These numbers now gave less occasion for apprehensiveness. More important, perhaps, the indispensable economic roles played by the Chinese were now being taken over by the Chinese mestizos (see box p 190). The mestizos lived in close proximity to the Malay Filipinos and, as promoters of Spanish and Filipino values and practices, were culturally compatible. They were Philippine-born, had few if any ties to China (some could not speak Chinese), and were not seen as a political threat. Some observers predicted that eventually the mestizos would completely replace the Chinese in the economy. Overshadowed now by the mestizos, the Chinese were at a level of size, concentration and nominal cultural proximity to be acceptable.

In the third period, 1850–1930, the Chinese population greatly increased and spread to all parts of the archipelago. The Chinese recovered their leading position in the economy. By the 1880s an anti-Chinese reaction had surfaced. The Chinese met this by organizing more powerful bodies than ever before to take care of their

A mestizo, General Emilio Aguinaldo, was President of the First Philippines Republic.

José Rizal, the national hero of part Chinese ancestry.

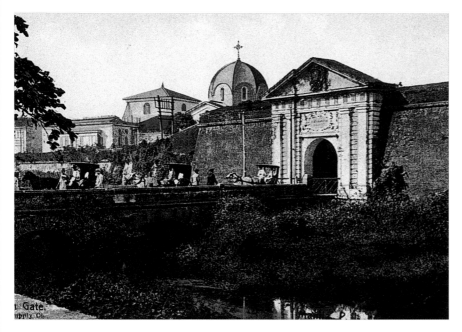

Gate of Parián with Franciscan church behind it, circa 1907.

being taught the long-term future and values of a modern Chinese nation, while Filipino youth were learning the civic and other lessons for a modern Filipino nation. The Chinese were again excluded.

In the fourth period, 1930–75, the Chinese continued to be excluded. In the 1930s Filipino and Chinese nationalisms reached their greatest conflict, with the Philippine Chinese caught in between. The Philippine Commonwealth Constitution and Naturalization Law affirmed that children of a Chinese father were to be Chinese citizens and naturalization would be difficult.

Meanwhile, Japan's invasion of Chinese territory brought new pressures on Philippine Chinese to support the 'fatherland.' China's Left versus Right politics now reached their most intense level in the Philippines. When the Japanese occupied the Philippines, 1942–45, Chinese guerrilla forces that opposed them were organized and joined on a Left-Right basis. The postwar and post-independence alliance of the Philippines with Taiwan was a victory for the Right, which now became the mainstream in Chinatown politics. The Left maintained itself as a non-mainstream group. The vast majority of Chinese, whatever their sympathies and preferences, were necessarily citizens of the ROC. More immigration of families from China in the 1930s had resulted in a larger number of children growing up in the Philippines. For them, in particular, the artificiality of being citizens of China but without access to the mainland origin points of their parents, was all too evident. So was the artificiality of being unable to be citizens in the land of their birth or early childhood.

The fifth period, 1975–present, offers the potential

own affairs, negotiate with the government, and appeal to China. By the early 20th century, China's nationalism and political parties had come to the Philippines, as had Chinese language newspapers, much of whose content, at that time, was about China's affairs. These Chinese institutions promoted Chineseness, Chinese nationalism and a focus on China at the same time as American-sponsored schools for Filipinos were promoting Filipino nationalism. As Chinese women and children were added to Philippine Chinese society, the youth were

MESTIZOS

Chinese-Filipino mestizos (see picture at left) have been a critically important element in the development of modern Philippine economy and society. Historically, they have been a major source of the modern Filipino economic, social and political élite. In the 20th century, Chinese mestizos are no longer a separate group. But for over 150 years in the Spanish period they were distinctly so. Chinese sojourners of that era were single males, whether or not they had families in China. There were many unions, legal or informal, with Filipinas. The mixed, or mestizo, offspring of these unions frequently combined business skills learned from the father with Catholicism and general Filipino cultural orientations from the mother.

Mestizos, as a group, were visible by the 1630s. By the 1740s local groupings of mestizos separated themselves from the Chinese into their own formal associations, or *gremios*. The most famous of these was in Binondo, then a suburb of Manila, and now the centre of Chinatown. As a part of Spanish attempts to control and convert the Chinese to Catholicism, Binondo had been developed by the Dominicans as a settlement for Christian Chinese and their children. Among those children was Lorenzo Ruiz, whose life and works earned him canonization in the 20th century as the Philippines' first saint. By the time Binondo became a part of the city of Manila, the mestizos had replaced the Chinese as the leading element among its residents. Mestizos were concentrated in and around Manila and the towns of Central Luzon, but were also found wherever else the Chinese had once settled. By 1810 there were approximately 120,000 of them in a Philippine population of about 2,500,000. Expulsions of Chinese in the 1750s

and 1760s gave the mestizos their chance to take over many of the economic roles hitherto exclusively Chinese: wholesaling, retailing, carpentry, printing, shoemaking, tailoring and many others. In Central Luzon they also became landowners.

By the early 19th century they were becoming the most powerful and influential group under Spanish rule – not as a special kind of Chinese but as a special kind of Filipino. The very term 'Filipino' was in part their creation. As urban society developed in the late 19th century, its culturally most creative and dynamic element was the Chinese mestizo. Members of this group, together with leading elements among Malay Filipinos, created a Hispanicized urban style of life and group identity as Filipinos. Increasingly, the Filipino élite came from this group. José Rizal (1861–96), the Filipino national hero, came from a Chinese mestizo background. Major financiers of the Philippine Revolution (1896–1902), like Mariano Limjap, Telesforo Chuidian, and Roman Ongpin, were Chinese mestizos. Most modern Filipino political leaders, including presidents, have been of at least partly Chinese mestizo background. When the Chinese began to immigrate again in larger numbers after 1850, they were able to oust the mestizos from many of their occupations. The mestizos now involved themselves increasingly in landholding and export crop agriculture, thereby becoming part of the landed élite of the modern Philippines.

By the end of the Spanish period the Chinese mestizos had disappeared as a separate group. The *gremios* were abolished and the children of mixed Chinese-Filipina marriages now were seen as either Filipino or Chinese. In the 20th century, as many Chinese women began to come to the Philippines, intermarriage rates probably decreased for a time. But after World War II, increasing contact between Chinese and Malay Filipino youth, especially in universities, has maintained a considerable level of intermarriage and thereby a substantial body of mestizos who are sometimes the majority in Chinese schools. But they occupy no special formal status with reference either to the Chinese or Filipino societies.

Edgar Wickberg

for inclusion. Ethnic Chinese are now nearly all citizens and provisions in recent Philippine constitutions (1973 and 1987) mean that persons of Chinese background now born in the Philippines will be citizens of it. While there is every indication that most ethnic Chinese are in the Philippines to stay and identify themselves with it, Filipino suspicions are still present. The opening of China to overseas Chinese investment and travel has stimulated some of the old fears that Chinese (despite their citizenship now) will turn again to China. But, as discussed below, developments in Philippine Chinese society suggest otherwise.

Economic roles

Between 1850 and the 1930s the Chinese assumed a commanding role in the economy. Suitable data is not available, but estimates from the 1930s indicate that the Chinese controlled much of the domestic economy, including over 75 per cent of both retail trade and the rice business. Their greatest achievement was the creation of networks of product distribution and sales that often extended to the farthest corners of the Philippines. In such places the local Chinese *sari-sari* store often served as collector and forwarder of local products, and retailer of imported daily-needs goods.

Credit advances to customers against future crop purchases were often a part of its operations. In rice surplus areas, Chinese millers and brokers often used credit arrangements to acquire control over lands, something mestizos had also done. But Chinese did not become landed producers of farm products, and they had almost no role in the rapidly growing sugar industry. The export goods they handled were chiefly abaca (Manila hemp) and coconut products. Their major imported good was textiles. Chinese were involved in a relatively minor way as actual importers and exporters. Their usual role was as distributors of goods others imported and collectors and forwarders of goods others exported.

In the American period, Chinese firms based in Manila entered all aspects of the newly developing lumber business. But with the exception of lumber, alcohol distilling and rice milling, the Chinese did little processing of primary goods; their role remained mostly one of purchasing, distribution and sales. Chinese hardware stores expanded, but typically did not manufacture but distributed American-made machinery. The founding of the China Bank in the 1920s did not herald the emergence of major entrepreneurs. The business leaders of 1900 and their descendants were still in place, but neither they nor others seemed eager to go beyond the role of commercial dominance in the domestic economy and an important role in certain goods for export. Meanwhile, Philippine Chinese remittances to China averaged US$6,400,000 per year during the 1930s, with perhaps 20 to 30 per cent of that being investments in Fujian.

In the early 1930s the Philippine Chinese were hit hard by the world Depression and by Japanese competition. The reduced domestic buying power caused by the Depression severely injured Chinese retail operations. In the case of the Japanese, their imported goods were mostly handled by Chinese. When the latter instituted a boycott in reaction to Japan's infringements on Chinese territory, the Japanese met this by establishing their own retail operations in the Philippines, selling the cheaper Japanese goods the Chinese – for a time, at least – would not handle. Expanding Japanese business in Mindanao also struck hard at Chinese interests there. By the late 1930s, as the economy improved, the position of the Chinese did also. But they now had to face nationalist economic measures passed by the Philippine Commonwealth government. The Japanese Occupation followed, after which further nationalist laws under an independent Philippines were promulgated.

Since the 1950s, the role of the Chinese has been reduced in some sectors (retailing, rice business, product distribution), but vastly diversified into other sectors. Although foreign estimates are sometimes over 50 per cent, recent estimates by Philippine researchers of the Chinese share of the economy range from 25 to 50 per cent, most often in the 25–35 per cent range. Diversification has been the result of Philippine government policies, a growing economy, new business skills, foreign investment and technology, and a response to globalization and its opportunities.

The economic élite in contemporary Philippine Chinese society are much different from previous élites. They are newcomers from the 1950s and after, and the fields of enterprise are also very different. Retail trade nationalization drove many Chinese out of that field. But those who possessed (or could obtain) the necessary resources shifted from retailing products to wholesaling or manufacturing them. This was facilitated by the government's import substitution programme of the 1950s and 1960s, which put up tariff barriers to encourage domestic manufacturers. Textiles, hardware, cigarettes, food products, pharmaceuticals and metal fabrication were all areas now entered by Chinese manufacturing entrepreneurs. Born in China or the Philippines, these people were new on the scene in the 1950s. Some had the advantage of advanced technical training in schools; others simply learned as they went. By the 1960s the most successful of these were emerging into new fields beyond these light- and medium-weight industries: wholesaling, finance, real estate and property development.

In the 1970s, the Marcos government's promotion of export-led development and its mass naturalization of the Chinese offered more new opportunities. Chinese professional engineers and architects appeared. The growing middle class, Chinese and Filipino, provided a customer base for the Chinese-owned department stores and huge shopping malls that now appeared. Chinese went beyond this into other new fields. By the early 1990s, Chinese controlled several of the most important English-language newspapers. Of the 35 commercial banks in the Philippines, at least ten were Chinese-owned, including the Metropolitan Bank, the fastest growing bank in the country. In newspapers, banking, property development and food processing – and even, to some extent, in agribusiness – the Chinese had become competitors of the long-standing Filipino/mestizo élite. Chinese 'tycoons' have now emerged, but, perhaps for historical reasons, they are, so far, neither as numerous nor as wealthy as those in several other Southeast Asian countries.

At the other end of the economic scale, perhaps 10 per cent of the ethnic Chinese are poor, but still better off than the poorest Filipinos.

Two Chinese tycoons: Lucio C. Tan (top) and John L. Gokongwei Jr. (bottom).

China, Chineseness and Filipinoness

China has always loomed large in the consciousness of Philippine Chinese, partly because of its geographic nearness but also because of its many meanings. China as a country, if strong and prestigious, can be a source of aid to Philippine Chinese society and individuals in it. Its defence and strengthening may be worth their contributions, sometimes even when that involves them in China's politics. China is also the site of their relatives' residence, the place where remittances are sent and contributions to schools or other local projects may be made, and investments are also possible. But this dimension of China is local and can conflict with concern for or identity with China as a country in the 20th century. A case in point was the deep involvement of some leading Philippine Chinese in Fujian's affairs during the era of the autonomous Fujian Republic of the early 1930s. One of those leaders, Eduardo Coseteng, was for a time mayor of Xiamen under the Republic.

China is also the source of social and cultural models and influences. The Chinatown organizations and institutions, for whatever Philippine reasons they are created, are based on models from China. The preservation of Chinese families and Chinese culture in the Philippines are Philippine issues, but with China dimensions. China thus has meanings that are political, economic, social and cultural, and they are often so mixed together that it is impossible to untangle them. Does a sustained interest in Chinese culture in the Philippines

Swearing in ceremony at the Manila Chinese Chamber of Commerce.

imply that the ethnic Chinese in question are politically loyal to China? Filipinos have long suspected that it does.

China, for its part, largely disregarded the Philippine Chinese until the last years of the 19th century. The 20th century has been different. As China began its struggle to overcome recent international humiliation and to become a strong, modern nation, it called upon Chinese overseas for aid. China established consulates in the Philippines to protect the lives and property of the Chinese there. It supported Chinese schools for their children. And Chinese governments and modern political parties brought Chinese politics to the Philippines.

Sun Yat-sen enjoyed some support among Philippine Chinese, although less so than in some other Southeast Asian countries, perhaps because of the dominance of Hokkiens – not fellow-Cantonese – there. The May Fourth Movement had its effect in Manila, where left-wing organizations began to develop in response to its influence. Most of these were labour unions. Given the absence of large industry, members of these bodies were employees of various kinds, including shop clerks. The Kuomintang victory of 1927–28 in China strengthened the Philippine branch of that party. But top-level Chinatown politics of the day was not dominated by the Kuomintang. Rather, it took the form of a power triangle involving the Kuomintang, the consulate and the Manila Chinese Chamber of Commerce, each struggling against and negotiating with the two others.

The Chamber had been founded in 1904–06 with assistance from China and was, in turn, a successor to the Gremio de Chinos of the late Spanish period. The Chamber was at the peak of its power in the 1920s and 1930s. Its leader, and the dominant force in Philippine Chinese society at the time, was Dee C. Chuan, a lumber baron and founder of the China Banking Corporation. The Chamber in the early 1920s had successfully fended off a Bookkeeping Act by the Philippine Legislature which would have been damaging to Chinese interests. An appeal against the law was made to the United States Supreme Court which ruled it unconstitutional. That appeal was the work of Albino SyCip, one of Dee's associates, who held a law degree from the University of Michigan. The Chamber also worked closely with the major charitable organization in Manila, Shanju Gongsuo (known in English today as the Philippine Chinese Charitable Association Inc.), which was established in 1877 and which was responsible for the Chinese hospital, cemetery and related properties.

In the 1930s, there were great pressures on all Chinatown organizations to put China's affairs ahead of Philippine concerns. These pressures were felt throughout the wide variety of associations that had emerged since 1900. In the climate of the 1930s, focusing on defending China also polarized the community in terms of Left or Right visions of China's future. Organizations lined up accordingly and even purely Chinatown issues became subject to the Left–Right polarization. Patriotism towards China, defence of ancestral localities and relatives in Fujian, and personal and community interests in the Philippines all became more mixed than ever. During the Japanese Occupation, the Chinese guerrilla forces opposing them were either 'pro-Kuomintang' or 'pro-Communist.' The most conspicuous of the latter was the left-wing Wha Chi, or 'Chinese Branch,' which,

in the post-Japanese independent Philippines, supported the Filipino Hukbalahap agrarian guerrillas in their attempted social revolution in Central Luzon.

When the Japanese Occupation ended and the new Philippine Republic was established, China's influence took a new turn. Within a few years, the Korean War and the subsequent American decision to support Chiang Kai-shek's government in Taiwan began the process of putting together a Taiwan-Philippine alliance as part of the American Cold War containment strategy. Taiwan now began to exercise a very strong influence upon the Philippine Chinese.

These international developments were paralleled by national ones. The Philippine government, with American aid, strenuously attempted to suppress the Hukbalahap and any other left-wing group believed to be a threat to the new Republic. In this climate the Chinese left-wing organizations – the Wha Chi and the labour associations that had been revived – had no chance of continuing to exist openly.

At the top in Chinatown there was now a revolution in power. Dee C. Chuan had died and the Manila Chamber found itself in difficulty trying to deal with the economic nationalizing policies of the Philippine government. This opened the way for a group of what had been second-line leaders to create a new and much more powerful organization, the Federation of Filipino-Chinese Chambers of Commerce and Industry, Inc. in 1954. Where the Manila Chamber had been only loosely affiliated with local Chinese Chambers of Commerce around the Philippines, the new organization was to be a tight federation of such bodies. Like the Chamber, its mandate was to deal with both commercial and more general affairs of the community – in other words, to be the umbrella organization for the Philippine Chinese. Not only did it have a tighter Philippine-wide organization than the Chamber, it also had good relations with both the ROC government in Taiwan and with the Office of the President of the Philippines. Together with the ROC Embassy (formerly consulate), the Federation lobbied for mitigating the effects of the nationalist laws.

Five pyramids of organizations were now created in the Chinese community. Paralleling the Federation's own business hierarchy, there were to be federations of Chinese schools, of Kuomintang organizations, of anti-Communist organizations, and of surname or clan associations. This last took the form of the Grand Family Association, to which all of the major surname associations belonged. All of this took place in the 1950s.

The Federation was at once both the apex of the business pyramid and the apex of the Chinese community's organizational structures. Its leaders and their policy direction had become the mainstream in Chinatown politics. The Chamber continued to exist, still with its associated organizations, the charitable Shanju Gongsuo and its cemetery and hospital. The Chamber's position was ambiguous. At times it was at least nominally under the umbrella of the Federation. But as often it played the role of a rallying point and alternative for the remnants of the Left, now visible as the non-mainstream, wanting not so much to overthrow the Federation and its leaders as to be independent of their – so it seemed – excessive control. Major organizations that clustered around the Chamber included some trade associations, the Hongmen Jinbu Dang, and the venerable musical association brotherhood, the Tiong Ho Sia which was founded in 1820.

From the mid-1950s to the mid-1970s, Chinatown politics appeared to be stable. But underneath, and in some cases separate from the pyramids of organizations, there was a great proliferation of small, Chinese-style organizations. Two kinds predominated: the brotherhood and the native-place association. Both kinds sought what they believed was now missing in larger organizations: close, dependable relationships of mutual aid and protection. Their appearance in such numbers was in part an expression of alienation from the Federation and other major associations that seemingly had become unconcerned with the needs of small businessmen and salaried employees, especially during the economically critical period of 1954–75.

Brotherhoods had long existed, usually in the form of musical associations which, among other things, interested themselves in *nanguan* or *nanyin* music, a type dating back to medieval Quanzhou. Most members, however, were not performers but joined for the comradeship, the mahjong and the oppositionist political stance in Chinatown politics that many such organizations assumed. Those of the 1960s, typically called *jieyi* or *jiemeng*, commonly used the term *yi* (righteousness) in their titles.

Native-place associations reflect, in their scope, the great concentration of village origins and major surnames of the Philippine Chinese. By breaking down larger organizations of broader scope one could form native-place associations referring to a small locality where a single surname predominated. These, then, became almost like fragments of an actual lineage kin group in a village in Fujian.

There were also sentiments about the preservation of Chinese culture and its transmission to the next generation. Some of those concerned about this identified Chinese culture with links to the ancestral home in China. They were concerned about what, by the 1960s, seemed to be a possibility that the new Philippine-born generation, with much greater exposure than preceding generations to local society as a whole, might be assimilated into Philippine society. Native-place associations were one way of trying to encourage a sense of Chineseness in this generation. Finally, although contact with ancestral localities in mainland China was supposedly cut off by severely limited immigration rules and an absence of any relations with the People's Republic of China, there had, in fact, continued to be both immigration and other relations.

Since early in the 20th century, Philippine Chinese had had very close relations with ancestral localities in Fujian. The 'dual family' system (see p 78) was an integral part of Philippine Chinese life. Chinese sojourners maintained a Chinese family in Fujian with remittances while a Philippine – mestizo – family was maintained in the Philippines. By the 1930s, Fujian affairs had become part of the daily life of the Philippine Chinese. Their remittances before World War II were one-third of all overseas Chinese remittances to Fujian, and in the period 1871–1949 their investments were one-quarter of all overseas Chinese investments in that province – this despite the fact that there were larger, and often more affluent, Hokkien populations in Malaya and Indonesia at the time. Nearly all remittances to Quanzhou prefecture were from the Philippines. Philippine Chinese surname and native-place associations – which proliferated during the 1930s – often intervened as mediators in disputes between lineages (localized kin organizations) in ancestral villages in Fujian.

After 1949, the Philippines had ruled out any direct immigration from Fujian or any direct contact with it. Remittances, investment and immigration should now have closed down completely. They did not. By the late 1950s, a substantial number of Hokkiens with relatives in the Philippines had managed to leave China (especially after special privileges for Overseas Chinese Dependants, Qiaojuan, began to be abolished in the mid-1950s) and to settle in the North Point neighbourhood of Hong Kong. Remittances to Fujian from Manila, which had never fully stopped, now began to be channelled through this new conduit. By the late 1950s two-thirds of the Philippine remittances were going to and through Hong Kong. The other one-third, which went directly to Fujian, continued at a constant level until at least the early 1960s.

There were also funds sent to aid in school repair and reconstruction. Investments also continued. In the mid-1950s, just as the mainland Chinese govern-ment was encouraging Chinese overseas to adopt the citizenship of their countries of residence, it was also encouraging them to invest in overseas Chinese home areas. Fujian established investment companies with that in mind, and the Philippine Chinese were among the participants. Even long-distance mediation of lineage disputes in Fujian, common in the 1930s, was not totally interrupted. In the 1960s the ROC ambassador in Manila became involved in two cases concerning direct intervention of Philippine Hokkiens in local disputes in Fujian.

The new North Point colony in Hong Kong was more than a conduit for funds. It was also one for immigration. Those in Fujian who could do so obtained permission to visit relatives in Hong Kong. They often remained there, overstaying their permits. Some of them then went on to visit relatives in Manila, where some among that group might also overstay, hoping that their status would be regularized at some point. They thus became one source of the 'illegals' problem in the Philippines, the others being Chinese smuggled in by Taiwan or Hong Kong gangs. Most 'illegals' have remained in Manila, where the Chinatown is so large that they are not readily visible to non-Chinese. Some 'illegals' have had their status regularized by an amnesty in 1988; a second took place in 1996. Besides the 'illegals,' there is a small flow of legal immigrants from Fujian, some of them under a programme which admits elderly relatives of Philippine Chinese who wish to retire in the Philippines.

Shortly after the Philippines established relations with the People's Republic of China in 1975, the new policy of 'reforms and opening' was declared in Beijing. Individuals and associations of all kinds in Manila and in Fujian now began to exchange visits. Manila's Hokkiens became involved in joint venture and other investments in Fujian. They continued their aid to schools and, once cultural policies were relaxed, Philippine Chinese became a major source of funds for rebuilding lineage halls in Jinjiang.

Given the uninterrupted connection to Fujian, it is not so surprising that native-place associations continued to be formed in Manila. At the national level, Taiwan had become a substitute for the mainland as 'China.' But even groups not on the Left in Manila knew that 'hometowns' were on the mainland and tried to stay in touch with them. When relations with the mainland were resumed in 1975 many such people were already organized into locally focused native-place associations and prepared to play a liaison role.

Since the Philippines' establishment of relations with mainland China in 1975, the rhetoric of discussion about alleged political orientation uses the terms 'pro-Taiwan' and 'pro-mainland.' Some 'pro-mainland' friendship organizations have been established in Chinese Manila, and the previous non-mainstream, or Left organizations, continue to use mainland connections in Chinatown politics. But distinctions are now blurred by the heavy investment of Taiwan entrepreneurs in Fujian and elsewhere on the mainland. The 'pro-Taiwan' partisans in Manila are, like the 'pro-mainland' ones, investors in Fujian and other parts of the mainland. Both readily travel on the mainland and visit ancestral localities. Some Philippine Chinese work in Fujian; others in Taiwan. But there is no measurable indication that any Philip-

Binondo, site of today's Chinatown in Manila.

Binondo Canal and lift bridge.   Manila, P. I.

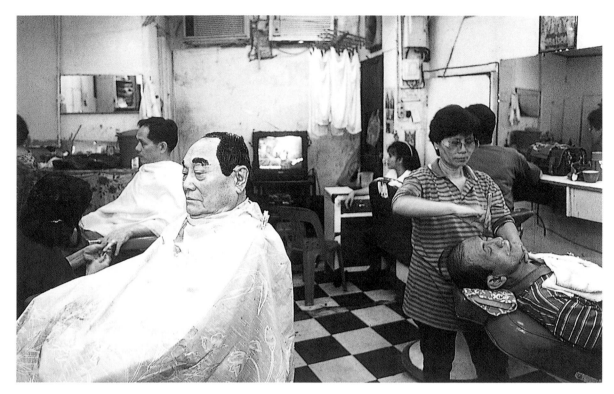

Hairdressing salon in Manila's Chinatown.

pine Chinese intend to reside permanently in either place should they decide to leave the Philippines. The Federation has lost some of the great power it formerly wielded. But it is still unchallenged as the most powerful single organization and the only one capable of speaking for all of Chinatown (if not necessarily all ethnic Chinese) on most issues.

Today there are about 1,000 ethnic Chinese organizations in the Philippines, the majority of them of the traditional Chinese type discussed above. Manila, with a Chinese population of 500–600,000, is overwhelmingly the centre of their activity. The proliferation of new organizations just described continues, but much more in Manila than anywhere else. While Manila's Chinatown remains vital, Chinatowns, as clusters of business and residence, have all but disappeared in most other places.

Cebu, the Philippines' second-largest city, with the second-largest Chinese population, has now about 40,000 ethnic Chinese and an organizational inventory of about 70. Davao, another important Chinese centre, has a population of about 13,000 served by about 25 organizations. Neither city now has a fully concentrated Chinatown, although there is some business and residential clustering of ethnic Chinese. And while Manila's Chinatown produces new organizations constantly, these cities' Chinese organizational list is stable. In these two places, as elsewhere, many of the local Chinese organizations are branches of ones established earlier in Manila. During the 1950s especially, several of Manila's organizations – particularly clan associations and Hongmen bodies – assisted in the creation of local branches around the Philippines. But these have only a loose association with the Manila branch.

The organizational developments described above are, then, mostly limited to Manila, and mostly to Hokkiens. Cantonese have had a different organizational history. Their largest centres are Manila and Baguio. As early as 1850 Cantonese created a general *huiguan* to look after their interests. Between the 1880s and 1941, 15 to 20 Cantonese clan associations were formed, plus a Hongmen organization, a small number of schools (notably, the Manila Chinese Patriotic School), and a few theatrical groups. Only a few organizations were created from 1945 to 1955 and none since. In the Shanju Gongsuo charitable association, the Cantonese continue to enjoy, as they have since its beginning, a representation of three out of 15 members of the executive committee. With a few conspicuous exceptions, Cantonese (who are mostly in the restaurant and hotel businesses) have not done well economically in the Philippines. Although not formally segregated, they have tended to cluster residentially, and in business terms, on certain streets in Manila's Chinatown.

Whether Cantonese or Hokkien, traditional-style Chinese organizations have been a force for Chinese cultural retention and the maintenance of Chinatown. But much has changed since 1975. Are they still viable? Demographic and socio-cultural trends seem to argue against it. Yet these traditional associations continue to proliferate today. Why so?

One factor is the very small but important influx of immigrants, legal or otherwise, from China and Hong Kong. They have the interest and the skills. They live in Chinatown, join traditional associations, and they help keep alive the five Chinese language newspapers that still exist.

Of more importance is the persistence, for the time-being at least, of an ethnic Chinese business system. This is one in which all participants are ethnic Chinese and have the necessary Chinese language and cultural skills to deal with prospective suppliers, customers or other associates. It is a system built on trust, which in turn is heavily dependent upon personal reputation. One component of reputation is officer status in Chinese-style organizations. A person whose name card reveals officer status in one or more of the larger or more prestigious traditional organizations is clearly someone to be taken seriously. Anyone whose business is mostly done in a Chinese context is at least partly involved or affected by this system.

Although it is centred on Chinatown in the Manila case, it operates whether there is a formal Chinatown or not. And its participants include those with suburban residence and cosmopolitan experiences, but whose business remains 'ethnic.' Thus, even a graduate of a professional course in university may end up not pursuing that profession but instead working in the family business in Chinatown and hence be influenced by these practices. As long as traditional associations are useful in this way they are likely to persist, unless some other kind of association turns out to be better for business networking and personal evaluation.

Chinese trade associations also continue to be valuable for mediation and for the defence of members who are doing business in a mostly Chinese environment. Member welfare is another major function of traditional associations. But since the mid-1970s that has become less important as general prosperity has prevailed for the Chinese and as native-place associations and brotherhoods in particular have assumed more of the load of whatever needs remain.

Chineseness in the Philippines has also been maintained by the system of Chinese schools. Begun in the early 20th century, these schools developed into a system of elementary and high school units with a single collegiate attachment to one of the latter. At their height in the 1950s, there were over 160 schools in the Philippines serving about 43,000 students. Their curriculum included, at that time, one-half subjects related to the Philippines and one-half related to Chinese culture. The latter courses were based upon curricula prepared for overseas Chinese students by the Overseas Chinese Affairs Commission in Taiwan. These stressed Chinese language, literature, civics (in relation to the ROC government and society) and Chinese cultural values. The version of Chineseness taught was clearly that sponsored in Taiwan. Textbooks were imported from Taiwan or Hong Kong and teachers came mostly from the former. Students were encouraged to prepare for university in Taiwan, if possible. Many did just that during the 1950s and early 1960s. Of these, most returned to the Philippines, often as teachers in the Chinese schools.

When the Chinese schools were filipinized in the early

1970s, the Chinese portion of the curriculum was radically reduced. In the case of language, only 120 minutes' instruction per day was allowed. The schools now underwent a great change. Student skills in language and language-related courses began to decline. At the same time, the mass naturalization of the Chinese opened many new economic opportunities in the general Philippine society. These were opportunities that often required a university education. They did not require Chinese skills. The result was that most of the graduates of top Chinese high schools like Chiang Kai-shek and Philippine Cultural (formerly Huaqiao Zhongxue) went on to university, but fewer than before took Chinese skills with them. Since few graduates of high schools now had the language skills to attend university in Taiwan and most preferred staying in the Philippines, this source of teacher recruitment now dried up. Supplying qualified teachers for the Chinese schools became a problem which educators and parents have tried to address with summer programmes involving either Taiwan or mainland China institutions.

The language problem was not only caused by filipinization of the Chinese schools. The Chinese middle class in the Philippines had expanded with the general prosperity of many Chinese families over the 1954–75 period. Such families had moved out of Chinatowns, lived in Filipino neighbourhoods and had Filipino house servants. It was Pilipino language that their children learned first as infants from their childminder (*yaya*). Hokkien might be spoken at home, but Mandarin, the language taught in Chinese schools, was an additional and, to children of this generation, artificial burden. Unlike in the 1950s and 1960s, their employment did not necessarily depend upon Chinese written language skills; it did depend upon English skills. Those parents whose business required Chinese language skills and who could afford to do so, sent children to Taiwan or mainland China for intensive language training. Others made the best of domestic facilities, which included, by the 1990s, courses in Chinese at some universities. Meanwhile, the Chinese schools have declined in number but not in enrolment. By the 1990s, there were only 129 schools for a student population which has greatly increased since the 1950s and which includes many non-Chinese.

The 1970s were also a watershed in the literature written by Chinese. All of it up to that time was written in Chinese; much of it since in English and Pilipino. The sojourning literature of the 1930s was followed by the writings of those who grew up in the Philippines but were well taught in Chinese language and culture by the Chinese schools. Their concerns were about Chinese life in the Philippines, but their guidelines and points of reference tended to be in Taiwan or Hong Kong. Only a small number of writers from that group, all over age 50, now remains. The younger writers lack both the skill and interest to follow their tradition. They have become oriented towards Philippine literature in English and Pilipino. It is this literature, developing since the 1970s, that is showing growth. Its points of reference are local and its interests are about how to be ethnically Chinese and Filipino in the face of generation gaps in the Chinese community and seeming marginality to Philippine society.

Chinese carving figure of Christ.

Chinese-style Catholic cathedral in Manila.

Religion has long been a major means of cultural expression for Philippine Chinese. Buddhism, Chinese Popular Religion (see p 80), Catholicism and Protestantism are all present. Chinese began to adopt Catholicism from early Spanish times. They were attracted to the faith by the special privileges given Chinese Catholics by the Spaniards; but it is clear that the power of the religion itself also attracted many. Today, one-third to one-half of the Chinese are said to be Catholic or nominally so, and the actual figure may be much higher. Historically, the Dominican parish of Binondo was the best known and developed Chinese Catholic unit. After World War II, as more Manila Chinese moved into middle-class neighbourhoods in Manila and suburbs, new parishes were added so that there are now four.

From the very beginning, Philippine Chinese Catholicism has commonly been syncretic. Individual Catholic saints and manifestations of the Virgin have been worshipped because of their particular saving power for Chinese, and their feasts have been observed in Chinese ways. Chinese popular deities – Guanyin and Mazu – are identified with one or another manifestation of the Virgin. The Virgin of Antipolo, identified with Mazu, is as much an object of pilgrimage for Chinese as for Filipinos. The Virgin of Caysasay, similarly identified, is worshipped in a Chinese temple in a Chinese fashion. Santiago (St James) is identified with Guan Gong and there is a temple to that effect in Manila's Chinatown. The Santo Niño, an image of the Christ Child enshrined in a Cebu Church, is believed by some Chinese to have power that can be tapped through a spirit medium in Manila's Chinatown.

It is common practice to venerate both Chinese Popular deities and Catholic saints, whether or not identifications between them are made. The general belief is that all have power that is accessible. Two or more religions may happily cohabit in a given household. Most often the parents are principally devoted to Chinese

GENERATIONS

As in any overseas Chinese community, generations are very important, especially in this case, where radical changes have marked so much of the period of these generations' lives. The three generations active in the Chinese Philippines in the 1990s differ greatly from one another. They will be called here the Oldest, Middle and Youngest Generations.

The Oldest Generation's members were born either in the Philippines or China; in the latter case, some were brought to the Philippines while very young. They came to maturity during the 1940s and 1950s. Their experiences mark and shape their cultural orientation. They are the generation that polarized itself over politics in China and Chinatown, fought the Japanese as guerrillas, endured the harassments and extortions of Philippine police and others, and survived the nationalist economic policies. Some in this group were able to move into new areas of the economy where such laws did not apply and to do well, a few even becoming the present group of Chinese-Filipino tycoons. These last have risen above the Chinese community and operate freely in touch with it but also with larger Philippine and international communities. Others, less fortunate, endured years of frustration until policies were changed.

In age, members of the Oldest Generation, by the 1990s, ranged from 55 upward. All had Chinese-language and cultural skills. For most, their decades of experience before the 1970s were the major shaping force. All had experienced being caught between China and the Philippines. Those decades have inclined them to focus upon Chinatown, its business system, its organizations and its politics. They are sustainers of what might be called a Chinatown culture – neither like China nor like the Chineseness of the Middle Generation. Those who fought as guerrillas did so for China but also for their future in the Philippines. Decades later, even the most radical of these, the Wha Chi (see main text), was recognized by the Philippine government as a defender of the Philippines and could once again operate openly. (China, too, has recognized these guerrillas as Chinese patriots, and reminiscences of some of them now fill certain publications in Guangdong and Fujian.)

Members of the Middle Generation were born in the Philippines in the 1940s and 1950s and reached maturity in the 1960s and 1970s. This is the generation whose members attended universities in substantial numbers, fought for citizenship, promoted integration rather than assimilation, and coined the expressions 'Chinese-Filipino' and 'Tsinoy' (see main text). Members have varying degrees of Chinese-language and other skills. They are decidedly Philippines oriented, not China or even Chinatown oriented. Their version of Chineseness is one that meshes with Philippine society as a whole, not the exclusive possession of a separated ethnic community.

The more active and articulate members of this generation sometimes express various frustrations with the Oldest Generation. The latter are seen as 'too Chinese,' or Chinese in the wrong ways (preoccupation with the Chinatown business system and with Chinese-style organizations). Realizing that time and demography are on its side, this generation would like broader acknowledgement of itself as a spokesman for the viewpoints of all ethnic Chinese in the Philippines. It is a source of some frustration to them that Philippine governments and other outsiders wishing to know 'what the Chinese think' still turn for this information to the heads of traditional Chinatown organizations. Sensitive to the historical tendency in the Philippines to view any interest in Chinese culture or in China as indicative of political loyalty to China, the Middle Generation spokesmen sometimes show concern about the impressions Chinatown, its organizations and its interests in China may be giving non-Chinese Filipinos. Because members of the Middle Generation share so much with middle-class Filipinos and are so much in touch with them, they seem to bear a responsibility to explain the Oldest Generation to the non-Chinese.

The Youngest Generation, born in the 1960s and 1970s, grew up with almost unrestricted opportunities in the Philippines. China, whether the mainland or Taiwan, is interesting but remote. Language and cultural skills in this group are greatly reduced. From the Middle Generation perspective, in contrast to the 'too Chineseness' of the Oldest Generation, this one is 'not Chinese enough.'

Edgar Wickberg

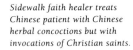

Sidewalk faith healer treats Chinese patient with Chinese herbal concoctions but with invocations of Christian saints.

beliefs while the children, often having been educated in Catholic schools, are at least nominally Catholic and largely uninterested in Chinese faiths. In cases such as these, the children's rooms may house Catholic saints while other parts of the house may be the abode of Chinese deities.

Such commonly seen gods of Chinese Popular Religion as Mazu, Guanyin and Tudi Gong are found in many temples. In the past, at least, Tudi Gong and Guan Gong were enshrined in trade association halls. Guan Gong is found in many temples, in brotherhood halls and in places of business. There is one territorial god temple in Manila's Chinatown – that of the City God (Cheng Huang) of the city of Shishi in the Quanzhou region.

Buddhism, in its pure form, is most conspicuously represented in the Seng Guan Temple of Manila. Founded in the 1930s, this temple is now quite large and impressive and continues to grow. Other Buddhist temples, and Popular Religion temples that include Buddhist deities, have been built in Manila and Cebu, especially since the 1960s. In the 1960s, perhaps in anticipation of Cultural Revolution damage, several god images kept in Fujian temples were brought to the Philippines and temples were built to house them. The other major cause of temple building in recent years seems to be related to business success – the result of a vow made by someone who has just prospered under the influence of a god to whom he made the vow.

The Chinese Cemetery in Manila has become a fa-

mous tourist site. Each tomb is an elaborate mansion in miniature, with equally elaborate facilities inside, as if in competition with its neighbours. The cemetery's streets are named after famous headmen, or *capitanes*, of the late Spanish period; Chinese consuls; and community leaders. There is a towering monument to Chinese diplomats martyred by the Japanese in the 1940s. Mass visits to tombs do not take place on Qingming Day in the spring, as Chinese tradition prescribes, but in parallel with Filipinos going to the adjacent Filipino cemetery, on All Souls Day in the autumn. In contrast to this arena of spectacle, the Cebu Chinese Cemetery, though also made up of above-ground tombs, is much more modest, as are the ceremonies of those who visit it on an All Souls Day.

Protestant Christianity entered the Philippines with the Americans, but also from Chinese churches in Fujian. Some of the best known Chinese schools have been operated by Protestant churches. Besides the mainline Protestant churches, there are charismatic evangelical ones. These are among the most dynamic, including the global and highly assertive churches of the Hong Kong-based Chinese Coordination Centre of World Evangelism (CCCOWE), which has held at least one of its conventions (1992) in Manila.

By the 1960s a new middle class was emerging. Its members were either born in the Philippines or brought there at an early age. Most of them were graduates of Chinese schools at a time when the schools could still provide good instruction in Chinese language. By the 1960s increasing numbers were attending and graduating from Philippine universities. They emerged at a time when the Filipino middle class was also growing in size – like the Chinese, the result of economic expansion in the Philippines and their own education-based opportunities. Chinese of the middle class entered new occupations, especially after 1975, when professions became open to them. Their appearance gave new diversity to the Chinese community. This was a group not fully a part of any Chinatown core: their residences were not in Chinatown and their business or profession might not be there either. Their way of life was increasingly like that of middle-class Filipinos. Even the kinds of Chineseness they expressed and the sources thereof were more diverse and offered more choices.

In the 1950s and 1960s Chinese culture had come mostly from Taiwan. After 1975, and especially after 1978, Taiwan was still accessible, but now so was mainland China. The cultural exchanges that had been possible with Taiwan organizations – schools, youth groups, sports teams and entertainment troupes – were now also possible with the mainland. And as Taiwan, by the late 1980s, opened up the field of Taiwanese local culture, Philippine Chinese could have exchanges with *nanguan* music troupes from both Fujian and Taiwan. As modern Chinese popular entertainment culture developed in Hong Kong and Taiwan, its products were readily available in the Philippines. Indeed, middle-class Chi-

Chinese couple wed at San Agustin Church in Manila.

nese organizations today sometimes present variety entertainment programmes that are intended for and appreciated by both middle-class Chinese and middle-class Filipinos.

This new middle class has also created Chinese organizations of a new, partly non-Chinese nature. These are Chinese organizations, in the sense that members are all ethnic Chinese and the organizations' interests are directed towards Chinese concerns. But the organizations themselves and their leadership styles draw upon Western models. Lions Clubs became popular in the 1960s. Like Lions everywhere, they are active in community service and in business networking among themselves. In the Philippine case, they are at once both exclusive and outreaching. Many of them use Chinese as their language, but they still welcome the networking possibilities of conventions involving non-Chinese and they readily participate in international Asian Lions meetings.

School alumni associations are another middle-class organization. Some of these refer to secondary schools in mainland China or Hong Kong; others to Philippine Chinese high schools. Since the 1950s there have been alumni associations of the major Chinese high schools in Manila. By the 1990s members of these had become generally successful, middle-class, culturally sophisticated ethnic Chinese. They organize at least some of their social life around these associations. The working part of their association activity focuses on raising funds to provide their school with superior facilities such as gymnasiums, computer rooms, audio-visual auditoriums, and the like. Another middle-class organization in Manila is the Fire Brigade. These provide equipment and volunteer firemen for Chinatown neighbourhoods. Some of them also operate weekly charity medical clinics staffed by ethnic Chinese medical and dental students. Typically, their clientele is mostly Filipino.

Finally, there is the Kaisa Para Sa Kaunlaran organization, made up of middle-class, university-educated professionals and business people. Kaisa is dedicated to integration and has provided, among other things, an award-winning children's television programme which shared Chinese culture and elementary language with its multicultural audience. In several of these middle-class organizations, women play a leading role.

The Kaisa Para Sa Kaunlaran is particularly important because of the issues it addresses and the visible leadership role it often plays in the public affairs of the Chinese community. The organization's names are interesting in themselves. The Pilipino name is an innocuous statement of alliance for progress. The Chinese version (Huayi Qingnian Lianhehui), translates as 'Local-born Chinese Youth Federation,' reflecting the ages of the founders in the mid-1980s. There is no English title for the organization. Its semi-monthly newspaper, *Tulay*, is mostly in English, with increasing amounts of Pilipino and small amounts of Chinese.

It is Kaisa in particular that has publicized and popularized the use of the expressions 'Chinese-Filipino' and 'Tsinoy.' The intent of the first term is to describe and identify Philippine Chinese of the contemporary era as Filipinos of partly Chinese background. Their cultural commitments are importantly Chinese, but their political identities and loyalties are completely Philippine.

Taking to the streets to protest kidnappings.

Kaisa's prescription for ethnic Chinese and Filipino relations is integration, not assimilation. Tsinoy is an amalgam of *Tsino*, for Chinese, and *Pinoy*, a slang term for Filipino. Kaisa sees itself and its publications as a bridge (*tulay*) between Chinese and Filipinos and between generations in the Chinese community. It maintains a library on the history and affairs of the Philippine Chinese and a Chinese heritage centre it has built houses its headquarters and a museum and library.

Kaisa has become increasingly a public spokesman for the rights of ethnic Chinese. Where the Federation, the titular head organization of the community, usually prefers to negotiate such issues in private, Kaisa has taken rights cases and public grievances of the ethnic Chinese to the press and to the streets. It was one of the leading groups in an unprecedented protest march of over 25,000 ethnic Chinese through Manila's streets in January 1993. The issue was the Philippine government's alleged failure to act vigorously against kidnapping gangs that particularly targetted ethnic Chinese.

Clearly, Kaisa and some other organizations are moving towards Filipinos. Are Filipinos reciprocating? Have they finally accepted the Chinese? The picture is unclear. There are still strong feelings by many that Chinese deserve no sympathy for their vulnerability to kidnapping and other problems because on the whole they do better economically than most Filipinos. The Chinese received their citizenship because of the strategies of Marcos, not as a result of a massive outpouring of Filipino sentiment for it. There are still suspicions that the Chinese exploit the Philippine economy without any commitment to the Philippine polity or society. During the Aquino presidency, Corazon Aquino emphasized her own Chinese background, even paying a ceremonial visit to her ancestral origin point in Fujian. For a time it seemed as if Chinese might be officially pictured as good Philippine citizens and contributors to the Philippine heritage. But in the Ramos presidency the emphasis seems to be again upon the necessary and usable economic power of the Chinese.

Edgar Wickberg

SINGAPORE

Thomas Stamford Raffles.

Overview

The Chinese in Singapore are a special case in the study of Chinese overseas: nowhere else, outside the People's Republic of China and Taiwan, do Chinese form the majority of the citizenry of a nation-state and hold the majority of positions at the highest levels of government.

The 1990 census numbers them at 2.1 million, or 77.7 per cent of a total resident population (of citizens and non-citizen permanent residents) of slightly more than 2.7 million. Malays (at 14.1 per cent) and Indians (at 7.1 per cent) are minority groups in the country. Chinese numerical predominance among the island's ethnic groups harks back to at least 1824, when the first census to be taken found that they numbered 3,317, a sizeable 31 per cent of the population. Thereafter the proportion climbed steadily, until it became more than 70 per cent by the turn of the century (see table 5.14).

Given its large Chinese population, it is not uncommon for Singapore to be considered a 'Chinese society' as that term is applied to China, Taiwan and Hong Kong. The inappropriateness of that description, however, is apparent the moment one compares the proportion of Singapore's non-Chinese population with those of the other 'Chinese societies': while Singapore's is more than 22 per cent, China's non-Han population of 'national minorities' is 7 per cent of its billion-plus population; Taiwan's aborigines are less than 2 per cent of its 21 million people, while Hong Kong's expatriates are no more than 2 per cent of its 6.4 million inhabitants. Thus Singapore is multi-ethnic and 'plural' to a degree not shared by these other societies. Furthermore, Singapore is located at the heart of the Malay Archipelago and not

Map 5.8

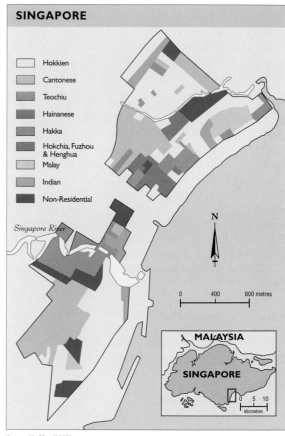

Source: Hodder (1953).

in that domain, generally referred to as East Asia and understood to cover Japan, Korea and Vietnam, whose civilization is traceable to ancient China. In addition, it is a completely independent state whose national identity has to be sufficiently broad to include ethnic groups other than Chinese. In the early years of nation-building, with its close neighbours Malaysia and Indonesia worrying about the subversive potential of ethnic Chinese in their midst, Singapore had to make it clear to the world that it was not a 'Third China.'

The peopling of the island has been a case of both immigration and natural increase, with the latter replacing the former as the dominant contributor to population growth some time after 1957. Statistics dating from 1881 show a continuous stream of Chinese immigration up to the Japanese Occupation, but also a continuous flow of return and secondary migration. Such movements persisted right up to the early 1960s, after which they dwindled. By 1990 the number of Chinese born in China, Hong Kong or Taiwan (that is, first-generation Chinese) had fallen to only 150,000, representing a mere 7 per cent of the resident Chinese population (see table 5.15). But because immigration was fairly heavy in the period leading up to World War II – the number of net

Table 5.14

PERCENTAGE DISTRIBUTION OF SINGAPORE'S TOTAL POPULATION BY ETHNIC GROUP

| YEAR | TOTAL POPULATION | CHINESE | PERCENTAGE OF TOTAL POPULATION | | | | TOTAL |
			MALAY	INDIAN	OTHERS		
1824	10,683	31.0	60.2	7.1	1.7		100
1830	16,634	39.4	45.9	11.5	3.2		100
1836	29,984	45.9	41.7	9.9	2.6		100
1840	35,389	50.0	37.3	9.5	3.1		100
1849	52,891	52.9	32.2	11.9	3.0		100
1860	81,734	61.2	19.8	15.9	3.1		100
1871	97,111	56.2	26.9	11.8	5.0		100
1891	181,602	67.1	19.7	8.8	4.3		100
1901	226,842	72.1	15.8	7.8	4.3		100
1911	303,321	72.4	13.8	9.2	4.7		100
1921	418,358	75.3	12.8	7.7	4.2		100
1931	557,745	75.1	11.7	9.1	4.2		100
1947	938,144	77.8	12.1	7.4	2.8		100
1957	1,445,929	75.4	13.6	8.6	2.4		100
1970	2,074,507	76.2	15.0	7.0	1.8		100
1980	2,413,945	76.9	14.6	6.4	2.1		100

'Total population' includes non-citizens and non-permanent residents in the post-independence censuses. 'Malays' is a generic category for various indigenous peoples of the Malay Archipelago. 'Indians' from 1970 onwards, include Sri Lankans or Ceylonese, previously classified under 'Others.'
Sources: Cheng (1985); Saw (1970); Singapore Census of Population 1990, Demographic Characteristics, 1992.

Map legend (Map 5.8 SINGAPORE):
- Hokkien
- Cantonese
- Teochiu
- Hainanese
- Hakka
- Hokchia, Fuzhou & Henghua
- Malay
- Indian
- Non-Residential

Singapore River

N

0   400   800 metres

MALAYSIA
SINGAPORE
0   5   10 kilometres

migrants, for example, was 172,604 in 1937, the year Japan stepped up its aggression against China – a significant proportion of Singapore-born middle-aged Chinese have China-born parents and are only second-generation. In other words, though Chinese settlement of Singapore dates back a century and a half, the generational 'depth' of the present-day Chinese population is fairly shallow.

In common with other overseas Chinese destinations, Singapore received few women before the 1870s, and none at all before 1853. Up to as late as 1901, there were almost four times as many men as women in Singapore, and it was not until the post-World War II period that the ratio more or less balanced.

In the 1980s and 1990s the need to widen the pool of talented manpower persuaded the political leadership to encourage immigration of Chinese from China and Hong Kong. From the latter, Singapore offered to take 25,000 would-be permanent residents in 1989. Highly trained immigrants from the People's Republic of China, particularly those armed with degrees from Western universities, have also been offered employment and permanent residence in Singapore. Figures for these arrivals are not made public, however. Asked for the total number of China-born immigrants who have become permanent residents since 1990, the Department of Population and Manpower Statistics confirmed that the chances of researchers obtaining such estimates were slim.

Historical formation

Singapore once had a Malay name, Temasek, rendered as Danmaxi in an account written in the first half of the 14th century by a Chinese traveller, Wang Dayuan. To that period date the fragments of ceramics which archaeologists have unearthed on the island and which provide evidence of early trading links with China. But Singapore before the colonial era did not have the commercial or strategic significance that it was to acquire under the British. It was, along with Riau and other islands, a node in the trading networks – of Malays, Bugis, Chinese and other peoples – that enveloped the Malay Archipelago. Indeed, some commentators argue that the history of the Chinese in Singapore had its beginnings not on the island itself but in Johor, the Malay maritime polity which included Singapore and the Riau islands. As many as 10,000 Chinese, many of them former coolies, were said to be settled on Bentan, a Riau island, as cultivators of gambier and pepper and to have remained there after the Malays and Bugis left.

Chinese converged upon Singapore when Thomas Stamford Raffles founded a British trading settlement there in 1819, in effect undermining Riau's erstwhile role as the key entrepôt in the archipelago. The phenomenal increase in gambier and pepper plantations in Singapore over the next 30 years – to a peak of 600 in the late 1840s – was an index of the speed with which Chinese cultivators, traders and labourers had moved into Singapore after 1819.

In an essay published in 1989, Wang Gungwu identified three types of Chinese among those who came to Singapore in the 1820s and 1830s. First, there were those acquainted with British and Dutch administrations through their sojourns in Malacca, Penang and other parts of the archipelago. Second, there were those whose intimate contacts with the Malay and Thai worlds across several generations of residence in the region had given them an understanding of native customs and ways of dealing with local rulers. The third group came directly from China, but were likely to have relatives with decades of trading experience in Nanyang. In summary, then, the early arrivals were by no means unfamiliar with the region. Furthermore, their purposes revolved around trading – this was true even of those who worked as cultivators or artisans – and they proved useful to the British in the latter's commercial activities.

From the 1840s onwards, however, the pattern changed, if only because of a greatly increased volume of labour migrants from China. As a particularly well-located entrepôt, Singapore received a larger number of these unskilled migrants than elsewhere, either absorbing them itself or serving as a transit point for those it funnelled to destinations further afield – Penang and elsewhere in the Malayan Peninsula; or northeast Sumatra, particularly Deli, where tobacco plantations needed large numbers of coolies; or farther away to Australia. The bulk of the labourers arrived through the credit ticket system (see p 61), indebted first to the labour brokers or junk masters who advanced them their passage money, and then to their employers, who took over their debt and whom they repaid by their labour.

By the 1850s the traffic, now grown international, had degenerated into the notorious coolie trade, the profits of which were shared by Western recruiting agents and Chinese secret societies. The merciless exploitation of the coolies called for regulation by the colonial authorities; this the latter sought to achieve in 1877 by establishing Chinese Protectorates in the Straits Settlements (of which Singapore was one along with Penang and Malacca). The first Protector, William Pickering, who read Chinese and spoke a number of Chinese dialects, controlled labour abuses by seeing to it that recruiting agents were licensed and employment contracts were registered. Policing by the Chinese Protectorate freed up the labour market, and firms looking to hire Chinese did not have to go through coolie brokers and secret societies. As a result, from the 1880s onwards, the number of Chinese arrivals increased dramatically.

The growth of a diversified community

Chinese immigrants differed not only in the timing of their arrival in Singapore. Comparing two Chinese settlers, Tan Tock Seng (1798–1850) and Seah Eu Chin (1805–83), brings out some of the other salient distinctions among the various groups of Chinese.

Tan Tock Seng was a Hokkien born in Malacca. He arrived in Singapore in the year of its foundation, when he was 21 years old, and started a business selling veg-

Table 5.15

RESIDENT POPULATION BORN IN CHINA, HONG KONG OR TAIWAN BY YEAR OF ARRIVAL AND SEX, 1990			
YEAR OF FIRST ARRIVAL	MALES	FEMALES	TOTAL
Before 1931	12,185	15,005	27,190
1931–40	20,157	23,056	43,213
1941–45	4,528	4,591	9,119
1946–50	11,327	9,830	21,157
1951–55	4,531	7,697	12,228
1956–60	5,794	8,566	14,360
1961–65	1,342	1,543	2,885
1966–70	1,248	1,245	2,493
1971–75	2,478	1,611	4,089
1976–80	1,856	1,625	3,481
1981–85	2,228	2,514	4,742
1986–90	1,935	3,077	5,012
Total	69,609	80,360	149,969

Source: Singapore Census of Population 1990, Demographic Characteristics, 1992.

William Pickering.

Tan Tock Seng.

etables, fruit and fowl. But it was not this which earned him his fortune but some speculations he made jointly with a British friend, Horrocks Whitehead of the firm Shaw, Whitehead & Co. His best-known act of philanthropy was to provide funds in 1844 for the establishment of the Chinese Pauper Hospital, which was later named after him. In 1846 he became the first Asian to be appointed a Justice of the Peace, a measure of the British regard for him.

Seah Eu Chin was born and educated in Shantou, Guangdong province. He arrived in Singapore in 1823 as a clerk on board a junk, a job which he continued to hold for five years on trading vessels plying the Straits of Malacca, the Riau Archipelago and the east coast of the Malayan Peninsula. Having acquired a knowledge of local ways, he worked as a bookkeeper and established himself as a commission agent, servicing the junks that passed through Singapore. With his profits he bought a vast tract of land and planted gambier and pepper, making a huge fortune at a time when prices were high.

In 1837 he married the daughter of the Chinese Kapitan of Perak and became the brother-in-law of Tan Seng Poh, the head of a Teochiu opium-farming syndicate in the 1860s and 1870s. Seah became a member of the Singapore Chamber of Commerce in 1840 and rendered public service frequently; among other things he helped manage the Tan Tock Seng Hospital and mediated in the Hokkien-Teochiu riots of 1854 (see below). He was appointed a Justice of the Peace in 1872. In addition, he was a scholar of Chinese literature; two articles he wrote in 1847 and 1848 on the Chinese in Singapore were translated and published in the *Journal of the Indian Archipelago and Eastern Asia*.

Two differences between Seah and Tan – the one China-born, the other not; the one hailing from one speech area (Teochiu), the other from another (Hokkien) – played important roles in the ordering of Singapore Chinese society. As a first-generation immigrant from China, Seah would have been called a *sinkeh*, a 'newcomer.' Tan, on the other hand, fell into the category 'Malacca Chinese,' itself part of the wider rubric 'Straits Chinese' or 'Straits-born Chinese.' In his 1848 article, Seah provided a rough breakdown of the occupations of an estimated 1,000 'Malacca Chinese' men in the population: 'Merchants and shopkeepers and their people' – 300; 'Cash keepers and others employed by Europeans' – 100; 'Householders employed variously' – 300;

Two faces of Singapore: Western and Chinese.

Seeking medical help at Tan Tock Seng Hospital.

'Petty traders' – 200, and 'Agriculturalists' – 100. In other words, practically none of them were labourers.

Later, the local-born descendants of China-born settlers in the Straits Settlements would also be considered 'Straits-born,' especially if they married into Straits Chinese families or became increasingly adapted to local ways. Straits Chinese were also known as Babas if male, and Nyonyas if female. Alternatively, Babas were referred to by the term used for the local-born in the Dutch territories, including the Riau islands. One Singaporean commentator, Lim Boon Keng (see box) described Chinese Peranakans as 'a new race . . . created by the fusion of Chinese and Malay blood,' and there was indeed some intermarriage between Chinese men and local women. Lim also observed that Peranakans has 'lost touch with China in every respect, except that they continued to uphold Chinese customs, and to practise, in variously modified forms, the social and religious practices of their forefathers.' But their modification of such practices and the fact that their speech was a patois combining Chinese and Malay led Lim to consider them 'a class by themselves.'

They were a class apart by virtue not only of cultural attributes but social and economic position. They were predominant in the commercial sectors and in closer contact with British administrators and merchants than other Chinese. Their social and economic influence was out of all proportion to their numbers: in 1848, for example, 'Malacca men' were only 2.5 per cent of the Chinese on the island, while in 1881, Straits Chinese numbered not more than 10,000, or 9.5 per cent of the Chinese population. They enjoyed the advantages that came with their knowledge of native ways, their experience of mixing and working with the British, and their command of the English language. These advantages made them useful as intermediaries between Europeans and local people, including Malays; and between them and the new arrivals.

Status distinctions apart, Chinese groups divided along speech lines. In his 1848 article, Seah, a Teochiu speaker himself, named five other speech groups: Hokkien, Cantonese (also called 'Macao Chinese'), Hakka and Hainanese. To these five may be added those who came to Singapore – in lesser numbers – from the speech areas of Henghua (Xinghua), Hokchia (Fuqing), Fuzhou and Sanjiang (that is, 'the three *jiang*': Jiangxi, Jiangsu and Zhejiang, the natives of whom were often commonly if inaccurately identified as 'Shanghainese' in Singapore).

The speech-based groupings into which the China-born community was fragmented – called *bang* in Chinese – were given spatial expression by colonial policy. As part of their divide-and-rule policy, the British had divided the central urban area into Malay, Indian and Chinese sections. The Chinese sections, in turn, were subdivided according to dialect groupings. Raffles had suggested as early as 1822 that in establishing the Chinese areas of the city, the authorities should consider that 'the people of one province are more quarrelsome than another, and that continued disputes and disturbances take place between people of different provinces.' Thus Hokkiens were concentrated on Telok Ayer and Amoy Streets, Teochius lived closer to the banks of the Singapore River, while Cantonese came to be associated with the Kreta Ayer area and so on. These spatial patterns could be clearly discerned right up to the 1950s; thereafter massive public housing and urban renewal programmes changed the face of the city. Raffles would not have been surprised by the civil disturbances of the sort which the Hokkien-Teochiu riots would exemplify in 1854.

Speech groups overlapped with those which turned on kinship, place of origin and occupation. According to

LIM BOON KENG

Called the 'sage of Singapore' upon his death, Lim Boon Keng (1869–1957) bridged the British and Chinese worlds in a way no Singaporean had done before.

His grandfather was a China-born Hokkien who arrived in Penang in 1839 and subsequently settled in Singapore. Both his grandmother and mother were Nyonya, the one hailing from Penang, the other from Malacca. Both his grandfather and father earned their living managing the spirit and opium farms of Cheang Hong Lim, whom the British recognized as a leader of the Hokkien community. Lim was educated first at a Hokkien clan temple and then at a government school in Cross Street. Promoted to Raffles Institution, he excelled in his studies, becoming the first Chinese to be awarded the Queen's Scholarship in 1887. At the University of Edinburgh he won a First Class Honours degree in medicine.

Lim Boon Keng, a man who straddled several worlds, in close-up (above) and seated in second car from left with friends on an outing (below).

At Edinburgh he was not accepted as a Chinese among fellow students from China and was piqued by his inability to translate a Chinese scroll presented by a lecturer. Upon returning to Singapore in 1893, he started to learn Mandarin and Cantonese and to read Chinese literature. English, however, remained the strongest language – as was evidenced by his reliance on an interpreter when he gave a speech at Amoy University in 1926.

His private medical practice at Telok Ayer Street established his reputation among Chinese and oriented him towards social reform. He maintained a private hospital for prostitutes and co-founded the Anti-Opium Society in 1906. He raised funds for the founding of the King Edward VII Medical School in 1905. A man of many parts, he was also active in business, particularly the rubber industry, shipping and banking. That he was one of the founders of the Singapore Chinese Chamber of Commerce, a body in which China took much interest, demonstrated his acceptance by the China-born community.

At the same time, he served as an adviser to the British in such institutions as the Legislative Council and the Chinese Advisory Board, professing allegiance to the colonial masters on occasions such as the Diamond Jubilee Celebrations in 1897, when he made a statement assuring them 'that to no other of Her Majesty's subjects will the Chinese of Singapore yield in loyalty and adhesion to Her Majesty.' He attended the coronation of King Edward VII in 1902 and that of King George V in 1911. During World War I he raised support among Straits Chinese for the Prince of Wales Relief Fund and also contributions towards the purchase of war planes. In recognition of his 'good work on behalf of war charities,' he was awarded the Order of the British Empire in 1918.

Lim co-founded the Straits Chinese British Association in 1900 and was twice elected president in the first two decades of its existence. He also founded the Chinese Philomathic Society, a Baba association devoted to the study of English literature, Western music and the Chinese language. He led the Straits Chinese Reform movement at the turn of the century and campaigned for the removal of the queue (pigtail) and against superstitious practices in Chinese folk-religious life. His promotion of education did not stop at the founding of the Singapore Chinese Girls' School; he urged the use of Chinese as a medium of instruction for Chinese children, and started Mandarin classes for Straits Chinese at his home. Between 1894 and 1911 he led the Confucian revival in Singapore and Malaya. A member of the anti-Manchu Tongmeng Hui, the predecessor of the Kuomintang, he became president of the Singapore branch of the latter party in 1913.

Tan Kah Kee praised him as one 'who was well-versed in Western materialistic sciences and Chinese cultural spirit.' At Tan's request, Lim became vice-chancellor of Amoy University in 1921–37, even though this was at the expense of his medical practice and business interests in Singapore. The university benefited from the funds he raised on its behalf from wealthy Chinese in Singapore, Malaya and Indonesia; from the medical school he set up and his efforts to make English a second language.

But his sympathy for Confucianism and the use of Classical Chinese did not go down well with the students, on whom the anti-traditionalism of the May Fourth Movement had had a decided influence. Only in retrospect, perhaps, would they see him not as an anachronism but as a modernizer in his own way.

Back in Singapore he was to suffer at the hands of the Japanese army of occupation, which, to pressure him into working for it (see main text), made his wife kneel under the scorching tropical sun for hours at a stretch in addition to bearing other hardships. Lim maintained his interest in the promotion of Chinese culture after the war, becoming the first president of the China Society in 1949 and remaining its patron until his death in 1957.

Kwok Kian Woon

Table 5.16

CHINESE RESIDENT POPULATION BY SPEECH GROUP, 1990		
DIALECT GROUP	NUMBER	PERCENTAGE OF CHINESE RESIDENT POPULATION
Hokkien	886,741	42
Teochius	461,303	22
Cantonese	319,322	15
Hakka	153,942	7
Hainanese	146,629	7
Fuzhou	35,883	2
Henghua	19,776	1
Shanghainese	16,676	1
Hokchia	13,065	1
Others	49,458	2
Total	2,102,795	100

Source: Singapore Census of Population 1990, Demographic Characteristics, *1992.*

a statistical profile of the occupations of Chinese in 1848, Hokkiens were strong in trading and general agriculture. This formed the basis for their subsequent dominance in rubber trading and banking. While Teochius – twice as numerous as Hokkiens at the time – were also well represented in trading and agriculture, more than half of them were in gambier and pepper planting, a sector which they monopolized until soil deterioration drove them to Johor in the 1850s. Both Hokkiens and Teochius were in economic sectors with significant rates of capital accumulation.

The Cantonese were skilled in carpentry, brick making, wood cutting, boat-building, baking, barbering, tailoring and shoemaking, and they also worked as house servants. The Hakkas shared many of the skills of the Cantonese; in addition to the many who were carpenters and wood cutters, large numbers were blacksmiths and goldsmiths, occupations which were exclusively Hakka. In the 1848 estimates, most of the 700 Hainanese were mainly general agriculturalists. When their numbers grew, Hainanese also provided catering and personal services in European establishments during the colonial era; later they became predominant in Singapore's catering and baking business. They also ran coffee-shops, as did those from Fuzhou, who arrived in significant numbers only from the early 20th century on. The Henghuas and Hokchias, arriving in the last two decades of the 19th century, around the time the rickshaw was introduced to Singapore, became rickshaw pullers. The Sanjiang people acquired a reputation in trades related to furnishing and clothing (including the laundry business), and in the selling of antiques, books, stationery and sundry goods.

Today, Hokkiens by far outnumber other speech groups. Teochius rank second and Cantonese third (see table 5.16).

Until the formation of the Chinese Protectorate, the British did not intervene directly in the affairs of the Chinese community at large. Instead the colonial authorities worked through the local élite, composed of recognized Straits Chinese and various *bang* leaders. These leaders usually assumed prominent roles in the plethora of clan, temple, trade and dialect-based associations which, alongside their other functions, served as Chinese self-regulating control mechanisms. It is to these 19th- and early 20th-century organizations that the thousand or so Chinese associations registered in present-day Singapore trace their origins. Consider, for example, the Ngee Ann Kongsi (Yi'an Gongsi) and the Hokkien Huay Kuan (Fujian Huiguan), both of which began life as temples, the Wak Hai Cheng Bio (Yuehaiqing Miao) and the Thian Hock Keng (Tianfu Gong) respectively. The Wak Hai Cheng Bio, located in Philip Street, near Boat Quay, was founded as a Teochiu communal organization around 1820 and housed the Goddess of

Immigrant woman working as housemaid.

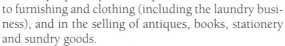

Priest from Thian Hock Keng Temple with worshippers.

the Sea, Tianhou, worshipped by the seafarers of southern China. The Thian Hock Keng temple, located in Telok Ayer Street, also honoured Tianhou, whose statue was brought to Singapore in 1840. The temple was completed in 1842 with funds from Tan Tock Seng and other wealthy Hokkiens. It and the Wak Hai Cheng Bio still stand on their original sites, a testimony to their significance in the history of the Chinese in Singapore.

There were other types of association. One was linked to the system of settlement, cultivation and landholding that prevailed in the river valleys opened up for pepper and gambier planting. A so-called *gangzhu* headed each settlement. He would recruit labourers on the basis of speech/native-place affiliation to settle and develop the plantations. He would be a member of an organization with secret society structures and initiation rituals; this was certainly the case with one such *gangzhu*, Chen Kaishun, who was a leader of the Ngee Heng (Yixing) Kongsi. (Confusingly, Chen also named one of the settlements he founded in Johor the Ngee Heng Kongsi.) Capital for *gangzhu* to develop plantations was advanced by Chinese shopkeepers and merchant entrepreneurs (*towkays*) in town, money the latter would have borrowed originally from European traders. Among the *towkays* were holders of the revenue farms for opium and spirit, the lucrative monopoly concessions granted by the colonial authorities.

Fights frequently broke out between rival *kongsi*, giving rise to much social disruption and violence: the outbreak of Hokkien-Teochiu riots of 1854 was one such instance. These riots might have been a spillover of conflicts connected to rebellions in China. However, in his book *Opium and Empire: Chinese Society in Colonial Singapore* (1990), Carl Trocki links the riots to the local struggle for the domination of the gambier and pepper economy and for opium revenue farms. Opium was the main item of trade in Singapore's early decades as a free port and a major contributor to the colony's annual revenue. The consumers were the poor gambier and pepper plantation labourers, many of whom went into debt to pay for their habit and had to commit to new labour contracts, postponing their plans to return to China.

The forms of solidarity commonly referred to as 'secret societies' provided a framework for the recruitment and control of the labouring masses. They were not at first treated as illegitimate organizations by the colonial authorities. They were so regarded, however, after 1889 when the Societies Ordinance outlawed them. Along with the passing of the Ordinance, Governor Cecil Clementi

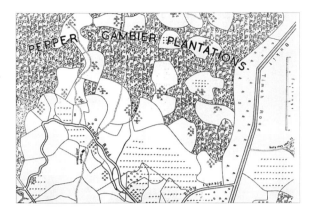

Smith created a Chinese Advisory Board with representatives drawn from the various speech groups. With these two measures the mechanisms of self-government among Chinese yielded to formal control by the colonial administration. In 1910 the opium farm was replaced by a government monopoly. Gambier was on its way out and rubber plantations employing Indian, rather than Chinese migrants, were becoming the way of the future.

Into the 20th century

Plans to return to China were harboured by the majority of Chinese during the 19th century. From then until about 1950, only the Straits Chinese, as Song Ong Siang (see below) has argued, 'could be considered as the "permanent" or "native" section of the Chinese population … [these people] have lived all their lives here and intend to find a resting-place for their bones in our soil. They are as jealous as the immigrant Chinese of their inherited Chinese customs, manners and prejudices, though, with the great majority of them, the feeling of patriotism or love for their fatherland is absolutely wanting.' Indeed, they identified politically with the British. In 1900 they formed the Straits Chinese British Association. During the visit of the Duke of York in 1901, they paid respect to his father, King Edward VII, in a loyal address, and attributed the colony's prosperity to 'the very liberal and benevolent policy of Her late Majesty the Great Queen Victoria of Blessed and Glorious memory.'

They posed a marked contrast to those whom the Chinese government cultivated. The latter, increasingly known as Huaqiao, were encouraged by the Chinese Consulate in Singapore and by visiting officials from China to transcend *bang* identities and unite as a coherent community. At the turn of the century, China's political cross currents impacted on Singapore. Both the reformist Kang Youwei, who took refuge in Singapore in 1900 during his exile, and the revolutionist Sun Yat-sen, who made eight visits to the island between 1900 and 1911, found followers among the colony's Chinese. The ideas of Kang and Sun were advanced through the establishment of Chinese cultural societies, newspaper and modern schools in Singapore. How much they meant to some Huaqiao may be seen in the case of Khoo Soek Wan.

Khoo Soek Wan (1874–1941), who signed his literary works with the pen-name *xingzhou yugong* (the Singapore resident), is credited with the first use of the Chinese name 'Xingzhou' for Singapore. Born in Fujian,

he arrived in Singapore at the age of seven in 1881 to join his father, a wealthy rice merchant. Seven years later, he was sent back to Fujian to receive a classical education and to prepare for the imperial examinations. He won a degree at the local level, but no further. Dejected by his failure, Khoo returned to Singapore in 1896.

On his travels in China he came into contact with people involved in the reformist movement for institutional change. Through the *Thien Nan Shin Pao* (*Tiannan xinbao*), a newspaper he had founded with Lim Boon Keng (see box p 203) and of which he was chief editor, Khoo promoted the ideas of the movement and rallied support for Kang Youwei, the leading reformist figure. In 1900, when Kang, exiled by the court's conservative opposition, visited Singapore, Khoo housed him, paid his expenditures and ensured his safety. Because of his connections to Kang and other major reformist figures, the Qing authorities arrested Khoo's family members in Fujian. Later he broke with Kang. In 1901 he was pardoned by the Chinese government and awarded an official title.

Increasing numbers of Huaqiao came to feel that China's future lay in Sun Yat-sen's revolutionary cause. In 1906 a branch of the Tongmeng Hui, the precursor of the Kuomintang, was set up in Singapore with Tan Chor Nam as chairman and Teo Eng Hock, Hsu Tzu Lin and Lim Nee Soon as office bearers. Following the inauguration of the Republic of China a branch of the ruling party, the Kuomintang, was established in Singapore in 1912. Huaqiao were eagerly receptive to the nationalist message from China. The new nationalism, rather than a general attachment to Chinese traditions or one's home village, came to form the basis of what it meant to be Chinese. And in the ensuing decades this sense of Chinese nationalism was complicated by the divide between the supporters of the Kuomintang and those of the Chinese Communist Party.

These developments, however, almost completely passed the Straits Chinese by. A 'King's Chinese' like Song Ong Siang (1871–1941), for example, identified fully with the British. Song was born and raised in a Chris-

Early map shows location of pepper and gambier plantations.

Adorned with flowers, hall awaits Sun Yat-sen's followers in Singapore.

tian Straits Chinese family; his father, a cashier with the Peninsular and Oriental Steam Navigation Company for more than four decades, had studied under James Legge, the famous translator of Chinese Classics who became Professor of Chinese at Oxford University. Song himself studied law at Cambridge University and was called to the English Bar in 1893.

While practising law he also served as a lay preacher and succeeded his father as a church elder. He represented the younger and progressive sector of the Straits Chinese community, calling for reform in customs and rituals. He was a member of the Legislative Council and was appointed to a variety of committees.

The Chong Hock Girls' School.

In 1923 he published *One Hundred Years' History of the Chinese in Singapore*, a massive work which recorded the lives and contributions of prominent Chinese so that future generations of Chinese in Singapore would, as he put it, 'get encouragement, incentive and stimulus to serve the Colony with equal public spirit, zeal and disinterestedness in their day and generation.' In 1936 he was created Knight Commander of the Order of the British Empire. It was perhaps just as well that he did not live to see the failure of the British to defend the island when the Japanese invaded and the subsequent waning of imperial power.

At home Song spoke Baba Malay, a blend of Malay and Hokkien, as well as English. Baba Malay evolved as a language of inter-ethnic communication throughout the Straits Settlements. However, the Straits Chinese's use of a written language based on Romanized Malay did not imply forsaking Chinese literary traditions completely. By the 1890s, for example, many Baba Malay translations of popular Chinese Classics had been published in Singapore. Of these, the translations of Chan Kim Boon – *Sam Kok* (*San Guo* or *The Three Kingdoms*, 30 volumes, 1892–96); *Song Kang* (*Shuihu Zhuan* or *Water Margin*, 19 volumes, 1899–1902), and *Chrita Seh Yew* (*Xi You Ji* or *Journey to the West*, 9 volumes, 1911–13) – stood out in terms of quality and quantity.

Mr and Mrs Song Ong Siang.

Chinese romances in Romanized Malay were popular with Peranakans.

In other ways, too, Babas remained traditionally Chinese, especially in the areas of family relations, everyday customs and folk-religious rituals. Indeed, it was in the process of modifying such practices through their encounter with local life that they managed to retain Chinese traditions, many which were, paradoxically, to be rejected and discarded in China itself in the course of revolutionary change in the first half of the 20th century. It is perhaps not altogether surprising that the Confucian revival movement in Singapore was forged not by a China-born Huaqiao but by a Straits Chinese graduate of a university in Britain, Lim Boon Keng (see box).

Lim was exceptional, though, in that the interest he took in studying Chinese after completing his English education enabled him to straddle the cleft between those educated in Chinese-medium schools and those educated in English. English education had a long his-

tory in Singapore; Raffles had encouraged Christian missionary work, one expression of which was a school for Chinese and Malay children established by the Reverend Samuel Milton in 1819. In the course of the century, 'mission schools' were founded by Protestant and Catholic missionaries and their organizations. The Singapore Institution was founded in 1823 (and renamed Raffles Institution in 1863). Both the English mission schools and Raffles Institution turned out young men for work in the junior ranks of government service and in mercantile offices, although, according to an official report in 1870, these youngsters were 'quite incapable of expressing themselves in writing, either grammatically or logically.' However, the improved standards of the English schools such as Raffles Institution were later impressively seen in the quality of the winners of the Queen's Scholarship (for higher study in Britain) initiated by Cecil Clementi Smith in 1889.

The intense development of modern Chinese education in Singapore paralleled the rise of nationalism. Early private schools taught classes in dialect; thus there was a Hokkien school at Pekin Street with 22 boys and a Cantonese school at Kampong Glam with 12 boys in 1829. After the establishment of the Chinese Republic, Mandarin replaced dialects as the medium of instruction. Textbooks and teachers came from China. Schools reflected the ideological contestations in China – between Kang Youwei and Sun Yat-sen in an earlier period, and between the Kuomintang and the Chinese Communist Party later. Following the intellectual ferment of the May Fourth Movement of 1919 – out of which emerged new styles of writing – school textbooks in the vernacular replaced those written in Classical Chinese, and the anti-traditionalistic ideas of the time gained some influence.

Chong Wen Ge, founded in 1849 by Tan Kim Seng, a wealthy philanthropist, is generally supposed to be Singapore's first Chinese-language school. Chinese community leaders apart, native-place associations and the Chinese Chamber of Commerce (most of whose leaders were Huaqiao merchants with little formal education) provided support to Chinese-language schools. Among the promoters of Chinese education and patrons of schools in Singapore were some great philanthropists –

the rubber magnates Tan Kah Kee (see box below) and Lee Kong Chian (1893–1967), to name just two.

English-medium schools, too, received donations from Chinese businessmen. The philanthropy of a single individual, Gan Eng Seng, a Malacca-born businessman, for example, created the Anglo-Chinese Free School. Starting life in 1886 in some shophouses in Telok Ayer Street, the school taught both English and Chinese. That it did not neglect Chinese earned it the approval of Governor Cecil Clementi Smith, who remarked at the opening: 'I am glad to know that a knowledge of Chinese will also be gained there, which to me appears an essential part of the education of a Chinese boy. The boys who grow up with a knowledge of that language and also attach to it a knowledge of English will prove better citizens than boys who throw off the language of the country to which they naturally belong, and adopt the English language simply from a utilitarian sense of

the time they are going to spend in the Settlement.'

What the governor deplored was the jettisoning of the Chinese language by those who, for purely utilitarian reasons, adopted English. The idea that an education in Chinese was of cultural importance was one upheld by the Chinese-language schools, while public thinking and official educational policy right up to the post-independence decades considered the learning of Chinese an 'essential' and 'natural' part of being Chinese and a knowledge of English of utilitarian value.

Economic expansion

As in language education, so in economic activity: while some Chinese merchants operated in an exclusively Chinese sphere – rice traders are a prime example – others expanded their activities through trading relations with Western capitalist institutions. The latter group, of whom Tan Tock Seng was an early exemplar, sold local

Gan Eng Seng.

TAN KAH KEE

No Chinese of renown came closer than Tan Kah Kee (1874–1961) to the model of the Huaqiao who made good abroad only to send all his money to China. The 'Henry Ford of Malaya,' as he has been called, used the fortune he made in Singapore to fund educational causes, founding not only schools in his natal Jimei, in Fujian's Tongan district, but, in a single-handed feat of philanthropy, the Amoy (Xiamen) University.

Upon arriving in Singapore in 1890, he worked in his father's rice business, then set up his own plant for pineapple canning and invested in pineapple planting after his father's firm failed in 1903. In 1906 he also moved into the rubber industry, becoming the 'Rubber King' of Southeast Asia with some 32,000 people working for him by 1925. He was much more than a mere businessman, however. In the 1920s and 1930s he attempted to reform Chinese society in Singapore and Malaya. He reorganized the Hokkien Huay Kuan in 1929 and made it more accountable to the Hokkien community it represented. He was also the first to champion the revision of the Singapore Chinese Chamber of Commence constitution, proposing that leaders be chosen by elections based on the candidates' merit rather than on their dialect-group alignments.

Tan's abiding concern was education. Under his leadership, the Hokkien Huay Kuan founded five primary and secondary schools in Singapore, chief among them the Chinese High School (Huaqiao Zhongxue). He also supported English education, giving various sums to the Anglo-Chinese School and Raffles College. In 1919 he donated millions of dollars to establish and endow Amoy University, for the vice-chancellorship of which he chose Lim Boon Keng (see box on p 203). (The university was handed over to the Chinese government and turned into a national university in 1937.)

During the Great Depression Tan fought hard to maintain his business empire. Although it collapsed despite his efforts in February 1934, he did not withdraw from the political arena. His leadership role in the Shandong Relief Fund Committee (1928–29), the Singapore China Relief Fund Committee (1937–41) and the Southseas China Relief Fund Union (1938–50) earned him a reputation for being a Huaqiao nationalist. Two weeks before the fall of Singapore to the Japanese army, Tan managed to escape to Sumatra, West Java, and then took refuge in East Java until 1945, looked after by the graduates of his schools in Jimei and of Amoy University even as the Japanese were trying to hunt him down. In Java he found time to write his memoirs. His safe return to Singapore was marked by a mass rally in Chongqing (the wartime capital in China). One of the congratulatory messages sent to that rally came from Mao Zedong; it read, 'The Huaqiao flag, the national glory.'

Tan continued to play a leadership role in Singapore's postwar construction, . To promote unity among the Chinese, he advocated the abolition of dialect-based schools, the centralization of educational authority and the

merging of the smaller native-place organizations. He also founded the Nan Ch'iao (Nanqiao) Girls High School in 1947. So that the Chinese part in the war be properly recognized, he took issue with Lieutenant-General A. E. Percival's February 1948 dispatch on the Malayan campaign, protesting the latter's suggestion that Asians were supportive of the Japanese and his silence on Chinese resistance. In a memorandum

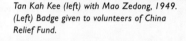

Tan Kah Kee (left) with Mao Zedong, 1949. (Left) Badge given to volunteers of China Relief Fund.

to the Secretary of State for War, Tan declared that unless amendments and an apology were made, the Malayan Chinese would compile its own report by way of giving a true picture of the campaign.

He made known his views on the constitutional changes to be effected in the run-up to Singapore's self-government, declaring himself in favour of giving Chinese a choice of either Chinese or Malayan citizenship, of safeguarding the special position and privileges of the Malays, and of parliamentary democracy based on popular elections. With the outbreak of civil war in China, however, he turned his attention to the political struggles on the mainland. Because of his open support for Mao and crusade against Chiang Kai-shek, the Kuomintang's supporters in Singapore and Malaya regarded him as an enemy. The bitter rivalry between those who supported Tan and those who opposed him was reflected in the struggle for control between the China Democratic League and Kuomintang factions in the Hokkien Huay Kuan, and in the mass rallies organized by the Left and the Right following Chiang's 1948 election as the president of China. The rivalry left deep political scars in the Chinese community.

In May 1950 Tan returned to settle in China. In 1961 he died in Beijing, aged 87. He was accorded a state funeral by the government of the People's Republic of China. Memorial services to honour him were held by Chinese in numerous cities in China, as well as in Hong Kong, Singapore, Rangoon, Jakarta, Semarang, Bandung, Surabaya, Palembang, Pontianak, Yokohama, Calcutta, Paris and Leipzig.

In the view of a biographer, C. F. Yong, Tan's legacy in China and Nanyang lies in 'his model of modernization through the promotion of education and industrial and technological development,' and in his 'pioneering spirit.' The latter extended beyond business enterprise to social reform and political action. But Tan's legacy as the bearer and perpetuator of Huaqiao identity proved short-lived, overtaken by the growing commitment among Chinese overseas to their countries of adoption.

Kwok Kian Woon

produce to Western merchants and bought Western goods from them. Then, in the early 20th century, some Chinese businesses began to bypass the locally based Western companies and to deal directly with manufacturers and traders in the West. Tan Kah Kee (see box p 207) pioneered such direct dealings in rubber trading.

Certain Chinese institutions emerged out of competition with Western business. Until the early decades of the 20th century, the financial needs of Chinese business – foreign exchange, short-term loans and so on – were met by European banks. However, as the economy expanded it became possible to mobilize capital within the Chinese community. Chinese banks emerged to provide services hitherto monopolized by European institutions, adapting successfully to the legal-institutional order established by the British. The Chinese Commercial Bank, for example, was the first Hokkien bank to be established (in 1912). Another was the Ho Hong Bank (1917), and a third the Oversea-Chinese Bank (1919). These three banks were to merge in 1932 to form the Oversea-Chinese Banking Corporation (OCBC), banding together to weather the hardships caused by the Depression. Under Lee Kong Chian and Tan Chin Tuan, who became the bank's chairman in 1966, the OCBC took over some of the most noted British-owned companies in Singapore.

Another enterprise to emerge all the stronger out of the Depression was Lee Rubber, also headed by Lee Kong Chian. Lee Rubber took over the factories of those rubber traders who, like Tan Kah Kee (Lee's father-in-law), fell on hard times during the Depression. The dynamism of Lee's undertakings in the postwar period is commonly attributed to his adoption of innovations and Western-style management practices.

The Japanese Occupation and decolonization

Huaqiao patriotic sentiment reached a climax with the Japanese invasion of China. This spirit was expressed in Singapore by boycotts of Japanese goods and in popular support for fund-raising efforts for disaster relief in China. When Singapore fell to the Japanese, therefore, the latter treated Chinese on the island with deep distrust and resentment. In the wake of the British surrender in February 1942, a *sook ching* ('purge through purification') operation mounted by the Japanese army exterminated thousands of Chinese on the island. Days after the British surrender, the Japanese ordered all Chinese males between the ages of 18 and 50 to report to 28 mass-screening centres; there they went through identification parades. Those suspected – on no evidence whatsoever – of being anti-Japanese were picked up for questioning and detention. Transported in lorries to 11 sites spread across the eastern half of the island, they were then massacred. The Japanese defendants at the 1947 War Crimes Trial admitted to killing a total of 5,000 Chinese, but local Chinese sources put the figure at 50,000. The Chinese who were not involved in the

pre-war anti-Japanese and Chinese nationalist movements but were suspected of helping the British were also arrested and tortured by the Kempeitai (Japanese military police).

In March 1942 the Kempeitai forced Lim Boon Keng to form the Overseas Chinese Association with the aim of collecting 50 million dollars – a crippling amount – from Chinese in Singapore and Malaya as a 'gift of atonement.' Donations were collected through the dialect groups (with a loan from the Yokohama Specie Bank covering the 22 million dollars by which it fell short). While promoting the social campaigns of the Japanese administration, the Overseas Chinese Association also helped to soften the impact of the Occupation by, for example, running a refugee home and repatriating destitute Chinese from the Malayan Peninsula.

The major part of anti-Japanese resistance came from the Chinese rather than from other ethnic groups. It was in some ways an extension of the war of resistance in China, fought by Communist and Kuomintang sympathizers in Singapore and Malaya. This may be seen in the heroism of a famous martyr, the Fujian-born Lim Bo Seng (1909–44). Lim, resident in Singapore since the age of 17, was educated at Raffles Institution and Hong Kong University. A prominent Hokkien businessman in pre-war Singapore, he was actively involved in establishing the China Relief Fund, in organizing anti-Japanese strikes and boycotts, and, with the help of the Malayan Communist Party (which controlled many labour unions), in mobilizing workers to participate in the anti-Japanese movement. With the outbreak of war he escaped from Singapore and made his way to Chongqing, the capital of wartime China, but turned up in Malaya in 1943 to work with the anti-Japanese underground there. He had joined a unit known as Force 136. Caught and tortured to death, he is remembered in Singapore by a memorial describing him as a 'Malayan patriot.' But, as the historian Eunice Thio observes, 'Whether it was primarily love for China (the land of his birth) or for Malaya-Singapore (his home) which led Lim to risk – and, in the event, to lose – his life, will remain unresolved.' George Yeo, Singapore's Minister for Information and the Arts, put this in another way when he said in 1995: 'When we honour Lim Bo Seng as a national or proto-national hero, we must not forget that Lim Bo Seng saw himself as a Chinese national fighting for Kuomintang China. Indeed, the rank

Female entertainers showed their patriotism by raising funds for China.

Lee Kong Chian.

Receipt issued to 'donors' to extortionate Japanese fund.

Japanese ten-dollar note.

LEE KUAN YEW AND CHINESE IDENTITY

Born in Singapore in 1923, Lee Kuan Yew is a fourth-generation Straits Chinese. He is of Hakka origin, his great-grandfather Lee Bok Boon having arrived in Singapore in 1863 from the Hakka-speaking county of Dabu in Guangdong province. In a typical sojourner pattern, Lee Bok Boon returned eventually to China and died there. But both he and his eldest son, Lee Kuan Yew's grandfather Lee Hoon Leong, married locally born women. Lee Hoon Leong, who attended an English school, worked as a purser in a Chinese shipping company; and it was during one of his regular trips to Indonesia that he met and married Ko Liem Nio, who came from Semarang, in Java. Their eldest son, Chin Koon, worked for the Shell Petroleum Company. Chin Koon's wife, Chua Jim Neo, gave birth to their first son, Lee Kuan Yew, when she was only 16.

Although Lee Kuan Yew's studies began with a two-year stint at the Choon Guan Chinese School, he completed his primary, secondary and tertiary education in English (successively at the Telok Kurau English School, Raffles Institution and Raffles College in Singapore; and, on a scholarship, at Cambridge University, England). 'I was,' as he later said, 'sent to an English school to equip me for an English university in order that I could then be an educated man – the equal of any Englishman – the model of perfection.' Both he and the woman he married, Kwa Geok Choo, studied Law at university.

By virtue of his British education, Lee did, as one of his biographers, Alex Josey, wrote, 'penetrate to the basic values of Western culture.' Lee certainly valued the British system of education and administration; Josey paraphrased him as saying in 1970 that 'learning by rote, as the Chinese did for two thousand years, was a system that was calculated to maintain stability and discourage innovation . . . The price of stability was the exclusion of imperial China from the great scientific and technological discoveries of the West, and the industrial revolution.' On the other hand, Lee said, 'when you have left the ancestral home, and are no longer governed by mandarins trained in the Analects, but by British administrators trained on General Orders which enjoined them to hold the ring fairly and honestly for all who live under their dispensation, it is that much easier to break out of the barren confines of the past.'

His grandfather, he recalled in 1956, 'had the greatest respect for the British Navy. He made a great deal of money because, he said, there was no piracy in Malayan waters. He lived until he saw the *Prince of Wales* sunk by Japanese aeroplanes.' His own admiration for the British colonial masters was dealt a heavy blow when Singapore fell to the Japanese. Yet he was to claim in 1956 that while he was brought up to be 'the equal of any Englishman,' he already felt at the time of his graduation that the whole set of the latter's values 'was wrong, fundamentally and radically wrong.' He thought himself quite the cultural equal of the imperial masters; referring to the flag on the limousine of the British High Commissioner in Kuala Lumpur, he said in 1965, 'Who is he to fly that flag? We kept quiet . . . He has got 400 years of empire, and my ancestors have got 4,000 years of written recorded history.'

His access to those thousands of years of recorded history was hampered by the fact that, as he himself put it in a speech in 1972, he had scrubbed what little Chinese education he had had from his mind when he switched to an English school. 'I was foolish enough,' he said, 'when I was young, not to listen to my grandmother who sent me to Chinese school to learn Chinese, because the method of teaching was wrong . . . They made me recite passages parrot-fashion.' With the language, he added, went the fables and proverbs, 'a whole value system, a whole philosophy of life.' The languages spoken in his parental home were mainly English and Malay.

Out of political necessity, he began to teach himself Mandarin in 1954; the People's Action Party was being formed and he needed the language to communicate with his potential allies and supporters, the mass of whom were Chinese-speaking. Besides, not knowing Chinese would make it hard to identify with the great tradition of a major civilization. As he put it in 1984, 'To be able to speak Mandarin and to read the Chinese script, is reassuring. To look at Chinese characters, see them as mysterious hieroglyphics, is to be psychologically disadvantaged . . . Only a Chinese Singaporean who cannot speak or read it, and who has been exposed to discomfiture or ridicule when abroad, will know how inadequate and how deprived he can feel. By then,

they would not be young enough to learn the language easily. I have personally experienced this. Therefore, I can state that its psychological value cannot be over-emphasized.'

To his fears of Singaporeans' 'deculturalization,' then, may be traced some of the impetus for the Speak Mandarin campaigns and the introduction of Confucianism in the school curriculum and public discourse (see main text). The part he has played in these movements recalls that of a prominent Singaporean Chinese of an earlier generation, Lim Boon Keng (see box p 203). Both men were educated in English and excelled at university in Britain. Both men started learning Chinese in adulthood. Both saw the need to relate themselves to the majority Chinese-speaking population. Both promoted the use of Mandarin and sought to revive Confucianism among Singapore's Chinese. But Lim lived at a time and in a political context in which it would not have been necessary to declare, as Lee did to refute any suggestion that Singapore might be a 'Third China,' that, having been born in Singapore and lived there for so long he had no links with China. Nor would Lim see any occasion to warn Singaporean Chinese against assertions of what has been labelled 'Chinese chauvinism.'

Alex Josey poses the question 'How much of a Chinese?' in his book on Lee. Physically, Josey writes, he is Chinese, but 'What is he intellectually, emotionally?' Josey himself attributes Lee's toughness of demeanour to his origins: 'Hakka Lee is an admixture of aggression and wary defence.' The significance of Lee's ancestry has also been invoked to explain other aspects of his character, but this has usually been based on a misunderstanding of Hakka history and ethnicity (see p 26). For example, the comment that 'Lee's physical structure demands a climate which is cold and dry, as it is in those parts of China where the Hakkas live,' subscribes to the Hakkas' self-mythologization as northerners from the Chinese heartland (this to counter Cantonese and other Chinese groups' characterization of them as non-Chinese barbarians).

Kwok Kian Woon

Lee Kuan Yew.

Lim Bo Seng

he held as major-general was conferred on him by the Chongqing government.'

Yet out of the battles concluded rose 'Malayan' nationalism and with it, the struggle for self-government. As in India and Indonesia, local nationalists were emerging from the war with the realization that colonial rule was not inevitable. However, while they had the experience of the Japanese Occupation in common, these nationalists took their ideological bearings from the nationalist struggles in the metropolitan countries. Thus, Malayan nationalism apart, there were sentiments of Chinese nationalism, Indian nationalism or Malay nationalism. For the Huaqiao, the polarization between supporters of the Kuomintang and the Chinese Communist Party deepened after the Japanese Occupation. What distinguished Chinese (or Indian or Malay nationalism) from 'Malayan' nationalism was that those who felt the latter included the English-educated of all these

ethnic groups. The nationalisms confined to specific ethnic groups, on the other hand, were condemned as 'chauvinism.'

Meanwhile Singapore underwent its transition to independence. The British held the ring as various groups competed for power. In 1959 the People's Action Party (PAP) came to power. This party was founded five years earlier by a young, multi-ethnic, English-educated anti-colonial and 'democratic socialist' group led by Lee Kuan Yew, a British-trained lawyer who was to become prime minister at the age of 35 (see box p 209).

Their English education won this group the support of the departing British, but the mass support it needed for its political ascendancy had to come from the Chinese-educated sector of the population. One of the PAP's links to that constituency was Ong Pang Boon, who, though educated in English at the university level, was a graduate of Chinese secondary school. Another was

LIM CHIN SIONG

The Singapore-born Lim Chin Siong (1933–96) summed up his role in his country's history by saying, 'In a way, Kuan Yew and I and others succeeded in arousing the people, uniting and organizing them to fight the colonial government. No one can deny our role, including my humble part, in this formative stage of our nation building.' When Lee Kuan Yew sought contacts in the Chinese trade unions during his early days in politics, he found the kind of people he wanted in Lim, someone 'able to communicate with the ground, able to muster people, but not motivated by greed.'

Lim had studied at the Chinese High School. In 1951 he was involved in the Anti-British League, an organization which 'a nationalist,' he later said, 'at that time, must join.' For his part in organizing a boycott of school examinations, he was detained by the Special Branch for a week. After his release, he was expelled from the Chinese High School. He found work as a paid secretary at the Changi Branch of the Singapore Bus Workers' Union. He later joined the Factory and Shop Workers Union and was elected secretary-general. His dedication won him great support, assisting his rise to prominence as a leader of 16 unions.

Lim was a founder member of the PAP in 1954. In 1955 he stood for election to the Legislative Assembly Election in Bukit Timah constituency and, at the age of 22, became the youngest assemblyman in Singapore history. In 1956, when the government, with British support, embarked on a pre-emptive purge of pro-Communists, Lim was again detained. He was released in June 1959, just before the PAP government was sworn into office.

In 1961, when Lee Kuan Yew was campaigning for merger with the Federation of Malaya, Lim voiced his opposition in a reflection of the deep differences between the stances of the mainly English-educated leadership and the Chinese-educated radical wing of the PAP. In June that year Lim was among those expelled from the PAP. This group then formed the Barisan Sosialis, a party of which Lim became the first secretary-general. In 1963 Lim and several others were rounded up and detained by internal security forces moving to forestall subversion against Malaysia (Operation Coldstore). While in prison and suffering severe depression, Lim attempted suicide. In July 1969 Lim resigned from the Barisan Sosialis and made public his intention to give up politics. That year he went into exile in London.

Lim returned to Singapore in 1984 and kept a low profile, living so unobtrusively with his wife and two sons that few of his neighbours knew who he was. But when he passed away in February 1996 some 700 people, including his former comrades in the PAP and Barisan Sosialis, turned up for his funeral. A memorial service held in Kuala Lumpur a few days later was attended by about 500 people. Lee Kuan Yew, in a statement about this former PAP cadre, said that Lim and his leftist colleagues taught him the meaning of dedication: 'He did not seek financial gain or political glory. He was totally committed to the advancement of his cause.' In a rare interview before his death, Lim, who was known to be a fiery orator, spoke of himself as one who always tried to calm people rather than incite them to violence. He spoke of his respect for Lee Kuan Yew, and made clear that his differences with Lee were political, not personal.

Kwok Kian Woon

Lim Chin Siong warmly welcomed by enthusiastic supporters (far left); large rally on his release from prison (above) and mourned by hundreds (left) on his death.

Lim Chin Siong (see box below).

Among those who joined the PAP around the time of its inception was the woman who was to become Ong Pang Boon's wife, Chan Choy Siong (1931–81). Fluent in Mandarin and Chinese dialects, Chan was one of Singapore's pioneer female activists, a commanding public speaker, and one of the PAP's biggest vote-getters. After serving as a City Councillor for two years, she won a seat in the 1959 general elections and became an MP. She was influential in pushing for the Women's Charter that was passed in 1961. In 1970 she retired at the age of 36 to make way for new blood, leaving a 14-year hiatus in which women were unrepresented in Parliament.

The struggle for power within the PAP in 1957 has been represented as an ideological one between the radical Left led by Lim Chin Siong and the 'moderates' led by Lee Kuan Yew. But it was also, as W. E. Willmott has written in *Management of Success*, 'a struggle between different communions, two groups with different and conflicting collective sentiments. Politically, it was a struggle between the leaders of the more numerous Chinese-educated community, who were trying to retain their power in Singapore, and the emerging English-educated professional class, who were trying to capture it.'

The extension of citizenship rights became an important issue as Singapore moved towards independence. In 1953, about 380,000 China-born Huaqiao were deemed 'aliens.' They had not qualified for British nationality, eligibility for which required a knowledge of the English language. The Chinese Chamber of Commerce campaigned vigorously against that requirement, which was indeed removed by the 1957 Singapore Citizenship Ordinance. The ordinance, which specified a residential requirement of only eight years, admitted the majority of those born in China to citizenship. During a visit to Indonesia in 1955, the Chinese Premier Zhou Enlai had renounced China's claim to the allegiance of Huaqiao who had adopted Indonesian citizenship. On a visit to Beijing the following year, David Marshall, who would become Singapore's Chief Minister, was reassured by Zhou that the Chinese government wished to see Chinese in Singapore acquire Singapore citizenship and give their exclusive loyalty to Singapore, and that any Chinese residing in Singapore who voluntarily adopted Singapore citizenship would immediately cease 'to have Chinese citizenship, though of course, his inherent racial and cultural affinity remains.'

In terms of cultural affinity, a 'Malayan' identity prevailed in the immediate postwar period; there was a magazine published in Kuala Lumpur in 1946–57 called *The Young Malayan*, one purpose of which was to 'help build up a body of loyal Malayan citizens who would always think of Malaya as their home – whether they happened to be Malays, Chinese, Indians or any other race.' The language which these people had in common and which underpinned their collective identity was English. As Lee Kuan Yew put it in 1961, 'Only the English-educated are completely Malayanized in their political outlook.' The 'Malayan' identity, then, was the possession particularly of the products (comprising members of all the ethnic groups) of the English-medium schools. It is of course true that many of those

Independence rally at airport, 1956.

educated in Chinese-medium schools were also Malayanized, but though they had made their homes in Malaya and Singapore, their political loyalty was questioned because of the China-orientation of their predecessors. What set the English-educated 'Malayans' apart from also the Babas was that they felt no affiliation to the British. That affiliation was, in any event, becoming increasingly irrelevant as British rule approached its end. With the departure of the British the 'golden age' of the Babas came to an end.

The English-language schools received the greatest support from the British. But while Chinese parents who could afford it sent their children to these élitist institutions, many more working-class Chinese went through the Chinese-language school system. What made the latter's nationalism different from that espoused by those who had attended English schools was that, the anti-colonial dimension apart, there was a strong wish to preserve things Chinese and, in some cases, to maintain political ties to China. Not all of them were working class, but because most of them were, while professionals tended to have been educated in English, the division by language overlapped that by class.

In everyday vocabulary and public discourse, Chinese identity came to be qualified by the terms 'Chinese-educated' and 'English-educated.' The bifurcation of the Chinese community into these two sectors broadly re-enacted that between the China-born *sinkeh* and the Straits-born Chinese of an earlier generation. However, unlike the illiterate *sinkehs*, the Chinese-educated transcended the particularism of dialect-based identities, speaking a common language (Mandarin) and interested themselves in the anti-colonial movement in Singapore in addition to the nationalist struggles in China. But like the China-born immigrants, most of the Chinese-educated did not have the command of English that the older Straits Chinese and those who went to English schools had.

In later years the Chinese language would be seen as a vehicle for transmitting 'traditional' Chinese values and for keeping Singaporeans in touch with their roots. However, such was not the view of those concerned with Chinese education in Singapore in the immediate post-

David Marshall.

war period. On the contrary, they were concerned with providing the modern education which schools in China were imparting, following the May Fourth Movement's agitations against 'feudal' habits and conceptions. The agitators' goal of ridding modern China of the shadow of its past was transplanted to those educated in the Chinese stream in Singapore. The May Fourth heritage, then, was 'the unique possession of the Chinese-educated,' as Sally Borthwick has written; 'its literature had formed their language studies, its thinkers set the parameters for attitudes towards the Chinese past and the international present.'

Moreover, while Chinese schools had strong nationalist tendencies, the education they provided was 'far more cosmopolitan than its English counterpart: higher-level students were familiar with Edison, Rousseau and Gorky, and even elementary pupils studied inspiring examples from Western history such as Lincoln and Columbus.' By contrast, 'English-medium courses contained no comparable figures from Asian history and culture.' The divide between the Chinese-educated and English-educated was not how many would see it today, as one between traditional Chinese and modern Western world-views.

On the other hand, the English-educated, like the Straits Chinese before them, did not need to travel the May Fourth route to modernity, for that process 'had been paralleled, duplicated and supplanted by the more accessible experience of Western adaptation' which had come with their English education. For them, 'the battle against feudalism, long over for the West, did not need to be refought on Singaporean soil.' By 1950, there had been a significant increase in the number of government-supported English-medium primary schools. This gradually led, Borthwick observes, to 'a de facto choice of English' by parents for their school-going children. The majority of Chinese schools, established and funded by local communities, offered much poorer facilities.

School leavers could go to China for advanced studies if they could afford it or, if not, enter the job market. The colonial occupational structure favoured the English-educated (especially in the civil service) and gave monolingual Chinese fewer opportunities. Thus the cultural divide between the two groups was reinforced by social inequality. Furthermore, just as opportunities for tertiary education were opening up for English school leavers with the establishment of the University of Malaya in Singapore in 1949, they were narrowing for the Chinese-stream students, whom the British colonial authorities would bar from re-entering Singapore if they were to go and study in the newly founded People's Republic of China. Those who identified with the New China – and therefore with socialism – returned or were deported, while for others the influence of China receded.

Where would Chinese-stream graduates go if not to mainland Chinese universities? Three Chinese community leaders – Tan Lark Sye (1897–1972), Lee Kong Chian and Ng Aik Huan – conceived the idea of setting up a Malayan Chinese university in 1946. In 1950 there were 281 Chinese schools, 76,200 students and 1,949 teachers in Singapore alone. At a Joint Meeting of the Executive and Supervisory Committee of the Singapore Hokkien Huay Kuan in January 1953, Tan Lark Sye, then president of the latter association, announced plans for the setting up of a local Chinese university. Tan, who was uneducated beyond a couple of years of school, donated five million Singapore dollars to the project.

His proposal, supported by the Singapore Chamber of Commerce and a wide range of Chinese associations in Singapore and Malaya, became a communal enterprise, gaining considerable momentum as money was enthusiastically raised from all sectors of the Chinese population, from wealthy merchants to the working masses. The display of enthusiasm and Chinese unity was famously illustrated by the contribution of a day's earnings from the island's 1,577 trishaw drivers in April 1954. On a 500-acre piece of land purchased and donated by the Hokkien Huay Kuan, Nanyang University (later popularly called Nanda, or Nantah in the local spelling), the first Chinese University in Southeast Asia, was formally inaugurated in March 1956 with an initial cohort of 330 students.

An article entitled 'From the Crisis in Chinese Education to the Mission of Nanyang University' captures the strong sentiments which underpinned the enterprise:

> For many years past, our Chinese-language education has continuously been in an unequal and despised position. This point will be acknowledged by all who still keep their people's tradition and have a conscience ... The Chinese language itself is treated with contempt ... If a Chinese has mastery of his own language, and through this linguistic tool gains other scientific knowledge and philosophic thought, that's not treated as knowledge. Because of this, the people trained by the Chinese-language education system find their talents neglected by others. This explains why many graduates of Chinese universities and Chinese high

Inauguration of Nanyang University.

schools find themselves uncertain, cast down, at a dead end. This is one aspect. Another aspect is those Chinese in society at large who are only thoroughly familiar with the Chinese language and who are therefore subjected by people everywhere to coldness, rudeness, ridicule, deception, harsh treatment and even insult. At the present time this forms a part of the life of countless Chinese.

The university came into existence at a time when activism in the Chinese middle schools was at its peak. The students, with the support of the trade unions, clashed with the police in a series of violent protests: against conscription on May 13, 1954 (the May Thirteenth or '513' Incident), on the first anniversary of the Hock Lee bus riots, and against government dissolution of the newly formed island-wide students' union in October 1956.

Decades later Lee Kuan Yew would recall the opening of Nanyang University as the 'most massive demonstration of emotional commitment to Chinese culture' Singapore had ever seen. Such a demonstration, when coupled with the mass student unrest of the time, makes it tempting to speak of Chinese education in the 1950s as a vehicle of both cultural chauvinism and political radicalism. It would not seem so simple, though, if it were seen in its proper context: the politics of decolonization and the Chinese-educated's bid for a place in Singapore society. Viewed in such a context, themes of nationalism, ethnic self-respect and aspirations for social uplift emerge. Nationalism meant a political orientation to developments both in China and in Malaya and Singapore, where many among the educated from different backgrounds dedicated themselves to the anti-colonial movement. Ethnic self-respect involved an identification with both ancestral culture and its modern transformations. Social uplift entailed both economic survival in the midst of inequality and political confrontation with the colonial authorities.

The making of a new nation

Singapore's nationalism had largely gestated in the labour movement, the militant anti-colonial unions providing fertile ground. Once independence was won, the PAP government moved to tame the unions and shrink the left wing's influence. It embarked upon an all-out drive for economic growth and efficiency, building an economy which combined local private enterprise, heavy state participation and increasing infusions of foreign investment. The government's attempts to instil patriotism and create a national identity included the preparation of primary school history textbooks telling the story of the immigrant peoples in Singapore, 'a romanticization,' as S. Gopinathan puts it, 'of the early pioneering spirit with successful businessmen cast as heroes. Perseverance and effort were the key values in these texts, and the rewards were financial prosperity and security.'

Singapore aimed at a meritocratic system whose rewards were based on performance and achievement rather than racial or religious criteria. This was linked to its avowal of giving equal treatment to the different races that made up the nation. The government pledged itself to a 'multiracial' and 'multilingual' policy, according equality of citizenship to all the races and making English, Chinese, Malay and Tamil official languages. Within this framework, ethnicity or race qualifies the idea of citizenship; hence the terms 'Chinese Singaporeans,' 'Malay Singaporeans' and 'Indian Singaporeans.' These became commonly accepted categories of identification by the state and by citizens.

In the early 1960s the British floated the idea of Singapore becoming independent as a state within a Malaysian Federation – Singapore seemed too small to be a viable nation-state. The merger, which occurred in 1963, was short-lived, however, and divorce followed in 1965. What with the PAP advocating a multiracial, multilingual and multicultural Malaysia (a 'Malaysian Malaysia,' as its slogan went), and the dominant political party in Malaysia insisting on Malay special rights and a Malay national identity, it is no wonder that the marriage did not last.

It was clear that any sense of Singapore identity the new nation evolved had to be sufficiently broad to include its different ethnic groups and their 'mother tongues.' An emphasis on Chinese ethnicity as the basis of nationhood would, to echo W. E. Willmott in his essay in *Management of Success*, have excluded a quarter of the population, exacerbated relations with neighbouring states, and contradicted the explicit ideology of the ruling party. Instead, a model was adopted in which all the component groups were promised cultural and linguistic equality. The desirability of equality between the ethnic groups – particularly between Chinese and Malays – became all the more apparent with the race riots of 1964.

In 1956 the All-Party Committee on Chinese Education had recommended equal treatment for Chinese, Malay, Tamil and English. In practice, English, the dominant working language in the legal and government sectors and supposedly the cultural property of none of the major ethnic groups, became the de facto national language. The report of the committee had also proposed bilingual education and the standardization of curricula in all schools under the jurisdiction and control of the

Students rush to protest meeting in May 1954.

To raise funds for Nanyang University, even dance hostesses played a part, 1953.

Ministry of Education. Under the PAP government, bilingual education first involved teaching English as a second language in Chinese-stream schools, and Mandarin, Malay and Tamil in English-stream schools. By the early 1970s, however, English was not only taught as a subject but also used as a medium of instruction. In line with official thinking, mathematics and science were taught in English and social studies subjects in the 'mother-tongue' languages. Chinese-stream schools, therefore, had to increase their students' exposure to the English language and to redeploy teachers to teach in English subjects formerly taught in Chinese.

The 'Chinese-educated'

The enrolment in Chinese-stream primary schools fell steadily as parents increasingly sent their children to English-medium schools. Between 1959 and 1978, the former's proportion of total primary school enrolment fell from nearly 46 per cent to about 11 per cent. Parents well understood the instrumental value of English, the possession of which improved one's chances of higher education and one's employment prospects.

Faced with the possibility of Chinese schools dying out, the Ministry of Education initiated a 'special assistance plan' in 1978. Under this plan, the best-known Chinese-stream secondary schools were reorganized as bilingual schools offering English and Chinese as first languages, and attracting top students from both language streams while maintaining their 'traditional' Chinese school environment. In the view of the education policy-makers, this strategy would allow Singapore to 'retain the best in Chinese education which the tide of events threatened to eliminate.'

Yet the tide of events did eliminate Chinese education at its highest level in the country. In 1975 Nanyang University adopted English as the medium of instruction – the long-standing practice at the University of Singapore. Nantah, judged a hotbed of resistance to the government, had in fact been under pressure for some time: Tan Lark Sye was eliminated in 1963, and some 237 students were arrested or expelled in the period 1964–66.

By a government initiative two years after the switch to English, first-year Nantah undergraduates were made to study with their counterparts at the University of Singapore with English as the main medium of instruction. Then, in 1980, the two universities merged to form the National University of Singapore. This move, in the words of an educationalist, 'effectively closed down a distinct achievement of the Chinese-educated and a powerful symbol of oppositional Chinese power.' The Nantah campus, a repository of sentiments and memories for many graduates, became the site of what would eventually emerge as the Nanyang Technological University. The name of this university, though, had no resonance for those who mourned what they saw as the effacement of the old Nanyang University.

Poster exhorting Singaporean Chinese to speak Mandarin.

By 1983 enrolment in Chinese primary schools had dwindled to only 2 per cent. By 1987, English had become the first language and main medium of instruction in all schools. Knowledge of English facilitated the absorption of science and technology and the conduct of international commerce. However, in line with the policy of multilingualism, the political leadership remained committed to the teaching of Mandarin as the 'mother tongue' of the Chinese and the language of cultural transmission, ensuring it a place, albeit a secondary one, in the school curriculum. Mandarin's perceived cultural function was linked to the authorities' constantly voiced fears of 'Westernization' and 'deculturalization' brought about by fast-paced economic development and modernization.

The Chinese-educated did not strongly or overtly protest the closure of Nanyang University. But this did not mean that they were unaffected by what many of them saw as the demise of the institutional foundations of their sense of personal and collective identity *vis-à-vis* the position of the English-educated and the status of English in Singapore society. The social and psychological struggles of the Chinese-educated were poignantly expressed in literary and non-fictional writings. A gamut of emotions emerged in numerous novels, short stories and poems by Chinese-educated writers. Some Chinese-educated intellectuals have referred to this body of writings as Singapore's own version of the 'literature of the wounded' (*shanghen wenxue*), borrowing the term used in China of writings evoking the tragedies and brutalities of the Cultural Revolution (1966–76).

One study has focused on an older generation of teachers, Nantah graduates included, who had taught Chinese or taught school subjects in Chinese. This was the group most directly affected by the decline of Chinese education. Themselves the products of Chinese education, they were now required by the changes in the educational system to teach in English, becoming what were called 'converted teachers.' The study finds a range of emotions in their personal accounts of this experience, including trauma, a sense of tragedy, feelings of bitterness at being discriminated against, and reluctant acceptance.

In another study, Lee Guan Kin (Li Yuanjin) looks at non-fictional writings – mainly Chinese newspaper editorials, articles, letters to the press, speeches and seminar discussions – and uncovers three kinds of response among the Chinese-educated between 1959 and 1987. The initial period was marked by hope, with appeals forcefully made for the resuscitation of Chinese education and emphasis laid on its cultural and moral value. In the early 1980s, however, a sense of helplessness and pessimism became evident, and the tone more cynical than condemnatory. By the end of the decade, feelings of grief and loss had given way to passivity and withdrawal, and the debates had more narrowly focused on such matters as the retention of standards in the teaching of the language. The overall stance was thus one of compromise. Lee attributed this to a combination of factors: the political sensitivity and fear (compounded in part by the historical association between Chinese education and left-wing politics) surrounding issues of language, culture and education, the weakened position of intellectuals in relation to the state, and the attitude captured in the Chinese phrase *ren ru fu zhong* – 'enduring humiliation in order to accomplish an important mission.'

Yet the Chinese-educated continued to see themselves as a marginalized group harbouring a 'deep feeling of hurt at being … excluded from the mainstream' (to quote the words of the editor of the main Chinese-language daily.) Their discontent seemed to be more than just a personal matter; it appeared to have political consequences. It was apparently expressed in votes cast against the PAP in the 1991 elections.

But Prime Minister Goh Chok Tong, among other Singapore leaders, urged them to put their sense of grievance behind them – they should, he said, rid themselves 'of this unnecessary psychological baggage.' Some leaders invoked 'the Nantah spirit' of the 1950s and 1960s – this identified not, as historically minded bystanders might suppose, with 'Chinese chauvinism' and 'Communism,' but perseverance amid adversity. And, as if to suggest that there was some continuity between the old Nantah and the present-day Nanyang Technological University, in 1996 the Nantah register was transferred, at the request of the Association of Nanyang University Graduates, the alumni body, from the National University of Singapore to the Nanyang Technological University.

All this might suggest that the Chinese-educated had indeed put their past behind them. But the past was not so easily buried, as events during the campaigns leading up to the January 1997 General Election showed. In the battle for the most keenly contested constituency (Cheng San), one of the Workers' Party candidates, Tang Liang Hong, a lawyer who had given voice to the marginalization of the Chinese-educated, came under attack by the PAP for being allegedly anti-English-educated and anti-Christian.

Tang, who speaks Chinese, English and Malay, was described as a Chinese chauvinist who endangered racial balance in multiracial Singapore. If allowed to spread, Lee Kuan Yew said at a party rally, the kind of views

Figure 5.1

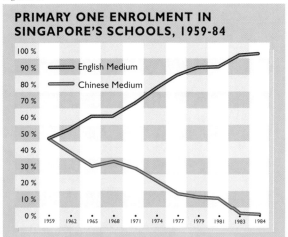

Tang represented would destroy the country; Singapore would 'go down like Beirut.' It mustn't be a 'China base,' as this was dangerous, while 'an ethnic Chinese base' was not. The Chinese-educated must decide what they want for their future: 'They can have peace and stability,' *The Straits Times*, on December 31, 1996, reported him as saying 'in which case they must accept English as the working language and have a spirit of give and take, or they can have a dominant Chinese society, which would lead eventually to collision.'

In the event the PAP won all but two of the country's 83 seats. In the months after the elections, PAP leaders, among them the prime minister, two deputy prime ministers and Lee Kuan Yew, brought 13 libel suits against Tang for remarks he had allegedly made against them during the campaign. Tang himself left the country after the election and for all practical purposes went into exile. The PAP leaders were later awarded a record sum amounting to more than S$8 million in damages.

Headline in The Straits Times *quotes Lee Kuan Yew on 'Chinese chauvinism.'*

These events left many with the impression, observed the editor of the main Chinese-language daily in 1997, 'that Tang's entry into politics represented a challenge by the Chinese-educated against the dominance of English.' Certainly, if the Chinese-educated felt themselves a beleaguered community, they felt hardly less so after the Tang affair. Yet, paradoxically, the marginalization and gradual disappearance of the older Chinese-educated group prompted official concern, expressed by the prime minister in his National Day Rally speech in 1997, that 'the Chinese community faced particular challenges in maintaining its roots, as there would be no new generation of Chinese-educated élite in 20 years.' Singapore needed a 'Chinese-proficient élite,' he told the nation, and for that it 'has to reproduce a core group of Chinese Singaporeans who are steeped in and knowledgeable about Chinese culture, history, literature and the arts.'

With the Chinese stream having been phased out by the 1990s, to be replaced by a younger bilingual generation, the 'Chinese-educated' has become a less well-defined category. Yet there remains, among this generation, a group of people who, though bilingual, are more comfortable speaking Chinese than English and to whom the term '*huaxiaosheng*' (graduates of Chinese-stream schools) has been loosely attached.

This group, however, is anxious to set itself apart from the Chinese-educated of its parents' generation and to break out of the old mould which equates the Chinese-educated with cultural 'chauvinism.' Interviewed at a seminar ('Identity: Crisis and Opportunity') in which this group explored their collective identity in 1996, a representative is quoted in *The Straits Times* of September 21, 1996, as saying: 'I sympathize with [the older generation], I understand them, and what I have today I inherited partly from them. But I know I have to be different from them – because I do not have the psychological and historical baggage that they have.'

How to be simultaneously Singaporean, Chinese and modern

Chinese opera draws few Singaporeans.

Until the 1980s it was widely believed, and not only in Singapore, that the last two constituents of the triad, namely 'Chinese' and 'modern,' did not go together. Western analysts of China's history of attempted modernization, for example, believed Chinese tradition, specifically Confucianism, to be a drag on Chinese progress and even to be an explanation for its backwardness.

A Singaporean scholar, C. J. W.-L Wee, has argued that for Singapore's political leadership, from the mid-1960s to the 1970s, the idea of being 'modern' entailed creating a society which was *not* predicated on 'retrogressive Asian values.' However, Wee believes, this earlier approach had changed by the early 1980s, perhaps because the leaders had found 'that the notion of "universal" values may not actually support the maintenance of a hardworking industrial society, as it led to social developments (a.k.a. 'Western decadence') that disrupted hard work.'

A few years earlier, in 1979, the government had launched the annual Speak Mandarin Campaign. This was not only because speaking Mandarin would facilitate communication across dialect lines, it was also seen to be a means of preserving Chinese identity. As Lee Kuan Yew put it at the opening of the 1984 campaign, 'English will not be emotionally acceptable as our mother tongue. To have no emotionally acceptable language as our mother tongue is to be emotionally crippled. We shall doubt ourselves. We shall be less self-confident. Mandarin is emotionally acceptable as our mother tongue. It also unites the different dialect groups. It reminds us that we are part of an ancient civilization with an unbroken history of over 5,000 years. This is a deep and strong psychic force, one that gives confidence to a people to face up to and overcome great changes and challenges.' In fact, about 85 per cent of Chinese pupils came from dialect-speaking homes, and to study Mandarin on top of the obligatory English meant that they were learning two new school languages (even though Mandarin was deemed their 'mother tongue').

As a result of the overhaul of bilingual education and the Mandarin campaigns in the 1980s, patterns of language use among Chinese greatly changed. Between 1980 and 1990 the percentage of Chinese above the age of four years in households in which English was the

'Non-descript' cultural 'mélange': Styrofoam Santa Claus in front of mall is pressed into service as God of Wealth as Christmas shopping gives way to Lunar New Year shopping.

predominant language spoken rose from nearly 8 per cent to 19 per cent. The increase in the use of Mandarin as the predominant household language was at a faster rate, from 10 per cent in 1980 to nearly 30 per cent in 1990. The increase in the use of English and Mandarin at home was accompanied by a significant drop in the use of Chinese dialects, from 81 per cent to 51 per cent

over the decade (see table 5.17).

English, foreign though it is supposed to be, is the mother tongue of nearly a fifth of the Chinese population. Moreover, it is widely spoken in the workplace. Indeed, perhaps nowhere in East and Southeast Asia is there such a large sector of the Asian population using English at home and at work. This makes Singapore, for all its official self-promotion as an Asian country, the most 'Westernized' country in Asia.

In the 1980s the emphasis on Mandarin was accompanied by the promotion of Confucianism. Earlier Lee Kuan Yew had said, 'The greatest value in the teaching and learning of Chinese is in the transmission of the norms of social or moral behaviour. This means principally Confucianist beliefs and ideas, of man, society and the state.' To guard against what the leader Goh Keng Swee called 'the dangers of secular education in a foreign tongue' and 'the risk of losing the traditional values of one's own people and the acquisition of the more spurious fashions of the West,' Religious Knowledge was introduced as a compulsory subject in secondary schools, with Buddhism, Christianity, Hinduism and Islam offered as options. Confucian Ethics was added to the list and received a disproportionate amount of attention and resources. The government-sponsored Institute of East Asian Philosophies was founded, and scholars of Confucianism, notably Tu Wei-ming of Harvard, were brought to Singapore to advise and lecture.

Confucianism, in an analysis by Eddie Kuo, a sociologist, 'was compatible with the dominant political culture in Singapore, specifically in terms of paternalism, communitarianism, pragmatism, and secularism. (To these a critic would add authoritarianism.) Indeed, the very manner in which the Confucian movement was initiated and promoted reflected a top-down pattern, similar to other "social engineering" programmes designed for various nation-building objectives.'

In the 1950s and 1960s the promotion of Chinese culture would have been tantamount to 'being pro-China and hence pro-Communist.' Now, with the official endorsement of Mandarin and Confucianism, 'the Chinese-educated population, including a small number of latent chauvinists, could safely jump on the bandwagon and promote Chinese culture by way of promoting Confucianism. To many Chinese and Chinese organizations, whether the movement was Confucian or not may have been secondary, for what was fundamentally important was that it served to promote Chinese culture, Chinese education, and hence Chinese identity. Confucianism hence served as a symbol of collective Chinese identity.'

The movement was not without unwelcome consequences. Non-Chinese minorities saw it as an officially sponsored sinicization which compromised the ideal of multiracialism and multilingualism. The Religious Knowledge programme was discontinued because the government grew anxious about the rise of 'religious revivalism.' Yet, while Confucian Ethics was phased out, Confucianist rhetoric persisted in public discourse, supported throughout the 1980s by the thesis, popularized by Western social scientists (see p 125), that Confucianism played a role in the economic growth of the 'four dragons' (South Korea, Taiwan, Hong Kong and Singapore). The thesis was welcomed in Singapore, where it

Table 5.17

PERSONS AGED FIVE YEARS AND OVER IN RESIDENT CHINESE HOUSEHOLDS BY PREDOMINANT LANGUAGE SPOKEN, 1980 AND 1990		
PREDOMINANT HOUSEHOLD LANGUAGE SPOKEN	1980	1990
Chinese households	100.0	100.0
English	7.9	19.2
Mandarin	10.2	29.8
Chinese dialects	81.4	50.6
Others	0.5	0.4

Source: Tham (1996).

Embodiments of 'Shared Values'?

served to reaffirm the political leadership's contention that 'traditional values' supported economic development and its repudiation of welfare dependence.

Confucianism could not, clearly, form the basis of the national ideology of a society that is not wholly ethnically Chinese. The 'Shared Values' which do form such a basis, according to a White Paper passed by Parliament in 1991, were defined as: the priority of nation or the community over the individual, the importance of the family, political consensus and racial and religious harmony. While criticizing the nepotism and 'strictly hierarchical' family relationships widely associated with Confucian practice, the paper maintained that many Confucian ideas were relevant to Singapore, and highlighted 'the concept of government by honourable men . . . (*junzi*), who have a duty to do right for the people, and who have the trust and respect of the population'; this 'fits us better,' it says, 'than the Western idea that a government should be given as limited power as possible, and should always be treated with suspicion unless proven otherwise.' Eddie Kuo has suggested that such a statement constituted 'a reversal of the earlier position that Confucianism as a political ideology must be distinguished from Confucianism as an ethical system that is to be promoted as the basis for moral growth and the building of character.'

In a speech to the Singapore Federation of Chinese Clan Associations and the Singapore Chinese Chamber of Commerce and Industry in 1991, Lee Kuan Yew said that the Shared Values do not 'make up a complete philosophy of life. The Chinese must draw on their traditional values in Confucianism, Daoism and Chinese folklore to complement them. The Malays must draw on Malay custom and Islam, the Hindus on their customs and the Hindu religion. If we try to put all these different background cultures into a blenderiser [*sic*], we will end up with a non-descript *mélange*.' In the early 1990s, the discourse on Shared Values dovetailed with the debate on 'Asian values,' which were claimed by their exponents, notably the leaders of Singapore and Malaysia, as being superior to 'Western values,' particularly liberal democracy and freedom. (Western observers thought their own scepticism vindicated when Southeast Asian economies came unstuck in 1997.)

Lee had attributed Singapore's success to the 'cultural values of the generation of the 1950s–70s,' which included self-sacrifice, hard work, thrift and a consciousness of one's obligations. These values had in fact coexisted with other (rejected) values, but as always with 'selective tradition,' as the British writer Raymond Williams has noted, only certain meanings and practices are emphasized and passed off as *the* tradition –

and not only emphasized but reinterpreted, diluted, or put into forms which support or at least do not contradict other elements within the effective dominant culture. When a reforming China presented business opportunities in the 1980s, Singapore placed a new premium on preserving Chinese identity and knowledge of the Chinese language. A boost was given to the annual Speak Mandarin campaign, which increasingly emphasized the economic value of the language.

By 1993 Singapore had become China's fifth largest investor. As well as being a significant node in the transnational flows of capital to Southeast Asia, Singapore now positioned itself as a 'gateway' to China, or an intermediary between that country and Western business.

The flagship project for pursuing this strategy was the China-Singapore Suzhou Industrial Park, a 70-square kilometre township where, jointly with the local municipal government, Singapore's image would be created. As well as capital, Singapore offered China management expertise and its ability to network with the world's leading multinational corporations. These companies would be invited to invest in the township, with Singapore helping to provide not only an international business ethos, but a familiarity with China based on the cultural and political values the two countries supposedly hold in common.

It soon became clear, however, that Singapore was no different from other foreign investors in finding it very hard to succeed in China. The Singaporean government's chief complaint was that the Suzhou municipal authorities were developing a competing economic zone and drawing away foreign investors from the one Singapore was building (in fact, the former zone was begun three years before Singapore came in). All in all, what Singapore's experience in Suzhou has made plain is the cultural gulf that exists between the two parties, the mismatch between the 'Chineseness' of Singapore and that of China. It is also clear that while capitalist development can be aided or hindered by cultural conditions, it ultimately runs on instrumental principles that transcend culture.

Kwok Kian Woon

Mandarin is accorded utilitarian value for Singaporeans who wish to do business in China.

THAILAND

Where the community begins and ends is one of the most challenging aspects of studying the Chinese in Thailand as a group. Estimates of their population today are at best guesswork. It would be hard to survey by surname, since most Sino-Thais (as they are often called) have taken Thai names. Enumeration is made all the harder by the high rate of intermarriage between Chinese and Thais. Estimates range from 4.5 to 6 million, or 10 per cent of the country's population of almost 60 million.

This statistical ambiguity is further complicated by the close relationship between Chinese and Thai culture, and the latter's incorporation of Chinese traditions as part of its own cultural heritage. Indeed, many observers see Sino-Thai (or 'Jek') culture as a constitutive part of Thai culture. There was a time in history, moreover, when Thais did not consider Chinese as foreigners. Yet, during the Cold War, when political ideology and security ties with the West kept China apart from much of Southeast Asia, the historical closeness of Thais and Chinese was downplayed. As non-Communist states like Thailand battled local Communist insurgencies backed by Beijing and relied on the United States for aid and security, the Chinese community assumed a low profile that obscured its cultural distinctiveness and lent weight to assimilationist arguments.

Migration history

Most historians now accept that Thais are descended in part from non-Han Chinese people who migrated southwards from areas of what is now China's Yunnan province. When contacts were first made by Thai academics with the Dai minority who live in the Yunnanese region known as Xishuangbanna in the mid-1970s, they were struck by its cultural similarities to the people of Laos and northern Thailand. Generally speaking, the Dai lived in wooden dwellings on stilts and spoke a dialect (called Daile in Chinese) intelligible to Thais.

Once established, the early Thai kingdom of Sukhothai maintained good relations with China, to which it stood as a tributary state. As the Thai historian Sarasin Viraphol showed in his seminal study of the tributary trade, the Siamese monarchy willingly sent tribute to China, not because it felt compelled to accept Chinese suzerainty. The profits to be made from the trade, which was exempt from normal tariffs and duties, were considerable. Those who detect China's influence beyond the purely commercial domain argue that King Ramkhamhaeng, the 13th-century Thai monarch, modelled his institutions closely on Chinese examples; and point to Thai traditions tracing ceramic wares produced at Sukhothai and Sawankhalok to potters brought back by Ramkhamhaeng when he went to China.

Chinese had been drawn first to the Malay peninsula,

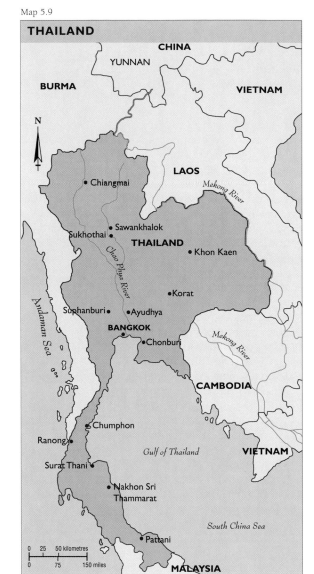

Map 5.9

Bowl from Sukhothai kiln.

visiting trading towns such as Chumphon, Surat Thani, and Nakhon Sri Thammarat (then known as Ligor) in the 13th and 14th centuries. Chinese tin miners were well-established in southern Siam when the first Westerners penetrated the area in the 16th century. A large Chinese settlement in the southern littoral town of Pattani is traced to Lin Daoqian, a notorious pirate, and those of his followers who fled there from Fujian in the 16th century.

Portuguese accounts of the period noted that Chinese merchants were 'everywhere established in Siam.' Chinese were the main competitors of the large contingent of Portuguese trading at the splendid new capital at Ayudhya. They had their own quarter in the city by the early 16th century, according to a contemporary Chinese chronicle, which also indicates the generational depth of their settlement when it notes that, 'In this country, people have no surnames. The Chinese at first retain their own surnames, but give them up after a few generations.'

The French ambassador at the court of Ayudhya, de la Loubere, put the Chinese population there in the mid-17th century at 3,000–4,000. G. William Skinner, author of the classic *Chinese Society in Thailand* (1957), estimates the number of Chinese in all Siam in the late-17th century at around 10,000, a little under 1 per cent of the total population. As for their origins, 17th-century sources make mention of people from the ports of southern Fujian and Canton.

Despite setbacks, Chinese became unrivalled in trade. They benefited from the decline of Japanese mercenary fortunes at the court of Ayudhya in the 1630s. They were quick to adapt to the Thai monarchy's interest in trade and profited from their role as the managers and agents of royal trade monopolies. Not being treated as foreigners gave them the edge over European traders. As a Chinese writer has observed, 'The inhabitants of Siam accept the Chinese very cordially; much better than do the natives of any other country that is really friendly to the Chinese.' During the siege of Ayudhya by the Burmese in 1766, resident Chinese reportedly played a heroic role in attempts to defend the city.

It so happened that the man who restored the shattered Thai kingdom after its defeat by Burma and eventually became king, presiding over the new capital at Bangkok, was half-Chinese. King Taksin's father was a Teochiu (Chaozhou) immigrant who reportedly held the gambling monopoly at the old court of Ayudhya; his mother was Thai. During his reign (1767–82), Taksin evidently encouraged more Teochius to emigrate and establish themselves as traders and plantation agriculturalists, growing sugar and pepper for export. The settlement he started grew up on the east bank of the Chao Phya, near the site of the present Grand Palace.

Taksin's reign was followed by that of Rama I, to whose planning was owed the siting of the Chinese trading hub in the area called Sampheng, still the heart of Bangkok's Chinatown today. Under Rama I and his successors, royal trading flourished as never before, and with it Chinese commercial involvement and immigration. Chinese enjoyed exemption from the system of slavery which bound Thai labour to the land; by contrast, the mass of Thais were not free to engage in commerce or work as individuals in the city. There was therefore a tremendous demand for foreign traders, artisans and even labourers. To the absolute monarchy of old Siam,

foreigners were useful and less of a hazard than Thais who, once they were entrusted with vital commercial tasks, might dilute the monarch's effective monopoly of trade and pose a threat to the throne. Traditionally, therefore, the courts of old Siam were replete with foreigners of all kinds. Both the old capital of Ayudhya and early Bangkok were cosmopolitan capitals with foreigners – not just Chinese – occupying prominent positions.

As the economy began to boom in the 1850s, so the pace of Chinese immigration quickened. From the seasonal influx of traders during the first half of the century, there grew the organized credit-ticket traffic of mass labour migration (see p 61) of the second half. By the late 19th century, there were enough of them in Thailand for a British explorer, Holt S. Hallett, to describe Chinese as 'ubiquitous.'

Bangkok grew on the backs of this immigrant Chinese workforce. By Skinner's reckoning, the city in the early 1900s was almost 50 per cent Chinese and had 'the stamp of a Chinese city.' But by no means all Chinese immigrants were city dwellers; others, notably the Hainanese, had fanned out in search of pioneering opportunities upcountry, possibly in retreat before Teochiu and Hokkien strength. Because they handled trade, many Chinese quickly established themselves at the middle level of society. But there were also Chinese who worked as labourers and poor agriculturalists, earning income little above that of the average Thai. Their mobility was much enhanced, however, because they handled money to a far greater extent than the average Thai, who still dealt in kind.

The overwhelming majority of Chinese immigrants came from Guangdong and Fujian provinces. Teochius predominated at 40 per cent of the Chinese population in the early 20th century, eclipsing Hainanese (18 per

Portrait of King Taksin in temple in Bangkok.

Chinese traders (here selling Buddha statuettes) were everywhere in Siam, 1920 (below left). (Box) Khaw Soo Cheang and his five sons.

AN EARLY THAI CHINESE DYNASTY

Khaw Soo Cheang (1797–1882) was a young Hokkien immigrant who arrived in Ranong, in southern Siam, after a stint as possibly a labourer in Penang. Rich in tin, the Ranong area had been mined by Chinese for generations. As the successful bidder for the tin tax farm, he built up a fortune. While the concession earned him wealth, his ability to deliver ever larger amounts of revenue to the Crown won him official recognition and appointment as governor.

Fathering many sons on his possibly Sino-Thai wives, sons who would intermarry with important Thais and Chinese and extend the family's influence over peninsular Siam, Khaw created an empire. As local strongmen owing allegiance to the political centre in Bangkok, the Khaws played a considerable role in the consolidation of Thai bureaucratic authority over the kingdom's southern periphery. They occupied something of a political vacuum, but one increasingly pressed upon by the colonial British in Malaya.

The family, as its chronicler Jennifer Cushman puts it, possessed 'a double identity' in being both the political representatives of the Thai court and entrepreneurs pursuing their own commercial interests. Foreshadowing the modern Thai Chinese, the Khaw family benefited greatly from being able to operate in two distinct domains, forging ties with the Thai nobility even as they maintained close links with the large Hokkien community in Penang.

The family's fortunes began to wane as Chinese business in Thailand as a whole was faced with Western competition and the withdrawal of state patronage. The family history thus captures how Chinese entrepreneurship and power evolved in an interplay of family and state relationships as these shifted in tandem with changes in the economic and political climate.

Michael R. J. Vatikiotis

cent), Hakkas (16 per cent), Hokkiens (16 per cent) and Cantonese (9 per cent). An important reason for Teochiu predominance beyond King Taksin's favouritism and the logic of chain migration was that the first of Bangkok's direct scheduled passenger steamer services to any port in the coastal sending areas in China was with Shantou.

Changes in economic fortune

Chinese played a key role in laying the economic foundations of the new Siam which emerged after the Burmese invasion. Until the 19th century, all trade was monopolized by the Crown. But with increasing Chinese immigration, Thai kings found they could relinquish their monopolies and farm them out as tax concessions to Chinese traders. By pledging a portion of the profits in tax to the Crown, the tax farmer collected taxes – in amounts greater than were due to the Crown – on an increasing range of goods and services, from cotton and birds' nests to opium and gambling. As Pasuk Phongpaichit and Chris Baker explain in their book *Thailand: Economy and Politics* (1995): 'Tax farming amounted to state-promoted entrepreneurship.' The king gave many of these tax farmers, or *nai akorn*, capital to establish plantations for export crops. To lend them authority, he granted them royal titles and administrative positions. In 1854, one successful tax farmer, Khaw Soo Cheang, was appointed governor of Ranong province in southern Thailand (see box p 219).

Thai historians have characterized the Chinese who prospered from this as 'bureaucratic capitalists' who exploited the feudal structure of Thai society and access to state power to become wealthy. In actual fact, it was a relationship of mutual benefit with the Thai élite. Fur-

Rice mills in Thailand.

thermore, it subordinated the Chinese to the Thai élite and ultimately led to a blending of the two groups through intermarriage.

After enjoying privileged commercial and political access for much of the mid-19th century, the Chinese began to experience declining fortunes after 1870 when the Crown moved to dismantle the tax farming system and build a revenue base of its own. By the early 1890s, most tax farming concessions had been placed under state management. The government continued to form joint ventures with Chinese merchants, but increasingly sought a range of other foreign partners.

The Bowring Treaty of 1855 gave Europeans an entrée to the rich trading opportunities in Thailand – and provided a useful means to balance Chinese commercial power. For by now there was a growing tide of resentment in Thai élite circles. Writing in 1916, a Thai aristocrat commented: 'In the old days, the Chinese ... always visited princes and nobles, or high officials, and were very close to the Thais .... Now they are different ... they see no need to visit or please anyone. They come in to pursue large businesses, investing in rice mills and trading firms with thousands or millions of baht [the Thai currency] without having to have connections with anyone.'

Those who suffered from the Crown's move to enhance its control over the economy included immigrant families who had acquired riches and powerful positions. Many moved out of tax-farming into rice milling, as by now intensive rice cultivation was becoming the mainstay of the country's export-led economy. Socially, they were forced to adapt as well, and in so doing became embedded more deeply in Thai society. Many of the old tax farmers sent their sons to schools founded under royal patronage and encouraged them to join the civil service. The legacy was a string of prominent families of Chinese origin who became the core of the bureaucratic élite in the 20th century – families like the Sarasin, Vejjajiva, Laohasetthi, na Songkhla, and Prachuapmoh.

The 1920s saw a new wave of successful Chinese enterprise sweep Thailand. A group of Chinese rice merchants burgeoned with the booming rice economy. At the same time, the growing domestic demand for consumer goods brought forth a group of Sino-Thai manufacturers and suppliers. Indeed, it was during this period that the foundations of modern Chinese business were essentially laid.

The rice network began with the upcountry Chinese (usually Teochiu) trader and ended with the Chinese (usually Teochiu) rice importer in Hong Kong and Singapore. Although many of the rice barons foundered in the post-1929 Depression, a handful who had built integrated businesses survived to spawn modern Thailand's industrial and commercial conglomerates. In the 1930s, the so-called Big Five families – Wanglee, Lamsam,

Home of the Chen clan in Guangdong.

WANGLEE

Wanglee's history goes back to Longdu, a Teochiu district in Guangdong province. There, in the mid-1840s, a fisherman called Chen Xuanyi joined his clansmen in working as a sailor on ships owned by a *nanbeihang* (general importer and exporter firm) in Hong Kong. Soon he had the means to buy a junk himself, and set himself up as a trader in Bonham Strand West, Hong Kong, shipping local products (including Siamese rice) between Southeast Asia, Shanghai, ports in northern China, Shantou and Hong Kong. His company, Kin Tye Lung, developed a sideline handling sojourning Chinese workers' remittances home.

His eldest son Cihong helped establish Wanglee in 1871 as Kin Tye Lung's associate company in Bangkok. Meanwhile, other members of the surname group set up other associate companies in Singapore (Tan Guan Lee), Shantou and Saigon. Then, 20 years later, Cihong retired to his hometown in China and left the business to his son Limei.

Limei went on to found a string of Wanglee's remittance agency branches – in Bangkok, Hong Kong, Penang, Saigon, Shantou and Singapore. As well as becoming the agent to Norway's BK Steamship Company, he acquired rice mills in Bangkok and became president of the Rice Mills Organization there. He extended his influence by acquiring shares in Tan Guan Lee and Kin Tye Lung. Later, he brought the latter's remittance business under the wing of Wanglee's Hong Kong branch and gave it to his son Shouhe to manage.

An elder son, Shouming, turned Wanglee's remittance agency in Bangkok into the modern Wanglee Chan Bank, and added insurance, tobacco and real estate to its interests. By the time he was assassinated (in Bangkok in August 1945), the Bonham Strand property had come into his possession and Wanglee had overshadowed the original parent, Kin Tye Lung.

Michael R. J. Vatikiotis

Bulasuk, Bulakun (Mahboonkrong), and Iamsuri – ruled the rice-trade roost (see box p 220). By and large they were the descendants not of the old tax farmers, but of immigrant traders who had started small. Instead of the royal patronage enjoyed by the tax farmers, they faced a government at best indifferent and at worst hostile, one which sought to balance Chinese economic power by favouring Western enterprise.

The emerging group of manufacturers and suppliers, too, had to contend with European competition. They formed trade associations, such as the Samosorn Phanit Jin Sayam (Sino-Siam Commercial Association), to exert pressure on the government to protect local products against foreign imports. Some of the great consumer business giants of today, such as the Boonrawd brewing family, made their mark during this period. But the fortunes of these *jao sua*, or great Chinese merchants, were not easily built.

The rise of Thai nationalism

In the first two decades of the 20th century, Siam felt (as did other Southeast Asian states) the nationalist currents blowing in from China. It was in this period that the Chinese there began to experience Thai prejudice and attempts to curb their cultural independence.

The roots of this anti-Chinese sentiment lay as much in developments in Thai society as it did in the Chinese community. King Vajiravudh, or King Rama VI, inherited the absolute monarchy from his father, Chulalongkorn, in a period of intense social and political change. Chulalongkorn, a king still greatly revered today, abolished slavery and established a modern bureaucracy. Political awareness was increasing. Vajiravudh turned to the new-fangled ideology of nationalism to boost support for the monarchy. In the absence of credible external threats, the Chinese became a ready target.

Anti-Chinese tracts he published included the famous one named *The Jews of the Orient*. In it he employed ethnic slander and prejudice to suggest that the Chinese were not loyal Thai subjects: 'Chinese are unwilling to recognize any obligation to the countries in which they reside, or to become citizens of such countries. In this characteristic, they are nowise different from the Jews.' Fortunately for the Chinese as well as the country as a whole, the kind of nationalism he preached was aimed at reinforcing the state rather than firing up the masses. The Chinese issue did not go away, however.

A general strike by Chinese workers in Bangkok in 1910 over new poll tax rates triggered many of the latent fears about Chinese commercial dominance. It was followed in 1913 by the Thai Nationality Law, which provided that any child born to a Thai parent anywhere was a Thai citizen and subject to Thai law. More importantly, the law stated that anyone born in the country, regardless of parentage, was Thai. The inclusiveness of the provisions was aimed at countering a new nationality law in China, which similarly stated that the offspring of a Chinese parent, wherever born, was a Chinese citizen (see pp 99–100).

Harder times then came with the worldwide Depression of 1929–34. Many of the trading empires built on the back of the agricultural export economy went to the wall. At the same time, the Japanese invasion of China brought the community's intense patriotic feelings towards the homeland to the fore. Once again, Chinese nationalist sentiment worried the Thai government.

Japanese aggression in China prompted the Chinese to take an unprecedented political stand in 1928: to the alarm of the government they launched a boycott of Japanese goods. The boycott lasted months, and was enforced by Chinese secret societies threatening businesses dealing with the Japanese. The disruption it caused brought home to the Thai authorities – though they hardly needed any reminding – the degree to which Chinese dominated the economy.

In 1932, a coup toppled the absolute monarchy. In the People's Party which came to power were military leaders keen to uplift the peasant, seen to be kept down by the urban capitalist class. This augured ill for Chinese, who were over-represented in that class. The government of Phibun Songkhram, the prime minister, moved to bring the economy under state control; this was tantamount to loosening the Chinese grip on private enterprise. Government unease could only have been increased by official statistics showing that in 1937 the Chinese repatriated to China an amount equivalent to 25 per cent of total government revenues for that year.

The 1930s and 1940s saw a rash of measures aimed at curbing Chinese activity. These included regulations excluding Chinese from 27 different professions, and the bringing of trades hitherto dominated by Chinese under government monopoly. The fee for a resident's permit was raised by almost 600 per cent between 1931 and 1937/38, an unprecedented step prompted by an influx from a China about to be overrun by the Japanese army (quotas, though, were not imposed until a decade later). Treason and riot laws were broadened; education laws, which limited the number of hours Chinese could be taught, were strictly enforced. The Hired Vehicle Act of 1939 allowed only Thai citizens to be taxi or bus drivers. Maritime fishing was also reserved for Thais, as was the legal profession.

Phibun, the prime minister who pushed through much of the anti-Chinese legislation, is not believed to have been anti-Chinese. His nationalism 'aimed to change the Chinese perhaps as much as it aimed to change the Thai,' suggests his biographer Kobkua Suwannathat-Pian. What he feared, it is argued, was the rise of Chinese nationalism. His policies hastened the process of assimiliation, favouring those who were prepared to take up Thai citizenship in return for being allowed to preserve and strengthen their economic position. His policies helped unfasten Chinese business from the old aristocratic clique and tied it to the military-backed government. This set the stage for the rapid rise of Chinese corporate interests under military protection in the postwar period.

Changes in 'Chinatown' society

By around 1905, Chinese accounted for approximately 10 per cent of the country's population of around 8.3 million people. Many immigrants settled and married local women. The offspring of Chinese fathers and Thai mothers, *lukjin*, on the whole identified themselves as Chinese. Continuous immigration kept Chinese hearts

Owyang Chi (1897–1988), son of a Chinese trader in Bangkok, as novice monk in Siam, 1907, and as graduate of Fudan University, Shanghai, 1921. His Siamese and Chinese experience later added to his effectiveness as Singapore's ambassador to Thailand.

Chinese Temple – Bangkok, 1987.

and minds fixed on China. The immigrant Chinese founded schools and temples, and paid for Mandarin-speaking teachers to come from China, or they sent their sons back to China for a proper education.

Immigrant labourers sought protection in secret societies like the Hongmen (called Hongzi and Laohong in Siam), the leaders of which would be the holders of the opium, liquor and gambling monopoly farms. Here as elsewhere, tax farming was inextricably linked to feuding among competing secret societies. Following the abolition of the farms from 1910 onwards, the secret societies faded quickly.

The character of the Chinese community was decisively affected by the fact that the years 1918–31 saw a massive wave of Chinese immigration. Not only were there now many more Chinese in Thailand, but the proportion of the China-born among them was now greatly increased. Even more importantly, with increasing numbers of women and families immigrating, Sino-Thai marriages declined.

Formal overseas Chinese organization became more pronounced. Chinese merchants banded together in increasing numbers of trade associations, the better to cope with the Depression and with Thai economic nationalism. The Chinese Chamber of Commerce, housed in a new building in Bangkok in 1930, rose in importance to become the most influential of all Chinese organizations. Mutual aid and Buddhist societies proliferated while the sick sought help in newly established Chinese hospitals and clinics. Same-surname and native-place associations underwent major reorganization in the decade from 1927. The Chinese Association, whose predecessor had started life at a meeting presided over by Sun Yat-sen in 1907, was formally set up in 1947.

Pre-eminent among the native-place associations was (and still is) the Teochiu Association, formally registered in 1938. The Hakkas, Cantonese, Hainanese and Hokkiens were organized into *huiguan*, as were the lesser groups from Jiangsu and Zhejiang, Guangxi and Yunnan; there was even a Taiwan Association. It is not known whether the list of 55 same-surname associations published in 1988 in Taipei (*Taiguo Huaqiao Gaikuang* by Shen Yingming) exhausts the total number. The earliest of these, dating to 1886, is the 10,000-strong Shen Clan Association.

It was mainly these associations which sponsored the first community schools. These schools began by teaching in dialect but presently switched to Mandarin as the medium of instruction. Here as elsewhere, Chinese nationalists introduced modern education. Schools proliferated, but in the face of government restrictions did not flower quite as luxuriantly as they did under the laxer colonial administrations of Indonesia and Malaya. A series of government measures – including eventually raids, closures and arrests of teachers – rigorously enforced from 1933 to 1955 succeeded in hobbling Chinese education in Thailand. As well as being an attempt to turn Chinese into Thais, these measures were part of

an anti-Communist drive to cleanse Chinese schools of their political colouring. Remembering this period as a boy in southern Thailand, a prominent Thai-Chinese businessman recalled how his parents made him learn Mandarin in the middle of the night to evade the scrutiny of local officials.

Chinese politics, specifically the republican cause, underpinned the publication of Bangkok's first Chinese newspapers in the 1900s. Later, voicing anti-Japanese sentiments in the local Chinese press was one means Chinese patriots employed to support China's war of resistance against Japan. However, during the Japanese occupation of Thailand, the Japanese army used one of the most important papers, *Zhongyuan bao*, to propagandize among the Chinese. Then, when the end of the war was in sight, a flurry of underground periodicals appeared. Between the pro-Communist and pro-Kuomintang papers was a struggle as intense in its way as the civil war in China. But the repression of Chinese activity by the Thai authorities in the late 1940s and early 1950s hit the Chinese press as hard as it did Chinese schools.

Bankrolling the generals

Bangkok, a city of almost 18 million in 1947, was home to as many as half a million Chinese. A contemporary account from a few years later argues that a casual visitor 'will find daily life in the capital of Bangkok dominated by the Chinese: the central business area solidly filled from one street corner to another with Chinese shops and houses, pushing out along arterial roads into neighbourhoods still predominantly Thai. The capital seems now half Chinese and considering the fervent energy of this minority, one can imagine the not far-distant future when, like Singapore, it may become a Chinese city.'

The imposition of an immigration quota, the Depression, the reduction of the quota and finally the Communist triumph in China – all helped to dry up Chinese inflows into Thailand. The Chinese community was now stabilized, and even though the 1940s heralded a period of Thai economic nationalism, Chinese business grew more robust.

Chinese entrepreneurs grew fat on the protection of local industries fostered by import tariffs introduced in the late 1930s. Industries and trade monopolies brought under state control formed joint ventures with Chinese entrepreneurs or simply appointed them to run the business. The managing director of the state-owned Thai Rice Company, for example, was Ma Bulakun, scion of a prominent Sino-Thai rice-trading family. The Lamsam family helped run the state trading firm Niyom Phanit.

A situation transpired in which Chinese big businessmen sat on the boards of state enterprises, while politicians became directors of Chinese companies.

Economic conditions created by the Pacific War and its aftermath also benefited Chinese and

Chinese businesses needed political patrons like Police General Phao Sriyanond.

created the seed capital for some of today's major Thai-Chinese business groups. A chain of events opened up opportunities for Chinese: the retreat of the colonial powers before the Japanese advance, the slowing down of European imports and the decline of the great European trading houses, the demand for goods stimulated by the Korean conflict and eventually the war in Indochina.

The coup which replaced Phibun with General Sarit Thanarat in 1957 heralded the ebbing of economic nationalism and the swelling of foreign investment (from the United States and then from Japan). 'The new entrepreneurs of the 1940s,' write Pasuk and Baker, 'grew quickly into the *jao sua* or merchant lords of the 1960s and 1970s.' Among those tracing their commercial origins to this period are Thai-Chinese business families like the Sophonpanichs (see box) and Chearavanonts. The latter family founded the Charoen Pokphand Group, Thailand's largest conglomerate (see p 113).

In his study of the Thai bureaucratic system in the 1960s, the American political scientist Fred Riggs has this to say about how the Chinese community was able to flourish under stricter conditions of state control. 'Each businessman received protection from an influential Thai official to carry out his business, and in return, the Chinese businessman paid his protector or patron for the service.'

Assimilation and assertion in modern Thai-Chinese society

The absorption of Chinese into Thai society is widely touted as a success story. But if many Chinese themselves say today that they are no longer Chinese but Thai, the road to integration had nevertheless been bumpy. Along the way, there were the two periods of Thai nationalism and the effects of tumultuous changes in China. The barrage of laws and regulations limiting Chinese cultural assertion introduced in the late 1930s, as well as the Communist takeover of China, helped sever, or at least severely limit, cultural ties with the homeland. For a period spanning the 1950s to the late 1970s, most

THE RISE OF THE BANGKOK BANK

Chin Sophonpanich (1910–88) was the eldest of five children born in Bangkok to a Teochiu father. The father, a sawmill clerk, sent him to China for his education. By all accounts Chin returned to Bangkok at the age of 17 and began working as, successively, an apprentice in a shop, on a boat travelling between Bangkok and Ayudhya, as a clerk in a construction company, and as a lumber trader. Chin was diligent and good with figures. He did well and eventually set up his own lumber company, soon diversifying into other products. At the end of World War II, he established Thailand's first finance company and became an influential foreign exchange dealer.

After the Pacific war, Chin expanded into trade with Hong Kong and the lucrative remittance business. The unstable economic situation after the war created a volatile but lucrative market for gold, which Chin imported to sell to local Chinese. Most Chinese settled in Thailand in this period continued to send money back to their families in China, often in the form of gold. In the past, remittances were handled by local dialect or clan associations. Chin helped to regularize – as well as to centralize – the remittance business, dressing it up in modern financial clothing through the use of telegraphic transfers. It was a clever way of making the system more efficient as well as more profitable, since commission could be charged at every stage in the process.

A conversation among a group of close friends from the Teochiu trading community led to the founding of the Bangkok Bank. These friends had joined together to engage in businesses ranging from import-export to banking. One of these enterprises developed into the successful banking operation from which emerged the Bangkok Bank in 1944. Chin's understanding of the financial world also gave him an entrée to the new ruling military clique, and he soon became a leading business contact for the military government that seized power in 1947.

The new bank fared well under Chin's guidance, as well as under the protection of his leading political patron, Police General Phao Sriyanon, a key figure in the Phibun Songkhram regime. After making a close study of how the big European banks worked, Chin established a solid financial service network, giving cheap credit to small merchants and lending at high rates of interest to bigger customers. The bank increased its equity by inviting the government's participation. Chin hired trained economists and professional bankers to help run the operation. He appointed senior military officers to the board, thereby enhancing the bank's political connections. By the mid-1950s, Bangkok Bank had established branches overseas, was running 16 domestic branches, and had declared assets approaching US$50 million. But when Chin's political patron General Phao Sriyanon was defeated in a coup by his rival General Sarit Thanarat, Chin was forced into exile in Hong Kong.

Whilst in Hong Kong, Chin developed his overseas banking connections and strengthened links with a wider pool of overseas Chinese business. Following a pattern later mimicked by other major Thai-Chinese business groups, Chin established an operation in Hong Kong and appointed a son, Robin Chan, to run the business.

On his return to Bangkok in 1964, Chin's overseas Chinese connections allowed him to steer the bank into offshore finance deals around the region, a move which fostered close links with leading ethnic Chinese entrepreneurs in Malaysia, Singapore and Indonesia. Until the early 1980s, for example, Bangkok Bank was a leading foreign bank in cities like Kuala Lumpur and Jakarta.

Back in Bangkok, Chin adopted a more cautious political profile. Instead of relying on a single political patron, the bank spread political risks by cultivating a wide range of government contacts. This shift from a single to multiple political connections was characteristic of a general trend among Thai-Chinese conglomerates. Chin hired successful businessmen and bureaucrats as senior executives, who in turn became actively involved in politics and government, producing some of the more successful technocrats in government today. One of the bank's directors, Boonchu Rajanasathien, became Finance Minister and played an active role in the Social Action Party. Amnuay Virawan (Chinese name: Lin Riguang), a former Bangkok Bank president, was hired from the finance ministry. He has held a variety of cabinet positions, and launched his own political party, the Nam Thai Party, in 1994.

The role played by Bangkok Bank in helping the Thai economy to expand from the 1950s cannot be underestimated. Utilizing connections based on clan and place of origin, the Bank extended credit to a host of small traders eager to cash in on new economic opportunities. The bank lent at high interest rates, but conditions were right and many of the businesses succeeded. The bank also helped underwrite the move from agribusiness into textiles in the early 1960s, and later bailed out the fledgling industry after the oil crisis of the 1970s. Over two decades from the 1960s, Bangkok Bank was financing over 40 per cent of the country's total exports and a little under 30 per cent of imports. In 1993, five years after Chin's death, Bangkok Bank was named one of the world's five most profitable banks by a leading British credit rating agency.

Michael R. J. Vatikiotis

THE YUNNANESE CHINESE AND THE KUOMINTANG REMNANTS

Tucked away off a narrow lane in the centre of the northern Thai city of Chiang Mai is the stately Wieng Ping mosque. The casual visitor might never notice that the mosque belongs to a thriving community of Chinese Muslims who came to the city from China's Yunnan province about a century ago. These Mandarin-speaking Muslims, also common in upper Burma

Chinese and Thai lessons in school run by Kuomintang in northern Thailand.

(see p 141), are designated one of the 55 non-Han 'minority nationalities' by the Chinese state but are seen to be 'Chinese' in Thailand. They do not fit the image of Southeast Asian Chinese as urban dwellers in that they are mostly engaged in agriculture.

Their first appearance in Chiang Mai was as traders who had travelled southward across the Shan states of Burma smuggling silk and opium under their wide coats and trousers. Known locally as 'Haw', a Shan word meaning 'to carry by horse or mule,' they were seen as bandits and soldiers. The first significant settlement in Chiang Mai may have come of a mass exodus to neighbouring Burma prompted by a Muslim uprising in Yunnan in the mid 1800s.

The Yunnanese, often surnamed Ma, quickly established a commercial presence in Chiang Mai. But they are by no means the majority of Chinese to have come from Yunnan. In 1949, the Communist victory in China sent units of the Nationalist Chinese army fleeing across the border into Burma (see p 142). Around 6,500 of these Kuomintang remnants were airlifted to Taiwan in 1953-4, but as many as 6,000 later decamped to Thai territory after a Sino-Burmese operation dislodged them from their stronghold in the Shan states in 1961. They became the last major wave of Chinese immigration to Thailand, arriving after the Teochiu flow had dried up.

At first, the alarmed Thai government called for their repatriation. Later it shifted towards accommodation and resettled the Kuomintang remnants, still in their uniforms and commanded by their officers, in 13 rural camps under the supervision of a special Thai army command. The Thai military was quick to grasp that having thousands of fanatically anti-Communist soldiers strung along the northern border offered a useful buffer against possible Communist infiltration. In the 1970s, the Kuomintang forces were widely used in operations against the Communist Party of Thailand, and to patrol the border with Burma. In the early 1980s, their number was officially estimated at around 12,000. A more realsitic unofficial estimate put them at more than 30,000, scattered mainly in the rural uplands of northern Thailand.

An estimated 25 per cent of the Kuomintang Chinese were granted Thai citizenship in 1971. But making them Thai culturally by enforcing strict education laws and curbing the teaching of Chinese in village schools proved difficult. One reason these Chinese villagers managed to retain their Chinese identity was by maintaining close links with the government in Taiwan. The old guard in Taiwan, searching for new blood to reinvigorate the Kuomintang in the early 1980s, began offering scholarships to these villagers with promises of a university education in Taiwan tied to periods of military service. These villagers, some without passports, found it easy to travel back and forth to Taipei through Bangkok, where their command of Mandarin made it attractive for local Thai-Chinese businesses dealing with Taiwan to hire them. Income in the villages remains significantly higher than in the average northern Thai village; the Kuomintang has organized efficient production of profitable cash crops such as potatoes and lychees. With the growth of tourism in the north, villages like Doi Mae Salong and Baan Nong Bua have begun to resemble prosperous tourist traps, rather than the remote army camps they once were.

Michael R. J. Vatikiotis

Food stall in Kuomintang village.

Thai Chinese had almost nothing to do with China, an experience that helped many of those born during this period to lose sight of their ancestral homeland. The anti-Communist tenor of successive Thai governments battling a Communist insurgency on Thai soil further attenuated Sino-Thai links to China.

Be that as it may, however, many Thai Chinese decided to naturalize and assume Thai names only after the defeat of the Kuomintang, or in the teeth of Phibun's anti-Chinese measures. Integration, then, has to some extent been the product of force, and perhaps only runs skin deep. Overt identification with political causes in China did give way to undivided loyalty to the Thai state, but many Thai Chinese continue to teach their children the Chinese language, and use their Chinese names in dealings with one another.

In what sense then are Chinese assimilated to Thai society? To tackle this question, it may be helpful to begin with what is espoused by Thai Chinese themselves. Sondhi Limthongkul, a newspaper publisher of Thai-Chinese ancestry, has this to say of his Hainan-born mother, settled in Thailand since she was 15 years old. 'Living 50 years under royal aegis,' he said of her, 'loving Thailand more than some native Thais. When she was very ill, we asked her whether she wanted to visit mainland China. She said that Thailand was her home and she did not want ever to leave the country. Today her children have thrived in Thai society.' The journalist Paisal Sricharatchanya says of Thai Chinese that 'Their patriotism lies with this country, though there is a sense of pride in their Chinese descent.' The late Kukrit Pramoj, a former prime minister closely related to the royal family but also of Chinese descent, put it this way: 'The Chinese came here with respect, not with egoism. They accept us …. And what we have here is acceptable to the Chinese. We have a monarchy which the Chinese respect. We have a history which the Chinese can be proud of. We have a way of life which the Chinese can adopt and enjoy.'

Sondhi Limthongkul's mother felt that Thailand, not China, was where she belonged. An attachment to a specific homeland may be one of the attributes of ethnic identity, but in her case that attachment was missing. For Paisal, political or national identification with Thailand need not override ethnic loyalty. What is implied in his statement is the recognition that national identity comprises two sets of dimensions, the one civic, the other genealogical; and that the two could be blended. With Kukrit Pramoj, more objective attributes enter the picture – history, ways of life and such symbols of national identity as the monarchy. What he was pointing to were the attractions Thai society offered the Chinese as sources of cultural and political identification.

But culture and polity are not necessarily congruent. The collective cultural identity of the Thai nation does not subsume all political differences. Against the nationalist ideal of unity, there is the fact of cultural and ideological heterogeneity. It is ironical that while the Thai state did succeed in turning second-generation Chinese into Thais, to speak Thai and to feel Thai, the first genuine Thai nationalist political action many Chinese undertook as Thai citizens and patriots was to rise up against the military government, thereby doing the exact opposite of what the state would have wanted them to do as 'Thais.' The student movements of the 1970s were led by Thai-Chinese students, many of whom fled to the jungle to become members of the Communist Party of Thailand after periods of violence in 1973 and 1976.

When right-wing extremists stormed the campus of Bangkok's Thammasat University on October 6, 1976, no one spoke openly about the anti-Chinese as well as anti-Communist sentiment that helped motivate the carnage. 'They singled out those students who wore spectacles,' recalls an eyewitness to the massacre. Perhaps hundreds of students were shot, hung from trees or burnt, or drowned trying to swim to safety across the Chao Phya River abutting the campus grounds. The rightist vigilantes who perpetrated the violent attack labelled the students as 'Yuan' or Vietnamese. This was a reference to the Communist leanings of the student movement. 'The ruling élite viewed us as un-Thai. We had to be crushed as a threat to the sovereignty of the state,' remembers a student leader 20 years on. For the perpetrators of the attack, to be Communist was to be Chinese (or Vietnamese) – that is, un-Thai. They made the issue turn on ethnicity when it was ideology that mattered. The experience bred in a generation of students, many of them Thai Chinese, a deep suspicion of the traditional boundaries of Thai culture, which make no room for the contribution of Chinese culture.

The 1976 upheaval was one example of the way Chinese identity remains a liability in times of stress. More recently, when Bangkokians took to the streets to protest a military government in May 1992, Chinese were again targeted as scapegoats. At the height of the protests and the ensuing violent crackdown by the army, anonymous leaflets appeared alleging that leaders of the Confederation of Democracy, a leading organizer of the protests, all had Chinese surnames.

Chinese identity became a political issue in another, perhaps less threatening, way, when it was deployed by the opposition in 1996 to defeat Prime Minister Banharn Silpa-archa in a censure debate. The opposition alleged that Banharn falsified immigration documents to hide the fact that he was born in China. Foreign birth disqualifies a Thai from being elected to parliament, but while the allegation was aimed at barring him from office, it was not perceived as an attack on Banharn's Chinese origins. After all, many of the opposition MPs pressing the charge against Banharn were themselves of Chinese descent. Rather, the episode, as well as the open way it was debated, is taken to mean that Chinese identity is no longer a bar to political activity. Yet it also shows how the legacy of discrimination against Chinese could be manipulated for political purposes.

The majority of Thai Chinese, as immigrants possessing a recent memory of confrontation with the state, have until very recently shunned politics. Yet with the slow growth of the country's parliamentary democracy since the 1980s, many Thai Chinese have entered the political system. About 30 per cent of the current parliament is composed of business people, most of them of Thai-Chinese descent. In the 1996 election campaign for the governor of Bangkok, several candidates openly canvassed for ethnic Chinese votes using their Chinese surnames. In a campaign marked by concerns about traf-

fic and pollution, by contrast Chinese-language advertisements coined a different pitch to Chinese voters: 'Creating happiness for the people and prosperity for Bangkok.' 'The Chinese community is entering a new era,' suggests a senior Thai journalist, himself of Chinese descent. He argues that politics and business are joined more explicitly than before, and that by entering the political fray, 'Chinese show that they are more confident about their standing in the country.'

On the one hand this phenomenon says much about the degree of assimilation in Thailand; but it also exposes the extent to which local business interests are dominated by Thai-Chinese merchant families. Simply put, politics in Thailand is business, and the Thai Chinese – whether at the corporate level in Bangkok, or in the provinces – have played a dominant role in underwriting political expenses, and deciding who gets elected.

Beyond domestic politics, sweeping transnational changes have affected the subjective significance of 'homeland' and other attributes of cultural identity. The first of these changes is the normalization of relations with Beijing in 1975. Three years later, the first Thai Chinese companies began to explore business opportunities in China. By the early 1980s, travel to China was easier (before then a stringent anti-Communist law virtually banned all travel to Communist countries), and cultural links could be safely restored. The end of the Vietnam War and later the Cold War removed the Communist stigma that long tainted the Chinese. With the onset of Deng Xiaoping's economic reforms in the 1980s, contacts were revived. More importantly, China was seen to offer lucrative business opportunities.

A poll conducted in 1995 by the local Chinese newspaper, *Sing Sian Yit Pao (Xing Xian ribao)*, found that 40 per cent of the readers it questioned had travelled to Hong Kong and 38 per cent to China on business or holiday within the past year. The Thai Chinese Chamber of Commerce hosted 278 delegations from China in 1994. The Charoen Pokphand Group (see p 113) is already the largest single foreign investor in China, and has begun matchmaking for Thai firms eager to invest in China.

The identities and discourses to which Thai Chinese adhere have also varied in importance and content with the transformation of the economy, specifically with the more or less uninterrupted economic boom enjoyed from the late 1970s to the late 1990s. Prosperity and social stability have catapulted Chinese into the vanguard of the burgeoning middle class. The sons and daughters of successful Chinese merchant families have diversified away from purely commercial pursuits and moved into the bureaucracy; others have taken up academic positions. All this has eroded the ethnic stereotype of Chinese as either shopkeepers or traders. In popular perception, affluence and élite status correlate highly with Chinese origin. Furthermore, Thai-Chinese identity has been affected by the popular representations of overseas Chinese upward mobility and East Asian economic success, seen to be paralleled at home by (to quote the scholar Craig J. Reynolds) 'the triumph of the Sino-Thai bourgeoisie as the national bourgeoisie.'

The quote comes from Reynolds's study of Thai society through its adaptation of a Chinese historical romance set in the last years of the Later Han dynasty, *San*

Sondhi Limthongkul.

Banharn Silpa-archa.

GODFATHERS AND POLITICIANS

The rapid growth of Thailand's economy in the 1960s and 1970s opened up lucrative opportunities in the provinces and saw the rise of provincial Thai-Chinese merchant families, many of whom have come to dominate local politics. The law did not stand in the way of the most successful, who made huge fortunes by operating both within and outside it. Known as *jao phor*, simply translated as 'godfathers,' these men wield considerable influence in politics at not only the local but national level. Local people look to these men for schools, roads and large temple donations, and the only people who could afford such things have tended to be successful Thai-Chinese business people.

As the government began to spend money developing services and infrastructure in the provinces, local Chinese entrepreneurs emulated their immigrant ancestors by becoming local agents, supplying the state with raw materials and services. As was the case with the tax farmers of old, the state was happy to contract out much of the development work. For this the local entrepreneurs charged exorbitantly high fees.

Fortunes built in this way became springboards for political careers. Banharn Silpa-archa, who served as prime minister from 1995–1996, grew rich from being the largest construction contractor to the Public Works Department in the 1970s. Born to Chinese immigrant parents in the central plains province of Suphanburi, Banharn started work as a humble tailor, turning to petty trade and eventually moving into construction. By the 1970s, his success in business had made him the richest and most influential man in Suphanburi. This in turn led him to politics and he served for many years as the secretary general of the Chat Thai party, eventually succeeding to the party leadership. Banharn, who led his party to electoral success at the polls in mid-1995, represents a breed of politician who traditionally wins votes by looking after his constituency. In Suphanburi, he lavished large sums of money on showcase infrastructure projects.

Some of the most lucrative sectors of the Thai economy are underground. Examples are the timber industry, forced underground by a logging ban; gambling; drugs; and smuggling along land border and coastal areas. Some of the richest and most prominent provincial businessmen made their fortunes from these illegal activities. One of the most notorious, Sia Leng (Charoen Pattanadamrongjit), was born in 1934 to immigrant Chinese parents in the northeastern town of Korat. After a perfunctory Chinese education, Sia Leng started to help his parents sell noodles. He excelled as a shop assistant and earned enough to learn more Chinese and study accountancy. At the age of 28, Sia Leng started his own business selling cash crops in the Khon Kaen area. From here, his business expanded into logging, real estate and mining. By the late 1970s, Sia Leng was managing a sprawling business empire that included an underground lottery. Needing protection, after surviving several assasination attempts, he cultivated politicians and generals in the army. 'I was a poor man before and did not have much education,' he once told a newspaper; 'Thus whatever I do I have to rely on friends and connections in politics.' Among his closest connections were two successive army commanders, one of whom went on to lead a political party. He coordinated a political campaign for the party in the northeast, where it won the lion's share of seats. By the early 1990s his political influence was so great that when he visited Bangkok, he could summon 'his' MPs to appear before him.

Somchai Kunpluem (alias Kamnan Po) made his fortune initially with a smuggling operation along the border with Cambodia. Later he came to dominate the business community of the eastern seaboard town of Chonburi, from where his sons became national-level MPs, and it was said that many others owed their seats to his influence. The business style of these provincial 'godfathers' is uncompromising; rivals and competitors are forced out of business, or simply murdered in dramatic gangland-style killings. Close connections with the local law enforcement authorities give them a more or less free hand. After one such killing, in which his chief rival lost his life, Kamnan Po denied any involvement, merely commenting that in Chonburi 'bad guys must die.'

Michael R. J. Vatikiotis

Guo Yanyi (*The Romance of the Three Kingdoms*). Known in Thai by its dialect transliteration, *Sam Kok*, and first translated into Thai at the end of the 18th century, the work became not only a school text but, in its innumerable incarnations, part of popular Thai reading and consumption. Serialized in the media, the story has been used to parody politicians and impart business acumen. It appears in one of its many versions, for example, as *War in Sam Kok: Strategies for Turning Things Around*.

It is thus 'not an imported cultural artifact so much as an instance of the reproduction of Chinese culture within Thailand.' Since the 1980s, Chinese culture in Thailand has been reproduced by the process which Reynolds, following other social scientists, refers as 'commodification.' Along with the packaging of aspects of Thai culture for tourist and marketing purposes, Chinese culture, he argues, has become another consumer product in Thailand, and as such must be seen as 'a subculture within the oficially recognized national culture schema.' This is exemplified by the way in which, by using *Sam Kok* as a 'how to' tool, 'the dynamic qualities of the Sino-Thai entrepreneurship mentality' have been 'packaged, sold and studied to learn the secrets of successful managers.'

The material success of Thai Chinese has bred a growing interest in Chinese culture among Chinese. Signs of a more assertive Chinese identity are not hard to detect. Since the 1980s, the popularity of imported Chinese soap operas and music has grown. Local TV stations have become less coy about showing Chinese-made dramas, for which they cite increasing popular demand. Some private cable TV stations have even begun airing programmes in Cantonese and Mandarin – though official sensitivity remains an obstacle to launching a fully Chinese-language station. At local video rental stores, while Hollywood movies are much in demand for entertainment, documentaries about Chinese history and culture dominate the serious sections. Pop culture is becoming as much Hong Kong as Western in origin. A major theme park has adopted Chinese culture as a main focus of its attractions; popular Thai-made movies draw on and distort Chinese mythology, transforming ancient fables into appealing stories.

The interest in Chinese culture has extended to a revival of the Chinese language. Although official regulations still restrict the teaching of the Chinese language in regular schools to seven hours a week, that has not stopped mature students taking up Chinese in their spare time at private schools. At the Sri Thabut Bamrung Chinese middle school in central Bangkok, weekend classes in Mandarin are over-subscribed. Here some 2,000 adults, mostly Chinese, have enrolled in classes taught by imported mainland Chinese. Enrolment in Chinese-language classes increased 30 per cent between 1993 and 1995. A Chinese studies centre at Bangkok's Chulalongkorn University, launched in 1995, managed to raise 5.5 million baht (US$220,000) in a three-month period. The dean of the new centre, Professor Umporn Panachet, attributes this generosity – stemming mostly from the Thai Chinese business community – to a new interest in China.

The resinicization upon which many Thai Chinese seem embarked calls to mind the words of the noted scholar of China, C. P. FitzGerald, in his book *The Southern Expansion of the Chinese People* (1972). As the overseas Chinese have assimilated, he observes, 'the level of transplanted Chinese culture has risen, not fallen, so that communities which were mainly illiterate only a century and less ago, are now steeped in the culture of their ancestral homeland, and unwilling to forego this heritage.' The resinicization is towards a Mandarin- (rather than southern dialect) speaking, Hong Kong- or globalized style of Chineseness than any local Thai-Chinese version. As one young Thai-Chinese professional puts it, 'Psychologically, most of the Chinese in

Thailand see their ancestors as coming from peasant stock, so believing in a culture is an upgrading for them.'

Burgeoning business opportunities in China are generally cited by students as the reason for the revival of Chinese studies. Knowing the language is seen to be a useful tool. At one major Thai bank, senior executives are taught Mandarin in the mornings. All this suggests the 'instrumental' use of ethnicity to further commercial ties and interests. 'My parents and I, we forgot that we were Chinese until now,' says a young Central bank official. 'I'm learning Chinese because we are entering a new era where China and the Chinese language are more important than before.' Now, this man says, 'I want to go back to being Chinese – it's useful.'

Knowledge of China is seen primarily, though perhaps not exclusively, as a resource. As elsewhere in the region, it is thought that overseas Chinese links to China can work to their adopted country's advantage. If China becomes a more important source of economic opportunity, Thailand is likely to press its ethnic advantage, using Thai Chinese to spearhead investment. In July 1995, when Thailand celebrated 20 years of bilateral ties with China, senior Thai officials spoke of the need to foster closer ties, embrace the Chinese language and position Thailand as a 'bridge to China' from the rest of Southeast Asia. Thailand is an enthusiastic supporter of the Greater Mekong development project, which plans to link the economies of Burma, Cambodia, Laos, Thailand and Vietnam to that of Yunnan province in southwest China.

In December 1995, the Thai Chinese Chamber of Commerce hosted the third gathering of the World Chinese Entrepreneurs Convention, earlier convened in Singapore and Hong Kong (see p 87). At the meeting the Chinese ambassador to Bangkok did what would have been unheard of two decades ago, which was to call openly on *all* Chinese to work towards the unity of China. The very fact that the conference could be held said much about the security and confidence of the Thai Chinese community, if not of the overseas Chinese in the rest of Southeast Asia.

At the same time, beyond the purely instrumental use of ethnicity, there is growing pride in China's achievements, a pride perhaps more easily expressed in Thailand than elsewhere in the region. Some Thai Chinese argue that Chinese culture should no longer be considered alien to the mainstream, but as an asset, indeed a facet of globalization. The acceptance of Chinese elements into Thai culture implies the overleaping of cultural boundaries entailed in globalization. Chineseness, suggests the Thai Chinese political scientist Kasian Tejapira, should be considered 'a kind of cultural capital and ethnic capital that will help Thailand grow in the region.' In a world which aspires to pluralism and cultural tolerance, should not the contribution of the Thai-Chinese be recognized? 'A society which is powerful,' writes the Thai-Chinese historian Nidhi Aeuisrivong, 'allows a variety in ways of life. The [Chinese] add to the cultural richness of Thai society.'

If business success has emerged as an important marker of Thai-Chinese identity, so has Chinese religion. Skinner's argument that religion is no hindrance to Chinese assimilation to Thai society is well known; 'The Chinese popular religion, with Mahayana elements,' he has written, 'is similar to Theravada Buddhism. Chinese religious sentiment is eclectic and syncretic rather than exclusivistic.' Indeed, Chinese religious customs are part Chinese and part Thai.

In the face of rapid economic change and new demands, and as the business environment becomes steadily more crowded and competitive, a greater interest in religion as a means of ensuring success has surfaced. Empowerment through ritual and magic runs strongly through Chinese culture. An abundance of cults and superstitions testifies to a religious revival in Thailand, none quite as striking perhaps as that revolving around the Buddhist Bodhisatva Guanyin, or Goddess of Mercy. The sheer size of the Guanyin temple in Bangkok's Lard Phrao district says much about the patronage of this cult, which has increased in popularity only since the mid-1980s. A five-storey building houses an elaborate shrine, complete with pillars elaborately decorated with stucco dragons. Outside stands a 21-storey pagoda.

To a 20-metre high statue of Guanyin erected outside Bangkok, patrons and worshippers appeal for good health and prosperity. Curiously, it is fashionable for many Theravada Buddhist temples to erect Guanyin shrines. Yet this devotional cult came from China, where it is a popular offshoot of the Mahayanist Buddhist church. Indeed, devotees at the Guanyin shrine read from Chinese-language texts, or Chinese transcribed into Thai script. Money rears its head here as elsewhere; steel safes complete with combination locks ensure that donations do not themselves become gifts from the Goddess of Mercy.

Perhaps the search for empowerment explains why Thai Chinese flock in large numbers to venerate the equestrian statue of Thailand's King Chulalongkorn, who died in 1910. Every Tuesday and Thursday, the bronze statue that stands in the centre of the spacious Royal Plaza becomes the focus of a popular and largely middle-class cult that expresses itself in elaborate offerings and prayers for luck and prosperity. The most common explanation for the popularity of King Chulalongkorn among Thai Chinese is that he represents the liberty and good government they desire. In the late 19th century, Chulalongkorn introduced reforms of the bureaucracy and education system, reforms which paved the way for modern Thailand to emerge.

Michael R. J. Vatikiotis

Bangkok Stock Exchange, part of Thai-Chinese business culture.

In Bangkok's Chinatown.

VIETNAM

Chinese in official robes attended by servant with umbrella.

While the official Vietnamese name for the Chinese is 'Hoa,' colloquial Vietnamese has two terms for them: *chu khach*, or 'uncle guest,' and *tau*, literally 'big ship.' By the term 'uncle guest,' the Vietnamese, with typical subtlety, politely but clearly distinguish themselves from Chinese. The second term is subject to differing interpretation, originally neutral but distinctly derogatory in certain contexts. Calling Chinese *tau* may evoke the big ships on which they came when they traded with Vietnam at a time when it had no major commercial centre. But it may also be related to *tau o*, a Vietnamese word for Chinese bandits active in the South China Sea in the early 19th century. Whatever their derivation, in their coexistence the two terms reflect mixed feelings towards Chinese – who are closely related to Vietnamese yet foreign; and who might bring good fortune or disaster.

China and Vietnam share a border of 1,306 kilometres. This contiguity makes the cross-frontier movements of Chinese somewhat different from those described by the modern terms 'emigration' and 'immigration.' Of even more importance was the fact that Chinese dynasties ruled northern Vietnam for more than ten centuries (see box). As a Chinese province, Vietnam adopted the Chinese writing system. This eased the way for Chinese migrants.

The settlement of Chinese – soldiers, political fugitives, administrators – spanned centuries, as did assimilation to Vietnamese society. Although there was some migration of Chinese women and children, intermarriage between Chinese men and Vietnamese women was generally the rule. Thus a Sino-Viet élite developed over the centuries, a process facilitated by the common writing system. From this group sprang such Vietnamese legends as the 6th-century independence leader Ly Bi, whose family came from northern China during disorders in the first century AD. There was also the Fujian-born Ly Cong Uan, who migrated to Vietnam and later became the founder and first king of the Ly dynasty (1009–1225). Although these

Sino-Viet élites were of Chinese origin, by and large, the scholar Keith Weller Taylor writes in his book *The Birth of Vietnam,* Chinese immigrants became members of the local society and, 'strictly speaking, were no longer Chinese. They developed their own perspective on Chinese civilization. They brought Chinese vocabulary and technology into Vietnamese society, but they developed a regional point of view that owed much to the indigenous heritage.'

Living in the shadow of China and its invasions, almost all Vietnamese dynasties restricted the entry of Chinese, particularly into the capital area (in today's Hanoi). To keep the Chinese at a safe distance from the capital, the Vietnamese opened Van Don, an island in the Gulf of Tonkin, to trade from the 12th to 16th centuries. Later, Pho Hien (in the centre of the Red River Delta) was established as the main trading town of the north, and Chinese were active there in the 17th century. In this way the Vietnamese rulers combined the advantages to be gained from Chinese trading activities with the strategic need to keep them away from the capital.

In addition to the traders and artisans in Pho Hien was a Chinese group living in the provinces of Lang Son, Tuyen Quang and Thai Nguyen on the Sino-Vietnamese border. These were copper, iron and silver mine workers from Guangdong province, many of them Teochius. As many as 10,000 Chinese labourers could be found working in a single mine, and there were 14 such mines at the time.

In the north, the Trinh lords (see box) repeatedly issued edicts in the 17th century to tighten control over the Chinese. By 1666 all Chinese desiring permanent residence in Vietnam had to be registered and to dress in Vietnamese style. Those temporarily resident had to live in designated areas segregated from Vietnamese.

The Nguyen lords in the south (see box) in the 17th and 18th centuries had a more relaxed attitude towards the Chinese, and this attracted migrants from Fujian and Guangdong provinces. Significant Chinese trading communities in Hue, Hoi An and Qui Nhon, and later in Saigon were established. In Hoi An alone the Chinese population was estimated at 4–5,000 in 1642, and by the end of the 18th century the Chinese population in southern Vietnam had probably reached 30–40,000.

In the late 17th century, the Nguyen wrested the Bien Hoa and My Tho areas in the Mekong Delta from Cambodia, largely with the help of two groups (totalling 3,000) of refugees from Guangdong. Fleeing the Manchu conquerors of Ming China, these people were led by Yang Yandi and Chen Shangchuan (Duong Ngan Dich and Tran Thuong Xuyen in Vietnamese). Also taken from Cambodia by a Chinese was Ha Tien, another strategically important port area. He was Mac Cuu (Mo Jiu), a refugee from Guangdong in the early 18th century. All these places were turned into prosperous towns attract-

Map 5.10

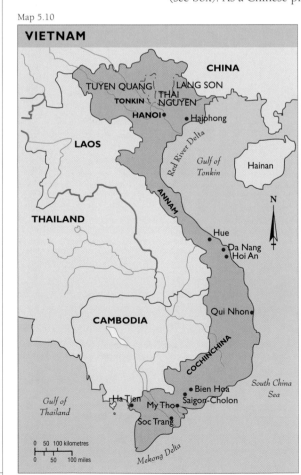

EVENTS BEARING ON THE CHINESE IN VIETNAM

China and Vietnam have been uneasy neighbours for more than two millennia. State-to-state relations between the two countries, sometimes amicable, sometimes antagonistic, have greatly impacted upon the fortunes of Chinese resident in Vietnam. The counterpoint to China's age-old predilection for intervening in Vietnam's affairs has been the persistence with which the latter has asserted both its political independence and its control over resident Chinese aliens. An important issue in the experience of the Chinese in Vietnam has been the depth and degree of the two countries' interaction.

In 111 BC, part of what is now Vietnam became a province of the Chinese empire. In 939 AD the Vietnamese succeeded in casting off the Chinese yoke and an independent Vietnamese kingdom was founded by the Ly kings (1009–1225), who established their capital in what is now Hanoi.

Except for a two-decade period in the 1400s, when China's Ming dynasty occupied the country, Vietnam managed to resist incorporation into the Chinese empire. During the 16th century, internal dissension, aggravated by China's intervention, troubled Vietnam and partitioned it into north and south. Regionally based rulers, the Trinh family in the north and the Nguyen family in what is now central Vietnam, vied for supremacy over the country.

By the middle of the 16th century, Hoi An, near the present-day city of Da Nang, had become a busy entrepôt trading centre where Portuguese, Dutch and English ships called on their way to China, Japan and other countries in Southeast Asia. By the middle of the 18th century, the Vietnamese, having driven out the Khmer from the Mekong Delta, had extended the country's frontiers to roughly what they are today.

In the 1770s and 1780s rebels rose in revolt. The Tay Son brothers, the most celebrated of these, ousted the ruling families. The emperor of China intervened by sending an army into north Vietnam, but the Tay Son rebels defeated it and established their own dynasty. This was toppled in 1802 by the prince Nguyen Anh, whose reign title was Gia Long. He built a new capital in the central city of Hue, modelling it after the Forbidden City in Beijing.

The Hue court appealed to China for help against a new threat, the French, in the 1870s. France had already absorbed southern Vietnam and turned it into a colony it called Cochinchina. Fighting the French incursion in the north were Vietnamese soldiers as well as Chinese 'Black Flags,' bands of Taiping rebels (see p 56) who had escaped over the border from southern China. But France's control over Indochina was assured when it defeated China in the Sino-French war of June 1884–April 1885.

Nationalist ideas imported from China (and later Mao Zedong's political thinking) played a part in the rise of Vietnamese revolutionaries and Communists. Indeed the Viet Minh (the Vietnamese Independence Brotherhood League), a Communist movement established by Ho Chi Minh, enlisted many ethnic Chinese in their struggle against the French.

Decolonization, when it finally came in 1954, was accompanied by the partition of the country into a Communist-run North Vietnam based in Hanoi and an anti-Communist, American-backed southern state based in Saigon. Thereafter, Vietnamization proceeded apace. China agreed to the naturalization of Huaqiao in the north (as part of the integration of ethnic Chinese into Vietnamese society) on the understanding that they would be treated fairly. Socialist transformation of the economy might have hit the Chinese there harder had more of them been merchants rather than fishermen and workers. Chinese in the south, wielding far greater commercial power, would have been fairer game. While Vietnamization in the north had a socialist cast, that in the south was nationalist.

Vietnam became a focal point for the Cold War between the world's superpowers. Helped by its Communist allies in China and the Soviet Union, North Vietnam fought the south until April 30, 1975, when Saigon fell to Hanoi's army. When the Communist forces entered Cholon, the Chinese quarter, that day, they found the streets lined with thousands of China's national flags and portraits of Mao Zedong. The Vietnamese authorities quickly ordered these to be withdrawn, seeing them as symbols of 'Chinese chauvinism.'

The Vietnamese approach to resident Chinese hardened when Vietnam's relations with China worsened. The country's tilt towards the Soviet Union, China's support of the Pol Pot regime in Cambodia (which was intensely hostile to Vietnam), rumours of war between Vietnam and China – all these developments made life harder for the resident Chinese. As part of the stream of 'boat people' leaving Vietnam, these Chinese caught world attention, and one of their community's distinguishing marks became its far-flung geographical dispersal following their re-migration to China, the US, Canada, France, Australia, Britain and other countries. At the receiving end of large numbers of such refugees in 1978, China, through the Overseas Chinese Affairs Office in Beijing, issued a statement accusing Vietnam of 'unwarrantedly ostracizing and persecuting Chinese residents in Vietnam, and expelling many of them back to China.' In 1979, worsening Sino-Vietnamese relations culminated in a brief but fierce war.

Vietnam abandoned doctrinaire socialism in 1986, when it decided to unfetter the economy and move towards a more open society. Doi moi, 'renovation,' the tag for the reforms, marks a new stage in the country's economic and political development.

Editor

Portrait of Ho Chi Minh looks down on Chinese family.

ing foreign trade at the expense of Cambodian interests. The Chinese lived there as merchants and artisans; some were appointed as official customs officers.

The Chinese played an intricate role in the Tay Son period in the 18th century (see box p 229). Both the Tay Son rebels and their opponent, Nguyen Anh, found the Chinese useful as both manpower and sources of wealth. In 1776, for example, the Tay Son robbed Dong Nai Dai Pho, the main Chinese trading centre in the Mekong Delta. It was most probably the Chinese there who, fleeing the rebels to today's Saigon region, established what was later to be known as Cholon ('great market'). Starting life as a cluster of villages to the southwest of modern Saigon, Cholon would become a thriving Chinese city. When the Tay Sons captured it in 1782, they massacred more than 10,000 Chinese.

Nguyen Anh, who triumphed over the Tay Son, recognized the semi-autonomous status of the Chinese in the Mekong Delta as early as 1698, and wisely registered them as permanent residents rather than regarding them as merchant sojourners. This made the Vietnamese the earliest among Southeast Asian regimes to take this measure.

As the descendants of Ming loyalists, the Chinese were called 'Minh Huong.' The term, *Ming xiang* in Chinese, meant '[maintaining] joss-stick for the Ming dynasty.' But in 1827 the Vietnamese court took it to mean 'Ming village' (the character for 'village' is a homophone of that for 'joss-stick'). Although originally applied to registered Chinese, in the 19th century the term 'Minh Huong' came to refer specifically to the offspring of Sino–Vietnamese intermarriage. Yet, unlike Peranakans in Malaya and the Dutch Indies, or mestizos in the Philippines, as a group the Minh Huong were not culturally distinctive; they did not develop a particular style of dress, cuisine or a language. The cultural distance to be traversed by the Chinese integrating into Vietnamese was shorter and smoother, and no intermediate group emerged.

In 1829 the Nguyen government prohibited Minh Huong families from going back to China, and in 1842 registered them separately from immigrant Chinese. This was not too high a price to pay; Minh Huong were allowed to take civil service examinations, which opened the door to higher social status. Throughout the 19th century the Minh Huong were remarkably active in Vietnamese politics. Among them were Trinh Hoai Duc (1765–1825) and Phan Thanh Gian (1795–1867), both cabinet ministers during the Nguyen dynasty and celebrated scholars. Tran Tien Thanh (1814–84), another Minh Huong Chinese, was made the Regent in 1883. Some observers hold that this list should also include Ngo Dinh Diem, the South Vietnamese president from 1954 to 1963 – he who tried forcibly to naturalize the Chinese and limit their economic prominence in 1956 (see below). For all their Chinese blood, the political outlook of the Minh Huong was unmistakably Vietnamese.

It was perhaps also this group that promoted the Vietnamese national form of writing. A script which appeared in the 10th century, Nom combines Chinese characters and Vietnamese forms. Under French rule, many books in Nom were printed not in Saigon, but in Foshan (Guangdong province) in the late 19th century.

It is said that as early as 1787, Nguyen Anh allowed Chinese settlers to administer their own affairs through dialect-based communities called *bang* (see Part III). Officers called *bang truong* were chosen by the members of each *bang* and accepted by the Vietnamese authorities. An indirect way of ruling the Chinese, this was also a pragmatic acceptance of a *fait accompli* of a particular time and place. The *bang* system was used under Emperor Minh Mang in the 1820s and 1830s to regulate Chinese immigration and control Chinese communities. It was to be extended by the colonial French, who gave the *bang truong* wide police and fiscal powers over their members.

Under the French

French authority over Vietnam, progressively imposed from 1858 to 1886, was exercised through three administrative divisions: Cochinchina, Annam, and Tonkin. In Cochinchina the number of Chinese rose from 44,000 in 1873 to 56,000 in 1889, with Cholon home to nearly 16,000 and Saigon to more than 7,000. In Tonkin and Annam Chinese were concentrated in Haiphong, Hanoi and Da Nang; but they did not become nearly as numerous there as they did in the south. Indeed, Vietnam's Chinese population had grown much less from overland crossings into the north than seaborne immigration to the south.

The easy passage between China and Vietnam facilitated both immigration and return migration. The volumes of the latter appear to be considerable: of the 1.2 million Chinese arrivals in 1923–51, for example, 850,000 went back to China. Yet, despite the geographical proximity, the size of Chinese settlement has been small compared to more distant Southeast Asian countries, whether in terms of absolute number or proportion. When the French left in 1954, for example, Chinese in Vietnam were estimated to be 2 per cent of the total population. In 1960, there were 800,000 Chinese in South Vietnam. Although this figure represented 85 per cent of the Chinese population in all Indochina, it was only a third of the Chinese in Thailand or Indonesia. The 5.6 per cent of total population they accounted for in South Vietnam pales beside, say, the 37 per cent Chinese represented in the Federation of Malaya, or even the 10 per cent in Thailand.

Up to a point, the French encouraged immigration, contracting Chinese labourers to work as miners, rubber tappers and railroad builders. In admitting only immigrants acceptable to the headman of their place-of-origin grouping, the French perpetuated the *bang* system instituted by earlier Vietnamese rulers, calling the groupings *congrégations*. The five *congrégations* – Cantonese, Teochius, Hakkas, Hokkiens and Hainanese – answered for their members, whose taxes they assessed and collected on behalf of the French authorities (see table 5.18). Outside the five groups lay Chinese immigrants from two Chinese provinces adjoining Vietnam,

Table 5.18

DISTRIBUTION OF CHINESE IN SOUTH VIETNAM BY SPEECH GROUP						
	1924		1950		1974	1989
	NUMBER	%	NUMBER	%	%	%
Cantonese	80,000	35	337,000	45	60	56.5
Teochiu	50,000	22	225,000	30	20	34.0
Hokkien	55,000	24	60,000	8	7	6.0
Hainanese	15,000	7	30,000	4	7	2.0
Hakka	15,000	7	75,000	10	6	1.5
Others	11,000	5	—	3	—	—

Source: Tran (1993).

namely Yunnan and Guangxi.

The activities of each *bang* were centred on the *huiguan* (native-place association) or community temple. The earliest *huiguan* was perhaps the Fujian one in Hoi An, established around 1690. The power exercised by native-place associations may be seen in the fact that it was they who issued entry permits to immigrants in the early French period. It was they too who saw to the pooling of funds, the setting up of schools and hospitals, and the management of graveyards. There were over 200 Chinese schools in South Vietnam in 1956 and six hospitals before 1975.

One view holds that the Chinese were of 'priceless help' to the French in the latter's colonial exploitation of Vietnam. The Chinese did indeed fill the French colonizers' manpower needs and provided revenue. It was Chinese who ran most of the revenue farms, especially opium, and these were the major source of financial support for the early French colonial bureaucracy and its projects. Yet the Chinese had cause when they repeatedly complained that French policies discriminated against them: a trading licence, for instance, would cost a Chinese twice as much as it would a Frenchman; and taxes were seven times as heavy for a Chinese coolie as for a Vietnamese. Since most Chinese shops kept their accounts in Chinese, which the French tax officer could not read, he would arbitrarily double the income claimed by the Chinese owner, and hence the taxes. Such measures were enough of a stumbling block to dampen immigration by the poorer Chinese.

There were occasions when Chinese reaction to French repressiveness took the form of uprisings. The most famous anti-French uprising in Vietnam was led by Phan Xich Long, the 'big brother' of the Heaven and Earth Society (*Tiandi Hui*), the Chinese secret society from Cholon. He was executed along with his 56 'brothers' by the French and buried in Cholon in 1916. The precursor of this event was the uprising against the French by the same society in 1879 in Soc Trang.

The French seemed to have arrogated most avenues of development to themselves, blocking all other ethnic groups. The Chinese could not invest in industry (with the exception of rice mills) as the French excluded locals and all foreigners from the industrial sector until 1930. Nor could they invest in mines, ownership of which by foreigners was prohibited by a colonial government edict. Instead, large French concessionary companies controlled all the mines (there were 123 from which Chinese had been extracting coal and other minerals for centuries, paying taxes to the Vietnamese court). This was in sharp contrast to British Malaya and even the Dutch Indies, where Chinese-owned mines constituted one of the major sources for Chinese capital accumulation.

Chinese merchants were also disadvantaged by the protectionism of French trade policy. While French products entered the country free of duty, foreign goods, especially imports from China and British India from the late 1880s, were heavily taxed. Indeed, it was not until 1930 that Chinese in Vietnam were allowed to participate in foreign trade.

The typical Chinese shaped by these French policies was a trader or an artisan, largely urban but also active in the countryside or in the mountainous regions, en-

Men set to work cleaning chickens.

gaging in retail and intermediate trade with the peasantry and uplanders. Self-employed artisans abounded in Cholon, of which a book on French Indochina by Charles Robequain (published in French in 1939) has this to say:

> Particularly at Cholon the variety of Chinese manufactures is extraordinary; there are buildings divided into seemingly identical compartments, which shelter the most diverse manufactures – food pastes, basketry, boots, paper boxes, brushes, candles, &c. Here is a duck raising establishment where the eggs are put into incubators filled with paddy chaff; when ready to hatch they are set out on a piece of screen where hundreds of ducklings emerge cheeping from their broken shells. In an old shed, glass makers are blowing paste through a long tube to make bowls, bottles, and lamps. Elsewhere looms placed side by side operate in crowded rooms.

However, very few Chinese, if any, rose to the heights achieved by entrepreneurs like Tan Tock Seng and Tan Kah Kee in Singapore, Oei Tiong Ham in the Dutch East Indies or Kim Seng Lee in Thailand. Nor do we find a Chinese working class analogous to the contract labour brought in to work on plantations and in mines in British Malaya and Dutch East Indies. The French did experiment with imported Chinese labour in the south in the early part of the 20th century, but there was always

French and Chinese appeals to 'Love and Justice' in religious mural.

a labour surplus in northern Vietnam and a Chinese coolie cost more than a Vietnamese one

The Chinese did dominate the rice trade, however. Saigon was established and flourished on the trade in rice, the leading export of colonial Vietnam. The greater part of the rice of French Indochina was exported from Saigon; and Cholon, the Chinatown adjacent to it, was where the rice merchants were concentrated. In 1876 the Chinese had their own mechanical mill, taking only seven years to catch up with the Europeans. By 1932, Chinese owned nearly all the 75 rice mills in Cholon, and large fleets of junks (some 3,000 in Cochinchina alone) to conduct the trade.

At the heart of Chinese commerce in Vietnam, the rice trade was the main index of Chinese prosperity. One can imagine the host of activities surrounding this trade all the year round: 'upstream,' the distribution of seed, fertilizer and credit to the countryside before the planting season; 'downstream,' the purchasing, transportation, storage and processing of paddy. All these were in Chinese hands. It was a trade which took Chinese agents from the commercial centres deep into the interior of the country. It was no doubt also the basis for Chinese speculation and wealth accumulation.

After independence

Following French withdrawal from Vietnam and the division of the country, some 40–45,000 Chinese quit the north for the south in 1954 (see box). Hanoi quickly moved to integrate the Chinese. In the south, it was a real blow to Chinese when, in 1956, the Saigon government headed by Ngo Dinh Diem barred non-nationals from 11 trades, including rice milling and transportation. By this act of economic nationalism, the government sought to eliminate what it believed was 'foreign' control of the economy. The result was that large quantities of rice were not collected and little was sold in Saigon, adversely affecting Vietnamese peasants. In a

matter of days large amounts of cash, equivalent to a sixth of the currency in circulation in South Vietnam at the time, were withdrawn from banks. Overseas, Saigon rice was boycotted by Chinese merchants in Hong Kong and Singapore. Within a few months the Vietnamese currency had dropped to a third of its former value.

On the positive side, indigenization of trade encouraged Chinese investment in industry, notably textiles, plastics, iron and steel works, chemical manufacturing and food processing. While as late as 1964 Chinese capital invested in industry was only 9 per cent of that of the French, ten years later it had jumped to four-fifths of the total. It was during this boom period that Chinese economic power rapidly caught up with that of their counterparts in other Southeast Asian countries. According to Vietnamese official data, by 1975 Chinese controlled 100 per cent of South Vietnam's domestic wholesale trade, 50 per cent of the retail trade, 70 per cent of foreign trade, and 80 per cent of industry. In banking Chinese were relatively late developers compared with, say, those in Thailand. But growth was rapid from 1964, with Chinese joining indigenous investors in arrangements not unlike the 'Ali-Baba' alliances of Indonesia and Malaysia (see p 159). The pre-1975 share of Chinese investment in banking in southern Vietnam is conservatively estimated to be about 50 per cent.

To assimilate the Chinese, the Saigon government successively decreed that children born to Chinese-Vietnamese couples were Vietnamese citizens, and that all Chinese born in Vietnam were (retroactively) Vietnamese citizens whether they liked it or not. Victor Purcell writes that this measure 'was generally regarded as the most drastic action yet taken by any Asian country to absorb an alien minority.' A number of Chinese who resisted compulsory naturalization left for Taiwan. Later, naturalization would turn out to be a beneficial move for the increasing numbers of Chinese who, by taking Vietnamese nationality, were able to conduct businesses barred to aliens.

Hanoi shows strong Chinese influence.

But disaster struck in 1975 (see box p 229). Chinese were stripped of their means of livelihood by the Hanoi government's 'anti-comprador bourgeoisie' and 'socialist transformation' campaigns, and two so-called 'currency reforms' between 1975 and 1978. The wealthy were arrested and had their properties confiscated. Losses suffered by Chinese investors were thought to amount to US$1–2 billion. All the Chinese newspapers in the south had to close down, as did all Chinese schools, hospitals and voluntary associations. As a group Chinese became scapegoats for Hanoi's inability to achieve socialism in the south. The journalist Nayan Chanda recalls a Vietnamese newspaper editor describing Cholon to him at the time as 'the capitalist heart beating within Vietnam's socialist body.'

The anti-Chinese campaign in the north was more racist than ideological. After suffering harassment and persecution, many were expelled by the Hanoi government, including veterans of the Vietnamese army and Party members who had served the cause of the Vietnamese with devotion. In 1978, waves of Chinese from northern Vietnam – numbering some 200,000 by year's end – crossed the border into China.

At about the same time, departures by sea from the south began to mount. These were the tides of what the world would call 'boat people.' Between 1978 and 1989 about a million refugees left Vietnam, 60–70 per cent of them Chinese. Some 10 per cent perished at sea. Those fortunate enough to have escaped pillage and murder by pirates and make it to neighbouring countries like Thailand, Malaysia and Singapore could still be pushed back to sea. Among the 68,678 boat people who reached Hong Kong safely between January 1 and August 15, 1979, the proportions of Chinese from northern and southern Vietnam were 56 and 26 per cent respectively.

A diminished economic role paralleled diminished numbers. Some surveys indicate that 34 to 50 per cent of traders in Saigon-Cholon were Chinese in 1982. In 1992, 40 per cent of Chinese families in Cholon were engaged in small business – that is, handicraft, cafes, restaurants and other services. Shortly after *doi moi* was announced in 1986 (see box), manufacturing ventures by the local Chinese developed rapidly. But the years of socialist antipathy to private enterprise have left their mark.

From overseas Vietnamese, principally ethnic Chinese, have come capital and know-how, but for local Chinese to regain the position they had achieved several decades back will be a slow and painful process.

They are still considered to be an asset by the government, which hopes their overseas relatives and connections will help to bring in foreign investment. There was indeed a surge of Southeast and East Asian Chinese capital into the economy in the first half of the 1990s, yet it is dubious whether the local Chinese were instrumental in attracting it. For intermediaries or local partners, the foreign Chinese conglomerates need not look to the resident Chinese, who can offer neither political connections nor useful networks.

In the absence of any systematic study, travellers' tales provide our only picture of Chinese today. One account, published in 1994 by Zhang Yu, a one-time resident of Saigon, tells of the revival of Chinese organizations among the 524,499 Chinese (about 425,000 fewer than before 1975) in Ho Chi Minh City. A Chinese-language evening school, opened in 1989, has been followed by scores of others (56 licensed, more than 70 unlicensed). To Zhang's surprise, half the students were Vietnamese; they were studying Chinese in the hope of getting coveted jobs in companies opened by foreign Chinese. *Huiguan* were allowed to reopen in 1988, and Zhang notes signs of life in a range of Chinese cultural and leisure activities, from art exhibitions to ping-pong contests. Of Chinese newspapers, however, only one remains, *Jiefang ribao* (*Liberation Daily*) – down from 22 during their heyday in the first half of 1965.

Li Tana

Scrambling to board an overloaded evacuation plane when Saigon fell in April 1975.

Teacher giving English lesson in former Chinese school (now privatized) in Hanoi (top). Chinese woman manning a pottery stall.

CANADA

Chinese labour on Canadian railroad, circa 1909.

Signs of the Chinese minority's dynamism abound in the Canada of the last quarter of the 20th century. The sheer increase in numbers is spectacular. According to census records, a resident Chinese population of 118,000 formed but 0.55 per cent of the total population in 1971. Primarily because of sizeable immigration, official statistics show it to have grown to 289,000 in 1981 and to 586,000 in 1991, a five-fold increase in 20 years. The 1991 census has further identified Chinese, after English and French, as the most spoken language in Canadian homes. Indeed, half a million people in Canada in 1991 reportedly named Chinese as their mother tongue.

Generally considered successful and aspiring, ethnic Chinese are also seen as key players in the economic future of Canada. This is in marked contrast to how they were regarded at the start of their 140-year history in Canada. Indeed, for over 100 years, until the 1950s and even the 1960s, Chinese suffered badly from racist rejection and discrimination as well as a lack of opportunities.

Overview of Chinese immigration and settlement

Historically, Chinese migration to Canada can be divided into the following stages: (1) the preliminary period of 1858–84; (2) the time of restricted entry from 1885–1923; (3) the exclusion era of 1923–47; (4) renewed but still limited immigration from 1947–67; and (5) the sustained and sizeable immigration since 1967. This periodization reflects largely the controlling effects of Canadian immigration policies and aspects of demographic, socio-economic and cultural changes among Chinese.

The Chinese migration to Canada was one stream of the massive outflow from southern China's Guangdong and Fujian provinces in the second half of the 19th century. It closely followed that to the United States and showed a similar pattern, pulled first by gold mining (along the Fraser River starting from 1858), and then by the chance of work in various construction projects (in the frontier setting of early British Columbia). The building of the Canadian Pacific Railway in 1880–84 alone brought in 17,000 Chinese; some of these Chinese had worked in the western United States, but the majority came directly from south China.

It is clear from the census records of the period that many gold miners, railroad workers and labourers soon returned to China or went elsewhere. Still, the presence of so many (several thousands) Chinese remaining, the competition they posed to other job-seekers and their perceived cultural difference were enough to engender an anti-Chinese movement among the white settlers. In 1885, the federal government in Ottawa responded to the demand of British Columbia politicians and imposed a head tax of C$50 each on the Chinese immigrants. The amount was later increased to C$100 in 1900 and then to C$500 by 1903. While imposing hardship on those seeking entrance to Canada, the financial deterrent alone had only a momentary effect, for some 82,000 Chinese reportedly arrived between 1886 and 1923 and paid C$23 million into the country's coffers.

After paying to get in, it was not uncommon for Chinese immigrants to return to China for a visit or go elsewhere for a short period of time. Still, their population grew steadily because of a net increase in immigration. By the early 1920s, there were some 40,000 ethnic Chinese residing in Canada, the majority of them in British Columbia. There they were found in many thriving mining towns on Vancouver Island and along the Fraser River in the interior. Many gravitated to Victoria, home to the first Canadian Chinatown, and especially to Vancouver, for jobs and also for the companionship, cultural comfort and security available in the ethnic neighbourhoods. Since the completion of the Canadian Pacific Railway, some Chinese had moved to Alberta, the Prairies, and

Map 5.11

Chinese coolies in panama hats arriving at quarantine station on Canadian coast, 1917.

further east, so that there were a string of Chinatowns from Victoria and Vancouver through Calgary, Edmonton, Moose Jaw, Regina, Winnipeg, to Toronto and Montreal.

As in the United States, the Chinese in Canada originated from a handful of counties clustering around the Pearl River Delta in Guangdong. The majority were natives of Siyi ('four districts': Taishan, Kaiping, Xinhui and Enping), predominantly Taishan. Others came mainly from Sanyi ('three districts': Panyu, Nanhai and Shunde) and the county of Zhongshan. Almost all spoke some local version of Cantonese, though a few were Hakka speakers from the same area. They gave the impression of having about a dozen common surnames, with certain surname groups coming preponderantly from certain counties.

Like some other immigrant groups in the New World, the Chinese were almost all males. The long and arduous sea journey from China, the physical labour required by mining and construction work, and later on the burdensome head tax ensured that only men in their prime and teenage boys ready to toil would come. If they had any hope of later sending for their families – a few actually did – they were stopped from doing so by the Chinese Immigration Act of 1923. Under this Canadian version of the exclusion laws (see p 262), no more than two dozen Chinese were admitted in the following 24 years. By the time the Great Depression struck, thousands of Chinese were ready to leave, and eventually many did during the exclusion era. The Chinese population shrank, and so did many Canadian Chinatowns. Chinese are the only immigrant minority in Canadian history to have had to pay a head tax and to have been singled out for exclusion.

The renewed but still restricted immigration of the next stage, begun in 1947, was entirely geared towards family reunion, with spouses and minor children arriving to join the old settlers. To qualify for admission, the applicants had first to make their way from mainland China to Hong Kong, then go through checking and security clearance procedures under the sponsorship of their relatives in Canada. Only in 1962, in response to the needs of the Canadian economy, was a category of independent migrants created whereby Chinese and others could apply for entry on the basis of merit, judged in terms of education or occupational skills. This was followed by a total revamping of the immigration system five years later, from which point on all applicants were screened and admitted according to a set of universal criteria – family reunion, educational qualifications, occupational skills and the like – without any reference to national origin, ethnicity, religion and so on.

A few observations on the differences between the pre- and post-1947 periods are worth making at this point. Prior to the end of exclusion, Chinese conjugal families were relatively few and they were confined by

Table 5.19

CHINESE POPULATION GROWTH IN CANADA			
YEAR	NUMBER	% INCREASE	% OF CANADA'S POPULATION
1881	4,383	—	0.10
1891	9,129	108.3	0.19
1901	17,312	89.6	0.32
1911	27,831	60.8	0.39
1921	39,587	42.5	0.45
1931	46,519	17.5	0.45
1941	34,627	-25.6	0.30
1951	32,528	-6.1	0.23
1961	58,197	78.9	0.32
1971	118,815	104.2	0.55
1981	289,245	143.4	1.20
1991	586,645	97.3	2.17

Sources: Censuses of Canada, 1881-1991; Lai (1988).

Table 5.20

SEX RATIO AND NATIVITY OF CHINESE IN CANADA		
YEAR	MALES PER 100 FEMALES	% OF NATIVE-BORN
1911	2,790	3
1921	1,533	7
1931	1,241	12
1941	785	20
1951	374	31
1961	163	40
1971	112	38
1981	102	25

Sources: Censuses of Canada, 1911–81, as adapted by Li (1988).

Table 5.21

DISTRIBUTION OF CHINESE POPULATION BY PROVINCE

Year	British Columbia	Ontario	Alberta	Quebec	Others
1901	86.0	4.2	1.4	6.0	2.4
1911	70.5	10.0	6.4	5.7	7.4
1921	59.4	14.2	9.0	5.9	11.5
1931	58.3	14.9	8.3	5.9	12.6
1941	53.8	17.1	9.0	6.9	13.2
1951	49.0	21.5	10.6	5.9	13.0
1961	41.6	26.0	11.9	8.2	13.2
1971	37.2	33.1	10.9	10.0	8.8
1981	33.5	41.0	12.8	6.7	6.0
1991	30.9	46.7	12.1	6.3	4.0

Sources: Censuses of Canada, 1901–91.

Table 5.22

INTENDED DESTINATIONS OF IMMIGRANTS FROM HONG KONG, MAINLAND CHINA AND TAIWAN BY PROVINCE, 1971–80

Destinations	Number of Immigrants			Total	% of Total
	Hong Kong	China	Taiwan		
Ontario	36,244	3,422	5,207	44,873	43.0
British Columbia	24,502	4,529	2,493	31,524	30.2
Alberta	11,042	1,059	609	12,710	12.2
Quebec	5,852	887	790	7,529	7.2
Others	6,272	787	654	7,713	7.4
Total	83,912	9,753	10,684	104,349	100

Sources: Immigration statistics, as adapted by Lai (1988).

Table 5.23

CHINESE POPULATION IN CENSUS METROPOLITAN AREAS

	1971	1981	1991
Vancouver	36,405	83,845	167,425
Toronto	26,285	89,590	231,820
Montreal	10,655	17,200	34,355
Edmonton	5,110	16,300	32,960
Calgary	4,630	15,545	32,515
Victoria	3,290	5,825	6,655
Ottawa-Hull	3,060	8,205	14,480
Winnipeg	2,535	6,195	10,445
Hamilton	1,380	3,405	5,985
Regina	1,275	1,835	2,490
Windsor	1,070	2,325	3,240
Saskatoon	975	2,410	3,155
London	820	1,960	3,230
Kitchener	565	1,710	3,340

Sources: Censuses of Canada, 1971–91.

and large to the merchant class. The 1911 ratio of 2,790 males to 100 females did improve somewhat but had still remained as high as 1,241 to 100 by 1931. Many immigrant men were in fact married, but lived in Canada without their spouses. That pattern changed first with gradual family reunions after 1947 and then with many couples and their children arriving in Canada as intact family units after 1967. Family separation also had the effect of delaying the arrival of Canadian-born offspring – so much so that by 1941, that is, more than 80 years after the onset of Chinese immigration, only one in five Chinese was born in the country. The proportion had doubled by 1961 because of family formation and local reproduction, but the trend was reversed in the following decades by sizeable immigration.

The early immigrants from Guangdong had a predominantly rural background. This remained the case after 1947, but only initially. Many of the new arrivals of the 1950s and 1960s were often people who had had several years of residence in Hong Kong prior to their

Chinese temple and shops on street in Victoria, circa 1892.

departure for Canada. From the 1970s, many newcomers were of a generation born or raised in Hong Kong. Direct immigration from mainland China was officially resumed after 1973, but by then ethnic Chinese from such other points of origin as Taiwan, the Philippines, Indochina, Malaysia, Singapore, India and South Africa were coming to Canada, attracted there by its more democratic and peaceful environment and supposedly greater economic opportunities.

The 1940s also saw a shift in the regional distribution of the Chinese population. British Columbia ceased to have more than half of all Chinese residents in the country. Eastern Canada's economic pull was especially felt by the post-1967 immigrants. By the end of the 1970s, Ontario had overtaken British Columbia as the province with the most Chinese, while Toronto had superseded Vancouver as the metropolitan area with the most Chinese. But what appears to be a shift in regional distribution was, on another level, the continuation of a trend for Chinese to concentrate in larger urban centres. The trend has been particularly pronounced since the 1980s. According to census information, 70 per cent of Chinese lived within the metropolitan areas of Vancouver, Toronto, Montreal, Calgary and Edmonton in 1971. The proportion increased to 75 per cent in 1981 and 85 per cent in 1991. The distribution being what it is, much of the discussion that follows will be based on Chinese experiences in the urban areas, particularly Toronto and Vancouver.

Discrimination and adaptation in early Chinatowns

White society's antipathy towards the Chinese and discriminatory legislation and practices were important conditioning factors in the lives of the early immigrants. Chinese were widely regarded as morally and culturally degraded aliens. While late 19th-century Canadians like Prime Minister John A. Macdonald and railroad contractor Andrew Onderdonk considered Chinese immigrants an economic necessity, in times of recession the cheap labour they rendered was seen to threaten the livelihood of the white working class and to signify Chinese inferiority.

Restricting immigration was but one aspect of Canadian racism. In 1875, a decade before the head tax was levied, the British Columbia legislature deprived Chinese of their vote in the provincial elections. This had the effect of disqualifying them from voting in any federal

*Delivery truck of Chinese
company in Vancouver, 1920.*

election, and when they were removed from the municipal voters' list in 1896, Chinese disenfranchisement in British Columbia was complete. Surprisingly, Saskatchewan, despite having only a small number of Chinese residents, was the other province where Chinese were barred from the ballot box.

Being Chinese was additionally an economic liability. In British Columbia, not having the vote excluded them from such choice professions as law and pharmacy, while numerous other restrictive employment regulations and punitive licensing requirements, targeted at Chinese by various provincial and municipal authorities, succeeded in marginalizing and segregating the Chinese labour force in the Canadian economy. In British Columbia, some Chinese were able to find work – for less pay than their white counterparts – at sawmills and salmon canneries. Others also laboured on farms to supply produce to city residents. However, a sizeable number of Chinese worked in restaurants, laundries and other service occupations, and such concentration was more pronounced in the rest of the country.

Within the major Chinatowns, a handful of élitist merchants engaged in import-export businesses, and, acting as labour contractors or agents for the Canadian Pacific Railway and major shipping companies, presided over the ethnic economy. Beneath them was a larger stratum of small businessmen and shopkeepers. While some of these were bona fide proprietors and managers, others were merely shareholders who contributed no more than their time and labour. Relying invariably on credit based on personal relationships and trust, the Chinese, even the mass of the working poor, aspired to become business partners one day. Not only did many see this

as the most desirable – and perhaps the only conceivable – channel of social mobility, but acquiring the 'merchant' status would, they believed, ease their admission and re-entry into Canada.

Many Guangdong natives arrived in Canada with a tremendous sense of responsibility towards the families they had left behind and a deep concern for the well-being of their native areas. Theirs was a sojourner's mentality, a part of established Chinese migratory behaviour reinforced by white discrimination. They hoped to work hard overseas, to send remittances home, to save up for an occasional visit, and eventually to retire back in the home village. But their marginal economic position, the intimidating and burdensome immigration regulations, plus the disorder in China, prevented most of them from realizing these dreams. Separated from their families, rejected by their Canadian hosts, they felt all the more nostalgic for their native areas and identified all the more closely with them.

Little wonder that native-place associations and clansmen organizations flourished in early Chinatowns. Part of the collective adaptation of ethnic Chinese, these mutual aid societies offered their members lodging, introductions to jobs, a circle of acquaintances, and some security in an otherwise completely alien country. They kept the migrants informed of developments in their places of origin, in whose affairs they could even participate by, say, coordinating fund-raising efforts to build a school or other modernizing projects. Moreover, locally, they provided members with a measure of assistance and protection from discrimination by non-Chinese and against competition from rival Chinese groups. By the exclusion period, these traditional organizations

Well-dressed Chinese in front of Legislative Buildings, Victoria, 1904.

Cartoon reflecting oppression of Chinese by politicians, 1860s.

could be found in Chinatowns across Canada.

Several other organizations deserve special attention because of their unique position in the various Chinatowns' internal politics and external relations. First and foremost was the Chinese Benevolent Association (CBA), the purpose of which was to serve as a community organization that addressed the general needs of the Chinese and acted as a spokesman for the group as a whole. The earliest CBA to appear was the one established in 1884 in Victoria. The one in Vancouver was founded about a decade later. By the 1920s, the Vancouver CBA had developed an elaborate leadership structure based on the representation of native-place associations and at-large elections. There were other regional CBAs, but no national organization ever evolved, no doubt because of the vast distances separating the various Chinese communities. If occasion arose for negotiations with Ottawa – an example is the protest against the implementation of the Chinese Immigration Act of 1923 and the subsequent campaign for its repeal – it was often the Chinese in eastern Canada, especially those in Toronto and Montreal, who took the lead rather than those in British Columbia.

Another Chinese organization of note was one with a colourful history, based as it was on the Hongmen tradition of secret brotherhood prevalent in 18th-century south China. The Zhigong Tang, known also as the Chinese Freemasons from about 1920, or its precursor, was set up by the Guangdong natives as early as 1863 in the mining town of Barkerville. Popular among workers and small businessmen rather than the élitist merchants who dominated the CBAs, the Zhigong Tang spread widely among the Chinese in early British Columbia, locating its headquarters first in Victoria and then in Vancouver. Later on, as some Chinese moved east, it was introduced to other parts of Canada, though its stronghold remained in western Canada.

The Zhigong Tang was a force to be reckoned with in Chinatown not just because of its pioneer status and entrenched position but because it was an important link between the Canadian Chinese and the politics of China. Confronting racial discrimination in Canada and the prospect of China's dismemberment by foreign powers, the immigrants were receptive to the respective reform and revolutionary messages of Kang Youwei and Sun Yat-sen (see p 101). With the rise of nationalistic sentiments, the Zhigong Tang lent its support to Sun Yat-sen; some of its organizations even mortgaged their properties to finance Sun's revolution.

As it turned out, this was only the beginning of decades of active engagement by immigrant Chinese in the politics of China. Factionalism and bitter rivalry split the Chinese community in Canada as elsewhere in the diaspora. The primary division was between the local supporters of Sun Yat-sen in the newly established Kuomintang and an indignant Zhigong Tang accusing Sun of reneging on his promise to reward its members with official appointments. The chaotic political situation

Table 5.24

PERCENTAGE AGE AND SEX DISTRIBUTION OF THE CHINESE POPULATION IN CANADA						
		1951			1961	
AGE GROUPS	MALE	FEMALE	TOTAL	MALE	FEMALE	TOTAL
0–9	5.50	5.09	10.59	11.90	10.91	22.81
10–19	9.39	4.17	13.56	5.97	4.38	10.35
20–34	6.72	5.55	12.27	17.30	10.92	28.22
35–44	7.74	3.10	10.84	3.08	3.23	6.31
45–54	12.86	1.80	14.66	4.43	4.13	8.56
55–64	21.00	0.94	21.94	6.20	2.85	9.05
65 & above	15.67	0.43	16.10	13.08	1.59	14.67
Total	78.88	21.08	99.96	61.96	38.01	99.97

Sources: Censuses of Canada, 1951 and 1961.

in China after the 1911 Revolution and the factional rivalries that plagued the Kuomintang before and after it formally assumed power in 1927 were reflected not only in armed fighting and political assassinations in Canadian Chinatowns but in local Chinese newspaper battles. Only the Japanese invasion of China in the 1930s generated some community-wide cooperation – in efforts to coordinate fund-raising and other activities to support the war in China. But even then, the deep-seated rivalries were merely muted, not dispelled.

However, the first generation of Chinese immigrants did not differ in their concern for China's fate as a modern nation and for the well-being of their native areas, nor in their experience of racist rejection by their host society. It was hard for them not to be conscious of themselves as ethnic Chinese and to recognize the limits to their future in Canada. Nor did prospects seem any brighter for even the small number of local-born Chinese, whose English education and Canadian citizenship (by birth) did little to improve their chances of finding jobs outside Chinatown or developing close social relationships with non-Chinese. Thus it was not only for nationalist and sentimental reasons that their parents insisted that they kept up their Chinese language skills and acquired some knowledge of Chinese subjects by attending supplementary Chinese schools in the late afternoons and evenings. Those who could afford it would send their children back to China for a native education.

The aftermath of exclusion

For the Chinese in Canada, the end of World War II was the beginning of a new era. The widespread goodwill and sympathy China earned during the war, the worldwide condemnation of racism in the wake of the Nazi genocide, and the repeal of the anti-Chinese exclusion laws by the United States Congress in 1943, paved the way for a similar repudiation of the 1923 Chinese Immigration Act by Canada in 1947. This was soon followed by the enfranchisement of the Chinese in British Columbia and Saskatchewan.

Chinese welcomed the end of formal exclusion not just as a matter of principle. The Communist revolution in China ended the sojourners' dream of returning to their native place. Instead, they sought to bring their families over from China. The Canadian government did not, as the US did after 1943, impose any quota on Chinese immigration, but initially it allowed only Chinese

with Canadian citizenship to sponsor their spouses and unmarried children up to the age of 18.

Chinese did two things to overcome or circumvent the restrictive regulations. First, they lobbied hard in Ottawa for concessions throughout the 1950s, with Vancouver's Chinese Benevolent Association launching a national campaign under the flamboyant leadership of Foon Sien Wong, who was widely considered by Chinese and non-Chinese alike to be the most effective spokesman for the community. It is said that Wong's persistent and much publicized efforts, blessed by good connections with the ruling Liberal Party and the mainstream media, led to the steady expansion of the admissible categories.

Secondly, some Chinese attempted to enter Canada by falsifying their ages, or simply by passing themselves off as somebody else, using the documents of, say, eligible applicants who had died, or immigrant slots which sponsoring relatives were willing to sell for a good price. In any event, illegal entry was a widespread practice which came to a head in May 1960, when the Royal Canadian Mounted Police raided many institutional premises and private homes. The crackdown on illegal immigration resulted in only a few convictions, but over 12,000 Chinese took advantage of the subsequent amnesty to rectify their status formally.

Clearly, the doors to non-European immigration were still not fully open. Nevertheless, the steady arrival of spouses, children and young adults could not but rejuvenate and replenish the ageing and dwindling Chinese population. The imbalance in sex ratio began to be righted, more conjugal families appeared, and new immigrant youth took form as a distinctive cohort in the gradually reviving Chinese minority. In Vancouver, where the effects of replenishment were the most pronounced, an estimated 13,000 Chinese newcomers arrived between 1947 and 1967. According to the census, the city's ethnic Chinese population subsequently increased from a mere 8,700 in 1951 to 15,000 in 1961 and to over 30,000 in 1971. At the same time, naturalization records show evidence of an increasing number of Chinese nationwide taking advantage of the greater access to Canadian citizenship to become settlers rather than transient sojourners.

In places with a large concentration of Chinese such as Vancouver, Toronto and Montreal, renewed immigration in the postwar period infused Chinatowns with vitality. There was now a larger clientele for ethnic food and services, as well as a timely supply of cheap young labour for Chinatown businesses. Chinese-language newspapers expanded their circulations, and many traditional organizations looked to the newcomers to join and energize them.

The Chinese communities seemed to be revitalized, but perhaps not in the way that the older settlers had expected. In tandem with the demographic changes in the 1950s, the first major inter-generational battle among ethnic Chinese erupted. On one side were the old-timers who had arrived in Canada before 1923. As pioneers and as parents, they naturally saw themselves as the prop of the community and asked for submission and respect from the incoming Chinese youth. But the latter were not so compliant. Inspired by youthful idealism and some modern Chinese education in China and Hong

Young Chinese fighting for Canada flanked by their proud parents.

Campaigning for Douglas Jung.

the immigrants to breach racial barriers and benefit from the decline in discrimination in Canadian society. In British Columbia, they were the first to enter such previously inaccessible professions as pharmacy, dentistry and law. Examples of educational and career accomplishments filled many pages of the English language magazine, *Chinatown News*, which began publication in Vancouver in 1953 as the mouthpiece of the Canadian-born Chinese. One of the most celebrated figures of the time was probably Douglas Jung, a lawyer elected from Vancouver to the Canadian Parliament as the first Chinese MP in 1957. The organizations set up by the Canadian-born Chinese also made their aspirations to upward social mobility and their orientation towards Canadian society quite apparent. For instance, the Chinatown Lions Club, formed in 1953 among up-and-coming professionals and businessmen, committed itself to public services and charities Western style, rather than to the mutual help and membership assistance typically rendered by the traditional associations.

The Canadian-born's perceived acculturation and loss of Chinese identity of course upset the older immigrants, but the elderly Chinese, as parents, were also gratified by their children's hitherto unknown success. In the end, it was the differences between the maturing local-born Chinese and the postwar immigrants that produced the most bitter arguments and greatest ill-feeling. The local-born were indignant about the newcomers' claim to being superior Chinese. In the eyes of the local-born, their own English education, language skills and Canadian experiences entitled them to lead the way towards wider acceptance of ethnic Chinese in Canada. That these newcomers spoke no English and did not know how to behave 'properly' was considered not only a source of embarrassment but a drag on progress. For their part, the new arrivals, especially the young among them, were no less outraged by the cultural pretensions of the local-born Chinese. These young immigrants were self-conscious about their initial ineptitude in Canada and mindful of their Chinese origins. In their role as cultural vigilantes, they condemned the apparent acculturation of the Canadian-born Chinese.

So after 1945 the Chinese minority was moving in the direction of greater internal diversity in terms of generation, cultural orientation and economic profile. Another notable development of the postwar period was the threat to the physical existence of Chinatowns across the country, though the causes and outcomes were not everywhere the same. Many lesser Chinese settlements on Vancouver Island and in the interior of British Columbia, already in decline since the exclusion era, were deserted altogether as the last survivors passed away. In one case, in Nanaimo in September 1960, Chinatown vanished in a fire. In larger cities like Vancouver, Toronto, Montreal, Calgary and Edmonton, matters appeared more complex. First, land speculation and rising real estate values discouraged many property owners from repairing and renovating their rundown properties; the rental income would not justify the cost and they would rather sell their buildings to developers offering good money to be allowed to tear them down. Moreover, in an age of urban redevelopment and expansion, city governments and urban planners saw the Chinatowns' occupation of valuable land in or near

Kong, they became severely critical of the 'backwardness' of the older generation and rejected their claim to leadership. Many youth societies sprang up in the 1950s and 1960s to organize cultural activities and sporting events outside the traditional associations. A few young people openly expressed their pride in the New China under Communist rule and thus drew the ire of the Kuomintang's supporters among the old-timers.

Another protagonist in this unfolding intramural conflict were Canadian-born Chinese who had come of age as a distinct generation from around the time of World War II. Many of them originated from the long-established and larger Chinatowns in Victoria and Vancouver, with a smaller number coming from other parts of the country. This group came into the limelight when some 500 of them were drafted into the Canadian armed forces in 1944. Upon their discharge, they formed the Chinese Veterans Organization in Vancouver, best known for its successful campaign for full citizenship on behalf of ethnic Chinese.

Generally, with their English education and language skills, the local-born Chinese were better equipped than downtown areas as unjustified. Finally, an 'internal' process was at work to depopulate Chinatowns: more and more Chinese themselves preferred to relocate to other neighbourhoods offering wider and better residential choices.

Starting from the 1950s, the three biggest Canadian Chinatowns, along with other smaller ones, all found themselves besieged by redevelopment projects. In time, Montreal's Chinatown was hemmed in by commercial and residential high-rises and left without any space for growth. Toronto's Chinatown was literally truncated to make room for the City Hall. In Vancouver, plans were afoot to level Strathcona, a residential area adjacent to the commercial part of Chinatown, when a dramatic bid to rescue Chinatown unfolded.

If implemented, the redevelopment plans would displace thousands of Strathcona residents, many of them Chinese. Among them were families with deep roots in Vancouver, elderly Chinese who lived together in communal housing without the company of their spouses, as well as post-1947 arrivals. The relocation of these people, it was argued, would devastate the Chinese community. Elderly and non-English speaking Chinese would not be able to partake of the cultural comfort and convenience of an ethnic neighbourhood. Families relocated to other parts of the city would not be able to send their children to Chinese schools, while their scattering would debilitate other Chinatown organizations. Similarly, businesses in Chinatown, particularly those dependent on an ethnic clientele, would lose their customers as well as workers. Unfortunately, the traditional Chinatown leadership under the Chinese Benevolent Association offered no effective opposition to the redevelopment plans. Adding to the confusion and frustration of the time was the voice of the *Chinatown News* representing the Canadian-born Chinese, which supported the redevelopment in the interest of furthering desegregation and acculturation.

A turning point finally came in the late 1960s, when the remaining residents established the Strathcona Property Owners and Tenants Association (SPOTA) to save their neighbourhood. A growing city-wide movement led by young academics, social workers, lawyers, other professionals and college students supported them. They also benefited from a new federal government under Pierre Trudeau, one sympathetic to grassroots democracy and wary of expensive and disruptive social policies. In a surprising turn of events in 1969, the SPOTA triumphed and, amid a display of popular support, was invited to join representatives from all three levels of the Canadian government (municipal, provincial and federal) to design and oversee a rehabilitation programme for the neighbourhood. The dramatic success of the SPOTA turned out to be twofold: not only did it stop the bulldozer from razing Strathcona, it engendered a new sense of community and political empowerment among Chinese as they entered the 1970s.

Becoming Chinese Canadian

Viewed in the larger context of the late 1960s and early 1970s, the SPOTA's campaign was but one of several pivotal events that together opened a new chapter in the history of the Chinese in Canada. First and fore-

most among these events was the formalization of multiculturalism as a Canadian national ideology in 1970, the culmination of a decade of soul-searching by Canadian political élites and a few minority groups. The Chinese did not play an active part in the soul-searching, but the official adoption of a multicultural policy could not but have a profound impact on the way they, along with other ethnic minorities, redefined their position in Canadian society. In brief, the idea of the new policy was that ethnicities, including Chinese ethnicity, were part and parcel of the Canadian mosaic. Remaining ethnically and culturally Chinese should no longer be held against Chinese in their claim to be part of Canada. To become Canadian, Chinese need not discard their cultural heritage; instead, such heritage should be preserved for the enrichment of Canadian life. These emergent multicultural sentiments were clearly behind the defence of Strathcona and the many preservation projects undertaken in Chinatowns in the succeeding years. In 1971 Vancouver's Chinatown was declared a special protected area under the provincial Archaeological and Historic Sites Protection Act, and the Chinatown Historic Area Planning Committee was formed in 1975 to coordinate various beautification efforts with Chinese participation. Other cities soon followed suit, taking steps to give their derelict Chinatowns a face-lift.

The redefinition of Chinatown from ghetto to treasured ethnic neighbourhood parallels a momentous change in cultural politics. In one of its about-faces, *Chinatown News* embraced multiculturalism and the new ethnicity, applauding the revitalization of Chinatowns and advocating the preservation of the Chinese language for the benefit even of the Canadian-born Chinese. Other efforts soon emerged in the 1970s to assert a place for Chinese culture in the new mosaic. Probably the best known vehicle for this was the Chinese Cultural Centre (CCC) in Vancouver.

The CCC was founded in 1973 by a broad coalition of groups to celebrate Chinese culture and to share it with non-Chinese Canadians. Its supporters were drawn from different generations of immigrant and local-born Chinese. Among the immigrants were a few of the surviving old-timers, but many more were post-1947 arrivals who considered the multicultural policy a vindication of their perseverance in maintaining Chinese culture. Together, they were able to solidify the much-needed support of the traditional organizations for the CCC. No less crucial to the CCC's rapid ascendancy in Chinatown was the participation of the Canadian-born Chinese, many of them seeking a new ethnic pride and re-identification with their ethnic community. The older and more established members of this group provided the leadership in the early stages of the CCC's growth, negotiating aggressively with Canadian officials for support. At the same time, the younger college and high school students infused the organization and its many activities with youthful enthusiasm and creativity.

Testifying to the CCC's popularity was its success in raising funds – particularly by garnering government recognition and support – for an ambitious building project. Even before its permanent premises were completed in 1980, it was running multifarious programmes (including English-language and Canadian citizenship classes, instruction in Chinese arts and crafts, legal aid,

Canadian multiculturalism: Caucasian rowers join Chinese in Dragon Boat race on Lake Ontario, near Toronto.

A part of Toronto that might be mistaken for Hong Kong.

translation and other services) and organizing public celebrations of Chinese New Year and other festivities. These activities were all indicative of a new level of cultural and social consciousness among Chinese. The CCC thus played a major role in renewing the centrality of Chinatown in the community life of the Chinese, at a time when the Chinese population was dispersing from such areas.

Thus official multiculturalism – and the general encouragement and institutional support it gave to the celebration of ethnic culture – energized the Chinese minority from the 1970s. Another important source of impetus was the widening of the door to immigration after the overhaul of government policy in 1967. With the final removal of the racial bias in immigration regulations (another example of Canada's commitment to the equal treatment of ethnocultural groups), new Chinese began to arrive in sizeable numbers.

Immigrants from Hong Kong made up the bulk of this new influx, which appeared at first glance to be a continuation of a trend already in motion. Like earlier immigrants, many were former residents of mainland China who had made their way to Hong Kong since 1949. But in other respects an increasing number of newcomers from Hong Kong were noticeably different from the earlier immigrants, who were predominantly rural in background, little exposed to Western culture and unable to speak English. Partly because the selective criteria of Canada's immigrant policy favoured the educated and highly skilled, and partly because of Hong Kong's postwar economic upgrading, many Chinese immigrants of the 1970s were people who could bypass the traditional ethnic economy of Chinatown to join the ranks of professionals and other occupations in the mainstream economy. The ability to do this was particularly marked in those who had initially come as students but who stayed on to work after graduating from Canadian universities. This resulted in a general elevation of the social and economic profiles of the ethnic Chinese and the solidification of a middle class.

The effects of this new stage of Chinese immigration were felt in big cities across the country. In the Greater Vancouver area, the population of Chinese increased from 36,000 in 1971 to just under 84,000 in 1981. Almost half of the Chinese there in 1981 had reportedly arrived within the preceding ten years. The proportion of recent immigrants was even larger in Metropolitan Toronto, which by the late 1970s was boasting the single largest Chinese population in the country. In Alberta, both Calgary and Edmonton tripled their number of Chinese residents during this decade. In all these places, the Chinese populations spread out from the former ethnic neighbourhoods in various directions and new clusters of Chinese grocery stores, restaurants and ethnic businesses emerged.

The new immigrants of the 1970s also distinguished themselves by the kinds of voluntary association they set up. The traditional Chinatown organizations had some success in recruiting new members from among arrivals from China, but much less so in the case of the newcomers from Hong Kong. Some of the latter, being bilingual in Chinese and English, could readily interact with both the earlier immigrants and the Canadian-born. However, for networking and support they seemed to prefer their own types of organization – alumni of prestigious schools in Hong Kong, merchant associations, professional groups and Christian churches. Especially notable were social service groups like the Toronto Chinese Community Services Association and the United Chinese Community Enrichment Services Society (known widely as SUCCESS) in Vancouver. Both were founded in 1973 by young professionals and social workers of Hong Kong background, and their mandates were identical: to ease the settlement and integration of the recently arrived Chinese immigrants, especially the less fortunate ones from mainland China and, later on, the refugees from Vietnam (see Part V: Vietnam).

Having grown in size, and able to draw on an enlarged social base and more diverse leadership resources, the Chinese minority became more assertive on public issues of collective interest. This could be seen in a national conference on immigration held in Vancouver in 1975, when the Chinese delegates challenged the federal government's Green Paper on Immigration and Population, which blamed the recent influx from Asia and the Caribbean for the escalation of racial tensions in many Canadian cities. Another instance of Chinese opposition to racism arose when a CTV public affairs television programme showed Chinese-looking 'foreign students' filling up university classrooms and depriving 'Canadians' of their rightful education. In Toronto, outraged young Canadian-born Chinese and immigrants joined hands in establishing the Chinese Canadian National Council. Through this civil rights organization (which has remained active ever since), they orchestrated a successful national campaign to demand redress and a public apology from the broadcaster.

As much as it was a time of unprecedented opportunity for the advancement of Chinese in Canada, the 1970s were also marked by some significant moments in their evolving relationship with China. Since 1949, they had been cut off from mainland China. Whatever contact they had with their native places had been channelled through the families and relatives settled in Hong Kong. At the official level, China meant Taiwan, which enjoyed Canadian diplomatic recognition because of the Cold War, but the support of the ethnic Chinese for the Nationalist regime shrank as the 1950s and the 1960s wore on. The long-standing rivalry in Chinatown politics between the Zhigong Tang and the Kuomintang might appear to linger on, and a small number of immigrant youth might have expressed enthusiasm for Communist China, but by and large the politics of China was beginning to seem archaic and remote.

Again, it was around 1970 that things changed dramatically. This came of China's rapprochement with the Western world. In particular, Canada's switch of diplomatic recognition from Taipei to Beijing in October 1970 ushered in a climate of openness in which ethnic Chinese could re-identify with China culturally and emotionally, followed by the renewal of direct contact with the native areas in Guangdong. The timing of these developments was important: this new pride in China and in being Chinese dovetailed at once with the rising

multicultural ethos in Canada.

Inevitably, Chinatown politics reflected these changes. The local Kuomintang had protested against the diplomatic switch, but to no avail, and afterwards saw its already declining influence further diminished by the jubilant and vocal pro-mainland China groups. In Toronto and elsewhere, the Kuomintang loyalists managed to hang on to their control of the CBA-type organizations, only to marginalize these supposedly community bodies from their diversified constituencies. However, it was in Vancouver that the Kuomintang had its biggest upset. Threatened by the CCC and by the fact that it looked to China and not Taiwan for models of Chinese culture, the Kuomintang and the CBA it controlled conspired to set up a competitive organization to divert Canadian government funding from the CCC. In retaliation, the CCC supporters staged a public campaign to discredit the CBA and took its executives to the provincial Supreme Court for failing to hold, as its own constitution required, open elections to its offices. On election day, thousands of Chinese showed up to cast their vote and the incumbents were swept out of office. The winners claimed to have democratized the CBA.

Thus, ironically, during this first decade of Canadian multiculturalism, China and its many levels of meanings – politics, ancestral culture, native place and so forth – seemed to loom larger in the consciousness of the ethnic Chinese than at any time since 1949. While most Chinese simply enjoyed the new pluralism in Canadian society, others, particularly some young Canadian-born Chinese, chafed at having 'China' attached to their ethnic identity. To celebrate the traditional and classical culture of China was fine but to do just that could be misleading, they insisted. The culture of their forefathers had its roots in village south China (not the locus of classical culture) and, more importantly, their

Table 5.25

LANDED IMMIGRANTS FROM HONG KONG, MAINLAND CHINA AND TAIWAN

Year	Hong Kong	Mainland China	Taiwan
1971	5,009	47	761
1972	6,297	25	859
1973	14,662	60	1,372
1974	12,704	379	1,382
1975	11,132	903	1,131
1976	10,725	833	1,178
1977	6,371	798	899
1978	4,740	644	637
1979	5,966	2,085	707
1980	6,309	4,936	827
1981	6,451	6,551	834
1982	6,542	3,572	560
1983	6,710	2,217	570
1984	7,696	2,214	421
1985	7,380	1,883	536
1986	5,893	1,902	695
1987	16,170	2,625	1,467
1988	23,281	2,778	2,187
1989	19,908	4,430	3,388
1990	29,261	7,989	3,681
1991	22,340	13,915	4,488
1992	38,910	10,429	7,456
1993	36,570	9,466	9,867

Sources: Immigration statistics, 1971–93.

Table 5.26

BRITISH COLUMBIA AND ONTARIO AS INTENDED DESTINATIONS OF IMMIGRANTS FROM HONG KONG, MAINLAND CHINA AND TAIWAN		HONG KONG	CHINA	TAIWAN
1981	Ont	2,679	2,008	438
	BC	1,598	2,655	196
1982	Ont	2,816	1,269	278
	BC	1,622	1,218	115
1983	Ont	3,074	924	296
	BC	1,774	746	142
1984	Ont	3,919	941	199
	BC	1,767	682	110
1985	Ont	3,400	816	269
	BC	1,803	591	160
1986	Ont	2,796	824	276
	BC	1,207	553	222
1987	Ont	8,701	1,213	564
	BC	3,514	733	410
1988	Ont	13,519	1,345	697
	BC	5,185	758	887
1989	Ont	10,798	2,097	1,026
	BC	4,848	1,141	1,391
1990	Ont	16,143	3,692	991
	BC	7,714	1,424	1,699
1991	Ont	11,220	5,910	1,090
	BC	6,301	3,544	1,447
1992	Ont	18,364	5,125	1,624
	BC	10,051	2,231	4,131
1993	Ont	15,918	4,920	2,098
	BC	11,426	2,190	5,975

Sources: Immigration statistics, 1981–93.

historical legacies were made up primarily of Chinese experiences in Canada. Hence their enthusiasm for plumbing the memories of old-timers and for pursuing creative works in music, visual art and literature that reflected their condition in Canada. Theirs appears to be a sharper definition of what it means to be Chinese Canadian.

Developments since the 1980s

While the institutional framework of state multiculturalism and the 'mosaic' rhetoric of the 1970s have largely persisted, the Chinese minority has changed profoundly, mainly because of further immigration at a very high level. Especially since the second half of the 1980s, Chinese immigration has been phenomenal. Hong Kong has sent the most people, ranking as number one among 'countries' of last permanent residence for every year since 1987. Meanwhile, mainland China and Taiwan made their way into the top ten in 1989 and 1992 respectively.

With almost no exception, all existing centres of Chinese population have expanded appreciably. The 1991 census put the numbers of Chinese in Montreal, Edmonton and Calgary at well above 30,000, but these are disputed as conservative estimates. Greater Vancouver has anywhere between 250,000 to 350,000, and the figure for Toronto is even higher. In these two locations especially, Chinese homes and economic activities have spilled over significantly

Chinese Canadian ballerina.

into neighbouring and formerly suburban municipalities. In the Toronto area, for example, Scarborough, North York and nearby Mississauga are considered choice areas of settlement by the Chinese. In the Lower Mainland of British Columbia, Burnaby, Richmond and even places farther away from Vancouver City (like Coquitlam and Surrey) have all seen notable increases in Chinese activity. The new immigrants prefer these areas because they are not as congested as the traditional city centres and housing is often more affordable there.

The new arrivals are usually characterized as relatively skilled, educated, culturally sophisticated and wealthy. As a generalization, this characterization fits those from Hong Kong and Taiwan, and others of middle-class background from elsewhere, but it ill fits many of those from mainland China. As a matter of fact, the social and economic profiles of the new immigrants can range widely. Some are indeed very rich, entering Canada under the business immigration programme as investors and entrepreneurs, but many others are of much more modest means. Some are sufficiently bilingual to feel comfortable in an English-speaking environment, but others have limited English proficiency or none at all.

The immigrants' numbers, aggregate wealth and resources have resulted in a new pattern of Chinese participation in the Canadian economy. Ethnic Chinese are now represented in a whole range of professions and occupational groups. Long gone are the days of virtual confinement to the Chinatown labour market or certain economic niches. Yet, far from shrinking, the Chinese sub-economy has become vibrant and multi-level, so big are the Chinese populations in places like Toronto and Vancouver, and so great their need for ethnic foods and services. Not only are there Chinese restaurants, bakery shops, hair salons, pharmacies and grocery stores, there are real estate companies, supermarkets, accounting firms, car dealers, property developers and banks managed and staffed by Chinese and, of course, patronized by Chinese. To reach out to customers in this sizeable 'internal' ethnic Chinese market, large Canadian corporations like airlines and long-distance telephone companies have begun in the 1990s to advertise in the Chinese media.

Places where signs of Chinese success may be detected include the campus of the University of British Columbia, where several new buildings and even an entire programme (in the school of journalism) now bear the names of their Chinese benefactors. A former chancellor of the University, Robert Lee, is a second-generation local-born Chinese, a very enterprising businessman in real estate. His good friend and former partner, David Lam See-chai, was Lieutenant-Governor of British Columbia. Lam and his family moved to Vancouver from Hong Kong in 1967, made a fortune in real estate and became a highly respected philanthropist.

In addition, the Chinese are also playing an important role in linking Canada with the Asia Pacific economies. Among Canada's new immigrants and off-shore investors are ethnic Chinese with capital, entrepreneurial skills and transnational business connections. That Raymond Chan, the only Chinese MP (for Richmond) elected in October 1993, was offered a cabinet position with responsibility for Asia Pacific Affairs in the Liberal government of Jean Chrétien is perhaps indicative of Canada's recognition that it would be a good idea to forge links to the global Chinese diaspora and to transnational ethnic Chinese capital.

Globalization is a theme we will return to later on, but for the moment let us consider localization and integration, both important facets of the Chinese experience in Canada. Here the new migrants are doing the same thing as their predecessors to ease their settlement and adaptation, except that they are more resourceful than the previous generations and Canadian society is more hospitable to Asian migrants.

Chinese continue to show considerable enthusiasm for institutional completeness. There are new Chinese newspapers, namely *Sing Tao* (1983), *Ming Pao* (1993) and *World Journal* (1991), all with local editions serving the western and eastern parts of the country; in early 1997 these had a combined circulation of 70,000 in Vancouver alone. Chinese homes in major urban areas can tune in to more than one radio station and television channel for programmes in Cantonese and Mandarin. Organizations remain an important strategy of immigrant adaptation. Not surprisingly, people from Hong Kong, Taiwan and mainland China gravitate to their own groups. Such in-group clustering and division are evident in the development of Chinese-majority Lions Clubs and in the proliferation of ethnic Christian churches. A 1993 study has found 97 Chinese Protestant churches in Toronto. A large majority consists of pastoral staff and members almost entirely of Hong Kong background, while the congregations of the remaining few are speakers of Mandarin and other dialects originating from Taiwan and elsewhere.

The immigrants from Taiwan deserve some attention because hitherto Chinese immigration to Canada has been basically a Cantonese undertaking. The US government's special post-1949 relationship with Taipei and the brain drain of graduate students and intellectuals from there to America had produced a distinctive Mandarin-speaking segment in the American Chinese population by the 1960s. By contrast, Canada remained relatively unattractive to Taiwan immigrants until the late 1980s. Among destinations within Canada, these immigrants seem to prefer British Columbia to Ontario, perhaps because their arrival coincided with the economic recession in eastern Canada. By 1997, the estimated number of Taiwan immigrants in the Vancouver area had reached some 40,000–50,000. It is hardly surprising then that the Taiwan government chose to locate its quasi-diplomatic body, the Taipei Economic and Cultural Office, in Vancouver in 1991, whereas its Hong Kong counterpart, the Hong Kong Economic and Trade Office, was set up in the same year in Toronto.

One especially visible group supported by Taiwanese is the Buddhist Compassion Relief Tzu Chi Foundation of Canada; this has a local team of 2,500 volunteers running charities with budgets of millions of Canadian dollars. Another group is the Taiwanese Canadian Cultural Society, heard in 1997 to be raising money for a C$4 million building to house itself.

Also indicative of Chinese integration is their increased involvement in Canadian politics. Since Douglas Jung's successful bid for a parliamentary seat in 1957, a handful of ethnic Chinese have been elected to public office at the municipal level. Good examples include Peter Wing, the mayor of Kamloops, British Columbia, in 1966–71; and the legendary Ying Hope, who served on the Toronto City Council for 16 years (1969–85). Meanwhile, Art Lee was elected MP for Vancouver East in 1974 (serving until 1979); and in 1987, the first ethnic Chinese was voted into the provincial legislature in

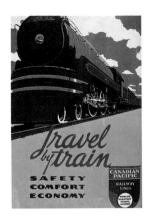

New immigrants differ radically from the earlier migrant labour that helped build the Canadian Pacific Railway.

Chinese Canadians march to protest discrimination.

Canadian stamp marks Chinese Year of the ox (1997) and bears character for 'good fortune.'

Ontario. All this notwithstanding, however, Chinese participation in Canadian electoral politics has been unremarkable. Chinese in Canada appeared not much affected by the 1960s Asian American movement across the border and the rise of ethnic political consciousness it entailed.

But signs of change may be detected in the 1990s, particularly in Toronto and Vancouver. Not only are there more Chinese candidates running for public office, Chinese involvement in Canadian party machineries and their attention to media coverage of elections and other public issues have risen noticeably. This was evident, for example, during the federal elections in 1993 and 1997. The 1997 election returned, for the first time, two ethnic Chinese (Raymond Chan and Sophia Leung), both from Greater Vancouver, to Parliament. Commentators take this to be a sign of Chinese resourcefulness – Chinese can more effectively pursue their self-interest through the ballot box now that there are more of them eligible for the vote. Others explain the trend by the new immigrants' background. Coming from places where political rights are restricted and democracy is slow to materialize, they are eager to claim political representation and fair treatment in their newly adopted country.

But even as they do this, powerful and seemingly countervailing forces complicate their adaptation to local society. The attachment to the place of former residence, whether Hong Kong or Taiwan, and the ability to keep alive trans-Pacific and transnational ties, appear to be at an all-time high in the history of the Chinese in Canada. Of course, this reflects the very recency of their arrival in Canada, but other factors, stemming from changing circumstances and global economic conditions, play a part. Some of the most recent Chinese immigrants, particularly those from Hong Kong and Taiwan, can perhaps be regarded as modern variants of the sojourner. Emigration for these people is not necessarily an irrevocable step and the option of return is seldom forfeited, especially as their financial means, no less than the convenience of modern jet travel and telecommunications, makes it easy to maintain long-distance contact.

Among those who had left Hong Kong out of a concern for the city's future under Chinese rule, a wait-and-see attitude prevails. A typical pattern is for the husband to return to his high-paying job or his business in his place of origin, leaving behind his wife and children in a female-headed household (see p 69). This so-called 'astronaut' phenomenon, with the husband flying frequently to visit his family in Canada, is a dramatic reversal of the 'bachelor society' of earlier Chinese migration history. The arrangement may seem eminently practical from a financial point of view, but its adverse effects on marital and parent-child relationships can scarcely be exaggerated.

The new immigrants' extra-local orientation comes also of the fact that many of them have found the business environment and employment situation uninviting compared to the familiar, vibrant and high-growth economies of East Asia. To minimize the economic sacrifices they have made in leaving for Canada, they quite understandably return to Hong Kong to work shortly after they have landed or obtained citizenship. Only time will tell whether this will be followed later by return

migration, but in 1997 the Canadian expatriate population in Hong Kong was estimated to be some 150,000 strong, a sizeable majority undoubtedly made up of the city's former residents.

Moreover, far from disapproving of it, the Canadian government seems to see the trend as fitting in nicely with its conscious reorientation to the Pacific Rim as a matter of the country's growth strategy in the 21st century. High-level official visits and trade delegations to the region abound. Other notable gestures, such as the hosting of Festival Canada in Hong Kong in 1991 and the reciprocal celebration of Festival Hong Kong the following year in five Canadian cities, all indicate official and corporate Canada's endorsement of strong ties with the region.

Hence, contemporary Chinese immigrant lives are shaped not just by the strategies of local adaptation in Canada but also by transnational links and practices that thrive on extra-local ties. For example, the Chinese-language media of the 1990s – characterized by rapid growth, increasing professionalism and energetic coverage of local issues and Canadian public affairs – keep Chinese abreast of what is happening or being debated in Hong Kong, Taiwan, China and the rest of the diaspora. Particularly noteworthy is the daily newspaper, Sing Tao, whose local edition is part of a global ethnic Chinese publishing concern producing local editions in Hong Kong, Southeast Asia, Australia and the United States.

International networking is also actively pursued by some Chinese organizations, especially churches and merchant groups. Reflecting the strategic importance of Vancouver in the Asia-Pacific and the growing economic power of the ethnic Chinese there, the Chinese Entrepreneurs Society of Canada played host to the Fourth World Chinese Entrepreneurs Convention in August 1997 (see p 87). Another transnational body already mentioned is the Tzu Chi Foundation; this runs charities on both sides of the Pacific and has sister organizations in at least 15 countries.

Finally, let us look at how the newest influx has been received by first, members of the longer-established Chinese minority and, secondly, the larger Canadian society. In neither case has adjustment been without friction, yet it has been relatively smooth considering how large the influx has been. The growth of Chinese economic power in Canada and the availability of many more ethnic goods and services have benefited the earlier Chinese arrivals. Their biggest complaint seems to be about the newcomers' perceived flamboyant lifestyle and their flaunting of wealth, their eagerness to re-create Hong Kong in their place of sojourn and their failure to show any genuine commitment to Canada.

Some issues have also been very divisive. One was the Tiananmen Incident of 1989. The public condemnation of Beijing by many new immigrants and their support for the cause of democracy in China ran up against the established interests of the pro-mainland China groups in Chinatown that had emerged out of the power struggle of the 1970s. At one point, the CCC in Vancouver became a battleground. During the election of the board of directors in 1993, the incumbents were challenged by a group consisting of many new immigrants, who contended that the programme the centre was running at the time was not representative of the diverse interests of the Chinese community. Unlike the battle over the Chinese Benevolent Association 15 years earlier, the contest this time was decided in favour of the incumbents, but such factionalism is likely to plague Chinese community politics for some time to come.

As for the mainstream society, reactions to immigration from Asia are by and large positive. It is often said that British Columbia was spared the recession eastern Canada suffered in the early 1990s thanks to the immigrants from Hong Kong and Taiwan and the considerable wealth they injected into the local economy. Heritage events and festival celebrations of Asian origin are likewise well-received. The Dragon Boat Festival,

launched in 1986 by the late Dr S. Wah Leung (founding dean of the Faculty of Dentistry at the University of British Columbia and long-time chairman of the CCC), has become a popular event enjoyed by Vancouverites of both Chinese and non-Chinese origin.

Yet there are sporadic outbursts of negative reactions which, if uncontained, may result in a more widespread and disruptive backlash. Immigrants from Asia, for example, have been blamed for driving up the value of real estate, and for building unneighbourly mansions, the so-called 'monster houses,' in the Vancouver area. In immigrant-heavy provinces like Ontario and British Columbia, complaints about newcomers straining the education system (especially the English-as-second-language programme) and other public resources are often heard. Such subtle and not so subtle immigrant-bashing has contributed to the rise of the Reform Party in the 1990s, a new factor in Canadian federal politics springing from British Columbia.

Chinese seem now to have entered a time in multicultural Canada when multiculturalism is being critically re-examined. The country's pluralistic ethos has allowed some members of the Chinese minority to emphasize their roots, some to display their ethnic and cultural consciousness, and others to simply enjoy the relaxed atmosphere. Is state multiculturalism producing the desired integration? Has it promoted sheer cultural permissiveness and condoned differences at the expense of national unity? Or is it just a benign variant of a racism that legislates 'otherness'? Whatever may be the form the public discourse takes to address these and other questions at the heart of Canadian identity, ethnic Chinese are not likely to be silent observers, let alone hapless victims.

Wing Chung Ng

Migrants re-create aspects of Hong Kong (left) in Vancouver (below).

THE CARIBBEAN

The Chinese community in the Caribbean is a product of two migrations: a 19th-century labour migration of semi-voluntary (indentured) workers – mainly for the sugar industry – and a 20th-century voluntary migration of working class, artisan and small trader elements. Because of the colonial and linguistic Balkanization of the islands (Spanish, English, Dutch, French), their actual histories have tended to be separate and isolated from one another, despite the existence of parallel social trends identifiable to an historian or region-wide social observer. This persistent complexity must be borne in mind in any discussion of the Chinese in the whole Caribbean region.

19th century and earlier

Chinese labourers first trickled into the Latin American region (New Spain and Peru) as early as the late 16th and early 17th centuries, a by-product of the Manila-Acapulco trade connection established after 1565 (see p 52). The writer Alexander von Humboldt, who travelled to Latin America between 1799 and 1804, certainly encountered Chinese in Cuba who apparently had gone there via the Manila galleons.

We do know that the first substantial settlement was an experimental import of 192 Chinese attempted in Trinidad in 1806, in the early years after the British takeover. The experiment was encouraged by British officials who had had experience of the Chinese migration to Penang in Malaya since the 1780s. Two hundred men were recruited in Macao, Penang and Calcutta, and were brought to Trinidad on a vessel of the East India Company called the *Fortitude*, along with a cargo of goods. They were dispersed over a number of sugar estates, and many remained on a small settlement just outside the capital Port of Spain where they became small cultivators and fishermen. Under the terms of their agreement, signed at Penang, they could claim free return passage to the East after a year. That was what most of them did, in fact. After three years, no more than 20 to 30 of the original 192 arrivals were still in Trinidad. These partly prospered and assimilated into ethnically and racially polyglot Trinidad society. Many also returned to the East at a later date. A similar experiment in Chinese migrant labour was also suggested for more developed Jamaica in the same decade, but that suggestion never bore fruit.

This isolated and failed experiment in Chinese settlement in the British West Indies before the end of slavery in 1834–38 was a foreshadow of the more organized attempts which would follow in the 1850s and 1860s, and had its roots in the same considerations: the gradual drying up, in the early 19th century, of traditional labour sources for the Caribbean sugar plantations with the abolition of the slave trade in 1807 and slavery itself in 1834–38. The unwillingness of the ex-slave population in the 1840s to confine themselves to labour on the sugar plantations, or to predictable wage levels or work performance even when they did remain on them, caused the idea of Chinese (and other) immigration to be revived.

The 1850s and 1860s were years of large-scale Chinese dispersal to various destinations in the expanding world economy of the mid-19th century, and Caribbean importers entered the scramble for labour very early on. The Spanish colony of Cuba began importing Chinese from Amoy in 1847. The British West Indies – mainly British Guiana (now Guyana) and Trinidad, marginally Jamaica – began again in the 1852–53 season. In contrast with the British colonies of the Caribbean, which were experiencing labour shortages owing to an African ex-slave exodus from the plantations, the Cubans (who did not abolish slavery until 1886) experienced labour shortages because of their overheated sugar economy, already the world's largest producer. They needed migrants to supplement, rather than substitute for, their black sugar workers. Processes similar to the British experience would engage the attention of the sugar planters of the French and Dutch West Indies after their own emancipations of 1848 and 1863.

In all these scenarios, the immigration experiment was multiracial in nature, beginning in fact with European labourers from various sources, such as England, Ireland, France, Germany, Malta and Portuguese Madeira. West Africans and black ex-slaves from other West Indian islands arrived as part of inter-island migration before the planters turned to the

Map 5.12

THE CARIBBEAN

UNITED STATES

BERMUDA

N

ATLANTIC OCEAN

Havana

CUBA

MEXICO

BELIZE

JAMAICA

GUADELOUPE

ANTIGUA

HONDURAS

MARTINIQUE

BARBADOS

Caribbean Sea

ARUBA

PACIFIC OCEAN

TRINIDAD

Arima

New Amsterdam

Port of Spain

San Fernando

Georgetown

PANAMA

GUYANA

SURINAM

Paramaribo

0   300   600 kilometres

0   300   600 miles

more fertile labour pools of the new Asian orbit of 19th-century imperialism – China, India and Annam (in present-day Vietnam) were sources for the French West Indies, while Indonesia was the recruiting ground in the case of Dutch Guiana, now Surinam. The voracious Cuban sugar industry relied on labour from Spain and the Canary Islands, Mayan Indians from Yucatan, as well as Chinese and a continuing flow of African slave labour until 1865.

Between 1847 and 1874, 347 vessels brought 125,000 Chinese to Cuba, while 51 vessels brought around 18,000 to the British West Indies between 1853 and 1884: 39 to British Guiana (13,539), eight to Trinidad (2,645), two to Jamaica (1,152), one to British Honduras (474), and one to Antigua (100). Most of the British West Indian vessels (all but four) arrived before 1866. Surinam also received about 2,640 between 1853 and 1874, and about 1,000 went to the French islands of Martinique and Guadeloupe in the 1860s. With the exception of about three vessels, all the migrants came under some form of indenture contract, even the women. The female contracts, however, were contracts of residence rather than contracts of labour as such – that is, fieldwork was optional (at least in the British colonies).

The major recruiting ground, as in most of the Americas, was within the classic sending districts of southern Guangdong: Siyi, Sanyi, Zhongshan and outlying districts (see Part I). The people were Punti and Hakka (see p 26 and 56). The Fujianese and Teochiu elements were there, especially in the earliest years, but as a small minority. The Cuban recruitment in the main was centred in Macao, the British recruited mainly out of Hong Kong and Canton, the Dutch out of Hong Kong and Java, while France obtained a few hundred labourers from the Shanghai as well as the Cantonese Pearl River Delta region. In 1860, there were almost as many Chinese in Cuba alone as there was in the United States (34,834 versus 34,933). A Cuban historian, Juan Pérez de la Riva, also claims that a few thousand Chinese were smuggled into Cuba from California via Mexico and New Orleans between 1865 and 1875.

The Chinese in the West Indies were employed on sugar plantations along with other free and indentured immigrants who arrived in the 1860s: Portuguese Madeirans, Indians and Black immigrants from the other West Indian islands and West Africa. They were widely dispersed in British Guiana and Trinidad: 116 out of 153 estates in the former, and 70–76 out of 153–58 estates in the latter. In Cuba, some estates had all Asian workers, but most were racially mixed. Chinese worked side by side with African slaves and with free labourers. A number of them also worked on coffee plantations. By the 1870s most Cuban plantations had a 60 per cent slave labour force, and a 40 per cent free and indentured labour force, the indentureds being mainly Chinese. In the 1860s and 1870s, the Chinese were about 2 to 3 per cent of the Cuban population.

The social conditions under which these indentured migrants laboured in the Caribbean varied widely. The Cuban immigration, like its Peruvian counterpart (see p 254), came in for the most criticism for the barbarity of both the recruitment and transportation process as well as subsequent plantation conditions. A Chinese appointed commission of enquiry, which reported in 1876 on Cuban conditions remains the classic exposé of life on the Caribbean sugar plantations for most of the indentureds. So harsh were Cuban work conditions that many indentureds ran away from the estates and, like the slaves, were hunted down and recaptured by *rancheadores* or professional slave-catchers.

Many Chinese also joined the anti-Spanish Cuban rebel force in the first War of Independence (1868–78), in exchange for promises of freedom from bondage. Conditions on the British Guiana plantations were also investigated in 1869–70 by a commission of enquiry. This effort produced an official report published as a parliamentary paper in 1871, as well as a dissenting independent publication by an ex-judge, Chief Justice Beaumont's *The New Slavery: An Account of the Indian and Chinese Immigrants in British Guiana*. While the Cuban atrocities were not duplicated in the British territories, these reports demonstrated that life was far from satisfactory for many of the Chinese who had migrated to the British colonies.

In addition to the harshness of plantation life, there was the restrictive atmosphere which prevented many from advancing their status in the post-indenture period. In Cuba, this was often due to conscious government attempts to coerce them into a state of permanent servitude, even after the end of their contracts. In British Guiana, it was due in the early years to monopoly competition from other ethnic groups like the Portuguese in the small-scale trading sector. Trinidad in the 1870s, probably because of its small population and relative underdevelopment, offered greater mobility opportunities to the ex-indentured Chinese, and indeed about 3,000 Chinese left Guiana and relocated mainly in Trinidad and Surinam in the 1870s and 1880s.

By the late 1880s, the Chinese in all the territories of the Caribbean region (except Cuba) had gravitated away from their original rural-labourer status to being artisans, fruit and vegetable cultivators, or small retail traders throughout their respective island homes. A few hundred had returned to China mainly at their own expense, since return passages were not included in their original indenture contracts. But most remained in the Caribbean, many (especially the Guiana-based) relocating to other territories. The China migration to the region continued, but as a trickle of individual voluntary migrants, often family members, although the last collective migration of contract workers actually arrived in Jamaica in 1884.

The 1891 census reports of Trinidad and British Guiana revealed the Chinese to be widely dispersed in their respective territories, urban- and rural-based, and mainly small shopkeepers. In British Guiana those living in rural districts outnumbered those living in the urban centres of Georgetown and New Amsterdam by 2,785 to 929 in a population reduced to 3,714. In Trinidad, the urban residents of Port of Spain, San Fernando and Arima were just under 50 per cent in a community of 1,006. This pattern continued until the 1946 census, when the urban percentage became quite marked in both territories, probably reflecting the impact of the new 20th-century migration, which will be discussed below.

The occupational transition from labourer to small trader was not quite as smooth in Cuba. The Cuban census of 1899 revealed that the Chinese population

Cartoons of Chinese pedlar (top) and cigar maker in Cuba.

had been reduced to only 14,863. The major occupations were still day labourers (8,033) and servants (2,754), followed by merchants (1,923). In 1919 under one third of a community of 16,146 (5,010) were based in Havana.

In the 19th century there were no exclusive Chinatowns comparable to those of California and New York, although parts of Georgetown in British Guiana – like Lombard Street in the depressed Werk-en-Rust district – contained clusters of influential and small Chinese businesses until a disastrous fire in 1913 led to a further dispersal. There was also a small settlement for ex-indentureds created in Hopetown, British Guiana, in the 1860s which functioned for a time as a rural Chinese ethnic settlement. Cuba in the 1860s also developed a small community of ex-indentureds on the outskirts of Havana in a district known as Zanja (the Ditch). Around this district a small Chinatown evolved, with restaurants and food shops, fruit and vegetable stores, and shops selling handicrafts, porcelain and traditional medicines. The community even established a Chinese theatre and three Chinese associations, one of them Hakka, and began publishing a newspaper in 1867 which has carried on into the 20th century.

Curiously, the most vibrant Chinese associations in British Guiana in the 19th century were centred around Christian Chinese worship, rather than traditional social activities. Anglican institutions, like the St Saviour's Church founded in the 1870s, for example, and numerous ethnic churches scattered throughout the countryside testified to the influence of Christianized Chinese who had come over in large numbers in the 1860s. Traditional community associations in both Guiana and Trinidad seemed to have become vibrant only in the early decades of the 20th century, with the second migration.

In the British and Dutch West Indies, a certain amount of family migration was encouraged. While it was not always as successful as planned, it did manage to introduce a certain amount of family stability among the migrants. There was also quite a lot of intermixing with the other racial groups (immigrants and blacks), leading to the emergence of a mixed Chinese community by the 1870s and 1880s. In Cuba, by contrast, where few women migrated, family life was almost non-existent in the 1870s, the 'bachelor society' reappearing in a plantation environment. The Cuba Commission of 1873 found two Chinese married to Chinese women, two married to white women, and about six married to mulattos and blacks. The Cuban census of 1877 enumerated 66 Chinese women in a Chinese population of 40,327.

Lyrics of Surinam national anthem rendered into Chinese.

20th century

The early years of the 20th century saw a new wave of migrants entering the Caribbean region. In the British and Dutch territories, they were mainly voluntary artisans and small traders responding to internal domestic turmoil in China just before and after the fall of the Qing dynasty in 1911, and probably to difficulties of access to traditional outlets like the United States since the exclusion laws of 1882 and after (see p 262).

Between 1900 and 1940, perhaps over 7,000 arrived in these colonies. The Chinese population of Surinam rose from 784 in 1920 to 2,293 in 1941; that of Jamaica from 2,111 in 1911 to 6,879 in 1943. The foreign-born Chinese alone of Trinidad rose from 832 in 1901 to 2,366 in 1946. Chinese numbers in British Guiana rose from 2,622 in 1911 to 3,567 in 1946, although there is evidence that the foreign-born component actually declined, and that Georgetown was rather a major transit point to other destinations, like Trinidad and Surinam. Many migrants actually arrived by a circuitous route, often residing in one or another American destination (including western Canada and Latin America) before eventually settling in their final island destination. There are many family stories still alive about the travels of these original migrants.

Noticeable in the new migration was the importance of new destinations like Jamaica, which had played a somewhat low-key role in the indenture period. (There was also a sizeable simultaneous migration to Panama). Cuba also lifted its earlier bans on Chinese migration imposed in 1874 and 1898 in order to accommodate a special influx of agricultural workers between 1917 and 1921, recruited to fill wartime labour shortages in the sugar industry. Altogether 12,537 entered under these arrangements, before restrictions were again imposed. Even so, lax law enforcement allowed another 5,000 to enter the island in the 1920s and 1930s, many of them women. By 1944, Cuba's 18,500 Chinese, while dispersed throughout the island, were 60 per cent urban, and 50 per cent Havana-based.

The growth of the Caribbean Chinese community from the 1940s to the 1990s is a unique variant of the Americanization process. Given the wide diversity of colonial and national jurisdictions under which they have found themselves evolving, this process has been many-layered, and often compartmentalized. There are social experiences among them that are hemispheric, many that are regional, and many that are island or colony-specific.

The majority of the Chinese in the 1990s are the descendants of the second wave of migrants in the 1920s and 1930s. There are many old families, especially among the Guyana-based or Guyana-derived, who can trace their origins back to a late-period indentured immigrant, but the phenomenon is not widespread, and collective memories have dimmed. Certainly, at the time of the 1946 censuses, the small professional class and many of the established large merchants in each territory would have been descended from the earlier indentureds, but the lines between 'old' and 'new' Chinese soon became blurred. The connection to the mid-19th century for many today is largely one of historical origins, for without a doubt both the first and second migrant waves originated in the same cluster of 'Cantonese' districts (or counties) in southern Guangdong which provided the human resource base for most of the Western Hemisphere Chinese diaspora, and a large portion of the worldwide diaspora.

After the 1940s, migration from Asia was reduced to a small, persistent (and unquantifiable) trickle somewhat similar to the migrations of the 1880s and 1890s. The 50-year period since then has therefore been years of assimilation and adjustment to their new host societies. Unlike the United States, where the development of the Chinese began in urban working-class ghettoes, and where their social transition and subsequent achievements have paralleled the 'immigrant' and specifically the 'minority' mobility story, the Chinese in the Caribbean have followed the 'minority middleman' path of development familiar to many Third World societies – that is, they have been a residentially dispersed, upwardly mobile, ethnically distinct, small and large merchant (and later professional) class, operating within the interstices of dependent colonial economies where the social and racial lines between the established élites and the working mass were clearly drawn long before their own arrival.

While the pace of their upward mobility has varied from territory to territory, the Chinese in the British and Dutch Caribbean – no more than 1 per cent of their host societies – are largely recognized as a successful upper-middle class, their members based not only in the traditional retail grocery trades but more in the import, service, manufacturing and professional sectors, their urban and suburban elements a distinctive subsector of the economic élite. In Cuba they have always remained a lower middle-class commercial sector. In the early 1950s, before the Cuban Revolution, when they were at the peak of their development, they controlled about 3,500 commercial enterprises, most of them small retail food stores, fruit and vegetable stores, laundries and restaurants, but unlike islands like Jamaica and to a certain extent Trinidad, they held no major monopoly in any sector.

Within the specific local and regional context, the pertinent questions here would be to what extent they have remained foreign immigrant communities, to what extent distinctive national ethnic minorities in post-colonial nation-states, to what extent indistinguishable socially and culturally from the mass of their fellow citizens. It would be accurate to say that all three trends are present in the Chinese community. The Chinese cultural connection has never been severed, but assimilation and local preoccupations have led to this community developing largely within the Western-colonial mould.

There are several generational traditions alive within families. The foreign-born small merchant is still here, side by side with Chinese who are about four generations removed from the original China contact. Chinese traditions have lived on in an eclectic manner, although Chinese ethnic distinctiveness still continues to persist, with varying degrees of approval from the broad majority culture. A substantial biological and cultural assimilation into the broad Caribbean Creole mainstream also exists side by side with these other trends. Many of these persons are counted in the census reports as 'mixed,' although self-identification and physical appearance can often lead to many also being included as 'Chinese.' Some of the older census reports even classify them as a distinct category.

The fate of the language best highlights the point. Chinese language of any variant is virtually non-existent, except among the foreign-born. While the Chinese script continues to flourish in small community news sheets, publications and association records (stronger in some territories than others), this is virtually confined to the foreign-born and elderly. Valiant attempts over time by the community associations to promote language schools and disseminate classical cultural traditions among the young have been partially successful only on the latter front.

Advertisement of Sheraton Chinese Restaurant in Surinam (top). Community gathering of the China Society in Trinidad.

This is the inevitable consequence of physical and cultural distance from China, the imperatives of functioning in a multiracial Westernized colonial and post-colonial environment, the educational system, broad social assimilation pressures from the host society (occasionally encouraged by zealous post-colonial regimes), and of course, individual choice by the young Chinese themselves as they assess the utility of the language (and other traditions) in a Western-American environment. On the other hand, Chinese cuisine (popular and gourmet) continues to flourish in all the territories, and is widely patronized by non-Chinese. Even among migrant communities like the Cuban Americans, there are to be found numerous Chinese-Cuban restaurants catering to these communities by Cuban Chinese who have themselves migrated to the USA.

The activities of community associations also illustrate the eclectic and transitional nature of the Chinese assimilation process. Three types of Chinese community association coexist in the region. There are the classic migrant place-of-origin associations found in all diaspora communities; there are those where origin-based organizations are fused into some kind of all-Chinese association; and there are those which are Chinese in form but not necessarily in content – that is, in their social and

Fruit and vegetable stall in Havana.

Table 5.27

CHINA-BORN IMMIGRANTS IN THE BRITISH CARIBBEAN

	1861	1871	1881	1891	1911	1921	1931	1946
B.Guiana	2,629	6,295	4,393	2,475	634	376	423	548
B.Honduras	1	133	68	52	27	12	na	42
Antigua	—	—	—	111	13	4	na	—
Trinidad	461	1,400	1,266	1,006	1,113	1,334	2,027	2,366
Jamaica	—	—	140	347	1,646	2,413	na	2,818
All Others	—	—	—	—	—	—	—	—
Total	3,091	7,828	5,867	3,991	3,433	4,139	na	5,774

Source: West Indian Census Report, 1946 (with corrections of 1946 figures).

Table 5.28

CHINESE COMMUNITIES (FOREIGN AND LOCAL-BORN) IN CARIBBEAN REGION

	1946	1960	1970	1980	1990
Jamaica	6,879	10,267	11,781	5,320	5,372
Trinidad	5,641	8,361	7,962	5,562	4,314
Guyana	3,567	4,074	3,402	1,842	1,338
Surinam	2,384	5,339	6,029	5,492	3,048
Belize	—	na	na	214	748
Cuba	15,822	11,834	5,892	na	7,000

These figures refer mainly to ethnically homogeneous Chinese, local and China-born. The large mixed Chinese populations in all the territories are sometimes enumerated as a distinct group, sometimes classified with the 'Mixed' category, and often also counted as Chinese.
Jamaica census dates are 1943, 1982, 1991. Surinam census dates are 1950, 1964, 1972, 1994. Cuba figures for 1946 and 1960 are actually for 1943 and 1953. The 1994 data are estimates limited to the urban areas of Paramaribo and Wanica, which contain 60 per cent of the Surinamese population.
Sources: Census data.

recreational observations. These latter include not only social clubs and associations, but also ethnic Christian churches or denominations.

Trinidad is strong on the first type of association, and all have associations of the second and third types. In Trinidad , there are the Taishan, San Wui (Xinhui), Sam Yup (Sanyi), Chungshan (Zhongshan), and Fui Toong On (Hui-Dong-An) associations (the last a Hakka association originating with migrants from Huiyang, Dongguan and Baoan). There is also the umbrella China Society, a loose federation of all the above. Cuba's Chinese also had many vigorous native-place associations in the downtown Havana Chinatown area in the 1950s, some of which may still survive today. The all-Chinese associations include two Hakka-dominated associations, Kong Ngie Tong Sang (Guangyi Tang Sheng) in Surinam and the Chinese Benevolent Association in Jamaica, plus the Chinese Association in Guyana. They include also Cuba's Casino Chung Wah (Zhonghua) Society, whose 3,000-plus members (one-fifth China-born) celebrated the association's centennial in 1993.

Of the Westernized recreational associations, there is a Chinese Association (mainly for the local-born) in Trinidad. And there is Guyana's distinct tradition of Chinese Christian church communities, which dates back to the 19th century. In Guyana there is even a Chinese freemasonry, centred around the Silent Temple Lodge, which was founded in 1907 after some of the Chinese business leaders were refused admission into the orthodox circles of freemasonry in the colony. Most of these clubs have sponsored modest Chinese-language publications and newspapers over the years, which circulate largely inside the foreign-born community and in the diaspora, mainly in the US, Canada, Hong Kong and Singapore.

Beyond all this, there is the reality that those Chinese who do participate in the life of these associations are a minority of their own communities. To the extent that most culture in the Caribbean is strongly impacted upon by colonial Westernization (and lately, Americanization)

biases, we can say that the Chinese too are a part of that process, assimilating and interpreting these broader influences in their own way. Thus it should come as no surprise that, despite the persistence over the years of the China influence in all its various expressions – including the return migration, education and relocation of many to China or Hong Kong – the major shaping influence in language and lifestyle, commerce and travel, even citizen loyalty, has been more the respective metropolitan power (or the nationalist alternative) than the ancestral homeland.

This phenomenon was already marked among the descendants of the indentureds as early as the 1900s, but has continued with the second-wave migrants. The fact of being an upwardly mobile ethnic minority, as opposed to a restricted or ghettoized working-class community, has encouraged the process. The most famous people produced by Caribbean Chinese have demonstrated this eclectic mingling of Western, Chinese and Caribbean traditions. There was the world famous Cuban artist Wifredo Lam, whose paintings have been exhibited in Paris and New York, with their Afro-Cuban and modernist motifs. There was the Trinidadian lawyer Eugene Chen (see box). There is the Guyanese classical Western concert pianist Ray Luck.

One important event which has silently impacted on Chinese attitudes since the 1960s, but particularly in the 1970s and 1980s, has been the rise of Left nationalist movements throughout the region, from the 1959 Revolution in Cuba at one end of the region all the way across to the events in Dutch Surinam in the 1980s. Between these dates, the British islands also experienced similar events, from the civil unrest and Burnham period in Guyana to the Williams (and anti-Williams) movements in Trinidad and the Manley period in Jamaica.

Even though the Chinese were nowhere singled out for special attention – though in Cuba the sweeping nationalization of small businesses impacted negatively on Chinese commerce – one consequence of all these related but separate developments in each territory has been a kind of small exodus of many Chinese businessmen and professionals out of the Caribbean towards new locations, like the United States and Canada (and the Netherlands in the case of Surinam). This has resulted in a marked numerical decline in most of these communities since the 1960s. Far from growing, these communities are all manifesting signs of transition. Cuba's Chinese community has dropped from 16,000 in the 1950s to around 7,000 in the 1990s, most members relocating to Florida, New Jersey and New York along with other Cuban exiles. Guyana's Chinese declined from 4,074 in 1960 to 1,338 in 1990; Jamaica's from 11,781 in 1970 to 5,372 in 1990; Trinidad's from 8,361 in 1960 to 4,314 in 1990; Surinam's from 6,029 in 1970 to less than 3,500 in 1990.

Given their social positions as partially assimilated 'middleman minorities' in the racial hierarchies of Caribbean societies, a certain amount of ethnic insecurity was inevitable during a period of Left nationalism (a period which seems to have lasted until the late 1980s, as in most of the post-colonial Third World). However, much of this relocation, especially from the British West Indies, has also had non-political roots. It has been the natural result of growing economic affluence and the attraction of the metropolitan environment to Chinese and non-Chinese alike in the Caribbean. In most cases, moreover, as with their fellow nationals, the relocation has not been absolute, because there continues to be a duality of place loyalty among most migrants, combined with a lot of travel between the new metropolitan locations (mainly Florida or Ontario) and the individual islands, where many family members continue to reside and do business.

Information about post-revolutionary Cuban Chinese is more difficult to come by, but there is evidence that island community life has dwindled somewhat from its former vibrancy, in part because of the heavy migration, in part also because of the ongoing cultural assimilation which has always been a strong feature of Cuban Chinese life. Travel between the metropolis and Cuba is also restricted, as it is for most Cubans. However, policy reversals since 1994 by the Cuban government towards small business, plus the growing diplomatic warming towards China, has contributed to a small economic and cultural revival of Havana's Chinatown district.

An interesting new development in the 1990s has been the growth of the tiny Chinese communities of some of the smaller Caribbean islands. Census statistics record very small but noticeable increases in countries like Belize, Aruba and Barbados. It is still too early to draw firm conclusions about these trends.

Walton Look Lai

'The Jungle' by Wifredo Lam, 1943. Gouache on paper mounted on canvas, 239.4 x 229.4 cm.

EUGENE CHEN

Born in Trinidad, Eugene Bernard Acham (1878–1944), better known as Eugene Chen, was a cocoa estate owner who went to China to join the Chinese nationalist movement as a protégé of Sun Yat-sen. A trained lawyer, he was appointed legal consultant to the Chinese Ministry of Communications in 1912, and later the editor of the English-language *Peking Gazette*. In 1917,

he was arrested for publishing revelations about the secret negotiations between the then Chinese Premier Duan Qirui and an expansionist Japan. Upon his release, he joined the new government of Sun Yat-sen, whose foreign affairs adviser and personal secretary he became.

A member of the Central Executive Committee of the Kuomintang, he was identified with the progressive wing of the party, of whose shortlived Canton- and Wuhan-based governments he was foreign minister. Following Chiang Kai-shek's coup against the Left in 1927, he became a major anti-Chiang figure. In 1933, he was expelled from the Kuomintang for participating in an anti-Chiang revolt in Fujian. Retirement to Europe was followed in 1938 by a sojourn in Hong Kong. Detained during the Japanese occupation of the colony, Chen was taken to Shanghai in 1942. Still under house arrest, he died of heart disease at the age of 66. The Chinese Communists who came to power in 1949 honoured him by transferring his ashes to Beijing's cemetery of the heroes of the revolution and erecting a memorial to his memory.

By his first wife, Agatha Ganteaume, who was of black-French descent, he had four children. After she died, he married the painter Georgette Chen (see p 130).

Lim Bee Leng

(Box) Eugene Chen painted by his wife Georgette. Oil on canvas, 46 x 38 cm.

SPANISH AMERICA

THE PRE-WORLD WAR II PERIOD

Chinese migration to the Spanish-speaking countries of Latin America (for names see table 5.29, p 258) before World War II occurred in two movements: a massive agricultural labour migration in the second half of the 19th century – the so-called coolie trade, known as *la trata amarilla* or 'yellow traffic' in Spanish – involving almost exclusively men. This was followed by a period of free immigration also dominated by single men, lasting until the Depression of the 1930s. By then, the Chinese population had become largely urban and commercial, most establishing residence and businesses in national and provincial capitals, as well as in mining and railroad towns and port cities.

This second flow paralleled the period of Chinese

exclusion in the United States, and took place in spite of the Chinese immigration restrictions passed by many Latin American countries. During this period, Mexico also witnessed severe anti-Chinese persecution resulting in the expropriation of Chinese businesses and properties as well as in outright expulsion. After World War II, Chinese immigration would be revived, although it never came close to the high levels of the 19th century. Among countries in Spanish America, Cuba, Peru and Mexico host the largest Chinese populations (for Cuba see Part V: The Caribbean).

Peru

A harsh fate awaited the Chinese in mid-19th century Peru, where slavery was abolished in 1854, and where a new coastal economy, comprising guano and sugar, attracted considerable foreign investment. The guano and sugar enterprises, both labour-intensive, went in search of cheap labour overseas. Following the example of British planters in the West Indies and Mauritius, and the sugar planters in Cuba, Peruvians turned to the importation of Chinese contract labourers or coolies. From 1849 to 1874, almost 100,000 coolies were transported across the Pacific Ocean to Peru. Finally, international outcry against this brutal human traffic abruptly terminated it in 1874, with the last contracts expiring by the 1880s.

Most Chinese worked on sugar plantations, but thousands also helped build the Andean railroad, and toiled and died in the extremely harsh conditions of the offshore guano mines south of Lima. Others were engaged in a variety of occupations – as domestic servants, artisans, unskilled labourers – in Lima, Callao and other towns. By the late 1860s, a few who had completed their contracts began entering commerce.

The coolies were legally bound to eight years' servitude. From the beginning, and deteriorating with time, the coolies were treated in exactly the same way as the African slaves before them, sometimes even worse. Upon arrival in Lima, they were physically examined in a humiliating way, then auctioned. On the plantations, they were housed in long slave quarters. The administrators and overseers resorted to the same methods of control and physical punishment as they had used with slaves – stocks and metal bars, leg chains or shackles, flogging, jails and lockups at night, even executions. Wages were not paid or were deducted for arbitrary reasons. Food and clothing were often not supplied, forcing the coolies to use their meagre savings to supplement inadequate provisions. The eight years were frequently forcibly extended on the grounds that the coolie, through prolonged illness or flight, owed time or money that had to be paid off with service. The result was that the coolies had very little to show for their years of bitter labour.

Map 5.13

The masters were seldom censured for the massive and flagrant violation of their obligations. The worst offenders were the sugar plantation owners and their surrogates, for on the large, often geographically isolated estates, their authority was absolute in the politically still disorganized environment of 19th-century Peru.

For their part, the coolies responded to the harshness and arbitrariness of the plantation regime much as slaves did before them. They rebelled, individually or collectively; they protested to the authorities whenever possible although usually to little avail; they ran away; they committed suicide. When, during the War of the Pacific (1879–82), the invading Chilean army sacked a number of coastal haciendas, they even allied with the invaders in return for their personal freedom.

They had practically no women among them. Until they left the plantations, few had the opportunity to form normal personal and family relationships. Diseases bred and spread among them, cramped and locked up as they were at night in their quarters. Opium smoking became one way to dull the pain. The Peruvian government actually encouraged the habit – among other effects, it inhibited collective resistance – by allowing its importation and sale on the plantations.

In one important respect, however, the coolies were more fortunate than the slaves before them. Should they survive their eight-year servitude, they did regain their freedom, at which time they had certain alternatives. Many chose to recontract themselves for another short term, from six months to no more than two years, usually with the same master. The practice was a means for planters to retain valuable workers on their estates, and a way for the coolies to accumulate more savings, leave the estate for good and move to a nearby town or a large urban area to enter commerce or take up a trade.

Around 1880, another form of recontracting appeared in Peru. Instead of individual recontracting agreements made between the planter and the coolie, the new system utilized a Chinese labour contractor who signed up and organized free Chinese into labour gangs (reminiscent of similar arrangements found in California, Baja California Norte, Cuba and Southeast Asia). This entire group was then hired out to a plantation for a specified period of time or for a specific piece of work. The Chinese contractor negotiated all the terms of work for his squad and handled all aspects of employment for the workers, including obtaining the advances from the planters, handing out tools, arranging for lodging and food, maintaining discipline, control and supervision. An important incentive to encourage enterprising Chinese to become contractors was concessions given them by large planters to operate stores on the estates that catered to the needs of the labour gangs.

The coolies (under original contracts or recontracted) liberated by the Chilean army during the War of the Pacific were eagerly hired as wage workers by other *hacendados* (landowners), usually by agreement with a Chinese contractor. Eventually, the contracting system gave way to a free or wage labour system, at first involving many Chinese until these died or moved out of agriculture into commerce and other urban occupations. They were succeeded by Peruvian highlanders contracted by labour brokers emulating the Chinese example.

An official inspection of the coastal provinces in 1887 located 8,503 Chinese, of whom the vast majority were ex-coolies, now free, who worked in agriculture, and who received the same wages and rations as other workers. Another 1,182 Chinese on the coast were individually recontracted, and only 838 were tied to a labour contractor. There were also 40 sharecroppers, 193 lessees, five shopkeepers and innkeepers. The commission located even one ex-coolie who had become an *hacendado* himself, and who hired 80 to 90 free Chinese to work for him.

Although the major imprint of the Chinese in Peru was unquestionably on the coastal export economy (guano and sugar) and later, in retail commercial development, they had also ventured into the largely Indian sierra as well as joined the pioneer efforts into the Peruvian Amazon. It is their contribution to Amazon settlement and resource development that the Chinese role has been least known and most neglected, deliberately suppressed in official Peruvian historiography owing to a prevailing 19th-century Peruvian attitude, as a 1983 study by Isabel Lausent suggests, that only European pioneers were capable of bringing civilization to the Amazonian jungle.

As early as 1873, Chinese colonies were established in the Amazon. By the end of the century, Chinese had built colonies in not only major towns such as Iquitos, Huánuco, Chanchamayo and Pucallpa, but scattered all over the Amazon region. Some of these first pioneers and settlers very likely were fugitives from coastal masters, joined later by coolies who had completed their contracts, and free immigrants.

These early colonies were small – around 100 persons each – but prosperous. They assumed a significance beyond their size in the sparsely populated, underdeveloped region. The Chinese acquired both urban lots and rural land; besides manufacturing basic consumer items, they grew food to provision the towns. In the towns and regional markets, as itinerant pedlars (muleteers) and shopkeepers, they not only sold their own cultivated produce (rice, and also beans, peanuts, sugar cane) and manufactured goods (clothing and shoes), but took on an intermediary role in the exchange of natural, artisanal and agricultural products between the highland and the jungle. When cash was not available, they bartered.

In these activities, they covered a great deal of territory, occasionally suffered Indian attacks, and also became much sought after as expeditionary guides and interpreters. Not only did they adapt with alacrity and facility to the Amazon environment, but as early pioneers and trailblazers they acted as cultural brokers between the Indian natives on the one hand and the Peruvian and European settlers on the other.

Rubber and gold in Loreto province, with its capital in Iquitos on the Amazon River, attracted Chinese from all over Peru, directly from China and from California. They spread out all over the vast jungle to tap the wild rubber trees; they washed for gold in the tributary rivers; and they established themselves in business in Iquitos. By 1899, the Chinese community of Iquitos, numbering 346, was the largest of the many foreign groups in that most cosmopolitan of Peruvian cities, isolated to be sure from the national capital of Lima, but well connected to Europe, the US and especially Brazil.

Mexico

For three centuries, the Manila galleon trade linked New Spain, now Mexico, to the East, whose luxury goods were exchanged for Mexican silver (see p 52). Not long after the trade was established, the first Asian colony in the Americas appeared. In 1635, a group of Spanish barbers in Mexico City complained about excessive competition from Chinese barbers in that colonial capital city. They petitioned the viceroy to remove these bothersome Asian barbers to special quarters on the outskirts of town so that they, the Spaniards, would not have to compete with the *chinos de Manila* for business. Although this early settlement of Chinese never grew into a large community during the colonial period, it did leave legacies now firmly entrenched in Mexican folklore. Notable among of these is the embroidered blouse known popularly as the *china poblana*, worn by Mexican women in central Mexico.

Colonial Mexico was a self-conscious, multi-ethnic society of whites, Indians and blacks, and all possible mixtures of the three races. Each racial combination had its own designation, from the familiar mestizo (white-Indian) and mulato (white-black) to at least 14 others. The lighter the skin, the more socially desirable. Interestingly, the word 'chino,' or Chinese, was sometimes used for the offspring of a mulato and an Indian woman – that is, a darker product, ranking 11th on a scale of 14. The concept of *chino*, it would seem, assumed particularly derogatory overtones.

With the ascension to national political power of General Porfirio Díaz in 1876, Mexico embarked on a course of rapid economic growth predicated upon foreign money, expertise and markets. The cost, however, was dictatorship and foreign immigration. Significant numbers of Chinese, chiefly young men, arrived between the 1880s and early 20th century. Most of them were concentrated in the northwest, bordering the Pacific.

The immigration accelerated after 1882, when the United States passed its first anti-Chinese exclusion act and Mexico became an attractive alternative (see p 262). Entering through the Pacific coast ports of Mazatlán and Guaymas, the Chinese spread themselves throughout Mexico, but primarily to the northern border states, no

Manila galleon brings men and goods from China to New Spain.

doubt attracted there by their proximity to the United States. However, an initial tendency to cross illicitly into the US abated, as they perceived and moved swiftly into a widening economic space in the rapidly developing frontier region, where the bulk of US investment was concentrated.

Mexico's Chinese population grew spectacularly from a little under 3,000 in 1910 to more than 24,000 in 1927, the growth owed primarily to continuous immigration from China rather than to natural reproduction within Mexico. By the same token, the gradual cessation of immigration explains the sharp demographic drop from 1927 to the 17,865 noted in 1930.

Very few Chinese women accompanied their menfolk overseas. However, Chinese men did form families with local women, usually of the common-law type. It is not known exactly how the mestizo offspring of these mixed unions were counted in the censuses. If tradition prevailed, whether the offspring were regarded as Mexicans or Chinese probably depended on whether they lived with their fathers (or both parents) and whether their fathers recognized their paternity. These children were most likely counted as Chinese, as were often the Mexican women who married Chinese men.

Unlike the Chinese in the American West, those in northern Mexico did not take up labouring jobs, which were filled by Mexicans, but rather entered commerce as small independent entrepreneurs, and occasionally in partnership with American mine and railroad owners in the company towns. Chinese shopkeepers quickly followed the trail of Yankee capital.

Nowhere was this pattern clearer than in the northwestern state of Sonora, which bordered the then territory of Arizona. Astutely avoiding competition with established European and Mexican merchants in old towns such as Guaymas and Hermosillo (the state capital), the Chinese ventured into some remote villages of the interior, but mostly to new working-class settlements that sprang up along railroad and mining sites; and later, to modern agricultural colonies. These were the new towns that grew in the wake of foreign, mainly US, investment in northern Mexico during the last quarter of the 19th century. The Chinese were often the first *comerciantes* to reach these new localities, thus the first shopkeepers to cater to the needs of the workers.

Within two generations, they had succeeded in monopolizing the small commercial sector of the state's economy. Far from being a hindrance, the Mexican Revolution of 1910–17 actually furthered their commercial growth in several ways. First, with most Mexicans engaged in civil conflicts, the revolution retarded the emergence of Mexican small businesses to compete with the Chinese. Second, even during these turbulent times, towns, including mining and railroad centres that continued to operate, needed to be supplied with goods and services.

Third, the various revolutionary armies needed to be provisioned. As aliens, the Chinese remained officially 'neutral' and willing to do business with all revolutionary factions. Although some of the sales were on 'forced loan' bases, whereby Chinese merchants were given a credit slip for future payment by revolutionary generals who commandeered goods and supplies, the Chinese considered these inconveniences to be part of the cost of doing business in the midst of chaos. Fourth, further solidifying the Chinese position in Sonoran commerce was the weakening of traditional trading links between Mexico and Europe during World War I, which coincided with the Mexican Revolution. Some of the departed German, French and Spanish commercial houses were replaced by Chinese firms, which turned to US suppliers, thereby forging new Mexican-US commercial ties. This in turn strengthened the existing symbiotic relationship between Chinese merchants and US interests in Sonora, and explains the actions frequently taken by US consuls to protect Chinese persons and businesses when they came under violent attacks by Mexicans.

Among the young, penniless Chinese arrivals was a small number of Chinese capitalists who came to set up merchant houses in Guaymas and Hermosillo, with branches in important new towns such as Magdalena along the Sonoran Railroad, and Cananea of the Greene Consolidated Copper Company. In some cases, they added factories next to the stores to manufacture cheap shoes and clothing. These large merchants hired almost exclusively fellow Chinese in the stores and factories. They also, significantly, extended goods on credit to enterprising but poor compatriots to peddle their wares in small, remote mining towns, and to set up new stores throughout the state.

By the 20th century, they controlled the trade in groceries, dry goods and general merchandise. Some Chinese engaged in market gardening on land they leased, then carted the fruits and vegetables to local markets, which were often dominated by Chinese-owned stalls. Other Chinese worked as artisans and small-scale manufacturers, producing shoes, clothing, brooms, *masa* (the corn dough used for making tortillas), pasta and sweets. In these multiple ways, the Chinese succeeded in creating a production, purchasing, supply and distribution network among themselves, a closed system with some clear characteristics of vertical integration that, in effect, became the state's first commercial infrastructure. This remarkable system endured until the early 1930s, when most of the Chinese were expelled from Sonora and their businesses nationalized.

Even with the sharp decline in their population, the Chinese maintained a solid hold on local small businesses throughout the state. Only a handful of traditional communities in Ures, Altar and Sahuaripa districts had no Chinese presence. What is important is that these towns had *probably no stores whatsoever*. In other remote communities with only one or a few commercial outlets, they were all Chinese-owned and run. Even more significant, the commerce of certain mining towns was also exclusively in Chinese hands. The same was true for rapidly developing commercial agricultural towns in the southern part of the state.

The Chinese monopoly was of the small commercial sector. It was not particularly alarming to the large Mexican capitalists who controlled the large commercial/industrial sector of the economy, but it would provide fodder for the average Mexican who could, and did, aspire to the small commercial sector that was firmly in Chinese hands. The ubiquitous nature of these Chinese *comerciantes* became a thorn on the side of middle- and working-class Mexicans.

Anti-Chinese persecution in Sonora first surfaced at the turn of the 20th century. It intensified during the violent years of the Mexican Revolution, continued sporadically during the post-revolutionary period of the 1920s, and culminated in the expulsion of the Chinese population in 1931 with the nationalization of local commerce.

Anti-Chinese attitudes prevalent in the 1880s in California and elsewhere in the US began filtering into Mexico. The Chinese, modest in fact but prosperous in comparison to ordinary Sonorans still struggling to improve their lives well after the Revolution that many of them fought in the name of social justice, reminded the locals just how much foreigners had historically controlled their destiny, and how much farther they would have to go to reclaim Mexico for the Mexicans. Understandably so, Mexican workers, landless peasants and their families formed the backbone of the campaign to remove the Chinese from their midst, dragging along a state and national political leadership that reluctantly gave in for political reasons.

Events in the Chinese community itself provided Sonorans with an excuse to organize anti-Chinese campaigns in 1922 and again in 1924–25. Rival Chinese political camps – the Kuomintang, represented by members of the Fraternal Union in Sonora, and the Chee Kung Tong (Zhigong Tang), with a more conservative political orientation – fought out their differences on Mexican soil. The 'tong wars', as these shoot-outs were called, provided a handy pretext for the Sonoran government to round up some 300 Chinese for deportation. In the event only a handful of the known leaders were deported. US consuls stepped forward to protect the Chinese: in the 1920s Chinese businessmen had become the major clients of American exporters of the Mexican West Coast.

Sonorans launched their final and successful campaign in 1929 during the Depression. Massive demonstrations, terrorization of Chinese shopkeepers, the invoking of the so-called '80 per cent labour law' stipulating that the work force of all foreign enterprises must be at least eight-tenths Mexican, a ban on Chinese-Mexican marriages – all these forms of persecution drove the Chinese to admit defeat in 1931 and to announce plans to quit the state.

Where did the expelled Chinese go? It is hard to trace their steps. Some tried to enter the US surreptitiously; some returned to China; and others resettled in more hospitable parts of Mexico, notably Baja California Norte, Mexico's last frontier.

The early development of Baja California Norte, especially the Mexicali Valley, was closely tied to the California-Mexico Land and Cattle Company and its parent company, the Colorado River Land Company. Its owners were the southern California tycoons and *Los Angeles Times* publishers Harrison Otis and his son-in-law, Harry Chandler. In deciding on extensive cotton cultivation for their land, Otis and Chandler chose as partners not local Mexicans, nor Mexicans from other parts of Mexico, but Chinese entrepreneurs from California and Chinese contract labourers imported directly from China.

Otis and Chandler did not plant the cotton themselves, but leased the land to others. Most of the lessees turned out to be Chinese. By 1920, these Chinese were raising 80 per cent of the Mexicali cotton crop. They

Mexican woman in china poblana.

Table 5.29

CHINESE POPULATIONS IN SPANISH AMERICA, 1950 AND 1967		
COUNTRY	1950	1967
Cuba	23,000	25,000
Peru	12,000	30,000
Mexico	12,000	10,000
Panama	2,700	8,000
Ecuador	1,000	4,200
Guatemala	1,000	4,000
Chile	1,329	2,000
Venezuela	1,300	3,000
Costa Rica	933	3,000
Nicaragua	650	1,000
Colombia	650	1,000
Dominican Rep.	561	1,000
Honduras	381	900
El Salvador	250	500
Argentina	250	300
Uruguay	60	100
Bolivia	30	50
Paraguay	10	10

Source: Ho (1967b).

did not baulk at the arduous, back-breaking task of clearing virgin land, and they easily solved the labour problem by contracting and importing coolie workers directly from China.

A few rich Chinese had their own capital to invest; most borrowed from Americans in southern California. They also raised capital from their own contract labourers by organizing them into cooperatives. Each man contributed whatever he could towards the collective enterprise, working for a share of the crops rather than straight wages. During the working season, the men received only clothing and food. This way, they had a stake in the business, were in effect partners with the lessee who had brought them to Baja California, and worked as hard as they could to make the venture a success. For the American landowner, it was a good deal indeed, for not only did he receive money at the outset for leasing out his land, but for no investment at all he saw his land cleared and, best of all, he usually received half of the year-end harvest from his lessees. Another beneficiary was the American cotton ginner who bankrolled the Chinese (by lending them money) and ginned their raw cotton.

Some of the Chinese planters in Mexicali also had commercial establishments serving Chinese and Mexicans alike. For mutual aid and protection, they had their own association, which included a hospital housed in its own building. This association, called Tuck Tong Society, facilitated negotiations between North Americans and Mexicans on the one hand and Chinese on the other. It maintained an American representative who was in close touch with Chinese interest in the US, particularly California's Chinatowns.

Chinese numbers grew dramatically, from 188 in 1910 to about 5,000 in 1918–19, cotton's best year in Baja California. However, during the succeeding two years the figure declined considerably as a result of a sharp drop in world cotton prices in 1920.

Mexicali apart, a colony of Chinese existed in Ensenada, the Pacific port and capital of Baja California.

Mexico City's Chinatown puts up decoration to mark Hong Kong's return to China, 1997.

Though very much smaller in size, the community was important in local commerce, mainly in retail food or groceries, hardware, clothing and general merchandise. The owners of these small businesses financed market gardening by small farmers, many of whom were probably Chinese. When Mexican nationalism and its correlate, anti-Chinese sentiment, reared its head, these well-entrenched traders were blamed for the inability of Mexican businesses to compete. 'We should not forget,' an anti-Chinese campaign leaflet said, 'that the competition of the Chinaman is mild, quiet, systematic, but extremely ruinous and dangerous.'

The anti-Chinese campaign, the declining importance of cotton and the continuous influx of internal Mexican migrants offering cheaper labour, were all pressures against Chinese immigration. During the 1930s, Mexico curtailed all foreign immigration and the Chinese population in Baja California, as throughout Mexico, declined steadily, reaching a low of 618 in 1940.

THE POST-WORLD WAR II PERIOD

Although far fewer in numbers, postwar immigration has been considerably more diverse in many ways: places of origin within and outside China; socio-economic, educational and occupational backgrounds; gender and age variations; political as well as economic 'push' factors. In choice of destination, too, the range has been wider.

The new immigrants arrived in countries already hosting considerable numbers of second- and third-generation, largely assimilated descendants of earlier immigrants, including many with non-Chinese, Latin American mothers. These children and grandchildren of Chinese immigrants should properly be viewed as Latin Americans of Chinese heritage, or *Chinos-Latinos*, not 'overseas Chinese.' As they call themselves, they are *tusan* (a word derived from the Chinese 'tusheng', meaning 'local-born'); most are non-Chinese speaking but endowed with Chinese surnames by patronymic practices. Immigrants and *tusan*, 'pure' and 'mixed' – all this explains the difficulty of determining the boundaries, membership, size, nature and characteristics of Chinese communities in Spanish America. Estimates run wildly from 100,000 to one million, depending on who is counting, who are considered Chinese and how the count is conducted. Unlike the United States, Latin American countries do not note the race or ethnicity of their citizens, while distinguishing between citizens and immigrants.

According to 1950 Latin American census figures, there was a total of 58,104 Chinese in Spanish America. A Taiwan-sponsored publication on the Chinese communities of all Latin America and the Caribbean, written by Ho Ming Chung and published in 1967, estimated 150,000 Chinese in this large region (including English, French and Dutch-speaking areas). Unfortunately, Ho did not make clear the source of his numbers (see table 5.29).

Both lists cover every Spanish-speaking country, thus testifying to the widespread distribution of the Chinese in postwar Latin America. Not all the Chinese in these countries came directly from China, but were re-migrants from other centres of Chinese concentration. Chinese from Peru, for example, re-migrated to Ecuador, Chile and Bolivia; from Panama, Mexico and Cuba, some Chinese went to Central America and Colombia.

The rounded figures are clearly gross estimates that underscore the lack of precise, accurate demographic data. As Latin American censuses typically do not enumerate by race or ethnicity, the Chinese counted in 1950 can probably be assumed to be immigrants who were not yet naturalized citizens of their respective countries of residence. Ho made no distinction between immigrant or native-born, citizen or alien, pure or mixed. Nor did he make clear the exact year his numbers were collected.

The case of Peru is illustrative of the difficulties of ascertaining the size of the Chinese population. Ho Ming Chung estimated in 1967 a Chinese population of 30,000, which was considerably higher than the 12,000 enumerated in Peru's own 1950 census. China's Xinhua News Agency estimated 100,000 in 1989, citing the Chinese Embassy as source. The Hong Kong daily *South China Morning Post* in 1992 provided a wildly improbable figure of 800,000, citing no source.

The Chinese communities in the immediate postwar period were ageing fast and very disproportionately male. For example, of the 10,915 Chinese officially counted in Peru's 1944 census, only 500 were women. Age and gender imbalances would be redressed somewhat with later, family-based patterns of immigration.

When Chinese immigration began to pick up slowly but perceptibly after World War II, among the first to arrive were political refugees from China looking for any country in the Americas which would give them temporary or permanent asylum. These were generally families, well-educated, perhaps with some personal wealth or capital, speaking Mandarin and Shanghainese (often English as well) rather than the Cantonese of the old Huaqiao.

By the 1950s and 1960s, they were joined by diplomats posted by the Taiwan government, some of whom or their family members might have stayed on after their terms of office expired. From the 1960s into the 1980s and 1990s, immigrants from the People's Republic of China (PRC), Taiwan, Hong Kong and Macao also arrived. Some came to join relatives already settled in Latin America; others came seeking better economic opportunities than were available at home; still others used Latin American countries as a springboard to their preferred final destination, the United States. A significant exception to this pattern was Cuba (see Part V: The Caribbean).

The children of the postwar immigrants to Spanish America tend to be educated and ambitious. While many, like their parents, have remained actively engaged in commerce, many others have found their way into the professions and government service. Whenever possible, they have moved from downtown commercial areas and Chinatowns to quiet, middle-class suburbs. They have also been more willing and more capable of assimilating into Latin American cultures, learning Spanish at school, adopting Catholicism, even entering electoral politics in some rare instances. They call themselves *tusan* (native-born) in direct challenge to the old concept of Huaqiao. Significant numbers have migrated to the United States and Canada, where they are identified, and self-identify, as both *Latinos* and *Chinos*, far more likely to speak fluent Spanish than much Chinese.

Beginning in the 1950s and all through the Cold War decades of the 1960s–80s, the government in Taiwan paid enormous attention to 'Huaqiao' communities everywhere, including Latin America, closely monitoring their leadership personnel as well as their social, cultural, political and economic activities. Political competition for the allegiance of these communities intensified in the 1980s, as Beijing turned its attention to what had been virtually an open field for Taipei.

Chinese Lion Dance in Lima's Chinatown.

During this decade, both the Xinhua News Agency of Beijing and the Central News Agency of Taipei diligently reported gatherings of 'patriotic' Chinese in various Latin American countries, usually when they were celebrating the PRC's national holiday of October 1, or Taiwan's Double Ten (October 10). In the case of pro-PRC demonstrations, the festivities were usually organized by the country's 'friendship society' with China (for example, Venezuela-China Friendship Association), typically chaired by a pro-Beijing Latin American (for example, Victor Ochoa of the Venezuela chapter).

During the 1980s, Beijing stepped up its diplomatic courtship of Latin American countries, succeeding in establishing diplomatic relations with 19 of them by 1987, which also meant that these countries severed relationships with Taipei. PRC leaders like the one-time Premier Zhao Ziyang used the occasion of many state visits to South America to rally the Chinese communities behind Beijing and its goal of 'reunification of Taiwan with the China mainland.'

For its part, Taiwan established a string of country-based 'Free Overseas Chinese' federations, coordinated by the Taipei-based Commission for Overseas Chinese Affairs. It also sponsored the country chapters of the 'Grand Alliance for Reunification of China.' Periodically during the 1980s, Taipei would convene several hundred 'overseas Chinese leaders' for pan-Latin American conventions in select countries, such as Chile in 1984, Paraguay in 1986, and Colombia in 1987. The Kuomintang also sponsored branch parties and schools.

By 1990, Taipei had seemingly conceded its inability to compete with Beijing on the diplomatic front, and so shifted its strategy to trade. In February 1994, the Secretary General of Taiwan's China External Trade Development Council announced plans to invest heavily in manufacturing plants in Mexico and Latin America, in order to take advantage of the North American Free Trade Agreement to export to the US.

These externally sponsored and funded organizations directed towards 'homeland' politics were not the only ones found in Chinese communities; in fact, much more authentic and long-lasting Chinese associations abounded wherever a critical mass existed. New ones arose as the nature and needs of the communities changed. Chinese organizations fell into three broad categories:

Chinese remains and epitaphs in a cemetery in Lima.

welfare and mutual aid; cultural, commercial, and educational; and political. This last category has already been discussed above. In general, they can be seen as rather short-lived products of the Cold War.

Welfare and mutual aid societies, usually founded and financed by the handful of prosperous merchants in the community, were typically established during the heyday of 19th-century labour migration. Prototypes were the Chinese Benevolent Society of Peru, and the Chinese Fraternal Union of Mexico. These benevolent societies were followed quickly by the formation of surname and native-place associations representing the almost exclusively Cantonese and Hakka speakers of this first wave immigration.

While providing the usual kinds of social service and welfare benefits to the sick and destitute among them, such closed and internally directed, privately funded ethnic immigrant organizations also acted as self-governing and self-policing agencies within the communities. They mediated disputes among Chinese while brokering relationships with the host society and government.

In the late 19th, early 20th centuries, when the Chinese moved away from wage labour and the countryside into urban areas, to owning their own businesses and hence greater prosperity, they established a variety of social clubs known locally by such names as *casino chino*. There, a range of social and recreational activities, including gambling, took place. Chinese chambers of commerce also appeared wherever Chinese businesses flourished.

Later in the 20th century, growing prosperity, improved literacy and greater self-confidence stimulated the establishment of Chinese newspapers and Chinese schools in those countries with large, settled Chinese communities, such as Peru. During the Cold War decades, when newspapers and schools served the needs and interests of the old Huaqiao as well as some of the new immigrants, they received considerable funding and support from Taiwan or from Beijing and thus were turned into political battlegrounds for the hearts and minds of the Chinese communities. In the late 20th century, with the younger generations unable to read much Chinese, newspapers such as Lima's *La Voz China* have seen their circulation drastically reduced.

With the postwar immigration, which brought over a more diverse group of Chinese representing more mid-

dle-class, professionally educated individuals with families, these early organizations have faded in importance, although they have not disappeared altogether. Postwar Mandarin- and Shanghainese-speaking immigrants have not followed the practice of the old Huaqiao in creating surname, native-place or comparable affinity groups, as their personal circumstances were significantly different and they encountered societies which received them under vastly different conditions. Together with some of the more assimilated second- and third-generation Chinese, including those with a non-Chinese parent, they have founded still other kinds of associations.

Common throughout Spanish American countries are social/cultural organizations with names like Unión China, Casino Chung-Wah, Asociación Tusan, Sociedad Central de la Colonia China, which sponsor activities such as 'Chinese Youth Day.' As more and more Chinese, especially the second generation, became Catholics, the Asociación Católica China was born. Spanish-language magazines, such as *Oriental*, published in Lima, appeared. At the same time, Chinese schools such as Lima's Colegio Juan XXIII (a Catholic school with a Chinese-speaking Jesuit principal) now provide their students the option of English rather than Chinese as the second language of instruction, along with Spanish. In the late 1980s, the parents' committee also established the Instituto Tecnológico Tusan within this school to offer more intense training in computers and information technology.

With their weak and deteriorating economic conditions, Latin American and Caribbean countries are not likely to attract significant numbers of immigrants from many places. The United States and Canada are without doubt much preferred destinations. However, given the US's and Canada's increasingly restrictive immigration policies, Hong Kong's absorption by China, and China's perennial population pressure, a handful of Chinese will continue to seek opportunities in Spanish America. In the 1990s, Mexico has also become a sometime entrepôt for Fujianese 'snakeheads' seeking to sneak their illicit human cargo into the US (see p 66).

Whether and to what extent Chinese will continue to migrate to Latin America, their forerunners have left indelible marks on Spanish American societies and cultures. Peru boasts several intellectuals of Chinese heritage: two examples are the late Pedro Zulen and Eugenio Chang-Rodríguez (currently an academic in the US), scholars known for their insightful analyses of Peruvian language, culture and politics. Not to be outdone, one of Mexico's most popular contemporary pop artists is the part-Chinese Ana Gabriel. Years after his death, Yon Sosa, the early guerrilla leader of Guatemala's war against military dictatorship and landed oligarchy, was joined in martyrdom by the courageous and indefatigable human rights activist and noted Guatemalan anthropologist, Myrna Mack. Both were of Chinese descent, and both fought passionately for dignity and social justice for the poorest of the Guatemalan people. In a more general sense, it is said that 15 percent of the Peruvian people have some Chinese blood. And Cuba's great writer, Alejo Carpentier, asserted that an authentic Cuban is one-third Spanish, one-third African, and one-third Chinese.

Evelyn Hu-DeHart

THE UNITED STATES

The Chinese in the United States are the largest Chinese community in the Western world. Their presence there dates back to the early years of the nation. American immigration policy, events in China and US-China relations have been the main factors in the community's growth in size and complexity.

The Pioneers: 1785–1848

In 1785, the *Pallas*, a China trade vessel from Canton, dropped anchor at Baltimore. The three Chinese in her crew were the first recorded Chinese arrivals on American soil. Occasional crewmen continued to stop briefly on the east and west coasts of North America. Others came as students, merchants, servants, circus performers and the like. But up to the mid-19th century, less than 50 Chinese lived in the continental United States.

The China trade also brought Chinese to Hawaii. By the late 1820s, 30 to 40 Chinese, many of them merchants, were living in Honolulu. Enterprising Chinese also installed small cane mills to start the sugar industry in the Islands. However, the Chinese population was still small at mid-century.

Unrestricted immigration: 1848–82

The discovery of gold in California in 1848 attracted a huge influx from places all over the globe, including China. California's Chinese population jumped from approximately 50 in the late 1840s to more than 25,000 by 1852. Immigration continued during the next three decades and by 1880, there were more than 100,000 Chinese on the US mainland. Many were Cantonese villagers from Guangdong's Pearl River Delta, with the majority hailing from Siyi, the 'Four Districts' on the delta's west flank (see Part I). The largest number originated from Siyi's Xinning (now Taishan) county. Many

Map 5.14

THE UNITED STATES

of those who became labourers came indentured by the credit-ticket system.

Many early Chinese went to the mining areas. As new gold strikes occurred during the last half of the 19th century, Chinese miners also migrated to different parts of the American west and even across the border to Canada. When the gold fever subsided in California at the end of the 1850s, the state turned to developing its economy using Chinese labour extensively. Since almost all were able-bodied males, the Chinese made up nearly 25 percent of California's physical labour force even though they were only about a tenth of the total population. Chinese labour was also used in other western states and territories, though to a lesser extent than in California, as they started to develop.

From the 1860s to the 1880s Chinese labour helped build the western sections of the transcontinental railroads, as well as trunk lines in the West. Upon completion of the railroads, many Chinese labourers settled in towns along the routes. Chinese also migrated via the transcontinental railroads to the central and eastern parts of America, so that by 1890 Chinese were in every state and territory.

In the west, particularly in California, Chinese labourers contributed greatly to the development of the economy. They reclaimed marshlands; constructed roads, rock walls, water flumes and reservoirs; worked borax deposits; mined quicksilver and coal. They were used extensively as farm labour. In many locations they were also tenant farmers, and commercial crops like

Section of transcontinental railroads worked on by Chinese labourers.

Table 5.30

YEAR	IMMIGRATION		POPULATION	
	UNITED STATES	**HAWAIIAN KINGDOM**	**UNITED STATES**	**HAWAIIAN KINGDOM**
1820	1	na		na
	IN DECADE PREVIOUS TO YEAR			
1830	2	na		na
1840	8	na		na
1850	35	na	725	71
1853				364
1860	41,397	672 (1852–60)	35,586	816
1866				1,306
1870	64,301	1,408	63,199	
1872				2,038
1878				6,045
1880	123,201	11,166	105,465	
1884				18,254
1890	61,711	21,276	109,776	16,752
1896				21,616
1900	14,799	22,198 (1891–99)	118,746	
1910	20,605		94,414	
1920	21,278		85,202	
1930	29,907		102,159	
1940	4,928		106,334	
1950	16,709		150,044	
1960	9,657		237,214	
1970	34,764		435,062	
1980	124,326		806,027	
1990	270,581		1,645,472	

CHINESE IMMIGRATION AND POPULATION GROWTH IN THE UNITED STATES

US population figures are for all states and territories. Alaska and Hawaii statistics are included only after they became US possessions. Alaska was purchased from Russia in 1867 but population statistics were unavailable until the 1890 census. Hawaii was annexed in 1898. Its population was included as part of total US population from 1900 on.
Sources: Char (1975); Historical Statistics of the United States: Colonial Times to 1970; Statistical Yearbook of the Immigration Naturalization Service, various years.

sugar beet and celery owed their success to Chinese horticultural skills. In addition to developing California's shrimp and abalone fisheries, Chinese were the mainstay of the Pacific Northwest salmon canneries. They also comprised the majority of workers in light industries such as woollen mills, shoe and boots, slippers, cigar-making and garment-making in the San Francisco Bay Area. Many other Chinese worked as domestics or laundrymen.

In Hawaii white planters began sugar production in the 1830s and soon dominated sugar manufacturing. To ease a labour shortage on the plantations as production increased, planters began importing Chinese contract labourers in 1852. As Hawaii's economy grew, stimulated by the flourishing sugar industry, it attracted many Chinese immigrants. Some worked as rice growers while others went into coffee, agricultural produce, fish, poultry and livestock. Still others were the shopkeepers and skilled workers of Hawaii's growing middle class. Unlike on the mainland, Chinese in Hawaii were predominantly from Xiangshan county (now Zhongshan, Zhuhai, Doumen), while a sizeable minority was from Hakka-speaking areas in the Pearl River Delta. From their native Guangdong province, Chinese introduced many plants to Hawaii.

Early Chinese immigrants customarily left their families in China. Thus most immigrants lived a bachelor's life. They would remit funds periodically to China to support families whom they would return to the village to visit every few years. Most intended to retire to China when they had accumulated sufficient savings, although many were unable to realize this dream. Among the small number of women were the wives of merchants and professionals, as well as some domestic servants, but a significant proportion were prostitutes. During this period most institutions in the Chinese community were patterned after those in traditional China, although a very small minority were influenced by Western concepts, usually acquired from Christian missionaries.

Chinese congregated and formed Chinatowns in many towns and cities. On the mainland, San Francisco became their economic, political, and cultural centre, the headquarters of a hierarchical structure consisting of native-place (huiguan) and clan associations (see Part III). Besides overseeing mutual aid and social control, native-place associations exhumed and shipped the bones of the dead back to ancestral villages for proper burial. They collectively formed the Chinese Consolidated Benevolent Association (CCBA), the so-called Chinese Six Companies that acted as a spokesperson for Chinese on mainland America. In Hawaii that role was played by the Honolulu and the United Chinese Society. Merchants and labour contractors provided the leadership in these organizations.

More egalitarian in spirit were the secret societies, also called 'tongs' on the US mainland. These were the chief challengers to the native-place associations' leadership of the community. Secret society members often had a hand in the businesses that flourished in a bachelor society, namely prostitution, gambling and narcotics, among other anti-social activities. On the mainland these organizations proliferated, and rival groups' struggles to control spheres of interest often erupted into the notorious 'tong wars.'

Local anti-Chinese sentiment had been evident since Chinese first appeared in California, but demonstrations of such feelings were limited until the economic depression of the 1870s left thousands unemployed and agitators blamed Chinese for taking jobs away. Labour unions spearheaded an anti-Chinese movement in California that soon enveloped the west. The political pressures it generated forced Congress to pass the first Chinese exclusion act in 1882. This banned the entry of Chinese labourers – exempting only diplomats, tourists, merchants, teachers and students (see box). Chinese were also barred from being naturalized as American citizens. During the next decades the law was extended with ever stricter provisions. After the US annexed Hawaii, exclusion was extended to the Islands.

Exclusion: 1882–1943

Exclusion reduced the influx, but many Chinese found a way round the laws. Some were smuggled in or jumped ship. More entered claiming exempt status or citizen status. In order to determine the validity of such claims, immigration officials detained and interrogated Chinese applicants at entry ports. At San Francisco, the principal port of entry, a detention facility established on Angel Island by the authorities processed thousands of arrivals between 1910 and 1940.

As labourers died or departed for China, numbers of

Chinese students headed for Massachusetts, Shanghai, 1872.

CHINESE STUDENTS IN AMERICA IN THE LATE 19TH AND EARLY 20TH CENTURIES

As part of its efforts at 'modernization' (see p 99), the late Qing government sanctioned initiatives to promote overseas study. One such initiative, championed by Yung Wing (Rong Hong, 1828–1912), was the Chinese Educational Mission to America. Yung had received a missionary education in Macao and studied in the US in 1847–54, becoming the first Chinese graduate of an American university (Yale). Influential officials such as Zeng Guofan and Li Hongzhang (see p 99) lent their support in the expectation that the students would acquire specialized training in such fields as military science, shipbuilding and engineering, and on their return they would help build railroads and telegraphs, develop modern mining, and establish an armaments industry. However, Yung Wing, who became a naturalized US citizen, entertained quite different hopes for the mission, seeing it as an opportunity for Chinese students to immerse themselves in Western culture and adopt its values.

Between 1872 and 1875, 120 Chinese boys (aged between 12 and 16) went to the US, where they were initially enrolled in high schools throughout the Connecticut valley in New England. The boys were supposed to stay for a period of 15 years, but conservative Chinese officials brought the mission to an abrupt end in 1881, and recalled the students before they had completely forsaken traditional Chinese values for American ones. Official Chinese ire at the US government's refusal to allow a select group of students to enter the naval and military academies at Annapolis and West Point had been exacerbated by a growing trend of anti-Chinese immigration legislation in America.

Only two students at the time had actually graduated from college; one of them, Jeme Tian Yau, became China's first railway engineer, although in subsequent years some former members of the mission entered the diplomatic service and took up posts in naval, mining and railway administration. One such former member was Tang Shaoyi, who entered government service during the last years of the dynasty and eventually became the first prime minister of the Chinese Republic in 1912.

A project which American officials and educators hoped would continue where the aborted mission had left off, facilitating the future peaceful expansion of American influence in China, arose from the United States government's decision in 1908 to remit the surplus of its Boxer Indemnity funds to fund Chinese government scholarships for overseas study in the US. The indemnities had been exacted for damages to foreign life and property suffered during the anti-foreign Boxer uprising in 1900. The American government had exacted a sum in excess of the total of legitimate claims, and it was this excess that was remitted in 1908.

Before 1908 the numbers of Chinese students had been small: 50 in 1903 and 150 in 1905. A number of American educational institutions had also individually offered scholarships to Chinese students; in 1907, for example, ten male Chinese students went to Yale and Harvard, while three Chinese women were able to attend Wellesley College. The Boxer scholarships helped to boost the Chinese student presence.

Competitive examinations were held in 1909, 1910 and 1911 to select students for such scholarships. One successful candidate in 1910 was Hu Shi (1891–1962), who was in the US for seven years, initially studying Agriculture and Botany at Cornell University before transferring to Columbia University to study Philosophy. A prominent advocate of literary reform during the May Fourth Movement, Hu was China's ambassador to the US in 1938–42. (He was to take up residence in New York upon the Communist takeover of China.)

In 1911 Qinghua College, a special school staffed by American instructors and teaching an American-style curriculum, was opened in Beijing to prepare Chinese scholarship holders for their sojourn in the US. It sent its first group of 16 graduates in 1912. By 1929, when the college was reorganized as an autonomous university and the practice of automatically sending all graduates to the US was ended, some 1,268 Qinghua graduates had studied in America. Overall, the Chinese student population in the US increased from 650 in 1911 to 2,600 in 1923. Since Qinghua graduates were all male, scholarships were separately offered to women on the basis of competitive examinations, and in 1914–29, 53 such scholarship holders went to the US. Overall, there were 640 women students there in 1925.

Qinghua students in the US during the period 1909–29 mostly studied engineering, the social sciences, science and business, a subject distribution that similarly prevailed amongst other Chinese students there. A large majority of those studying there before 1945 hailed from the prosperous coastal provinces of Guangdong, Jiangsu and Zhejiang. Furthermore, students primarily came from the business, professional and governing classes.

Paul Bailey

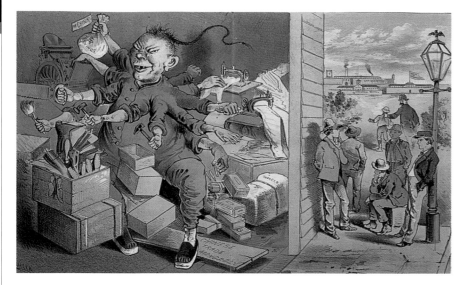

Cartoon of Chinese with numerous hands grabbing all the jobs and leaving White Americans (right) unemployed, 19th century.

Chinese men intermarried with Hawaiian women in multi-ethnic Honolulu.

vegetables for the market. In the San Francisco Peninsula, they turned to cut flowers, specializing in asters and chrysanthemum. However, on the mainland the dwindling Chinese labour force could no longer play a significant role in Californian agriculture. Similarly, in Hawaii other Asian immigrants supplanted Chinese plantation labour and farmers.

At the turn of the century, some Chinese entrepreneurs began to shift from commerce to industrial and financial enterprises. However, a lack of capital and an unfriendly environment made it hard for major enterprises to compete and survive. San Francisco's Canton Bank (founded 1907) failed in 1926, and Hawaii's Chinese American Bank (founded 1915) had to reorganize in 1933. Similarly, the San Francisco-based China Mail Steamship Company went bankrupt in 1923. Canneries operating in the San Francisco Bay Area at the turn of the century were gone by the 1930s.

Among the few major mainland enterprises to flourish were the National Dollar Stores (which established a chain of department stores) and Wah Chang Corporation (which traded in antimony and tungsten from China). In Hawaii, where white sugar interests dominated the developing economy but Asians formed a majority of the population, many Chinese enterprises were able to compete and flourish. One successful entrepreneur was Chun Quon, whose firm C. Q. Yee Hop went from selling meat at the turn of the century to being a large conglomerate in the 1930s, one which included a cattle ranch, a hardwood products company, a brewery and a realty company.

During this period the increasingly American-born Chinese population was greatly influenced by Western institutions, particularly the public schools and Christian churches. A Chinatown subculture mixing features of Chinese and Western societies began to emerge. The American-born also formed their own social organizations, patterning them after Western models. Meanwhile, American-born women, influenced by Western concepts of women's equality, exhibited a greater degree of independence and social consciousness than women in traditional Chinese society.

In multi-ethnic Hawaii, Chinese began entering the professions, and a Western-educated Chinese middle class started to emerge at the turn of the century. By the 1920s a majority were citizens and had begun to take an active part in civic affairs. In 1926 Yew Char and Dai Yen Chang became the first Chinese to be elected to Hawaiian public office. On the more colour-conscious mainland, however, Chinese found it harder to enter the professions or even get clerical work in mainstream society. Nor did citizens become a majority in the population until 1940. Participation in the American political process lagged correspondingly.

Yet some Chinese were able to transcend the racial discrimination isolating them from the larger society. At the beginning of the century, Ng Poon Chew frequently lectured on the Chautauqua and Lyceum circuits and to American organizations on China and the Chinese. In the 1920s and 1930s Yun Gee became a well-known figure in art circles in San Francisco, New York and Paris. In the 1920s the cinematographer James Wong Howe and actress Anna May Wong carved out careers in the film industry, although Howe's artistry was not officially

Chinese declined, reaching their nadir in 1920 on the mainland. The drop in the predominantly male labour population, plus the growth of an American-born generation, led to a gradual decrease of the male/female ratio on the mainland from a high of 2,679:100 in 1890 to 285:100 by 1940. Chinese became increasingly concentrated in urban areas, and were at their most numerous in California, Hawaii and New York.

At the turn of the century, the Chinese community began to establish institutions patterned after Western models such as chambers of commerce and civic organizations. As the bachelor society gradually changed to one based on family, the power of secret societies, native-place and clan associations waned. A sense of community gradually came into being, and many communities established CCBAs to deal with matters of common concern.

During this period many employers refused to hire Chinese. On the mainland Chinese were concentrated disproportionately in the service industry, and domestics and laundrymen became stereotypical Chinese occupations. Others entered the restaurant business, where chop suey and later fortune cookies became well-known items on menus. The Chinese also operated stores selling groceries, agricultural produce and meat to non-Chinese, especially non-white, customers. These operations were particularly numerous in California, Hawaii, the American southwest and the Mississippi Delta region. Some communities also had a flourishing underground economy consisting of gambling and the lottery.

From the turn of the century through the 1930s, there were Chinese who purchased apple crops for processing in areas such as Sebastopol and Watsonville. In the Stockton area, Chinese farmers produced quantities of potatoes, and one Chin Lung was known as the Chinese potato king. Other farmers continued growing fruits and recognized until he won an Oscar in 1955. In 1940 Dong Kingman won acclaim for his water-colours. During the 1930s and the war years, the China-born immigrant Lin Yutang wrote a stream of novels, translations and non-fictional works that helped mould the image of China and Chinese in the minds of many Americans.

Other Chinese, however, were frustrated by the apparent lack of a future in America. They empathized with the rising nationalism in China, and participated in the reform and revolutionary movements in the hope that a strong China would help improve their status abroad (see Part IV). Many supported the Kuomintang, the party that eventually became the dominant political force in China and in overseas Chinese communities. Some Chinese Americans went to China to join government or military service, or to work as professionals. Others invested in businesses and enterprises in Hong Kong and mainland China. They also donated generous sums to build schools, libraries, roads and hospitals, usually in their native areas.

The interest in events in China was reflected in a lively Chinese-language press in San Francisco, Honolulu, New York and Chicago; these expressed a range of political opinions. By the 1930s radio broadcasts had also started in Honolulu and San Francisco. Chinese schools helped to nurture nationalist sentiments, countering somewhat the Americanization of the younger generation. A small minority went to China for their education.

Chinese Americans were particularly supportive of China in its attempt to resist foreign aggression. In the 1930s, Chinese in America not only donated money to support China's fight against the Japanese but also demanded that the Kuomintang government halt the civil war and unite the nation to resist Japan. After the outbreak of the Sino-Japanese War in 1937, Chinese in America dug even deeper into their pockets to provide much-needed financial support for the mother country.

Restricted immigration: 1943–65

World War II was a turning point for Chinese Americans. Many served in the American armed forces or in the merchant marine. Thanks to the wartime labour shortage, Chinese were hired for skilled and technical positions formerly closed to them. By this time the Chinese were a small minority, no longer the prime target of American racism. Moreover, China's resistance to Japanese aggression had created a favourable image of the Chinese among Americans. In a move designed to counter the propaganda of the Axis powers and to encourage China to continue to fight Japan, Congress repealed the Chinese exclusion acts in 1943. Although the law assigned only a token annual immigration quota of 105 to Chinese, Chinese regained the right of naturalization. After the war Congress passed legislation allowing war veterans to bring Chinese wives to America. From 1945 to 1950, almost 8,000 Chinese women, comprising the overwhelming majority of Chinese arrivals, entered the country.

In the meantime, the Communists won the civil war in China against a Kuomintang government beset by inflation and corruption. But instead of recognizing the newly inaugurated People's Republic of China (PRC), America continued to have diplomatic relations with the Nationalist regime in Taiwan. Furthermore, in both the Korean and Vietnam Wars, the PRC and the US were on opposing sides. The hostility between the two nations, together with the anti-Communist hysteria in America, enabled the Taiwan government to strengthen its control over the Chinese there.

With the change of government in China, Congress passed legislation allowing several thousand Chinese students, visitors and seamen to remain in America. Subsequent legislation admitted about 30,000 Chinese refugees between the 1950s and the early 1960s. Many were non-Cantonese professionals, entrepreneurs, intellectuals and ex-government officials of Nationalist China. Beginning in the late 1950s, many Taiwan and Hong Kong students also came seeking higher education. When they completed their studies, most sought to stay in America.

Restricted to an annual immigration quota of 105 after World War II, many Chinese resorted to entering America under fraudulent identities. The federal government began investigating and prosecuting such cases during the late 1940s. In 1955 Hong Kong consul Everett Drumright issued a report charging Chinese with organized immigration fraud. But this practice had been so pervasive that the government faced the prospect of tying up the courts for years if it were to prosecute such cases. Instead, immigration authorities, together with community leaders, eventually worked out a programme under which Chinese confessing their true identities to immigration authorities would be allowed to gain legal immigration status. Some 20,000 Chinese went through this programme.

During the same period discriminatory barriers in American society against the Chinese and other minorities were gradually lifted. In the postwar boom Chinese began to find job and business opportunities in mainstream society. The number of Chinese entering professional and technical

Anna May Wong.

Chinese woman working the switchboard at the Chinatown Telephone Exchange, 1920s.

Oakland-based Chinese raised funds to relieve wartime suffering in China, 1939 (below).

I. M. Pei as a Harvard student.

Tsung-dao Lee (top) and Chen-Ning Yang, 1961.

occupations increased by two and a half times between 1940 and 1950, and by three and a half times between 1950 and 1970, becoming some 26 per cent of all working Chinese. In 1970 another 21 per cent were in sales and clerical occupations.

Many made their way to the pinnacle of their field. Among the most outstanding were I. M. Pei, the world-famous architect (see p 62); and Chen-Ning Yang and Tsung-Dao Lee, joint winners of the Nobel Prize in Physics in 1957.

Others achieved a reputation in writing and music. In the 1950s, mainstream publishing houses brought out the autobiographical writings of American-born Pardee Lowe and Jade Snow Wong. C. Y. Lee's *Flower Drum Song*, a novel which addressed the cultural conflicts faced by Chinese Americans, became a Broadway musical in 1958 and a motion picture in 1961. In 1953, Hawaii-born Dai Keong Lee, who first became known in the 1930s, composed the music for the stage production *Teahouse of the August Moon*. Singer Yi-kwei Sze and composer Chou Wen-chung also launched their careers in the 1950s.

About a third of the Chinese, however, worked in low-paying service occupations such as laundries and restaurants, or were machine operators in garment factories. Except in Hawaii, few Chinese worked in skilled blue-collar jobs because craft unions resisted the entry of minorities. But by the 1950s and 1960s, public pressure had forced some unions to admit token numbers of minorities.

In the post-World War II period, the businesses most accessible to Chinese were those requiring only modest capital outlays namely laundries, grocery stores and restaurants. Before the advent of automatic washing machines and permanent press fabrics in the 1950s, there were about 10,000 hand laundries in the US in 1949. In 1949, there were approximately 2,000 Chinese-owned grocery stores. In the postwar boom many of these expanded into supermarkets, particularly in the American southeast and southwest, in California's Central Valley and Hawaii. In California, the southwest and Hawaii, some grew into shopping malls.

The restaurant business grew from about 4,300 eating places in 1949 to about 5,900 in the mid-1970s, about half of them in California and New York. Upscale restaurants catering to the middle class arose. Eateries offering regional styles of cooking other than the long-established Cantonese cuisine, became more numerous.

Garment making has long been a major Chinatown industry. San Francisco was its centre, but with the increase in immigration – and therefore labour supply – after the mid-1960s, many garment factories opened in other Chinatowns, and by the 1970s their number in New York had exceeded that in San Francisco.

Many Chinese Americans chose higher education as the road to upward mobility. In addition, many Taiwan and Hong Kong students and scholars stayed in the country. Thus by 1970, a quarter of the Chinese-American men had college degrees, twice the US average. During the postwar boom, some became entrepreneurs, establishing industries based on high technology. One was Wang Laboratories; founded in 1951 by An Wang, this became a leader in marketing mini-computers and word processing equipment in the 1970s.

Hawaii-Chinese businesses also flourished. A 1972 survey showed that Chinese-owned firms in Hawaii grossed an average of US$162,807 per firm, almost double that of the US$82,250 earned per mainland firm. Hung Wo Ching, for example, was a major entrepreneur who took over the bankrupt Trans-Pacific Airlines in 1958 and transformed it into the profitable Aloha Airlines. Chinn Ho and his Capital Investment Company (founded 1945), played a major role in land development. The rise of Chinese and other Asian financial interests put pressure on existing white-dominated institutions to appoint more Asians, including Chinese, to managerial positions.

Only a few Chinese survived in the agricultural sector. A few farmers in California, Florida, New Jersey and Long Island in New York still grew vegetables, principally for the Chinese-American market. There were also some big farmers. In the San Francisco Bay Area Chinese flower nurseries enjoyed a measure of prosperity until imported cut flowers and increasing production costs brought about a decline in the 1970s.

Reflecting increasing investment activity in the community, new Chinese-American financial institutions were set up, often in partnership with non-Chinese investors, on the mainland and in Hawaii. These were small to medium in scale and their financial dealings were usually limited in scope.

As their economic and social status improved, many Chinese began to live outside the ethnic neighbourhood, among the general population. Chinatowns declined, while the power and influence of the traditionalist Chinese associations continued to recede. Even as these organizations groped for ways to be relevant to the changing Chinese community, the younger generation was rapidly losing its knowledge of the Chinese language and Chinese customs. Chinese schools and Chinese newspapers declined. This change was particularly rapid among Chinese in Hawaii and those living in mainland suburbs and in small towns.

The sojourner mentality was replaced by a Chinese-American outlook. Traditional Chinese observances lost their religious significance, but gained a commercial purpose as Chinese Americans started exploiting Chinese customs to promote business. In 1950, for example, the Honolulu Chinese Chamber of Commerce organized the Narcissus Festival to attract visitors to Chinatown during Chinese New Year. This was followed by the inauguration of the Chinese New Year Festival in San Francisco in 1953.

Chinese Americans continued to play prominent roles in Hawaiian politics. When Hawaii attained statehood in 1959, Hiram Fong was elected senator. Up to the mid-1990s this was the highest electoral position reached by Chinese Americans. On the mainland, some Chinese Americans also began to be appointed to minor city commissions and judgeships. In 1946 Wing Ong in Arizona became the first Chinese on the mainland to be elected state assemblyman.

Immigration on an equal basis: after 1965

In the half century after World War II ended, the Chinese population in America grew more than tenfold. This growth was particularly rapid after Congress

The Chinese-American Dream: having three sons at Harvard.

dropped the country's racially discriminatory immigration policy and passed the Immigration Act of 1965. The act granted applicants from all nations, including China, equal treatment, with an annual immigration quota of 20,000 each. In 1982 Congress passed legislation assigning a separate 20,000 immigration quota to Taiwan; and in 1987 it gave a 5,000 quota to Hong Kong.

Many students from these two places obtained permanent-resident, then citizen, status. During the 1980s the Taiwanese community in the US grew more than tenfold, from less than 20,000 to more than 200,000 in the mid-1990s. Many continued to come on student visas. In the 1990s the number of Taiwan students consistently exceeded 30,000, and Taiwan ranked third among countries sending students to the US in 1996. Visitors from Taiwan also arrived and stayed. Firms and governments in Hong Kong and Taiwan sent representatives to America as commercial ties expanded.

From the 1960s onwards, thousands of ethnic Chinese relocated to America from troubled spots like Cuba, Central America, Peru, Burma, Philippines, Thailand, Malaysia and Korea. The biggest influx was from Vietnam, Cambodia and Laos (see pp 233, 148 and 170). By 1990 almost a million Indochinese refugees had arrived in America, about 30 to 40 per cent of them ethnic Chinese. A high percentage of these refugees belonged to the Cantonese and Teochiu speech groups, but there were also a significant number of Hakka, Hokkien and Hainanese speakers. The flow from other Southeast Asian countries was similarly polyglot, reflecting the linguistic composition of the Chinese population in each sending country. Immigration from Latin America was mostly Cantonese. The few who emigrated from Korea, however, were Mandarin speakers tracing their origins to Shandong and other provinces in northern China (see p 341).

Direct immigration from mainland China, down to a trickle for almost three decades, greatly increased from the late 1970s, spurred by the normalization of US-China relations and the relaxation of the latter's emigration policy. As cultural exchanges between the two countries developed, students and visiting scholars, too, arrived from China to study alongside their Taiwan and Hong Kong counterparts. The size of this group exceeded 40,000 in the early 1990s, and ranked first among foreign students of all nationalities in 1992. In 1992, in response to the June 4, 1989 Tiananmen Incident, Congress passed legislation enabling China students who had arrived before April 11, 1990 to apply for permanent-resident status. By the June 30, 1993 deadline, the US Immigration and Naturalization Service had received more than 50,000 applications. Additionally, expanding commercial and cultural ties between the two nations led to the stationing of numerous representatives and staff members of PRC agencies and corporations in the US.

Students apart, peasants and working class Chinese have found their way from China to America. Most arrived as legal immigrants; others were smuggled in by a clandestine worldwide network involving secret societies (see box p 268 and Part II).

Up to the mid-1960s, the Chinese-American community consisted overwhelmingly of Cantonese from the Pearl River Delta. The post-1965 immigration drastically changed that profile. The great influx of newcomers, many of whom were lacking fluency in English, has created a number of sub-communities differing in regional origin. Cantonese, Mandarin and English are the languages most often used in inter-group communication.

For the distribution of Chinese by speech or place of origin, no accurate figures exist, only orders of magnitude. Although the Cantonese are no longer as overwhelmingly dominant as before, they still accounted for the largest group in the

Industry publication with An Wang and his company's new product on the cover, 1969.

LITTLE FUZHOU

In ten short years, from 1985 to 1995, the Fuzhou community in New York grew from a tiny enclave at the junction of East Broadway and Division Street in lower Manhattan into the largest and most concentrated Chinese speech group in the city. The two-block stretch of East Broadway running from Confucius Plaza, under the Manhattan Bridge overpass to the intersection with Pike Street is what some call Little Fuzhou, the axis through which all immigrants, the vast majority brought by people-smuggling networks, have passed before settling in the immediate vicinity, in satellite communities up and down the east coast, or in isolated outposts – generally restaurants – throughout the country.

It is here, next to the traditionally Cantonese Chinatown with which it competes for space, that one finds clusters of mostly men gathered outside employment agencies scrutinizing Chinese-language blackboard listings for dish-washing and garment-assembly jobs; the banks, some of them underground, that hold savings and send remittances back to China; the all-purpose *fuwu gongsi*, or 'service companies,' ranging from those that help clients navigate American government bureaucracies to those that sell forged and fraudulent documents; the native-place associations; the travel agents, immigration lawyers, restaurants and other businesses which utterly depend on a Fuzhou-speaking clientele.

Little Fuzhou would probably still function more or less as it does had its population somehow come by legal means, especially since most of those arriving before mid-1994 acquired – through general immigration amnesties, fraud and benefits offered only to PRC citizens – the right to work and reside in the United States. Besides, the sewing machine operator without an employment authorization card (an excellent facsimile of which, in any case, has always been easily obtained from black-market document vendors) has never earned appreciably more than a worker with one. Both are paid by the piece.

With a 15- to 20-fold income differential between Fuzhou and America, a year's labour in an American restaurant or sweatshop becomes a strong magnet indeed. There have been two principal changes in the pattern of employment, one in individual careers, and the other in the type and location of jobs. The objective of most non-skilled, clandestine migrants has remained constant, namely to move through three stages of work as quickly as possible: first, to reimburse relatives and friends whose loans were used to pay professional smugglers; second, to then save as much capital as possible; three, to bring relatives to the US (by any means available) and to start one's own business, graduating from wage labourer to entrepreneur. What has changed is the amount of time it takes to complete these phases.

The initial group of seed migrants, men who arrived between World War II and 1970, wound up working as waiters, dishwashers and cooks, often in non-Chinese restaurants. Most had no smuggling fees to pay since they had jumped ship, but they needed several decades to raise sufficient capital to proceed to stage three. The next wave of migrants paid off their relatively modest interest-free smuggling debts in about two years, and were able to accumulate enough cash – working 12–14 hours a day, six days a week, with savings rates typically 90 per cent – to bring family and start a business within a decade.

The most recent wave of smuggled Fuzhou speakers, beginning around 1991, have faced several additional hurdles. The cost of passage increased so much that it soon took four or five years, rather than two, to pay back debts that now often carried interest rates of 20–25 per cent. Higher expenses – despite living eight to a room, sleeping in shifts and subsisting on noodles – meant lower savings rates, and an influx of job seekers during the peak migration years of 1991–93 meant depressed wages, which bottomed out at about US$800 a month for an entry-level position in a restaurant or garment factory in 1993.

The second change over time has been in the kind and location of work available. With the arrival of more women after 1979, the number of registered garment factories in New York's Chinese communities increased to over 500 by the early 1990s, creating an important interface with the mainstream US economy. The other important shift was the territorial expansion of Chinese restaurants, especially fast-food or take-out joints,

first into the greater New York area, and then into every state in the Union, including Alaska. This geographic growth ensured that a continuing flow of unskilled labour would be able to find jobs, albeit in far-flung outposts that made these workers expatriates twice over, first from Fuzhou, and then from Little Fuzhou. Wages, at least, were 20 to 40 per cent higher than in New York to compensate for such isolation.

When yet another employment opportunity emerged, it was not without a certain irony. Starting in the early 1990s, hundreds of Chinese peasants who had escaped the back-breaking drudgery of agricultural work in China found themselves working on vegetable farms in New Jersey, including several owned by a Fuzhou businesswoman named Zheng Cuiping, whose other interests included real estate, banking (sending back remittances) and – a line of work from which she claims to have retired – people smuggling.

There are two umbrella groups competing for the fealty of the community, the Fukien American Association (Meidong Fujian Tongxianghui), and the United Fujianese of America Association (Fujian Gongsuo). The first, established in the early 1940s by a group of ten men, is by far the larger, with some 20,000 dues-paying members, each representing a household, in 1996, 80 per cent of them in the greater New York area. The membership of both associations is 99 per cent Fuzhou natives, mostly from towns and villages (such as Changle) in the countryside around Fuzhou (see p 33). Association officials estimate that there are 150,000 Changle residents alone in the US, and acknowledge that 'over half of them' came by clandestine means, certainly an underestimate. They also point out, with some pride, that Fuzhou speakers are to be found in all 50 states and Puerto Rico.

Besides offering services typical of community associations – modest scholarships for exceptional students, a trust fund for the family of fireman killed while on the job in the neighbourhood, small loans to individuals in distress – the Fukien American Association also functions in the traditional role of a Chinatown 'tong,' one affiliated with a street gang called upon from time to time to act as enforcer or protector. The association's hired muscle, according to the FBI and Immigration and Naturalization Service investigators, was and may continue to be the Fuk Qing, or 'Fuzhou Youth,' most of whose leadership was convicted in 1994 of crimes ranging from extortion to murder.

One of the primary sources of income for the Fuk Qing, and other splinter gangs that have filled the vacuum after the 1994 convictions, is holding newly arrived clandestine immigrants and collecting the outstanding portion of their smuggling debt, generally 90 per cent of a fee that escalated from US$10,000 in 1980 to US$40,000 in 1996. A few days, a week, a month – depending on when payment is made – in a deliberately threatening and uncomfortable 'safe house' is a tribulation that nearly all smuggled migrants have endured, but almost all have survived. Beginning in 1994, gangs added kidnapping-for-ransom to their criminal repertoire, demanding that payments be made in China by victims' relatives to gang confederates. These crimes became so common in 1995 as to create an atmosphere of terror, which abated somewhat – as did the number of kidnappings – after a joint Sino-US investigation led to the highly publicized arrest of gang members who were later convicted of killing one of their captives.

There are also many village-based groups, including the Sanshan, Mawei and Houyu associations. In the case of Houyu, a two-surname coastal village in Changle at the mouth of the Min River, there are two associations representing the 70 per cent of the village population that has reconvened in Manhattan and Long Island, with scattered families in Philadelphia and Washington. Indeed, the Zheng and Zhang clans brought not only their families but their centuries-old feud with them to America, a tension that has flared periodically into violence over the years, including armed clashes during the Cultural Revolution and the aftermath of an ill-fated, cross-clan betrothal in New York in 1993 that was cancelled after a dispute over the seating arrangements at the banquet. Some Houyu natives have even based applications for political asylum on fear of persecution by opposing clan members. In general, relations between rival associations are complicated and tense, but cordial – all groups invite each other's representatives, for example, to elaborate Chinese New Year banquets.

Marlowe Hood

mid-1990s. Chinese from Taiwan were next. People of Fuzhou ancestry number about 150–200,000. Teochius, Hakkas and Chinese from Guangxi number about 100,000 each. The Hainanese and Hokkien groups (excluding those from Taiwan) each numbers 30–40,000. The remainder trace their ancestry to other regions in China.

Eligible newcomers swelled the ranks of existing native-place and other voluntary associations. Those originating elsewhere formed new native-place associations. Chinese also established organizations based on the country where they last resided. A few new clan associations also appeared. All these served primarily a social function; however, they also facilitated the newcomers' adjustment to the American environment by providing mutual help and support. The increasing number of educated immigrants is reflected in the growing number of clubs formed by the alumni of universities and middle schools in mainland China, Taiwan and Hong Kong. Alumni clubs facilitated networking also among Chinese from other countries, especially those from Vietnam and Burma.

From the mid-1960s to the mid-1990s, the Chinese population grew to an estimated two million, making it the largest Asian group in America, though still only about 0.7 percent of the total population. Among destinations, California, home to four out of every ten Chinese in America, consistently ranked first throughout the postwar decades. Hawaii had ranked second for many decades, but was bumped into third place in 1970 by New York, where about a fifth of the total Chinese population settled. None of the other 47 states has more than 5 per cent of the total Chinese population.

Contemporary Chinese are overwhelmingly urban. Whereas 75.2 per cent of the total US population lived in urban areas in 1990, 97.6 per cent of the Chinese did. However, only 53.5 per cent of the Chinese lived in the central cities. With the great influx of newcomers, many Chinatowns that had declined as Chinese moved out to other areas became bustling places in the late 1960s and early 1970s. The number of Chinese in the New York and Los Angeles metropolitan areas grew rapidly enough to rival that of the San Francisco Bay Area. New concentrations of Chinese businesses arose in locales such as Los Angeles County's San Gabriel Valley, Orange County's Westminster, New York's Flushing and Brooklyn, Bellaire near Houston, Richardson near Dallas, Chamblee near Atlanta, and San Diego.

San Francisco and Honolulu were the only two metropolises where Chinese were more than 10 per cent of the population. The highest percentages, however, were found in the suburban cities of Monterey Park, Alhambra and Rosemead in Los Angeles' San Gabriel Valley.

With the high influx of immigrants, the ratio of foreign- to local-born rose between the mid-1960s and mid-1990s from about half to seven-tenths of the Chinese population. For Chinese aged 16 and over, the proportion is even higher at eight out of every ten. Of the foreign-born, 56.8 per cent were newcomers who had arrived in the United States in the ten years before 1990. According to the census, six out of ten Chinese reported not being able to speak English very well, and 82.9 per cent of those five years and older also spoke a language other than English. The immigration of more females

Table 5.31

TEN STATES WITH THE LARGEST CHINESE POPULATIONS			
1960	1970	1980	1990
California	California	California	California
Hawaii	New York	New York	New York
New York	Hawaii	Hawaii	Hawaii
Illinois	Illinois	Illinois	Texas
Massachusetts	Massachusetts	Texas	New Jersey
Washington	New Jersey	Massachusetts	Massachusetts
Texas	Washington	New Jersey	Illinois
New Jersey	Texas	Washington	Washington
Pennsylvania	Pennsylvania	Maryland	Maryland
Michigan	Maryland	Florida	Florida

Sources: Census of Population, General Population Characteristics, *various years.*

than males since the end of World War II has resulted in a continuous decline of the male/female ratio from 189.6:100 in 1950 to 99.3:100 in 1990.

The high proportion of new immigrants explains why the Chinese have been less given to interracial marriages than such other Asian groups as the Japanese and Filipinos. Still, out-marriages have increased markedly since the late 1960s, especially among the more Westernized. They were at their highest among the predominantly American-born Chinese in Hawaii, where as early as the 1980s approximately three out of four marriages were to partners other than Chinese. In Los Angeles during the same period, the proportion was about half, while in New York, where the population was predominantly first-generation, it was less than three in ten.

The decades since the 1960s have seen the growth of a Chinese-American middle class with a strong presence in managerial, professional and white-collar occupations. In Hawaii, the rise of Asians as important components of the business establishment in the 1970s, narrowed the gap between the proportion of Asians, including Chinese, and that of whites in decision-making positions. On the mainland, however, the Chinese

Photos of relatives left behind in China prominently displayed in immigrant's home in New York.

still have lower incomes and job responsibilities than those of white colleagues with similar qualifications. Many Chinese ascending the corporate ladder soon hit a 'glass ceiling' that prevents further progress to top managerial positions. Equality of opportunity still has to be fought for.

In the mid-1960s the push for equal rights by minorities forced the federal government to launch the War on Poverty. Many communities initiated programmes targeting their social and economic problems. In the Chinese community the increase in immigration coincided with the onset of the federal programme. There was a scarcity of adequate housing, jobs, child and health care as well as a pressing need to help the newcomers adjust to their new surroundings. In many immigrant families, anti-social and criminal behaviour among the young greatly increased as cultural and generational conflicts exacerbated the deterioration in parental discipline and authority.

Programmes to tackle these problems were initiated and staffed by Western-educated professionals and activists. Many were Hong Kong immigrants or were of the generation raised in America after World War II. As these people gained experience organizing the community and dealing with the mainstream establishment, they became a significant force in the community. Some of these activists soon went beyond community programmes to make common cause with the emerging Chinese-American middle class to pursue equal opportunities in the mainstream.

This common pursuit was reflected in heightened feelings of community and ethnicity. Many became concerned with Chinese-American issues and the Chinese-American image. Groups such as Chinese for Affirmative Action (founded 1969) and Organization of Chinese Americans (founded 1973) emerged to fight for civil rights and affirmative action. In 1974 San Francisco Chinese activists won a US Supreme Court ruling in a landmark case – the decision in Lau versus Nichols led to a nationwide mandate for bilingual/bicultural education not only for the Chinese but for other non-English speaking minorities.

In their bid for improved political and social status, Chinese Americans formed political coalitions with other minorities, particularly as groups of Asian Americans. On the Pacific Coast students pushed for Asian American Studies programmes to be established in universities. In that climate of activism, students from Hong Kong and Taiwan were spurred to organize the Protect Diaoyutai Movement in 1970 to protest Japanese claims

to the Diaoyutai (islands also claimed by China). Some activists from this short-lived movement went on to join forces with others – those tackling local issues in the Chinese community.

Pressures brought to bear during the 1970s by activist groups resulted in changes in mainstream American institutions. Doors began to open for Chinese and other minorities in television and radio, journalism, law enforcement, the performing arts and other fields. Increasing numbers of qualified Chinese Americans were promoted to managerial or prominent positions in mainland institutions and businesses during the 1980s. Among the most visibly successful was Connie Chung, a broadcast journalist who became an anchor for national news coverage on television.

Chinese Americans also became more visible in mainstream officialdom. Many became members of municipal and county government boards and commissions. Others were appointed to municipal, state and federal judgeships. Still others became state and federal officials (although Chinese have yet to attain full cabinet rank). In the military a few were promoted as senior officers.

As Chinese Americans became increasingly active in mainstream politics, many formed coalitions to campaign successfully for local electoral office. A few were elected to state offices. Until the mid-1990s the highest elected office attained by a Chinese on the mainland was Gary Locke, who became Washington's state governor in 1996. As yet no other Chinese has followed Senator Hiram Fong to the US Congress.

As is natural for first-generation immigrants, the politics of the sending country continues to command attention. The contest between Taiwan and China, each with its partisan supporters, had polarized the community. But as tension in the Taiwan Straits relaxed during the 1980s, so did that in the community. Kuomintang repression on Taiwan had forced dissidents to take refuge abroad in the US and other countries. In America some Taiwanese worked with American politicians to pressure the Taiwan regime into democratizing the island. Others lent their energies to the Taiwan independence movement. Some Chinese Americans of Taiwan origin actively supported the various political factions that burgeoned after Taiwan lifted martial law in the late 1980s and allowed political parties other than the Kuomintang on the island.

A few dissidents came to the US from China in the 1980s. Their ranks were augmented by the flood of dissidents taking refuge abroad after the Tiananmen Square Incident of June 4, 1989. However, disunity and power struggles within their ranks as well as the improving economic picture in China have prevented them from being more than just a minor irritant to China.

Economic life

By the 1970s the laundry business was declining. By the 1980s the garment manufacturing industry was also retreating before the competition posed by imports. However, in 1995 there were still 2,300 small garment factories concentrated in New York, Los Angeles, San Francisco Bay Area and other large cities. The restaurant business, meanwhile, has continued to flourish and

Jeffrey Yang, Chinese-American founder of Yahoo! Inc., an Internet media company.

expand. Of the estimated 20,000 restaurants in the mid-1990s, most, though not all, served Chinese food, with some offering Japanese, Western and other cuisines. There were also Chinese running fast food chain operations. One of the largest, comprising Panda Express and Panda Inn, had 138 outlets in 18 states in 1994.

The increasing Asian immigrant population gave rise to a greater demand for Asian goods. Chinese businesses were among those importing large quantities of Asian, particularly Chinese, food items, house wares and utensils. First Taiwan and Hong Kong immigrants, then Chinese from Indochina, established supermarkets and shopping malls offering a rich variety of Chinese, Southeast Asian and American groceries. A few grew to be chain operations. One of the largest is the Ranch 99 supermarket chain; founded in 1984, this was operating 19 branch stores in California and one in Nevada by the mid-1990s.

Real estate has remained a favourite object of ethnic Chinese investments. That had been the case with Chinese Americans when they improved their economic status during the 1950s and 1960s. By the 1970s and 1980s, new immigrants, as well as Taiwan, Hong Kong and Southeast Asian sources, were injecting even larger amounts of capital into this sector. The real estate business boomed in many regions receiving ethnic Chinese investment. The competition for land use led to rent increases and inflated real estate prices in some areas. Investments also led to the rapid development since the 1970s and 1980s of new concentrations of Chinese businesses.

Chinese-American entrepreneurs are now found in practically all sectors of the American economy, although there remain areas where they are particularly concentrated. Beginning in the early 1970s, many Taiwan immigrants entered the hotel and motel business in Southern California. By 1987 they were operating about 500 such businesses, accounting for about 40 per cent of the motels in the region. Chinese Americans, mostly new immigrants, founded numerous electronic, computer, high-tech and engineering firms. The largest is Computer Associates International, a software company founded by Charles Wang. Many of these corporations have established ties to entrepreneurs and companies in the Far East.

Another sector penetrated by Chinese Americans in the 1970s is the trade in semi-precious stones. Of this, their share had grown to 10 per cent by 1990. Yet another example of the breadth of Chinese-American involvement in the US economy is the successful thrust of Chinese-owned Nautica Enterprises and La Chine Chassie into the respective mainstream markets for men's and women's wear. Agriculture, on the other hand, has attracted few Chinese, and newcomers to the field have chosen to market specialty crops such as mushrooms, ginseng and *longan*.

The improved economic status of the Chinese; their known propensity for saving; the increased business links with, and the continued influx of large amounts of capital from, the Pacific Rim countries – all this has not only caught the attention of American financial institutions but also stimulated the establishment of Chinese-owned banks. Since the early 1970s new banks have appeared in San Francisco, New York and Los Angeles,

Table 5.32

PERCENTAGE OF 16 AND OVER WORKING POPULATION IN DIFFERENT OCCUPATIONAL CATEGORIES, 1990		
OCCUPATION	PERCENTAGE	
	TOTAL CHINESE WORKING POPULATION	TOTALS WORKING POPULATION
Managerial and professional specialty occupations	35.9	26.4
Managerial occupations	15.2	12.3
Professional specialty occupations	20.7	14.1
Technical, sales and administrative support	31.2	31.7
Technical, sales	17.6	15.5
Administrative support, including clerical	13.5	16.3
Service occupations	16.5	13.2
Farming, forestry and fishing occupations	0.4	2.5
Precision production, craft and repairs occupations	5.6	11.3
Operators, fabricators and labourers	10.6	14.9
Machine, operators, assemblers, inspectors	7.6	6.8
Transportation and material moving occupations	1.2	4.1
Handlers, equipment cleaners, helpers, labourers	1.8	3.9

Sources: 1990 Census of Population, General Population Characteristics; 1990 Census of Population, Asians and Pacific Islanders in the United States.

followed by those set up in the 1980s and 1990s in smaller communities such as Houston, Boston and Chicago. Investments in these institutions have come from both domestic and foreign sources, not all of them ethnic Chinese.

Businesses from the Far East have also followed the flow of capital across the Pacific. Their local partners have often been Chinese Americans. Apart from firms such as Taiwan's Acer Computer and Formosa Plastics, these businesses have included hotels, real estate, and the American branches of major Taiwan, Hong Kong, mainland Chinese and Southeast Asian banks.

Continuing the trend since the 1960s, 1990 figures show that the Chinese population aged 25 years and over in 1990 had a high education level, with 40.7 per cent having a bachelor or higher degree as compared with 20.3 per cent among the total population. Similarly, the percentage of the Chinese working population in higher income professional specialty occupations was almost one and a half times that of the population as a whole. Chinese were especially numerous in health and dental care, engineering and technology, academia and education. Many stand out. Two examples are Samuel Ting, winner of the 1976 Nobel Prize for Physics; and Yuan T. Li, co-winner of the 1986 Nobel Prize for Chemistry.

Professional specialty occupations, together with managerial, technical, sales, and administrative support (including clerical occupations) accounted for about two-thirds of the Chinese working force, a proportion surpassing that of the population at large. Little wonder that some observers in the academic and mainstream press have characterized Chinese (and other Asian Americans) as a 'model minority' that has bettered itself by perseverance and hard work. In doing so they have helped fuel a new stereotype.

About a quarter of the Chinese workers, mainly first-generation immigrants, did not have a high school education. Of these, many men ended up working in unskilled occupations such as those in the service sector, while women found employment as machine operators in the garment industry. Owing to past exclusionary practice by unionized labour, Chinese, except those in Hawaii, are grossly under-represented in the categories of skilled workers and craftsmen.

Charles Wang.

Cultural activities

The flood of newcomers reversed the decline that Chinese cultural and recreational institutions had been suffering since the 1950s. Chinese cuisine, fashion, popular and traditional music, choral singing and karaoke, operatic and vernacular drama, martial arts and kung fu, lion and folk dances, tai chi and *qigong* found constituencies in the community and even in mainstream society. Cultural groups proliferated. In some communities multi-purpose facilities were established for Chinese recreational activities.

Chinese religious institutions also enjoyed a revival. To the few surviving joss houses were added temples dedicated to Huang Daxian, Che Gong and Guan Gong, deities transplanted from Hong Kong. These were joined by shrines to the Queen of Heaven and Bentougong, deities introduced by the Chinese from Vietnam.

Chinese Buddhism has also expanded greatly. Earlier Buddhist institutions in America included the Chinese Buddhist Association of Hawaii and Buddha's Universal Church of San Francisco. But the number proliferated with the arrival of Taiwan and Southeast Asian newcomers. Generous donations, from Taiwanese in particular, went into the construction of the Hsi Lai Monastery in

Hours of piecework being put in by women workers in New York's Chinatown.

Parade in Los Angeles Chinatown.

Los Angeles County in 1988, among other such places. Another active group, the Buddhist Compassion Relief Tzu-Chi Foundation, founded an American branch in 1985. This Taiwan organization actively supported many charitable causes and by the 1990s had established offices in several American cities.

There were many Christians among the new immigrants, and as the Chinese population increasingly diversified, some churches scheduled services in different Chinese dialects as well as in English to serve their congregations better. New churches conducting services in Cantonese, Mandarin, Hokkien and other varieties of regional speech also appeared. Evangelical in character, many of these did not engage in the social action of the older churches.

Chinese-language newspapers, whose readership shrank in the 1950s and 1960s, have enjoyed a new lease of life. By starting a North American edition in the early 1960s, Hong Kong's *Sing Tao Daily* became the first foreign-owned newspaper to establish a beachhead in the United States and Canada. The venture proved a success when the paper's circulation expanded with increased immigration in the 1970s.

Drawing on a talent pool readily provided by immigrants and students literate in the Chinese language, Chinese newspapers improved both in literary style and reporting. San Francisco and New York have remained the two principal centres of Chinese journalism, with Los Angeles laying claim to third place by the 1980s. During the 1970s and 1980s, numerous papers competed for a share of the rapidly growing Chinese market. However, by the late 1980s many community-based dailies had ceased publication in the face of soaring costs and limited returns. In the 1990s *Sing Tao* and *World Journal* (*Shijie ribao*, a subsidiary of Taiwan's leading newspaper *United Daily News*, or *Lianhe ribao*), dominated the market, with separate editions published in several North American communities. Two other papers competing for the national market are *China Press* (*Qiao bao*), connected to China interests; and *International News* (*Guoji ribao*), originally founded with capital from Taiwan but sold to an Indonesian-Chinese immigrant during the 1990s.

Many community-based publications chose not to compete directly with the national dailies. Instead they targeted niche audiences, publishing less costly weekly or monthly editions. Such papers, proliferating in smaller communities, have been able to succeed where dailies would have failed. Also published are a few magazines. Some papers focus on community news and events,

others advocate a particular political line. The range of publications is wide. Chinese from Indochina have their own newspapers (the *Vietnam-Chinese Newspaper*, founded in 1980 in Los Angeles, being one of the first to appear), as do dissidents from Taiwan and China. And just as the PRC students, visiting scholars and immigrants who settled in the US in the early 1990s issued their own newsletters or periodicals, so did Buddhists, evangelical Christians and other interest groups.

Journalists and novelists writing in Chinese can find a market for their work in Hong Kong, Taiwan and even China. Two of the first Chinese-American novelists to reach a wide audience in East Asia are Helen Yu, better known to her readers as Yu Lihua; and Kenneth Pai, better known in the Chinese world as Bai Xianyong (see box in Part IV), both of Taiwan origin. Immigrants from China and Indochina have also added to the literary output. In some communities in America writers have formed different literary and poetry societies to maintain liaison and provide mutual support.

The growth of the Chinese population has fostered the rapid expansion of the Chinese-language media. Chinese television programmes were started in the early 1970s in Los Angeles, New York and San Francisco. By the next decade such programmes had also appeared in other communities. The programming material (mostly serial drama) on which Chinese-language radio and television has relied heavily, used to come from Taiwan and Hong Kong, but by the 1980s and 1990s, PRC and even Southeast Asian productions were being broadcast. Chinese-language television programmes have also stimulated the opening of videotape rental and sales outlets. As a result, Chinese cinemas, a legacy of the 1930s, are no longer the thriving places they were in the 1950s and 1960s.

No less than their predecessors, new immigrants want their progeny to preserve their Chinese heritage. Chinatown Chinese-language schools, in decline since the 1950s, revived. New schools, often formed on the initiative of concerned parents, emerged in Chinese communities outside Chinatowns. By the mid-1990s the number of Chinese schools had increased to more than 600 from the 40 or so that had existed in the 1950s.

Since many Chinese resident outside Chinatowns do not live within easy walking distance of the schools, many schools operate on weekends only. Mandarin rather than Cantonese is the language of instruction in most schools. Most schools taught traditional Chinese characters, but since the early 1990s a growing number of schools is favouring the simplified script or is teaching both forms.

In the 1990s the language curriculum of some Chinese schools succeeded in gaining recognition from local boards of education as being equivalent to language courses offered in local public high schools. In 1994 Chinese also became one of the foreign languages in which college applicants could choose to be examined in the Scholastic Aptitude Test (SAT). Language apart, school subjects cover also Chinese culture, knowledge of which cannot be taken for granted among pupils highly assimilated to American society.

Since the 1960s, the numbers of both American- and foreign-born Chinese showing a high degree of acculturation to Western society have grown significantly. Yet while these people's behaviour and aspirations conform to norms set by mainstream American society, they themselves are set apart by their physical appearance. This has enhanced group consciousness and interest in Chinese-American history. The need felt by many to define the place of the Chinese American in American society and culture has manifested itself in the formation of such groups as San Francisco's Chinese Historical Society of America (founded 1963) to research and promote the contributions of Chinese to American history, and the Chinese Culture Foundation (founded 1965) to promote Chinese and Chinese-American culture.

The interplay of Chinese and American elements has produced a culture, which, when considered together with the experiences and traditions of other Asian minorities, is often described as 'Asian American.' Among vehicles for this culture are Los Angeles's East West Players (founded 1965), New York's Basement Workshop (founded 1971), San Francisco's Kearny Street Workshop (founded 1972) and Asian American Theatre Company (founded 1973).

American- and foreign-born immigrants alike have contributed to the definition of this evolving culture. Chinese-American themes are explored in the work of fiction writers such as Maxine Hong Kingston (see box in Part IV, p 135) and Amy Tan. Numerous other writers have expressed their feelings as Chinese Americans in poetry. Yet others have written for the stage. In 1972 Frank Chin's *Chickencoop Chinamen* became the first play by a Chinese American to be performed in the mainstream theatre.

Christine Choy, Loni Ding and Arthur Dong won awards in the 1980s for producing documentaries probing aspects of the Asian-American experience; while the work of the feature film director Wayne Wang has succeeded in crossing the boundary between Chinese-American and mainstream American cinema (see p 132).

In dance and music, too, some Chinese artists have aimed at cultural integration. Chiang Ching and Lily Cai, both dancers of PRC origin, have synthesized Chinese and American forms and techniques in their choreography. Asian-American heritage inspired the performances of Taiwan immigrant H. T. Chen (Chen Xuetong) and his contemporary dance company, Chen and Dancers, in the 1980s and 1990s. Experimentation with American jazz and Chinese music characterized the work of Jon Jang in the 1980s.

Some Chinese Americans are part of the mainstream cultural scene. The renowned cellist Yo-Yo Ma was from the start a player on the world stage, not a 'Chinese' musician but an international performer. Nor is the work and reputation of the Shanghai-born film actress Joan Chen confined to purely Chinese circles. The 1988 Tony Award for best play and best performance went respectively to David Henry Hwang's *M. Butterfly* and the actor B. D. Wong. Dennis Dun's reputation as a film and television actor in the 1980s went beyond the Asian-American theatre. Maya Lin won mainstream recognition as the architectural designer of the Vietnam Veterans' Memorial in 1982. Ding Shaoguang, a first-generation immigrant, was commissioned by the United Nations to design several commemorative stamps and first-day envelopes in the 1990s.

Him Mark Lai

Joan Chen.

Yo-Yo Ma.

AUSTRALIA

Chinese migration to Australia has been concentrated in two periods: the latter half of the 19th century and the three decades since the 1960s. In the intervening years, continuity was provided by the Australian-born Chinese community. Despite the continuity, the contemporary Chinese community is very different from that of last century. So also is Australian society.

The periods of major Chinese immigration have coincided with watersheds in Australian history. In the first, Australia's population grew rapidly and the associated development of nationalism culminated in the federation of the six former British colonies into the Australian nation in 1901. In the second period, multiculturalism replaced assimilation as the official policy on inter-ethnic relations, which had become more diverse following extensive non-British immigration after World War II. In addition there has been a major restructuring of Australia's economy and a growing Australian economic and political involvement with newly independent and fast-growing Asian countries.

Engraving dated 1856 shows Chinese miners heading for the diggings.

19th-century migration and settlement

Archaeological evidence suggests that Chinese traders may have reached the coast of northern Australia before European colonization, and there were limited schemes to recruit Chinese agricultural labour, 3,000 or whom arrived after 1847. But the first substantial influx of Chinese migrants only commenced after the discovery of gold in 1851. The Chinese were a significant and very visible section of the transitory populations of the New South Wales and Victorian gold-fields, constituting 60 per cent of the former and 25 per cent of the latter in 1861.

They soon became the targets of violent attacks and the object of discriminatory legislation similar to that experienced by the Chinese in North America. The first attempt to limit Chinese arrivals was the 1855 Victorian legislation imposing a poll tax on Chinese arrivals and limiting the numbers carried on ships. Legislation limiting Chinese access to new gold-fields and requiring them to live in separate residential areas was also part

Family in car in Darwin, 1927 (bottom right).

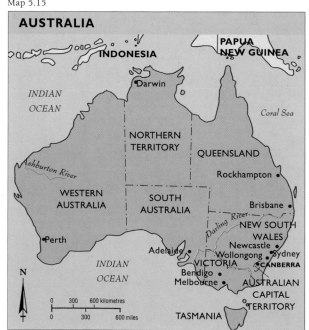

Map 5.15

of the restrictions adopted in a number of the other colonies as discoveries of gold attracted Chinese immigrants (see Chronology, opposite).

With the decline of individual gold-fields, many Chinese left the New Gold Mountain, as they called Australia, to return to China. Others remained, gaining a living as agricultural labourers and, in some cases, operating rural stores. Earlier fears of Chinese competition for gold were transferred to workers' fears of cheap Chinese labour. The strength of the workers' trade union movement resulted in a successful anti-Chinese seaman's strike in 1878, and in legislation aimed to restrict Chinese workers in the furniture trade. These discriminatory measures and reduced economic opportunities, aggravated by a major Depression in the 1890s, encouraged the departure of more Chinese. At the time of the federation of the Australian colonies in 1901, Chinese were less than 1 per cent of the total population, a marked contrast to their 3.3 per cent in 1861.

The federation was a watershed for Chinese settlement. A major factor leading to federation had been the desire to control non-European, especially Chinese, immigration, and the Immigration Restriction Act was one of the first to be passed by the new Commonwealth Parliament. This Act, which provided the legislative base for the White Australia Policy, restricted entry by providing for a dictation test in any European language to be given to those arriving without a Certificate of Ex-

emption. Apart from returning residents, such certificates were limited to Chinese coming as managers of existing businesses or with the skills needed by Chinese businesses (such as chefs and clerks). The wives and children of Chinese merchants were also allowed short-term entry. While the federation removed previous opportunities for Chinese to become naturalized citizens, one advantage for Chinese residents was that they were able to move freely across State and Territory borders.

By 1901, two Chinese groups could be distinguished. The larger consisted of single men, working in a variety of rural and urban labouring activities. Through market gardening, one of their major occupations, Chinese dominated the supply of fresh vegetables in Australian cities and towns.

Far smaller was the group of successful Chinese professionals and businessmen, some of whom had established international business connections. Australian Chinese capital, for example, was important in the founding of the three major Chinese department stores – Wing On, Sincere and Sun – in Hong Kong and Shanghai. The businessmen also mixed in non-Chinese business and social circles and established families in Australia. Often their wives were European women since, as late as 1901, there were still 61.5 Chinese men for every Chinese woman in Australia, although the sex ratio among the 3,090 part-Chinese offspring of these unions was equal.

Towards unrestricted migration

For the next half century, the Chinese population continued to decline as the older immigrants died and restrictions reined in immigration. World War II saw the arrival of Chinese refugees from New Guinea and the Pacific Islands, and by 1947, the Chinese population was just over 12,000.

In the 1950s and 1960s, a gradual easing of the White Australia Policy allowed Australian citizens to bring in their non-European spouses, and overseas-born Asians to become once again naturalized citizens whose spouses could be admitted. Restrictions on the entry of part-Europeans and highly skilled non-Europeans also ended. The Chinese population expanded, but its size remained unremarkable.

By 1971, just prior to the complete abandonment of the White Australia Policy, the Chinese population, excluding those who were part-Chinese, was not much changed from the 1960s at 26,000. A third of the Chinese were Australian-born, a quarter had been born in China and another 40 per cent had been born elsewhere in Asia. The majority of the latter were Chinese students from Southeast Asian countries, studying in Australia under educational aid programmes initiated after World War II.

On their arrival these students found a small but well-established community of Australia-born Chinese. Over the years, the contacts of this community with Chinese culture had been attenuated, and there had been extensive assimilation into the larger population. Indicative of these changes, Darwin, the major city in the Northern Territory with a long-established Chinese population, elected Australia's first Chinese mayor in 1966.

CHRONOLOGY

1848	120 Chinese labourers arrive from Amoy
1851	Gold discovered
1855	Victoria passes legislation to restrict Chinese immigration. Repealed 1863
1857	South Australian legislation to restrict Chinese immigration
1857	Buckland River anti-Chinese riots
1861	Lambing Flat anti-Chinese riots
1861	New South Wales passes legislation to restrict Chinese immigration. Repealed 1867
1877	Queensland anti-Chinese legislation
1878	Anti-Chinese seaman's strike
1886	Western Australia anti-Chinese legislation
1896	Victoria and New South Wales legislation to restrict Chinese in the furniture-making industry
1901	Immigration Restriction Act
1903	Asians lose right to be naturalized
1957	Non-Europeans allowed to apply for citizenship after 15 years' residence and, subsequently, to bring spouses and children to Australia
1958	Immigration Restriction Act repealed and limited entry allowed for 'distinguished and highly qualified' persons
1966	Residence period for naturalization reduced to five years and a wider range of individuals admitted under the 'distinguished and highly skilled' category
1973	Adoption of non-discriminatory immigration selection. Residence period for naturalization of all non-British immigrants shortened to 3 years and then, in 1984, to 2 years. Papua New Guinea gains self-government followed by independence from Australia in 1975
1975	Arrival of refugees from East Timor after Indonesian invasion
1976	Arrival of first group of Vietnamese 'boat people'
1989	PRC students in Australia given a four-year extension on the temporary entry visas following the Tiananmen Incident
1993	A majority of the PRC students with visas extended in 1989 allowed to apply for permanent residence in Australia

Contemporary Chinese migration and settlement

The election of a Labor government in 1972 was followed by the final abandonment of the White Australia Policy and the introduction of a non-racially discriminatory immigration and naturalization policy. Another important decision for the Chinese community was the diplomatic recognition of the People's Republic of China (PRC). This reopened contacts and removed the final barriers to significant Chinese entry, even though a slow but steady increase in ethnic Chinese immigration had already been occurring before 1973, mainly from Malaysia, Singapore and Hong Kong.

Various Australian government policy decisions and complex international developments explain the composition and characteristics of the contemporary Chinese population, which was some 450,000 in 1996. Chinese migrants come in search of not so much the New Gold Mountain as political and personal security, and a less physically polluted environment.

The granting of independence to Papua New Guinea in 1975 led to the settlement in Australia of several thousands of the former Australian colony's Chinese; these Chinese were already Australian citizens (see p 297). Shortly after, with the ending of the Vietnam war, the Australian government began grudgingly to accept refugees from Indochina, many of them ethnic Chinese (see p 229). At the end of the 1970s, an increased focus on

(Box) 19th-century Chinese ceramic fragments unearthed from Northern Territories goldfields in 1993.

Australian Chinese investor in department stores in Hong Kong and Shanghai.

accepting family-reunion immigrants allowed existing Chinese residents to bring in more family members. Newer migration streams were opened up during the 1980s as immigration policy became more economically oriented and sought to attract highly skilled professionals, technicians and managers as well as business migrants with capital and entrepreneurial skills. By 1986, the Chinese population of Australia was about 200,000 or 1.3 per cent of the total population (see table 5.33). It was also highly diverse. The Australian-born Chinese had declined to a fifth of the population, while nearly a fifth was from Indochina. Malaysia (15.4 per cent), China (15.2 per cent), and Hong Kong and Macao (13.0 per cent) were also important source countries. Among the 4.7 per cent born in Indonesia, nearly half were from East Timor. Chinese from Singapore were 3.6 per cent, while nearly another 2 per cent were from the Pacific region, mainly Papua New Guinea.

The growth in Chinese immigration continued throughout the late 1980s, and by 1991 the Chinese population had increased to approximately 350,000. Over the same period, those speaking a Chinese language had also increased 88 per cent (from 139,100 to 261,648), becoming the third largest non-English speaking group in Australia. Diversity increased with the growth in numbers. Numerous Hong Kong professionals, managers and technical workers, concerned about their post-1997 future, entered Australia as highly skilled independent and business migrants, especially following the Tiananmen Incident of June 4, 1989. From the mid-1980s, Taiwan-born Chinese began to enter as business immigrants. Most significant has been the arrival of large numbers of Chinese from the PRC. Some entered with the support of relatives in Australia, but Australia's 1985 decision to sell places in Australian universities and English-language classes to overseas students brought in the larger number. Many were more interested in coming to Australia to work than to study English. Before the 1989 Tiananmen Incident, 20,000 PRC students arrived and a further 25,000 followed in the two years after the Incident.

Following the Incident, the prime minister gave an undertaking that these students would not be forced to leave Australia and, accordingly, they were given a special four-year extension to their temporary entry permits. By December 1992, many of the 34,800 post-Tiananmen arrivals had sought asylum in Australia. In response to an extensive lobbying campaign, the government announced in November 1993 that the majority would be granted effective refugee status and permanent residence. By February 1996, permanent residence had been granted to nearly 37,000. This gave them the right to bring in immediate family members. In 1995–96 nearly 10,000 such immigrants (constituting 10 per cent of the total Australian intake for the year) arrived.

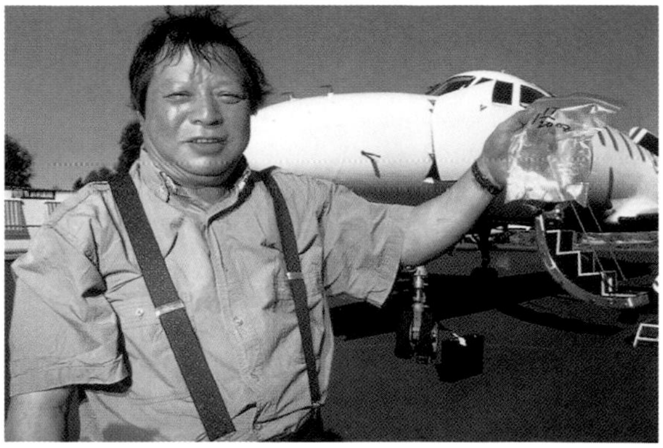

Shanghai-born entrepreneur prospers from digging opals from outback.

Between 1991 and 1996, there was a sizeable growth in immigration from Hong Kong, China and Taiwan, and continuing inflows from countries such as Malaysia and Singapore. Immigration from Indonesia, which includes ethnic Chinese, has also increased. Census figures for 1996 show an increase in the population of the PRC-born to 111,000, the Hong Kong-born to 68,400 and the Taiwan-born to 19,500; these indicate growth rates since 1991 of 42.5 per cent, 19 per cent and 56 per cent respectively. While the numbers arriving from Hong Kong and Taiwan have since slowed, strong growth in the numbers of PRC-born family immigrants is expected. This will further change the place-of-origin balance between the different groups in the Chinese community.

From sojourner to wayfaring resident

The extensive movement of temporarily resident Chinese between Australia and Asia is very different from those of earlier sojourners. The revolution in communications has made it possible to reside in one country and simultaneously conduct business in another, while extensive travel has grown in tandem with the emergence of a middle class in Asia and that region's expanding international trade with Australia.

Apart from tourists, the major group of Chinese who are officially resident in Australia on a temporary basis are students. In 1994–95, 39 per cent of the 51,358 student visas issued went to students from Indonesia (11.7 per cent), Singapore (8.6 per cent), Malaysia (7.4 per cent), Hong Kong (6.4 per cent) and Taiwan (4.8 per cent). Because PRC students frequently overstayed and/or did not comply with their visa conditions, their entry has been severely restricted since 1992. In 1994–95 just over 1,000 gained student visas compared with 22,420 in 1988–89. Another group of Chinese living in Australia on temporary visas are those entering as skilled workers (Australia has long discouraged temporary, unskilled migration). The numbers involved are, however, small and none of the countries with large Chinese populations were among the top ten source countries which in 1994–95 accounted for some 70 per cent of the 77,300 visas.

Hence the majority of Chinese in Australia are either Australian-born or immigrants with rights to permanent residence and eligible for Australian citizenship after two years' residence. A very high proportion of Chinese immigrants, especially those from Hong Kong, have taken up the option of Australian citizenship as soon as it has

Figure 5.2

CHINESE BY BIRTHPLACE, 1986

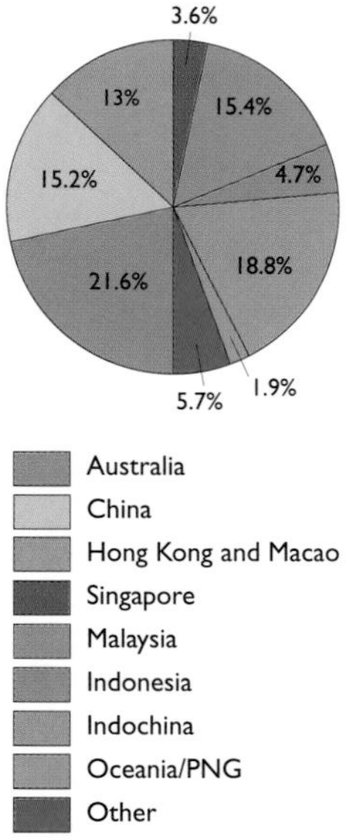

Table 5.33

CHINESE IN AUSTRALIA

YEAR	CHINESE	PART-CHINESE	TOTAL CHINESE	% OF AUSTRALIAN POPULATION
1901	29,627	3,090	32,717	0.78
1911	22,753	3,019	25,772	0.58
1921	17,157	3,669	20,826	0.39
1933	10,846	3,503	14,349	0.21
1947	9,144	2,950	12,094	0.16
1954	12,878	2,680	15,558	0.17
1961	20,382	3,186	23,568	0.22
1966	na	na	26,723	0.23
1971	26,198	na	26,198	0.21
1976	na	na	36,638	0.27
1986	169,141	27,206	196,347	1.30

Definition of 'Chinese' has changed from census to census. Figures for 1971 apparently exclude part-Chinese.
Sources: Census data.

become available. The only two source countries where there has been an increase in those who are eligible but who do not become citizens are Malaysia and the PRC.

Citizenship is not necessarily an indication of the intention to settle permanently. Rather, as in the case of many individuals from Hong Kong, and increasingly the PRC, which in 1994–95 was the third largest source of permanent departures, it may be a form of insurance. While approximately nine out of every ten Hong Kong- and Taiwan-born permanent departures return to their birthplace, less than half of those born in the PRC or Malaysia do so. Hong Kong is an especially popular destination for many departing Australian residents, many of whom may be Chinese born elsewhere.

Far larger than the numbers of Chinese indicating they are leaving Australia permanently are those who leave for relatively lengthy periods, often in connection with their employment. This is especially common among Hong Kong Chinese, particularly those without young children, who have gained Australian citizenship. These people's longer-term settlement intentions are often uncertain and dependent on developments in Hong Kong after July 1997.

The 'astronaut' phenomenon found among Chinese in the US and Canada – where husbands leave their families abroad while they themselves return to their job or business in their place of origin – also exists in Australia, especially among Hong Kong and Taiwan businessmen and highly skilled workers. The arrangement, which inverts and modernizes the older sojourner pattern, creates tensions whose resolution varies from family to family.

The changing composition of the Chinese

In contrast to the predominantly male migration of the 19th century, the numbers of Chinese men and women in Australia were almost the same in 1986 (100.5 men for every 100 women) and 1991 (just over half of all Chinese speakers were males). There were, however, variations according to place of origin. Those born in the PRC had a higher percentage of males, for example, than those born in Taiwan, probably because a larger proportion of those who came from the PRC to study were men unaccompanied by their families, while more husbands in the Taiwan group were likely to be 'astronauts.' The imbalance among the PRC arrivals is already beginning to change as they take advantage of permanent residency to bring in wives and families.

With the large-scale immigration of relatively young individuals, only 5.1 per cent of all Chinese speakers were aged over 64 in 1991, while 43.2 per cent were aged between 25 and 44. The long-established China-born Cantonese group had a much larger proportion of

the elderly (nearly a fifth) than the China-born Mandarin speakers (only 4.7 per cent). In age structure, the Mandarin group differed from the student-migrants from Hong Kong and Southeast Asia in having relatively small numbers in the 16–24 age group.

Intermarriage with partners outside the Chinese community, extensive among the earlier groups of Chinese settlers, has steadily declined among the China- and Hong Kong-born from 1923 through to 1992, a period of increased immigration from those places. Among the PRC-born, more men (28.4 per cent) than women (a fifth) married out in 1991–92. Census data for 1991 suggest that among the Singapore- and PRC-born, those with Australian spouses tended to have higher economic and educational qualifications, which may have facilitated a higher level of social mixing outside their own regional groupings.

Malaysian Tan Chin Nam at 1996 Melbourne Cup.

As numbers grew, so did the community's geographical, linguistic and social heterogeneity. In the 19th century, Guangdong and Fujian supplied most of the immigrants, including the small numbers who came via Singapore. While Siyi ('four districts') groups were prominent in Melbourne, Brisbane had mainly migrants from Zhongshan, whereas Sydney had a more diverse Chinese population. The arrival of non-Cantonese Chinese students from Southeast Asia after World War II added to the regional and linguistic diversity (though numbers of these had, like the Australian-born, been educated in English rather than in Chinese), as did the influx of Indochinese refugees, many of whom were Chinese educated in Mandarin. The number of Mandarin speakers has also risen with the immigration from

Australian wife and mixed offspring of immigrant (surnamed Lee) in Cairns.

History of Chinese in Australia portrayed in scroll by Chinese artist Mo Xiangyi.

Taiwan and the PRC, the latter sending significant numbers from east and north China, areas not previously represented in Australia.

By 1991, of the 261,648 Chinese-language speakers, 62.2 per cent spoke Cantonese as the first language at home, 20.8 per cent spoke Mandarin, 5.7 per cent spoke another Chinese language and 11.2 per cent indicated simply that they spoke 'Chinese.' The continuing prominence of Cantonese and the growing significance of Mandarin are evident from the enrolments in the government's English language, Adult Migrant Education Programme in 1994 and 1995. Of these enrolments, Cantonese were 38.7 per cent, Mandarin speakers were 43.1 per cent, Hakkas (mostly from East Timor) were 1.2 per cent, Teochius (mostly from Cambodia) were 0.4 per cent, Hokkiens (mostly from China) were 0.2 per cent, while those who spoke 'Chinese' were 16.3 per cent.

Residential patterns

Australia is one of the most highly urbanized countries in the world and Chinese, like other recent migrants, are even more highly concentrated in the cities. New South Wales and its capital, Sydney, Australia's largest city and its financial centre, attract over 40 per cent of all recent immigrants, and an even higher percentage of those from Asian countries. Not all the Chinese are, however, equally likely to settle in New South Wales, even though, as figure 5.3 shows, it is home to half of all Australia's Chinese.

In 1996, over half of all those born in the PRC, Hong Kong and Macao, were settled in New South Wales, while smaller proportions lived in Victoria and the other states

and territories. The Taiwan-born's first choice was Queensland, then New South Wales. Singaporeans favoured Western Australia, followed by New South Wales and Victoria. The major centre of Malaysian settlement was Victoria, followed by New South Wales and Western Australia. New South Wales and Victoria were major centres of settlement by those born in Vietnam, Cambodia and Laos. Among the smaller groups of overseas-born Chinese, figures for 1991 show that those from Papua New Guinea favoured Sydney and the Brisbane region. By contrast, the East Timorese Chinese were concentrated in Melbourne, Sydney and Darwin. A city of less than 80,000 people, Darwin has a Chinese community established in the 19th century. In addition to the relatively large Australian-born Chinese community, Darwin's Chinese population has been augmented by those from East Timor and other parts of Southeast Asia, especially Singapore.

The geographical distribution of Chinese reflects the diverse educational, kinship, geographical and economic networks which have moulded settlement patterns and, in the case of the Indochinese refugee groups, the role of government resettlement policies. As is illustrated by Sydney, the largest centre of Chinese settlement, Chinese, like the rest of the Australian population, have moved into the suburbs, and Chinatowns are not major residential centres, even though they have expanded with the increase in Chinese numbers. Residential 'ghettoes' are not a feature of Australian cities, and even in Ashfield, the Sydney municipality with the highest concentration of Chinese speakers, Chinese are only 10.2 per cent of the population. Elsewhere, the percentage of the Chinese in the suburban areas is much less.

Over the years, as permanent settlers have replaced students as the main group in the immigrant Chinese population, the centres of settlement have moved away from areas close to the University of New South Wales. Hong Kong groups are now settled extensively in the middle- and upper-middle class areas on the North Shore and in the newer middle-class areas of the Hills District, as well as around Hurstville and Sylvania in the south. Middle-class Taiwanese groups have also favoured the Upper North Shore and Hills district. The predominantly middle-class Malaysians and Singaporeans have settled on the North Shore and in the Epping, Ryde and Denistone areas. By contrast with these groups, the more recently arrived PRC-born have settled in the cheaper areas around Ashfield and Auburn. To these areas, and to Marrickville, the Indochinese arrivals, originally settled in Fairfield and Cabramatta, have also relocated.

In other large cities, similar patterns of residential concentration distinguish the wealthier, middle-class

Figure 5.3

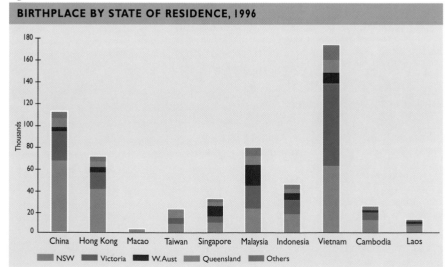

BIRTHPLACE BY STATE OF RESIDENCE, 1996

Thousands (y-axis: 0, 20, 40, 60, 80, 100, 120, 140, 160, 180)

China, Hong Kong, Macao, Taiwan, Singapore, Malaysia, Indonesia, Vietnam, Cambodia, Laos

Legend: NSW · Victoria · W.Aust · Queensland · Others

Hong Kong, Taiwan and Southeast Asian Chinese from those who have come as refugees or as recent arrivals from the PRC.

Economic activity and situation

By the 1960s, Chinese had already begun to move out of niche occupations in market gardening and restaurants into the professions and white collar work. This trend has been continued by the substantial numbers of Chinese arriving from Malaysia, Singapore and Hong Kong; highly educated professionals, fluent in English, with educational qualifications readily recognized in Australia, these Chinese pose a contrast to the refugees from Indochina and East Timor and the large numbers of students from the PRC. Although often highly educated, the PRC students have been disadvantaged, like the Indochinese refugees, by their limited English and lack of locally recognized qualifications and work experience, and so have found it hard to achieve an employment status commensurate with their education.

In 1991, during a major recession, when the national level of unemployment was 7.1 per cent, 13.6 per cent of the recently arrived Mandarin speakers from the PRC were unemployed. Within the Chinese community, only those who came as refugees from Vietnam, Cambodia and Laos fared worse. The major group of Chinese with unemployment below the national average was the Singapore-born (6.7 per cent), while the rate among the Australian-born Chinese was the same as the national average.

Among those employed in 1991, there were significant occupational differences between those born in Hong Kong, the PRC and Taiwan. Those from the PRC were concentrated in low status, unskilled, blue collar, occupations, with a quarter working as labourers, a tenth as machine operators, and a fifth in various skilled trades; in this last sector, the chief concentration was in Chinese-owned restaurants.

By contrast, a third of the Hong Kong-born worked as either professionals or para-professionals (especially in accounting, computing and other business-related professions), while a tenth worked as managers. A similar concentration in high-status occupations was also evident among those born in Taiwan, except that they were more likely to be employed as managers than professionals or para-professionals.

Self-employment, often in niche occupations serving the general population or in businesses catering to the ethnic community, is one way of overcoming discrimination or difficulties in gaining employment, and is a route that has been followed by Chinese in Aus-

tralia. To judge from 1991 figures, there was again considerable variation within the Chinese community, with the predominantly Cantonese speaking Chinese from Papua New Guinea showing the highest rate (15 per cent) of self-employment, bringing to Australia their established strategy of self-employment as traders. Chinese of Cambodian, Laotian and non-East Timorese Indonesian origin were also more likely to be employers or self-employed, but not the Taiwan-born, who must have found it hard to establish businesses in a deep economic recession. Of all the Chinese language groups, the ones with the fewest employers/self-employed were the Mandarin-speaking PRC former students and the Singaporeans. Among the Australian- and Vietnamese-born Chinese, only those who spoke Mandarin had markedly high levels of self-employment.

As the large Chinese commercial telephone directories in Sydney and other centres illustrate, the growth of the Chinese population has certainly created renewed opportunities for businesses catering for Chinese customers' needs – groceries, travel, videos and a range of financial and personal services. Many such businesses are owned by Chinese, but others are not, although they often employ Chinese-speaking staff. Less visible than shops and other small businesses is the Chinese investment in residential and commercial property. This has been very common among wealthy local and overseas-based Chinese family groups and public companies. Instead of being sourced in Australia and invested overseas, as was the case in the 19th century, now much of the wealth being invested by Chinese comes from overseas, non-resident Chinese.

Property was the commonest source of the wealth of the richest 200 Australians named in a 1996 listing. Included in the list are three Chinese. Allegedly the wealthiest is Fu Hsien-ta, who immigrated from Taiwan in 1992. In Brisbane, where he settled, he has invested in shopping centres while also retaining business interests in Taiwan. Bernard Chan was born in New Guinea, where his father and uncles had investments in plantations and trading activities dating from the German period (see Part V: The South Pacific). After World War II the family began to invest also in Australia, following the common route of first providing accommodation for family members on holiday in Sydney, and then branching into other areas of property investment, including

Advertisement in Singapore paper promotes Melbourne property.

Hong Kong's airline Cathay Pacific locates its data centre in Sydney.

Chinese restaurants proliferate in Sydney.

shopping centres. By the end of the 1980s they had relocated their major business activities to Australia. Different again is the story of Daniel Chen, a Teochiu who came to Australia just before World War II. While property has been an important part of his investment strategy, Chen's range of business interests also includes garment manufacturing and importing, as well as wine-making.

In addition, food processing, computers and leisure activities have attracted overseas and Australian Chinese investment. However, agriculture, the resource industry, engineering and manufacturing have not been popular. Encouraged by the Australian government policy of increasing Australia-Asia trade, many Chinese, especially individuals and small groups from the PRC, have engaged in trading activities with their places of origin. But the success of these is not always clear.

The transformation of community institutions and culture

The expansion of Chinatowns

Accompanying the rapid growth of the Chinese population has been the revitalization and restructuring of community institutions and organizations. One highly visible sign of these changes has been the growth of ex-

Malaysian money has restored the once-decrepit Queen Victoria Building in Sydney.

isting and new Chinatowns. On top of being the focuses for commercial, community and welfare services catering for the Chinese population, Chinatowns – such as the older ones in the capital cities and Cabramatta in Sydney – have been promoted by local governments and business organizations as Chinese 'cultural' precincts to attract tourists and non-Chinese visitors. The preference for the low- and medium-density suburban housing typical of Australian cities means that few Chinese actually live in the downtown Chinatowns. The main exception is Sydney, and to a lesser extent Melbourne, where non-resident Chinese are among those purchasing new, luxury, high-rise downtown apartments for use on their visits to Australia or for investment. Given the large middle-class component in the Chinese population, many of the new 'Chinatowns' are now located within existing middle-class shopping centres in suburbs such as Chatswood (Sydney), Box Hill (Melbourne) and Sunnybank (Brisbane).

The media

Another highly visible expression of community change is the rebirth of the local Chinese press after earlier Chinese newspapers ceased publication in the 1920s. The first of the new Chinese newspapers, *Sing Tao Jih Pao* (*Xingdao ribao*), began publication in 1982 and was followed by the *Australian Chinese Daily* in 1987. Since the mid-1980s, three further daily Chinese newspapers, the *Chinese Age*, the *Independence Daily* and the *Chinese Herald*, have begun publication, and others are planned. In addition to these five dailies, which are all published in Sydney but distributed nationally, there are many weekly and monthly newspapers, and a plethora of more informal newsletters and publications produced by former PRC students as a way of earning a living. Advertising is an important source of revenue for these publications, most of which are distributed free.

Complementing the print media are radio and television. In addition to the government funded Special Broadcasting Service, which provides radio and television programmes in Cantonese and Mandarin, private Chinese language radio stations now exist in Sydney, Melbourne, Brisbane and Adelaide. Chinese groups offer programmes on community television in Sydney and Melbourne. Two of the new commercial cable television suppliers offer nationally available Chinese-language programmes. Galaxy offers New World Television, which sources most of its programmes from Hong Kong, with general programming in Cantonese and some Mandarin. The other supplier, Optus, offers two channels via satellite transmission from Hong Kong and Beijing. These channels offer mainly Mandarin programmes with an emphasis on news and public affairs. The media outlets are an important source of information about developments affecting the Chinese in Australia and, also, internationally. They also serve as a source of entertainment, complementing both specialist cinemas screening Chinese films and the extremely popular Chinese videos readily available from local stores.

Chinese associations

By the end of the 1960s, most of the surviving Chinese associations had become largely moribund, with their main support coming from the elderly China-born population. Now there is a large and flourishing range of Chinese voluntary associations, the majority of them newly established, the rest reinvigorated versions of older organizations. One example of the latter is the Chinese Youth League, founded in Sydney in 1939 to raise funds for the war against Japan and to look after the welfare of Chinese seamen stranded in Australia. From 1945 until Australia re-established diplomatic relations with China in the 1970s, the League was active in promoting relations between Australia and the PRC. It then became involved in organizing Chinese-language classes and now undertakes a range of cultural and sporting activities. Slightly different is the Melbourne Kong Chew (Gangzhou) Society, a native-place association founded in the 1850s and now active in staging Cantonese Opera performances.

The contemporary organizations vary markedly in size, structure and function, as well as in their level of activity and stability. A 1996 government list of the larger organizations with a social welfare, educational or political role contains the names of 138 organizations. New South Wales had the largest number (57), followed by Victoria (38), Queensland (15), South Australia (9), Northern Territory (7), Western Australia (5), the Australian Capital Territory (4) and Tasmania (3). These apart, several hundred organizations cater for specific groups or interests within the Chinese community.

In type, some Chinese associations are large, multi-function social welfare organizations; others have a narrower focus, catering, for example, for the elderly. Still others are commercial in orientation. In this last group fall Chambers of Commerce, the Australian Chinese Academics and Professionals Association and the Chinese Restaurateurs Association of Victoria. There is also a wide array of other special-purpose organizations bringing together individuals whose common interests range from photography to being the alumni of overseas schools or colleges.

The large multi-function organizations have the highest profile both inside and outside the Chinese community. One such body, the Sydney-based Australian Chinese Community Association (ACCA) – whose nearly 6,000 members are primarily Hong Kong, Singapore and Malaysian professionals – provides a range of community services catering for newly arrived immigrants, the aged, women and youth groups in a number of suburbs. It has also begun an employment service and runs a Chinese-language school. Advocacy work and representations to government organizations are important elements in achieving its aim of building links between the Chinese and wider Australian society. Funding for these activities partially comes from membership fees and donations, but many of the welfare and educational activities receive government assistance.

Other similar Sydney organizations include the Chinese Australian Social Services Society and the Chinese Migrant Association of New South Wales, the latter catering for Chinese from the PRC. The role of providing community service, particularly emphasized by the Sydney associations, is assumed in Melbourne by the Federation of Chinese Associations and the Chinese Community Social Services Centre. Comparable organizations elsewhere are the Cathay Club in Brisbane, the Chung Wah (Zhonghua) Society in Perth, the Chinese Welfare

Sydney's Chinese Youth League dragon boat team.

Services of South Australia and the Overseas Chinese Association of South Australia in Adelaide. In both Sydney and Melbourne, community groups run hostels and nursing homes for elderly Chinese, and there are organizations whose primary function is to serve the needs of the growing numbers of elderly Chinese.

Many groupings are based on place of origin. In the 19th century this would have been a district or speech area in south China; today it could be a region like Indochina. However, associations based on the last place of previous residence coexist with native-place organizations – examples are the Hainanese Association, the Australian Chinese Teo Chew (Teochiu) Association in Sydney, and the Fujian Association of Victoria representing mainly recent immigrants.

The concerns of the organizations vary with the social and economic circumstances of the regional group they represent. Thus those catering for refugee groups – such as the Sydney-based Chinese Descendants Mutual Association, the New South Wales Indochina Chinese Association, the Timor Ethnic Chinese Community in Victoria and the Indochina Ethnic Chinese Association of Victoria – focus mainly on welfare and social service provision. In pursuing these aims they often receive considerable financial support from the government.

Representing a different kind of community, one of primarily business immigrants, the Taiwan associations – such as the Australian Taiwanese Friendship Association, which consists of about 1,000 families, and the Taiwan Women's League in Queensland – organize social activities and language classes. Associations catering for the professional, English-speaking Malaysian and Singaporean community also tend to place a greater emphasis on cultural and social activities rather than on welfare. In contrast, groups developed by PRC students after 1989 often aimed specifically at lobbying the Australian government for permanent residency. With this aim largely achieved, many of these groups lost their *raison d'etre* and no longer operate.

Australia does not have formal diplomatic links with Taiwan, but economic and cultural interests are represented by semi-official trade offices. Inevitably, there are organizations

Chinese cinema in Sydney.

Siyi Buddhist temple in Sydney.

whose primary concern is with political developments involving Taiwan or the PRC. The aim of maintaining links with the country of origin similarly lies behind the support given to the various Singapore clubs by the Singapore government through the Singapore International Foundation. Other groups, such as the Sydney-based Australian Chinese Forum, are more concerned with Australian rather than place-of-origin political developments, especially as they affect local Chinese and their relations with non-Chinese communities.

Attempts to bring the plethora of groupings together within a unifying structure or umbrella organization at either the national or local level have so far been unsuccessful. The diversity of interests and backgrounds, together with personal competition, has made it difficult to develop an organizational structure acceptable by all, and to identify individuals able to represent, or speak on behalf of, the Chinese community as a whole.

Religion

In the 19th century, despite the transitory nature of their sojourn, Chinese built joss houses or temples, sponsored often by native-place associations. These places of worship accommodated not only the tablets of deceased sojourners and their bodies awaiting repatriation to China, but also new arrivals, the elderly or indigent.

Christian churches also played an important part in the Chinese community as places of worship, as sources of English language education and as intermediaries with the Anglo-Australian society. By the 1960s, with many Chinese having become Christians, joss houses were actively maintained only in Sydney (the Sze Yap [Siyi] and Yiuming temples), Melbourne (the oldest continuous temple, the See Yup [Siyi] temple dating from 1866) and Darwin.

As the Chinese population has grown, so too, have new Christian and Buddhist congregations. The older Chinese joss houses have been renovated, sometimes by non-Chinese heritage groups. Figures for 1986 show the breakdown of Chinese by religious affiliation as follows: a third Christian, a sixth non-Christian, and the remainder either indicated that they had no religion or gave an equivocal response. Half of those born in Australia, Singapore and Indonesia, especially East Timor, were Christian; nearly half of the non-Christians were Buddhists from Indochina, while a fifth were Buddhists from Malaysia and Brunei. Two-thirds of those from China and Hong Kong and 55 per cent of those from Indochina claimed no religious affiliation.

By 1991, a quarter of the Chinese speakers described themselves as Christians, nearly half of them Catholics. One in eight was Buddhist. Half claimed that they had no religion, while almost 10 per cent failed to answer. Birthplace was a source of variation here as in other spheres of Chinese life: few Chinese born in the PRC and Vietnam described themselves as Christians. But,

while over a third of the Vietnamese-born Chinese were Buddhists, less than 10 per cent of those from the PRC were. Two-thirds of the PRC-born stated they had no religion, and well over half of those born in Hong Kong agreed. Those least likely to report they had 'no religion' were the Malaysian and Singaporean Chinese. Among both groups over a third professed themselves to be Catholics or to belong to other Christian religions. A quarter of the Malaysian Chinese also described themselves as Buddhists, a rate that was even higher than among the Taiwan-born.

Paralleling the growth in individual adherents has been an increase in the numbers of individual religious institutions, especially in Sydney and Melbourne. Whereas only a few Chinese Christian congregations existed in the 1970s, by 1989 some 50 existed in Australia – with 20 in Sydney and 18 in Melbourne. By 1996, 51 churches in Melbourne were associated with the Chinese Inter-Church Committee (CIC), while over 80 churches in Sydney were affiliated with the United Evangelism Committee (UEC). In addition to churches attached to the Anglican, Presbyterian, Baptist or other major denominations, there were numerous independent congregations; these had a strong evangelical or pentecostal ethos and recruited their pastor directly from overseas.

Despite the significant number of Chinese Catholics, there were only a few Catholic congregations; this suggests that Catholics were more likely than Chinese Protestants to worship in their local neighbourhood churches. More than a place for worship, these church congregations provide a wide range of social and cultural activities, including Chinese-language classes and, very importantly for many new arrivals, a support network and sense of community. Attendance at Sunday services is often a prelude to lunch and participation in a range of activities.

The arrival of Indochinese refugees was a watershed in the expansion of Buddhism, now the fastest growing religion in Australia, increasing 300 per cent between 1981 and 1991. In 1991, Vietnamese speakers were a third (31.3 per cent) of Australia's Buddhists, while Chinese speakers were only slightly fewer (Cantonese 16.2 per cent, Mandarin 6.2 per cent, other Chinese 6.2 per cent). A majority of the Chinese Buddhists are from Indochina and they have developed their own temples and shrines. As in the Christian churches, affiliation varies according to origins and this is reflected in language usage – Cantonese, Mandarin, and in some cases Vietnamese or English.

Buddhist services are held in individual homes and in temples. Institutions vary widely, from the Bright Moon temples in Melbourne and Sydney supported by the local Vietnamese Chinese community, to the more lavish ones built with international support from Hong Kong and Taiwan. The most notable example of international support is the Nan Tien (Nantian) Temple, which was opened in 1995 in Wollongong, 75 kilometres south of Sydney. Claimed to be the largest Buddhist temple in the southern hemisphere, it belongs to the Fokuangshan (Foguangshan), a sect which has other temples in Brisbane, Sydney, Melbourne and Perth, and whose educational, cultural and religious activities are designed to serve both Chinese and non-Chinese.

As with Buddhism, the older syncretist temples are now increasingly supported, and major new temples, such as the Heavenly Queen Temple in Melbourne catering for those from Indochina, are planned. International links also exist with the Hong Kong-based Ching Chung (Qingsong) Daoist Association now operating in both Brisbane and Sydney.

The transmission and transformation of Chinese culture

Chinese-language education

The children of the early Chinese settlers learned their Chinese either from private tutors or at schools in China. Inevitably, many of the Australian-born Chinese grew up with only a limited knowledge of Chinese. This became an embarrassment to the many whose ignorance of Chinese was disdained by the more recent Chinese immigrants.

By the 1970s, Australian government educational policy was supporting the incorporation of 'migrant' or 'community' languages within the regular school curriculum. Chinese-language curricula were developed for primary and secondary schools, and students could study Mandarin for their university entry examinations (although it was mainly overseas-educated students who did so) Specialist Chinese-language teachers were appointed to selected government primary schools to offer transition bilingual programmes, usually in Mandarin, the mother tongue of in fact only a small proportion of Chinese students.

Chinese community groups also began to organize their own supplementary Cantonese and Mandarin language classes in 'ethnic schools' operating outside normal school hours. Since the late 1970s, the schools run by non-profit organizations have received government funding, although their curriculum and staffing are not subject to any government control. Government subsidies have undoubtedly contributed to the expansion of these schools, most of whose students are of primary school age. In states such as Victoria, some of these ethnic schools are also accredited to teach courses for the end-of-secondary-school certificates, and for entrance to universities and post-secondary education.

In 1996, Sydney had the largest number of Chinese ethnic schools (37), with two others in the major regional cities of Wollongong and Newcastle. These schools had 538 teachers and an enrolment of 8,660 students, a marked increase on the 1,600 students attending Chinese ethnic schools in the early 1980s. In Melbourne in 1995, 25 organizations taught Chinese to 6,300 students. In other states with smaller Chinese populations, there were fewer Chinese ethnic schools – nine in Brisbane and another one in the regional city of Rockhampton, five in Perth, four in Adelaide, three in Canberra and one each in Tasmania and Darwin.

The enrolments of the schools and the number of their campuses vary considerably. In Sydney the smallest school in 1996 enrolled 20 students, while the largest enrolled nearly 1,500 students. The schools' links with the various community organizations ensure that they attract different groups of students. While the schools' locations play some part in their enrolments, more important is whether they teach Mandarin or

Cantonese, complex or simplified characters and, linked to these considerations, what role their sponsoring organization plays in community or international politics. This last factor determines whether or not the school uses textbooks supplied free by the Taiwan government or obtained from the PRC or Singapore.

The schools may also cater primarily for students from specific areas such as Indochina, Taiwan or East Timor. In the early 1980s in Sydney, Cantonese classes were more popular among the Australian-born Chinese families or those from Hong Kong. Since then, there has been a shift towards Mandarin; of the 39 schools operating in New South Wales in 1996, only four taught solely Cantonese, whereas 14 taught only Mandarin and a majority (21) taught both Mandarin and Cantonese. And only 30 per cent of the students were enrolled in Cantonese classes. The shift reflects not only the changing composition of the Chinese population, but also Hong Kong parents' increasing interest in their children acquiring a knowledge of Mandarin.

While some ethnic schools are operated by separate educational organizations, most come under the aegis of multifunction community organizations. One trend, particularly noticeable in Sydney, is for religious groups to sponsor classes, which are held on Sundays to coincide with religious services. Of the 39 organizations running schools in New South Wales, 11 are Christian churches and another two are Buddhist groups.

Since the early 1980s in Sydney, many of the tensions between Chinese-language schools, reflecting wider tensions in the Chinese community, have moderated, and they have come together in an umbrella organization, the Chinese Language Education Council of New South Wales. Apart from playing an administrative role, this body develops curriculum and lobbies for Chinese-language education in the state. In Melbourne, the development of such an umbrella is being explored.

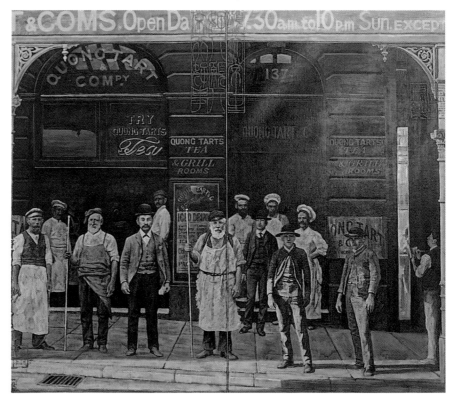

Shen Jiawei paints scene from Australian history, oil on canvas, 122 x 142 cm.

Film director Clara Law (top) and Dr John Yu, Australian of the Year.

The arts

For the 19th-century sojourners, touring Cantonese opera groups were the main form of Chinese cultural activity. Traditional music continued to interest the Chinese, but proved difficult to sustain in isolation from China; and by the early 1900s, the Australian-born Chinese were becoming increasingly interested in Western forms. But after 1945, with the arrival of new Chinese immigrants, Chinese musical expression underwent a renaissance. This was especially the case from the late 1980s, when, with the arrival from the PRC of professional musicians, the Chinese Song and Dance Ensemble, the Australian Chinese Opera Association, the East-West Philharmonic Orchestra, the New Continental Orchestra and the Australian Chinese Music Ensemble were established. An ongoing issue for Chinese musicians is the relationship between traditional Chinese and Western music, as well as the modern developments in both musical traditions. Varying emphases and syntheses of these traditions co-exist within the contemporary Chinese community.

Similar diversity and tensions exist in other areas of the arts. Paintings which run the gamut of traditional Chinese forms and abstract modernism show evidence of this, as does the diversity in the work of visual artists belonging to the Association of Australian Chinese Artists (founded in 1981). Among visual artists whose work has departed from older traditions and who have gained prominence outside the Chinese community are Guan Wei in Sydney and Zhou Xiaoping in Melbourne. In a thematic departure from the heroic oils which won him recognition during the Cultural Revolution (by, among others, Mao Zedong's wife Jiang Qing), the Shanghai-born painter Shen Jiawei has tackled Australian historical subjects since his settlement in Sydney.

The arrival of Chinese from Indochina first led to the development of a group of Australian-based authors writing in Chinese and the founding of literary journals like *Chinese Culture* and *Otherland* (*Yuan xiang*). Reflecting the individuals' diverse backgrounds, different genres and themes are discernible – from the writings of Indochinese on their refugee experience to the 'overseas student literature' (*liuxuesheng wenxue*) of the PRC students. Drawing extensively on their experiences settling in Australia are Sang Ye, who writes in Chinese; and Lillian Ng, who writes in English. As is exemplified by *Floating Life*, an award winning feature movie directed by Clara Law, the themes of migration and settlement also interest Chinese film-makers.

However, when Chinese artists venture outside the confines of the Chinese community and the use of traditional Chinese forms, they find their work labelled as 'Chinese' or 'multicultural' instead of being assessed in universalistic terms. The regular staging of Chinese and Asian Arts Festivals increasingly highlights the vitality of local Chinese artistic expression, but also

Chinese protest racism at Town Hall, Sydney.

the tension between very traditional expressions of Chinese culture and those forms, less readily identified as 'Chinese,' which incorporate more diverse cultural references.

Australian Chinese today

By the middle 1990s, in the space of only three decades, the small Chinese population had grown to become the second largest (after the Italian) non-English speaking ethnic group in Australia. The rapidity of this growth coincided with the decline of Europe as a major source of Australia's immigrants. From the 1980s, the Australian economy also experienced a number of deep recessions and historically high levels of unemployment. During this period there was widespread concern about continuing high levels of immigration and a breakdown in the bipartisan political support for immigration as a fillip to the country's economic development.

Public concerns about extensive immigration all too often turned into anti-Asian hostility reminiscent of the 19th century. Adding to the hostility was a perception by sections of the community that the Australian government's emphasis on the importance of economic and political ties with the Asian region was at the expense of the country's traditional European links and heritage. The first major expression of the hostility was the anti-Asian immigration 'debate' of 1984. This and other public debates, which inevitably affected the Chinese, continued into the 1990s. The 1996 election of two independent federal parliamentarians hostile to immigration and Asians, as well as to government policies on multiculturalism and Aborigines, aroused concern among the Chinese. These concerns were fuelled by a perception of the government's failure to counter the parliamentarians' racist statements and by an increased incidence of hostility directed at Asians.

Despite this hostility, by the mid-1990s Chinese had begun to make their mark in a number of areas of public life. Most state parliaments have a member of Chinese background, and Senator Bill O'Chee represents Queensland in the Australian Senate. These parliamentarians belong to both major political parties and do not represent specifically Chinese interests or constituencies. In local government, the most prominent Chinese councillor is Henry Tsang, the Deputy Lord Mayor of Sydney. In the media and the arts, prominent Chinese include the novelist Brian Castro, the television presenter Annette Shun Wah and the choreographer and dancer Kai Tai Chan. Both the Presbyterian and Uniting Churches Synods in New South Wales have elected Chinese heads (Right Reverend John Ting, 1994–95 and Reverend Dr Tony Chi, 1992–93), while Bishop George Tung Yep was head of the Anglican Church in Northern Queensland. Chinese play a prominent role in academia and the professions, especially in medicine (an example being the Shanghai-born heart surgeon Dr Victor Chang). In 1996, Dr John Yu, the head of Sydney's New Children's Hospital, was named Australian of the Year.

Certain areas of Chinese culture have also been adopted with considerable enthusiasm by non-Chinese. Apart from Chinese food, two areas of Chinese culture which have gained increasing popularity outside the Chinese community are traditional medical practices and the martial arts. This interest has created new opportunities and markets for Chinese and non-Chinese practitioners alike. Acupuncture and other services are now provided by Chinese and locally trained practitioners. By 1996, moves to set up formal registration procedures, comparable to those for Western medical practice, were well advanced. Actively promoting these changes was the National Traditional Chinese Medicine Liaison Committee, which represented 16 practitioner associations, both Chinese and non-Chinese.

All this affects the way individuals view their own identity as Chinese. At the same time, in a world where traditional cultural forms are under extensive pressure from modernization and globalization, the nature of individual Chinese identity has become more difficult to define. While it is true, as the film-maker Daniel Zhu has remarked, that for many Australian Chinese, 'Chinatown as a symbol of Chinese culture is dead,' it is not altogether clear what has taken its place.

Australia has two Chinese museums depicting Chinese culture and identity: the Museum of Chinese Australian History in the Melbourne Chinatown area; and the Golden Dragon Museum in Bendigo, a former gold-mining town in Victoria. The latter in particular locates the experience of Chinese in Australia in the context of traditional Chinese culture. In doing so, it expresses the interest among members of the established Australian-born Chinese community in tracing their ancestral roots as part of their search for identity. Illustrating this search is the public video made of their family history by the descendants of the 19th-century herbalist, Kwong Sue

Duk, as well as the museum collections developed by Chinese communities in cities such as Darwin.

A common theme in the writing of the Australian-born Chinese is how their families strove to become assimilated into Australian society. Now, with Australian society's increasing diversity and with the political shift from assimilation to multiculturalism, these people's personal quest for identity is being undertaken in a very different context. They are also encountering many highly confident and successful immigrant Chinese who deride their lack of knowledge of Chinese culture, especially of the written and spoken language. Furthermore, the Australian-born Chinese sometimes feel marginalized by the prominent role of recent Chinese immigrants in community activities, and the way they themselves are treated as immigrants (that is, newcomers) by the majority population.

The post-1970s immigrants are able to maintain close personal contact with developments in their homelands and internationally in a way unimaginable in an earlier generation. Such contact is legitimized by multiculturalism and the state and federal governments' emphasis on close ties with Asia. Reinforcement is further provided by the presence in Australia of numerous branches of the Chinese media, religious organizations and economic enterprises – all these link the local Chinese community with the wider Chinese diaspora. Chinatown and the ancestral village in China no longer constitute the effective boundaries of the community's 'Chinese' world.

However, while these circumstances support the maintenance of a Chinese identity among the Australian Chinese population, there is such diversity that it is difficult to pinpoint what constitutes its components. The most visible elements are a symbolic reference to a historically distant shared ancestry and cultural heritage, although for many, the immediate 'homeland' is not China. There is also, potentially, the Chinese's shared experience in Australia of hostility and discrimination. Even the latter may be responded to very differently.

The extensive segmentation of the Australian Chinese population – by source country, by economic and linguistic differences and variations in residential patterns, religion and media usage – means that there is little to unite the Chinese population at the level of everyday social encounters. One of the most isolated groups is that from East Timor, which, after two decades in Australia, is only gradually developing contacts with other Chinese. Those from Indochina have a little more contact with other Chinese, as have those from the PRC. The latter, like those from Taiwan, lack the tradition of being part of an international immigrant community.

There is little indication that Chinese migration will cease. The effect of this migration will be a continuing dynamism in the Chinese community as it adjusts to the newcomers as well as to the larger Australian society.

Christine Inglis

Multicultural taste.

Catalogue of exhibition on Chinese families compiled by Museum and Art Gallery of the Northern Territory.

NEW ZEALAND

Appo Hocton.

Map 5.16

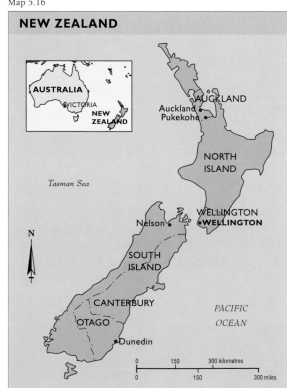

After New Zealand came under British sovereignty in 1840, the first known Chinese settler arrived. Called Appo Hocton (the latter two syllables a corruption of his Chinese given name), Wong Hoc Ting came to Nelson in 1842 as a steward on the immigrant ship *Thomas Harrison*. By 1852 he was naturalized and able to buy land for cattle and sheep farms.

In the following year, Edward Gibbon Wakefield, known for his success in settling the colony with British small farmers, formulated detailed plans to bring in Chinese 'to become valuable servants, as shepherds and stock-keepers, mechanics   workers in the dairy, sawyers, fishermen, gardeners, cooks, grooms, footmen, etc.' But nothing came of the scheme, labelled a conspiracy to overrun the innocent Colony with 'ignorant, slavish and treacherous' Chinese 'slaves.'

In 1861, gold was discovered in Otago in the South Island. The place attracted large numbers of European miners and became a hive of activity. However, it suffered a slump when the adventurers flocked to a newly discovered gold-field on the west coast in 1864. To fill the gap, the Dunedin Chamber of Commerce arranged with Ho A-mei, a Hong Kong Chinese merchant based in Melbourne, Australia, for Chinese miners to be recruited from the gold-fields in nearby Victoria. The Chinese, it was thought, were hardworking and inoffensive, and they did not mind reworking abandoned claims. The first shipment of 12 men thus landed in Dunedin in 1866. More came directly from China within a year, and by 1867 over 1,000 Chinese had arrived in what they would call the 'New Gold Mountain.'

Thus early migration to New Zealand followed the same broad pattern as that to San Francisco (the 'Old Gold Mountain'), British Columbia and Victoria in Australia; it was part of the mid-19th century gold-rush to the various Pacific Rim mines. The immigrants often moved from one gold-field to another throughout the Pacific Rim. Poll tax records reveal that New Zealand's early Chinese came not only from Australia but also from Canada and California. The migration was also part of a global phenomenon, the recruitment of labour by the European colonists of the New World (see Part II).

The Chinese came from the Pearl River Delta in Guangdong province – the majority (67 per cent) from Panyu county to the north of Canton, the rest from Siyi, Zhongshan, Zengcheng and Dongguan (see Part I). Oral history accounts of Chinese elders trace the earliest departures to the mid-1850s Red Turban revolt, a failed challenge to a dynasty beset by European imperialist aggression. Reality might have been less dramatic: land paucity and over-subdivision of farmland meant that the majority of the Cantonese were tenant farmers vulnerable to usurers and natural calamities. With its sparse population and plentiful opportunities, New Zealand beckoned to Chinese and Anglo-Saxon immigrants alike. However, unlike the latter, the Chinese intended only to be sojourners, not settlers.

Chinese immigrants all came under the credit ticket system (see Part II). A guarantor – either a relative, employer or broker – advanced the fare and frequently the exorbitant poll tax as well (see below). Although the credit ticket system was frequently exploitative, there has not been any suggestion that this was the case with immigration to New Zealand. Indeed, many guarantors seemed to have inspired gratitude for their genuinely philanthropic efforts to help fellow-villagers. Even so, most Chinese immigrants to New Zealand had to work for at least four to five years before they could repay their debts. While native-place associations – Poon-Fah (Panyu and Huaxian), Szeyap (Siyi), Tsang-shing (Zengcheng), Kwong Chew (Gangzhou, the classical name for Xinhui) – frequently acted as guarantors, individual merchants like Sew Hoy in Dunedin, William Kwok in Wellington, Ah-Chee and Thomas Wong Doo in Auckland often sponsored aspiring immigrants and also advanced fares.

Chinese dwellings in the Otago gold-fields were usually grass-sod huts with mud-and-stone walls. Contemporary photographs show them with vegetable plots outside and roof-tops covered with rice-bag sacking.

The majority of the men would have married before emigration, leaving wives at home to look after their (the men's) parents. Since they worked on abandoned claims and since the gold was largely depleted by the 1900s, most miners failed to strike it rich. James Ng's studies (*Windows on a Chinese Past*) paint a grim picture of the Chinese: ageing, poverty-stricken, marginalized and stranded in an alien land. Women were very few: only nine to 4,995 men in 1881, for example. By 1901, some 13 per cent of the men were over 60, and a great majority of them had not been back to China for 20 years, no doubt because they could not afford the passage. Out of a total Chinese population of 1,761 in Otago in 1896, 22 were inmates of mental asylums.

The gold depleted, many either left New Zealand

(from 1882 to the 1920s, annual departures exceeded annual arrivals) or drifted to urban centres to seek alternative means of livelihood – as laundrymen or market gardeners interacting minimally with mainstream society. Wherever they went, Chinese excited a degree of hostility far beyond their numbers, which steadily declined to a nadir of only 2,147 in 1916. But even worse was to come.

Anti-Chinese sentiment and legislation, 1881–1920

Australia was the main source of the anti-Chinese songs and cartoons purveyed in New Zealand, which seemed to have imported the White supremacists' prejudice and fear wholesale. One cartoon depicted the Chinese as an octopus strangulating furniture traders; this had some relevance in Melbourne, where Chinese carpenters did indeed do well, but it had no meaning at all in New Zealand.

Popular xenophobia supported the anti-Chinese sentiments of politicians like George Grey (Governor 1845–53 and 1861–68), who saw the Chinese as a threat to his mission to turn New Zealand into a purified replica of England in the South Pacific. Similarly, leading politicians William P. Reeves and Richard Seddon (Prime Minister 1893–1906) spoke of Chinese in the most derogatory terms, ranging from 'these animals' to 'specimens of an effete race which might very well be left to die out.'

Immediately after World War I, 'We fought not for the Chinese but for a White New Zealand' became a popular slogan of the Returned Servicemen's Associations. Seen to be taking away jobs, Chinese were scapegoated also by the Grocers' Assistants' Union and the Furniture Trade Industrial Union of Workers. The Auckland Watersiders Union threatened to boycott any ship which brought in Asian passengers. The White New Zealand League was formed in 1925 and newspapers were full of the 'Yellow Peril.' In the mid-1920s, market gardeners in Pukekohe stirred up anti-Chinese agitation, though Chinese were so downtrodden and so small in number (30 in Pukekohe Borough and Franklin County combined) that they seemed hardly worth the fuss.

Against this background of racist hostility, a series of laws discriminating against Chinese was passed. The first of the Chinese Immigrants Acts, passed in 1881, limited the number of Chinese who could be landed to

one for every ten tons of each ship's cargo. This so-called 'tonnage ratio' would be revised to one to 100 in 1888 and halved again in 1896. Furthermore, every Chinese immigrant had to pay a poll tax, raised from ten to 100 pounds in 1896.

At around the same time, the Australian states' attempts to legislate 'coloured' people out provoked Japan into denouncing the 'White Australian Policy' and making it known all over the world. Highly embarrassed, Britain had to teach its colonies a way of handling immigration matters less crudely. In 1897, Joseph Chamberlain, the British Secretary of State, told the colonies that while mother Britain sympathized with their desire to keep their lands white, any future exclusion acts must not be seen to be based on race and colour. This was the background to the 1907 legislation which introduced an additional 'reading test' to the Chinese. Immigrants were required to read 'to the satisfaction of customs officials at the port of entry' 100 English words picked at random.

Legislation discriminating against Chinese already resident in New Zealand was also introduced. In 1908, the cabinet denied naturalization – and even permanent residence – to all Chinese. Moreover, Chinese, even New Zealand-born babies, had to be thumbprinted and have re-entry permits upon their return to New Zealand from a trip abroad. And the police could enter any Chinese premises without a search warrant if it suspected gambling or opium smoking there (such raids took place as recently as the 1960s).

Finally, the 1920 Immigration Restriction Amendment Act, by requiring every aspiring immigrant (other than people of British and Irish descent) to apply for a special permit, succeeded in bringing 'to a successful end,' writes P. S. O'Connor in his 1968 article, 'the long search for an instrument of policy which would ... keep New Zealand White.'

In 1935, the government set a quota of ten entry permits a year for families of New Zealand-born Chinese – to which was added five more annually for families of naturalized Chinese in 1940. A new category of visas admitted young Chinese on student permits for a year at a time.

Seen by local trade unions to be taking jobs away from New Zealand grocers.

Two men about to return to China in 1903 after long residence in Otago.

Diggers in front of their dwellings in Otago gold-fields.

Family gathers at forebear's grave on Chinese All Souls' Day.

Marginal existence in White New Zealand, 1920–52

Chinese social associations, the earliest of which were the native-place organizations formed by the gold-miners in the late 1860s, mushroomed during this period. The Poon-Fa Association, for people from Panyu and Fah County, was resurrected in 1916. The Kwong Chew Club, for Xinhui people, was founded in Auckland in 1920. The Tung-Tsang Association, for Dongguan and Zengcheng natives, was founded in Wellington in 1924. Finally the Szeyap Association was founded in Wellington in 1936. Thus all the major home counties of Chinese New Zealanders were represented.

Chain migration, a process allied to the credit ticket system, had brought to New Zealand kinsmen from the same home locality. One major routine function of native-place associations was to organize – in lieu of the families left behind – the annual Qingming ceremonies honouring the dead. In certain cemeteries in Dunedin and Wellington, each native-place association had its own burial ground. The Chinese associations also organized banquets to mark other festivals. And most had reading rooms where members could meet, read and chat.

Exclusion from New Zealand life attached the Chinese all the more firmly to homeland politics, a matter of concern to the many who believed they would go back there one day. There were two main political organizations: the Chee Kung Tong (Zhigong Tang or Chinese Freemasons, founded 1907) and the Tongmeng Hui (the precursor of Kuomintang, founded 1905). Both aimed at overthrowing the Manchus and strengthening China.

From the start, the Chee Kung Tong tended to be more conservative; supporting Yuan Shikai (see p 101), the military leader who snatched power when the Qing dynasty was toppled. Because of its Triad origins, the society tended to have adherents from humbler artisan-peasant backgrounds. The Kuomintang, by contrast, had members who were comparatively well-educated, usually more conversant with Western ways and more politicized. Supporters of Sun Yat-sen, they launched the *Man Sing Times* (*Minsheng Times*), the first Chinese language newspaper in New Zealand, in 1922 in Wellington.

China had entered a period of warlordism following the fall of the Manchus. The rivalry between the government in Beijing and a secessionist regime based in Canton was echoed in New Zealand, where the Chee Kung Tong supported the former and the Kuomintang the latter. The two sides clashed openly over which flag

to fly at the Double Tenth (Chinese National Day) celebration in 1927. However, with the triumph of Chiang Kai-shek's offensive against the north in 1928, the Kuomintang's claim to being *the* Chinese political party in New Zealand was assured.

In 1928, the Kuomintang moved quickly to establish an umbrella organization over all the regional associations. The first pan-Chinese association had been founded with the encouragement of the first Chinese consul Hwang Yung-liang (Huang Rongliang) in 1909. Called the *Chong Wah Hui Koon* (Zhonghua Huiguan, Chinese Association), it had ceased to function with the demise of the Qing dynasty. Now, representatives from 16 regions met in Wellington to form the New Zealand Chinese Association. In 1935 the Association was expanded to include the representatives of 26 branches from all around the country.

The association was destined to become very powerful. In 1937, when war broke out between Japan and China, New Zealand Chinese answered the call to support the motherland on a wave of patriotic fervour. The Association leadership made it mandatory for every able-bodied Chinese man to donate money. Those who failed to do so risked social ostracism or being denounced as 'traitors' by notices placed in Chinese newspapers. Whether from coercion or spontaneous generosity, New Zealand Chinese, in spite of being comparatively poor, ranked second among overseas Chinese communities across the world in the amount they donated per capita in 1937–44. The very smallness of the community no doubt made fee collection easier.

Once World War II was over, patriotism waned and the resentment felt against the high-handed measures of the association leadership came to a head. For many years afterwards the office-bearers of the various branches quarrelled over what to do with the leftover donations, and the authority of the association suffered a setback from which it never quite recovered.

In 1943, a Labour government motivated partly by visions of a more united Chinese community and partly by the wish to organize market gardening (by now the chief occupation of the Chinese) to ensure regular provision to the American Pacific fleets, encouraged the formation of the Federation of Chinese Commercial Growers. A *New Zealand Chinese Growers Monthly Journal* was started in 1949 and became the voice of the Chinese. Instead of being focused exclusively on China, this covered New Zealand events, farming and horticultural topics as well as local Chinese community news. As well as being the most influential, it was the longest running Chinese paper, maintaining its pan-Chinese and all-New Zealand appeal right up to 1972.

War War II gave Chinese a chance to become settlers. In 1939, Chinese men working in New Zealand were joined by their families, who were issued with temporary war refugee permits, but who stayed beyond their allotted two years because the war did not end until 1945. By then, the refugee Chinese women and children were well-accepted by New Zealand society; and it would not look good to be forcibly deporting Chinese at a time when Europeans were being wooed with assisted-migration schemes to bolster the country's scanty population. Besides, the Dunedin Presbyterian Church, under the leadership of Reverend McNeur, diligently lobbied politicians on behalf of the Chinese. Finally, in 1947, the government granted permanent residence to the wives and children who came as war refugees in 1939; children born to those women in New Zealand; and students and temporary residents who had been in the country for over five years. A total of 1,323 Chinese gained residence in this way.

Subsequently, in 1949 and then 1950, 50 Chinese families who had been in New Zealand for over 20 years were allowed to apply for the rest of their family members to join them. Thereafter, Chinese men resident in the country for over 20 years could also apply for family reunion. The entry of women thus marked the point at which an itinerant male labour force became a group of families, or a true community.

Yet government policies towards the Chinese continued to be influenced by the predominant desire for the country to develop as a 'European community,' one that did not welcome 'Asiatics.' With the Communist victory in China, Chinese already settled in New Zealand were looked upon with a new wariness, their allegiance to their new home once again suspect. In April 1951, the government decreed that Certificates of Registration issued to Chinese and Indians permanently resident in New Zealand were to be valid for re-entry into the country for a period of 18 months from the date of issue only. It was also stated that 'Chinese' were to be regarded as all persons of Chinese extraction whatever their nationality.

Towards the matter of nationality, the cabinet approved a cautious policy in 1951. This specified, on top of the normal requirements for naturalization, that the Chinese must renounce their Chinese nationality and give proof that they were 'closer to the New Zealand way of life than to the Chinese.' A prerequisite was a good knowledge of English, the test for which was so stringent that out of an initial 400 applications, only 20 cases were considered worthy. Ten other persons qualified in 1953, and another ten in 1954. Most of the successful applicants were young and well-educated, to judge from their occupations – engineers, public servants, interpreters, radio servicemen and so on, as opposed to market gardeners and laundrymen.

Oral history sources reveal that many older Chinese were extremely reluctant to renounce their Chinese citizenship unilaterally. Proving themselves 'closer to the New Zealand way of life' than to the Chinese was also a huge hurdle, not only because it was inherently difficult but because it was psychologically alienating.

Assimilation: 1950s–1980s

During this period, the Chinese community remained largely self-contained, placid and self-absorbed. New Zealanders were generally confident that the country was racially harmonious. 'New Zealand had no racial problem worth mentioning' was the accepted myth. In the two decades after World War II, New Zealand enjoyed a high standard of living. Normalcy, security and prosperity were the watchwords of the day. The Chinese seemed quite content to remain on the fringe of the mainstream, and counted themselves lucky to have the chance to raise their families as intact units in a land of plenty.

In those monocultural years the 1920 permit system continued to govern immigration – that is, applicants were or were not admitted on merit and no reason need be given. In 1961, the Immigration Amendment Act ended British subjects' privileged exemption from having to get permits, but immigrants continued to come from the narrowly selected traditional sources of Britain and Western Europe.

Chinese population gradually rose from 6,731 in 1956 to 10,283 in 1966. This was thanks largely to natural increase and the admission of some spouses and dependent children. The Chinese community had become strongly indigenous by then, with over 75 per cent of its members locally born. It was also a young community, more than half of it below the age of 25. As a small ethnic minority, Chinese New Zealanders appeared to be on the verge of being assimilated.

Parents looked to Chinese-language schools to keep their New Zealand-born children Chinese in speech and culture. Although these schools mushroomed – major centres such as Dunedin, Wellington and Auckland all had them – none of them enjoyed much success. The government saw them as retarding assimilation and withheld entry permits to Chinese teachers. Lacking funds and properly trained teachers, Chinese schools operated only on weekends or after school. Tired children soon dropped out. However, sports teams of Chinese youngsters, transcending language differences, flourished.

By the 1970s, most of the local-born could only speak limited functional Chinese, their vocabulary confined to food and home activities. Formal addresses at community meetings were made in English because community leaders no longer had a good enough command of Chinese, nor was it widely understood. Chinese festivals, including Chinese New Year, went largely unobserved.

Those years saw the Chinese advancing in income,

National tournament of Chinese New Zealanders, 1950.

Figure 5.4

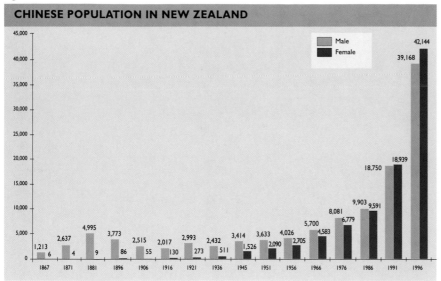

CHINESE POPULATION IN NEW ZEALAND

Sources: New Zealand censuses, 1871 to 1996.

Figure 5.5

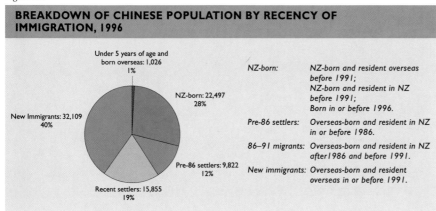

BREAKDOWN OF CHINESE POPULATION BY RECENCY OF IMMIGRATION, 1996

Sources: Unpublished figures from 1991 and 1996 censuses.

Attending Festival of Asia, Auckland, 1996.

social standing, and educational and professional accomplishment. In the 1960s, many Chinese qualified as doctors, lawyers, accountants and architects. However, few gained leadership positions. Most were self-employed managers of small to medium-sized concerns, running companies that their immediate family could oversee. There were no Chinese directors on the boards of international corporations, and no policy-makers in government. The American civil rights movement had no parallel in New Zealand, and Chinese seemed untroubled by issues of ethnicity and identity.

They hardly featured in the statistics of accident, crime and prison. Nor were they prominent users of public funds. Figures for Chinese hospitalization and welfare dependency were similarly low. As a group they existed in such an unobtrusive way that they were hardly noticed. Social mixing with mainstream society usually stopped at the level of birthday parties and office gatherings. The norm was to marry within the community, and up to the early 1970s, young Chinese travelled to Hong Kong or Taiwan to find suitable Chinese spouses – there were simply too few Chinese New Zealanders to choose from.

A study carried out in those years by Andrew Trlin revealed their considerable social distance from mainstream European New Zealanders. While most of the latter did not mind having a Chinese workmate or colleague, they felt less keen about having a Chinese neighbour. Few had Chinese friends and most did not favour intermarriage with Chinese.

During those years the Chinese earned the epithet 'model minority' because they were so unobtrusive, law-abiding and undemanding. Numerically they only made up about 0.6 per cent of the total population. In the 1980s Chinese were a largely middle-class, well-educated and low-profile group numbering only 19,000 people. Proportionally small and politically silent, most were unprepared for the rapid changes of the next decade.

A decade of dynamic change, 1986–96

The Labour government which came to power in 1984 embarked boldly upon a programme of economic restructuring aimed at stimulating the local economy and attracting international investment. Forming a part of the restructuring was the 1987 Immigration Act, the vehicle for a change of policy geared to offsetting the effects of a net annual migration loss averaging 18,000 in 1976–86.

The act provided for the selection of new immigrants on criteria of personal merit without regard to race, national or ethnic origin. This opened the country to non-traditional immigrants, including re-migrants from the Chinese diaspora. Census returns in 1991 show Chinese numbers to have risen to about 40,000, or 1.1 per cent of the country's total population of 3.2 million.

By 1996, the Chinese population had doubled yet again, to 81,309 or about 2 per cent of the country's population of 3.6 million. This figure includes the 20 per cent who are part-Chinese – that is, European-Chinese, Maori-Chinese or Samoan-Chinese. A marked feature of the Chinese population is its 'rawness,' with overseas-born arrivals in the preceding ten years (60 per cent) far outnumbering both the locally born (about 28 per cent) and the overseas-born who had been in New Zealand for more than a decade (about 12 per cent). The main territories which sent new arrivals between 1968–96 were Taiwan, the People's Republic of China and Hong Kong. A smaller number came from Malaysia and Singapore.

Thanks to the immigration policy's bias towards 'quality' immigrants, most of these newcomers hailed from cities in their countries of origin, and are highly educated professionals, technocrats or business people. Thus they are very different from their late 19th- or early 20th-century predecessors from rural south China. Nor were they economic refugees in search of a higher standard of living, but people leaving homelands offering greater economic opportunities than New Zealand. Hong Kong migrants mostly came in search of a political haven ahead of the colony's return to Chinese sovereignty in 1997. Taiwan migrants shared similar, if less immediate, political worries. In 1995, when China started its series of missile practices after President Lee Teng-hui visited the

United States, applications for New Zealand residence visas shot up. Many also came in search of a more relaxed lifestyle and a less competitive education system for their children.

The 1996 age and gender profiles show the Chinese to be significantly younger than the national average. This is to be expected of a community with a preponderance of new immigrants brought in by a selective immigration policy favouring the young and skilled. Most of the Chinese are below 50 and of working age. However, closer examination of the gender mix reveals some worrying features. For the first time in history, the female population (42,144) has exceeded the male (39,168). This imbalance is especially pronounced in the 20–29, 30–39 and 40–49 age cohorts, and is a reflection of the 'astronaut' pattern, in which men return to their place of origin to continue their business, supporting their families from overseas. The imbalance goes back only a few years: the 1991 census showed a healthier sex ratio (of 99 Chinese males to 100 Chinese females), one which closely resembled New Zealand's population as a whole.

From the employment status profile of 1996, it may be seen that many of the newcomers (those arriving in 1986–96) have found it hard to find work in New Zealand. Although only 8 per cent reported that they were officially 'unemployed and actively seeking work,' more than 60 per cent were 'not in the labour force.' Only 15 per cent of the newcomers were 'full-time wage and salary earners' and 7 per cent were self-employed. The frustration felt by these people, who were highly qualified professionals in their country of origin, is likely to lead to the exodus of the breadwinners, usually the men.

Figure 5.7

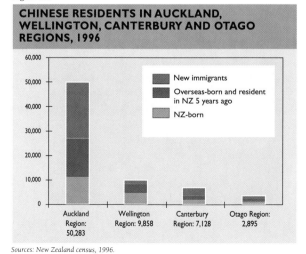

CHINESE RESIDENTS IN AUCKLAND, WELLINGTON, CANTERBURY AND OTAGO REGIONS, 1996

Legend:
- New immigrants
- Overseas-born and resident in NZ 5 years ago
- NZ-born

Auckland Region: 50,283
Wellington Region: 9,858
Canterbury Region: 7,128
Otago Region: 2,895

Sources: New Zealand census, 1996.

Nevertheless, the personal income of Chinese as a whole does not compare too badly with that of the general population, though over 17 per cent reported 'loss or zero income' as compared to 5 per cent in the general population. Among employed Chinese, the cohorts classified as professionals (13 per cent), technicians and associate professionals (10 per cent), and clerks (11 per cent) are very close to the national averages. The Chinese have more 'legislators, administrators and managers' and a significantly higher percentage of 'service and sales workers' than the rest of the population.

Chinese are mostly urban dwellers, about 63 per cent of them living in Auckland, North Island's commercial centre. A preference for certain suburbs is apparent. In Auckland they are remarkably concentrated in affluent suburbs like North Shore, Epsom, Remuera and Howick-Pakuranga. The last named, a newly developed area in the east, has earned the name 'Far Eastern suburbs.' As has been the case in America, the well-heeled new immigrants and local-born Chinese congregate in the affluent suburbs, leaving the old Chinatowns to the very old early settlers and the poorer illegal immigrants.

Opinions on the new Asian immigrants are polarized. On the one hand there is the Business Roundtable, representing New Zealand's largest international trading companies, pushing for a wider opening to Asia's entrepreneurs and investment capital. On the other hand there is the New Zealand Defence Movement, which claims to protect the common interests of the indigenous Maori and Pakeha minorities, against the 'invasion' of Asian capitalists.

The politicians waver unsurely in the middle. How is their belief that Asia is where New Zealand's future lies to be reconciled with their preference for immigrants from the 'traditional sources'? The introduction of MMP (Mixed-Members-Proportional), a system which favours small parties and divergent groups, has made vacillating policies towards Asian immigration all the more likely.

However, for better or for worse, New Zealand can no longer remain the monocultural country it has been for 150 years. New Zealanders' wariness about the new immigrants is but a manifestation of their own underlying quest for a national identity. Weaned from a Britain preoccupied with the European Union, it has to decide what it will become. With a strong British culture and largely homogeneous European population, how is New Zealand to come to terms with its geopolitical position as an Asian-Pacific nation? The physical presence of the new Asian immigrants is a constant reminder of this challenge. The numerous outbreaks of racial tension are less symptoms of any organized racist revival than the teething troubles of a newly multi-ethnic society.

Manying Ip

Because of large Chinese homes like this in Howick, the Auckland suburb has been nicknamed 'Chiwick.'

Figure 5.6

CHINESE POPULATION BY SEX AND AGE GROUP, 1996

Age groups: 70 Years and Over, 60-69 Years, 50-59 Years, 40-49 Years, 30-39 Years, 20-29 Years, 15-19 Years, 5-14 Years, Under 5 Years

Legend: Female, Male

Sources: New Zealand statistics.

THE SOUTH PACIFIC

Chinese entered the South Pacific in the first half of the 19th century as carpenters and cooks aboard the ships of traders searching for sandalwood for the Canton market. When that resource was exhausted, traders turned to *bêche-de-mer*, tortoise shell and nacre (pearl shell), and began to set up trading stations on the various islands themselves. The first Chinese to settle in the islands were such traders, many of them working as agents for Chinese companies in Sydney. Copra soon became their major export.

Sydney was the hub of Chinese trade in the Pacific, but Tahiti, Levuka and Rabaul became auxiliary centres for the dispersion of agents and goods. The few Chinese who settled in Tahiti in the 1850s spread trading stations throughout what is now French Polynesia and the Cook Islands over the next half-century. Similarly, the Chinese in Levuka established trade networks throughout the Fijian islands early in the 20th century. Rabaul, where a Chinese merchant settled in about 1880, was the centre for an area that covered what is now Papua New Guinea and the Solomon Islands. Often these isolated traders took indigenous wives, with the result that many Polynesians and some Melanesians have Chinese ancestry, although they do not claim Chinese identity or participate in a Chinese community.

In the late 19th and early 20th centuries, Chinese contract labour was introduced into a number of colonies, starting with Tahiti in 1865. Indentured Chinese

Table 5.34

ESTIMATED CHINESE POPULATION IN THE PACIFIC ISLANDS, 1996			
COUNTRY	NUMBER OF CHINESE	TOTAL POPULATION	%
French Polynesia	8,800	218,000	4.1
Fiji	5,000	774,800	0.6
Papua New Guinea	1,500	4,042,400	0.04
Solomon Islands	900	367,800	0.2
Nauru	600	10,500	5.7
New Caledonia	400	182,200	0.2
Vanuatu	300	164,100	0.2
Tonga	200	98,200	0.2
American Samoa	150	54,800	0.3
Western Samoa	100	163,400	0.1
Wallis & Futuna	50	14,400	0.3
Kiribati	10	78,400	0.01
Cook Islands	2	19,100	0.01
Total	18,012	6,188,100	0.3

labourers worked for a short time in New Caledonia in the 1880s before they were replaced by workers from Vietnam and Java. The Germans began recruiting Chinese labour for their copra plantations in New Guinea in 1898 and Samoa in 1903. In 1906, the British Phosphate Company brought Chinese labour to their mines on Nauru and somewhat later on Banaba. Chinese banana planters in Fiji hired a few contract labourers during the first two decades of the 20th century. By the beginning of the war in the Pacific, however, only Western Samoa, Banaba and Nauru still had Chinese indentured labour. Altogether, between 1865 and 1941, some 20,000 Chinese went to the South Pacific as indentured labourers. Today, a few hundred Chinese are on contracts in the South Pacific, including skilled craftsmen and clerks for the Nauru Phosphate Company, garment workers in Fiji, construction workers for Chinese builders and cooks for Chinese restaurants in various countries.

By the 1920s, Chinese traders were found on islands in every corner of the South Pacific except Tonga, the Ellice Islands (now Tuvalu), Tokelau, Niue and New Caledonia. This spread diminished after the Pacific War, when some countries indigenized local trade through cooperatives. Today most of the Chinese in the Pacific live in urban centres.

The 18,000 Chinese in the South Pacific today are spread through a dozen countries (see table 5.34). There is little communication between the various communities, each of them connected instead to metropolitan centres on the Pacific Rim: Sydney, Auckland, Vancouver, Honolulu or Los Angeles. The largest communities are in Tahiti, Fiji and Papua New Guinea. Smaller communities exist in six other countries. There are descendants of Chinese traders in Kiribati and the Cook Islands, as elsewhere, although most of them do not identify themselves as Chinese.

Chinese communities in these countries vary greatly

Map 5.17

THE SOUTH PACIFIC

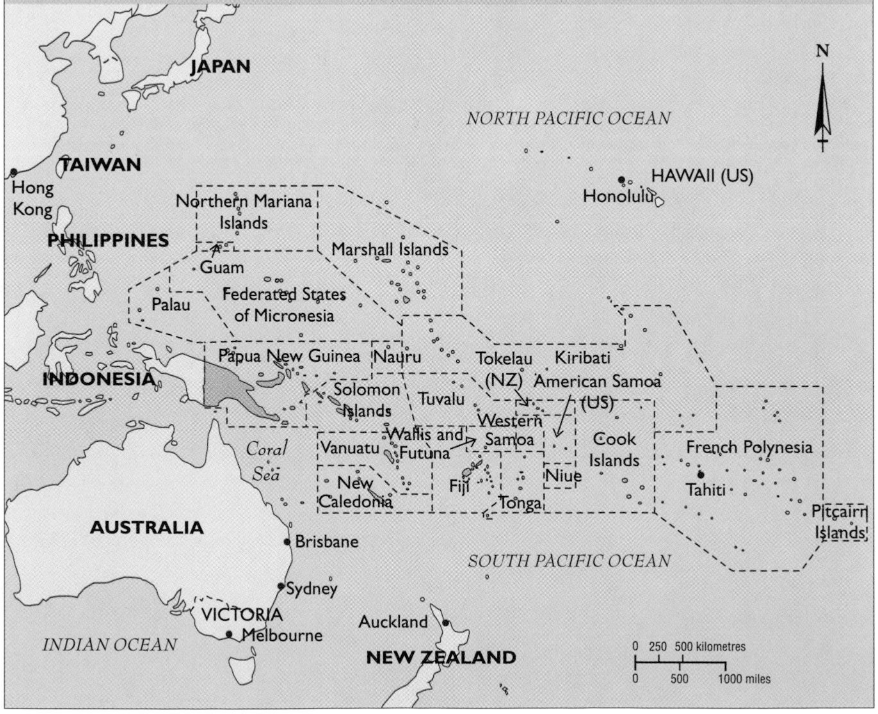

by size, provenance, colonial experience and economic activity. Their relations with China also vary: the Solomon Islands, Nauru, Tonga and Tuvalu have ambassadors from the government in Taipei, while the rest recognize the People's Republic of China. There are Peoples' Republic of China embassies in Fiji, Vanuatu and Kiribati. Both Taiwan and the People's Republic of China have aid programmes in the Pacific Islands, including hospitals, agricultural stations, construction companies and teachers for Chinese schools.

FIJI

Fiji, which won independence from Britain in 1970, is a multi-ethnic country in which the original Melanesians make up roughly half the population, and Indians (the descendants of labourers brought to work on sugar plantations) the other half. Chinese are only 0.6 per cent of the population.

After elections seated a coalition government dominated by Indians and ethnic tensions intensified, a coup led by Army Colonel (later Prime Minster) Sitiveni Rabuka, an ethnic Melanesian, overthrew the civilian government and introduced preferential policies favouring indigenes. However, relations between indigenes and Chinese have been mostly cordial throughout the latter's 150-year history in Fiji, and there has been some intermarriage. Their participation in the political life of the country is evident in the presence of Chinese in public positions, both elected and appointed.

History

Chinese first visited Fiji in the early years of the 19th century as cooks and carpenters on Australian and American ships seeking sandalwood for the Canton market. When, by about 1820, Fiji had been stripped of sandal wood, adventurers turned to *bêche-de-mer*, and some Chinese entered that trade. The first Chinese trader arrived in 1855, the second in 1872, both natives of Taishan in the Siyi district of Guangdong province. With the 1868 discovery of gold on Viti Levu, a sudden increase in the foreign population provided Chinese with an opportunity to engage in import and export, and a small Chinese community became established at Levuka.

These Chinese settlers came from Melbourne, as did most of the other foreigners, so connections with Australia remained the predominant overseas link until well into the 20th century. The Chinese found a niche in the service trades (carpentry, cooking, supplying vegetables, retail) in Levuka and later in Suva, but some undertook itinerant trade with the indigenous villagers throughout the islands, exchanging imported goods for *bêche-de-mer*, tortoise shell and later copra. A few set up banana plantations in the Rewa and Sigatoka valleys.

In 1900, the Chinese in Fiji numbered less than 100, but the expanding banana trade soon brought plantation workers recruited from China and Australia, so that the 1911 census (the first to count Chinese as a separate category) found 305 Chinese, only 29 of them women. Turmoil in southern China following the 1911 Revolution provoked large-scale emigration, and Chinese without any connections began to arrive from Zhongshan, Panyu and the Siyi counties (Taishan, Kaiping, Xinhui

and Enping). Although the colonial government encouraged Chinese immigration for economic reasons, it refused repeated requests from local Chinese (and later British) planters for Chinese indentured labour. This was provided to Fiji's British plantations by India from 1879 until 1920, when the indenture system officially ended. After that, many Indians became retail traders.

In 1919 the banana trade was badly blighted, and some of the larger Chinese companies in Suva turned to copra, settling agents throughout the islands to trade it for imported commodities. Chinese companies controlled 25 per cent of the copra trade before the Pacific War, causing some Australian and British companies to complain about Chinese competition. Companies such as Joong Hing Loong (Zhongxinglong), Kwong Tiy (Guangtai), Sang On Tiy (Yongantai), Fong Sam, Kwong Sang (Guangshang) and Zoing Chong (Yingchang) established shops in all the small towns on Viti Levu, Vanua Levu, and most of the smaller islands.

Some of these companies were branches of Chinese companies in Australia or New Zealand, others were indigenous to Fiji. The extent of their trade can be exemplified by Zoing Chong, which imported Chinese goods and exported *bêche-de-mer*, copra, pearl shell and wood to China, ran a furniture factory and a rice mill in Fiji, and grew bananas and rice for export, along with fruits and ginger, to Australia and New Zealand.

Between the two world wars, the largest companies served as *gaaifong* (*jiefang*), social centres providing welfare, temporary accommodation, credit and social facilities for countrymen from a particular district in China. They came under the umbrella of the Kuomintang, which was founded in Suva in 1916. No secret society existed, nor were there any clan or native-place associations in Fiji.

In 1929 a Chinese vice-consulate under the direction of the Sydney consul general was opened in Suva. Seven years later a Chinese school was established, by which time there were 1,751 Chinese in Fiji, 275 of them women. This was the zenith of Kuomintang activity, with party branches in Suva, Lautoka, Ba, Tavua and Labasa. The headquarters building in Suva served as the community centre for the whole Chinese community; almost all Chinese men belonged to the party, and its executive committee provided leadership for community activities.

During the Pacific War, Chinese business prospered from provisioning the numerous military personnel stationed in Fiji. More Chinese women and children came after the war until China curbed emigration in 1951, by which time there were over 3,000 Chinese, rising to a maximum of over 5,000 in 1966. At the same time, the rise of copra cooperatives sponsored by the government and competition from Indian retailers pushed many Chinese out of the hinterland to congregate at Suva.

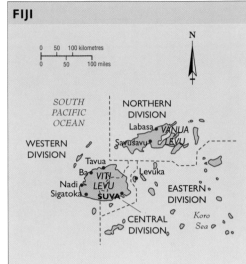

Map 5.18

FIJI

Wedding in Fiji.

As the Suva Chinese community grew by both internal migration and immigration, Chinese cultural activities flourished. A Fiji Chinese Arts Club was formed in 1960 and frequently presented Cantonese operas and concerts. Films from Hong Kong and Taiwan were shown regularly in downtown cinemas. The British colonial administration, however, was suspicious of any Chinese community activity for fear of Communist subversion. An incident in October 1961, when a Chinese in Ba was taken to court merely for possessing several magazines from Beijing, became the excuse to register all Chinese aliens and permit deportation on suspicion and without formal charge.

In 1965, a Chinese association was established to lobby for the vote before a commission that was considering a constitution for Fiji. When the Chinese were finally enfranchised as 'General' electors (along with Europeans and other non-Indian, non-Fijian citizens), the association helped to elect the first Chinese member of the legislature, Mr H. W. (Bill) Yee (Yu Hanhong). Although the association soon died, Yee continued in the legislature for 16 years.

At this time, the prospect of Fijian independence provoked substantial emigration of Chinese from Fiji, primarily to Canada, which had liberalized its immigration criteria in 1966, but also to Australia and New Zealand. This trend continued after independence in 1970, so that in 1981 there were only 4,600 Chinese in Fiji, more than half of them in the Suva region. Although emigration did not abate – and was especially marked just after the 1987 coup – immigration has since augmented the population.

Population

There are about 5,000 Chinese and part-Chinese in Fiji. Almost all live in and around Suva, for long the favoured destination. Elsewhere, there are about 300 Chinese in Lautoka, 200 in Nadi, dozens in Sigatoka, Savusavu, Labasa and Ba, and a few individuals on the outer islands.

The great majority are Cantonese, but others are now coming from elsewhere on the mainland as well as from Hong Kong, Taiwan and, in smaller numbers, from Malaysia. Most of the Cantonese are from the Siyi region, notably from Taishan, with smaller proportions from Kaiping and very few from Xinhui or Enping. About 500 come from Dongguan, significant numbers from Zhongshan, and a few from Panyu. In earlier times, these locality/dialect groups kept more separate, marrying only within their own group, but today they mingle freely, and the differences between them are diminishing. Differences in dialect are kept alive by new immigrants.

Chinese-owned garment factories established in the 1990s have brought in several hundred Mandarin-speaking workers (mainly women) recruited by labour agencies in various parts of China. In addition, Taiwan immigrant families are now found in various kinds of business in and around Suva.

In January 1995, a proposal by Prime Minister Rabuka to bring 28,000 Chinese immigrants to Fiji to foster investment and economic development met serious objections from various sectors of the population, including Chinese. It became one of the issues that sparked a mass demonstration in February, when 12,000 Fijians marched down Suva's main street. Nothing came of the scheme, but Chinese immigration continues unabated.

It is impossible to determine what proportion of the Chinese in Fiji are from mixed marriages. In the interwar years, some Chinese took Fijian wives, and a few married European or part-European women. Mixed marriages between Chinese and Indians was rare. Estimates of Chinese with mixed parentage range from one-fifth to one-half of the Chinese. Several prominent citizens – including a government minister, a retired senator, a high school principal and a retired army officer – are part-Chinese. Depending often on whether their Chinese fathers had arranged a Chinese education for them, some place more emphasis on their Chinese side, others on their Fijian.

Today, mixed marriages occur more frequently among the younger generation, with both men and women marrying Fijians, Indians, Europeans, and the children of mixed marriages. Because Fijian law divides citizens into 'racial' categories according to their paternity, this means that, while children of Chinese fathers are Chinese whatever their mother is, children of Chinese mothers are Chinese only if their fathers are also Chinese.

Economic role

As elsewhere in the Pacific, Chinese in Fiji are prominent in the commercial and service sectors of the economy, but also in manufacturing (furniture, clothing, soft drinks and biscuits). Chinese commercial enterprises include retail shops, import-export companies, hotels, financial services and travel agencies. In Suva, most of the restaurants, coffee shops and takeaway bars are Chinese. There is a sprinkling of Chinese businesses in Lautoka and Nadi, and in Savusavu and Labasa on Vanua Levu as well. Spreading up the hillsides all around Suva are ginger and vegetable farms started by Chinese. Chinese staff many of the stalls in the municipal market, selling vegetables, bananas, ginger and other edibles.

Many Chinese in Suva are now in professional occupations – as engineers, lawyers, doctors, civil servants, teachers, librarians and accountants. These are the descendants of the pioneers, many of whom were uneducated but struggled to ensure that their children received tertiary education.

There is now very little evidence of Chinese from different native places specializing in particular lines of enterprise, although Chinese from Dongguan still appear to be concentrated in market gardening.

Recent immigrants, with much more capital than the earlier pioneers could muster, have founded larger companies in a variety of sectors. Chinese companies from China, Taiwan, Hong Kong and Malaysia are also investing in Fiji, with resident managers and some of the workforce recruited from China. The garment factories are a major example, employing hundreds of workers, many of them contract labour from China. Four construction companies from China are fulfilling building contracts, bringing some of their labour from China. Taiwan interests have invested in different enterprises, including light manufacturing, import-export and ginger processing.

Several of the largest hotels are owned by Hong Kong, Singaporean or Malaysian Chinese companies. In 1994,

Malaysia Borneo Finance opened branches in Fiji and bought Carpenters, which owns the Morris Hedstrom department store chain; in 1996 they sold it to Sateras, another Malaysian company. In 1996 also, Fujian province began negotiations for a major investment in sugar production. Forestry is another potential sector for ethnic Chinese investment, mainly from Malaysia.

Organizations

The oldest Chinese association in Fiji is the Kuomintang, which continues to hold social and cultural activities in its room in downtown Suva. It has a lending library and a lion dance team, and also brings visitors (such as a children's choir, dance troupes and acrobats) from Taiwan for cultural performances.

No organization aspired to represent the Chinese community as a whole – a role the Kuomintang served for 30 years, 1916–46 – until 1992, when the Fiji Chinese Association (Feiji Huaren Xiehui) was founded by several Chinese professionals. Educated in Australian and New Zealand universities, few of the younger professionals are fluent in Chinese, but they nevertheless take an active interest in the Chinese community, and as a result membership is growing. Among other concerns, such as organizing rituals at Qingming (the day ancestors' graves are visited), and supporting the Father Law Old People's Home, where several indigent elderly Chinese reside, it seeks to represent Chinese interests in researching social problems like rural violence, and to monitor new legislation before Parliament.

Other associations group different categories of Chinese, linked together informally through overlapping memberships and executive committees. An organization that recruits community-wide in Suva is the China Club, on whose premises sporting, cultural and social activities are held and members can enjoy a bar and other facilities. Founded in 1955, this club has a broad membership among Suva's professionals, including many non-Chinese associate members.

The Chinese Youth Social and Cultural Association (Zhonghua Qingnian Shehui Wenhua Xiehui) was founded in Suva in 1971 with the primary purpose of organizing social events for young Chinese. Prominent Chinese elders serve as its patrons. The association has waxed and waned over the years, depending on the enthusiasm of its leadership, but it continues to organize recreational and cultural activities, including performances (at both Chinese community events and on civic occasions) of classical Chinese dance by a women's group taught by a succession of dancers from Taiwan. A Western Association of Chinese Youth was established in Lautoka in 1980, and together these two groups run sports competitions in soccer, volleyball and basketball.

At the heart of the Chinese community in Suva is the Yat-sen School. Originally established as a primary school with 24 Chinese pupils in 1936, it served the dual aim of teaching English to new Chinese immigrant children and preserving the Cantonese language of Fiji-born children. It was managed by K. W. March (Yu Jinrong), the leader of the Chinese community at the time, supported by a board chaired by the Chinese vice-consul. In 1952 it moved to a new building and expanded its roll.

As the Chinese grew in number and concentrated in Suva, the school became a community responsibility with the establishment of the Chinese Education Society Inc., which elects the school's board of directors at an annual general meeting open to anyone of Chinese paternity. It began teaching in Mandarin at about 1970 when a teacher from Taiwan arrived. From 1977, the intake of the school included non-Chinese pupils, and their proportion has grown since then.

Headquarters of the Kuomintang in Suva, about 1941, since destroyed.

The Chinese Education Society opened a secondary school on the same site in 1986; the enrolment then was 720. Today the Yat-sen School has over 1,000 pupils, of which 360 are in the secondary school. About half are Chinese, the remainder Fijian, Indian, European, Pacific Islanders and children of mixed marriages.

Another Chinese school was opened in Lautoka soon after the war and taught in Cantonese as recently as 1976. Today it teaches in English and is no longer controlled exclusively by Chinese, and its Chinese character has diminished somewhat.

For many years, the Yat-sen School hired Catholic teachers, and its graduates went to Catholic high schools because they had the highest academic standards. Consequently, many of the Chinese in Suva are Catholics today, particularly among the 40- to 60-year-olds. A minority has joined Protestant churches. Whether Christian or non-Christian, the Chinese continue to celebrate traditional festivals such as Qingming, Chongyang (ninth day of the ninth lunar month, marked by hill climbing), the Mid-Autumn Festival and Chinese New Year.

Relations with China

When the British government recognized the People's Republic of China in 1951, the Kuomintang consulate in Suva closed and the vice-consul returned to Taiwan. Soon after, however, Taiwan opened a trade mission which served as a conduit for Chinese culture, providing visiting teachers and dance instructors. During the next two decades, the Cold-War climate precluded any relationship between the Chinese in Fiji and their homeland, although there were two waves of immigration during difficult times in China, in 1958–59 (Great Leap Forward) and in 1965–66 (start of the Cultural Revolution).

Independent Fiji established diplomatic relations with the People's Republic of China in 1976, and the latter's embassy was opened in Suva with a resident ambassador. However, the Taiwan trade mission continued to operate under a euphemistic name, and since the 1987 coup has been allowed to call itself Trade Mission of the

Republic of China.

Thus, both Beijing and Taiwan maintain active links with the Chinese community. The National Days of both, October 1 (China) and October 10 (Taiwan), are celebrated by the Chinese in Suva, with public events and cultural performances organized by the respective official representatives. October 10 also happens to be Fiji Independence Day, so it tends to have larger celebrations. The Yat-sen School benefits from a regular supply of teachers – the primary school teachers from Taiwan, the secondary from the mainland. This creates some problems for the pupils, who begin their study with old-style Chinese characters and Wade-Giles romanization, then shift to simplified characters and Pinyin when they enter high school. The school's board of directors, however, manages this compromise effectively.

NAURU

The economy of the small island state of Nauru, with a total population of only 10,000, is based entirely on mining by the Nauru Phosphate Corporation. This company brings workers from Kiribati, Tuvalu and the Solomon Islands for the unskilled jobs once done by Chinese indentured labour, and hires Chinese as mechanics, skilled craftsmen and bookkeepers. Many of the Chinese working for the corporation have sponsored their relatives to open restaurants and retail shops. Each hamlet around the island has a small Chinese restaurant, and there are several shops and restaurants close to the compound (known as 'the Location') where all the non-European foreign employees reside.

Most of the Chinese come from Siyi, notably Taishan and Enping. Native-place associations (*tongxianghui*) existed earlier but have disappeared. A Chinese association known as the Huaren Kangle Shi represents Chinese interests to the corporation and government and organizes a lion dance at Chinese New Year and a banquet on October 10 (the National Day of the Republic of China on Taiwan).

The Taiwan government runs a small agricultural research station with a staff of four, and its embassy has a small staff as well.

NEW CALEDONIA

The last New Caledonian census recorded no Chinese because they were all counted as Tahitian. In the period 1957–63, when Tahiti was suffering an economic recession, many Tahitians, including several hundred Chinese, moved to Nouméa, the capital of New Caledonia. The Chinese opened various kinds of shop and Chinese restaurants. Today Chinese own supermarkets, shopping centres, clothing and general stores, hotels and restaurants as well as import-export companies.

Apart from a few chefs recently hired from Hong Kong, the Chinese in Nouméa are all French citizens of Hakka origin, and almost all are Catholics. Their children speak French and English, no Chinese, and many of them are sent to Australia for higher education. Some of them maintain relations with Chinese in Tahiti.

A Chinese association (Communauté Chinoise) was established in 1978 but has no headquarters. Most of its officers are women, unusual among Chinese com-

munity associations around the world. They organize a picnic at Christmas, dinner-dances at Chinese New Year, Mother's Day, Bastille Day and the Autumn Moon Festival, and special events for visiting dignitaries.

Among those who have trading connections with Nouméa are the few Hong Kong Cantonese families who live on Wallis and Futuna, two islands thousands of kilometres away.

W. E. Willmott

PAPUA NEW GUINEA

The original Chinese community had developed over nearly a century of settlement. During that period, Papua New Guinea was successively under German (1884–1914) and Australian administration, becoming independent in 1975. After World War I, Australia took over German New Guinea as a League of Nations mandated territory administratively separate from Papua, but in 1945 combined the two into the Territory of Papua and New Guinea with the common capital at Port Moresby, administering the mandate from 1946 as a United Nations Trust Territory.

The first Chinese arrived in German New Guinea as indentured labourers to work on ill-fated plantations, but then became an important source of skilled labour providing the mechanics, carpenters and tailors required in the colonial economy. Only a handful was allowed to operate plantations. A few started small commercial enterprises and were involved in recruiting indigenous plantation labour, bird of paradise hunting and operating small stores trading in copra. But it was not until after World War II, with the expansion of the cash economy, that the Chinese became concentrated in the commercial sector. There they played an important role as middlemen servicing the needs of the growing, indigenous urban population.

Prior to independence from Australia in 1975, Papua New Guinea had a population of some 3,000 Chinese and part-Chinese, three-quarters of whom were the locally born descendants of those who had come before 1914 to work in German New Guinea (see table 5.35). Virtually all the remainder were their kinsmen and long-established residents. Until the 1970s, the community was divided along a line separating 'Methodists' from 'Catholics.' Methodists, predominantly Hakkas and those surnamed Seeto (Situ) in the Cantonese-speaking group, were Kuomintang followers. The Cantonese-speaking Catholics, however, were from long-established and often wealthy families.

Employees of German firm in Papua New Guinea included Chinese (centre).

With the approach of independence, many Chinese feared for their future safety and livelihood. Under citizenship laws adopted at independence, few Chinese, even those locally born, were eligible for provisional citizenship. Only a small number of Chinese applied for naturalization, preferring instead to retain their recently acquired Australian citizenship. Many relocated to Australia. In 1986, over 3,000 Papua New Guinea-born Chinese were living in Australia. This resettlement, and also their relocation to Port Moresby and other parts of the Australian Territory of Papua, had only been possible after 1967, when the Chinese, who then all lived in the United Nations Trust Territory of New Guinea, were allowed to apply for Australian citizenship.

Upon independence certain occupations, including small trade stores, were restricted to Papua New Guinea nationals. Nevertheless, ongoing businesses were allowed to continue operating under their existing non-national ownership. Some of the Chinese who moved to Australia maintained their business by renting it to a newly arrived Chinese or by going into partnership with a Papua New Guinea national. Those who remained have redirected their businesses out of general retailing into wholesaling; manufacturing, especially of clothing and food stuffs; and specialist niches such as electronics and computers.

Two decades after independence there have been dramatic changes in the numbers, origins and composition of the Chinese population. These changes are a direct result of economic and political changes in both Papua New Guinea and the Asian region. The departure of many Chinese from the newly independent country left a vacuum in commerce. This was partially filled by those who remained but also by new arrivals from Asia. The latter are closely linked to such aspects of economic globalization as multinational and international investment, as well as investments associated with international aid programmes.

In the mid-1990s Papua New Guinea had a Chinese population of approximately 1,500 out of a total of 3.7 million (30,000 of whom are non-citizens). Less than 15 per cent of the Chinese belong to the former homogeneous 'local' population. The term 'local' is applied to the long-established Chinese to distinguish them from the new arrivals, who are called 'overseas' Chinese. Malaysia is now the major birthplace of those commonly referred to as 'overseas' Chinese, followed by the People's Republic of China, Singapore, Taiwan and Hong Kong. A very small proportion of the Philippines- and Indonesian-born population included among the noncitizens shown in the table are also ethnic Chinese. Uncertainty about the size of the Chinese population, which some estimates place as high as 4,000, stems from the diversity in the Chinese population, which now includes many short-term, temporary residents who work in remote logging camps and similar sites and have limited contacts with the urban Chinese.

Port Moresby is the major centre of Chinese settlement, while smaller numbers live in Lae and other towns. Before independence Rabaul, the centre of Chinese settlement from the German period, was already losing its Chinese population to newer growth centres such as Port Moresby, Lae and towns in the Highlands. The decline of Rabaul's Chinese population increased with the relocation of many of the 'local' Chinese to Australia at independence. A devastating earthquake in 1994 made the town and its adjacent areas even less attractive to Chinese settlers.

Among the most numerous group of new arrivals – from Malaysia – two distinct patterns of migration exist. The first, which differs little from earlier waves of migration and business expansion, involved chain migration by the relatives of a brother and sister from Peninsular Malaysia who had married into a local Chinese family. The local family was unusual in that it lacked kinship ties with the rest of the Chinese community and had few economic resources. However, the Malaysian brother and sister, with their Papua New Guinea Chinese spouses, prospered by setting up small stores and then expanding into larger businesses. The businesses began to flourish at the time of independence and within two decades the initial store of the original immigrant (the Malaysian brother) had grown into a series of supermarkets and other businesses. He then sponsored other Malaysian relatives to come and manage his stores. These in turn became independent proprietors themselves but retained close business ties with their sponsor.

In contrast to this classic pattern of individuals with limited economic resources seeking their fortune through self-employment, the second type of Malaysian Chinese migrant came under the aegis of large multinationals, as skilled staff accompanying these companies' investments. The importance of this second pattern of Malaysian migration has increased since the late 1980s, when the government aimed its 'Look North' policy at strengthening

Map 5.19

PAPUA NEW GUINEA

Table 5.35

CHINESE AND NON-CITIZEN POPULATION OF PAPUA NEW GUINEA					
COUNTRY OF BIRTH	**1914a CHINESE**	**1947b CHINESE**	**1971c CHINESE**	**1980d NON-CITIZEN**	**1990e NON-CITIZEN**
Papua New Guinea	na	na	1,991	12,227	5,168
Australia	na	na	103	4,443	3,170
China	na	na	580	200	183
Hong Kong	na	na	na	93	60
Malaysia	na	na	na	201	674
Philippines	na	na	na	2,332	1,600
Singapore	na	na	na	101	106
Taiwan (f)	na	na	na	less than 105	less than 204
Indonesia	na	na	na	455	5,995
Other	na	na	86		
Total Chinese	1,424	2,074	2,760	na	est 1,500
Total non-indigenous		54,526		na	na
Total non-citizens			na	32,670	25,621
Total population		2,489,935	3,010,727	3,607,954	

a) Figures are for 'Chinese' in German New Guinea.
b) Figures are for New Guinea (2,043 Chinese) and Papua (31).
c) Figures are for New Guinea (2,080) and Papua (680).
d) Figures based on race are not available. Only 1,126 'citizens' were born abroad.
e) Figures based on race are not available. Only 702 'citizens' were born abroad. The 1990 figures exclude the North Solomons Province, which in 1980 had a 'non-citizen' population of 3,300 and a 'citizen' population of 126,506. The estimates for Chinese are derived from birthplace figures.
f) Figures for Taiwan-born are based on an estimate.
Sources: Report on Military Occupation of German New Guinea, 1914–21; 1947, 1971, 1980 and 1990 censuses.

ties with Asian countries while lessening reliance on the Australian economy and investment.

The largest of these multinationals is Rimbunan Hijau, which, along with other Malaysian Chinese companies, dominates the logging industry (an industry which contributed US$545.9 million to the national economy in 1994). The diverse interests of these companies extend into property development and finance as well as the media. In 1993 Rimbunan Hijau set up Papua New Guinea's second daily newspaper, *The National*. In addition to these large multinationals, a number of smaller Singaporean and Malaysian firms have also brought in their own supervisory staff after setting up branches or acquiring an interest in a range of manufacturing and other ventures.

SIR JULIUS CHAN AND PAPUA NEW GUINEA POLITICS

Sir Julius Chan, twice Prime Minister of Papua New Guinea (1980–82 and 1994–97), entered politics in 1968 when elected to the colonial House of Assembly. He retained his seat in the post-independence Parliament and has been a member of successive coalition governments for half of the two decades since independence.

Such a sustained career is unusual in Papua New Guinean politics. The fact that only his mother is of indigenous ancestry, contrasting Sir Julius with other major political figures, makes it all the more remarkable. His father, Chin Pak (Chen Bo), was born in China (in Taishan) and migrated to Papua New Guinea with his brother and other kinsmen in the German period. He became a trader and one of the few Chinese to lease a plantation near Namatanai on New Ireland. Sir Julius was born in 1939 on nearby Tanga Island, the area where his mother's family is located and where his political base is. His electorate is Namatanai Open, and the People's Progress Party, which he co-founded in 1970 and of which he remains the leader, is strongest in the New Guinea islands and coastal region.

Until he entered politics in 1968, Sir Julius's life was similar to that of his Chinese and part-Chinese contemporaries. During the wartime Japanese occupation of New Guinea, the family were placed in a Japanese work camp near Namatanai and then resettled in Rabaul. Primary school in Rabaul was followed by boarding school and university in Brisbane, Australia. After an accident interrupted his studies, he returned in 1960 to Papua New Guinea, where he worked for the Australian administration. Differential pay scales and the continuation of discrimination, even after gaining Australian citizenship, discouraged young Chinese from seeking a career in the colonial administration or European private sector. Like many contemporaries, Sir Julius left the administration service in 1962 to work in the successful family business. In addition to coastal shipping, the business had an interest in a Rabaul shipbuilding company operated by a group of Chinese partners.

Prior to independence no Chinese was ever appointed by the Australian administration to non-elective positions in the Legislative Council or House of Assembly, though some were appointed to the Town and District Advisory Councils. Many Chinese feared taking a role in politics in case it provoked a backlash. However, when elections were introduced prior to independence, some young Chinese stood successfully for election to local councils. Another Chinese-Indigenous man joined Julius Chan in the 1972 House of Assembly. Although both men stood in areas where their families had long-established kinship and business connections, the relatively small numbers of Chinese voters meant that neither's election was dependent on the Chinese vote. Since independence, any potential which the Chinese population might have had for influencing politics through the electoral process has all but disappeared, since so few are citizens with the right to vote.

Kinship and regional ties play an important part in the volatile local politics. While Chan's own links in New Ireland have been important in giving stability to his political career, his linkages with the Chinese community, which are often perceived as lacking a strong commitment to Papua New Guinea, provide a basis for critics to question his political credentials. However, the criticisms are couched in terms of his linkages to Australia rather than to Chinese interests in Asia. He is fluent in Cantonese, but commentators see him as having put little push into the 'Look North' shift of economic ties from Australia to Asia.

Christine Inglis

The smaller numbers of Chinese from Taiwan and the People's Republic of China reflect their more limited economic interests in Papua New Guinea, although Taiwanese have extensive investments in the offshore fishing industry. Both countries have had aid programmes partially staffed by their own nationals, some of whom, especially those from the People's Republic, have remained. This latter group has found employment in factories run by other Chinese, or else in businesses such as takeaway food shops or small trade stores requiring little capital. It is noteworthy that Hong Kong migrants and investment are absent, though one would expect some from the fact that the original Chinese were from Guangdong and the links they maintained with China were directed through Hong Kong.

The changing composition of the Chinese population and the high proportion of temporary residents makes it impossible to refer in any meaningful way to the existence of a Chinese community in Papua New Guinea today. To the extent that this community continues to exist, it is based in Australia in areas such as Sydney and the Gold Coast. The Cathay Club in Port Moresby, whose management continues to be dominated by local Chinese, still exists as a symbol of Chinese community, but the membership now includes many European and middle-class Papua New Guinean families.

'Local' and 'overseas' Chinese are distinguished by more than birthplace and period of settlement. A cultural and social divide separates the locally born Cantonese speakers, who have been extensively influenced by contacts with Australians and other Europeans, from the new arrivals, few of whom speak Cantonese and who have much closer links with traditional Chinese culture. This is epitomized by the Chinese New Year, an event celebrated by overseas Chinese but whose traditions had been transferred to the January 1 New Year by local Chinese. Among overseas Chinese the differences in country of origin are further compounded by differences in social class, language, economic interests and lifestyle. The fact that the short-term, contract residents leave their families in their places of origin means that there is a high masculinity ratio. The law and order problems in towns like Port Moresby, where expatriates avoid going out at night, discourage family settlement and work against the development of a viable Chinese community.

The small disunited Chinese population has limited political influence as a group. Nevertheless, individual Chinese businessmen, especially those associated with the large multinational companies, are widely perceived to use their considerable influence to further their economic interests. Corruption is a widely acknowledged problem. But local Chinese point out that its occurrence has coincided with the advent of 'overseas' Chinese, especially those from Malaysia. They also argue that because of their long and close contacts with the indigenous population, as well as their knowledge of the local language and customs, the image of the 'ugly Chinese' (or 'Asian') raised in the media and general discussion does not encompass them. Whatever validity the distinction they draw may have in parts of New Guinea with a long history of Chinese settlement – such as West New Britain and New Ireland – it means little in areas (such as those recently opened up to logging) where the indigenous population's first contact has been with Chinese from Malaysia and elsewhere.

After over a century of settlement Chinese are now more marginal legally and socially than they were in the 1970s. The relocation of many to Australia was seen as symbolizing a lack of commitment to the country. Meanwhile, foreigners, especially those with a high economic profile and with a temporary status in the country, easily become potential scapegoats for the country's economic and political crises (the latter revolving around the long-running secessionist rebellion in Bougainville and other provinces). Whether Chinese will continue to live and work in the country in substantial numbers may ultimately depend on whether they can see some economic benefit accruing to themselves. Certainly at present, few would feel that they can have a long-term future there.

Christine Inglis

THE SOLOMON ISLANDS

Most of the Chinese in the Solomon Islands came from the Siyi county of Kaiping in Guangdong province, many of them named Guan. Their number grew steadily to about 1,600 in 1975, but several hundreds left when the country became independent in 1978. The population has since been augmented by workers from China, and large mining and timber companies from Malaysia and Singapore.

Almost all of the approximately 900 Chinese live in the metropolitan area of Honiara, with a few families at Gizo and Auki and some individuals on other islands. Chinese general stores line the two streets of Honiara's Chinatown, across the river from the city centre. Chinese are also active in inter-island trade and shipping, food processing, restaurants, hotels, automobile repairs, sales and rentals. A number of Chinese are found in professions such as accounting, medicine and teaching. Chinese serve on several of the boards of major government agencies and banks.

Most of the older Chinese belong to the Chinese Association (Zhonghua Zonghui), which serves as a liaison with government and organizes events for the Chinese community at Qingming (when ancestors' graves are tended) and the New Year (January 1). It also looks after the Chinese section of the municipal cemetery. A

Map 5.20

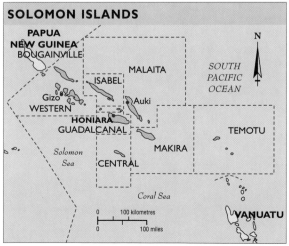

SOLOMON ISLANDS

Headstone in cemetery at Honiara, Solomon Islands, indicates deceased's native place: Kaiping, Guangdong.

Chinese Youth Association organized sports and social events until the late 1990s, when it became moribund.

Chinese run a private primary school, originally established by the Chinese Association; today 90 per cent of its pupils and teachers are non-Chinese, although Mandarin is taught by a teacher from Taiwan. Many Chinese in Honiara send their children to Australia for further schooling.

The Taiwan government has funded a hospital and an agricultural research station at Honiara, each of which has a small staff of Chinese. Several Malaysian Chinese companies are logging on various islands, and fishing boats from Taiwan also operate in the Solomons.

TAHITI

French Polynesia comprises scores of islands spread over five archipelagoes (Society, Marquesas, Tuamotu, Gambier, and Austral) in the south-eastern Pacific. While individual Chinese are scattered in all five archipelagoes, almost all live on Tahiti (where most of the population of French Polynesia is to be found).

History

The first Chinese trader to settle in Tahiti arrived in 1851 and was joined by others in 1856, when several miners from Victoria, Australia, on their way to the California gold-fields decided to stay in Tahiti instead. This small Chinese community was suddenly enlarged in 1865 by the arrival from Hong Kong of 1,000 indentured labourers for the Atimaono cotton plantation, almost all of them Hakka. When the plantation declared bankruptcy in 1873, hundreds of these workers opted to remain in Tahiti to develop market gardens and other businesses. About 30 went to the Marquesas and a few to the Gambiers to work on plantations there. Most returned to China in the following years.

At the 1892 census only 320 Chinese remained in the French colony. There was only one Chinese woman, indicating that many of the Chinese had taken Tahitian wives. A third of the Chinese were in agriculture, the rest divided among labourers, merchants and craftsmen. The 1902 census counted 412 Chinese in French Polynesia, 365 of them on Tahiti and 43 in the Marquesas. Some of these came from California, where gold mining

Chinese arrivals at Papeete, 1911.

had dried up and life became difficult for the Chinese.

Throughout the last decades of the 19th century, controversy raged among French settlers about the Chinese presence. While most were happy to have Chinese domestic servants and market gardeners in the colony, French traders feared Chinese competition in commerce and proposed harsh taxes on their businesses and restrictions on further immigration. Charges of 'Chinese invasion,' 'immorality,' 'unsanitary conditions,' 'gambling and opium' and 'unfair competition' filled the local press. Public meetings protested the 'Yellow Peril,' at least one of them organized by the famous painter Paul Gauguin. In response, the French colonial authorities decreed a poll tax and an immigration fee, but preferred to encourage Chinese business in the interests of the colony as a whole. Following their practice in Indochina, they divided the Chinese into two *congrégations*, Hakka and Cantonese (Punti), and appointed two *chefs de congrégations* with responsibilities for taxes and maintaining order.

In the period 1907–14, when hundreds of thousands fled disorder in China, 2,500 Chinese came to Tahiti, including over 200 women. This marked the beginning of a Chinese community based on family rather than solely men. Another peak of female migration occurred in 1921–28, when 500 of the 2,200 Chinese immigrants were women. The opening of a direct steamship line between Hong Kong and Papeete in 1924 allowed for easier movement of Chinese in both directions. The Chinese population of French Polynesia rose to over 4,000 by 1928, 4,600 by the start of the Pacific War, about 4,000 of whom were on Tahiti itself. Chinese businessmen at that time had a well-developed network of retail stores around the island and were engaged in exporting copra, pearl shell and vanilla.

This community was served by a number of associations, none of which embraced the entire Chinese population. From 1913 the colonial authorities treated Chinese as a single *congrégation* with only one *chef* until 1933, when the system was terminated. A mutual aid society had existed since 1872, officially registering in 1911 as Si-Ni-Tong (Xinyi Tang). It administered the Chinese cemetery at Arue, on the outskirts of Papeete, and looked after the small Chinese temple that had been established in 1866. In 1921, l'Association Philanthropique Chinoise, or Chinese Benevolent Society (Zhonghua Huiguan) was founded by a prominent Chinese merchant banker, Chin Foo (Chen Shichong) and his friends, who were in conflict with Sun Yat-sen's younger supporters, who wanted the Si-Ni-Tong to pursue the republican cause. A branch of the Kuomintang was opened in 1918, and a branch of the Chee Kung Tong (Zhigong Tang, known elsewhere as the Chinese Freemasons) in 1937. All three of these associations ran Chinese schools teaching in Hakka. In 1925 the Cantonese minority set up the Nam Hoi Kon On Woi (Nanhai Guang'an Hui) to represent their interests.

Chinese business prospered during the Pacific War. Far from the combat zone, Tahiti's Chinese were nevertheless involved in provisioning and providing logistical support for a large American base on the island of Bora-Bora. In 1942 personality and political dissension fractured the Tahiti Kuomintang into two branches distinguishing themselves as the Kuomintang and the Kuo Men Tong (same Chinese characters romanised differently), or, as the Chinese call them, 'KMT 1' and 'KMT 2.' Yet another branch was established at Uturoa. All three branches collected money from patriotic Chinese for the war effort in the motherland. A Chinese consulate was opened in 1944.

After the war, about 800 elderly Chinese returned to China. Although immigration virtually ceased, the Chinese population continued to grow naturally. Of the 7,465 Chinese counted in the 1956 census, almost a third were born in Tahiti, a proportion that rose steadily thereafter. The rising price of vanilla on the world market encouraged more Chinese into production, although the majority was still in retail trade and import-export, where they competed with French firms. Growing and marketing vegetables, butcheries and bakeries were in Chinese hands. Few Chinese were as yet in professional occupations.

Three events in the 1960s caused major changes in the Chinese community. First, the Tahitian economy received a huge boost when the French moved their nuclear testing site from Algeria to Mururoa in 1963. This provided boom conditions for the rapid growth of Chinese business. Second, France recognized the People's Republic of China in 1963. This eroded the power of the Kuomintang branches and increased the status of the Chinese Benevolent Society, which had remained neutral throughout China's civil war. Third, in moves to encourage assimilation in 1964, the French forced all the Chinese schools (four at the time) to close and introduced easier naturalization, with the result that many Chinese opted for French citizenship. After 1973 citizenship was granted to everyone born in the colony; well over half of the Chinese at that time were eligible. Chinese were now able to buy land, receive scholarships for overseas study, and enter fully into the political life of the colony.

During the 1970s, as the proportion of French citizens rose among Chinese, they began to play an active part in local politics. The first Chinese in public office was Dr Yen Howan, who became mayor of Papeete in 1971. Michel Law was elected to the Territorial Assembly in 1972, and Arthur Chung in 1977. Each formed a political party and continued in territorial politics for some years, Law's favouring French rule and Chung's tending towards Tahitian autonomy. Charlie Ching, a prominent activist in the independence movement at the time, was not part of the Chinese community although of Chinese ancestry.

Map 5.21

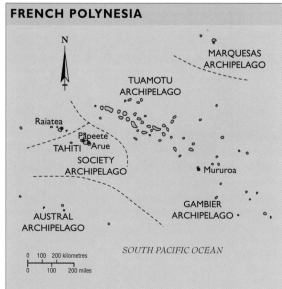

FRENCH POLYNESIA

N

MARQUESAS ARCHIPELAGO

TUAMOTU ARCHIPELAGO

Raiatea

Papeete
TAHITI Arue
SOCIETY ARCHIPELAGO

Mururoa

AUSTRAL ARCHIPELAGO

GAMBIER ARCHIPELAGO

SOUTH PACIFIC OCEAN

0   100   200 kilometres
0   100   200 miles

Population

The nearly 9,000 Chinese in French Polynesia represent about 4.1 per cent of the total population. They are found in all the archipelagoes of French Polynesia, but the vast majority lives on Tahiti, where they constitute about 6 per cent of the total population. Less than 500 Chinese live at Uturoa on Raiatea, another of the Society Islands, while scattered individuals make their homes in the Marquesas, Gambier, Tuamotu and Austral archipelagoes.

More than 90 per cent of the Chinese were born in French Polynesia, less than 500 born in China. Small numbers of chefs have been recruited from Hong Kong on short-term visas, and a few families have brought relatives from China. Apart from this, there is very little immigration.

Almost all the Chinese in Tahiti are of Hakka origin, two-thirds of them from Huiyang and others from Dongguan and Baoan. The smaller number of Cantonese, less than 15 per cent, came mainly from Nanhai and Siyi. Hakka is the lingua franca within the Chinese community in Papeete, although French is taking over, as few of those under 40 have studied Chinese. On the other islands, most Chinese speak the local Polynesian language in their homes and businesses.

The 1988 census revealed that 14 per cent of the Chinese had mixed parentage, almost all of them with Polynesian mothers. The total number of people claiming some Chinese ancestry was over 20,000, but most of these did not consider themselves Chinese. There were 110 males for every 100 females, and the population was ageing as families became smaller and more youth opted for Tahitian identity. Intermarriage is becoming common in Tahiti today.

Economic role

Since the 1960s the economy has been sustained by the French nuclear testing programme, which has provided opportunities for Chinese businessmen to diversify and develop their commercial activities. Today they are prominent in all three sectors of economic activity, namely, agriculture, manufacturing and services. The end of French testing in 1996 and the consequent removal of personnel and plant severely challenge the economy and will no doubt adversely affect much Chinese business in the archipelago.

Large Chinese companies are typically diversified into many enterprises. Some export vanilla, copra, pearl shell, black pearls or fish, although vanilla and copra are far less significant than previously. Most of these companies are also involved in importing a wide range of goods, including food items, clothing, shoes, electronic equipment, durable goods, automobiles and industrial machinery. Some also engage in light industry, manufacturing soap, coconut oil, juices or soft drinks.

Retail trade is largely in Chinese hands, especially outside central Papeete. Chinese also provide services such as carpentry, equipment and auto repairs, transport, butchery and baking. Some restaurants and hotels are owned by Chinese, although they compete in this sector with French and 'demis' (French–Polynesian mixed-parentage). Chinese gardens provide most of the vegetables in the Papeete market. Chinese are engaged in inter-island transportation and some commercial fishing. The few Chinese living on other islands run pearl farms, vanilla plantations or local retail shops.

New in this generation is a professional class of several hundred Chinese including doctors, teachers, lawyers, accountants and dentists. They are well educated and often trilingual in Chinese, French and English. Many qualified in California, the preferred destination for Chinese going abroad for higher education. Real estate is another recent profession for Chinese.

Community organization

None of the Chinese associations represents the community as a whole, although four of them have buildings and organize community events and activities. The largest of these, the Chinese Benevolent Society, holds regular Chinese classes, social and cultural events, as do KMT 1, KMT 2 and the Zhigong Tang. Some rivalry exists between these three associations, although they cooperate in some of the projects initiated by the Si-Ni-Tong.

The Cantonese minority is organized into a number of less formal native-place associations, none of which has a headquarters building. Together they are known as the Seven Villages Association (Qixiang Huiguan), although this is not a registered society. No formal clan associations exist in Tahiti, although several of the most prominent lineages call their families together now and then to organize visits to the cemetery or care for indigents.

Two recently established associations represent new trends in the community. In 1977, Te Vahine Porenetia (Polynesian Woman) was organized by several Chinese women who saw a need for a women's service club across ethnic lines. Most of its members are Chinese, however. The other association, Wen Fa (Wenhua), was founded by several professional Chinese with the intention of strengthening Chinese culture in Tahiti. Its members meet regularly and together have sponsored prizes for language students, organized events at the Chinese New Year, and sponsored meetings for visiting Chinese personalities. It has edited an important book on the history of the Chinese in Tahiti, *Histoire et Portrait de la Communauté Chinoise de Tahiti*.

Because most of the Chinese in Tahiti are Catholics, the Catholic church has built a Chinese Catholic Centre, where various social and cultural activities take place. A Chinese priest administers the centre, together with leading Chinese laymen and women. A small number of Chinese adhere to various Protestant denominations, most of them fundamentalist in orientation. Other Chinese remain believers in traditional Chinese religions, including some Buddhists. The community regularly celebrates Qingming (day when ancestors' graves are tended) with visits to the large Chinese cemetery at Arue, but Chongyang (ninth day of the ninth lunar month,

(Left) Chin Foo, banker and Si-Ni-Tong's president, with wife and children. (Top) Public notice of meeting called by painter Paul Gaugin, left 1900, to determine measures to 'halt the Chinese invasion' and Polynesian-Chinese girl.

Kuomintang flag and portrait of Sun Yat-sen decorate hall in Papeete.

Tahitians of mixed Polynesian-Chinese ancestry.

marked by hill climbing) has been replaced by All Saints Day (November 1) because of the many Catholics in the community.

The Si-Ni-Tong, the oldest Chinese association in Tahiti, owns considerable capital and is therefore the scene of some political conflict within the community. Its board was increased from seven to 35 members in 1950 to accommodate the Chinese Benevolent Association, the two branches of the Kuomintang, the Zhigong Tang and the Seven Villages Associations. Each of these groupings has had seven members on the Si-Ni-Tong until the latter underwent further restructuring, from which it will probably emerge as more genuinely representative of the whole Chinese community.

On the Si-Ni-Tong's initiative, the Kanti Temple (Guandi Miao) was built at Mamao in Papeete in 1984 (see box p 303). On the same property, the Si-Ni-Tong administers a home for elderly Chinese without families. This home was enlarged in 1981 to house women as well as men. The Si-Ni-Tong also oversees the Chinese cemetery and built a pavilion for communal ritual near the ceremonial gate.

A neo-Polynesian identity

Many younger Chinese in Tahiti consider themselves Polynesian today, though this does not mean rejecting their Chinese identity. Chinese foresee the emergence of a neo-Polynesian culture that includes aspects of all the cultures found in the country. Stressing the distinctiveness of a Chinese community may lead to a marginalization Chinese are concerned to avoid. For example, when the Wen Fa association considered presenting an annual prize for the best student of Chinese, they decided to enlarge the contest to include four languages (French, English, Tahitian, and Chinese) to avoid being seen as parochial. Similarly, the Chinese women who organized Vahine Porenetia intended it for women

of all ethnicities. Two Chinese sports clubs, the Dragon Football Club and the Phoenix Basketball Club, have become multi-ethnic and are no longer considered to be Chinese associations.

The fact that most Chinese in French Polynesia are French citizens allows them to enter completely into local Tahitian politics, society and culture, unlike in those countries where they continue to be identified socially and legally as non-indigenous. Some Chinese are pro-French rule while others are pro-Tahitian independence, as are many citizens in the other ethnic groups.

TONGA

The Kingdom of Tonga is the only region in the South Pacific that escaped becoming a colony of an outside power. However, from 1869, a German firm headquartered in Samoa controlled the copra trade. As it excluded Chinese traders from the archipelago, no Chinese settled in Tonga until the 1970s, when Tonga recognized the government in Taipei. The rate of Chinese (and other) immigration rose sharply in the late 1980s, especially after Tonga began selling 'Tongan National Passports' in 1989.

Today there are about 200 Chinese resident in Tonga, all of them in Nuku'alofa. Most come from various parts of mainland China, with a few from Taiwan or Hong Kong. About 10 per cent are Tongan citizens, the remainder on temporary visas. Chinese run restaurants, hotels, retail stores, food stalls and snack bars. A large airport hotel is being built by a Taiwanese businessman with a workforce from Tianjin.

In 1989, the Chinese in Nuku'alofa founded the Kingdom of Tonga Chinese Association (Dongjia Wangguo Zhonghua Huiguan), with officers elected annually. It rents a house on the main street, where it runs Mandarin classes for children.

VANUATU

The 1989 census in Vanuatu counted 261 Chinese residents, but since that time a number of children and elderly have moved to Australia, while new immigrants have raised the numbers to about 300 in all. Two-thirds of them live in the capital, Vila, the remainder at Luganville on Esperitu Santo. Recent immigrants came from China, Hong Kong, Taiwan and Malaysia, while the older residents are Cantonese, almost all of them from Dongguan and Zengcheng counties in Guangdong province.

Chinese are engaged primarily in retail and wholesale of imported goods, with some involved in restaurants, inter-island shipping, hotels, supermarkets, food processing and exports. Several large Malaysian, Chinese and Taiwanese companies are logging on different islands, and Chinese companies are constructing public and private buildings and a dam on Malakula.

In Vila, the shops and restaurants originally in Chinatown have dispersed throughout the city and suburbs. In contrast, the main street of Luganville is lined with nearly 40 Chinese general stores. There is a Chinese association in both centres, although the one in Vila no longer has a headquarters building and is inactive. The Santo Chinese Association (Shengdu Zhonghua

THE KANTI TEMPLE

The Kanti Temple (Guandi Miao) is the largest Chinese temple in the South Pacific. It was inaugurated on May 30, 1987 with a day-long celebration that involved several Chinese associations. The temple replaces a smaller one built in 1866, soon after the Chinese indentured labourers arrived on the island. When this burned down in 1981, the Si-Ni-Tong mobilized community resources to build a replacement on a much grander scale, this time incorporating a number of other deities, including Guanyin; the Gods of Wealth (Caifu Shen); the ancestor of all overseas Chinese (Huaqiao Zhugong); and a shrine to a local Chinese martyr, Chim Soo (Shen Xiugong), who was beheaded at Atimaono in 1869. Following a riot among the Chinese labourers against their miserable conditions, Chim Soo allegedly accepted the blame to save the lives of others implicated. Commemorative rituals are practised at Qingming before his large grave in the Chinese cemetery.

The People's Republic of China donated a pair of stone lions for the temple, while the Overseas Chinese Commission in Taipei contributed a pair of carved dragons on the pillars, as well as carvings and a plaque.

When the Si-Ni-Tong was running lotteries to build the temple, Archbishop Coppenrath, Catholic primate of Tahiti, condemned them as sinful and urged Chinese Catholics to oppose the temple as anti-Christian. Despite this, many Chinese Catholics contributed money and effort to the project, because they saw it as part of a Chinese cultural revival. The same view was expressed by non-Catholic Chinese who were also not believers in traditional Chinese religions.

The temple is used for various traditional, non-Christian Chinese religious practices. Its presence reminds younger Chinese of aspects of Chinese heritage they might otherwise ignore completely. It is intended to be the centrepiece of a Chinese cultural centre that will eventually include other buildings for cultural and social activities.

While the previous Kanti Temple faced the sea, this one faces inland, on the advice of a Taiwanese geomancer. Some elderly Chinese blame the orientation of the temple for misfortunes the Chinese have experienced since its construction.

W. E. Willmott

Gonghui) has a clubroom and holds annual elections for its executive committee.

When Vanuatu was jointly administered by the British and French as the New Hebrides, Chinese immigrants had to opt for one jurisdiction or the other. Most opted for the British, so English speakers outnumber French speakers today. Most of them have become citizens of Vanuatu, and a few have converted to Catholicism or Presbyterian Christianity. The vast majority send their children to Australia for higher education, although a small number go to Nouméa. In neither place do they become literate in Chinese, although efforts are made to teach them the language. Older Chinese retire to Sydney, where there is a growing community of Chinese from Vanuatu.

Aid from the People's Republic of China has provided the country's parliament buildings, built by a Chinese company with Chinese contract labour.

WESTERN SAMOA

The Chinese in Western Samoa live in and around Apia, the only urban centre. Most of the general stores are owned by Chinese, including the largest department store. Several restaurants, a hotel and two bakeries are also ran by Chinese. Even after the Pacific War, they operated village stores scattered throughout the country, many of which are now owned by their part-Chinese descendants.

The original Chinese traders who settled in Apia were Hokkiens from Xiamen in Fujian Province. However, all the indentured labour came through Hong Kong, most of whom were from the Siyi districts, notably Enping. Today all the Chinese are Cantonese, including the few recent immigrants, almost all of whom are the relatives of residents.

Although there are many Samoans with Chinese ancestry, few of them are now involved in the Chinese community unless they were sent to China for education. The lack of anti-Chinese prejudice among Samoans makes it possible for Chinese and part-Chinese to participate fully in Samoan society, to become civil servants and elected members of parliament. The boundaries of the community are therefore vague, with some Samoans recognizing their Chinese heritage and others ignoring it.

Every two years the Samoan Overseas Chinese Association (Sayao Huaqiao Gonghui) elects an executive of two parts, four Chinese officers and four part-Chinese officers. Because the Chinese are faced with few issues in Samoa, interest in the association has waned in recent years. Its large hall is now used primarily to show films and as a venue for boxing matches.

Some of the Chinese in Western Samoa have relatives in American Samoa, but generally there is little communication between them. The Chinese in American Samoa have connections to Hawaii rather than to their nearest neighbour.

W. E. Willmott

Chinese general store in Luganville, Vanuatu.

BRITAIN

Table 5.36

THE CHINA-BORN POPULATION IN ENGLAND AND WALES	
YEAR	POPULATION
1851	78
1861	147
1871	202
1881	665
1891	582
1901	387
1911	1,319
1921	2,419
1931	1,934

Sources: Censuses of England and Wales.

Pre-war Chinese settlement

The history of the Chinese in Britain is closely tied to that of the British Empire in East Asia and subsequently shaped by British immigration controls. The first documented Chinese presence in Britain can be traced to the 18th century, when vessels conducting Britain's growing maritime trade with East Asia brought Chinese seamen to the ports of London and Liverpool. 'Very resolute' Chinese men, for example, were reported to be involved in a scuffle with a crowd of locals in Stepney, East London, by the *Morning Chronicle* newspaper of July 27, 1782. Throughout the 19th century, Chinese seamen originating mainly from the southern coastal provinces of China, in particular Guangdong, clustered around the dockland areas of Limehouse (East London) and Liverpool, forming a transient population. Census figures show just how small this highly mobile, seafaring population was before 1945 (see table 5.36).

The Chinese presence in early 20th-century Britain was marked by the demonization of certain places, in particular the Chinese settlement in Limehouse, first dubbed 'Chinatown' in 1902 by an investigative journalist called George Sims. Home to a community of Chinese seafarers, a number of them with white female partners and Anglo-Chinese children, Limehouse was routinely the subject of lurid portrayals in newspapers and popular fiction before its destruction in World War II. Today, the only traces of this early Chinese settlement are some of the street names: Ming, Canton and Pekin Streets.

The anti-Chinese agitation of sections of the popular press and of the British working class partly explains the confinement of Chinese to a limited range of occupations such as running hand laundries and grocery shops. There were recurrent attacks on Chinese property and people. In these hostile circumstances the Chinese turned to organizations such as the Chinese Freemason Society, or Chee Kong Tong (Zhigong Tang) in Chinese; the Chinese Mission in Pennyfields and the Zhonghua Chinese Language School, established in 1935 with Sir Robert Hotung, a rich half-Chinese businessman in Hong Kong, as one of its patrons.

The Chinese contribution to the British war effort is a little known chapter of the British-Chinese story. During World War I, France and Britain shipped about 100,000 men from Shandong province in north China to serve on the Western front as trench diggers, cooks and machine repairers. Given China's neutral stance, these men were not directly involved in fighting, but still some 2,000 of them died. Most lie in graves in France and Belgium, but some were buried in England – for example, at Egg Buckland cemetery in Plymouth.

After the war, the British government was keen to deport the surviving Chinese. Government documents reveal the existence of an Aliens and Nationality Committee that met regularly throughout 1919. The minutes of June 21,1919 warn that the Chinese presence 'may at any moment lead to racial riots which are to be avoided at any costs.' In World War II Chinese seamen operating out of Liverpool played an important part in maintaining Britain's supply lines and once again were deported for their trouble.

Throughout the 20th century, a steady stream of students and diplomats augmented the Chinese population. In the 1930s the president of the Central Union of Chinese Students, Szeming Sze, estimated a population of 450 Chinese students in Britain. The famous Beijing author Lao She taught Chinese at London University from 1924 to 1930 and set one of his novels, *The Two Mas*, in the city.

Chinese communities in postwar Britain

The small Chinese population entered a new phase after 1945, with Britain's postwar boom increasing the

Map 5.22

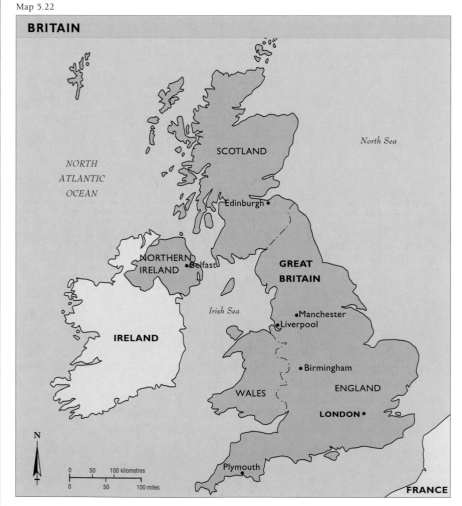

BRITAIN

NORTH ATLANTIC OCEAN

SCOTLAND

North Sea

Edinburgh

NORTHERN IRELAND
Belfast

GREAT BRITAIN

Irish Sea

Manchester
Liverpool

IRELAND

Birmingham

WALES

ENGLAND

LONDON

N

Plymouth

FRANCE

| 0 | 50 | 100 kilometres |
| 0 | 50 | 100 miles |

demand for labour and prompting an upsurge of immigration from the British Commonwealth. Numbers have to be guessed at as the decennial censuses categorized them by country of birth rather than ethnic origin. These show a steady growth in the numbers of people from China, Hong Kong, Singapore and Malaysia (see table 5.37). Most of these would be ethnic Chinese.

The postwar demand for labour accounts for the substantial increase in Chinese numbers. Furthermore, under the 1948 British Nationality Act, Commonwealth citizens had the right to settle in Britain. The colonial status of Hong Kong, Singapore and Malaysia (then Malaya) facilitated easy migration to the metropolitan country.

A key source of Chinese migration has been the New Territories of rural Hong Kong. There, Hakka villagers' livelihood as subsistence rice growers was undermined by a combination of factors. The vast numbers of refugees fleeing China in 1949 were putting pressure on the land. Many of these newcomers were skilled agriculturalists offering stiff competition to the local Hakka peasants. At about this time, cheap rice was being imported into Hong Kong from Thailand, undercutting local growers. Meanwhile, the urbanization of Hong Kong was drawing new generations into the city. A settled way of life was disturbed and emigration seemed a viable solution. Britain's expanding economy and the fact that the New Territories villagers were born in the British colony and so were Commonwealth citizens explained their choice of destination.

With servicemen returning from various parts of the Empire, one consequence of the war had been the development of a taste for new cuisines. The rebuilding of the country, the development of suburban lifestyles and the rise in the number of women workers combined to boost the practice of 'eating out' once postwar rationing had ended. In the restaurant trade, immigrant Chinese found a niche which was labour-intensive and which required little knowledge of English. From the 1950s onward, the number of Chinese eating establishments around the country grew swiftly. Initially, the catering staff was almost exclusively male. As James L. Watson shows in his book *Emigration and the Chinese Lineage: The Mans in Hong Kong and London* (1975), many of the new arrivals were connected by ties of kinship and locality in Hong Kong.

In contrast to the immigrants from Hong Kong, the Chinese from Malaysia and Singapore tended to be better qualified and to possess a higher standard of English. Large numbers came as nurses and students.

In the early 1960s Britain's immigration laws again intervened to reshape Chinese migration decisions. The 1962 Commonwealth Immigrants Act withdrew the automatic right of citizenship. An employment voucher system was initiated, followed in 1971 by work permit quotas. The requirement of having a job secured in advance furthered the concentration of Chinese settlers in catering, with

Table 5.37

BRITISH RESIDENTS BORN IN EAST AND SOUTHEAST ASIA					
YEAR	CHINA	HONG KONG	SINGAPORE	MALAYSIA	TOTAL
1951	8,636	3,459	3,255	4,046	19,396
1961	9,192	10,222	9,820	9,516	38,750
1971	13,495	29,520	27,335	25,680	96,030
1981	17,569	58,917	32,447	45,430	154,363

Sources: Censuses of England and Wales.

restaurant owners filling openings in their businesses by recruiting newcomers through family and village connections. Back in Hong Kong, many families became dependent on regular remittances from Britain.

From the late 1960s onward, dependants became an important source of new labour in Chinese catering businesses. What was initially intended as a period of sojourning developed into extended residence. The formation of family units consolidated settlement and provided the basis for the setting up of small catering businesses. Family labour was an important means of countering the new competition from American fast-food chains. Types of catering outlets grew in the 1970s, with the Chinese family takeaway (and even fish-and-chip shops) becoming a familiar sight in every British town. The dispersal of the Chinese population in Britain reflects the need for each business to have a wide catchment area and to move away from competitors.

Contemporary demographic profile

The most comprehensive official source on the Chinese in Britain is the 1991 census, which for the first time included a question on ethnic origin and had 'Chinese' as one of its categories. This allows for a more accurate estimation of the Chinese population than previous statistics.

Chinese Freemason Society in Limehouse, 1926-28.

Schoolgirls in Limehouse, 1930s.

Figure 5.8

DISTRIBUTION BY AGE AND GENDER, 1991

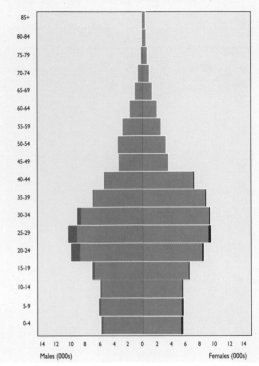

85+
80-84
75-79
70-74
65-69
60-64
55-59
50-54
45-49
40-44
35-39
30-34
25-29
20-24
15-19
10-14
5-9
0-4

14 12 10 8 6 4 2 0 2 4 6 8 10 12 14

Males (000s)   Females (000s)

The dark shading at the end of each bar represents the additional numbers which should be added to compensate for under-counting in the 1991 census.
Source: Coleman and Salt (1996).

The total Chinese population was reported as 156,938, with 77,669 males and 79,269 females. However, census forms were not available in Chinese and Chinese community organizations question the data's validity. The demographers themselves now regard the figures as an underestimate, putting the adjusted total at approximately 162,400. Three features stand out from the data.

First, the Chinese population is relatively youthful; the age-gender pyramid (see figure 5.8) bulges between the ages of 20 and 44. Secondly, the Chinese population is widely dispersed. Although more than half lives in the southeast of England, there are no areas of concentrated settlement even there. In no district does the Chinese population exceed 2 per cent of the total.

The 1991 census figures do not cover Northern Ireland, which is part of the United Kingdom but not Britain (see box p 310). Chinese there are the largest visible ethnic minority. The Northern Ireland Chinese Welfare Association estimates that there are 7,000 Chinese in the province, most of them in the greater Belfast area.

Viewed from Britain, Chinese there suffer two disadvantages peculiar to Northern Ireland. First. they face racial harassment without the protection of the race relations legislation operating in the rest of the United Kingdom. Second, their position as an ethnic minority in the context of severe religious conflict between Protestants and Catholics is at times uniquely vulnerable.

The third important feature is country of origin. Hong Kong predominates, followed by the locally born, those sometimes called BBC, or British-born Chinese (see figure 5.9). The China-born form the next largest segment, followed by those from Malaysia. Chinese numbers were augmented by refugees from Vietnam in the late 1970s and early 1980s, many of them ethnic Chinese.

Since 1989, there has been an increase in applications for political asylum by people from mainland China and a rise in the number of Chinese students extending their stays. In the aftermath of the 1989 Tiananmen Incident in June 1989, grave concern about the future of Hong Kong after 1997 eventually forced the British government to pass the British Nationality (Hong Kong) Act of 1990; this offered citizenship to 50,000 Hong Kong heads of households and their families. All this means that the Chinese population is growing, at precisely what rate it is hard to tell, as the basis of the census compilation has altered.

The census does not provide information about language use. In 1985 the Department for Education and Science estimated that 70 per cent were Cantonese speakers, 25 per cent Hakka and 5 per cent Mandarin. Research by Li Wei in northeast England shows that the younger generations tend to speak English to each other, but retain some proficiency in speaking Chinese to their parents. A national survey by the Policy Studies Institute of London, published under the title *Ethnic Minorities in Britain: Diversity and Disadvantage* in 1997, puts those able to speak a Chinese language at 77 per cent.

VOICES FROM THE CHINESE COMMUNITY IN CONTEMPORARY BRITAIN

On the takeaway
Melissa: *I wake up about one or two, have something to eat, go to the takeaway, start work. You know, peel the onions, wash the mushrooms, clean the plates, get prepared the food and stuff. It's just like that every single day. It's boring, it's not stimulating enough.*
May: *My mum insisted I stay on the counter right until we closed which is after the pubs close up to midnight ... and I used to get racial abuse, sexual harassment, I used to get everything ... saying we were this and that and the other ... I hated it, they just used to make me feel so small.*
Tania: *I think I have to do something more. Because once you're stuck in a takeaway you don't have any free time ... You feel that your being will just die if you do this, you know, all your life.*

On the generation gap
Sylvia: *When my parents came over it was about 30 years ago. They brought over the values of Chinese culture in Hong Kong of the 1960s and they're stuck in that time warp.*

(Box) *Dragon Inn Takeaway, Birmingham.*

On discrimination
Lily (a newly qualified accountant): *Some of them are quite startled that you are capable of holding down a professional job, seeing you in a suit. Apparently when I was recruited one of the comments in the office was, 'This girl, can she actually read and write? Can she speak proper English?'*

On identity
Sui: *In England you never feel a sense of belonging because ... it's like the white people's place, isn't it? And if you look at yourself and think about it, you're not one of them. But then if you think ... are you a Chinese person? The Chinese people reject you because, like, you're Westernized. So you don't really belong to any slot. You belong in a slot of your own in the middle ... I think we have to establish our own identity.*

Of these, Cantonese speakers represent 66 per cent, Hakkas 11 per cent, Mandarin speakers 10 per cent and Hokkiens 2 per cent (another 6 per cent of the Chinese surveyed spoke Vietnamese).

One theme that will gain prominence in the future is that of mixed relationships. Census data shows that about 26 per cent of Chinese women have non-Chinese partners compared to 13 per cent of Chinese men. The number of mixed-race children is likely to grow over time, helped by the population's geographical dispersal.

Economic profile

According to estimates by the House of Commons Home Affairs Select Committee in their 1985 report on Chinese in Britain, 90 per cent were in the catering or related trades, and as many as 60 per cent in family-owned takeaways. More recent research places this figure a little lower, but still highlights the dependence of the majority of Chinese families on the catering economy. An analysis by David Owen of a 2 per cent sample of records of the 1991 census reveals that 53.8 per cent of Chinese men and 36.8 per cent of women are in the two categories most likely to cover catering employment (that is managers in services and personal service occupations).

The family-owned catering business has shaped the lives of most Chinese families. The most obvious feature of life in Chinese takeaways is the long working hours. The hard labour apart, those working on the takeaway counter (often young women) are exposed to drunken racist customers late at night. Research has revealed just how commonplace mild forms of harassment are in such interactions. When customers are drunk, fights can break out and windows get broken. Chinese families have grown accustomed to the police arriving late when such incidents occur. It is little wonder that young people can't wait to leave the confines of the takeaway (see box).

As the postwar migrant generation begins to retire from catering, Chinese find themselves at a crucial turning point. The hopes of the second and third generations centre on whether they will escape the confines of the catering trade. The 1991 census showed that 7.3 per cent of Chinese men in employment worked in science and engineering, and 11.3 per cent of Chinese women in the health associate professionals category (which includes nursing). The unemployment rate for Chinese in April 1991 was only 9.3 per cent, compared to 8.8 per cent for white people and 18.3 per cent for ethnic minorities as a whole. Such figures suggest a relatively prosperous community. However, great care must be taken in interpreting these statistics, as they include a large number of temporarily resident students from East and Southeast Asia.

The results of the Policy Studies Institute survey published in 1997 show the Chinese (as well as Indians and Asians from Africa) to have slightly fewer households in the lowest income band, slightly more in the top band and a slightly higher average income than the white comparison group. Indeed, Chinese average weekly incomes were the highest among the ethnic groups surveyed. However, whites count many more pensioners among them than the other groups, and once these are taken out of the figures, Chinese household incomes were found to be no different from those of the whites.

Educationally, the emerging generations seem to be doing well. In 1995 approximately three-quarters of Chinese students applying for entry to higher education institutions in Britain were successful, a greater proportion than any other ethnic group. The 1991 census showed that 25.8 per cent of Chinese people over 18 had higher-level qualifications, compared to 13.4 per cent of white people. In theory, education is a route to social mobility, but in a country with a high unemployment rate and a labour market with a potential for discrimination, gaining a university degree is no guarantee of a professional career. Young people escaping the catering trade still face racism, even in the professions.

British perception of Chinese mobility is sometimes skewed by the visibility of well-known Chinese with a background different from that of the locally raised catering group. For example, the best-selling author Jung Chang, whose book *Wild Swans* has captured the public imagination, arrived in Britain in 1978 from China armed with a university education. Ivan Heng, a Singaporean Chinese who performed when resident in London, is a lawyer turned actor. Because London is a world city, many writers and artists move to it from environments which afford them a smaller or less appreciative audience for

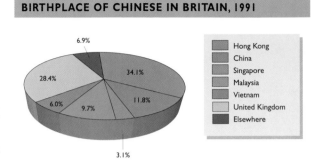

Figure 5.9

BIRTHPLACE OF CHINESE IN BRITAIN, 1991

- Hong Kong
- China
- Singapore
- Malaysia
- Vietnam
- United Kingdom
- Elsewhere

6.9%
34.1%
28.4%
6.0%
9.7%
11.8%
3.1%

Source: 1991 census.

Ivan Heng.

Chinese arch in London's Chinatown.

the display of their talents. British schools and universities also draw some of the brightest Chinese in Asia, Chinese who often stay on – at least for a duration – after they graduate.

British-Chinese politics

There are two main strands of political activity: the male-dominated networks of Chinatown business élites, and community action in the public and voluntary sectors.

A number of major British cities in the 1980s reacted to the changing structure of the economy by implementing policies which use public and private sector partnerships to regenerate inner-city areas. These policies involved the promotion of cultural diversity as a tourist attraction, resulting in redesigned Chinatown areas with gift shops, restaurants and pagoda-style telephone kiosks. Examples of the 'make-over' of Chinatowns include the decoration and pedestrianization of Gerrard Street in London, the construction of a Chinese archway in Manchester, and the development near Birmingham's Chinatown of the Arcadian centre, a shopping and leisure complex which incorporates a 'Chinese street' of restaurants, businesses and community centres.

Local Chinese businessmen played an important role in these projects. The need for organized representation penetrated the previously atomized catering trade, resulting in the formation of the Chinese Takeaway Association. The increasing political involvement has a symbolic cultural consequence in the growth of Chinese New Year celebrations as public spectacles in several large British towns; these are organized by Chinese groups, supported by local councils and increasingly enjoyed by non-Chinese people.

A very different strand of Chinese political action is evident in the network of Chinese community centres that has developed through a mixture of voluntary effort and public sector support since the mid-1970s. These centres organize advice sessions and English language classes, and mediate with outside institutions for older Chinese people whose knowledge of English is often limited. The best example of an organization which campaigns for the community is the Chinese Information and Advice Centre in London (CIAC). Renowned for its past campaigns in support of Chinese women facing deportation or suffering domestic violence, CIAC continues to offer much needed services. Domestic violence in Chinese families has been the subject of very little published research. In terms of strategies to address the problem, one pioneering venture has been the Chinese Women Refuge Group in London. Founded in 1989, the Group has offered support to Chinese women who have suffered domestic violence or sexual abuse.

An issue that has come to the fore is the care of elderly Chinese people, most of whom speak little or no English. In the 1990s, sheltered housing schemes specifically for Chinese old people were developed in several cities. In partnership with housing associations and local government, these schemes employ Chinese wardens and counter the isolation that the Chinese elderly might otherwise suffer. One example is Connaught Gardens in Birmingham, which opened in 1990 and is a thriving community of over one hundred.

The distinctive experiences of young Chinese people in Britain are today also giving rise to new social institutions. Hitherto, aside from the supplementary Chinese-language schools which young people have attended at weekends up to the age of 16 with varying degrees of enthusiasm, there has been no formal gathering point for Chinese youth to meet. However, since the mid-1980s, organizations such as Tower Hamlets Chinese Youth Project and Birmingham Chinese Youth Project have developed a range of cultural, educational and social services for Chinese teenagers. Notable here is the participation of British-born Chinese, who provide services to their peers and help gather an otherwise scattered and potentially isolated population. Out of these developments came the first national Chinese youth conference in Birmingham in November 1995, and the award of $500,000 by the National Lottery for a three-year programme of activities to the Birmingham Chinese Youth Project in June 1996.

Hitherto, Chinese representation within the British party political system has been scant. Councillor Ng Mee Ling, from Malaysia, is the most prominent of a tiny number of Chinese people elected to office in Britain. Ng, who arrived in Britain in 1968 and has an academic background in environmental studies, is a Labour councillor and deputy leader of Lewisham Council in London. According to her, there is more scope for Chinese involvement in local government. 'People are pushing at the door,' she has said, 'and it is opening . . . It is time to move from community politics to party politics.'

Although there is little evidence of political mobilization in the British-educated generation, some Chinese professionals in their twenties have formed Chinese Link, a London-based forum for discussing social issues. Despite such initiatives, a survey of Chinese young people found that less than half definitely saw their future in Britain, suggesting a weak sense of belonging.

The Hong Kong connection

Hong Kong rather than China has been the prominent focal point for most of the British Chinese. Hong Kong popular culture is a vital if often overlooked element in

London Chinatown telephone kiosks (top), fruit store (middle) and party at Chinese community centre, London.

the identity formation of young overseas Chinese. Bereft of Chinese role models in the Western media, many turn to the contemporary icons of Hong Kong music, film and television. The popularity of Hong Kong culture has helped to establish Cantonese as the lingua franca of Chinese in Britain and encouraged Chinese children to retain a connection with Hong Kong; without it the younger generation would have lost their command of the Chinese language faster.

For home entertainment since the early 1980s, late-night Chinatown cinema in Britain has been largely replaced by video cassettes rented from specialist Chinatown outlets and, increasingly, by Chinese satellite and cable TV. Two Chinese cable and satellite channels, Chinese News and Entertainment, and The Chinese Channel, are now available. They mainly import programmes from Hong Kong and China, although they show a small amount of local British-Chinese community news.

More conventional channels of communication persist in the form of Chinese newspapers. *Sing Tao* is the main Chinese-language daily, and the Chinese Information Centre in Manchester publishes the monthly newspapers *Siyu Chinese Times* and *Chinese Business Impact*. All these different media keep Hong Kong in the minds of Chinese in Britain and feed the desire for journeys home. The 1997 Policy Studies Institute survey estimated that 60 per cent of Chinese people in Britain had visited their country of origin in the previous five years, the highest figure for any minority community.

To younger generations, Hong Kong can be more than just a holiday destination. Research suggests that several hundred British-raised Chinese returned to Hong Kong during Britain's recession in the early 1990s. Irene Li, a former community worker in Britain, outlines the reasons for 'going back': 'I think in Hong Kong they like the fact that you're from abroad. You have a different accent from everybody else yet you're still Chinese. So you can speak Chinese and you can speak English. . . A lot of Chinese people think they can't get much career progression in England. There's still racial discrimination. Whereas you come to Hong Kong and you're suddenly being given jobs which you would never get in England.'

Li has helped to establish a social club called Overseas Chinese Connection, which appeals to young Chinese returnees to Hong Kong from North America and Australasia as well as Europe. Educated British-Chinese young people with Chinese-language skills may be well-placed to progress in the Hong Kong labour market. Their possession of a British passport provides them with some insurance against any adverse political developments, but as with all residents of Hong Kong they face an uncertain future.

British-Chinese identity

Aside from a small movement back to Hong Kong, most Chinese have settled in Britain. Owing to their small numbers and scattered distribution, they are unlikely to achieve the political visibility of their Black and South Asian British counterparts. Indeed, they have been portrayed as a silent minority, shunning the limelight and therefore bypassed by commentators and politicians. In

1977, James L. Watson wrote, 'I doubt that the relative imperviousness of the Chinese in Britain will last beyond the first generation. As yet, however, an Anglo-Chinese or Sino-British culture has not materialized.' Today, with the growth of a sizeable British-born population, new forms of political activity and cultural creativity are developing a British-Chinese identity.

(Top) Chinese bridge and pagoda in Birmingham.

(Bottom) Camden Chinese community centre, London.

British-Chinese themes have emerged in a range of artistic productions. The first Chinese actor to star in a British television series was David Yip in *The Chinese Detective*, first shown in 1981. This breakthrough was not followed up, however, and images of Chinese people continued to fall into the well-worn caricatures of Charlie Chan, Triad gangsters and takeaway owners. However, a new generation of artists is offering fresh perspectives. Kevin Wong, a British-born Chinese writer, has had a film set in Liverpool's Chinese community in the 1960s, *Peggy Su*, commissioned by the BBC for broadcasting on national television. Two collections of writing published by Lambeth Chinese Community Association, *Exploring Our Chinese Identity* (1992) and *Another Province* (1994), give expression to a variety of British-Chinese experiences.

In the performing arts, the Mu Lan Theatre company, set up in 1988 to provide greater opportunities to East Asian artists and writers, has promoted several performances, including a one-woman show by Anna Chen, an actress of mixed Chinese-English parentage. This show, *Suzy Wrong – Human Cannon,* premiered at the 1994 Edinburgh Festival. Chen sets out to expose Western stereotypes of Chinese women. Her comments explain not just her own work, but that of an emerging generation of British-Chinese artists. 'Rather than obliterating the Chinese culture within us,' she says, 'we are creating a new third thing out of our twin heritage and that's very exciting.' The struggle from the margins to the mainstream will continue into the next century.

David Parker

Anna Chen.

NORTHERN IRELAND

Six counties of Ulster, to the north of the island of Ireland, form part of the United Kingdom of Great Britain and Northern Ireland. This means that migrants and foreign students have the same right of abode there as in Great Britain.

Relatively isolated and suffering three decades of the 'Troubles' (civil violence instigated by Republican and Unionist terrorist groups), Northern Ireland has rarely been a first-choice destination. Students from Malaysia and Hong Kong, however, have seen lower living costs and moderate university fees as incentive enough to come to Belfast to further their education. From the 1950s to the 1970s the Chinese population numbered anything from a few dozen to several hundred, and nearly all were at university. In the 1980s and 1990s overseas student numbers steadily rose: along with many UK universities, the two Northern Ireland colleges actively recruited overseas students, the higher fees charged to foreign students being one of the main reasons for this exercise. The businesslike approach to education is most clearly manifested in the growth industry of education fairs, which are held several times a year in Malaysia, Singapore, Hong Kong and Taiwan. On a much smaller scale, Northern Ireland grammar schools offer boarding places to overseas secondary-level students, and have formed a partnership to promote boarding places in some of the top schools.

The 1990s has also seen the introduction of the second-generation student – the sons and daughters of alumni coming to Northern Ireland for their secondary and tertiary education. Maintaining links has been facilitated by the formation of Asia-based branches of alumni associations and the networking of the Northern Ireland Partnership, administered by the Industrial Development Board.

The few students who have become long-term residents are generally Malaysian nationals, with some Singaporeans and Hong Kongers. Usually their spouse is Northern Irish and they assimilate easily into local life, with their children viewing themselves, and in turn being seen, not as Chinese but as Ulster people with a 'Chinese Daddy or Mammy.' As graduates, most work in the professions and, after encountering the inevitable promotion-limiting glass ceiling that comes with such an insular society, some re-migrate back to Asia or elsewhere. This assimilated group also includes the Chinese spouses, usually wives, of expatriates returning from the Far East.

Since the 1980s, with a surge of new arrivals from a Hong Kong destined to return to Chinese sovereignty and a push-on effect on inward migration from the rest of the UK, there has been a huge growth in the six counties' Chinese population. Estimated to be about 8,000 in 1996, Chinese are now Ulster's largest ethnic minority. Hong Kongers apart, most of the other arrivals were mainland Chinese, with small numbers of Vietnamese coming as refugees. The majority of Hong Kong Chinese work in catering; the first Chinese restaurant opened in 1962, but while numbers have lagged behind those in Great Britain, not least because of demands for protection money from paramilitaries (mostly proscribed organizations of a military nature),

(Clockwise from right) Half-Chinese Miss Northern Ireland, 1984; Chinese in front of his boutique hotel in Belfast; Ulster university alumni officer with returned students from the UK in Taipei; Ulster university representative with student at recruitment fair in Hong Kong, 1996.

Chinese takeaways are now seen everywhere in Ulster.

Until about 1980, Chinese or quasi-Chinese organizations were attached to the universities. The Malaysian Students' Society is the longest established, with Chinese at one time forming the majority of its members; the Chinese Cultural Society and an association of Hong Kong students, active until the 1980s, no longer exist. Both the Singapore Students' Society, which dates from 1989, and the more recently formed People's Republic of China Students' Association have clearly identifiable national and cultural agendas and interests. In 1983 the Chinese Chamber of Commerce was constituted by Hong Kong businessmen, who also formed the Chinese Welfare Association (CWA) in 1986, with aims that included the promotion of Chinese culture and language.

The CWA also places great emphasis on race relations, and indeed played a leading role in the campaign for the introduction of the Race Relations Order in 1997. Race relations legislation was at one time thought unnecessary, given Northern Ireland's history of sectarianism based on religious and political background. During the peak of the 'Troubles' in the 1970s and 1980s, being a racial minority was often seen as an advantage; as one Chinese put it:

'I can go up the Falls Road [Nationalist area] one day and down the Shankill [Unionist area] the next. My face makes me neutral.' But today racial prejudice is highlighted by Chinese numbers. Chinese restaurant staff are easy targets for abusive behaviour and physical attacks. Late-night opening to catch the closing-time trade from pubs makes for large numbers of drunken customers. The squeeze on locations has also resulted in takeaways being sited in areas where many locals would fear to go.

Problems are often exacerbated by the limited English of the recent arrivals. The CWA provides assistance through an interpreting service, language classes, tuition and projects with youth and the elderly. On the other hand, second and now third generations, speaking with the distinctive Northern Ireland twang, have integrated into the local community with varying degrees of success, though few have escaped the 'Ching-chong Chinaman' chants of the playground. Surveys have yet to be undertaken to establish how many of these local-born Chinese continue to work in the catering industry because it is the family business or because they have encountered discrimination in the mainstream workplace. Re-migration to more cosmopolitan parts of the UK or overseas, long a feature of the Northern Ireland Chinese population, will no doubt continue in the future.

Rosemary Lim

FRANCE

Ties between France and China go back to the early trade in silk, the French city of Lyon being one of the termini of the Silk Road, a great commercial network through which, over the centuries, goods and knowledge were exchanged between China and Europe. Among the earliest Chinese to travel to the West were a few who arrived in France in the 18th century. One was Arcadius Huang (1679–1716), the son of a Fujianese who had been converted to Catholicism by French missionaries. In 1702 Huang accompanied one of these missionaries to Paris, where he remained until his death and where he earned a living as a translator in the King's Library. He married a French woman, began work on a Chinese-French dictionary, and was used as a source of information on China by the young Montesquieu.

Migratory movements

1900–40

Chinese migration leading to settlement dates only as far back as World War I. The first movement was of Chinese contract workers recruited by France and Britain (one of France's allies) during World War I (see Part II). Acutely short of labour, the French government turned to foreign manpower to free French workers for the battlefields. Between 1916–18, Britain recruited about 100,000 Chinese for France, while France itself recruited almost 40,000. The Chinese workers were employed in all sorts of tasks: building barracks, cleaning roads, unloading ships, making ammunition and exhuming dead soldiers.

After the hostilities, the great majority of Chinese were repatriated. About 3,000 workers remained, including 1,850 qualified men who signed new contracts to work in the metallurgical industries. Other workers found employment in the mechanical or aeronautical sectors in the suburbs of Paris. Coming from all parts of China (but particularly from the northern provinces), most of those who stayed behind were natives of Shandong, Hebei, Hubei and Anhui.

This war migration was immediately followed by the so-called 'work-study movement' (see box, p 318). Of the students brought by this movement, some 400 to 500 stayed behind for good, contributing to the emergence of a Chinese community. Although work-study students were phased out, young Chinese continued to trickle into France for training.

A third wave of Chinese immigration occurred in the inter-war period. This brought people from Wenzhou and Qingtian in Zhejiang province (see Part I). Initiated by Zhejiang natives recruited during World War I, this migration went on accelerating in the late 1920s until World War II slowed it down. Faced with the 1930s Depression, the newcomers took to itinerant trading to make ends meet.

Since World War II

In the postwar period, Chinese migration to France was spurred by major political events in East Asia: the Communist takeover of China in 1949, the decolonization process in Indochina in 1954, the restoration of French-Chinese diplomatic ties in 1964, the collapse of the American-backed South Vietnamese regime in 1975, and the opening up of China in the 1980s.

In the aftermath of World War II, once lines of communication had been restored, many of the Chinese who had settled in France, especially the traders, fled hard times (food rationing) in France and returned to China, accompanied by their children and French wives. Others went to the Netherlands, Belgium or Italy to join their relatives. After the Communist triumph in 1949, the homeward movement included intellectuals, teachers and technicians enthusiastic about going back to work for the new China.

It was a two-way flow, however. The years 1949–55

Chinese workers unloading artillery changes in France, about 1917.

Map 5.23

Identity card and certificate issued to Chinese workers during World War I.

saw a reverse influx of journalists, traders, teachers and artists as well as Chinese or ethnically mixed Franco-Chinese families with links to France. Most of these families were natives of former French concessions or leased territory in Tianjin, Fuzhou and Guangzhouwan.

Then, just as the Chinese population was about to stabilize, war between the colonial French and the Viet Minh (the Vietnamese Independence Brotherhood League) ended. The armistice signed in Geneva in 1954 required French withdrawal from Indochina and divided Vietnam at the 17th parallel. Afterwards the colonial French administration evacuated its nationals, including some Chinese who possessed French nationality. On October 26, 1955, the chief of state in the southern part proclaimed a Republic of Vietnam. There, by a decree promulgated in 1956 and applied retroactively, all Chinese born in Vietnam were automatically to become Vietnamese citizens. This was an attempt to assimilate the Chinese, as was a decree enforcing all Vietnamese citizens to take Vietnamese names. As a result, many Chinese families quit Vietnam for France during 1955–60 (see Part V: Vietnam).

Shortly afterwards, migration from China resumed with the normalization of ties between China and France in 1964. Among the agreements signed between the two countries was one permitting Chinese in France to bring in their families. The main beneficiaries of this provision were Wenzhou and Qingtian groups who had settled in Hong Kong or Macao since 1949. When, three years later, the spillover of the Cultural Revolution in China shook Hong Kong, Chinese settled in France were joined by immigrants from the British territory.

The dramatic collapse of the Saigon regime in 1975 gave impetus to another migrant flow. Following the US defeat in what used to be French Indochina, and as communism changed Vietnamese and Laotian society, hundreds of thousands – including large numbers of ethnic Chinese – left those countries. Worse still was the situation in Cambodia (see Part V: Cambodia). The escalation of the Vietnam-China conflict into open warfare further swelled the exodus of ethnic Chinese from Vietnam. According to French Home Ministry data, from

Chinese marries French, 1948.

1975 to 1987 France officially received 145,000 refugees from Indochina, 50 to 60 per cent of whom were of Chinese ancestry.

Finally, since the 1980s, a conjunction of social, economic and political factors has led to new immigration from China, Hong Kong, Macao, Taiwan, Malaysia, Thailand and other Southeast Asian countries. The new migrants include diverse categories of individuals who have settled in France for a range of reasons.

Characteristics of the Chinese community

Population trends

The interwar Chinese population was estimated at 2,863 in 1926, 3,660 in 1931 and 2,794 in 1936 (see table 5.38). The numbers are almost certainly an underestimate. Inadequacies of data collection techniques, foreigners' mistrust of census officers, under-reporting in response to the prevailing xenophobia of French society in the 1930s – all these flawed the population censuses of 1920–40.

For the period from the 1950s to the 1990s, the statistics are even less accurate. They counted only Chinese nationals, leaving out the large numbers of ethnic Chinese who have come from Southeast Asia since the mid-1950s. The census figures given in the table are clearly a gross underestimate.

It is possible to arrive at a more accurate figure. Until 1975, the year of the influx from Vietnam, the number of Chinese in France was normally set at 20,000.

Surveys estimate that between 50 to 60 per cent of the 145,000 refugees France received from Indochina between 1975 and 1987 were of Chinese descent. The number of Chinese coming from Indochina can therefore be estimated at 75,000 people. Adding to this figure the 20,000 individuals already present in France before 1975, and the few thousand who have since immigrated from China, Hong Kong, Macao, Taiwan and elsewhere (Malaysia, Singapore, Thailand), we arrive at a figure of between 120,000 and 150,000 ethnic Chinese. Out of a total population of 56.2 million (1990), people of Chinese descent make up just under 2.9 per cent.

One of the main features of the first waves of Chinese migration to France was the numerical imbalance of the sexes. From the 1920s to the 1940s, Chinese women represented on average only 8 per cent (7.8 per cent in 1926; 8.7 per cent in 1931 and 8.3 per cent in 1936) of the total Chinese population (see table 5.38). The pattern is familiar: if wives joined their emigrant

Table 5.38

DISTRIBUTION OF CHINESE CITIZENS IN FRANCE BY SEX										
YEAR	1911	1921	1926	1931	1936	1946	1954	1968	1975	1982	1990
Male	246	13,084	2,640	3,342	2,563	1,686	1,880	1,668	1,880	2,920	7,415
Female	37	139	223	318	231	244	440	812	1,235	2,040	6,636
Total	283	13,223	2,863	3,660	2,794	1,930	2,320	2,480	3,115	4,960	14,051

Sources: Institut National de la Statistique et des Etudes Economiques; population censuses.

Teochiu-speakers around the world gather in Paris, 1991.

husbands, they did so several years later and in only a small number of cases. The pattern persisted until well after World War II. Chinese women represented only 12.6 per cent of the total population in 1946; 19 per cent in 1954; 32.7 per cent in 1968 and 39.6 per cent in 1975. Only the arrival of the Chinese refugees after 1975 helped establish a balance.

Linguistic groups

The diversity of the countries of origin is paralleled by the variety of local Chinese origins and therefore dialects spoken. The earlier phases of immigration originated in Zhejiang province, but the larger part of the Chinese population today is made up of Southeast Asian Chinese of predominantly Guangdong origin (Cantonese, Teochiu, Hakka and Hainanese).

The 'northerners,' from Beijing, Tianjin and other points north, are Mandarin speaking, as are Chinese from Taiwan. The first northerners were the World War I contract workers from Shandong, Hebei, Shanxi and other Mandarin-speaking provinces. Most of these are either dead or have returned to China. The sprinkling of Mandarin-speaking Chinese from Taiwan, mostly students, did not appear until the 1960s.

The first of the Wenzhou-Qingtian immigrants came to France as contract workers during World War I. Hawkers from the 1920s to the 1940s, they are now dealers in leather goods around the Arts-et-Métiers area in Paris. Renewed migration from Zhejiang in the 1990s has faced the community with an influx of mostly young and mostly urbanized fellow-townsmen. The arrival of this new group, with its strong drive to succeed, has resulted in a breach in the generations.

The 'Shanghainese' originated in Suzhou, Yangzhou and towns situated near the Yangzi River or the lake of Taihu. The earliest migrants opened shops selling Chinese exotica in Paris before World War I (see below). In the 1960s and 1970s, they became restaurant owners in the 16th *arrondissement* (district, hereafter

arrondissement) or in the business areas of Paris. Nowadays, they are found in diverse economic sectors (export-import, catering, foodstuff trading and so on).

The Cantonese originated from Guangzhou, Zhongshan, Hong Kong and Macao. The first ones to arrive were recruited as specialized workers in Hong Kong and Macao during World War I. From the 1920s to the 1940s, they worked in catering in the Latin Quarter in Paris. After 1955, the Cantonese of Vietnam joined them in the Latin Quarter in opening restaurants. Since 1975, the massive influx of refugees from Southeast Asia has buttressed their number.

The Teochius come mainly from Laos, Cambodia and Vietnam, the first ones arriving from Vietnam in the 1950s. Only a handful arrived before 1975, but massive numbers moved in with the Indochinese refugee exodus. Of all Chinese speech groups in France, the Teochius are the most sizeable and, economically speaking, the most highly organized and powerful. Their numerous networks in France, Southeast Asia, China and elsewhere give them an unbeatable comparative advantage in business.

The Hakkas and Hainanese, long established in Southeast Asia, came to France as refugees from 1975 onwards. Hakkas and Hainanese live by foodstuff trading, catering, garment manufacturing, arts and crafts, and services.

Urban settlement

The fact that the Chinese came to France as economic migrants has largely dictated their pattern of settlement, with its concentration in the great urban centres, chiefly Paris, Marseilles and Lyon. In France as elsewhere, 'Chinatowns' cannot be dissociated from Chinese economic activities. By and large the overseas Chinese have always set up residence near their commercial premises.

As many as three-fifths of the Chinese in France live in Paris and its suburbs, drawn like other foreign minorities to the national capital by the wide choice of

Le Lotus Pub in Paris.

employment and multiple opportunities it offers.

Before 1975, the histories of Chinese settlement and Chinese economic pursuits were intertwined. The factory workers of the inter-war years settled in the suburbs to the northwest and southwest of Paris (Cormeilles-en-Parisis, Boulogne-Billancourt), the hawkers near the railway station, Gare de Lyon (12th arrondissement), and the students and restaurateurs in the Latin Quarter (5th arrondissement). The Chinese neighbourhoods of that period spread along two or three lanes lined with old, buildings (5th and 12th arrondissements, Boulogne-Billancourt). Badly appointed, the decaying houses were transit stops rather than permanent dwellings. Many Chinese lived in hotels, or else in blocks where Chinese formed the majority of tenants, the other apartment buildings being occupied by French and foreign populations (Russian, Polish, Italian, Armenian, North African and so on).

Two developments marked the postwar period: one, the emergence of a new Chinese neighbourhood in the 3rd arrondissement; and two, the reinforcement of the Chinese settlement in the 5th arrondissement (Latin Quarter) by the influx of Sino-Vietnamese from Indochina. Before the urban renewal programmes of the 1960s and 1970s, these areas were very much like the Chinese neighbourhoods of the inter-war years – with lanes, time-worn buildings and the strong presence of immigrant populations.

Some years later, the massive immigration of refugees from Southeast Asia further led to the growth of new Chinese neighbourhoods in the 13th, 19th and 20th arrondissements of Paris, and in its eastern suburbs (Marne-la-Vallée). The Chinese concentration in certain areas of the 13th, 19th and 20th arrondissements stemmed not from commercial considerations or gregariousness so much as the availability of housing and/or commercial sites there. In the 1960s, the French government and the municipal authorities decided to restore the older parts of Paris. The centre (1st–3rd–4th arrondissements), the south (13th arrondissement) and the northeast (19th–20th arrondissements) all underwent urban renewal. In the course of all this the first tower blocks of the 13th arrondissement (the Porte de Choisy and Porte d'Ivry areas) were erected in the early 1970s. Shunned by the Parisians for their unattractiveness and their high rental cost, these high-rises provided ready accommodation to the Asian refugee arrivals in 1975.

At the same time, the old residential buildings in the northeast corner were being renovated (the Belleville area in the 19th and 20th arrondissements) and part of the inhabitants, mostly foreign immigrants, were expelled to the suburbs. The Southeast Asian Chinese moved into the area in the early 1980s.

In Marseilles, the Chinese never congregated in any particular area, with the exception of the 1920–40 period when a small group of hawkers set themselves up just behind the Saint-Charles railway station. No real Chinese neighbourhood evolved and Chinese live dispersed in the city, where they mainly work in the restaurant business or as traders supplying Asian foods.

In Lyon, on the other hand, a small Chinese neighbourhood – in the 7th arrondissement, along Pasteur Street – evolved in the 1980s out of the Indochinese refugee immigration. Previously a small Chinese community lived dispersed in the city. Typically, the Chinese quarter today is home to food shops, restaurants, video-cassette rental stores and an association.

Economic pursuits

Before 1975

Chinese work in sectors as varied as computing, medicine, paramedical services, art, publishing and so on. However, this article will examine six of their chief occupations. It will be seen from the survey that before 1975 the Chinese were predominantly self-employed, operating small trades and workshops.

The first Chinese to engage in commerce in France were dealers in Chinese products – porcelain, lacquer, furniture, fabrics, trinkets and other Chinese exports for which there was a European craze. The fashion for 'Chinese ornament' appeared in Europe in the 17th century, fed by imports started by the Dutch, English, and French East India Companies. First reaching France under the reign of Louis XIV, such products became very fashionable during the first half of the 18th century, then declined in the second half of that century. Nevertheless, the liking for Chinese products had not completely disappeared in the Paris of the *belle époque* when Shanghainese tradesmen Lu Jiatu and Zhang Renjie opened the first shop in 1904. Their success was copied by other Chinese, and the years 1920–40 saw more such shops open. These were in Chaussée d'Antin, Madeleine and Faubourg-Montmartre, centres of commerce, with big department stores, and also financial districts.

Second, Chinese worked as pedicures or chiropodists. The first Chinese pedicure salon opened under the name 'Beijing Gongsi' just before World War I in rue de la Paix, only a couple of minutes from the Opéra. The

Map 5.24

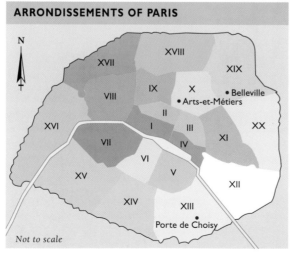

ARRONDISSEMENTS OF PARIS

N

XVIII
XVII
XIX
IX
VIII
X
• Belleville
• Arts-et-Métiers
II
XVI
I
III
XX
VII
IV
XI
VI
V
XV
XII
XIV
XIII
• Porte de Choisy

Not to scale

number of such centres increased between 1920 and 1940 to almost 20. They were initially set up in the area between the 1st and 2nd arrondissements (the Opéra quarter, Faubourg Saint-Honoré) before expanding towards the 8th, 9th and 10th arrondissements in 1920–40. Today, only a few such centres survive.

Chinese were also hawkers. The Wenzhou and Qingtian migrants arriving in 1925–35 turned to hawking to weather the Depression and unemployment. The Gare de Lyon area became an assembly point for these hawkers. Through door-to-door and street trading, these migrants interacted with the French more than they might otherwise have done.

Chinese have been leather craftsmen and dealers. The manufacture and sale of leather products have always been in the hands of the Wenzhou and Qingtian migrants. They took up the trade when Jewish leather craftsmen, whose specialization it previously was, were deported to Germany during World War II. The trade evolved when, at the end of the 1950s, the Wenzhou and Qingtian migrants moved from the Gare de Lyon area (12th arrondissement) to that of the Arts-et-Métiers (3rd arrondissement). Since the mid-1980s, with the influx of labour provided by the new Zhejiang arrivals, this sector has reached saturation point. From among these arrivals a new and more aggressive generation of craftsmen and tradesmen has emerged; reduced hourly rates, prolonged working hours and lower sale prices have made life tougher all round.

Chinese have worked as cabinet-makers since the mid-1930s. To earn their keep, former students began by restoring furniture, then started to manufacture and sell furniture that was easy to assemble: coffee tables, bedside tables, small chests of drawers and so on. The trade took off when World War II interrupted transport links between Europe and Asia and European importers could no longer bring these goods in from the Far East. Chinese in France stepped in to satisfy the pent-up French demand for Chinese furniture. In the 1980s they found themselves in cut-throat competition with the waves of Chinese from Southeast Asia and Zhejiang who penetrated the business in the 1980s. None could rise above the competition and today the craft is all but collapsing. Only a few workshops and stores remain, surviving as best they can. In terms of area of settlement, the Chinese cabinet-makers have always plied their trade in the 11th and 12th arrondissements (rues Saint Nicolas, Charonne, Lappe), and in the Faubourg Saint-Antoine quarter known as the 'temple of furniture in France.'

Chinese have long been restaurateurs. The first Chinese restaurants opened in Paris before World War I. Between 1920–40, almost 40 such establishments were set up, of which at least 15 were still open on the eve of World War II. However, it was only in the late 1950s and early 1960s, following the post-1954 decolonization arrival of the Sino-Vietnamese, that Chinese restaurants began to proliferate in the Latin Quarter. However, saturation point was reached within a few years, 1955–65, and Chinese restaurants were forced to expand towards other districts.

The wave of Southeast Asian Chinese refugees further crowded the market. A Home Ministry survey of central Paris counted 97 Chinese restaurants in 1960, 187 in 1970 and 270 in 1977 out of a total of 709 Asian restaurants, of which 400 were Vietnamese. In 1990, the author of this article counted more than 728 Chinese catering businesses in Paris and almost as many in the suburbs – that is, a total of 1,400 restaurants in the Greater Paris area.

The waves of Southeast Asian Chinese migration after 1975 have widened the range of economic pursuits by the Chinese community. Commercial firms have multiplied and entrepreneurs have ventured into previously uncharted territory: the hotel business, real estate, printing, transport and travel, dealing in meat, food retail (supermarkets, greengrocers), general trade (jewellery, garment manufacturing, decoration, shoemaking), stockbroking, services and so on.

1980s–90s

Since the early 1980s, the highest concentrations of Chinese economic activity have been in the Porte de Choisy area, in the 13th arrondissement of Paris. In 1990, this area alone accounted for 20.5 per cent of the economic activity of the entire Parisian Chinese community. The Belleville quarter (19th–20th arrondissements) ranked second (18 per cent), followed by Arts-et-Métiers (3rd arrondissement) at 11.2 per cent. These three urban areas together account for almost half (49.7 per cent) of all Parisian Chinese economic activities, the other half being dispersed in other districts. As for the economic activities themselves, they are either the traditional ones (restaurants, leather crafts) pursued before 1975, or those more recently developed (jewellery, bakery, real estate, garment manufacturing and so on).

Classified ads in Chinese paper published in Paris.

Outside a Chinese restaurant in Paris.

Table 5.39

BREAKDOWN OF CHINESE ECONOMIC ACTIVITIES IN PARIS, 1992		
CATERING		
Cafés and bars		7
Fast-foods (self-service, delicatessens)		114
Restaurants		728
	Sub-total	849
FOODSTUFF TRADING		
Butchers		12
Bakers (pastry)		12
Delicatessens		15
Frozen foods		17
Supermarkets, Grocers		62
	Sub-total	118
GENERAL TRADING		
Books		2
Clothes (sales)		28
Decoration (artif. flowers, elect. signboards)		13
Editing		4
Flowers		7
Furniture		29
Garments (manufacturing)		54
Gifts, souvenirs		36
Jewellery (gold)		52
Jewellery (costume)		25
Leather goods		87
Newspapers		4
Optics, glasses		2
Computer systems (sales)		18
Printing		9
Radio, Hi-Fi, TV		11
Restaurants (equipment for)		22
Sewing machines (sales)		14
	Sub-total	417
SERVICES		
Automobile (repairs)		3
Banks		3
Beauty-care centres		12
Driving schools		8
Entertainment (clubs)		4
Estate agents		15
Experts, consultants (accountancy, finance)		34
Filling stations (petrol)		2
Hairdressing		32
Hotels		3
Insurance		6
Laundry & ironing		3
Medical practice (GPs and specialists)		68
Studios (photographic)		10
Financial services (agencies, moneylenders)		3
Travel agencies		19
Video shops (rentals)		24
Works (installations and repairs)		13
	Sub-total	262
	Grand-total	1646

Sources: Guide de la Communauté Chinoise en France, 1992; *and fieldwork by Live Yu-Sion.*

The most spectacular expansion has been in the restaurant/catering business (see table 5.39). This represented 44.2 per cent of all Chinese economic activity in the 1990s. If fast-foods, such as self-service shops and takeaways, at 7.4 per cent, were added, then the sector would account for 52 per cent of all Chinese economic pursuits in Paris. It was partly thanks to the new tastes and flavours which the Southeast Asian Chinese have given Asian gastronomy in France that the sector has expanded so rapidly.

General trading comes second at 25.3 per cent. Of the categories of general trade, leather craft (20.9 per cent), garment manufacturing (13 per cent) and gold jewellery (12.5 per cent) are the three most important. Services come third at 15.9 per cent. These chiefly break down into medicine and health (26 per cent), financial and legal services (13 per cent), and hairdressing salons (12.2 per cent).

Paradoxically, foodstuff trading ranks last (7.2 per cent) among Chinese economic activities. Of this, fresh food retail represents 52.5 per cent, frozen products 14.4 per cent, butchers 10.2 per cent and delicatessens 12.7 per cent. The impression that a large number of Chinese food shops exists is a misleading one, created by their dense urban concentration and the high visibility of their predominantly Asian clientele. In actual fact, the sector is dominated by two or three supermarkets – exemplified by Tang Frères (the Tang Brothers) and Paris-Store – which import and distribute products from China, Taiwan, Singapore, Thailand, Japan, Malaysia and elsewhere.

Associations and networks

The oldest Chinese associations were those set up after World War I by some intellectuals. Educational in purpose, they aimed to eliminate illiteracy among the Chinese workers who had stayed behind in France after the hostilities. Their leaders set out to impart a basic knowledge of Chinese, French, arithmetic, geography and history to their countrymen. The most representative is the Association Générale des Travailleurs Chinois en France (General Association of Chinese Workers in France). Created on November 11, 1919 and funded by members' subscriptions, it grouped together the Chinese workers of Greater Paris, the Creusot, Bordeaux, Dunkerque and elsewhere. It started an evening school for workers and published the *Journal Chinois Hebdomadaire* (*Weekly Chinese Journal*).

This organization was, however, not typical of the general run. The more familiar Chinese association was the kind based on native-place/language ties. In the Paris of the 1930s, the Zhejiang community (Wenzhou and Qingtian) set up its association in rue Chalon (12th arrondissement). After World War II, it moved its premises to the Arts-et-Métiers area. The Association des Résidents Chinois du Zhejiang en France (Zhejiang Chinese Residents Association in France) organized, among other activities, group outings, sports meetings and the screening of Chinese films. It was located on rue Au Maire until the early 1980s, when it moved to rue du Temple.

Before 1981, Chinese associations were rare: the Chinese community was quite small, and a French statutory order dating from 1939 restrained and regulated the right of association of foreigners the better to control their activities. Since October 1981, when the socialist government abolished this measure, Chinese associations of all kinds have multiplied. There are around 60 in France as a whole, some 40 of them in Paris and Île de France (the belt of suburbs and commuter towns surrounding Paris), the majority located in the Chinese neighbourhoods. The main activities of these associations revolve around preserving Chinese language and culture: Chinese classes, Chinese cuisine classes, calligraphy, chess competitions, organizing the major traditional festivals, organizing religious ceremonies and so on. But they also ease members into French society by running French classes.

For some years now, religious practice has been on the rise. This is a rallying point for some associations. Chinese from Indochina have built temples or places of worship within their association premises, using donations from members, devotees and above all from traders and restaurateurs. In these shrines several gods are often placed alongside each other on the same altar, or else on different altars but within the same religious space. So Buddhas of different nationalities – Indian, Chinese or Thai – may be worshipped simultaneously, as may a female deity like Guanyin, without any apparent feeling of conflict or confusion on the part of the devotees.

The family remains the pivot of many networks. Family ties, which have always played an important part in migration and in mutual aid among expatriates, link Chinese in France to both their places of origin and to other Chinese diasporas. Letter-writing, visits, remittances, marriage, investments and so on have helped them to maintain their ties to China, while visits have kept them in touch with relatives or friends settled in other European countries, whether Holland, Belgium, Italy, Spain or Portugal. With Southeast Asia added to the sources of immigration since 1975, these networks have extended to Hong Kong, Macao, Bangkok, Singapore, Taiwan and other major cities in Asia. The intensification of such connections has resulted in a revival of Chinese cultural practices in the Chinese community in France.

For migrants of the first generation, emigration does not imply a breach with the home country. For the younger generations, ties to China continue to have meaning. This is suggested by a university research survey (published by this author in 1991) on links to China and the Chinese diaspora. Of the Chinese interviewed, 51.2 per cent maintain some links with the family left behind in China, 24.9 per cent have not kept any and 23.9 per cent did not answer the question. Those in constant contact with their family are China-born, married to a Chinese partner and meet other Chinese regularly in their daily life. They came to France after 1975, and belong to the middle and lower social strata (that is, they are workers, artisans, petty traders, service staff).

Asked if they wished to visit China, 43.9 per cent of the foreign-born replied in the affirmative; 7.8 per cent said no; and the rest, 48.3 per cent, did not answer. Those who said they wished to visit China divide by birthplace into France, Southeast Asia and other countries in fairly similar proportions. They fall into two distinct age groups: 20–29 years, or 40–49 years.

The wish to visit China is particularly strongly expressed by those who speak only French or who speak only a little Chinese. These are people who lead lives outside the Chinese milieu without, however, severing ties with it. Their cultural models are both French and Chinese, and they feel a dual sense of belonging. In their everyday experiences, their cultural identity appears more French than Chinese. Visiting China would presumably compensate for a psychological vacuum on the Chinese side and help restore the balance between the two identities.

Chinese in France have also maintained links with their closest relatives in the diaspora: 53.2 per cent declare having kept some links with their families overseas; 5.9 per cent have not; and 41 per cent did not reply because they did not have any relatives living outside China. The first group comprises more women than men. They are either French-born and fall into the 20–29 age group; or they are Southeast Asia-born, 40–49 years old, and occupationally and socially humble (workers, employees in the services sector). They are among those most deeply imbued with Chinese cultural values. Family solidarity matters to these people, all the more so, it seems, because of their relatively low socio-economic level.

However, any discussion of cultural identity must take into account not only the emergence of younger generations born and educated in France but the fact that, since the opening of the European frontiers in 1993, an increasing number of Chinese have moved into neighbouring countries with pre-existing Chinese communities. As the younger generations integrate into French society, the Chinese, like other minorities in France and the rest of Europe, meanwhile find themselves caught in the transformations attendant upon regional integration into larger economic and political communities.

Live Yu-Sion

News-stand in Paris selling both French and local Chinese dailies.

Parisian-born Chinese financial analyst.

THE WORK-STUDY MOVEMENT

The work-study movement (1919–21), which brought more than 1,500 Chinese students to France, was founded by Li Shizeng (1881–1973). Li had studied agriculture at the Ecole Pratique d'Agriculture in Montargis (south of Paris) and biology at the Institut Pasteur in Paris. During this initial sojourn he not only became an enthusiastic Francophile and devotee of anarchist ideals but also established a wide network of contacts amongst French intellectuals and politicians.

The work-study scheme was prefigured by a school attached to the bean curd factory he opened outside Paris in 1908. In the school, the 30 workers he had recruited from his native village in north China were taught Chinese, French and general science. So that more students could be sent to France, in 1912 Li helped found the Association for Frugal Study in France (Liu Fa Jianxue Hui). In 1912–13 some 100 'frugal study' students arrived, most of them placed in schools and colleges in Paris and Montargis, where they were expected to dress and eat simply and to live communally, sharing all menial tasks.

When the French and British governments began recruiting Chinese labour for war-related work in France (see main text and Part II), Li sought to expand his project, seeing a unique opportunity for Chinese students to interact with both French and Chinese workers. With the support of the

Sino-French Education Association (Hua Fa Jiaoyu Hui), established in 1916 by prominent French and Chinese intellectuals (Li included) to promote mutually beneficial cultural relations, schools were opened in Beijing, Baoding and Chengdu to prepare potential students for France.

Between March 1919 and December 1920, 17 groups of work-study students totalling almost 1,600 arrived in France. Many of the students (whose ages ranged from 16 to 25) came from the poorer inland provinces of Sichuan (378) and Hunan (346), in marked contrast to the predominance of Zhejiang and Jiangsu students amongst those who went to Japan and the US. While candidates for government scholarships to study abroad had to be graduates of universities or higher specialist schools, many of the work-study students had not progressed beyond middle or primary school. Li's scheme thus gave more people the chance to study overseas. Once in France, the Sino-French Education Association helped place students either in factories (iron, steel and armaments) or in schools in the Paris region.

While late-19th century conservative Chinese officials viewed overseas study strictly in terms of technical training, Li looked to it to inculcate the new values which returning students would need to effect fundamental social change in China. To study in France, which Li extolled as a country free of the corrupting influences of monarchy and religion, was to imbibe progressive republican ideals. It was also an ideal opportunity to narrow the gap between mental and manual labour. It would, Li and his fellow champions believed, liberate students from the shackles of a traditional élitism that had accorded superior status to the literary scholar; on their return to China they would help to achieve social

harmony and equality.

The students themselves, many of whom had been active in the organization of public lectures and evening classes in the wake of the May Fourth Movement, were fired by similar ideals. One group that responded eagerly to the movement was the New People's Society (Xinmin Xuehui), established in Hunan by Mao Zedong and Cai Hesen in 1918; 18 members of the society (though not Mao himself) were to make the trip to France. French politicians and educators were also enthusiastic, seeing the Chinese students as a future conduit of French influence in China.

Some students were later to become important leaders of the Chinese Communist Party (Zhou Enlai, Deng Xiaoping, Li Lisan, Chen Yi and Li Fuchun), while others became famous Communist 'martyrs' – namely Cai Hesen (1890–1931), Zhao Shiyan (1900–27) and Xiang Jingyu (1895–1928), the first director of the party's Women's Bureau.

The hopes of the scheme's promoters, however, were not to materialize. The Sino-French Education Association was unable to cope logistically with the large number of students. The Depression in France led to increasing unemployment and the Chinese students, with a poor grasp of French and little or no experience of factory work, were particularly vulnerable. In 1920 Zhou Enlai (who regularly reported on the life of Chinese students in France for a newspaper back home) noted the existence of 700 students in the Paris region unable to attend school (from a lack of money) or find a job. By early 1921 the association had cut its subsidies to the impoverished students and begun to dissociate itself from the movement altogether.

Following an angry student demonstration in February 1921 outside the Chinese Legation in Paris, French political and business representatives, together with the Chinese Embassy, established a special committee (Comité Franco-Chinois de Patronannage) to provide emergency funds and to persuade firms and schools to accept (or retain) students.

However, increasing student politicization gradually aroused the hostility of French and Chinese authorities. In August 1921 over 300 Chinese students in Paris protested against a proposed French government loan to China whose terms were seen as infringing Chinese sovereignty. During the following month over 100 students forcibly occupied the newly opened Sino-French Institute in Lyon, whose aim – to admit academically more advanced students from China – was seen to be an abandonment of the ideals of the work-study movement. The demonstrating students insisted that the institute enrol (without conditions) the destitute and less academically qualified work-study students already in France. As a result of this protest, over 100 students were deported.

Thereafter the movement was wound down. Most students had returned to China by the beginning of 1926, although not before some had created the Chinese Communist Youth Party in Europe (Lü Ou Zhongguo Shaonian Gongchandang) in June 1922. Many students were later to claim that their interest in Marxism and socialist revolution had first been stimulated during their sojourn in France. Their radicalization had also resulted in an increasingly vociferous opposition to imperialist encroachment in China. Such

Chinese periodical hot off the press (above). Li Shizeng (top right). Deng Xiaoping (last row, third from left) with other socialists in France.

opposition came to a head following the May 30 Incident (1925), when Chinese workers protesting against the brutality of a Japanese factory owner in Shanghai were fired on by a police force under British command. Chinese students, together with those Chinese workers who had remained in France after their contracts had expired in 1922, organized mass protest meetings calling for an end to foreign privilege in China and the withdrawal of all foreign troops from Chinese soil. Over 40 students were arrested, 17 of whom were eventually deported.

Paul Bailey

ITALY

Migration history

Since the legendary journeys of Marco Polo in the 13th century and the Jesuit missions in Asia at the end of the 16th century, China has held a special place in the imaginations of Italians. In the letters home of the famous missionary Matteo Ricci, who lived in China from 1583 to 1610, detailed accounts of Chinese life and thought appeared. Today, with Chinese having become Italy's sixth largest immigrant community and with *i quartieri cinesi*, Chinese quarters, developing into thriving communities, Italians are being brought into still greater contact with China.

Three main waves of immigration brought Chinese to Italy in the 20th century: (1) from the 1920s and 1930s to 1972, (2) from 1972 to 1985, and (3) from 1986 to the present. The first Chinese in Italy came via France, settled in Milan, and became street vendors selling ties. Before World War II, the Chinese numbered 40–50, mainly students, diplomats and tradesmen, the majority residing in Milan. Many of these people did not arrive directly from China, but had lived elsewhere in Europe before moving to Italy. In this earlier phase and throughout the 1950s, the Chinese community was composed primarily of single, fairly well-educated males, many of whom would later marry Italian women. With accumulated wealth from China or the other European countries in which they had resided before settling in Italy, and from their earnings in the restaurant and leather industries, these men became small businessmen and opened small shops and restaurants. The demographic profile changed as the immigrants' relatives (including women) and more Chinese from other European countries began arriving in the 1960s. By the end of the 1960s, the Chinese population had increased to between 600 and 700.

The second wave was of a higher volume. In the 1970s, entire families with capital to invest, Chinese from elsewhere in Europe as well as people from China migrated to Italy. Interviews revealed that by the late 1970s, Chinese numbers had increased to 8–9,000. (Official data recorded only 375 Chinese in 1980.) As with the first wave, the majority of these newcomers found work in restaurants or in leather firms. They settled primarily in the established communities in Milan, Florence, Bologna and Rome. Also like the first wave of immigrants, many Chinese who arrived after 1972 originated in southern China and Hong Kong.

The third and largest wave of immigration transformed the character of the Chinese communities in Italy. These communities have not been well-documented and official records lag behind reality. Available sources conflict both as to the size of the settlements and their location, and the discussion which follows is based on a general consensus developed from a combination of interviews, documents and other materials.

Map 5.25

Unlike many of the communities in other European countries, the most recent Chinese immigrants to Italy did not come from the poorer mountainous regions of Zhejiang but from the wealthier plains around Wenzhou (see p 40). A great number entered the country through irregular means, buying passage aboard boats that promised them safe transportation to Italy (see below). Four main factors form the background to the growth of both illegal and legal Chinese migration. The Act of Indemnity of 1986 provided for the regularization of Chinese already arrived in Italy and gave newly legal residents the right to apply for family reunification. Second, in 1990 Chinese were again granted regularization, and autonomous, independent workers or relatives who arrived 'spontaneously/illegally' to join their families were given legal status in Italy. As word spread, other illegal Chinese immigrants from France, England and Holland came to Italy to qualify for legality under the Acts of Indemnity. Regularization also removed the fear of detection and deportation that had stopped Chinese parents from sending their children to the local schools.

A third background factor was the Italian-Chinese Treaty of 1985, which aimed to intensify economic co-operation and to create favourable conditions for investment and business ventures by one country in the other. After the Tiananmen Square Incident of 1989, the Italian government halted, but did not annul, the agreement. Over 1,000 people – students and tourists – were

Chinese pedlar of necklaces and bracelets in Milan, circa 1928.

Chinese immigrant with Italian wife and children, 1920s.

Table 5.40

DISTRIBUTION OF CHINESE ENTERPRISES IN THE FLORENCE – PRATO AREA, 1995			
	FLORENCE	PRATO	CAMPI BISENZIO
Leather	124	2	—
Clothing	14	261	81
Other types of manufacturing	—	2	—
Total manufacturing	138	265	81
Commercial	2	3	51
Restaurants	27	—	—
Other commercial activities	8	2	—
Total commercial activities	37	5	51
Grand total	175	270	132
No of registered Chinese	1,141	1,483	349

Source: Tomba (1996).

granted permission to remain in Italy after the Incident. Finally, Italian consumer demand for Chinese food products made investments in restaurants and grocery stores increasingly profitable.

According to official data, Chinese numbered 1,500 before 1986. After the first Act of Indemnity (1986), numbers soared to 9,880. Following the second Act of Indemnity (1990), numbers rose again to 19,237. At the end of 1993, 22,875 Chinese legally resided in Italy. In 1992, the population of legal immigrants was 63 per cent male and 37 per cent female. In age, 65 per cent of the legal population were between 25 and 44. In terms of education, while the older people in the Chinese community had moderate to advanced schooling, the younger members had poor to moderate schooling. Of the Chinese children in the Italian public educational system, 1,706 were in elementary school, 641 in pre-school, 570 in middle and high school, and 448 at university.

In 1992 the Chinese were concentrated in the larger metropolitan areas in the regions of Lombardy (Milan), Tuscany (Florence) and Lazio (Rome), with smaller communities in Emilia-Romagna (Bologna) and Piedmont (Turin). They were different from other immigrant communities in that many owned businesses that employed family, friends and other Chinese. This peculiarity strengthened the tendency of the Chinese to concentrate in specific areas, creating *i quartieri cinesi*. Compared to other immigrant communities, the Chinese also held a higher number of *permessi di soggiorno* (residence permits) with independent worker status. Of the *permessi* given, 18 per cent claimed independent worker status, 55 per cent claimed dependence, 8 per cent family reasons, and 5 per cent study purposes. The status of the other permits is unknown.

Those people who did not work in Chinese-owned businesses usually worked as domestic servants, construction workers, street and market vendors, or loaders and unloaders of products in the central markets.

Chinese vendor at a flea market in Milan.

The people who worked in the Italian section of the labour market number approximately 2,000. Most people, approximately 17,000, worked long hours in Chinese-owned businesses in the restaurant, leather or clothing industries as owners or workers, the latter for very low salaries.

Many forms of locally based associations exist. Like the mutual assistance groups in Milan and Florence, these groups attempt to organize the spare time of the young Chinese, offer courses on the Italian language, aid the Chinese in dealing with Italian bureaucracy by getting the proper documents, and provide general support for new immigrants.

Exact numbers of Chinese illegal immigrants in Italy are unknown; however, approximately 25,000 *clandestini* (illegals) are estimated to reside in the Florence metropolitan area alone. Italian officials believe the clandestine immigration to have been organized by a trafficking business that has branches in the United States, Spain, Holland, Germany and France. Milan, with over 200 Chinese restaurants and 600 leather firms, serves as one of the most important centres of this business. According to some accounts, before arrival in Milan or Florence/Prato, the clandestine immigrant will have travelled from Shanghai to Moscow and detoured through France, Yugoslavia or Albania. The police believe that Italian criminal organizations in Puglia are working in conjunction with their Chinese counterparts by providing boats that transport immigrants from Albania to Italy. The trip from China costs 15–20 million lire (US$10,000–13,000), the amount paid in advance to the trafficking organizations by businesses in Italy seeking *clandestini* labour. Such labour, producing goods at less than half the cost of those made by Italian workers, helps increase the employers' profits. After a long and arduous journey, the arrivals are taken to Italian cities by truck and are locked in huge sheds in terrible conditions, forced into indentured servitude. The *clandestini* work for years before paying their debts in full to their employers.

The main communities

Whatever their mode of entry, Chinese are making a place for themselves in Italy, establishing businesses and adjusting to their new environment. They have formed several organizations to provide social, cultural, economic and political support and to mediate between Chinese (very few of whom speak Italian well) and Italians. Since most Chinese lead lives very isolated from Italian society, the regional and linguistic fragmentation within the Chinese communities is not appreciated by the mainstream society, which assumes a homogeneity which does not in fact exist.

Just as Chinese have had to learn to adjust to Italy, so Italians have worked to adapt to the growing ethnic diversification of their country. Many Italian organizations offer free Italian language courses to new immigrants. Several education projects aim to help Chinese children maintain their knowledge of their native language and culture on the one hand, and expose Italian children to cultural differences on the other. In certain classrooms in Milan, Italian and Chinese students are taught by two teachers, one Italian and one Chinese. These teachers introduce the idea of cultural, linguistic and historical diversity. Advocates of this programme insist that exposing children to the equal value of individual cultures helps to ameliorate future racial tensions. They hope to stimulate both groups of children by encouraging curiosity, participation and interest in each other's cultures.

Milan was the site of the first Chinese settlements in Italy in the 1920s. The first Chinese restaurant, La Pagoda, opened in 1962. Until the end of the 1970s, there were few such restaurants, but in the 1980s, numbers rose to the hundreds and the 1990s saw them increase sharply and spread to other provinces and regions. Other businesses soon followed, selling everything from Chinese food products to assorted trinkets and *objets d'arts*.

Chinese associations, offering different networks of support, are much more established in Milan than in places of relatively recent Chinese settlement. Chinese have found other meeting points in Chinese libraries, associations, Chinese cinemas and karaoke clubs. One association in particular, Associazione Cinesi a Milano (the Chinese Association in Milan) has provided support for the education of Chinese children. In collaboration with the elementary school Giusti and the middle school Panzini, the association has promoted a cross-cultural learning experience for Chinese and Italian students. Another association, Associazione Italia Cina, has organized exhibits, lectures, language and cooking courses, as well as movies and theatre for both Chinese and Italians.

Although the community in Milan has a higher standard of living than the other communities in Italy, one can still find pockets of exploitation, *clandestini* and poverty. In 1995, the police found 90 Chinese 'slaves' in Bréscia locked up in a building and forced to sew clothes for 15 hours a day for food and a mattress. Official records count only 400 Chinese in Bréscia, but considering 90 illegals were discovered in just one raid, officials believe the number of illegal Chinese immigrants in the Milan metropolitan area to be extremely high.

Rome has the largest Chinese community in Italy. Unlike in Milan, no Chinese quarter exists in Rome, as the community is spread throughout the city. Before 1949, most of the immigrants originated from mainland China. After 1949 however, more and more Chinese arrived from Hong Kong and Taiwan intending to invest money in Italy. The diversity of origin makes the Roman Chinese community different from those in Milan and Florence. But as in the latter two cities, the leather and restaurant industries are the two main employers of Chinese. The leather industry is widespread throughout the city, particularly in the outskirts of the city. Italian observers point to the existence of gambling and instances of crime and extortion, connecting these activities with what is called the *mafia gialla* (yellow or Chinese Mafia).

The Chinese in Tuscany have been studied by, among others, the Department of Social Sciences at Florence University. No less than 82 per cent of the Chinese there live in the Florence and Prato areas. About 90 per cent of them originated in the Wenzhou municipality, Yueqing and Rui'an districts in Zhejiang province. Influxes of any size were unknown until the beginning of the 1980s, when the municipalities of Campi Bisenzio and Signa as well as the western suburbs of Florence (Brozzi and

Inside a leather goods sweatshop.

Peretola) received many Chinese migrants arriving not directly from Zhejiang but from other European countries, particularly France and Holland. In 1989, 1,239 Chinese obtained residence permits; and in 1995, 3,228 registered Chinese were officially counted as living in the Florence/Prato area. The actual number is far higher, Florence having the highest percentage of *clandestini* in Italy. In some of the communes around Florence, the Chinese and Italian populations are virtually equal in number. One neighbourhood in particular, San Donnino, has the dubious distinction of being known as San Pechino (San Beijing). Illegal Chinese immigrants are estimated to be around 25,000 in the greater metropolitan area – Prato, San Donnino, Pistoia, Empoli, Campi Bisenzio and Florence.

To judge from the proportion of residence permits issued between 1987 and 1989 to family members – which, at 20 per cent, is higher than that found in any of the non-European Economic Community countries – Wenzhou migrants diverge from others in not being overwhelmingly single males. It is as though the transplantation were not so much of individuals as of the small, informal family businesses that have underpinned the rapid economic development of Wenzhou itself. In Florence these Wenzhou households are predominantly engaged in the manufacture of leather handbags, while in Prato they are mainly involved in the garment industry. In 1993, for example, 132 out of 223 officially registered Chinese enterprises in the municipality of Campi Bisenzio worked in leather production. In Prato, most of the Chinese businesses became sub-contractors (in such low-end jobs as assembling or label sewing) to the ready-to-wear manufacturers of that city (see table 5.40).

The production of leather goods and clothing has been a postwar Tuscan speciality, one characterized by concentration, small business, and family and social solidarity. The Chinese arrived at a time when this local economy was undergoing structural changes and facing the internationalization of competition. The niche these changes created for the production of low-quality and low-price goods was quickly filled by the Chinese.

While many Chinese businesses are registered, their employees are not. This is illegal under Italian law, but the fact that the 'employees' are family members makes prosecution or proof of exploitation very difficult. Nor have the authorities succeeded in moving part of the migrant community to less congested areas. However, the social isolation of the communities is palliated to some extent by the emergence of a second-generation of Italian-educated Chinese.

Aliza S. Wong

THE NETHERLANDS

Organization of peanut vendors in the 1930s. On far right, student and founder Oey Kang Soey.

The Netherlands has been at the crossroads of many different Chinese immigration waves to Europe. As a result, this small country is host to one of largest Chinese populations on the continent (only the French, British and Russian Chinese communities are larger). The Dutch Chinese population is sharply divided into several independent communities.

History and composition of the Dutch Chinese population

Before World War II

At the beginning of the 20th century, the first *peranakan* Chinese students from the Dutch East Indies came to the Netherlands for their university training. In 1930, their number had grown to 150. In 1911, they established their own association, the Chung Hwa Hui (Zhonghua Hui), which published the Dutch-language periodical *Chung Hwa Hui Tsa Chih* (*Zhonghua hui zazhi*). These Peranakans spoke Malay or another Indonesian language as their mother tongue and, having been educated in Dutch-medium schools, they were fluent in Dutch.

As elsewhere in Europe, the number of pedlars from the area around the port city of Wenzhou and the inland town of Qingtian in southern Zhejiang grew rapidly in the Netherlands after World War I. Immigrants from Wenzhou and Qingtian, which are Wu-speaking areas, often still have only an imperfect command of Mandarin, though the latter is supposed to be their lingua franca.

Cantonese-speaking seamen from Guangdong were brought over from Britain by Dutch shipping companies in 1911 to break a seamen's strike. After the strike, some continued to work on Dutch ships and gradually replaced Dutch stokers. Dutch seamen saw them as rivals and scabs and one union

ran an inflammatory campaign against the 'yellow peril.' As a result of the recruitment of more and more Chinese seamen by Dutch companies, small Chinatowns sprang up in Rotterdam and Amsterdam. The community was extremely fragmented, with the seamen organized in regional groupings.

In the wake of the Great Depression of 1929, many Chinese seamen were laid off. Changes in shipping practice lessened their chances of work at sea. Originally, many were hired as coal-stokers, but the switch to oil rendered large numbers redundant, and furthermore Dutch unions refused to let the Chinese work above deck.

In 1931, an unemployed seaman began making and selling *pindakoekjes* (peanut-cakes): small cakes made of peanuts and caramelized sugar. Other seamen and Zhejiang peddlers, equally hard hit by the Depression, quickly turned to this trade as well. As a result, the Chinese *pindaman* (peanut-man) became a familiar sight throughout the Netherlands.

Despite the temporary relief brought by the peanut trade, the Chinese in the Netherlands lived in often miserable circumstances throughout the 1930s; steadily, their numbers fell. Most Cantonese sooner or later signed back on again as seamen, while many of the Zhejiang pedlars returned to China or moved on to other countries. But the fall in numbers came not only from the economic crisis. The police, particularly in Rotterdam, carried out raids on Chinatown that resulted in the deportation of several hundred Chinese.

When World War II broke out, fewer than 1,000 Chinese remained in the Netherlands. Alongside these Chinese from China, there were more than 100 Peranakan students in 1940.

After World War II

In 1949, Indonesia became independent. Over the next few years, a quarter of a million 'East Indies Netherlanders' were repatriated, among them people of Chinese origin. By 1957, there were 1,400 Peranakans in the Netherlands. Others followed, particularly after the anti-Chinese pogroms in Indonesia between 1959 and 1968 (see Part V: Indonesia).

Knowing no Mandarin, Cantonese or any other Chinese dialect, most Peranakans in the Netherlands have hardly any contact with other groups of Chinese. Many are academics and professionals: a strikingly large proportion works in the medical sector (as doctors, dentists, specialists or pharmacists). After the winding-up of the Chung Hwa Hui in 1962, there were no major Peranakan organizations until the 1980s, when more and more Peranakans, now nearing retirement, became interested in exploring their historical and cultural background. At present, Peranakan associations (such as Inisiatip, De Vriendschap, Huayi Xieshanghui and

Map 5.26

THE NETHERLANDS

N

0 10 20 kilometres

0 10 20 miles

North Sea

AMSTERDAM

The Hague   THE NETHERLANDS

Rotterdam

Tilburg

Eindhoven

GERMANY

BELGIUM

Lianyihui) together have some 800 members.

After the war, the other Chinese communities also grew spectacularly, spurred by the emergence of the Chinese-Indonesian catering trade. The immediate cause of the Chinese-Indonesian restaurant boom was Indonesia's independence. Members of the Dutch colonial élite brought back a taste for eastern cooking. The Chinese restaurateurs were quick to add Indonesian dishes to their menu and called their restaurants 'Chinese-Indonesian.'

Viewed over a longer term, the rising standards of living in the Netherlands after the war were even more important in driving the restaurant boom. Unlike the French, the Dutch lack an indigenous tradition of affordable restaurants for ordinary people, and in the immediate postwar period, Chinese faced virtually no competition from other ethnic restaurants.

The growth in the number of restaurants led to the immigration of progressively larger numbers of Chinese, and thus to the expansion of not only the original communities of Cantonese and Zhejiang Chinese but of Chinese not belonging to those groupings. The latter, made up mostly of Chinese from Hong Kong's New Territories, with smaller contingents from Singapore and Malaysia, arrived in much larger numbers. They supplied the labour which might have been sourced from the home communities of the Chinese already settled in the Netherlands, had the restrictive emigration policies of the People's Republic not cut it off; only from 1974 onward were many of the obstacles to emigration removed and the flow resumed.

The Hong Kong Chinese, of whom a sizeable community already lived in Britain, were the first to grasp the opportunity. Very quickly, Cantonese- and Hakka-speaking Hong Kong Chinese took root in the Netherlands. By the late 1960s, they were the dominant group, making standard Cantonese the lingua franca for the majority of the Dutch Chinese. Only the Peranakans, Zhejiangese, and Surinamese Hakka remained, each in their way, independent from the Cantonese and resistant to any compulsion to learn standard Cantonese.

The Singaporean and Malaysian Chinese have never been able to copy the success of the Hong Kong Chinese. The first immigrants from these countries came 10 to 15 years later than the Hong Kong pioneers, and could not profit from the presence of a substantial community already present in Britain. These pioneers had

Table 5.41

CHARACTERISTICS OF MAIN CHINESE GROUPS IN THE NETHERLANDS

GROUP	PLACE OF ORIGIN	FIRST LANGUAGE	MAIN PERIODS OF IMMIGRATION	LINGUA FRANCA
Peranakan	Indonesia	Malay, Dutch	1949–70	Dutch
Cantonese	Hong Kong, Guangdong	Cantonese, Hakka, Dutch	1911–30, 1950–present	Standard Cantonese, Dutch
Zhejiangese	Zhejiang	Southern Wu, Dutch	1920–30, 1974–present	Mandarin, Dutch
Singaporean/ Malaysian	Singapore, Malaysia	Hokkien, Hainanese, Teochiu, Cantonese, Hakka, Dutch	1965–80	Cantonese, Mandarin, Dutch, English
Surinamese	Surinam	Hakka, Dutch	1975–80	Dutch
Vietnamese	Vietnam	Cantonese, Dutch	1975–82	Cantonese, Mandarin, Dutch
Fujianese	Eastern Fujian	Eastern Fujianese	1985?–present	Mandarin, Cantonese? Dutch?

no network of relatives and friends to provide the necessary loans to purchase restaurants. By the time some of them were ready to start their own businesses, the number of restaurants in the Netherlands was fast reaching saturation point, and business opportunities were far less plentiful than before. By and large, they continued to be employed by the more established communities of Cantonese and Zhejiang Chinese. This is also reflected linguistically. The Singaporean Chinese in the Netherlands are chiefly speakers of Hokkien, Mandarin and English; Malaysian Chinese are Cantonese speakers. Singaporean Chinese who did not know standard Cantonese had to learn it upon arrival to communicate with Cantonese employers and colleagues.

Besides the Chinese from Hong Kong, Zhejiang and Guangdong provinces, Indonesia, Taiwan, Malaysia and Singapore, three other groups of migrants have established themselves in the twenty-odd years before 1996. These are the Surinamese Chinese, the Vietnamese Chinese, and the Fujianese Chinese.

The Chinese in Surinam, a former Dutch colony, are Hakkas from many different areas in Southeast China, Hong Kong, and even Southeast Asia. Approximately 4,000 Surinamese Chinese currently live in the Netherlands. They left Surinam shortly before its independence in 1975, because they felt unsure of the future and feared Creole domination.

Between 1975 and 1982, the Dutch government accepted 6,000 Vietnamese political refugees, 24 per cent of whom are ethnic Chinese whose main languages are Cantonese and Vietnamese. Since 1982, Vietnamese immigration (mainly new refugees and relatives of refugees already in the Netherlands) has slowed. Unlike the Surinamese Chinese, who have no separate organizations in the Netherlands, the Vietnamese Chinese began to form associations shortly after their arrival. They have a national organization, a member of the European and global Vietnamese Chinese organizations, and their own periodical, *Viet Hoa* (Vietnamese Chinese).

Immigrants from eastern Fujian province appeared in Europe in the second

A Chinese peanut vendor in Holland.

Figure 5.10

IMMIGRATION OF MAIN CHINESE GROUPS TO THE NETHERLANDS

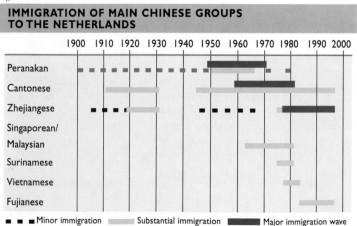

■ ■ ■Minor immigration   ▬▬▬ Substantial immigration   ▬▬▬ Major immigration wave

Kong Hing restaurant in Amsterdam, 1930s.

half of the 1980s as a direct consequence of the activities of human traffickers, or 'snakeheads' (*shetou*). Other than that its size has grown rapidly, little is known about this group (see p 63).

The Chinese population in the 1990s

On the basis of municipal population-registration data, the scholar Y. Zhao concluded that at least 59,000 ethnic Chinese lived in the Netherlands on January 1, 1990. Among the 59,000, we estimate that the number from the People's Republic of China and Hong Kong is roughly 19,000 each.

The immigration of Zhejiang, Guangdong and Hong Kong Chinese is primarily a product of a specialized culture of migration that has been firmly established in certain villages. This pattern is also reflected in the immigration data. In the 1980s, despite the continuing growth of the Hong Kong economy and the slump in the Dutch catering trade (see below), Hong Kong Chinese continued to migrate to the Netherlands in significant numbers. Although the number of Hong Kong Chinese immigrants between 1984 and 1990 (from 300 to 400 a year) was about half that between 1976 and 1979, it was still far higher than the number of emigrants. (The average yearly net immigration between 1984 and 1986 of people born in Hong Kong was 212. Between 1976 and 1979, it was 529.)

Even more telling is the revival of emigration from the People's Republic of China, and, more specifically, from the Wenzhou and Qingtian areas. Inflows from these areas to western and southern Europe rapidly gained momentum after the Chinese government started allowing emigration in the early 1970s. Despite the crisis of the Dutch Chinese catering trade in the Netherlands, there is no sign that immigration from these areas is levelling off.

Geographical distribution, employment and social structure

Although Amsterdam has a district known as Chinatown or *Chinese buurt*, it is not a Chinatown in the usual sense of the word – that is, a compact residential community of Chinese people. Amsterdam's Chinatown is a commercial and recreational centre, but most Chinese who frequent it live elsewhere.

The geographical dispersion of Chinese in the Netherlands results from their specialization in the restaurant trade. Chinese opening new restaurants generally do so in areas where they will have least competition.

Some 50 to 60 per cent of Dutch Chinese work in catering. In the late 1980s, another 15 or 20 per cent were registered as unemployed and seeking work as cooks, waiters or restaurant managers. No other ethnic group in the Netherlands has specialized in one sector of the economy to the degree that the Chinese have.

This specialization was caused above all by the culture of migration and the logic of chain migration. More mundane factors also helped. Unskilled immigrants with little or no Dutch cannot find jobs outside catering that would earn them comparable wages. Even Chinese partly educated in the Netherlands (the 'intermediate generation') end up as waiters, managers or proprietors.

Nevertheless, Chinese are increasingly active in other sectors of the economy as well. A small number are engaged in the ethnic sector – that is, grocery stores, video shops, bookshops, and import-and-export companies that cater for the Dutch Chinese community. The rapidly growing second generation, educated in the Netherlands, is especially reluctant to enter the catering trade. No research has yet been done on the employment structure of this second generation. However, the fact that these Chinese have succeeded in the Dutch educational system bodes well for their competitiveness in the labour market.

For the Chinese as a whole, day-to-day social contacts are restricted to a small circle of acquaintances. This restriction is partly imposed by the restaurant business: long working hours (often 11 or 12 hours a day), lack of holidays, a dispersed pattern of settlement, and the large degree of independence that comes with the ownership of a restaurant. As a result, the community is fragmented. There is little active participation in organizations, and restaurant workers or owners depend on friends and acquaintances for work, staff, premises and other needs. Yet working in restaurants also inhibits social integration in Dutch society. Waiters and owners meet and address Dutch customers, but the contact is brief and superficial. The restaurants remain isolated pockets of Chinese life.

The catering trade

Until the late 1970s or early 1980s, the number of restaurants grew by about 18 per cent a year. At first, the growth took place in the western cities of Amsterdam,

Rotterdam and the Hague, the cradle of the Chinese-Indonesian catering trade. Gradually, the number of restaurants in this region reached saturation point and Chinese started moving elsewhere, first to the south and then to the north and east.

In the early 1980s, however, the boom ended. The market throughout the Netherlands became saturated and there was little room left for new restaurants, save at the cost of old ones in the same district. The general economic crisis in the 1980s led to a decline in eating out. At the same time, the number of non-Chinese foreign restaurants increased rapidly. Scandals about hygiene and complaints about the quality of the food in Chinese-Indonesian restaurants, together with reports of organized Chinese crime, harmed the reputation of the Chinese-Indonesian restaurants and, to a lesser extent, of the Chinese as an ethnic group.

The Chinese community seemed incapable of adjusting to the changes. Because of their specialized niche in catering, many have a poor grasp of the Dutch language, Dutch administration and culture, and are ill-equipped to strike out in new directions. Increasing numbers of Chinese became jobless and were obliged to turn to the authorities, particularly the government-run job centres. Until then, Chinese in the Netherlands had been well known for regulating their own affairs; the catering crisis, combined with a growing attention in the Netherlands to minorities, led to an increasing Chinese visibility.

Faced with decreasing turnover in the 1980s, most restaurant owners chose to cut costs. In 1982, a restaurant employed on the average 4.6 workers; in 1987, the average had dropped to 2.7. This practice resulted in a rate of unemployment that in 1987 probably reached between 20 and 25 per cent. (This compares badly with the national unemployment rate of 14 per cent but less poorly with those of other minorities: Moroccans, 39; Spaniards, 19; Turks, 41 and Yugoslavs, 24.) Many of the unemployed were elderly cooks who had become a burden to their employers.

Over the same period, the number of restaurants dropped only slightly. Reducing the wage bill was not simply a matter of firing redundant employees. Sometimes, workers were replaced by (much cheaper) illegal immigrants or people officially registered as unemployed, who did not show up in the statistics. More often, however, the owner and his family simply worked longer hours than previously.

Yet restaurants that are no longer viable and whose owners are forced to sell can always find buyers among new chain-migrants who, against all odds, still dream of being their own boss. Moreover, one reason for the restaurants' profitability had been the steady influx of cheap and docile chain-migrants. Paradoxically, the flow of new blood into the Chinese community is a strongly conservative force that preserves an old-fashioned style of entrepreneurship.

It is therefore unlikely that the crisis in the Dutch Chinese community is over for good. At first glance, this assertion may seem to be contradicted by the resumption of growth (albeit at a still far slower rate than in the 1960s and 1970s) in the number of restaurants in the early 1990s. But a closer look fails to turn up any signs that the underlying causes of the crisis of the 1980s

have been removed. No new areas in Holland can be opened up by Chinese caterers and most Chinese restaurants have failed to improve their business practices. Rather, their expansion seems to reflect the robust growth of the Dutch economy as a whole between 1987 and 1992.

Nevertheless, a minority of entrepreneurs has embarked on an alternative strategy. The new type of Chinese restaurant that emerged in the 1980s was no longer first and foremost a family enterprise but a calculated business venture aimed at profit maximization, catering for specific new markets such as business lunches and dinners, exclusive parties and receptions. Many of these new-style entrepreneurs were intermediate-generation Chinese for whom the restaurant is a first step to more ambitious projects.

The elderly, children and schools

With the ageing of the Chinese population in the 1980s and 1990s, care of the elderly has become an issue of some concern to the Chinese community. Today, many elderly Chinese live alone, either because they want to or because their children's homes are too small. The municipal governments of the Hague and Amsterdam responded in the 1990s by subsidizing experiments with old people's homes catering specially for elderly Chinese. These projects have reportedly been most successful; more are likely to follow.

With the increase in the number of Chinese children since the 1970s, many Chinese (Cantonese) schools have been set up throughout the Netherlands; they provide an alternative to sending children back to China. They operate mainly on Wednesday afternoons and Saturdays when the children are free from their Dutch school. About half of the total number of children attend a Chinese school.

Chinese schools have been set up by a variety of local and national Chinese organizations independent of Dutch authorities. Many of these organizations owe their existence almost exclusively to the demand for Chinese education. Dutch authorities consider the schools a matter for the Chinese themselves and exercise no control over the quality and content of the education on offer.

Chinese organizations

In 1965, Chinese from Zhejiang founded the Lü He Huaqiao Zonghui, or the Algemene Chinese Vereniging in Nederland (General Chinese Association in the Netherlands). This strove to represent the

Table 5.42

PLACE OF ORIGIN, 1990	
COUNTRY OR TERRITORY	**NUMBER**
Mainland China, Hong Kong, Taiwan, Macao	39,000
Indonesia	16,000
Surinam	4,000
Singapore	3,000
Malaysia	1,000
Double count	- 4,000
Total	59,000

Based on data collected by the Dutch Central Bureau of Statistics on January 1, 1990. 'Country' refers to nationality. Country of birth, father's or mother's (or both parents') country of birth, or to two or three of these categories.

Table 5.43

CHINESE-INDONESIAN RESTAURANTS			
TOTAL NUMBERS FOR SELECTED YEARS			
YEAR	**NUMBER**	**CHANGE**	**AVERAGE YEARLY CHANGE (%)**
1960	225		
1970	618	+ 393	+ 17
1982	1,916	+ 1,298	+ 18
1987	1,842	- 74	- 1
1991	1,988	+ 146	+ 2

PERCENTAGE OF TOTAL IN FOUR DIFFERENT REGIONS FOR SELECTED YEARS							
YEAR	**1960**	**1965**	**1970**	**1975**	**1982**	**1987***	**1991**
North	5	5	5	5	9	9	8
East	13	12	13	13	16	18	18
West	70	68	63	55	50	48	49
South	12	15	19	26	25	25	25
Total	**100**	**100**	**100**	**99**	**100**	**100**	**100**

The regional distribution for 1987 was calculated only for the 1,708 restaurants out of a total of 1,842 that had an ethnic Chinese owner.
Sources: For 1960–82, Bedrijfschap Horeca (1983); Pieke (1988a); for 1991, Bedrijfschap Horeca (1992).

Dutch police levying fine, circa 1975

interests of the entire Chinese community. The association is on good terms with the Embassy of the Peo ple's Republic of China and publishes a semi-monthly newspaper, *Huaqiao Tongxun / Overzeese Chinezen Bulletin* (Overseas Chinese Bulletin). The composition of the General Chinese Association, despite its statutes, is by no means an accurate reflection of the Chinese population. However, although it represents mainly Zhejiangese, especially from Wenzhou, it has been quite successful in attracting members. It has branch associations in eight regions and at least 800 members.

The General Association is not the only traditional-style regional organization in the Netherlands. Chinese from in and around Qingtian have their own community organization, as do the Cantonese speakers. In addition, there are several Cantonese regional and lineage organizations.

In the 1980s, many other types of association were formed, ranging from small recreational and sports clubs to associations of Chinese businessmen in Rotterdam and Amsterdam. Most visible among them were associations chiefly concerned with social work and education among the Chinese. The most important of these associations is the Helan Zhonghua huzhuhui/Stichting Chinese Cultuur, Recreatie en Maatschappelijk Werk (CCRM, Foundation for Chinese Culture, Recreation and Social Work), spawned by a Hong Kong missionary church in Rotterdam. The CCRM has links with the government in Taiwan, which makes it the natural rival of the China-supported General Association. Publishing the bilingual newspaper *Banyuebao/De Chinese Half-maandelijkse Infokrant* (The Chinese Semi-monthly), it has headquarters in Rotterdam and branches and Chinese schools in many other Dutch cities. More recently, the CCRM set up national organizations for the elderly, women and youth, and a regional foundation for Chinese in Rotterdam. Regional organizations similar to but independent from the CCRM exist in the Hague, Amsterdam, Tilburg, Eindhoven, and several other Dutch cities and towns.

In 1987, the leaders of traditional organizations such as the General Chinese Association and the more modern associations concerned with social work and education joined hands in an umbrella organization, the QuanHe Huaren shetuan lianhehui/Stichting Landelijke Federatie van Chinese Organisaties in Nederland (National Federation of Chinese Organizations in the Netherlands). In 1987, the federation began publishing the bilingual *Lianhui Qikan/Federatie Periodiek* (Federation Journal). The aim of the federation was to coordinate the efforts of member organizations and represent Chinese interests and opinions to the Dutch government. Its history has not been a peace-

ful one. In 1990, personal and ideological conflicts came to the boil, whereupon the CCRM, a principal force in the Chinese community, decided to discontinue its membership.

From being poorly organized until the early 1980s, the Chinese have since seen a manifold increase in their associations. In 1995, more than 80 organizations had either joined the National Federation or had informally registered with the CCRM. The reasons for this increase are many; they include the crisis in the catering trade, the need to provide Chinese-language education for the second generation, the growth of a new élite of educated first- and second-generation Chinese, and the coordination of the lobby for government recognition and subsidy.

The Chinese in the Netherlands are undergoing a not entirely harmonious transition. Until the early 1980s, they tried to solve their problems by themselves and seldom appealed for outside help. The older Chinese, most of whom originated from outside Hong Kong and settled in the Netherlands before the main wave of Chinese migration, have an attitude towards work and authority that one rarely finds among the newcomers. These veterans have often experienced hard times in Europe. They learned the value of, not to say the need for, self-reliance. But new leaders with a different political agenda are now emerging from the ranks of the second generation and more recently arrived immigrants.

Two factors influence the thinking of this new group of leaders. First, a change in Dutch attitudes towards ethnic minorities calls for new strategies and approaches by the minorities. Second, the home societies of the new immigrants have little in common with the old China that the earlier generations left behind.

The Chinese: an ethnic minority?

In the mid-1980s, the Dutch government and parliament embarked on a reappraisal of its ethnic minority policies. The question was asked as to whether any additional ethnic groups should be officially recognized as minorities under the government's minority policies. At exactly the same time, the Chinese community encountered increasingly serious problems.

The question of whether or not the Chinese were a minority like any other had never been posed before because of the image of the Chinese held by Dutch people and the Chinese themselves. Chinese seemed to be well off; they rarely made any claim on the authorities.

Around the early 1980s, however, it became clear to an increasing number of Chinese leaders that the old strategy of self-reliance would no longer suffice. In particular, almost all Dutch Chinese saw the urgent need for Chinese-language schools for the rapidly growing second generation. Chinese organizations, as we have seen, were quick to enter this new market; in the course of just a few years, they established schools throughout the Netherlands. As a result, these organizations, which had remained small and relatively insignificant until then, grew in size, number and importance.

In the late 1970s and early 1980s, leaders of the resuscitated traditional organizations and especially of the cultural centres had established contacts with local and national Dutch politicians and officials and had become quite fluent in the language of Dutch minority politics. The National Federation of Chinese Organizations in the Netherlands, together with other Chinese organizations and leaders, pointed to rising unemployment, language difficulties, and the general lack of integration of the Chinese. In Dutch minority-policy discourse, such problems are all-important indicators of disadvantage. Such disadvantage would qualify the group in question for minority status, but only if the government was also deemed to have borne 'special responsibility' for the presence in the Netherlands of the group.

Yet, in 1986, politicians of several parties decided that such a policy would lock ethnic and social boundaries into the shapes and patterns that they had formed in the early 1980s. The case of the Chinese, a modest, hard-working, but apparently seriously disadvantaged minority, became one of their main arguments against government policy. The Chinese, who only a few years earlier had been a model (that is, invisible) minority, suddenly found themselves caught in the limelight of Dutch minority politics.

The Dutch Government promised to commission a study on whether or not the Chinese community was disadvantaged. After a prolonged period of lobbying and infighting between 1984 and 1988, and partly on the basis of a research report written by Frank N. Pieke (the author of this article), the government in the end declined to grant minority status to the Chinese. The reason it gave was that the Chinese were not sufficiently underprivileged in terms of income, employment, education and housing. The report also pointed out that a minority status may have the unintended effect of stigmatizing an ethnic group, whose enjoyment of minority benefits could all too easily be seen as freeloading by the majority population. But the government allowed local authorities to subsidize services and organizations catering for the local Chinese population, thereby in effect sanctioning existing practice. Ironically, the main (but never officially stated) reason for not giving national minority status was that this would have entitled the Chinese to national subsidies for education, by far the most expensive of all officially sponsored minority facilities. What had initially prompted the Chinese to ask for minority status thus turned out to be the principal cause of the lobby's eventual defeat.

The 1988 discussions left permanent scars on the Chinese community. In the early 1980s, the leaders of Chinese cultural centres and traditional organizations had used the promise of subsidized Chinese-language education to put an end to decades of invisibility and self-reliance that had been articles of faith of the older generation. After the publication of the Pieke report in March 1988 but a few months before the government announced its decision, the older generation reasserted themselves. Going along with Dutch minority discourse, they argued, had tainted the image of the Chinese community. The report and the ensuing public debate had not only suggested that Chinese were incapable of solving their own problems but had exposed large-scale illegal immigration, low pay and bad working conditions in the restaurants, and generational conflict; as a result, the image of Chinese was now hardly better than that of stigmatized minorities like the Turks, Moroccans and Surinamese. Referring to their own bitter experiences

in the 1930s, they pointed to the risk of future discrimination and the loss of a position in the Dutch economy that had been built up over decades. These arguments carried so much weight that a meeting in 1988 of leaders of Chinese organizations on the Pieke report decided against urging the Dutch Government to grant minority status to their community.

The 1980s taught the Chinese community that the Dutch perception of ethnic minorities can indeed be a minefield, and at the same time laid bare some of the structural cleavages in the Chinese community. The unity of the 1980s had been largely a product of Dutch minority policies, which favour unified ethnic groups. Under the current circumstances, the power and influence of the younger generation of Chinese leaders again depend not on government policies but on the patronage of local government and individual Dutch politicians and officials. This has resulted in a proliferation of Chinese organizations that, now more than ever, serve local or particular interests such as Chinatown shop owners, restaurateurs, the elderly, women, or the second generation. As a rule, these organizations cooperate only on specific, often semi-ritual, occasions – for example sports meetings, political debates on the position of the Chinese, election rallies and celebrations of Chinese New Year.

This development may, in the long term, prove positive. The community's interests were little served by the minority policies of the 1980s, which to a large extent subsidized and thus indirectly encouraged existing structures of ethnic segregation and stratification. The community seems therefore well positioned to take full advantage of the current change in Dutch minority policy. For since 1990, the government has turned away from a policy of preserving ethnic identities and of integrating and emancipating ethnic groups as groups, and has tried to break through the ossified ethnic interests shaped by the earlier approach. Instead, it now stresses integration through individual effort and concentrates its resources where they are most needed, for example, in helping new immigrants and poorly educated or unemployed members of the second generation.

If this trend persists, the Chinese community's essential lack of coherence may become an asset rather than a liability. This lack of internal coherence means that the many different Chinese organizations are independent and flexible enough to deal with specific and changing conditions at both the national and local levels. Such adaptability and elasticity is frequently lacking in bodies representing officially recognized minorities, which are often both a product of and locked into a rigid bureaucratic structure.

Frank N. Pieke

Four generations of the Thio family in Rijswijk. Born in Indonesia, Mr Thio (seated right) worked as a civil servant before his retirement.

RUSSIA

Before the 1990s

The Chinese community in Russia is one of the oldest in Europe, the first Chinese having settled in Siberia in the 15th century or earlier. A key factor in the history of migration from China to Russia has been the two countries' geographical proximity and long common land border. The three main Chinese areas on the border abutting Russia are: Xinjiang province to the far west, Inner Mongolia, and what Europeans have called 'Manchuria' in the northeast. Until the frontiers were properly demarcated, Chinese hunters, herders, fishermen and ginseng diggers travelled freely to what is now Russian territory.

Map 5.27

CHINA'S BORDER WITH RUSSIA, 1840

Source: Schwartz, 1964.

In 1689, by the Treaty of Nerchinsk, the Moscow government reluctantly recognized the entire Amur basin as Qing territory, but up to the mid-19th century few Chinese subjects inhabited the right bank of the Amur, and fewer still the left bank. Russia took advantage of Qing inattention to settle and strengthen its presence in eastern Siberia at China's expense; and in 1860, by the Sino-Russian Treaty of Beijing, it succeeded in extending its political and commercial influence throughout the entire northern frontier of the Qing empire, from Manchuria to Xinjiang. However, migrant Chinese continued to pursue seasonal work in the areas ceded to Russia.

This was the first phase of the Chinese diaspora's history in Russia. The second stage, spanning the first half of the 20th century, saw the recruitment of Chinese labour (see box) and the expansion of Chinese settlements in the central and western parts of Russia. In this period, too, Chinese came to study in Russia, many at the Sun Yat-sen University of Working Chinese established with Chinese funding in Moscow in 1925 to train Communist cadres for the future Chinese revolution. In China itself, the October Revolution had mesmerized a whole group of intellectuals. Among the Chinese alumni of the Sun Yat-sen University were Chiang Ching-Kuo (one day to become the president of Taiwan), Deng Xiaoping, as well as young Communists who entered the history of the Chinese revolution as the '28 Bolsheviks' (Moscow's emissaries who, as returned students in China, would come to be known as 'China's Stalin Section' and who were to be overshadowed by Mao Zedong in the Chinese Communist Party). Students apart, Chinese merchants came to Russia, engaging in small businesses in places such as Vladivostok and Khabarovsk.

Map 5.28

RUSSIA

With the collapse of Tsarist power in 1917, the repatriation of the Chinese workers recruited by the fallen government became a pressing concern. Protracted negotiations between China and Russia ensued, with the latter pleading financial incapacity. Many Chinese were reduced to mendicancy, begging their way homeward along the Trans-Siberia Railway. Others joined the Red Army. It was only when the Red Cross, Britain, France and other Western countries came to their aid that Chinese workers were eventually provided with the means to return to China. However, sizeable numbers remained in settlements in the Soviet Far East.

To help organize the repatriation, Chinese students, merchants and worker representatives had founded an organization, the Zhonghua Lü E Lianhehui. The students were led by Liu Zerong, a second-generation Russian-educated Chinese, the son of an immigrant tea producer of Guangdong origin. In 1918, the organization was transformed into a workers' association; and as such it served to propagate Communist ideas through its publications.

Chinese labour was made welcome once more in 1928–32, a time of rebuilding and development in the Soviet Far East, notably around Vladivostok. Working by day, Chinese labourers were made to study by night (socialism was one of the subjects taught). In Moscow, which was host to a Chinese community of about 8,000 people in the 1920s, an organization named Zhongguo Fuxing She (Society for the Revival of China), or Obshestvo vozrozhdenia Kitaya in Russian, was set up with the backing of the Soviet government. This was not only a support group for the local Chinese but a political organization aimed also at training pro-Russian Chinese cadres for future revolutionary work in China. Children of the Comintern's cadres and leading members of foreign Communist parties, including those from China, attended a special boarding school established under the aegis of this association in Ivanovo (near Moscow). Some of the pupils of this school – the offspring of Wang Ming (one of the 28 Bolsheviks), for example – became permanent residents. The association was also concerned with organizing and regulating Chinese trade in Russia.

The 'great friendship' with the Soviet Union forged by the Chinese Communists shortly after they took power in China in 1949 marked the third phase in the history of the Chinese in Russia. In 1950–55, the Chinese community there numbered about 350,000. When relations between the two countries degenerated towards the end of the 1950s into a bitter ideological quarrel and fierce border skirmishes, Chinese in the Soviet Union came under suspicion as 'spies' and 'fifth-columnists.' So long as the Chinese believed that the Soviet Union constituted the greatest threat to their country, it held little attraction as an immigrant destination.

Chinese traders in Vladivostok.

The 1990s

All this changed with the collapse of the political system and the liberalization of Russian society at the end of the 1980s, when the fourth phase of the history of the Chinese in Russia began. Chinese were one of many ethnic groups to arrive in the country when it opened the doors to aliens. In the 1990s, before Russia had had the opportunity to create immigration laws, it experienced an explosive growth in immigration from not only the countries of the former Soviet Union but Africa, the Middle East and China.

Before 1992, when President Boris Yeltsin created the Federal Migration Service, Russia had no immigration legislation. In 1994, the Russian Parliament passed two resolutions directing the Federal Migration Service to implement policies to prevent the occurance of illegal immigration, the conditions for which, given Russian inexperience in regulating migratory flows, were particularly favourable.

The number of Chinese immigrants granted residence permits has been small. One report, *Itogy* (The Results), published by the Russian Centre for the Study of Public Opinion in 1997, puts the number of Chinese applying officially for such permits in 1995 at only 83. Similarly, official Chinese statistics give the number of Chinese living around the Amur River and in Khabarovsk at 87 Chinese and 75 families respectively. But the Russian Ministry of Foreign Affairs and its local departments in the Russian Far East are convinced that the actual numbers of Chinese are far higher – some estimates put them at four to six million.

In 1993, about 2.5 million Chinese visited Russia, dwarfing the numbers of visitors from other countries. A spot check revealed that at least one third of these arrivals were keen to stay in Russia for a long period and a quarter declared that they would be able to do so. A 1994 report by the International Organization for Migration (IOM) in Brussels alludes to an expert estimate of 200,000 Chinese, the majority living in the eastern part of Russia or Siberia with some 10,000 in Moscow and thousands in other large cities.

Of the 309 migrants of African, Middle Eastern and Asian origin questioned by the IOM, only the Chinese and Vietnamese interviewees (who together made up 15

CHINESE WORKERS IN RUSSIA, 1860s–1917

From the 1860s to the early years of the 20th century, huge numbers of Chinese migrant workers (principally from the northeastern provinces as well as Shandong) had freely moved throughout the Russian Far East and Siberia, clearing forests, building and repairing railroads (especially the Trans-Siberian railroad during the 1890s), exploiting gold-mines north of the Heilongjiang river and constructing the harbour at Vladivostok. Although from the 1860s, and particularly after the turn of the century, the Russian government began to place restrictions on Chinese immigrants and to discourage further entry (out of strategic concerns as well as its desire to satisfy the demands of a growing Russian population in the area), Chinese seasonal migration continued unabated. The Chinese population of Russia's Maritime Province, for example, increased from 47,390 in 1906 to 68,355 in 1908; in the spring of 1907 alone, over 1,000 seasonal workers sailed to Vladivostok from the Chinese ports of Weihaiwei and Qingdao. Excluding short-term residents, one estimate puts the Chinese population of the Russian Far East at just over 111,000 in 1911.

World War I led to acute shortages of labour in Russia and this prompted a change of government policy. In 1915 it sanctioned the recruitment of Chinese indentured labour, to be used throughout the country rather than just the Russian Far East. Although such recruitment was to be based on clearly defined contracts stipulating location and wages (and approved of by Chinese local officials), the pressing Russian need for labour meant that much of the process was unregulated and unsupervised, leading to abuses similar to those of the notorious coolie trade of the 19th century (see p 61). Estimates of the total number of Chinese workers recruited by the Tsarist government between 1915 and 1917 vary from 30,000 and 100,000 to 500,000.

Many worked on the repair of the Murmansk railroad in the north (where 400 died of cold and hunger); others toiled in the oilfields in Georgia and coalmines in the south. Despite officials' guarantees that Chinese labour would not be used in combat zones, many Chinese workers were in fact sent to European Russia close to the front line. Up to 7,000 may have been killed by German fire.

Paul Bailey

Chinese labour building the Trans-Siberian Railway.

per cent of the sample) had evidently gained from coming to Russia, having achieved the main purpose of their migration, which was to work. None of the 23 Chinese interviewees was unemployed or suffering financial difficulty, and the main reason given for leaving China was the very low wages there. Six out of the eight married respondents had left their families in China and two had left children in China. Despite having relatives and friends in many parts of the world, most of the Chinese were unlike the other ethnic groups in that they were not 'transit migrants' using Russia as a stepping stone to another country so much as classic sojourners intending to earn money and then return home. Only four said that they would like to go to the West (two to the United States, one to Hungary and one to any other European country).

All had a visa, 14 claiming to have paid between US$100 and US$150 for theirs. Only two had come via a third country (Kazakhstan and Belarus), the majority having entered Russia directly. Compared to the interviewees from other ethnic groups, the Chinese were particularly guarded, those engaged in trade most of all. Traders apart, the main groups of Chinese surveyed were students, labourers and office clerks. Nine had come as students, and experts believe that the 'student channel' was widely used by Chinese to enter Russia: once entry was achieved, few appeared at their educational institutions or kept up their studies before embarking on business activities.

Geographical distribution

Historically, the Russian Far East has been the favoured location of Chinese settlement. Although the main sites of Chinese settlement there are Vladivostok, Khabarovsk, Irkutsk, Ulan-Ude and Chita, it may be more accurate today to speak of 'plural centres' since there has been a movement towards the western regions and to big cities

Chinese traders travel to Moscow every month on the Trans-Mongolia Railway.

such as Moscow and St Petersburg.

Official statistics put the number of Chinese in Moscow in 1989 at 11,335, but police and other sources have arrived at estimates of between 50,000 to 200,000, the majority of them unregistered residents. They are scattered through a number of districts, but if any part of Moscow may be identified as a core Chinese area, that part is to the north, between the Medvedkovo and Rechnoy vokzal underground stations. The dilapidated houses previously serving as the local universities' dormitories have become their apartments and offices. The Chinese are at their most concentrated in the All-Russian Exhibition Centre, a huge complex comprising exhibition pavilions, parks, fountains and pedestrian precincts. A third of the pavilions are occupied by Chinese small traders or owned by Chinese or Chinese-Russian joint ventures.

Since the mid-1990s, small cities in the central European part of Russia such as Nizhny Novgorod, Voronezh and Tula have attracted Chinese migrants. Not only is it cheaper to live in these places, the opportunities to strike (often illegal) business deals with the local administration are greater.

Social and economic profile

A clear distinction may be made between the old settlers, those who came to Russia decades ago and consider themselves 'native Russian Chinese,' and the newcomers, who are often intensely disliked by the former. The influence of the leading members of those who arrived in the 1950s is, if not directly thwarted, decidedly circumscribed. The mediating role is assumed by the Association of Moscow Chinese Overseas (Mosike Huaqiao Huaren Lianhehui), which began publishing a Chinese-language newspaper, Russian-Chinese Bulletin (*Zhong E xinxi bao*) in 1996. In that year, too, the Haiwai Huashang Gonghui, an association of overseas Chinese businessmen (with a membership of 25,000 in 1997), was established in Moscow.

The biggest group of Chinese consists of wholesale merchants and their families. In Moscow, 503 Chinese companies were registered in 1997, but such official statistics are often meaningless because so much Chinese business is unlicensed. For example, whether they make a living from teaching martial arts and *qigong* (Chinese yoga), or from treating patients, the Chinese do so without a licence or official registration. From trading, the more successful members of the Chinese community have moved into banking and finance. Meanwhile, for certain private banks in Moscow, Khabarovsk and other cities, Chinese have become especially important clients.

Ethnic businesses exist to supply Chinese with food, reading matter and other goods from China. In Moscow

Leather jackets and other Chinese goods displayed for Russian wholesale traders visiting this centre, which hosts the biggest community of Chinese in Moscow, the only real 'Chinatown.'

and Khabarovsk, Chinese have opened casinos catering exclusively to a Chinese clientele. However, the restaurants and fast-food joints commonly associated with Chinese elsewhere in Europe are not particularly prevalent, and there are no more than a dozen such places in Moscow and half a dozen in St Petersburg.

What has formed the background to the Chinese pursuit of economic opportunities, often described as illegal, has been the interpenetration of crime, government and business in Russia itself. The arbitrary power of bureaucrats and the burden of federal and local taxes, no less than the plethora of permits and bribes needed to do anything, has made it almost impossible to run a business entirely legally even if one wanted to, and even if one could find law-abiding government officials with whom to collaborate.

Many Russians in border towns, watching Chinese chalk up sales in the markets, believe they are witnessing a commercial invasion from the south. While some see economic benefits to encouraging Chinese trade – a pro-Chinese faction based mainly on financial interest has developed in Russian politics – others fear unregulated Chinese expansion, estimating that in the eastern regions of Russia, Chinese immigrants could form the majority of the population within 20 years.

Alexei Maslov

Chinese businessman in Moscow.

JAPAN

Although the Chinese are the second largest foreign group in Japan (after the Korean), they numbered only 234,264 in 1996, less than 0.19 per cent of a total population of 125.9 million. A smaller number still, 33,578, are counted as residents, and of these only 30,376 have gained permanent resident status. Neither the geographical proximity of China and Japan, nor the importance of the contribution of each to the other's cultural and modern transformation, seems to have led to the growth of a sizeable Chinese settlement. Many of the reasons lie in the strict enforcement of regulations governing the residence and employment of foreigners in Japan which has use only for people and goods it considers economically, socially and culturally necessary. As a result, a particular regionally based group (or *bang*) of Chinese, one able to offer services and goods in demand, gained power in Japan.

Nagasaki

Among early Chinese immigrants to Japan were scribes, potters, weavers and metal workers. From these the Japanese acquired technical skills, knowledge of the Chinese script, Confucianism and Buddhism. Owing to China's restrictive trade policies during the Ming and Qing

Map 5.29

dynasties (see p 99), much of the commerce between the two countries was illegal, conducted by Japanese and Chinese merchant adventurers and pirates (Wako, the Japanese pronunciation of a Chinese term, *wokou*) whose raids were a scourge to East Asian coasts from the 13th to the 17th centuries. To judge by the records of the licensed trade conducted between the early 15th and the mid-16th centuries, the goods exchanged were silks, porcelains and copper cash from China and copper, sulphur, painted folding fans and swords from Japan. The Chinese government's efforts to crush these raiders drove some of them to seek refuge and perhaps settlement in Japanese ports. Kyushu, which the pirates used as their base, probably supported sojourning communities of Hokkien Chinese.

But the comings and goings of Chinese did not fall into an enduring pattern until the start of the Tokugawa shogunate (1603–1867), when the port of Nagasaki began to host a small settlement of Chinese merchants. In the early and mid-17th century, Chinese ships – notably those owned by the Hokkien merchants, Li Dan, Zheng Zhilong and his son Zheng Chenggong by a Japanese wife – linked Japan with the newly opened up island of Taiwan as well as with Fujian and Manila (see p 49).

The trade ships which arrived at Nagasaki had come from the coasts of not only Fujian but Zhejiang, Jiangsu and Jiangxi (collectively known as Sanjiang, or 'Three Jiangs'), all areas of resistance against the alien Qing dynasty that had replaced the Ming. To suggest that they were not Qing subjects, the traders called themselves Tangren ('Tang people'), or Tojin in Japanese, and their ships were known as 'Tang ships' or Tosen. The master mariners and mates were largely Hokkien or of Sanjiang origin, while the crews tended to be Hokchia (natives of Fuqing, in Fujian province), who were remunerated by being allowed to bring small cargoes of their own for trading at their destination.

The port was a home base for intermittent seasonal traders, sojourners-turned-stayers and permanent residents. In 1604, the Japanese authorities appointed the first of the Chinese commissioners, Feng Liu, to serve as a liaison and to oversee the Chinese community. Feng married a Japanese and died in Nagasaki. Most of his successors were the offspring of Chinese fathers and Japanese mothers.

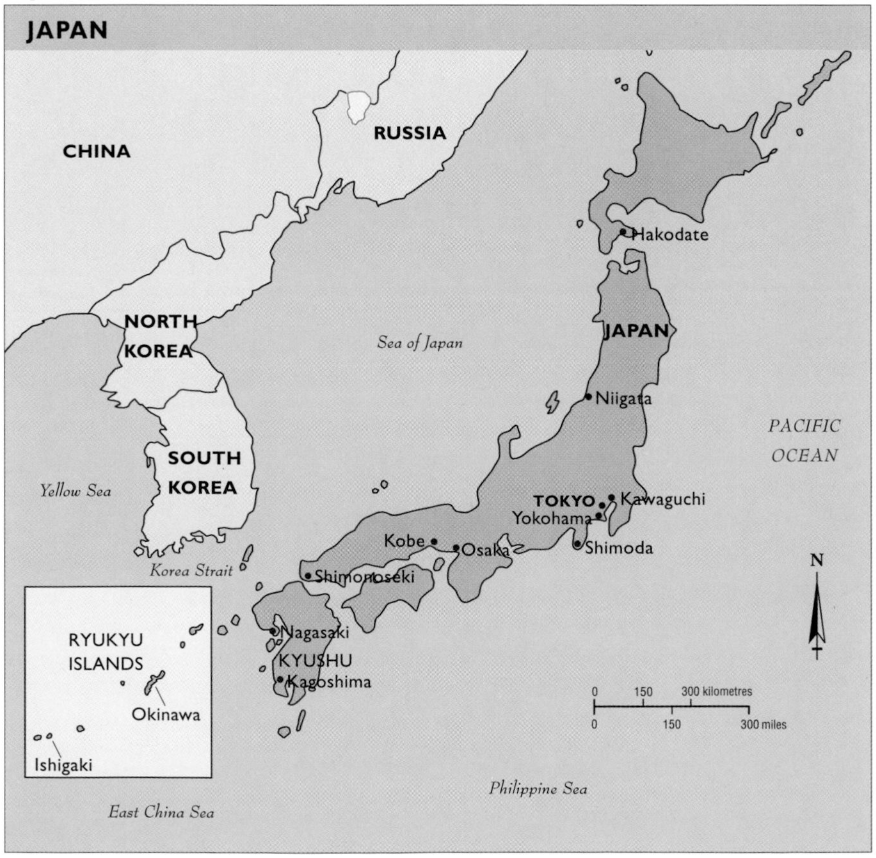

One of these commissioners' responsibilities was to prevent the practice of the Christian religion, regarded by the Tokugawa as a subversive foreign influence. From 1612 onwards all Christian missionary activity was banned and suspected Christians persecuted. To make clear their religious affiliation, Chinese erected Buddhist temples, each place-of-origin group – or *bang* – building their own: the Sanjiang group the Xingfu Monastery in 1623, the Hokkiens the Fuji Monastery in 1628, and the eastern Fujianese (mainly Fuzhou and Hokchia speakers) the Chongfu Monastery in 1629. (The Cantonese, whose heyday had yet to come, built their Shengfu Monastery nearly 50 years later.) These temples have remained sites of historical interest in Nagasaki, while contemporary festivities marked by dragon dances in October and dragon boat racing in May hark back to the days when, to the sound of gongs and dragon dancing, merchant seamen carried images of Mazu, Empress of Heaven (Tianhou), from their ships and placed them in the four temples for the duration of their sojourn in the port. The temples served both as places of worship and as community associations responsible for ritual, burial and welfare matters and for mediating disputes among the Chinese.

Chinese also raised a temple to Confucius in 1647. This was damaged by bombs during World War II, rebuilt in 1967 and again in 1980, the second time with the help of the Confucius Temple in Qufu, the sage's birthplace in Shandong province. Ceremonies marking Confucius's birthday are still held there today. A primary school in the temple ran classes for both boys and girls for more than 80 years until diminishing Chinese numbers forced it to close in 1988.

In 1639 the shogunate ushered in two centuries of national seclusion, during which Japan's foreign trade contacts were limited to the Koreans, Dutch and Chinese. In contrast to the dozen Dutch trading vessels that might dock at Nagasaki each year, between 30 (during 1611–47) and 49 (1648–61) Chinese merchant junks arrived annually, the number increasing after the lifting of the Qing ban on overseas trade. In a peak year, 1688, 193 ships arrived, bringing 9,128 people. Fujianese ships were numerically dominant, no fewer than 86 out of the 193, while Zhejiang sent 40, Guangdong 30, and Taiwan and Southeast Asia 14.

To slow the outflow of copper, the Tokugawa encouraged the export of seafood in exchange for Chinese silk, set limits on copper exports (thereby giving rise to smuggling) and eventually restricted the number of Chinese ships allowed in, first to 70 and then, in 1715, to only 30, distributed as follows: ten from Nanjing (in Jiangsu), 11 from Ningbo (Zhejiang), two from Amoy (southern Fujian), two each from Taiwan and Guangdong and the rest among motley others. Furthermore, by specifying that each ship must only carry the products of its own source locality, the Tokugawa gave the silk-producing areas of Jiangsu and Zhejiang an advantage at the expense of the Fujianese, who had been conducting a profitable coastal trade shipping sugar northwards and picking up

silk at Jiangsu and Zhejiang for shipment and sale in Japan. Conflict between the two groups resulted, from which the Jiangsu-Zhejiang group emerged the stronger, eclipsing the Fujianese dominance in Nagasaki, and becoming in time the chief dealer in Japanese marine products.

The initial Chinese right to live anywhere in the city was progressively curtailed until, in 1688, the entire community was confined to a 9,373-*tsubo* (about 31,025 square metres) Chinese enclosure. Chinese chafed at their ghettoization, and on occasion they and their Japanese guards would come to blows. It was not until the early 19th century that restrictions were relaxed and Chinese pedlars could be seen in the streets of the city.

The opening of Japan

A turning point in Japanese history, the country's opening to the West in 1858, set off a chain of events that culminated in the Meiji Restoration, the series of political, economic and social changes that turned Japan into a unified modern state. Treaties concluded with the United States and European powers successively opened the ports of Shimoda, Hakodate, Kanagawa (modern Yokohama), Nagasaki, Niigata, Hyogo (modern Kobe), Edo (today's Tokyo) and Osaka to Western residence. As in the treaty ports in China, Westerners enjoyed extraterritoriality in the foreign concessions, a status which permitted them to be tried by their own courts and laws. The resident Chinese, however, were not accorded that status until a Sino-Japanese treaty – opening eight ports to Chinese trade and residence – was signed in 1871. Before that date, the Japanese government regarded them as aliens living under its jurisdiction. After that date, the Chinese were properly registered (and assigned according to their income to classes: three in Yokohama and two, upper and lower, in Kobe).

The majority of the Western merchants that appeared in these ports had run businesses in China, and when they established branch firms in Japan, they brought with them their Chinese employees and servants, who lived in the foreign concessions as the Westerners' 'affiliates.' These Chinese, many of them compradors, were crucial intermediaries between these Europeans, who spoke no Japanese, and the locals, who spoke no foreign language and lacked any experience of dealing with Europeans – so much so that these Chinese have been described as 'agents of Westernization' in Japan. Since the Japanese had adopted the Chinese script, they could communicate with even non-Japanese speaking Chinese by doing so in writing.

The Cantonese, of all Chinese speech groups the most conversant with Western ways (thanks to Canton's early opening to the West), at last came into their own as the interface between the local and foreign communities, and additionally as commission merchants commercially connected to Guangdong, Hong Kong and Southeast Asia. An even larger number of Chinese not 'affiliated' to Westerners also arrived in the ports following their opening, many of them becoming nominal dependants of Europeans by paying the latter a fee and renting property in the foreign concessions.

The Japanese resented the Western domination of Japan's foreign trade and also the part which Chinese

Japanese artist's impression of Chinese trader in the Qing dynasty.

Chinese compradors in Yokohama.

Table 5.44

CHINESE POPULATION IN JAPAN, 1876–1942

Year	Total	Year	Total	Year	Total	Year	Total	Year	Total
1876	2,266	1891	5,344	1904	9,411	1919	12,294	1932	18,471
1877	2,218	1892	5,574	1905	10,388	1920	14,258	1933	20,599
1878	2,810	1893	5,343	1906	12,425	1921	15,056	1934	23,968
1879	3,281	1895	3,642	1907	12,273	1922	16,936	1935	28,000
1880	3,046	1896	4,533	1908	10,847	1923	12,843	1936	29,671
1884	4,143	1897	5,206	1910	8,420	1924	16,902	1937	17,584
1885	4,071	1898	6,130	1911	8,145	1926	22,272	1938	17,043
1886	4,130	1899	6,359	1913	11,867	1927	23,934	1939	18,622
1887	4,209	1900	6,890	1915	12,046	1928	29,297	1940	20,284
1888	4,805	1901	7,730	1916	11,869	1929	31,827	1941	18,078
1889	4,975	1902	8,027	1917	13,755	1930	31,890	1942	19,195
1890	5,498	1903	7,423	1918	12,139	1931	19,135		

Numbers include inhabitants of Manchukuo but not those of Taiwan.
Sources: For 1876–1927, Nagata Goro. 'Ryunichi kakyo no jinko to shokugyo.' In Keizai to boeki 83 (Sept. 1963): 46–53. Yokohama Siritsu Daigaku Keizai Kenkyusho. For 1928–42, Naimusho Keihokyoku, ed. Gaiji keisatsu gaikyo. Fuji Shuppan, 1989 Fukkoku 6 (1928–40): 332; 7 (1941): 463; 8 (1942): 807.

Table 5.45

CHINESE POPULATION IN JAPAN, 1946–96

Year	Total	Year	Total	Year	Total	Year	Total	Year	Total
1946	30,847	1955	43,865	1964	49,174	1973	46,642	1982	59,122
1947	32,889	1956	43,372	1965	49,418	1974	47,677	1983	63,164
1948	36,932	1957	44,710	1966	49,387	1975	48,728	1984	67,895
1949	38,241	1958	44,789	1967	49,592	1976	47,174	1986	84,397
1950	40,481	1959	45,255	1968	50,445	1977	47,862	1988	129,269
1951	43,377	1960	45,535	1969	50,816	1978	48,528	1990	150,339
1952	42,147	1961	46,326	1970	51,841	1979	50,353	1992	195,334
1953	43,778	1962	47,096	1971	52,333	1980	52,896	1994	218,585
1954	43,282	1963	47,827	1972	48,089	1981	55,616	1996	234,264

Sources: For 1947–79, Homusho Nyukoku Kanrikyoku, ed. Shutsunyukokukanri no kaiko to tenbo – Nyukan hossoku 30 Shunen o kinen shite, 1980. For 1980–96, Homusho Nyukokukanrikyoku,ed. Zairyu gaikokujin tokei.

Nanking Road in Yokohama.

in China as the writer Su Manshu, was brought up by Kawai in Yokohama until he was taken back to Guangdong as a six-year-old in 1889. However, in 1898, Su Manshu returned to Yokohama to study at the Datong School (see below). Later he enrolled at the Seijo Gakko Academy and joined a number of revolutionary organizations set up by Chinese students in Tokyo (see box), but it was back in China, primarily Shanghai, that he found his *métier* as a translator (he was the first to introduce Byron to China), poet and writer of fiction (some with Japanese characters).

In Nagasaki, a fire had burned down the Chinese enclosure in 1869. In its vicinity, in Hirobaba and Shinchi, many Chinese settled with their families. The census of 1880 counted 549 Chinese residents in the city, 490 men and 59 women. In Hirobaba, the Cantonese built their temple-cum-community association in 1871. The ambiguity between temple and guild association disappeared when the Sanjiang and Fujian groupings began establishing *gongsuo*, or guild houses (see p 77), and native-place organizations (or *huiguan*) in the late 1880s.

Of the Chinese merchants who prospered in Nagasaki, the most prominent was Chen Shiwang (1869–1940), a Fujianese from Quemoy whose father Chen Guoliang had arrived in the port before 1850 and initiated a business network linking Japan, China and Nanyang. The family business, Taiyi Hao, greatly expanded during the lifetime of the second generation, with Chen Shiwang's brother, Shike, establishing a branch firm in Kobe. The voluminous company records, donated to a museum by the descendants, have become a valuable source of study by both Japanese and Chinese historians.

Nagasaki, having lost its position as Japan's only international seaport, declined in importance, and its Chinese settlement, one of three 'Chinatowns' in Japan, paled before those of Kobe and Yokohama. The latter city, with its Chinatown located within the foreign settlement, had the largest registered Chinese population: 1,002 in 1869; 2,169 (including 306 women) in 1880 and 3,644 in 1907. The bulk hailed from Guangdong, principally the Pearl River Delta counties of Xiangshan (now Zhongshan), Nanhai and Shunde. Records (part of which were destroyed in an earthquake and during World War II) show that Cantonese merchants, traditional *qianzhuang* bankers, foodstuff dealers and other trades established their own association in 1898. After steamship lines were opened between Yokohama and Shanghai in 1875, the numbers hailing from Jiangsu, Zhejiang and Fujian increased, but never sufficiently to challenge the dominance of Cantonese.

Yokohama's Chinatown, founded in 1873, remains the largest in Japan, with 260 restaurants attracting some 12 million visitors a year. Its Guandi Temple, inaugurated in 1876, has been damaged three times but, refurbished in 1990 with the help of donations and the support of both Japan and China, has become a popular tourist site.

Yokohama had Japan's first umbrella Chinese organization, the Chinese Huiguan, established in 1873. It also had the first Chinese school, the founding of which was closely tied to the opening of the Yokohama branch of Sun Yat-sen's anti-Qing, revolutionist organization, the Revive China Society, or Xingzhong Hui, the chief

compradors and merchants played in that domination. Conflicts arose additionally from the Japanese authorities' attempts to suppress Chinese opium smoking. But the pattern of Chinese-Japanese social relations mingled discord and distance with closeness, and many Chinese men formed liaisons with Japanese women beyond those recorded by the number of permits taken out for intermarriage. To cite just one example, a Cantonese comprador, Su Jiesheng, the manager of a British-owned tea trading company in Yokohama, had a Japanese concubine, Kawai, and a half-Japanese son by her maid (and possibly niece). His son, one day to become renowned

CHINESE STUDENTS IN JAPAN IN THE EARLY 20TH CENTURY

Japan's defeat of Russia in 1905 strengthened the country's appeal as a destination for overseas study since it was seen as confirmation that an Asian country could successfully modernize by promoting Westernizing change while retaining indigenous values. Overseas study in Japan at this time was thus considered a convenient short-cut for the acquisition of Western knowledge (via Japanese translations). It was also officially encouraged as a means of producing a future corps of government administrators, teachers and military officers. When the Confucian-based civil service examination system was abolished in 1905, a modern education acquired either in the new schools within China or overseas in Japan and the West gained a new legitimacy.

Although Chinese had begun to go to Japan as early as 1896 (when 13 attended the Tokyo Higher Normal School), the numbers increased dramatically after 1901. In 1902 there were between 400 and 500 Chinese students in Japan; by 1906 the total had reached nearly 9,000. Overall, during the period 1898–1911, an estimated 25,000 Chinese students went to Japan for some kind of schooling. The significance of Japan as a location for overseas study before 1911 is also evident from by the fact that of the 1,388 foreign-educated Chinese students who passed the new civil service examinations between 1906 and 1911, 90 per cent were graduates of Japanese institutions. By 1903 Chinese students came from every province in China (with the exception of Gansu), although those from the more prosperous central-south provinces of Jiangsu and Zhejiang predominated. Figures from 1903 indicate that of the 663 students for whom information was available, 67 per cent were aged between 17 and 25 years; most came from scholar-official families and had received a classical Confucian education. Not surprisingly, given the social background of the students, as many as 60 per cent were self-financing while the remaining 40 per cent were recipients of central/provincial government scholarships or sponsored by business/merchant associations. Reflecting the Qing dynasty's emphasis after 1901 on government, educational and military reform, the majority of Chinese students in Japan enrolled in liberal arts, teacher training and military study programmes. Most of these programmes, however, were only short-term (some of which were especially established for Chinese students by the Japanese authorities and of dubious quality); in 1907, for example, of the 7,000 Chinese students listed, 60 per cent were enrolled in short-term courses while only 3–4 per cent were attending higher specialized schools.

Japanese government officials and educators from the beginning welcomed the influx of Chinese students. Motives ranged from an altruistic desire to contribute to China's modernization to the more pragmatic ambition of enhancing Japan's influence in China. The latter was symbolized in 1898 by the creation of the To-A Dobunkai (East Asia Common Culture Society), a Japanese government-subsidized organization that promoted Sino-Japanese cultural and educational links, collected intelligence-gathering data on China and lobbied for a more active government policy in East Asia. In 1902 it established a preparatory school for Chinese students in Japan, the Tokyo Dobun Shoin, one of a number of schools especially set up in Japan for incoming Chinese students. These included preparatory military schools (the Seijo Gakko and Shinbu Gakko) to train Chinese students for the prestigious Japanese Army Officers School (Rikugun Shikan Gakko) and the Kobun Institute (Kobun Gakuin), founded in 1902 to provide training in the Japanese language as well as the elements of a middle school education.

Significantly also, provision was made for Chinese female students when Shimoda Utako (1854–1936) in 1902 accepted seven Chinese women to

Revolutionaries among Fujian students in Japan.

study at her Women's Practical Arts School (Jissen Jogakko), which she had founded in 1899. The school subsequently enrolled 20 women from Hunan province in 1904 and 21 from Fengtian province in 1907 for teacher training, and in 1908 opened a separate Chinese division. More than 200 Chinese women were trained at Shimoda's school up to 1914. Although the number of Chinese female students in Japan was always small compared to that of male students (their numbers grew from 11 in 1903 to 100 in 1907, when they constituted about 1 per cent of the Chinese student population), their presence nevertheless was a pathbreaking phenomenon. Hitherto the only Chinese female students to have gone abroad were the few sponsored by missionaries to study medicine in the US at the end of the 19th century. It is also interesting to note that formal education for girls within China itself was not officially sanctioned until 1907, although a number of primary and vocational schools for girls had already been opened by local gentry and officials before then.

The differing hopes cherished by the Qing dynasty and Japanese authorities concerning overseas study were not entirely fulfilled. Chinese students remained aloof from Japanese society (in later memoirs some were to refer bitterly to the condescending and sometimes contemptuous attitudes demonstrated by the host society towards their 'backward' Chinese guests) and very few returned to China harbouring special feelings of affinity with Japan. During their sojourn many Chinese students became highly politicized, publishing journals and magazines that not only discussed modern political concepts (nationalism, republicanism) and radical ideologies (anarchism, socialism) – often via translations from Japanese works – but also condemned the Qing government's reform programme as a sham and its stance in the wake of growing foreign encroachment in China as vacillating and even treasonous. Students also created their own associations and became involved in political protest (for example, calling for resistance against Russia in 1903 when it became clear that Russian troops that had entered Manchuria were delaying their evacuation of the area) or demonstrations against attempts by Chinese and Japanese authorities to enforce a stricter supervision and control of the Chinese student body.

In 1905 up to 4,000 Chinese students participated in protests against Japanese government regulations restricting the number of students who could reside off-campus and preventing students from enrolling in an educational institution if they had been expelled from another. In the wake of these protests 2,000 students returned home and the numbers of Chinese overseas students in Japan declined in subsequent years. By 1910 there were just over 2,000. Some students, having joined Sun Yat-sen's anti-Manchu organization, the Tongmeng Hui (Alliance League), when it was established in Tokyo in 1905, became activists on their return to China, either disseminating anti-dynastic propaganda in the new schools or forging revolutionary links with the new army units (many of whose Japanese-trained younger officers were likewise influenced by nationalist and republican ideals) and the more traditional secret societies. By the time the 1911 Revolution had overthrown the monarchy and led to the formal establishment of a Republic in 1912, only 1,400 Chinese students remained in Japan.

Although Chinese students continued to go to Japan after 1912 – on the eve of the Sino-Japanese War in 1937, for example, their numbers were 5,000–6,000 in total – the enormous attraction the country had exerted as a destination for overseas study during the first years of the 20th century was not sustained in the 1920s and 1930s against the background of an increasingly aggressive Japanese encroachment in China. Also, as modern educational institutions proliferated in China (many of which were staffed by foreign-trained Chinese teachers), the need to seek western knowledge abroad became less urgent. Finally, other countries such as the US and France became major destinations for Chinese overseas students in the 1910s and 1920s.

Paul Bailey

Guandi Temple, Yokohama.

1921, and after the Huaqiao School's destruction by the 1923 earthquake, this was combined with the other two to form what came to be known as the Chinese Public School (Zhonghua Gongli Xuexiao). Later, as a result of the conflict between the Kuomintang and the Communists, the school split into two; the pro-Kuomintang school, enjoying generous funding, is today housed in a five-storey, well-equipped building.

Chinese moved to Kobe, some from Nagasaki, after it opened and 516 Chinese, including 91 women, were found to be living there in 1880, the number rising to 1,800 by 1911. The community was predominantly Cantonese, whose trading operations spanned southern China, Nanyang, Hawaii and California and who were regarded as competitors by the Western traders. Although these Westerners repeatedly complained that, as China was not a treaty power, these Chinese were trading illegally, they demurred when the Japanese authorities asked them to report those not 'affiliated' to them.

The Cantonese set up their own *gongsuo* in 1876, the premises of which moved a number of times until they came to rest at the spot occupied today by the Kobe Chinese Chamber of Commerce, one floor of which houses a small museum of overseas Chinese history. Among Cantonese who prospered was Mai Shaopeng (1861–1910), who inherited a business house, Yihe Hao, which his father had set up in Japan when the latter arrived as a 20-year-old from his natal Guangdong. Among other business pursuits, he exported matches, an important item of Kobe's foreign trade with China and Southeast Asia. However, speculative losses in the stock market later forced him to leave Kobe for Southeast Asia. Taken ill in Singapore, Mai Shaopeng died in Hong Kong in 1910.

Kobe also hosted a smaller community of people from Jiangsu and Zhejiang, the merchants of which cultivated their corporate identity through the Sanjiang Gongsuo and made their money trading with northern and central China. Among them the most successful was Wu Jintang (1854–1926), who arrived in Nagasaki in 1885 from Zhejiang and moved from there to Kobe five years later, establishing the Yisheng Shanghao trading company to import cloth, soybean and bean cakes and export seafood and matches. Later, he bought a majority share in a Japanese textiles company, Kanebo; contributed to Sun Yat-sen's cause, supported welfare and educational causes both in Japan and in his native Zhejiang. Decorated by the Japanese government, he became a naturalized Japanese citizen in 1904, but five years after he died his body was shipped to his native place in China for burial.

Leading merchants such as Wu and Mai all sat on the board of the Kobe-Osaka Chinese Huiguan (see below) and donated to the renovation of its premises. So did Wang Jingxiang, the son of Wang Mingyu, an immigrant from Quemoy, Fujian, who founded the family firm Fuxing Hao. In 1913, Wang Jingxiang became the comprador of a bank, Yokohama-Shokin Ginko. His wife, Lin Zhenyu, was the granddaughter of a Singapore Chinese community leader, Lin Lu. His son and heir was named Zhongshan by Sun Yat-sen, whose revolutionary cause he ardently supported. During World War II he stayed for a period in Saigon, Vietnam, but

local movers of which were two Cantonese brothers, Feng Jingru and Feng Zishan. In a reflection of the politics of China, one dimension of which was the rivalry between Sun Yat-sen and the monarchist reformer Kang Youwei (see p 101), when the Feng brothers came under the latter's influence, the school became strongly biased towards the Emperor Protection Society (which Kang had founded). Named Zhongxi by Sun in 1897, the school was subsequently renamed Datong, 'Great Unity,' Kang's vision for the future as set forth in his book *Datong Shu* (*The Book of the Great Unity*). It had hoped to have Kang's renowned disciple, Liang Qichao, as its headmaster, but Liang was too busy to accept and suggested another of his mentor's disciples, Xu Qin, instead. The school's pupils, it has been reported, were required to bow to the image of Confucius every Sunday and risked expulsion if they refused. Apart from Chinese, the pupils learned English, taught by graduates of Hong Kong's Queen's College.

That the school taught classes in Cantonese was one reason the Sanjiang *bang* set up their own school in 1898, one which used Shanghainese as the medium of instruction. Another noteworthy school was the pro-Republican Huaqiao School, established with the support of the newly founded revolutionary party Tongmeng Hui (see box p 335). A third, privately funded, was founded in later returned to Kobe. Now into its sixth generation in Japan, the Wang family continues to interest itself in the affairs of the Chinese community.

Many of the merchants in Kobe were in fact re-migrants from nearby Osaka, which had 116 Chinese in 1880. At the instigation of the Chinese consul, and with a view to breaking down narrow native-place ties and strengthening cross-*bang* and inter-city connections, the Chinese established the Kobe-Osaka Chinese Huiguan in 1892. Representation on the board, however, reflected the relative commercial strengths of the various regional groups, with Kobe Cantonese, for example, occupying the largest number of seats and Osaka traders of southern origin occupying the fewest.

Cantonese were also the first Chinese to trade and settle in Hakodate, arriving as the compradors and interpreters of Western merchants. The Sanjiang contingent which followed them was to dominate the trade in marine products – of which Hakodate was a considerable producer – defeating their Japanese competitors (whom the government advantaged by its market regulations) by making it more attractive for local producers to sell to them rather than to the Japanese dealers. This they did by offering cash advances and guaranteeing purchases.

The Chinese Huiguan in Hakodate is the only one in Japan to have survived World War II. In the postwar period its exclusivity was successfully challenged by Chinese of Hokchia (Fuqing) origin, who, occupying a lower rung of Chinese society, had not previously been admitted to its membership.

The imperial ordinance 352

The extensive programme of reform and modernization which characterized the early Meiji period would bear fruit in the emergence of Japan as the dominant power in East Asia. In a landmark war against China in 1894, one concluded with the Treaty of Shimonoseki in 1895, Japanese forces utterly defeated China, which from then on became an object of Japanese exploitation and imperialist ambition. With the abolition of foreign settlements and extraterritoriality thereafter, the war marked the end of a brief period in which Chinese in Japan enjoyed parity with Westerners as privileged foreigners. A wave of nationalistic boycotts of Japanese goods in China hurt the interests of those engaged in the China trade, which in time fell increasingly into the hands of the Japanese.

Owing largely to a series of ordinances governing the entry of Chinese of selective occupational categories, the composition of the Chinese population changed significantly after the war. The Japanese government issued Ordinance 352 restricting the admission of foreign labourers. Those who drafted and deliberated the ordinance were in fact targeting Chinese immigrants. However, the Privy Council which debated the issue decided to exempt petty traders from those prohibited entry, probably because pedlars were everywhere welcome in Japan and because China itself hosted many expatriate Japanese either living by that trade or engaging in espionage for the military disguised as pedlars.

The effect of the ordinance was to encourage the growth of the Hokchia community, whose tradition of peddling harked back to the days when, as has been

mentioned earlier, they came as sailors bringing small cargoes of their own to sell on arrival at Nagasaki. The small contingent of Shandong pedlars offered them little competition as they came to monopolize petty trading, working either alone or with one other person, who could either be their employer or a creditor to whom they made interest payments of about 6 or 7 per cent. A characteristic of Hokchias was that they did not trespass on each other's territory, so that latecomers to the market would venture further and further afield until, in time, the networks of Hokchia vendors had spread far and wide.

After 1918, when regulations barring certain categories of foreigners from entering Japan were issued, many Hokchia petty traders were refused admission on the grounds that they fell into one of the categories, namely poor persons in need of relief. Indeed, how to distinguish labourers (by their big feet and thick arms, according to one set of instructions) became a preoccupation of Japanese officials at the various ports of entry. However, Japanese discrimination against petty traders did not diminish Hokchia numbers, which make up a tenth of the total number of Chinese permanent residents today.

A further exemption allowed in domestic servants, cooks and other service occupations. As had been the case with Chinese 'affiliated' to Westerners at the time of Japan's opening, this was dictated by the needs of Japan's American and European residents. 'Affiliated' Chinese included not only domestic servants but tailors, barbers and cooks, for Chinese in places like Shanghai and Canton had learned to make Western

Headquarters of the Chinese Huiguan in Hakodate.

Labels of match boxes distributed and exported by Chinese.

Wielder of one of the 'three knives.'

Momofuku Ando.

suits, give Western-style haircuts and prepare Western dishes earlier than the Japanese. The encouragement the entry regulations gave to the immigration of people providing these services gave rise to the occupational identification of Chinese in Japan with what is called *sanba dao*, 'three knives' – the barber's razor, the cook's cleaver and the tailor's scissors (named 'scissor-knife' in Chinese). A relaxation of the regulations in 1912 made it possible to approve the admission of hairdressers and cooks by a local rather than a higher-level authority. The relaxation did not apply to tailors, presumably because Japanese tailors had now taken the place of Chinese, and this is reflected in the occupational breakdown of Chinese in 1924, which gives 1,956 hairdressers, 1,509 cooks and 465 tailors.

The northern traders

After its victory over China – and later over Russia in 1905 – Japan developed spectacularly. Its first modern industry was textiles, and Japanese cotton was venturing into the world market on a significant scale at a time when its economic penetration of Manchuria, where it had won predominant rights, was expanding. Furthermore, World War I benefited Japanese manufacturers by greatly increasing the demand for Japanese goods in Asian and other markets severed from their usual European sources of supply. In 1915–20 the export of cotton goods almost doubled.

The new opportunities for gain this opened up were quickly seized by a group of Chinese, the northern *bang* of traders whose travel and relocation were greatly facilitated by the inauguration in 1899 of direct steamship sailings between Osaka, the old centre of the cotton trade, and the northern Chinese ports of Tianjin, Niuzhuang and Chefoo. Because they were located in Kawaguchi, the former foreign settlement area, the Japanese called them Kawaguchi-kasho, 'Kawaguchi Chinese merchants.' Numbering 307 in 1927, they lodged in inns-cum-brokers' storehouses, of which there were 16, six of them belonging to traders from Ningbo (Zhejiang), and the rest to those from the northern provinces.

Southern Chinese were second to these northerners in both number and financial strength. Their *gongsuo*, established in 1887, at first included the northerners in its membership, but as their numbers increased the latter set up their own separate trade association in 1895, one known from 1916 as the Chinese Northern Bang Gongsuo. In 1936, Chinese numbers in Osaka totalled 3,200, of whom 1,466 lived in Kawaguchi and about 400–500 were Hokchia petty traders.

Solidarity among fellow-regionals, combined with the support of their common-origin and common-trade *gongsuo*, made the northern Chinese traders' operations highly cost-effective and more than competitive against those of the Japanese. In 1936, the year before full-scale war broke out between China and Japan, Osaka's proportion of Japan's exports of cotton goods to China was 95.7 per cent. Of this, 28.4 per cent was handled by the Chinese traders. In 1935, of Osaka's exports of cotton goods to Manchuria, northern China and central China, these traders handled 58.4 per cent, 70.8 per cent and 35.9 per cent respectively. Although they were not active for long – from the late 19th century to 1937 – their

trade practices have rubbed off on the native Japanese merchants of Osaka – one reason, perhaps, for the reputation the latter enjoy as Japan's toughest businessmen.

Taiwanese

The Japanese invasion of China in 1937 led to a sharp fall in the size of the Chinese population in Japan, but by the conclusion of the Pacific War, it had more than rebounded (see tables 5.44 and 5.45). The composition of the Chinese community changed radically during the war years, with people from Taiwan – Formosans, as they are also called – accounting for the population's largest portion. Official statistics collected in 1940 show that they numbered 22,499 out of a total Chinese population of 20,284. In the immediate postwar period, they accounted for half the Chinese community. Taiwan had been a Japanese colony since its cession to Japan by the 1895 Treaty of Shimonoseki, and by virtue of that fact Taiwanese were Japanese nationals.

The Taiwanese population of postwar Japan fell mainly into five groups: students, traders, workers, teenage labour and demobilized troops. Official figures for 1930 give a total of 1,600 students in Tokyo, representing 64 per cent of Taiwanese resident in that city, the home of half the total Taiwanese population. These students were a vital force in the negotiations between the Chinese community, the Japanese government and the Allied (effectively American) powers which occupied Japan between 1945 and 1952.

The traders dealt mainly in Dajia straw mats (so called because they were chiefly produced in Dajia, Taiwan). The Japanese, monopolizing the commerce in other local products (sugar, rice and bananas), left little room for Taiwanese traders; how little may be seen from the fact that straw mats formed only 0.1 per cent of the value of Japan's imports from Taiwan. Imported mats were made into panama hats and exported to America and other countries. Though these traders tried to branch out into other lines of business, they lacked the experience and resources to succeed. However, they did do well in such sectors as food, real estate and entertainment. The most successful was a manufacturer of instant noodles, the Nissin company, whose Taiwan-born founder Wu Baifu (b. 1910), named Momofuku Ando in Japanese, turned a speciality of his native place, noodles with shredded chicken, into a product sold in markets worldwide.

The third category, workers, comprised young men who arrived in Japan to work in munitions factories during the war. Only by being employed in arms manufacture could young Taiwanese escape military conscription. They mostly concentrated in Osaka, where they had relatives. The fourth group comprised 14- and 15-year-old Taiwanese who had been brought to Japan to take the place of young Japanese who, by leaving for the front, had caused a shortage of labour at home. They were selected for their good scholastic performance, supposedly for technical training in Japan, but once there they were assigned to labouring jobs in munitions factories, where they were cruelly and harshly treated. When war ended, they were left, ill-clothed and hungry, to fend for themselves – which many of them could only do by theft and robbery. Finally, there were the demobbed Taiwanese soldiers who arrived with the returning Japanese troops; some were returned to Taiwan but many stayed.

The Occupation administration treated these five groups differently from those of mainland China origin. The latter were deemed nationals of the United Nations and enjoyed rights and special food rations denied to 'nationals of countries formally under the domination of Japan.' However, in 1946 the Republic of China held out to these people the prospect of enjoying the same rights as United Nations nationals when it offered them citizenship. Because the Japanese authorities raised certain objections, the matter was not resolved until, in 1947, the Occupation administration handed them a 'Memorandum concerning Registration of Chinese Nationals,' notifying them that 'The Chinese Mission in Japan has undertaken the registration and documentation of persons in Japan who claim Chinese nationality and has issued registration certificates ....' the legitimate bearers of which 'will be respectively considered as Chinese subjects and hence United Nations Nationals for purposes of the exercise of criminal jurisdiction by the Japanese authorities.'

One effect of the incorporation of Taiwanese in Chinese society was the obliteration of the former division between the wealthy merchant class and those who wielded the 'three knives.' Trading apart, many Taiwanese pursued careers in the professions, as doctors, lawyers, writers and artists. Another effect was to turn Tokyo into the chief city of Chinese residence. There, in 1946, for the first time in the history of the hitherto fragmented Chinese community, a pan-Japan Chinese Federation was established. The encouragement of the Chinese Mission was no doubt instrumental in its formation, but so were three other factors. One, as nationals of a victor country, the Chinese felt like giving expression to their nationalistic sentiments. Two, it was the culmination of an ongoing trend towards cooperation during the war years, when the various regionally and occupationally based groups would confer together on how best to respond to international developments. And three, once disunited by the variety of regional speech, Chinese were now able to transcend group boundaries by their possession of a common language, Japanese.

Thereafter, two lines of development may be discerned: the politicization of the federation as it asserted its role in community-wide leadership, and its fission into pro-Kuomintang and pro-Communist camps with the ascendancy of the People's Republic of China.

1980s and 1990s

Japan's economic boom in the late 1980s led to severe shortages of labour, especially in the construction and service industries. This development, coupled with the appreciation in the value of the yen, attracted large influxes of male foreign workers from Asian countries such as China and the Philippines. These workers did what the Japanese spurned, namely the so-called 3K jobs (those that are *kitsui, kitanai, kiken*, difficult, dirty, dangerous). As manual workers are in theory not allowed entry, many Chinese came on student visas or as clandestine immigrants.

Part-time work by students is officially limited to four hours a day, but this restriction is widely flouted by the so-called 'pre-college students' (*shugakusei*), who, unlike the 'college students (*ryugakusei*), are enrolled in Japanese-language schools but who in fact spend the greater part of their time working. Much to the concern of their Japanese neighbours, many of them economize by sleeping four or five to a room, and because they have little time and inclination to keep their lodgings clean, Japanese landlords have baulked at accepting these students as tenants.

In 1988, the influx of these 'pre-college students' reached a peak – visa applications reached 40,000 in Shanghai alone. A count at the end of 1996 found 20,001 'pre-college students' and 33,120 'college students' in Japan. The influx has caused enough of a concern for the Japanese to have taken it up with the Chinese government.

The fate of clandestine immigrants in Japan resembles that of those in America and other countries (see p 63). Examples reported in the press include the arrival of 160 Chinese 'boat people' at Goto, Nagasaki, in 1989; and the discovery of the corpses of two (possibly drowned) Chinese women washed ashore on the island of Ishigaki in 1993. The main source areas of clandestine Chinese migrants have been Changle and Hokchia (Fuqing) in eastern Fujian. Registration of personal identity is required of all persons residing in Japan for more than 90 days who do not hold Japanese citizenship, and employers hiring illegal foreign workers are subject to penalties, but the severe labour shortage has made these means of control less than completely effective, and considerable numbers of illegal Chinese have successfully evaded them.

A third category of Chinese came under the *kensiu*, or 'trainee' scheme, whereby qualified foreign recruits are brought in through official channels to satisfy the staffing needs of various enterprises. The keen competition for these slots among candidates has resulted in highly skilled Chinese arriving in Japan, but the jobs they then find themselves doing frequently turn out to be fairly low-grade ones located in ill-equipped factories in the remote countryside. In 1996 there were 11,449 Chinese 'trainees.'

A fourth category comprises orphans of Japanese or half-Japanese parentage stranded in China – mainly in the former Japanese-controlled Manchuria – after World War II ended. The government has brought them back in batches with their families from Heilongjiang, Liaoning and Jilin provinces to be reunited with their families in Japan. Raised in China, non-Japanese speaking, these largely middle-aged newcomers have found it hard to adjust to their newly found relatives and vice versa.

The rate of intermarriage involving Japanese and Chinese has greatly increased – the figure for end-1996 was 39,948 such marriages – partly because of the matchmaking efforts of 'international marriage agencies.' These agencies profit from introducing Japanese men – usually farmers or fishermen of sometimes advanced age – to Chinese women, frequently young Shanghainese eager to go abroad. The results have been variously comical and tragic.

Syukushin Kyo (Shu-zhen Hsu)

Advertisement of 'international' marriage bureau.

CHINESE VOICES IN YOKOHAMA

Interviews conducted with the residents of Yokohama's Chinatown in the mid-1990s by a Japanese photographer, Murakami Reiichi, were compiled into a book, *Yokohama Chukagai teki Kakyo-den* (*Lives of Yokohama's Overseas Chinese*), and published in 1997 in Tokyo. These excerpts convey a range of Chinese experiences.

Wu Leji

When Wu, a scholarship student who had been prevented from returning to China by the war, became the principal of the Chinese School in 1951, a messenger from the consulate of the Republic of China came to order him to campaign against Communism. '*I said, this is an overseas Chinese school. A place of study, no politics is needed ... Politics is what the students should choose for themselves when they grow up. I know neither Mao nor Zhou Enlai. You [the Kuomintang government] were in control of education in China; why on earth did so many Communists pop up under your educational system? They said I was a rebel, and got quite nasty.*'

Zhu Maolin

Captured by the Japanese in China and sent to labour on a construction site in Japan in 1944, Zhu was digging shelters when told on August 15, 1945 that the war had ended. '*We were pleased ... we were to be released. But I thought, I was brought here to have a God-awful time for doing nothing wrong so I'll have my revenge on Japan and stay on. But as I stayed and worked in Japan, I gradually realized that not all Japanese were evil. The war had been as hard on them as on us. And I ceased to resent them. I came to Tokyo to earn my living. Menial jobs, gangsterism, jail – I've done it all.*'

Chen Fupo

Following his family to Japan, Chen studied at Meiji University, worked in Taiwan as an official, then returned in 1961 to Japan, where he studied at Tokyo University and eventually became the owner of a restaurant and the chairman of the Yokohama Chinese Association. '*When Japan severed diplomatic relations with Taiwan and switched recognition to the People's Republic in 1972, I was ideologically troubled ... It's painful to think of China divided into two nations. The overseas Chinese, of whom I am one, feel this keenly –* 130,000 *of us in Japan and* 30 *million overseas Chinese worldwide know what democracy is. We are away from [China] and can see things more clearly.*'

Xu Jiang Yueqin

Her father is an unknown Japanese named Kato. She arrived in Japan with her mother in 1946 and went to his home in Kagoshima. '*He didn't accept us. I don't remember him well. We had a terrible time, with no money and not speaking the language. We went to a car repairer we came to know on the ship. We lived by nursing babies and working in the black market, carrying big bags of sugar. We would hide whenever the police showed up. I couldn't afford to go to school. How to eat was a daily problem.*' Hearing there were many Chinese in Yokohama, she and her mother moved there. Her mother remarried a Chinese tailor and she herself married a Chinese cook. '*A wonderful man. Gentle and hardworking.*' A restaurant they opened is now managed by their eldest son. '*It was so hard before. But now my children run the restaurant well and I have grandchildren. I'm thankful I am healthy and happy.*'

Yang Yongshou

Since being interviewed, he has closed down his tailor shop and let it to a restaurant. Originating in Shanghai, where his brother still runs the family tailor shop, Yang had come to Japan after a stint in Hong Kong. '*I bought this house with all my savings – 50,000 yen. I had nothing, and the living was hard. It still is. Just enough to live. I have no hobby. Nothing but work ... I'm going to quit soon, maybe in three months. My eyesight is no good. It's hard to thread a needle. I'm so tired. Really tired.*'

Li Shifu

His band, the Lee Seifuku Connection, has played in Yokohama and abroad. Of his immigrant father, he says: '*At first he was selling chocolate and things in Chinatown. The supply must have come from GHQ [the Tokyo headquarters that carried out the Allied responsibilities for the Occupation of Japan and US military responsibilities]. He has done a lot of other things, such as running bars for foreigners.*' Li Shifu (second left) attended the Chinese School, then switched to a Japanese one because he was an excellent ping-pong player but Chinese schools were not eligible to enter official school tournaments. As a boy, he hung around the American military bases and found himself drawn to Western pop music. '*I played brand-name guitars, and when I was 15, I bought a 150,000-yen Fender. I got a discount for it at the American base ... We used to play at the weekend parties of our friends at the base. Twist and jive were popular then.*'

Translated from the Japanese by Kazuko Asakura

KOREA

1882–1910

The Tumen and Yalu rivers form a natural common border between Korea and China, and territorial adjacency made migratory movement easy. It has been a two-way movement; and if, as is claimed by the scholar Yang Zhaoquan, Korea was the first country in the world to host a Huaqiao community, China is also home to a large Korean minority (one numbering 1.9 million in 1990).

In Ming and Qing times, Korea's relations to China were those of a tributary state living under the latter's political and cultural shadow. Beyond China and to a lesser extent Japan, Korea maintained so few foreign contacts that Westerners called it the Hermit Kingdom. In 1882, to guard against the imperialist challenge Japan posed to its influence over the country, China stationed six battalions in Korea and signed a treaty for the development of private maritime and overland commerce between the two countries.

The treaty assigned a Chinese commercial consul to Seoul and established commercial offices in Inchon, Pusan and Wonsan, three ports opened to international trade as part of Korea's adaptation to a world changing under Western expansion. The treaty, which authorized Chinese merchants to live and trade in these ports, was followed by a series of others, the net effect of which was to make Korea and China increasingly open to each other's merchants. These agreements paved the way for the growth of a Huaqiao community of traders, workers and farmers. Korea's agreement to the establishment of a Chinese concession, first at Inchon and then at Pusan and Wonsan, was a further fillip to Chinese immigration. In 1885, the China Merchants' Steam Navigation began scheduled sailings between Shanghai, Yantai (in Shandong province) and Inchon.

Between then and 1893, China's position in Korea was dominant, with its Resident there, Yuan Shikai, directing not only diplomatic but also domestic affairs. However, in 1894, Japan challenged that position in a series of battles around Seoul and Pyongyang. By the terms of the 1895 Treaty of Shimonoseki which concluded the Sino-Japanese war, China had to agree to the termination of tribute and to recognize the full independence of Korea.

In the meantime, the Chinese population in Korea had grown more than thirteen-fold in the ten years between 1883 and 1893 (see table 5.46). Chinese resided mainly in Seoul and the three open ports. The bulk of them were from Shandong province, with smaller numbers originating in Zhejiang, Guangdong, Jiangsu and Hubei – half of Seoul's Chinese population in 1883, for example, was of Shandong origin. Chinese merchants were to be divided into three main regional groupings, each with its own native-place organization or *huiguan*: the northern *bang* (of people from Shandong and Hebei), the Guangdong *bang*, and the southern *bang* (of people from Zhejiang, Jiangsu and other central and southern Chinese provinces). Women were a small minority, and were to remain so for decades.

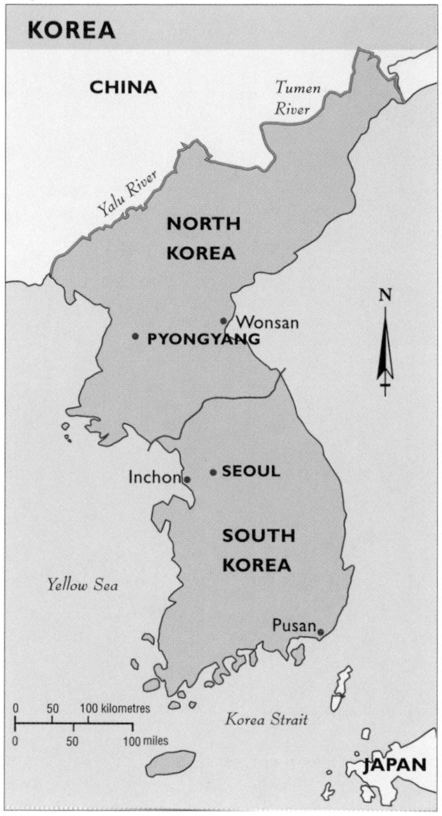

Occupationally, merchants formed the majority, while smaller proportions worked as market gardeners and labourers. Thanks to these merchants, trade between Korea and China greatly expanded. Korean customs records show that while Japan dominated the export trade, China was able to increase its share of the import trade at Japan's expense from 19 per cent in 1885 to 40 per cent in 1891. Between them, Japanese and Chinese merchants monopolized Korea's foreign trade.

Resident Chinese wholesalers distributed the imported merchandise to either Huaqiao or Korean retailers or to shops owned by Japanese. The most famous of the Chinese trading firms in the late 19th century was Tongshuntai, started by Tan Jiesheng, who arrived in Korea as a 20-year-old in 1874. With branches not only in various Korean cities but also in Shanghai, Canton, Hong Kong and Nagasaki, Tongshuntai was Korea's biggest trading company, dealing chiefly in Chinese silk, medicine and Korean ginseng.

Trading apart, the Chinese ran eating places, sundry goods stores, medicine shops and *qianzhuang* (traditional, Chinese-style banks), the latter providing credit and facilitating remittances. They also owned rice mills, oil-press workshops and liquor distilleries, as well as foundries producing farming implements and household utensils. Another area of Chinese endeavour was transport. With the support of Yuan Shikai and the Qing government, Tongshuntai and other Chinese businesses put up the capital to launch a steamship company in 1893. In the same year, Chinese merchants set up a company to provide horse-drawn carriages for transporting cargoes between Seoul and Inchon.

Map 5.30

Leaders of early Chinese community in Seoul in front of commemorative shrine for admiral who brought the first group of Chinese immigrants to Korea.

Table 5.46

NUMBER OF CHINESE IN KOREA, 1883–1910	
YEAR	TOTAL
1883	162
1884	666
1885	264
1886	468
1891	1,489
1892	1,805
1893	2,182
1906	3,661
1907	7,902
1908	9,978
1909	6,568
1910	11,818

Source: Yang and Sun (1991).

1910–31

Korea, already effectively a Japanese protectorate, was formally annexed by Japan in 1910. A development that would also affect the lot of the Chinese in Korea was Japan's growing aggression in the Chinese provinces immediately to Korea's north, a region (called Manchuria by Europeans) which the Japanese army openly invaded in 1932. Meanwhile, in Korea, Chinese numbers grew sixfold between 1910 and 1930 (see table 5.47) Even so, though theirs was the biggest of the foreign non-Japanese communities in colonial Korea, they were a tiny minority, only a little over 0.3 per cent of a total population of about 20.2 million in 1930.

As the population grew, so did the range of Chinese economic activity. Commerce continued to predominate, its expansion from 1910–27 discernible in the rising number of Chinese proprietors and traders (which doubled, for example, in the ten years between 1912 and 1922), and in the growing range and size of Chinese-owned shops. Per capita, the Chinese contributed higher property and household taxes than either the Koreans or the Japanese, the highest rate of all being paid by Tan Jiesheng. In manufacturing, their output value per enterprise exceeded that of Koreans and Japanese. As labourers (many recruited by the Japanese colonial government from northeastern China and Shandong), they worked on the big infrastructure projects started by the Japanese government in the 1920s – road building, bridge and railway construction, port expansion and so on. Koreans, being mostly farmers, were unfit for work requiring some degree of familiarity with civil engineering. Chinese coolies, paid at a lower rate than their Japanese counterparts, provided the labour needed to build everything from the Governor-General's office to the Yalu River Steel Bridge, something of a wonder in those days. They worked in teams, using double-handled saws to cut timber quickly and efficiently.

But whether as labourers or merchants, Chinese were increasingly constrained by Japanese restrictions. For instance, in 1917 the colonial government limited the number of Chinese labourers allowed to be employed at any one job site to no more than a third of the workforce. From 1923 onwards, it steeply raised import duties on Chinese textiles, and eventually banned the import of Chinese silks altogether. Hard hit by this, Chinese traders and shopkeepers were further harassed by attacks on their shops and properties by Koreans (themselves exploited and oppressed by the Japanese). Anti-Chinese feeling ran particularly high in 1927, fuelled by newspaper allegations that the Korean minority in China was being harshly treated.

Koreans in China were overwhelmingly settled in Jilin, the province on the Chinese side of the Tumen river. There, what came to be known as the Wanbaoshan Incident – a fracas over a waterway being dug with Korean farm labour – occurred in July 1931. Incensed by reports that Chinese farmers and police attacked, wounded and killed Korean settlers at Wanbaoshan, and unaware that these stories were based on a distortion of the facts by Japanese-owned newspapers, thousands

Table 5.47

NUMBER OF CHINESE, 1910–30		
YEAR	NUMBER	NO OF WOMEN
1910	11,818	1,089
1911	11,837	692
1912	15,517	924
1913	16,222	987
1914	16,884	1,139
1915	15,968	1,254
1916	16,904	1,408
1917	17,967	1,726
1918	21,894	1,630
1919	18,588	1,691
1920	23,989	2,607
1921	24,695	2,783
1922	30,826	3,203
1923	33,654	3,707
1924	35,653	4,459
1925	46,196	5,669
1926	45,291	5,471
1927	50,056	6,883
1928	52,044	8,216
1929	56,672	9,446
1930	67,794	11,821

Sources: Yang and Sun (1991); Wang (1958).

of Koreans in Inchon, Pyongyang and Seoul took to the streets chanting 'Death to the Chinese!'

In what was the first racial riot to have occurred in Korean history, a virulent, week-long series of attacks by Koreans left about 142 Chinese dead, 546 seriously injured, and hundreds of Chinese shops and properties torched and looted. In his book *My 60 Years in Korea,* Ching You-kuang (Qin Yuguang), who served repeated terms as the president of the Overseas Chinese Association of Seoul (Hancheng Huaqiao Xiehui) and who witnessed the riots as a teenager, blames the Japanese for fomenting the violence.

Nearly a thousand Chinese fled to China by ship from Inchon, while some 16,800 sought safety at the Chinese consulate in Seoul. The riots left a wound in the psyche of many, now elderly, Chinese immigrants, permanently hardening their suspicions of Koreans as a hostile people ready to pounce on them at the slightest provocation. For their part, many Koreans see China as a predatory neighbour which must forever be kept at arm's length. Chinese commentators blame local history textbooks for much of the anti-foreign sentiment among Koreans, whose resentment is fuelled by accounts of Korean kings being forced to kowtow before Qing emperors and to send tributes of women and slaves to buy peace from China.

Post-1931 developments

The year 1931 had seen a halving of the Chinese population, from 67,794 in 1930 to 36,778. However, Chinese returning from China to resume their business in Korea pushed the population back up to 49,334 in 1934. In the 1930s, the fortunes of the Chinese in Korea were an aspect of the deteriorating relations between China and Japan. In 1931, Japan overran Manchuria, and in the following year it created the puppet state of Manchukuo. Then, in the summer of 1937, full-scale war erupted between the two countries, ending any chance that Chinese residents in Korea might have had of regaining their earlier economic strength. Indeed their position was now precarious and they lived in an atmosphere of intimidation, for the Japanese police could accuse them of being spies and arrest them. Their numbers fell to 20,000, but as wartime conditions in China itself worsened, many returned to Korea, raising numbers to about 60,000 on the eve of the Japanese surrender in 1945.

The vacuum created by the collapse of Japanese colonial control resulted in the two Cold War rivals, the Soviet Union and the United States, moving in. Korean territory was divided into a zone of Soviet influence to the north and one of American influence in the south along the 38th parallel. In June 1950, North Korea invaded the South, starting a three-year war. Mao Zedong sent about a million troops to fight on the side of the Communist north. Resident Chinese suffered huge losses and large numbers returned to China or relocated from Seoul and Inchon to other Korean towns.

In 1958, there were 14,351 Chinese in North Korea, the bulk of them making a living as market gardeners. Since the 1960s the community has shrunk, and only 8,000 were counted in 1990. Numbers were higher in South Korea, 22,734 in 1957, the majority running small businesses and restaurants. An estimate puts the Chinese population there at around 21,000 in 1997.

Chinese numerical and economic decline stemmed at least in part from the discrimination they suffered under both Syngman Rhee, president from 1948 to 1960, and Park Chung Hee, president from 1961 to 1979. The former enforced the localization of all domestic business activities, and under the guise of cracking down on smuggling, he more or less removed Chinese businessmen from the foreign sector. 'I remember watching Korean policemen raiding Chinese warehouses and seizing goods at random,' recalls Yu Xinchen, grandson of Yu Xiguang, the man who established Gonghechun, the first grand-style Chinese restaurant in Inchon.

Both presidents implemented currency reforms that depleted Chinese savings. In 1967, restrictions on foreign land ownership and other policies ended up dispossessing Chinese engaged in various cottage industries. Some Chinese acquired Korean citizenship to stay in business, but many closed down their shops and factories. Nor did the Chinese feel only economic disadvantage: they were shocked and insulted when, shortly after the Korean War, part of the space occupied by their community cemetery in Inchon was taken over by a politically well-connected school for what community leaders say was token compensation. In the 1970s, about 10,000 Chinese quit Korea and re-migrated to the United States, Canada, Australia and Brazil.

The classic sojourning pattern, greatly facilitated by China's geographical proximity, was undermined by the severing of Korea's ties with Communist China, relations with which were not normalized until 1992. Since the renewal of diplomatic ties between the two countries, however, there has been a relaxation in Korean officialdom's attitude towards the Chinese community. Chinese born in Korea may choose to be Korean (or Chinese) nationals upon reaching the age of 18.

Korean companies began to recruit graduates of the Overseas Chinese School in Seoul for postings to China and Southeast Asia. Leading this trend was the Samsung group, Korea's biggest electronics conglomerate. The company was offering 60 million won (US$71,429) a year in scholarships to the school. Pupils who received a grant almost automatically found jobs – about 30 a year – with the company. Many Chinese feel that the worst chapter of their history in Korea has closed. 'We're no longer seen as threatening the local economy,' says Sun Shuyi, the Taiwan-educated school's principal.

However, inside the company, a Chinese can still find himself handicapped by his ethnic background when it comes to job assignment or promotion. Foreigners are discriminated against in Korea, and the Chinese are disadvantaged by their exemption from military service, a key condition of employment by prestigious companies. Running up against these barriers, some quit in mid-career to start their own businesses – opening language institutes, travel agencies and so on. An increasing number has turned once again to trading with China – and now also Southeast Asia – exporting garments and electronics. Others have moved to Shandong for jobs in manufacturing firms receiving Korean investment.

But the story of the Chinese in Korea is essentially one of decline. There are many invisible barriers to their joining mainstream society. About a dozen gain Korean citizenship each year, but more than 90 per cent live as foreigners holding Taiwan passports; to become nationals they have to have at least 50 million won (US$62,400) in cash, a decent job and a South Korean sponsor. As non-nationals, they have to apply for alien registration every five years and obtain re-entry permits before going abroad. While they have not been singled out for special disfavour, as foreigners they are barred from buying houses exceeding 200 *ping* (66 square metres) in size or shop space exceeding 50 *ping* per person. Bank loans, scarce even for locals, are hard to come by for Chinese. Because of restrictions on land ownership, Chinese can only own factories if they do so as foreign investors going halves with local partners. Even to publish community newspapers, Chinese must find Korean sponsors, for foreigners are not allowed to invest in the media industry. With access to the bureaucracy and the banking system practically closed to foreigners, they have to bring in large amounts of capital from overseas. Thus most Chinese make do with running small eating places or herbal medicine shops; indeed the restaurant business is their mainstay. 'We are condemned to making a living selling noodles,' one Chinese commentator remarks in a Korean-language magazine.

The commentator, Ju Boling, runs a small bookstore in the heart of the ever-shrinking Chinatown near the Myongdong shopping area. Born and raised in South Korea (and therefore second-generation), he is completely bilingual and boasts university degrees from both Korea and Taiwan. Ju does not have a licence to import the books and magazines he sells. These are imported through a Korean agent; a law guarding against subversive literature prohibits foreigners from freely importing publications. His Chinese neighbours occupy the most expensive real estate in the country, but that does them little good because to buy or sell property, they need the approval of half a dozen government offices ranging from the Ministry of Construction and the tax authority to the police. Indeed, they cannot even rent out part of their house without government approval.

Yet an observer will not gain a rounded picture of the Chinese in the 1990s without looking in at the Overseas Chinese School in the Yonhidong district. Out of the 1,100 students, 300 have Korean mothers, a sign that intermarriage has become more common, not only because of closer contacts between Chinese and Koreans but because family properties are better protected if they are in the name of the Korean spouse. Acculturation has accelerated. As was noted by the periodical mentioned earlier, the school's playgrounds 'now resound with Korean as much as they do with the Shandong dialect common among many Chinese immigrants in South Korea.' The pupils no longer speak pidgin Korean. Looking like Koreans and speaking the language without an accent, they are indistinguishable from the average Korean youngster. Rather than run restaurants, a younger generation of Chinese have become doctors, engineers, architects and even entertainers (one of the country's most popular songstresses is half-Chinese).

Shim Jae Hoon

Construction of Chinese community school in Seoul.

INDIA

Leather shoes handmade by Chinese in Calcutta.

History

Chinese settlement in India dates back to the 18th century, when a Chinese sailor, referred to as Atchew or Acchi in English and as Yang Dazhao in Chinese, arrived on a ship from Guangdong province to Calcutta in the 1770s.

According to a popular story frequently told by Indian Chinese, this sailor outwitted Warren Hastings, the British governor-general of Bengal. Hastings agreed to grant Acchi as much land as could be covered on horseback in a day. However, he apparently underestimated Acchi's riding abilities, and Acchi succeeded in covering so much territory that he secured for himself a large tract of land on the banks of the Hooghly River, downstream from Calcutta. It is said that he then recruited workers from China to grow sugar cane.

After a few years, however, Acchi began to have problems with the Chinese labourers he had recruited, and

Map 5.31

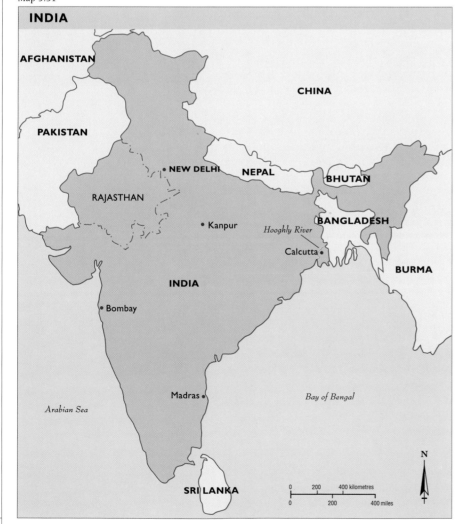

he complained in a 1781 letter to Hastings that most of these labourers had escaped upstream to Calcutta. From that time onward, Calcutta became the centre of Chinese settlement in India. New Chinese immigrants always came to Calcutta first, and the much smaller settlements of Chinese in other Indian cities, even to this day, are the result of further migration from the Calcutta Chinese community rather than direct migration from China itself.

The first references to Chinese residence in Calcutta date from the period during which Acchi's settlement was established. In a 1784 advertisement in *The Calcutta Gazette*, for instance, a Chinese man referred to as Tom Fatt offered his services as a cleaner of water tanks. He was also said to own a rum works, cabinet works and to make sugar candy.

Relationships between Chinese and the government in this early period seem to have been somewhat similar to those that existed between diaspora Chinese and colonial governments throughout much of Southeast Asia, where the Kapitan system provided the structure by which Chinese and the government related to each other. In this arrangement, an intermediary from the Chinese community, one who was agreeable both to the community and to the colonial administration, handled all communications between the authorities and the Chinese.

However, throughout the 19th century, the numbers of Chinese in Calcutta remained low: an 1858 article in the *Calcutta Review* estimated the Calcutta Chinese population to be around 500 only. The population was overwhelmingly male: in the same article, the author alludes to the lack of Chinese women and to the fact that local Chinese men cohabited with Indian or Anglo-Indian women. The offspring of these unions, however, retained their Chinese identity, and the Chinese community in India has never exhibited any tendencies to acculturate or assimilate to any of the ethnic groups within the host society.

During the first few decades of the 20th century, the Chinese community in India began to grow, as did the numbers of Chinese women. Between the years 1911 and 1931, the ratio of Chinese men to women was reduced from eight to one to four to one. In succeeding decades, especially during the 1930s and 1940s, when the tumultuous events in China caused a rapid increase in emigration, the proportion of women in the Chinese population of Calcutta increased considerably. The number of Indian Chinese accounted for in the census of 1951 was over 9,000, and by the time of the Sino-Indian conflict in 1962 (see below, p 345), the population of Indian Chinese had exceeded 14,000, of which 6,000 were female. By this time, the census also noted that there were approximately 2,000 Chinese residents in Bombay.

However, the revolution in China in 1949 and the Sino-Indian conflict of 1962 reversed the trend of continuing increases in the Indian Chinese population. After the revolution in China, it was extremely difficult for mainland Chinese to travel abroad. Only after China embarked on its 'reforms and opening' after 1978 did renewed contact occur between Indian Chinese and their relatives in China. In isolated cases, some of these relatives have emigrated to India to join families from whom they were long separated.

In India, the 1962 conflict with China was also extremely significant in reversing the growth of the Indian Chinese community. Several thousand Chinese were deported, or else they returned voluntarily to China at that time. In addition, by the late 1960s, emigration by Indian Chinese to Europe, Australia and North America had begun, and this trend continues at an increasingly rapid rate today. Thus, by 1971, the population of Chinese in India had decreased to 11,000.

Occupational specialization

The Chinese of India are currently subdivided into three sub-ethnic groups: Hakka, Cantonese, and Hubeinese. Although the census has never differentiated among these sub-groups, the numerical dominance of the Hakka is clear both to knowledgeable outside observers as well as to the Chinese themselves. Because the Hakkas are preponderant, many Cantonese and Hubeinese learn to speak Hakka so that they may communicate effectively with this group. The Hakkas themselves all have their origins within one area in China: Meixian in Guangdong province (see p 39).

These three Chinese sub-ethnic groups have long been associated with particular occupational specialities. The Hakkas are concentrated in shoemaking and tanning; the Cantonese in carpentry; and the Hubeinese, the smallest community, are dentists. In addition, both Cantonese and Hakkas run restaurants; the Hakkas own and operate beauty parlours, and until the early 1950s, Chinese women in the tanning district of Calcutta were in the illicit liquor business. Finally, Cantonese were renowned as shipfitters until the conflict of 1962. (Since they were considered a security risk in the strategic river port area, they were barred from working there.)

These occupational niches emerged very early. For instance, Chinese skills as carpenters are mentioned in a 1784 advertisement in *The Calcutta Gazette*. And in a *Calcutta Review* article of 1857, the Chinese are also referred to as shoemakers. This same article also mentions that it is the Hakkas who are shoemakers and the Cantonese who are carpenters.

Although the Hakka community in India has long been associated with leather work, the tanning community is of more recent origin. The first Chinese tanners came to Dhapa, a swampy area on the eastern periphery of Calcutta, around the year 1910. They began tanning as an adjunct to shoemaking, but soon the process of tanning took precedence, owing to its profitability. In addition, because tanning is the work of Untouchables in India, the Chinese faced very little competition from Hindus, owing to the belief in its polluting nature in Hindu ideology. (The tanning industry in India has three main centres: Kanpur, Madras, and Calcutta. In the first

two centres, it is controlled by Muslim Indians, and in Calcutta, it is dominated by Chinese).

In the beginning, these Chinese tanners used methods much like the village tanners throughout India, but World War I provided the original Chinese tanners in Calcutta with an opportunity to purchase the requisite machinery. Several European firms had liquidated and transferred their capital to England at the end of the war, enabling the Chinese to buy their machinery cheaply.

Since World War I, when there were ten such Chinese tanning businesses in Calcutta, the number has grown to over 300. Undoubtedly, the Chinese practices of living in their factories, utilizing family labour and running the machinery nonstop helped them economize. The growth in tanneries occurred as the result of three processes: first, migrants from other parts of Calcutta moved to the tanning district as word of its profitability spread; second, many tanners who began as tenants in other's factories gradually succeeded and went into business on their own; and third, the number of businesses in the community increased when single businesses were divided among the descendants of the original owner.

(Top) Typesetter at the Chinese Journal of India. *(Bottom) Chinese hairdressers in Calcutta.*

Impact of the Sino-Indian conflict

No account of the Indian Chinese would be complete without examining the profound impact of the border disputes resulting in armed conflict between India and China in 1962. The conflict influenced family and business strategies, community life and relations with the host society.

Before 1959, when Sino-Indian relations were good, identification with the Communist government in China was more acceptable within the Chinese community of India than identification with the Kuomintang government of Taiwan. Many Chinese businesses received loans from the Bank of China, and the Indian government looked favourably on Indian Chinese who acquired Chinese passports. Those Chinese who were not citizens of China were either Indian citizens or considered stateless. It is important to emphasize that Chinese born in India after 1950, when the new constitution took effect, were citizens of India, and at the time of the 1962 conflict there were 900 such citizens.

Nonetheless, during this conflict even Indian citizen-

One of two dailies published in Calcutta.

ship could not protect the Indian Chinese. Anyone who was a descendant of a country which was at war with India was denied citizenship through a 1962 act of the Indian Parliament. Further, over 2,000 Indian Chinese were interned in a camp in the Indian state of Rajasthan. Others were jailed or served with a notice to 'quit India.' Additionally, some Chinese who were employed in factories lost their jobs, and over 2,500 Chinese were repatriated to China.

Although most Indian Chinese born in India after 1950 are now citizens, they still do not feel secure. The 1962 conflict changed family strategies, and now most families try to send at least a few family members abroad so that they will have links they can utilize should they need to leave India in the future. The city of Toronto in Canada is now host to several thousand Indian Chinese. A process of chain migration is well under way, and every year these families are joined by more family members from India. However, since tanning remains lucrative, it is likely that at least in the near future, some community members will remain in Calcutta to run their businesses.

Organization of the Chinese community

Among the Indian Chinese, language group, native place and surname serve as the most critical internal divisions within the community. Distinctions based on language are most critical. On that account, the Hakka, Cantonese and Hubeinese have few institutions in common. At present, only the Overseas Chinese Association and one of the two Chinese newspapers have clientele or members who cross speech-group lines.

In Calcutta, where the largest community of Indian Chinese lives, there are now three Chinese schools which are affiliated with a pro-Taiwan faction of the community, one which also controls the Overseas Chinese Association. (A school run by a pro-mainland faction of the community was closed after the 1962 conflict). Two of these Chinese schools are Hakka and one is Cantonese. In addition, there is a Chinese school run by the Catholic

Indian Chinese relocated to Toronto.

church. However, the enrolment in all three schools has diminished considerably since most Chinese parents now prefer to send their children to schools in which the medium of instruction is English.

Below the level of language group, each Chinese sub-group has organized itself along different lines. For Hakkas, surname has been the primary basis of segmentation within the community, while for the Cantonese, segmentation has been according to native place. The Hubeinese, on the other hand, are the smallest Chinese community, and have only one association, the Hubeinese Association.

Amongst the Hakkas there are more than 15 different surnames, and each of these is associated with a group that elects officers, raises funds, mediates members' disputes and assumes certain responsibilities during major life-cycle events, as well as for festivals in the annual ritual cycle. For instance, surname group officers might mediate in a dispute between brothers who wish to divide their assets and property. Or they might plan a banquet for surname group members after the annual visit to ancestors' graves. At times, they have also intervened in disputes between a husband and wife, or have given small loans to community members in their surname group.

Links to the world beyond

The Indian Chinese are linked to family members across continents. In addition to the many who have emigrated to Toronto, there are also smaller numbers who have emigrated to Australia, Austria, Sweden, Hong Kong, Taiwan and the United States. A small number of emigrants to these countries, as well as Canada, have also returned to India. Most of these returned migrants are workers who have lost their jobs, and have come back to their family tanning businesses in Calcutta.

In addition, since China embarked on its 'reforms and opening' in 1978, large numbers of Indian Chinese have also returned to their native villages in China for visits. Frequently, these visits involve donations to local schools or the local ancestral temple. They almost always involve a banquet for relatives in their native villages.

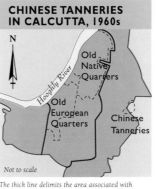

CHINESE TANNERIES IN CALCUTTA, 1960s

Not to scale

The thick line delimits the area associated with higher castes and classes. Low castes and classes are concentrated in a greater number of wards to the right of this border.
Source: Oxfeld (1993).

Map 5.32

Finally, as the number of Calcutta Chinese has grown in Toronto, the community has begun to reorganize under new conditions. It is not uncommon for the wedding of a community member to draw over 400 guests, almost all of them Calcutta Hakkas. But while the ethnic organization of Calcutta encouraged the Chinese there to retain many of their native customs (weddings and funerals, for instance, are strikingly similar to those in Meixian, from where their ancestors emigrated), the host society of Canada may not be so conducive to such cultural insularity. The fate of the 'Indian Chinese' in their new host societies, however, most await the passage of time before any definitive conclusions can be reached.

Ellen Oxfeld

MADAGASCAR

Madagascar is situated to the southwest of the Indian Ocean, 430 kilometres from the coast of Africa. Portuguese sailors were the first Europeans to sight it (in 1500); the Dutch, British and French tried to settle it, but it was the French who finally (in 1643) established a trading post there. This was at Fort-Dauphin, to the south of the island. Madagascar became a French colony in 1896 and, after a spell as a self-governing member of the French Community, when it was known as the Malagasy Republic, it gained full independence in 1960. Home to 14 million inhabitants (according to a 1995 estimate), the republic of Madagascar – comprising the Madagascar Island ('Big Island') and several small islands – is peopled by groups of African, Arab, Malayo-Indonesian, European, Indian and Chinese ancestry. The Chinese number some 18,000, or about 0.15 per cent of the total population.

Since the 1980s, Madagascar has been counted among the world's poorest countries. The country's ills, particularly its political instability, corruption and public insecurity, have militated against the growth of a dynamic Chinese community there.

Migratory movements

Two types of migration account for the Chinese presence in Madagascar: indentured labour migration from Indochina and China, and spontaneous immigration from China, Reunion and Mauritius.

In 1896–1902, Chinese and Indian labourers were brought in to meet the manpower needs created by the exploitation of the resources of the Big Island following its annexation by the French. Foreign labour seemed a better proposition than either European and Creole workers, who demanded a higher salary, or labourers of Malayo-Indonesian origin, who were harder to train.

The first contingent, of 499 Chinese hired at Moncay (Tonkin), landed in 1896 at Tamatave (east Madagascar), followed by three other batches within a little over a year. In total, 3,003 coolies came to Madagascar in less than two years. They were employed in excavation works, road and bridge building, and the transport of materials. But the living and working conditions were so hard and unhealthy that a number of coolies fell ill or even died. The Chinese refused to continue working in such conditions, and from 1897 onwards, the survivors were sent back to their country of origin, those who were sick following in 1898.

The first recruitment exercise thus proved a failure. But Chinese labour was in demand once again a few years later. The colonial authorities arranged for the arrival of two new Chinese contingents, one from Indochina, the other from China. The first batch of 500 Cantonese (of Shunde and Nanhai origin), hired in Haiphong, reached Diégo-Suarez (north Madagascar) in

1900 and was put to work building roads and improving the fixtures in the city's naval base. The second batch, of 764 coolies recruited at Fuzhou, landed in Tamatave in 1901. They were employed in building the Tamatave-Tananarive (Antananarivo) railway.

The difficulty the two groups had in adapting to the harsh and unhygienic physical environment was compounded by the authorities' bad management. Shortly after their arrival, some of the workers fell ill; others simply died. A Labour Inspection Report on railway construction mentions that at the end of only ten months of work, almost 77 per cent of the coolies were decimated by illness. The colonial administration had no choice but to send the Chinese back to their countries of origin. In any case, a number had already deserted their jobs.

Except for some individuals arriving directly from China or Southeast Asia before the 19th century, voluntary Chinese migrants to Madagascar came mainly from Reunion or Mauritius. Ties, especially of a commercial nature, had linked the Mascarene Islands (Mauritius, Reunion, Seychelles, Madagascar) from the start of the Chinese presence there. Cantonese-speaking, these Chinese and their descendants are the ones who form the Madagascar Chinese community today.

During his travels in the Big Island, Ellis, an English missionary, came upon a Chinese chandler's shop established in Tamatave in 1862. Other Chinese settled in Nosy Bé (north Madagascar) in 1866, and then in Tamatave in 1870. At the beginning of 1880, a Cantonese who had left Mauritius by ship in search of sea cucumbers ended up in Tamatave, where subsequently many of his fellow-countrymen joined him. By that time, Chinese were already settled in Diégo-Suarez (north), Antalaha

Chinese grocer's shop in Tamatave, 1906.

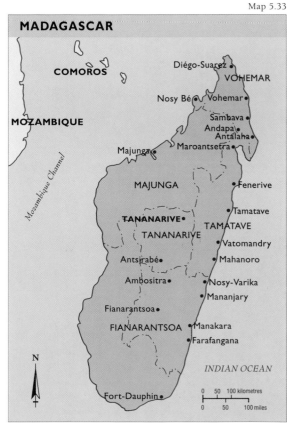

Map 5.33

Table 5.48

CHINESE NUMBERS IN MADAGASCAR, 1893–1941											
Year	1893	1896	1897	1902	1904	1921	1929	1931	1933	1936	1941
Men	—	—	—	—	443	808	1,657	1,804	—	—	—
Women	—	—	—	—	3	29	191	237	—	—	—
Children under 15 years	—	—	—	—	6	119	377	475	—	—	—
Total	40	50	190	284	452	956	2,225	2,516	2,246	2,785	3,637

Sources: Grandidier (1908): Galliéni (1905); Annuaire de Madagascar et Dépendences, 1899, 1905, 1937; Bulletin de l'Agence Générale des Colonies, Nov 1931; Bulletin de l'Académie Malgache, 1947–48.

and Sambava (northeast). But it was with French colonization that Chinese migrants from Mauritius and Reunion started arriving in large numbers.

From 1896 to 1898, 378 Chinese left Mauritius for Tamatave. Similarly, in 1900, there were 36 departures from Mauritius to Diégo-Suarez and 114 in 1901. These were mainly small merchants who settled around the camps of Chinese workers, selling sundry articles. Some of those who had deserted the construction of the Tamatave-Tananarive railway joined the small Chinese community from the Mascarene islands. They started out by seeking employment with their fellow-countrymen. Once they had saved enough money, they became self-employed, opening small shops on their own account. Later on, they sent for their wives (whom they had married during one of their journeys to China), relatives or friends.

According to the French colonial administration's first reliable census – that of 1904 – there were at that time 452 Chinese in Madagascar, including three women and six children under 15 years of age (see table 5.48). The 1905 population census listed 460 Chinese in Madagascar – probably an underestimate. From 1900 to 1950, about 5,000 Chinese settled for good in Madagascar, 3,182 from China, 1,311 from Mauritius and 502 from Reunion. It has to be remembered that Chinese have migrated continuously from one island of the Mascarene group to another. Women were few. Their proportion in the Chinese population grew with the passing years, but only in the 1960s did it approach that of the men, reaching 44.3 per cent in 1967 (see table 5.49).

To the colonial authorities, the increasing inflows of Chinese felt like an invasion. To slow them down (and also those of Indian immigrants), they implemented a series of measures in the three decades leading up to World War II: in 1903, they subjected incoming Chinese to passport control and demanded that a deposit be paid upon arrival; and in 1913, they decreed restrictions on the issue of licences to Asian merchants. However, the big colonial enterprises (Compagnie Lyonnaise, Compagnie Marseillaise, Société Industrielle et Commerciale de l'Emyrne and so on) needed the services of Chinese merchants. From 1920, they encouraged the Chinese to migrate to Madagascar to work as middlemen, collecting local products from Malagasy farmers. Thus from 1921 to 1929, the Chinese population more than doubled (see table 5.48).

Faced with this influx, the authorities passed a decree on October 12, 1929 stipulating that any immigrant landing in Madagascar had to (1) prove that he was the owner of a commercial venture or that he possessed 25,000 francs, or that he was the holder of a job contract with a creditworthy employer; (2) remit to the authorities at the port of disembarkation a sum amounting to 3,800 francs for possible repatriation charges and another 600 francs for possible hospital expenses if he had no specific employer. Finally, a decree of June 21, 1932 prohibited Asians from practising several professions without prior authorization (hotelier, arms and munitions trader, stockbroker or goldsmith, banker, public transport contractor, customs or immigration agent, political activist, among others).

These barriers proved less than wholly effective in 1932–40, when Japanese aggression in China provoked the outflow of thousands of Chinese abroad. Since this happened at a time when the big French companies in Madagascar were still in need of Chinese go-betweens, Chinese already established there arranged for family members, friends or fellow-villagers to join them. Thus 573 Chinese entered Madagascar in 1937, and 726 between March 1938 and May 1939.

The colonial administration reacted by issuing a decree (on November 19, 1932) raising the licence fees payable by Asian merchants. With the outbreak of World War II, no foreigner could enter without special authorization by the governor. The applicant had to declare his identity in his own language and fill, in his own hand, an anthropometric form which was then forwarded to the Central Bureau of Foreigners run by the Public Security Department. All these legal measures considerably slowed down Chinese arrivals in Madagascar. From 1940 to 1960, the year of Madagascar's independence, only about 200 Chinese entered the Big Island.

The restrictions on Chinese and Indian immigration outlasted French colonial rule. They continued to be applied during the 12 years (1960–72) of the first Malagasy Republic. Thereafter, the island was plunged into political and economic turmoil. The economic and social insecurity trailing this in the 25 years since 1972 prompted the departure of more than 3,000 Chinese for France, Canada or Reunion (where today they number about 2,000, 1,000 and several hundreds respectively, with traders and students forming the two largest categories). In 1972, Chinese in Madagascar totalled approximately 20,000; today, their strength is anywhere between 17,00 to 18,000. Two other reasons the Chinese left for brighter prospects elsewhere from 1972 onwards were the nationalization of economic activities and the replacement of French by the Malagasy language as the medium of instruction in schools.

The second Malagasy Republic severed diplomatic relations with the Nationalist government in Taiwan in 1972. Concrete results of its new ties to the People's Republic of China may be seen in the latter's provision of training, health and technical assistance, as well as in the factories, dams and so on which China has constructed in Madagascar. But no agreement on the issue of immigration has been signed between the two countries. Nevertheless, following China's post-1979 economic

Table 5.49

CHINESE NUMBERS IN MADAGASCAR, 1951–75								
Year	1951	1957	1959	1961	1963	1965	1967	1975
Men	3,466	—	—	—	—	—	5,052	2,397
Women	1,434	—	—	—	—	—	4,017	1,642
Total	4,900	7,349	8,032	8,901	8,066	9,008	9,069	4,039

Sources: Population Census 1951. Bilbao (1965); Institut National de la Statistique et de la Récherche Économique, 1974–75.

liberalization, migration of Chinese – albeit a trickle – has resumed. Family reunion apart, this has involved the settlement of new merchants specializing in the sale of finished goods from China, in catering or in the travel business. In the 1990s, about ten students from China were enrolled at the University of Antananarivo (Tananarive).

Community characteristics

The 12 years of the first Malagasy Republic, which maintained diplomatic relations with the government on Taiwan rather than with the People's Republic of China, loosened the ties of the Chinese in Madagascar to their native country. As holders of Taiwan passports, many of them had trouble keeping in touch with their relatives in mainland China.

During French colonial rule, most of the Chinese remained Chinese citizens. Those opting for French nationality numbered eight in 1949–54, 150 in 1956 and several hundreds in 1961. Shortly before independence, applications for French nationality by both Chinese and Indians mounted, but the French kept them to a limit by tightening naturalization procedures. Nor were Chinese encouraged to take out Malagasy nationality when the country became self-governing in 1960.

However, Chinese children of part Malagasy descent have Malagasy nationality (this is why they do not appear in the statistics for foreigners). Many Chinese males of the first generation – that is, those arriving in Madagascar before World War II – lived with Malagasy women who gave birth to children of mixed blood. The researcher Léon Slawecki counted some 10,000 mixed Chinese in 1970, whereas pure Chinese are thought to number between 7,000 to 8,000. What is special about the mixed Chinese is that the majority of their fathers saw to it that they acquired a Chinese education. Thus they are culturally mixed: Chinese and Malagasy. By contrast, the offspring of parents of mixed blood do not go to Chinese schools. Sino-Malagasy men often marry Sino-Malagasy women or simply Malagasy women.

By the late 1990s, the first generation were in their 70s. The well-to-do had left and the second generation, born in Madagascar before or just after World War II, were in their 50s. Living for the most part by trade, these were the people most affected by the country's political and socio-economic troubles. The third generation, born in the 1950s and 1960s, usually stayed on for good in the countries where they had gone to pursue higher studies, namely France and Canada.

Linguistically, the community is overwhelmingly Cantonese. Chinese community leaders – that is, the heads of the Chinese congrégations (see below) – made sure that it stayed that way, warding off any Hakkas, the Cantonese's historical rivals, who might have relocated from Mauritius and Reunion.

Geographically, the Chinese are dispersed. Until scheduled flights to Madagascar began in the 1960s, Chinese chiefly entered the country at the port of Tamatave, and it was here, and in the districts surrounding it – namely Fenerive, Vatomandry and Mahanoro – that the Chinese originally settled. They then fanned out along the cities and villages of the east coast (Sambava, Vohemar, Maroantsetra), to Diégo-Suarez and Majunga in the north and also the south-eastern cities of Manakara, Farafangana and Mananjary. Later on, they moved to the central plateau of the Big Island (Tananarive, Antsirabé, Ambositra, Fianarantsoa).

The three major centres of Chinese settlement are the central plateau (which harbours 43 per cent of the total), the east coast (36.2 per cent), and the north (Diégo-Suarez, 18 per cent). Among cities, Tamatave has always ranked first; it was the site of the first Chinese shop, school, temple, newspapers and associations.

The geographical dispersal, coupled with the smallness of Chinese numbers, has militated against social and cultural association. Organizations are few, and largely confined to big cities like Tamatave and Tananarive. Cultural activities are limited to domestic rituals: the celebration of the Chinese New Year, eating 'moon cakes' during the Mid-Autumn Festival, and paying homage to ancestors on All Souls' Day. Outside Tamatave, Diégo-Suarez and Mananjary, temples are rare; in the last two cities, they are mere ruins. The one in Tamatave is the only one that is maintained and visited, often only by old ladies.

What does remain more or less active is the Chinese congrégation. The French colonial authorities had responded to rising Asian arrivals (452 Chinese and 1,560 Indians in 1904) by instituting, from the end of 19th century onwards, checks on foreigners entering the country. A decree of November 3, 1896 obliged the Chinese and Indians to set up a congrégation grouping all their compatriots living in the same administrative area. Each group was presided over by a leader appointed by the area officer upon the group members' recommendation. The leader had to assist the colonial administration in monitoring the Chinese population, providing information on changes of address, arrivals, departures and so on. In exchange, he was granted the right to police protection. In 1947, there were 27 Chinese congrégations in Madagascar of which eight were located in Tamatave. Though much diluted since the mid-1970s, the monitoring of the community has persisted to this day.

Established by the French, the congrégation system was half-heartedly embraced by the Chinese. They had their own means of social organization and mutual aid: the traditional, regionally based association they called kongsi (and not huiguan or tongxianghui). The first of these, the Nan-Shun Association, representing

Altar to ancestors in Chinese temple in Tamatave.

Medical certificate issued by a doctor of the French consulate in Hong Kong to a Chinese woman going to Madagascar in 1938.

Items belonging to Mauritius-born Chinese woman married to a Chinese man in the 1920s in Vatomandry.

the natives of Nanhai and Shunde, was set up in 1906 in Tamatave. Like the *congrégations*, there is a *kongsi* in every Malagasy city harbouring a Chinese community. Indeed, in many cities, the two institutions are located under the same roof.

Xingwen was the first Chinese school in Tamatave. Founded in 1938, it had 629 students in 1954, and closed in 1978. As had happened in Reunion, the French colonial authorities made the teaching of French compulsory in the Chinese schools in Madagascar. Xingwen was pro-Kuomintang, but in 1950, a second Chinese school, the pro-Communist Huati, was started in Tamatave. Political rivalry apart, the two schools competed against each other in sport and cultural activities. A third school, the Chinese Catholic Centre (1953–72), was created by a French Catholic priest aiming to convert young Chinese to Catholicism.

Pupils from the outlying areas of the island boarded at the schools in Tamatave. But not all parents liked to send their children away to boarding school, and so Chinese schools closer to home were also founded, in Vatomandry, Fenerive-East, Manakara, Mananjary, Farafangana, Antalaha, Andapa and Fianarantsoa. Between 1940 and 1960, a dozen primary schools opened in Madagascar.

Since the 1960s, more and more parents have preferred to send their children to French schools, and there is no Chinese school in Madagascar today (Xingwen has been transformed into a coeducational French-medium school since 1978). Moreover, young Chinese have been leaving the country to continue their studies in France since 1972.

Economic activities

The earliest Chinese traders in Madagascar were those coming from Mauritius and Reunion. Before French colonization, small groups of traders had already penetrated the entire eastern (Tamatave, Antalaha, Maroantsetra, Mananjary, Manakara) and northern (Diégo-Suarez, Nosy Bé) parts of the island. Under French rule, they moved to the centre (Tananarive, Antsirabé, Fianarantsoa), and then to the west (Majunga). These traders would come several times a year to sell such basic products as salt, sugar, soap, petrol, cloth and so on, returning with tropical goods like vanilla, coffee, raffia, pepper, cloves and the like. To them, Madagascar, sizeable in territory and population (it had 2,600,000 inhabitants in 1904), represented an extensive new market and frontier of opportunity.

Chinese engaged in both rural and urban trade. Rural Chinese were both shopkeepers and collectors of tropical products (clove, vanilla, coffee, rice). They bought the products from the

The Congrégation Chinoise, a benevolent society in Tamatave.

Malagasy peasants, sorted them out before packing them in sacks and forwarding them to Chinese traders in the cities, who then sold them to the big colonial companies. They did what Europeans were reluctant to do, travelling across the roadless countryside and working and living in isolation in the bush. During the collection season, they would work non-stop 12 to 13 hours a day. Off-season, the Chinese shop was not only a purchasing point but also a meeting place for the whole village. The inhabitants would go there to chat, have a drink, listen to and exchange village or country news. Furthermore, the Chinese shop served as a creditor to the peasants, giving them loans against future harvests, thereby fulfilling a fundamental economic function and playing a key role in the rural Malagasy economy.

Today, with the prolonged slump of the local economy and with young Chinese leaving the bush to study, rural trade has declined, but it has not disappeared. Indeed, whereas there were about 1,600 Chinese shops at the end of the 1950s, they numbered about 2,000 in the 1990s. Rural Chinese who did not trade cultivated coffee, vanilla or cloves or raised cattle on their own holdings, or else they engaged in fish-farming.

In the urban sector, Chinese operated mainly wholesale/retail businesses. These were started during World War II, most of them limited to retail or wholesale/retail sale of foodstuff and manufactured goods. These businesses not only supplied the small retailers with goods but also collected the local tropical products. The wholesalers handled the export and import of goods. Chinese were not as specialized in this sector as the Indians, except for vanilla exportation, where they were strong until the mid-1970s – since then, however, this activity has been controlled by the government. In 1949, there were only 15 Chinese export/import companies; today, they number by the hundreds. Trading apart, Chinese ran restaurants, flour mills, travel agencies, hotels, bars or transport businesses. They also owned bakeries and medium-sized factories producing candles and fizzy drinks.

During the colonial period, big French companies complained about the competition they had to face from the Chinese and Indian companies. They therefore sought to restrict Asian business activities. After independence (1960), the Malagasy authorities continued to apply colonial restrictions to foreigners. For example, a decree of June 6, 1962 aimed at limiting the immigration of Asians, the acquisition of state-owned lands, and prohibiting the practice of some professions (arms dealer, insurance agent, hotelier, theatre and cinema owners, transport contractor, printer, bookseller, goldsmith, among others).

Nowadays, Madagascar is home to barely 2,000 Chinese firms, of which 1,800 are sole proprietorships, and about 150 are limited liability companies. Contrary to general opinion, the Chinese do not play an important role in the Malagasy economy. However, since the economic liberalization of Madagascar at the end of the 1990s, there has been a revival of the business relationships among the Chinese of the Mascarene islands. These ties are likely to be intensified, especially since the setting up of 'duty-free zones' in Madagascar at the beginning of 1990s.

Live Yu-Sion

MAURITIUS

The growth of the community

Situated in the western Indian Ocean, the independent state of Mauritius was first colonized by the Dutch (1638–1710). It was settled in 1715 by the French, who named it Ile de France. In 1810 Britain annexed the island, and administered it until Mauritius became independent in 1968. Despite 158 years of British administration, however, French language and culture have remained predominant. Under successive governments, slaves and contract labourers were imported to help develop the island, and it was in this context that Chinese agricultural labourers first landed on Mauritius, brought in by force from the Dutch Indies or recruited from Singapore and Penang. However, compared to African or Indian labour, Chinese contribution to the island's agricultural development was insignificant. Chinese labourers whom the French forcibly brought in and maltreated, for example, asked to be repatriated almost as soon as they arrived in the colony.

By contrast the settlement of Chinese free immigrants is a success story. The presence of Chinese merchants dates back to the second half of the 18th century. Chinese arrived on the island as partners of French merchants active in the Canton trade. However, it was Robert Farquhar, who had had experience of Chinese immigration when he worked in Penang and who championed it in Mauritius when he became its first British governor, who laid the ground for permanent Chinese settlement in the western Indian Ocean. By a proclamation in 1817, he introduced police measures to control immigrant populations. In the scheme he adopted, one akin to the Kapitan system used in the Dutch Indies, one man had to assume responsibility for his fellow countrymen. As the person who stood surety for free Chinese immigrants, the 'Chinese captain,' in his view, would have to be 'conversant with the British character, speak English and have very liberal allowances.'

The first Chinese to present himself for this role was Hayme – or, as he was also known, Hahyme Choisanne or Log Choi Sin (?–1874) – a native of Fujian well-versed in both European and Chinese languages and the owner of a shop in Port Louis, the capital. In 1821, Hayme obtained permission to proceed to China to bring in a few of his countrymen at his own expense. He returned five years later accompanied by Whampoo, Hankee, Nghien, Hakhim and Ahim, five men for whom he stood surety and who must have been, if not relatives, at least co-provincials.

In 1839 Hayme petitioned the governor for permission to build the island's first Chinese temple on a piece of land he owned in the western suburbs of Port Louis. The Cohan Tai Biou, as the temple was called, had an administrative board presided over by Hayme. Board members judged cases of Chinese transgressions against the law and provided material help to the needy. From that temple proceeded a pageant, a dragon dance watched by the entire population, the governor included, on the eve of Hayme's departure from the island to return to China in 1872. Two years later Hayme died in his homeland.

The island lived mainly by sugar exports. When the slaves who worked on the plantations were emancipated in 1835, the planters turned to an alternative source of labour: Indian migrants. As emancipation neared, proprietors faced with the prospect of losing their slaves began to sell their plantations at any price. In an attempt to limit land speculation, the colonial government, by a proclamation dated June 21, 1842, deprived all aliens of the right to purchase, own or inherit landed or immovable properties. As a consequence Chinese immigrants, who were non-British subjects, found their activities restricted to the narrow field of trade and artisanal work.

It happened that retail trade was little developed at the time, for hitherto, the slaves representing half of the total population had been fed and clothed by their masters, who bought provisions in bulk. After emancipation, people had to provide for themselves and to learn to manage a cash economy. The emancipated population was also leaving the sugar estates and forming embryonic villages all over the island. All this represented a chance for the Chinese pedlars and shopkeepers to spread themselves out and carve out a place for themselves in the host society. The increasing number of traders among Chinese migrating to the island from 1847 onwards is a measure of the commercial opportunities available to them. In 1847–60, traders totalled 1,164, while seamen and marine carpenters numbered 158 and agricultural workers 252. By the end of the century, traders were 81.3 per cent of the Chinese population. Chinese immigration was facilitated after 1850 by the frequent traffic between India and Mauritius: Chinese could easily obtain a passage on vessels carrying Indian labourers from Calcutta to Mauritius.

Up to 1860, Mauritius received only Fujianese and Cantonese, and the two groups lived in complete harmony under the leadership of Hayme, who exercised both temporal and spiritual powers over the community from the Cohan Tai Biou. But 1860 proved a turning point in the history of the Chinese in Mauritius, for that was the year the first Hakka immigrants arrived. The latter were escaping the harsh fate meted out to supporters of the Hakka-led Taiping Rebellion when it was finally quashed

Hayme.

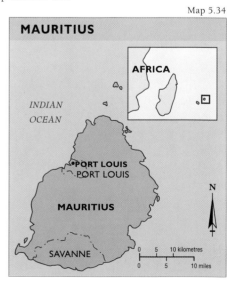

Map 5.34

by the Qing government in China (see p 56). The Beijing Convention was also signed that year, and by extending the freedom to emigrate to the whole empire, it greatly facilitated departures (see p 55). On July 27, 1860, the *Ville de Paris* landed seven Hakkas – Chan Heyou, Chin Ton, Tan Chow, Chan See, Ong Hassan, Le Bow and Chan Buck, all hailing from Meixian (see p 39) – at Mauritius.

These early arrivals were followed by members of a Lee clan, and within two or three years, Hakkas had grown into a strong enough group to spurn Hayme's authority, acknowledging Athion, a member of that clan and a merchant based in Port Louis, as their leader instead. They gave Athion power of attorney to buy a piece of land at Motais Street, about 200 metres from the Cohan Tai Biou, and contributed funds to build a temple there, one dedicated to Guandi, the God of War. They also established an organization, the Liong See Tong, for the purpose of bringing in more Hakkas to the island, particularly those belonging to the Lee clan. Hakkas were aggressive and enterprising, and those who opened shops not only ventured into country districts neglected by others, but offered customers a broader array of goods than the Cantonese retailers – haberdashery, perfume, shoes, cutlery, crockery, glassware, ornaments and fancy merchandise. Cantonese prejudices against them were reflected in the October 17, 1903 issue of the local paper *Le Radical*, which noted that the Hakkas were 'considered as people of mixed blood' and were called 'Macayah,' a common label used of the group by those who intended a slur on Hakka speech, *macayah* being the Hakka pronunciation of the interrogative 'what.'

It was a Cantonese who emerged to assume Hayme's mantle in the 1880s. Affan Tank Wen

(1842–1900), the son of Tan Kouan, an immigrant from Canton, first worked as a shopkeeper in the country district of Savanne; later, after his marriage to a Mauritian woman, Elizabeth Athow, the daughter of one of the wealthiest Chinese merchants in Port Louis, he moved to town to become assistant manager to his father-in-law. In 1873 he became naturalized as a British subject and then began to take an active interest in politics, becoming a member of the Comité pour la Reforme, which was campaigning for a greater Mauritian representation in government. He was appointed to an advisory committee on constitutional affairs, and recognised as the leader of the Chinese community by the then governor, John Pope Hennessy.

Although he himself was baptised a Catholic upon his marriage to Elizabeth Athow, he was a prime mover in the erection of a Chinese temple; dedicated to Tianhou, the goddess widely worshipped by seamen, this was inaugurated in 1896. Nor did his position as the spiritual leader of the Chinese community prevent him from working closely with Mother Barthelemy, a Catholic who was proselytizing among the Chinese. At her death he had a monument built to her memory, in recognition of her devotion to the poor of the community. When, in 1899, a plague broke out in Port Louis, he instigated the creation of the Chou Fa Iyon Plague Hospital for the treatment of Chinese patients, modelling it on the Tung Wah Hospital in Hong Kong (see p 106). Known during his lifetime as the 'protector of the poor,' Affan Tank Wen died suddenly in 1900 without issue.

From 1860 onwards, the colonial government had begun to ease restrictions on immigration; one relaxation was the removal in 1862 of the legal requirement for the Chinese Captain to stand surety for every new immigrant. With the removal of all immigration controls in 1877, Chinese arrivals, mostly Hakkas, had mounted. This, coupled with the island's slide into a phase of unprecedented economic depression caused by natural calamities, a malaria epidemic and a slump in the sugar market, had given Affan Tank Wen cause for concern. He had thus arranged for part of the Chinese arrivals to be redirected to destinations further afield – first to Reunion, Seychelles and Madagascar, and then to South Africa.

Thus up to the onset of World War II, Port Louis came to play the same role for the Indian Ocean as Singapore had for Southeast Asia, as a funnel for the Chinese diaspora. With the movement to the neighbouring islands well underway by 1888, the governor, whose years of service in Hong Kong had predisposed him to the Chinese people, could counter the Legislative Council's motion to curb Chinese immigration with the observation that the number of departures had exceeded that of arrivals by 443.

The balance which the community leaders tried to maintain between old-timers and newcomers ensured that, until the end of the 19th century, the Chinese population never exceeded 3,600. Newcomers were subjected to 'screening' by the community leaders, who had arranged for procedures to be set up in China for investigating the backgrounds of prospective migrants, of whom only those issued with a certificate of good conduct could be admitted to Mauritius. Those not in possesion of such a document would be sent back to China, the local Chinese community paying their return fare.

One control measure the government took was to divide immigrants into 'desirables' and 'undesirables,' the former to be armed with a certificate, or 'passport,' issued by the authorities at Hong Kong or Singapore, their first port of call. It worked none too well and in 1907 the government enacted an ordinance to restrict 'the introduction of destitute persons likely to become chargeable to the colony and of vicious and criminal persons.' To speed up the reception of new arrivals, the government empowered the local Chinese Chamber of Commerce (see below) to endorse passports and obtain visas for the 'desirables.' What the government termed 'pauper charges' on destitute immigrants were paid out of a fund to which the whole community of Chinese traders contributed.

Up to the first quarter of the 20th century, immigrants were overwhelmingly male (see table 5.50). The arrival of the first Chinese woman is recorded in the port registers of 1860; named Bway, she was 22 years old and originated from Amoy. It seemed she had left China clandestinely, disguised as a man, for she declared herself a trader, just like the 40 Chinese men who arrived on the same boat as she. Although few Chinese men contracted legal marriages with local women, liaisons were fairly common. The women were from an ethnically mixed group termed 'Free Coloured,' or 'gens de couleur' (now designated 'General Population') who looked to the whites for their model and identified social prestige with

Table 5.50

YEAR	MEN BORN IN: MAURITIUS	CHINA/HONG KONG	TOTAL	WOMEN BORN IN: MAURITIUS	CHINA/HONG KONG	TOTAL
1850	—	—	586	—	—	—
1861	—	—	1,550	—	—	2
1871	—	—	2,284	—	—	3
1881	—	—	3,549	—	—	9
1891	—	—	3,142	—	—	9
1901	19	3,438	3,457	—	58	58
1911	266	3,047	3,313	221	134	355
1921	1,116	4,117	5,233	1,074	438	1,512
1931	1,835	4,508	6,343	1,511	1,069	2,580
1944	3,096	3,712	6,808	2,893	1,181	4,074
1952	6,485	3,936	10,421	6,038	1,391	7,429
1962	9,154	3,500	12,654	8,987	1,417	10,404
1972	10,077	2,772	12,849	9,968	1,267	11,235

NUMBER OF CHINESE IN MAURITIUS

Separate enumeration by place of origin began only in 1901.
Sources: Blue Books of the Colony of Mauritius and census reports.

lightness of skin colour and material prosperity. In a letter written in 1871, Governor Arthur Gordon remarked that the Chinese, 'who are thorough citizens of the world,' have none of the Indian immigrants' 'prejudices of race' when it came to Creole women, and 'they rapidly assume the manners, dress, and (in name at least) the religion of the country they inhabit.' Well-to-do Chinese shopkeepers were considered a good catch by local country women. In the urban setting, local women were status conscious and, unlike Chinese women, would not consent to living on the shop premises.

Chinese men did not hesitate to take their Creole wives to their native places to visit; nor, if these women proved unacceptable to their kin back home, to abandon them in Hong Kong. There were cases of such women having to be repatriated by the Hong Kong colonial government, which naturally asked the Mauritian government for reimbursement. The Chinese in Mauritius saved the day by suggesting that a fund be set up for such eventualities, the money to be raised by the government taking a levy of 5 per cent on all licences

In their Sunday best.

Sino-Mauritian woman.

issued to Chinese traders.

Children of mixed parentage had to learn Chinese and traditional Chinese ways, but as a concession to the Mauritian mothers, they were baptised in the Catholic religion. In the decade between 1911 and 1921, the number of Chinese Catholics more than doubled from 207 to 520. In the latter year, there were 386 children born of the union of Chinese with 'General Population' women, and 148 born of the union of Chinese with Indian women. Raised away from the shop premises, the children tended to imbibe their mothers' notions of social prestige and so were inclined to jobs in the civil service or the professions. Attending English- or French-medium schools, they grew up with little knowledge of the Chinese language and only a blurred conception of their fathers' merchant culture.

Community differentiation

The Chinese community grew not only larger but more complex with the influx of Hakkas. The death of Affan Tank Wen in 1900 gave Hakkas the chance to challenge Cantonese hegemony. The Cantonese hailed largely from Nan-Shun, short for Nanhai and Shunde. Conflict between them and the Hakkas smouldered for two years

During the Republican period intellectuals and Kuomintang followers arrived in Mauritius.

and then erupted in violence in 1903 during the election campaign for the presidency of the Cohan Tai Biou. The struggle, reminiscent of the Punti-Hakka feud in China (see p 27), cost many Chinese lives. It went on for five years, and as no solution acceptable to all parties could be found, the community appealed for the first time to the Supreme Court, which decreed on June 21, 1906 that the presidency be rotated annually between the rival groups. The management was to be by a 15-member committee composed of five Cantonese, five Hakkas and five Fujianese. With the formation of this committee, the era of the Chinese captain's pre-eminence closed and that of shared responsibility began.

Broad, cross-dialect representation also underlay the Chinese Chamber of Commerce which the Chinese in Mauritius established in 1909. Called the Vasiong Kwong Sow Society, the institution was modelled on the ones which had been created in Shanghai and Singapore. Cantonese and Hakka presidents elected from the respective constituencies took turns in running it, while the secretary was a permanent appointment. The latter saw to the admission or repatriation of 'destitutes,' working closely with the Commissioner of Police. Thus Adrien Konfortion, who held the post for 29 years, performed many of the functions normally discharged by a consular official. As a letter from the president to the government put it in 1925, 'It has always been our policy to see that our people should not go astray, and our special duty has ever tended towards helping our folks and sup-

porting them by our own means and at our own expense whenever they are in difficult circumstances.' Later the chamber became the official seat of the Kuomintang party. In 1948 its life came to an end when, following the colony's constitutional changes, Jean Ah-Chuen, the then president of the chamber, was nominated to the Legislative Council (see below).

Meanwhile the commercial interests which the Chamber aimed to advance diversified. Hakkas took the lead, branching from trade into small-scale industries. The most lucrative was the rum industry, the profits of which helped finance the Chamber's activities. Hakkas also manufactured aloes bags (used to transport sugar). At the end of the first quarter of the 20th century, Hakkas like Ng Cheng Hin, Venpin, Leung Pew and Ah-Fat were the main producers of cigarettes, owning seven out of the eight manufacturing plants set up on the island. Until the Hakka footwear manufacturer Ah-Piang et Cie opened in 1911, only imported shoes were sold in Mauritius, but once Hakkas like Ng Chen Hin and Ng Thow Hing came into the picture, even boots for Mauritian soldiers and policemen were supplied locally. By 1940, Chinese commercial success would be apparent to anyone taking a walk along Farquhar and Queen Streets, each lined with the premises of wholesalers and merchants of Hakka origin.

Constitutional development and Chinese representation

Up to 1936, the Chinese showed little interest in local politics, as qualifications for enfranchisement were so high that there were only 11,800 voters in a population of 400,000. But constitutional changes introduced in 1947 enlarged the electorate by making a simple literacy test the qualification for the vote. Jean Ah-Chuen was nominated to the 1948 Legislative Council as the representative of the Chinese community. Born in 1911 to a Hakka trading family, Ah-Chuen spoke Hakka, Mandarin, French and English. Under his direction, the family store grew to be one of the most popular groceries on the island. He took a keen interest in public affairs, and it was on his initiative that a Chinese Contingent Home Guard was created to help defend the island when World War II was declared. As the president of the Chinese Chamber of Commerce, he also headed the Chinese Resistance Relief Fund to raise money for a China suffering from Japanese aggression.

In 1960, further constitutional changes ushered in adult universal suffrage. To safeguard the rights of minorities, who were in danger of being precluded from representation in the Legislative Council, Jean Ah-Cheun attended the 1960 constitutional conference in London to vigorously defend those rights and to obtain adequate guarantees for their preservation in the new constitution. In the 1963 elections, he was elected to the Legislative Council as the head of the independant Union Sino-Mauricienne party. In 1959–68, Hindus dominated the Legislative Council. As independence approached, the fear of the emergence of an Indian-controlled government drove some Chinese, as members of an ethnic minority, to seek greater security in Europe, America or Australia.

When elections were fought in 1967, the stakes were

between either independence or association with Great Britain. Ah-Cheun campaigned for the latter cause under the banner of the PMSD (Parti Mauricien Social Démocrate) and regained his seat, although it was the party favouring independence which won the elections. In the coalition government formed thereafter, he was appointed Minister for Local Government, a portfolio he held until 1976.

He lost his seat in the 1977 elections, however, when young voters (enfranchised by the lowering of the voting age to 18) repudiated the aging élite and supported a new Left-leaning party, the MMM (Mouvement Militant Mauricien). Creoles, Muslims and Chinese supported the MMM, but clashes over economic policy brought its government down in 1983 and its period in power proved brief. The ensuing election campaign was dominated by the Alliance Party, a coalition of older parties appealing to the Hindu element in Mauritian society. The new prime minister, Aneerood Jugnauth, led the country through an unprecedented economic boom, but because he favoured Hindu primacy in the civil service and key economic spheres, his policies exacerbated ethnic tensions and contributed to his downfall in the 1995 elections.

Chinese representation in the National Assembly stands poised on a delicate balance in a tug of war between the big political parties. The Chinese community is roughly 2.9 per cent of the total population, and victorious parties, aware of the importance of its support, would always include a Chinese candidate. In 1995, for example, the 62 elected members of parliament were ethnically distributed as follows: Hindus 35, General Population 17, Muslims nine and Chinese one, while the breakdown of the 22 ministers was 12 Hindus, five General Population members, four Muslims and one Chinese.

The Chinese community, however, is fully conscious that with only one representative in government, the scope for the defence of their interests is limited. They are aware that as a constituency they are too small to carry any political weight, and that to gain bargaining power, they must create their own opportunity and basis for political influence. This they sought in the sphere of economic development.

The economy's heavy reliance on the sugar industry has been mentioned. This has been the preserve of Franco-Mauritians, the descendants of the white settlers, since the 19th century. During colonial days, the General Population dominated the civil service and middle-ranking employment in the private sector, while the Indian community controlled the small agricultural plantations, and the Chinese the retail trade. After independence, as part of an attempt to diversify the economy, an export processing zone was established to attract both local and foreign investment. This was where the Chinese could come into their own, and indeed it was a Chinese, E Lim Fat, who initially advocated establishing the zone and introduced the model developed in Taiwan and Singapore.

Starting life in 1971 and producing knitwear, garments, textiles, footwear, TV sets, refrigerators, soft toys and plastic products for markets in the European Economic Community and the US, the zone developed so rapidly that in 15 years it overtook the sugar industry as the country's chief employer and exporter. The contribution of ethnic Chinese to that growth has been conspicuous. This has been both local and foreign; in terms of the latter, Hong Kong has been the most important, accounting for three-fourths of all foreign investment, and Taiwan the second most important. As for China, the main contribution to the Mauritian economy has been in the form of the supply of qualified female migrant labour. The importance of the export processing zone to the health of the economy has validated the local Chinese claim to a place in the Mauritian sun.

The government is eager to develop links with Asia and believes that ethnic affinities would greatly facilitate this. Hence it appointed E Lim Fat as the chairman of the Mauritius Free Port Authority, which was created to help the country weather the challenges of increasing competition from low-wage producers in Asia and Africa and the loss of protection afforded by agreements giving the country's products preferential access to European and American markets. To the government's moves to involve them in its efforts to expand international trading, the Chinese have eagerly responded. In other ways, too, the Chinese are a definite part of the Mauritian mosaic, 95 per cent of them having gained Mauritian citizenship and some 80 per cent of them having embraced Catholicism while still retaining a sense of their Chinese ancestry.

Huguette Ly-Tio-Fane Pineo

Busy street in Port Louis (top). Chinese students play traditional instruments by way of preserving their cultural identity.

REUNION ISLAND

Reunion is a small island situated to the southwest of the Indian Ocean, 880 kilometres east of Madagascar. Although the official French claim to the island (named Bourbon to begin with) dates back to 1642, permanent settlement started only in 1663. Except for a period of British occupation in 1810–15, it remained a French colony until 1946, when administrative reform in France changed its status to that of an Overseas Department of the metropolitan country and, in 1973, an administrative region.

The ethnic mixture of Reunion's population is the result of successive migratory movements from the 17th century onwards. Today, that population, estimated at 679,198 in 1996, breaks down as follows: (1) Creoles of African origin called 'Cafres' (35.5 per cent), who are descendants of former slaves from Senegal, Guinea and Mozambique; (2) white Creoles (29 per cent), mainly of European origin, who further divide into the 'Gros-Blancs,' former sugar cane plantation owners, and the 'Yabs,' pauperized whites living in the high plateaux of the island; (3) Tamils, called 'Malabars' (20 per cent), who were recruited during the 19th century on the Malabar coast to work in the sugar cane plantations; (4) metropolitan French (6.5 per cent), working mainly as civil servants, professionals or entrepreneurs; (5) Muslims from India, called 'Z'arabes' (5.5 per cent), descended from those who came to Reunion from Gujarat around 1870 as traders; (6) Chinese (3.5 per cent) recruited during the 19th century also to work in the sugar cane plantations.

Sugar cane plantation.

Migration history

Faced with the abolition of slavery (1848), plantation owners and administrators resorted to foreign indentured labour. This explains the presence of Chinese and Indians in Reunion: they came in as indentured labour-

Map 5.35

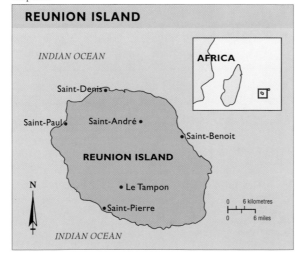

REUNION ISLAND

INDIAN OCEAN

AFRICA

Saint-Denis

Saint-Paul • Saint-André •

•Saint-Benoit

REUNION ISLAND

N

• Le Tampon

•Saint-Pierre

0   6 kilometres
0   6 miles

INDIAN OCEAN

ers under contractual arrangements termed 'engagement.'

The first batch of Chinese was recruited in 1844–46, the next in 1901–07. The first, recruited in Malaya, arrived in Reunion in 1844, followed two years later by contingents from Penang and Singapore. Some of these men were of Fujian origin; others were natives of Guangdong and Macao. Assigned jobs in agriculture, forestry or dam building, they were treated no better than slaves by plantation owners who were after profitability at all costs. The working and living conditions were appalling enough for labourers to rise in violent rebellion. As early as 1846, the colonial authorities had cause to suspend the recruitment of 'black sheep.'

In 1848, Chinese numbered 728; this figure fell by more than half in the 15 succeeding years. Some indentured labourers stayed on after their contracts ended; others chose to move to Mauritius, leaving only 547 of their fellows in Reunion in 1896. Throughout the 19th century, with the exception of 1872, Chinese numbers never exceeded 1,000.

Almost half a century later, the colonial authorities turned once again to Chinese labour, this time to help diversify the island's economy, particularly by renewing tea cultivation. In October 1901, a group of 812 Chinese workers recruited in Fuzhou arrived in Reunion. Again, labourers were badly treated: contracts were not honoured, payments were deferred, food rations were insufficient. Most of them left the island in 1907, following the rioting they had started on the various plantations.

Manpower shortage remained a problem. To meet the needs of the developing sugar industry, and at the request of the big land owners, the colonial authorities decided to authorize Chinese immigration at the same time as setting out the rules and regulations governing their employment and residence on the island. A decree of June 12, 1862, for example, defined immigrants as travellers not bound by any indenture (*libre d'engagement*). They had to secure a residence permit and pay a corresponding tax if they wanted to stay on the island. A supplementary piece of legislation promulgated 20 years later (on August 27, 1882) allowed all immigrants to apply to the governor for the right to remain on the island after the termination of their employment contract. This law also authorized family reunion and the immigration of women.

As a result, from 1862 onwards, different groups of Chinese workers from the provinces of Fujian or Guangdong (Nanhai, Shunde, Meixian) came to the island: free labourers, traders, chain migrants joining their families. Besides, from 1898 onwards, a sea passage having opened between Hong Kong and the three Mascarene islands (Madagascar, Mauritius, and Reunion), immigrants could enter Reunion directly, without having to stop over in Mauritius.

In the wake of World War I, a new phase of prosperity into which the sugar industry entered was matched by a resumption of migration from China and India. Some of the Chinese who had left for Mauritius or Madagascar or elsewhere (Seychelles, France, Indochina and so on) returned; others continued to bring in their wives and children as well as other close relatives from China. Besides, during the 1930s, events such as the China-Japan war further propelled migration. From 1907 to 1941, Chinese numbers rose steadily (see table 5.51). Since then they have remained more or less stable, the community managing to survive only through the birth of younger generations.

In 1946, because Reunion was made an Overseas Department of France, immigration rules and regulations and legislation in force in France were also applied to the island. From 1950 onwards, the French authorities allowed only those Chinese who had been born or who were employed locally to enter the island. In any case, emigration all but ended with the Communist victory in China in 1949. The establishment of diplomatic relations between France and the People's Republic of China in 1964 did not pave the way to a renewal of immigration, and it was only with the emergence of a new era in China's politics in the 1980s that Chinese immigrants came to Reunion. Some came to be reunited with their families, others to work – this time for Chinese employers – as professional cooks or restaurant employees.

From 1950 onwards, it became harder and harder to arrive at accurate figures for the size of the Chinese community. One reason is that, in Reunion as in France, population censuses do not count by ethnic origin. Until World War II, the majority of Chinese retained their Chinese citizenship, French nationality being granted only to those judged sufficiently assimilated to French culture; but later, as they naturalized as French citizens, they ceased to be counted as Chinese. Another reason statistics are questionable is that they do not reflect departures for Mauritius and Madagascar. According to an official count, out of the 2,042 foreigners living on Reunion on October 1, 1989, Chinese numbered 145. But if ethnic and demographic criteria were used, one might arrive at an estimate of 20,000 to 25,000.

The first unindentured Chinese women – nine of them – arrived on the island as early as 1864. Until the 1920s, their number never exceeded a hundred; thereafter it rose rapidly, from 105 in 1921 to 1,183 in 1941. In the intervening period, they numbered 277 in 1926, 466 in 1931, and 616 in 1936.

Economic activities

Once freed from their labour contract, the first batch of indentured Chinese switched to itinerant trading. They brought items of everyday necessity to the high plateaux of Reunion and bartered them for food products (vegetables, salads, tropical fruits and so on) or local cottage industry goods (brushes, broomsticks and so on). They then took these products to sell in the cities. A few years later, they started setting up shops.

The first Chinese shop was set up by a Cantonese from Shunde, Chen Zhangman, at La Possession in 1858. Chinese businesses first appeared in the big cities (Saint-Denis, Saint-Paul, Saint-Pierre, Saint-Benoit), then spread to the island's high plateaux from 1890 onwards. Businesses were particularly concentrated in Saint-Denis, which boasted 75 Chinese businesses at a time (at the turn of the century) when the island as a whole had only 547 Chinese traders. In 1900, a Chinatown developed in Saint-Denis. And in foodstuff trading, the Chinese had established a near monopoly.

White Creoles reacted violently to this monopoly. They made their hostility felt, first by instituting (through the decree of June 17, 1887) a residence tax for foreigners, and then by waging a press campaign (lasting from 1894 until World War I) denouncing the 'invasion' of Reunion by the Chinese. In racist terms, the newspapers of that period portrayed Chinese as the 'Yellow Peril' and demanded that they be deported.

After World War I, Chinese economic activity continued to expand. But it slowed down considerably during the Depression of the 1930s, at which time another press campaign against Chinese traders started. In 1932, under a series of administrative measures taken by the colonial government, foreigners were issued with individual identity cards and made to pay a deposit of 150 francs each to stay in Reunion. Furthermore, they were barred from a range of jobs: no foreigner could be a publisher, a manager or editor of newspapers or other publications, a show business or cinema operator, a public transport contractor, an arms dealer, banker, goldsmith or money-changer, let alone pursue such public sector professions as customs and immigration officers. Foreigners had to refrain from any political activity. Nor did they have any political rights.

After World War II, Chinese economic activity developed faster than that of the island as a whole. Upon becoming a Department in 1946, Reunion received a massive

Table 5.51

NUMBER OF CHINESE IN REUNION	
YEAR	NUMBER
1902	1,378
1907	810
1911	884
1921	1,052
1926	1,626
1931	2,242
1936	2,845
1941	3,853

Sources: Population censuses and statistics.

Chinese shop in Saint-Denis.

Tomb of Chinese born in Shunde, Guangdong.

Chinese corner shop.

infusion of funds from France (7.5 million francs In 1950; 44 in 1957; 325 in 1964). This inflow of capital gave a boost to Chinese retail businesses, which noticeably expanded between 1945 and 1960. A survey conducted by local Chinese researchers in 1962 shows the Chinese to be mainly concentrated in the food distribution sector. A more detailed breakdown of economic activity was as follows: 87 per cent were retail traders, 3.2 per cent were wholesalers, while 1.7 per cent were wholesale and retail traders. Restaurateurs (1.7 per cent), drivers (1.4 per cent), photographers (1 per cent) and bakers (0.9 per cent) made up the bulk of the rest (see table 5.52).

Chinese shops were usually located at street corners, where the potential customer traffic was likely to be at its densest. They usually sold food (sugar, oil, salt, rice, coffee, tinned food and so on) and a large range of non-food goods (hardware, fabric, soaps, candles, hats and so on). They also played a social role, serving as places for locals to meet, talk and, for men particularly, to while away their leisure hours drinking and exchanging gossip. Chinese shops rarely employ people from outside the family. As a rule, the entire family lives on the floor above the shop. Since the 1970s, these shops have been disappearing not only because of competition from supermarkets but because the younger generations would rather study than carry on the family business.

Between the French or Asian (China, Hong Kong, Japan) supplier and the Reunionese retailer or consumer stands the Chinese wholesaler or importer. In 1974, out of the island's 34 importers, 19 were Chinese, while 12 were white Creoles and three were Z'arabes. Foodstuff apart, imports range from electrical household appliances, furniture, hi-fi systems, clothes and manure to motor cars and spare parts. From the 1970s onwards, the emergence of an urban population – made up of rural-to-city migrants and the ever larger numbers of civil servants arriving from metropolitan France – raised living standards in Reunion. This led to the replacement of the Chinese corner shop by modern self-service stores (mini-markets) and supermarkets. In 1980, out of 95 mini-markets found on the island, 75 were owned by Chinese; and out of a total of 18 supermarkets, 10 belonged to Chinese. Most supermarkets are franchised by large chains in France (such as Le Prisunic), which supply them with fresh products and introduce modern management methods for a share of the revenue. To rationalize imports and reduce costs, Chinese retailers began in 1972 to organize themselves into purchasing groups, those in the north forming the CRAD (Coopérative Réunionnaise d'Achat des Détaillants Réunionnais, or Reunion Purchasing Cooperative of Reunionese Retailers), and those in the south establishing the CADR (Coopérative d'Achat des Détaillants Réunionnais, or Reunionese Retailers Purchasing Cooperative).

In May 1981, François Mitterrand brought the French Left to power. This had political, economic and social repercussions for life in Reunion. For a start, so much did social security benefits increase under Mitterrand that by the 1990s, not only was 40 per cent of the population living on welfare but state handouts were accounting for as much as half the income of the Reunionese. All this translated into the increase of consumer market potential. Bidding for supermarket sites became more and more competitive. But the Chinese, despite banding together in purchasing cooperatives to improve their competitiveness, lost ground to the 'hypermarkets' started by the white Creoles. Neither the wholesale business nor many of the mini-markets survived the onslaught of the hypermarkets.

In the background lay political changes. At the end of 1982, the French government modified Reunion's status and gave it a measure of autonomy. With the devolution of power to Reunionese, land sales – to developers of hypermarkets, for example – came to be decided by the mayors of the big cities. As is revealed by a scandal which came to light in the courts in 1996, the so-called 'Saint-Denis affair,' such decisions could be swayed by secret contributions to political parties campaigning for municipal elections.

Beyond the commercial sector, Chinese are notably successful in printing and the media. For example, the owner of the daily *Le Quotidien*, which started publishing in 1976 and enjoys the highest circulation among newspapers, is Chinese. Since the 1970s, the younger generations (that is, those born after World War II) have moved increasingly to jobs in the administrative sector and in the professions. Civil servants apart, they tend to become primary and secondary school teachers, auditors, doctors, dental surgeons and architects.

Social and cultural organization

Only two regional speech groups may be identified in the Chinese community. The Cantonese, originating from villages in the neighbourhood of Canton (Nanhai, Shunde, Shajiao) were the first to reach Reunion, in 1880. They settled mainly in the northern part of the

Table 5.52

DISTRIBUTION OF CHINESE ECONOMIC ACTIVITY, 1962	
Type of activity	**No of units**
Retailers	702
Wholesale dealers	26
Wholesale-retail traders	14
Caterers (restaurants)	14
Drivers	11
Photographers	8
Bakers	7
Transport concerns	4
Cigarette manufacturers	3
Car mechanics	3
Jewellers	3
Soft drinks manufacturers	3
Wine sellers	2
Drinks/ice-cream parlours	2
Supermarkets	2
Flour millers	1
Pharmacists	1
Total	806

Source: Huaqiao zhi bianzuan weiyuanhui (1966).

island: Saint-Denis, Saint-André, Saint-Benoit. Other Cantonese had, however, already started moving from Mauritius to Reunion as early as 1850. The other speech group is Hakka. The first Hakkas came from Meixian or Mauritius between 1885 and 1890. A few years later, others arrived from the French colonies in Indochina. They settled in the south of the island (chiefly Saint-Pierre, Le Tampon), away from the Cantonese, apparently because of the animosity which the two groups felt towards each other and which had been amply displayed in the Hakka-Punti wars in China (see pp 27 and 56).

Cantonese associations in Saint-Denis – based both on clan and place of origin – go back to 1877. As a rule, new associations arose with each wave of migration, or in response to important events both in Reunion and China. For a population as small as Reunion, a remarkably large number of organizations evolved between the two world wars: the Chan Surname Association, Foyer de l'Amitié et de l'Equité (Lianyi Tang), Fondation Nan-Shun (Nan-Shun Tang, based on origins in Nanhai and Shunde), Foyer d'Union et de la Victoire (Liansheng Tang), among others. During World War II, when news of the atrocities committed by Japanese troops reached Reunion, the Chinese there were spurred by patriotic sentiment to form organizations to collect money to help their native country.

Today, the 15 or so associations on the island survive with great difficulty. Their activity intensified during the 1980s, when Reunionese of all ethnic origins took an interest in 'roots.' But the Chinese associations espouse no cultural mission and do little beyond organizing Chinese language and cooking classes, sports activities, group outings and parties.

The first Chinese school was founded in 1927 in Saint-Denis. But it had to close for lack of teachers. Teachers came from either Mauritius or China, and taught in either Cantonese or Hakka. Schools were founded with the support of the Chinese Chamber of Commerce, itself funded mainly by Chinese traders' contributions. Seen by the colonial authorities to be hindering assimilation to French culture, Chinese schools which existed before World War II had to teach fewer hours of Chinese than French. By way of adapting to these strictures, Reunion's Chinese created Franco-Chinese bilingual schools, the first one opening in 1942 at Saint-Denis. Schools in both Saint-Denis and Saint-André were highly regarded, thanks to the quality of their teaching and their large enrolment; together they accounted for about 80 per cent of young locally born Chinese schoolchildren.

After World War II, with Reunion becoming a French Overseas Department, education in French schools became compulsory. This hastened the decline of Chinese education, as did the perception among parents that knowledge of Chinese was no longer essential now that the option of returning to China was no longer open. Thus, instead of attending the bilingual schools, children born in the 1950s went to French primary and secondary schools. As a result, those aged 40 years or so no longer speak Chinese, except for a few who had learned Mandarin at the University of Reunion or in France, or who had visited and stayed in China or Taiwan. For these people, learning the Chinese language

was a means to retrieving their lost Chinese cultural identity.

Immigration from China ended in 1950, and from that time until 1964, Chinese in Reunion maintained only limited contact with the People's Republic of China. The majority were holders of Taiwan passports, and it was only when China and France normalized relations in 1964 that they could visit their ancestral homeland (usually by obtaining a visa in Hong Kong). With the French Left coming to power in 1981, cultural policy became more pluralist, encouraging Chinese acrobats, painters, musicians, chefs and athletes to visit the island and stage performances there.

The early 1980s also marked a step forward for the Chinese in politics. Although Chinese have sat on various municipal councils since as early as the 1960s, the election of André Thien-Ah-Koun, a Reunionese Chinese, as the mayor of the city of Tampon in 1983, and then as a Member of Parliament in 1989, was something of a political landmark for the Chinese community.

Meanwhile, the generation born after World War II was heading towards an identity crisis. With Reunion becoming an administrative division of France, acculturation to French culture – and the downgrading of Chinese language and culture – became the order of the day, so much so that these Chinese even felt ashamed of being Chinese. Today, they are identified as Chinese or as people of Chinese descent, look Chinese and are considered Chinese by society as a whole; yet they possess neither the Chinese language nor knowledge of Chinese culture. Their lingua franca is Creole but they feel neither Creole nor French and do not participate in Creole or French cultural activities, having, in fact, not assimilated to either culture. On a personal level, there is much engagement with the question of where they belong and to what they belong, and how they might comfortably put the Chinese, French and Creole bits and pieces of their lives together.

Live Yu-Sion

Signboard advertising supermarket '2000' during Chinese New Year at Saint-Denis, 1997.

Front entrance of the Saint-Charles French-Chinese School at Saint-Paul.

SOUTH AFRICA

The Chinese in South Africa form one of the smallest ethnically identifiable communities in the country. Although they have been part of South African history since shortly after the commencement of European settlement, they have generally preferred to maintain an inconspicuous position within the racially stratified and complex South African society. This has however not exempted them from the impact of discriminatory race legislation and the effects of Apartheid (a racially based segregationist policy). On the contrary, until the onset of democratic changes of the new South Africa in 1994, Chinese occupied a marginal position between a white dominant minority and a black subordinate majority. As Melanie Yap and Dianne Leong Man put it in their book, *Colour, Confusion and Concessions* (1996), the Chinese 'have lived in limbo, neither dark enough to be black nor light enough to be white.'

Since the first official census in South Africa in 1865, the Chinese have only once been listed as a distinct 'ethnic group.' This is partly because their numbers were considered too small to warrant separate attention, and for the better part of the 20th century their immigration into South Africa was prohibited. They have therefore mainly been categorized as 'mixed' or 'other' or, together with the larger Indian population, as 'Asian.' It is thus impossible to create detailed statistical profiles of the community size, growth rates and immigration and emigration patterns.

We have figures for one of the territories in South Africa for a limited period: Chinese in the Cape Colony numbered 215 in 1891, 1,380 in 1904, 812 in 1912, 781 in 1913 and 732 in 1921. In the early 1960s Chinese numbered about 6,000. Since the 1980s, however, there has been an influx of immigrants from Taiwan and, in lesser numbers, from mainland China and Hong Kong. At present the Chinese community numbers between 20,000 to 25,000, or about 0.05 per cent of the total South African population.

Traditionally the Chinese have settled in the six main metropolitan regions: Gauteng (Johannesburg-Pretoria region), Port Elizabeth-Uitenhague, Cape Peninsular, Kimberley, East London and Durban. This is linked to their involvement in the business and professional sectors. With the influx of new immigrants in the 1990s, Chinese have also settled in various other areas.

Many locally born Chinese trace their descent from Chinese who arrived in South Africa in the 19th century from principally two areas in Guangdong province: the Cantonese-speaking counties of Nanhai, Shunde and Panyu; and the Hakka-speaking Meixian (see Part I).

Historical development

There is some evidence that the first contact between the Chinese and southern Africa was made some 60 years before the Portuguese rounded the Cape of Good Hope. Zheng He, the famous Ming Dynasty mariner (see p 48), sailed down the east coast of Africa in the early 15th century and apparently passed the Straits of Mozambique to reach what was probably Kerguélen Island in the Antarctic Ocean.

However, the first Chinese to arrive in South Africa came to the Cape during the Dutch East Indian Company period (1652–1795). Within two months of the establishment of the refreshment station, the Dutch commander made numerous requests for Chinese artisans and workers to be imported to farm and develop the settlement, appeals which were repeated by his Dutch successors as well as the British officials who administered the Cape in the 19th century. Although the respective authorities did not concede, numerous Chinese did arrive at the Cape. Some were convicts and ex-convicts from mainly Batavia; others were independent merchants from mostly Canton and the Hakka homeland, Meixian, coming sometimes via Madagascar or Mauritius; and still others were individuals who came

Map 5.36

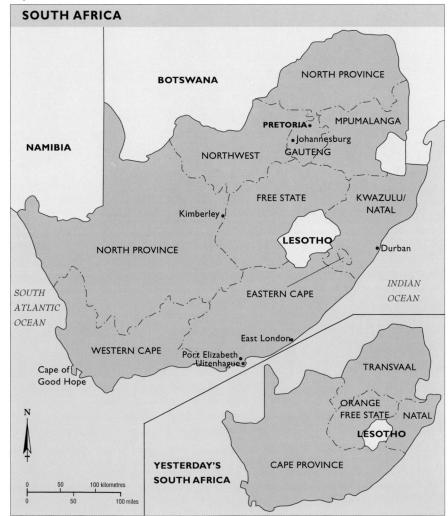

ashore from passing ships. Chinese convicts were generally treated as slaves, and on the expiration of their sentences became part of the 'free black community' – a term used to refer to all free persons wholly or partly descended from Africans or Asians.

Although the numbers of these early Chinese arrivals were very limited, never exceeding 50 to 100 at any one time, they had a relatively significant impact on early Cape society. Many of them were small-scale traders dealing in commodities such as tea, Eastern fabrics, chinaware, fish, baked products and vegetables grown on their own plots of land. Some were involved in crafts such as chandlering, while others kept small but successful eating houses. It is evident that a number of the Chinese were reasonably wealthy as they were listed as being owners of slaves and property. During the Dutch East India Company period, their prosperity aroused hostility from the Dutch settlers, who petitioned against their competition and had legislation instituted which prevented Chinese from continuing with some of their commercial activities.

Chinese immigration remained negligible until after the middle of the 19th century, when diamonds and gold were discovered. This mineral revolution coincided with the mass international emigration from China in the mid-19th century. Although Africa was one of the last continents to which these Chinese migrated, the numbers in South Africa increased markedly, first in diamond-producing Kimberley (in the 1870s), and then mainly in the gold-mining town of Johannesburg and its vicinity (1880s). Many of the new arrivals were from southern China, primarily Fujian, Guangdong and Hainan Island, while others came from Chinese communities in the Straits Settlement and Malaysia.

The Chinese who came to the diamond- and gold-fields arrived there not to mine, this being prohibited by law, but rather to establish various trade and service businesses. It was estimated that by the end of the 19th century there were at least 3,000 Chinese in the Johannesburg region operating six large import firms, 250 grocery stores, laundries and market gardens. At this time various restrictive regulations were introduced in the four South African territories as regards citizenship, residential areas, trading licences and the carrying of passes. Although these laws were directed primarily against the increasing influx of ex-indentured Indian labourers from the Natal sugar plantations, as fellow-Asians the Chinese were also affected.

With the outbreak of the South African War (also known as the Anglo-Boer War, 1899–1902), many of the Chinese who did not return to China left the mining areas for the less turbulent coastal towns of Port Elizabeth and East London. After the war some decided to settle in these areas, but the majority returned to the gold-mining regions.

The gold-mining industry on which the Transvaal economy was based was devastated by the work stoppage and labour dispersal caused by the war. The mine owners campaigned to import Chinese indentured labour as a means to reconstruction. Despite the widespread resistance which this proposal elicited both locally and abroad, the British Conservative government, which now controlled the Transvaal Colony, sanctioned the scheme. After negotiations with the Chinese, the

Chinese junk, the first that rounded the Cape of Good Hope, 1848.

Labour Importation Ordinance was passed in 1904, and the first consignment of indentured labourers arrived on the SS *Tweeddale* in 1904. A total of 34 shipments brought 63,695 Chinese indentured labourers to work on the gold-mines during the 1904–10 period. As a result of disputes with the officials in China's southern provinces, only three shipments were brought from there, with the remainder (62,006 or 97.4 per cent) coming from the northern provinces. The labourers contracted for a period of service not exceeding three years, with the right of renewal for a further two, after which they were to be returned to their country of origin.

The Labour Importation Ordinance was described as the 'most unpopular of all unpopular measures.' Of its 35 sections, half were purely restrictive and aimed at confining the labourers' employment, preventing their escape, prohibiting permanent settlement and precluding competition with the white working class. The other sections included regulations on the compounds, diet and medical care. The Foreign Labour Department was formed for the sole purpose of carrying out the stipulated provisions, and a Chinese Consulate-General was established in Johannesburg to see to the protection of the contracted labourers as well as the other Chinese in South Africa.

The regulations notwithstanding, the management, white miners and the Chinese police abused the Chinese flagrantly. Corporal punishment was often inflicted and fighting was a regular occurrence underground. The Chinese responded to this treatment, the arduous work

Chinese mine workers and interpreters.

Cartoon of African pulling queue of Chinese indentured mine labourer.

and frustrating captivity in various ways. The most common was desertion, which often led to house-breaking and sometimes murder. The Chinese also responded by showing solidarity with fellow-workers no matter how trivial the cause. They would combine in refusing to work, attacking the compound officials, fighting African workers or destroying property. Within the first six months of Chinese employment, 16 incidents requiring police intervention were reported. These developments account for the two extreme perceptions of the Chinese indentured labour system: 'Chinese Slavery' and the 'Yellow Peril.'

Yet the mining industry described the Chinese as the 'most efficient [group of labourers] that has ever been known on these fields.' This benefit was however short-lived. As a result of opposition by the Liberal government in England and the *Het Volk* party in the Transvaal, both of which effectively used the Chinese labour issue as part of their respective election drives, the scheme was terminated. In November 1906 further recruitment was prohibited and the renewal of contracts disallowed. By 1910 the last of the Chinese indentured labourers had been repatriated.

The increased presence of Chinese in the Transvaal from 1904, combined with other anti-Asian sentiments, had a long-term detrimental effect on the free Chinese community throughout the four territories of South Africa. This was despite the fact that during the public furore which preceded the introduction of the indentured labour, the free Chinese community in the Transvaal had made it quite clear that they were 'neither interested nor concerned with the introduction or otherwise of Chinese labour for the mines.'

Regulations to curb and control Asian activities and prevent further immigration were intensified under the post-South African war British administration. In 1904 the Cape Colony introduced the Chinese Exclusion Act; this effectively prohibited admission of all save those able to produce a certificate of exemption. Certificates were granted to Chinese who were British subjects or resident in the Cape at the time of the passing of the Act. The Colony of Natal perpetuated its restrictions on Asian immigration with the infamous language test, while the Orange River Colony endorsed its pre-

Leung Quinn.

war legislation prohibiting entry to 'Asian coloureds.' In the Transvaal, an Asiatic department was created to monitor *Asian* activities, and the Receiver of Revenue was instructed not to grant new annual trading permits unless proof of pre-war trading was submitted. The Chinese community responded with letters to the press, petitions and deputations to the government, all of which were to no avail.

In 1906 legislation was drafted which further exacerbated the position of the free Chinese in the Transvaal. The Asiatic Registration Act, or 'Black Act' as it became known, demanded the compulsory registration of all Asians over the age of eight. A new certificate of identification had to be issued and required information such as marks of identification as well as finger and thumb impressions. This certificate was a prerequisite for the granting of trading licences and the penalty for failing to comply ranged from a fine to a gaol sentence or deportation. The Chinese community resolved to send a deputation to the British government. Although this coincided with an Indian delegation, initially the Chinese were acting quite independently. As a result of these initiatives the enactment of the bill was temporarily delayed. But, in 1907 when the Transvaal was granted responsible government and the *Het Volk* party came into power, it became law.

Together with the rest of the Indian community, Mahatma Gandhi, who was practising law in Johannesburg in the early 1900s, resolved to offer the government a compromise: they were prepared to submit to voluntary rather than compulsory re-registration. If, however, the offer was not accepted, the Indians would resort to *satyagraha*, that is, passive resistance. Within two weeks of this decision 900 members of the Chinese community, under the leadership of Leung Quinn, decided to support the Indian resolution and took an oath to submit themselves to the 'extreme penalty of the law, namely liability to imprisonment and to boycott the permit office.' A period of close cooperation between Gandhi and the Chinese community began when the government rejected the compromise.

Chinese solidarity was evident throughout the first phase of the campaign, and at one stage there were more Chinese in gaol than Indians. In 1908, while both Quinn and Gandhi were imprisoned, they offered the government a second compromise of voluntary registration. The proposal was accepted and although the Chinese still objected to the fingerprint requirement, virtually the whole of the community registered. Contrary to expectations, the Transvaal government did not repeal the Asiatic Registration Act and the compulsory clause was maintained. This resulted in a split in the ranks of the Chinese regarding the continuance of the campaign, with the majority deciding to suspend action.

The Chinese were the only non-Indian group to participate in the passive resistance campaign. This was also the first and last time in South African history that the Chinese were directly active in political agitation. The Chinese community was often praised by Gandhi and he commended their exemplary role in the campaign to his own people. He complimented the Chinese Association on the way they ran their finances and admired their meeting hall as well as the Cantonese club, remarking that the Indians could do well to imitate this. He praised the way in which the Chinese community maintained political unity and encouraged the Indians to follow suit. He also spoke highly of the Chinese on an international level, referring to their use of boycott to protest the introduction of legislation unfavourable to Chinese by powers like the United States of America and Japan, commending this as an aspect of *satyagraha*.

Yet even though Mahatma Gandhi admired the Chinese, and in particular their commitment to the campaign, he was not prepared to concede an alliance between the two communities, claiming that it was 'adversity [which] had made them strange bedfellows in the struggle.' The Chinese for their part also made it apparent to the British authorities that they objected to being treated in the same way as 'British subjects coming from India,' indicating that 'while it may be proper for the British government to treat its Indian subjects as it pleases … subjects of the Chinese Empire should not be treated in a manner derogatory to the dignity of the [Chinese] Empire …. '

The position of the Chinese did not improve with the formation of the Union of South Africa in 1910, since the new political authority merely perpetuated the restrictive nature of the former colonies' legislation. Immigration was virtually prohibited, making the size of the Chinese community dependent on natural increase and special-permit entrants. Owing to their limited numbers (a total of about 4,000 by the 1940s), they maintained a relatively low profile until the National Party government came to power in 1948. According to its Apartheid policies, the Chinese were subjected to a range of discriminatory laws aimed at enforcing racial segregation. Not only did the legislation inconvenience the Chinese, but because it was applied inconsistently, it made them feel uncertain and insecure.

The Apartheid system was based on the Group Areas Act (1950), which identified three main groups for the purpose of segregated residency. Besides the 'white' and 'black' group, there was a more inclusive 'coloured group,' subdivided into Malay, Indian and Chinese. Although the Chinese had asked to be classified as 'white,' they accepted being constituted as a separate group provided that it did not mean segregation in the trade and commercial sector on which the majority of the community depended. Three Chinese group areas were initially proclaimed, but in 1969 they were replaced by a permit system effectively giving the Chinese the unique position of access to all racial areas for the purposes of trade and residence. Besides the humiliating implications of the permit measure, numerous Chinese were also forcibly relocated to accommodate the proclamation of areas for different groups.

Other Apartheid legislation which affected the Chinese directly included the prohibition of mixed marriages, disenfranchisement and separate amenities. Although the Chinese increasingly tended to live as part of white society, in terms of the law they were classified as non-white and subject to licence. They resided in white areas, belonged to white churches, attended predominantly white private schools as well as white tertiary institutions. However, the emigration of 60 per cent of Chinese graduates during the period 1964–84 was indicative of just how untenable the situation was.

Chinese support Indians in passive resistance campaign, Johannesburg.

In the 1980s and 1990s

Towards the end of the 1970s, the National Party government began to change its attitude towards the Chinese for reasons of political and economic expediency. The Republic of China (Taiwan) and South Africa, both increasingly isolated internationally, developed trade and diplomatic relations. These ties had some beneficial consequences for the South African Chinese community, prompting the repeal of certain restrictive laws; and in 1980 the State President nominated a Chinese member to the newly constituted President's Council. In view of the contentious nature of the appointment and the racial bias of the government, the Chinese community declined the position, stating they 'preferred to remain invisible.'

Instead of becoming involved in government politics, the six regional Chinese organizations, which had generally acted independently on local issues since the turn of the century, deemed it necessary to form a national organization. In 1981 the Chinese Association of South Africa (CASA) was formed to act as the official mouthpiece for the community.

In the face of South Africa's increasing economic isolation during the late 1980s and early 1990s, private and government initiatives were taken to attract potential entrepreneurs from Hong Kong and Taiwan to boost the flagging economy. Regions were identified where up to 500 (wealthy) immigrant Chinese families could be settled. CASA declared its opposition to the creation of such racially exclusive areas – against which they had lobbied over the years – resulting in some of the projects being discontinued. With the advent of a more democratic South Africa, CASA persisted in emphasizing its impartiality both in terms of party politics as well as the status of the two Chinas represented in South Africa. In 1994 the Chinese finally became part of the non-racial dispensation in South Africa after centuries of marginalized and ambivalent status.

Karen Leigh Harris

Chinese and African children playing together at school.

TIMELINES

Currents of political, demographic, economic, social and cultural changes in China with a bearing on the story of the overseas Chinese.

DATES	HISTORIC EVENTS	LONG-TERM CHANGES
618–907	**TANG DYNASTY**	
668	Tang unifies Korea under its tributary, the state of Silla.	People from all over Asia throng Chang'an, the imperial capital.
		Indian Buddhism flourishes under imperial patronage. The Chan (Zen) sect appears. Chinese Buddhist pilgrims visit Southeast Asia.
		Introduced from Southeast Asia, the use of tea as a drink spreads.
		Chinese institutions are copied by Korea and Japan.
906	Empire splits into several independent kingdoms.	Chinese population pushes further into the south and southeast (today's Fujian and Guangdong), driving out or absorbing non-Han aborigines.
		Full development of system of recruiting civil servants by examination spells the triumph of the bureaucratic society over the aristocratic.

Tang Taizong, founder of the Tang.

DATES	HISTORIC EVENTS	LONG-TERM CHANGES
907–960	**FIVE DYNASTIES**	
935	Korea breaks free from China.	
939	Vietnam becomes independent.	
960–1127	**NORTHERN SONG**	
1012	The big family clan comes into its own. The reformer Fan Zhongyan (989–1052) establishes rules for 'estates of equity' – special, inalienable lands whose income is to be used for the clan's common needs, such as education and welfare.	Varieties of early-ripening rice imported from Champa (on Vietnam's southeast coast) double harvests and land under cultivation.
1125	Jurchen tribes from Manchuria overrun North China.	
1127–1279	**SOUTHERN SONG**	
1127	Court takes refuge south of Yangzi and inaugurates Southern Song dynasty. Settlement and sinicization of southeast China intensifies.	
11th–13th c.		Population passes the 100 million mark.
		China undergoes a 'commercial revolution,' with an upsurge in overland and overseas trade.
		Porcelain, textiles and lacquer production is perfected. Printing and publishing spread.
		Long-distance travel – by civil servants, merchants, sailors, boatmen and carters – intensifies. Urbanization advances, with trades, men of substance, vagabonds and impoverished peasants moving to towns. Merchant associations (*hang*) multiply, as do associations (*hui*) formed by upper class as well as ordinary people.
		The practice of foot-binding spreads, crippling countless women.
		Confucianism comes into full bloom under Neo-Confucianists like Zhu Xi. Neo-Confucianism, stressing relations of authority, obedience and benevolent paternalism, is established as orthodoxy.
1225		*Zhu Fan Zhi*, compiled by Zhao Rukuo, depicts Southeast Asia and the Indian Ocean from the viewpoint of the trading port of Quanzhou.

Song dynasty porcelain bowl.

Song naval vessel.

DATES	HISTORIC EVENTS	LONG-TERM CHANGES
1279–1368	**YUAN DYNASTY**	

1279	Mongols conquer China.	Mongol rule greatly facilitates Arab trade. Arab merchants live under their own customs and headmen in Chinese seaports like Canton and Zayton (Arab name for the Fujian port of Quanzhou).

Mongol Emperor Kublai Khan.

While numerous foreigners come to China, movement in the opposite direction takes Chinese as far as Russia and Persia. While many Chinese things – medical remedies, art motifs and gunpowder among others – diffuse westward, China is in turn influenced by Arab-Turkish culture.

Islam takes permanent root in China.

End-13th c.	Mongol expeditions to Vietnam, Cambodia, Burma and Java probably spur the Chinese peopling of Southeast Asia.
1271	Unsuccessful naval expedition is launched against Japan.
1281	Naval expedition against Japan fails.
1285	Champa and Cambodia recognize Mongol suzerainty. 
1288	Vietnam recognizes Mongol suzerainty.
1292–93	Expedition against Java.
1368	Chinese rebel hero Zhu Yuanzhang seizes Beijing and proclaims himself emperor.

Yuan dynasty brush washer.

1368–1644	**MING DYNASTY**

A hierarchical system of foreign relations, the tributary system, is refined into high ritual – with envoys sent to, and missions coming from, Korea, Japan, Annam (Vietnam), Burma, Champa, Tibet and other states.

1371	The emperor forbids all private overseas trade.
1403–24	Reign of Yongle.
1405–33	Imperial ambitions to incorporate South and Southeast Asian states into the tribute system are expressed in seven spectacular maritime expeditions led by a Muslim court eunuch named Zheng He.
1406–27	Vietnam incorporated once more into the Chinese empire.
1427	Vietnam once again gains independence. 
1433	Imperial ban on informal or private trade, repeated with increasing penalties in 1449 and 1452.
1514	Portuguese reach China by sea, the first Europeans to do so.
1550s	Harassment of the China coast by Japanese and Chinese pirates culminates in outright invasions.
1567	A system of licensed private trade replaces the imperial ban on all private overseas commerce.
c.1570	Silver first imported from Spanish America. 
1592–98	Japan and China clash over Korea.
1624	The Dutch establish posts on Taiwan coast, forcing out the Japanese and later the Spaniards and signalling the arrival of Europeans in East Asian waters.
1570–1640	
1644	Ming falls to the Manchus.

The Yongle emperor.

Macao's St Paul's Church, relic of early Portuguese presence.

Chinese junk.

The Chinese junk trade flourishes as never before, and Chinese traders enjoy a boom in business at Southeast Asian ports.

DATES	HISTORIC EVENTS	LONG-TERM CHANGES
1644–1911	**QING (MANCHU) DYNASTY**	
1645–60s	Growth in naval-commercial power on the littoral climaxes in the emergence of a Fujianese maritime empire under the buccaneer-commander Zheng Chenggong (Koxinga).	
1656	Imperial edict bans sea navigation.	
1661	Koxinga drives the Dutch out of Taiwan.	Chinese settler population on Taiwan, chiefly from Fujian, reaches 50,000.
1661–62	To crack Koxinga's defence, forced coastal evacuations move inhabitants 16–26 kilometres inland. Terrible suffering ensues.	
1668	Chinese are barred from Manchuria.	
1673	Southern provinces secede from the Qing.	
1677	Qing reconquers Fujian.	
1680		Settler population on Taiwan rises to well over 100,000.
1683	Taiwan is annexed by Qing.	
1684	Maritime ban is rescinded.	
1699	British trading post or factory is established at Canton.	
1717	Imperial edict once more restricts maritime activity, albeit partially.	
1727	Maritime ban is lifted.	
1757	The Qing court restricts all foreign trade to the port of Canton. Europeans have to trade under the 'Canton system,' which confers a monopoly on a group of Chinese firms.	
1762		Census records 200 million inhabitants.
1770s	British traders ship Indian opium to offset trade deficits hitherto paid for by silver bullion in exchange for Chinese silks, porcelains and teas.	
1788–89	Qing expeditions to Vietnam.	
1793	Macartney embassy sent by the East India Company and King of England fails to persuade the Qianlong emperor to lift trade restrictions.	
1812		Census records 361 million inhabitants.
1820–25	East India Company's increasing exports of opium to China drive the Chinese balance of trade into deficit.	Opium addiction and smuggling spread rapidly.
1830		Census records 394,780,000 inhabitants.
1840	First Opium War begins.	
1842	Treaty of Nanjing cedes Hong Kong to Great Britain and opens five Treaty Ports – Amoy (Xiamen), Canton, Fuzhou, Ningbo and Shanghai – to Western trade and residence.	
1846		Census records 421,340,000 inhabitants.
1850s–60s	Taiping Rebellion led by the Hakka 'God Worshipper' Hong Xiuquan devastates southern China. Large and small revolts shake the empire.	
1856–60	France and Britain defeat China in the Second Opium War.	
1860–84	The Self-Strengthening Movement and a bid for 'wealth and power' lead to the adoption of Western techniques and the development of modern enterprise.	
1885–90	China enters the most tragic period of its history: humiliation in wars with France (resulting in the loss of Vietnam) and Japan foreshadows dismemberment by aggressive foreign powers and the dissolution of the Chinese world.	
1895	Treaty of Shimonoseki ceding Taiwan to Japan is signed.	

The emperor Kangxi (r. 1662–1722).

Canton factories.

Opium poppy flower.

DATES	HISTORIC EVENTS	LONG-TERM CHANGES
(cont'd) 1644–1911 QING (MANCHU) DYNASTY		

1900	The dynasty is too far gone to be saved by a massive programme of Meiji-type reforms. The Boxer Rebellion is followed by the Allied nations' occupation of Beijing.	
1905	Revolution is organized abroad and in the foreign concessions of the Treaty Ports. The Republican Tongmeng Hui, precursor of the Kuomintang, is born in Japan.	
1911	Dynasty is overthrown by revolutionists led by Sun Yat-sen.	

Sun Yat-sen (seated right) in Hong Kong, 1911.

1912–49	**REPUBLIC OF CHINA**	
1912	A government national in name only is established under Sun Yat-sen, who soon surrenders power to the militarist Yuan Shikai.	
1914–18	World War I.	
1916–28	Yuan Shikai dies and China enters the 'warlord era.'	
1919	Cultural and revolutionary currents coalesce in the intellectual upsurge named the May Fourth Movement, sparked off by passionate opposition to the terms (very unfavourable to China) of the Versailles Peace Conference.	
1927	A national revolution combining a drive to unify China and the rise of Chiang Kai-shek succeeds in installing the new Kuomintang government in Nanjing.	
1931-32	Japan invades and occupies Manchuria.	
1937	Japanese invasion sparks an upsurge of resistance. The Kuomintang withdraws to the interior, while Japan occupies part of China.	
1941	Pearl Harbor rolls the Sino-Japanese War into World War II.	
1945–49	Following Japanese surrender, Nationalists and Communists slide into civil war. Communism triumphs, and the Kuomintang retreats permanently to Taiwan.	

Chiang Kai-shek.

La Jeunesse, one of the influential May Fourth era periodicals.

Mao Zedong leads Communists to victory.

1949–	**PEOPLE'S REPUBLIC OF CHINA**	
1958–62	The Great Leap Forward trails famine on a staggering scale. The Sino-Soviet rupture parts two socialist behemoths. Fighting breaks out between Chinese and Indian border troops.	
1966–76	The Cultural Revolution unleashes violent tensions in Chinese society.	
1972	US President Nixon's visit marks China's re-opening.	
1976	The deaths of Zhou Enlai and Mao Zedong pave the way for Deng Xiaoping's ascendancy.	
1979	China's transition from socialism – called 'reforms and opening' – begins. Special Economic Zones are established along the coast.	
1982		Census shows China's population has passed the one-billion mark.
1984	China and Great Britain agree on the return of Hong Kong to Chinese sovereignty in 1997.	
1989	On June 4, armed tanks smash their way through to Tiananmen Square, where political protestors and hunger strikers are assembled, to wreak a massacre that shocks the world.	
1997	After 156 years as a British colony, Hong Kong is reincarnated as a Special Administrative Region of China.	

Last British governor and Beijing's representative in Hong Kong.

ACKNOWLEDGEMENTS

For help of one kind or another with research and the procurement of pictures, the Chinese Heritage Centre is indebted to the following individuals and institutions:

In Australia, Museum and Art Gallery of the Northern Territory;

In Britain, Charlotte Havilland of John Swire and Sons; J. J. G. Brown of Matheson and Company, London;

In Canada, British Columbia Archives; Anthony B. Chan;

In Denmark, Mette Thunoe;

In Italy, Daniele Cologna, Yap Eng Guan;

In Japan, Kazuko Asakura, Yokohama Archives of History;

In Malaysia, Sarawak Museum, *Sin Chew Jit Poh*;

In the Netherlands, the Amsterdams Historisch Museum;

In New Zealand, James Ng, Otago Heritage Books;

In the Philippines, Jonathan Best, Teresita Ang See of Kaisa Para Sa Kaunlaran, Inc.;

In Singapore, Boon Yoon Chiang of Jardines Matheson (S) Ltd, Canadian Tourism Commission, Centre for Chinese Language and Culture (Nanyang Technological University), Meileen Choo, Goh Ee Choo, Ch'ng Kim See, Aileen Lau, Lee Chee Keng, Lim Guan Hock, Lise Young Lai, Singapore National Archives, Ni Yibin, Singapore Art Museum, *The Straits Times* Editorial Library, Tan Siew Eim, Lucas Tettoni, Yee Siew Pun;

In Suriname, J. A. Tjin Wong Joe;

In Sweden, Gerhard Joren;

In the United States, Darrell Corti, National Archives and Records Administration, The MIT Museum, The Pacific Bell Museum.

PICTURE CREDITS

Part I

p 18 Zheng Dehua; p 21 Science Press; p 26 Chen Hanmin (top), Wang Gangfeng (bottom); p 28 Zheng Dehua (all); p 29 Zheng Dehua (all); p 30 Victoria and Albert Museum, (bottom); p 32 Zeng Ling; p 33 Courtesy of China Information Centre; p 34 The Nineties Monthly/Going Fine Limited (top); p 35 Zheng Dehua (all); p 36 Liu Yilin (top), courtesy of Matheson and Company (middle); p 37 Zheng Dehua (top), Goh Eck Kheng (bottom); p 38 Courtesy of Persatuan Thoong Nyien (Hakka) Johor Bahru (middle upper), Zheng Dehua (middle lower); p 39 Courtesy of Mette Thunoe (top), courtesy of Information Office of Wenzhou Municipality People's Government (bottom); p 40 Courtesy of Mette Thunoe (top), Victoria and Albert Museum (bottom); p 41 Wang Miao; p 42 Courtesy of Singapore Kiung Chow Hwee Kuan (top), Wang Miao (middle, bottom); p 43 Courtesy of Singapore Kiung Chow Hwee Kuan (middle).

Part II

p 44 Mary Evans Picture Library; p 46 Nanjing University (middle); p 47 *Yazhou Zhoukan*/Huang Qindai; p 48 Antiques of the Orient (middle left), Jan Adkins (bottom); p 50 Sumarah Adhyatman (top, middle left); p 51 Sumarah Adhyatman (top), Antiques of the Orient (bottom); p 53 Chicago Historical Society; p 54 Joint Publishing (Hong Kong) Company (top), Urban Council of Hong Kong from the collection of Hong Kong Museum of Art (bottom); p 55 Antiques of the Orient (top left), Urban Council of Hong Kong from the collection of Hong Kong Museum of Art (top right), National Geographic/Sisse Brimberg (middle), Mary Evans Picture Library (bottom); p 56 Roger Viollet (bottom); p 57 Courtesy of Matheson and Company; p 58 Agence-France Presse,

Hong Kong (top), Li Zhensheng (bottom); p 59 Getty Images/Louis Chu; p 60 Antiques of the Orient; p 61 Courtesy of John Swire and Sons (bottom), p 62 *Yazhou Zhoukan*; p 63 Daisy Kwok (top), courtesy of National Archives and Records Administration, United States/90-G-124-479 (bottom); p 64 Roger Viollet; p 67 The Nineties Monthly/Going Fine Limited; p 68 Reuters/Jonathan Drake; p 71 Hans van den Boogaard (top, middle).

Part III

p 72 National Archives, Singapore; p 74 FormAsia Books Limited; p 75 National Palace Museum (top); p 76 Nigel Hicks (top); p 77 Courtesy of Library of Congress/Arnold Genthe (top), National Archives, Singapore (bottom); p 79 Southeast Asian Ceramics Society; p 80 Harry Gruyaert (top), National Archives, Singapore (bottom); p 81 Philip Little (top left), Michael Liew (top right), Michael Vatikiotis (bottom); p 84 Courtesy of British Columbia Archives/G-01130 (top); p 85 Ho Khee Tong (top); p 86 Courtesy of Singapore Federation of Chinese Clan Associations (top); p 87 Courtesy of Archives Association Mémoire Collective (bottom); p 90 Courtesy of Bishop Museum/On Char Collection (bottom); p 92 Courtesy of Oversea-Chinese Banking Corporation, Singapore (top), courtesy of Meileen Choo (bottom); p 93 Enny Nuraheni; p 94 Raghu Rai.

Part IV

p 96 Zhang Hongtu; p 99 National Archives, Singapore (middle); p 100 Courtesy of Tai-Wu Yulin (middle), Urban Council of Hong Kong from the collection of Hong Kong Museum of History (bottom); p 102 Hans van den Boogaard (top); p 103 Snark International (top); p 104 Courtesy of *The Bangkok Post*; p 105 Natural History Museum (top), Joint Publishing (Hong Kong) Company (middle), courtesy of Library of Congress/Arnold Genthe (bottom); p 106 Joint Publishing (Hong Kong) Company (all); p 107 Joint Publishing (Hong Kong) Company (top), courtesy of Meileen Choo (middle); p 108 Bank of China (middle); p 109 Patrick Zachmann; p 110 Patrick Zachmann; p 112 Zeng Ling (top); p 113 Michael Vatikiotis; p 114 Courtesy of Matheson and Company (middle), Vancouver Public Library (bottom); p 115 Singapore History Museum (top), courtesy of Singapore Turf Club (bottom); p 116 National Archives, Singapore, courtesy of Jonathan Best; p 117 National Archives, Singapore (top), Victoria and Albert Museum (bottom); p 118 Courtesy of Anthony B. Chan (top), courtesy of Leo Suryadinata (bottom); p 119 Courtesy of Leo Suryadinata; p 120 Associated Press (top), courtesy of National Archives and Records Administration, United States (bottom); p 121 National Archives, Singapore (top), courtesy of Matheson and Company/Coats Crafts (bottom); p 122 Courtesy of Felicia Lowe (top), M. Photo (bottom); p 123 Singapore Art Museum (top), courtesy of Yeoh Jin Leng/Fine Arts Press (bottom); p 124 Liu Shengqia; p 125 Associated Press; p 126 Xu Zongmao (top), Metropolitan Museum of Art, New York (bottom); p 127 Antiques of the Orient (middle); p 128 Singapore Art Museum/Cheong Leng Guat (middle), Urban Council of Hong Kong from the collection of Hong Kong Museum of Art/C.C. Wang (bottom left), Singapore Art Museum/Lee Ee Ling (bottom right); p 129 Courtesy of Zao Wou-ki/Raffles City Private Limited (top), courtesy of Hung Liu (middle left), courtesy of Tseng Yuho (middle right), courtesy of Gu Wenda (bottom); p 130 Courtesy of Singapore Art Museum/Lee Foundation (top left), courtesy of Singapore Art Museum/Tan Swee Hian

(top right), courtesy of Sanit Khewhok (bottom); p 131 Courtesy of Singapore Art Museum/Chong Fah Cheong (middle left), courtesy of Singapore Art Museum/Wong Hoy Cheong (middle right), courtesy of Singapore Art Museum/Lao Lian Ben (middle lower), courtesy of Singapore Art Museum/Goh Ee Choo (bottom left), courtesy of Singapore Art Museum/Baet Yeok Kwan (bottom right); p 132 Courtesy of Meileen Choo (top); p 133 Scarlet Cheng (top, left), M. Photo (top, right), courtesy of Columbia Pictures/Clive Coote (middle), Wee Khim (bottom, left); p 134 *Yazhou Zhoukan* (bottom).

Part V: Communities

p 136 Kenneth Wayne Heller

Southeast Asia

p 139 Wang Miao; p 141 Bertil Lintner (top), Hseng Novug Lintner (bottom); p 142 Bertil Lintner; p 143 Goh Eck Kheng (top), David Devoss (bottom); p 144 Courtesy of Eleanor Mannikka; p 145 Serge Dubuisson/Centre des archives d'Outre-Mer (top), Toyama Museum of Fine Art (bottom); p 146 W. E. Willmott; p 147 Darren Whiteside; p 149 Ira Chaplain; p 150 Tim Hall (all); p 152 Antiques of the Orient (top), Haags Gemeentemuseum (bottom); p 154 Los Angeles County Museum of Art (all); p 156 Antiques of the Orient; p 157 Koninklijk Instituut voor Taal-, Land-en Volkenkunde, Leiden; p 158 *Forbes Zibenjia* (bottom); p 159 *Forbes Zibenjia* (all); p 160 Editions Didier Millet; p 161 Sectie Militaire Geschiedenis Landmachtstaf; p 163 Courtesy of *Sin Chew Jit Poh*, Malaysia (bottom); p 166 Associated Press (top); p 167 Philip Little; p 168 Courtesy of *Sin Chew Jit Poh*, Malaysia (top), Agence-France Presse, Hong Kong (bottom); p 169 Photobank; p 170 Ng Shui Meng; p 172 British Library (middle); p 174 Courtesy of Tai-Wu Yulin (top), courtesy of Alice Scott-Ross (middle); p 175 National Archives, Singapore; p 176 Courtesy of Pacific Bank Berhad (middle left), National Archives, Singapore (bottom); p 177 LLG Cultural Development Centre Bhd (top); p 178 Courtesy of Lim Kit Siang (top), courtesy of Lim Chong Eu (middle left), Utusan Melayu (Malaysia) Berhad (middle right, bottom); p 179 Philip Little; p 180 *Forbes Zibenjia* (all); p 181 Ling Liong Sik; p 182 *Yazhou Zhoukan*/Chan Looi Tat (all); p 183 Courtesy of Elizabeth Choy; p 184 Courtesy of Sarawak Museum; p 186 Courtesy of Wee Cho Yaw; p 188 Courtesy of Jonathan Best; p 189 Courtesy of Kaisa Para Sa Kaunlaran, Inc. (top, middle); p 190 Courtesy of Jonathan Best (top), Geronimo Berenguer de los Reyes Jr. Museum (middle); p 191 *Forbes Zibenjia* (all); p 192 Associated Press; p 193 Courtesy of Kaisa Para Sa Kaunlaran, Inc.; p 194 Courtesy of Jonathan Best; p 195 Leong Ka Tai; p 196 Tara Sosrowardoyo; p 197 Courtesy of Kaisa Para Sa Kaunlaran, Inc.; p 198 Catherine Karnow (top), Rio Helmi (bottom); p 199 Melvyn Calderon; p 201 National Archives, Singapore (middle), courtesy of Tan Tock Seng Hospital (bottom); p 202 National Archives, Singapore (top), courtesy of Tan Tock Seng Hospital (bottom); p 203 National Archives, Singapore (all); p 204 National Archives, Singapore (middle), Raffles Hotel (bottom); p 205 National Archives, Singapore (all); p 207 Courtesy of Tan Kok Kheng (middle), National Archives, Singapore (bottom); p 208 National Archives, Singapore (middle), courtesy of Oversea-Chinese Banking Corporation, Singapore (bottom); p 209 *The Straits Times* Editorial Library; p 210 National Archives, Singapore (top, middle, bottom left); p 211 *The Straits Times* Editorial Library (top); p 213 *The Straits Times* Editorial Library (top), courtesy of Lim Guan Hock (bottom); p 216 Philip Little (top), *The Straits Times* Editorial Library (bottom); p 217 Courtesy of Susan Tan Pin Pin (top); p 218 Sten Sjostrand; p 219 Michael Vatikiotis (top), Musée Guimet, Paris (bottom); p 220 Photobank (top), Zheng Dehua (middle); p 221 Courtesy of Owyang Hsuan (all); p 222 Wang Miao (top), Courtesy of *The Bangkok Post* (bottom); p 223 Courtesy of *The Bangkok Post*; p 224 Hseng Novug Lintner (top), Michael Vatikiotis (bottom); p 225 *Forbes* (top), Bureau Bangkok (bottom); p 227 *The Nation* (top), Wang Miao (middle); p 228 Leonard de Selva; p 229 Patrick Zachmann; p 231 Tapabor (top), Peter Korniss (bottom); p 232 Paul Chesley; p 233 United Press International (top), courtesy of Gerhard Joren (middle), Tim Hall (bottom).

The Americas
p 234 Vancouver Public Library / 1773; p 235 Courtesy of British Columbia Archives / G-01591; p 236 Courtesy of British Columbia Archives / D-05246; p 237 Courtesy of British Columbia Archives / C-02398; p 238 Courtesy of British Columbia Archives / PDP01873, D-08817; p 239 Courtesy of Anthony B. Chan; p 240 Vancouver Public Library; p 242 *Asia Inc.* / Ron Watts (top), *Asia Inc.* / K. Straiton (bottom); p 244 *Yazhou Zhoukan*; p 245 Canadian Pacific Ltd (top), courtesy of Anthony B. Chan (bottom); p 246 Canada Post Corporation; p 247 Kevin Bishop (middle), courtesy of Canadian Tourism Commission (bottom); p 251 Walton Look Lai (middle), Rolando Pujols (bottom); p 253 Museum of Modern Art, New York / S. D. O. Wifredo Lam (top), courtesy of Singapore Art Museum / Lee Foundation (bottom); p 256 *National Geographic* / Roger Morris; p 257 SERPOL; p 258 Xinhua News Agency; p 259 Bjorn Klingwall; p 260 Lynn Pan (all); p 261 Union Pacific Museum Collection; p 263 Hai Feng Publishing Co.; p 264 Courtesy of The Bancroft Library (top), Bishop Museum / On Char Collection (bottom); p 265 Courtesy of National Archives and Records Administration, United States / 208-PU-223-DD-F5-2791-1 (top), courtesy of The Pacific Bell Museum (middle), Sylvia Sun Minnick (bottom); p 266 Courtesy of The MIT Museum (top), courtesy of Fudan University (middle upper, middle); p 267 Patrick Zachmann (top); p 269 Catherine Karnow; p 270 *The Straits Times* Editorial Library; p 271 M. Photo / Tomas Muscionico; p 272 Harvey Wang (top), Santi Visalli (bottom); p 273 Russel Wong (top), M. Photo (bottom).

Australasia and Oceania
p 274 National Library of Australia (top), Roy Cheong (bottom); p 275 Courtesy of Museum and Art Gallery of the Northern Territory (top); p 276 David Paul Morris; p 277 Courtesy of Dato Yap Lim Sen (top), courtesy of Edmond Lee (bottom); p 278 Australia-China Friendship Society; p 279 Australia-China Friendship Society (top), Gary Ede (bottom); p 280 Gary Ede (top), courtesy of Dato Yap Lim Sen (bottom); p 281 Fairfax Photo Library (top); p 282 Benaji; p 283 Courtesy of Dato Yap Lim Sen; p 284 M. Photo / Southern Star (top), courtesy of University of Sydney (middle), Fairfax Photo Library (bottom); p 285 Courtesy of *Far Eastern Economic Review* / Morgan Chua (top), Museum and Art Gallery of the Northern Territory / Evelyn Yuen (middle); p 286 Nelson Provincial Museum / W. E. Brown Collection; p 287 Alexander Turnbull Library, Wellington, New Zealand (top), courtesy of Otago Heritage Books / James Ng (middle), Kirkland Collection (bottom); p 288 Courtesy of Otago Heritage Books / James Ng; p 289 Alexander Turnbull Library, Wellington, New Zealand; p 290 Asia2000 Foundation of New Zealand; p 291 Sinorama Magazine; p 293 W. E. Willmott; p 295 Fiji Overseas Chinese Cultural Centre; p 296 *Deutsche Kolonialzeitung*; p 298 Sir Julius Chan; p 299 W. E. Willmott; p 300 Auckland Institute; p 301 L' Association Wen Fa (top left, top right), Bernard Hermann (middle); p 302 Bernard Hermann (all); p 303 W. E. Willmott (all).

Europe
p 305 Hulton Deutsch (all); p 306 Terry Lo; p 307 *The Star,* Malaysia (middle), Grace Lau (bottom); p 308 Grace Lau (all); p 309 Terry Lo (top), Grace Lau (middle), Anna Chen (bottom); p 310 The University of Ulster (top, middle right), John Harrison (middle left), Belfast Telegraph (bottom); p 311 University of Minnesota; p 312 Courtesy of Archives Association Mémoire Collective (all); p 313 Patrick Zachmann; p 314 Courtesy of M. Bordry; p 315 Courtesy of Archives Association Mémoire Collective (top), Laurent Kalfala (bottom); p 317 Live Yu-Sion (top), M. Photo / Liu Heung Shing (bottom); p 318 Bibliothèque municipale de Lyon (all); p 319 Civico Archivo Fotografico di Milano (middle); p 320 Marco Costa; p 321 Christian Novak; p 322, 323, 324 Courtesy of Amsterdams Historisch Museum; p 326 Louis van Paridon; p 327 Cor Jaring; p 329 National (Russian) Scientific Library of the Far East; p 330 Roger Viollet (middle); p 331 Alexei A. Maslov (top), M. Photo / James Hill (bottom).

East Asia
p 333 (all), 334 Courtesy of Yokohama Archives of History (all); p 337 Courtesy of Yokohama Archives of History (bottom); p 338 Courtesy of Yokohama Archives of History (top), Nissin Foods (middle); p 340 Reiichi Murakami (all); p 341, 343 Courtesy of Ching You-kwang.

Indian Ocean and Africa
p 345 *The Straits Times* Editorial Library (top); p 346 *The Straits Times* Editorial Library (top), Ellen Oxfeld (bottom); p 347 Live Yu-Sion; p 349 Live Yu-Sion (all); p 350 Live Yu-Sion (all); p 351, 352, 353, 354 Huguette Ly-Tio-Fane Pineo (all); p 355 Paul Chesley (top), Yves Pitchen (middle); p 357 Danielle Jay (middle), Live Yu-Sion (bottom); p 358 Live Yu-Sion; p 359 Live Yu-Sion (all); p 361 Africana Museum (top), Transvaal Archives Depot / 4031 (bottom); p 362 *The Reef* (top), *Indian Opinion* (bottom); p 363 *Transvaal Weekly Illustrated* (top), Ruth Motau (bottom).

Timelines
p 364 National Palace Museum (top), Nanjing Museum (middle); p 365 Courtesy of Soobin Art Gallery (top), Nanjing Museum (middle upper), Hu Chui (middle lower); p 366 Hu Chui (top), Urban Council of Hong Kong from the collection of Hong Kong Museum of Art (middle), E. T. Archive (bottom); p 367 Horstman Godfrey (top), Hai Feng Publishing Co. (middle upper), Museum of the Chinese Revolution (middle), Frank Fischbeck (middle lower), Yazhou Zhoukan / Huang Qindai (bottom).

p 400 Editions Didier Millet.

While every effort has been made to trace copyright holders, the publishers would like to apologize to anyone who has not been formally acknowledged.

CHINESE CHARACTER LIST

A Cheng 阿城
Acham, Eugene Bernard (see Chen, Eugene)
Ah-Chee 陈达枝
Ah-Chuen, Jean 朱梅麟
Amnuay Virawan (see Lin Riguang)
Amoy (see Xiamen)
Anhui 安徽
Ann Kway (see Anxi)
Anxi 安溪
Aw Boon Haw (see Hu Wenhu)
Baet Yeok Kwan 麦毓权
Bai Xianyong 白先勇
baishen 拜神
Ban Hin Lee 万兴利
bang 帮
banghui 帮会
hangzhang 帮长
Banyuebao 半月报
Baoan 宝安
Baoding 保定
Baohuang Hui 保皇会
Baoshan 保山
Bei Dao 北岛
Beijiang 北江
Beijing 北京
bendi 本地
Bentougong 本头公
Bian Chiang 联昌
Bihua Taishang Jingmao Xiehui 比华台商经贸协会
Bincunshan 彬村山
Boen Bio (see Wen miao)
Boen Tjhiang Soe (see Wenchang Ci)
Boluo 博罗
Bu shi Lushan zhen mianmu/Zhi yuan shen zai ci shan zhong 不识庐山真面目，只缘身在此山中
C. Q. Yee Hop 思乔义合
Cai Hesen 蔡和森
Cai, Lily 蔡福丽
Caifu Shen 财富神
Canton 广州
cha 茶
Chan, Bernard 陈秉达
Chan Choy Siong 陈翠嫦
Chan, Jackie 成龙
Chan, Julius 陈仲民
Chan Kai Tai 陈启泰
Chan Kim Boon 曾锦文
Chan, Raymond 陈卓愉
Chan, Robin 陈有庆
Chang Dai Yen 郑帝恩
Chang, Eileen (see Zhang Ailing)
Chang Jung 张戎
Chang, Terence 蒋家骏
Chang, Victor 张任谦
Chang'an 长安
Changhou Tang 昌后堂
Changle 长乐
Changxian 长限
Chaoan 潮安
Chao-Shan 潮汕
Chaoyang 潮阳
Chaozhou 潮州
Char Yew 谢有
Che Gong 车公
Cheang Hong Lim 章芳林
Chee Kung Tong (see Zhigong Tang)
Chefoo 芝罘
Chekiang (see Zhejiang)
Chen, Anna 陈云西
Chen Bo 陈柏
Chen Cihong 陈慈黉
Chen, Daniel 陈锡恩
Chen, Eugene 陈友仁

Chen Fupo 陈福坡
Chen, Georgette (see Zhang Liying)
Chen Guoliang 陈国梁
Chen H. T. (see Chen Xuetong)
Chen Hansheng 陈翰笙
Chen, Joan 陈冲
Chen Kaige 陈凯歌
Chen Kaishun 陈开顺
Chen Limei 陈立梅
Chen Shangchuan 陈上川
Chen Shichong 陈世崇
Chen Shike 陈世科
Chen Shiwang 陈世望
Chen Shouhe 陈守河
Chen Shouming 陈守明
Chen Ta 陈达
Chen Xuanyi 陈宣衣
Chen Xuetong 陈学同
Chen Yeliang 陈业良
Chen Yi 陈毅
Chen Yuanfeng 陈元丰
Chen Zhangman 陈璋满
Chen Zhiping 陈支平
Chen-chou (see Zhenzhou)
Cheng Huang 城隍
Cheng San 静山
Chengdu 成都
Chenghai 澄海
Cheong Soo Pieng 钟四宾
Cheung, Maggie 张曼玉
Chi, Tony 徐文章
Chia Ek-chor (see Xie Yichu)
Chia Tai (see Zhengda)
Chiang Ching 江青
Chiang Ching-Kuo 蒋经国
Chiang Kai-shek 蒋介石
Chie Nun (see Xu Neng)
Chim Soo (see Shen Xiugong)
Chin Foo (see Chen Shichong)
Chin, Frank 赵健秀
Chin Lung 陈康大
Chin Pak (see Chen Bo)
Chin Peng 陈平
Chin Sophonpanich 陈弼臣
Ching Chung (see Qingsong)
Ching Hung Wo 程庆和
Ching You-kuang (see Qin Yuguang)
Chixi 赤溪
Chong Fah Cheong 张华昌
Chong Hock 崇福
Chong Wah Hui Koon (see Zhonghua Huiguan)
Chong Wen Ge 崇文阁
Chongfu 崇福
Chongqing 重庆
Chongyang 重阳
Choo Eng Choon 朱永春
Choo Kok Leong 朱国亮
Choon Guan 俊源
Choo Meileen 朱美莲
Chop Bian Hong 联芳号
chop suey 杂碎
Chou Wen-chung 周文中
Choy, Christine 崔明惠
Chua Jim Neo 蔡认娘
Ch'üan-chou (see Quanzhou)
Chun Quon 陈滚
Chung, Arthur 钟富刚
Chung, Connie 宋毓华
Chung Hua Hui (see Zhonghua Hui)
Chung Hwa Hui (see Zhonghua Hui)
Chung Hwa Hui Tsa Chih (see Zhonghua hui zazhi)
Chung Wah (see Zhonghua)
Chungshan (see Zhongshan)

Chung-Wah 中华
Chuqu 处衢
Cixi 慈禧
Cohong (see gonghang)
Coseteng, Eduardo 许友超
cukong 主公
Dabu 大埔
Dagang 大港
Dai 傣
Daile 傣仂
Dajia 大甲
dan 石
Danxian 儋县
Dapeng 大鹏
Datian 大田
Datong 大同
Datong Shu 大同书
daxing 大姓
Dee C. Chuan 李清泉
Deguo Hanbao Zhonghua Huiguan 德国汉堡中华会馆
Dehua 德化
Deng Xiaoping 邓小平
Dhanin Chearavanont (see Xie Guomin)
Diaoyutai 钓鱼台
Ding Dawei 丁大为
Ding, Loni 丁碧兰
Ding Shaoguang 丁绍光
diqu 地区
Dong, Arthur 曾奕田
Dong Jioa Zong (see Dongjiaozong)
Dong, Kingman 曾景文
Dongguan 东莞
Dongjiang 东江
Dongjiaozong 董教总
Dongshan 东山
dou 斗
Doumen 斗门
dsui hua 掇画*
Duan Qirui 段祺瑞
Duanhua 端华
Dun, Dennis 江演恒
Dunhuang 敦煌
Duoduo 多多
Duong Ngan Dich (see Yang Yandi)
Eng Keng 英抗
Enping 恩平
Fah (see Huaxian)
Fan Zhongyan 范仲淹
Fangshan 方山
Feiji Huaren Xiehui 斐济华人协会
Feng Jingru 冯镜如
Feng Liu 冯六
Feng Zishan 冯紫珊
Fengcaitang 风采堂
fengshui 风水
Fengshun 丰顺
Fengtian 奉天
Fo 佛
Foguangshan 佛光山
Fokuangshan (see Foguangshan)
Fong, Hiram 邝友良
Foochow (see Fuzhou)
Foshan 佛山
Fu Hsien-ta 傅显达
Fu'an 福安
Fui Toong On (see Hui-Dong-An)
Fuji 福济
Fujian 福建
Fujian Gongsuo 福建公所
Fujian Huiguan 福建会馆
Fuk Ching (see Fuqing)
Fuk Qing 福清
Fu-Ning 福宁

Funü Lianyihui 妇女联谊会
fuqi 福气
Fuqing 福清
fuwu gongsi 服务公司
Fuxing Hao 复兴号
Fuzhou 福州
gaifong (see jiefang)
Gan 赣
Gan Eng Seng 颜永成
Gan Yangzi 赣扬子
Gang-Ao 港澳
Gangzhou 冈州
gangzhu 港主
Gansu 甘肃
Gao Shengzhi 高绳芝
Gao Xingjian 高行健
Gaoyang 高阳
Gee Yun 朱源芷
Ghee Hin 义兴
Goh Chok Tong 吴作栋
Goh Ee Choo 吴一主
Goh Keng Swee 吴庆瑞
Gong Li 巩俐
gongguan 公馆
gonghang 公行
Gonghe 公和
Gonghechun 共和春
gongsi 公司
gongsi heying 公私合营
gongsuo 公所
Goulou 勾漏
Gu Cheng 顾城
Gu Wenda 谷文达
Guan Gong 关公
Guan Wei 关伟
Guandi 关帝
Guangdi Miao 关帝庙
Guangdong 广东
Guangfu 广府
Guangsheng 广生
Guangtai 广泰
Guangxi 广西
Guangyi tang sheng 广义堂生
Guangzhou 广州
Guangzhouwan 广州湾
Guanhua 官话
guanxi 关系
Guanyin 观音
Guanyin Dashi Ye 观音大势爷
Guanyin Ting 观音亭
gui 归
Guiqiao 归侨
Guizhou 贵州
Guo Songyi 郭松义
Guoji ribao 国际日报
Gutian 古田
Hai San 海山
Haicheng 海澄
Haikou 海口
Hainan 海南
Haiwai Huashang Gonghui 海外华商公会
haiwai 海外
haiwai siren huikuan fuwu chu 海外私人汇款服务处
Haiyang 海阳
Hakka 客家
Han 韩
Han 汉
Hanbao Zhonghua Haiyuan Zhi Jia 汉堡中华海员之家
Hancheng Huaqiao Xiehui 汉城华侨协会
hang 行
Hangzhou 杭州
Hanyu 汉语
haoming 好命
He Dong 何东
He Qi 何启
He Xiangning 何香凝
Hebei 河北
Hehe 和合
Heilongjiang 黑龙江
Helan Zhonghua Huzhuhui 荷兰中华互助会
Heng, Ivan 王爱仁
Henghua (see Xinghua)
Heshan 鹤山

Ho A-mei 何亚美
Ho Chi Minh 胡志明
Ho Chinn 何清
Ho Hong 和丰
Ho Kai (see He Qi)
Ho Ming Chung 何名忠
Ho Ping-ti 何炳棣
Hoa 华
hoan'a 番仔
Hochiu (see Fuzhou)
Hock Hua 福华
Hock Lee 福利
Hokchia (see Fuqing)
Hokchiu (see Fuzhou)
Hokkien 福建
Hokkien Huay Kuan (see Fujian Huiguan)
Hoklo 福佬
Hong Kingston, Maxine 汤婷婷
Hong Ying 虹影
Hongmen Jinbu Dang 洪门进步党
Hongmen 洪门
Hoo Ah Kay 胡亚基
Hoo Hap (see Hehe)
Hotung (see He Dong)
Houguan 侯官
Houyu 侯屿
Hsi Lai 西来
Hsu Tzu Lin 许子麟
Hu Jianliang 胡健良
Hu, King 胡金铨
Hu Shi 胡适
Hu Wenhu 胡文虎
Hu Xuanze 胡璇泽
Hua 华
Hua Zhi 华支
Huafa jiaoyu hui 华法教育会
Huai 淮
Huang Daxian 黄大仙
Huang Rongliang 黄荣良
Huang Zunxian 黄遵宪
huangcao 黄草
Huangdi 黄帝
huangniu bei 黄牛背
huang-ts'ao (see huangcao)
Huaqiao 华侨
Huaqiao Tongxun 华侨通讯
Huaqiao Zhongxue 华侨中学
Huaqiao Zhugong 华侨主公
Huaren 华人
Huaren Kangle Shi 华人康乐室
Huashang 华商
Huashang ribao 华商日报
Huati 华体
Huaxian 花县
huaxiaosheng 华校生
Huayi 华裔
Huayi Qingnian Lianhehui 华裔青年联合会
Huayi Xieshanghui 华裔协商会
Huayu 华语
Hubei 湖北
hui 会
Hui 徽
Hui 回
Hui, Ann 许鞍华
Hui-Dong-An 惠东安
huiguan 会馆
Huilai 惠来
Huimin 惠民
Huiwen 会文
Huiyang 惠阳
Huizhou 惠州
hukou 户口
hun hui gutu 魂回故土
Hunan 湖南
Hwang, David Henry 黄哲伦
Hwang Yung-liang (see Huang Rongliang)
jao sua (see zuo shan)
Jeme Tian Yau (see Zhan Tianyou)
jia 家
jiang 江
Jiang Qing 江青
Jiangmen 江门
Jiangsu 江苏

Jiangxi 江西
Jianpuzhai Huaren Lishihui 柬埔寨华人历史会
Jiaoling 蕉岭
Jiaying 嘉应
jiefang 街坊
Jiefang ribao 解放日报
jiemeng 结盟
Jieyang 揭阳
jieyi 结义
jiguan 籍贯
Jilin 吉林
Jilong 吉龙
Jimei 集美
Jin 晋
Jinan 济南
Jinan 暨南
Jinjiang 晋江
Jinmen 金门
jinshan 金山
jinshan daihai 锦山带海
jinshanzhuang 金山庄
Jintian 今天
Jishan Tang 继善堂
jitian 祭田
Jiulong 九龙
Jon Jang (see Hu Jianliang)
Joong Hing Loong (see Zhongxinglong)
Ju Boling 鞠柏岭
juan 眷
Jung, Douglas 郑天华
junzi 君子
Kaiping 开平
Kasian Tejapira 郑卓峰
Kang Youwei 康有为
Kanti (see Guangdi)
Kejia 客家
Kejia yanjiu daolun 客家研究导论
ketou 客头
Khaw Soo Cheang 许泗漳
kheh-tau (see ketou)
Kheng Leong 庆隆
Khoo Soek Wan 邱菽园
Kiangsi (see Jiangxi)
Kim Seng Lee 金成利
Kin Tye Lung (see Qiantailong)
Kong Chew (see Gangzhou)
Kong Koan (see gongguan)
Kong Ngie Tong Sang (see Guangyi tang sheng)
kongsi 公司
Koo Men Tong 国民党
Kowloon 九龙
Koxinga (see Zheng Chenggong)
Kuo, Eddie 郭振羽
Kuok, Robert 郭鹤年
Kuomintang 国民党
Kwa Geok Choo 柯玉芝
Kwee Tek Hoay 郭德怀
Kwok, William 郭期颐
Kwong Sang (see Guangsheng)
Kwong Sue Duk 邝仕德
Kwong Tiy (see Guangtai)
Kwong Yik 广益
Kwong-Chew 冈州
Lam, David See-chai 林思齐
Lanfang Kongsi 兰芳公司
Lao She 老舍
Laohong 老洪
laoke 老客
Lau Hui Kang 刘会干
Lau Pak Khuan 刘伯群
Lauw Chuan Tho 刘泉道
Law, Clara 罗卓瑶
Law, Michel 刘月林
Lee Ang 李安
Lee, Art 李桥栋
Lee Bok Boon 李沐文
Lee, Bruce 李小龙
Lee C. Y. 黎锦扬
Lee Chin Koon 李进坤
Lee Dai Keong 李帝强
Lee Guan Kin (see Li Yuanjin)
Lee H. S. 李孝式
Lee Hoon Leong 李云龙

Lee Kong Chian 李光前
Lee Kuan Yew 李光耀
Lee Man Fong 李曼峰
Lee, Robert 李亮汉
Lee San Choon 李三春
Lee Teng-hui 李登辉
Lee Tsung-Dao 李政道
Lehui 乐会
Leizhou 雷州
Leong Man, Dianne 梁瑞来
Leong Sow-Theng 梁肇庭
Leong Yew Koh 梁宇皋
Leung Quinn 梁佐銮
Leung S. Wah 梁苏华
Li 黎
Li Dan 李旦
Li Fenglan 李凤兰
Li Fuchun 李富春
Li Hongzhang 李鸿章
Li Ka Shing 李嘉诚
Li Lisan 李立三
Li Minghuan 李明欢
Li Peng 李鹏
Li Rong 李荣
Li Shifu 李世福
Li Shimin 李世民
Li Shizeng 李石曾
Li Wei 李嵬
Li Wenzheng 李文正
Li Yuan T. 李远哲
Li Yuanjin 李元瑾
Li'ao 丽岙
Lianfanglou 联芳楼
Liang Jianmao 梁建茂
Liang Qichao 梁启超
Liang Shiyi 梁士诒
Liang You 良友
lianhe paisong chu 联合派送处
Lianhe Qikan 联合期刊
Lianhe ribao 联合日报
Lianjiang 连江
Liansheng Tang 联胜堂
Lianyi Tang 联义堂
Lianyihui 联谊会
lianying chu 联营处
Lianyou Huzhu She 联友互助社
Liao Chengzhi 廖承志
Liao Hui 廖晖
Liao Zhongkai 廖仲凯
Liaoning 辽宁
Lie Kim Hok 李金福
Liem Sioe Liong (see Lin Shaoliang)
Lim Bo Seng 林谋盛
Lim Boon Keng 林文庆
Lim Chin Siong 林清祥
Lim Chong Eu 林苍佑
Lim Goh Tong 林梧桐
Lim Jock Seng 林玉成
Lim Kit Siang 林吉祥
Lim Lian Geok 林连玉
Lim, Michael 林运生
Lim Nee Soon 林义顺
Lim Teck Hoo 林德甫
Limjap, Mariano 林合
Lin Ching Hsia 林青霞
Lin Dagu 林大姑
Lin Daoqian 林道乾
Lin Jinzhi 林金枝
Lin Lu 林露
Lin Maoxiang 林茂祥
Lin, Maya 林璎
Lin Riguang 林日光
Lin Shaoliang 林绍良
Lin Yutang 林语堂
Lin Zhenyu 林珍玉
Ling Liong Sik 林良实
Ling Shan 灵山
Lingnan 岭南
Lishan 李山
Liu Binghong 刘秉洪
Liu Binyan 刘宾雁
Liu Fa Jianxue Hui 留法俭学会
Liu Hong 刘虹

Liu Keguang 刘克光
Liu Suola 刘索拉
Liu Zerong 刘泽荣
liudong 流动
Liuniwang dao Huaqiao zhi 留尼旺岛华侨志
liuwang wenxue 流亡文学
liuxuesheng wenxue 留学生文学
Locke, Gary 骆家辉
Log Choi Sin 陆才新
Loke Wan Tho 陆运涛
Loke Yew 陆佑
longan (see longyan)
Longdu 隆都
Longling 龙陵
Longxi 龙溪
Longyan 龙岩
longyan 龙眼
Lowe, Felicia 刘咏嫦
Lowe, Pardee 刘裔昌
Lü Fa Qingtian Tongxianghui 旅法青田同乡会
Lü He Huaqiao Zonghui 旅荷华侨总会
Lu Jiatu 卢家图
Lü Ou Lincun Tongxianghui 旅欧林村同乡会
Lü Ou Wenshi Zongqinhui 旅欧文氏宗亲会
Lü Ou Zhonggong Shaonian Gongchandang
旅欧中共少年共产党
Luo Fangbo 罗芳伯
Luo Xianglin 罗香林
Luo Xinhan 罗新汉
Luxia 庐下
Ly Bi 李秘/李贲
Ly Cong Uan 李公蕴
lychee 荔枝
Ma Yo-Yo 马友友
Mac Cuu (see Mo Jiu)
Mai Shaopeng 麦少彭
Man Sing (see Minsheng)
Manchus 满族
Mao Zedong 毛泽东
March, K. W. (see Yu Jinrong)
Mawei 马尾
Mazu 妈祖
Meidong Fujian Tongxianghui 美东福建同乡会
Meixian 梅县
Miao 苗
Min 闽
Ming 明
Ming 命
Ming Bao 明报
Ming xiang 明香/明乡
Minh Huong (see Ming xiang)
Minhou 闽侯
Minnan 闽南
Minqing 闽清
Minsheng 民声
minxinju 民信局
Mo Jiu 莫玖
Mo Xiangyi 莫祥义
Mosike Huaqiao Huaren Lianhehui 莫斯科华侨华人联合会
mu 亩
Mu Lan 木兰
Nam Hoi Kon On Woi (see Nanhai Guang'an Hui)
Nan Ch'iao (see Nanqiao)
Nan Tien (see Nantian)
Nan'an 南安
nanbeihang 南北行
Nanda 南大
nanguan 南管
Nanhai 南海
Nanhai Guang'an Hui 南海广安会
Nanhua 南华
Nanjing 南京
Nanqiao 南侨
Nan-Shun 南顺
Nantah (see Nanda)
Nantian 南天
Nanyang 南洋
nanyin 南音
Neo Yee Pan 梁维泮
Ng Aik Huan 黄奕欢
Ng Fae Myenne 伍慧明
Ng, Lilian 黄贞才
Ng Mee Ling 吴美玲

Ng Poon Chew 伍盘照
Ng Teck Hock 黄迪福
Ngee Ann Kongsi (see Yi'an Gongsi)
Ngee Heng (see Yixing)
Ngo Dinh Diem 吴庭艳
Nian 捻
Nie Hualing 聂华苓
Niezi 孽子
Ningbo 宁波
Ninglong 宁龙
Niuzhuang 牛庄
Oei Tiong Ham 黄仲涵
Oei Tjong Hauw 黄宗孝
Ong Pang Boon 王邦文
Ong Siew Eng 王秀英
Ong Tiang Swee 王长水
Ong Wing 邓悦宁
Ongpin, Roman 王彬
Onn Siew Siong 温瑞祥
Ou 瓯
Ou Hua Nianhui 欧华年会
Ouhua Lianhui 欧华联会
Oujiang 瓯江
Ouzhou Huayi Xinxiu Gechang Bisai
欧洲华裔新秀歌唱比赛
Ouzhou Huaqiao Huaren Shetuan Lianhehui
欧洲华侨华人社团联合会
Ouzhou Huaqiao Tuanti Lianyihui 欧洲华侨团体联谊会
Ouzhou Huaren Xuehui 欧洲华人学会
Ouzhou Huashang Jingmao Xiehui 欧洲华商经贸协会
Ouzhou Qingtian Tongxianghui 欧洲青田同乡会
Ouzhou Taiwan Shanghui Lianhe Zonghui
欧洲台湾商会联合总会
Owyang Chi 欧阳奇
Pai, Kenneth (see Bai Xianyong)
Pan, Lynn 潘翎
Pang Boon Ting 方文珍
Panyu 番禺
Paua, José Ignacio 侯阿保/刘亨赙
Pei I. M. 贝聿铭
Peking (see Beijing)
Peng Chia Fu 彭家福
Peng Chia Sheng 彭家声
Pengmin 棚民
Phan Thanh Gian 潘清简
Phan Xich Long 潘赤龙
Pheung Kya-fu (see Peng Chia Fu)
Pheung Kya-shin (see Peng Chia Sheng)
piaobo 漂泊
ping 坪
Pinghua 平话
Pingtan 平潭
pinyin 拼音
pixinju 批信局
Po Leung Kuk 保良局
Poon-Fah 番花
Poon-yu (see Panyu)
Pukou 浦口
Puning 普宁
Punti (see bendi)
Putian 莆田
Putonghua 普通话
Putuoshan 普陀山
Pu-Xian 莆仙
Qianlong 乾隆
Qiantailong 乾泰隆
qianzhuang 钱庄
Qiao bao 侨报
qiao 侨
Qiaoban 侨办
qiaohui 侨汇
Qiaojuan 侨眷
Qiaoling 侨领
qiaowu 侨务
qiaoxiang 侨乡
Qidu 七都
qigong 气功
Qin Yuguang 秦裕光
Qing 清
Qingdao 青岛
Qinghua 清华
Qinglan 清澜
Qingming 清明

Qingsong 青松
Qingtian 青田
Qinlian 钦廉
Qiongdong 琼东
Qionghai 琼海
Qiongshan 琼山
Qiong-Wen 琼文
Qiongzhou Huiguan 琼州会馆
Qiu Linxiang 邱鳞祥
Qixiang Huiguan 七乡会馆
qiyun 气运
Quangsee (see Guangxi)
QuanHe Huaren Shetuan Lianhehui 全荷华人社团联合会
Quan-Zhang 泉漳
Quanzhou 泉州
Quek Leng Chan 郭令灿
Quemoy 金门
Qufu 曲阜
Raoping 饶平
ren ru fu zhong 忍辱负重
Riady, James 李白
Riady, Mochtar (see Li Wenzheng)
Rong Hong 容闳
Rui'an 瑞安
Ruili 瑞丽
Sam Kauw (see san jiao)
Sam Kok 三国
Sam Yup (see Sanyi)
Samyap (see Sanyi)
San guo yanyi 三国演义
san jiao 三教
San Wang 三王
San Wui (see Xinhui)
sanba dao 三把刀
Sang On Tiy (see Yongantai)
Sang Ye 桑晔
sangley 生理/商旅
Sangqing yu Taohong 桑青与桃红
Sanjiang 三江
Sanshan 三山
Sanyi 三邑
Sayao Huaqiao Gonghui 萨么华侨公会
Seah Eu Chin 佘有进
See Hiang To (see Shi Xiangtuo)
See Yup (see Siyi)
Seeto (see Situ)
Seiyap (see Siyi)
Seng Guan 信愿
Sew Hoy 徐肇开
Shajiao 沙滘
Shandong 山东
Shanghai 上海
Shanghen wenxue 伤痕文学
Shanju Gongsuo 善举公所
Shankou 山口
shantang 善堂
Shantou 汕头
Shanxi 山西
Shaojiang 邵将
Shaonan 韶南
She 畲
shen 神
Shen Jiawei 沈加蔚
Shen Xiugong 沈秀公
Shen Yingming 沈英名
Shengdu Zhonghua Gonghui 圣都中华公会
Shengfu 圣福
shenshi 绅士
Shenyang 沈阳
Shenzhen 深圳
shetou 蛇头
Shi Xiangtuo 施香沱
Shijie ribao 世界日报
Shijie Taiwan Shanghui Lianhe Zonghui 世界台湾商会联合总会
Shishi 石狮
Shouning 寿宁
Shuihu Zhuan 水浒传
shuike 水客
Shun Wah, Annette 周瑞兰
Shunde 顺德
Siauw Giok Tjhan (see Xiao Yucan)
Sichuan 四川

Sihui 四会
Sin Po (see Xin bao)
Sing Dao 星岛
Sing Sian Yit Pao (see Xing Xian ribao)
Sing Tao 星岛
Sing Tao Jih Pao (see Xingdao ribao)
Si-Ni-Tong (see Xinyi Tang)
sinkeh (see xinke)
sinseh 先生
Situ 司徒
Siyi 四邑
Siyu 丝语
Sondhi Limthongkul 林明达
Song 宋
Song Kim Keow 宋金娇
Song Ong Siang 宋旺相
Soong Mei-ling 宋美龄
Su Dongpo 苏东坡
Su Jiesheng 苏杰生
Su Manshu 苏曼殊
Sumet Jiaravanon (see Xie Zhongmin)
Sun 大新
Sun Shuyi 孙树义
Sun Yat-sen 孙逸仙
Suzhou 苏州
Swatow (see Shantou)
SyCip, Albino 薛敏老
Sze Yap (see Siyi)
Sze Yi-kwei 施义桂
Szeyap (see Siyi)
Taiguo Huaqiao gaikuang 泰国华侨概况
Taihu 太湖
Taipei 台北
Taiping 太平
Taishan 台山
Taiwan 台湾
Taiyi Hao 泰益号
Taizhou 台州
Ta-kong (see Dagang)
Tan, Amy 谭恩美
Tan Chee Koon 陈志勤
Tan Cheng Lock 陈祯禄
Tan Chin Nam 陈振南
Tan Chin Tuan 陈振传
Tan Chor Nam 陈楚楠
Tan Guan Lee 陈元利
Tan Jiesheng 谭杰生
Tan Kah Kee 陈嘉庚
Tan Kim Seng 陈金声
Tan Koon Swan 陈群川
Tan Lark Sye 陈六使
Tan, Lucio 陈永栽
Tan, Raymond 陈树杰
Tan Seng Poh 陈成宝
Tan Siew Sin 陈修信
Tan Swee Hian 陈瑞献
Tan Tock Seng 陈笃生
Tan, Vincent Chee Yioun 陈志远
Tang 堂
Tang 唐
Tang Kung Suk 邓恭叔
Tang Liang Hong 邓亮洪
Tang Shaoyi 唐绍仪
Tang Tingshu 唐廷枢
Tangjia Wangguo Zhonghua Huiguan 汤加王国中华会馆
Tangren 唐人
Tangrenjie 唐人街
Tangshan 唐山
Tanka 疍家
tau 艚
te (see cha)
Tengyun 腾云
Teo Chew (see Teochiu)
Teo Eng Hock 张永福
Teochew (see Teochiu)
Teochiu (see Chaozhou)
Tham Nyip Shen 谭业成
Thian Hock Keng (see Tianfu Gong)
Thien Nan Shin Pao (see Tiannan xinbao)
Thien-Ah-Koun, André 曾宪建
Thio Thiau Siat (see Zhang Bishi)
Tian Gong 天公
Tian 田

Tiananmen 天安门
Tiandi Hui 天地会
Tianfu Gong 天福宫
Tianhou 天后
Tianjin 天津
Tiannan xinbao 天南新报
Tin Fook 天福
Ting, John 丁崇麟
Ting, Samuel 丁肇中
Tingzhou 汀州
Tiong Ho Sia 长和郎君社
Tiong Hoa Hwee Koan (see Zhonghua Huiguan)
Tiong Xiao King 张晓卿
Tionghoa (see Zhonghua)
Tjan Tjoe Siem 曾祖沁
Tjan Tjoe Som 曾祖森
Tjong A Fie (see Zhang Hongnan)
Tjong Yong Hian (see Zhang Yunan)
Toisan (see Taishan)
Tong King-sing (see Tang Tingshu)
Tongan 同安
Tongbao 同胞
Tonggu 铜鼓
Tongji 同济
Tongmeng Hui 同盟会
Tongshuntai 同顺泰
tongxianghui 同乡会
tongye gonghui 同业公会
towkay 头家
Tran Thuong Xuyen (see Chen Shangchuan)
Tran Tien Thanh 陈践诚/陈养钝
Trinh Hoai Duc 郑怀德
Tsang, Henry 曾筱龙
Tsang-shing (see Zengcheng)
Tseng Yuho (see Zeng Youhe)
Tsui Hark 徐克
Tu Wei-ming 杜维明
Tudi Gong 土地公
Tumen 图们
Tung Chai (see Tongji)
Tung Wah 东华
Tung Yep, George 余瑞良
Tung-koon (see Dongguan)
Tung-Tsang 东增
tusan (see tusheng)
tusheng 土生
Ty, George 郑少坚
Tzu Chi 慈济
Vasiong Kwong Sow 华商公所
Wah Chang 华昌
Wak Hai Cheng Bio (see Yuehaiqing Miao)
Wanbaoshan 万宝山
Wang An 王安
Wang C. C. (see Wang Jiqian)
Wang, Charles B. 王嘉廉
Wang Dayuan 汪大渊
Wang Gungwu 王赓武
Wang Jingxiang 王敬祥
Wang Jiqian 王己千
Wang Ming 王明
Wang Mingyu 王明玉
Wang, Peter 王正方
Wang, Wayne 王颖
Wanglee Chan 黄利栈
Wanglee 黄利
wangluo 网络
Wanning 万宁
Wee Cho Yaw 黄祖耀
Wee Hood Teck 黄佛德
Wee Kheng Chiang 黄庆昌
Wee Tee Yah 黄智爷
Weihaiwei 威海卫
Wen Fa (see Wenhua)
Wen miao 文庙
Wenchang Ci 文昌祠
Wenchang 文昌
Wencheng 文成
Wen-chou (see Wenzhou)
Wenhua 文化
Wenzhou 温州
Wha Chi (see Hua Zhi)
Wing On 永安
Wing, Peter 吴荣添

wokou 倭寇
Wong, Anna May 黄柳霜
Wong B. D. 黄亮荣
Wong Foon Sien 黄文甫
Wong Hoc Ting 王鹤亭
Wong Hoy Cheong 黄海昌
Wong, Jade Snow 黄玉雪
Wong, James Howe 黄宗沾
Wong Nai Siong 黄乃裳
Wong Siu-lun 黄兆伦
Wong, Thomas Doo 黄梓
Woo, John 吴宇森
Wu Baifu 吴百福
Wu Bang Gongsuo 五帮公所
Wu Jintang 吴锦堂
wu ke bu shan, wu shan bu ke 无客不山，无山不客
Wu Leji 乌勒吉
Wu Liande 伍连德
Wu Lien-teh (see Wu Liande)
Wu Tianming 吴天明
Wu Tingfang 伍廷芳
Wu, Vivian 邬君梅
Wu Zaimin 吴在民
Wuhan 武汉
Wuhua 吴化
Wuyi 武夷
Wuyi 万邑
Wuzhou 婺州
Xi You Ji 西游记
Xia 夏
Xiamen 厦门
xian 县
Xiang 湘
xiang 乡
Xiang Jingyu 向警予
Xiangshan 香山
Xianyou 仙游
Xiao Yucan 萧玉灿
Xie Guomin 谢国民
Xie Yichu 谢易初
Xie Zhongmin 谢中民
xiedou 械斗
Xietai 协泰
Xietiangong 协天公
xieyi 写意
Xijiang 西江
Xin bao 新报
Xin'an 新安
Xing Xian ribao 星暹日报
Xingdao 星岛
Xingdao ribao 星岛日报
Xingfu 兴福
Xinghua 兴化
Xingwen 兴文
Xingzhong Hui 兴中会
Xingzhou 星洲
xingzhou yugong 星洲寓公
Xinhua 新华
Xinhui 新会
Xinhui 新惠
Xinjiang 新疆
xinke 新客
Xinmin xuehui 新民学会
Xinning 新宁
Xinyi Tang 信义堂
xinyong 信用
Xu Jiang Yueqin 徐江月琴
Xu Neng 徐能
Xu Qin 徐勤
Xuanzhou 宣州
Xue Fucheng 薛福成
Yalu 鸭绿
Yan Zhizhao 严志昭
Yang Chen-Ning 杨振宁
Yang Dazhao 杨大钊
Yang Li 杨力
Yang Lian 杨炼
Yang Shangkun 杨尚昆
Yang Yandi 杨彦迪
Yang Yongshou 杨永寿
Yang Zhaoquan 杨昭全
Yangwen 杨文
Yangzhou 扬州

Yangzi 扬子
Yanluo 阎罗
Yantai 烟台
Yao 瑶
Yap Ah Loy 叶亚来
Yap, Melanie 叶慧芬
Yat-sen 逸仙
Yazhou ribao 亚洲日报
Ye Xiaodun 叶小敦
Yee, Bill H. W. (see Yu Hanhong)
Yen Chih Chao (see Yan Zhizhao)
Yen, Howan 邓仁广
Yeo, George 杨荣文
Yeoh Jin Leng 杨仁龄
Yeoh, Michelle 杨紫琼
Yi'an Gongsi 义安公司
Yihe Hao 怡和好
Yim Ho 严浩
Ying Hope 刘英光
Yingchang 英昌
yinhao 银号
Yisheng Shanghao 怡生商号
Yiuming 洪圣宫
Yixing 义兴
yizhuang 义庄
Yong C. F. 杨进发
Yong Teck Lee 杨德利
Yongantai 永安泰
Yongchun 永春
Yongding 永定
Yongjia 永嘉
Yongle 永乐
Yongxun 邕浔
You jian zonglü 又见棕榈
youshen 游神
Youzhu 油竹
Yu Hanhong 余汉宏
Yu, Helen (see Yu Lihua)
Yu Huang 玉皇
Yu Jinrong 余锦荣
Yu, John 余森美
Yu Lihua 於梨华
Yu, Ronny 于仁泰
Yu Xiguang 于希光
Yu Xinchen 于心辰
yuan 元
Yuan 元
Yuan 院
Yuan Shikai 袁世凯
Yuan xiang 原乡
Yuan Yang 袁养
Yuanxiao 元宵
Yue 粤
Yuebei 粤北
Yuehaiqing Miao 粤海清庙
Yueqing 乐清
Yuetai 粤台
Yuezhong 粤中
Yugui 于桂
Yuhu 玉壶
Yuhuatai 雨花台
yun 运
Yung Wing (see Rong Hong)
Yunnan 云南
Zao Wou-ki (see Zhao Wuji)
Zeng Guofan 曾国藩
Zeng Youhe 曾佑和
Zengcheng 增城
Zhan Tianyou 詹天佑
Zhang Ailing 张爱玲
Zhang Bishi 张弼士
Zhang Daqian 张大千
Zhang Hongnan 张鸿南
Zhang Hongtu 张宏图
Zhang Liying 张荔英
Zhang Renjie 张人杰
Zhang Xun 张勋
Zhang Yimou 张艺谋
Zhang Yu 张俞
Zhang Yunan 张煜南
Zhangzhou 漳州
Zhanjiang 湛江
Zhao Liang 赵亮

Zhao Rukuo 赵汝适
Zhao Shiyan 赵世炎
Zhao Wuji 赵无极
Zhao Ziyang 赵紫阳
Zhaoan 诏安
Zhaoqing 肇庆
Zhejiang 浙江
zhen 镇
Zheng Chenggong 郑成功
Zheng Cuiping 郑翠萍
Zheng He 郑和
Zheng Zhilong 郑芝龙
zhengchangtian 蒸尝田
Zhengda 正大
Zhenzhou 真州
Zhigong Tang 致公堂
Zhili 直隶
Zhong E xinxi bao 中俄信息报
Zhongguo Fuxing She 中国复兴社
Zhonghua Gongli Xuexiao 中华公立学校
Zhonghua Hui 中华会
Zhonghua hui zazhi 中华会杂志
Zhonghua Huiguan 中华会馆
Zhonghua Lü E Lianhehui 中华旅俄联合会
Zhonghua 中华
Zhonghua Qingnian Shehui Wenhua Xiehui
中华青年社会文化协会
Zhonghua Shanghui 中华商会
Zhonghua Zonghui 中华总会
Zhongkui 钟馗
Zhongshan 中山
Zhongshan Xuehui 中山学会
Zhongxi 中西
Zhongxinglong 中兴隆
Zhongxue 中学
Zhongyuan bao 中原报
Zhou Daguan 周达观
Zhou Enlai 周恩来
Zhou Xiaoping 周小平
Zhouning 周宁
Zhu Fan Zhi 诸蕃志
Zhu Maolin 朱茂林
Zhu Xi 朱熹
Zhu Yuanzhang 朱元璋
Zhuang 壮
zhudong 住冬
zhufan 住番
Zhuhai 珠海
Zoing Chong (see Yingchang)
Zongyi 综艺
Zou Rong 邹容
zu 族
zuo shan 座山

*The Chinese character is normally pronounced 'duo,' but
Tseng Yuho has borrowed it to create the compound 'dsui hua'
to refer to her form of art.*

BIBLIOGRAPHY

ORIGINS

Chen Bin. 'Zui zao dao Ouzhou de Qingtian ren' (The Earliest Qingtian Arrivals in Europe). *Qingtian wenshi ziliao* (Qingtian Cultural and Historical Materials) 6 (1995).

Chen Han-seng. *Landlord and Peasant in South China*. New York: International Publishers, 1936.

Chen Li'te. 'Qingtian ren chuguo dao Ouzhou de jingguo' (The Migration of Qingtianese to Europe). *Qingtian wenshi ziliao* (Qingtian Cultural and Historical Materials) 6 (1995).

Chen Ta. *Emigrant Communities in South China: A Study of Overseas Migration and its Influence on Standards of Living and Social Change*. New York: Institute of Pacific Relations, 1940.

Chen Zhiping. *Kejia yuanliu xin lun* (Hakka Origins Revisited). Guilin: Guangxi Jiaoyu Chubanshe, 1997.

Cohen, Myron L. 'The Hakka or "Guest People": Dialect as a Sociocultural Variable in Southeastern China.' *Ethnohistory* 15, 13 (1968): 237-92.

Eberhard, Wolfram. *Social Mobility in Traditional China*. Leiden: E. J. Brill, 1962.

Faure, David. *The Rural Economy of Pre-liberation China: Trade Expansion and Peasant Livelihood in Jiangsu and Guangdong, 1870 to 1937*. New York: Oxford University Press, 1989.

Feng Chongyi, and David S. G. Goodman. *China's Hainan Province: Economic Development and Investment Environment*. Western Australia: University of Western Australia Press for Asia Research Centre on Social, Political and Economic Changes, Murdoch University, 1995.

Feng Ziping. *Zouxiang shijie de Hainan ren* (Towards Hainanese Globalization). Beijing: Zhongguo Huaqiao Chubanshe, 1992.

Fujiansheng difang zhi bianwei hui (The Editorial Committee of the Gazetteer of Fujian Province), ed. *Fujiansheng zhi. Huaqiao zhi* (Gazetteer of Fujian Province. History of the Chinese Overseas). Fuzhou: Fujian Renmin Chubanshe, 1992.

Gan Xianqiong, ed. *Qionghai xianzhi* (Gazetteer of Qionghai County). Guangdong Keji Chubanshe, 1995.

Gardella, Robert. *Harvesting Mountains: Fujian and the China Tea Trade, 1757-1937*. Berkeley: University of California Press, 1994.

Ge Jianxiong, Cao Shuji, and Wu Songdi, eds. *Jianming Zhongguo yimin shi* (A Brief History of Chinese Migration). Fuzhou: Fujian Renmin Chubanshe, 1993.

Godley, Michael R. *The Mandarin-capitalists from Nanyang: Overseas Chinese Enterprise in the Modernization of China 1893-1911*. New York: University of Cambridge, 1981.

Goodman, David S. G., ed. *China's Regional Development*. London and New York: Routledge for the Royal Institute of International Affairs, 1989.

Guangdongsheng difang zhi bianzuan weiyuanhui (The Editorial Committee of the Gazetteer of Guangdong Province), ed. *Guangdongsheng zhi. Huaqiao zhi* (Gazetteer of Guangdong Province. History of the Chinese Overseas). Guangdong: Guangdong Renmin Chubanshe, 1996.

Han Yifeng. 'Shaba Hainan ren zhiye xingshi zhi yanbian' (The Occupational Changes of Hainanese in Sabah). *Nanyang xuebao* (Journal of the South Seas Society) 28, 1 & 2 (1973): 1-16.

Huang Shouchang, ed. *Wenchang tonglan* (A General Survey of Wenchang). Wenchang Xian Difang Shi Zhi Bangongshi, 1994.

Jinjiang diqu Huaqiao lishi xuehui choubei zu (Jinjiang Overseas Chinese History Society Preparatory Committee), ed. *Huaqiao shi* (Overseas Chinese History) 2 (1983) and 3 (1985).

Kulp, Daniel H. *Country Life in South China: The Sociology of Familism*. New York: Bureau of Publications, Teachers College, Columbia University, 1925.

Leong Sow-Theng. *Migration and Ethnicity in Chinese History: Hakkas, Pengmin, and their Neighbors*. Stanford, Calif.: Stanford University Press, 1997.

Li Minghuan. '"To Get Rich Quickly in Europe!" – Reflections.' Paper presented at the 'European Chinese and Chinese Domestic Migration' Workshop, Oxford, July 3-5, 1996.

Li Rong. 'Hanyu fangyan de fenqu' (The Regional Distribution of Dialects). *Fangyan* (Dialects) 4 (1989): 241-59.

Lin Jinzhi, and Zhuang Weiji. *Jindai Huaqiao touzi guonei qiye shi ziliao xuanji: Fujian* (Fujian: Selected Historical Materials on the Investments of Modern Overseas Chinese Enterprises). Fuzhou: Fujian Renmin Chubanshe, 1985.

———. *Jindai Huaqiao touzi guonei qiyeshi ziliao xuanji: Guangdong* (Guangdong: Selected Historical Materials on the Investments of Modern Overseas Chinese Enterprises). Fuzhou: Fujian Renmin Chubanshe, 1989.

———. 'Haiwai Huaren zai Chao-Shan diqu de touzi' (Overseas Chinese Investments in Chao-Shan). *Nanyang wenti yanjiu* (Southeast Asian Affairs) 1 (1994): 18-27.

Luo Xianglin. *Kejia yanjiu daolun* (Introduction to the Study of the Hakkas). Xingning: Xishan Shucang, 1933.

Mei, June. 'Socioeconomic Origins of Emigration: Guangdong to California, 1850-1882.' *Modern China* 5, 4 (1979): 463-501.

Myers III, Willard H. 'The Dynamic Elements of Chinese Irregular Population Movement.' Paper presented at the 'Asian Migrant Trafficking: The New Threat to America's Immigration Tradition' Conference, Honolulu, July 25-27, 1996.

Naquin, Susan, and Evelyn S. Rawski. *Chinese Society in the Eighteenth Century*. New Haven and London: Yale University Press, 1987.

Ng Chin Keong. *Trade and Society: The Amoy Network on the China Coast, 1683-1735*. Singapore: Singapore University Press, 1983.

Ng, Peter Y. L. *New Peace County: A Chinese Gazetteer of the Hong Kong Region*. Hong Kong University Press, 1983.

Norman, Jerry. *Chinese*. England: Cambridge University Press, 1988.

Skinner, G. William. *Chinese Society in Thailand: An Analytical History*. Ithaca, N. Y.: Cornell University Press, 1957.

———. 'Mobility Strategies in Late Imperial China: A Regional Systems Analysis.' In *Regional Analysis*, edited by Carol A. Smith, vol. 1. New York: Academic Press, 1976.

———. 'Regional Systems in Late Imperial China.' Paper presented at the 2nd Annual Meeting of the Social Science History Association, Ann Arbor, Michigan, 1977.

———. 'Presidential Address: The Structure of Chinese History.' *Journal of Asian Studies* 44, 2 (February 1985): 271-92.

Tang Wenji, ed. *Fujian shi lun tan* (A Discussion of Fujian History). Fuzhou: Fujian Renmin Chubanshe, 1992.

Tang Wing-shing. *Urbanisation in China's Fujian Province since 1978*. Hong Kong: Hong Kong Institute of Asia-Pacific Studies, 1995.

Thunoe, Mette. 'Origin and Causes of Emigration from Qingtian and Wenzhou to Europe.' Paper presented at the 'European Chinese and Chinese Domestic Migration' Workshop, Oxford, July 3-5, 1996.

Watson, James L. *Emigration and the Chinese Lineage: The Mans in Hong Kong and London*. Berkeley: University of California Press, 1975.

Woon, Y. F. 'An Emigrant Community in the Ssu-yi Area, Southeastern China, 1885-1949: A Study in Social Change.' *Modern Asian Studies* 18, 2 (1984): 273-306.

Wu Tai, ed. *Jinjiang Huaqiao zhi* (The History of Jinjiang's Overseas Chinese). Shanghai Renmin Chubanshe, 1994.

Wurm, S. A., and Li Rong, et al., eds. *Language Atlas of China*. Hong Kong: Longman, 1987.

Xia Chenghua. *Jindai Guangdongsheng qiaohui yanjiu, 1862-1949* (The Study of Remittances in Contemporary Guangdong Province, 1862-1949). Singapore: Nanyang Xuehui, 1992.

Yang Li, and Ye Xiaodun. *Dongnanya de Fujian ren* (Fujianese in Southeast Asia). Fuzhou: Fujian Renmin Chubanshe, 1993.

Yeung Yue-man, and David K. Y. Chu. *Development Corridor in Fujian: Fuzhou to Zhangzhou*. Hong Kong: Hong Kong Institute of Asia-Pacific Studies, 1995.

Zheng Dehua, and Cheng Luxi. *Taishan qiaoxiang yu Xinning tielu* (Taishan and Xinning's Railroad). Zhongshan Daxue Chubanshe, 1991.

Zheng Liangshu, ed. *Chaozhou xue guoji yantaohui lunwenji* (Collected Papers on Teochiu Studies from an International Symposium). Guangzhou: Jinan Daxue Chubanshe, 1994.

Zo, Kil Young. 'Emigrant Communities in China, Sze-Yap.' *Asian Profile* 5, 4 (August 1977): 313-23.

MIGRATION

Bailey, Paul. *Reform the People: Changing Attitudes towards Popular Education in Early Twentieth Century China*. Edinburgh: Edinburgh University Press, 1990.

Baker, Hugh D. R. 'Branches All Over: The Hong Kong Chinese in the United Kingdom.' In *Reluctant Exiles? Migration from Hong Kong and the New Overseas Chinese*, edited by Ronald Skeldon. Armonk, N. Y.: M. E. Sharpe; Hong Kong: Hong Kong University Press, 1994.

Blick, J. 'The Chinese Labor Corps in World War I.' *Harvard Papers on China* (August 1955): 111-45.

Campbell, Persia Crawford. *Chinese Coolie Emigration to Countries within the British Empire*, with a preface by W. Pember Reeves. London: Frank Cass, 1971.

Cannell, Michael. *I. M. Pei: Mandarin of Modernism*. New York: Carol Southern Books, 1995.

Chan Kam Wing. *Cities with Invisible Walls: Reinterpreting Urbanization in Post-1949 China*. Hong Kong: Oxford University Press, 1994.

———. 'Internal Migration in Post-Mao China: A Dualistic Approach.' Paper presented at the 'European Chinese and Chinese Domestic Migration' Workshop, Oxford, July 3-7, 1996.

Chan S. 'European and Asian Immigration into the United States in Comparative Perspective, 1820s to 1920s.' In *Immigration Reconsidered: History, Sociology, and Politics*, edited by V. Yans-McLaughlin. New York: Oxford University Press, 1990

Chen Hansheng, ed. *Huagong chuguo shiliao huibian* (Historical Materials on the Emigration of Chinese Labourers). 10 volumes. Beijing: Zhonghua Shuju, 1981 & 1984.

Chen Sanjing. *Huagong yu Ouzhan* (Chinese Workers and World War I). Taipei: Institute of Modern History Studies, Academia Sinica, 1986.

Chen Ta. *Chinese Migrations, with Special Reference to Labor Conditions*. Washington: Government Printing Office, 1923.

Chi, Madeleine. *China Diplomacy 1914-1918*. Cambridge, Mass.: Harvard University Press, 1970.

Cross, G. *Immigrant Workers in Industrial France*. Philadelphia: Temple University Press, 1983.

Curtin, Philip D. *Cross-cultural Trade in World History*. New York: Cambridge University Press, 1984.

Davis, Ralph. *The Rise of the Atlantic Economies*. New York: Cornell University Press, 1973.

Destefano, Athony M. 'Immigrant Smuggling through Central America and the Caribbean.' Paper presented at the 'Asian Migrant Trafficking: The New Threat to America's Immigration Tradition' Conference, Honolulu, July 25-27, 1996.

Fairbank, John King. *Trade and Diplomacy on the China Coast: The Opening of the Treaty Ports 1842-1854*. Cambridge, Mass.: Harvard University Press, 1953; reprint 1969.

Fang Shan. 'Mainland China's Overseas Construction Contracts and Export of Labor.' *Issues and Studies* 27, 2 (1991): 65-75.

Fawcett, James T., and Benjamin V. Carino, eds. *Pacific Bridges: The New Immigration and the Pacific Islands*. Staten Island: Center for Migration Studies, 1987.

Gernet, Jacques. *A History of Chinese Civilization*, translated by J. R. Foster. New York: Cambridge University Press, 1982. (A translation of *Le monde Chinois*.)

Guo Songyi. 'Qingdai de renkou zengzhang he renkou liuqian' (Population Growth and Mobility in the Qing Dynasty) *Qingshi luncong* (Essays on the Qing History) 5 (1984): 103-38.

Hicks, George, ed. *Overseas Chinese Remittances from Southeast Asia 1910-1940*. Singapore: Select Books, 1993.

Hobsbawm, Eric J. *The Age of Capital 1848-1875*. London: Cardinal, 1989a.

———. *The Age of Empire 1875-1914*. London: Cardinal, 1989b.

Horne, John. 'Immigrant Workers in France during World War I.' *French Historical Studies* 14, 1 (Spring 1985): 57-88.

International Office for Migration. *Chinese Migrants in Central and Eastern Europe: The Cases of the Czech Republic, Hungary and Romania*. Brussels: Migration Information Programme, 1995.

Kane, Hal. *The Hour of Departure: Forces that Create Refugees and Migrants*. Washington, D. C.: Worldwatch Institute, 1995.

Kuhn, Philip A. 'Why should Sinologists Study the Chinese Overseas?' Unpublished paper, 1997.

Levathes, Louise. *When China Ruled the Seas: The Treasure Fleet of the Dragon Throne 1405-1433*. New York: Simon & Schuster, 1994.

Lin C-P. 'China's Students Abroad: Rates of Return.' *The American Enterprise* 5, 6 (1994): 12-14.

Look Lai, Walton. *The Chinese in the West Indies 1806-1950: A Documentary History*. Jamaica: University of the West Indies Press, 1998.

MacNair, H. F. *The Chinese Abroad*. Shanghai: Commercial Press, 1933.

Myers III, Willard H. 'The Dynamic Elements of Chinese Irregular Population Movement.' Paper presented at the 'Asian Migrant Trafficking: The New Threat to America's Immigration Tradition' Conference, Honolulu, July 25-27, 1996.

Ng Chin Keong. *Trade and Society: The Amoy Network*. Singapore: Singapore University Press, 1983.

Nugent, W. Crossings. *The Great Transatlantic Migrations, 1870-1914*. Bloomington: Indiana University Press, 1992.

Pieke, Frank N., and Gregor Benton, eds. *The Chinese in Europe*. Basingstoke: Macmillan Press; New York, N. Y.: St. Martin's Press, 1998.

Poston, Dudley L., JR, Michael Xinxiang Mao, and Mei-Yu Yu. 'The Global Distribution of the Overseas Chinese around 1990.' *Population and Development Review* 20, 3 (September 1994): 631-45.

Purcell, Victor. *The Chinese in Southeast Asia*. Rev. ed. London: Oxford University Press, 1965.

Ravenstein, E. G. 'The Laws of Migration.' *Journal of the Statistical Society* 48 (1885): 167-227.

———. 'The Laws of Migration.' *Journal of the Statistical Society* 52 (1889): 214-301.

Reid, Anthony, ed. *Sojourners and Settlers: Histories of Southeast Asia and the Chinese*. St. Leonards, N. S. W: Allen & Unwin for Asian Studies Association of Australia, 1996.

Sanchez-Albornoz, Nicolas. *The Population of Latin America: A History*. Berkeley: University of California Press, 1974.

Sassen, Saskia. *The Global City: New York, London, Tokyo*. Princeton, N. J.: Princeton University Press, 1991.

Segal, Aaron. *An Atlas of International Migration*. London: Hans Zell Publishers, 1993.

Skeldon, Ronald, ed. *Reluctant Exiles? Migration from Hong Kong and the New Overseas Chinese*. Armonk, N. Y.: M. E. Sharpe; Hong Kong: Hong Kong University Press, 1994.

———, ed. *Emigration from Hong Kong: Tendencies and Impacts*. Hong Kong: The Chinese University Press, 1995.

Skinner, G. William. 'Mobility Strategies in Late Imperial China: A Regional Systems Analysis.' In *Regional Analysis*, edited by Carol A. Smith, vol. 1. New York: Academic Press, 1976.

———, ed. *The City in Late Imperial China*. Stanford, Calif.: Stanford University Press , 1977.

Spence, Jonathan. *God's Chinese Son: The Taiping Heavenly Kingdom of Hong Xiuquan*. London: HarperCollins, 1996.

Summerskill, M. *China on the Western Front: Britain's Chinese Work Force in the First World War*. London: Michael Summerskill, 1982.

Thunoe, Mette. 'Origins and Causes of Emigration from Qingtian and Wenzhou to Europe.' Paper presented at the 'European Chinese and Chinese Domestic Migration' Workshop, Oxford, July 3-7, 1996.

Tinker, Hugh. *A New System of Slavery: The Export of Indian Labour Overseas 1830-1920*. London: Oxford University Press, 1974.

Twitchett, Denis, and John K. Fairbank, eds. *The Cambridge History of China*, vol. 10 & 11: *Late Ch'ing 1800-1911*, pt. 1 & 2. New York: Cambridge University Press, 1978 & 1980.

———, and Frederick W. Mote, eds. *The Cambridge History of China*, vol. 7 & 8: *The Ming Dynasty, 1368-1644*, pt. 1 & 2. New York: Cambridge University Press, 1988 & 1998.

Wang Gungwu. *China and the Chinese Overseas*. Singapore: Times Academic Press, 1991.

———. *Community and Nation: China, Southeast Asia and Australia*. St. Leonards, N. S. W: Allen & Unwin for Asian Studies Association of Australia, 1992.

Wang Sing-wu. 'The Attitude of the Ch'ing Court toward Chinese Emigration.' *Chinese Culture* 9 (December 1968): 87-99.

Watson, James L. *Emigration and the Chinese Lineage: The Mans in Hong Kong and London*. Berkeley: University of California Press, 1975.

World Bank. *The East Asian Miracle: Economic Growth and Public Policy*. New York: Oxford University Press, 1993.

Wou P. *Les travailleurs Chinois et la Grande Guerre* (Chinese Labourers and the Great War). Paris, 1939.

Wu Ze, ed. *Huaqiao shi yanjiu lunji* (Collected Research Papers on Overseas Chinese History). Shanghai: Huadong Shifan Daxue Chubanshe, 1984.

Xie Jiaxiao. *Zhang Daqian zhuan* (The Biography of Zhang Daqian). Taipei: Xidai Shu Ban, 1993.

Yen Ching-hwang. *Coolies and Mandarins: China's Protection of Overseas Chinese during the Late Ch'ing 1851-1911*. Singapore: Singapore University Press, 1985.

Zhao Heman, ed. *Guangxi ji Huaqiao Huaren ziliao xuanbian* (Selected Materials on Overseas Chinese of Guangxi Origin). Guangxi Renmin Chubanshe, 1990.

Zhu Guohong. 'A Historical Demography of Chinese Migration.' *Social Sciences in China* 12, 2 (Winter 1991): 557-84.

———. *Zhongguo de haiwai yimin: Yi xiang guoji qianyi de lishi yanjiu* (Overseas Emigration from China: A Historical Study of International Migration). Shanghai: Fudan Daxue Chubanshe, 1994.

Zweig, David, and Chen Changgui. *China's Brain Drain to the United States: Views of Overseas Chinese Students and Scholars in the 1990s*. Berkeley, Calif.: Institute of East Asian Studies, 1995.

INSTITUTIONS

Brown, Rajeswary Ampalavanar. *Capital and Entrepreneurship in South-East Asia*. Basingstoke: The Macmillan Press; New York: St. Martin's Press, 1994.

———, ed. *Chinese Business Enterprise in Asia*. London and New York: Routledge, 1995.

Chen Ta. *Emigrant Communities in South China: A Study of Overseas Migration and Its Influence on Standards of Living and Social Change*. New York: Institute of Pacific Relations, 1940.

Cheng Jia. 'Haiwai Huaren shetuan de xin dongxiang' (New Trends in Chinese Overseas Organizations). *Huaren yuekan* (Chinese Monthly) 4 (April 1990): 29-3l and 5 (May 1990): 24-25.

Cheng Lim-Keak. *Social Change and the Chinese in Singapore*. Singapore: Singapore University Press, l985.

Cohen, Myron L. 'Development Process in the Chinese Domestic Group.' In *Family and Kinship in Chinese Society*, edited by Maurice Freedman. Stanford, Calif.: Stanford University Press, 1970.

Crissman, Lawrence W. 'The Segmentary Structure of Urban Overseas Chinese Communities.' *Man* 2, 2 (l967): 185-204.

Deng Tuo. *Lun Zhongguo lishi de ji ge wenti* (On a Number of Questions in Chinese History). Beijing: Sanlian Shudian, 1963.

Freedman, Maurice. *Lineage and Organisation in Southeastern China*. London: The Athlone Press, 1958.

———. *The Study of Chinese Society*. Stanford, Calif.: Stanford University Press, 1979.

Geertz, Clifford. 'The Rotating Credit Association: An Instrument of Development.' *Economic Development and Cultural Change* 10 (1962): 243-62.

Hershatter, Gail, Emily Honig, Jonathan N. Lipman, and Randall Stross . *Remapping China: Fissures in Historical Terrain*. Stanford, Calif.: Stanford University Press, 1996.

Hicks, George, ed. *Chinese Organisations in Southeast Asia in the 1930s*. Singapore: Select Books, 1996.

Ho Ping-ti. *The Ladder of Success in Imperial China: Aspects of Social Mobility, 1368-1911*. New York: University of Columbia Press, 1962.

———. *Zhongguo huiguan shilun* (A Historical Survey of Landsmannschaften in China). Taiwan Xuesheng Shuju, 1966.

Kulp, Daniel H. *Country Life in South China: The Sociology of Familism*. New York: Bureau of Publications, Teachers College, Columbia University, 1925.

Lai, Him Mark. 'Chinese Organizations in America Based on Locality of Origin and/or Dialect-Group Affiliation, l940s-l990s.' In *Chinese America: History and Perspectives, 1996*. San Francisco: Chinese Historical Society of America, l996.

Lang, Olga. *Chinese Family and Society*. New Haven: Yale University Press, 1946.

Li Minghuan. *Dangdai haiwai Huaren shetuan yanjiu* (Contemporary Ethnic Chinese Overseas Organizations). Xiamen: Xiamen Daxue Chubanshe, l995.

———. 'Transnational Links among the Chinese in Europe: A Study on European-wide Chinese Voluntary Associations.' In

The Chinese in Europe, edited by Frank N. Pieke and Gregor Benton. Basingstoke: Macmillan Press; New York, N. Y.: St. Martin's Press, 1998.

Liu Wu-chi. *Su Man-shu*. New York: Twayne, 1972.

Ma, L. Eve Armentrout. 'Urban Chinese at the Sinitic Frontier: Social Organizations in United States' Chinatowns, 1849-1898.' *Modern Asian Studies* 17, 1 (1983): 107-35.

Mak Lau Fong. *The Sociology of Secret Societies: A Study of Chinese Secret Societies in Singapore and Peninsular Malaysia*. Kuala Lumpur and New York: Oxford University Press, 1981.

Murray, Dian H. *The Origins of the Tiandihui: The Chinese Triads in Legend and History*. Stanford, Calif.: Stanford University Press, 1994.

Ownby, David, and Mary Somers Heidhues, eds. '*Secret Societies' Reconsidered*. Armonk, N. Y.: M. E. Sharpe, 1993.

Qin Baoqi. *Qing qianqi Tiandi Hui yanjiu* (The Study of Tiandi Hui in the Early Qing). Beijing: Zhongguo Renmin Chubanshe, 1988.

Redding, S. Gordon. *The Spirit of Chinese Capitalism*. Berlin and New York: Walter de Gruyter, 1993.

Rowe, William T. *Hankow: Commerce and Society in a Chinese City, 1796-1889*. Stanford, Calif.: Stanford University Press, 1984.

Rush, James R. *Opium to Java: Revenue Farming and Chinese Enterprise in Colonial Indonesia, 1860-1910*. Ithaca, N. Y.: Cornell University, 1990.

Scott-Ross, Alice. *Tun Dato Sir Cheng Lock Tan: A Personal Profile*. Singapore: Alice Scott-Ross, 1990.

See Chinben. 'Feilübin Huaren wenhua de chixu: Zongqin yu tongxiang zuzhi zai haiwai de yanbian (Persistence and Preservation of Chinese Culture in the Philippines: The Development of Clan and Hometown Associations in an Overseas Chinese Community). *Bulletin of the Institute of Ethnology, Academia Sinica* 42 (l976): 1l9-206.

Skinner, G. William, ed. *The City in Late Imperial China*. Stanford, Calif.: Stanford University Press, 1977.

Smith, Richard J. *China's Cultural Heritage: The Qing Dynasty, 1644-1912*. Rev. ed. Boulder: Westview Press, 1994.

Song Ong Siang. *One Hundred Years' History of the Chinese in Singapore*, introduced by Edwin Lee. Singapore: Oxford University Press, 1984.

Tan Chee Beng. *The Baba of Melaka: Culture and Identity of a Chinese Peranakan Community in Malaysia*. Petaling Jaya, Selangor: Pelanduk Publications, 1988.

Trocki, Carl A. *Opium and Empire: Chinese Society in Colonial Singapore, 1800-1910*. Ithaca, N. Y.: Cornell University, 1990.

Wang Tai Peng. *The Origins of Chinese Kongsi*. Petaling Jaya, Selangor: Pelanduk Publications, 1988.

Wickberg, Edgar. 'Some Problems in Chinese Organizational Development in Canada.' *Canadian Ethnic Studies* 11 (1979): 88-98.

———, ed. *From China to Canada. A History of the Chinese Communities in Canada*. Toronto: McClelland and Stewart, 1982.

———. 'Chinese Organizations and Ethnicity in Southeast Asia and North America since 1945: A Comparative Analysis.' In *Changing Identities of the Southeast Asian Chinese since World War II*, edited by Jennifer Cushman and Wang Gungwu. Hong Kong: Hong Kong University Press, l988.

———. 'Chinese Organizations in Philippine Cities since World War II: The Case of Manila.' *Asian Culture* 17 (June 1993): 91-105.

———. 'Overseas Chinese Adaptive Organizations, Past and Present.' In *Reluctant Exiles? Migration from Hong Kong and the New Overseas Chinese*, edited by Ronald Skeldon. Armonk, N. Y.: M. E. Sharpe, 1994.

Willmott, D. E. *The Chinese of Semarang: A Changing Minority Community in Indonesia*. Ithaca, N. Y.: Cornell University Press, 1960.

Willmott, W. E. *The Political Structure of the Chinese Community in Cambodia*. London: Athlone Press, 1970.

Wong P., S. Applewhite, and J. M. Daley. 'From Despotism to Pluralism: The Evolution of Voluntary Organizations in Chinese American Communities.' *Ethnic Groups* 8 (1990): 215-33.

Wong Siu-lun. 'The Chinese Family Firm: A Model.' *The British Journal of Sociology* 36, 1 (1985): 58-70.

Wu Fengbin, ed. *Dongnanya Huaqiao tongshi* (General History of the Overseas Chinese in Southeast Asia). Fuzhou: Fujian Renmin Chubanshe, 1993.

Yen Ching-hwang. *A Social History of the Chinese in Singapore and Malaya, l800-1911*. Singapore: Oxford University Press, l986.

Yoshihara Kunio, ed. *Oei Tiong Ham Concern: The First Business Empire of Southeast Asia*. Kyoto: Kyoto University, 1989.

Yung, Judy. *Unbound Feet: A Social History of Chinese Women in San Francisco*. Berkeley: University of California Press, 1995.

Zhou Nanjing, ed. *Shijie Huaqiao Huaren cidian* (Dictionary of Overseas Chinese). Beijing: Beijing Daxue Chubanshe, 1993.

Zhou Zhaojing. *Chaozhou huiguan shihua* (History of Chaozhou Huiguan). Shanghai Guji Chubanshe, 1995.

RELATIONS

Ah Cheng. *Three Kings*, translated by Bonnie S. McDougall. London: Collins Harvill, 1985. (A translation of *San Wang*.)

Asia/America: Identities in Contemporary Asian American Art. New York: Asia Society Galleries, 1994.

Backman, Michael. *Overseas Chinese Business Networks in Asia*. Canberra: East Asia Analytical Unit, Department of Foreign Affairs and Trade, 1995.

Bai Xianyong. *Niezi* (Crystal Boys). Taipei: Yuanjing Chuban Gongsi, 1983.

Barfield, Claude E., ed. *Expanding U.S.-Asian Trade and Investment: New Challenges and Policy Options*. Washington D. C.: American Enterprise Institute, 1997.

Brown, Melissa J., ed. *Negotiating Ethnicities in China and Taiwan*. Berkeley: China Research, Institute of East Asian Studies, University of California, 1996.

Browne, Nick, Paul G. Pickowicz, Vivian Sobchack, and Esther Yau, eds. *New Chinese Cinema: Forms, Identities, Politics*. Cambridge: Cambridge University Press, 1994.

Cai Kejian. 'Fangwen Bai Xianyong' (An Interview with Bai Xianyong). In *Di liu zhi shouzi* (The Sixth Finger), edited by Bai Xianyong. Beishi: Erya, 1995.

Campbell, Persia Crawford. *Chinese Coolie Emigration to Countries within the British Empire*, with a preface by W. Pember Reeves. London: Frank Cass, 1971.

Chan Kwok Bun, and Tong Chee Kiong. 'Modelling Culture Contact and Chinese Ethnicity in Thailand.' *Southeast Asian Journal of Social Science* 23, 1 (1995): 1-12.

Char Tin-yuke. *The Sandalwood Mountains: Readings and Stories of the Early Chinese in Hawaii*. Honolulu: The University of Hawaii Press, 1975.

Chen, Edward K. Y., and Teresa Y. C. Wong. 'Economic Synergy: A Study of Two-way Direct Foreign Investment Flow between Hong Kong and Mainland China.' In *The New Wave of Foreign Direct Investment in Asia*, compiled by Nomura Research Institute and Institute of Southeast Asian Studies. Singapore: Institute of Southeast Asian Studies, 1995.

Chen Hansheng, ed. *Huagong chuguo shiliao huibian* (Historical Materials on the Emigration of Chinese Labourers). 10 volumes. Beijing: Zhonghua Shuju, 1981 & 1984.

Chen Ta. *Emigrant Communities in South China: A Study of Overseas Migration and Its Influence on Standards of Living and Social Change*. New York: Institute of Pacific Relations, 1940.

Chen Tain-Jy, Ying-Hua Ku, and Meng-Chun Liu. 'Direct Investment in Low-wage and High-wage Countries: The Case of Taiwan.' In *Corporate Links and Foreign Direct Investment in*

Asia and the Pacific, edited by Edward K. Y. Chen and Peter Drysdale. Australia: Harper Educational Publishers, 1995.

Cheu Hock Tong, ed. *Chinese Beliefs and Practices in Southeast Asia*. Petaling Jaya, Selangor: Pelanduk Publications, 1993.

Chi, Schive. *Taiwan's Economic Role in East Asia*. Washington, D. C.: The Center for Strategic and International Studies, 1995.

Chia, Jane. *Georgette Chen*. Singapore: Singapore Art Museum, 1997.

Chia Oai Peng. *Malaysian Investment in China*. Tokyo: Institute of Developing Economies, 1996.

Chirot, Daniel, and Anthony Reid, eds. *Essential Outsiders?* Seattle: University of Washington Press, 1997.

Clark, John. 'Into the Woods: Yeoh Jin Leng, Malaysia's Distinguished Teacher and Artist.' *Art and Asia Pacific* 1, 2 (April 1994): 61-65.

Constable, Nicole, ed. *Guest People: Hakka Identity in China and Abroad*. Seattle: University of Washington Press, 1996.

Cushman, Jennifer, and Wang Gungwu, eds. *Changing Identities of the Southeast Asian Chinese since World War II*. Hong Kong: Hong Kong University Press, 1988.

Douw, Leo M. 'Overseas Chinese Entrepreneurship and the Chinese State: The Case of South China, 1900-49.' In *Chinese Business Enterprise in Asia*, edited by Rajeswary A. Brown. London and New York: Routledge, 1995.

———, and Peter Post, eds. *South China: State, Culture and Social Change during the 20th Century*. Amsterdam and New York: North-Holland, 1996.

Dsui Hua: Tseng Yuho. Hong Kong: Hanart TZ Gallery, 1992.

Duara Prasenjit. 'Nationalists among Transnationals: Overseas Chinese and the Idea of China, 1900-1911.' In *Ungrounded Empires: The Cultural Politics of Modern Chinese Transnationalism*, edited by Aihwa Ong and Donald Nonini. New York: Routledge, 1997.

Eng-Lee, Seok Chee. *Inspired Gifts: Donated Works in the Singapore Art Museum*. Singapore: Singapore Art Museum, 1995.

Espiritu, Yen Le. *Asian American Panethnicity: Bridging Institutions and Identities*. Philadelphia: Temple University Press, 1992.

Faure, David, and Helen Siu, eds. *Down to Earth: The Territorial Bond in South China*. Stanford, Calif.: Stanford University Press, 1995.

———, and Tao Tao Liu, eds. *Unity and Diversity: Local Cultures and Identities in China*. Hong Kong: Hong Kong University Press, l996.

Fitzgerald, Stephen. *China and the Overseas Chinese: A Study of Peking's Changing Policy, 1949-1970*. Cambridge: Cambridge University Press, 1972.

Fujiansheng difang zhi bianwei hui (The Editorial Committee of the Gazetteer of Fujian Province), ed. *Fujiansheng zhi. Huaqiao zhi* (Gazetteer of the Fujian Province: History of the Chinese Overseas). Fuzhou: Fujian Renmin Chubanshe, 1992.

Fukuda Shozo. *With Sweat and Abacus: Economic Roles of Southeast Asian Chinese on the Eve of World War II*, edited by George Hicks. Singapore: Select Books, 1995. (A translation of *Kakyo keizai-ron*.)

Fung K. C. 'Mainland Chinese Investment in Hong Kong: How Much, Why, and So What?' *Journal of Asian Business* 12, 2 (1996): 20-38.

Gao Xingjian. *Ling Shan* (The Magic Mountain). Taipei: Lianjing Chubanshe, 1990.

Godley, Michael R. *The Mandarin-capitalists from Nanyang: Overseas Chinese Enterprise in the Modernization of China, 1893-1911*. Cambridge, England: Cambridge University Press, 1981.

Goodman, Bryna. *Native Place, City, and Nation: Regional Networks and Identities in Shanghai, 1853-1937*. Berkeley: University of California Press, l995.

Graham, Edward M., and Paul R. Krugman. 'The Surge in

Foreign Direct Investment in the 1980s.' In *Foreign Direct Investment*, edited by Kenneth A. Froot. Chicago: University of Chicago Press, 1993.

Guangdongsheng difang zhi bianzuan weiyuanhui (The Editorial Committee of the Gazetteer of Guangdong Province), ed. *Guangdongsheng zhi. Huaqiao zhi* (Gazetteer of Guangdong Province. History of the Chinese Overseas). Guangdong: Guangdong Renmin Chubanshe, 1996.

Guangdongsheng jiyou xiehui (The Philatelic Association of Guangdong Province), ed. *Chao-Shan qiaopi lunwenji* (Collected Essays on Remittances in the Chao-Shan area). Beijing: Renmin Youdian Chubanshe, 1993.

Handley, Paul. 'Growing Fast, the CP Way.' *Institutional Investor*. October 1996.

Harvey, David. *The Condition of Postmodernity*. Oxford: Blackwell, 1990.

Hay, John. *Boundaries in China*. London: Reaktion Books, 1994.

Hicks, George L., ed. *Overseas Chinese Remittances from Southeast Asia 1910-1940*. Singapore: Select Books, 1993.

Hong Kingston, Maxine. *The Woman Warrior*. New York: Knopf, 1976.

Hong Ying. *Summer of Betrayal: A Novel*, translated by Martha Avery. London: Bloomsbury, 1997. (A translation of *Luo wu dai*.)

Huntington, Samuel P. 'The Clash of Civilizations?' *Foreign Affairs*, 72, 3 (Summer 1993): 22-49.

———. *The Clash of Civilizations and the Remaking of World Order*. New York: Simon & Schuster, 1996.

Jomo, K. S. 'A Specific Idiom of Chinese Capitalism in Southeast Asia: Sino-Malaysia Capital Accumulation in the Face of State Hostility.' In *Essential Outsiders?*, edited by Daniel Chirot and Anthony Reid. Seattle: University of Washington Press, 1997.

Kahn, Herman. *World Economic Development: 1979 and Beyond*. London: Croom Helm, 1979.

Kaiser, Stefan, David A. Kirby, and Ying Fan. 'Foreign Direct Investment in China: An Examination of the Literature.' *Asia-Pacific Business Review* 2, 3 (Spring 1996): 44-65.

Kasian Tejapira. 'Imagined Uncommunity: The Lookjin Middle Class and Thai Official Nationalism.' In *Essential Outsiders?*, edited by Daniel Chirot and Athony Reid. Seattle: University of Washington Press, 1997.

Kohsaka Akira. 'Interdependence through Capital Flows in Pacific Asia and the Role of Japan.' In *Financial Deregulation and Integration in East Asia*, edited by Takatoshi Ito and Anne O. Krueger. Chicago: University of Chicago Press, 1996.

Kotkin, Joel. *Tribes: How Race, Religion, and Identity Determine Success in the New Global Economy*. New York: Random House, 1992.

Krämer, Oliver. 'No Past to Long for? A Sociology of Chinese Writers in Exile.' Unpublished paper.

Kwok Kian Chow. *Channels & Confluences: A History of Singapore Art*. Singapore: Singapore Art Museum, 1996.

Lau, Emily. *Runaway: Dairy of a Street Kid*. Toronto: HarperCollins, 1989.

Lee, Gregory B. 'Contemporary Chinese Poetry, Exile and the Potential of Modernism.' In *Chinese Writing and Exile*, edited by Gregory B. Lee. Chicago: The Center for East Asian Studies, University of Chicago, 1993a.

———, ed. *Chinese Writing and Exile*. Chicago: The Center for East Asian Studies, University of Chicago, 1993b.

Lever-Tracy, Constance, David Ip, and Noel Tracy. *The Chinese Diaspora and Mainland China: An Emerging Economic Synergy*. Basingstoke: Macmillan Press, 1996.

Li Minghuan. '"To Get Rich Quickly in Europe !" — Reflections.' Paper presented at the 'European Chinese and Chinese Domestic Migration' Workshop, Oxford, July 3-5, 1996.

Lim, Linda Y. C., and L. A. Peter, eds. *The Chinese in Southeast Asia: Identity, Culture and Politics*, vol. 2. Singapore: Maruzen Asia, 1983.

Lim, Shirley Geok-lin. 'Immigration and Diaspora.' In *An Interethnic Companion to Asian American Literature*, edited by King-kok Cheung. Cambridge: Cambridge University Press, 1997.

Lin Jinzhi, and Zhuang Weiji. *Jindai Huaqiao tuozi guonei qiye shi ziliao xuanji: Fujian* (Fujian: Selected Historical Materials on Modern Overseas Investments in Enterprises in Fujian). Fuzhou: Fujian Renmin Chubanshe, 1985.

———. *Jindai Huaqiao tuozi guonei qiye shi ziliao xuanji: Guangdong* (Guangdong: Selected Historical Materials on Modern Overseas Investments in Enterprises in Guangdong). Fuzhou: Fujian Renmin Chubanshe, 1989.

Lin Jinzhi. *Huaqiao touzi guonei qiye gailun* (An overview of the Investments of Modern Overseas Chinese Enterprises in China). Xiamen: Xiamen Daxue Chubanshe, 1988.

———, ed. *Huaqiao Huaren yu Zhongguo gemin he jianshe* (Overseas Chinese and China's Revolution and Construction). Fuzhou: Fujian Renmin Chubanshe, 1993.

Liu Wu-chi. *Su Man-shu*. New York: Twayne, 1972.

Liu Zuoren. 'Jinshanzhuang de yanjiu' (The Study of 'California Traders'). *Zhongguo jingji* (The Chinese Economy) 101 (February 1959): 20-22.

Lone, Stewart, and Gavan McCormack. *Korea since 1850*. New York, N. Y.: St. Martins Press, 1993.

Lu, Sheldon Hsiao-peng. *Transnational Chinese Cinemas: Identity, Nationhood, Gender*. Honolulu: University of Hawaii Press, 1997.

MacFarquhar, Roderick. 'The Post-Confucian Challenge.' *The Economist*. February 9, 1980.

Mak Lau Fong. *Fangyan qun rentong: Zaoqi Xing Ma Huaren de fenlei faze* (Dialect Group Identity: A Study of Chinese Subethnic Groups in Early Malaya). Taipei: Institute of Ethnology, Academia Sinica, 1985.

———. *The Dynamics of Chinese Dialect Groups in Early Malaya*. Singapore: Singapore Society of Asian Studies, 1995.

Mao Qixiong, and Lin Xiaodong. *Zhongguo qiaowu zhengce gaishu* (China's Overseas Chinese Policies). Beijing: Zhongguo Huaqiao Chubanshe, 1993.

Mo, Timothy. *Sour Sweet*. London: Andre Deutsch, 1982.

———. *An Insular Possession*. London: Chatto & Windus, 1986.

Naisbitt, John. *Global Paradox*. New York: W. Morrow, 1994.

Ng Fae Myenne. *Bone*. New York: Hyperion, 1993.

Ng Wing Chung. 'Taiwan's Overseas Chinese Policy from 1949 and the Early 1980s.' In *East Asia Inquiry: Selected Articles from the Annual Conferences of the Canadian Asian Studies Association 1988-1990*, edited by Larry N. Shyu, Chen Min-sun, Claude-Yves Charron and Matsuo Soga. Montreal: CASA, 1991.

———. 'Ethnicity and Community: Southern Chinese Immigrants and Descendants in Vancouver, 1945-1980.' PhD diss., University of British Columbia, 1993.

Nie Hualing. *Sangqing yu Taohong* (Mulberry and Peach). Taiwan: Youlian Chubanshe, 1976.

Oey, Eric M. 'Sustenance for the Soul: The Religious Writings of Kwee Tek Hoay.' *Asian Culture* 17 (June 1993): 41-63.

Pan, Lynn. *Sons of the Yellow Emperor*. London: Secker & Warburg, 1990.

Parker, David. *Through Different Eyes: The Cultural Identities of Young Chinese People in Britain*. Aldershot: Avebury Ashgate Publishing Ltd., l995.

Pieke, Frank N. 'Four Models of China's Overseas Chinese Policies.' *China Information* 2, 1 (1987): 8-16.

Pomerantz-Zhang, Linda. *Wu Tingfang, 1842-1922: Reform and Modernization in Modern Chinese History*. Hong Kong: Hong Kong University Press, 1992.

Redding, S. Gordon. *The Spirit of Chinese Capitalism*. Berlin: Walter de Gruyter, 1990.

Remer, C. F. *Foreign Investments in China*. New York: Macmillan, 1933.

Rowe, William T. *Hankow: Conflict and Community in a Chinese City, 1796-1895*. Stanford, Calif.: Stanford University Press, l989.

Sabapathy, T. K., ed. *Modernity and Beyond: Themes in Southeast Asian Art*. Singapore: Singapore Art Museum, 1996.

Salmon, Claudine. *Literature in Malay by the Chinese of Indonesia*. Paris: Association Archipel, 1981.

———, ed. *Literary Migrations: Traditional Chinese Fiction in Asia 17-20th Centuries*. Beijing: International Culture Publishing Corporation, 1987.

Schiffrin, Harold Z. *Sun Yat-sen and the Origins of the Chinese Revolution*. Los Angeles: University of California Press, 1968.

Seagrave, Sterling. *Lords of the Rim*. London: Bantam Press, 1995.

Sheares, Constance. *Art in the City: The Raffles City Collection*. Singapore: Raffles City Pte. Ltd., 1995.

Shi Xiangtuo. *Xiangtuo cong gao* (Xiang Tuo's Manuscripts). Singapore: Wanli Shuju, 1989.

Sinn, Elizabeth. *Power and Charity: The Early History of the Tung Wah Hospital, Hong Kong*. Hong Kong: Oxford University Press, 1989.

———. 'Emigration from Hong Kong Before 1941: General Trends.' In *Emigration From Hong Kong*, edited by Ronald Skeldon. Hong Kong: Chinese University Press, 1995a.

———. 'Emigration from Hong Kong Before 1941: Organization and Impact.' In *Emigration From Hong Kong*, edited by Ronald Skeldon. Hong Kong: Chinese University Press, 1995b.

Siu, Paul C. P. *The Chinese Laundryman: A Study of Social Isolation*, edited by John Kuo Wei Tchen. New York: New York University Press, 1987.

Skinner, G. William. *Leadership and Power in the Chinese Community of Thailand*. Ithaca, N. Y.: Cornell University Press, 1958.

———. 'Creolized Chinese Societies in Southeast Asia.' In *Sojourners and Settlers: Histories of Southeast Asia and the Chinese*, edited by Anthony Reid. St. Leonards, N. S. W.: Allen and Unwin for Asian Studies Association of Australia, 1996.

Song Ping. 'An Analysis of Models: How Schools are Run by Overseas Chinese in South Fujian.' In *South China: State, Culture and Social Change during the 20th Century*, edited by Leo M. Douw and Peter Post. Amsterdam and New York: North-Holland, 1996.

Suryadinata, Leo, ed. *Chinese Adaptation and Diversity: Essays on Society and Literature in Indonesia, Malaysia & Singapore*. Singapore: Singapore University Press, 1993a.

———. 'Literature of the Ethnic Chinese in Indonesia and the United States.' *Asian Culture* 17 (June 1993b): 32-40.

———, ed. *Southeast Asian Chinese: The Socio-cultural Dimension*. Singapore: Times Academic Press, 1995.

———, ed. *Ethnic Chinese as Southeast Asians*. Singapore: Institute of Southeast Asian Studies, 1997.

Tan Chee-Beng. 'The Preservation and Adaptation of Tradition: Studies of Chinese Religious Expression in Southeast Asia.' *Contributions to Southeast Asian Ethnography* 9 (December l990): 1-145.

Tradition and Innovation: Twentieth Century Chinese Painting. Hong Kong: Urban Council of Hong Kong, 1995.

Tsou Jung. *The Revolutionary Army: A Chinese Nationalist Tract of 1903*, introduced and translated, with notes by John Lust. The Hague, Paris: Mouton, 1968. (A translation of *Geming jun*.)

Tu Wei-ming, ed. *The Living Tree: The Changing Meaning of Being Chinese Today*. Stanford, Calif.: Stanford University Press, 1994.

Wang Gungwu. *China and the Chinese Overseas*. Singapore: Times Academic Press, 1991a.

———. *The Chineseness of China: Selected Essays*. Hong Kong: Oxford University Press, 1991b.

———. *Community and Nation: China, Southeast Asia and Australia*. St. Leonard, N. S. W.: Allen & Unwin for Asian Studies Association of Australia, 1992.

———. 'Among Non-Chinese.' In *The Living Tree: The Changing Meaning of Being Chinese Today*, edited by Tu Wei-ming. Stanford, Calif.: Stanford University Press, 1994.

Wang Singwu. *The Organization of Chinese Emigration 1848-1888: With Special Reference to Chinese Emigration to Australia*. San Francisco: Chinese Materials Centre, 1978.

Wong, Cynthia Sau-ling. 'Chinese American Literature.' In *An Interethnic Companion to Asian American Literature*, edited by King-kok Cheung. New York: Cambridge University Press, 1997.

Woon Yuen-fong. 'The Guan of Kaiping County in the 1990s: Still a Cohesive Group?' In *South China: State, Culture and Social Change during the 20th Century*, edited by Leo M. Douw and Peter Post. Amsterdam and New York: North-Holland, 1996.

Wu Chun-hsi. *Dollars, Dependents and Dogma: Overseas Chinese Remittances to Communist China*. Stanford, Calif.: The Hoover Institution on War, Revolution and Peace, 1967.

Wu Fengbin, ed. *Dongnanya Huaqiao tongshi* (General History of the Overseas Chinese in Southeast Asia). Fuzhou: Fujian Renmin Chubanshe, 1993.

Wu Lien-teh. *Plague Fighter: The Autobiography of a Modern Chinese Physician*. Cambridge, England: W. Heffer, 1959.

Wu Yu-lin. *Memories of Dr Wu Lien-teh: Plague Fighter*. Singapore: World Scientific, 1995.

Yang Songnian, and Wang Kangding, eds. *Dongnanya Huaren wenxue yu wenhua* (Southeast Asian Chinese Literature and Culture). Singapore: Singapore Society of Asian Studies, 1995.

Yang, William. 'I Ask Myself, Am I Chinese?' *Art and Asia Pacific* 1, 2 (April 1994): 89-95.

Yen Ching-hwang. *The Overseas Chinese and the 1911 Revolution*. Kuala Lumpur and New York: Oxford University Press, 1976.

———. *Studies in Modern Overseas Chinese History*. Singapore: Times Academic Press, 1995.

Yu Lihua. *You jian zonglü, you jian zonglü* (To See the Palm Tree Again, To See the Palm Tree Again). Hong Kong: Tiandi Tushu, 1980.

Zhao, Henry Y. H., and John Cayley, eds. *Under-sky, Under-ground: Chinese Writing TODAY*, 1. London: Wellsweep, 1994.

Zhuang Guotu. *Zhongguo fengjian zhengfu de Huaqiao zhengce* (The Huaqiao Policies of the Chinese Government). Xiamen Daxue Chubanshe, 1989.

COMMUNITIES

SOUTHEAST ASIA
Brunei
Blundell, Peter. *The City of Many Waters*. London: J. W. Arrowsmith, 1923.

Niew Shong Tong. *Sha, Wen, Sha dili lunwenji* (Essays on Sarawak, Brunei and Sabah). Sarawak: Poluozhou chubanshe, 1976.

———. *Wenlai Huazu huiguan shi lun* (A History of the Chinese Clan Associations of Brunei Darussalam). Singapore: Singapore Society of Asian Studies, 1991.

———. 'Chinese Society in Brunei.' In *Southeast Asian Chinese: The Socio-cultural Dimension*, edited by Leo Suryadinata. Singapore: Times Academic Press, 1995a.

———. 'Luodishenggen: Haiwai Huaren wenti yanjiu wenji' (Selected Papers on Overseas Chinese Studies). Sibu: Sarawak Chinese Cultural Association, 1995b.

Tan Pek Leng. 'A History of Chinese Settlement in Brunei.' In

Essays on Modern Brunei History. Brunei Darussalam: Universiti Brunei Darussalam, 1992.

Burma (Myanmar)
Bo Yang. *Golden Triangle: Frontier and Wilderness*, translated by Clive Gulliver. Hong Kong: Joint Publishing, 1987. (A translation of *Jinsanjiao*.)

Chakravarti, Nalini Ranian. *The Indian Minority in Burma: The Rise and Decline of an Immigrant Community*. London: Oxford University Press, 1971.

Christian, John Leroy. *Burma and the Japanese Invader*. Bombay: Thacker, 1943.

Forbes, Andrew D. W. 'The Chin-Ho (Yunnanese Chinese) Caravan Trade with North Thailand during the Late 19th and Early 20th Centuries.' Unpublished paper, 1985.

Linter, Bertil. *Land of Jade: A Journey through Insurgent Burma*. Edinburgh: Kiscadale Publications, 1990.

———. *Burma in Revolt: Opium and Insurgency since 1948*. Boulder: Westview Press, 1994.

Purcell, Victor. *The Chinese in Southeast Asia*. Rev. ed. London: Oxford University Press, 1965.

Smith, Martin. *Burma: Insurgency and the Politics of Ethnicity*. London: Zed Press, 1991.

———. 'Burma (Myanmar).' In *The Chinese of Southeast Asia*, edited by Minority Rights Group. London: Minority Rights Group, 1992.

Taw Sein Ko. *Burmese Sketches*, vol. 1 & 2. Rangoon: British Burma Press, 1913 & 1920.

Thompson, Virginia, and Richard Adloff. *Minority Problems in Southeast Asia*. Stanford, Calif.: Stanford University, 1955.

Cambodia
Chou Ta Kuan (Zhou Daguan). *Notes on the Customs of Cambodia*, translated into English from the French version by Paul Pelliot of Chou's Chinese original by J Gilman d'Arcy Paul. Bangkok: Social Science Association Press, 1967. (A translation of *Zhenlai fengtu ji*.)

Edwards, Penny. 'Shifting Boundaries: A Century of Chineseness in Cambodia.' Paper presented at the 48th Annual Meetings of the Association for Asian Studies, Honolulu, 1996.

Furnivall, J. S. *Colonial Policy and Practice: A Comparative Study of Burma and Netherlands India*. Cambridge: Cambridge University Press, 1948.

Nguyen Quoc Dinh. *Les congrégations Chinoises en Indochine Française* (Chinese Congrégations in French Indochina). Paris: Librairie du Recueil Sirey, 1941.

Wertheim, W. F. *East-West Parallels: Sociological Approaches to Modern Asia*. The Hague: W van Hoeve, 1964.

Willmott, W. E. 'History and Sociology of the Chinese in Cambodia Prior to the French Protectorate.' *Journal of Southeast Asia History* 7, 1 (March 1966): 15-38.

———. *The Chinese in Cambodia*. Vancouver: University of British Columbia Press, 1967.

———. *The Political Structure of the Chinese Community in Cambodia*. London: Athlone Press, 1970.

———. 'The Chinese in Kampuchea.' *Journal of Southeast Asian History* 12, 1 (March 1981): 38-45.

Indonesia
Blussé, Leonard. *Strange Company: Chinese Settlers, Mestizo Women and the Dutch in VOC Batavia*. Dordrecht: Foris for Koninklijk Institut voor Taal-, Land-en Volkenkunde, 1986.

———. *Tribuut aan China: Vier eeuwen Nederlands-Chinese betrekkingen* (Tribute for China: Four Centuries of Netherlands-Chinese Relations). Amsterdam: O. Cramwinckel, 1989.

Brown, Iem. 'Religions of the Chinese in Indonesia.' In *The Ethnic Chinese in the ASEAN States: Bibliographical Essays*, edited by Leo Suryadinata. Singapore: Institute of Southeast Asian Studies, 1989.

Carey, Peter. 'Changing Javanese Perceptions of the Chinese Communities in Central Java, 1755-1825.' *Indonesia* 37 (April 1984): 1-47.

Castles, Lance. 'The Ethnic Profile of Djakarta.' *Indonesia* 3 (April 1967): 153-204.

Cator, W. J. *The Economic Position of the Chinese in the Netherlands Indies*. Oxford: Blackwell, 1936.

Coppel, Charles A. 'Mapping the Peranakan Chinese in Indonesia.' *Papers on Far Eastern History* 8 (September 1973): 143-67.

———. 'The Origins of Confucianism as an Organized Religion in Java, 1900-1923.' *Journal of Southeast Asian Studies* 12 (1981): 179-96.

———. *Indonesian Chinese in Crisis*. Kuala Lumpur: Oxford University Press for the Asian Studies Association of Australia, 1983.

———. 'From Christian Mission to Confucian Religion: The Nederlandsche Zendingsvereeniging and the Chinese of West Java, 1870-1910.' In *Nineteenth and Twentieth Century Indonesia: Essays in Honour of Professor J. D. Legge*, edited by David P. Chandler and M. C. Ricklefs. Clayton, Victoria: Southeast Asian Studies, Monash University, 1986.

Diehl, F. W. 'Revenue Farming and Colonial Finances in the Netherlands East Indies, 1816-1925.' In *The Rise and Fall of Revenue Farming: Businesss Élites and the Emergence of the Modern State in Southeast Asia*, edited by John Butcher and Howard Dick. New York and London: St. Martin's Press, 1993.

Groot, J. J. M. de. *Het kongsiwezen van Borneo: een verhandeling over den grondslag en den aard der Chineesche politieke vereenigingen in de kolonien* (The Kongsis of Borneo: A Treatise on the Basis and the Nature of Chinese Political Associations in the Colonies). The Hague: M. Nijhoff, 1885.

Guillot, Claude. 'Banten en 1678' (Banten in 1678) *Archipel* 37 (1989): 119-52.

———, H. Ambary, and J. Dumarcay. *The Sultanate of Banten*. Jakarta: Gramedia Book Pub. Division, 1990.

Hadiluwih, Subanindyo. *Cina Medan: Studi tentang masalah Tionghoa di Indonesia* (The Chinese of Medan: Study of the Chinese Problem in Indonesia). Medan: Pemda Tingkat I Sumatera Utara; Fakultas Hukum UISI, 1990.

Heidhues, Mary F. Somers. *Bangka Tin and Mentok Pepper: Chinese Settlement on an Indonesian Island*. Singapore: Institute of Southeast Asian Studies, 1992.

———. 'Kongsis and Hui in 19th Century West Borneo and Bangka.' In *'Secret Societies' Reconsidered*, edited by David Ownby and Mary Somers Heidhues. Armonk, N. Y.: M. E. Sharpe, 1993.

———. 'Chinese Settlements in Rural Southeast Asia: Unwritten Histories.' In *Sojourners and Settlers: Histories of Southeast Asia and the Chinese*, edited by Anthony Reid. St. Leonards, N. S. W.: Allen and Unwin for Asian Studies Association of Australia, 1996a.

———. 'The Hakka Gold Miners of Kalimantan after the End of the Kongsi Era.' Paper presented at the 3rd International Conference on Hakkaology, Singapore, 1996b.

Heringa, Rens, and Harmen C. Veldhuisen. *Fabric of Enchantment: Batik from the North Coast of Java*. Los Angeles: Museum Associates, Los Angeles County Museum of Art, 1996.

Kahin, George. *Nationalism and Revolution in Indonesia*. Ithaca, N. Y.: Cornell University Press, 1952.

Kwee Tek Hoay. *The Origins of the Modern Chinese Movement in Indonesia*, translated and edited by Lea E. Williams. Ithaca, N. Y.: Southeast-Asia Program, Dept. of Asian Studies, Cornell University, 1969. (A translation of *Atsal moelahnja timboel pergerakan Tionghoa jang modern di Indonesia*.)

Lasiyo. 'Agama Khonghucu (The Confucian Religion): An Emerging Form of Religious Life among the Indonesian Chinese.' PhD diss., University of London, 1992.

Lohanda, Mona. *The Kapitan Cina of Batavia, 1837-1942*. Jakarta: Djambatan, 1996.

Maxwell, Robyn. *Textiles of Southeast Asia: Tradition, Trade and*

Transformation. Canberra: Australian National Gallery; Melbourne: Oxford University Press, 1990.

Ng Chin-keong. *The Chinese in Riau: A Community on an Unstable and Restrictive Frontier*. Singapore: Nanyang University School of Humanities and Social Sciences, 1976.

Nio Joe Lan. *Riwajat 40 taon dari Tiong Hoa Hwe Koan-Batavia, 1900-1939* (The History of Forty Years of the Tiong Hoa Hwe Koan of Batavia, 1900-1939). Batavia-(Jakarta): Tiong Hoa Hwe Koan, 1940.

Oetomo, Dédé. 'The Chinese of Indonesia and the Development of the Indonesian Language.' *Indonesia* (Special Issue on the Role of the Indonesian Chinese in Shaping Modern Indonesian Life) (1991): 53-66.

Ricklefs, Merle Calvin. *A History of Modern Indonesia since c. 1300*. Rev. ed. Stanford, Calif.: Stanford University Press, 1993.

Rush, James. *Opium to Java: Revenue Farming and Chinese Enterprise in Colonial Indonesia, 1860-1910*. Ithaca, N. Y.: Cornell University Press, 1990.

Salmon, Claudine, and Lombard Denys. *Les Chinois de Jakarta: Temples et vie collective: The Chinese of Jakarta: Temples and Communal Life*. Paris: SECMI, 1977.

Salmon, Claudine. *Literature in Malay by the Chinese of Indonesia*. Paris: Association Archipel, 1981.

———. 'Ancestral Halls, Funeral Associations, and Attempts at Resinicization in Nineteenth-century Netherlands India.' In *Sojourners and Settlers: Histories of Southeast Asia and the Chinese*, edited by Anthony Reid. St. Leonards, N. S. W.: Allen and Unwin for Asian Studies Association of Australia, 1996.

———. 'La communauté Chinoise de Surabaya. Essai d'histoire, des origines à la crise de 1930' (The History of the Chinese in Surabaya). *Archipel* 53 (1997): 121-206.

Sidharta, Myra. 'The Indonesia Chinese and the Batik Trade: Where Business and Creativity Meet.' In *Di semua lini, di semua waktu: Bunga rampai 50 tahun Ardiyanto* (In All Lines, in All Times: Collection Presented for the 50th Birthday of Ardiyanto), edited by Hariadi Saptono. Yogyakarta: Panitia Peringatan 50 Tahun Ardiyanto Pranata, 1994.

Skinner, G. William. 'The Chinese Minority.' In *Indonesia*, edited by Ruth T. McVey. New Haven: HRAF Press for Southeast Asia Studies, Yale University, 1963.

Somers, Mary F. 'Peranakan Chinese Politics in Indonesia.' PhD diss., Cornell University, 1965.

Suryadinata, Leo. *Eminent Indonesian Chinese: Biographical Sketches*. Rev. ed. Singapore: Institute of Southeast Asian Studies, 1995.

The Siauw Giap. 'Religion and Overseas Chinese Assimilation in Southeast Asian Countries.' *Revue du Sud-Est Asiatique* (Journal of Southeast Asia) 2 (1965): 67-83.

———. 'Group Conflict in a Plural Society.' *Revue du Sud-Est Asiatique* (Journal of Southeast Asia) 1 (1966): 1-31 and 185-217.

Williams, Lea E. *Overseas Chinese Nationalism: The Genesis of the Pan-Chinese Movement in Indonesia, 1900-1916*. Glencoe, Illinois: The Free Press, 1960.

Laos

Freedman, Maurice. *The Study of Chinese Society: Essays*, selected and introduced by G. William Skinner. Stanford, Calif.: Stanford University Press, 1979.

Halpern, Joel M. *Population Statistics and Associated Data*. Los Angeles: University of California, 1961.

Mouhot, Henri. *Travels in Siam, Cambodia and Laos 1858-1860*, introduced by Michael Smithies. Singapore: Oxford University Press, 1989.

Purcell, Victor. *The Chinese in Southeast Asia*. Rev. ed. London: Oxford University Press, 1965.

Robequain, Charles. *The Economic Development of French Indo-China*, translated by Isabel A. Ward. London: Oxford University Press, 1944. (A translation of *L'évolution économique de l'Indochine Française*.)

Su Zi. *Liaoguo zhilue* (A Brief History of Laos). Taipei, 1961.

Malaysia

Anand, Sudhir. *Inequality and Poverty in Malaysia: Measurement and Decomposition*. Washington, D. C.: World Bank, 1983.

Associated Chinese Chambers of Commerce and Industry Malaysia (ACCCIM). Papers presented at the Malaysian Economic Conference, Kuala Lumpur, 1978.

———. *The Second Malaysian Chinese Economic Congress Report*. Kuala Lumpur, 1992.

Backman, Michael. *Overseas Chinese Business Networks in Asia*. Canberra: East Asia Analytical Unit, Department of Foreign Affairs, 1995.

Baring-Gould, Sabine, and C. A. Barrpfylde. *A History of Sarawak under Its Two White Rajahs 1839-1908*. London: Sotheran, 1909.

Bowie, Alasdair. 'Redistribution with Growth? The Dilemmas of State-sponsored Economic Development in Malaysia.' *Journal of Developing Societies* 4 (1988): 28-45.

Brooke, Sylvia. *Queen of the Head-hunters: The Autobiography of H. H. the Hon. Sylvia Lady Brooke, Ranee of Sarawak*. London: Sidgwick & Jackson, 1970.

Cheah Boon Kheng. *Red Star over Malaya: Resistance and Social Conflict during and after the Japanese Occupation, 1941-1946*. Singapore: Singapore University Press, 1983.

Chew, Daniel. *Chinese Pioneers on the Sarawak Frontier 1841-1941*. Singapore: Oxford University Press, 1990.

Chin, John M. *The Sarawak Chinese*. Kuala Lumpur: Oxford University Press, 1981.

Demery, D., and Demery, L. *Adjustment and Equity in Malaysia*. Paris: Development Centre of the Organization for Economic Co-operation and Development, 1992.

Faaland, Just, Parkinson J. R., and Rais Saniman. *Growth and Ethnic Inequality: Malaysia's New Economic Policy*. London: Hurst & Co., 1990.

Heng Pek Koon. *Chinese Politics in Malaysia: A History of the Malaysian Chinese Association*. Singapore: Oxford University Press, 1988.

Jesudason, James V. *Ethnicity and the Economy: The State, Chinese Business, and Multinationals in Malaysia*. Singapore: Oxford University Press, 1989.

Jomo, K. S., ed. *Malaysia's New Economic Policies: Evaluations of the Mid-term Review of the Fourth Malaysia Plan*. Kuala Lumpur: Malaysian Economic Association, 1985.

———. *Growth and Structural Change in the Malaysian Economy*. London: MacMillan, 1990.

———. *U-turn?: Malaysia Economic Development Policies after 1990*. Australia: Centre for East and Southeast Asian Studies, James Cook University of North Queensland, 1994.

Ko, Joseph Tee Hock. 'Chinese Dialect Groups in Sarawak: Composition and Growth between 1947 and 1983.' *Sarawak Gazette* 112, 1498 (December 1986): 8-16.

Lim, Linda Y. C., and L. A. Peter Gosling, eds. *The Chinese in Southeast Asia: Ethnicity and Economic Activity*, vol. 1. Singapore: Maruzen Asia, 1983.

Loh, Francis Kok Wah. *Beyond the Tin Mines: Coolies, Squatters and New Villagers in the Kinta Valley, Malaysia, c. 1880-1980*. Singapore: Oxford University Press, 1988.

Malaysian Chinese Association. *Report of the MCA National Task Force on Deviations in Implementation of the New Economic Policy (NEP)*, 1988.

———. *Secretary-general's Report 1993 and 1994*.

Means, Gordon P. *Malaysian Politics: The Second Generation*. Singapore: Oxford University Press, 1991.

Niew Shong Tong. *Sha, Wen, Sha dili lunwenji* (Essays on Sarawak, Brunei and Sabah). Sarawak: Poluozhou chubanshe, 1976.

———. 'Dongma Huaren de lishi ji qi fazhan' (The History and Development of Chinese in East Malaysia). In *Malaixiya Huarenshi* (The History of Chinese in Malaysia), edited by Lim

Chooi Kwa and Loh Cheng Sun. Petaling Jaya, Selangor: The Federation of Alumni Association of Taiwan University, 1984.

———, and Tian Yingcheng, eds. *Shalaoyue Huazu yanjiu lunwenji* (A Study of the Chinese in Sarawak). Sarawak Chinese Cultural Association, 1992.

Osman-Rani, H. 'Malaysia's New Economic Policy: After 1990.' In *Southeast Asian Affairs 1990*. Singapore: Institute of Southeast Asian Studies, 1990.

Purcell, Victor. *The Chinese in Southeast Asia*. Rev. ed. London: Oxford University Press, 1965.

Ratnam, K. J. *Communalism and the Political Process in Malaya*. Singapore: University of Malaya Press, 1965.

Runciman, Steven. *The White Rajahs: A History of Sarawak from 1841 to 1946*. Cambridge: Cambridge University Press, 1960.

Slimming, John. *Malaysia: Death of a Democracy*. London: John Murray, 1969.

Snodgrass, Donald R. *Inequality and Economic Development in Malaysia*. Kuala Lumpur: Oxford University Press, 1980.

Tregonning, K. G. *A History of Modern Sabah 1881-1963*. Singapore: University of Malaya Press, 1964.

Vasil, R. K. *The Malaysian General Election of 1969*. Singapore: Oxford University Press, 1972.

Zainal Aznam Yusof. 'Growth and Equity in Malaysia.' In Malaysia Development Experience: Changes and Challenges. Kuala Lumpur: National Institute of Public Adminstration, 1994.

The Philippines

Ang See, Teresita. 'Integration and Identity: Social Changes in the Post-World War Philippine Chinese Community.' *Asian Culture* 14 (April 1990a): 38-46.

———. *The Chinese in the Philippines: Problems and Perspectives*. Manila: Kaisa Para Sa Kaunlaran, 1990b.

———. 'Philippine-Chinese Literature in English and Filipino: An Introduction.' *Asian Culture* 17 (June 1993): 83-90.

———. 'The Chinese in the Philippines: Continuity and Change.' In *Southeast Asian Chinese: The Socio-cultural Dimension*, edited by Leo Suryadinata. Singapore: Times Academic Press, 1995.

Blaker, James R. 'The Chinese in the Philippines: A Study of Power and Change.' PhD diss., Ohio State University, 1970.

Chen Liefu. *Feilübin de minzu wenhua yu Huaqiao tonghua wenti* (Philippine National Culture and the Chinese Assimilation Problem). Taipei: Zhengzhong Shuju, 1968.

Felix, Alfonso, ed. *The Chinese in the Philippines*. 2 vols. Manila: Solidaridad Publishing House, 1966-69.

Go Bon Juan, and Teresita Ang See, eds. *Heritage: A Pictorial History of the Chinese in the Philippines*. Manila: Kaisa Para Sa Kaunlaran and Prof. Chinben See Memorial Trust Fund, 1987.

Guldin, Gregory E. 'Overseas at Home: The Fujianese of Hong Kong.' PhD diss., University of Wisconsin, 1977.

Huang Zisheng, and He Sibing. *Feilübin Huaqiao shi* (History of the Philippine Chinese). Guangzhou: Guangdong Gaodeng Jiaoyu Chubanshe, 1987.

Liu Zhitian. *Zhong Fei guanxi shi* (History of Sino-Philippines Relations). Taipei: Zhengzhong Shuju, 1964.

McBeath, Gerald. *Political Integration of the Philippine Chinese*. Berkeley: South and Southeast Asian Studies, University of California, 1973.

Omohundro, John T. *Chinese Merchant Families in Iloilo: Commerce and Kin in a Central Philippine City*. Quezon City: Ateneo de Manila University Press; Athens, Ohio: Ohio University Press, 1981.

Palanca, Ellen H. 'Chinese Business Families in the Philippines since the 1890s.' In *Chinese Business Enterprise in Asia*, edited by Rajeswary Ampalavanar Brown. London and New York: Routledge, 1995.

See Chinben. 'Feilübin Huaren wenhua de chixu: Zongqin yu tongxiang zuzhi zai haiwai de yanbian' (Persistence and Preservation of Chinese Culture in the Philippines: The Development of Clan and Hometown Associations in an Overseas Chinese Community). *Bulletin of the Institute of Ethnology, Academia Sinica* 42 (1976): 119-206.

————. 'Chinese Clanship in the Philippine Setting.' *Journal of Southeast Asian Studies* (Special Issue on Ethnic Chinese in Southeast Asia) 12, 1 (March 1981): 224-47.

————. 'Chinese Organizations and Ethnic Identity in the Philippines.' In *Changing Identities of the Southeast Asian Chinese since World War II*, edited by Jennifer Cushman and Wang Gungwu. Hong Kong: Hong Kong University Press, 1988.

————. 'The Ethnic Chinese in the Philippines.' In *The Ethnic Chinese in the Asean States: Bibliographical Essays*, edited by Leo Suryadinata. Singapore: Institute of Southeast Asian Studies, 1989.

————, and Teresita Ang See. *The Chinese in the Philippines: A Bibliography.* Manila: De La Salle University Press, 1990.

————. *The Chinese Immigrants: Selected Writings of Professor Chinben See*, edited by Teresita Ang See. Manila: Kaisa Para Sa Kaunlaran and Chinese Studies Program, De La Salle University, 1992.

Sy Yinchow. 'Xuyan: Liushi nian lai de Fei Hua wenxue' (Preface: 60 Years of the Philippine Chinese Literature). In *Fei Hua wenyi* (Philippine-Chinese Literary Arts), edited by Sy Yinchow. Manila: Philippine-Chinese Literary Arts Association, 1992.

Tan, Antonio S. *The Chinese in the Philippines 1898-1935: A Study of their National Awakening.* Quezon City: R. P. Garcia Press, 1972.

————. 'The Chinese Mestizos and the Formation of Filipino Nationality.' In *Chinese in the Philippines*, edited by Theresa Carino. Manila: De La Salle University, 1985.

Tan, Susie L. 'Chinese Language Literature in the Philippines, Past and Present.' *Asian Culture* 17 (June 1993): 73-82.

Tulay. Manila: Kaisa Para Sa Kaunlaran, Inc., June 1988. Monthly Chinese-Filipino Newsdigest. Fortnightly since August 1995.

Weightman, George H. 'The Philippine Chinese: From Aliens to Cultural Minority.' *Journal of Comparative Family Studies* 16, 2 (Summer 1985): 161-79.

Wickberg, Edgar. 'The Chinese Mestizo in Philippines History.' *Journal of Southeast Asian History* 5, 1 (March 1964): 62-100.

————. *The Chinese in Philippine Life, 1850-1898.* New Haven: Yale University Press, 1965.

————. 'Some Comparative Perspectives on Contemporary Chinese Ethnicity in the Philippines.' *Asian Culture* 14 (April 1990): 23-37.

————. 'Chinese Organizations in Philippine Cities since World War II: The Case of Manila.' *Asian Culture* 17 (June 1993): 91-105.

————. 'Anti-Sinicism and Chinese Identity Options in the Philippines.' In *Essential Outsiders?*, edited by Daniel Chirot and Anthony Reid. Seattle: University of Washington Press, 1997.

Yoshihara Kunio. *Philippine Industrialization: Foreign and Domestic Capital.* Quezon City: Ateneo de Manila Press; Singapore: Oxford University Press, 1985.

Yung Li, Yuk-wai. *The Huaqiao Warriors: Chinese Resistance Movement in the Philippines, 1942-45.* Hong Kong: Hong Kong University Press, 1995.

Zhou Nanjing. *Feilübin yu Huaren* (The Philippines and Ethnic Chinese). Manila: Kaisa Para Sa Kaunlaran, 1993.

Singapore
Benjamin, Geoffrey. 'The Cultural Logic of "Multiracialism".' In *Singapore: Society in Transition*, edited by Riaz Hassan. Kuala Lumpur: Oxford University Press, 1994.

Bloodworth, Dennis. *The Tiger and the Trojan Horse.* Singapore: Times Books International, 1986.

Borthwick, Sally. 'Chinese Education and Identity in Singapore.' In *Changing Identities of the Southeast Asian Chinese since World War II*, edited by Jennifer Cushman and Wang Gungwu. Hong Kong: Hong Kong University Press, 1988.

————. 'Chinese Education and Employment in Singapore.' In *Zhanhou haiwai Huaren bianhua: Guoji xueshu yantaohui lunwenji* (The Postwar Transformation of Overseas Chinese: Collected Papers of an International Symposium), edited by Guo Liang. Beijing: Zhongguo Huaqiao Chubanshe, 1990.

Chelliah, D. D. *A History of the Educational Policy of the Straits Settlements with Recommendations for a New System Based on Vernaculars.* Kuala Lumpur: The Government Press, 1948.

Cheng Lim-Keak. *Social Change and the Chinese in Singapore: A Socio-economic Geography with Special Reference to Bang Structure.* Singapore: Singapore University Press, 1985.

Chew, Melanie. *Leaders of Singapore.* Singapore: Resource Press, 1996.

Chia, Felix. *The Babas Revisited.* Singapore: Heinemann Asia, 1994.

Cui Gui Qiang. *Xinjiapo Huaren: Cong kaibu dao jianguo* (The Chinese in Singapore: Past and Present). Singapore: EPB Publishers, 1994.

Goh Keng Swee, and the Education Study Team. *The Report on the Ministry of Education 1978.* Singapore: Ministry of Education, 1979.

Gopinathan, S. 'Education.' In *A History of Singapore*, edited by Ernest C. T. Chew and Edwin Lee. Singapore: Oxford University Press, 1991.

————. 'Language Policy Changes 1979-1992: Politics and Pedagogy.' In *Language, Society and Education in Singapore: Issues and Trends*, edited by S. Gopinathan, Anne Pakir, Ho Wah Kam and Vanithamani Saravanan. Singapore: Times Academic Press, 1994.

Han Fook Kwang, Warren Fernandez, and Sumiko Tan. *Lee Kuan Yew: The Man and His Ideas.* Singapore: Singapore Press Holdings and Times Editions, 1998.

Hodder, B. W. 'Racial Groupings in Singapore.' *Malayan Journal of Tropical Geography* 1 (1953): 25-36.

Josey, Alex. *Lee Kuan Yew: The Struggle for Singapore.* Rev. ed. Singapore: Angus & Robertson Publishers, 1980.

Ke Mulin, ed. *Xin Hua lishi renwu liezhuan* (Biographies of Singapore Chinese Historical Figures). Singapore: EPB Publishers, 1995.

Kuo, Eddie C. Y. 'Confucianism as Political Discourse in Singapore: The Case of an Incomplete Revitalization Movement.' In *Confucian Traditions in East Asian Modernity: Moral Education and Economic Culture in Japan and the Four Mini Dragons*, edited by Tu Wei-ming. Cambridge, Mass.: Harvard University Press, 1996.

Kwok Kian Woon. 'Social Transformation and the Problem of Social Coherence: Chinese Singaporeans at Century's End.' *Asiatische Studien/Études Asiatiques*, 49, 1 (1995): 217-41.

Lam, Jenny Lin, ed. *Voices & Choices: The Women's Movement in Singapore.* Singapore: Singapore Council of Women's Organisations and Singapore Baha'I Women's Committee, 1993.

Lee, Edwin. 'Community, Family and Household.' In *A History of Singapore*, edited by Ernest C. T. Chew and Edwin Lee. Singapore: Oxford University Press, 1991a.

————. *The British as Rulers: Governing Mulitiracial Singapore 1867-1914.* Singapore: Singapore University Press, 1991b.

Lee Ting Hui. 'Chinese Education in Malaya 1894-1911: Nationalism in the First Chinese Schools.' In *The 1911 Revolution: The Chinese in British and Dutch Southeast Asia*, edited by Lee Lai To. Singapore: Heinemann Asia, 1987.

Leifer, Michael, ed. *Letters from Mao's China by David Marshall.* Singapore: Singapore Heritage Society, 1996.

Li Yuanjin. 'Xinjiapo Huawen jiaoyu bianqian xia zhishifenzi de bao gen xintai, 1959-1987.' (Changes in Chinese Education

in Singapore and the Attitude of Intellectuals towards the Preservation of Roots, 1959-1987). In *Chuantong wenhua yu shehui bianqian* (Tradtional Culture and Social Change), edited by Yang Songnian. Singapore: Tung Ann District Guild, 1994.

Lianhe Zaobao. Lee Kuan Yew: A Pictorial Biography. Singapore: Singapore Press Holdings, 1994.

Lim Jim Koon. 'Forget the Sedan Chair, Let's Get on a Jetliner – Together: A Chinese-educated's View on the Tang Liang Hong Affair.' Speech delivered at the 3rd National Education Seminar, Singapore, January 23, 1997.

Lin Meng. 'Cong Huawen jiaoyu weiji shuo dao Nanda de renwu' (From the Crisis in Chinese Education to the Mission of Nanyang University). In *Yi jiu wu san niandu quan xing Huawen zhongxue biyeban wei Nanda choumu jijin youyi dahui tekan* (Commemorative Magazine of All-Singapore Chinese High Schools' Fund Raising for Nanda in 1953), 1954.

Liu Peifang. 'Lishi changhe zhong de yi duan jiyi.' (A Section of Memory in the Long River of History). *Lianhe Zaobao.* September 25, 1994.

Loy Teck Juan, Seng Han Tong, and Pang Cheng Lian, eds. *Lee Kuan Yew on the Chinese Community in Singapore.* Singapore: Singapore Federation of Chinese Clan Associations and Singapore Chinese Chamber of Commerce & Industry, 1991.

Pendley, Charles. 'Language Policy and Social Transformation in Contemporary Singapore.' *Southeast Asian Journal of Social Science* 11, 2 (1983): 46-58.

Pitt Kuan Wah. 'Chinese Coolie Immigrants in Nineteenth Century.' *Review of Southeast Asian Studies (Nanyang Quarterly)* 14 (June 1984): 31-59.

Qiu Xinmin. *Qiu Shuyuan shengping* (The Life of Qiu Shuyuan). Singapore: Seng Yew Book Store, 1993.

Rudolph, Jürgen. 'Reconstructing Identities: A Social History of the Babas in Singapore.' PhD diss., University of Erlangen-Nüremberg, 1994.

Sai Siew Yee. 'Post-Independence Educational Change, Identity and Huaxiaosheng Intellectuals in Singapore: A Case Study of Chinese Language.' *Southeast Asian Journal of Social Science* 25, 2 (1997): 79-101.

Saw Swee-Hock. *Singapore Population in Transition.* Philadelphia: University of Pennsylvania Press, 1970.

Siah U Chin. 'Annual Remittances to China.' *Journal of the Indian Archipelago and Eastern Asia* 1 (1847): 35-37.

————. 'The Chinese of Singapore.' *Journal of the Indian Archipelago and Eastern Asia* 2 (1885): 283-90.

Song Ong Siang. *One Hundred Years' History of the Chinese in Singapore*, introduced by Edwin Lee. Singapore: Oxford University Press, 1984.

Tan Beng Luan, and Irene Quah. *The Japanese Occupation: 1942-1945: A Pictorial Record of Singapore during the War.* Singapore: Times Editions, 1996.

Tan Chee-Beng. *Chinese Peranakan Heritage in Malaysia and Singapore.* Kuala Lumpur: Penerbit Faja Bakti Sdn. Bhd., 1993.

Tan Kah-Kee. *The Memoirs of Tan Kah-Kee*, translated and edited by A. H. C. Ward, Raymond W. Chu and Janet Salaff. Singapore: Singapore University of Singapore, 1994. (A translation of *Nanqiao huiyilu*.)

Tang Eng Teik. 'Uniqueness of Malayan Chinese Literature: Literary Plemic in the Forties.' *Asian Culture* 12 (1988): 102-15.

Tham Seong Chee. *Multi-Lingualism in Singapore: Two Decades of Development.* Singapore: Department of Statistics, 1996.

Thio, Eunice. 'The Syonan Years, 1942-1945.' In *A History of Singapore*, edited by Ernest C. T. Chew and Edwin Lee. Singapore: Oxford University Press, 1991.

Turnbull, C. M. *A History of Singapore 1919-1975.* Kuala Lumpur: Oxford University Press, 1977.

Trocki, Carl A. *Prince of Pirates: The Temenggongs and the Development of Johor and Singapore, 1784-1885.* Singapore: Singapore University Press, 1979.

————. *Opium and Empire: Chinese Society in Colonial Singapore, 1800-1910*. Ithaca, N. Y.: Cornell University Press, 1990.

Wang Gungwu. 'A Short Introduction to Chinese Writing in Malaya.' In *Bunga Emas: An Anthology of Contemporary Malaysian Literature (1930-1963)*, edited by T. Wignesan. Kuala Lumpur: Rayirath (Raybooks) Publications, 1964.

————. *China and the Chinese Overseas*. Singapore: Times Academic Press, 1991.

Wang Ruming, ed. *Chen Liushi bainian dan jinian wenji* (Tan Lark Sye: A Commemorative Collection on His Hundredth Birth Anniversay). Singapore: Nanda Shiye Youxian Gongsi; Hong Kong: Xianggang Nanyang Daxue Xiaoyou Hui, 1997.

Warren, James Francis. *Rickshaw Coolie: A People's History of Singapore (1880-1940)*. Singapore: Oxford University Press, 1986.

Wee, C. J. W.-L. 'Contending with Primordialism: The "Modern" Construction of Postcolonial Singapore.' *Positions* 1, 3 (Winter 1993): 715-44.

Williams, Raymond. *Marxism and literature*. Oxford: Oxford University Press, 1977.

Willmott, W. E. 'The Emergence of Nationalism.' In *Management of Success: The Moulding of Modern Singapore*, edited by Kernial Singh Sandhu and Paul Wheatley. Singapore: Institute of Southeast Asian Studies, 1989.

Wong, John. 'Promoting Confucianism for Socioeconomic Development.' In *Confucian Traditions in East Asian Modernity: Moral Education and Economic Culture in Japan and the Four Mini-Dragons*, edited by Tu Wei-ming, Cambridge, Mass.: Harvard University Press, 1996.

Xu Yunqiao, and Cai Shijun, eds. *Xin Ma Huaren kang Ri shiliao* (Malayan Chinese Resistance to Japan 1937-1945: Selected Source Materials). Singapore: Cultural & Historical Publishing House, 1984.

Yen Ching-hwang. *A Social History of the Chinese in Singapore and Malaya 1800-1911*. Singapore: Oxford University Press, 1986.

————. *Community and Politics: The Chinese in Colonial Singapore and Malaysia*. Singapore: Times Academic Press, 1995.

Yeo Song-Nian, and Leung Yuen Sang. 'In Search of Identity: Chinese Literature in Malaysia and Singapore 1991-1983, *Asian Culture* 5 (1985): 18-23.

Yong C. F. *Tan Kah-kee: The Making of an Overseas Chinese Legend*. Singapore: Oxford University Press, 1987.

————. *Chinese Leadership and Power in Colonial Singapore*. Singapore: Times Academic Press, 1991.

Thailand
Brown, Ian. *The Élite and Economy in Siam c.1890-1920*. Singapore: Oxford University Press, 1988.

Coughlin, Richard J. *Double Identity: The Chinese in Modern Thailand*. Hong Kong: Oxford University Press, 1960.

Cushman, Jennifer. *Family and State: The Formation of a Sino-Thai Tin-mining Dynasty, 1797-1932*. Kuala Lumpur: Oxford University Press, 1991.

FitzGerald, C. P. *The Southern Expansion of the Chinese People*. Bangkok: White Lotus, 1972.

Hall, D. G. E. *A History of Southeast Asia*. London: MacMillan, 1968.

King Vajiravudh. 'The Jews of the Orient.' In *The World of Southeast Asia: Selected Historical Readings*, edited by H. Benda and J. Larkin. New York: Harper Row, 1967.

Pasuk Phongpaichit, and Chris Baker. *Thailand: Economy and Politics*. Oxford: Oxford University Press, 1995.

Purcell, Victor. *The Chinese in Southeast Asia*. Rev. ed. London: Oxford University Press, 1965.

Reynolds, Craig. 'Tycoons and Warlords: Modern Thai Social Formations and Chinese Historical Romance.' In *Sojourners and Settlers: Histories of Southeast Asia and the Chinese*, edited by Anthony Reid. St. Leonards, N. S. W.: Allen and Unwin for Asian Studies Association of Australia, 1996.

Shen Yingming. *Taiguo Huaqiao gaikuang* (Chinese in Thailand). Taipei: Zhengzhong Shuju, 1988.

Skinner, G. William. *Chinese Society in Thailand: An Analytical History*. Ithaca, N. Y.: Cornell University Press, 1957.

————. *Leadership and Power in the Chinese Community of Thailand*. Ithaca, N. Y.: Cornell University Press, 1958.

Viraphol Sarasin. *Tribute and Profit: Sino-Siamese Trade 1652-1853*. Cambridge, Mass.: Harvard University Press, 1977.

Yoshihara Kunio. *The Rise of Ersatz Capitalism in Southeast Asia*. Singapore: Oxford University Press, 1988.

Vietnam
Amer, Ramses. *The Ethnic Chinese in Vietnam and Sino-Vietnamese Relations*. Kuala Lumpur: Forum, 1991.

Butcher, John, and Howard Dick, eds. *The Rise and Fall of Revenue Farming*. New York: St. Martin's Press, 1993.

Chen Ching-Ho. *A Brief Study of Family Register of the Trans: A Ming Refugee Family in Minh Huong Xa, Thua Thien (Central Vietnam)*. Hong Kong: Southeast Asia Studies Section, New Asia Research Institute, Chinese University of Hong Kong, 1964.

————. *Historical Notes on Hoi-An (Faifo)*. Carbondale: Center for Vietnamese Studies, Southern Illinois, 1974.

Crawfurd, John. *Journal of an Embassy to the Courts of Siam and Cochin China*, introduced by David K. Wyatt. Singapore: Oxford University Press, 1967.

Dai Nam thuc luc chinh bien (Chronicle of Nguyen Dynasty). Tokyo: The Oriental Institute, Keio University, 1963.

Dubreuil, R. *De la condition des Chinois et de leur rôle économique en Indochine* (The Condition of the Chinese and their Economic Roles in Indochina). Bar-sur-Seine: Imprimerie C. Caillard, 1910.

Fujiwara Riichiro. 'The Regulation of the Chinese under the Trinh Regime and Pho Hien.' In *Pho Hien: The Centre of International Commerce in the 17th and 18th Centuries*. Hanoi: The Gioi Publishers, 1994.

Grant, Bruce. *The Boat People: An 'Age' Investigation with Bruce Grant*. Harmondsworth: Penguin, 1979.

Huaqiao zhi bianzuan weiyuanhui (The Editorial Committee of the Huaqiao History). *Yuenan Huaqiao zhi* (History of the Chinese in Vietnam). Taipei: Huaqiao Zhi Bianzuan Weiyuanhui, 1958.

Khoo Joo Ee. *The Straits Chinese: A Cultural History*. Amsterdam and Kuala Lumpur: The Pepin Press, 1996.

Li, Tana, and Anthony Reid, eds. *Southern Vietnam under the Nguyen*. Singapore: Institute of Southeast Asian Studies, 1993.

Mac Duong. *Xa hoi nguoi Hoa o Thanh pho Ho Chi Minh sau nam 1975* (The Chinese Community in Ho Chi Minh City after 1975). Ho Chi Minh City: Khoa Hoc Xa Hoi, 1994.

Marr, David G. *Vietnamese Anticolonialism: 1885-1925*. Berkeley: University of California, 1971.

Murray, Martin. *The Development of Capitalism in Colonial Indochina (1870-1940)*. Berkeley: University of California Press, 1980.

Nguyen Huyen Anh. *Viet Nam danh nhan tu dien* (A Dictionary of Famous Figures in Vietnam). Saigon: Khai Tri, 1967.

Nguyen Khac Vien. *Contemporary Vietnam: 1858-1980*. Hanoi: Red River Press, 1981.

Nguyen Van Huy. *Nguoi Hoa tai Viet Nam* (The Chinese in Vietnam). Costa Mesa: NBC Press, 1993.

Nguyen Van Sang. 'Nguoi Viet goc Hoa va kinh te Viet Nam' (The Vietnamese Chinese and Vietnam's Economy). MA diss., Quoc Gia Hanh Chanh, 1974.

Purcell, Victor. *The Chinese in Southeast Asia*. Rev. ed. London: Oxford University Press, 1965.

Robequain, Charles. *The Economic Development of French Indo-China*, translated by Isabel A. Ward. London: Oxford University Press, 1944. (A translation of *L'évolution économique de l'Indochine Française*.)

Skinner, G. William. 'Creolized Chinese Societies in Southeast Asia.' In *Sojourners and Settlers: Histories of Southeast Asia and the Chinese*, edited by Anthony Reid. St. Leonards, N. S. W.: Allen and Unwin for Asian Studies Association of Australia, 1996.

Taylor, Keith Weller. *The Birth of Vietnam*. Berkeley: University of California Press, 1983.

Tran Khanh. *The Ethnic Chinese and Economic Development in Vietnam*. Singapore: Institute of Southeast Asian Studies, 1993.

Tran Trong Kim. *Viet Nam su luoc* (A Brief History of Vietnam), vol. 2. Saigon: Trung Tam Hoc Lieu, 1971.

Tsai Maw-kuey. *Les Chinois au Sud-Vietnam* (The Chinese of South Vietnam). Paris: Ministère de l'Éducation Nationale, Comité des Travaux Historiques et Scientifiques, Bibliothèque Nationale, 1968.

Wu Yuan-li, and Chun-hsi Wu. *Economic Development in Southeast Asia: The Chinese Dimension*. Stanford, Calif.: Hoover Institution Press, 1980.

Xu Shanfu. 'Lun Huaqiao zai Yuenan jingji zhong de diwei zuoyong ji qita, 1919-1939 (On the Chinese Role in Vietnam's Economy, 1919-1939). *Huaqiao yanjiu* (Chinese Overseas Studies (1988): 181-200.

Zhang Yu. 'Chong fang Yuenan' (Vietnam Revisited). *Bagui qiaoshi* (Bagui's Overseas Affairs) 22, 2 (1994): 54-58.

THE AMERICAS
Canada
Adilman, Tamara. 'A Preliminary Sketch of Chinese Women and Work in British Columbia, 1858-1950.' In *Not Just Pin Money: Selected Essays on the History of Women's Work in British Columbia*, edited by B. Latham, R. Latham and R. Pazdro. Victoria: Camosun College, 1984.

Anderson, Kay J. *Vancouver's Chinatown: Racial Discourse in Canada, 1875-1980*. Montreal: McGill-Queen's University Press, 1991.

Baureiss, Gunter A. 'Ethnic Resilience and Discrimination: Two Chinese Communities in Canada.' *The Journal of Ethnic Studies* 10, 1 (1982): 69-87.

Canada and Hong Kong Research Project. *Canada and Hong Kong Update*, 1-13 (1990-95).

Chan, Anthony. 'The Myth of the Chinese Sojourner in Canada.' In *Proceedings of the Asian Canadian Symposium II*, edited by Gordon Hirabayashi and Victor Ujimoto. Ottawa: Multiculturalism Directorate, 1978.

————. *Gold Mountain: The Chinese in the New World*. Vancouver: New Star Books, 1983.

Chan Kwok Bun. *Smoke and Fire: The Chinese in Montreal*. Hong Kong: Chinese University Press, 1991.

Cheng, Tien-fang. *Oriental Immigration in Canada*. Shanghai: The Commercial Press, 1931.

Cho, George, and Roger Leigh. 'Patterns of Residence of the Chinese in Vancouver.' In *Peoples of the Living Land*, edited by J. Minghi. Vancouver: Tantalus, 1972.

Chong, Denise. *The Concubine's Children: Portrait of a Family Divided*. Toronto: Viking, 1994.

Con, Harry (Jian Jianping). *Zhongguo Hongmen zai Jianada* (The Chinese Freemasons in Canada). Vancouver: Chinese Freemasons Canadian Headquarters, 1989.

Creese, Gillian. 'Organizing against Racism in the Workplace: Chinese Workers in Vancouver before the Second World War.' *Canadian Ethnic Studies* 19, 3 (1987): 35-46.

Evans, Paul, and Michael Frolic, eds. *Reluctant Adversaries: Canada and the People's Republic of China, 1949-1971*. Toronto: University of Toronto Press, 1991.

Goldberg, Michael. *The Chinese Connection: Getting Plugged into Pacific Rim Real Estate, Trade and Capital Markets*. Vancouver: University of British Columbia, 1985.

Hawkins, Freda. *Canada and Immigration: Public Policy and Public Concern*. Montreal: McGill-Queen's University Press, 1972.

Hoe Ban Seng. *Structural Changes of Two Chinese Communities in Alberta, Canada*. Ottawa: National Museum of Man, 1976.

Huang, Evelyn. *Chinese Canadians: Voices from a Community*. Vancouver: Douglas and McIntyre, 1992.

Johnson, Graham. 'Chinese Family and Community in Canada: Tradition and Change.' In *Two Nations, Many Cultures*, edited by Jean Elliot. Scarborough, Ontario: Prentice-Hall of Canada, 1979.

———. 'Chinese-Canadians in the 1970s: New Wine in New Bottles?' In *Two Nations, Many Cultures*, edited by Jean Elliot. Rev. ed. Scarborough, Ontario: Prentice-Hall of Canada, 1983.

———. 'Ethnic and Racial Communities in Canada and Problems of Adaptation: Chinese Canadians in the Contemporary Period.' *Ethnic Group* 9 (1992): 151-74.

Lai, David Chuen-Yan. *Chinatowns: Towns within Cities in Canada*. Vancouver: University of British Columbia Press, 1988.

———. *The Forbidden City within Victoria: Myth, Symbol and Streetscape of Canada's Earliest Chinatown*. Victoria: Orca Book Publishers, 1991.

Lee, Carol. 'The Road to Enfranchisement: Chinese and Japanese in British Columbia.' *BC Studies* 30 (Summer 1976): 44-76.

Lee, David Tung-hai. *Jianada Huaqiao shi* (A History of the Chinese in Canada). Taipei: Zhonghua Dadian Bianyinhui, 1967.

Li, Peter S. 'Chinese Immigrants on the Canadian Prairie, 1910-1947.' *Canadian Review of Sociology and Anthropology* 19 (1982): 527-40.

———. *The Chinese in Canada*. Toronto: Oxford University Press, 1988.

———. 'The Emergence of the New Middle Class among the Chinese in Canada.' *Asian Culture* 14 (1990): 187-94.

——— 'Chinese Investment and Business in Canada: Ethnic Entrepreneurship Reconsidered.' *Pacific Affairs* 66 (1993): 219-43.

Ma, L. Eve Armentrout. *Revolutionaries, Monarchists and Chinatowns: Chinese Politics in Americas and the 1911 Revolution*. Honolulu: University of Hawaii Press, 1990.

Roy, Patricia. *A White Man's Province: British Columbia Politicians and Chinese and Japanese Immigrants, 1858-1914*. Vancouver: University of British Columbia Press, 1989.

Stanley, Timothy. 'Schooling, White Supremacy and the Formation of a Chinese Merchant Public in British Columbia.' *BC Studies* 107 (Autumn 1995): 3-29.

———. ' "Chinamen, Wherever We Go": Chinese Nationalism and Guangdong Merchants in British Columbia, 1871-1911.' *Canadian Historical Review* 77, 4 (December 1996): 475-503.

Sugimoto, Howard Hiroshi. 'The Vancouver Riots of 1907: A Canadian Episode.' In *East across the Pacific,* edited by Hilary Conroy and Scott Miyakawa. Honolulu: University of Hawaii Press, 1972.

The Women's Book Committee, and Chinese Canadian National Council. *Jin Guo: Voices of Chinese Canadian Women*. Toronto: Women's Press, 1992.

Thompson, Richard. 'Ethnicity Versus Class: An Analysis of Conflict in a North American Chinese Community.' *Ethnicity* 4, 4 (1979): 306-26.

———. *Toronto's Chinatown: The Changing Organization of an Ethnic Community*. New York: AMS Press, 1989.

Tsang, Henry, ed. *Self Not Whole: Cultural Identity and Chinese-Canadian Artists in Vancouver*. Vancouver: The Chinese Cultural Centre, 1991.

Ward, Peter. *White Canada Forever: Popular Attitudes and Public Policy towards Orientals in British Columbia*. Rev. ed. Montreal and Kingston: McGill-Queen's University Press, 1990.

Wickberg, Edgar. 'Chinese Organizations and the Canadian Political Process: Two Case Studies.' In *Ethnicity, Power and Politics in Canada*, edited by Jorgen Dahlie and Tissa Fernando. Toronto: Methuen, 1981.

———, ed. *From China to Canada: A History of the Chinese Communities in Canada*. Toronto: McClelland and Steward, 1982.

Willmott, W. E. 'Chinese Clan Associations in Vancouver.' *Man* 64 (1964): 33-37.

———. 'Some Aspects of Chinese Communities in British Columbia Town.' *BC Studies* 1 (Winter 1968-69): 27-36.

———. 'Approaches to the Study of the Chinese in British Columbia.' *BC Studies* 4 (Spring 1970): 38-52.

Yee, Paul R. *Teach Me to Fly, Skyfighter! and Other Stories*. Toronto: James Lorimer, 1983.

———. *The Curses of Third Uncle*. Toronto: James Lorimer, 1986.

———. *Saltwater City: An Illustrated History of the Chinese in Vancouver*. Vancouver: Douglas and McIntyre, 1988.

———. *Breakaway*. Toronto: Groundwood, 1994.

The Caribbean
Campbell, Persia Crawford. *Chinese Coolie Emigration to Countries within the British Empire*, with a preface by W. Pember Reeves. London: Frank Cass, 1971.

Chia, Jane. *Georgette Chen*. Singapore: Singapore Art Museum, 1997.

Clementi, Cecil. *The Chinese in British Guiana*. Georgetown: Argosy, 1915.

Crespo, Mercedes. *Cong kuli dao zhurenweng—Jinian Huaren dao Guba 150 nian* (Commemoration of 150 Years of the Chinese Emigration to Cuba), translated by Liu Zhenli and Wang Shuxiong. Beijing: Shijie Zhishi Chubanshe, 1997. (A translation of unpublished manuscript.)

Guanche Perez, Jesus. *Componentes etnicos de la nacion cubana* (Ethnic Components of the Cuban People). Habana: Fundacion Fernando Ortiz y Ediciones Union, 1996.

Helly, Denise. *Idéologie et ethnicité: Les Chinois Macao à Cuba, 1847-86* (Ideology and Ethnicity: Macao Chinese in Cuba, 1847-86). Montréal: Presses de l'Université de Montréal, 1979.

Look Lai, Walton. *Indentured Labor, Caribbean Sugar: Chinese and Indian Migrants to the British West Indies, 1838-1918*. Baltimore: Johns Hopkins University Press, 1993.

———. *The Chinese in the West Indies 1806-1995: A Documentary History*. Jamaica: University of the West Indies Press, 1998.

The Cuba Commission Report: A Hidden History of the Chinese in Cuba. The Original English Language Text of 1876, introduced by Denise Helly. Baltimore: Johns Hopkins University Press, 1993.

Spanish America
Bao, Daniel. *No Hay Sangre Fresca Aqui* (There is No Fresh Blood Here*): The Chinese Community in Montevideo, Uruguay*. Unpublished paper, 1987.

Chen Kwong Min. *The Chinese in the Americas*. New York: Overseas Chinese Culture Pub. Co., 1950.

Ching Chieh Chang. 'The Chinese in Latin America: A Preliminary Geographical Survey with Special Reference to Cuba and Jamaica.' PhD diss., University of Maryland, 1956.

Chiu, Fabiana. *Beyond the Chinese Coolie: From Salsa to Chifa*. Unpublished paper, 1994.

Ho Ming Chung. *Milu Huaqiao shouce* (The Manual of the Overseas Chinese in Peru). Taipei, 1967a.

———. *Nanmei guojia ji Huaqiao shiye jianjie* (Overseas Chinese Enterprises in South America). Taipei, 1967b.

Kwong, Alice Jo. 'The Chinese in Peru.' In *Colloquium on Overseas Chinese*, edited by Morton Fried. New York: Institute of Pacific Relations, 1958.

La Honorable Colonia China en la República Mexicana (The Honourable Chinese Community in Mexico). Mexico: Ediciones 'Roco', 1957.

Lausent-Herrera, Isabel. *Pequeña propriedad, poder y economia de mercado* (Small Holdings, Power and Market Economy). Lima: Instituto de Estudios Peruanos, 1982.

———. 'Lima: Au coeur de la villa, le quartier Chinois' (Lima: The Heart of the City, the Chinese Quarter). *Problème d'Amérique Latine* (Latin American Problems) 4 (1994): 311-19.

Li He. 'Chinese Immigration to Peru.' *Ibero-Americana: Nordic Journal of Latin American Studies* 20, 2 (1990): 3-16.

Millones, Luís. *Minorías etnicas en el Perú* (Ethnic Minorities in Peru). Lima: Pontifica Universidad Católica de Perú, 1973.

Oriental (Lima, Peru) 639 (March 1986).

The United States
Bailey, Paul. 'The Chinese Work-study Movement in France.' *China Quarterly* 115 (September 1988): 441-61.

Barringer, Herbert, Robert W. Gardner, and Michael J. Levin. *Asians and Pacific Islanders in the United States*. New York: Russell Sage Foundation, 1993.

Char Tin-yuke, ed. *The Sandalwood Mountains: Readings and Stories of the Early Chinese in Hawaii*. Honolulu: University Press of Hawaii, 1975.

Chen, Jack. *The Chinese of America: From the Beginning to the Present*. San Francisco: Harper & Row, 1980.

Chin Ko-lin. 'Safe House or Hell House? The Experience of Newly Arrived Undocumented Chinese.' Paper presented at the 'Asian Migrant Trafficking: The New Threat to America's Immigration Tradition' Conference, Honolulu, July 25-27, 1996.

Chinn, Thomas W., Him Mark Lai, and Philip P. Choy, eds. *A History of the Chinese in California: A Syllabus*. San Francisco: Historical Society of America, 1969.

Destefano, Anthony M. 'Immigrant Smuggling through Central America and the Caribbean.' Paper presented at the 'Asian Migrant Trafficking: The New Threat to America's Immigration Tradition' Conference, Honolulu, July 25-27, 1996.

Glick, Clarence E. *Sojourners and Settlers: Chinese Migrants in Hawaii*. Honolulu: University Press of Hawaii, 1980.

LaFargue, T. *China First Hundred: Educational Mission Students in the US 1872-1881*. Pullman: Washington State University Press, 1993.

Lai, Him Mark, Joe Huang, and Don Wong. *The Chinese of America, 1785-1980: An Illustrated History and Catalog of the Exhibition*. San Francisco: Chinese Culture Foundation, 1980.

Lai, Him Mark. 'Historical Development of the Chinese Consolidated/Huiguan System.' In *Chinese America: History and Perspectives*. San Francisco, Calif.: Chinese Historical Society of America, 1987.

———. 'The Chinese Press in the United States and Canada since World War II: A Diversity of Voices.' In *Chinese America: History and Perspectives*. San Francisco, Calif.: Chinese Historical Society of America, 1990.

———. 'Chinese Organizations in America Based on Locality of Origin and/or Dialect Group Affiliation, 1940-1990s.' In *Chinese America: History and Perspectives*. San Francisco, Calif.: Chinese Historical Society of America, 1996.

Lew Ling. *The Chinese in North America: A Guide to Their Life and Progress*. Los Angeles: East-West Culture Publishing Association, 1949.

Liu Ningrong. *Zhongguo renshe chao* (China's Clandestine Immigrants). Hong Kong: The Nineties, 1996.

Mai Liqian (Him Mark Lai). *Cong Huaqiao dao Huaren: Ershi shiji Meiguo Huaren shehui fazhan shi* (From Overseas Chinese to Chinese American: The Evolution of Chinese American Society in the Twentieth Century). Hong Kong: Joint Publishing Co., 1992.

Mark, Diane M. L., and Ginger Chih. *A Place Called Chinese America*. Washington, D. C.: Organization of Chinese Americans, 1982.

Meidong Fujian tongxianghui: Wushi zhounian jinian te ce (Fujian American Association: 50th Anniversary Commemorative Yearbook), 1993.

Myers III, Willard H. 'The Dynamic Elements of Chinese Irregular Population Movement'. Paper presented at the 'Asian Migrant Trafficking: The New Threat to America's Immigration Tradition' Conference, Honolulu, July 25-27, 1996.

Ng, Franklin, ed. *Asian American Encyclopedia*. New York: Martin Cavendish, 1995.

Report of the Interagency Workshop (US Federal Government). '*Presidential Initiative to Deter Alien Smuggling.*' December 1995.

Wang Y. C. *Chinese Intellectuals and the West 1872-1949*. Chapel Hill: University of North Carolina Press, 1966.

AUSTRALASIA AND OCEANIA
Australia
Adam, Enid, and Philip J. Hughes. *The Buddhists in Australia*. Canberra: Australian Government Publishing Service, 1996.

Ata, Abe I. Wade, ed. *Religion and Ethnic Identity: An Australian Study*. Richmond, Victoria: Spectrum, 1989.

Backman, Michael. *Overseas Chinese Business Networks in Asia*. Canberra: East Asia Analytical Unit, Department of Foreign Affairs and Trade, 1995.

Chang J. 'Contemporary Chinese Writing in Chinese in Australia.' Paper presented at the 'Chinese in Australasia and Oceania' Conference, Melbourne, September 1996.

Choi Ching-yan. *Chinese Migration and Settlement in Australia*. Sydney: Sydney University Press, 1975.

Dang T., and A. Borowski. *Split Family Migration among Business and Skilled Migrants*. Canberra: Bureau of Immigration Research, 1991.

Giese, Diana. *Astronauts, Lost Souls and Dragons: Conversations with Chinese Australians*. St. Lucia: Queensland University Press, 1997.

Huck, A. *The Chinese in Australia*. Melbourne: Longmans, 1967.

———. *The Assimilation of the Chinese in Australia*. Canberra: Australian National University Press, 1974.

Inglis, Christine. 'The Chinese in Australia.' *International Migration Review* 6 (1972): 266-81.

———, et al., eds. *Asians in Australia: The Dynamics of Migration and Settlement*. Singapore: Institute of Southeast Asian Studies, 1992.

———. 'The Hong Kong Chinese in Sydney.' In *Reluctant Exiles?: Migration from Hong Kong and the New Overseas Chinese*, edited by Ronald Skeldon. Hong Kong: Hong Kong University Press, 1994.

Ip, D. 'Gold Mountain No More: Impressions of Australian Society among Recent Chinese Immigrants.' Paper presented at the 'Last Half Century of Chinese Overseas: Comparative Perspective' Conference, Hong Kong, December 19-21, 1994.

Jacobs, B., and Yu O. *Bitter Peaches and Plums: Two Chinese Novellas on the Recent Chinese Student Experience in Australia*. Melbourne: Monash Asia Institute, 1995.

Jupp, J., ed. *The Australian People: An Encyclopedia of the Nation, Its People and Their Origins*. Sydney: Augus and Robertson, 1988.

Lever-Tracy, Constance, et al. *Asian Entrepreneurs in Australia : Ethnic Small Business in the Chinese and Indian Communities of Brisbane and Sydney*. Canberra: Australian Government Publishing Service, 1991.

Lyng, J. *Non-Britishers in Australia: Influence on Population and Progress*. Victoria: Melbourne University Press, 1927.

Markus, Andrew. *Australian Race Relations*. Sydney: Allen and Unwin, 1994.

Price, C. *The Great White Walls are Built: Restrictive Immigration to North America and Australasia 1836-1888*. Canberra: Australian National University Press, 1974.

Rolls, Eric. *Sojourners: The Epic Story of China's Centuries Old Relationship with Australia: Flowers and the Wide Sea*. St. Lucia: Queensland University Press, 1992.

———. *Citizens*. Brisbane: University of Queensland Press, 1996.

Ryan, J. *Chinese in Australia and New Zealand: A Multidisciplinary Approach*. New Delhi: New Age International Publishers, 1995.

Shu J., and Hawthorne, L. 'Asian Student Migration to Australia.' *International Migration* 34, 1 (1996): 65-96.

Travers, Robert. *Australian Mandarin: The Life and Times of Quong Tart*. Kenthurst: Kangaroo Press, 1981.

Wang Sing-wu. *The Organization of Chinese Emigration 1848-1888: With Special Reference to Chinese Emigration to Australia*. San Francisco: Chinese Materials Center, 1978.

Willard, M. *History of the White Australia Policy*. Victoria: Melbourne University Press, 1923; reprint 1967.

Wilton, J. *Hong Yuen: A Country Store and Its People*. Armidale: Armidale C. A. E., 1988.

Yarwood, A. *Asian Migration to Australia: The Background to Exclusion, 1896-1923*. Victoria: Melbourne University Press, 1964.

Yong Ching Fatt. *The New Gold Mountain: The Chinese in Australia 1901-1921*. Australia: Raphael Arts, 1977.

New Zealand
Ip Manying. 'From Sojourners to Citizens: Metamorphosis of the New Zealand Chinese since World War II.' *Asian Culture* 14 (April 1990a): 195-204.

———. *Home Away from Home*. Auckland: New Women's Press, 1990b.

Leckie, Jacqueline. 'In Defence of Race and Empire: The White New Zealand League at Pukekohe.' *The New Zealand Journal of History* 19, 2 (October 1985): 103-29.

Sedgwick, Charles P. 'The Organisational Dynamics of the New Zealand Chinese: A Case of Political Ethnicity.' In *Tauiwi: Racism and Ethnicity in New Zealand*, edited by Paul Spoonley et al. Dunedin: Dunmore Press, 1984.

———. 'Persistence, Change and Innovation: The Social Organisation of the New Zealand Chinese 1866-1976.' *Journal of Comparative Family Studies* 16, 2 (1985): 205-29.

Stanbridge, Julia M. 'The Chinese Lessons in New Zealand Chinese Growers Monthly Journal.' MA diss., University of Auckland, 1989.

Trlin, Andrew D., and Paul Spoonley, eds. *New Zealand and International Migration: A Digest & Bibliography no. 2*. Palmerston North: Department of Sociology, Massey University, 1992.

The South Pacific
Cahill, P. 'The Chinese in Rabaul: 1914-1960.' MA diss., University of Papua New Guinea, 1972.

Chen Hansheng, ed. *Huagong chuguo shiliao huibian* (Historical Materials on the Emigration of Chinese Labourers), vol. 8, 9 &10. Beijing: Zhonghua Shudian, 1984.

Coppenrath, Gérald. *Les Chinois de Tahiti, de l'aversion à l'assimilation 1865-1966* (The Chinese in Tahiti: Discrimination and Assimilation, 1865-1966). Paris: Musée de l'Homme, 1967.

Fong, Alison. *A Chinese Community in Fiji*. Suva: South Pacific Social Sciences Association, 1974.

Greif, Stuart. *The Overseas Chinese in Fiji*. Taipei: College of Chinese Culture, 1977.

Inglis, Christine. 'Chinese.' In *Encyclopedia of Papua New Guinea*, edited by P. Ryan. Victoria: Melbourne University Press, 1972.

———. 'Particularism in the Economic Organization of the Chinese in Papua New Guinea.' *Anthropological Forum* 4 (1975-76): 69-76.

———. 'Social Structure and Patterns of Economic Action: The Chinese in Papua New Guinea.' PhD diss., University of London, 1978.

———. 'Women and Trade: A Chinese Example from Papua New Guinea.' In *An Old State in New Settings: Studies in the Social Anthropology of China in Memory of Maurice Freedman*, edited by Hugh D. R. Baker and S. Feuchtwang. Oxford: JASO, 1991.

Kumekawa, Eugene Seiichi. 'Person, Group and Context: The Foundations of Ethnic Identity among the Chinese in Fiji.' PhD diss., San Diego, University of California, 1988.

Laracy, Hugh. 'Unwelcome Guests, the Solomons' Chinese.' *New Guinea and Australia, the Pacific and South-East Asia* (January 1974): 27-37.

Laubreaux, Janine. *Les Asiatiques en Nouvelle-Calédonie* (The Asians in New Caledonia). Faculté de lettres et sciences humaines, Université de Montpellier, 1965.

McInnes, D. *Julius Chan and Namatanai*. Port Moresby: Morauta, 1995.

Moench, Richard U. 'Economic Relations of the Chinese in the Society Islands.' PhD diss., Harvard University, 1963.

Moore, Clive, Jacqui Leckie, and Doug Munro, eds. *Labour in the South Pacific*. Townsville: James Cook University Press, 1990.

Ramsden, Eric. 'William Stewart and the Introduction of Chinese Labour in Tahiti.' *Journal of the Polynesian Society* 55, 3 (September 1946): 187-214.

Souvenir Magazine in Commemoration of the 50th Anniversary of the Yat Sen Primary School, 1936-1986, and the Establishment of the Yat Sen Secondary School. Suva: Chinese Education Society Inc., 1986.

Tom, Nancy Y. W. *The Chinese in Western Samoa 1975-1985*. Apia: Western Samoan Historical and Cultural Trust, 1986.

Tung Yuan-chao. 'The Political Participation of the Chinese in French Polynesia.' *Bulletin of the College of Liberal Arts* 41 (June 1994): 251-67.

Vognin, Sophie Titania. 'La population Chinoise de Tahiti au XIXe siècle' (The Chinese Population of Tahiti in the 19th Century). In *Le peuplement du Pacifique et de la Nouvelle-Calédonie au XIXe siècle* (The Peopling of the Pacific and the New Caledonia in the 19th Century), edited by Paul de Deckker. Paris: Éditions L'Harmattan for Université Française du Pacifique, 1994.

Wen Fa, and B. Hermann. *Histoire et portrait de la communauté Chinoise de Tahiti* (The History and the Portrait of the Chinese Community in Tahiti). Barcelona: Industrias Graficas MIBA, 1979.

Willmott, W. E. 'Economic Role and Cultural Identity of Chinese in Pacific Island Countries.' In *Studies of Ethnic Chinese Economy: Collected Papers of International Symposium on Ethnic Chinese Economy*, edited by Xiao Xiaoqin and Li Dingguo. Shantou: Shantou University 1996a.

———. 'Origins of the Chinese in the Pacific Islands.' In *Histories of the Chinese in Australasia and the South Pacific*, edited by Paul Macgregor. Melbourne: Chinese Australian Museum, 1996b.

Willson, Margaret E. 'The Generous Face: Concepts of Personhood and Trade among the Papua New Guinea Chinese.' PhD diss., University of London, 1989.

———, Clive Moore, and Doug Munro. 'Asian Workers in the Pacific.' In *Labour in the South Pacific*, edited by Clive Moore, Jacqui Leckie and Doug Munro. Townsville: James Cook University Press, 1990.

Wong, Judith A. 'The Distribution and Role of the Chinese in Fiji: A Geographical Study of an Immigrant Group in the Plural Society of Fiji.' MA diss., University of Sydney, 1963.

Wood, M. 'White Skins, Real People, and Chinese in Some Spatial Transformations of the Western Province, PNG.' *Oceania* 66 (1995): 23-50.

Wu, David Y. H. 'An Ethnic Minority: The Adaptation of Chinese in Papua New Guinea.' PhD diss., Australian National University, 1974.

————. 'Chinese as an Intrusive Language.' In *New Guinea Area Languages and Language Study*, edited by S. A. Wurm, vol. 3, pt. 2. Canberra: Australian National University Press, 1977.

————. *The Chinese in Papua New Guinea: 1880-1980*. Hong Kong: Hong Kong University Press, 1982.

Yee Hoy Shang. *Three Score Years and Ten: Achievements and Leisurely Reflections*. Suva, undated.

Yee Sin Joan. *The Chinese in the Pacific*. Suva: South Pacific Social Studies Association, 1974.

EUROPE
Britain
Blick, J. 'The Chinese Labor Corps in World War I.' *Harvard Papers on China* (August 1995): 111-45.

Chen Sanjing. *Huagong yu Ouzhan* (Chinese Workers and World War I). Taipei: Institute of Modern History Studies, Academia Sinica, 1986.

Chen Ta. *Chinese Migrations, with Special Reference to Labor Conditions*. Washington: Government Printing Office, 1923.

Chung Yuen Kay. 'At the Palace: Researching Gender and Ethnicity in a Chinese Restaurant.' In *Feminist Praxis*, edited by Liz Stanley. London: Routledge, 1990.

Clegg, Jenny. *Fu Manchu and the 'Yellow Peril.'* Stoke on Trent: Trentham Books, 1994.

Coleman, David, and Salt John, eds. *Ethnicity in the 1991 Census: Demographic Characteristics of the Ethnic Minority Populations*, vol. 1. London: HMSO, 1996.

House of Commons. *Home Affairs Select Committee Report on the Chinese Community in Britain*. January 1985.

Joint Council for the Welfare of Immigrants (JCWI). *A Matter of Honour: The Nationality Question in Hong Kong*. London: JCWI, 1989.

Kohn, Marek. *Dope Girls: The Birth of the British Drug Underground*. London: Lawrence and Wishart, 1992.

Lacy, Michelle, Lili Man, and Jessie Lim, eds. *Exploring Our Chinese Identity*. Lambeth Chinese Community Association, 1992.

Li Wei. *Three Generations, Two Languages, One Family: Language Choice and Language Shift in a Chinese Community in Britain*. Clevedon: Multilingual Matters Ltd, 1994.

Lim, Jessie, and Li Yan, eds. *Another Province: New Chinese Writing from London*. Lambeth Chinese Community Association and SiYu Chinese Times, 1994.

MacNair, H. F. *The Chinese Abroad*. Shanghai: Commercial Press, 1933.

Mama, Amina. 'Woman Abuse in London's Black Communities.' In *Inside Babylon: The Caribbean Diaspora in Britain*, edited by W. James and C. Harris. London: Verso, 1993.

Menski, Werner, ed. *Coping with 1997: The Reaction of the Hong Kong People to the Transfer of Power*. Stoke on Trent: Trentham Books, 1995.

Owen, David. *Ethnic Minorities in Great Britain: Settlement Patterns*. Coventry: Centre for Research in Ethnic Relations, University of Warwick, 1992.

————. *Ethnic Minorities in Great Britain: Economic Characteristics*. Coventry: Centre for Research in Ethnic Relations, University of Warwick, 1993.

————. *Chinese and 'Other' Ethnic Minorities in Great Britain*. Coventry: Centre for Research in Ethnic Relations, University of Warwick, 1994.

Parker, David. *Through Different Eyes: The Cultural Identities of Young Chinese People in Britain*. Aldershot: Avebury, 1995.

Summerskill, Michael. *China On the Western Front*. London: Michael Summerskill, 1982.

Sze Szeming. 'Chinese Students in Great Britain.' *The Asiatic Review* 27 (1931): 311-20.

Taylor, Monica. *Chinese Pupils In Britain*. London: National Foundation for Educational Research, 1987.

Waller, Philip. 'The Chinese.' *History Today* 35 (September 1985): 8-14.

Watson, James L. *Emigration and the Chinese Lineage: The Mans in Hong Kong and London*. Berkeley: University of California Press, 1975.

————. *Between Two Cultures*. Oxford: Basil Blackwell, 1977.

Wong, Lornita Yuen Fan. 'The Hong Kong Chinese Speech Community.' In *Multilingualism in the British Isles: Africa, the Middle East, Asia*, edited by S. Alladina and V. Edwards. London: Longman 1991.

————. *Education of Chinese Children in Britain and the USA*. Clevedon: Multilingual Matters Ltd, 1992.

France
Archaimbault, Charles. 'En marge du quartier Chinois de Paris' (On the Fringe of the Chinese Neighbourhood in Paris). *Bulletin de la Société des Études Indochinoises* (Bulletin of the Society of Indochinese Studies) 28, 3 (1952): 275-94.

Bailey, Paul. 'The Chinese Work-Study Movement in France.' *China Quarterly* 115 (September 1988): 441-61.

————. *Reform the People: Changing Attitudes towards Popular Education in Early Twentieth Century China*. Edinburgh: Edinburgh University Press, 1990.

Barman, Geneviève, and Nicole Dulioust. 'La France au miroir Chinois' (France in the Chinese Mirror). *Les Temps Modernes* (Modern Times) (January 1988): 32-67.

Blick, J. 'The Chinese Labor Corps in World War I.' *Harvard Papers on China* (August 1955): 111-45.

Chen Sanjing. *Huagong yu Ouzhan* (Chinese Workers and World War I). Taipei: Institute of Modern History Studies, Academia Sinica, 1986.

Chen Ta. *Chinese Migrations, with Special Reference to Labor Conditions*. Washington: Government Printing Office, 1923.

Condominas, George, and Richard Pottier. *Les réfugiés originaires de l'Asie du Sud-Est* (The Refugees Originating from Southeast Asia). Paris: La Documentation française, 1982.

Cross, G. *Immigrant Workers in Industrial France*. Philadelphia: Temple University Press, 1983.

Guide de la communauté Chinoise 1991-92 (Guide to the Chinese Community). Paris: Éditions les Cent-fleurs.

Hassoun, Jean-Pierre. 'Le Chinois: Une langue d'émigrés' (The Chinese: A Language of Emigrants). In *Vingt-cinq communautés linguistiques de la France* (Twenty-five Linguistic Communities in France), vol. 2, edited by Geneviève Vermes. Paris: CNRS/L'Harmattan, 1988.

Horne, J. 'Immigrant Workers in France during World War I.' *French Historical Studies* 14, 1 (Spring 1985): 57-88.

LaFargue, T. *China and the World War*. New York: Howard Fertig, 1973.

Leung, John K-C. 'The Chinese Work-Study Movement: The Social and Political Experience of Chinese Students and Students Workers in France.' PhD diss., Brown University, 1982.

Levine, Marylin. 'The Found Generation: Chinese Communism in Europe 1919-1925.' PhD diss., University of Chicago, 1985.

Live Yu-Sion. 'Du quartier Latin à Billancourt: Une école de la politique' (From the Latin Quarter to Billancourt: A Political School). In *Presse et mémoire* (Press and Memory). Paris: Éditions ouvrières/Génériques, 1990.

————. 'La diaspora Chinoise en France: Immigration, activités socio-économiques, pratiques socio-culturelles' (The Chinese Diaspora in France: Immigration, Socio-economic Activity, Socio-cultural Practices). PhD diss., École des Hautes Études en Sciences Sociales, 1991.

————. 'Les Chinois de Paris depuis le début du siècle: Présence urbaine et activités économiques' (The Chinese in Paris since the Beginning of the 20th Century: Urban Presence and Economic Activities). *Revue Européenne des Migrations Internationales* (European Review of the International Migration) 8, 3 (1992): 155-73.

————. 'Les Asiatiques à Belleville: Immigrations et représentations' (Asians in Belleville: Immigration and Representations). *Hommes et Migrations* (Man and Migrations) 1168 (September 1993): 31-37.

————. 'Attitudes et opinions de la population Française à l'égard des réfugiés de l'Asie du Sud-Est' (French Opinions and Attitudes towards the Refugees from Southeast Asia). In *Les réfugiés en France et en Europe* (Refugees in France and Europe). Fontenay-sous-Bois: Ofpra, 1994a.

————. 'Les Chinois de Paris: Groupes, quartiers, réseaux' (The Chinese in Paris: Groups, Neighbourhoods and Networks). In *Le Paris des étrangers depuis 1945* (Foreigners' Paris since 1945). Paris: Publications de la Sorbonne, 1994b.

————. 'Image des Chinois en France: Une introduction diachronique' (The Image of the Chinese in France: An Diachronic Introduction). *Cahiers d'Anthropologie et Biométrie Humaine* (Journal of Anthropology of Human Biometrics) 13, 3/4 (1995): 453-64.

————, and Costa-Lascoux Jacqueline. *Paris XIIIe, lumières d'Asie*. (Paris the XIIIth Arrondissement: Light of Asia). Paris: Éditions Autrement, 1995.

MacNair, H. F. *The Chinese Abroad*. Shanghai: Commercial Press, 1933.

Ponchaud, François, and François Bonvin. *Les réfugiés du Sud-Est-asiatique, leur insertion en région Parisienne* (The Refugees from Southeast Asia: Their Settlement in Paris Area). Paris: Fondation pour la Recherche Sociale, 1980.

Shu Xincheng. *Jindai Zhongguo liuxue shi* (A History of Chinese Students Abroad in Modern China). Shanghai: Zhonghua Shuju, 1933.

Tsien Tsi-Hao. *L' Empire du Milieu retrouvé* (The Middle Empire Rediscovered). Paris: Flammarion, 1979.

Wang, Nora. 'Paris-Shanghai: Débats d'idées et pratique sociale; Les intellectuels progressistes Chinois 1920-1925' (Paris-Shanghai: Debates of Ideas and Social Practice; The Progressive Chinese Intellectuals 1920-1925). PhD diss., University of Paris VIII, 1986.

Wang Y. C. *Chinese Intellectuals and the West 1872-1949*. Chapel Hill: University of North Carolina Press, 1966.

Wou P. *Les travailleurs Chinois et la Grande Guerre* (Chinese Labourers and the Great War). Paris, 1939.

Italy
Carchedi, Francesco. 'I Cinesi' (The Chinese). In *L'arcipelago immigrazione. Caratteristiche e modelli migratori dei lavoratori stranieri in Italia* (The Immigration Archipelago. Characteristics and Migratory Patterns of Foreign Workers in Italy), edited by Giovanni Mottura. Roma: Ediesse, 1992.

————. 'La presenza Cinese in Italia. Direzionalità dei flussi, dimensioni del fenomeno e caratteristiche strutturali' (Chinese Presence in Italy. Directions of the Flows, Dimensions of the Phenomenon and Structural Characteristics). In *L'immigrazione silenziosa. Le comunità Cinesi in Italia* (The Silent Immigration. The Chinese Community in Italy), edited by Giovanna Campani and Francesco Carchedie e Alberto Tassinari. Turin: Edizioni della Fondazione Giovanni Agnelli, 1994

Donelli, Maurizio. 'Prato del Dragone' (Prato of the Dragon). *Corriere della Sera*. February 13, 1995.

Galli, Susanna. 'Le comunità Cinesi in Italia: Caratteristiche organizzative e culturali' (The Chinese Communitiy in Italy: Organizational and Cultural Characteristics). In *L'immigrazione silenziosa. Le comunità cinesi in Italia* (The Silent Immigration. The Chinese Community in Italy), edited by Giovanna Campani and Francesco Carchedie e Alberto Tassinari. Turin: Edizioni della Fondazione Giovanni Agnelli, 1994.

Tomba, Luigi. 'Exporting the "Wenzhou Model" to Beijing and Florence: Ideas for a Comparative Perspective on Labour and Economic Organisation in Two Migrant Communities.' Paper presented at the 'European Chinese and Chinese Domestic Migrants' Workshop, Oxford, July 3-5, 1996.

Orlandi, Ranieri. 'Colpo alla mafia gialla' (Strike of the Yellow Mafia). *Corriere della Sera.* March 15, 1995.

Pasolini, Caterina. 'Tagliata la testa del serpente' (Sever the Head of the Dragon). *La Repubblica.* March 15, 1995.

Vallini, Nunzia. 'Novanta schiavi nei sotterranei. É la Chinatown di Brescia. Lavorano gratis pure i bambini' (Ninety Slaves Underground. It is the Chinatown of Brescia. Even the Children Work for Free). *Corriere della Sera.* September 26, 1995.

The Netherlands

Archaimbault, Charles. *Boeren en Landlopers: Migranten uit Oost-China* (Peasants and Tramps: Migrants from East China). In *De Chinezen* (The Chinese), edited by Gregor Benton and Hans Vermeulen. Muiderberg: Coutinho, 1987.

Bedrijfschap Horeca. *Chinees-Indische restaurants* (Chinese-Indonesian Restaurants). The Hague: Bedrijfschap Horeca, 1983.

———. *Chinees-Indische restaurants: Onderzoeksresultaten* (Chinese-Indonesian Restaurants: Research Data). The Hague: Bedrijfschap Horeca, 1992.

Directoraat Welzijn, Ministerie van Welzijn, Volksgezondheid en Cultuur. *Investeren in integreren: Het WVC-minderhedenbeleid* (Investment in Integration: The Minorities Policies of the Ministry of Welfare, Popular Health, and Culture). Rijswijk: Ministerie van Welzijn, Volksgezondheid en Cultuur, 1994.

Galen, Kees van. 'Geschiedenis van de Chung Hwa Hui 1911-1962: Indo-Chinese studenten en Peranakan politiek in Nederland' (History of the Chung Hwa Hui 1911-1962: Indonesian Chinese Students and Peranakan Politics in the Netherlands). MA diss., Universiteit van Amsterdam, 1989.

Heek, F. van. *Chineesche Immigranten in Nederland* (Chinese Immigrants in the Netherlands). Amsterdam: Emmering, 1936.

Hoeven, Erik van der, and Henk de Kort. *Over Vietnamezen in Nederland: Een beschrijving van 720 Vietnamese vluchtelingen, interimverslag II* (Concerning the Vietnamese in the Netherlands: A Description of 720 Vietnamese Refugees, Interim Report II). The Hague: Coördinatiecommissie Wetenschappelijk Onderzoek Kinderbescherming, 1983.

Kleinen, John, and Martin Custers. 'De Hoa's: Chinese vluchtelingen uit Vietnam' (The Hoas: Chinese Refugees from Vietnam).' In *De Chinezen* (The Chinese), edited by Gregor Benton and Hans Vermeulen. Muiderberg: Coutinho, 1987.

Pieke, Frank N. *'De Positie van de Chinezen in Nederland'* (The Position of the Chinese in the Netherlands). Leiden: Documentatiecentrum voor het Huidige China, 1988a.

———. 'The Social Position of the Dutch Chinese: An Outline.' *China Information* 3, 2 (1988b): 12-23.

———. 'Chinese Educational Achievement and "Folk Theories of Success".' *Anthropology and Education Quarterly* 22, 2 (1991): 162-80.

———, and Gregor Benton. 'The Chinese in the Netherlands.' In *The Chinese in Europe,* edited by Frank N. Pieke and Gregor Benton. Basingstoke: Macmillan Press; New York, N. Y.: St. Martin's Press, 1998.

Pop, Margot M. *Werkloosheid onder Mediterranen in Nederland, 1986* (Unemployment among Mediterraneans in the Netherlands, 1986). Utrecht: Nederlands Centrum Buitenlanders, 1987.

Prins, C. J. M. 'Registertelling naar nationaliteit en geboorteland, 1 Januari 1990' (Population by Nationality and Country of Birth, Count Based on the Municipal Population Registers, 1 January, 1990). *Maandstatistiek van de Bevolking* 1 (1991): 18-37.

Rijkschroeff, B. R. A. C. Verlaan, and G. A. Kwa. *Oudere Peranakan Chinezen in Nederland* (Elderly Peranakan Chinese in the Netherlands). Capelle aan den IJssel: Labyrinth, 1992.

Sciortino, R. M. E., A. Wessels, and H. B. Teng. *Chinese ouderen in Amsterdam: Verslag van een onderzoek naar de leefsituatie van Chinese ouderen in Amsterdam* (Chinese Elderly in Amsterdam: Report of an Investigation into the Life of Chinese Elderly in

Amsterdam). Amsterdam: Stichting voor Toegepaste Gerontologie, Vrije Universiteit Amsterdam, 1993.

Wieringa, Frouke. *Dongfeng–Oostenwind: Chinezen in Nederland* (Dongfeng–East Wind: Chinese in the Netherlands). Amsterdam: Amsterdams Historisch Museum, 1990.

Wubben, Henk J. J. *'Chineezen en ander Aziatisch ongedierte': Lotgevallen van Chinese immigranten in Nederland, 1911-1940* ('Chinese and other Asian Vermin': The Vicissitudes of Chinese Immigrants in the Netherlands, 1911-1940). Zutphen: De Walburg, 1986.

Zhao Y. 'Chinezen in Nederland, 1 Januari 1990' (Chinese in the Netherlands, 1 January, 1990). *Maandstatistiek van de Bevolking* 6 (1992): 17-23.

Russia

Chi, Madeleine. *China Diplomacy 1914-1918.* Cambridge, Mass.: Harvard University Press, 1970.

Chen Sanjing. *Huagong yu Ouzhan* (Chinese Workers and World War I). Taipei: Institute of Modern History Studies, Academia Sinica, 1986.

He Ping. 'Eguo yuandong dichu Huagong wenti zhi chutan' (A Preliminary Exploration of the Chinese Worker Question in the Russian Far East). *Haiwai Huaren yanjiu* (Journal of Overseas Chinese Studies) 3 (1995): 77-124.

'Itogy' (The Results), 18 (1997): 58.

International Office for Migration. *Chinese Migrants in Central and Eastern Europe: The Cases of the Czech Republic, Hungary and Romania.* Brussels: Migration Information Programme, 1995.

LaFargue, T. *China and the World War.* New York: Howard Fertig, 1973.

Larin, Alexandra G. 'Chinese Immigration in Russia, 1850's-1920's.' *Zhongyang Yanjiuyuan, Jindaishi Yanjiusuo jikan* (Bulletin of the Modern History Studies, Academia Sinica) 24, 2 (1995): 843-92.

Li Yongchang. 'Zhongguo jindai fu E Huagong shu lüe' (An Account of Chinese Workers in Russia in the Modern Period). *Jindaishi yanjiu* (Modern History Studies) 38, 2 (March 1987): 214-30.

Miasnikov, V. S. 'Ethno-cultural Aspects of Interaction between Russia and China and their Influence upon the Soviet-Chinese Relations.' *Sino-Soviet Affairs* 15, 4 (1991-92): 87-103.

———. 'Chinese People in Russia: Ethnic-Psychology Dimensions.' Paper presented at the 'Chinese Immigration in the Russian Far East' Conference, Atlanta, December 12-13, 1994.

Schwartz, Harry. *Tsars, Mandarins, and Commissars: A History of Chinese-Russian Relations.* Philadelphia: Lippincott, 1964.

Sheng Yueh. *Sun Yat-sen University in Moscow and the Chinese Revolution: A Person Account.* New York: Paragon Book Gallery, 1971.

Tinguy, Anne de. 'Chinese Immigration to Russia: A Variation on an Old Theme.' In *The Chinese in Europe,* edited by Gregor Benton and Frank N. Pieke. Basingstoke: Macmillan Press; New York, N. Y.: St. Martin's Press, 1998.

Voskresenski, A. D. *The Difficult Border: Current Russian and Chinese Concepts of Sino-Russian Relations and Frontier Problems.* New York: Nova Science, 1996.

Wood, Alan, ed. *The History of Siberia : From Russian Conquest to Revolution.* New York: Routledge, 1991.

EAST ASIA
Japan
Harrell, Paula. *Sowing the Seeds of Change: Chinese Students, Japanese Teachers 1895-1905.* Stanford, Calif.: Stanford University Press, 1992.

Hishitani Buhei. *Nagasaki gaikokujin kyoryuchi no kenkyu* (A Research on Foreign Residents in Nagasaki). Kyushu Daigaku Shuppankai, 1988.

Huang Fuqing. *Qingmo liu Ri xuesheng* (Chinese Students in Japan in the late Qing). Taipei: Institute of Modern History

Studies, Academia Sinica, 1975.

Ichikawa Nobuchika, and Dai Yifeng, eds. *Jindai lü Ri Huaqiao yu Dongya yanhai diqu jiaoyiquan: Changqi Huashang 'Taiyi Hao' wenshu yanjiu* (Chinese Sojourners in Modern Japan and Business Networks in East Asia's Coastal Areas: A Documentary Research on a Chinese Concern – 'Taiyi Hao' in Nagasaki). Xiamen Daxue Chubanshe, 1994.

Ito Izumi. *Yokohama Chukagai: Kaiko kara shinsai made* (Yokohama Chinatown: From Opening of Treaty Ports to the Earthquake Calamity). Yokohama Kaikoshiryokan, 1994.

Japan: An Illustrated Encyclopedia. Tokyo: Kodansha, 1993.

Kamachi Noriko. 'The Chinese in Meiji Japan: Their Interactions with the Japanese before the Sino-Japanese War.' In *The Chinese and the Japanese: Essays in Political and Cultural Interactions,* edited by Akira Iriye. Princeton, New Jersey: Princeton University Press, 1980.

Kobe shigakukai. 'Tokushu Kobe no Kakyo' (Special Issue: Kobe's Chinese). *Rekishi to Kobe* (History and Kobe) 5, 4 (1966).

Liu Wu-chi. *Su Man-shu.* New York: Twayne Publisher, 1972.

Murakami Reiichi. *Yokohama Chukagai teki Kakyo-den* (Lives of Yokohama's Overseas Chinese). Tokyo: Shimpusha, 1997.

Nagasaki Kakyo Kenkyukai. *Nenpo* (Annual Report) 1-6 (1985-90).

Nakamura Tadasu. *Kinsei Nagasaki boekishi kenkyu* (A Study of Nagasaki Trading in Modern Times). Yoshikawakobunkan, 1992.

Reynolds, Douglas. *China, 1898-1912: The Xinzheng Revolution and Japan.* Cambridge, Mass.: Harvard University Press, 1993.

Shiba Yoshinobu. *Kakyo* (Overseas Chinese). Iwanami Shinsho, 1995.

Shigeto Takeo. *Nagasaki kyoryuchi to gaikoku shonin* (Foreign Merchants and Residential Areas for Foreigners in Nagasaki). Kazamashobo, 1967.

Shu Tokuran. *Nagasaki Kasho boeki no shiteki kenkyu* (A Historical Study of Chinese Trading in Nagasaki). Fuyoshobo, 1997.

Shu Xincheng. *Jindai Zhongguo liuxue shi* (A History of Chinese Students Abroad in Modern China). Shanghai: Zhonghua Shuju, 1933.

Sugawara Kazutaka. *Yokohama Chukagai no kenkyu* (A Study of Yokohama Chinatown). Nippon keizai shinbunsha, 1988.

Kyo Syukushin. 'Kawaguchi Kasho nitsuite' (Chinese Merchants in Kawaguchi). In *Kindai Nippon to Aijia* (Modern Japan and Asia). Tokyo Daigaku Shuppankai, 1984.

———. 'Nippon ni okeru rodoimin kinshiho no seiritsu' (The Imperial Ordinance: Restriction on Foreign Labourers). In *Higasi Ajia no ho to shakai* (The Laws and Societies of the East Asia), edited by Koichi Matuda. Kyukosyoin, 1990a.

———. *Rodoimin Kinshiho no shiko o megutte* (The Enactment of the Imperial Ordinance on Foreign Labourers). *Shakaigaku Zasshi* (Journal of Sociology) 7 (March 1990b): 102-19.

———. 'Nippon ni okeru kakyo juyo no hensen' (Changing Attitudes towards the Chinese in Japan). In *21seiki Ajia no kokusaikankei* (Asia's International Relationship), edited by Kenichiro Hirano. Harashobo, 1996.

Uchida Naosaku. *Nippon Kakyoshakai no kenkyu* (A Study of the Chinese Community in Japan). Dobunkan, 1949.

Yamada Nobuo, ed. *Nipponkakyo to bunkamasatsu* (Cultural Conflict and Chinese in Japan). Gennando, 1983.

Yamaoka Yuka. *Nagasaki Kasho keiei no shiteki kenkyu* (A Historical Study of Nagasaki Chinese Merchants). Mineruvashobo, 1995.

Yamawaki Teijiro. *Nagasaki no Tojin boeki* (Chinese Trading in Nagasaki). Yoshikawakobunkan, 1964.

———. *Kinsei Nicchu boekisi no kenkyu* (A Study of Japan-China Trading Relations in Modern Times). Yoshikawakobunkan, 1969.

Yasui Sankichi, ed. *Kinhyakunen Nicchu kankei no shiteki tenkai to hanshin Kakyo* (The Development of Japan-Chinese relations and the Chinese in Kobe-Osaka Region in the last Century). Kagakukenkyuhi Kenkyu Seika Hokokusho, 1997.

Korea

Chang, Cecilia. 'Aliens in their Adopted Land.' *Free China Review* (July 1989): 33-36.

Liao Xiaojian. 'Jinri Hanguo Huaqiao' (Chinese in Korea Today). *Qiaoyuan* (Chinese Overseas Information) 4 (1997): 32-33.

Lone, Stewart, and Gavan McCormack. *Korea since 1850*. New York: St. Martins Press, 1993.

Qin Yuguang. *Liushi nian jianwen lu* (60 Years of Observations). Publisher unknown; undated.

The Economist. 'The Vanishing of Chinatown.' August 3, 1996.

Wang Qiamin. *Hanguo Huaqiao zhi* (History of the Chinese in Korea). Taipei: Huaqiao Zhi Bianzuan Weiyuanhui, 1958.

Yang Zhaoquan, and Sun Yumei. *Chaoxian Huaqiao shi* (History of the Chinese in Korea). Beijing: Zhongguo Huaqiao Chubanshe, 1991.

INDIAN OCEAN AND AFRICA

India

Berjeaut, Julien. 'La communauté Chinoise de Calcutta 1780-1997' (The Chinese Community in Calcutta, 1780-1997). Université Paris VIII-St-Denis. École Normale Supérieure de Fontenay-St-Cloud, Paris, 1997.

Chatterjee, Gouri. 'Goodbye Chinatown: Calcutta's Chinese are Forced to Move – Again.' *Far Eastern Economic Review*. May 16, 1996.

Oxfeld, Ellen. *Blood, Sweat and Mahjong: Family and Enterprise in an Overseas Chinese Community*. Ithaca, N. Y.: Cornell University Press, 1993.

Madagascar

Bardonnet, Daniel. 'Les minorités Asiatiques à Madagascar' (Asian Minorities in Madagascar). *Annuaire Français de droit International* (French International Law Directory) 10 (1964): 127-224.

Bilbao, René. *Le droit Malgache de la nationalité* (The Nationality Law in Madagascar). Paris: Cujas, 1965.

Bousiges, Jacques. 'Les étrangers à Madagascar' (Foreigners in Madagascar). Thesis, Rennes University, 1956.

Chen Hansheng, ed. *Huagong chuguo shiliao huibian* (Historical Materials on the Emigration of Chinese Labourers), vol. 8, 9 & 10. Beijing: Zhonghua Shuju, 1984.

Donque, Gérald. 'Les minorités Chinoise et Indienne à Madagascar' (Chinese and Indian Minorities in Madagascar). *Reveue Française d'Études Politiques Africaines* (French Review of African Political Studies) 25 (1968): 85-103.

Fang Jigen. *Feizhou Huaqiao shi ziliao xuanji* (Selected Historical Materials on Chinese in Africa). Beijing: Xinhua Chubanshe, 1986.

Gallieni, Joseph-Simon. *Madagascar de 1896 à 1905* (Madagascar 1896-1905). Tananarive: Imprimerie Officielle, 1905.

Gayet, Georges. 'Immigrations asiatiques à Madagascar' (Asian Immigrants in Madagascar). Civilisations 5, 1 (1955): 54-65.

Grandidier, Alfred. *Histoire physique, naturelle et politique de Madagascar* (Physical, Natural and Political History of Madagascar), pt. 2. Paris: Imprimerie Nationale, 1908.

Guérin, Jean. 'Les minorités Asiatiques et Comoriennes à Madagascar' (Asian and Comoran Minorities in Madagascar). D. E. S. Law diss., Tananarive University, 1961.

Le Bourdiec, Paul. 'L'implantation des minorités étrangères à Madagascar avant 1972' (Settlement of Foreign Minorities in Madagascar before 1972). Annuaire des Pays de l'Océan Indien (Directory of the Indian Ocean Countries) 3 (1978): 37-67.

Ly-Tio-Fane Pineo, Huguette. *Chinese Diaspora in Western Indian Ocean*. Mauritius: Éditions de l'Océan Indien and Chinese Catholic Mission, 1985.

Slawecki, Léon. *French Policy towards the Chinese in Madagascar*. Hamden: The Shoe String Press, 1971.

Triviere, Léon. 'L'émigration Chinoise vers Madagascar et l'Afrique' (Chinese Emigration to Madagascar and Afica). Reveue Économique Française (French Economic Review) (October 1964).

Tsien Tche-Hao. 'La vie sociale des Chinois à Madagascar' (Social Life of the Chinese in Madagascar). *Comparative Studies in Society and History* 3, 2 (1961): 170-81.

Mauritius

Chen Hansheng, ed. *Huagong chuguo shiliao huibian* (Historical Materials on the Emigration of Chinese Labourers), vol. 8, 9 & 10. Beijing: Zhonghua Shuju, 1984.

Fang Jigen. *Feizhou Huaqiao shi ziliao xuanji* (Selected Historical Materials on Chinese in Africa). Beijing: Xinhua Chubanshe, 1986.

Ly-Tio-Fane Pineo, Huguette. *Chinese Diaspora in Western Indian Ocean*. Mauritius: Éditions de l'Océan Indien and Chinese Catholic Mission, 1985.

Reunion Island

Chen Hansheng, ed. *Huagong chuguo shiliao huibian* (Historical Materials on the Emigration of Chinese Labourers), vol. 8, 9 & 10. Beijing: Zhonghua Shuju, 1984.

Coppenrath, Gérard. *Les Chinois de Tahiti: De l'aversion à l'assimilation, 1865-1966* (The Chinese in Tahiti: From Aversion to Assimilation 1865-1966). Paris: Musée de l'Homme, 1967.

Durand, Dominique, and Hin-Tung Jean. *Les Chinois de la Réunion* (Chinese of Reunion). Capetown: Australes Éditions, 1981.

Fang Jigen. *Feizhou Huaqiao shi ziliao xuanji* (Selected Historical Materials on Chinese in Africa). Beijing: Xinhua Chubanshe, 1986.

Fock-Yee, Jeanne. 'Les Chinois à la Réunion' (The Chinese in Reunion). MA diss., Université de Toulouse, le Mirail, 1974.

Gérard, Gilles. 'Les Réunionnais d'origine Chinoise' (Reunionese of Chinese origin). MA diss., Bordeaux III University, 1989.

Helly, Denise. 'Des immigrants Chinois aux Mascareignes' (Chinese Immigrants in the Mascarene Islands). *Annuaire des Pays de l'Océan Indien* (Directory of the Indian Ocean Countries) 3 (1976): 103-24.

Huaqiao zhi bianzuan weiyuanhui (The Editorial Committee of the Huaqiao zhi), ed. *Liuniwangdao Huaqiao zhi* (Chinese in Reunion). Taipei: Huaqiao Zhi Bianzuan Weiyuanhui, 1966.

Lee-Tin, Richard. 'Les Chinois à la Réunion: Parcours d'adaptation socio-économique et ethnicité' (Chinese in Reunion: Socio-economic Adaptation and Ethnicity). MA diss., Reunion University, 1989.

Live Yu-Sion. 'La diaspora Chinoise en France: Immigration, activités socio-économiques and pratiques socio-culturelles' (Chinese Diaspora in France: Immigration, Economic Activities and Socio-cultural Practices). PhD diss., École des Hautes Études en Sciences Sociales, Paris, 1991.

———. 'Sociologie de la Réunion: Mutations, paradoxes, représentations, migrations' (Sociology of Reunion: Mutations, Paradoxes, Representations, Migrations). In *Colloque 20 ans d'Anthropologie à la Réunion, May 1995* (Colloquium 20 years of Anthropology in Reunion, May 1995). Saint-Denis: Harmattan Publications for Réunion University, 1997.

Ly-Tio-Fane Pineo, Huguette. *Chinese Diaspora in Western Indian Ocean*. Mauritius: Éditions de l'Océan Indien and Chinese Catholic Mission, 1985.

Marimoutou, Michelle. *Les engagés du sucre* (The Indentured Workers of the Sugar Industry). Saint Denis: Éditons du Tramail, 1990.

Slawecki, Léon. *French Policy towards the Chinese in Madagascar*. Hamden: The Shoe String Press, 1971.

Wong, Édith Hee-Kam. *La diaspora Chinoise aux Mascareignes: Le cas de la Réunion* (Chinese Diaspora in the Mascarene Islands: Case Study of Reunion). Paris: L'Harmattan Publications, 1996.

Wong-Cheng, Jacqueline. 'Les Chinois à la Réunion' (The Chinese in Reunion). *Cahiers d'Études Chinoises* (Notes on the Chinese Studies) 6 (1987): 13-37.

South Africa

Chen Hansheng, ed. *Huagong chuguo shiliao huibian* (Historical Materials on the Emigration of Chinese Labourers), vol. 8, 9 & 10. Beijing: Zhonghua Shuju, 1984.

Duyvendak, J. J. L. *China's Discovery of Africa*. London: Probsthain, 1949.

Fang Jigen, ed. *Feizhou Huaqiao shi ziliao xuanji* (Selected Historical Materials on Chinese in Africa). Beijing: Xinhua Chubanshe, 1986.

Harris, Karen Leigh. 'Rand Capitalists and Chinese Resistance.' *Contree* 35 (1994a): 19-31.

———. 'The Chinese in South Africa: A Preliminary Overview to 1910.' *Kleio* 26 (1994b): 9-26.

———. 'Chinese Merchants on the Rand, c.1850-1911.' *South African Historical Journal* 33 (November 1995): 155-68.

———. 'Gandhi, the Chinese and Passive Resistance.' In *Gandhi in South Africa*, edited by Judith Brown and Martin Prozesky. Pietermaritzburg: Natal University Press; New York: St. Martin's Press, 1996.

Huang Tsen-ming. *The Legal Status of the Chinese Abroad*. Taipei: China Cultural Service, 1954.

Human, Linda. *The Chinese People of South Africa: Freewheeling on the Fringes*. Pretoria: University of South Africa, 1984.

———, Fok K. Y., and Chorn N. 'Marginality and Competitive Advantage: The Implications of the Opening of the CBDS for Chinese Businesses.' *South African Journal of Business Management* 18, 1 (March 1987): 133-44.

Ly-Tio-Fane Pineo, Huguette. *Chinese Diaspora in Western Indian Ocean*. Mauritius: Éditions de l'Océan Indien and Chinese Catholic Mission, 1985.

Richardson, Peter. *Chinese Mine Labour in the Transvaal*. London: Macmillan Press, 1982.

Snow, Philip. *The Star Raft: China's Encounter with Africa*. Ithaca, N. Y.: Cornell University Press, 1988.

Yap, Melanie, and Dianne Leong Man. *Colour, Confusion and Concessions: The History of the Chinese in South Africa*. Hong Kong: Hong Kong University Press, 1996.

INDEX

Maps, figures, tables, captions and boxes
are indicated by page numbers in italics.